Influences of

Forest and Rangeland Management
on Salmonid Fishes and Their Habitats

Major Funding for publication of this book
was provided by the

U.S. Department of Agriculture, Forest Service

Pacific Northwest Research Station
and
Forest Environment Research

Influences of
Forest and Rangeland Management
on Salmonid Fishes and Their Habitats

Edited by

William R. Meehan

U.S. Department of Agriculture
Forest Service

American Fisheries Society Special Publication 19

Bethesda, Maryland, USA
1991

The American Fisheries Society Special Publication series is a registered serial. Suggested citation formats follow.

Entire book

Meehan, W. R., editor. 1991. Influences of forest and rangeland management on salmonid fishes and their habitats. American Fisheries Society Special Publication 19.

Chapter within the book

Swanston, D. N. 1991. Natural processes. American Fisheries Society Special Publication 19:139–179.

Address orders to

American Fisheries Society
5410 Grosvenor Lane, Suite 110
Bethesda, Maryland 20814, USA

Contents

3   Salmonid Distributions and Life Histories 47

W. R. MEEHAN AND T. C. BJORNN

4   Habitat Requirements of Salmonids in Streams 83

T. C. BJORNN AND D. W. REISER

8 Road Construction and Maintenance 297
M. J. FURNISS, T. D. ROELOFS, AND C. S. YEE

9 Water Transportation and Storage of Logs 325
J. R. SEDELL, F. N. LEONE, AND W. S. DUVAL

Contributors

Calvin O. Baker (Chapter 15): U.S. Forest Service, Fernan Ranger District, 2502 Sherman Avenue, Coeur d'Alene, Idaho 83814, USA.

Peter A. Bisson (Chapter 14): Weyerhaeuser Technical Center WTC-2H4, Weyerhaeuser Company, Tacoma, Washington 98477, USA.

Theodore C. Bjornn (Chapters 3 and 4): Idaho Cooperative Fish and Wildlife Research Unit, College of Forestry, Wildlife and Range Science, University of Idaho, Moscow, Idaho 83843, USA.

Paul Brouha (Chapter 17): American Fisheries Society, 5410 Grosvenor Lane, Suite 110, Bethesda, Maryland 20814, USA.

Thomas W. Chamberlin (Chapter 6): Ministry of the Environment, Bag 5000, Smithers, British Columbia V0J 2N0, Canada.

Roger N. Clark (Chapter 13): U.S. Forest Service, Pacific Northwest Research Station, 4043 Roosevelt Way, N.E., Seattle, Washington 98105, USA.

Wayne S. Duval (Chapter 9): Environmental Sciences Ltd., 1155 Robson Street, Suite 407, Vancouver, British Columbia V6E 1B5, Canada.

Fred H. Everest (Chapter 6): U.S. Forest Service, Pacific Northwest Research Station, 3200 S.W. Jefferson Way, Corvallis, Oregon 97331, USA.

Roger D. Fight (Chapter 16): U.S. Forest Service, Pacific Northwest Research Station, Post Office Box 3890, Portland, Oregon 97208, USA.

Harvey L. Forsgren (Chapter 18): U.S. Forest Service, Intermountain Region, 324 25th Street, Ogden, Utah 84401, USA.

Michael J. Furniss (Chapter 8): U.S. Forest Service, Six Rivers National Forest, 507 F Street, Eureka, California 95501, USA.

Dave R. Gibbons (Chapter 13): U.S. Forest Service, Alaska Region, Post Office Box 21628, Juneau, Alaska 99802, USA.

Stanley V. Gregory (Chapter 7): Department of Fisheries and Wildlife, Oregon State University, Corvallis, Oregon 97331, USA.

James D. Hall (Chapters 14 and 15): Department of Fisheries and Wildlife, Nash Hall 104, Oregon State University, Corvallis, Oregon 97331, USA.

R. Dennis Harr (Chapter 6): U.S. Forest Service, Pacific Northwest Research Station, 3200 S.W. Jefferson Way, Corvallis, Oregon 97331, USA. *Present address*: College of Forest Resources AR-10, University of Washington, Seattle, Washington 98195, USA.

Tracii L. Hickman (Chapter 15): U.S. Forest Service, Pacific Northwest Research Station, Corvallis, Oregon 97331, USA. *Present address*: U.S. Forest Service, Estacada Ranger District, 595 N.W. Industrial Way, Estacada, Oregon 97023, USA.

Brendan J. Hicks (Chapter 14): Department of Fisheries and Wildlife, Oregon State University, Corvallis, Oregon 97331, USA. *Present address*: Ministry of Agriculture and Fisheries, Fisheries Research Centre, Post Office Box 6016, Rotorura, New Zealand.

Daniel D. Huppert (Chapter 16): National Marine Fisheries Service, Southwest Fisheries Center, La Jolla, California, USA. *Present address*: School of Marine Affairs HF-05, University of Washington, Seattle, Washington 98195, USA.

Jeffrey L. Kershner (Chapter 18): U.S. Forest Service, Fish Habitat Relationships Program, Fish and Wildlife Department, Utah State University, Logan, Utah 84322, USA.

Frank N. Leone (Chapter 9): U.S. Forest Service, Pacific Northwest Research Station, 3200 S.W. Jefferson Way, Corvallis, Oregon 97331, USA. *Present address*: 102 North Moffat Street, Prince George, British Columbia V2M 3C3, Canada.

Harold W. Lorz (Chapter 7): Oregon Department of Fish and Wildlife, 170 N.E. Vandenberg Avenue, Corvallis, Oregon 97330, USA.

Michael L. McHenry (Chapter 12): U.S. Forest Service, Intermountain Research Station, 316 Myrtle Street, Boise, Idaho 83702, USA. *Present address*: Northwest Indian Fisheries Commission, Post Office Box 1029, Forks, Washington 98331, USA.

William R. Meehan (Editor; Chapters 1, 2, 3, and 18): U.S. Forest Service, Pacific Northwest Research Station, Post Office Box 20909, Juneau, Alaska 99802, USA.

Michael L. Murphy (Chapter 2): National Marine Fisheries Service, Auke Bay Fisheries Laboratory, Post Office Box 210155, Auke Bay, Alaska 99821, USA.

Rodger L. Nelson (Chapter 12): U.S. Forest Service, Intermountain Research Station, 316 Myrtle Street, Boise, Idaho 83702, USA.

Logan A. Norris (Chapter 7): Department of Forest Science, Peavy Hall 154, Oregon State University, Corvallis, Oregon 97331, USA.

William S. Platts (Chapters 11 and 12): U.S. Forest Service, Intermountain Research Station, 316 Myrtle Street, Boise, Idaho 83702, USA. *Present address*: Don Chapman Consultants, Inc., 3180 Airport Way, Boise, Idaho 83705, USA.

Gordon H. Reeves (Chapter 15): U.S. Forest Service, Pacific Northwest Research Station, 3200 S.W. Jefferson Way, Corvallis, Oregon 97331, USA.

Dudley W. Reiser (Chapter 4): EA Engineering Science and Technology, Inc., 8577 154th Avenue N.E., Redmond, Washington 98052, USA.

Terry D. Roelofs (Chapters 8 and 15): Department of Fish and Wildlife, Humboldt State University, Arcata, California 95521, USA.

Donald C. Schmiege (Chapter 10): U.S. Forest Service, Pacific Northwest Research Station, Post Office Box 20909, Juneau, Alaska 99802, USA. *Present address*: 1800 Evergreen Avenue, Juneau, Alaska 99801, USA.

James R. Sedell (Chapters 9 and 14): U.S. Forest Service, Pacific Northwest Research Station, 3200 Jefferson Way, Corvallis, Oregon 97331, USA.

Douglas N. Swanston (Chapter 5): U.S. Forest Service, Pacific Northwest Research Station, Post Office Box 20909, Juneau, Alaska 99802, USA.

Rudolph N. Thut (Chapter 10): Weyerhaeuser Technical Center WTC-2H2, Weyerhaeuser Company, Tacoma, Washington 98477, USA.

Carlton S. Yee (Chapter 8): Department of Forestry, Humboldt State University, Arcata, California 95521, USA.

Preface

An awareness that management activities on forest and range lands can affect the productivity of salmonid habitats has increased during the last 30 years. Before then, timber harvest and processing, road construction, livestock grazing, mining, and other commercial and recreational activities on both public and private lands took place without much concern about their consequences for other resources, in particular for fish habitats. As this awareness developed, resource scientists and managers accelerated their efforts to understand the often complex relations between land-use activities and aquatic resources. In recent years, forest and range managers have come under increasing pressure to assure that fish habitats on public lands remain productive and that fish populations are maintained at levels that meet commercial, recreational, and subsistence demands. These are not easy tasks. Political pressures from various interest groups often put the manager "between a rock and a hard spot." Multiple-use management is often thought to mean that all resources on a piece of land are managed so that all the users of these resources obtain their desired products. In reality, all the resources may be considered, but not necessarily equally. Constraints will be applied in some fashion, either to manage for maximum production of one resource to the exclusion of some or all of the others, or to manage all resources so that everybody gets something, but nobody gets everything he or she would like. All the timber in a watershed, for example, cannot be cut down without seriously affecting water quality and hence fish production. Fishery managers will not accept this, and campers and backpackers will complain bitterly about the aesthetic degradation of the landscape. Maintaining all productive lands in a pristine condition is likewise not a viable option; our society demands products of the land to maintain its standard of living. So we must strike some kind of compromise that allows us to obtain natural commodities without reducing the productivity of the land. Land, in this context, includes the water and aquatic resources associated with it.

Much knowledge, though incomplete, exists to help resource managers plan for the protection and enhancement of salmonid habitats, but it is widely scattered throughout the scientific literature and the files of resource agencies. To be of use to managers and researchers, this information must be summarized and assembled into a source document that is readily available, understandable, and usable. As a start, the Pacific Northwest Research Station of the U.S. Forest Service published a series of reports between 1979 and 1985 entitled "Influence of Forest and Rangeland Management on Anadromous Fish Habitat in Western North America." The 14 reports summarized the information then available on the relation between western forest and range management activities and anadromous fish habitats. The primary audiences for those publications were forest managers and fishery biologists. The series was well received and used extensively by managers, researchers, and other persons interested in the conservation and management of natural resources on public and private lands.

The evident interest in this type of documentation led to a decision by the U.S. Forest Service and the American Fisheries Society to revise, update, and expand the information in the original reports. This book is the result. We have added chapters that describe stream ecosystems and how they relate to salmonid habitats, life histories and distributions of salmonids throughout North America, responses of fish populations to the changes brought about by land-management activities, planning strategies used to integrate fish habitats into natural resource management, and general approaches to managing salmonid habitats. The chapters corresponding to the original series have been extensively revised and updated. The tremendous amount of new information that has become available in this area during the last few years has been incorporated. The extensive reference section alone should be an invaluable compilation. In addition to managers and researchers, we hope the book will become a primary reference for students in fisheries, forestry, and other natural resource disciplines. Although the book still emphasizes anadromous fish and their freshwater habitats in western North America, we have included information on resident salmonids and have attempted to expand the applicability of the discussions to other regions of North America. Much of the information that focuses directly on western conditions applies to anadromous salmonids in the Atlantic and Great Lakes states and provinces, as well as to resident trout and char populations throughout North America. Likewise, much of the information describing the effects of forest management on fish habitats is relevant to habitat changes caused by road construction, mining, or some other activity.

This book is certainly not the last word on the interrelations between salmonid production and the management of forest and range lands. Many of the problems facing resource managers have not been solved, and some probably have not even been identified. But we cannot place a moratorium on the harvest and use of natural resources while we learn precisely how all components of the environment will respond. We must manage our lands using our current knowledge while we continue to identify and explore better ways to accomplish this task and still protect, and where possible enhance, our valuable fishery resources. I hope this book will expedite our progress.

William R. Meehan

Acknowledgments

Many people, in addition to the authors and their colleagues, contributed to the preparation of this book. Special thanks go to Martha H. Brookes, who reviewed much of the material in the book and suggested innumerable ways to make it a better product, and to Delbert E. Thompson, who prepared many of the final figures and generally oversaw the artwork. Shirley N. Dalton, Barbara E. Streveler, Dawn H. Crossley, Michelle M. Haffner, Lori J. Erbs, Beth Ann Hoback, Kimberly Comet, Carol A. Ayer, Dwynne Kromarek, and Deborah J. Anderson helped to find original publications cited by the authors and to prepare the extensive list of references. I am especially indebted to Tawny A. Blinn and James D. Hall for assisting me in the awesome task of checking the nearly 2,000 references for accuracy and for consistency among chapters. James J. Rogers not only kept my word-processing systems functioning but identified and developed programs that made my editing and communications tasks easier and more efficient. Elaine M. Loopstra modified and prepared many of the final figures. George R. Snyder and his staff at the National Marine Fisheries Service's Auke Bay Fisheries Laboratory gave me a place to work and many helpful suggestions during the book's early development. Kenneth H. Wright was instrumental in arranging time for me to work on this project, and Fred H. Everest and Mason D. Bryant took over many of my regular administrative duties during the book's preparation. Particular thanks are due to the U. S. Department of Agriculture, Forest Service, for contributing funds for the book's publication.

Several authors also wish to acknowledge the help they received as they prepared their respective chapters.

William R. Meehan greatly appreciates the assistance of Richard L. Lantz in preparing an early draft of Chapter 1.

Michael L. Murphy and William R. Meehan thank Elmer Landingham for his excellent job of preparing the final figures for Chapter 2.

Theodore C. Bjornn and Dudley W. Reiser appreciate the reviews of Robert Kendall, Paul Eschmeyer, Steve Leider, Bruce Shepherd, and Cleve Steward, and the assistance of Gwynne Chandler in preparation of the figures for Chapter 4. Their chapter is Contribution 352 from the Forest, Wildlife and Range Experiment Station, University of Idaho.

Thomas W. Chamberlin, R. Dennis Harr, and Fred H. Everest appreciate the excellent discussions with Kate Sullivan on channel morphology that greatly enhanced Chapter 6.

Logan A. Norris, Harold W. Lorz, Stanley V. Gregory, and William R. Meehan greatly appreciate the time and effort expended by Andris Eglitis in reformatting and synthesizing much of the information in Chapter 7, particularly the many lengthy and detailed tables. The Forest Pest Management staff of the U.S. Forest

Service, Washington, D.C., compiled the Pesticide Use Reports referred to in this chapter.

Michael J. Furniss, Terry D. Roelofs, and Carlton S. Yee thank Leslie Reid, Mark Smith, Jeff Patty, William Weaver, Danny Hagans, Ray Rice, Joseph Moreau, Nancy Reichard, and Kerry Overton for their valuable review comments on Chapter 8.

James R. Sedell, Frank N. Leone, and Wayne S. Duval thank Judy Bufford for constructing the tables, drawing the log transfer figures, and performing archival research for Chapter 9. They also thank Sue Hanneman for unflagging help and archival assistance, Martha Brookes and Tawny Blinn for insightful editing and bibliographic help, and Delbert Thompson for saving time and money in the final figure preparation. Rose Davies, Phyllis Taylor-Hill, and Dee Safley provided overtime effort and enormous grace and humor while typing the several drafts of this chapter. Tim Slaney, Mary Jo Duncan, Gary Vigers, Ian Webster, Morris Zallen, Gary Birch, W. Richard Olmsted, and Jean Coustalin provided the basic literature searches that went into this chapter.

Rudolph N. Thut and Donald C. Schmiege thank Don McLeay and Tim Hall for their critical reviews of the first draft of Chapter 10.

Roger N. Clark and Dave R. Gibbons acknowledge the assistance of Gilbert B. Pauley in preparing an earlier version of Chapter 13.

Brendan J. Hicks, James D. Hall, Peter A. Bisson, and James R. Sedell appreciate the very thorough review of Chapter 14 by Michael L. Murphy, and the ideas provided by Carl J. Cederholm, A. Espinosa, Christopher A. Frissell, Gordon F. Hartman, and J. Charles Scrivener. Their chapter is Technical Paper 8451, Oregon Agricultural Experiment Station.

Paul Brouha thanks Robert Dewey for information used in Chapter 17 on Alaska Cooperative Fisheries Plans, Lynn Starnes for descriptive material concerning fisheries on the National Refuge System, and Michael Crouse for assistance in documenting planning processes for fisheries used by the U.S. Bureau of Land Management.

Jeffrey L. Kershner, Harvey L. Forsgren, and William R. Meehan appreciate the help of Donald A. Duff, Ronald L. Dunlap, Dave R. Gibbons, David A. Heller, Charles M. Holstine, C. Kerry Overton, and Fred M. Stowell in developing an outline and providing ideas for Chapter 18. James M. Meehan refined the figures.

In addition to internal reviews, all technical chapters were subjected to formal peer reviews by the American Fisheries Society. The following people substantially improved the chapters assigned to them: Carl L. Armour, Don K. Bartschi, Charles R. Berry, Jr., N. Allen Binns, Max L. Bothwell, Carl J. Cederholm, Derek V. Ellis, Kurt D. Fausch, Thomas J. Hassler, David A. Heller, Wayne A. Hubert, Gary L. Larson, Steven A. Leider, John B. Loomis, David Lorence, Ronald Marcoux, Douglas J. Martin, G. Wayne Minshall, Lee A. Mulkey, Robert J. Naiman, Glenn R. Phillips, Basil M. H. Sharp, Bradley B. Shepard, Bruce G. Shepherd, Courtland Smith, Virginia G. Thomas, Harold M. Tyus, Phyllis K. Weber, Thomas A. Wesche, and Warren W. Wiley.

At the American Fisheries Society, Robert L. Kendall, Sally M. Kendall, Catherine W. Richardson, and Elizabeth A. Mitchell contributed editorial improvements in the final manuscripts and saw the book through production. Robert R. Gabel prepared the index.

And finally, I wish to express my deepest thanks to my wife, Sandra, whose unswerving patience, understanding, and encouragement saw me through the times when I doubted the wisdom of taking on the task of putting this book together.

William R. Meehan

List of Fish Species

The colloquial names of many fish species have been standardized in *Common and Scientific Names of Fishes from the United States and Canada*, 5th edition, American Fisheries Society Special Publication 20, 1991, and *World Fishes Important to North Americans*, American Fisheries Society Special Publication 21, 1991. Species listed in those publications are cited only by common name in this book. Their respective scientific names follow below; names in parentheses are those by which the species were formerly known. Names of cutthroat trout subspecies are those of R. J. Behnke, American Fisheries Society Symposium 4:1–7, 1988.

Albacore . . . . *Thunnus alalunga*
Alewife . . . . *Alosa pseudoharengus*
Apache trout . . . . *Oncorhynchus apache* (*Salmo apache*)
Arctic char . . . . *Salvelinus alpinus*
Atlantic salmon . . . . *Salmo salar*

Black bullhead . . . . *Ameiurus melas* (*Ictalurus melas*)
Blacknose dace . . . . *Rhinichthys atratulus*
Blennies . . . . Families Blenniidae, Clinidae
Bluegill . . . . *Lepomis macrochirus*
Bonneville cutthroat trout . . . . *Oncorhynchus clarki utah*
Brook trout . . . . *Salvelinus fontinalis*
Brown trout . . . . *Salmo trutta*
Bullhead catfishes . . . . Family Ictaluridae
Bull trout . . . . *Salvelinus confluentus*

Capelin . . . . *Mallotus villosus*
Carps . . . . Family Cyprinidae
Central stoneroller . . . . *Campostoma anomalum*
Channel catfish . . . . *Ictalurus punctatus*
Cherry salmon . . . . *Oncorhynchus masou*
Chinook salmon . . . . *Oncorhynchus tshawytscha*
Chubsuckers . . . . *Erimyzon* spp.
Chum salmon . . . . *Oncorhynchus keta*
Clinids . . . . Family Clinidae
Coastal cutthroat trout . . . . *Oncorhynchus clarki clarki*
Cods . . . . Family Gadidae
Coho salmon . . . . *Oncorhynchus kisutch*
Combtooth blennies . . . . Family Blenniidae
Common carp . . . . *Cyprinus carpio*

Cutthroat trout .... *Oncorhynchus clarki (Salmo clarki)*

Dolly Varden .... *Salvelinus malma*

Eastern mudminnow .... *Umbra pygmaea*
Emerald shiner .... *Notropis atherinoides*
English sole .... *Pleuronectes vetulus (Parophrys vetulus)*
Eulachon .... *Thaleichthys pacificus*
European perch .... *Perca fluviatilis*

Fathead minnow .... *Pimephales promelas*
Fourhorn sculpin .... *Myoxocephalus quadricornis*
Freshwater eels .... FAMILY Anguillidae

Gila trout .... *Oncorhynchus gilae (Salmo gilae)*
Gizzard shad .... *Dorosoma cepedianum*
Golden shiner .... *Notemigonus crysoleucas*
Golden trout ... *Oncorhynchus aguabonita (Salmo aguabonita)*
Goldfish .... *Carassius auratus*
Grass carp .... *Ctenopharyngodon idella*
Green sunfish .... *Lepomis cyanellus*
Guppy .... *Poecilia reticulata*

Herrings .... FAMILY Clupeidae

Inconnu .... *Stenodus leucichthys*

Killifishes .... FAMILY Cyprinodontidae
Kokanee .... *Oncorhynchus nerka*

Lahontan cutthroat trout ...... *Oncorhynchus clarki henshawi*
Lake chubsucker .... *Erimyzon sucetta*
Lake trout .... *Salvelinus namaycush*
Lampreys .... FAMILY Petromyzontidae
Largemouth bass .... *Micropterus salmoides*
Livebearers .... FAMILY Poeciliidae
Longfin smelt .... *Spirinchus thaleichthys*
Longnose killifish .... *Fundulus similis*

Medaka[a] .... *Oryzias latipes*
Medakas .... FAMILY Adrianichthyidae
Minnows .... FAMILY Cyprinidae
Mosquitofish[b] .... *Gambusia affinis*
Mudminnows .... FAMILY Umbridae

Northern pike .... *Esox lucius*
Northern redbelly dace .... *Phoxinus eos*

Pacific cod .... *Gadus macrocephalus*
Pacific herring .... *Clupea pallasi (Clupea harengus pallasi)*

---

[a]Now Japanese medaka.
[b]Now western mosquitofish.

Pacific sand lance .... *Ammodytes hexapterus*
Perches .... FAMILY Percidae
Pikes .... FAMILY Esocidae
Pink salmon .... *Oncorhynchus gorbuscha*
Pumpkinseed .... *Lepomis gibbosus*
Pupfishes .... *Cyprinodon* spp.

Rainbow trout .... *Oncorhynchus mykiss* (*Salmo gairdneri*)
Redside shiner .... *Richardsonius balteatus*
Righteye flounders .... FAMILY Pleuronectidae
Roach .... *Rutilus rutilus*
Rockfishes .... *Sebastes* spp.
Ronquils .... FAMILY Bathymasteridae
Ruffe .... *Gymnocephalus cernuus*

Sand lances .... FAMILY Ammodytidae
Scorpionfishes .... FAMILY Scorpaenidae
Sculpins .... FAMILY Cottidae
Sea lamprey .... *Petromyzon marinus*
Searcher .... *Bathymaster signatus*
Sheepshead minnow .... *Cyprinodon variegatus*
Shiner perch .... *Cymatogaster aggregata*
Slimy sculpin .... *Cottus cognatus*
Smallmouth bass .... *Micropterus dolomieu*
Smelts .... FAMILY Osmeridae
Sockeye salmon .... *Oncorhynchus nerka*
Speckled dace .... *Rhinichthys osculus*
Steelhead .... *Oncorhynchus mykiss* (*Salmo gairdneri*)
Sticklebacks .... FAMILY Gasterosteidae
Stonerollers .... *Campostoma* spp.
Striped bass .... *Morone saxatilis*
Suckers .... FAMILY Catostomidae
Sunfishes .... FAMILY Centrarchidae
Surfperches .... FAMILY Embiotocidae
Surf smelt .... *Hypomesus pretiosus*

Temperate basses .... FAMILY Percichthyidae
Threespine stickleback .... *Gasterosteus aculeatus*
Trouts .... FAMILY Salmonidae

Walleye .... *Stizostedion vitreum*
Westslope cutthroat trout .... *Oncorhyncbus clarki lewisi*
Whitefishes .... *Coregonus* spp., *Prosopium* spp.

Yellowfin sole .... *Pleuronectes asper* (*Limanda aspera*)
Yellow perch .... *Perca flavescens*
Yellowstone cutthroat trout ..... *Oncorhynchus clarki bouvieri*

List of Trees and Shrubs

The colloquial names of plant species have not been fully standardized. The common names of woody species listed below and used in this book follow A. A. Beetle's *Recommended Plant Names*, University of Wyoming Agricultural Experiment Station Journal 31, Laramie, 1970, and S. L. Welsh's *Anderson's Flora of Alaska and Adjacent Parts of Canada*, Brigham Young University Press, Provo, Utah, 1974.

Alaska-cedar . . . . *Chamaecyparis nootkatensis*
Alder . . . . *Alnus* spp.
Ash . . . . *Fraxinus* spp.
Aspen . . . . *Populus* spp.

Baldcypress . . . . *Taxodium distichum*
Bigleaf maple . . . . *Acer macrophyllum*

Ceanothus . . . . *Ceanothus* spp.
Common bladdersenna . . . . *Colutea arborescens*
Common waterwillow . . . . *Decodon verticillatus*

Douglas-fir . . . . *Pseudotsuga menziesii*

Fourwing saltbush . . . . *Atriplex canescens*

Giant sequoia . . . . *Sequoiadendron giganteum*
Golden willow . . . . *Salix aurea*

Juniper . . . . *Juniperus* spp.

Pignut hickory . . . . *Carya glabra*
Ponderosa pine . . . . *Pinus ponderosa*

Quaking aspen . . . . *Populus tremuloides*

Red alder . . . . *Alnus rubra*
Red-osier dogwood . . . . *Cornus stolonifera*
Redwood . . . . *Sequoia sempervirens*
Rhododendron . . . . *Rhododendron macrophyllum*

Salmonberry . . . . *Rubus spectabilis*
Shining willow . . . . *Salix lucida*
Siberian peashrub . . . . *Caragana arborescens*
Silky dogwood . . . . *Cornus amomum*
Sitka spruce . . . . *Picea sitchensis*
Sugar maple . . . . *Acer saccharum*

Symbols and Abbreviations

The Système International d'Unites (SI), the universal system of metric notation, is followed in this book. The SI symbols and other abbreviations listed below are used without further definition in the text. Also undefined are standard mathematical, chemical, and atomic (elemental) symbols and chemical acronyms given in standard dictionaries.

A	ampere	N	north; normal
AC	alternating current	N	sample size
°C	degrees celsius	NS	not significant
	([°Fahrenheit − 32]/1.8)	n	nano (10^{-9}, as a prefix)
cm	centimeter (0.394 inch)	o	ortho (as a chemical prefix)
Co.	Company	P	probability
Corp.	Corporation	p	pico (10^{-12}, as a prefix)
d	day	p	para (as a chemical prefix)
DC	direct current	pH	negative log of hydrogen ion activity
D.C.	District of Columbia		
E	east	R	multivariate correlation or regression coefficient
e	base of natural logarithms (2.71 . . .)	r	univariate correlation or regression coefficient
e.g.	(exempli gratia) for example		
et al.	(et alia) and others	S	siemens (for electrical conductance; = mho, 1/ohm); south
etc.	et cetera		
g	gram (0.0353 ounce)	SD	standard deviation
h	hour	SE	standard error
i.e.	(id est) that is	s	second
Inc.	Incorporated	tonne	metric ton (1,000 kg, 2,200 pounds, 1.1 short tons)
k	kilo (10^3, as a prefix)		
kg	kilogram (2.20 pounds)	UK	United Kingdom
km	kilometer (0.622 mile)	U.S.	United States (as adjective)
L	liter (0.264 gallon, 1.06 quarts)	USA	United States of America
log	logarithm	USSR	Union of Soviet Socialist Republics
Ltd.	Limited	V	volt
M	molar (as a suffix or by itself)	W	watt, west
m	meter (as a suffix or by itself; 1.09 yards, 3.28 feet, 39.4 inches); milli (10^{-3}, as a prefix)	μ	micro (10^{-6}, as a prefix)
		o	degree (angular)
min	minute	%	per cent (per hundred)
mol	mole	‰	per mille (per thousand)

1 hectare = 2.47 acres

Chapter 1

Introduction and Overview

W. R. Meehan

The value of salmonid fishes to the people of North America is well over US$1 billion annually. The demands of commercial fishermen, recreational anglers, and consumers of fish products continually push this value higher. All salmonid species require relatively pristine freshwater habitats during part or all of their life cycles. Most such habitats still available to them are on public lands that have not been heavily developed for agricultural, industrial, or urban purposes. Traditionally, however, public lands have been managed for nonfishery resources, chiefly timber and livestock, and little attention has been paid to the quality of associated aquatic habitats—until recently. During the last 20 years or so, as the great value of fish and other wildlife has become apparent, and as biologists have learned more about the detailed habitat requirements of salmonids and other animal species, the management of public natural resources has begun a fundamental evolution away from maximization of single resources toward optimization of resource complexes. This book is a product of that evolution and, I hope, will reinforce it.

The salmonid resources of western North America depend greatly on the condition of surrounding forests and rangelands. Human management of these lands can have serious effects on aquatic resources, especially when—as now—managers are under increasing pressure to produce more and more commodities and amenities from a given piece of land. This book is based on the premise that one role of management is to keep future options open; one of the book's purposes, therefore, is to help managers and landowners understand the complex interactions of fish and habitat, so that they may deal more effectively with the responsibilities of managing aquatic resources.

The condition of the watersheds that make up forests and rangelands controls the physical and chemical makeup of the streams that drain them and of the lakes that lie within them. The geology, climate, vegetation, soils, topography, hydrology, and other characteristics of watersheds influence the suitability of aquatic habitats for salmon, trout, and char. The habitat requirements of salmonids are rather precise, and activities that affect water quantity, quality, or regimen—either directly or indirectly through various watershed processes—can alter fishery productivity.

Because fish production is influenced by the management of adjacent lands as well as of the streams themselves, protection and maintenance of high-quality fish habitats should be among the goals of all resource managers. Preservation of good existing habitats should have high priority, but many streams have been damaged

Influences of Forest and Rangeland Management on Salmonid Fishes and Their Habitats
American Fisheries Society Special Publication 19:1–15, 1991

and must be repaired. The productivity of streams can be reduced by catastrophic natural processes that occlude spawning gravels or block access by fish (for example), but many stream problems, especially in western North America, have been caused by poor resource management practices of the past. Enough now is known about the habitat requirements of salmonids and about good management practices that further habitat degradation can be prevented, and habitat rehabilitation and enhancement programs can go forward successfully.

Historical Perspective

In the middle of the last century, the resources of western North America were considered by many to be inexhaustible. The fallacy of this idea has been well demonstrated. For example, it took only about 50 years, to the early 1900s, for the livestock industry to completely exploit the vast grasslands of the western USA. Overgrazing had become a serious concern by the late 1920s, but the detrimental effects of livestock grazing continued. Management by allotment became the accepted practice by the mid-1960s, but the effects of grazing on aquatic ecosystems were still given little attention. Only in the 1970s did the importance of riparian vegetation to wildlife receive serious emphasis, and it was still later before the interactions between livestock and fisheries gained notice. The timber and mining industries have had similar histories of rapid exploitation and slow appreciation of other resource values. Ideas and attitudes change slowly, and today—even when the consequences of excessive or improper resource use are known—changes in outlook and policy are extremely slow. Since World War II, demands on natural resources have increased dramatically, and stewardship and wise management are more essential now than ever before.

Since forests and ranges first became used commercially, most of the habitats of salmonid fishes on these lands have been altered in subtle to drastic ways. Activities associated with logging, road construction, mining, and livestock grazing have affected the quality of fish habitat by (for example) changing streambank morphology, producing sediment, altering water temperature, influencing the food supply of rearing fish, and blocking access to spawning areas. Even noncommercial uses such as recreation can have these effects.

Historically, as the nations of North America developed, political support lay with commodity production and short-term economic considerations, not with a more balanced, multiple-use approach to resource management. As the USA and Canada became developed to a considerable extent, people began to take a longer view toward both economics and resource conservation. Public concern for the environment has been expressed in both countries for many years, but most forcefully since the 1960s, and it is now embodied in many laws at all levels of government throughout the USA and Canada. Litigation has increased accordingly as interest groups have begun to influence the course of resource management. Many resource management agencies, educational institutions, and industrial organizations have created and funded programs in response to this increased concern for environmental quality, especially during the last 20 years. They have often worked cooperatively to identify ways in which resources can be used, singly or in combination, with minimal degradation of other resources. Their goal is to prevent habitat damage, rather than to rely on litigation or mitigation to

resolve problems after damage has occurred. Their approach is increasingly integrative and interdisciplinary, as reflected by several recent conferences that addressed interrelations of the many resources found on a piece of land and the effects of resource use and management on these relationships.

Much has been learned during the past 20 years about the effects of forest and rangeland management on salmonid habitats. Some of this information can be found in the published literature, but a considerable amount has not been formally published. Resource management agencies frequently conduct administrative or management studies that are not planned and reported in a research format: monitoring programs, field surveys and inventories, and sampling programs done in connection with other studies. The reports are reviewed internally by the sponsoring agency and then filed. A wealth of information can also be found in theses and dissertations that have not been published as scientific papers. One of the reasons for assembling this book is to bring together much of this unpublished information, which describes failures as well as successes, and to make it available to resource managers, researchers, students, and the interested public.

The Situation Today

Two means of protecting natural stocks of salmonids are available to resource managers—limiting the numbers of fish caught, and maintaining adequate habitats. Harvest regulations address catch limits through actions of regional fishery management councils and other regulatory bodies. A detailed discussion of this aspect of stock protection is outside the scope of this book, but harvest control and habitat management must be addressed simultaneously to assure continued production of salmonid stocks. Because management activities on forest and rangelands have already altered the habitats of salmonids extensively, maintaining productive habitats on most such lands can only be accomplished through a combination of protection, rehabilitation, and enhancement.

Most public lands are now managed to provide multiple benefits, although some are still managed more for dominant uses. Private lands are managed to meet landowners' objectives. Lands of different ownership are often adjacent to each other and intermixed. Streams flow through them without regard to ownership, and although the objectives of private and public owners usually are different, some degree of consistency in management practices is desirable. Private ownership does not carry with it the right to damage public resources. Therefore, a strong case can be made for establishing more standardized habitat-protection criteria that satisfy the needs of both public and private owners. Enhanced understanding of the options available and of the species and habitats affected should bring this objective closer to fruition.

Attempting to address such a broad array of land management issues over a large geographic area presents a paradox: these issues and their interactions are complex, but the solutions to the issues must be simple so they will be broadly applied by people who may not understand all the complexities. This paradox i another reason to seek standardized criteria that can be applied to differe ownerships.

Much is known about how to protect or enhance fish, wildlife, timb livestock, and other resources, but political pressures often result in confl

among resource uses. When several important resources occur in the same management unit, all cannot receive the same degree of attention that proponents of each would like. For example, the best timber stands often occur in valley bottoms adjacent to productive salmonid streams. Because cutting riparian vegetation may cause degradation of stream habitats, maximizing timber removal and maximizing fish production may be incompatible management options. The resource use with the greatest amount of political support will usually receive the most consideration during land-use planning, and the other resources may suffer as a result. Thus advocacy is an important part of resource management, and a certain amount of adversarial politics is likely to accompany most management planning and activity.

From this general and historical background, I turn to an overview of the book's contents. Each of the topics that follow is treated much more completely in one or more subsequent chapters.

Salmonids and Their Environments

Stream Ecosystems

Before the effects of resource management on fish habitat can be measured, we must have a thorough understanding of how the physical, chemical, and biological components of a stream system interact to form and control the habitats of salmonids. From a fishery manager's standpoint, salmonid production is the end product of the energy that is routed through the stream ecosystem by two general processes: photosynthesis within the stream's plant community, and transfer of organic material to the stream from adjacent terrestrial environments. A third source of nutrients in some streams is the carcasses of spawned-out anadromous salmonids.

A stream's channel and energy sources change from headwaters to mouth, and its biological community adapts accordingly. These changes along the stream system are controlled by climate, geology, vegetation, and adjacent land-use practices; consequently they vary considerably among systems.

Salmonid Life Histories and Habitat Requirements

Salmonids need several kinds of habitat during their lifetimes. All salmonids need spawning, incubation, and rearing habitats. Resident populations also need adult feeding habitats; anadromous populations need an estuary and the ocean or a large lake. Migrants must pass through several distinct habitats on their way to and from feeding and breeding areas. The importance of each of these habitat types differs among fish species. Pink and chum salmon fry, for example, migrate to the sea shortly after emerging from the gravels, so they have little need for a freshwater rearing habitat. Resident trout populations, on the other hand, may spend 5 or 6 years in fresh water, and rearing habitat is a major factor in their life cycles. Lakes are important components in the life history of sockeye salmon and some populations of trout and char. Migration routes assume greater importance for anadromous forms than for nonanadromous populations. Management of forests and rangelands can affect all of these habitats, as will be noted later in this and subsequent chapters.

Natural Processes

Salmonid habitats are products of the geology and soils, topography, vegetation, climate, and hydrology of a watershed. For the most part, these watershed characteristics remain fairly constant, and so does the productivity of the aquatic habitats. Any change in these conditions, however, can bring about changes in habitats that may greatly affect fish production. Such changes may be caused by human activities such as logging, road construction, livestock grazing, and mining, or by natural events such as floods, mass soil movements, wind, and fire.

Changes in weather are the primary causes of changes in hydrologic processes. Extreme changes in the amount of precipitation cause floods or droughts that can severely affect other watershed features, including fish habitats. Floods can cause heavy sedimentation of streambeds and damage to channels. Floods also can reposition the large woody debris that helps form pools, provides cover for young fish, and releases nutrients for stream productivity. Abnormally low streamflow can restrict movements of fish and reduce the amount and quality of rearing habitat; shallow and slow-moving water usually is warmer as well.

Mass soil movements usually occur when soils are saturated with water, particularly on steep slopes. When earthflows reach streams, they bring large quantities of sediment to the channel and may scour the streambed down to bedrock. In the area of scour, spawning gravels are lost as well as the cover provided by woody debris, boulders, and undercut banks. Farther downstream, gravels and the fish embryos they contain become smothered with sediment, and habitats used by invertebrate organisms, the primary food of rearing salmonids, becomes degraded.

Strong winds can uproot trees, disturbing the soil, reducing the stabilizing influence of tree roots on steep slopes, and substantially increasing the potential for mass soil movements. Windthrow frequently occurs along streams because winds tend to follow the natural pathways provided by the drainage system. Windthrow may be beneficial if it is moderate and at staggered intervals, because it is the primary source of the large woody debris that is so important to fish productivity. If all the riparian vegetation blows down at once over a long stretch, however, short-term benefits to the stream will be followed by a long-term shortage of wood to replace the debris that washes away or decays.

Natural or "wild" fires can destroy root masses and, like strong winds, lead to slope failure and stream sedimentation. Fire can also alter the nutrient properties of the soil and hence the nutrients available to streams. Destruction of the riparian vegetative canopy opens up streams to increased solar radiation, which can be either harmful or beneficial depending on the background temperature of the water and the degree of change in thermal loading.

The influences of these kinds of natural processes must be well understood before the effects of human activities on forest and rangelands can be evaluated.

Land-Use Activities

Various land-use and management activities can affect salmonid habitats. Although the activities themselves may differ widely, the environmental alterations they produce generally affect fish habitats in similar ways. The effects of increased sedimentation on spawning gravels, for example, will be the same whether the sediment resulted from road construction, logging, mining, or livestock grazing. The same is true for other habitat variables such as water temperature, quantity and distribution of instream cover, channel morphology, and dissolved oxygen concentration.

Timber Harvesting

The timber industry on the west coast of North America essentially began in the middle of the 19th century. By the early 1880s, most timber at the edges of saltwater bays and large rivers had been felled and floated to nearby sawmills. Loggers then began to search for timber farther inland, and streams and rivers became the natural transportation routes to the mills.

Small streams were cleared of obstructions, and splash dams were constructed on many of them. These dams impounded water that was released periodically to sluice logs down the waterways. The surges of water and logs gouged stream channels, destroyed banks, scoured out spawning gravels and incubating salmonid embryos, and caused heavy siltation. When the dams were closed, water flows often were so low that eggs and alevins desiccated and died. Streams were cleared of the large woody debris, boulders, undercut banks, and other forms of cover that we know today are essential components of salmonid habitats. By the late 1800s and early 1900s, hundreds of dams had been constructed; almost any stream that was capable of floating logs was used to float them. Evidence of the early log drives can still be seen today.

The effects of timber harvesting and silvicultural treatments (planting, thinning, burning, mechanical site preparation, and application of chemicals) on stream ecosystems are complex. These activities can influence the productivity of salmonid habitats both positively and negatively, illustrating that the land–water ecosystem must be managed as an integrated whole. Small streams support a large proportion of salmonid production and help maintain habitat quality downstream, but they are also the streams most easily altered by human activities. Timber harvesting may change the distribution of precipitation that reaches the ground (and the evaporation rate from the ground), the amount that is intercepted or evaporated by foliage, and the amount that can be stored in the soil. These hydrological properties, as well as the density of road or surface-drainage networks and the physical structure of the soil, govern the rate and pathways of movement of water to stream channels.

The principal aquatic consequences of timber felling and yarding are changed rates of sediment and nutrient delivery, and altered levels of temperature and dissolved oxygen. Harvest activities on upslope areas can alter soil structure as soils are disturbed, exposed to the elements, compacted, and—in the case of roads—graded and drained. Tree cutting alone can reduce soil strength by eliminating root structures, and the yarding process can expose mineral soil to accelerated surface erosion. Mass soil movements and accelerated runoff are likely results, and streams will be affected as already described. Stream degradation can be relatively long-lasting, and the homogenization of stream channel configurations from harvesting activities is a particularly long-term threat to fish habitats. Therefore, prudent managers strive to minimize soil exposure and compaction, identify and avoid slopes that are at or near their stability thresholds, and maintain vigorous root networks.

The value of maintaining a buffer strip of streamside vegetation to ameliorate the direct effects of logging activities has been well documented. Streamside vegetation stabilizes streambanks and channels, provides cover, and maintains stream temperatures within fairly well-defined limits. When streamside vegetation is removed, summer water temperatures generally increase in direct proportion to the amount of increased sunlight on the water surface. Smaller streams that were completely shaded can warm more, and have greater diel temperature fluctuations, than larger streams once the riparian canopy is removed. The breakdown of streambanks is among the most persistent results of riparian harvesting, and it is among the most difficult to avoid when streamside felling or skidding and cross-stream yarding occur. Therefore, although measures exist for protecting streambanks, often the only way to avoid extensive bank damage is to avoid working in the riparian zone altogether.

Dissolved oxygen concentrations within gravels may drop if logging causes fine organic debris to accumulate on and in streambeds; however, overzealous cleaning of logging debris from stream channels can damage habitats even more. Nutrient concentrations in streams may increase after logging, but usually by moderate amounts and for short periods.

Chemical Applications

Many chemicals are used on forest and rangelands to protect, rehabilitate, or enhance resources. These chemicals can be grouped into three major categories: pesticides, fertilizers, and fire retardants. Chemicals are used to control many specific groups of pests (rodents and fungi, for example), but the majority of pesticides used on forest and rangelands are herbicides and insecticides. Fertilizers are applied to commercial forest lands that are deficient in nitrogen or, less often, in phosphorus. The fire retardants most used today are composed primarily of ammonium compounds.

These toxic chemicals can affect salmonids directly, if they contact the fish, or indirectly, if they reduce the amount of riparian cover, the abundance of insects that fish eat, or otherwise change fish habitats. Most chemicals are applied from aircraft, and their most common route of entry to streams and lakes is by aerial drift from target areas during application. Chemicals that settle in ephemeral channels also may be washed into permanent streams during freshets. Lesser amounts move into stream channels by overland flow and leaching.

Once chemicals enter the water, they may bioaccumulate throughout the food chain from bacteria and algae through invertebrate animals to fish at one or more trophic levels. Potential direct and indirect toxic effects must be carefully considered when chemical applications to a watershed are planned, particularly if the applications will be by aerial spraying.

Road Construction and Maintenance

Forest transportation systems can harm salmonids and their habitats because of the sediments they release to streams. Sediment generated by road construction reaches streams through surface erosion and mass movements of destabilized soil, and the effects can be dramatic and long-lasting.

Thorough reconnaissance, good planning, and wise route selection are the keys to minimizing the impacts of roads on streams; ad hoc protective steps taken during or after construction are much less effective. After the route is selected, measures to reduce erosion can be incorporated into the road design. Excavations should be minimized. Cut-and-fill slopes should be stabilized with vegetation or artificial structures. Bridges and drainage structures such as culverts should be properly placed and appropriately sized to accommodate runoff. The timing of construction with respect to seasonal watershed dynamics can be especially critical. Completed roads should be kept in good condition with an active maintenance program.

Bridges and culverts can block fish migrations, and this is one of the most serious difficulties for fish in western forests; one poorly designed and installed culvert can affect the fish population of an entire stream drainage. Common problems include outfall drops that are too great, lack of resting pools below culverts, and excessive water velocities through or insufficient water depth within culverts. Bridges usually disturb streams less than culverts do, but they may be uneconomical or impractical on low-volume forest roads; culverts then become necessary. Culverts must be big enough to pass maximum flows, and a single large culvert is usually preferable to several smaller ones.

Water Transportation and Storage of Logs

Most logs are stored and transported on land today, but water still is used for these purposes in some areas. Extensive river drives are no longer common, but large rafts of logs may be stored in big rivers and in saltwater bays and coves until they are towed or barged to the mills. Much bark is lost when logs are dumped into the water and hoisted back out onto barges or at mill sites, and the sometimes extensive accumulations of bark on the bottom of a bay or river sharply raises the local biochemical oxygen demand in the water. Marine shellfish may be adversely affected by these debris mats, and salmonids may be indirectly affected by a reduction in the benthic invertebrate populations that are a major source of food. The logs themselves can physically disrupt habitats if they are stored or moved in shallow water or if they break free of confinement and become grounded along the shoreline.

It is best to avoid storing and transporting logs on water whenever these functions can be accomplished on land without other harm to aquatic habitats. If such operations have to be conducted on water, they should be sited away from sensitive habitats, logs should be eased (not dumped) into the water, dislodged bark should be collected and properly disposed of, and logs should be rafted in bundles that are made up before logs are placed into the water.

Processing Mills

Since the early days of the timber industry, many western sawmills and pulp and paper mills have been located on saltwater bays, on tidal estuaries, or near the mouths of large rivers. These aquatic areas are important to anadromous salmonids for feeding, rearing, and migration to and from the sea. Thus, the fish frequently come into contact with effluents from the mills.

How mill wastes affect salmonids depends on the volume and concentration of pollutants, the degree to which the wastes have been treated, the ability of the estuary or river to dilute the discharge, the behavior of the fish populations exposed to the effluent, and the duration of exposure. Poorly treated effluents and accidental spills of waste can be acutely or sublethally toxic to fish and to the organisms that support them, and the toxicants can bioaccumulate throughout the food chain. Mill wastes can affect the reproduction, physiology (including white and red blood cell counts), growth, and behavior of salmonids.

Treated mill effluents often have elevated concentrations of nitrogen and phosphorus. At low concentrations in nutrient-poor waters, these nutrients can enhance algal and periphyton populations and thus increase total system productivity. At high concentrations, however, they stimulate so much algal growth that spawning grounds and invertebrate habitats are smothered. The best defenses against effluent toxicity and eutrophication are to treat mill wastes properly and to take all possible precautions against accidental waste spills.

Livestock Grazing

Wherever livestock grazing occurs in western North America, it poses a potential threat to the integrity of salmonid habitats. The literature amply demonstrates that improper livestock grazing degrades streams, riparian environments, and fish populations. On uplands, soil is compacted and the vegetative composition is changed, which increase runoff and erosion. Closer to the stream, streambank vegetation and stability decline when livestock concentrate near water. The combination of upland erosion, loss of riparian canopies, and breakdown of streambanks lowers local water tables and causes streams to become wider but more shallow, warmer in summer but colder in winter, and poorer in instream structure but richer in nutrients and bacterial populations. All these effects can adversely influence salmonid populations.

Research has also shown that aquatic ecosystems are resilient and can restore themselves over time if properly protected under intensive livestock management programs; the cost of this protection is generally less than would be required for installation of artificial stream-improvement structures. The challenge is to identify and develop grazing systems that are compatible with local aquatic habitats and to persuade landowners and livestock managers to implement them. Persuasion has been difficult, and change has occurred slowly. Existing laws, regulations, manuals, land-use plans, and allotment guides have not enabled land management agencies to fully protect and restore aquatic habitats affected by livestock grazing. Stronger management direction for these agencies is needed.

Mining

Mining on public lands has had high legislative priority for well over a century. Although mining retains this priority, mining activities now must meet official water quality standards that protect aquatic environments in most areas—although work force limitations make monitoring and enforcing these regulations difficult. In addition, a plan outlining potential environmental damage and proposed rehabilitation usually is required before permission to mine a site is granted. Posting of a reclamation performance bond to cover damages is also necessary.

Many mining methods exist, and the one selected depends primarily on the mineral sought and site-specific conditions such as the amount of overburden.

Effects on aquatic environments vary with the method used, the toxicity of minerals present, and the manner in which mine waste piles, haul roads, tailings ponds, stockpiles, and processing plants are developed and operated. Pollution from abandoned mines can be as serious as pollution from active mines, and it can continue for decades after a mine is abandoned.

Mining can pollute streams and lakes by releasing suspended and bed-load sediments, toxic heavy metals, and acids, and it often causes changes in stream channels and water flow. Suspended sediment reduces light penetration and thus photosynthesis and primary production, delays fish migration, disrupts fish feeding and thus growth, interferes with respiration through the gills, and increases gill irritation and thus infection by fungi and bacteria. Deposition of excessive bedload sediment eliminates habitats for the invertebrates on which fish feed, reduces the permeability of spawning gravels, and blocks the interchange of subsurface and surface waters. Sediments contain nutrients such as nitrogen and phosphorus that can, when in excess, cause blooms of undesirable algal and plankton species. Sediments can also act as a sink for metals; bottom-feeding aquatic insects concentrate these metals and move them into the food chain.

Acid is a major pollutant from mine drainage. The alkaline soils that occur in much of western North America can ameliorate some but not all of the potential damage from acid drainage, and precautions should be taken to restrict the amount of drainage from the mine site or to treat effluents. At low pH levels, sensitive species may be eliminated, whereas tolerant, less-desirable species may proliferate; overall, the density and diversity of aquatic organisms is reduced. As acidity increases, so does the incidence of abnormal fish behavior, and the reproductive capacity of adult salmonids, as well as the viability of eggs and alevins, is reduced. Although the effects of sublethal acidity are not cumulative in fish, they reduce the ability of fish to detoxify other poisons such as heavy metals.

During some types of mining, vegetation is stripped off the land or streams are dredged or channelized. These disruptions of land and channel increase sedimentation rates in streams, produce higher peak flows during storm runoffs, and reduce base flows during dry periods. Streamflows decrease when water is diverted for milling and mining operations.

Mitigative techniques for mining are like those for other activities that disrupt lands and streams. Access roads should be constructed properly. Drainage from waste heaps and settling ponds should be controlled, and effluents should be treated whenever possible. Stripped lands and degraded streams should be rehabilitated at the first opportunity. The costs of these treatments are markedly reduced if mining operations are planned from the beginning with pollution control and environmental recovery in mind.

Recreation

Fishing is a major recreational use of lakes and streams, but many other activities—swimming, boating, hiking, riding, camping—can damage riparian and aquatic habitats as well. The most effective control of such damage lies with managing access to streams and concentrations of people along them. Both access and concentration are strongly influenced by other, concurrent uses of watershed resources. For example, logging roads lead recreationists into backcountry areas that might otherwise be inaccessible, and the placement of those roads—whether they cross streams frequently or infrequently, whether they run along ridgetops or valley bottoms—determines in large measure the kinds and intensity of uses that will be made of streams. Thus, planning and managing recreation require a multiresource perspective if aquatic habitats are to be protected and if user conflicts are to be prevented or resolved.

Fish and Habitat Management

Salmonid Responses to Habitat Change

As the preceding accounts have shown, diverse activities on forest and rangelands can affect salmonid habitats in broadly similar ways. The responses of salmonid populations to these changes, however, vary with species, life stage, season, and geographic location, complicating the management of fish resources in altered streams and lakes. For example, a summer temperature increase may enhance coho salmon production in a northern stream but depress it in a southern one. Adults often can avoid conditions that kill less-mobile young. Anadromous and resident populations may respond differently to a habitat change. Species that rear in fresh water may react one way to a perturbation, species that only spawn and incubate there another. These many differences mean that resource managers must be both knowledgeable about the populations in their care and flexible in their management prescriptions.

Habitat Rehabilitation and Enhancement

Protection of aquatic habitats should be the primary goal of resource managers. However, managers also need rehabilitation techniques to enhance the natural recovery processes of disturbed rivers and streams.

Fish habitats have been rehabilitated and enhanced for over 50 years. Many techniques now used on western waters stem from successful work on trout streams in eastern and central North America, although much trial and error was needed to adapt them to the more variable hydrology of western streams. These methods of habitat management are ecologically sound but sometimes expensive. Enough now is known about the biology and habitat requirements of salmonids, and about the pitfalls of various rehabilitation techniques, that habitat management can be more effective than previously. It should be reiterated, however, that habitat protection should always be the primary goal of responsible land managers.

Fundamental to habitat management is identification and mitigation of limiting factors—factors that limit production. Limiting factors differ among species and life stages, and change over space and time. They are always present, even in unmodified ecosystems; when one limit is relieved, another comes into play, and several can act simultaneously. Examples are summer temperature, winter flow, abundance of spawning gravel, amount of cover, and accessibility to key habitats. Most aquatic habitat management deals with limiting factors that have been imposed by human activities in a watershed. Sometimes, however, habitats can be altered to enhance fish production even in unexploited watersheds.

Instream habitat improvements can significantly increase the abundance of salmon and trout. Common techniques are to clean, trap, or emplace gravels that improve spawning opportunities, to install woody debris or other structures that increase the amount of cover for young fish, and to remove or surmount barriers that impede access to habitats. Some improvements serve several purposes simultaneously. For example, a properly installed series of gabions can enhance spawning and rearing areas, reduce streambank erosion, and improve fish passage.

Evidence increasingly shows that the quality and quantity of winter habitats control the production of salmonid smolts in some stream systems. Intermittent side pools, back channels, and other areas of relatively still water are especially valuable overwintering areas for juveniles. Where stream gradients are not low enough for such slow-water areas to occur, such as along the Pacific coast, construction of ponds and side channels adjacent to streams has considerable potential for enhancing salmonid abundance.

Stream improvement techniques would evolve faster if more projects were thoroughly evaluated and if more evaluations were made accessible to others. Many costly mistakes have been repeated because earlier projects had not been evaluated at all or the evaluations had ended prematurely. These shortcomings usually are attributed to lack of funds and personnel, but short-term savings have created great long-term costs in terms of both money and management ability. Evaluation should be an integral part of most habitat improvement projects, and it should be planned and budgeted before projects begin.

Systemwide Management

Economic Considerations

In recent years, commercial salmon fishing in the western USA and Canada has grossed US$300–700 million annually, and the wholesale market value of finished salmon products has exceeded $1 billion. The economic importance of recreational fishing is more difficult to measure, because there are no market prices comparable to those of commercial fishing, but annual expenditures for salmon sportfishing in the northwestern USA have been estimated at upwards of $160 million. Subsistence fishing, especially by Native Americans along the north Pacific coast, is an important economic consideration, as are the employment and other economic benefits that fishing brings to thousands of people in associated and support industries.

Because each watershed contains a complex mix of tangible resources (water, fish, land, wildlife, timber, grass, minerals) and intangible ones (recreational opportunities, esthetic and existence values), managers should try to increase the total net value of all resource uses. But some uses—fishing, timber harvest, and livestock grazing, for example—may affect the potential values of others, and optimal management of forests and rangelands must establish a balance among competing uses. To achieve this, managers need to know the net values of fisheries and other resources as well as the more easily measured values of timber and livestock products. As with all natural resources, the net commercial and recreational value of a given stream habitat varies from place to place because of local geographic and economic factors.

The actual choice of management policies may be severely constrained by political requirements established at local, state, provincial, federal, or international levels. Such limitations may, in turn, constrain the economic objectives of management. Nevertheless, managers must achieve the most efficient possible use of natural habitats by balancing net economic values among the various resource uses, and by distributing the economic gains fairly among resource users.

Planning

All resource management programs should be carefully planned, whether they relate to stream sections, watersheds, or entire forests. It is in the planning stage that management objectives and procedures are determined, political and economic constraints are accommodated, and cooperation among participating individuals and agencies is established. If projects are not carefully planned, they are likely to go over budget, to encounter unexpected opposition from governmental or public groups, and to fall well short of expectations.

Most management agencies now have comprehensive planning protocols that incorporate issue identification, data collection, examination of management alternatives, plan implementation, monitoring, and evaluation. Although the planning steps are broadly similar among agencies and projects, the complexity of each step increases rapidly with the size of a project. Large projects such as multiuse forest management typically require several years to plan and implement.

Now that many public lands have been designated for multiple-use management and managers generally are required by law to consider the broad environmental implications of their work, planning allows resource advocates to press their case in forums that once were closed to them. Until recently, for example, fishery matters were rarely considered when logging, grazing, or mining permits were issued. Today, fishery biologists and managers and the fishing public usually can make fish and their habitats integral parts of systemwide management plans. Indeed, planners do well to seek out and involve all interested parties, for months or years of hard work can be compromised by an influential agency's last-minute veto or a public group's expensive litigation.

With enhanced opportunities to influence resource plans and policies come several obligations. One is to persevere through the long planning process. It does little good to inject a resource issue into a plan at an early stage if one is not around later to defend it when inevitable compromises have to be made with other resource users. Another obligation is to be well informed. If a resource's social and economic values cannot be stated convincingly, and if the resource's needs cannot be presented clearly and in detail, that resource is unlikely to fare well when the final plan is implemented. Finally, one must develop public and governmental constituencies for one's resource or position. Planning is partly politics, and a chorus is more likely to be heeded than a solo voice.

Management Principles

A good fisheries or fish habitat management progam should consist of three major components: planning, implementation, and evaluation. All too often in the past, fish habitat management prescriptions or projects have been carried out without adequate planning and follow-up evaluation to determine whether or not the program accomplished the objectives for which it was designed.

The planning stage may well be the most important part of the management process. In the planning stage, the objectives of the management program as they relate to fish and fish habitat productivity must be clearly defined and stated, and procedures to track the management plan must be identified to ensure that the stated objectives retain their visibility during the implementation phase. Careful consideration must be given during the planning phase to projected costs and benefits of the program to assure that it can be accomplished in a cost-effective manner. It is important that not only fishery biologists, but personnel in other related disciplines are included in the planning process. Potential users of the fisheries resources, as well as users of other resources that may be influenced by the management program, should be brought into the planning process at its beginning to ensure that support for the program is established and will continue throughout its implementation.

At the end of a specific short-term operation, such as a stream rehabilitation project, or at intervals throughout a longer-term management scheme, the results of the program should be evaluated. If interim evaluation of a long-range program indicates that the stated objectives are not being met, the plan should be revised—or terminated if no other reasonable procedures can be identified. Thorough evaluation will determine whether or not the specific management plan was successful; if it was, future projects with similar objectives will be more readily accepted by users and agency administrators, and if it was not, time, effort, and funds will not be wasted on additional programs that will probably end in similar failure.

For broad management activities related to fish and fish habitat productivity that could affect the aquatic system, such as timber harvest or livestock grazing, the entire watershed or drainage basin should be considered, rather than merely the specific reaches of a stream adjacent to a planned activity. A management activity in the area of a headwater tributary, for example, may not have undesirable effects on the adjacent stream reach, but the cumulative effects of several similar activities in adjacent subbasins on downstream aquatic habitats may be significant.

The basic premise for any fisheries or fish habitat management program should be that protecting the habitat from any management effects that would degrade it is preferable to mitigating the effects or rehabilitating the habitat after resource damage has occurred. Habitat protection is generally less costly in the long run than habitat restoration, and is usually effective in maintaining the quality and productivity of the habitat; rehabilitation of damaged habitat may not necessarily restore it fully to its original condition.

Summary

The interrelations among salmonid fishes and their habitats are complex; the cumulative effects of seemingly insignificant habitat alterations, whether caused by natural processes or by human activities, can dramatically change the diversity and productivity of fish populations. Before intelligent decisions can be made about the effects that uses and management of forest and rangeland resources have on fish and their habitats, managers must understand these interrelations and the potential consequences of manipulating them.

In this introductory chapter, I have discussed very generally the potential conflicts between forest and rangeland use and salmonid habitat productivity. The following chapters address the specific influences of resource management on salmonid habitats and, when possible, provide guidelines for uses that are compatible with optimum productivity of salmonid habitats. The extensive reference section will help resource managers and other interested readers to locate sources of further information on the various aspects of resource use and management.

Chapter 2

Stream Ecosystems

M. L. Murphy and W. R. Meehan

Like every area of nature where living organisms interact with their environment in an exchange of energy and materials, a stream is an ecological system, or ecosystem, composed of a biological community, the community's resources, and its physical and chemical context (Warren 1971). Activities of the stream community, as it carries out photosynthesis, consumption, and decomposition, direct the flow of energy from sunlight and organic matter through the food web. As predators, salmonids are influenced by energy-flow processes operating at all levels in the stream ecosystem, from primary production to decomposition, as well as by physical conditions of the habitat.

To best manage salmonid habitat, a full understanding is needed of the ecosystem processes that underlie stream productivity. Use of the land frequently affects both physical and biological conditions in streams, and effects on salmonid populations depend on changes in physical habitat as well as on changes in lower trophic levels. Thus, streamside management must take into account both physical and energy-flow processes of stream ecosystems in any effort to maintain or enhance salmonid habitats. In this chapter, we describe (1) the structure, function, and dynamics of stream ecosystems, (2) relationships between ecosystem processes and salmonid populations, and (3) implications of these relationships for managing salmonid habitats.

Ecosystem Structure and Function

Every ecosystem has structure and function. Structure of an ecosystem refers to the arrangement of its three components—the biological community, energy and material resources, and physical habitat—in relation to one another. Function of an ecosystem refers to the collection of biological, chemical, and physical processes that govern the flow of energy and material through the ecosystem.

Structure of a stream's biological community can be described in terms of ecological dominance (Colinvaux 1973), species diversity (Reger and Kevern 1981), or various other models. Ecosystem productivity, however, is best addressed if structure and function are considered simultaneously. Classification of organisms into functional groups (Cummins 1973) accomplishes this by relating the organisms directly to processes of energy flow. Members of each functional group perform a similar process (Figure 2.1). Plants fix energy from sunlight, and fungi and bacteria decompose organic matter. Consumer functional groups,

17

Influences of Forest and Rangeland Management on Salmonid Fishes and Their Habitats
American Fisheries Society Special Publication 19:17–46, 1991

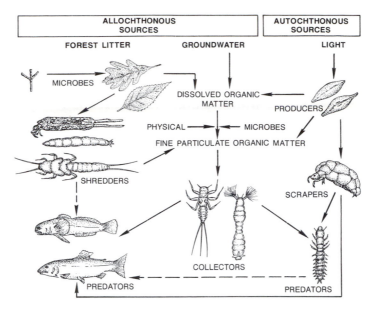

FIGURE 2.1.—Energy sources for, energy-flow pathways in, and the trophic structure of woodland stream ecosystems. Deciduous leaves, photosynthesis by diatoms, and dissolved organic matter in groundwater are major energy sources. Genera that typify consumer functional groups are the shredders *Pteronarcys* (above), *Tipula*, and *Pycnopsyche*; the collectors *Stenonema* (left) and *Simulium*; the scraper *Glossosoma*; and the predators *Nigronia* (lower right), *Cottus*, and *Salmo* (left). Litter microbes are characterized by hyphomycetes fungi. The dashed arrow indicates infrequent exchange. Organisms are not drawn to scale. (Adapted from Cummins 1974; reproduced with permission from the American Institute of Biological Sciences.)

including invertebrates and fish, use energy from plants and microbes and are grouped according to how they feed (Table 2.1). Shredders chew large particles like leaves of terrestrial plants or aquatic macrophytes, scrapers rasp periphyton or microbes from rock or wood substrate, and collectors filter suspended fine particles from the water or gather particles from deposits. Predators obtain energy by preying on other consumer groups, as well as on terrestrial animals that fall into the stream.

Various types of organic matter and inorganic nutrients stored in or passing through the stream form the resource component of ecosystem structure (Figure 2.1). By convention, organic matter is grouped according to particle size: dissolved organics (<0.5 μm), fine particulates (0.5 μm–1 mm), and coarse particulates (>1 mm). Because of its physical effects on channel morphology, large woody debris (>10 cm in diameter) is often considered separately. Any separation of organic matter by size is arbitrary, because particle sizes form a continuum ranging from molecules in solution to large woody debris.

The physical and chemical features of an ecosystem's structure provide the framework for development of the biological community and its resources. A stream's physical habitat is determined mainly by associated hill slopes and riparian vegetation (Sullivan et al. 1987). The principal factors that control channel morphology are water discharge, sediment load, solid elements such as

TABLE 2.1.—Consumer functional groups of stream animals. (Adapted from Cummins 1973; Merritt and Cummins 1978.)

Functional group	Subdivision based on feeding mechanisms or dominant food	Representative taxa
Shredders	Detritivores: decaying vascular plant tissue	Trichoptera (*Hydatophylax*, Lepidostomatidae) Plecoptera (Peltoperlidae, Pteronarcidae) Diptera (*Holorusia*)
	Herbivores: living vascular plant tissue	Trichoptera (*Phryganea, Leptocerus*) Lepidoptera (Pyralidae) Coleoptera (Chrysomelidae) Diptera (*Polypedilum, Lemnaphila*)
Scrapers	Rock substrate	Ephemeroptera (Heptageniidae, Baetidae, Ephemerellidae) Trichoptera (Glossosomatidae, *Neophylax*) Lepidoptera (*Parargyractis*) Coleoptera (Psephenidae) Diptera (Thaumaleidae, Deuterophlebiidae)
	Wood substrate	Ephemeroptera (Caenidae, Leptophlebiidae) Trichoptera (*Heteroplectron*) Snails (*Juga*)
Collectors	Filter feeders	Ephemeroptera (*Isonychia*) Trichoptera (Hydropsychidae, Brachycentridae) Diptera (Simuliidae, *Rheotanytarsus*, Culicidae)
	Deposit feeders	Ephemeroptera (Ephemeridae, *Baetis, Paraleptophlebia*) Diptera (Chironomini, Psychodidae)
Predators	Swallowers of whole animals	Odonata Plecoptera (Perlidae) Megaloptera Trichoptera (Rhyacophilidae) Coleoptera (Amphizoidae) Diptera (Tanypodinae, Empididae) Fish (salmonids) Birds (kingfishers, mergansers) Mammals (otters, bears)
	Piercers of tissue fluids	Hemiptera (Belastomatidae, Notonectidae) Coleoptera (Dytiscidae) Diptera (Tabanidae)

woody debris, bedrock, and boulders, and bank characteristics. Flowing water and sediment mold the channel around the resistant solid elements. Stream channels are shaped primarily during storms, when flow is high enough to move sediment lining the channel bed. Scoured areas become pools in nonstorm periods, and depositional areas become riffles. Stable channels are in dynamic equilibrium where streams balance sediment influx by carrying sediment away.

Pools and riffles may change location, but an average balance of channel features is maintained.

The physical consequences of large woody debris are particularly important to salmonids (Bisson et al. 1987; Sullivan et al. 1987). Large woody debris, especially trees that have fallen into the stream with root wads still anchored to the streambank, provides physical structure that creates pools and undercut banks, deflects and breaks up streamflow, and stabilizes the stream channel. Woody debris benefits all life stages of salmonids. Although log jams sometimes block spawning migrations of adult salmon, debris usually aids migration by creating pools and cover where salmon can rest and conserve energy for spawning. By forming small dams, debris helps to prevent spawning gravels from washing downstream. For juveniles, the slack water around debris offers good opportunities for drift feeding, and debris provides essential cover from predators and from freshets of autumn and winter.

The stream and terrestrial ecosystems are closely linked. The flow of water, sediment, nutrients, and organic matter from the surrounding watershed shapes physical habitats and supplies energy and nutrient resources for the stream community. Riparian vegetation strengthens streambanks, contributes woody debris, and governs the influx of light and organic matter to the stream. Along the continuum from headwaters to lowland rivers, the terrestrial influence weakens as water discharge and sediment load increase and physical structures become less common. Generally, headwater streams are confined by valley walls and shaped by bedrock, woody debris, and coarse sediment; lowland rivers meander across floodplains of fine sediment and are shaped by scour and deposition at meander bends (Sullivan et al. 1987). As streams widen, the canopy opens to allow more light, and the importance of riparian litter to the stream's energy base decreases, outweighed by the influx of residual organic matter from upstream.

Thus, the stream fauna and flora, organic matter and nutrients, and the physical and chemical environment form the structure of a dynamic, open ecosystem, closely linked to riparian vegetation and changing progressively from headwaters to river mouth. Energy from sunlight and organic matter flows into, through, and out of the ecosystem; by processing these inputs, the stream community obtains energy for activity, growth, and reproduction.

Energy Sources

Energy becomes available to the stream community from two main sources: photosynthesis by aquatic plants in the stream itself (autochthonous sources) and decomposition of organic matter imported from outside the stream (allochthonous sources) (Figure 2.1). The mix of energy sources has a major influence on the structure and function of stream ecosystems.

Autochthonous Sources

Aquatic plants occur in three basic forms—phytoplankton, periphyton, and vascular macrophytes—each requiring different habitats and sending its energy through different pathways in the ecosystem (Wetzel 1975). Each form characterizes streams of different size, gradient, and exposure to sunlight.

TABLE 2.2.—General distribution of stream and river flora in relation to current velocity. (Adapted from Wetzel 1975.)

Basic form	Current velocity (m/s)	Representative taxa
Phytoplankton	<1	Diatoms (*Stephanodiscus*) Green algae (*Ankistrodesmus*)
Periphyton	≤1	Diatoms (*Navicula, Eunotia*) Macroalgae (*Chara, Ulothrix*)
	>1	Diatoms (*Achnanthes, Meridion*) Macroalgae (*Cladophora, Hildengrandia*)
Vascular macrophytes	0.2–1	*Elodea, Hippuris, Potamogeton*
	0.5–2	*Ranunculus, Apium, Fontinalis*

"True" phytoplankton is normally restricted to slow-flowing rivers and sloughs, and typically does not occur in small streams. In streams, nearly all suspended algae are the detached and drifting cells of benthic algae (Swanson and Bachmann 1976). Centric diatoms and small green algae represent the true phytoplankton of slow rivers (Table 2.2). Plankton is often flushed downstream as the river rises, and most plankton production is used by collectors.

Periphyton consists of algae attached to the stream bottom and submerged debris, usually with bacteria, fungi, and adherent organic matter in a complex association called "aufwuchs." Periphyton has two forms: macroalgae (green, blue-green, and red algae) that have filamentous, sheet, or mat-like morphology; and unicellular algae, especially diatoms, that form thin, cohesive layers on stream substrates. Macroalgae usually dominate in low-gradient, open streams, whereas diatoms dominate in higher-gradient, shaded streams (Minshall 1978). Species and growth forms usually change seasonally and segregate according to water velocity (Table 2.2).

Macroalgae generally produce maximum biomass in spring and early summer, and subsequently die and detach from the streambed in late summer and autumn (Minshall 1978). Macroalgae often accumulate during periods of low streamflow when velocity slows, and then wash downstream as streamflow rises. Even in slow currents, the underlying layers of a thick algal mat will decay, allowing the mat to float away (Naiman 1976). Daily net production of macroalgae (Table 2.3) ranges from about 300 mg C/m^2 in a forest stream in summer to over 3,000 mg C/m^2 in a Mohave Desert stream. Macroalgae generally are not harvested by invertebrates. Some blue-green algae are avoided by consumers because they produce toxins, and many are poorly digested and provide poor nutrition (Arnold 1971). Although some invertebrates readily consume macroalgae, most production by these plants is consumed as detritus after the algae die (Minshall 1978).

Periphytic diatoms are usually kept at a low standing biomass by stream scour, invertebrate grazing, and forest shade (Minshall 1978). Because diatoms reproduce rapidly (i.e., they have a fast turnover), however, their production is often many times greater than their standing biomass. The consumer biomass supported by diatom production may be more than 15 times the standing biomass of diatoms (McIntire 1973). Peak diatom production generally is in spring before riparian vegetation leafs out and in autumn after leaves have fallen. Daily net production

TABLE 2.3.—Daily net primary production (gross photosynthesis minus respiration) of macroalgae and periphytic diatoms in various streams. Dominant taxa, if reported, are in parentheses.

Site (dominant taxon)	Net primary production (mg C/m^2)	Reference
Macroalgae		
Mature hemlock and spruce forest, southeast Alaska, Jul, third-order stream (*Ulothrix*)	324	Murphy (1984)
Sonoran desert, Arizona, Jul–Aug (*Cladophora*)	907	Busch and Fisher (1981)[a]
Thermal artesian stream, Mohave desert, California, annual average (*Oscillatoria*)	3,250	Naiman (1976)[a]
Periphytic diatoms		
Mature Douglas-fir forest, western Cascade Mountains, Oregon, seasonal range: winter–summer		
First-order stream	0–267	Naiman and
Third-order stream	200–400	Sedell (1980)[a]
Mature hemlock and spruce forest, Carnation Creek, Vancouver Island, British Columbia, 2-year average (*Achnanthes*)	170	Stockner and Shortreed (1976)[a]
Southeast Alaska, Jul–Aug, first- to second-order streams		
Mature hemlock–spruce forest	467–640	Duncan and
4-year-old clear-cut	589–837	Brusven (1985b)[a]
12-year-old clear-cut	595–795	

[a] Authors' data reported as ash-free dry matter (AFDM) or in oxygen units were converted to mg carbon by the equations 1 mg AFDM = 0.5 mg C, and 1 mg O_2 = 2.7 mg C.

of periphytic diatoms in small forest streams (Table 2.3) is lowest in winter and averages 200–650 mg C/m^2 in summer. Most diatom production is used by invertebrates that scrape the diatom film or collect detached cells.

Invertebrates that scrape the diatom film can limit primary production and affect species composition of the algae. Snails, caddisflies, and isopods can graze periphyton to such a low standing biomass that primary production is reduced (Elwood and Nelson 1972; Lamberti and Resh 1983; Murphy 1984). An increase in algal productivity per unit biomass partially offsets the decrease in biomass because remaining algae compete less for light and nutrients. Grazers also can influence the kinds of algae that make up periphyton. Heavy grazing, for example, prevents filamentous algae from becoming established (Jacoby 1985). Some caddisflies (*Leucotrichia* spp.) actively remove the blue-green *Microcoleus* alga without ingesting it, thereby preventing it from encroaching on preferred diatoms (Hart 1985).

Diatoms that detach from the streambed are strained from the water by filter feeders like the net-spinning caddisfly *Hydropsyche* sp. or are collected after they settle by deposit feeders like the chironomid *Paratendipes* sp. (Hawkins and Sedell 1981). Such detached algae are important food for invertebrates, and the chlorophyll content of fine detritus is a good indicator of high food quality.

Drifting diatoms are often of paramount importance to net-spinning caddisflies (Fuller and Mackay 1981), and growth of deposit-feeding chironomids may increase sharply after a diatom bloom (Ward and Cummins 1979).

Vascular macrophytes have four main growth habits: emergents rooted below water but with aerial leaves, such as cattails (*Typha* spp.); floating-leaved plants with submerged roots, such as water lilies (*Nuphar* spp.); unattached plants, such as duckweed (*Lemna* spp.); and submerged plants attached to the stream bottom, such as river weeds (*Potamogeton* spp.) (Westlake 1975). Macrophyte species and growth forms, like those of periphyton, segregate according to water velocity (Table 2.2). A river may be lined by emergents, have floating-leaved plants in shallow water, and have submerged plants in midstream. Macrophytes commonly dominate in low-gradient streams with open canopies. Mosses (*Fontinalis* spp.) are the only abundant macrophytes in small, densely shaded streams, but also are abundant in some fast rivers (Naiman and Sedell 1980). Emergent parts of live macrophytes are consumed by invertebrates, but submerged parts generally are not consumed because of their tough cell walls, lignified structures, and low nitrogen contents (Gregory 1983). Peak production of macrophytes is in spring and early summer. Most of this production remains intact and accumulates until the plant dies in late summer and autumn, when it becomes available to consumers as detritus (Mann 1975; Minshall 1978). Macrophytes decompose faster than terrestrial leaves: dead macrophytes lose about 50% of their weight in a week, compared to 5–25% for terrestrial leaves (Anderson and Sedell 1979).

Allochthonous Sources

Outside sources contribute allochthonous organic matter to a stream by four main pathways: litterfall from streamside vegetation; groundwater seepage; soil erosion; and fluvial transport from upstream (Figure 2.1). Animal activities, such as migrations of anadromous salmonids (and decay of their carcasses if they die), also can provide important amounts of organic matter and nutrients in some streams. Organic matter from these sources differs in when and how it enters the stream, how it decays, and where it predominates.

Litter from streamside vegetation.—Streamside vegetation provides large quantities of organic matter when leaves, needles, and woody debris fall or blow into the stream. In temperate regions, leaves and needles are shed in annual cycles (Figure 2.2; Anderson and Sedell 1979), whereas woody debris enters the stream at irregular intervals as whole trees or branches are felled by wind and bank erosion (Bisson et al. 1987). Leaves and needles usually contribute most of the readily usable organic matter in woodland streams, often more than 1 kg/m^2 annually (Table 2.4).

Leaves and needles decay in four phases: they are leached by water, conditioned by microbes, and shredded by invertebrates and physical abrasion; then residual fine particles are recycled within the benthic food chain by microbes and invertebrates (Figure 2.3). Rate of decay depends on chemical composition and is directly related to temperature (Figure 2.4). Generally, the greater the nitrogen and phosphorus content, the faster leaves and needles decay (Kaushik and Hynes 1971). Differences in temperature can override chemical composition because decay-resistant leaves, such as those of white oak, decay faster in warm water

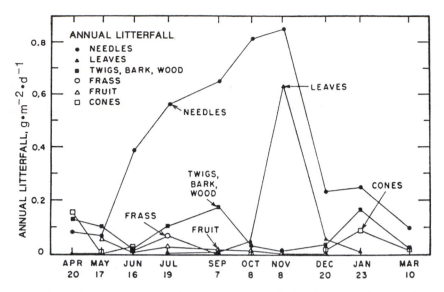

FIGURE 2.2.—Seasonal inputs of various types of riparian litter into a first-order woodland stream in western Oregon. (Adapted from Sedell et al. 1974.)

than do more labile leaves in cold water. Pignut hickory leaves lose about 50% of their weight in the first month in a stream at 5°C but nearly 100% at 20°C.

During the first few days, leaves lose about 15% of their weight as soluble matter is leached into the stream (Figure 2.3; Petersen and Cummins 1974). With a carbon:nitrogen (C:N) ratio less than 5:1, leachate is highly labile and about 80% is quickly assimilated by stream bacteria. Hourly microbial uptake of leachate during autumn ranges from 16 to 207 mg/m^2 of streambed (Wallis 1981) and may be greater than 1 g/m^2 during a large input of leachate (Lush and Hynes 1978). Leachate is taken up faster from deciduous leaves than from coniferous needles. Almost all (98%) red alder leachate, for example, is removed from the water within 2 d, whereas only 35–60% of Douglas-fir leachate is removed in that time (Dahm 1984). The more resistant compounds are gradually depleted over several

TABLE 2.4.—Annual inputs of leaf and needle litter into small woodland streams. Annual inputs are in terms of total dry matter (DM) or ash-free dry matter (AFDM) per square meter of streambed.

Stream	Annual input (g/m^2)	Reference
WS10, western Oregon	912 (DM)	Sedell et al. (1974)
Bear Brook, New Hampshire	511 (DM)	Fisher and Likens (1973)
Unnamed stream, Georgia	1,533 (DM)	Cummins et al. (1973)
Unnamed stream, eastern USA	1,095 (DM)	Vannote (1969)
Shaheen Creek, southeast Alaska (mature hemlock and spruce forest)	89 (AFDM)	Duncan and Brusven (1985a)
Shaheen Creek, southeast Alaska (3-year-old clear-cut)	52 (AFDM)	Duncan and Brusven (1985a)
Staney Creek, southeast Alaska (11-year-old clear-cut)	295 (AFDM)	Duncan and Brusven (1985a)

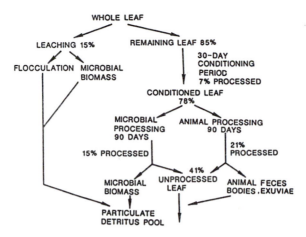

FIGURE 2.3.—A generalized processing budget for leaf packs in woodland stream ecosystems, showing the approximate percentages of the original leaf lost to leaching, microbial biomass and respiration, and invertebrate consumption during 3 months of processing. (Adapted from Petersen and Cummins 1974; reproduced with permission from Blackwell Scientific Publications.)

months (Figure 2.5). Thus, most leaf leachate is retained and rapidly processed in headwater streams, but some moves downstream without much processing.

Chemical reactions cause some leachate to flocculate or adsorb to clay and form fine particles (Figure 2.3). In the laboratory, 3–30% of sugar maple leachate precipitates with cations, especially calcium (Lush and Hynes 1973), and about 20% of red alder leachate adsorbs to clay (Dahm 1981). Flocculation is enhanced by an alkaline pH and turbulence, and the rate of flocculation influences where leachate becomes available as food for invertebrate collectors. In acidic water, potential food is lost downstream because flocculation is delayed, but in alkaline water, more remains available because flocculation is nearly immediate.

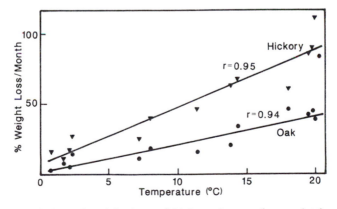

FIGURE 2.4.—Relation of weight loss of hickory leaves (inverted triangles) and oak leaves (dots) to stream temperature after 1 month in a Michigan stream; r is the correlation between weight loss and temperature. (From Suberkropp et al. 1975; reproduced with permission from the International Association of Theoretical and Applied Limnology.)

FIGURE 2.5.—Declines in the concentration of labile (LDOC) and refractory (RDOC) dissolved organic carbon compounds in the leachate of hickory and sugar maple leaves because of bacterial uptake. $T_{1/2}$ is the number of days for one-half of the DOC to be removed from solution. (From Wetzel and Manny 1972; reproduced with permission from the American Society of Limnology and Oceanography.)

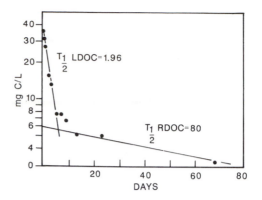

Leaves and needles must be "conditioned" by microbes for about 30 d before invertebrates will consume them (Figure 2.3; Petersen and Cummins 1974), although at least one invertebrate, the chironomid *Brillia flavifrons*, grows well on fresh green leaves (Stout and Taft 1985). During conditioning, fungi and bacteria colonize the leaf, and fungal hyphae penetrate and begin to digest it. About 7% of leaf weight is lost because of microbial activity during conditioning. Conditioning increases concentrations of nutrients in leaf detritus because microbes use nitrate and phosphate from stream water and carbon compounds from the leaf to build their own proteins, thereby decreasing the C:N ratio of the detritus (Mulholland et al. 1984). The microbes themselves cause the increased nutrients in the detritus, and a flourishing microbial population usually is a prerequisite for invertebrate consumption.

After being conditioned, leaves and needles are shredded by invertebrates (Figure 2.3). Typical shredders include large, case-building caddisflies (genera *Heteroplectron* and *Lepidostoma*), stoneflies (families Pteronarcidae and Peltoperlidae), and craneflies (Tipulidae). Some shredders (e.g., *Oecetis* spp.) have cellulase enzymes in their guts, either from symbionts or from ingested microbes, and they obtain some nutrition from leaf tissue (Sinsabaugh et al. 1981). Generally, however, invertebrates prefer and grow better on leaves with active microbes, and nutrition comes from the microbes, not from the leaf tissue (Anderson and Cummins 1979). By consuming litter and excreting residues, shredders convert leaf litter to fine particles and make more food available for collectors (Short and Maslin 1977). Although microbes can decompose litter completely in the absence of shredders, shredders accelerate litter decomposition by about 20% (Petersen and Cummins 1974).

Because leaves and needles of various species decay at different rates, they form a continuum from fast to slow decay (Table 2.5). Red alder leaves, for example, decay 50% in less than 2 months, whereas Douglas-fir and western hemlock needles may take more than 9 months to decay that much (Sedell et al. 1975). New food for invertebrates is added continually through the year as different species of leaves and needles are conditioned and become functionally available (Petersen and Cummins 1974). Within 1 year, most leaves are completely reduced to fine particles, though substantial portions (15–40%) of some slow-decaying species may remain intact.

TABLE 2.5.—Processing coefficients of different species of leaves and needles, arranged from fast- to slow-decaying groups; calculated numbers of days for 50% to be reduced to fine particles (t_{50}; i.e., biological half life); and percentages remaining after 1 year (%R_{365}). The decay coefficient (k) is derived by least-squares fit to the exponential model $W_t = W_0 e^{-kt}$; W_t is weight at time t in days and W_0 is initial weight (Petersen and Cummins 1974).

Decay group	k	t_{50} (d)	%R_{365}
Fast			
Red alder[a]	0.0124–0.0168	41–56	0–1
White ash[b]	0.0120	58	1
Silky dogwood[b]	0.0115	60	2
Medium			
Common waterwillow[b]	0.0101	69	2
Pignut hickory[b]	0.0089	78	4
Shining willow[b]	0.0078	89	6
Vine maple[a]	0.0068–0.0201	34–102	0–7
Slow			
White oak[b]	0.0052	133	15
Quaking aspen[b]	0.0046	155	19
Douglas-fir and			
western hemlock[a]	0.0025–0.0131	53–277	1–34

[a]Data are ranges for two streams in western Oregon (Sedell et al. 1975).
[b]Data are for fall–spring in a small woodland Michigan stream (Petersen and Cummins 1974).

As decomposition proceeds, litter becomes progressively smaller and more refractory (resistant to breakdown). Leaf particles lose weight primarily from decomposition of cellulose and hemicellulose, while such refractory components as lignin accumulate (Triska et al. 1975; Suberkropp et al. 1976; Ward 1984). Cellulose and hemicellulose, about one-third of fresh leaf litter, disappear gradually and continually, while the proportion of lignin increases from about 10% in fresh leaves to 30% in leaf residues.

Residual fine particles from litter and other sources are recycled many times in the benthic food chain. Microbes colonize the particles; invertebrates then collect them, digest the microbes, and excrete residues; and microbes recolonize the particles to restart the cycle. In contrast to leaves that are colonized internally and surficially by fungi and bacteria, fine particles are colonized only on the surface by bacteria (Anderson and Cummins 1979). By reworking fine detritus, invertebrates provide space for further microbial activity (Anderson and Sedell 1979). Collector invertebrates have a central role in processing fine detritus. Typical collectors are black flies (Simuliidae), which catch suspended particles (seston) with specialized mouthparts; hydropsychid caddisflies, which strain seston with nets; and ortho-clad chironomids, which gather particles in deposits. They gain nutrition mainly from bacteria on the particles rather than from the particles themselves. These invertebrates assimilate only about 5% of the material they ingest, and must pass large quantities of food through their guts. Larval black flies, for example, refill their guts every 20–30 min (Ladle et al. 1972). Bacteria quickly recolonize egested particles and reach maximum activity on feces 2–3 d after egestion (Hargrave 1976).

Woody debris can be extremely abundant in streams (Table 2.6), even if it is not added very rapidly, because it decays slowly. Boles usually make up most of the woody debris in a stream, but branches and twigs, in aggregate, constitute a greater annual input. Woody debris decays mainly within a thin surface layer less

TABLE 2.6.—Amount of large woody debris (>10 cm in diameter) in some stream channels in undisturbed forests. Data reported in volume units were converted to mass, based on an assumed specific weight of organic debris of 0.5 g dry weight/cm^3 (Swanson et al. 1984).

| Forest | Woody debris | | Reference |
	kg/m^2	m^3/100 m^2	
Western Oregon, old-growth Douglas-fir (5 first- and second-order streams)	39–76	7.8–15.2	Murphy (1979)
Western Washington, old-growth western hemlock and Sitka spruce (7 streams)	20–44	4.0–8.8	Grette (1985)
Southeast Alaska, old-growth western hemlock and Sitka spruce			
4 streams	3–12	0.6–2.3	Swanson et al. (1984)
32 stream reaches	2–54	0.3–10.9	Murphy et al. (1987)
Georgia, mature baldcypress			
Fourth-order stream	8	1.7	Wallace and Benke (1984)
Sixth-order river	7	1.5	Wallace and Benke (1984)

than 1 cm deep (N. H. Anderson et al. 1978, 1984). Because of their greater surface:volume ratio, branches and twigs decay faster than boles (Triska et al. 1975). Woody debris decays slowly because of its high C:N ratio (>1,000:1), and large trees take hundreds of years to completely decompose (Harmon et al. 1986). Bacteria offset the wood's low nutritional quality by fixing nitrogen gas dissolved in the stream, in combination with carbon from the wood, to build their own proteins. Nitrogen fixation on woody debris can contribute substantial amounts of usable nitrogen to a stream: 700 mg N/m^2 annually, compared to 900 from needles and 450 from deciduous leaves (Buckley and Triska 1978).

Wood decay is accelerated by invertebrates, which can annually consume 1–2% of the wood in a stream (Anderson et al. 1978). Only a few invertebrate species directly consume decaying wood. The caddisfly *Heteroplectron* sp. and the snail *Juga* sp. scrape wood surfaces; the beetle *Lara* sp. gouges surficial grooves; and the cranefly *Lipsothrix* sp. tunnels into soft, rotten logs. These invertebrates receive most of their nutrition from microbes on the wood; their guts contain no symbiotic bacteria to aid digestion of cellulose. Consumption of wood by invertebrates, as well as physical abrasion by the stream and suspended sediment, produce large quantities of fine particles, often several times the amount from leaves and needles (Ward and Aumen 1986).

Groundwater and soil erosion.—As much as one-quarter of a stream's total allochthonous organic matter may enter dissolved in groundwater (Fisher and Likens 1972). Sometimes, geochemical conditions of the groundwater zone (low oxygen content, cold temperature, low pH) do not favor complete decomposition of dissolved organic matter (DOM), which can be processed further in streams where conditions suit microbial growth (Wallis 1981). The microbial slime that covers streambed sediments can remove large amounts of DOM from percolating groundwater. Most DOM in groundwater, however, is of low nutritional value, consisting mostly of refractory residues of terrestrial litter already thoroughly processed by

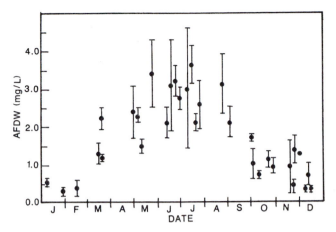

FIGURE 2.6.—Concentration of suspended organic particles (ash-free dry weight, AFDW) in a North Carolina stream during nonstorm periods. Each point is the mean of 2–9 samples from the same date, over a period of 6 years. Error bars are 95% confidence intervals for dates with more than two samples. (From Webster and Golladay 1984; reproduced with permission from the International Association of Theoretical and Applied Limnology.)

soil microbes. Most is used slowly and incompletely over a long distance, passing through the stream without much processing and contributing little energy to the stream community (McDowell and Fisher 1976; Klotz and Matson 1978).

Soil erosion in the form of surface erosion, soil creep, and root throw can add organic particles directly to a stream (Ward and Aumen 1986). Depending on characteristics of streamside erosion, inputs of organic matter can outweigh those from litterfall. As with DOM in groundwater, particles derived from soil erosion also consist mostly of refractory residues of terrestrial litter.

Fluvial transport from upstream.—Organic matter exported from a stream reach becomes an allochthonous input to downstream reaches. The importance of such fluvial transport increases with stream size. Upstream reaches supply about one-third of the total allochthonous input to small streams but nearly all the allochthonous organic matter in large rivers (Vannote et al. 1980). The source of fluvial transport depends on upstream processes. Most seston in woodland streams is generated in the stream itself by invertebrate processing of detritus (Webster and Golladay 1984). In streams with open canopies, much seston consists of algal cells and cell fragments detached from the streambed (Swanson and Bachmann 1976).

Most transport of organic particles occurs during high streamflows associated with storms, but biological activity controls the amount of seston transported during periods of base streamflow (Figure 2.6). Invertebrate feces alone account for most nonstorm seston in small woodland streams (Webster 1983). Peak nonstorm seston production in these streams is in spring when well-conditioned detritus is abundant, periphyton production is peaking, and rising temperature stimulates biological activity.

Input from animal activities.—Animals transport organic matter to streams in numerous ways. Terrestrial insects drop into streams and are eaten by fish. Drift of immature aquatic insects exports matter downstream, and flight of mature

TABLE 2.7.—Indexes of nutritional quality of various types of organic matter.

Type of organic matter	C:N ratio	Lignin (%)
Woody debris (Douglas-fir)[a]		
Twigs	235	34
Bark	324	10
Wood	1,343	48
Needles[a]		
Douglas-fir	97	14
Leaves		
Pignut hickory[b]	14	
Red alder[a]	23	10
Willow and ash[c]	26	
White oak[b]	34	
Bigleaf maple[a]	62	17
Vine maple[a]	77	8
Fine detritus		
Fresh (<2 months)[d]		8–17
Natural[b,d]	18	30–35
Insect feces[b]	40	
Aquatic macrophytes		
Rorippa nasturtium-aquaticum[c]	8	
Ranunculus calcareous[c]	13	
11 species[e]	13–69	
Periphyton[f]	1–11	

[a]Anderson et al. (1978).
[b]Ward and Cummins (1979).
[c]Dawson (1980).
[d]Ward, unpublished data referred to in Ward (1984).
[e]Calculated from data of Boyd (1970).
[f]McMahon et al. (1974).

stages can move matter upstream. Beavers carry woody debris to streams, and grazing and browsing mammals, such as cattle and deer, transfer matter by feeding in uplands and defecating in a stream's floodplain. Fish movements within a stream network also transfer matter from one stream reach to another. Annual spawning runs of anadromous salmonids can bring large amounts of organic matter and nutrients into a stream. Carcasses from an average run of pink salmon in one Alaska stream, for example, deposit 200 g of organic matter (dry weight), 70 g of nitrogen, and 0.7 g of phosphorus per square meter (Walter 1984).

Nutritional Quality of Organic Matter

The total quantity of organic matter in a stream is not, by itself, an accurate measure of the productive capacity of the ecosystem. More important is the nutritional quality of the organic matter; it controls how fast the community can extract energy (Ward and Cummins 1979). Most animals require food with a C:N ratio less than 17:1 (Russell-Hunter 1970). Almost all forms of allochthonous organic matter have a higher C:N ratio, so they require microbial processing to enhance food quality. The quality of various forms of organic matter varies widely, as measured by the C:N ratio or the percentage of lignin (Table 2.7). At the low end of the spectrum are woody debris and conifer needles; at the high end are periphyton,

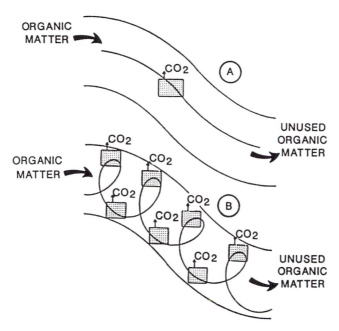

FIGURE 2.7.—Organic matter spiralling in stream ecosystems (A) without retention structures and (B) with many retention structures. Each spiral represents a period when organic matter is retained and processed to yield energy and CO_2. The tighter the spirals, the more frequently the organic matter is retained, and the more efficiently it is used. (Adapted from Wallace et al. 1977; reproduced with permission from the International Association of Theoretical and Applied Limnology.)

macrophytes, and fast-decaying deciduous leaves. A large reservoir of decay-resistant organic matter usually is stored in the stream channel throughout the year (Ward 1984). Between fresh inputs, the most labile detritus is metabolized, while refractory portions accumulate and steadily decline in nutritional quality.

Against this background of abundant but biologically inert material come the fresh inputs of highly nutritious detritus from algal blooms and leaf fall. These seasonal inputs induce peaks in stream production, and many stream invertebrates have evolved to take advantage of them to complete their life cycles (Otto 1981; Ward 1984). Growth patterns of invertebrates are controlled by food quality and temperature (Ward and Cummins 1979). Life cycles of many shredders, for example, are keyed to the autumnal leaf fall, and these animals grow most during late autumn and winter. Collectors such as *Paratendipes* spp. grow fastest after algal blooms and leaf fall when microbial biomass on fine detritus is highest and temperature is favorable. Larval black flies, which filter seston, grow most during spring when temperature is optimal and the seston's chlorophyll content and microbial respiration are highest (Merritt et al. 1982).

Export and Retention of Organic Matter

On their way from the headwaters to the river mouth, organic matter and nutrients are repeatedly transported, retained, metabolized, and exported in a cycling process called "spiralling" (Figure 2.7; Newbold et al. 1982). To contrib-

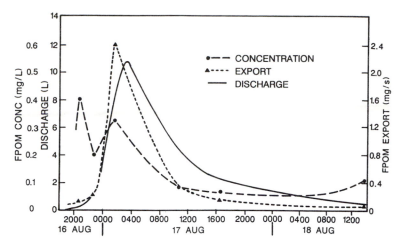

FIGURE 2.8.—Changes in concentration and export of fine particulate organic matter (FPOM; <1 mm) and in stream discharge during a summer storm. (From Bilby and Likens 1979; reproduced with permission from the American Society of Limnology and Oceanography.)

ute energy to the food web of a stream reach, organic matter must first be retained in the channel where it can be processed. Export and retention, therefore, determine the contribution of organic matter and nutrients to a stream ecosystem.

Export of organic matter depends on hydraulic power of the stream, size of the particle, and retentive capacity of the channel (Sedell et al. 1978; Speaker et al. 1984). Stream power (the product of discharge, channel gradient, and density of water) is a measure of a stream's ability to entrain material. Organic particles have low specific gravity and move more readily than inorganic sediment. The smaller the particle, the more easily it moves. Little power is needed to move fine organic particles, but much greater power is required to move large woody debris.

Particles retained in the stream channel remain there, available for processing, until stream power increases enough during storms to transport them downstream. During a summer storm, transport of fine organic particles starts as soon as rain begins to fall (Figure 2.8; Bilby and Likens 1979). The concentration of suspended particles peaks shortly after rainfall begins and then declines because of dilution as stream discharge rises. The total amount of organic particles in transport, however, parallels the increasing stream discharge, but transport peaks and begins to decline sharply before the stream discharge peaks. The amount exported during a storm increases with time since the last storm. Thus, the rising stream unloads fine particles from storage sites where they had accumulated since the last storm.

A stream's capacity to retain organic matter is a function of both hydrologic and biotic features (Minshall et al. 1983; Speaker et al. 1984). Interstices in the streambed and roughness elements (e.g., boulders and woody debris) in the channel promote retention, as do macrophytes and filter-feeding invertebrates (Sedell et al. 1978; Young et al. 1978; Dawson 1980). Dissolved organic matter is retained when it is flocculated (under alkaline conditions), adsorbed by clay, or assimilated by microbes (Lush and Hynes 1973; Dahm 1981). Inorganic nutrients are retained when they are taken up by plants and by microbes on decomposing organic detritus (Gregory 1978; Mulholland et al. 1984).

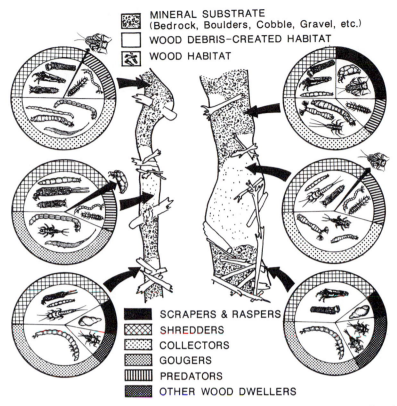

MINERAL SUBSTRATE
(Bedrock, Boulders, Cobble, Gravel, etc.)
WOOD DEBRIS-CREATED HABITAT
WOOD HABITAT

SCRAPERS & RASPERS
SHREDDERS
COLLECTORS
GOUGERS
PREDATORS
OTHER WOOD DWELLERS

FIGURE 2.9.—Relative abundances of wood-created habitats and associated invertebrates in first- to second-order (left) and third- to fourth-order (right) forested streams. (From Anderson and Sedell 1979; reproduced with permission from Annual Reviews.)

Large woody debris has a key role in the retention of organic detritus. Woody debris often determines the distribution of both detritus and invertebrates that consume the detritus (Figure 2.9). Debris alters stream and river morphology, creating pools, multiple channels, sloughs, backwaters, and even lakes (Sedell and Froggatt 1984; Triska 1984). Debris dams also trap sticks and branches that effectively retain leaves. Carcasses of anadromous salmonids also are retained mostly by woody debris (Cederholm and Peterson 1985). Because large boles resist decay and transport, they provide stable storage sites in small streams, where one-half of the streambed may be composed of woody debris and detritus (Anderson and Sedell 1979).

Small stream ecosystems generally are efficient at retaining litter and processing it to DOM and fine particles. Almost all leaves that fall into small streams are retained within the next 10–1,000 m downstream (Speaker et al. 1984). About 60–90% of the carbon exported from streams is dissolved (Dahm 1981), and 80% of exported particles are minute (<50 μm) residues of detritus (Figure 2.10; Sedell et al. 1978). As streams get larger, however, they retain less detritus because retention structures, such as woody debris, rapidly decline in abundance (Minshall et al. 1983).

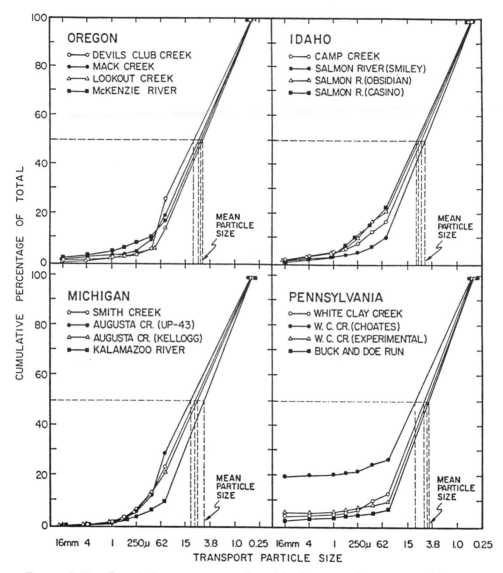

FIGURE 2.10.—Cumulative percentages of particle sizes annually transported in streams and rivers in four regions of the USA. Particle size classes are arranged on the horizontal axes in order of decreasing size from particles greater than 16 mm to particles 0.25–0.99 μm (μ) in diameter. (From Sedell et al. 1978; reproduced with permission from the International Association of Theoretical and Applied Limnology.)

The River Continuum

As energy sources change from headwaters to lowland rivers, the biological community adjusts to its different resources and to the physical conditions of the channel (Figure 2.11). Progressing downstream, biological activity reduces leaves, needles, and woody debris—the major inputs to headwater streams—to DOM and fine particulate residues—the major inputs to rivers. Such trends are embodied in the river continuum concept (Vannote et al. 1980), which portrays

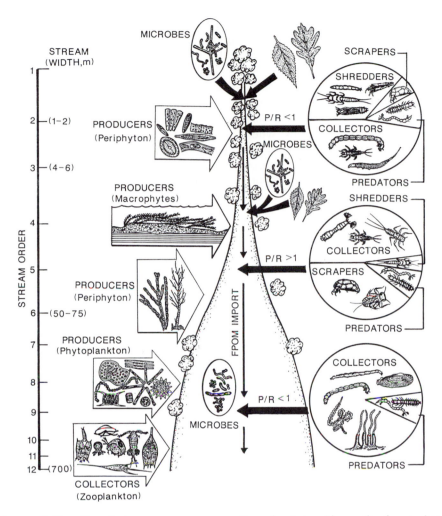

FIGURE 2.11.—Trends in energy sources, ratios of autotrophic production to hetero-trophic respiration (P/R), and functional groups along a river continuum. FPOM is fine particulate organic matter. (From Vannote et al. 1980; reproduced with permission from the Canadian Journal of Fisheries and Aquatic Sciences.)

the entire drainage network as an integrated system. Theoretically, the biological community that develops in each segment along a river continuum assumes processing strategies that efficiently use energy inputs and minimize "leakage" downstream. Most energy from forest litter that falls into headwater reaches, for example, is used by microbes and invertebrates in the headwaters, and only about 25% "leaks" downstream (Sedell et al. 1974).

Along a river continuum, energy sources and processes change systematically (Figure 2.11; Vannote et al. 1980). In headwater streams, decay of riparian litter provides most of the community's energy, and the ratio of autotrophic production to heterotrophic respiration (P:R) is low (<1). In midsize streams, primary production under the more open canopy may exceed heterotrophic decomposition (P:R >1). In large rivers, shade is reduced, but turbidity and increased water depth reduce light penetration to the river bed, and primary production usually is outweighed by microbial respiration stimulated by large influxes of DOM and fine organic particles from upstream (P:R <1).

Consumer functional groups also change systematically from headwaters to river mouth, responding to the shifts in energy sources (Figure 2.11; Hawkins and Sedell 1981; Minshall et al. 1983). Shredders and collectors, which use riparian litter and its residues, are dominant in the headwaters. Scrapers peak in abundance in midsize streams, where periphyton production is high. Collectors—important in headwater reaches—are even more important downstream because of the increased downstream abundance of fine particulate residues of algae and riparian litter. Prominent in large rivers are collectors that burrow into soft sediment (Beckett et al. 1983), such as burrowing mayflies (*Hexagenia* spp.), sand-dwelling chironomids (*Robackia* spp.), and clams (*Sphaerium* spp.). Predators constitute a similar proportion of the community in all segments along the continuum.

The river continuum is modified by climate, geology, and vegetation. The typical continuum in forested lands often differs from those in other vegetation systems (Minshall et al. 1983). Meadow and desert streams, for example, obtain much of their energy from autochthonous sources; hence, they differ fundamentally from small woodland streams. In addition, local features, such as rock outcrops, may disrupt the general pattern within a river system. These forces are superimposed on the tendency for stream ecosystems to change progressively and predictably from headwaters to mouth.

Controls on Energy Flow

The productivity of stream ecosystems usually is controlled by the availability of materials and energy. Limiting factors, in the strict sense, are sources of material and energy that, when in short supply, limit photosynthesis and decomposition (Ruttner 1971). By Liebig's "law of the minimum," productivity is limited by the factor in least supply. Thus, a rich supply of nitrogen (N, primarily as nitrate) promotes photosynthesis only if light and phosphorus (P, primarily as phosphate) also are in good supply. If the limiting factor is supplied in surplus, the next scarcest factor becomes limiting.

Aquatic primary production usually is limited by either low light or low nutrient supplies (Ruttner 1971). If nutrients suffice, primary production can increase with increased light up to an optimum, or saturation level, of about 1–2 lumens/cm^2 (McIntire 1975), which is about 10–20% of full sunlight (Figure 2.12). Above this optimum, photosynthesis may be partly inhibited by photooxidation of enzymes. In small woodland streams, dim light under the forest canopy usually limits primary production (Gregory 1980). As streams widen or riparian vegetation is removed, light increases and photosynthesis can accelerate. Some streams, however, have so little N or P that nutrients limit photosynthesis and removal of the forest canopy does not increase primary production (Stockner and Shortreed 1978).

Energy flow from decomposition of organic matter usually is limited by the abundance of decomposable organic compounds and the concentrations of N and P in the stream (Kaushik and Hynes 1971; Elwood et al. 1981). For example, experimental addition of sucrose to a stream increased bacterial, invertebrate, and

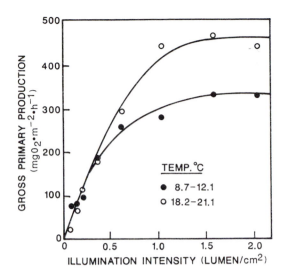

FIGURE 2.12.—Relation between light intensity and rate of primary production for periphyton assemblages in laboratory streams, as influenced by temperature. (From McIntire 1975; reproduced with permission from Blackwell Scientific Publications.)

cutthroat trout production (Warren et al. 1964). Addition of leaf leachate also can increase bacterial production (Cummins et al. 1972). Most allochthonous organic matter, however, is more resistant to decay than leachates are. Addition of N or P to a stream can promote the decomposition of these organics (Figure 2.13) because microbes can absorb nutrients from the water to metabolize carbon compounds. Decomposition in several streams, for example, accelerated after N and P were added from carcasses of spawning kokanees and alewives (Richey et al. 1975; Durbin et al. 1979).

The mechanism of nutrient limitation in streams is different from that in lakes, where biomass can increase until a nutrient is exhausted (Elwood et al. 1981). Streams receive a continual supply of nutrients from upstream, but concentrations often are so low that nutrient uptake is limited by the rate of diffusion through the boundary layer around algal and microbial cells (Klotz 1985). Under such a diffusion limitation, photosynthesis and decomposition are limited by the concentration of nutrients in stream water, even though nutrient supply is continuous.

Either N or P may limit production, depending on their relative abundance. Optimal N:P ratios for decomposition and photosynthesis range from 1.5:1 to 31:1 (Elwood et al. 1981). A ratio lower than about 1.5:1 indicates N is limiting; a ratio higher than about 31:1 indicates P is limiting. Streams may be under dual N and P limitation as the N:P ratio fluctuates above or below optimum. Low N:P ratios (N limitation) favor growth of N-fixing algae, such as the blue-green algae of the genera *Nostoc* and *Oscillatoria*. The capacity for N fixation by many microbes and algae may render streams P-limited, even when the supply of N is low.

Besides these limiting effects of light and nutrients, other controlling, lethal, and accessory factors (Fry 1947) also influence energy flow. Controlling factors, of which temperature is most important, regulate metabolism without entering the metabolic chain; lethal factors affect productivity by killing organisms; and accessory factors modify effects of others. High temperature, for example, can increase photosynthesis (Figure 2.12), but too high a temperature may be lethal. Turbidity acts as an accessory to limit photosynthesis by clouding the water (Iwamoto et al. 1978). Streambed scour and invertebrate grazing are lethal factors

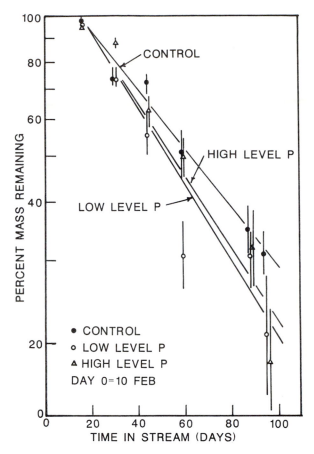

FIGURE 2.13.—Mass loss of oak leaf packs in phosphorus-enriched and control sections of Walker Branch, Tennessee. Concentrations of PO_4-P were <10 µg/L in the control section, 100 µg/L in the low-P enriched section, and 1,000 µg/L in the high-P enriched section. Plotted are geometric means (±2 SE) of 4–10 leaf packs and associated regression lines. (From Elwood et al. 1981; reproduced with permission from the Ecological Society of America.)

that can reduce primary production by keeping algal biomass low. Certain pollutants, such as acid runoff, reduce decomposition by killing invertebrates and microbes (Hall et al. 1980; Burton et al. 1985).

Salmonids in the Ecosystem

A salmonid's relation to the stream ecosystem depends on its life stage. A typical life cycle of an anadromous salmonid consists of several stages, each with different habitat requirements. Among other things, adults require spawning gravel and cover from predators; eggs and alevins require stable gravel and cool, oxygenated water; and rearing juveniles require food and cover. Thus, stream-rearing juveniles and nonanadromous adults relate to both physical habitat and energy flow in a stream; other stages relate solely to physical habitat. Salmonid habitat requirements are described fully by Bjornn and Reiser (1991, this volume). In this chapter, we emphasize aspects of physical habitat required for successful stream rearing.

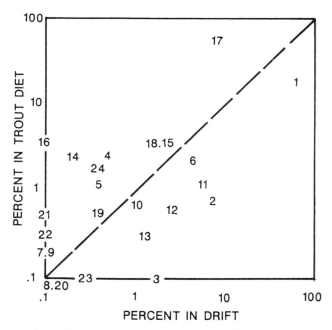

FIGURE 2.14.—Relation between percent composition of prey items consumed by brook trout (N = 44) and percent composition of drift in Cement Creek, Colorado, June 1977. Total recognizable prey = 2,135. Spearman's correlation r_s = 0.46; $P < 0.05$. 1 = *Baetis bicaudatus*, 2 = *Cinygmula* sp., 3 = *Epeorus longimanus*, 4 = *Rhithrogena hageni* and *R. robusta*, 5 = *Ephemerella infrequens*, 6 = *E. coloradensis*, 7 = *E. doddsi*, 8 = *Paraleptophlebia vaciva*, 9 = *Ameletus velox*, 10 = *Alloperla* spp., 11 = *Zapada haysi*, 12 = Perlodidae, 13 = other Plecoptera, 14 = *Brachycentrus* sp., 15 = *Rhyacophila* sp., 16 = other Trichoptera, 17 = Simuliidae, 18 = Chironomidae, 19 = other Diptera, 20 = *Heterlimnius* sp., 21 = other Coleoptera, 22 = Acari, 23 = emerging aquatic insects, and 24 = terrestrial invertebrates. (From Allan 1981; reproduced with permission from the Canadian Journal of Fisheries and Aquatic Sciences.)

Salmonids are opportunistic predators that eat a wide variety of aquatic invertebrates, as well as terrestrial invertebrates that fall into the stream (Mundie 1969). Although salmonids can forage on both drifting prey in stream currents and epibenthic prey on the stream bottom (Tippets and Moyle 1978), they feed predominantly on drift in streams (Elliott 1973).

Drift consists of invertebrates being carried downstream in the water column or on the stream surface; the animals drift for both accidental and behavioral reasons (Hynes 1970). Immature insects may be washed out of the substrate by turbulence or they may leave the bottom of their own volition. Mature insects drift during their passage from the stream to mate. Drift generally is greater at night, especially shortly after sunset, because invertebrate activity is inhibited by light. More drift occurs from turbulent riffles than from quiet pools, and drift increases sharply during freshets. Although variable, the amount of drift is roughly proportional to invertebrate production in riffles (Waters 1961).

The salmonid diet usually reflects the composition of the drift (Figure 2.14), and availability of drift determines time of feeding (Griffith 1974). Early night is the major feeding period (Johnson and Johnson 1981). To feed, salmonids station themselves in eddies and dart into the current to catch prey (Bachman 1984; Wilzbach 1985). Drift feeders probably do not deplete populations of benthic invertebrates (Allan 1982), whereas benthic feeders in pools can eliminate conspicuous taxa or harass them into hiding (Stein 1977; Hemphill and Cooper 1984).

Because salmonids are generalist predators, all functional groups of invertebrates are potential prey, but scrapers, collectors, and predators usually are eaten most because of their propensity to drift. Baetidae, Chironomidae, Simuliidae, and Hydropsychidae, which are scrapers, collectors, or predators, are common in both the drift and salmonid diet (Figure 2.14; Johnson and Ringler 1980; Koski and Kirchofer 1984). These insects generally are small, and their populations turn over rapidly. Production is often 2–10 times standing biomass (Waters 1969). Many shredders (e.g., Limnephilidae, Lepidostomatidae) and some scrapers (e.g., Glossosomatidae), by comparison, are uncommon in salmonid diets (Jenkins et al. 1970; Griffith 1974). Their advanced instars are large, heavy, and armored with wood or stone cases so that they do not often drift and are hard for fish to ingest. Many insects that do not drift as larvae, however, can become important prey when they mature and emerge.

Salmonids usually are territorial, and the amount of food they can obtain depends on their territory size and the food in or passing through it (Allen 1969). Territory size is determined by such factors as fish size, current velocity, and cover. Suitable territories have one or more stations with slack water where fish can wait for drift while expending little energy (Bachman 1984; Fausch 1984). Because such stations usually are in limited supply, salmonids habitually occupy only a small part (often <15%) of the entire habitat available to them, and population size may be limited by the number of suitable foraging sites (Bachman 1984).

The period of highest mortality of juvenile anadromous salmonids is usually during the first few months in spring and summer, when newly emerged fry establish territories and the population achieves equilibrium with carrying capacity (Figure 2.15). Soon after emerging from the redd, fry begin to defend territories (Mason and Chapman 1965). Where fish are numerous, their territories may cover all suitable parts of the streambed and surplus fish, unable to hold territories, are displaced, drift downstream, and presumably are lost to predators (Chapman 1962a; McFadden 1969). Coho salmon fry sometimes move downstream in large numbers shortly after emergence; some go to the estuary and presumably perish, because they do not return as adults (Crone and Bond 1976; Hartman et al. 1982).

Abundant food and cover can increase carrying capacity because more fish can occupy a given area and fewer emigrate (Mason and Chapman 1965). Salmonids are thought to adjust their territory size according to food abundance by altering their aggressive behavior (Symons 1968; Dill et al. 1981). When food is scarce, they attack intruders at a greater distance, and their territories expand; when food abounds, aggression subsides and territories shrink (Figure 2.16). Abundant cover also reduces territory size: a scattering of debris visually isolates fish and reduces aggression (Dolloff 1986). Thus, food abundance, physical habitat, and salmonid behavior interact to determine carrying capacity of a stream for salmonids.

In many streams, the relative importance of food and physical habitat depends on the season. Food often overrides cover in determining fish abundance in

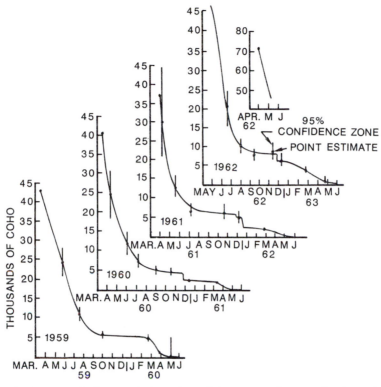

FIGURE 2.15.—Trends in population size of four year-classes of coho salmon from emergence to seaward migration in Deer Creek, Oregon. (From Chapman 1965; reproduced with permission from the American Fisheries Society.)

summer, but cover overrides food in winter (Mason 1976; Wilzbach 1985). As streams become cold in autumn, young salmonids eat less and seek cover from the high stream velocities common during autumn and winter storms. Important types of winter cover include large woody debris, deep pools, coarse substrate, and

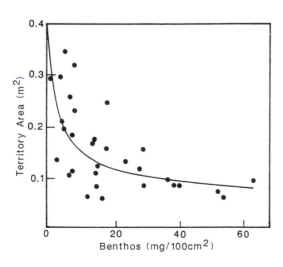

FIGURE 2.16.—Relation between area of coho salmon territories and abundance of benthic prey in the territories. (From Dill et al. 1981; reproduced with permission from the Canadian Journal of Zoology.)

undercut banks (Heifetz et al. 1986). Salmonids that cannot find cover may be washed downstream, and populations appear to decline over winter depending on amount of cover and severity of winter conditions. Thus, food availability may limit salmonid abundance in summer through density-dependent mortality, but freshets and freezing conditions can deplete populations in autumn and winter through density-independent mortality (Murphy et al. 1984b). Exceptions to this general scheme, however, are numerous. Physical habitat often is of overriding importance in summer when young salmonids need cover from bird or fish predation. Likewise, excessively high stream temperature in summer can make even the most productive habitats unsuitable.

Implications for Managing Salmonid Habitat

Historical Perspective

Most streams and salmonid populations in the Pacific Northwest have undergone extensive change over the last 150 years and often do not exhibit the productivity that was present under pristine conditions (Sedell and Luchessa 1982). Old cannery records in Oregon, for example, document that streams once supported salmon runs that far exceeded present runs or even management goals after habitat rehabilitation. Without an understanding of pristine streams as a point of reference, present protection and enhancement efforts may lack an adequate context to assure success.

Historical records document how pristine streams interacted with forests (Sedell and Luchessa 1982; Sedell and Froggatt 1984; Triska 1984). Historically, wild fish stocks evolved with streams that were obstructed by fallen trees, beaver dams, and vegetation growing in and alongside the channels. Rivers as large as seventh order had numerous fallen trees in their channels and frequently were obstructed by drift jams. Main river channels contained abundant gravels and fine sediments, and habitat complexity was enhanced by multiple channels and sloughs and by scour around boulders and snags.

Over the last 150 years, the character of streams and rivers throughout the Pacific Northwest has changed dramatically (Sedell and Luchessa 1982; Sedell and Froggatt 1984). From the middle 1800s to 1920, rivers were cleared of debris to improve navigation, and floodplain forests were cleared for agriculture, timber, and fuel wood. After years of snag removal and riparian forest clearing, most major rivers were confined to single channels with few downed trees and greatly reduced slough and shoreline habitats. These major changes occurred before flood control and irrigation projects began in the 1930s, which closed off vast areas to migrating anadromous fish and inundated or dewatered habitats.

Logging has affected stream habitats in the Pacific Northwest for more than 100 years (Sedell and Luchessa 1982). From the 1880s to 1915, small rivers and streams were used to drive logs to the mills. To drive logs, splash dams were used to augment flow, sloughs and low banks were blocked off, and debris and other obstructions were cleared from the channels. Logging debris was a major problem in streams during the 1920s to 1970s, when trees were felled into streams and large quantities of slash were left in the channels. Beginning in the 1940s, debris avalanches from roads and clear-cuts, and scouring of small stream channels, increased as timber harvest moved to steeper slopes. In the 1970s, forest practices acts in several states sought to remedy logging problems but frequently resulted in overzealous stream clean-ups that left streams devoid of debris. Trees left in buffer strips were salvaged as quickly as they blew down. The primary activity for improving fish habitat was removal of debris jams to allow fish to pass, and little consideration was given to salmonid rearing habitats or downstream effects of released sediments. Increasing demand for wood fiber and more efficient use of timber has left less debris available for streams.

Natural disturbances have lesser effects on stream ecosystems than does logging (Sedell and Luchessa 1982). Streams in areas burned by wildfire have higher sediment loads than they do in old-growth forests, but habitats recover faster than in logged and cleared streams. Fires often do not burn riparian zones, which usually are wetter than upland zones; even when a riparian zone is burned, most fires do not consume large wood pieces, and large woody debris remains available to streams as the burned stand regrows (Swanson and Lienkaemper 1978).

Today there remain few examples of the full, natural interaction of complete, large river systems with adjacent forests. In the Pacific Northwest, most undisturbed streams are restricted to small, high-gradient examples in inaccessible and mountainous areas. The salient features of a stream in old-growth forest are an abundance of large woody debris, a mix of deciduous and coniferous leaf and wood litter, and large gaps in the canopy that allow algae to grow. These elements provide a stable, highly interactive stream–riparian zone ecosystem with a diversity of food and physical habitat that historically sustained a high productivity of wild salmonids.

Influence of Riparian Vegetation

Because of the close linkage between the stream and terrestrial ecosystems, logging, livestock grazing, mining, and other activities can have numerous effects on the stream ecosystem and its salmonid populations. Most effects of land uses on streams are mediated through changes in riparian vegetation. More detailed discussions of effects of land uses on salmonids are provided by Hicks et al. (1991, this volume).

Riparian vegetation has many influences on the stream ecosystem. In addition to contributing leaf detritus, riparian vegetation produces insects that fall into the stream and supplement the salmonid diet. Riparian vegetation also contributes logs and branches that shape channel morphology, retain organic matter, and provide essential cover for salmonids. Its roots stabilize stream banks and maintain undercut banks that offer prime salmonid habitat. Riparian vegetation forms a protective canopy, particularly over small streams, that helps maintain cool stream temperature in summer and insulate the stream from heat loss in winter. The riparian canopy, however, also limits light penetration to the stream and may suppress aquatic primary production. In regions where livestock grazing is an important activity, brush and grasses along the stream can influence fish habitat in ways similar to those of trees in forested regions. By their dense roots, brush and sod reduce soil erosion, stabilize streambanks, and form undercut banks. A full discussion of the relationships between riparian vegetation and salmonid habitats in rangelands is given by Platts (1991, this volume).

The influence of riparian vegetation diminishes as streams get larger (Meehan et al. 1977). In the headwaters, small trees and brush can effectively shade the stream; farther downstream, even large trees may not provide effective shade. Small streams receive more of their organic matter from local riparian vegetation than do larger streams, although secondary channels of large streams and rivers often function like small streams and receive matter directly from local vegetation (Sedell and Froggatt 1984). The role of woody debris also changes with stream size. In small streams, debris is distributed where it fell and influences most of the stream channel. In larger streams that can float whole trees, debris is clumped in logjams or pushed onto the banks. Even in large rivers, however, debris provides essential salmonid habitat by "capping" side channels (Sedell et al. 1983) and by causing scour of deep holes in shallow river braids (Siedelman and Kissner 1988). Historically, logjams on pristine rivers created extensive secondary channels and off-channel sloughs and marshes, effectively increasing habitat complexity and total rearing area (Sedell and Froggatt 1984; Triska 1984).

Effects of Altering Riparian Vegetation

Because of the numerous ways that riparian vegetation influences the stream ecosystem, effects of land uses can be multiple and varied, depending on type of land use, degree of disturbance to streamside vegetation, size of stream, physical setting, and succession after disturbance. Where streamside trees are removed by logging or where streambanks are denuded by livestock grazing, increased light may stimulate production of periphyton. Such increase in production generally is greater in small streams than in larger streams that are naturally more open to sunlight (Murphy and Hall 1981). Changes in primary production also may depend on the type of bedrock and nutrient supply in the watershed. If nutrients remain scarce after disturbance, primary production may not increase even when the canopy is opened (Shortreed and Stockner 1983).

Increased periphyton production after canopy removal sometimes increases the abundance of invertebrates and fish, mainly by enhancing the quality of detritus. When algae—a higher-quality food than leaf and needle litter—detaches from the streambed, it enhances the quality of seston and deposited detritus (Hawkins and Sedell 1981; Hawkins et al. 1982). This enhanced detrital quality increases the abundance of invertebrate collectors and, in turn, increases the abundance of predators, including salmonids (Murphy et al. 1981; Hawkins et al. 1982). With some notable exceptions in Oregon (Moring and Lantz 1975) and British Columbia (Culp and Davies 1983; Scrivener and Andersen 1984), unshaded streams from California to Alaska have shown greater invertebrate and salmonid abundances in summer than have shaded streams (Chapman and Knudsen 1980; Murphy and Hall 1981; Hawkins et al. 1983; Bisson and Sedell 1984; Murphy et al. 1986). Opening the canopy, however, can cause stream temperature to increase to levels that are lethal to salmonids (Hall and Lantz 1969), nullifying any potential benefit of increased food production.

Cumulative effects of increased water temperature and sediment from numerous disturbances in a watershed also can nullify any beneficial effects of increased food production. Increases in temperature and sediment are not just local problems restricted to a particular stream reach, but problems that can have adverse cumulative effects throughout the entire basin (Sedell and Swanson 1984).

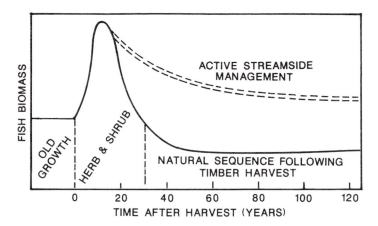

FIGURE 2.17.—Theoretical long-term response of a salmonid population to harvesting of old-growth forest. Active streamside management of riparian vegetation to maintain an open canopy and the abundance of large woody debris may sustain a higher-than-normal fish biomass in a stream reach. (From Sedell and Swanson 1984.)

Models of thermal loading (Brown 1969) show that an increase in water temperature in the upper basin can have serious effects on salmonid habitats in downstream areas. The total amount and locations of disturbed areas and the distribution of critical fish habitat within a basin will influence the magnitude of effects from cumulative thermal and sediment loadings. Thus, salmonid biomass may increase in a local area of stream when the canopy is opened and food production is increased, but cumulative downstream effects from many such openings may reduce overall salmonid production in the watershed.

As riparian vegetation recovers after disturbance, the canopy closes again, nutrient input decreases, and aquatic primary production declines (Murphy and Hall 1981). Canopy is denser in even-age, second-growth forest than in old-growth forest. Thus, as succession proceeds, aquatic primary and secondary production may initially increase for about 20 years and then decline to levels lower than those in old-growth forest for a much longer time (Figure 2.17). Streamside thinning is a possible way to maintain canopy openings in second-growth forest (Sedell and Swanson 1984); in some cases, thinning second-growth vegetation along a stream can enhance fish production (Figure 2.17; Hunt 1979). Selective cutting of mature riparian vegetation is another way to create openings in the canopy that will enhance primary production, but this must be done in a manner that assures continued sources of large woody debris and does not limit the rearing habitat necessary for maximum salmonid production.

Land uses that alter riparian vegetation also change allochthonous sources of organic matter for the stream (Duncan and Brusven 1985a). Streamside logging in coniferous forests switches the type of litter that enters the stream—from mostly conifer needles under mature forest, to deciduous leaves in early succession, to needles again in later years. The total input of riparian litter to a stream may increase after timber harvest because of increased growth of deciduous shrubs and trees. Disturbance of woody debris and salvage of merchantable logs from the stream channel reduce the amount of structure in a stream, and, if all trees are

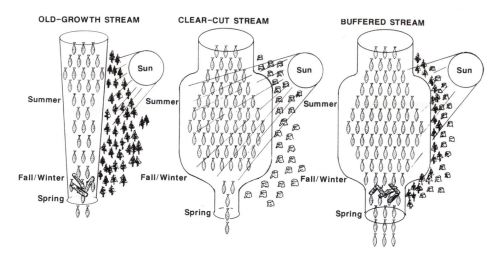

FIGURE 2.18.—''Bottlenecks'' (i.e., limiting factors) in stream production of coho salmon in old-growth forest and in areas logged with and without buffer strips. In old-growth forest streams, low primary production limits coho salmon populations in summer, and abundant cover helps survival over winter. In streams in clear-cut areas, high primary production increases fry abundance in summer, but poor cover decreases survival over winter. In streams with buffer strips, moderate primary production increases fry abundance in summer, and good cover maintains survival over winter. (From Koski et al. 1984.)

removed from the stream bank, no new debris will be available to replace large old pieces as they decay (Bryant 1983; Bisson et al. 1987). Such long-term reductions in large debris lower the retentive capacity of the channel for organic matter (Gurtz et al. 1980; Bilby 1981) and reduce cover for rearing salmonids.

Response of a salmonid population to such changes in energy sources and physical habitat depends on how the changes affect ''bottlenecks'' in fish production (Figure 2.18; Koski et al. 1984). Bottlenecks represent the most restrictive phases of the salmonid life cycle; they limit production and must be relieved to increase production. For example, increased primary production after canopy removal allows increased fry abundance in summer, but this increase may be nullified by a shortage of winter cover (Murphy et al. 1986). Removal of debris decreases essential winter cover and destabilizes the stream channel, which can cause high winter mortality of salmonid eggs, alevins, and juveniles (Bisson et al. 1987).

Conclusion

When assessing the effects of land uses, resource managers should consider both trophic and physical aspects of the stream ecosystem. Land uses often have multiple effects, and salmonids will respond in various ways to the changes in lower trophic levels and physical habitats. Increased food sometimes will enhance salmonid abundance in spring and summer, but adverse changes in physical habitat can reduce populations, especially over winter. Therefore, an increase in energy flow through the food web can enhance salmonid production only if physical habitat also is favorable. The riparian zone must be managed to provide both food production and suitable physical habitats for fish. Both are necessary to sustain salmonid production.

Chapter 3

Salmonid Distributions and Life Histories

W. R. Meehan and T. C. Bjornn

Several terms are used to describe assemblages of salmonids: stocks, runs, populations, races, and demes. We believe "stock," "race," and "deme" are essentially synonymous; they describe a group of fish that are genetically self-sustaining and isolated geographically or temporally during reproduction (see Volume 38, Number 12 of the *Canadian Journal of Fisheries and Aquatic Sciences* for papers on the stock concept). We prefer *stock*. *Run* usually refers to a group of fish migrating in a river (most often a spawning migration) that may be made up of one or many stocks, depending on the location. *Population* usually refers to a group of fish found in a particular location at a given time; a population often is made up of more than one stock. For example, the chinook salmon that begin migrating up the Columbia River in April and May are referred to as the spring chinook salmon run, which is made up of many stocks destined for natal headwater streams throughout the drainage. The cutthroat trout in Yellowstone Lake make up a population of many stocks that originate in the tributaries to the lake and outlet river.

General Distribution

The anadromous salmonids are distributed from about latitude 32°N to 70°N (mid-California to the Arctic Ocean) on the west coast of North America, and from latitude 41°N to 60°N (Connecticut to northern Newfoundland) on the east coast (McDowall 1987). On the west coast of North America, some anadromous salmonids migrate short distances out into the Pacific Ocean from the mouths of their home streams, but others migrate long distances (Healey and Groot 1987). On the east coast, the Atlantic salmon migrates north to the Labrador Sea and the west coast of Greenland (Reddin and Shearer 1987).

The mechanisms anadromous fish use to migrate to the oceans and then return to their natal streams appear to vary, depending on the segment of their migration. Healey and Groot (1987) contended that juveniles migrating from stream mouths to ocean feeding areas use some form of compass orientation, and that adults on their return migrations use compass orientation to reach the coast but may require bicoordinate orientation (Griffin 1955) to find their way along the coast to the river mouth, where the fish then switch to local environmental cues.

Populations of native nonanadromous salmonids are distributed throughout the USA and Canada, and a few populations (e.g., rainbow trout) are found as far

Influences of Forest and Rangeland Management on Salmonid Fishes and Their Habitats
American Fisheries Society Special Publication 19:47–82, 1991

south as Mexico. Many populations have been introduced into suitable waters where they were previously absent.

General Life History Patterns

Most of the salmonids we discuss are part of the small proportion of fish species (about 1%; McDowall 1987) that are diadromous (migrate between fresh water and salt water). Of those of our species that are diadromous, all are anadromous (they mature at sea and return to fresh water to spawn), and two (Dolly Varden and Arctic char) may be considered amphidromous (they migrate between fresh water and salt water for reasons other than spawning). The tendency toward anadromy varies from none (lake trout), to a few stocks (brook trout), to many stocks (steelhead and coastal cutthroat trout), to nearly all stocks (e.g., pink and chum salmon). A period of saltwater residence is probably not obligatory for any of the species, but migration to the sea occurs in virtually all natural stocks of some species. Maturation of fish from anadromous stocks that stay in fresh water is rare for pink and chum salmon (except in the Great Lakes), common (but mostly among males) for chinook salmon, and not unusual for steelhead, coastal cutthroat trout, and sockeye salmon (lacustrine stocks of sockeye salmon are called kokanee).

For those salmonids that are anadromous, migration to the sea can take place within days after emergence from the redd (typical of pink and chum salmon) or after an extended period of rearing in streams (coho and chinook salmon, steelhead, Atlantic salmon, cutthroat trout) or lakes (sockeye salmon). Figure 3.1 represents the typical life cycle of anadromous salmonids; variations of this general life cycle are sometimes found in particular populations, and are discussed later in the section on specific life histories. The length of time these fish spend in fresh water before migrating to the sea is regulated by both genetic and environmental factors (Randall et al. 1987). Anadromous salmonids undergo a physiological preparation for the change from fresh to salt water before migrating to the sea; the preparation involves interactions between internal and external regulators (Baggerman 1960).

Migratory behavior of salmon and trout may be under general endogenous control (Wagner 1974; Groot 1982); environmental factors such as photoperiod and temperature exert a synchronous or secondary controlling influence. In species like the chum and pink salmon, the seaward migration appears to be primarily under genetic control; these fish migrate soon after they emerge from their redds regardless of conditions in their natal stream. For other species, genetics dictate that the fish attain a certain size before migration and the environment regulates how long it takes to attain that size. In cold infertile streams, it may take four or more years to attain smolt size.

Movements of newly emerged salmonids to feeding areas or of smolts to the sea occur primarily at night in the spring and early summer for most stocks, but the timing for specific stocks is related to environmental conditions (avoidance of predators, abundance of food, temperature) that provide the highest chance of survival (Godin 1982). Length of time at sea or in feeding areas other than natal streams, as well as age and the size at which adults return to fresh water or to

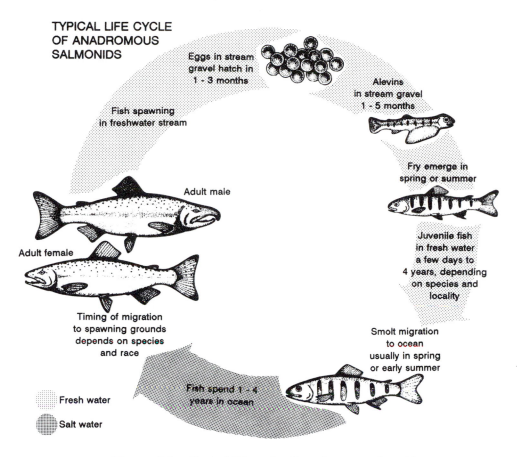

TYPICAL LIFE CYCLE OF ANADROMOUS SALMONIDS

Eggs in stream gravel hatch in 1 - 3 months

Alevins in stream gravel 1 - 5 months

Fish spawning in freshwater stream

Fry emerge in spring or summer

Adult male

Juvenile fish in fresh water a few days to 4 years, depending on species and locality

Adult female

Timing of migration to spawning grounds depends on species and race

Smolt migration to ocean usually in spring or early summer

Fish spend 1 - 4 years in ocean

Fresh water

Salt water

FIGURE 3.1.—Typical life cycle of anadromous salmonids.

breeding areas within streams to spawn, vary with species and stock, and can be influenced by growth rates (Bilton et al. 1982; Peterman 1982).

It is not known if the ancestral form for present-day salmonids was a marine or a freshwater fish, but the behavior patterns of salmonids are probably linked to their origins. Some (Day 1887; Regan 1911; Mottley 1934; Balon 1968, 1980a) have argued for a marine progenitor that invaded fresh water; others (Tchernavin 1939; Neave 1958; Hoar 1976) have proposed that the freshwater forms were the more primitive and those that adopted an anadromous life history were more advanced. If the origin was in fresh water, the anadromous life history may have evolved to take advantage of a more abundant food resource in the sea than in fresh water (Gross 1987; Gross et al. 1988). A similar migration pattern exists in many stocks of nonanadromous salmonids that migrate downstream into lakes or larger rivers to grow and mature before returning to natal streams to spawn.

Rounsefell (1958) and Hoar (1976) discussed the origin and migratory behavior of salmonids. One end of the spectrum includes species that spend their entire lives in fresh water (lake trout) and the other includes species these authors labeled as "obligatory anadromous": pink, chum, and chinook salmon. Although the latter three species are invariably anadromous in their native range, pink and chinook salmon have been transplanted to the Great Lakes and other freshwater lake systems where they have established successful reproducing populations.

The dynamics of anadromous salmonid abundance can be complex; survival, growth, or maturation can depend or not on density in one or more of the various life history stages. The relative importance of factors operating on freshwater or marine life stages varies with species and location. In general, the first year of life is critical for all species whether in fresh water or the sea, for that is when the fish are most vulnerable to various forms of predation that may limit their abundance. For species that migrate to the sea soon after emergence (<40 mm in length) and tend to remain in schools (pink and chum salmon), the egg-to-fry stage in fresh water is important (Wickett 1958). Survival and growth, however, can also be regulated in a density-dependent manner during the initial year at sea (Peterman 1987). The freshwater life stages appear to be relatively more important for the species that spend more time in fresh water and attain a larger size before migrating to the sea (Rago and Goodyear 1987). Atlantic salmon and steelhead are examples of species that spend considerable times (usually 2–4 years) in fresh water before migrating to the sea and attain relatively large size (150–225 mm in length) so that they are less vulnerable to predation in the ocean. During their stay in fresh water, however, their abundance has been regulated by various forms of density-dependent and density-independent mortality (Bjornn 1978; Chadwick 1982). Figure 3.2 illustrates the general length of time (by life stage) that representative species of anadromous salmonids remain in fresh water and in salt water during their lives.

During winter, salmonids in interior streams change behavior from mostly feeding, as they had done all summer, to hiding and conserving energy. Fish that had been territorial in summer may congregate in large pools in winter, move into areas with woody debris and brush, or move into the interstitial spaces in the substrate (Chapman and Bjornn 1969; Bustard and Narvar 1975a). The number of fish that can or will stay in a stream over winter can vary with quality of the winter habitat (Bjornn 1978) and the severity of the winter weather (Seelbach 1987). If the habitats in small streams are not suitable and the weather is severe, the fish move to larger rivers in the fall and early winter (Bjornn and Mallet 1964; Bjornn 1978). A reverse behavior pattern has been observed in coastal streams (Cederholm and Scarlett 1982): young coho salmon, cutthroat trout, and steelhead move upstream into small tributaries from main-stem rivers in fall and winter. Coastal and inland rivers differ in water temperatures and flow patterns; coastal rivers are warmer than inland rivers and carry freshets during winter, whereas flows are relatively stable in inland rivers.

The timing of migrations and the distributions of salmonids have been changed in some areas because of construction of dams, selective harvesting, water diversions, and changes in habitat (Atkinson et al. 1967). Distributions have expanded when construction of fish-passage facilities over or around falls and other obstacles has opened (or reopened) streams to anadromous fish and when runs have been established through the release of hatchery fish into streams where they did not previously occur.

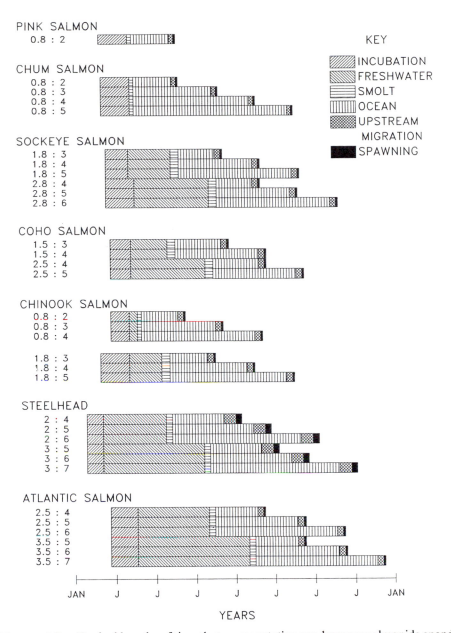

FIGURE 3.2.—Typical lengths of time that representative anadromous salmonids spend in various developmental stages and in fresh water or the ocean during their lives. Numbers under the species names are age keys indicating years spent rearing in fresh water, egg to smolt, in relation to the total age of the fish. For example, 2.5:5 indicates a fish in its 5th year of life that had spent 2.5 years incubating and rearing in fresh water before migrating to sea. The Pacific salmon (pink, chum, sockeye, coho, and chinook) invariably die after their first spawning. Adults of other anadromous species may spawn twice or more, returning to the sea between times.

Pink Salmon

FIGURE 3.3.—North American distribution of pink salmon. The Great Lakes populations have been introduced.

Specific Distributions and Life Histories

Pink Salmon

Pink salmon occasionally enter the Russian River of central California and some rivers in Oregon, but their regular spawning distribution extends from the Puyallup River, Washington, northward to central Alaska and eastward to the Mackenzie River in the Northwest Territories, Canada (Figure 3.3; Neave et al. 1967). Although they extend into the northern Bering Sea and Arctic Ocean, being reported regularly from tributaries as far north as Kotzebue Sound and occasionally from rivers along the northern coast of Alaska, most of their far-northern runs are small. Centers of abundance for pink salmon are the Kodiak, Cook Inlet, and Prince William Sound areas in Alaska, but the importance of these areas is overshadowed by the pink salmon runs of southeastern Alaska (Atkinson et al. 1967).

Pink salmon are the most abundant of the Pacific salmon species spawning in British Columbia waters (Aro and Shepard 1967). A large part of the province's pink salmon spawning (75%) takes place in 57 rivers or streams, about 8% of all streams used by pink salmon in British Columbia.

In their southern breeding areas around Puget Sound, pink salmon spawn only during the odd-numbered years; farther north, there are even-year runs as well. Populations of even- and odd-year-spawning pink salmon have been established in the Great Lakes (Figure 3.3), where 3-year-old adults are present in addition to the normal 2-year-olds (Kwain 1987). In their natural range, however, pink salmon mature almost invariably at 2 years of age (Figure 3.2). Throughout the Pacific Northwest, adult pink salmon enter fresh water from July to October, spawn soon thereafter, and die.

Young pink salmon emerge from the gravel after absorbing their yolk sacs and migrate directly to sea. They return as adults after 12–18 months in the ocean. Because of their strict adherence to a 2-year life cycle, there is nearly complete genetic separation of stocks spawning in even- and odd-numbered years. The spawning behavior of stocks established in the Great Lakes is indistinguishable from that of sea-run fish along the Pacific coast of North America (Hart 1973; Scott and Crossman 1973).

Pink salmon do not exhibit the preciseness in homing found in other species of anadromous salmonids such as sockeye salmon (Helle 1966). If adult salmon on their spawning migration identify their home streams through perception of some environmental characteristics imprinted during their natal freshwater existence, it seems reasonable that the length of freshwater residence of the juveniles would be related to the precision with which the adults returned to their natal areas. Sockeye salmon, because of their longer association with natal freshwater areas, would be expected to be more precise than pink salmon in their homing ability.

Survival of pink salmon in fresh water appears to be affected by the timing of spawning, density and distribution of adults on spawning grounds relative to characteristics of the stream, quality of the intragravel environment, predation on eggs and alevins, and stream discharge during spawning and incubation (Heard 1978). In Sashin Creek, southeastern Alaska, survival of progeny from adults spawning early was usually higher than that of progeny from late spawners. Merrell (1962) noted that odd-year pink salmon spawned in Sashin Creek an average of 12 d earlier than even-year fish, and that freshwater survival was usually higher for progeny of odd-year spawners. He also noted that survival of eggs and alevins was higher in the upper portion of the stream than in the lower sections, possibly due to fewer fine sediments and better water quality in the upper portion (McNeil 1966a, 1968). However, the upper areas were used extensively only when many spawners were present; in years when few were present, they spawned mostly in the lower portion of the stream (Merrell 1962). Thus, both habitat and fish behavior contributed to differences between stocks in Sashin Creek: the odd-year runs of pink salmon were considerably larger than the even-year runs (Heard 1978), entered the stream earlier, and used more of the upper reaches of the stream; their progeny were larger and survived better than those of even-year runs, and thereby sustained a larger population size.

The timing of upstream migration and spawning by pink salmon is related to water temperatures in the spawning areas. The earliest runs of pink salmon in southeastern Alaska occur in cold streams along the mainland or on the larger islands in the north, and the latest runs occur in warmer streams along the outer channels and coastal areas (Sheridan 1962a). Noerenberg (1955) noted that 72–76% of even-year pink salmon in Prince William Sound, Alaska, spawned in the intertidal zone and that they spawned later than fish that spawned further upstream. Sheridan (1962a) concluded that the time of spawning was related to cumulative temperature requirements for development of embryos and to the temperature of water in the spawning area necessary for optimum survival of the offspring. Vernon (1962) reported that the early segment of pink salmon that entered the Fraser River, British Columbia, spawned mainly in waters that originated in the interior of the province and were subject to low winter temperatures, whereas the late segment spawned in lower tributaries in the more moderate coastal climate. Pink salmon originating in the southern part of their range have adapted to the high temperatures found there by returning to natal streams and spawning later, incubating for a shorter period, and entering the ocean earlier than northern stocks (Takagi et al. 1981).

The lower limit of temperature necessary for normal development of pink salmon embryos in southeastern Alaska was reported to be 4.5°C by Bailey and Evans (1971). The majority of pink salmon fry migrate to sea at temperatures between 4 and 5°C, even though they may have been subjected to quite different incubation temperatures (Wickett 1962).

Pink salmon, like all the anadromous salmonids, live in a variety of salinities during their life cycle (Takagi et al. 1981): fish hatch out in the rivers, migrate downstream, feed and mature in the ocean, and then return to the rivers to spawn and die. Pink salmon have developed the ability to withstand the transition from fresh water to full-strength sea water even before they are old enough to emerge from the redd (Bailey 1966). The establishment of land-locked runs in the Great Lakes, however, demonstrates that pink salmon can survive and mature in fresh water (Takagi et al. 1981).

Pink salmon fry that migrate short distances to the sea or to the Great Lakes from spawning areas generally do not feed, but may do so during longer migrations (Hart 1973; Takagi et al. 1981; Kwain 1982). Food organisms typically found in the stomachs of fry that did feed in streams were larvae, nymphs, and pupae of aquatic insects such as midges (Chironomidae), stoneflies (Plecoptera), mayflies (Ephemeroptera), caddisflies (Trichoptera), two-winged flies (Diptera), and bugs (Hemiptera), and well as small crustaceans such as copepods and cladocerans.

In Lake Superior streams, few stomachs of adult pink salmon examined immediately before and during spawning contained food. In those that did, fish (smelt and other unidentifiable species) and insects were the predominant items, and zooplankton were the next most-frequently eaten prey (Kwain 1982).

Chum Salmon

Chum salmon have the widest natural distribution of any of the Pacific salmon in North America (Figure 3.4). They have spawned and reared in streams from the Sacramento River in California northward to the arctic shore of Alaska and eastward to the Mackenzie River on the arctic coast of Canada (Bakkala 1970).

Most chum salmon spawn in the fall as 3-, 4-, or 5-year-old fish (Figure 3.2; Beacham and Starr 1982; Helle 1984). They tend to spend more time in salt water in the northern latitudes and spawn at an older age (Helle 1984). Chum salmon

Chum Salmon

FIGURE 3.4.—North American distribution of chum salmon.

rarely spawn in North America at age 2, but if they do, it is largely in the southern part of their range. The few chum salmon that spawn as 6-year-olds are found in the northern areas. In the last few months of life, chum salmon move from offshore feeding grounds to coastal waters in June to September. Early-run (summer) fish move upstream to spawning grounds from July to early September and spawn in August and September. Late-run (autumn) fish enter and spawn in streams from October to January (Bakkala 1970). In the northern part of the species' range, almost all chum salmon spawners are summer-run fish; in the most southerly parts of their range, autumn and later spawning is the rule (Bakkala 1970; Helle 1984). In the central part of their range, such as southeastern Alaska and northern British Columbia, most chum salmon spawn in summer and early autumn, but a few runs spawn later.

Most chum salmon spawn within the lower reaches of streams and frequently within the tidal zone. Some, however, spawn considerable distances from the sea—more than 2,500 km up the Yukon River of Alaska and Canada, for example (Bakkala 1970). Eggs are deposited in loose gravels in which there is sufficient water flow to deliver oxygen to developing embryos and remove metabolites, usually at depths of 15 to 30 cm. Water temperatures at spawning range from 4 to

16°C (Neave 1966). The time from fertilization to hatching can range from about 1.5 to 4.5 months.

Fry emerge from the gravel in March through May, spend a few days to several weeks in the stream, and then move downstream to the sea at lengths of 35–40 mm (Healey 1980). Although they may be found in streams from March through July, most fry leave fresh water in April and May (Bakkala 1970).

Survival of chum salmon from the egg to fry stage is usually less than 10% (Bakkala 1970), and it is related to flows and temperatures during incubation. In past studies, survival tended to be highest when the winter was relatively warm and dry (Beacham and Starr 1982). The greatest cause of mortality of eggs and embryos was fluctuation in streamflow, which alternately dewatered redds, shifted gravels and dislodged eggs, and deposited sediments on and in the gravels, impeding intragravel water flow (Bakkala 1970). Lethal water temperatures for fry in fresh water are about −0.1°C and above 24°C; fry have shown a preference for temperatures of 12–14°C (Brett 1952).

Two density-dependent factors that appear to limit population size of chum salmon in fresh water are redd superimposition during spawning and mortality associated with density of eggs in the streambed. At any particular spawning density, however, fluctuations in fry production are attributed to density-independent factors such as flooding, freezing, and drought (McNeil 1966b). The optimum density of spawners may vary with streambed permeability (Wickett 1958).

Chum salmon alevins remain in the gravel until their yolk sacs are completely or almost completely absorbed; during that time, the yolk sac is the main source of food, but some alevins will also take small food items such as Diptera larvae, diatoms, and copepods (Bakkala 1970). In fresh water, chum salmon fry feed primarily on benthic organisms, chiefly aquatic insects. Chironomid larvae and mayfly nymphs are important food items, and to a lesser extent, stonefly nymphs, caddisfly larvae, black fly (Simuliidae) larvae, and terrestrial insects are eaten (Bakkala 1970). Chum salmon adults stop feeding when they enter fresh water, and obtain energy for upstream migration and spawning from body fat and protein (Bakkala 1970).

Although predation and lack of food are probably the primary causes of mortality of chum salmon fry in fresh water, they do not appear to regulate abundance (Bakkala 1970). Predation is probably a more serious source of mortality than is lack of food. Larger salmonids and fish-eating birds are the primary predators. Bears (Ursidae) prey on chum salmon spawners in Alaska, and seals (Phocidae) take adults in the lower reaches of streams and rivers.

Sockeye Salmon and Kokanee

In North America, sockeye salmon are distributed from the Columbia River in the south to northern Alaska (Figure 3.5). The most important stocks occur in rivers tributary to Bristol Bay in western Alaska and in the Fraser River system in British Columbia (French et al. 1976).

The salmon *Oncorhynchus nerka* occurs in two forms: the anadromous sockeye salmon, and the nonanadromous kokanee. Anadromous sockeye salmon typically spend their first year of life (sometimes longer) in a lake before migrating to the ocean to rear and mature. Kokanee, on the other hand, originated as residual

Kokanee and Sockeye Salmon

FIGURE 3.5.—North American distribution of sockeye salmon (anadromous form) and kokanee (nonanadromous freshwater form of sockeye salmon). Populations east of the main distribution have been introduced.

sockeye salmon that failed to migrate to the sea, and they usually spend their entire life in fresh water, although some have become anadromous. Kokanee usually mature at a smaller size than do anadromous sockeye salmon because there is usually less food in the lake environments than in the ocean (Foerster 1968). In a few river systems, there occur stocks of sockeye salmon that spawn in streams without associated lakes. In some of these cases, the fry may migrate directly to the sea and are termed "ocean-type" sockeye salmon, as opposed to "lake-type" fish that rear for a year or more in lakes or "river-type" fish that rear for a year or more in river channels (Wood et al. 1987).

Sockeye salmon usually spend 2 or 3 years in the ocean, although in some river systems minor parts of the run return to fresh waters after 1 or 4 years at sea (Figure 3.2). Maturing fish return to their rivers of origin between May and October, most of them in July, August, or September. A variable amount of time may be spent in the lakes or streams prior to spawning.

Spawning generally occurs in late summer and autumn, August–November. The time of arrival at individual areas is quite consistent from year to year

(Foerster 1968). Spawning takes place either in small streams flowing into lakes, in the gravel areas along lake shores with seepage flows (underground springs), or in the upper reaches of lake outlet streams. A less common occurrence is for the adults to spawn in a tributary to a lake outlet; the fry must move downstream to the outlet and then upstream in the outlet to reach the lake, where they rear for a year or more. Spawning usually coincides with water temperatures of 3–7°C (French et al. 1976).

Spawning sites selected by sockeye salmon generally contain medium- to small-sized gravel, with a limited amount of coarse sand, through which a good flow of water can be maintained. Any small amounts of silt, fine sand, and detritus that overlie or are interspersed with the coarser gravels will be removed by the fish as they excavate the redd (Foerster 1968).

Kokanee, like sockeye salmon, spawn in the late summer or fall. Fish that spawn in tributary streams usually do so earlier than those that spawn along lake shores. In Redfish Lake, Idaho, kokanee spawned in August in tributary streams, but sockeye salmon spawned in October along the lakeshore (Bjornn et al. 1968). In two streams tributary to Flaming Gorge Reservoir, Wyoming, the peak of kokanee spawning occurred in mid-September in water temperatures of 7–15°C; the fish were predominantly 4 years of age (Parsons and Hubert 1988). In the Odell Lake system, Oregon, stream-spawning kokanee selected the slower-flowing riffle areas near stream margins with gravel that ranged from 1.3 to 1.9 cm in diameter; spawning gravels along the lakeshore ranged from 0.3 to 2.5 cm in diameter (Averett and Espinosa 1968).

The period of egg incubation for both kokanee and sockeye salmon depends primarily on the temperature of the water flowing through the redd and may vary from 80 to 140 d. The fully formed, free-swimming fry emerge from the gravel in early spring (April and May; Foerster 1968).

After emergence, the fry usually move from the spawning areas into a lake. There they rear to maturity for up to 3 years before migrating to the ocean in April to June if they are anadromous, or for up to 6 years if they are nonanadromous. Most sockeye salmon spend 1 or 2 years in a lake, then migrate to the sea and remain there 2–3 years before returning to spawn as 4- to 6-year-old fish. Age at maturity for kokanee is predominantly 3 years in some southern populations, but usually 4 or 5 years (Rieman and Bowler 1980).

The most important foods of young sockeye salmon and kokanee in lakes are planktonic crustaceans, particularly copepods and cladocerans (Foerster 1968). They feed on zooplankton at all times of the year, selecting the largest or most abundant prey items; their growth rate depends on zooplankton abundance (Lorz and Northcote 1965; Rieman and Bowler 1980). *Daphnia* sp. is a preferred food when it is available; *Bosmina* sp., *Cyclops* sp., and other zooplankton are eaten when *Daphnia* populations are not available or are low in numbers. Though changing food availability can affect growth and result in higher mortality over time, a scarcity of food at time of emergence and entry of fry into the lake may result in high mortality (Rieman and Bowler 1980). For example, in Pend Oreille Lake, Idaho, kokanee fry emergence begins in May and peaks in June; food items such as *Daphnia* and *Bosmina*, however, have not become abundant until July in recent years, because of introductions of *Mysis relicta* (Rieman and Bowler 1980).

A serious competitor with young sockeye salmon for food in many lakes is the threespine stickleback. It subsists on the same planktonic crustaceans eaten by sockeye salmon, inhabits the same areas of the lake, and is often very abundant. Each adult stickleback consumes more than half as much food as a young sockeye salmon; therefore, a large crop of actively feeding sticklebacks can have a serious effect on the growth and well-being of a population of juvenile sockeye salmon in a lake (Foerster 1968). Removal or reduction of the stickleback population in a lake ought to be a way to enhance sockeye salmon growth and survival. A complicating factor is that Dolly Varden frequently inhabit sockeye salmon rearing lakes and feed on sticklebacks (Foerster 1968). The sticklebacks may buffer the young sockeye salmon from predation by Dolly Varden, but the relations among sticklebacks, Dolly Varden, and young sockeye salmon should be defined.

Intraspecific competition for food in a lake is also a potential problem for rearing sockeye salmon. Each yearling or older sockeye salmon consumes about 270 g of *Cyclops* during the year, or about 3.7 times the amount eaten by underyearling fish (Foerster 1968). If kokanee are abundant in the lake, they compete with young sockeye salmon for food.

The most important predators on juvenile sockeye salmon and kokanee are Dolly Varden, Arctic char, rainbow trout, and lake trout; arctic terns (*Sterna paradisaea*) and glaucous-winged gulls (*Larus glaucescens*) also take large numbers of migrants (Hartman et al. 1967). The farther the young fish must migrate to a lake or the sea, the higher will be the mortality in fresh water due to predation. Migrating fry generally do not travel in well-formed schools, whereas smolts are usually schooled during migration. Fry and smolts migrate mainly at night, which lessens the chances of predation.

Coho Salmon

Coho salmon are taken readily by sport anglers and caught in large numbers by commercial fishermen from California to Alaska. Natural production of coho salmon is limited by the carrying capacity of streams where the young fish spend the first year or two of life. Hatcheries have been used to supplement natural stocks of fish and to create hatchery stocks during the past 30 years.

Coho salmon are native to many drainages around the Pacific rim from California to Alaska (Figure 3.6) and westward to Japan. They have been introduced to other areas, and substantial fisheries have developed in the Great Lakes and other freshwater lakes that have been sustained by artificial propagation or natural production. Coho salmon are found in a broader diversity of habitats than are any of the other anadromous salmonids, from small tributaries of coastal streams to lakes to inland tributaries of major rivers. Groups of stocks in close proximity appear to be similar, as would be expected, but groups of stocks from one area differ from groups in other areas (Utter et al. 1973; Olin 1984; Wehrhahn and Powell 1987).

Adult coho salmon return from the ocean as early as July in northern areas and during the fall in southern areas. Spawning occurs in the fall to early winter, young fish emerge from the redds in spring, and the juveniles rear in fresh water for one or more years before migrating to the sea. The length of freshwater rearing depends on the growth rate, which in turn depends on productivity and temper-

Coho Salmon

FIGURE 3.6.—North American distribution of coho salmon. Populations east of the main distribution have been introduced.

ature of the natal streams. After they emerge in the spring, young fish spread into the available rearing space, some moving upstream but most moving downstream. In streams, the young fish feed mainly on aquatic and terrestrial insects (Mundie 1969); in lakes, they may feed on *Daphnia* and available forage fish. Water velocity and the presence of other fish are important constraints on the habitat that can be used by the young fish, which often must remain in shallow fringe areas of pools and runs until they become large enough to compete successfully for more-favored sites in deeper, faster water.

Most anadromous coho salmon spend 2 or 3 years at sea and reach 3–6 kg in weight, although fish weighing more than 12 kg have been caught. Survival of smolts at sea is greater when smolts enter the ocean at a larger size and at times when food is abundant, which usually occur later in the emigration season (Bilton et al. 1982; Martin and Wertheimer 1987). In many coastal streams, the fish move into small tributaries to spawn with the onset of fall rains and increased flows. The embryos are in the redds over winter and may be subjected to disturbance by freshets.

Chinook Salmon

FIGURE 3.7.—North American distribution of chinook salmon. Great Lakes and Maine populations have been introduced.

In fall, as stream temperatures decline, young coho salmon become more security conscious, change their behavior, and seek areas with more cover than the areas they used in summer. They may move into side channels, sloughs, and beaver ponds for the winter, and they are usually found close to various forms of woody debris, roots, and overhanging brush that provide cover in water of low velocity (Hartman 1965; Bustard and Narver 1975a).

Chinook Salmon

The chinook salmon, sometimes referred to as the king, tyee, spring, and quinnat salmon, is another species much sought after by sport and commercial fishermen. Like coho salmon, chinook salmon are indigenous to the northern half of the Pacific coast of North America (Figure 3.7). They are most abundant in the larger river systems (Sacramento, Klamath, Rogue, Columbia, Fraser, Skeena, Strikine, Taku, Chilkat, Kenai, and Yukon rivers), and although they occur in many of the smaller coastal and island river systems, they are absent from many that are used by coho salmon. They have also been transplanted to large lakes (including the Great Lakes), where they have grown to large size when forage fish were abundant, matured despite retention in fresh water, and in some cases reproduced successfully.

The distribution and migration routes of chinook salmon in the ocean vary with the stock. In general, most of the fish head north along the Pacific coast after they enter the ocean, but many fish in some stocks go south (Wahle and Vreeland 1978; Wahle et al. 1981). The distance traveled in the ocean from the river mouth also varies among stocks; some Oregon and Washington stocks stay mainly in the vicinity of those states whereas some migrate north to the Gulf of Alaska.

The chinook salmon is the largest of the Pacific salmon; individuals may reach 50 kg or more, though most weigh less than 18 kg. The number of years the fish spend at sea (or in fresh water, if confined there) before maturing varies by stock. Some stocks are made up mostly of large fish that stay in the ocean for three or more years. At the other end of the spectrum are stocks with a high proportion of "jacks," or fish that spend only 1 year at sea.

Natal streams for chinook salmon may be relatively short coastal rivers or tributaries at the head of major drainages hundreds of kilometers from the sea. The time that adults return to their natal river systems depends primarily on the distance to the spawning grounds and the date the fish must spawn. Fish that migrate long distances and spawn earliest generally enter the large rivers first in the spring. For example, chinook salmon that will spawn in the headwaters of Idaho's Salmon River in August (nearly 1,500 km from the ocean) enter the Columbia River in April and May. In contrast, chinook salmon that will spawn some 1,000 km downstream in the Columbia River in October and November enter that river in August and September. The precise time of entry into small coastal rivers may depend on rainfall and increased streamflows, which usually occur within a range of time that allows adults to reach the spawning grounds when they should. The many stocks that enter large rivers may be grouped for management purposes by the timing of migration. Early-migrating fish in the Columbia River, for example, are referred to as the spring run, which is made up of many stocks destined for headwater tributaries throughout the basin.

Chinook salmon spawn as early as July in northern areas (McPhail and Lindsey 1970) and as late as January in the south (Burck and Reimers 1978), but spawning by any given stock occurs mostly during a 3- to 4-week period determined by the temperature regime of the natal stream. Fish spawn early in northern and high-elevation streams that cool early in the fall and are likely to have ice in the winter. In the Sacramento River in California, where temperature and flow regimes have been altered by water developments, and in Lake Superior (Kwain and Thomas 1984), where chinook salmon have been introduced, fish have been observed spawning in the spring.

Young chinook salmon emerge from the redds in spring except in some river systems where water-storage projects may have altered temperature regimes and the time of spawning. The young rear successfully in a wide variety of environments from small infertile streams to large rivers or impoundments.

Age at migration to the sea is variable in chinook salmon. Juveniles of summer- or fall-run stocks migrate to the ocean during their first year of life (Figure 3.2), usually after 3–6 months of rearing and after attaining a size of 70–90 mm total length. The young of spring-run stocks move seaward during the spring of their second year (sometimes the third year in cold streams). Healey (1983) studied some British Columbia stocks and referred to the subyearling migrants as ocean-type salmon (the first annulus on scales is formed in the ocean) and the yearling or older migrants as stream-type salmon (first annulus formed in fresh water). Healy claimed that the ocean-type fish remained in nearby coastal waters throughout their ocean life and that the stream-type migrated far offshore. He postulated that the ocean-type chinook salmon were found only in the southern portion of the species' range (south of about latitude 56°N) and that they were the most abundant form of chinook salmon in nearly all of those river systems. The Columbia River (about latitude 46°N) has stocks of chinook salmon that migrate to the ocean during their first year of life and those that migrate as yearlings. Of those stocks that enter the ocean as subyearlings, the lower-river, fall-run stocks appear to stay south of northern Vancouver Island, British Columbia, while in the ocean, but certain upriver stocks (also classed as fall-run fish) migrate as far north as Alaska (Parker and Kirkness 1956; Van Hyning 1973).

In some inland rivers, juvenile chinook salmon that do not enter the ocean until the spring of their second year may migrate down out of natal streams in the late summer and autumn and spend the winter in larger rivers before resuming their seaward migration in the spring (Chapman and Bjornn 1969; Bjornn 1971; Fessler et al. 1977). Like the other salmonids in streams that get cold in winter, the behavior of chinook salmon juveniles changes from mainly feeding in summer to hiding and close association with cover in winter.

Rainbow Trout and Steelhead

Rainbow trout and steelhead (the anadromous form of rainbow trout) are native to the drainages of Pacific North America (Figure 3.8) and Asia (Behnke 1966; McPhail and Lindsey 1970), but they were not as widely distributed as the cutthroat trout and chars. Rainbow trout have been transplanted to many temperate-zone waters in both the northern and southern hemispheres and have developed self-sustaining populations in many areas. Some forms of the rainbow trout (commonly referred to as kamloops and steelhead) are relatively long-lived, feed on forage fish in lakes (Hartman 1969) or the ocean, and attain large size (more than 15 kg). Other populations, however, live in streams their entire lives, feed mainly on insects, and are not especially large at maturity (often less than 2 kg).

Juveniles of the anadromous steelhead, like those of coho salmon and many chinook salmon, spend an extended period in fresh water before migrating to the sea. Steelhead smolts are usually larger (15–20 cm total length) and rear longer in fresh water (up to 4 years) than those of coho and chinook salmon (7–12 cm for those that rear a year or longer in fresh water). Migration to the sea usually occurs in the spring and the steelhead remain in the ocean for up to 4 years, their ultimate size depending on the length of their ocean residency.

Some drainages of the Pacific coast have two types of steelhead population, summer and winter, so named for the time of year and state of maturity when the fish return to fresh water from the ocean (Smith 1969). Summer-run fish return to fresh water during June through September, migrate inland toward spawning areas, overwinter in the larger rivers, resume migration in early spring to natal streams, and then spawn. Winter-run fish return to fresh water in autumn or winter, migrate to spawning areas, and then spawn in late winter or spring. Adults

Rainbow Trout and Steelhead

FIGURE 3.8.—North American distribution of steelhead (anadromous form of rainbow trout) and rainbow trout (nonanadromous freshwater form). Populations east of Pacific drainages have been introduced.

do not enter some coastal streams until spring, however, just before spawning. The time of spawning is usually consistent from year to year in a given stream but it can differ by a month or more among streams in the same region, depending on local environments. Steelhead may use small headwater streams for spawning, and they may use the same areas used by salmon, which spawn at another time of year.

Steelhead do not invariably die after spawning as do the Pacific salmons, but the same senescense and physiological processes that occur in salmon lead to substantial postspawning mortality of adult steelhead (Robertson et al. 1961). In small coastal streams, up to 30% of the adults may survive to spawn a second or third time, but in large drainages where fish migrate long distances, the proportion of fish that spawn more than once is much lower. Sex ratios of adult steelhead and rainbow trout vary widely, from about 65% females for steelhead returning to Dworshak National Fish Hatchery in Idaho to about 43% females for rainbow trout spawning in the Lardeau River in British Columbia (Irvine 1978).

In the Chilliwack River of British Columbia, 13 different combinations of stream and ocean ages of steelhead (1 year in the stream and 1 year at sea to 4 years in the stream and 3 years at sea) were present in samples from the 1948–1953 sport fishery analysed by Maher and Larkin (1955). Most (96%) of the fish were in four age combinations: 2 or 3 years in streams and 2 or 3 years at sea. Sixty percent of the young fish migrated to the sea at age 2 (16.5 cm) and 35% at age 3 (20.0 cm). In the Green River, Washington, 73% of the returning adults had migrated to the sea as age-2 smolts and most of those had spent 2 or 3 years at sea (Pautzke and Meigs 1941).

Fecundity of steelhead is related to length and age of the fish, but it varies among stocks and locations (Bulkley 1967). Fish about 55 cm long may have fewer than 2,000 eggs, whereas fish 85 cm long can have 5,000 to 10,000 eggs, depending on the stock.

In drainages open to anadromous salmonids, young steelhead often compete with young coho and chinook salmon, cutthroat trout, Dolly Varden, and bull trout for food and space. Segregation of the species in the use of habitat has been observed when more than one species or age-group of fish was present in the same section of stream (Hartman 1965; Peterson 1966; Fraser 1969; Andrusak and Northcote 1971; Everest and Chapman 1972; Glova 1984). Some investigators believed the segregation was selective (an evolutionary adaptation: Nilsson 1967); others thought it resulted mainly from interactions between fish, the outcomes of which were determined by the size, aggressiveness, and capabilities (e.g., swimming performance) of the fish.

Young rainbow trout and steelhead, as well as other trout and salmon, have a variety of migration patterns that vary with local conditions; control mechanisms appear to range from mostly genetic to mostly environmental (Northcote 1969a). In some populations, fish may spend their entire lives in a limited area of a small stream, but in others, they may migrate upstream or downstream soon after emergence from the redds to enter lakes (Lindsey et al. 1959) or other rearing areas. The time when steelhead smolts migrate to the sea appears to be controlled primarily by photoperiod (Bjornn 1971), but it is influenced at times by other environmental factors such as flow, temperature, and lunar phase. Once in the sea, steelhead may stay close to their home stream, as do the "half pounders" of some Oregon and California stocks (Everest 1973), or they may migrate far offshore, as do some stocks that have been caught in the Japanese high-seas fishery in the Gulf of Alaska (C. K. Harris 1988).

Survival rates have been assessed for the various life stages of steelhead and summarized in a report by Bley and Moring (1988). Survival of embryos in redds depends on the amount of fine sediments present, the degree to which redds are disturbed by freshets, maintenance of adequate flows, and other factors. Survival from egg to emergent fry can be high under ideal conditions, but is usually less than 50%. Relatively few fish (<20%) survive their first year in the stream (Burns 1971; Bjornn 1978; Allen 1986); the small, newly emerged fish are particularly vulnerable to predation, and severe winter and spring conditions can cause high losses in some streams (Seelbach 1987). Steelhead that become smolts after 2 or 3 years in streams usually represent less than 10% of the eggs deposited in redds. Survival from smolt to adult for steelhead varies annually and from area to area. Survival rates can be relatively high (10–20%) for fish that return to coastal streams or low (<2%) for fish that must surmount dams and travel long riverine distances to natal streams.

Cutthroat Trout

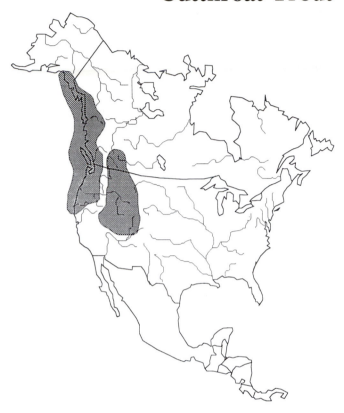

FIGURE 3.9.—North American distribution of cutthroat trout. The discontinuous distribution represents subspecific differentiations.

Cutthroat Trout

Cutthroat trout are distributed widely, but not uniformly, from southern Alaska to northern California along the Pacific coast and inland from the Saskatchewan south to the Rio Grande drainages (Behnke and Wallace 1986; Behnke 1988) (Figure 3.9). They are often found above as well as below barriers, and frequently in association with bull trout and mountain whitefish. Recent invaders such as salmon and steelhead are usually restricted to the areas downstream from barriers.

In 1930, Jordan et al. (1930) suggested there were 16 species of cutthroat trout, but Miller (1950) combined groups and listed 12 subspecies. In a recent review, Behnke and Wallace (1986) described 13 subspecies; of these, the coastal, westslope, and Yellowstone subspecies are most abundant at present, and the continued existence of some others is considered threatened.

Cutthroat trout have evolved under a wide array of competitive situations. They may be the only salmonid present, as in Yellowstone Lake (Gresswell and Varley 1986), or they may have to compete with up to five other species of anadromous and nonanadromous salmonids. The cutthroat trout has coexisted with a wide variety of other species in a variety of habitats by occupying different parts of the habitat than do the other species (Hartman and Gill 1968; Hanson 1977; Nicholas 1978; Nilsson and Northcote 1981; Johnston 1982; Glova 1984, 1986). Introductions of nonnative salmonids, coupled with habitat degradation and overexploitation, have led to the demise of many local stocks of cutthroat trout (Griffith 1986b).

Throughout their range, cutthroat trout spawn in the spring or early summer, usually in small streams (Irving 1955; Johnson 1963; Johnston 1982). Spawning fish may be as small as 15 cm and females may contain less than 100 eggs in cold headwater streams, but they may exceed 5 kg in lake systems where the fish are piscivorous, such as Bear Lake, Idaho–Utah, and Pyramid Lake, Nevada. In most populations, however, mature fish are 25–50 cm long and the females have 500–2,000 eggs (Cramer 1940; Irving 1955; Johnson 1963). Their progeny emerge from redds in summer. They may then move downstream into lakes or stay in the natal streams for extended periods, but they commonly rear in streams for two or more years and then migrate downstream, mainly in the spring, to larger rivers, lakes, or the ocean (coastal cutthroat trout) for a final period of rearing before reaching maturity. Coastal fish remain at sea for a summer. The spawning migration usually occurs in the spring for nonanadromous cutthroat trout but coastal fish return between late summer and winter, depending on stock, and overwinter in streams before spawning or merely returning to sea the following spring (Giger 1972; Johnston 1982).

Migrations of cutthroat trout vary widely with subspecies and locality. The fish in some populations remain in a small area of a stream their entire lives (Miller 1957), whereas fish in others migrate from natal streams to lakes (Bjornn 1961), larger rivers, or the sea, and then back to the streams when they mature. Coastal cutthroat trout usually enter the ocean in spring at age 2 to 4, do not migrate far from their home stream (usually staying within 50 km of it), and return in autumn or winter. If mature, they spawn in late winter or early spring. The kelts and fish that did not mature during their first summer at sea leave natal streams soon after spawning and reenter the ocean. Cutthroat trout, like other salmonids, have well-developed homing abilities that allow them to return to natal streams (McCleave 1967; Johnston 1982).

The behavior of cutthroat trout, as of most other salmonids, changes between summer and winter. In summer the fish are widely dispersed and mainly interested in feeding; in winter they hide, enter the interstices of substrates, form large schools in large rivers, and are much more wary than in summer (Lewynsky 1986). Some migrate downstream in autumn (as much as 160 km) and back upstream in the spring, probably in response to winter conditions (Bjornn and Mallet 1964; Johnson 1977).

The subspecies of cutthroat trout vary in their propensity to feed on forage fish and attain large size. The westslope subspecies is one of the least likely, the Lahontan and Bonneville subspecies the most likely, to do so. In lakes with abundant kokanee as forage, westslope cutthroat trout rarely exceed 1 kg (Bjornn and Liknes 1986), but the other two subspecies reach 5 kg or more (Gerstung 1986; Nielson and Lentsch 1988). Cutthroat trout feed extensively on *Daphnia* when it is available (McMullin 1979); in some infertile lakes, however, other fish species (e.g., kokanee) apparently reduce the abundance of *Daphnia* to such low levels

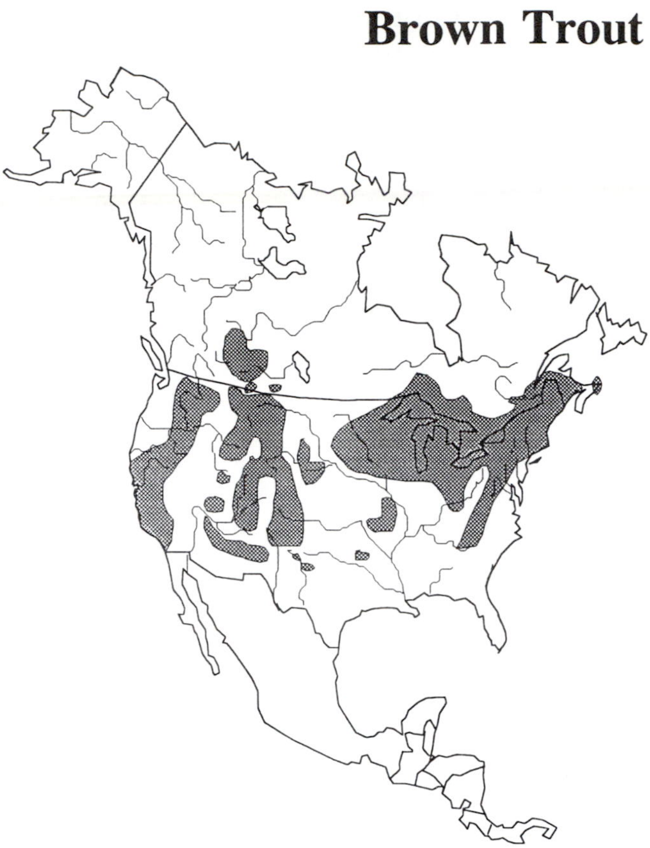

Brown Trout

FIGURE 3.10.—North American distribution of brown trout. The species is Eurasian and all North American populations stem from introductions.

that the cutthroat trout feed mainly on littoral-zone insects (Bjornn 1957). In streams, cutthroat trout feed mainly on aquatic and terrestrial insects (Griffith 1974).

Brown Trout

Brown trout are indigenous to Europe and have been introduced into several drainages throughout North America, where self-sustaining populations have developed (Figure 3.10). In Europe, both anadromous and nonanadromous populations are present (Solomon 1982), and both forms are sometimes present in the same lake or river system (Jonsson 1985). Most of the populations in North America, however, remain in fresh water throughout their lives.

Brown trout spawn in the fall and early winter; their progeny emerge from redds in late winter or spring, depending on the temperature regime of the natal stream. After emergence from the redd, young brown trout disperse to feeding areas, become territorial in streams, and colonize the available rearing areas (Solomon 1982). In some drainages, the fish may rear for one or more years and then migrate to larger rivers, lakes, or (in Europe) the sea, where they spend one or more years, mature, and then return to spawn. In a Norwegian lake, fish that remained in fresh water were up to 10 years old and 47 cm long, and males outnumbered females (Jonsson 1985). For the anadromous segment, smolts were 2–7 years old (14–29 cm long), adults were 3–9 years old (29–67 cm long), and females were more abundant than males. Those fish that migrated to the sea at age 2 appeared to grow faster than those that migrated at older ages. Growth, survival, and density depend on the same factors that regulate those variables in other salmonids.

In northern Norway and Iceland, brown trout smolts migrate to the sea in spring at about the same time as do Atlantic salmon, spend the summer feeding, and then return to fresh water to spend the winter, whether they are mature or not (Berg and Jonsson 1989; Gudjonsson 1989). If mature, the fish home to their natal streams with a high degree of accuracy, but if immature, they may not return to their natal stream for the winter.

In an Oregon stream, brown trout growth was limited by the low fertility of the stream and a high density of conspecifics (Lorz 1974). Adults were abundant enough to produce surplus progeny, and abundance was related to quality of the habitat in the stream.

Atlantic Salmon

Atlantic salmon reproduce in streams from about 43°N to 59°N latitude on the east coast of North America (Figure 3.11), in Greenland and Iceland, from about 43°N to 71°N latitude on the western and northern coasts of Europe, and in arctic Russia (Thorpe and Mitchell 1981). In their oceanic migrations, the fish of some stocks stay relatively close to their natal stream, those of other stocks migrate long distances along the North American or European coasts, and fish of still other stocks from both sides of the Atlantic migrate to feeding grounds near Greenland before returning to spawn (Reddin and Shearer 1987; Berg and Jonsson 1989).

The life cycle of Atlantic salmon, like that of steelhead, has many variations, which provides an extra measure of insurance that small stocks will persist despite reproductive failures in any one year (Saunders and Schom 1985). Young fish typically spend 2–4 years in streams before becoming smolts and migrating to the sea, and they spend up to 6 years at sea (Figure 3.2). Atlantic salmon may reproduce first as 2- or 3-year-old fish that mature prematurely in fresh water (these usually are males) or after they have spent time at sea; they may also spawn in more than one year (repeat spawners). The fish spawning in any year can come from several prior year-classes; conversely, fish of a given year-class may spawn in several future years, depending on the time spent in the streams and in the ocean before maturity.

Schaffer and Elson (1975) found a tendency for the mean age of Canadian Atlantic salmon ascending long streams to be older than the age of fish ascending shorter streams. They also found that age of first spawning was related to marine growth rate, and that mean age at first spawning was younger in Maine and Ungava, the southern and northern ends of the North America range, than in most of the intervening areas.

Adult Atlantic salmon may enter rivers in spring, migrate to upstream areas, and remain there until autumn. Such timing may allow the fish to avoid thermal barriers in the estuary or in the lower ends of rivers in summer (Hawkins 1989). Spawning in the fall is cued by river temperature (Heggberget 1988).

Atlantic Salmon

FIGURE 3.11.—North American distribution of Atlantic salmon.

Atlantic salmon stocks of far-northern Ungava Bay in Canada have a life history that appears to be modified by the ice conditions and cold water in the bay (Power et al. 1987). Smolts enter the estuary in July but may not migrate through the bay to the Atlantic Ocean until September (later than more southern stocks), if ice and low water temperatures persist in the bay until then. Likewise, adult migrations through the bay and into natal rivers can be delayed by these unfavorable conditions.

Osterdahl (1969) found that most Atlantic salmon naturally produced in a Swedish stream spent 2 or 3 years in the stream before migrating to the ocean, mainly in late May or June. The early-season migrants were older than the later migrants and they moved mostly at night, whereas the later migrants moved mostly during daylight. Males made up 35–40% of the smolts, and about 50% of the young males matured before smoltification.

In river systems with lakes, Atlantic salmon juveniles may spend part of their freshwater rearing period in the lakes before going to the ocean (Ryan 1986). Nonanadromous populations of Atlantic salmon exist in scattered locations throughout its range, usually in landlocked lakes without access to the sea.

Survival of Atlantic salmon during the various life stages varies with locality, but is generally similar to that of other salmonids (see literature cited in Bley and Moring 1988). The survival rate of embryos in hatcheries is often as high as 90%, but survival in redds is frequently less than 25% because of less-than-optimum conditions. Survival from recently emerged fish to smolts has ranged up to 12%, but is more often in the 2–4% range. Smolt-to-returning-adult survival varies annually and between localities, ranging from less than 1% to 26%.

Predation by American mergansers (*Mergus merganser*) and belted kingfishers (*Megaceryle alcyon*) can be an important cause of mortality of juvenile Atlantic salmon in streams. On the Miramichi River in New Brunswick, parr eaten by mergansers amounted to more than two-thirds of the number of smolts produced each year (White 1957). Elson (1962) estimated that control of mergansers and kingfishers along the Pollett River in New Brunswick could result in a fivefold increase in the number of smolts produced.

Atlantic salmon shift behavior and habitat use with change of season, like other salmonids. In winter they are less interested in feeding and seek cover more than they do in summer (Rimmer et al. 1984), and they may leave some streams in autumn and move downstream to larger rivers that are more suitable for overwintering (Riddell and Leggett 1981).

The food of young Atlantic salmon in streams is primarily a function of the availability and size of the prey. In streams on both sides of the Atlantic Ocean, the young fish feed on invertebrates drifting in the water or found on the stream bottom (Allen 1940; Lillehammer 1973; Williams 1981). Larval or pupal forms of black flies, midges, mayflies, and stoneflies are often used as food along with cladocerans, if available.

Arctic Char

The Arctic char is one of several species of *Salvelinus* native to western North America. It has a varied life history adapted to the freshwater and marine environments of the northern circumpolar region, where it is the only salmonid that has become widely established in arctic waters. The coastline of the Arctic Ocean forms the present day locus of the Arctic char's distribution (Figure 3.12) and the species reaches its maximum size and density there (Johnson 1980). Southward along the North American coast the anadromous form extends to the approximate limit of sea ice in winter. South of this limit only nonmigratory stocks occur. Most of the fresh waters presently occupied by Arctic char are of recent, postglacial origin.

Around the margins of the polar basin, melting snow caused by the continuous sunshine of May and June augments the flow of rivers that flow continuously under the ice throughout the winter. In spring or early summer, anadromous Arctic char leave the still-frozen lakes and migrate to the sea as the sea ice begins to melt and open water develops between land and the permanent ice pack. Within this lead, there is a surge of biological activity that provides abundant food for the fish for a brief period of time. After a relatively short period (up to 9 weeks) of intensive feeding, Arctic char return to fresh water in mid-August or early September, well in advance of the formation of new sea ice that begins in October (Mathisen and Berg 1968; Johnson 1980; Gyselman, 1984; Dempson and Kristofferson 1987; Berg and Jonsson 1989; Gudjonsson 1989).

Arctic Char

FIGURE 3.12.—North American distribution of Arctic char.

Even immature Arctic char, once they have reached the smolt stage, make annual migrations to salt water (Johnson 1980). Mature fish usually return to their natal stream to spawn and spend the winter, but immature fish often spend the winter in other than their natal stream. Both immature and maturing fish return to fresh water each fall because the ocean temperatures are too cold for overwinter survival in much of the species' range. Because of their repeated movements between fresh water and the sea to take advantage of food and avoid unsuitable temperatures, Arctic char can be termed amphidromous.

Arctic char spawn in late summer and autumn in a wide variety of environments in the lakes of the high arctic and in the lakes and rivers of the subarctic and north temperate regions. Water depths at which Arctic char spawn in lakes vary from 1–3 m along shorelines to 100 m (Johnson 1980). Arctic char usually spawn on gravel and frequently on small to large cobbles with or without a mixture of coarse sand. Incubation time of eggs and embryos varies from 35–40 d at 12°C (Swift 1965) to 180 d at 0.75–1.5°C (Schindler et al. 1974). In some amphidromous stocks (e.g., in the Northwest Territories of Canada), maturing fish may not migrate to the sea in the year they will spawn. Maturing fish that do migrate restrict their movements in the ocean and are the first to return to fresh water (Dempson and Kristofferson 1987).

Movements of Arctic char at sea appear to be more restricted than those of some salmon and trout. Although some travels of 200–300 km in a summer have been recorded, most Arctic char appear to stay within 100 km of their home stream (Dempson and Kristofferson 1987; Berg and Jonsson 1989).

Arctic char are able to home to their natal streams, but there is evidence that they may stray at a higher rate than the anadromous salmon and trout. Tagged fish often have been recaptured in streams other than the one in which they were originally captured, evidence that Arctic char readily enter and may spend one or more winters in nonnatal streams. Most such records involve immature fish, however, and the evidence for a high rate of straying by spawners is less convincing (Dempson and Kristofferson 1987).

Arctic char show a wide range of variation with respect to age at first spawning, spawning season, and spawning time (Johnson 1980). After hatching and before reaching sexual maturity, the young spend several years in fresh water, followed by two to four seasons of migration to the sea for feeding. The anadromous form of Arctic char may spawn in either lakes or rivers, but autumn appears to be their only spawning season. Nonanadromous populations may spawn in lakes in autumn or spring, but apparently spawn in rivers only during autumn (Johnson 1980). The choice of lake or river spawning seems to depend on the suitability of available sites with respect to substrate quality, continuous presence of nonfreezing water, and low temperatures.

Many individuals in anadromous populations live to a considerable age and therefore may be expected to spawn several times during their life. Arctic char older than 30 years have been found (Hunter 1976).

Living in regions where food is relatively limited both in season and in diversity, Arctic char must be less selective than species living in more productive environments. In arctic lakes, the variety of available food is relatively small, and primary food items may consist of chironomids, large crustacean plankton, harpactacoid copepods, ostracods, amphipods, mysids, and mollusks (Johnson 1980). Plankton is an important food source in some lakes. In general, the diet of Arctic char seems wide-ranging and opportunistic. In most arctic lakes, other fish are not plentiful, and most piscivory by Arctic char would be cannibalistic (Johnson 1980).

In most environments they occupy, Arctic char are virtually immune from predation once they have reached a certain size, and they can be considered the terminal predators. Fish-eating birds take a few Arctic char, particularly young fish in shallow waters (Johnson 1980).

Dolly Varden

Dolly Varden, another species of *Salvelinus* native to western North America, are similar to the Arctic char in that they migrate often between fresh water and the sea (i.e., they are amphidromous), they do not migrate long distances into the ocean, they overwinter in fresh water and spawn in the fall, and they spawn more than once (i.e., they are iteroparous). Although the fish move into and may overwinter in nonnatal streams, Armstrong and Morrow (1980) and Armstrong (1984) believed that spawners stray little.

Dolly Varden

FIGURE 3.13.—North American distribution of Dolly Varden.

Two forms of Dolly Varden, a northern and a southern form, have long been recognized in North America. Anadromous stocks of northern Dolly Varden occur in streams along the north coasts of Alaska and Canada east to the McKenzie River delta (Armstrong and Morrow 1980). The southern form is found as far south as Oregon and Washington (Figure 3.13).

Dolly Varden usually attain maturity at 5 or 6 years of age. Fish that have reached maturity may spawn each year, but most anadromous Dolly Varden in northern Alaska spawn only every second year (Armstrong and Morrow 1980). Most of the maturing fish that entered Lake Eva in southeastern Alaska, and fish that had completed spawning there, were of ages 5, 6, and 7 (Blackett 1968).

Spawning may occur as early as latter August or as late as November, but most of it occurs in September and October. Favored spawning areas are main channels, usually in fairly strong current at depths of 0.2 m or more, or in springs. Development of the eggs to hatching requires 7 or 8 months in rivers of northern Alaska, and the alevins remain in the gravel of the redd until the yolk sac has been absorbed, a period of 60–70 d. Emergence of fry from the redds occurs from April to June. Alevins of anadromous stocks in Hood Bay Creek, southeastern Alaska, emerge from the gravel in May and juveniles remain in the stream for 2–4 years (Armstrong 1970).

Growth is most rapid from July to August. By mid-September, most young Dolly Varden have attained lengths of about 60 mm and weights of about 2 g. Most adult fish reach 7 to 9 years of age, although a few older fish have been observed. Northern Dolly Varden remain in their natal streams for the first several years, migrating at times between the natal rearing areas and other parts of the drainage. Beginning at about age 2, smoltification takes place in the spring and the fish migrate to the sea to feed along with older fish.

Armstrong (1974) hypothesized that fish that originate in streams without lakes enter the sea as smolts in spring and autumn at ages 3 to 4, and that the fish then search for a stream with a lake wintering area; during this search they may enter and leave several streams. The following spring they return to the sea and if they are still immature, they repeat the movements of the previous year. At maturity, they enter their natal stream from July to October to spawn in September to November. Shortly after spawning, the survivors return to the sea and seek out a lake system in which to overwinter.

In the Keogh River on northern Vancouver Island, British Columbia, Smith and Slaney (1980) found Dolly Varden that were immigrating from the ocean were 110–470 mm long (average, 280 mm) and 2–9 years old. Adults averaged 340 mm and made up 40% of the run, which entered the river from July to October; the other 60% were "subadults" that averaged 220 mm in length and were returning from their first migration to the ocean.

Freshwater growth of Dolly Varden in the Keogh River was slow (Smith and Slaney 1980); fry required an average of 3 years to reach the smolt stage at an average length of 139 mm. Growth in the ocean, however, was rapid; first-time smolts gained 74 mm in length and 98 g in weight in 107 d, on average.

In the Keogh River, Dolly Varden fry and parr were found mostly in higher-velocity habitats (fry: 54% in riffles, 40% in runs, and 6% in pools or slack water; parr: 64% in riffles, 22% in runs, and 14% in pools and slack water). About 79% of the smolts were produced in the mainstem river (86 smolts/km) and 21% in tributaries.

Seaward migration from the Keogh River occurred from March to June. Adults moved from the lakes to the river and into the ocean first, followed by first-time smolts (Smith and Slaney 1980). The older fish remained in the ocean an average of 157 d before returning to fresh water, the smolts an average of 107 d.

The survival of Keogh River Dolly Varden was 0.4–0.6% from egg to smolt, 12% from fry to smolt, and 44% from smolt to subadult (Smith and Slaney 1980). Overwinter survival of subadults was about 56%. Survival of adults that returned to the ocean was about 70% over 150 d in the ocean; survival of adults that overwintered in the river was 61%.

On emergence, Dolly Varden fry are about 25 mm long; they feed primarily on chironomids and mayflies, as well as on other insects and small crustaceans. Most of the food is taken on or near the stream bottom (Armstrong and Morrow 1980). At ages 1–3, Dolly Varden feed on insects and the eggs and young of other fish; pink and chum salmon fry are eaten in April to June, if available (Armstrong and Morrow 1980). Insects consumed by Dolly Varden are primarily aquatic species

Bull Trout

FIGURE 3.14.—North American distribution of bull trout.

taken from the substrate and the drift and terrestrial forms taken at or near the surface (Armstrong and Morrow 1980).

Northern Dolly Varden are apparently not subject to heavy predation in arctic Alaska during their freshwater residency, although a few fish may be taken on the spawning grounds by bears, wolves, otters, and birds.

Bull Trout

Bull trout are native to western North America, once present in most drainages from northern California to the headwaters of the Yukon River and from the coastal rivers east to the Saskatchewan, Peace, and Liard rivers that drain the east side of the continental divide (Figure 3.14). The bull trout was formally recognized as a distinct species of the genus *Salvelinus* in 1978 (Cavender 1978). Prior to that date, most populations that are now known as bull trout were called Dolly Varden. Bull trout are generally nonanadromous, but they are similar to Arctic char and Dolly Varden in appearance and in many aspects of life history and behavior.

Bull trout often occur together with cutthroat trout and mountain whitefish upstream from barriers in many drainages, an indication of early colonization. In drainages colonized later by salmon and steelhead, bull trout have coexisted successfully, occupying a different niche than the trout and salmon, and using the salmon as food.

Bull trout live in a variety of habitats including small streams, large rivers, and lakes or reservoirs. In some drainages, the fish spend their lives in cold headwater streams. In others, they spend the first 2–4 years in small natal streams and then migrate into larger rivers, lakes, or reservoirs to spend another 2–4 years before maturing (Bjornn 1961). Bull trout that stay in cold headwater streams their entire lives usually do not exceed 25 cm in length when mature, whereas those that move to lakes where forage fish are plentiful can attain weights of more than 10 kg.

In some stocks of bull trout, maturing adults may begin migrating to the spawning grounds in the spring or early summer even though they do not spawn until late August through October (Bjornn 1961; Fraley and Shepard 1989). The early spawning migration has been observed most often in stocks with large spawners that migrate from lakes into relatively small tributaries. The bull trout that live their lives in small headwater streams migrate relatively short distances to spawning sites.

Female bull trout may deposit as few as a hundred or up to 5 or 10 thousand eggs in the redds they build, depending on their size. The embryos incubate during the fall, winter, and spring and the surviving fry emerge from the redds in April and May. The rate of embryo development is temperature-dependent, and bull trout in the Flathead River drainage of Montana must accumulate about 635 temperature units (centigrade degree-days above 0°C) between spawning and emergence (Fraley and Shepard 1989).

After they emerge, young bull trout disperse up and down the stream to find suitable areas to feed. Juveniles differ from those of many other trout and salmon in that they stay close to the stream substrate and do not take up positions in the water column.

Bull trout that leave natal streams to rear elsewhere for part of their lives may migrate extensively. Some fish spend their first 2–4 years in tributary streams, then migrate to lakes (if any are available), where they feed for another 2–4 years before spawning for the first time. The migration back to the natal streams may be several kilometers long (Bjornn 1961; Fraley and Shepard 1989). In a common variant of this pattern, the fish migrate downstream to large rivers rather than to lakes, and then move up and down the river seasonally. In the Middle Fork of the Salmon River in Idaho, bull trout have been observed moving as much as 100 km downstream to wintering areas during the fall and back upstream to summer feeding areas in the spring (Bjornn and Mallet 1964).

Young fish feed primarily on aquatic invertebrates in the streams during their first 2 or 3 years but become more piscivorous, given the opportunity, as they get larger. Bull trout that move into lakes feed almost exclusively on forage fish, including kokanee if they are abundant. Growth of fish in the lakes is usually much faster than that of fish that remain in the colder natal streams.

The bull trout has been eliminated from some of its native range and seriously reduced in abundance in most of the remaining drainages, and its range has not been expanded to our knowledge. Excessive exploitation, habitat degradation, and introductions of exotic species are probably the major causes of the declines.

Brook Trout

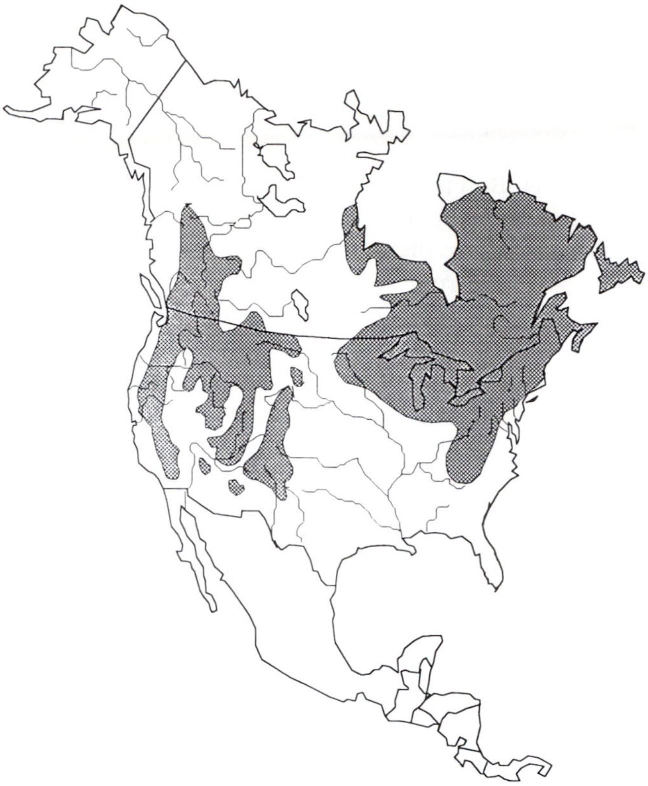

FIGURE 3.15.—North American distribution of brook trout. Populations west of the main eastern distribution are introduced.

Artificial propagation of bull trout is in its infancy and has not been used on a large scale to supplement or replace damaged stocks.

Brook Trout

The brook trout is indigenous to eastern North America. In its native range, it is particularly abundant in the Canadian provinces of Ontario, Quebec, New-foundland, Labrador, New Brunswick, and Nova Scotia, and in the states of Maine, Vermont, New Hampshire, and upper New York (Figure 3.15). It naturally occurs along the Hudson Bay coast into northern Manitoba, around the Great Lakes, and southward in headwater streams of the Appalachian Mountains to Tennessee and Georgia (Power 1980).

During glacial times, brook trout populations existed farther south on the Atlantic coast and perhaps in the upper Mississippi Valley (McPhail and Lindsey 1970). Postglacial dispersal northward was coastal and across the interior of the Quebec–Labrador plateau. Penetration to headwaters of river systems was aided by changes in sea level, streamflow patterns, and isostatic changes in land elevation (Power 1980). Brook trout have also been introduced into many suitable waters of western North America (Figure 3.15).

The brook trout has long been a favorite of anglers, who are concerned about the declining numbers of this species in eastern North America. Habitat destruction by agricultural and forestry practices, industrial water use, dams, and pollution were responsible for this decline (Power 1980).

The brook trout has the shortest life span of all the *Salvelinus* chars; in many areas it rarely lives until its fourth year. The maximum age is 9 years (Power 1980).

Brook trout spawn in the autumn when day length and temperature are decreasing. In the north and at high elevations farther south, spawning occurs in late August or September. Over most of the range, October is the usual time of spawning but in southern areas, spawning may not occur until December (Power 1980). The redd is usually constructed in gravel but if upwelling ground water is present, brook trout will spawn on sand or silty–sandy bottoms.

Although most brook trout live their entire lives in relatively short reaches of streams or in small lakes, a few migrate to the sea. Migration to a lake or the sea usually provides more living space and results in better growth, lower mortality, and larger fish (Power 1980). In stream and river habitats, movement is minimal. Alevins disperse from redds into shallow waters until they have established territories. As the fish grow larger, they occupy bigger territories, usually in deeper water. Brook trout that are hatched in streams and later move to lakes usually do so during their second or third summer when they have reached lengths of 80–150 mm (Power 1980). Most seaward migration takes place in autumn, and most migrations from salt to fresh water occur in April to early July.

The upper lethal temperature for yearling brook trout is approximately 25.3°C (Power 1980). The normal range of water temperatures found in brook trout habitats is 0–20°C, depending on the season, and the preferred temperature range is 10–12°C. Summer temperatures occasionally may exceed this, but the fish move into cooler waters when they do.

Dominant foods of brook trout in lakes are plankton (largely *Daphnia* sp.) and fish (mainly northern redbelly dace, other minnows, yellow perch, and pumpkinseeds). In other habitats, important food items are aquatic and terrestrial insects, including Diptera (primarily Chironomidae), Trichoptera, Plecoptera, Orthoptera (grasshoppers), and Hymenoptera (ants) (Power 1980; Fraser 1981). Foods of lesser importance include Odonata (dragonflies), Ephemeroptera, Coleoptera (beetles), leeches, mollusks, and crustaceans (including crayfish). The diets of small and large brook trout are generally similar, although the order of importance of prey sometimes differs. Food of terrestrial origin is relatively unimportant in midwinter, but it is a predominant part of brook trout diets during the summer in some streams (Lord 1933).

Among the predators of brook trout are American mergansers, belted kingfishers, great blue herons (*Ardea herodias*), and mink (*Mustela vison*).

Lake Trout

Native lake trout, like brook trout, are confined to North America, particularly its northern parts (Figure 3.16). In Canada, the species is found in all the provinces and territories except Prince Edward Island and insular Newfoundland. In the USA, native populations occur in Alaska, Montana, Minnesota, Wisconsin, Michigan, Maine, Vermont, New Hampshire, New York, and Pennsylvania.

Lake Trout

FIGURE 3.16.—North American distribution of lake trout. Isolated populations in the western USA have been introduced.

Before they were extirpated from Lakes Michigan and Erie, lake trout were also in Indiana, Illinois, and Ohio. The species has been successfully introduced into California, Nevada, Colorado, Washington, Oregon, Idaho, Utah, Wyoming, Massachusetts, and Connecticut (Martin and Olver 1980).

The major factor regulating the natural range of lake trout has been the geologic history of northern North America. The lake trout's distribution lies almost totally within the boundaries of Pleistocene glaciation (Lindsey 1964). The most recent major ice sheet, the Wisconsinan, displaced the *Salvelinus* chars from all of Canada and from parts of the northeastern USA. It has been proposed that multiple refugia, including unglaciated Alaska and the Yukon Territory, provided sanctuary for the lake trout during this time of glacial activity. Recolonization in Canada and the northern USA from these refugia probably took place in several ways (Martin and Olver 1980): by following the retreating ice front via temporary pondings; by migrations into the large Pleistocene glacial lakes, such as Agassiz, Peace, and Tyree, and their outlets; and by migration through the arctic waters, which had lower salinities than some of the eastern seas (Lindsey 1964). The lake trout is primarily a freshwater species and the least likely of the North American salmonids to go to sea (Rounsefell 1958), but it may occasionally be found in waters of low salinity.

The age of lake trout at first maturity may vary from 4 to 13; corresponding lengths and weights are 28–65 cm and 0.5–2.5 kg (Martin and Olver 1980). Although primarily fall spawners, lake trout are known to reproduce in each of the months from June to January (Martin and Olver 1980). Peak spawning in several Ontario lakes occurs from late September to early November (MacLean et al. 1981). In Great Slave Lake, some lake trout mature at age 5 and most are mature by age 10; spawning takes place in late summer and early autumn (MacLean et al. 1981). In general, northern stocks spawn earlier than those in more temperate regions. Intermittent spawning by lake trout sometimes occurs, particularly in northern populations. Females ripen only every second or third year in some lakes (L. Johnson 1972).

Lake trout usually spawn in lakes, and rarely spawn in streams (Martin and Olver 1980). In most cases, they do not build redds, but spawn along exposed shorelines off points or islands or on midlake shoals. The substrate is usually broken rubble or angular rocks 3–15 cm in diameter, which commonly are interspersed with large boulders. Depths of spawning areas range from 15 cm to more than 90 m (Eschmeyer 1964); in most smaller inland lakes, shoals are generally less than 6 m deep (Martin and Olver 1980). Stream spawning, although rare, may occur in the arctic (Martin and Olver 1980).

At least 50% of lake trout embryos survive to hatching in some lakes (Martin and Olver 1980). Incubation lasts about 4 months in the more southern lakes of the lake trout's range, but is generally shorter for stream-spawning stocks.

The distribution of lake trout throughout a body of water depends on season, size and age of fish, spawning or feeding activities, and physical and chemical conditions such as temperature, light, and dissolved oxygen (Martin and Olver 1980). Lake trout make extensive vertical and horizontal movements in response to these and other influences. Those that live in large lakes can move great distances. Eschmeyer (1964) believed that lake trout juveniles moved from spawning areas to deep water about 1 month after hatching, or at the time the yolk sac was fully absorbed, generally before mid-May. During the period of lake stratification, lake trout become concentrated in the colder waters below the thermocline (Martin and Olver 1980). As surface waters cool in autumn and thermal stratification breaks down, the lake trout move back to shallower water, still on or close to the bottom. Lake trout are often found in shallow shoreline areas in spring and early summer until the surface waters of lakes become too warm.

The lake trout is omnivorous in its food habits and will take most available forage including annelids, crustaceans, insects, arachnids, mollusks, fishes, and small mammals. In some instances, they may even take plant materials (Martin and Olver 1980). For their first few years of life, lake trout rely heavily on invertebrate foods; as they grow older, invertebrates become less important and forage fishes are preyed upon to a greater extent (Martin and Olver 1980). In large lakes, lake trout are primarily piscivorous; their prey includes alewives, ciscoes, kokanee, sculpins, whitefish, sticklebacks, smelts, and cyprinids. When invertebrates are taken by lake trout in large lakes, they are frequently mysids and amphipods. In mountain lakes in the western USA and in the smaller lakes in the eastern part of its range, lake trout feed on suckers, whitefish, sculpins, chubs, smelts, yellow perch, ciscoes, and other salmonids (Wales 1946; Van Wyhe and Peck 1968; Frantz and Cordone 1970). Invertebrates taken in these smaller lakes include crayfish, mysids, Diptera larvae, caddisfly larvae, ants, and grasshoppers. As lake trout become larger, they usually concentrate on larger members of a prey species instead of eating greater numbers of small individuals (Frantz and Cordone 1970).

Lake trout are top predators for most of their lives and they live in deep waters, so competition with other species for food is not extensive (Martin and Olver 1980). The only important predator on adult lake trout is the sea lamprey, which has decimated lake trout in the Great Lakes (Martin and Olver 1980).

Summary

Certain aspects of the distribution and life history of the trout, salmon, and chars are shared by most species. They are all found in the northern temperate region of North America and their distributions have been affected by recent glaciation, mountain building, and volcanic activity. All but the rainbow and cutthroat trouts typically spawn in the fall, and all but the lake trout build redds in which to deposit their eggs. None of the species defend their young. Species that have lived together for long periods in the same stream or lake have adapted by using slightly different parts of the habitat. The young fish are generally opportunistic and feed mostly on available invertebrates.

Chapter 4

Habitat Requirements of Salmonids in Streams

T. C. Bjornn and D. W. Reiser

Habitat needs of salmon, trout, and char in streams vary with the season of the year and stage of the life cycle. The major life stages of most salmonid species are associated with different uses of fluvial systems: migration of maturing fish from the ocean (anadromous fishes), lakes, or rivers to natal streams; spawning by adults; incubation of embryos; rearing of juveniles; and downstream migration of juveniles to large-river, lacustrine, or oceanic rearing areas. We present information from the literature and from our own research on the range of habitat conditions for each life stage that allow the various species to exist. When possible, we attempt to define optimum and limiting conditions. Anadromous salmonids of the Pacific drainages of North America are our primary focus, but we have included information on other salmonids to illustrate the ranges of temperature, water velocities, depths, cover, and substrates preferred by salmon, trout, and char in streams. The scientific names of species identified by common names here are listed in the book's front matter.

Upstream Migration of Adults

Adult salmonids returning to their natal streams must reach spawning grounds at the proper time and with sufficient energy reserves to complete their life cycles. Stream discharges, water temperatures, and water quality must be suitable during at least a portion of the migration season. Native stocks of salmon, trout, and char that have evolved in stream systems with fluctuations in flow, turbidity, and temperature have often developed behaviors that enable survival despite the occurrence of temporarily unfavorable conditions. Native salmonids usually have sufficient extra time in their maturation, migration, and spawning schedules to accommodate delays caused by normally occurring low flows, high turbidities, or unsuitable temperatures. When upstream migration is not delayed, the fish in some stocks that migrate long distances arrive in the spawning areas 1–3 months before they spawn. Some stocks of fish that migrate short distances may not move into natal streams until shortly before spawning, but they must often wait in the ocean, lake, or river for flows or temperatures in the spawning streams to become suitable.

The flexibility in maturation and migration schedules observed in many stocks of native salmonids is not unlimited and has evolved for the specific environment

Influences of Forest and Rangeland Management on Salmonid Fishes and Their Habitats
American Fisheries Society Special Publication 19:83–138, 1991

TABLE 4.1.—Water temperatures (Bell 1986) and depths and velocities (Thompson 1972) that enable upstream migration of adult salmon and trout.

Species of fish	Temperature range (°C)	Minimum depth (m)	Maximum velocity (m/s)
Fall chinook salmon	10.6–19.4	0.24	2.44
Spring chinook salmon	3.3–13.3	0.24	2.44
Summer chinook salmon	13.9–20.0	0.24	2.44
Chum salmon	8.3–15.6	0.18	2.44
Coho salmon	7.2–15.6	0.18	2.44
Pink salmon	7.2–15.6	0.18[a]	2.13
Sockeye salmon	7.2–15.6	0.18	2.13
Steelhead		0.18	2.44
Large trout		0.18	2.44
Trout		0.12	1.22

[a] Estimate based on fish size.

of each stock. Natural or human-caused changes in the environment can be large enough to prevent fish from completing their maturation or migration to spawning areas; the proportion affected depends on the extent of the change. Transplanted stocks of fish may be less successful than native stocks in reproducing themselves if they do not possess the flexibility in migration timing required in their new environment.

Temperature

Salmon and trout respond to stream temperatures during their upstream migrations. Delays in upstream migration because natal streams were too warm have been observed for sockeye salmon (Major and Mighell 1966), chinook salmon (Hallock et al. 1970), and steelhead (Monan et al. 1975). Bell (1986) reported that Pacific salmon and steelhead have migrated upstream at temperatures between 3 and 20°C (Table 4.1).

Streams can be too cold as well as too warm for upstream-migrating salmonids. Cutthroat and rainbow trout have been observed waiting for tributaries to warm in spring before entering them to spawn. Adult steelhead that return from the sea in summer and autumn, and then spend the winter in inland rivers before spawning the following spring, overwinter in larger rivers downstream from their natal streams because the smaller headwater streams are often ice-choked during winter. We believe adult steelhead overwinter in the larger rivers because survival is higher there and the slightly higher temperatures in the rivers enable timely maturation (Reingold 1968).

Stream temperatures can be altered by removal of streambank vegetation, withdrawal and return of water for agricultural irrigation, release of water from deep reservoirs, and cooling of nuclear power plants. Unsuitable temperatures can lead to disease outbreaks in migrating and spawning fish, altered timing of migration, and accelerated or retarded maturation. Most stocks of anadromous salmonids have evolved with the temperature patterns of the streams they use for migration and spawning, and deviations from the normal pattern could adversely affect their survival.

Dissolved Oxygen

Reduced concentrations of dissolved oxygen (DO) can adversely affect the swimming performance of migrating salmonids. Maximum sustained swimming speeds of juvenile and adult coho salmon at temperatures of 10–20°C were reduced when DO dropped below air-saturation levels, and performance declined sharply when DO fell to 6.5–7.0 mg/L, at all temperatures tested (Davis et al. 1963). Swimming performance of brook trout declined similarly (Graham 1949). Low DO may also elicit avoidance reactions (Whitmore et al. 1960; Hallock et al. 1970), and may halt migration. Hallock et al. (1970) observed that adult migration ceased when DO fell below 4.5 mg/L, and did not resume until it exceeded 5 mg/L. Minimum DO recommended for spawning fish (at least 80% of saturation, and not even temporarily less than 5.0 mg/L) should provide the minimum needs of migrating salmonids.

Turbidity

Migrating salmonids avoid waters with high silt loads, or cease migration when such loads are unavoidable (Cordone and Kelley 1961). Bell (1986) cited a study in which salmonids did not move in streams where the suspended sediment concentration exceeded 4,000 mg/L (as a result of a landslide). Timing of arrival at spawning grounds by chinook salmon that migrate upstream during snowmelt runoff can vary by a month or more, depending on the concentration of suspended solids in rivers along their migration route (Bjornn 1978). In the lower Columbia River, the upstream migration of salmon may be retarded when secchi disk readings are less than 0.6 m (Figure 4.1).

High turbidity in rivers may delay migration, but turbidity alone generally does not seem to affect the homing of salmonids very much. In studies after the eruption of Mount St. Helens in 1980, Whitman et al. (1982) found that salmon preferred natal stream water without volcanic ash in an experimental flume, but that they recognized their natal streams despite the ash and attempted to ascend them. Quinn and Fresh (1984) reported that the rate of straying of chinook salmon to the Cowlitz River Hatchery was low and unaffected by the 1980 eruption, but that many coho salmon in the Toutle River, the Cowlitz River tributary most affected by the eruption, did stray to nearby streams in 1980 and 1981. Olfaction is a primary sense salmonids use for homing during upstream migration (Hasler and Larsen 1955; Hasler et al. 1978). Each stream may have a unique bouquet, and the extent to which that bouquet can be altered—by the addition of exotic chemicals, trans-basin diversions, and unnatural suspended sediments—without affecting the homing of salmonids is not known.

Barriers

Waterfalls, debris jams, and excessive water velocities may impede migrating fish. Falls that are insurmountable at one time of the year may be passed by migrating fish at other times when flows have changed. Stuart (1962) determined in laboratory studies that leaping conditions for fish are ideal when the ratio of height of falls to depth of pool below the falls is 1:1.25 (Figure 4.2). Given suitable conditions, salmon and steelhead can get past many obstacles that appear to be barriers. Both Jones (1959) and Stuart (1962) observed salmon jumping over

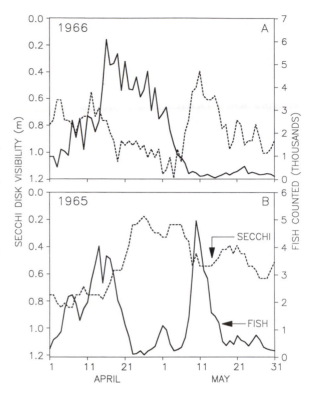

FIGURE 4.1.—Secchi disk visibility (broken line) and number of chinook salmon adults (solid lines) migrating up the Columbia River past Bonneville Dam during April and May of 1965, when high turbid flows interrupted the migration, and of 1966, when turbidities were low and the timing of migration was normal.

obstacles 2–3 m in height. Powers and Orsborn (1985) analyzed barriers to upstream-migrating fish in terms of barrier geometry, stream hydrology, and fish capabilities. They reported the abilities of salmon and trout to pass over barriers depended on the swimming velocity of the fish, the horizontal and vertical distances to be jumped, and the angle to the top of the barrier (Figure 4.3). Reiser and Peacock (1985) computed maximum jumping heights of salmonids on the basis of darting speeds; these heights ranged from 0.8 m for brown trout to more than 3 m for steelhead (Table 4.2).

The swimming abilities of fish are usually described in three categories of speed: cruising speed, the speed a fish can swim for an extended period of time, usually ranging from 2 to 4 body lengths/s; sustained speed, the speed a fish can maintain for a period of several minutes, ranging from 4 to 7 body lengths/s; and darting or burst speed, the speed a fish can swim for a few seconds, ranging from 8 to 12 body lengths/s (Watts 1974; Bell 1986; Table 4.2). According to Bell (1986), cruising speed is used during migration, sustained speed for passage through difficult areas, and darting speed for escape and feeding. Water velocities of 3–4 m/s approach the upper sustained swimming ability of large fish like salmon and steelhead.

Debris jams, whether natural or caused by human activities, can prevent or delay upstream migration. Chapman (1962b) cited a study in which a 75% decrease in number of spawning salmon in one stream was attributed to blockage by debris. On the other hand, many debris jams can be easily passed by fish and they often form pools and provide cover for fish. Removal of debris barriers

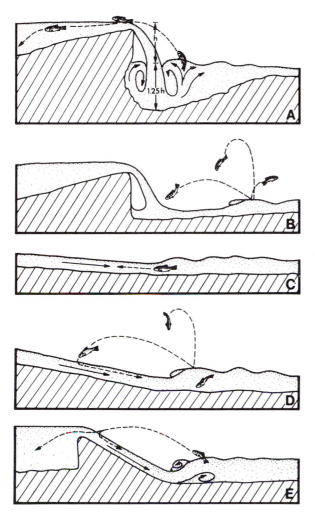

FIGURE 4.2.—Leaping ability of salmonids. (From Eiserman et al. 1975, diagrams drawn after Stuart 1962). (A) Falling water enters the pool at nearly a 90° angle. A standing wave lies close to the waterfall, where fish can use its upward thrust to leap the falls. Plunge-pool depth is 1.25 times the distance (h) from the crest of the waterfall to the water level of the pool. (B) The height of fall is the same as in A, but pool depth is less. The standing wave is formed too far from the ledge to be useful to leaping fish. (C) Flow down a gradual incline is slow enough to allow passage of ascending fish. (D) Flow over an incline steeper than fish can negotiate. Fish may even be repulsed in the standing wave at the foot of the incline. They sometimes leap futilely from the standing wave. (E) A shorter barrier with outflow over a steep incline may be ascended by some fish with difficulty.

should be done with care to avoid sedimentation of downstream spawning and rearing areas and loss of hydraulic stability.

Streamflow

Fish migrating upstream must have streamflows that provide suitable water velocities and depths for successful upstream passage. A variety of techniques have been used to estimate the flows required for migrating fish. Baxter (1961) reported that salmon needed 30–50% of the average annual flow for passage through the lower and middle reaches in Scottish rivers and up to 70% for passage up headwater streams. Thompson (1972) developed a procedure for estimating minimum flows required for migrating fish on the basis of minimum depth and maximum velocity criteria (Table 4.1) and measurements in critical stream reaches, usually shallow riffles. Stream discharges that provide suitable depths and velocities for upstream passage of adults can be estimated by the techniques he described (Thompson 1972):

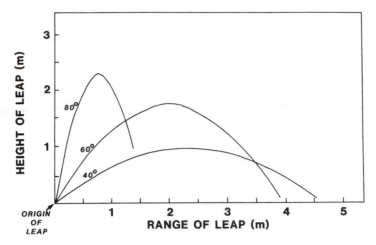

FIGURE 4.3.—Leaping curves for chinook, coho, and sockeye salmon swimming with a maximum burst speed of 6.8 m/s and jumping at various angles. (Adapted from Powers and Orsborn 1985.)

... shallow bars most critical to passage of adult fish are located and a linear transect marked which follows the shallowest course from bank to bank. At each of several flows, the total width and longest continuous portion of the transect meeting minimum depth and maximum velocity criteria are measured. For each transect, the flow is selected that meets the criteria on at least 25% of the total transect width and a continuous portion equaling at least 10% of its total width.

The mean selected flow from all transects is recommended as the minimum flow for passage.

Sautner et al. (1984) reported that passage of chum salmon spawners through sloughs and side channels of the Susitna River, Alaska, depended primarily on water depth, length of the critical stream reach, and size of substrate particles. Fish could successfully pass any stream reach of reasonable length if the depth was greater than 0.12 m when substrate particles averaged larger than 7.6 cm in diameter, or if the depth was greater than 0.09 m when particles were less than 7.6 cm.

TABLE 4.2.—Swimming (Bell 1986) and jumping abilities (Reiser and Peacock 1985) of average-size adult salmonids.

Taxon	Swimming speed (m/s)			Maximum jumping height (m)
	Cruising	Sustained	Darting	
Chinook salmon	0–1.04	1.04–3.29	3.29–6.83	2.4
Coho salmon	0–1.04	1.04–3.23	3.23–6.55	2.2
Sockeye salmon	0–0.98	0.98–3.11	3.11–6.28	2.1
Steelhead	0–1.40	1.40–4.18	4.18–8.08	3.4
Trout	0–0.61	0.61–1.95	1.95–4.11	
Brown trout	0–0.67	0.67–1.89	1.89–3.87	0.8

Spawning

Substrate composition, cover, water quality, and water quantity are important habitat elements for salmonids before and during spawning. The number of spawners that can be accommodated in a stream is a function of the area suitable for spawning (suitable substrate, water depth, and velocity), area required for each redd, suitability of cover for the fish, and behavior of the spawners. Cover is important for species that spend several weeks maturing near spawning areas.

The amount of suitable stream substrate for spawning varies with the size (order) of the stream and species of salmonid using it, as Boehne and House (1983) learned from study of two coastal and two Cascade Range watersheds in Oregon. First-order streams (small headwater streams without tributaries) were not used by salmonids. Less than half the second-order streams (streams resulting from the junction of two or more first-order streams) were used by salmonids; those that were contained nonanadromous cutthroat trout. Most of the third-order streams (steams resulting from the junction of two or more second-order streams) in the coastal watersheds, but only 37% of those in the Cascade Range drainages, were used by cutthroat trout. The larger anadromous steelhead, coho salmon, and chinook salmon spawned in a few third-order streams, but most were found in fourth- and fifth-order streams. As stream order increased, gradient decreased but stream length, width, and depth increased. The amount of spawning gravel per kilometer of stream was greatest in fourth-order coastal watersheds and fifth-order Cascade Range watersheds. Platts (1979b) found similar relations between stream size (order) and use of the streams by fish in an Idaho drainage.

Streamflow

Streamflow regulates the amount of spawning area available in any stream by regulating the area covered by water and the velocities and depths of water over the gravel beds. D. H. Fry (in Hooper 1973) summarized the effect of discharge on the amount of spawning area in a stream.

> As flows increase, more and more gravel is covered and becomes suitable for spawning. As flows continue to increase, velocities in some places become too high for spawning, thus cancelling out the benefit of increases in usable spawning area near the edges of the stream. Eventually, as flows increase, the losses begin to outweigh the gains, and the actual spawning capacity of the stream starts to decrease. If spawning area is plotted against streamflow, the curve will usually show a rise to a relatively wide plateau followed by a gradual decline.

Relations between flow and amount of suitable spawning area have been assessed or predicted by methods based primarily on measurements of water depths and velocities in areas with suitable substrate. Collings (1972, 1974) used a process of depth and velocity contouring to determine the area suitable for spawning at a given discharge. Thompson (1972) quantified the width of the stream at cross-channel transects on spawning bars that met minimum criteria of depth (18 cm) and velocity (0.3–3.0 m/s) at different flows. When measurements have been taken over a wide range of flows, a graph can be plotted of flow versus suitable spawning areas (Figure 4.4) or usable width (Figure 4.5). A method

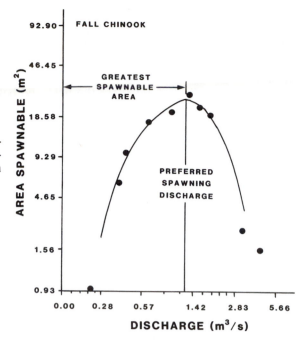

FIGURE 4.4.—Usable-area technique for selecting preferred spawning discharge, North Nemah River. (From Collings 1972.)

similar to that used by Waters (1976), termed the instream flow incremental methodology (IFIM), was developed by U.S. Fish and Wildlife Service personnel to estimate the amount of suitable habitat (for spawning, in this instance); the method relates variations in a stream's water velocity, depth, substrate, and other variables to use of the stream by fishes (Stalnaker and Arnette 1976b; Bovee 1978, 1982, 1986; Bovee and Milhous 1978; Trihey and Wegner 1981). An IFIM analysis results in an index of suitable habitat (weighted usable area, WUA) for a range of streamflows (Figure 4.6). Wesche and Rechard (1980) and EA Engineering, Science and Technology, Inc. (1986) reviewed and evaluated a variety of methods that could be used for estimating the quantity and quality of spawning habitat for salmonids.

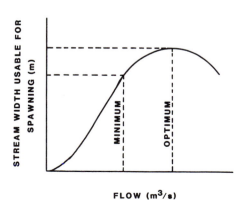

FIGURE 4.5.—Usable-width technique for determining spawning flow. (From Thompson 1972.)

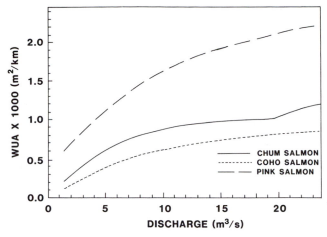

FIGURE 4.6.—Relation of available chum, coho, and pink salmon spawning habitat (weighted usable area, WUA) to streamflow, Upper Tunnel Creek. (From Reiser and Ramey 1984.)

Temperature

Timing of salmonid spawning has likely evolved in response to water temperatures in each stream before, during, and after spawning, and, in some streams, to the occurrence of flows that allow upstream migration of maturing adults. Salmonids have spawned when water temperatures have ranged from 1.0 to 20.0°C, but the favorable range of temperatures for spawning is much narrower (Table 4.3). In British Columbia (Shepherd et al. 1986b), salmon were observed spawning over a wide range of temperatures, but most of the pink, chum, and

TABLE 4.3.—Recommended temperatures for spawning and incubation of salmonid fishes (Bell 1986).

Species	Temperature (°C)	
	Spawning	Incubation[a]
Fall chinook salmon	5.6–13.9	5.0–14.4
Spring chinook salmon	5.6–13.9	5.0–14.4
Summer chinook salmon	5.6–13.9	5.0–14.4
Chum salmon	7.2–12.8	4.4–13.3
Coho salmon	4.4–9.4	4.4–13.3
Pink salmon	7.2–12.8	4.4–13.3
Sockeye salmon	10.6–12.2	4.4–13.3
Kokanee	5.0–12.8	
Steelhead	3.9–9.4	
Rainbow trout	2.2–20.0	
Cutthroat trout	6.1–17.2	
Brown trout	7.2–12.8[b]	

[a] The higher and lower values are threshold temperatures beyond which mortality increases. Eggs survive and develop normally at lower temperatures than indicated, provided initial development of the embryo has progressed to a stage that is tolerant of cold water.

[b] From Hunter (1973).

sockeye salmon spawned in water of 8–13°C, chinook salmon in water of 10–17°C, and coho salmon in water of less than 10°C (mode, 5–6°C).

Each native fish stock appears to have a unique time and temperature for spawning that theoretically maximizes the survival of their offspring. Temperatures before and during spawning must allow the spawners to survive and deposit their eggs, but temperatures during incubation of the embryos (which regulates timing of juvenile emergence from the redd) may be the primary evolutionary factor that has determined the time of spawning (Heggberget 1988). In the case of fall spawners, newly spawned embryos must reach a critical stage of development before the water becomes too cold (Brannon 1965), and emergence of fry must occur at a suitable time during the following spring (Sheridan 1962a; Miller and Brannon 1982; Godin 1982; Burger et al. 1985; Heggberget 1988). Spring spawners must not spawn before the water has warmed sufficiently to permit normal development of embryos, but there may be a survival advantage for the fish to spawn as early as possible to allow the offspring to emerge and grow before the onset of winter. Support for the latter hypothesis can be found in Idaho streams, where steelhead usually spawn before the peak of the snowmelt runoff in spring (thereby risking destruction of their redds by the high flows) rather than after the peak, which would delay the emergence of their offspring until late summer.

Areas with upwelling groundwater have been selected as spawning areas by salmonids such as chum salmon, brown trout, and brook trout (Benson 1953; Bakkala 1970; Witzel and MacCrimmon 1983; Vining et al. 1985). Use of areas with groundwater flow may have survival advantages if the water quality (suitable temperatures and dissolved gases, and lack of damaging heavy metals and sediments) in such areas is more suitable than in areas without groundwater.

Space

The amount of space required by salmonids for spawning depends on the size and behavior of the spawners and the quality of the spawning area. Large fish make large redds; tolerance of nearby fish varies by species; and poor-quality spawning areas may force females to make several redds. Redds range in size from 0.6 m² to more than 10 m² for anadromous salmonids, and from 0.09 m² to 0.9 m² for smaller nonanadromous trout and salmon (Table 4.4).

Many salmonids prefer to spawn in the transitional area between pools and riffles (Hazzard 1932; Hobbs 1937; Smith 1941; Briggs 1953; Stuart 1953). Tautz and Groot (1975) reported that chum salmon spawned in an accelerating flow, such as that found at a pool–riffle transition. By placing crystals of potassium permanganate on the gravel surface, Stuart (1953) demonstrated the presence of downwelling currents in these transitional areas (Figure 4.7) and noted that the gravel there was easy to excavate and relatively free of silt and debris. Vaux (1962, 1968) reported that downwelling currents normally occurred in areas where the streambed was convex (such as the pool–riffle transition), and upwelling currents occurred in concave areas (such as the downstream end of a riffle).

The density of redds in streams depends on the amount of stream area suitable for spawning, the number and size of spawners, and the area required for each redd. In two Lake Michigan tributaries with alternating pool–riffle habitat, the densities of spawning chinook salmon ranged from about 80 to 250 fish per hectare of stream area (Carl 1984). The average velocities at the preferred spawning sites in the two streams

TABLE 4.4.—Average area of salmonid redds and area recommended per spawning pair of fish in channels.

Species	Average area of redd (m^2)	Area recommended per spawning pair[a] (m^2)	Source
Chinook salmon	9.1–10.0		Neilson and Banford (1983)
Spring chinook salmon	3.3	13.4	Burner (1951)
Spring chinook salmon	6.0		Reiser and White (1981a)
Fall chinook salmon	5.1	20.1	Burner (1951)
Summer chinook salmon	5.1	20.1	Burner (1951)
Summer chinook salmon	9.4		Reiser and White (1981a)
Coho salmon	2.8	11.7	Burner (1951)
Chum salmon	2.3	9.2	Burner (1951)
Sockeye salmon	1.8	6.7	Burner (1951)
Pink salmon	0.6	0.6	Hourston and MacKinnon (1957)
Pink salmon	0.6–0.9		Wells and McNeil (1970)
Steelhead	5.4		Orcutt et al. (1968)
Steelhead	4.4		Hunter (1973)
Steelhead	4.4		Reiser and White (1981a)
Rainbow trout	0.2		Hunter (1973)
Cutthroat trout	0.09–0.9		Hunter (1973)
Brown trout	0.5		Reiser and Wesche (1977)

[a] Modified from Clay (1961).

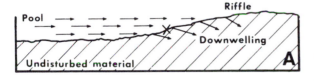

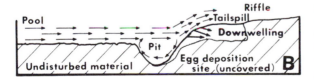

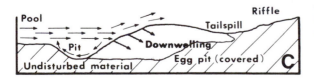

FIGURE 4.7.—Longitudinal sections of a spawning area. (From Reiser and Wesche 1977.) (A) Convexity of the substrate at the pool–riffle transition induces downwelling of water into the gravel. The area likely to be used for spawning is marked with a ×. (B) Redd construction results in negligible currents in the pit (facilitating egg deposition) and increased currents over and through (downwelling) the tailspill. (C) Egg-covering activity results in the formation of a second pit upstream, which may also be used for spawning. Increased permeability and the convexity of the tailspill substrate induces downwelling of water into the gravel, creating a current past eggs. The current brings oxygen to the eggs and removes metabolic wastes.

were 0.42 m/s and 0.50 m/s—similar to those reported by Burner (1951) in the Toutle River, Washington. In the Nechako River, British Columbia, Neilson and Banford (1983) reported that the area of chinook salmon redds averaged 9.1 and 10.0 m^2 and that densities were 1 redd per 235 m^2 and 1 per 112 m^2 in two areas with water depths of at least 0.45 m (the shallowest water in which redd construction was seen). Water depth in the deepest part (pit) of 47 completed redds was 0.46–1.20 m (mean, 0.87 m). Water velocity over the pit of the redds was 15–100 cm/s (mean, 56 cm/s). In a small Oregon coastal tributary, coho salmon constructed 1.7 redds per female and produced a density of 194 redds per hectare of stream (R. A. House, U.S. Bureau of Land Management, unpublished data).

The number of redds that can be built in a stream depends on the amount of suitable spawning habitat and the area required per spawning pair of fish (Reiser and Ramey 1984, 1987; IEC Beak 1984; Reiser 1986). The area suitable for spawning (defined by water depth, velocity, and size of substrate) is usually less than the total area of gravel substrate in the stream, and spatial requirements for each spawning pair may exceed the area of a completed redd. Surface areas of redds can be readily measured, but the spatial requirement for each spawning pair may require additional information such as area of suitable spawning habitat, number of spawners in a given area, and the size and behavior of spawners. Burner (1951) suggested that a conservative estimate of the number of salmon a stream could accommodate could be obtained by dividing the area suitable for spawning by four times the average area of a redd.

In an Oregon stream, gravel substrate made up 25% of the total stream area, but only 30% of that gravel substrate was suitable for spawning by coho salmon (R. A. House, unpublished data). The main stem of the Tucannon River in southeastern Washington contained nearly 200,000 m^2 of gravel substrate (D. W. Kelley and Associates 1982); however, only a small fraction of the river bed was suitable for anadromous fish spawning in the judgment of one of us (T.C.B.), who surveyed 9,000 linear meters of the river and estimated that 3,200 salmon or steelhead redds could be constructed without serious superimposition of redds. If the total area of gravel substrate in the stream (200,000 m^2) had been divided by the average size of salmon or steelhead redds (about 5 m^2), the capacity of the river would have been erroneously estimated to be about 40,000 redds. If Burner's (1951) formula (four times the average redd area) had been used, the estimate would be about 10,000 redds. Much of the river was unsuitable for spawning because water depths and velocities were outside the range acceptable to spawning salmon.

Water Depth and Velocity

Preferred water depths and velocities for various spawning salmonids have been determined from measurements of water depth and velocity at redds (Cope 1957; Sams and Pearson 1963; Orcutt et al. 1968; Thompson 1972; Hooper 1973; Hunter 1973; Smith 1973; Reiser and Wesche 1977; Reiser and White 1981a; Neilson and Banford 1983; Shepherd et al. 1986b). Water depths measured at redd sites varied with species and size of fish and ranged from 6 to 300 cm. In general, the water was at least deep enough to cover the fish during spawning; large salmon required 15–35 cm and smaller trout 6–10 cm (Table 4.5). Many fish spawned in water deeper than necessary to submerge them, but it is not known if the fish preferred the greater depths or were merely using what was available. Water

TABLE 4.5.—Water depth, velocity, and substrate size criteria for anadromous and other salmonid spawning areas.

Species	Depth (cm)	Velocity (cm/s)	Substrate size (cm)	Source
Fall chinook salmon	≥24	30–91	1.3–10.2[a]	Thompson (1972)
Spring chinook salmon	≥24	30–91	1.3–10.2[a]	Thompson (1972)
Summer chinook salmon	≥30	32–109	1.3–10.2[a]	Reiser and White (1981a)
Chum salmon	≥18	46–101	1.3–10.2[a]	Smith (1973)
Coho salmon	≥18	30–91	1.3–10.2[b]	Thompson (1972)
Pink salmon	≥15	21–101	1.3–10.2[a]	Collings (1974)
Sockeye salmon	≥15	21–101[b]	1.3–10.2[a]	[b]
Atlantic salmon	≥25	25–90		Beland et al. (1982)
Kokanee	≥6	15–73		Smith (1973)
Steelhead	≥24	40–91	0.6–10.2[c]	Smith (1973)
Rainbow trout	≥18	48–91	0.6–5.2	Smith (1973)
Cutthroat trout	≥6	11–72	0.6–10.2	Hunter (1973)
Brown trout	≥24	21–64	0.6–7.6[c]	Thompson (1972)

[a] From Bell (1986).
[b] Estimated from criteria for other species.
[c] From Hunter (1973).

velocities at the redd sites ranged from 3 to 152 cm/s, but most were from 20 to 100 cm/s (Table 4.5).

Measurements of depth and velocity were usually taken at the upstream edge of the redd because that point most closely approximated conditions before the redd was constructed and reflected the depths and velocities selected by the fish. Two locations in the water column have been used for making estimates of preferred velocity: 0.6 × depth from the surface to the streambed, and nose velocity (which approximates the location of the fish close to the bed surface). Most velocity criteria have been developed for 0.6 × depth. The ranges of preferred depths and velocities have been defined in a variety of ways. Thompson (1972) used the depths and velocities within a 90–95% confidence interval. Hunter (1973) used the middle 80–90% of the measurements. Smith (1973) used a two-sided tolerance limit within which there was 95% confidence that 80% of the measurements would occur within a normal distribution. Others have simply listed the ranges of depth and velocity measured.

More recently, investigators have developed a series of index curves to depict the suitability of selected variables for different species of fish and life history stages (Figure 4.8). Such curves, used primarily in IFIM, have usually been developed from empirical measurements of depth, velocity, and substrate at the redd site. The curves were based on the assumption that fish select areas in a stream with optimal combinations of physical and hydraulic conditions. The development and limitations of these types of curves were discussed by various investigators (Bovee and Cochnauer 1977; Waters 1976; Baldridge and Amos 1982; Bovee 1982, 1986; Theilke 1985; EA Engineering, Science and Technology, Inc. 1986).

Substrate

The suitability of gravel substrate for spawning depends mostly on fish size; large fish can use larger substrate materials than can small fish. Bell (1986) stated that substrate for anadromous salmon and trout should range from 1.3 to 10.2 cm

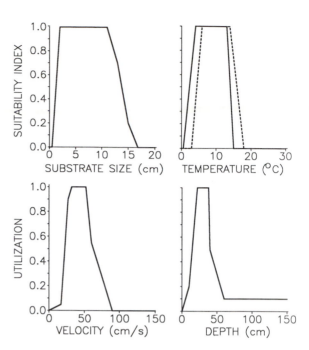

FIGURE 4.8.—Suitability index curves for average substrate particle size and temperature, and use curves for mean current velocity in the water column and water depth, in a spawning area used by chinook salmon. Solid line indicates spawning, dashed line incubation. (Redrawn from Raleigh et al. 1986.)

in diameter (Table 4.5). For smaller fish, other investigators have recommended that the materials not exceed 5.2 or 7.6 cm, depending on size of the fish. The criteria presented above are in general agreement with the sizes of substrate particles found in redds (Orcutt et al. 1968; Hooper 1973; Hunter 1973; Smith 1973; Reiser and Wesche 1977). Salmon have been observed spawning in areas with substrate particles larger than 30 cm, but most often in areas where the majority of particles were smaller than 15 cm (Shepherd et al. 1986b).

To determine the composition of substrate used by salmonids, investigators have collected substrate samples from active redds or known spawning areas and graded them through a series of sieves (Burner 1951; Cope 1957; Warner 1963; Orcutt et al. 1968; Hunter 1973; Reiser and Wesche 1977; Tagart 1976; Corley and Burmeister 1979; Huntington 1985). In such studies, various techniques have been used for the collection of substrate materials (McNeil and Ahnell 1964; Tagart 1976; Walkotten 1976; Platts and Penton 1980; Lotspeich and Everest 1981) and for their characterization (Platts et al. 1979b; Lotspeich and Everest 1981; Shirazi and Seim 1981; Tappel and Bjornn 1983). The particle makeup of redds or spawning areas has been characterized by the proportions within specified size ranges (Tappel and Bjornn 1983), the geometric mean particle diameter (dg: Shirazi and Seim 1981), and the Fredle index (Fi: Lotspeich and Everest 1981).

Substrates used in artificial spawning channels represent the particle sizes best suited for selected species in the judgment of those who designed the channels. Gravel from 2 to 10 cm in diameter was used in the Robertson Creek (British Columbia) spawning channels for pink, coho, and chinook salmon (Lucas 1960). Gravel from 0.6 to 3.8 cm was used in the Jones Creek (British Columbia) spawning channel for anadromous fish (MacKinnon et al. 1961). The Tehama–Colusa spawning channels in California, designed primarily for chinook salmon, contained gravel 1.9–15.2 cm in diameter (Pollock 1969). Bell (1986) stated that, in general, up to 80% of the substrate in artificial spawning channels should be gravel with diameters of 1.3–3.8 cm; the balance should be of sizes up to 10.2 cm.

Cover

Cover for salmonids waiting to spawn or in the process of spawning can be provided by overhanging vegetation, undercut banks, submerged vegetation, submerged objects such as logs and rocks, floating debris, deep water, turbulence, and turbidity (Giger 1973). Cover can protect fish from disturbance and predation and also can provide shade. Some anadromous fish—chinook salmon and steelhead, for example—enter freshwater streams and arrive at the spawning grounds weeks or even months before they spawn. If the holding and spawning areas have little cover, such fish are vulnerable to disturbance and predation over a long period. Nearness of cover to spawning areas may be a factor in the selection of spawning sites by some species. In three studies, for example, brown trout selected spawning areas that were adjacent to undercut banks and overhanging vegetation (Johnson et al. 1966; Reiser and Wesche 1977; Witzel and MacCrimmon 1983).

Incubation

Although incubation is inextricably tied to spawning, the habitat requirements of embryos during incubation are different from those of spawning adults and thus warrant a separate discussion. When an adult fish selects a spawning site, it is also selecting the incubation environment. Successful incubation of embryos and emergence of fry, however, depend on many extragravel and intragravel chemical, physical, and hydraulic variables: DO, water temperature, biochemical oxygen demand (BOD) of material carried in the water and deposited in the redd, substrate size (including the amount of fine sediment), channel gradient, channel configuration, water depth (head) above the redd, surface water discharge and velocity, permeability and porosity of gravel in the redd and surrounding streambed, and velocity of water through the redd. Chapman (1988) reviewed the literature and discussed the primary factors involved in the incubation of salmonid embryos.

The relations between number of spawners, eggs deposited in redds, and juveniles that emerge from the redds take a variety of forms, depending on the species, life history, stream, and incubation conditions. The number of eggs deposited may increase linearly with the number of spawners as long as the amount of suitable spawning area is not limiting, but level off when suitable habitat becomes in short supply. Usually the number of fry emerging is directly related to the number of eggs deposited; if these two numbers are plotted against each other, differences in the linear slope between areas or streams probably reflect differing qualities of the incubation environment. Some species such as pink or chum salmon occasionally aggregate in extraordinarily large numbers on limited spawning grounds; if redds are superimposed and high egg densities result in oxygen depletion and poor incubation conditions, the number of emerging fry could be inversely related to the number of spawners.

Substrate

Streambed particles in the redd at the end of spawning, and organic and inorganic particles that settle into the redd and surrounding substrate during incubation, affect the rate of water interchange between the stream and the redd, the amount of oxygen available to the embryos, the concentration of embryo wastes, and the movement of alevins (especially when they are ready to emerge from the redd). During redd construction and spawning, the spawners displace streambed particles, deposit eggs and sperm in one or several pockets (Hawke 1978; Chapman 1988), and then cover the embryos with hydraulically displaced particles. During this process, fine sediments and organic materials in the stream substrate tend to be washed downstream; consequently the redd environment is as favorable for the embryos immediately after construction as it will ever be. Conditions for embryos within redds may change little or greatly during incubation depending on weather, streamflows, spawning by other fish in the same area at a later time, and fine sediments and organic materials transported in the stream.

Redds may be disturbed by late-spawning fish constructing redds, or by floods that displace the streambed containing the redd. Redds that remain intact during incubation may become less suitable for embryos if inorganic fine sediments (Figure 4.9) and organic materials are deposited in the interstitial spaces between the larger particles. The fine particles impede the movement of water and alevins in the redd, and the organic material (or the microbe community on it) consumes oxygen during decomposition; if the oxygen is consumed faster than the reduced intragravel water flow can replace it, the embryos or alevins will asphyxiate.

The redd construction process reduces the amounts of fine sediments and organic matter in the pockets where eggs are deposited (McNeil and Ahnell 1964; Ringler 1970; Everest et al. 1987a). If fine sediments are being transported in a stream either as bedload or in suspension, some of them are likely to be deposited in the redd. The amount of fine sediment deposited and the depth to which it intrudes depend on the size of substrate in the redd, flow conditions in the stream, and the amount and size of sediment being transported (Cooper 1965; Beschta and Jackson 1979). In general, intrusion into the redd increases as particle size decreases. When fine sediments are large relative to the spaces (pores) between gravel particles in the redd, they may only settle into the surface layer of the redd, where they can block other sediments from the deeper egg pockets (Hobbs 1937; Beschta and Jackson 1979; Chapman 1988). Under certain conditions, a layer of fine sediments may form above the egg pocket during redd construction or later. Such a layer can be beneficial (if it prevents deposition of fine organic or inorganic materials in the pocket), detrimental (if it impedes emergence of the alevins), or both. Deposition of fine sediments in redds may reduce survival more if it occurs early rather than late in the incubation period (Wickett 1954) because young embryos take up oxygen less efficiently than advanced embryos (Shaw and Maga 1943; Reiser and White 1988).

Depth of the egg pockets below the surface of the streambed varies with the size of fish and the size of streambed material. Large fish like chinook salmon may dig as deep as 43 cm below the streambed surface, but average pocket depths are in the 20- to 30-cm range (Hobbs 1937; Hawke 1978; Chapman 1988). The egg pockets of smaller fish tend to be closer to the streambed surface. Hawke (1978)

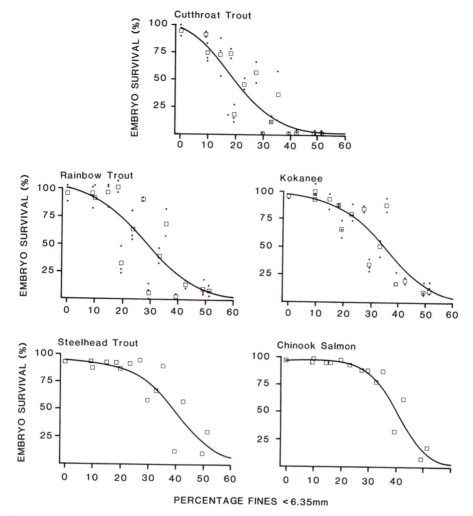

FIGURE 4.9.—Relation between embryo survival and percentage of substrate particles smaller than 6.35 mm for several salmonid species. Chinook salmon and steelhead data are from Tappel and Bjornn (1983); the others are from Irving and Bjornn (1984). Curves were fitted to the data by exponential equations. Squares indicate mean values and dots denote individual replicates.

and Everest et al. (1987a) found that the eggs tended to be near the bottom of the pocket and adjacent to the undisturbed streambed at the bottom of the redd.

During incubation, sufficient water must circulate through the redd as deep as the egg pocket to supply the embryos with oxygen and carry away waste products. Circulation of water through redds is a function of the porosity (ratio of pore space to total volume of redd) of the particles in the redd, hydraulic gradient at the redd, and temperature of the water. Porosity is highest in newly constructed redds and declines during the incubation period as the interstitial spaces acquire fine sediments. The hydraulic gradient through a redd is enhanced by the mounded tailspill created during construction (Figure 4.7). Permeability (ability of

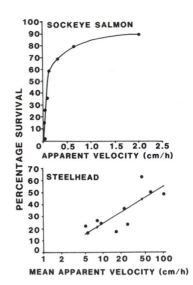

FIGURE 4.10.—Relations between rate of flow of water through a gravel bed and the survival of eyed sockeye salmon eggs (redrawn from Cooper 1965) and steelhead embryos (from Coble 1961).

particles in the redd to transmit water per unit of time) and apparent velocity (volume of water passing through a given area of redd per unit of time) are two commonly used measures of the suitability of a redd for successful incubation of salmonid embryos (Wickett 1954, 1958; Pollard 1955; Terhune 1958; Coble 1961; Vaux 1968). When the permeability and apparent velocity of water in the redd have been too low, reduced embryo survival has been measured for sockeye salmon (Pyper in Cooper 1965), steelhead (Coble 1961), chinook salmon (Gangmark and Bakkala 1960), pink salmon (Wickett 1958), and coho salmon and steelhead (Phillips and Campbell 1961). Survival of embryos decreases as apparent velocities (an indication of the amount of DO reaching the embryos) decrease (Figure 4.10).

Interchange of water between a stream and its streambed particles (Figure 4.7) has been repeatedly demonstrated (Stuart 1953; Sheridan 1962b; Vaux 1962; Cooper 1965). Sheridan (1962b) showed that groundwater in salmon spawning areas in southeast Alaska contains little oxygen, and that the oxygen content of intragravel water decreases with gravel depth. He concluded that the major source of oxygen in intragravel water was the interchange of that water with the surface flow. Cooper (1965) used dyes to demonstrate the influence of streambed configuration on intragravel flow patterns (Figure 4.11). Wells and McNeil (1970) attributed the high intragravel DO in Alaskan pink salmon spawning beds to high permeability of the substrate and to stream gradient. McNeil and Ahnell (1964) reported high permeabilities (>24,000 cm/h) in salmon spawning areas when sands and silts smaller than 0.84 mm made up less than 5% of the particles, and lower permeabilities (<1,300 cm/h) when they made up more than 15%. In sloughs of the Susitna River in central Alaska, Vining et al. (1985) noted that DO concentrations in intragravel water were consistently lower than in surface waters; in the main channel, however, differences in DO concentrations between surface and intragravel waters were slight.

Apparent velocity of water in redds may increase or decrease with the depth (and quantity) of the surface water (Reiser and White 1981a). Early evidence of

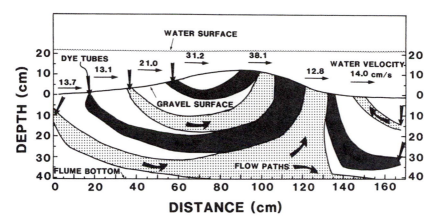

FIGURE 4.11.—Water flow through homogeneous gravel in a flume with a surface similar to that of a new salmon redd. Shadings indicate dispersions of injected dyes. (Redrawn from Cooper 1965.)

this was reported by Wickett (1954), who found a direct relation between gage-height readings in a stream and subsurface flow. Chapman et al. (1982) also observed decreases in apparent velocity when flow decreased from 1,982 to 1,019 m³/s in the Columbia River.

Salmonid embryos have survived dewatering of redds when the dewatering occurred before hatching, temperatures were kept within a suitable range, fine sediment concentrations did not impede air flow, and humidity was maintained near 100% in the redds (Reiser and White 1981b, 1983; Becker et al. 1982; Stober et al. 1982; Becker and Neitzel 1985; Neitzel and Becker 1985). In a moist environment, unhatched embryos are able to get the oxygen they need from air in the redds (Figure 4.12). Several examples have been reported. Hobbs (1937) found that 80% of the brown trout eggs he observed were still alive in redds that had had no surface flow for 5 weeks, and Hardy (1963) found similar results in brown trout redds after 2–5 weeks of dewatering. Chinook salmon embryos survived in redds that had been dewatered for 3 weeks (Hawke 1978). Steelhead and chinook salmon embryos tolerated 1–5 weeks of dewatering (water flowed through the gravel 10 cm below the eggs) with no significant reduction in survival to hatching, alevin quality, growth rate, or quality of emerged fry (Reiser and White 1983). Survival through hatching of dewatered eggs of chinook, chum, pink, and coho salmon and steelhead was high during a study by Stober et al. (1982). Chinook salmon embryos survived 24 h of dewatering when relative humidity was kept at 100%, but all died if humidity was lowered to 90% (Neitzel and Becker 1985).

In streams with substantial groundwater inflows, DO concentrations and flow patterns of intragravel water may not relate in the usual way to substrate composition and permeability (Hansen 1975; Sowden and Power 1985). Upwelling areas are reportedly favored for spawning by chum, sockeye (Lister et al. 1980; Wilson 1984; Vining et al. 1985), and pink salmon (Krueger 1981). Embryo incubation is improved because upwelling reduces the chances that embryos will become dewatered or frozen, provides a stable incubation environment, and increases the water exchange rate past the embryos, thereby enhancing the

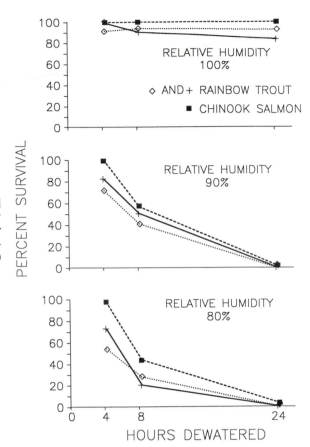

FIGURE 4.12.—Percent survival for dewatered embryos of rainbow trout and chinook salmon under conditions of reduced relative humidity. (From Becker et al. 1986.)

replenishment of DO (if the upwelling water has sufficient amounts) and removal of metabolic waste (Vining et al. 1985).

Egg densities in natural redds are relatively low compared to those in artificial culture facilities; they typically do not affect embryo and alevin survival unless the incubation environment is of marginal quality. If a large chinook salmon deposited 5,000 eggs in a single redd that covered 10 m^2, the density in that redd would be 500 eggs/m^2. However, the density in the actual egg pocket or pockets would be higher, perhaps as high as 2,000–5,000 eggs/m^2 if most of the eggs were deposited in one or two pockets. McNeil (1969) reported that production of pink salmon fry approached 500 fry/m^2 of spawning area when egg deposition was 2,000–3,000 eggs/m^2. In shallow matrix incubators, Kapuscinski and Lannan (1983) found that chum salmon could be incubated at densities as high as 43,000 eggs/m^2 without sacrificing quality of the fry produced.

Once incubation is complete and the alevins are ready to emerge from the redd and begin life in the stream, they must move from the egg pocket up through interstitial spaces to the surface of the streambed. Nunan and Noakes (1985) concluded that emergence of salmonid alevins was a response primarily to gravitational cues rather than to light or intragravel water flow. Emergence can be a problem if the interstitial spaces are not large enough to permit passage of the alevins. In laboratory studies, alevins of chinook salmon and steelhead (Bjornn

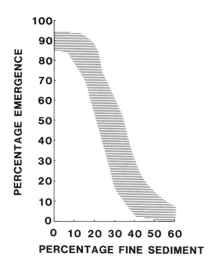

FIGURE 4.13.—Percentage emergence of swim-up fry placed in gravel–sand mixtures in relation to the percentage of sediment smaller than 2–6.4 mm in studies by Bjornn (1968), Phillips et al. (1975), Hausle and Coble (1976), and McCuddin (1977). The stipled area includes data from eight tests on brook trout, steelhead, and chinook and coho salmon.

1968) and coho salmon and steelhead (Phillips et al. 1975) had difficulty emerging from gravel-filled troughs when the percentage of fine sediments exceeded 30–40% by volume (Figure 4.13). Particle sizes that reduce embryo survival and impede emergence have been defined as those less than 6.4 mm (Bjornn 1968; McCuddin 1977), less than 4.6 mm (Platts et al. 1979b), less than 3.3 mm (Koski 1966), less than 2.0 mm (Hausle and Coble 1976), and less than 0.84 mm (McNeil and Ahnell 1964; Hall and Lantz 1969; Cloern 1976; Tagart 1976). Witzel and MacCrimmon (1981) tested rainbow trout in vertical-flow incubators filled with particles of 2, 4, 8, 16, and 26.5 mm, and found that emergence was impeded when particles were less than 8 mm in diameter. Stowell et al. (1983) defined the harmful size range of particles as those less than 6.4 mm, when at least 20% were less than 0.84 mm in diameter. As we previously mentioned, the particle size composition of redds can be characterized in numerous ways (Platts et al. 1979b; Lotspeich and Everest 1981; Shirazi and Seim 1981; Tappel and Bjornn 1983).

Fine sediments that impede intragravel flow and alevin movements may also affect the size of emergent fry (Koski 1966, 1981; Phillips et al. 1975; Tappel and Bjornn 1983; Tagart 1984; MacCrimmon and Gots 1986) and the time of emergence (Koski 1966, 1975; MacCrimmon and Gots 1986), but such effects were not seen in all studies (Hausle and Coble 1976; McCuddin 1977). Silver et al. (1963) reported that the size of newly emerged steelhead and chinook salmon depended on apparent velocities, even at velocities as high as 740–1,350 cm/h. Shumway et al. (1964) found that reduced velocities (3–10 cm/h) resulted in decreased size of fry at all DO levels tested (2.5–11.5 mg/L), and that hatching was delayed at low DO concentrations.

Dissolved Oxygen

Critical concentrations of DO that barely satisfy respiratory demands have been experimentally determined for salmonid embryos at different developmental stages (Table 4.6). Alderdice et al. (1958) found that embryos generally were most sensitive to hypoxial conditions during the early stages of development, when they had received 200–390 temperature units (a temperature unit is one degree

TABLE 4.6.—Critical levels of dissolved oxygen (DO; minimum that satisfies respiratory demand) for salmonid embryos at various stages of development.

Species	Stage of development	Age (d)	Critical DO (mg/L)
Chum salmon	Pre-eyed	0	0.72
(Wickett 1954)	Pre-eyed	5	1.67
	Pre-eyed	12	1.14
	Faintly eyed	85	3.70
Chum salmon		<1	0.72[a]
(Alderdice et al.		<1	1.67[a]
1958)		4	1.14[a]
		12	3.96
		16	3.70[a]
		27	5.66
		35	6.60
	Nearly hatching	45	7.19
Atlantic salmon	Died		0.76
(Lindroth 1942)	Nearly hatching		5.80
	Hatching		10.00
Atlantic salmon	Eyed	25	3.1
(Hayes et al. 1951)	Hatching	50	7.1

[a] From Wickett (1954).

above zero for one day). Wickett (1954) showed that larval development during the early stage of development depended wholly on diffusion for satisfying oxygen requirements. Once the circulatory system is functional, oxygen transfer to the embryo becomes more efficient.

Embryos may survive when DO concentrations are below saturation (but above the critical level), but their development often deviates from normal. Doudoroff and Warren (1965) found that when DO was below saturation throughout development, embryos were smaller than usual and that hatching was either delayed or premature. Alderdice et al. (1958) showed that low DO concentrations in the early stages of development of chum salmon delayed hatching and increased

FIGURE 4.14.—Relation between mean length of steelhead sac fry when hatched and dissolved oxygen concentration at which the embryos were incubated, for several water velocities during incubation and a temperature of 9.5°C. (From Silver et al. 1963.)

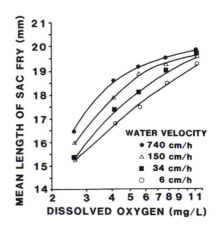

TABLE 4.7.—Characteristics of sockeye salmon alevins at hatching after embryos were incubated in water at three oxygen concentrations. (From Brannon 1965.)

Characteristic	O_2 concentration (mg/L)		
	3.0	6.0	11.9
Temperature units[a] to 50% hatching	670	670	670
Length (mm)	16.3	18.6	19.7
Yolk-sac shape	Spherical	Longitudinal	Longitudinal
Pigmentation	Lightly on head	On head and starting on back	On head and back
Visibility of the dorsal and anal fin rays	Not visible	Distinguishable	Readily visible
Caudal fin development	Forming	Forming	Well advanced

[a] Degree-days above 0°C.

the incidence of morphological anomalies. Silver et al. (1963) reported that newly hatched steelhead and chinook salmon alevins were smaller and weaker when they had been incubated as embryos at low and intermediate DO concentrations than when they were incubated at higher concentrations (Figure 4.14). Shumway et al. (1964) found that reduced DO lengthened the incubation period of coho salmon embryos, which hatched into smaller alevins than normal. Brannon (1965) found differences in length and other anatomical features among newly hatched sockeye salmon fry that had developed at three DO levels (Table 4.7); however, weights of the emergent fry were similar among treatment groups.

In field studies, survival of steelhead embryos (Coble 1961) and coho salmon embryos (Phillips and Campbell 1961) was positively correlated with intragravel DO in redds (Figure 4.15). Phillips and Campbell (1961) concluded that intragravel DO must average 8 mg/L for embryos and alevins to survive well. Stober et al. (1982) and Fast and Stober (1984) reported that newly hatched alevins in the gravel are able to detect oxygen gradients and migrate to areas containing more DO.

Intragravel DO concentrations are functions of many factors: water temperature, surface and intragravel water interchange, apparent velocity of water flow in

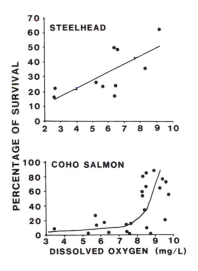

FIGURE 4.15.—Relation between dissolved oxygen concentration and survival of steelhead embryos (from Coble 1961) and coho salmon embryos (Phillips and Campbell 1961) in natural redds.

the redd, permeability of the substrate, and oxygen demand of organic material in the redd, among others. Hall and Lantz (1969), Ringler and Hall (1975), and Moring (1975a) reported that intragravel DO concentrations were reduced in some Oregon streams after adjacent areas had been logged. They attributed such reductions to elevated stream temperatures after removal of the riparian canopy and to increased concentrations of fine sediment that reduced substrate permeability and apparent velocity. Tagart (1976) and Reiser and White (1981b) found direct relations between DO and permeability and inverse relations between DO and percentage of fines in stream substrates. Coble (1961) generalized his experience with this subject by stating that when apparent water velocities are low, DO is low; when they are high, DO is usually high.

All streams transport particulate and dissolved organic matter. The amount transported and the timing of transport varies with the productivity of the stream, the source and type of organic matter, and streamflow (Fisher and Likens 1973; Hobbie and Likens 1973; Liaw and MacCrimmon 1977; Naiman and Sibert 1978; Bilby and Likens 1979; Dance et al. 1979; Naiman and Sedell 1979). Organic matter that settles into redds can reduce the DO concentration as it decomposes; the extent of oxygen depletion depends on the amount and type of organic debris (Hargrave 1972) and the chemical, physical, and hydraulic characteristics (DO content, temperature, permeability, and reaeration capability) of the stream and its substrate. Excessive recruitment of organic material to a stream can result in reduced DO concentrations and intragravel water flow, leading to reduced survival of incubating embryos (Olssen and Persson 1986).

Although DO concentrations required for successful incubation depend on both species and developmental stage, we recommend that concentrations should be at or near saturation, and that temporary reductions should drop to no lower than 5.0 mg/L, for anadromous salmonids. Apparent velocities of water flowing through redds also must be maintained at acceptable rates because high DO alone does not guarantee optimum embryo development. In redds with similar DO concentrations, but different apparent velocities, embryonic development may be better in the redds with the higher rate of water exchange (Coble 1961). Mathematical models have been developed to estimate apparent velocity in redds (Bovee and Cochnauer 1977) and to assess transfer of DO between the stream and substrate (Chevalier and Carson 1985), concentrations of intragravel DO (Chevalier and Murphy 1985), salmonid egg respiration (Carson 1985), and fry emergence (Miller 1985).

Temperature

Water temperature during incubation affects the rate of embryo and alevin development and the capacity of water for dissolved oxygen, and (beyond certain limits) survival of the young fish. There are upper and lower temperature limits (thresholds) for successful incubation of salmonid eggs (Table 4.3). In general, the higher the temperature (within the acceptable range), the faster the rate of development and the shorter the incubation period and time to emergence. The amount of time required for embryos to hatch and for alevins to emerge from redds varies by species and perhaps by location. For example, time to 50% hatch for Pacific salmon species ranges from 115 to 150 d at 4°C and from 35 to 60 d at 12°C; coho salmon require the least time and sockeye salmon the most (Alderdice

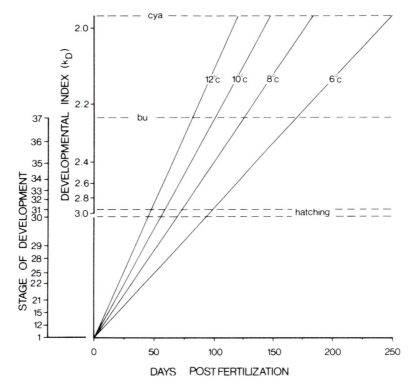

FIGURE 4.16.—Effect of temperature on the development of chinook salmon according to Vernier's (1969) stages of development and Bams's (1970) developmental index (k_D) in a graph from Heming (1982). In the graph, bu = button-up stage of development and cya = complete yolk absorption.

and Velsen 1978; Tang et al. 1987; Velsen 1987). Steelhead and rainbow trout require about 85 d at 4°C and 26 d at 12°C to reach 50% hatch. Heming (1982) graphed stage of development against time (Figure 4.16) for chinook salmon raised experimentally at several temperatures; from these graphs, he estimated emergence at 192 d at 6°C and 85 d at 12°C, about twice the time to 50% hatch. In field studies on the Columbia River, Chapman et al. (1982) found that Heming's curves were reasonable predictors of the time chinook salmon fry emerge. Time to hatch for lake trout is similar to that of chinook salmon, 80–90 d at 6°C (Dwyer 1987).

In many streams in which salmonids spawn, winter temperatures are lower than the 4.4°C minimum recommended for incubation in Table 4.3, but the eggs develop normally because spawning and initial embryo development occur when temperatures are within the suitable range. Combs and Burrows (1957) and Combs (1965) reported that pink and chinook salmon embryos could tolerate long periods of low temperature if the initial temperature was above 6.0°C and embryogenesis had proceeded to a critical developmental stage before the onset of lower water temperatures. Combs and Burrows (1957) believed that salmon produced from eggs deposited in water colder than 4.5°C would be less viable than fish produced from eggs spawned in warmer water. Wangaard and Burger (1983) reported 3.4°C as the temperature below which some newly spawned chum and pink salmon embryos would be killed. Bailey and Evans (1971) defined the lower threshold temperature for pink salmon embryos as 4.5°C. In a summarization of available data, Velsen (1987) reported high mortalities for all Pacific salmon and steelhead when water temperatures were lower than 2–3°C after fertilization. Jungwirth and Winkler (1984) reported that embryos of fall-spawning fishes develop more slowly at any temperature, and have lower upper lethal incubation temperatures, than progeny of spring spawners. Incubation temperatures can also affect the size of newly hatched alevins. When Beacham and Murray (1985) incubated chum salmon eggs at temperatures of 4, 8, and 12°C, the newly hatched alevins incubated at 4°C were the longest, and those at 12°C were the heaviest, but there was no difference in size at emergence. Reiser and White (1981b) observed similar early differences among chinook salmon, which then reached equivalent sizes after 57 d of rearing.

Intragravel water temperatures are influenced by temperatures of the surface water, the thermal mass of the substrate, and the interchange rate of surface and intragravel water. Ringler and Hall (1975) observed that temperatures of intragravel water reached diurnal maxima 2–6 h after those of surface waters in an Oregon stream. Chapman et al. (1982) observed temperature lags of 2–8 h between surface and intragravel waters. There are seasonal as well as daily differences: intragravel water temperatures often are lower than surface water temperatures during summer, and higher during winter (Shepherd et al. 1986a). When salmonids spawn in areas close to groundwater inflows (Hansen 1975; Witzel and MacCrimmon 1983; Wilson 1984; Vining et al. 1985), embryos experience reduced extremes in water temperatures than they would otherwise.

Incubating embryos and alevins can be killed when frazil or anchor ice forms in streams and reduces water interchange between the stream and the redd. Anchor ice normally forms in shallow water typical of spawning areas and may completely blanket the substrate. Ice dams may impede flow or even dewater spawning areas. When such dams melt, the released water may, floodlike, displace the streambed and scour the redds. In an experiment by Reiser and Wesche (1977), eggs placed in plastic-mesh boxes 15 cm below the surface of the streambed completely froze even though the stream above was more than 13 cm deep. Anchor ice had formed at least twice during the incubation period. Neave (1953) and McNeil (1966b) also reported that embryo survival was poor at freezing temperatures.

Rearing in Fresh Water

The abundance of juvenile salmon, trout, and char in streams is a function of many factors, including abundance of newly emerged fry, quantity and quality of suitable habitat, abundance and composition of food, and interactions with other fish, birds, and mammals. Fausch et al. (1988) reviewed many of the models developed in recent years to predict the abundance of fish in streams from habitat variables. We next discuss variables of habitat quantity and quality, and where possible, list the preferences of juvenile salmonids.

The abundance of older fish generally increases as the abundance of juveniles increases until an upper limit (here termed carrying capacity) is reached. We believe that the relation between the seeding level—the number of young fish emplaced in a stream by adult fish or humans—and the abundance of older fish is

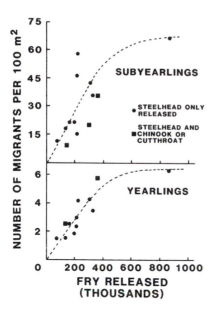

FIGURE 4.17.—Relation between the number of steelhead fry released in Big Springs Creek, Idaho, and the number of subyearling and yearling rainbow trout and steelhead per 100 m^2 that migrated from the stream. Each point represents one of the 1962–1974 year-classes (1962–1973 for yearlings); curves were fitted by inspection. (From Bjornn 1978.)

asymptotic for most salmonids that spend an extended period in streams. At relatively low seeding levels, environmental conditions that set the carrying capacity of a stream for a given age group of fish will place little constraint on the abundance of juveniles and older fish. As spawner abundance (or stocking) approaches that needed for full seeding, the biotic or physical factors that set the carrying capacity come into full play. Habitat variables we discuss here may set the carrying capacity of streams for salmonid fishes, but interactions among many of the relevant physical and biotic variables have not been well defined. In addition, variables that are important in one stream or season may be relatively unimportant in another.

Changes in spawner abundance and variation in the success of incubation and emergence affect the number of young fish entering a stream. Changes in the abundance of newly emerged fry can result in large or insignificant changes in abundance of older fish, depending on the shape of the reproduction curve and actual fry abundance. In two productive Idaho streams, the abundance of older steelhead was primarily a function of the number of newly emerged juveniles placed in the stream at seeding rates up to about 6 fish/m^2 (Bjornn 1978) (Figure 4.17). When steelhead were stocked at a rate of 12/m^2 in Big Springs Creek (right-most point in Figure 4.17), no more subyearlings or yearlings were produced than when 6/m^2 were stocked—evidence that the carrying capacity had been reached. In the Lemhi River, about the same number of steelhead smolts were produced (75,000–80,000) from releases of 2.5 and 4.6 million newly emerged juveniles—additional evidence that carrying capacity had been achieved. The carrying capacity for chinook salmon in the Lemhi River was not reached during 12 years of study in which natural egg-deposition rates ranged from 2 to 8/m^2 (Figure 4.18).

In less-productive Idaho streams, seeding rate (abundance of spawners) was the main factor regulating the abundance of juvenile steelhead (Figure 4.19) and chinook salmon when spawner abundance was relatively low. In Marsh Creek,

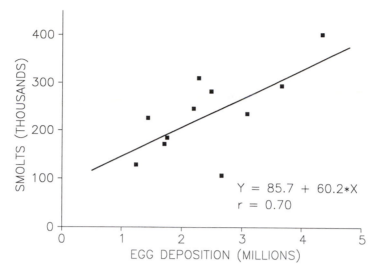

FIGURE 4.18.—Egg deposition *(X)* by adult chinook salmon in the upper Lemhi River, Idaho, and number of smolt-sized fish *(Y)* that later migrated past the Lemhi River weir during fall, winter, and spring, 1963–1973. (From Bjornn 1978.)

one of the relatively unproductive streams, the density of juvenile chinook salmon, monitored irregularly over 12 years, was related to spawner abundance over a nearly 20-fold range (Figure 4.20). Sekulich (1980) presented evidence that the summer carrying capacity for naturally produced salmon in the relatively unproductive streams was 2–3 g/m^2, lower than the carrying capacity of at least 13 g/m^2 in the relatively productive Lemhi River (Bjornn 1978). In Pacific coast streams, the biomass of coho salmon averaged 2–3 g/m^2 in several studies (Cederholm and Reid 1987).

The number of chinook salmon smolts produced in two Lake Michigan tributaries with alternating pool–riffle habitats was independent of the threefold difference in spawner densities that occurred in 2 years of study (Carl 1984). Even at their lower density, spawners apparently seeded the rearing area fully (about 80 spawners per hectare, 0.7–2.9 newly emerged fish per square meter).

For a given level of seeding, what factors in the stream environment regulate abundance or set the carrying capacity for juvenile salmonids? Density-independent environmental factors (amount of suitable habitat, quality of cover, productivity of the stream, and certain types of predation) set an upper limit on the abundance of juveniles, and the population is held to that level by interactions that function in a density-dependent fashion (competition and some types of predation). Carrying capacity, and hence fish production, may vary yearly if controlling habitat components, such as streamflow, vary widely from year to year at critical periods such as late summer (Smoker 1955). The carrying capacity of a stream may also vary with the season, differing, for example, between winter and summer (Bjornn 1978), and it may differ for the various life stages of fish.

Environmental factors can affect the distribution and abundance of juvenile salmonids throughout a stream or drainage or within specific segments of streams.

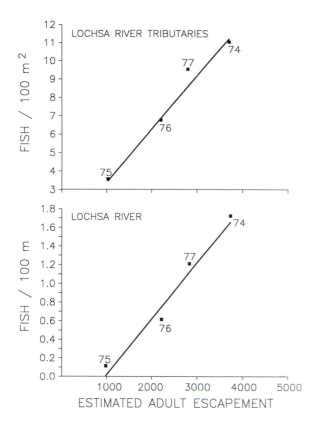

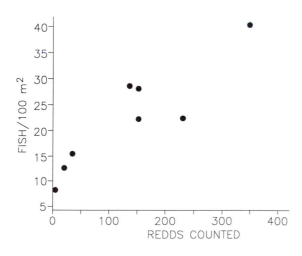

FIGURE 4.19.—Observed density of age-1 steelhead in relation to estimated number of adults returning to the Lochsa River and its tributaries, Idaho, 1974–1977. (Redrawn from Mabbott 1982.)

Temperature, productivity, suitable space, and water quality (turbidity, DO, etc.) are examples of variables that regulate the general distribution and abundance of fish within a stream or drainage. Factors to which fish respond at specific locations in a stream are velocity, depth, substrate, cover, predators, and competitors. Fish often spawn in limited parts of a drainage (sometimes in ephemeral streams), but

FIGURE 4.20.—Relation between chinook salmon redds counted and density of age-0 juveniles the following summer in an Idaho stream. (Authors' original data.)

the juveniles spread out and occupy most of the areas that are suitable and accessible (Everest 1973; Leider et al. 1986).

All of the general factors must be within suitable ranges for salmonids during the time they use a stream segment; otherwise, no fish will be present and there will be no concern about site-specific factors. Rarely, if ever, are most factors optimum for salmonid production. Often some factors may be near optimum while others are suboptimum but still in a suitable range.

Temperature

Salmonids are coldwater fish with definite temperature requirements during rearing. Water temperature influences the metabolism, behavior, and mortality of fish and the other organisms in their environment (Mihursky and Kennedy 1967). Although fish may survive at temperatures near the extremes of the suitable range, growth is reduced at low temperatures—because all metabolic processes are slowed—and at high temperatures—because most or all food must be used for maintenance. Many salmonids change behavior with increases or decreases in temperature.

Normal water temperatures in salmonid streams vary daily, seasonally, annually, and spatially. Humans have altered temperature patterns by changing riparian zone vegetation, diverting water, building reservoirs, and discharging hot water from power plants. Alterations of natural light and temperature patterns in streams can be beneficial or detrimental, depending on the situation, but the consequences of marked changes in the temperature regime of a stream are not fully understood. Small streams in dense forests of the Pacific Northwest, for example, might be too cold in summer for maximum growth of salmonids (Chapman and Knudsen 1980), but warming the stream by altering the riparian vegetation (Gray and Edington 1969; Narver 1972a; Moring 1975a; Moring and Lantz 1975; Murphy et al. 1981; Johnson et al. 1986; Murphy et al. 1986; Beschta et al. 1987) might not enhance growth unless food abundance can satisfy the increase in fish metabolism and other needs of the fish are met (Brett et al. 1969; Hughes and Davis 1986; Hartman et al. 1987; Holtby 1988a). Care must be taken to avoid unwanted warming of downstream waters and excessive loss of cover (both overhead bank and instream) that may be important in winter as well as in summer (Murphy et al. 1986). In many large streams, temperatures become too warm for salmonids in summer for a variety of reasons, including excessive exposure to the sun.

Temperatures that can be tolerated by fishes have been defined and determined in two ways (Brett 1952; Becker and Genoway 1979): slow heating of fish (to reveal the critical thermal maximum, CTM), and abrupt transfer of fish between waters of different temperature (to show the incipient lethal temperature, ILT). In general, upper lethal temperatures determined by the CTM procedure tend to be higher than those established with the ILT technique. The upper ILT for anadromous Pacific salmon, Atlantic salmon, trout, and char range from about 23 to 29°C, depending on species and acclimation temperature (selected examples are in Table 4.8). Half of the upper lethal values presented in Table 4.8 were taken from Brett (1952), who acclimated fish at 20°C and used 50% mortality at 1,000 min as the end point. Lee and Rinne (1980) reported CTM values of 29–30°C for hatchery stocks of rainbow, brown, and brook trout stocked in Arizona and two

TABLE 4.8.—Lower lethal, upper lethal, and preferred temperatures (°C) for selected species of salmon, trout, and char based on techniques to determine incipient lethal temperatures (ILT) and critical thermal maxima (CTM).

Species	Lethal temperature (°C)		Preferred temperature (°C)	Source	Technique
	Lower lethal[a]	Upper lethal[b]			
Chinook salmon	0.8	26.2	12–14	Brett (1952)	ILT
Coho salmon	1.7	26.0	12–14	Brett (1952)	ILT
		28.8[c]		Becker and Genoway (1979)	CTM
Sockeye salmon	3.1	25.8	12–14	Brett (1952)	ILT
Chum salmon	0.5	25.4	12–14	Brett (1952)	ILT
Steelhead	0.0	23.9	10–13	Bell (1986)	
Rainbow trout		29.4		Lee and Rinne (1980)	CTM
		25.0		Charlon et al. (1970)	ILT
Brown trout		29.9		Lee and Rinne (1980)	CTM
		26.7		Brett (1952)	ILT
Gila trout		29.6		Lee and Rinne (1980)	CTM
Apache trout		29.4		Lee and Rinne (1980)	CTM
Brook trout		29.8		Lee and Rinne (1980)	CTM
		25.8		Brett (1952)	ILT
			14–16	Graham (1949)	
Cutthroat trout	0.6	22.8		Bell (1986)	
Atlantic salmon		27.1		Brett (1952)	ILT
		27.8		Garside (1973)	ILT
Lake trout		25.0		Brett (1952)	ILT

[a] Acclimation temperature was 10°C; no mortality occurred in 5,500 min.
[b] Acclimation temperature was 20°C unless noted otherwise; 50% mortality occurred in 1,000 min.
[c] Acclimation temperature was 15°C.

native trouts (Gila trout and Apache trout) when these fish were acclimated at 20°C and subjected to a temperature change rate of 1.2°C/h. Although some salmonids can survive at relatively high temperatures, most are placed in life-threatening conditions when temperatures exceed 23–25°C, and they usually try to avoid such temperatures by moving to other areas.

Lower lethal temperatures for salmonids depend somewhat on previous acclimation (Brett 1952) but they probably are no lower than −0.1°C (Brett and Alderdice 1958). Temperatures in the range of 1 to 4°C can be lethal if fish acclimated in warmer water are transferred abruptly into the cold water. Under natural conditions, fish are not subjected to cold water (<4°C) without prior acclimation in gradually decreasing temperatures, and thus lower lethal temperatures for most species are near 0°C.

Daily summer temperatures can fluctuate more than 15°C in small streams with flows less than 1 m³/s and little or no shade (Meehan 1970; Bjornn 1978).

Temperatures can increase rapidly in a short distance under direct sunlight: 6°C in 1,000 m within a stream flowing at about 1.4 m³/s in central Idaho, for example (Bjornn et al. 1968). As stream size and water mass increase, daily temperatures of streams fluctuate less and tend to reflect the local climate near the stream.

Many populations of native salmonids respond to natural temperature patterns in streams by moving upstream or downstream when water temperatures become unsuitable. Fish may use a section of stream during one season of the year, but move to other sections at other seasons because temperatures become unsuitable. Salmonids may not always avoid unsuitable temperatures, however, especially if the temperatures change rapidly and are not part of the normal pattern in which the fish evolved. Munson et al. (1980) found that rainbow trout accustomed to feeding in a certain location continued to enter the area after temperatures had been changed to a lethal level.

In small streams where daily maximum temperatures approach upper incipient lethal values, salmonids can thrive if the temperature is high for only a short time and then declines well into the optimum range. In an Idaho stream with daily maximum temperatures up to 24°C that lasted less than 1 h and minimums of 8–12°C, juvenile chinook salmon and steelhead maintained high densities and grew normally (Bjornn 1978). In larger Idaho streams where summer maximum temperatures were 24–26°C, but the minimums were relatively high (15–16°C), most young salmon and trout moved upstream or into tributaries where temperatures were lower (Mabbott 1982).

As water temperatures in temperate-zone streams decline in autumn, salmonids change behavior from mostly feeding and defending territory to hiding and schooling. The winter behavior patterns appear to us to be motivated by security. Fish that were curious and easily approached by divers in summer become wary and often dart from view in winter. Winter water temperatures in streams can range from freezing to relatively moderate, according to geographic and groundwater influences. Temperatures in coastal streams often are moderated by maritime climates. Inland, streams can become filled with flow ice, anchor ice, and ice jams during extreme cold spells. The temperature at which the change in behavior occurs apparently varies by species. Chapman and Bjornn (1969) reported that most of the steelhead and chinook salmon juveniles they tested in winter were visible above the substrate at 6°C but hid at 4°C (Figure 4.21). In a British Columbia stream, juvenile coho salmon and steelhead began shifting to winter positions at about 7°C (Bustard and Narver 1975a). Gibson (1978) found that Atlantic salmon began entering the interstitial spaces of rubble substrate in autumn when water temperatures dropped to 10°C, and most had disappeared at 9°C.

The response of salmonids to the lower temperatures that occur in autumn and winter in temperate streams can vary by species and size of fish. Small fish (<15–20 cm) tend to hide in interstitial spaces in the substrate of streams, or in other forms of cover if available, and may move to shallower water (Bustard and Narver 1975a; Gibson 1978), whereas larger fish may join together in schools and move long distances to find suitable winter habitat. In the Lemhi River drainage, Idaho, a large fraction of the young chinook salmon and steelhead moved downstream from rearing areas after their first summer (Bjornn 1971). The chinook salmon moved down into the Salmon River and even the Snake River

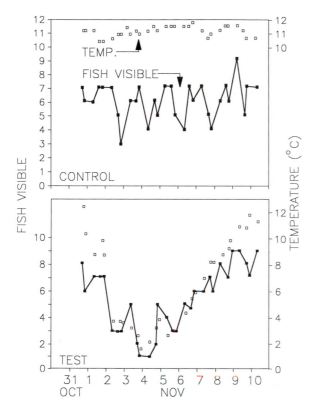

FIGURE 4.21.—Water temperature and number of age-0 steelhead visible above the substrate in test and control vats. (From Chapman and Bjornn 1969.)

(50–200 km) to spend the winter before continuing to the ocean as smolts the following spring. The steelhead moved downstream out of a tributary with a high summer carrying capacity (at least 12 g/m²) but a lower winter carrying capacity, and spent the winter, the next summer, and the following winter in the larger stream before going to the ocean the following spring. Both the chinook salmon and steelhead moved downstream in response to low winter temperatures and a lack of winter cover. Fish migrating downstream in the fall ceased moving when placed in channels with large rock piles (which contained interstitial spaces used in winter) but continued moving downstream when placed in channels without the rock piles (Bjornn and Morrill 1972). In contrast, few juvenile cutthroat trout moved downstream in autumn in tributaries of other Idaho streams where densities were lower (2.1 g/m²) and adequate amounts of suitable winter cover were apparently present (Mauser 1972). On sunny autumn days, the cutthroat trout could be seen in the stream in the afternoon when temperatures approached the daily high (8–10°C), but were not visible in the morning when temperatures were low (3–5°C).

Larger fish that may not be able to use voids in the substrate to hide in winter have been observed joining together in large schools (600 fish) and in some cases moving long distances in fall and spring. In the Coeur d'Alene River of Idaho, Lewynsky (1986) counted fish along transects throughout the summer, fall, and winter; in winter, larger (>20 cm) cutthroat trout moved from dispersed summer feeding stations throughout the river to a few large pools, where they became much more wary and difficult to approach. The extent of seasonal movements of fish in response to temperature is illustrated by migrations of cutthroat and bull trout more than 100 km downstream in autumn and back upstream in spring and early summer in the Salmon River, Idaho (Bjornn and Mallet 1964). Winter temperatures and ice conditions apparently were unsuitable in the upper portions of the Middle Fork drainage and most of the fish larger than 15 cm moved. Temperatures in the main-stem rivers became marginal in summer for salmonids.

Temperature is one of the factors that contribute to quality of habitat for fish. If temperature is in a tolerable range for the fish, the question of optimum temperature becomes pertinent. Optimum temperature could be defined in relation to a variety of population or individual variables, including temperature preference, growth, efficiency of converting food to tissue, standing crops, and swimming performance. When Brett (1952) placed five species of Pacific salmon in a vertical temperature gradient, they all tended to congregate in the 12–14°C stratum.

Optimum temperatures, measured in terms of fish growth rate and food conversion efficiency, vary with the amount of food available. Brett et al. (1969) reported that growth of yearling sockeye salmon was highest at about 5°C when the daily ration (percent of body weight) available was 1.5%, but shifted to about 15°C when the ration was 6%. At highest temperatures, the growth rate declined regardless of food abundance. Food conversion efficiency peaked at 8–11°C (Brett et al. 1969)—lower than the 15°C associated with maximum growth, optimum metabolic scope for activity, greatest tolerance of oxygen debt, and maximum sustained swimming speed (Brett 1964). After tests with Atlantic salmon, Dwyer and Piper (1987) reported that maximum growth with unlimited food was attained at 16–19°C, but that growth efficiency was highest at 10–16°C.

Similar relations—with variations in the optimum temperature or temperature range—probably exist for other species. The optimum temperature for brook trout, for example, appears to be 14–16°C. Graham (1949), as reported in Mihursky and Kennedy (1967), listed 14–16°C as the temperature preferendum for brook trout, and Beamish (1964) gave 15°C as the temperature for maximum spontaneous activity. Dwyer et al. (1983) reported that brook trout grew most efficiently at 10 and 13°C. Jensen and Johnsen (1986) presented evidence that stocks of fish may be able to adapt to temperatures that might otherwise make their existence unlikely.

Brett et al. (1958) reported that the optimum temperature for sustained swimming was 15°C for sockeye and 20°C for coho salmon (Figure 4.22), and that maximum sustained swimming speeds at these temperatures were 35 and 30 cm/s, respectively. Sustained swimming performance was reduced to about 12 cm/s for sockeye salmon and to 6 cm/s for coho salmon at temperatures near 0°C. Davis et al. (1963) also found that the maximum sustained swimming speed of underyearling coho salmon was higher at 20°C than at 15 or 10°C. In a study of the critical swimming speeds of yearling rainbow trout as a measure of temperature preference, Schneider and Connors (1982) found no significant differences at 10, 15, or 20°C, but swimming performance was reduced at 25°C. The 25°C test temperature was 2°C less than the ILT measured for rainbow trout by Charlon et al. (1970).

The effect of water temperature on fish behavior and the regulation of densities in streams is not well understood, but there is some evidence that densities or

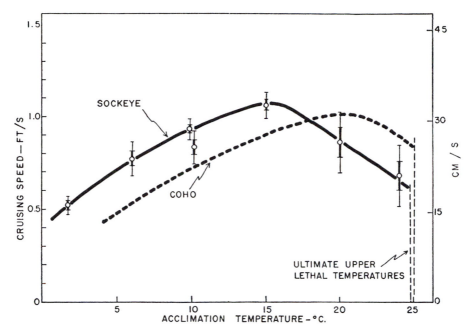

FIGURE 4.22.—Variation in cruising speed among temperature-acclimated underyearling sockeye and coho salmon, adjusted to common mean lengths of 6.9 cm and 5.4 cm, respectively. The fish were cultured under similar conditions and were 4 to 6 months of age. The sockeye salmon data are means (circles), standard errors (heavy vertical bars), and standard deviations. (From Brett et al. 1958.)

even production of fish may be less at high (but suitable) temperatures than at lower ones. In laboratory stream studies, Hahn (1977) found that twice as many steelhead fry remained in channels with daily temperature fluctuations of 8–19°C or a constant temperature of 13.5°C than in a channel held at a constant 18.5°C. At constant 8.5°C, the density of fish was twice that found in channels held at 13.5°C. Hughes and Davis (1986), who studied coho salmon and steelhead in laboratory streams, concluded that a moderate (4°C) increase in temperature could decrease the productivity of streams for those species when food is limiting. Glova (1986) found that habitat use by juvenile coho salmon and cutthroat trout in summer, when temperatures were 13°C, was different from that in winter, when temperatures were colder. When tested separately in summer, most fish of both species took up residence in pools, but, when tested together, most of the coho salmon stayed in pools and cutthroat trout remained in riffles. In winter at temperatures of 3°C, both species, whether together or separate, preferred pools and overhead cover.

Changes in water temperatures resulting from land and water use may affect fish indirectly as well as directly. In a small Vancouver Island stream, coho salmon emerged earlier when winter water temperatures became higher after logging, and detrimental downstream movement of the newly emerged fish occurred when freshets took place soon after emergence (Scrivener and Andersen 1984). Growth rate of coho salmon juveniles was inversely related to density in the stream, and the fish were larger in autumn after logging than before because of the earlier

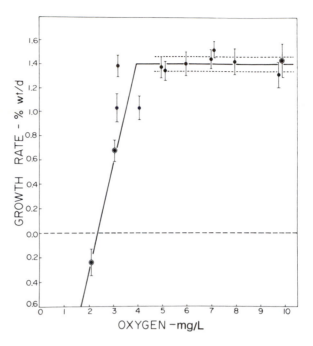

FIGURE 4.23.—Specific growth rate (percent of body weight per day ± SE) of fingerling coho salmon (5–10 g) in relation to oxygen concentration at 15°C. (From Brett and Blackburn 1981.) Dotted lines are 95% confidence limits for values with dissolved oxygen above 6 mg/L. Sloped line (fitted by eye) defines the zone of dependence of growth on dissolved oxygen.

emergence and longer period of growth. A dam on the Rogue River, Oregon, altered flows and temperatures in both summer and winter, and changed the timing of salmon and steelhead fry emergence, adult migration, fish distribution in the river, and adult mortality (Cramer et al. 1985).

Dissolved Oxygen

The waters of most natural salmonid streams have enough DO for juveniles, although concentrations in small streams may be reduced by large amounts of organic debris when temperatures are high and flows low (Hall and Lantz 1969). Streams downstream from deep, productive reservoirs may have marginally low DO concentrations at times if the discharge comes from the hypolimnion. The DO must be above a critical level for salmonids to exist in streams. Rainbow trout have survived laboratory tests at DO concentrations of less than 2 mg/L (Alabaster et al. 1957), and the survival threshold concentration for Atlantic salmon smolts is about 3.3 mg/L (Alabaster et al. 1979), but growth rate (Figure 4.23) and food conversion efficiency (Figure 4.24) are probably limited by concentrations less than 5 mg/L. Davis (1975), who reviewed information on incipient DO response thresholds and developed oxygen criteria related to concentration, water temperature, and percent saturation (Table 4.9), concluded that salmonids would not be impaired at concentrations near 8 mg/L (76–93% saturation), and that initial symptoms of DO deprivation would occur at about 6 mg/L (57–72% saturation). Davis et al. (1963) and Dahlberg et al. (1968) found the maximum sustained swimming performances of coho and chinook salmon decreased when DO concentrations were much below air-saturation levels (about 8–9 mg/L at 20°C).

In summary, salmonids may be able to survive when DO concentrations are relatively low (<5 mg/L), but growth, food conversion efficiency, and swimming

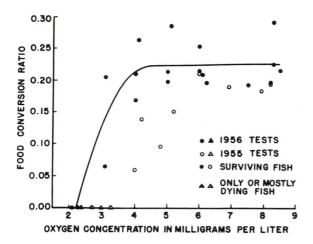

FIGURE 4.24.—Food conversion ratio (weight gained by fish/weight of food consumed) for frequently fed age-0 coho salmon in relation to dissolved oxygen concentration. A food conversion ratio of zero (not a negative ratio) has been assigned to each group of fish that lost weight. The curve has been fitted only to the 1956 data. (From Herrmann et al. 1962.)

performance will be adversely affected. High water temperature, which reduces oxygen solubility, can compound the stress on fish caused by marginal DO concentrations.

Most data on the oxygen requirements of salmonids come from laboratory studies. Brett and Blackburn (1981) appropriately urged caution when such data are extrapolated to fish in natural streams. Water qualities and the biological activities necessary for survival may differ between laboratory and field environments.

Turbidity

In most streams, there are periods when the water is relatively turbid and contains variable amounts of suspended sediments. Larger juvenile and adult salmon and trout appear to be little affected by ephemerally high concentrations of suspended sediments that occur during most storms and episodes of snowmelt (Cordone and Kelley 1961; Sorenson et al. 1977). Bisson and Bilby (1982) reported, however, that juvenile coho salmon avoided water with turbidities that exceeded 70 NTU (nephelometric turbidity units), which may occur in certain types of watersheds and with severe erosion. Berg and Northcote (1985) reported that feeding and territorial behavior of juvenile coho salmon were disrupted by short-term exposures (2.5–4.5 d) to turbid water (up to 60 NTU).

Newly emerged fry appear to be more susceptible to even moderate turbidities than are older fish. Turbidities in the 25–50-NTU range (equivalent to 125–275 mg/L of bentonite clay) reduced growth and caused more young coho salmon and steelhead to emigrate from laboratory streams than did clear water (Sigler et al.

TABLE 4.9.—Response of freshwater salmonid populations to three concentrations of dissolved oxygen. (Modified from Davis 1975.)

Response	Dissolved oxygen (mg/L)	Percent saturation at temperature (°C)					
		0	5	10	15	20	25
Function without impairment	7.75	76	76	76	76	85	93
Initial distress symptoms	6.00	57	57	57	59	65	72
Most fish affected by lack of oxygen	4.25	38	38	38	42	46	51

1984). Juvenile salmonids tend to avoid streams that are chronically turbid, such as glacial streams or those disturbed by human activities (Lloyd et al. 1987), except when the fish have to traverse them along migration routes.

Productivity of Streams

Streams vary in productivity due largely to the nutrients and energy available. The rates of primary and secondary production largely determine the amount of food available to fish. A detailed discussion of energy sources and processes is presented by Murphy and Meehan (1991, this volume).

The amount of food available to fish is one of the factors that set the salmonid carrying capacity of streams. In many infertile streams, summer fish production appears to be food-limited. A change in fish production, density, or growth when food availability increases or decreases is proof of food limitation. More coho salmon could be produced in a small Vancouver Island stream during summer when Mason (1976) increased the amount of food available. In another Vancouver Island stream, Slaney et al. (1986) added inorganic fertilizers (phosphorus and nitrogen) to a 29-km section and found large increases in primary production, no significant changes in invertebrate abundance and fish density, and significant increases in trout growth. The increased growth allowed steelhead to become smolts at a younger age; because this period of juvenile mortality was reduced, the stream produced more smolts.

Positive correlations between stream productivity and production, standing crops, and growth of brown trout were observed by McFadden and Cooper (1962). In Idaho streams that differed in conductivity by a factor of 10 (40 to 400 $\mu S/cm^3$), the production and standing crop of age-0 chinook salmon differed by a similar factor (T. C. Bjornn, unpublished data). Konopacky (1984) found juvenile chinook salmon and steelhead lost weight and eventually left laboratory streams when no food was supplied; he also found proportionate increases in production, but not in density, in response to two levels of daily ration. Wilzbach (1985) reported that most cutthroat trout left laboratory channels when they were given a daily ration of frozen brine shrimp equal to only 5% of their body weight, whether cover was provided or not, but they stayed when given a 15% ration.

Brett et al. (1969) defined the daily rations needed for maximum growth of sockeye salmon at various temperatures. If this relation is similar for other species of salmon and trout, a yearling salmonid in a stream with daily mean temperature of 10°C would need a daily food supply equivalent to 6–7% of its body weight to attain maximum growth. In streams that are food-limited, maximum growth rates may not be achieved by the fish because that may not be the most efficient use of resources. The social interactions that fish use to regulate densities and respond to food abundance may result in more fish growing at less-than-maximum rates, rather than fewer fish growing at maximum rates.

Juvenile salmonids can consume a large fraction of the invertebrates drifting during daylight in the streams they occupy (Allan 1982; Wilzbach et al. 1986), but fish do not appear to regulate the abundance of benthic or drifting invertebrates in streams except in very limited situations of time and space (Allan 1983). Production of aquatic invertebrates that juvenile salmonids eat depends on the amount of organic material available in streams. Bilby and Likens (1980) showed the importance of debris dams in small streams for the accumulation of coarse particulate organic matter. Nearly 75% of the organic matter deposited in first-order streams was associated with the dams, versus 58% in second-order streams and 20% in third-order streams. Fish also eat terrestrial invertebrates that are associated with vegetation surrounding streams.

Space

Space suitable for occupancy by salmonids in streams is a function of streamflow, channel morphometry, gradient, and (in many instances) various forms of instream or riparian cover. Suitable space for each salmonid life stage has water of sufficient depth and quality flowing at appropriate velocities. The addition of cover (extra depth, preferred substrates, woody debris, etc.) increases the complexity of the space and usually the carrying capacity. The addition of certain types of cover (overhead, for example) may make some areas in streams suitable for fish that would not otherwise be used.

The space an individual fish needs and uses—in some instances a territory—is a part of the total suitable space available. Food abundance (Chapman 1966), the competitors (Fausch and White 1981, 1986) and predators present, and the complexity of the habitat determine what part of the available suitable space an individual fish uses.

Fish densities in streams provide a measure of the spatial requirements of juvenile salmonids, but the wide variation in observed densities illustrates the diversity of habitat quantity and quality and other factors that regulate fish abundance. In a productive Idaho stream, end-of-summer densities of age-0 chinook salmon (9.6 g mean weight) have been as high as 1.35 fish/m^2 and 12.9 g/m^2 (Bjornn 1978). With the age-0 steelhead (4.5 g) also produced in the stream, the combined densities were 2.05 fish/m^2 and 16.1 g/m^2. These salmonids were not uniformly distributed throughout the length of the stream and densities in some sections were as high as 3.4 fish/m^2 (21.8 g/m^2). Total salmonid density, including the age-1 and older fish, has been as high as 3.5 fish/m^2 and 27.0 g/m^2. Spring-to-fall production (tissue elaborated) by age-0 chinook salmon and steelhead has been measured at rates as high as 20.3 g/m^2.

In less productive third- and fourth-order streams in Idaho, age-0 chinook salmon were less dense (usually <0.8 fish/m^2), the fish grew slower (end-of-summer weight, about 5 g), biomass standing crops were only 1–3 g/m^2, and few fish of other species were produced. Summer production was 1–2 g/m^2 (T. C. Bjornn, unpublished data). In coastal and inland British Columbia streams, Shepherd et al. (1986b) reported overall maximum densities of 0.14 age-0 chinook salmon/m^2 (five streams) and 0.41 age-0 and age-1 coho salmon/m^2 (nine streams).

Salmonids, especially the juveniles, also use the space available in side channels for rearing. Mundie and Traber (1983) found higher densities of steelhead (0.66 smolts/m^2 and 9.94 g/m^2) and coho salmon (0.85 smolts/m^2 and 12.8 g/m^2) in side-channel pools than are commonly found in the main channels of Pacific coastal streams. Peterson (1982a, 1982b) reported coho salmon moving into side-channel pools for the winter.

The amount of space needed by fish increases with age and size. Allen (1969) assembled data on densities for a variety of salmonids and found a positive relation between area per fish in streams and age (Figure 4.25) or length. For the streams he evaluated, 7–10-cm fish (which had completed the first year of life)

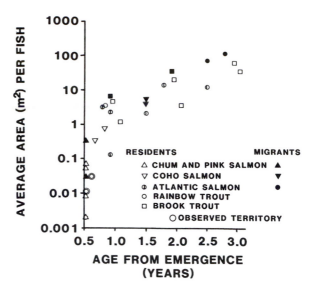

FIGURE 4.25.—Average area per fish (on a logarithmic scale) versus age for several salmonids in streams. (Redrawn from Allen 1969.)

were found at densities of 0.1 to 1.0 fish/m^2 (10-cm fish averaged 0.17 fish/m^2 and 1.7 g/m^2). Densities of larger and older fish were usually less than 0.1 fish/m^2.

Based on the foregoing, the summer space requirements of juvenile salmonids during their first year in streams probably range from 0.25 to 10 m^2 of stream per fish, depending on such things as the species and age composition of fish present, stream productivity, and quality of the space. The space required in winter has not been as well defined.

The presence of abundant space does not necessarily mean there will be large numbers of fish. The space must be in the right context with other needs of the fish. For example, the abundance of age-0 chinook salmon in some infertile Idaho nursery streams appeared to be asymptotically related to the size of pools (Figure 4.26). In pools up to about 200 m^2 in area (volume, 150 m^3), the number (or biomass) of fish observed was directly related to size of the pools. In larger pools, however, much of the space in the downstream portions was unused, despite the presence of suitable depths and velocities. Fish abundance was probably food-limited in these streams and thus the fish were concentrated in the upper portions of each pool, close to the incoming food supply.

The effect of reducing space available to fish in small pools of third-order streams was illustrated by Bjornn et al. (1977) in a stream sedimentation experiment. When sand was added to a natural pool, reducing pool volume by half and surface area of water deeper than 0.3 m by two-thirds, fish numbers declined by two-thirds.

Streamflow.—Streamflow, one of the basic determinants of the amount of space available for fish, varies seasonally in ways that depend on geography and climate. In coastal streams, flows are often high in winter because of heavy rain and snowfall. In inland areas, flows are most often high in spring as a result of snowmelt, but rain-on-snow events occasionally cause high flows in winter. In most unregulated salmonid streams of North America, flows are usually lowest in late summer, fall, or winter (Stalnaker and Arnette 1976a). Diversion of water

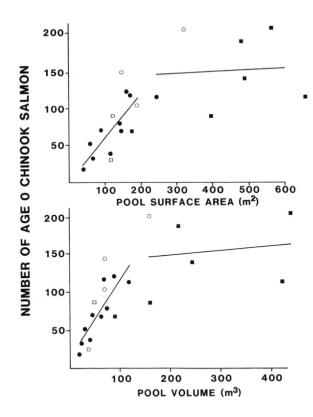

FIGURE 4.26.—Relation between pool surface area or volume in several Idaho streams (denoted by different symbols) and number of juvenile chinook salmon per pool. (Redrawn from Konopacky 1984.)

from streams and storage of water for municipal, agricultural, flood control, and hydropower uses usually lead to altered streamflows and potential changes in the carrying capacity of streams for salmonid fishes. The relation between streamflow and carrying capacity could vary with channel geometry and surrounding land forms; it probably differs, for example, between streams consisting mostly of riffles in a V-shaped canyon and streams with alternating pools and riffles in a broad valley. In general, the relation must start at the origin (no flow, no fish), increase (perhaps not uniformly) with increases in flow up to a point, and then level off or decline if flows become excessive. The relation between flow and carrying capacity is difficult to assess directly in natural streams, however, and there are few studies for reference. The roles of flow magnitude and seasonality in setting the carrying capacity of a stream have not been well defined.

Kraft (1972) diverted water from a 520-m section of natural stream channel in Montana for 3 months in summer and found that both physical stream characteristics and resident brook trout were more affected in runs than in pools. After a 90% reduction from normal summer flows (about 1.0 m^3/s), depth in runs decreased 38%, average water velocity decreased 73%, and cover decreased 50%; decreases were smaller in pools. The response of brook trout to the 90% flow reduction was variable, but many fish in the dewatered section moved from runs into pools; the number of fish decreased an average 62% in dewatered runs compared with 20% in runs that were not dewatered (Figure 4.27).

In an Oregon flume studied by White et al. (1981), water velocities, depths, wetted perimeters, and surface areas in runs declined with decreases in flow, as

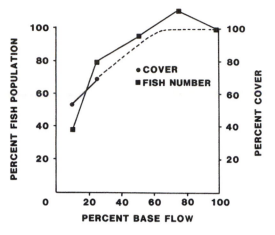

FIGURE 4.27.—Relations of fish number and cover to reductions in summer base flow in three runs in Blacktail Creek, Montana. (Data from Kraft 1968, as plotted by White 1976.)

did the abundance of wild steelhead juveniles, but the researchers were unable to determine the relative influences of the physical features on fish abundance. The authors also calculated an index (weighted usable area, WUA) of the amount of suitable habitat in the flumes for juvenile steelhead, based on IFIM. Their estimates of WUA from suitability curves for velocity and depth did not correspond closely with the number of fish remaining at each flow.

The IFIM, although controversial and incompletely validated, is a modeling procedure designed to help evaluate the importance of differing streamflows to the production of fish. The procedure generates a relation between WUA and flow. Typically, WUA increases asymptotically with flow (Figure 4.28), but the estimates can vary widely depending on the velocity and depth suitability indexes used. In an Idaho stream, WUA estimates for age-0 chinook salmon were highest at flows that occurred near the end of summer, and decreased when flows were higher or lower. The WUA values based on velocity and depth were highest for pools, followed by runs, and then riffles.

For IFIM models to be useful, there must be a definable relation between WUA index values and the standing crop or production of fish in a stream. Such relations can exist only if the physical variables included in the model (velocity, depth, substrate, cover, etc.) are the factors that regulate abundance. Stalnaker (1979) found that standing crop of brown trout was strongly correlated with WUA in 19 sections of 8 Wyoming streams. Orth and Maughan (1982) and Conder and Annear (1987) had less success in relating WUA index values to standing crops of fish or to another habitat quality index. Conder and Annear (1987) discussed the use of the IFIM to estimate changes in fish production in streams as related to streamflow. Nickelson et al. (1979) reported on studies of models that could be used to evaluate streamflow requirements of salmonids in Oregon streams. After several years of study, they recommended use of the IFIM with the addition of variables for pool volume and cover.

Smoker (1955) found a correlation between the commercial catch of coho salmon and annual runoff, summer flow, and lowest monthly flow in 21 western Washington drainages 2 years previously; the data covered the years 1935–1954. In the last two decades, hatchery production of coho salmon smolts has increased markedly and made such comparisons more difficult, but Mathews and Olson (1980) analyzed data

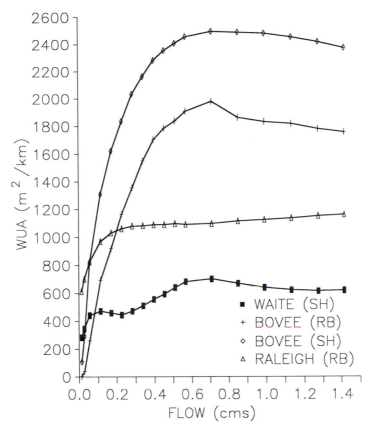

FIGURE 4.28.—Indices of suitable area (weighted usable area, WUA) versus flow (cubic meters per second) for juvenile steelhead (SH) and rainbow trout (RB) in a California stream based on different probability-of-use curves devised by Waite, Bovee, and Raleigh. (Ian Waite, unpublished data.)

from Washington for the years 1952–1977 and found that summer streamflow still had an important influence on total coho salmon production in Puget Sound area streams. Scarnecchia (1981) found that the coho salmon catch off the Oregon coast for the years 1942–1962 was correlated with total flow in five coastal rivers during the salmon's freshwater existence; however, the catch was poorly correlated with the 60-d period of lowest flow in these rivers. Nickelson (1986), in an analysis of coho salmon survival from smolt to adult off the Oregon–California coast, concluded that survival at sea was variable (related to upwelling), but density independent. The implication of the above studies is that the abundance of adult coho salmon is a function of the number of smolts produced, which is in turn related to streamflow and the other factors that regulate the production of smolts.

Velocity.—Given flow in a stream, velocity is probably the next most important factor in determining the amount of suitable space for rearing salmonids (Chapman 1966; deGraaf and Bain 1986); if the velocities are unsuitable, no fish will be present. Natural streams contain a diversity of velocities (Figure 4.29) and depths,

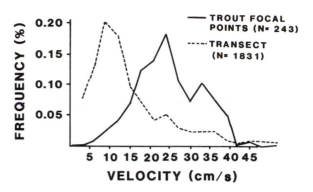

FIGURE 4.29.—Frequency of velocities at sites (focal points) occupied by trout in three sections of Uvas Creek, California, and frequency of velocities measured along transects in the stream. (From Smith and Li 1983.)

some of which are suitable for most salmonids. The velocities required and used by juvenile salmonids vary with size of fish, and sometimes with species. Some juvenile salmonids, as they grow, select sites in streams with increasingly faster velocities (Chapman and Bjornn 1969; Everest and Chapman 1972; Rimmer et al. 1984; Moyle and Baltz 1985), presumably to gain access to more abundant food (Chapman and Bjornn 1969; Fausch 1984). Sites used for feeding over long periods and the size of food items eaten may be selected largely to maximize net energy gain (Bachman 1984).

Water velocities required by fish of various sizes have been estimated from studies of the sites fish occupy in streams and of the swimming performance of fish in laboratories. Use of data from so-called field microhabitat studies to establish velocity and depth requirements has limitations because the sites selected by fish in natural streams are influenced by factors other than their velocity and depth preferences. Interactions with other fishes and the presence and location of cover alter sites selected by fish (Fausch and White 1981, 1986). Wild brown trout placed in a flume shifted position to stay within a suitable velocity range when flows were increased (Baldes and Vincent 1969). In a study by Shirvell and Dungey (1983), velocity was the most important factor determining the preferred sites of large brown trout (42 cm), but the fish often chose compromise positions to be close to food or cover.

Velocity and depth preferences may change seasonally. Chisholm et al. (1987) noted that brook trout selected areas of lower velocity (<15 cm/s) and deeper water (>30 cm) in winter than in summer, but showed no preference for substrate. Tschaplinski and Hartman (1983) noted similar shifts by coho salmon in winter to

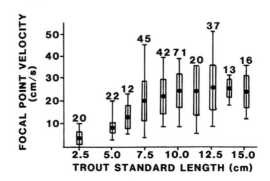

FIGURE 4.30.—Water velocities at focal points (means, ranges, and 95% confidence intervals) for trout of different standard lengths in a California stream. Numbers above data points are sample sizes. (From Smith and Li 1983.)

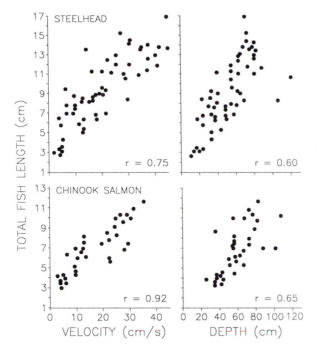

FIGURE 4.31.—Correlations between length of juvenile steelhead and chinook salmon and velocity and depth of water at sites (focal points) used by the fish in two Idaho streams. (Redrawn from Everest and Chapman 1972.)

sites (deep pools, undercuts, debris jams, side sloughs) with low velocity (<30 cm/s) but good cover.

Newly emerged fry (20–35 mm long) of salmon, trout, and char require velocities of less than 10 cm/s, based on studies of sites selected by the fish in streams (Chapman and Bjornn 1969; Everest and Chapman 1972; Griffith 1972; Hanson 1977; Smith and Li 1983; Konopacky 1984; Pratt 1984; Bugert 1985; Moyle and Baltz 1985; Sheppard and Johnson 1985). Larger fish (4–18 cm long) usually occupy sites with velocities up to about 40 cm/s (Figures 4.30, 4.31, 4.32; Table 4.10). Velocities at the sites occupied (focal points) by juvenile steelhead in a California stream were higher than the modal velocities in the stream (Figure 4.29), increased asymptotically with fish length (Figure 4.30), increased with temperature, and were less than the velocities at their usual feeding sites (Smith and Li 1983). Because invertebrate drift abundance increased with velocity across a stream section, there was a potential energetic benefit from feeding in the fastest water possible. In Idaho streams, young chinook salmon and steelhead occupied deeper and faster water as they increased in size (Figure 4.31), presumably to gain better access to food. By the end of summer, young chinook salmon (4–10 cm long) were found in the full range of available depths, but in velocities that were on the low end of those available (Figure 4.32).

Swimming performance as measured in the laboratory provides a measure of the ability of a fish to swim under specified conditions, but may not reveal velocities preferred by the fish. Brett et al. (1958) reported cruising speeds (speeds a fish could maintain for at least 1 h under stimulation) of juvenile coho salmon increased with fish size and temperature (Figure 4.33). At 10°C, cruising speeds

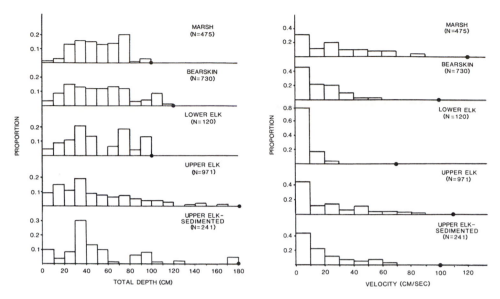

FIGURE 4.32.—Distribution of age-0 chinook salmon (77–89 mm mean total length) relative to water depth and velocity in pools of Idaho streams in August 1979. Dots indicate maximum water depth or velocity observed in the pools surveyed. (From Konopacky 1984.)

were 20–25 cm/s for 5-cm coho salmon and 35–40 cm/s for 9-cm fish; at 20°C, the speeds were 5–6 cm/s faster. Cruising speeds of fish are lower than speeds at which fish can swim for short bursts, but may be higher than water velocities observed at focal points selected by fish in streams. In a southeast Alaska stream, the mean velocity at focal points selected by age-0 (<7 cm long) and yearling (up to 12 cm long) coho salmon averaged 13–14 cm/s (T. C. Bjornn, unpublished data). Brett (1967) reported that juvenile sockeye salmon (136 mm mean length) could swim for 300 min in velocities up to about 37 cm/s (at 15°C) without becoming fatigued; at increasingly higher velocities, all fish eventually became fatigued (Figure 4.34). Velocities that did not produce fatigue in 300 min (<37 cm/s) were about half the cruising speed for fish of a given size.

Depth.—The depth of water juvenile salmonids use depends on what is available, the amounts and type of cover present, and the perceived threat from predators and competitors. Young trout and salmon have been seen in water barely deep enough to cover them and in water more than a meter deep. Densities (fish/m^2) of some salmonids are often higher in pools than in other habitat types (runs, riffles, pocket waters; Figure 4.35), but that may reflect the space available (there is more volume in pools per unit of surface) rather than a preference for deep water, especially for smaller fish (<15 cm long).

Fish usually are not uniformly distributed at all depths in a stream. Raleigh et al. (1986) presented index curves for chinook salmon in which suitabilities for newly emerged fry and juveniles were highest at depths of 25–60 cm. The curves were constructed from observations of fish distributions in streams. Everest and Chapman (1972) found significant correlations between size of fish and total water

TABLE 4.10.—Depths and velocities at sites used by salmonids in streams.

Species and source	Age[a] or size	Depth (cm)	Velocity (cm/s)
Steelhead			
Bugert (1985)	31–44 mm	24	40
Everest and Chapman (1972)	0	<15	<15
	1	60–75	15–30
Hanson (1977)	1	51 mean	10 mean
	2	58 mean	15 mean
	3	60 mean	15 mean
Moyle and Baltz (1985)	0	35	7.3
	Juvenile	63	19.4
	Adult	82	28.6
Sheppard and Johnson (1985)	37 mm	<30	<25
Smith and Li (1983)	25 mm		4
	50 mm		8
	75 mm		18
	100 mm		24
	150 mm		24
Stuehrenberg (1975)	0	<30	14 (range, 3–26)
	1	>15	16 (range, 5–37)
Thompson (1972)	0	18–67	6–49
Chinook salmon			
Everest and Chapman (1972)	0	15–30	<15
Konopacky (1984)	77–89 mm	55–60	12–30
			18 (dawn)
			12 (midday)
			25 (dusk)
Stuehrenberg (1975)	0	<61	9 (range, 0–21)
	1	<61	17 (range, 5–38)
Thompson (1972)	0	30–122	6–24
Steward and Bjornn (1987)	78–81 mm	40–58	8–10
Coho salmon			
Bugert (1985)	40–50 mm	24	39 (flume)
	0		15
	1		18
Nickelson and Reisenbichler (1977)	0	>30	<30
Pearson et al. (1970)	0		9–21
Sheppard and Johnson (1985)	62 mm	30–70	<30
Thompson (1972)	0	30–122	5–24
Cutthroat trout			
Hanson (1977)	1	51 mean	10 mean
	2	56 mean	14 mean
	3	57 mean	20 mean
	4	54 mean	14 mean
Pratt (1984)	<100 mm	32	10
	>100 mm	62	22
Thompson (1972)	0, 1	40–122	6–49
Atlantic salmon			
Rimmer et al. (1984)	40–100 mm		30
	100–150 mm		38
Bull trout			
Pratt (1984)	<100 mm	33	9
	>100 mm	45	12

[a] Ages are in years or life stages, without units.

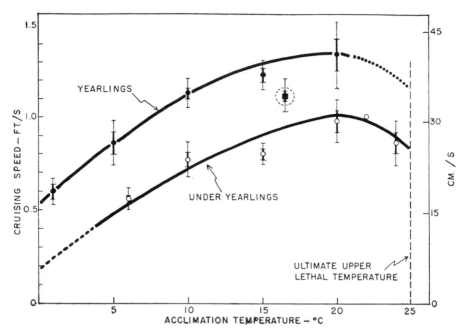

FIGURE 4.33.—Variation in cruising speed for temperature-acclimated underyearling and yearling coho salmon, adjusted in each age group to common mean lengths of 5.4 cm and 8.9 cm, respectively. The circled point between two curves is for exercised underyearling coho salmon acclimated to 16.5°C. Standard deviation (thin vertical bar) and standard error (heavy bar) are indicated for each sample. (From Brett et al. 1958.)

depth at sites (focal points) occupied by juvenile chinook salmon and steelhead (Figure 4.31). Correlations were poor between fish size and distance of focal point from the bottom; most fish, regardless of size, were near the bottom. In two Newfoundland Rivers, water depth was an unimportant factor in site selection by juvenile Atlantic salmon (deGraaf and Bain 1986).

If fish have a preferred depth of water, we believe it is readily subjugated to the needs for suitable velocities, access to food, and security from predators. Sites that fish select in streams must satisfy all the basic needs to enable the fish to survive. In laboratory streams, chinook salmon fry 30–40 mm long occupied a wide variety of

FIGURE 4.34.—Percentage of young sockeye salmon that became fatigued within 300 min at 15°C when forced to swim at the velocity indicated. The mean total length of the 104 fish in the sample was 13.6 cm. (Redrawn from Brett 1967.)

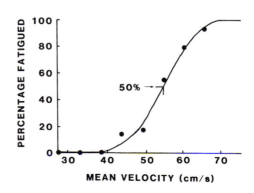

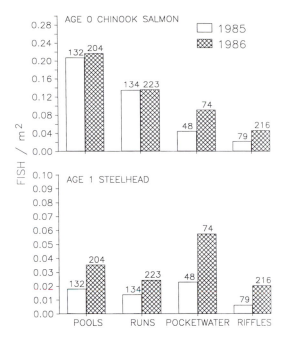

FIGURE 4.35.—Densities of age-0 chinook salmon and age-1 steelhead in various types of habitat in 22 Idaho streams. Numbers above bars represent the number of units of each type of habitat surveyed. (Authors' original data.)

sites (including the deepest water) when they were the only fish present, but only restricted areas when they shared the streams with yearling steelhead 70–120 mm long (T. C. Bjornn, unpublished data). The newly emerged fry were distributed throughout the water in both small pools (0.6 m wide, 1.2 m long, 0.32 m deep) and larger pools (1.5 m wide, 2.5 m long, 1.1 m deep) when no other fish were present and there was no threat of bird predation. The presence of only two yearling steelhead in a 4.8-m section of the smaller stream (two pools, two riffles, one run) changed the behavior of and site selection by the chinook salmon fry: some left the stream and those that remained stayed close to the bottom in the pools or moved into the interstitial spaces of the gravel substrate. When larger numbers of yearling steelhead were present, all chinook salmon fry left the stream or were eaten. In the larger stream, the fry moved to shallow water (<6 cm deep) above a sand bar, left the stream, moved into the substrate, or were eaten when yearling steelhead were present. A simulated kingfisher flight over the sand bar frightened the fry into the pool where they were vulnerable to predation by steelhead.

The relation between water depth in streams and fish numbers has not been empirically defined, but depends on the mixture of fish species and sizes, types and amounts of other cover present, and size of stream. In second- to fourth-order salmon streams, we suspect the relation is asymptotic, fish abundance increasing with increases in depth (more space) up to a point. We see no reason why fish that form schools in pools should become less abundant in extra deep water, but territorial fishes and those that select sites close to the substrate may not be as abundant in deep pools as in shallower types of habitat (runs and pocket water; Figure 4.35).

Substrate.—The substrates of salmonid streams are important habitats for incubating embryos and aquatic invertebrates that provide much of the food of

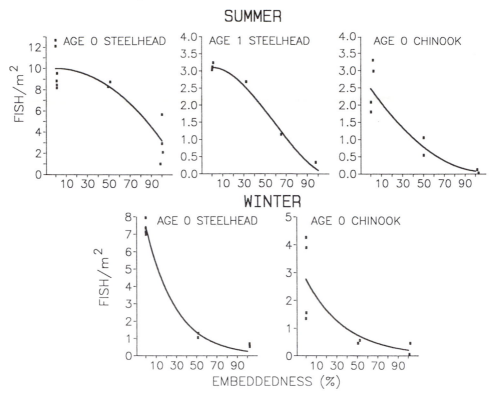

FIGURE 4.36.—Densities of chinook salmon and steelhead juveniles remaining in laboratory stream channels after 5 d during winter and summer tests to evaluate the effects of sedimentation. The channels had alternating pool–riffle configurations; fine sediments (<6 mm) were added to pools and riffles to embed the cobbles and boulders from 0 to 100%. (From Bjornn et al. 1977.)

salmonids, and they provide cover for fish in summer and winter. Silt and sand substrates have little or no value as cover for fish. Larger substrate materials (up to 40 cm in diameter) provide visual isolation and their interstitial spaces are often the primary cover, along with depth and water turbulence, in some streams.

Salmonids will hide in the interstitial spaces in stream substrates, particularly in winter, when the voids are accessible (Chapman and Bjornn 1969; Bjornn and Morrill 1972; Gibson 1978; Rimmer et al. 1984; Hillman et al. 1987). Newly emerged fry can occupy the voids of substrate made up of 2–5-cm diameter rocks, but larger fish need cobble and boulder-size (>7.5-cm diameter) substrates. The summer or winter carrying capacity of the stream for fish declines when fine sediments fill the interstitial spaces of the substrate (Figure 4.36). In a laboratory stream experiment, Crouse et al. (1981) found that production (tissue elaboration) of juvenile coho salmon was related to the amount of fine sediments in the substrate. When large substrate particles (>12 mm in diameter) were covered (embedded) with various amounts of fine sediments (<2 mm in diameter), fish production was reduced in direct proportion to the degree of embeddedness (expressed as a substrate score or geometric mean size of particles). In another laboratory stream study, Bjornn et al. (1977) found that the density of juvenile steelhead and chinook salmon in summer and winter was reduced by more than half when enough sand was added to fully embed the large cobble substrate (Figure 4.36).

Much of the food eaten by salmonid fishes in streams is produced in the substrate. Particles that make up stream substrates, and thus the habitat of aquatic invertebrates, vary widely from silts and sands to boulders and barely fractured bedrock. Invertebrates differ in their ability to thrive in various types of substrates. Chironomids of various species do well in silts and sands, but the larger ephemeropterans, trichopterans, and plecopterans prefer a mixture of coarse sands and gravels. The addition of fine sediments to stream substrates as a result of watershed disturbances and erosion is worrisome because sedimentation may reduce the abundance of invertebrates. In streams where food is limiting for fish, a reduction in aquatic invertebrate abundance would lead to reduced fish production.

The influence of fine sediments on aquatic invertebrates and ultimately on fish has been investigated, but has not been clearly defined. Cordone and Kelley (1961) reported that fine sediments were detrimental to aquatic organisms. Brusven and Prather (1974) found that invertebrate abundance was reduced when larger streambed particles were fully embedded in fine sediments. Bjornn et al. (1977) found that many ephemeropterans, trichopterans, and simuliids were less abundant in riffles fully embedded with fine granitic sediments than in less-embedded riffle substrates. Hawkins et al. (1983) found decreasing numbers of invertebrates in shaded riffles as the percentage of fine sediments increased, but no such correlation existed in unshaded riffles. In seminatural laboratory streams, benthic and drifting invertebrates (mostly chironomids and ephemeropterans) were more abundant in sections with sand–pebble substrate than in sections with large gravel (Konopacky 1984).

Summer and winter carrying capacities of streams for salmonids may differ markedly because of the substrate present. For example, more than half the steelhead and chinook salmon that reared in two Idaho streams in summer left during fall and winter, but ceased migrating downstream when they encountered areas with larger substrate (Bjornn 1978). In laboratory experiments, fall and winter migrants stopped migrating downstream when placed in channels with large rocks, but continued migrating when put in channels with small gravel (Bjornn and Morrill 1972). After piles of large rock were added to provide cover in sections of a stream with small gravel, more juvenile steelhead stayed there in winter than previously (Chapman and Bjornn 1969). In summer, substrates contribute to a stream's carrying capacity by providing habitat for invertebrates that fish eat and, perhaps less importantly, by providing cover. In winter, the substrate is more important as a source of cover than as a source of food.

Cover

Cover is an important, but difficult to define, aspect of salmonid habitats in streams. Some of the features that may provide cover and increase the carrying capacity of streams for fish are water depth, water turbulence, large-particle substrates, overhanging or undercut banks, overhanging riparian vegetation, woody debris (brush, logs), and aquatic vegetation. Cover provides security from predation for fish and allows them to occupy portions of streams that they might not use otherwise. The needs of fish for cover may vary diurnally, seasonally, by species, and by size of fish (Kalleberg 1958; Hartman 1963, 1965; Chapman 1966; Ruggles 1966; Butler and Hawthorne 1968; Edmundson et al. 1968; Allen 1969; Chapman and Bjornn 1969; Everest 1969; Lewis 1969; Wesche 1973; Hanson 1977; Cunjak and Power 1986). Cover is usually an important variable in models developed to estimate the standing crop of salmonids that could be expected in streams (Binns and Eiserman 1979; Conder and Annear 1987).

Fish abundance in streams has been correlated with the abundance and quality of cover. Standing crops of cutthroat trout in summer were correlated with the indices of cover (Figure 4.37) and surface area used by Wesche (1974). Juvenile steelhead and chinook salmon responded to various types (Figure 4.38) and amounts (Figure 4.39) of cover in winter by either staying in or leaving outdoor laboratory streams (T. C. Bjornn and C. R. Steward, unpublished data). More fish remained in channel pools with a combination of deep water, undercut bank, large rocks, and a bundle of brush than in pools with less cover. The number of chinook salmon remaining in pools increased with increasing amounts of cover (Figure 4.39).

The addition of structures or large boulders to streams to create pools and cover can increase the abundance of salmonids if the amount of suitable habitat is limiting the fish population. When gabions were added to an Oregon stream after logging, debris removal, and floods, the number, depth, and total volume of pools increased, as did the biomass of salmonids (House and Boehne 1985).

Large woody debris originating from riparian timber is a form of cover in many streams and its importance has become more widely known in recent years (Bisson et al. 1987; Holtby 1988a). For example, coho salmon production declined when woody debris was removed from second-order streams in southeast Alaska (Dolloff 1983). More large woody debris and juvenile coho salmon were found in

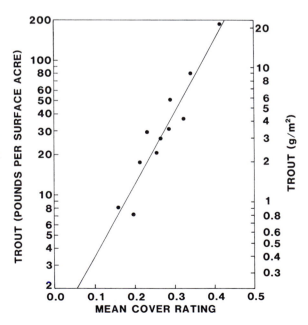

FIGURE 4.37.—Relation between mean trout cover rating and standing crop estimate of trout for 11 study areas. (From Wesche 1974.)

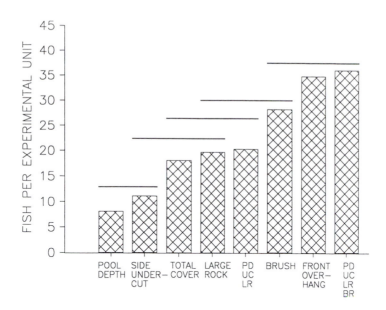

FIGURE 4.38.—Number of yearling steelhead that remained in sections of an outdoor laboratory stream in winter in pools that contained various types of cover. (T. C. Bjornn and C. R. Steward, unpublished data.) Bars not covered by the same horizontal lines were statistically different ($P < 0.05$).

streams surrounded by mature, mixed-conifer forest than in streams lined by red alder that had grown in a 20-year-old clear-cut (House and Boehne 1986). When wood debris was removed from a stream, the surface area, number, and size of pools decreased, water velocity increased, and the biomass of Dolly Varden decreased from 12.5 to 3.9 g/m^2 (Elliott 1986). In another stream, young steelhead were more abundant in clear-cut than in wooded areas in summer but moved to areas with pools and forest canopy in winter (Johnson et al. 1986). Bryant (1983, 1985)

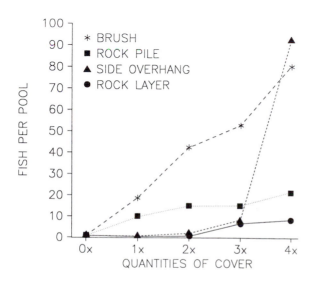

FIGURE 4.39.—Response (number remaining in pools) of yearling chinook salmon to various amounts of different types of cover in an outdoor laboratory stream during winter. (C. R. Steward and T. C. Bjornn, unpublished data.)

proposed guidelines for woody debris management in streams after he found a gradual loss of large debris from streams where riparian timber had been removed.

Overhead cover (including undercut banks, overhanging vegetation, logs, and debris jams) is often an important component of fish habitat in streams. Boussu (1954) reported increases in trout standing crop after the addition of overhanging brush as cover, and decreases when brush and overhanging banks were removed. Overhead bank cover, in association with water depths of at least 15 cm, was the single most important type of cover for brown trout in Wyoming streams (Wesche et al. 1985, 1987). In a small Lake Erie tributary, the distribution of subyearling rainbow trout, brown trout, and coho salmon was related to bank and instream cover (Gordon and MacCrimmon 1982). Brusven et al. (1986) found that 82% of age-0 chinook salmon preferred sections of a small stream channel with one-third overhead cover to sections without such cover. With the same stream channel, Meehan et al. (1987) showed that the fish preferred shade from artificial canopies to open areas, especially in the shallow reaches. Juvenile Atlantic salmon and brook trout were attracted to shaded areas of a shallow flume, but moved to deeper water when given the opportunity (Gibson 1978). Wilzbach et al. (1986), however, found that cutthroat trout foraged more effective on experimentally introduced invertebrate prey in pools within a recently logged area than in forested pools, presumably because light levels were higher in the logged area. Growth of trout was higher in pools of the logged section, but the investigators thought differences in foraging efficiency alone did not fully account for the slower growth in the forested pools.

Use of stream habitat and cover by juvenile salmonids may depend on the presence of other fish. Glova (1986) reported evidence of interactive segregation between juvenile coho salmon and cutthroat trout in summer. When tested separately, most fish of both species were found in pools, but when tested together, most coho salmon were in pools and cutthroat trout were in riffles. In winter, Glova (1986) found that both species, whether together or separate, preferred pools and overhead cover. Similar interactive segregation in summer has been demonstrated for coho salmon and steelhead: salmon used the pools and steelhead the riffles when the species were together in the same streams (Hartman 1965). In southeast Alaska streams, cover affected habitat use by coho salmon, steelhead, and Dolly Varden with respect to depth, position in the water column, and water velocity. Coho salmon and steelhead selected lower positions in the water column in pools without cover than in pools with overhead bank cover or instream cover (Bugert 1985). The presence or absence of Dolly Varden 10–20 cm long in pools caused shifts in habitat use by age-0 steelhead and coho salmon, even when some forms of cover were provided.

Seaward or Lakeward Migration

In some populations of salmonids, the fish spend their entire lives in a limited reach of stream (Miller 1954, 1957; Hunt 1974; Bachman 1984). In many other populations, however, juveniles may live in their natal streams for a few days to more than 3 years and then move to other areas to complete their maturation. Nonanadromous salmon, trout, and char may move downstream into lakes (upstream in some cases) or larger rivers. The anadromous salmonids eventually migrate to the sea, but in some cases spend extended periods rearing or overwintering in streams (or lakes) other than their natal sites (Bjornn 1978; Leider et al. 1986). Regardless of the destination of the juvenile migrants, flows and water quality must be suitable for the migration to be successful.

The timing of most lakeward or seaward migrations of salmonids that rear for an extended period in steams appears to be regulated primarily by photoperiod, but streamflow, water temperatures, and growth may play a role in some areas. Chinook salmon and steelhead smolts migrated seaward from an Idaho stream at slightly different times, but the timing for each species was similar each year, and was modified only slightly by flow and moon phase (Bjornn 1971); water temperatures were similar each year. In a Norwegian river, water temperature (increase and general temperature in spring) accounted for most of the variation in timing of the seaward migrations of Atlantic salmon (Jonsson and Ruud-Hansen 1985); streamflow, cloudiness, and lunar cycle were not correlated with the migration.

Streamflows are usually adequate in unaltered streams because seaward migration commonly occurs in the spring. Seaward migration has been altered in streams and rivers from which large amounts of water are diverted or along which large reservoirs have been created. Streamflows that were sufficient before construction of dams become inadequate in large reservoirs. There is evidence that smolts depend on river currents during their downstream migration (Fried et al. 1978), and they have difficulty finding their way through large reservoirs with barely perceptible currents. The time required for a smolt to travel the 517 km from the Salmon River in Idaho to The Dalles Dam in the lower Columbia River increased by about 30 d during years with low flows after completion of six intervening dams. The poor success of smolts moving down through large reservoirs with low flows may be due in part to the suppression of some parr-to-smolt physiological processes; Adams et al. (1973) observed this condition when fish were held in relatively high water temperatures (15–20°C). The parr-to-smolt transition is often incomplete when fish begin to migrate and may fail to develop fully if the fish encounter high temperatures and reservoirs without perceptible currents.

Another hazard created at some dams is supersaturation of dissolved gases, particularly nitrogen, which can cause gas bubble disease in both upstream- and downstream-migrating salmonids (Ebel 1970; Ebel and Raymond 1976). Salmon may be more successful than steelhead in sensing and avoiding highly supersaturated waters (Stevens et al. 1980), but most salmonids migrating in the rivers are susceptible to gas bubble disease.

The magnitude of the effect dams and associated reservoirs can have on anadromous fishes is evident in data from the Columbia River drainage. Salmon and steelhead must pass up to nine dams in the Columbia and Snake rivers during their migrations to and from the sea. Smolt-to-adult survival rates declined from more than 4% before 1968 to less than 1.5% in the mid-1970s when all the dams were completed (Raymond 1988). In years with low flows (such as 1973 and 1977), smolt mortality averaged 45% at each dam and reservoir, compared to 15% in years with higher flows. In recent years, smolt-to-adult survival rates of steelhead and chinook salmon from the Snake River have increased to 2–5% with the help of spillway deflectors to reduce gas supersaturation, fish bypasses around turbines, transportation around dams, and supplemental spills at dams without bypasses (Raymond 1988).

Summary

In the foregoing discussion of habitat variables, each factor was addressed separately, but the reader should keep in mind that fish usually respond to the combined effect of two or more of the physical, chemical, and biological variables in their environment. The fish may respond physiologically (altered growth and health) and behaviorally (site selection and interactions) to the array of environmental features they encounter. In streams where fish live and reproduce, all the important factors are in a suitable (but usually not optimum) range throughout the life of the fish. The mix of environmental factors in any stream sets the carrying capacity of that stream for fish, and the capacity can be changed if one or more of the factors are altered. The importance of specific factors in setting carrying capacity may change with life stage of the fish and season of the year.

Low streamflows, high water temperatures, and excessive turbidities impede adult salmon, trout, and char on their migration to spawning areas. These impediments occur even in pristine environments on occasion, but more often in drainages with irrigation, extensive agriculture, hydropower, surface mining, forest harvesting, and flood control projects. Once in the spawning areas, the amount and suitability of stream substrate and flows in the spawning areas are key factors. During incubation of the embryos and alevins, conditions within the redd dictate the number of young fish that will emerge into the stream. Adequate flows of well-oxygenated water and relatively small amounts of fine sediments (organic and inorganic) will allow a high percentage of the young fish to survive and emerge from the redd.

As soon as the young fish begin rearing in the stream, they become subject to predation by other fish, birds, and mammals, and they interact with the other fish present for choice feeding sites and cover. Given adequate numbers of young fish to use all the available habitat, the number and size of fish that can be produced in a stream is governed by the quantity and quality of space available, productivity of the stream, and the presence of competitors and predators. In summer, juvenile fish are primarily concerned with feeding and they select sites in streams that optimize the opportunity to obtain food, yet provide acceptable security from predation. In winter where water temperatures are low, the fish appear to be primarily concerned with security; they hide in cover or adopt behavior patterns that may have security benefits (such as gathering in large schools) and they are less interested in feeding. Because the requirements of salmonids and their use of habitat in winter are different from those in summer, the carrying capacity of streams or stream reaches may not be the same during both seasons. The changes in carrying capacity that result from alteration of stream features depend on the roles those features play in establishing the carrying capacity—roles that can change with time.

Chapter 5

Natural Processes

D. N. Swanston

Freshwater habitats for salmonids are, in part, the products of interactions among climate, hydrologic responses of watersheds, and hillslope and channel erosion processes. Together with the kind and extent of vegetation cover, these processes control streamflow, input of allochthonous materials to the channel, channel stability, and the development and persistence of channel structures suitable for spawning, incubation, and rearing of fish. In the absence of major disturbance, these processes produce small, but virtually continuous changes in the natural environment, resulting in a constant background level of habitat variability and diversity against which the manager must judge the modifications produced by nature and human activity.

Major disruption of these interactions can drastically alter habitat conditions. The result may be movement and redistribution of spawning gravels, addition of new sediment and woody debris to the channel system, changes in accessibility to fish of viable spawning habitats, changes in availability of food organisms, and changes in seasonal and diurnal water temperatures.

A more detailed accounting of stream ecosystem processes (Murphy and Meehan 1991), habitat requirements of salmonids (Bjornn and Reiser 1991), and the biological response of salmonids to changes in habitat (Hicks et al. 1991) are presented elsewhere in this volume. In this chapter, I discuss the interactions of climate, hillslope, and channel processes in their natural (undisturbed) context, and point out the resulting environmental changes and potential effects on the condition of salmonid habitats.

Intensity and Timing of Events

The actual effect on habitat quality and productivity of any of these processes depends largely on the intensity and timing of disrupting events. Some events are regular and cyclical in occurrence, distributed over the broad spectrum of climatic and geomorphic regions within which anadromous fish habitats occur (seasonal and annual precipitation, moderate streamflows, and freezing and ice formation). Others are sporadic and difficult to predict, triggered by extreme storms, earthquakes, major vegetation disturbances, and regional climatic change (floods, landslides, windthrow, fire, insects, disease, faunistic channel alterations). Once such an event occurs, it may significantly alter local channel configuration and gradient, bed composition, and degree of sediment and woody debris loading.

Influences of Forest and Rangeland Management on Salmonid Fishes and Their Habitats
American Fisheries Society Special Publication 19:139–179, 1991

TABLE 5.1.—Approximate ranges of recurrence of major disrupting events and the effects of these events on channel and habitat conditions in streams.

Event	Range of recurrence (years)	Channel changes	Habitat effects
Daily to weekly precipitation and discharge	0.01–0.1	Channel width and depth; movement and deposition of fine woody debris; fine sediment transport and deposition	Minor siltation of spawning gravels; minor variation in spawning and rearing habitat; increased temperature during summer low flows
Seasonal precipitation and discharge; moderate storms; freezing and ice formation	0.1–1.0	Increased flow to bank-full width; moderate channel erosion; high base-flow erosion; increased mobility of in-channel sediment and debris; local damming and flooding; sediment transport by anchor ice; gouging of channel bed; reduced winter flows	Changes in pool:riffle ratio; siltation of spawning gravels; increased channel area; increased access to spawning sites; flooding of side-channel areas; amelioration of temperatures at high flows; decreased temperatures during freezing; dewatering of gravels during freezing; gravel disturbance by gouging and anchor ice
Major storms; floods; rain-on-snow events	1.0–10	Increased movement of sediment and woody debris to channels; flood flows; local channel scour; movement and redistribution of coarse sediments; flushing of fine sediments; movement and redistribution of large woody debris	Changes in pool:riffle ratio; shifting of spawning gravels; increased large woody debris jams; siltation of spawning gravels; disturbance of side-channel rearing areas; increased rearing and overwintering habitat; local blockage of fish access; filling and scouring of pools and riffles
Debris avalanches and debris torrents	5.0–100	Large, short-term increases in sediment and large woody debris contributions to channel; channel scour; large-scale movement and redistribution of bed-load gravels and large woody debris; damming and obstruction of channels; accelerated channel bank erosion and undercutting; alteration of channel shape by flow obstruction; flooding	Changes in pool:riffle ratio; shifting of spawning gravels; siltation of spawning gravels; disturbance of side-channel rearing areas; blockage of fish access; filling and scouring of pools and riffles; formation of new rearing and overwintering habitat
Activities of beavers	5.0–100	Channel damming; obstruction and redirection of channel flow; flooding of banks and side channels; ponding of streamflow; siltation of gravels behind dams	Improved rearing and overwintering habitat; increased water volumes during low flows; slack-water and backwater refuge areas during floods; refuge from reduced habitat quality in adjoining areas; limitation on fish migration; elevated water temperatures; local reductions in dissolved oxygen

TABLE 5.1.—Continued.

Event	Range of recurrence (years)	Channel changes	Habitat effects
Major disturbances to vegetation	10–100		
Windthrow		Increased sediment delivery to channels; decreased litterfall; increased large woody debris in channel; loss of riparian cover	Increased sedimentation of spawning and rearing habitat; increased summer temperatures; decreased winter temperatures; increased rearing and overwintering habitat; decreased fine organic debris
Wildfire		Increased sediment delivery to channels; increased large woody debris in channels; loss of riparian vegetation cover; decreased litterfall; increased channel flows; increased nutrient levels in streams	Increased sedimentation of spawning and rearing habitat; increased summer temperatures; decreased winter temperatures; increased rearing and overwintering habitat; decreased availability of fine woody debris; increased availability of food organisms
Insects and disease		Increased sediment delivery to channels; loss of riparian vegetation cover; increased large woody debris in channels; decreased litterfall	Increased sedimentation of spawning and rearing habitat; increased summer temperatures; decreased winter temperatures; increased rearing and overwintering habitat
Slumps and earthflows	100–1,000	Low-level, long-term contributions of sediment and large woody debris to stream channels; partial blockage of channel; local baselevel constriction below point of entry; shifts in channel configuration	Siltation of spawning gravels; scour of channel below point of entry; accumulation of gravels behind obstructions; partial blockage of fish passage; local flooding and disturbance of side-channel rearing areas
Climatic change	1,000–100,000	Major changes in channel direction; major changes in channel grade and configuration; valley broadening or downcutting; alteration of flow regime	Changes in type and distribution of spawning gravels; changes in frequency and timing of disturbing events; shifts in species composition and diversity

Important natural events and activities that control and contribute to physical habitat change, approximate range of recurrence, and associated channel and habitat effects are shown in Table 5.1.

Short-Term Changes

In the short term (days, weeks, months), the resulting channel changes and increases in availability, transport, and deposition of sediment and woody debris cause a variety of disruptions of aquatic organisms and their environments (Swanson 1980). For example, fine sediment deposited over organic detritus can render primary production unusable by bottom fauna, decreasing the availability of bottom fauna as a food source to fish. Accumulations of fine sediment in the interstices of spawning gravels may restrict flow of oxygenated waters to eggs and decrease the opportunities for fry to move from subsurface gravels to open water once they have hatched. High flows and rapid additions of sediment and large woody debris to the channel may cause scour of the channel bed and shifting of bedload gravels, which can seriously reduce the availability of food and habitat.

Long-Term Changes

In the long term (years, decades), the channel changes produced may actually improve habitat quality and productivity by stabilizing the channel system, increasing the total area available for spawning, increasing both summer and winter rearing habitat, and improving access to fish.

Even when major disrupting events markedly reshape stream channels and change the distribution of aquatic habitats, the actual effects of such changes on aquatic organisms appear to be short-lived. Organisms survive high floods by finding protected sites in gravel, behind logs, among roots and flooded vegetation, and in the lower portions of low-gradient tributary streams. Many insects have life cycles with terrestrial phases during periods when major flooding is likely. Thus, streams can be rapidly colonized following major events by organisms from terrestrial and aquatic refugia (Swanson 1980). Preliminary work on habitat changes following landslide disturbances in the Oregon Coast Range (Everest and Meehan 1981b) suggested that the total effect of debris torrents may be positive, although spawning and rearing habitat may be initially degraded. In the long term, torrents created habitat diversity by adding boulders, rubble, gravel, and woody debris to the channel and by increasing both quantity and quality of habitats for juvenile and adult coho salmon. In this study, productivity of coho salmon returned to pre-landslide levels within 3 years, due mostly to increased rearing and spawning habitats behind piles of landslide debris.

Influence of Climate and Hydrologic Processes on Water Delivery to Channels

Hydrologic Cycle

Water is introduced to the land surface as part of the hydrologic cycle in the form of rain, atmospheric moisture (fog), or snow. Precipitation in any form falling on a watershed reaches the ground or stream surfaces directly or is intercepted by vegetation. Some of this intercepted water evaporates; the remainder reaches the ground by dripping through the canopy and leaf cover or by moving downward along stems of understory and overstory vegetation (stem flow). The amount of precipitation "lost" to evaporation or "delayed" in its passage to the ground by these interception processes depends on the amount and extent of vegetation cover and on the intensity and duration of the storm that produces the precipitation (Figure 5.1). Watershed size, channel gradient or steepness, the amount and distribution of vegetative cover, and seasonal and short-term (daily and weekly) changes in precipitation are major factors controlling streamflow and the occurrence of natural disturbances that may affect salmonid habitats.

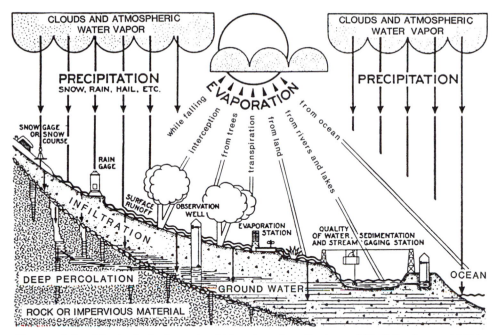

FIGURE 5.1.—The hydrologic cycle. (After American Society of Civil Engineers 1949.)

Precipitation Input

The quantity and timing of streamflow is largely determined by the amount and duration of water input and the dominant hydrologic processes operating within the contributing watershed.

Rain-dominated zones.—In the rain-dominated zone along the Pacific coast and at lower elevations in the Cascade and Coast ranges of British Columbia, snow is rare; fall and winter precipitation is almost exclusively rain. In these areas, the streamflow regime closely follows annual precipitation patterns (Figure 5.2). Moderate- to high-intensity storms during the fall and winter months produce rapid increases in streamflow and occasional floods that disturb channels. At higher elevations (above 1,200–1,400 m), rapid melting of shallow snowpacks during storms may greatly augment these streamflow increases (Harr 1979). Over most of this zone, little rainfall occurs during the summer and summer flows are usually low. First-order streams commonly go dry. At the northern end of the zone (Alaska and the north coast of British Columbia), moderate rainfall continues through the spring and summer, maintaining substantial streamflows throughout the year.

Snow-dominated zones.—In snow-dominated areas of interior western North America, most winter precipitation falls as snow and most snow melts during a short, predictable period in the spring. Heavy rainfall is not common during winter months in this zone, but moderately high rainfall may occur during the late fall. Occasional high-intensity rainfall occurs during the summer associated with thunderstorms. Low streamflows are common in the summer after snowmelt ceases, and some first-order streams may go dry (Figure 5.3).

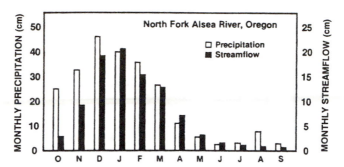

FIGURE 5.2.—Distribution of annual precipitation and streamflow for a site in the rain-dominated zone: North Fork Alsea River, Oregon, 1976. (After Harr 1979.)

Transient-snow zones.—In a transition zone between these rain- and snow-dominated hydrologic systems, beginning at the Sierra Nevada Mountains in California and extending through the Cascade and Coast ranges of Oregon and Washington to the coastal mountains of British Columbia and Alaska, there are local areas where both rain and snow are common during most winters (Harr 1979). In this transient-snow zone, runoff closely follows precipitation during the fall and early winter, and maximum flows generally occur from November to January (Figure 5.4). At higher elevations where proportionately more snow falls, a second period of high flow may occur in the spring when snow melts. Except at the northern end of the rain-dominated zone, summer flows are usually low and some first-order streams commonly go dry.

Modifying Influence of Snowpacks

Snow is subject to the same interception phenomena as rain and in about the same proportions (Dunford and Niederhof 1944; Rowe and Hendrix 1951; Sartz and Trimble 1956; Hart 1963). In addition, where substantial snowpacks develop, water may be detained for considerable periods in its passage through a watershed and into the channel system. Snowpacks contribute to such surface storage both in the frozen phase and as free water held in the pore spaces of the snow (Anderson et al. 1976). The volume and duration of detention, and thus the timing of release and subsequent channel and habitat modifications, depend on such

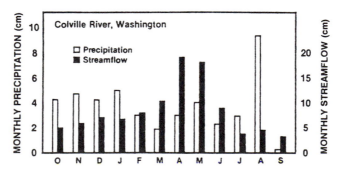

FIGURE 5.3.—Distribution of annual precipitation and streamflow at a site in the interior snow-dominated zone: Colville River, Washington, 1976. (After Harr 1979.)

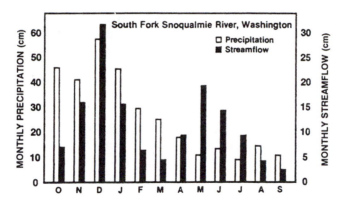

FIGURE 5.4.—Distribution of annual precipitation and streamflow at a site in the transient-snow zone: South Fork Snoqualmie River, Washington, 1976. (After Harr 1979.)

conditions as snow depth, air temperature, pore space, initial free-water content, and occurrence of warm-rain-on-snow events (U.S. Army Corps of Engineers 1956; Smith and Halverson 1969; Smith 1974; Harr 1986). Greatest detention of water is in the warm snowpacks of the Sierra Nevada and the west slopes of the northern Rocky Mountains, where most of the water falling as snow or rain on snow is detained over the winter and released when snow melts. It is common for such melting to occur over a short time span in spring due to rapidly warming air temperatures; the abundant meltwater saturates hillslope soils and induces high streamflows that impart instability to channel systems and cause habitat alterations.

Watershed vegetation shades snow, delays its melting, and thus extends the time that a snowpack is held in surface storage. Vegetation also influences the rate of snowmelt. For example, although snow under forest cover melts later and persists longer than snow in the open, it may melt more rapidly once melting begins because temperatures may be much higher later in the season (Anderson et al. 1976). If a watershed has a mixture of vegetated and open areas, however, snow will melt at different times and the amount of water released at any one time may be lower than it would be if the vegetation were homogeneous.

Aspect may also influence melting. Snow on south-facing slopes may disappear before much of the snow melts on northerly aspects.

Interception, Evapotranspiration, and Storage of Water

Rain-dominated zones.—In humid, heavily vegetated, old-growth forest areas within the influence of intense Pacific storm systems, interception losses of precipitation are substantial in the spring and summer, when major storms are infrequent and may account for more than 25% of summer rainfall in areas subject to summer drought (western Oregon, southwest Washington, northern California; Rothacher 1963; Patric 1966). Between low precipitation inputs, high interception losses, vigorous plant growth, and active transpiration by understory and overstory vegetation, the amount of water in the soil mantle is reduced. As a result, summer base flows (discharges entering stream channels from groundwater or sources of delayed runoff) and associated streamflows are reduced and hillslope and streambank erosion processes are less active. Under these conditions, the input of allochthonous materials (both organic and inorganic) is reduced, stream temperatures are higher, levels of dissolved oxygen may be reduced, fish migration is restricted, and spawning, incubation, and rearing areas are reduced or become unavailable. Influences of physical habitat on ecosystem structure and function are discussed in more detail by Murphy and Meehan (1991).

Interception and evapotranspiration have less overall effect on water in the soil mantle during fall and winter due to cooler temperatures, reduced transpirational activity of vegetation, loss of leaves and increased litterfall from deciduous vegetation, and frequent high-intensity, long-duration storms. During these rainy months (generally between September and February), streamflows are high and the water content of hillslope soils is at or near saturation. As a result, base flows are high, channels are increasingly mobile and subject to scour and redistribution of bed materials, hillslopes have a greater landslide hazard, and exposed channel banks are prone to increased lateral erosion and undercutting. These variations in seasonal flow are illustrated in the old-growth Douglas-fir forests of western Oregon. Rothacher (1963) found that nearly 100% of the precipitation from storms of less then 0.13 cm (which typically occur during the spring and summer) was intercepted and evaporated, but less than about 5% of the precipitation from storms of more then 20 cm (which typically occur during fall and winter) was lost by these means. Under the latter conditions, the input of allochthonous materials (both organic and inorganic) to stream channels is substantially increased, levels of dissolved oxygen are higher, water temperatures are reduced, and available areas for spawning, incubation, and rearing are increased. Also associated with the increases in flow are potential increases in turbidity (amount of sediment in suspension), bedload movement, and redistributions of large woody debris.

Snow-dominated zones.—In the interior areas of the west during the spring, summer, and fall months when dry conditions prevail, interception and evapotranspiration losses, although considerably less than on the Pacific coast (2–4% of total annual rainfall, according to Anderson 1976), strongly affect the total amount of water entering the soil and the total available for streamflow. The low levels of precipitation and high evapotranspiration withdrawals leave dry hillslope soils and low streamflows. The resulting habitat conditions will be similar to those described for the spring and summer low-rainfall periods along the Pacific coast, but they probably are more severe because of the generally lower levels of annual rainfall. When rapid snowmelt or an occasional high-intensity storm does occur (for example, in association with spring chinook winds or summer thunder storms), interception and evapotranspirational effects become negligible because the amount of water dumped on the surface is so great. As a consequence of the resulting high streamflows and saturation of hillslope soils, the entire hillslope channel system may become mobilized and subject to extensive allochthonous inputs, increases in turbidity and channel erosion, and redistribution of sediment and organic debris.

Transient-snow zones.—At higher elevations in the Cascade and Coast ranges of northern California, Oregon, Washington, British Columbia, and Alaska, and locally within interior portions of western North America where both rain and snow are common during winter months, occasional high runoff and associated channel disturbances result from rapid snowmelt during warming trends coupled with prolonged heavy rainfall (Waananen et al. 1971; Harr 1979). Within the transient-snow zone, where most precipitation occurs as rain, thin snowpacks are common and may remain for extended periods during the winter months. Occasionally a snowpack may persist for 1–3 months, but in most years it usually melts within 1–3 weeks and may recur several times during the winter. During these winter snowmelt periods, the large amount of water released generally overwhelms evapotranspirational effects and the ability of the soil to absorb water. Streamflows tend to be higher and hillslopes more susceptible to landslides and surface erosion. Sediment and woody debris in the channel become mobilized and substantial amounts of allochthonous materials are added to the channel.

The magnitude and timing of these winter rain-on-snow events can be important to fish habitat. For example, if a flow of sufficient volume to mobilize bed-load materials occurs, many eggs and alevins may be destroyed.

Movement of Soil Water

If the soil is not already saturated, new water reaching the soil surface will infiltrate pore spaces in the soil. When water arrives at a rate that exceeds the soil's infiltration capacity, some flows overland. In undisturbed forests, infiltration rates of soils generally accommodate average levels of water input, so except during long rains or rapid snowmelt, most of the moisture reaching the ground directly or after interception enters the soil.

Upon entering the soil, water is subject to gravitational and capillary forces that cause it to move and frictional forces that restrict movement. Because of the high gradient of most western watersheds, and because soils generally conduct less water at depth, water entering the soil begins to move downslope as it moves deeper into the soil. The direction and rate at which the water moves depend on the rate at which water reaches the ground and the permeability (capacity for transmitting water) of the receiving soil. Both rate and direction of movement vary considerably over the course of a storm (Harr 1977). Maximum rates of soil water flow, however, are low and frequently are about equal to the average rate of rainfall during moderate storms. This slow-moving soil water is subject to evaporation and depletion by plants through transpiration. The rate at which plants withdraw water is largely a function of the energy available for water vaporization in leaves and the availability and ease with which water may be withdrawn from the soil. Thus, during spring and summer when the growing season is at its peak, evapotranspirational withdrawals are high. In areas characterized by a summer dry season, where little additional water is added to the soil as the growing season progresses, soil moisture decreases and the remaining water becomes more tightly held by the soil. The result is a decrease in base flows to the channel and a net reduction in streamflow. This condition is alleviated after the first storms in the fall recharge the soil water deficit.

Influence of parent material.—Infiltration capacity of a soil, soil water storage capacity, and soil water transmission rates are strongly influenced by the depth, size, and shape of pore spaces and the extent, size, and shape of the interconnections among pores. These variables are a product of the soil's origin and composition.

Coarse-grained soils derived from colluvium, alluvium, or glacial tills are highly permeable. Their infiltration capacities and soil water transmission rates are high, so overland flows (surface runoff from unchanneled surfaces) are limited to major storm and snowmelt events. Water transport to channels is primarily by subsurface flow and base flows are a major sustaining source of water to the channel between storms. Little water is held in long-term soil storage, however, so base flows into streams during dry periods tend to be small and short-lived. These soils thus moderate the flow responses to moderate storms, and potentially destructive high flows occur primarily during major storms. Flows are minimal during summer drought and large areas of viable spawning area may become dewatered.

Fine-grained soils derived from glacial, marine, or lacustrine materials, or from weathered siltstones, sandstones, and volcaniclastic rocks, generally have low permeabilities. Infiltration capacities and soil water transmission rates are low, so overland flows may develop even during moderate rainfalls. Water that does enter the soil may be held for extended periods and may produce steady, low-level base flows throughout much of the year. The net effect on channels developed in these materials is more rapid development of potentially destructive high flows during even moderate storms, and maintenance of moderate low flows for extended periods during summer drought.

Streamflow

In the simplest model, streamflow—on an annual or longer basis—is the difference between precipitation and evapotranspiration losses (Harr 1976). Variations in soil water storage and temporary storage of water in the snowpack may alter the directness of this relationship; further, some water may also seep deep into the subsoil and bedrock and thus not contribute to streamflow in the immediate drainage basin. Generally, however, water not removed by plants ultimately moves downslope as overland flow or as saturated and unsaturated base flow to supply streams.

In the rain-dominated zone, annual runoff to streams is generally high because annual precipitation is high (Table 5.2). Most small mountain channels respond quickly to individual precipitation events, exhibiting rapidly increasing streamflow and an expanding channel network shortly after rainfall begins (Harr 1977). As the channel network expands, drainage density increases and the watershed becomes more efficient at producing runoff. If precipitation continues at a relatively high rate, streamflow will also continue at a high rate. When rainfall in montane areas decreases or ceases altogether, streamflow peaks almost immediately and then decreases rapidly as soil water on steep slopes drains rapidly into the channel (Figure 5.5). During a western winter rainy season, this sequence of events may occur 10 to 20 times or more, depending on the frequency of storms entering the region from the Pacific Ocean (Harr 1979).

In the snow-dominated zone, annual runoff to streams is considerably less and quite variable because annual precipitation is lower and high-intensity storms are infrequent (Table 5.2). Small mountain channels in this zone typically respond to individual precipitation events (chiefly summer thunderstorms) like streams in the rain-dominated region, but most of the water for streamflow comes from snowpacks that accumulate in the winter and melt in the summer.

TABLE 5.2.—Mean annual precipitation and runoff to streams for selected forested watersheds. (Modified from Anderson et al. 1976.)

Location	Area (hectares)	Midarea elevation (m)	Precipitation (mm)	Runoff to streams (mm)	Climatic zone
Fraser Experimental Forest, Colorado	289	3,170	558.8	304.8	Snow-dominated
Sierra Ancha Experimental Forest, Arizona (Middle Fork)	207	2,179	812.8	76.2	Snow-dominated
Three Bar Experimental Watersheds, Arizona (Watershed D)	32	1,295	685.8	50.8	Snow-dominated
H. J. Andrews Experimental Forest, Blue River, Oregon (Watershed 2)	60	762	2,387.6	1,549.4	Rain-dominated

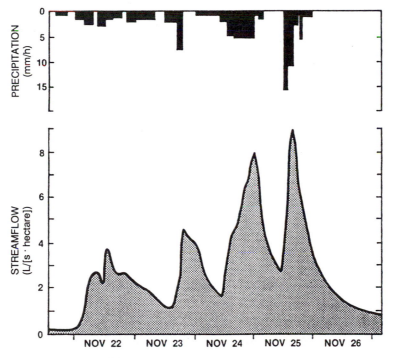

FIGURE 5.5.—Precipitation and streamflow in a small mountain watershed on the H. J. Andrews Experimental Forest, Oregon, November 21–24, 1977. Note the rapid response of streamflow to precipitation and the rapid decrease in streamflow once precipitation ceased. (After Harr 1979.)

In the transient-snow zone, annual runoff to streams is variable but tends to be high. Elevated flows occur at frequent intervals during the winter after warm-rain-on-snow events.

Peak flows.—The larger the precipitation event, the greater is the amount of water going into the system and the larger the potential streamflow. As a watershed responds to precipitation or other water input, streamflow increases to maximum levels known as peak flows. Each storm or water-producing event creates a peak flow, reflecting the interaction of the event with the physical characteristics of the watershed. High or sustained rates of water input contribute to greater runoff and higher peak flows.

The magnitude of streamflow is highly variable. It depends on the antecedent moisture content of the hillslope soils (how much was there before the onset of an event) and the characteristics of the water-producing event. Increases in streamflow of at least two orders of magnitude between the start and the peak of storm runoff often occur. Peak flows of similar or greater magnitude result from rain-on-snow events, when a substantial portion of streamflow comes from rapid snowmelt concurrent with storm precipitation.

Modifying factors.—The quantity of water and the rate at which it reaches the channel and passes through the channel system during a particular hydrologic event are influenced by storm and watershed size, vegetation cover, and certain topographic considerations.

Watershed size influences the quantity of streamflow and the size and timing of peak flows during any particular storm. Generally, the smaller the watershed, the more rapid are the streamflow increases in response to rainfall. In small watersheds in the western Cascade Range of Oregon, for example, maximum rates of runoff have approached 80% of the average rate of rainfall during the previous 12–24 h and 75% of the maximum 6-h rainfall (Rothacher et al. 1967). As watersheds increase in size, total water yields increase (a larger area is being drained), but peak flows become less marked and their response times to rainfall lengthen due to larger areas of interception, evapotranspiration, and temporary storage.

The influence of vegetation on streamflow is greater for small storms than for large ones. Interception and evapotranspiration account for a large proportion of small-storm precipitation, and soil water retained against gravity by plant roots accounts for a greater proportion of water entering and remaining in the soil. As precipitation increases or is supplemented by snowmelt, these withdrawals become relatively less important. Streamflow resulting from extreme events is minimally influenced by these withdrawal processes, although a forest cover does detain some portion of any rainstorm and thus somewhat reduces flood discharge and peak flows.

Quantity and timing of streamflows are also related to hillslope position. Higher-elevation watersheds generally receive a larger quantity of water per storm because of orographic effects (more precipitation falls at higher elevations because of the cooling and condensation of moisture from rising air masses). Because these watersheds are small, soil water retention and evapotranspirational losses are less influential, and runoff and peak flows tend to be higher than in the larger, lower watersheds. Studies in North Carolina (Hewlett 1967) showed that forested primary ridges at 1,524 m delivered almost 457 mm of direct runoff per

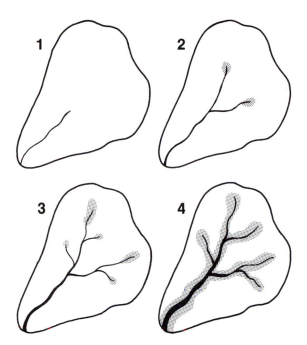

FIGURE 5.6.—Time-lapse view of a small watershed showing expansions of the channel network and the source area of storm runoff (shaded area) as a storm progresses. (After Harr 1979.)

year, but forest land at lower elevations delivered only about 63 mm. A December rainfall that dropped 213–274 mm of water on three watersheds above 914 m produced 127–223 mm of direct runoff and maximum peaks of 68–167 m³/s. The rainfall on three watersheds below 914 m ranged from about 172 mm to 178 mm; direct runoffs were 40–58 mm and peak flows were 22–32 m³/s (Hoover and Hursh 1943).

Variable source area of storm runoff.—The concept that may be the most important one for understanding the hydrology of watersheds and the potential effects of high runoff and peak flows on channel conditions and fish habitat is the "variable source area of storm runoff," described by Harr (1976). This concept relates high-runoff events to a dynamic source area that expands and contracts according to rainfall, other water-input characteristics, and the capacity of the soil mantle to store and transmit water (Hewlett and Nutter 1970). Thus, as an event progresses and more water is added to the system, the water collection network expands along ephemeral channels and linear hillslope depressions to many times its perennial dimensions and streams become both longer and wider (Figure 5.6). As a result of the increasing source area for streamflow, flow quantities, depth, cross-sectional area, and both transport and erosion power of water can increase dramatically over the life of the event. The stream channel represents a temporary depository of variable area for sediment and organic debris stored above the limits of the perennial channel. As the channel system expands, this stored debris, and any material in a semistabilized position within the channel, become mobilized. If the flow volumes and velocities become large enough, and if enough sediment and large woody debris are mobilized, major shifts in channel structure and gravel distribution will occur.

Hillslope and Channel Processes

Habitat alterations resulting from transport and deposition of fine sediment, from bed-load movement and redistribution, and from movement and redistribution of large woody debris are closely linked to storm flows and to large-scale random events such as landslides that add large quantities of material to the channel system over short time periods.

Mean annual concentrations of sediment in streams of undisturbed watersheds are generally low, but the amount of sediment transported during individual storms can be substantial. For example, Fredriksen et al. (1975) reported mean annual stream concentrations of sediment from undisturbed watersheds in the western Cascade and Oregon Coast ranges of 1.3–44.6 mg/L and 1.4–21.4 mg/L, respectively. In contrast, mean maximum concentration that occurred during major storms ranged from 11 to 15 times the annual rate for the western Cascade Range watershed and from 39 to 85 times the annual rate for the Coast Range watershed. Much of this increase was the direct result of soil mass movements (landslides) into the stream channels and of sediment mobilized from channel margins by storm flows.

Surface Erosion

Surface erosion is essentially a two-stage process in which soil particles are first detached and then transported. The size and density of surface soil particles and the degree of protection afforded by plant and litter cover control the detachment process. Transport is influenced by rainfall intensity and duration, slope gradient and length, and soil infiltration rate.

Two hydrologic processes are principally responsible for surface hillslope erosion. One is channelized erosion by restricted flows—rilling and gullying. The other is sheet erosion, in which particles are detached and moved downslope by raindrop splash, by nonchannelized overland flow, or by gravitational movement (rolling and sliding) of dry particles.

Surface erosion of forested sites usually results from intense rainstorms or excess surface flows after the soil is bared by landslides, fire, overgrazing, logging, or other causes. Interception increases splash erosion because drops falling from the canopy have greater mass and kinetic energy than raindrops (Tsukamoto 1966). Increases in both sheet erosion and rill and gully erosion result when soils lose infiltration capacity due to compaction by logging or other equipment, herds of livestock or other animals, or raindrops. Fire also can reduce infiltration rates by inducing near-surface water-repelling layers in the soil (Debano et al. 1976).

In areas characterized by coarse, cohesionless soils and periods of drought, dry creep and sliding of materials from denuded slopes may be an important source of local surface erosion.

Sediment delivery.—In an undisturbed watershed, delivery of sediment and woody debris to channels by surface erosion is generally low, but extremely variable from year to year. These variations are driven by weather patterns,

TABLE 5.3.—Annual variability in sediment yield from undisturbed watersheds in a rain-dominated and a snow-dominated zone. (From Larson and Sidle 1981.)

Water year	Sediment yield (tonnes/km^2 of watershed)					
	Rain-dominated watershed[a]			Snow-dominated watershed[b]		
	Suspended	Bed load	Total	Suspended	Bed load	Total
1966	2.2	18.2	20.4	0.8	0.8	1.6
1967	2.1	0.0	2.1	2.2	2.2	4.4
1968	3.0	0.5	3.5	0.8	0.8	1.6
1969	7.3	4.9	12.2	1.4	1.4	2.8
1970	4.9	4.9	9.8	1.6	1.6	3.2
1971		8.4		4.6	4.4	9.0
1972	27.5	1.8	29.3	6.1	5.8	11.9
1973	0.9	2.1	3.0	1.2	1.1	2.3

[a]Watershed 2, Blue River drainage, of the H. J. Andrews Experimental Forest in the Cascade Range of western Oregon. The watershed has an area of 0.61 km^2, an elevation range of 526–1,067 m, and a mean slope of 61%. It is completely forested and underlain by interbedded andesite flows and tuffs and breccias. Soils are shallow, sandy silts. The mean precipitation is 2,286 mm.

[b]Main Fork Horse Creek, Horse Creek Experimental Watershed, in the Selway River drainage of the western Bitterroot Range in north-central Idaho. The watershed has an area of 16.7 km^2, an elevation range of 1,250–1,737 m, and a mean slope of 31%. It is completely forested and underlain by sedimentary and metamorphosed sedimentary rocks, primarily gneisses. Soils are moderately deep, well-drained sands and silts. The mean precipitation is 1,143 mm.

availability of materials, and changes in exposed surface area. Table 5.3 illustrates this variability in sediment delivery from two watersheds in distinctly different climatic zones.

Amounts vary locally as well, because of differences in inherent erodibility of local soils and differing patterns of geology, climate, landform, and vegetation. Table 5.4 illustrates this local variability with examples of mean annual suspended-sediment yields from selected undisturbed watersheds scattered across climatic zones. Sediment yields tend to be higher in rain-dominated than in snow-dominated areas.

Soil Mass Movements

Soil mass movements are major components of hillslope erosion and sediment transport to stream channels in mountainous regions. Where and when landslides occur, their size, and the amount of material transported are controlled by hillslope gradient, quantity of water in the soil, composition of parent materials, depth and degree of weathering, and certain microtopographic features such as linear depressions that serve to concentrate and focus groundwater flows.

Soil mass movements tend to be episodic in occurrence and add substantial quantities of sediment and organic debris to stream channels over intervals ranging from a few minutes to many years. The materials added can markedly alter the channel for 300 m downstream; the effects include rapid increases in bed- and suspended-sediment loads, shifts and redistribution of existing channel-bed sediments, and partial or complete blocking of the channel by large woody debris. If entry velocities and channel gradient are high enough, and if the entrained soil, rock, and organic debris expand in volume sufficiently (bulking effect), extensive scour may occur below the point of entry and channel alteration will extend considerably farther.

TABLE 5.4.—Local variability in mean annual suspended sediment yield from undisturbed, forested watersheds in rain- and snow-dominated climatic zones. (From Larson and Sidle 1981.)

Location	Watershed	Period of record (years)	Area (km^2)	Mean precipitation (mm)	Suspended sediment yield $(tonnes/km^2)$
Rain-dominated watersheds					
Oregon	Flynn Creek	1959–1965	1.98	2,540	40.7
Coast Range,	Deer Creek	1959–1965	2.97	2,540	38.5
Alsea River	Needle Branch	1959–1965	0.69	2,540	21.8
Willamette Valley near Corvallis, Oregon	Oak Creek	1978–1980	7.11	1,524	11.6
H. J. Andrews Experimental Forest, western Cascade Range, Oregon	Watershed 2	1957–1976	0.61	2,286	21.7
Bull Run watershed, western Cascade Range, Oregon	Fox Creek	1970–1979	2.48	2,540	2.0
Snow-dominated watersheds					
Entiat	Fox Creek	1967–1970	5.03	584	39.9
River, east	Burnes Creek	1967–1970	5.51	584	6.1
Cascade Range, Washington	McCrea Creek	1967–1970	4.65	584	4.9
Horse Creek, north-central Idaho	East Fork	1966–1978	14.12	1,143	2.6
	Main Fork	1966–1978	16.54	1,143	1.6
Silver Creek drainage, central Idaho	Cabin Creek	1966–1974		711	8.1
	Ditch Creek	1966–1974		711	117.1

The mechanics of failure, the types of soil mass movement, and the factors that control and contribute to development of landslides on forested terrain are well described in the literature (Swanston 1969, 1971, 1974; Swanston and Swanson 1976; Swanson et al. 1987). Three groups of general processes are the principal contributors to habitat change: slumps and earthflows, debris avalanches, and debris torrents.

Slumps and earthflows.—Slumps and earthflows typically develop in deeply weathered siltstones, sandstones, mudstones, and volcaniclastic rocks where groundwater movement is restricted due to low soil permeabilities and the particle size of solids and weathered bedrock is dominated by the clay-size fraction. Such landslides generally develop as the result of long-term water accumulation in the soil and rock (seasonal, annual) and are not directly influenced by individual storms.

Slumps originate as backward rotations of blocks of soil and weathered rock along a curved failure surface; there is little downslope displacement. *Earthflows* usually begin with a slump or series of slumps; by a combination of true

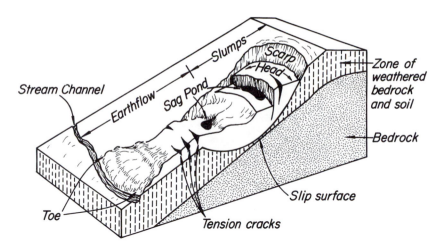

FIGURE 5.7.—Diagram of a typical slump and associated earthflow developed in deeply weathered bedrock and surficial materials. (After Swanston and Swanson 1976.)

rheological flow of the clay fraction and slumping and sliding of individual blocks, the earth moves downslope with a continuity of motion resembling the flow of a viscous fluid (Figure 5.7).

Earthflow processes are generally slow moving. Measured rates in Oregon and northern California, where these processes have been monitored extensively (Swanston and Swanson 1976; Kelsey 1978; Swanston et al. 1988), are quite variable and range from 2.5 to 2,720 cm/year. The highest rates have been measured for earthflows along major anadromous fish streams that drain the Coast Range of northern California (Kelsey 1978; Table 5.5).

Sediment delivery to stream channels can be high. Based on studies of 19 earthflows entering the Van Duzen River basin in northern California, Kelsey (1978) estimated that the annual yield of sediment to the river by earthflow processes was 41,455 m^3 or about 2,182 m^3 per failure. In contrast, studies at

TABLE 5.5.—Rates of movement of active earthflows in the western Cascade Range, Oregon (Swanston and Swanson 1976), and the Van Duzen River basin, northern California (Kelsey 1978).

Location	Period of record (years)	Movement rate (cm/year)	Method of observation
Western Cascade Range			
Landes Creek	15	12	Deflection of road
Boone Creek	2	25	Deflection of road
Cougar Reservoir	2	2.5	Deflection of road
Lookout Creek	1	7	Strain rhombus measurements across active ground breaks
Van Duzen River basin			
Donaker earthflow	1	60	Resurvey of stake line
Chimney Rock earthflow	1	530	Resurvey of stake line
Halloween earthflow	3	2,720	Resurvey of stake line

FIGURE 5.8.—The Drift Creek slide in the west-central Coast Range of Oregon, a combined slump and earthflow in nearly horizontal sandstones and siltstones. The lower end has dammed Drift Creek to form a lake more than 12 m deep.

Lookout Creek in the western Cascade Range of Oregon yielded estimated annual yields from a single earthflow of only 340 m^3 (Swanston and Swanson 1976).

Earthflow movement in unstable western terrains is predominantly seasonal: most displacement occurs after fall and winter storms have thoroughly wetted the slopes. Movement may continue over several seasons when the water content of the moving mass is maintained by altered drainage conditions or long-term changes in precipitation (Swanston et al. 1988).

Where earthflows intersect streams, their influence may be exerted upstream as well as down; in extreme cases, they may dam the stream (Figure 5.8). Downstream, they are intermittent to continuous long-term sources of sediment and organic debris for the channel. During periods of movement, the toe of the earthflow protrudes into the channel and is gradually eroded away by high winter flows. Slumping, due to the undercutting of the protruded material by storm flows, may abruptly add large quantities of soil, rock, and organic debris to the channel. If flows are high enough, the smaller fractions of newly added sediment (cobbles, gravel, sand) and organic detritus are transported almost immediately down-

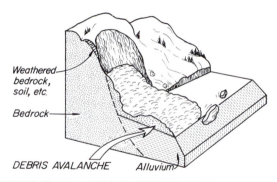

Weathered
bedrock,
soil, etc.

Bedrock

DEBRIS AVALANCHE   Alluvium

FIGURE 5.9.—Debris avalanche failures: (upper) a typical debris avalanche in shallow, semi-cohesionless soils; (lower) massive debris avalanche track developed in shallow colluvium near Wrangell, Alaska.

stream. Bedload materials are commonly deposited as wedges of coarse sediment behind barriers and at channel bends, creating new or revitalizing existing spawning habitats. Materials carried in suspension are transported farther downstream and are frequently distributed as blankets and windrows of fine sediment and organic detritus overlying existing spawning gravels. Larger rock and organic debris may remain behind at the earthflow intrusion as a residual lag deposit, forming a tangled mass of boulders and logs behind which gravels and sediment from up-channel may accumulate to form new spawning areas. This lag deposit armors the channel and frequently creates a temporary base level or "nickpoint"; the result is a sharp increase in channel gradient through the accumulation zone and the formation of pools below it.

Debris avalanches.—Debris avalanches constitute some of the most common soil mass movements on steep, forested terrain. They are shallow, rapid landslides resulting from the failure of a block of soil, rock, and organic debris along a more-or-less planar or flat surface parallel to the slope (Figure 5.9).

TABLE 5.6.—Debris avalanche erosion in forested, clear-cut, and roaded areas. (From Swanston and Swanson 1976.)

Site	Period of record (years)	Area (km²)	Slides (number)	Annual debris avalanche erosion (m³/km²)	Rate of debris avalanche erosion relative to forested areas
Stequaleho Creek, Olympic Peninsula, Washington (Fiksdal 1974)					
Forest	84	19.3	25	71.8	1.0
Clear-cut	6	4.4			
Road	6	0.7	83	11,825.0	165.0
Alder Creek, western Cascade Range, Oregon (Morrison 1975)					
Forest	25	12.3	7	45.3	1.0
Clear-cut	15	4.5	18	117.1	2.6
Road	15	0.6	75	15,565.0	344.0
Selected drainages, Coast Mountains, southwest British Columbia					
Forest	32	246.1	29	11.2	1.0
Clear-cut	32	26.4	18	24.5	2.2
Road	32	4.2	11	282.5[a]	25.2
H. J. Andrews Experimental Forest, western Cascade Range, Oregon (Swanson and Dyrness 1975)					
Forest	25	49.8	31	35.9	1.0
Clear-cut	25	12.4	30	132.2	3.7
Road	25	2.0	69	1,772.0	49.0

[a]Calculated from O'Loughlin (1972) with the assumption that the area of road construction inside and outside clear-cuttings was 16% of the area clear-cut.

Because of the roughness of the slope surface and the narrowing of the landslide path below the point of initiation, approximately 40% of the initial debris avalanche volume remains stored on the slope. The remainder is deposited at the base of the slope or enters first-order channels, where the debris is incorporated into the channel flow and moves rapidly down channel as a *debris torrent*.

The rate of debris avalanche occurrence, and therefore the rate of debris torrent occurrence, is controlled by the general stability of the landscape and the frequency of storms severe enough to trigger initial failures. Swanston and Swanson (1976) reported annual rates of debris avalanche erosion from six forested study sites in Oregon, Washington, and British Columbia that ranged from 11 to 72 m³/km² (Table 5.6).

Debris avalanches have rather consistent characteristics in the various rain-dominated geologic and geomorphic settings from northern California to southeast Alaska and eastward toward the snow-dominated zone (Bishop and Stevens 1964; Dyrness 1967a; Swanston 1970, 1974; O'Loughlin 1972; Colman 1973; Fiksdal 1974). In these rain-dominated areas, debris avalanches occur in shallow (<2 m), coarse-grained soils with high permeabilities. The slopes on which they occur have gradients near or above the maximum stable angle of the mantling soil materials (30–36°). In addition, most begin after a high-intensity storm or a rapid snowmelt has created a temporary water table and associated high pore-water pressures in the soil.

In the Cascade Range of western Oregon, storms with intensities great enough to initiate debris avalanches and debris flows have a return interval of 7 years or less (Swanston and Swanson 1976). Storms correlated with accelerated debris avalanche occurrences in coastal Alaska have return intervals of 5 years or less (Swanston 1969).

Critical intensities of rainfall have been reported in the range of 76 to 152 mm or more in 24 h. Whether or not a particular intensity becomes critical depends strongly on local topographic and climatologic variables. These variables include presence of linear depressions for groundwater accretion (concentration of subsurface flow), total storm precipitation, and antecedent moisture (moisture in the soil prior to the storm) (Sidle et al. 1985).

In the interior west, the correlation of debris avalanche and debris torrent occurrence with individual storm intensities and return intervals is not as clear-cut. There, snowpacks and warm-rain-on-snow events influence the timing of water storage and release to soils.

Debris avalanches leave scars, broad rectangular strips, and spoon-shaped depressions extending downslope toward the valley floor or intervening drainage channel. Once the sliding mass reaches a linear hillslope depression or first-order drainage, its confinement and channelization produce characteristic long tails below the failure scar along which debris volumes of less than 10 m^3 to as much as 10,000 m^3 have been transported (Swanston and Swanson 1976). Average initial failure volumes of debris avalanches in forested areas in the Pacific Northwest range from 1,540 to 4,600 m^3.

Because debris avalanches are shallow failures, timber and other vegetation cover, whose roots anchor soil but whose above-ground structures transfer wind stress to the soil mantle, significantly affect where and when debris avalanches occur. An added factor in areas of even occasional seismic activity is the lateral stress applied to the soil mantle by ground shaking during earthquakes. Seismic activity helped trigger soil mass movements in Alaska (Bishop and Stevens 1964) and in the central Rocky Mountains (Bailey 1971). In the Queen Charlotte Islands, British Columbia, the most seismically active area in Canada (Sutherland-Brown 1968) and also one of the best salmon-producing areas on the Pacific coast, a direct correlation between earthquakes and high landslide activity has been postulated (Alley and Thomson 1978).

Debris torrents.—Debris torrents are rapid movements of large volumes of water charged with soil, rock, and organic debris down steep stream channels (Figure 5.10). Debris torrents typically occur in steep-gradient second- and higher-order channels. These events are triggered during extreme storm flows by addition of debris avalanche materials from adjacent hillslopes or by the breakup and mobilization of debris accumulations in the channel. The initial slurry of water and associated debris commonly entrains large quantities of additional sediment, as well as living and dead organic material from the streambed and banks. Some debris torrents are triggered by debris avalanches of less than 100 m^3, but may ultimately include 10,000 m^3 of debris intrained along the track of the torrent (Swanston and Swanson 1976).

The main factors controlling the occurrence of debris torrents are the quantity and stability of debris in channels (supplied by earlier debris avalanches and debris flows), steepness of the channel, stability of adjacent hillslopes, and peak-discharge characteristics of the channel (flow volume, cross-sectional area).

The concentration and stability of debris in channels reflect the history of stream flushing and the health and stage of development of the surrounding timber

FIGURE 5.10.—Debris torrent developed in pumice on the north slope of the Entiat Valley, east-central Cascade Range, Washington. The torrent resulted from a temporary damming of the channel at peak flows by debris avalanches from the channel side slope. The hillslope had been destabilized by massive wildfire the previous year.

stand (Froehlich 1973). High concentrations of old debris indicate infrequent flushing and stable hillslopes.

Channel steepness controls the rate at which debris is delivered and transported, and the dominance of erosion or depositional processes during a particular event. Scouring generally occurs above channel gradients of 10° and deposition begins below this gradient. Velocity reduction and major deposition of debris

TABLE 5.7.—Debris torrent occurrences in selected areas in western Oregon. (From Swanston and Swanson 1976.)

Site	Period of record (years)	Area (km^2)	Debris torrents			Annual number per km^2	Rate of debris torrent occurrence relative to forested areas
			Triggered by debris avalanches (number)	With no associated debris avalanche (number)	Total		
H. J. Andrews Experimental Forest, western Cascade Range, Oregon							
Forest	25	49.8	9	1	10	0.008	1.0
Clear-cut	25	12.4	5	6	11	0.036	4.5
Road	25	2.0	17		17	0.340	42.0
Alder Creek drainage, western Cascade Range, Oregon							
Forest	90	12.3	5	1	6	0.005	1.0
Clear-cut	15	4.5	2	1	3	0.044	8.8
Road	15	0.6	6		6	0.667	133.4

FIGURE 5.11.—Channel scoured to bedrock by a debris torrent in the Oregon Coast Range.

torrent material occur when channel gradients drop below about 7 or 8° (12–14%) (Thurber Consultants 1983; Benda 1985a).

Velocities of debris torrents on the order of 20 m/s have been calculated, based on channel gradients and estimates of total volume transported (Thurber Consultants 1983). The rates of occurrence, however, have been systematically documented in only two small areas of the Pacific Northwest, both in the western Cascade Range of Oregon (Morrison 1975; Swanston and Swanson 1976). In these studies, annual rates of occurrence were 0.005 and 0.008 events/km² for forested areas (Table 5.7). Torrent tracks in forested areas ranged from 100 to 2,280 m long and averaged 610 m of transport channel length.

Although debris torrents occur substantially less frequently than debris avalanches (see Tables 5.6, 5.7), debris torrents can cause marked changes in fish habitat when they reach a stream. Because of the high velocities and large

FIGURE 5.12.—Debris jam in an anadromous fish stream in the Oregon Coast Range. The jam resulted from a debris torrent that entered the stream from an adjacent slope.

volumes of entrained soil and debris, the erosive power generated as the debris torrent moves downstream can scour hundreds of meters of channel to bedrock (Figure 5.11). Fortunately, such scour usually occurs above spawning areas or other important fish habitats. When the torrent flow loses momentum, a tangled mass of large woody debris is deposited in a matrix of sediment and fine organic detritus that covers areas up to several hectares (Swanston and Swanson 1976) (Figure 5.12). The effect of such events can be the obliteration of entire spawning reaches and major shifting and redistribution of sediment and large woody debris. At the point of deposition, the channel may be blocked or rerouted, and new pools and riffles develop behind obstructing debris.

The channel changes produced by debris torrents may dominate local channel morphology for centuries and exert a strong influence on aquatic ecosystems downstream from point of entry (Benda 1985b). Because debris flows develop primarily during storm flows, much of this material is transported almost immediately away from the entry point and deposited in large accumulations at scattered sites downstream, where it causes local channel scour and aggradation.

Work by Benda (1985a, 1985b) in the Oregon Coast Range suggests that the actual behavior of debris torrents and their effects on streams result from a combination of geomorphic and hydrologic factors including junction angle, channel gradient, and magnitude of stream discharge. Debris torrents that reach second-order channels at a low angle of incidence (70–90°) tend to deposit debris at the tributary junction. At this point, channel gradients are decreasing, channel widths are increasing, and an abrupt change in flow direction occurs. How long this deposit remains in place depends on the drainage area above the deposit and the volume of flow in the tributary at the time the torrent arrived. Debris torrents that enter second-order channels at a high angle of incidence tend to travel further and may reach third- and higher-order channels before debris is deposited or dispersed. Channel slopes also control erosion and deposition once debris flows enter the stream. Debris torrents generally scour first- and second-order channels with gradients above 10°. At lesser gradients, erosion rates are reduced, and substantial deposition begins when gradients drop below 6°. As debris flows move into higher-order channels, deposition and erosion are reduced as the magnitude of streamflow increases.

The effects of debris torrents are alteration of channel cross section and profile, changes in pool:riffle ratio, alteration of the availability and viability of spawning and rearing areas, and development of new habitat areas. New large woody debris dams and sediment wedges are commonly created at, and immediately below, points of entry; bed-load shifts alter habitats of resident fish and benthic organisms; and availability and distribution of oxygen-bearing intragravel water is substantially altered. Over the long run, such effects tend to concentrate biological processes at debris-flow deposition sites (Sedell and Dahm 1984). For example, Everest and Meehan (1981b) initially found decreased spawning and rearing habitats and decreased fish biomass immediately below recent debris flow deposits: a 90% reduction of salmonid biomass in small streams and a 55% reduction in large streams. Within 3 years after the debris flow, however, productivity had returned nearly to preflow levels. Pools created by the new debris supported increased fish populations and created more spawning and rearing habitats than had existed previously. These pools produced underyearling coho salmon at rates 10 times greater than did reaches with no debris flow pools.

In-Channel Transport and Deposition

Once sediment and woody debris reach the channel, or become mobilized within the channel system, their downstream movements and ultimate effects on fish habitat are dictated by the morphology of the channel, the quantity and size of introduced materials, and the frequency and magnitude of high flows.

Channel shape and structure.—Channel morphology is determined by structural constraints within the channel (bedrock outcrops, imbedded large woody debris, sediment wedges) and by sediment and water input. It is formed during storm events when flow is great enough to transport the coarse sediments that line the channel bed (Sullivan et al. 1987). The resulting channel shape has a sequence of recognizable units, including riffles, pools, runs, glides, scour pools, and boulder cascades (Figure 5.13). Water flowing downstream is continually forced to adjust its velocity and depth, which control the ability of the stream to transport sediment. In riffles and cascades, for example, flows are shallow and fast; suspended and bedload sediment are generally transported through such units, and the units themselves remain in a stable position until flows of great enough magnitude occur to mobilize the dominant stream-bottom materials. In pools, flows are deep and slow; suspended and bed-load sediments generally are deposited in these units.

Obstructions such as large woody debris (trees), boulders, imbedded rootwads, and bedrock outcrops produce additional variations in channel velocity and direction, frequently creating pools, gravel bars, and side-channel rearing areas. These structural features are vitally important in managing forested watersheds to preserve fish habitat because they store and sort sediment, enhance scour and

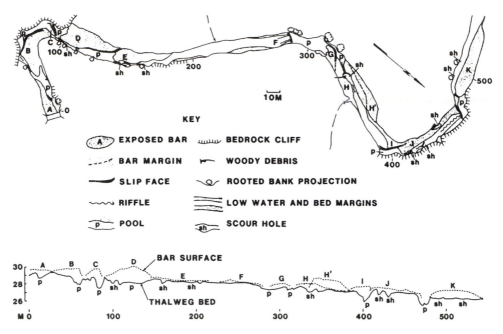

FIGURE 5.13.—Map and longitudinal profile of Jacoby Creek, northwestern California, showing the relationship between stream channel units and their association with obstructions and bends. (After Lisle 1986b.)

deposition of bed material, diversify velocity and depth, and fix the position of bars and pools (Lisle 1986b). The presence of obstructions is determined by local geology and active hillslope- and channel-erosion processes. Woody debris is supplied by debris flows and debris torrents, windthrow, fire, insects, disease, and local channel erosion.

Streambed composition and sediment movement.—Sediment within streams moves either in suspension or by sliding, rolling, and bouncing along the bottom (collectively called bed-load transport; Figure 5.14). The dominant mode of transport is determined by particle size and by velocity of flow (Figure 5.15). During low flows, bed-load transport is minimal and suspended sediment is limited to silt and clay-sized particles (<0.05 mm in diameter). As flows increase, sand-sized particles (<2.0 mm in diameter) become incorporated into the water column. During storm flows, extensive bedload movement may occur, involving particles in excess of several centimeters if the energy imparted to the channel bed is great enough.

The transport of suspended sediment occurs over a wide range of flow conditions, but because the turbulence required to keep these particles in suspension is relatively low, once entrained they move rapidly downstream and tend to remain in suspension unless major reductions in stream energy occur. Very small particles, such as silt and clay, can be moved by virtually any flow. Sand-sized particles (often referred to as fine sediment by fisheries biologists), however, can only be suspended during higher flows and remain stored in and on the streambed between storms (Sullivan et al. 1987).

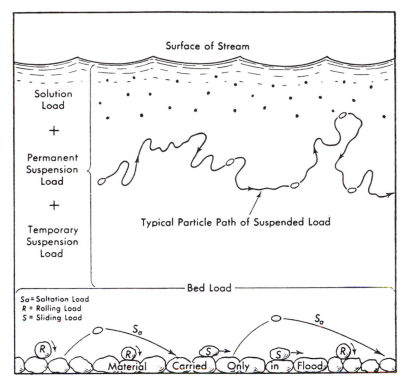

FIGURE 5.14.—Schematic diagram showing the types of load carried by a stream. (After Garrels 1951.)

In short mountain streams, sediment suspended during storm flows may pass completely through the channel system without being deposited unless a major reduction in stream energy occurs. When energy is reduced, most commonly at obstructions and channel bends, suspended sediments settle to the channel floor. Some of the fine materials infiltrate relatively clean, porous gravels on the channel bed, where they may reduce intragravel flow of oxygenated water and block emergence of fry. Scrivener and Brownlee (1989) found that when pore size was reduced by the intrusion of fine sediments large coho and chum salmon alevins had a greater mortality than small alevins in Carnation Creek, British Columbia.

Intrusion of fine sediments (primarily sand) is limited initially to the upper 10–15 cm of the streambed (Beschta and Jackson 1979; Hartman et al. 1987), and subsequent higher flows may flush the fine sediment from the gravel. If the source of fine materials persists, however, and if flows of sufficient energy to flush the sediments do not occur, increasing amounts may settle deeper into the gravels and subsequently reduce the viability of the spawning site. Studies at Carnation Creek (Hartman et al. 1987) indicate that sudden pulses of fine sediment entering a stream tend to be deposited and then cleaned away in a few years, provided that the stream system is not overloaded with sediment and that erosion sources have healed. If sediment sources are persistent and fine sediments intrude deeper into the streambed, it may take many years for them to be cleaned out.

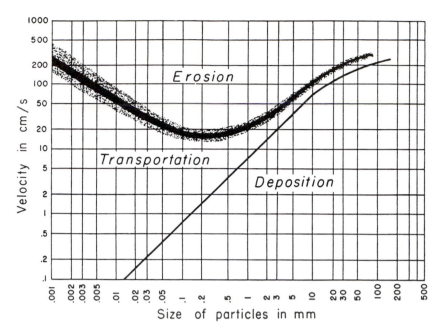

FIGURE 5.15.—Velocities at which different sizes of sediment are eroded, transported, or deposited in a stream. (After Hjulstrom 1935.)

The movement of bed-load sediment is controlled by interactions between particle size, channel morphology, and flow conditions (Leopold et al. 1964). In general, coarse sediment particles move through the stream system discontinuously, being alternately stored or mobilized over varying periods that differ with the type of storage location (i.e., riffle, pool, cascade), size of particle, and magnitude of flow. Gravel, cobbles, and boulders (bed load) can be moved only by larger storms, and thus are stored for long periods in streams, mainly as gravel bars (Sullivan et al. 1987). Bars form best where the channel is wide enough to accommodate them (bank-full width:depth ratios greater than about 12:1; Jaeggi 1984) and the stream gradient is low enough to allow deposition (less than about 2%; Ikeda 1975; Florsheim 1985). Bars usually grow and shrink seasonally because of local imbalances between deposition and erosion, but tend to keep the same location as long as channel boundaries remain intact and obstructions remain in place (Leopold et al. 1964; Lisle 1986b).

Sediment storage.—Coarse materials temporarily stored in the channel are generally sorted and arranged by streamflow to form an "armoring" layer on the channel bed. Because relatively high flows are required to disrupt the armor layer of gravel-bedded streams, significant bed-load transport in many streams may be limited to only a few days each year. It is during these brief periods of "flushing" flows that important and long-term changes in channel morphology and composition of the bed material occur. The resulting overturn and mixing of the upper layers of streambed gravel flushes fine sediments, redistributes bed-load materials (forming new pools and riffles), and leads to local accumulations of large fluvial sediment deposits or "wedges" behind obstructions and at points of reduced gradient along the thalweg (Church 1983; Figure 5.16). These sediment wedges are

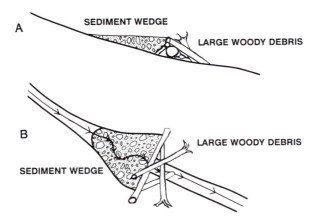

FIGURE 5.16.—Diagrams of sediment wedges deposited behind woody debris in a coastal spawning channel: (A) longitudinal profile; (B) plan view.

generally superimposed upon previous channel morphology and frequently result in expanded gravel areas of low gradient suitable for spawning. These wedges may become dry during low-flow summer months, however. Little quantitative work has been done on the origin and deposition of these wedge deposits. Preliminary investigations in coastal streams in the Queen Charlotte Islands, British Columbia (Roberts 1987), indicate that such wedges are common in channels subject to recurrent landslides. They are most frequent and extreme in harvested watersheds where sediment volumes produced by landslides may be augmented by bank erosion or lateral retreat of streambanks destabilized by logging.

Importance of woody debris.—Woody debris—including material resulting from fire, disease, and decomposition—is delivered to the stream by wind, streambank undercutting, and soil mass movements. Once in the stream, it may be deposited almost immediately in or along the channel margins or transported considerable distances down the channel to be deposited as windrows of small organic detritus and piles or jams of mixed logs and smaller organic debris. The point of deposition and the distance of travel depend largely on the originating process and the volume of flow in the channel at the time of deposition. Streams of all sizes are affected by debris, but the density of debris per unit area of stream bottom decreases as stream size increases. In small headwater streams (up to third- and fourth-order channels), trees generally lie where they fall and are only moved as a result of decomposition or by catastrophic events such as extreme storm flows or debris torrents. As streams within a watershed expand in response to storm runoff, they become wider and deeper. Large woody material (logs) may float and accumulate at channel obstructions, forming concentrated collections of debris or debris dams. In rivers, where a tree bole of any size can be floated, large woody debris usually is left by flood flows at bends or along channel margins (Swanson et al. 1976).

Woody debris deposited and redistributed during storm flows and soil mass movements is a common and important channel feature with both physical and biological consequences for fish habitat. Work in Oregon (Keller and Swanson

1979; Sullivan 1986), California (Keller and Tally 1979), British Columbia (Toews and Moore 1982b; Hogan 1986), and New Zealand (Mosley 1981) has demonstrated the substantial influence of large organic debris on stream channel form and process. Large woody debris alters the longitudinal profile and reduces the local gradient of the channel, especially when log dams create slack pools above or plunge pools below them, or when they are sites of sediment aggradation. Small to intermediate channels with only small amounts of entrained woody debris tend to have straight, long riffles and infrequent small, rounded pools. Channels with large quantities of woody debris seem to have small, distorted pools and frequent short, step-like riffles. Woody debris in streams protects banks from erosion at some sites but diverts high-velocity flow into banks elsewhere, and thus is an important determinant of local bank erosion and pool formation (Sullivan et al. 1987).

The size of large woody debris strongly affects the stability of debris accumulations (Toews and Moore 1982b; Bryant 1983; Bilby 1984; Grette 1985; Bilby and Ward 1989). The length of a piece of wood relative to channel width is the most important factor (Bisson et al. 1987); short pieces can stabilize narrow channels, but longer pieces are needed to stabilize wider channels (Figure 5.17). The diameter of pieces is also important because thicker pieces require greater discharges to move, withstand heavier impacts and static loads, and resist decay longer than smaller pieces.

Orientation and degree of burial also strongly influence stability. Pieces oriented less than 30° to the axis of flow appear to be more stable then those angled more then 60° (Bryant 1983). Pieces that have both ends anchored in the streambed or bank or that are almost completely buried in the channel floor are more stable than those with only partial anchoring or burial (Toews and Moore 1982b; Bilby 1984; Grette 1985).

Large jams in channels of any size sometimes block the passage of migrating fish and effectively close off areas to spawning (Meehan 1974). Such jams also may form a temporary base level in the channel, which becomes wider, more shallow, and a site of sediment deposition on the upstream side and extensively scoured downstream. If the stream breaks through the blockage, it may cut down through the sediment wedge, dewatering large areas of potential spawning habitat. Or, if the wedge is large enough, the stream may form a new channel around the obstruction, causing extensive bank erosion and bypassing the wedge and sections of spawning habitat downstream.

Woody debris forms abundant storage sites for sediments in forest streams as large as fourth order (20–50-km^2 drainage area), where storage is otherwise limited by steep gradients and confinement of channels between valley walls (Sullivan et al. 1987). Studies of this storage function in Idaho (Megahan and Nowlin 1976) and Oregon (Swanson and Lienkaemper 1978) indicated that annual sediment yields from small forested watersheds are commonly less than 10% of the sediment stored in channels. More recent work in Redwood Creek, northwestern California (Pitlick 1981), indicated a similar relationship between sediment storage and debris, and further suggested a distinct difference in storage function with the type of forest cover. Debris produced by redwood forests decomposes more slowly than logs from Douglas-fir forests and thus lasts longer, is more abundant, and stores more sediment. Pearce and Watson (1983) found that a volume of sediment

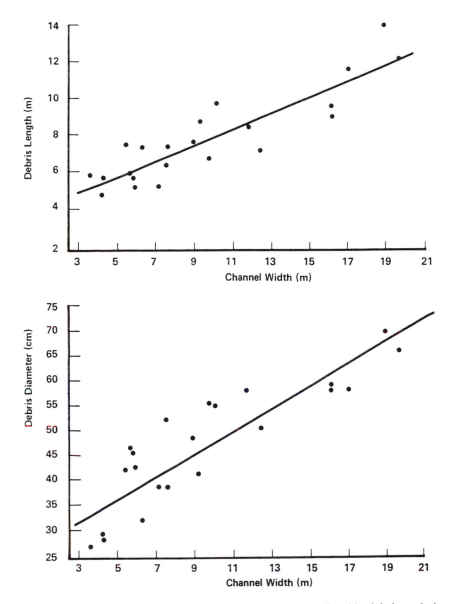

FIGURE 5.17.—Relationships between length and diameter of stable debris and channel width. Each point represents the geometric mean length or diameter of logs not held in place by other debris in study streams in western Washington. (After Bilby and Ward 1989.)

equivalent to 50 to 220 times the average annual input remained stored behind debris dams in a New Zealand stream 5 years after the debris was introduced by a landslide event.

The gravel trapped and stored behind debris may provide excellent spawning habitat. In addition, wood embedded in the channel frequently provides a "stepped" channel profile, along which much of the gradient drop is over short wood-created falls that alternate with low-gradient pools. This gives a large portion of the stream a lower gradient and more acceptable spawning and rearing habitat than might otherwise be available. Unless flushed by major flows, fine sediment trapped by this debris tends to be routed through the system slowly as the wood accumulations decompose.

The biological community also benefits from such stream debris (Hicks et al. 1991; Murphy and Meehan 1991). Debris accumulations provide cover for resident and anadromous fish (Narver 1971; Hall and Baker 1975) and retain organic detritus entering the stream system. Before it is acceptable to detritus-feeding invertebrates, detritus of terrestrial origin must first be conditioned by microbes in the stream (Triska and Sedell 1975). The conditioned detritus becomes the base of a food chain that includes insects and fish, and the debris accumulations provide the necessary physical characteristics and habitats to retain all these stream ecosystem components in the same area.

Accessory Processes

Certain accessory events and processes may significantly influence the hillslope and channel dynamics that cause habitat change. These events include windstorms, infestations of insects and disease, activities of animals (particularly beavers), and wildfire—all of which influence the input of woody debris and sediment to forest channels—and freezing and ice formation—which alter the timing and extent with which that debris moves through the channel system.

Wind

Strong winds occur primarily during storms and frequently blow down trees in a forested area. This can have both direct and indirect effects on fish habitat. If such a "windthrow" occurs on a steep slope, the uprooting of trees may substantially increase the slope's susceptibility to landslides, and thus indirectly increase the likelihood of debris delivery to the stream channel. Windthrow in the riparian zone affects fish habitat directly when trees are blown into streams or streamside cover is removed.

Windthrow has been recognized for many years as a widespread natural phenomenon in forested regions throughout the USA (Lutz and Griswold 1939; Stephens 1956). Storms with winds of hurricane force (velocities in excess of 33 m/s) may cause an entire stand to be uprooted. More commonly, however, scattered individuals or groups of trees are knocked down (Figure 5.18). Studies of windthrow in virgin forests of the Oregon Coast Range (Ruth and Yoder 1953) indicate that the process is most severe in areas with a high water table or with very shallow soils in which roots are unable to establish firm anchoring.

Windthrow on sloping sites tends to open the mineral soil to direct ingress of water, and it destroys the anchoring and reinforcing effect of tree roots at unstable sites. If windthrow occurs on a slope that is nearly or fully saturated with water, the impact of falling trees and the instantaneous development of pore-water pressure this causes can directly stimulate soil mass movements (Swanston 1967).

Apart from major floods and soil mass movements, windthrow is one of the principal ways for large woody debris to enter streams (Swanson and Lienkaemper 1978). For the most part, windthrow adjacent to streams is beneficial to fish

FIGURE 5.18.—Natural windthrow in the riparian zone along Kook Creek, Chichagof Island, Alaska.

habitat, adding logs, limbs, and rootwads directly to the channel. Extensive windthrow affects streams of all sizes, but it probably has greater relative importance for small to medium-sized streams. Along large rivers, undermining of trees by bank erosion probably supplies more large woody debris than windthrow does (Keller and Swanson 1979).

Windthrown debris (often whole trees) generally bridges narrow channels or enters the channel complete with branches and portions of the rootwad. In contrast, large woody debris carried into the stream by landslide processes becomes broken into smaller pieces (Swanson and Lienkaemper 1978). From a fish habitat standpoint, a nearly intact tree provides more stability, hydraulic diversity, and cover than fragments of the stem and limbs (Bisson et al. 1987). The benefits of large debris elements and the effects large debris has on channel processes were noted in the previous section.

Windthrow in the riparian area opens up or removes the tree canopy adjacent to the stream. The amount of direct solar radiation available to a stream increases accordingly. In summer, the mean monthly maximum temperature of Pacific Northwest streams increases 3–8°C (Beschta et al. 1987). Evidence so far, however, suggests that these increases rarely exceed the tolerance levels of resident fish species. In the drier interior, temperature increases may be greater because periods of solar radiation are more extended during summer low flows.

Sections of exposed stream may experience large diurnal fluctuations in summer-time temperature. The magnitude of temperature increase depends on surface area of the exposed reach and stream discharge. Streams with small discharges and large exposed areas generally experience the greatest temperature increases (Sheridan and Bloom 1975). These elevated temperatures will not decrease appreciably as the stream passes through shaded reaches unless mixing with cooler water occurs (Beschta et al. 1987).

During winter, streams may experience reduced temperatures when canopy is removed because more energy is lost to evaporation, convection, and long-wave radiation from the stream surface (Beschta et al. 1987). This is probably not important in coastal streams within the rain-dominated zone, where cloud cover and relatively warm nighttime temperatures preclude major cooling effects. In the interior snow-dominated zone, at northern latitudes, and at higher elevations in the rain-dominated and transient-snow zones, where significant reductions in winter temperatures occur, such cooling may be important, but little quantitative information is available.

Water temperature changes and increased levels of light can significantly affect the availability of food for fish, the timing of spawning and incubation of embryos, and the egg-to-fry survival (Bjornn and Reiser 1991). Increased light availability and elevated temperatures in clear-cuts have been linked to increased algal production and higher invertebrate production, which makes more food available to fish (Murphy and Hall 1981; Bisson and Sedell 1984). Elevated temperatures during low-flow periods may alter the temperature environment in redds, increasing mortality of eggs and affecting morphological characteristics of fish during embryonic development (Orska 1963). Temperature increases can also lead to earlier emergence of fry, longer growing seasons, and increased survival. A possible negative effect of earlier emergence of fry is that conditions in the stream (or estuary, in the case of pink and chum salmon fry, which move downstream to the ocean soon after emergence) may be less favorable than they would be at a later date.

Overstory canopy removal along channels also influences snow accumulation and melting. Snow accumulates to a greater extent in forest openings, primarily because it is recruited from adjacent forest canopy by wind and by the air turbulence associated with the openings themselves (Troendle and Leaf 1980). An additional gain results because less snow is intercepted and evaporated away than in canopied areas (Haupt 1979). Although little information is available about snow accumulations in natural openings, Anderson et al. (1976) reported increases of snow in logged areas of the snow-dominated zone; the increases ranged from 10% to 40%, depending on the degree of harvest activity. Added snow cover over exposed stream sections may insulate the channel and prevent redds from reaching lethal low temperatures, gravels from freezing, and extensive anchor ice from forming. In the spring, snow in these openings melts earlier and more rapidly then does snow within the forest because more radiation can reach the surface (Garstka et al. 1958).

Insects and Disease

The killing of trees by insects and disease affects the forest and ultimately the stream environment much like windthrow, but generally much less frequently.

Interception and evapotranspiration are reduced or stopped, but infiltration of water that reaches the soil surface is usually not affected (Anderson et al. 1976). The loss of overhead cover near stream channels by defoliation causes local water temperatures to increase. The weakened root systems of dead trees make the affected timber much more susceptible to windthrow, which promotes soil disturbances and mass movements.

U.S. Forest Service (1958, 1977d) data indicate that insects kill far more trees than disease does. Damage from insect and disease infestations is scattered. Mortality in an area is usually confined to a single tree species and not all the individuals of that species are infected. In mixed-forest types, this has practically no effect on erosion and streamflow because canopy, surface cover, and root systems are maintained. Under those conditions, the only influence on fish habitats results from the death of streamside trees, which opens the channel to direct sunlight and increases woody debris loading from falling litter and limbs. Occasionally, large areas do become infested (usually because one tree species dominates) and substantial portions of the timber cover are destroyed. On the White River drainage in Colorado (Love 1955; Bethlahmy 1974), bark beetles killed most of the trees in a 1,974-km^2 area, and total streamflow increased by about 22%. The effects of increased flow, sediment, and organic debris in the channel on fish habitats was unrecorded but probably followed the principles discussed earlier in this chapter.

Animal Activities

Ungulates.—Large herbivores such as deer *Odocoileus* spp., elk *Cervus elaphus*, and moose *Alces alces* can cause changes in riparian areas that could affect fish habitat. Ungulates affect plant community structure by two processes: forage consumption and trampling (Hanley and Taber 1980). Recent studies have shown that heavy browsing tends to reduce the abundance of shrubs in understory vegetation; the abundance of conifers and grasses increases as competition with shrubs becomes reduced (Hanley and Taber 1980; Hanley 1987). In situations where shrubs provide cover and nutrients, ungulate browsing could influence fish productivity. When large mammals are concentrated in the riparian zone, streambank trampling could also occur. Elk and moose probably cause more of this type of stream habitat disturbance than do other species. The effects of livestock grazing in this regard are undoubtedly more dramatic than those of wild ungulates, and are discussed in detail by Platts (1991, this volume).

Beavers.—Beavers *Castor canadensis* are common in many forested areas in North America. Typically they inhabit low-gradient riparian zones along rivers and streams, where they construct dams and diversions to impound water. The ponds they create, and the associated flooding and side-channel formation in and adjacent to anadromous fish streams, can dramatically affect physical habitat condition and diversity (Figure 5.19). Spawning areas are covered with deep water and may become blanketed with fine sediment, but flooding of adjacent banks and rerouting of channels may create new rearing and over-wintering areas for juvenile and resident salmonids. The silt that accumulates in ponds behind dams can increase the standing crop of bottom fauna (Gard 1961b). The ponds are sediment traps; B. H. Smith (1980) reported that stream sedimentation below beaver dams was reduced as much as 90%.

FIGURE 5.19.—Beaver dam constructed across Puyallup Creek, an anadromous fish stream on Prince of Wales Island, Alaska.

In low-gradient streams and rivers that cross floodplains, beaver ponding tends to cover streambed gravels, reducing habitat diversity and available spawning area (Churchill 1980). In small mountain streams, beaver ponds may provide up to 400% more rearing habitat, which is often more limiting to salmonid production than spawning habitat (Gard 1961b). In streams larger then fourth order, beavers have little influence on channel characteristics because the dams are temporary and other hydraulic forces have a greater influence on the channel.

Water temperatures are also altered by dam construction. Temperatures tend to be higher in ponds during the summer and autumn (Reid 1952; Adams 1954; Bryant 1984), probably due to accumulated heat from direct radiation to the pond surface and the lack of cooling base flows. Fish populations living in marginally high water temperatures could be adversely affected. Populations normally living in colder headwaters, however, could benefit from increased basic biological productivity.

Recent work in southeast Alaska (Bryant 1984) indicates that beaver ponds provide important salmonid rearing habitat, particularly with respect to winter conditions and seasonality of streamflow. Higher densities of coho salmon are generally found in both ponds and adjacent areas than in channel systems without ponds. Seasonal movements between the pond and both upstream and downstream areas are common during periods of deteriorating habitat quality. During low-flow periods, ponds provide needed water volumes, but levels of dissolved oxygen may be low. Fish avoid these areas of reduced water quality by moving upstream. Dewatering may also occur downstream from the dam. During high flows, beaver ponds provide slack-water areas and backwater refuges during floods. Fall freshets tend to flush ponds, providing good-quality water through the fall and winter. At high water, dams can usually be breached by adult salmon on their way to upstream spawning areas. Most dams also have "leaks" that permit movement of juveniles during increased flows.

Overwinter survival of coho salmon appears to be significantly improved in beaver ponds (Bryant 1984). This may be due to larger surface areas of water, deeper water, and increased cover provided by bank features and associated debris and overhanging brush.

Wildfire

Burning of forests destroys the covering vegetation on slopes and along stream channels and may locally alter the physical properties of the surface layers of soil. The immediate effects are to increase both total water yield and storm-flow discharge from the watershed. The water surface is exposed to direct sunlight, increasing water temperatures, and substantial quantities of woody debris from falling limbs, litter, and trees enter the channel. Fire also exposes the bare mineral soil to increased surface runoff and surface erosion. Surface runoff from burned areas generally imports more dissolved nutrients than usual to streams.

Surface erosion processes—including raindrop and rill erosion and dry ravel (tumbling, rolling, and bounding of single particles downslope) during wetting–drying and freezing–thawing cycles—transport large volumes of sediment and organic debris from the slope to the channel (Figure 5.20). Fire also increases the potential for landslides up to 5 years after the event due to the decay of anchoring and reinforcing root systems (Swanston 1974; Ziemer and Swanston 1977).

Intensive drying of soil, combustion of organic matter that binds soil aggregates, loss of litter cover, and strong convective winds produced by the fire's heat all contribute to debris movement down slopes during hot fires. In steep terrain, rolling rocks and logs released by destruction of roots and other supportive organic matter trigger downslope movement of additional material, greatly increasing the concentration of large woody debris at unstable sites on slopes and within and adjacent to stream channels (Swanson 1981).

Effects of snow hydrology in burned ecosystems have received little study, particularly in terms of fire-induced changes in groundwater regime (Swanson 1981). Speculation on this subject is complicated by the great contrasts between cold, dry and warm, wet snow types and between long-term snowpack and multiple accumulation–melt regimes. Several investigators have shown that spring snowmelt is more rapid in forest openings than in areas under a forest canopy (U.S. Army Corps of Engineers 1956; Berndt 1965; Rothacher 1965; Gary and Coltharp 1967; Haupt 1979). This is due mainly to direct solar radiation, but Anderson (1967) suggested that back-radiation by trees at exposed boundaries may augment the effect. It is likely that fire scorching of ground materials and boles of trees would increase long-wave radiation to the snowpack and accelerate these snowmelt rates even more (Tiedemann et al. 1979). This has been documented by Smith (1974) and others, who described melt zones around blackened snags and rapid condensation melting in areas characterized by a warm snowpack. Some of this water infiltrates the soil, but most is probably carried directly to

FIGURE 5.20.—Dry ravel, or dry creep and sliding, of surface materials downslope after a fire along the Klamath River in northern California.

streams on fire-formed impermeable surfaces, producing higher streamflows and associated channel instability.

Fire affects nutrient availability and subsequent nutrient loading of streams in several ways. Nutrients incorporated in vegetation, litter, and soil can be volatilized during pyrolysis and combustion, mineralized during oxidation, or lost by ash convection (Grier 1975). After the fire is out, nutrients can then be redistributed by leaching of the ash layer and soil, and transported to the stream by surface erosion, soil mass movement, or solution transport. Studies of nutrient transfer to streams after wildfire and controlled fire in the western Cascade Range of Oregon and in north-central Washington indicated that levels of organic nitrogen within the first year were about twice those recorded before the fires (Fredriksen 1973; Tiedemann 1973; Tiedemann et al. 1979). The cause of this increase was believed to be greater flows that displaced organic detritus from areas adjacent to the streams. Striking increases in nitrate-nitrogen were also observed in stream water within the first year after fire, although no measurements exceeded the recommended U.S. Environmental Protection Agency (1973b) level of 10 mg/L. These elevated nitrate concentrations subsided as revegetation progressed. A flush of ammonium nitrogen occurs immediately after a fire but generally dissipates within the first few weeks. Small, temporary

increases in phosphorus levels in stream water have also been reported (Tiedemann 1973; Grier 1975).

The effects of these changes in nutrient concentration on fish habitat are not
well known. The levels of increased nutrients reported in streams after fire appear
to be below toxic thresholds for aquatic organisms and dissipate rapidly with
stream dilution and flushing. Gibbons and Salo (1973) pointed out that the addition
of nutrients to a stream my actually be beneficial, especially to relatively sterile
streams, by supporting additional plant and animal life that are food sources for
fish. Such results have remained difficult to predict, however, and excessive
nutrient loading, particularly in low-flow channels, may result in eutrophication.

By far the most significant effects of fire on channel morphology are the
well-documented increases in water, sediment, and debris delivered to stream and
river systems. Studies of fire-denuded watersheds in west-central Washington
(Klock and Helvey 1976a, 1976b) have shown that maximum streamflows were
double the rate of flows before the fires. In addition—the combined result of rapid
snowmelt, high-intensity rainstorms, and destruction of covering and anchoring
vegetation—massive debris torrents occurred 2 years after the burn with frequencies 10 to 28 times greater than before the fire. Nobel and Lundeen (1971) reported
an annual postfire erosion rate of 413.3 m^3/km^2 for a portion of the South Fork
Salmon River—seven times the rate on similar but unburned lands in the vicinity
(Megahan and Molitor 1975). In northern California, Wallis and Anderson (1965)
reported sediment discharges 2.3 times greater from burned than from unburned
areas.

These large increases in volumes of sediment and debris, frequently delivered
to the channel system by rapidly moving episodic events such as storm flows and
landslides, may seriously overload the channel transport mechanisms and cause
significant changes in habitat. Additions of large woody debris tend to improve
habitat diversity by providing cover and creating new spawning, incubation, and
rearing areas. Movement and redistribution of bed-load materials can destroy eggs
and displace alevins already in the channel, but gravels are also flushed of
entrained fines and new spawning areas are created. Fine sediments entering the
channel system may blanket spawning gravels in areas of reduced flow velocity,
but for the most part, attendant high flows in the main channel tend to carry most
of this material entirely through the system.

Freezing and Ice Formation

In the more northern latitudes, and at higher elevations in the interior
snow-dominated zone, freezing temperatures and the development of ice on
hillslopes and within stream channels may substantially reduce the rate of
streamflow and increase sediment contributions from bare hillslope areas. If the
channel freezes over, subsequent melting and ice breakup may cause flooding and
extensive bank and channel erosion; the channel is mechanically plowed by the
ice and sediments are transported by anchor ice that had attached to bottom
sediments during freeze-up.

In areas where extensive ice formation in channels is rare, freezing temperatures tend to have their greatest effect by accelerating transport of surface
sediment to the channel. "Concrete frost"—wet soil solidly frozen—probably
occurs only sporadically on forested slopes in interior areas of the northwest

(Anderson et al. 1976). In the Pacific coastal mountains, it is generally absent. Where present, it may prevent infiltration and cause local overland flow. Its frequency of occurrence is so low, however, that it probably has very little effect on water flows in adjacent stream channels. Much more important is the development of "needle ice." Needle ice is produced by the growth of frost crystals beneath pebbles and soil particles on unvegetated slopes during diurnal cycles of freezing and thawing (Sharpe 1960). The particles are lifted perpendicular to the slope surface. When the needle ice begins to melt, the ice crystals and their loads of earth, pebbles, and organic debris fall downslope and may continue to slide and roll for some distance. Such "surface creep" is an important local contributor to sediment transport from bare mineral-soil areas to small streams throughout the mountainous areas of western North America.

In areas where extensive channel ice is formed, freezing supercools the water, producing nuclei of "frazil ice" particles (spicules and thin plates of ice suspended in the water) and anchor ice around stones and gravel particles along the channel bottom (Gilfilian et al. 1973; Michel 1973). Ice begins to form along stream banks in areas of nonturbulent flow. Through accumulation of frazil ice along the rough streamside edges of the initial (static) ice, slush and ice flows eventually form a continuous ice cover.

Anchor ice forms along the channel bottom from the accumulation of frazil ice particles on the rough surfaces of coarse bottom sediments and on the lee sides of pebbles, cobbles, and boulders. During ice formation, anchor ice frequently breaks loose from the bottom and is carried, with gravel and coarse bottom sediments still attached, to the surface downstream. The resulting disruption of channel-bed sediments may disturb or destroy spawning and incubation areas and cause extensive redistribution and downstream transport of bottom materials.

Wide, shallow streams are more susceptible to anchor-ice formation than are deep, narrow ones because supercooled water develops more rapidly. There is also a tendency for anchor ice to form more readily in uncanopied stream sections where more rapid cooling can occur. This latter effect may be offset if enough snow accumulates to insulate the stream before temperatures drop too low; channel icing then tends to be less severe in openings than in canopied areas with less snow.

In small streams subject to extensive channel-ice formation, the conversion of water to ice removes a substantial volume of water from winter streamflow. Kane and Slaughter (1973) estimated that winter icing of Gold Stream—a stream near Fairbanks, Alaska, that is used by anadromous fish—locks up nearly 40% of the winter streamflow. Habitat changes from these icing conditions can range from lowering of intragravel water temperatures and freezing of near-surface eggs to dewatering of spawning gravels and mechanical destruction of any eggs or alevins contained in the gravel. Also, ice jams that form during freeze-up can cause flooding that diverts flow into side channels, scours spawning reaches, and redistributes woody debris. This could seriously reduce suitable habitat for overwintering fish in these colder environments.

The breakup of ice cover in the spring generally follows melting of the seasonal snow pack, when rising water in the channel cracks the ice by vertical hydrostatic pressure; the resultant blocks and plates of ice are carried downstream as ice flows. The movement of these flows is intermittent and jerky, resulting in periodic damming and flooding of low areas near the channel, extensive gouging and mechanical erosion of the channel banks, and transport and redistribution of bottom gravels. During this period, side-channel overwintering areas are again subject to disruption, and extensive alterations to spawning habitat can occur.

Summary

The natural processes and modifying events described in this chapter may operate separately or in combination to create limiting habitat characteristics in a particular stream section or system. Human activities in the stream and its parent watershed may profoundly affect these events, their frequency, and their magnitude. These modifying influences are discussed in detail in subsequent chapters.

A firm understanding of the natural physical processes that interact to control habit conditions is thus essential if we wish to improve salmonid habitat quality and effectively limit quality reductions resulting from forest and rangeland management practices. Critical to this understanding is a knowledge of the events and processes leading to significant habitat change.

Streamflow, channel configuration, the quantity and distribution of materials in the channel, and the frequency and rate of delivery of sediment and organic debris to the stream system control the viability of a stream for fish habitat. Storm flows and landslides are the dominant random events that cause physical habitat change. In addition, certain accessory events and processes may significantly influence habitat conditions. These processes include windstorms, wildfire, activities of animals, and infestations of insects and disease, which influence woody debris and sediment input to forest channels; and freezing and ice formation, which alter the timing and extent of debris movement through the channel system.

Chapter 6

Timber Harvesting, Silviculture, and Watershed Processes

T. W. Chamberlin, R. D. Harr, and F. H. Everest

Waters in forested lands of western North America are major producers of anadromous salmon and trout. The size of the fishery resource is large, but it is diminishing as a result of human activities and currently is only a fraction of its original size. Western forested watersheds also produce an array of other natural resources, including a variety of wood products. Areas that produce both timber and salmonids coincide over much of western North America (Figure 6.1), and the increasing public demand for both of these resources creates frequent management conflicts. Under most circumstances, both timber and fish can be successfully managed in the same watershed if measures to protect water quality and fish habitat are carefully coordinated with timber management operations.

This chapter is confined to the effects of timber management activities on stream ecosystems, particularly streams with anadromous salmonids. Lakes and estuaries are also vital to the life cycle of many anadromous salmonids, but consideration of those realms is left to other authors (e.g., Tschaplinski 1988).

Timber management activities discussed in this chapter include felling and yarding of trees, site preparation by burning or scarification, fire hazard reduction, forest regeneration by planting or seeding, reduction of competition by brush removal and tree thinning before commercial harvest, and some effects of road building on the hydrologic and sediment systems discussed in the chapter. Other chapters of this book treat road building (Furniss et al. 1991) and forest chemicals (Norris et al. 1991) in detail.

Numerous models allow the standing crop of fish to be estimated from habitat variables. Fausch et al. (1988) reviewed 99 models of various types, and Hicks et al. (1991, this volume) summarize the response of salmonids to changes in habitat. The diverse habitat requirements of many salmonids are discussed in this volume by Bjornn and Reiser (1991). We will concentrate, therefore, on how timber management influences hydrologic and sediment transport processes and thereby affects the amount and quality of flowing water, gravel substrates, cover, and food supplies required by all salmonid species.

Relations between Timber Management and Salmonid Habitat

Because the several species and life phases of salmonids have diverse habitat requirements, streams that support them productively must sustain a varied complex of hydraulic and geomorphic conditions (Sullivan 1986) that are distrib-

181

Influences of Forest and Rangeland Management on Salmonid Fishes and Their Habitats
American Fisheries Society Special Publication 19:181–205, 1991

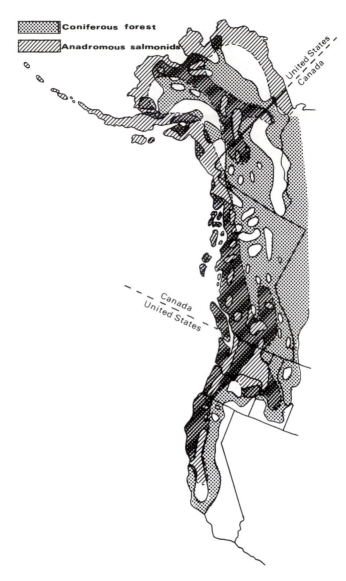

FIGURE 6.1.—Areas of timber and anadromous salmonid production in western North America.

uted along the stream continuum (Vannote et al. 1980). The close relation between watershed (basin) properties and stream characteristics has been repeatedly emphasized (Lotspeich 1980), and serves as a good approach for understanding how forest management influences fish habitat.

Figure 6.2 is a conceptual model of the linkages between timber management activities and fish. In this model, the influences of these activities are transmitted through changes in watershed processes and structures that, in turn, modify the habitat elements described by Bjornn and Reiser (1991). Hartman (1988) provided an excellent synthesis of these complex relationships for the watershed of

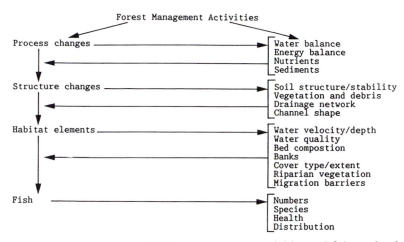

FIGURE 6.2.—Linkages between timber management activities and fish production.

Carnation Creek, British Columbia, and reemphasized the importance of understanding basic watershed processes.

Water plays a central role in watershed processes, but equally important are the sediments it moves and the structure imposed on stream channels by bedrock and the trees, roots, and logs of the riparian ecosystem. The land–water ecosystem must be managed through space and time as an integrated whole if productive fish habitat is to be maintained.

Importance of Small Streams

Salmonids occupy a wide variety of streams that range in size from tiny headwater tributaries to the mainstream Columbia River. Some species even migrate to, and spawn and rear for a while in, first-order streams that may become intermittent or dry in summer.

Most spawning and rearing in forested watersheds, however, takes place in second- to fourth-order streams; coho salmon and trout often are found further upstream than other salmonid species. Such small streams account for the majority of total aggregate stream length available to salmonids in most watersheds.

Even when small streams are not accessible to migrating fish because of barriers or steep gradients, they are vitally important to the quality of downstream habitats. The channels of these streams carry water, sediment, nutrients, and wood debris from upper portions of the watershed. The quality of downstream habitats is determined, in part, by how fast and at what time these organic and inorganic materials are transported.

Small streams are responsible for a high proportion of salmonid production in a basin, and they influence the quality of habitat in larger tributaries downstream. They also are the streams most easily altered by forest management activities. Small streams are intimately associated with their riparian zones and are highly responsive to alterations in riparian vegetation and the surrounding watershed.

Vegetative crown cover is often complete over first- through third-order streams. Because small streams depend largely on litter fall for organic energy input (Murphy and Meehan 1991, this volume), any manipulation of the canopy or streambank vegetation will influence the stream's energy supply. Likewise, road building or other activities that increase sediment supplies or modify local runoff may have greater effects on smaller streams than they would on larger systems.

Although larger streams generally have a greater capacity to buffer the effects of changes to the riparian zone, salmonid fry often preferentially inhabit the lower-velocity margins and back channels of such streams (Ptolemy 1986). Forest harvesting and other land-use impacts can accumulate over time to cause substantial changes in stream-edge environments, even along very large rivers (Sedell and Froggatt 1984).

Hydrologic Effects

Water defines fish habitat more than any other factor does. Hence, changes in the quantity, quality, or timing of streamflow caused by timber harvesting and silviculture are a primary focus for timber–fish interactions. The basic components of the hydrologic cycle—precipitation, infiltration, evaporation, transpiration, storage, and runoff—have been introduced by Swanston (1991) in this volume. Here we discuss how timber management activities influence those components and some of the consequent effects on salmonid habitats.

Regional Variations in Streamflow Response

Regional differences in runoff patterns, ranging from rain-dominated to snow-melt-dominated systems, are illustrated by Swanston (1991). Coastal watersheds with high-elevation ranges may have a mixture of runoff types with gradual transition zones; as one moves from south to north along the Pacific coast, the summer "dry" period becomes increasingly wet.

This regional variability makes it very difficult to generalize about the hydrologic effects of forest management, but can help resource managers to focus on those parts of the hydrologic cycle that will have the most influence on fish habitats in their areas. For example, in rain-dominated coastal systems, frequent high winter floods make the maintenance of side channels a primary habitat protection activity. In interior snow-dominated watersheds, by contrast, management practices to augment low late-summer rearing flows are encouraged.

Regional variation in streamflow behavior will also influence management practices related to sedimentation. In the interior basins, spring breakup and snowmelt are responsible for most of the movement of road and channel sediments, but, along the coast, frequent rains provide sufficient energy to transport material during many months of the year.

In general, forest management activities influence salmonid habitats when they alter the normal regional streamflow pattern at the extremes—that is, by increasing or decreasing the normal levels or occurrences of very high or very low flows. Management actions to manipulate these changes in beneficial directions may be possible, and are furthered by an understanding of how timber harvesting affects each component of the water balance.

Influences on the Water Balance

Timber management activities do not normally change the total amount of precipitation entering a watershed. A possible exception occurs in areas where fog drip from forest foliage adds substantially to water input but is lost when forest vegetation is removed (Harr 1982). Harvesting may, however, substantially alter the spatial distribution of water and snow on the ground, the amount intercepted or evaporated by foliage, the rate of snowmelt or evaporation from snow, the amount of water that can be stored in the soil or transpired from the soil by vegetation, and the physical structure of the soil that governs the rate and pathways by which water moves to stream channels. Within this complex of elements in the water balance, the effects of harvest and silviculture can be grouped into three major categories that form the basis for most runoff analyses: influences on snow accumulation and melt rates; influences on evapotranspiration and soil water; and influences on soil structure that affect infiltration and water transmission rates.

Snow accumulation and melt.—The forest canopy intercepts snowfall, redistributes snow, shades the snowpack, and lowers wind velocities. Harvesting affects these processes in various ways, depending on the temperature, precipitation, and wind patterns characteristic of a region.

In the colder, drier winter climate of the interior, intercepted snow is easily blown from the canopy. During prolonged windless periods, snow may sublimate and be lost from the snowpack.

In warmer, more moist climates of the transient-snow zones, snow is wetter and sticks longer in the forest canopy. Warm air (above 0°C) melts intercepted snow, causing it to reach the ground as meltwater or in wet clumps. Snowpacks under mature forest are thus variable in depth, discontinuous, and wetter than snowpacks in the open (Berris and Harr 1987). Under younger tree canopies, however, snow may be deep because tree branches are more flexible and bend downward, causing snow to slide off onto donut-shaped piles around individual boles (Berris 1984).

Forest openings alter wind patterns and trap snow. Small openings (up to eight tree heights in diameter) trap snow more effectively than large ones, although more snow will be available for melt even in large openings than in forested terrain. In the West Kootenays of British Columbia, snow accumulation in openings up to 42 tree heights in diameter was 37% greater than in the forest and melted 38% faster (Toews and Gluns 1986). Troendle and King (1985) found that peak snow water equivalent (depth of water that results when snow melts completely) averaged 9% higher, and peak snowmelt flows averaged 20% greater, after a forest was logged in small patches.

In dry interior climates, the rate at which snow melts from openings depends principally on energy from shortwave solar radiation (i.e., sunshine). Hence, the loss or creation of shade patterns can significantly affect the rate of melt and the timing of runoff peaks. During cloudy, rainy, and windy weather characteristic of winter storms on the Pacific coast, in contrast, sunshine is a minor heat source for melt compared to the convective transfer of sensible and latent heat from moist air to the snowpack. When rain falls on snow, the melt rate increases in proportion to the wind speed and the air temperature (U.S. Army Corps of Engineers 1956).

Forest harvesting that opens up stands to stronger winds can thus increase the melt rate. For example, Harr (1986) and Berris and Harr (1987) found that more heat was available to melt snow in a recent clear-cut than in an adjacent old-growth Douglas-fir stand during a rain storm of an intensity that recurs at roughly 2-year intervals. The greater amount of heat, coupled with 2–3 times more water in the snowpack, resulted in 22% more water (rain plus snowmelt) flowing from the clear-cut than from the forested plot. Likewise Golding (1987) documented a 13.5% increase in peak winter storm flows after only 19.2% of a coastal British Columbia watershed was clear-cut.

Whether increased water outflow from a logged site causes an increase or a decrease from the whole basin depends on where the site is with respect to other elevations, aspects, and distances from the channel mouth. Shallow snow in the transient-snow zones melts and runs off fairly quickly during rain storms, for example, but deeper snowpacks such as those in the Sierra Nevada may not translate melt into runoff changes as directly (Kattelmann 1987). In the snow zone, models such as those of Leaf and Brink (1973) and Kattelmann (1982) can help forest managers design logging plans that synchronize or desynchronize the runoff of snowmelt at different locations in a basin, and thereby contribute to fishery management objectives.

In the transient-snow zones of the Pacific coast, the effects of harvest on runoff are variable and not well documented, primarily because the montane relief and meteorology are themselves so variable. Still, plot studies on both small and large paired watersheds have shown increases in the size of peak flows after logging (Harr and McCorison 1979; Christner and Harr 1982; Harr 1983), suggesting that timber harvests can affect fish habitat in these areas as well.

Influences on evapotranspiration and soil water.—Clear-cutting, shelterwood cutting, or thinning eliminates or reduces a substantial area of leaves and stems that would otherwise intercept precipitation and allow it to be evaporated when sufficient energy was available. Likewise, fewer tree roots reduce the amount of water that would otherwise be extracted from the soil and hence be unavailable for streamflow. These two factors cause soil water content (and sometimes groundwater) and runoff to be higher in logged than in unlogged areas, and the effect increases as the percentage of stems removed increases. When stands are only thinned, the residual stand may increase its use of water (Hibbert 1967), so changes in streamflow following thinning are likely to be less than might be expected from counts of trees alone.

Table 6.1 shows some examples of changes in annual runoff that have been observed after timber harvesting. The increases have been largest (in absolute terms) during the growing season, when substantial precipitation also occurs. In western Oregon, the greatest portion of the annual increase occurred during the early part of the fall–winter rainy season, when rain rapidly filled the soil pores in cleared areas and then had to run off as surface flows (Rothacher 1971; Harr et al. 1979). Later in the rainy season, even soils under mature canopies became saturated, so runoff from logged and unlogged areas was roughly the same.

These generalizations apply to clear-cut areas that have not been further disturbed by roads, yarding, or burning, and that are not subject to major rain-on-snow events. Compounding effects of such physical disturbances are discussed in the next section.

TABLE 6.1.—Examples of changes in annual runoff after timber harvest. (From Hibbert 1967.)

Location	Species	Treatment	Increase in water yield in the first year (%)
Coweeta, North Carolina	Hardwoods	100% clear-cut	40
Coweeta, North Carolina	Hardwoods	35% selective	40
H. J. Andrews, Oregon	Conifers	40% clear-cut	[a]
Wagon Wheel Gap, Colorado	Mixed	100% clear-cut	22
Fool Creek, Colorado	Conifers	40% clear-cut	30

[a] Small increase in low flow.

Increased late-summer or fall runoffs can increase available fish habitat. They may also moderate the increases in stream temperature that result from removal of shade vegetation. Summer flows have doubled and tripled immediately after clear-cutting and broadcast burning of logging slash in small watersheds (Rothacher 1971; Harr et al. 1979), although increases were short-lived. Rapid regrowth of riparian vegetation may reduce summer streamflows below prelogging levels (Harr 1983).

Increases in soil water content and groundwater levels can indirectly affect fish habitat in other ways. On logged hill slopes, moist soil is vulnerable to mass movements (O'Loughlin 1972; Swanston 1974). On the other hand, higher groundwater levels after harvesting may expand the area of floodplain habitats accessible to fish, particularly during summer low-flow periods (Hetherington 1988).

Influences on soil structure.—The third group of influences that timber harvesting and silviculture can have on the water balance involves the entry of water into soil and its downslope movement to streams. Most undisturbed forest soils can accept water much faster than normal rates of rainfall or snowmelt (Dyrness 1969; Harr 1977), and virtually all water that reaches such soils enters them and follows subsurface routes to stream channels. Substantial surface runoff occurs only when storms are unusually heavy or rainy seasons are especially long, as noted above for western Oregon.

Forest management activities that disturb the soil such as road building, yarding, burning, or scarification can alter the pathways water takes to stream channels, and hence increase (or decrease) the volume of peak streamflows. Soil can be compacted by logging equipment (Greacen and Sands 1980) or by logs dragged over the ground during yarding and site preparation (Dyrness and Youngberg 1957). When surface soils are exposed, their pores can be clogged by fine sediment and their structure can be broken down by the energy of falling raindrops (Lull 1959). If the infiltration capacity of the soil is sufficiently reduced, water runs off over rather than through the soil. Higher peak flows and increased sediment transport result.

In general, yarding exposes the least amount of soil when it is done with balloons or helicopters, and the most when logs are skidded with tractors (Figure 6.3). In steep terrain, high-lead cable yarding has disturbed soils over

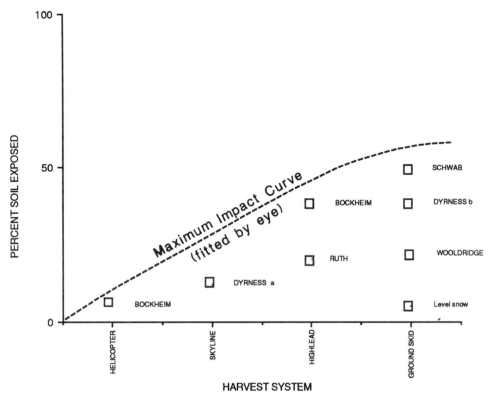

FIGURE 6.3.—Areal extent of mineral soil exposed by alternative yarding techniques. Squares represent empirical studies by the authors indicated and the well-known protection afforded soils by snow cover. Logs moved by helicopter and skyline cables do not touch the ground during transportation. In high-lead yarding, one end of a log is suspended from an overhead cable and the other end drags along the ground. Ground-skidded logs are dragged full length over the terrain. References: Bockheim = Bockheim et al. (1975); Dyrness a = Dyrness (1967b); Dyrness b = Dyrness (1965); Ruth = Ruth (1967); Schwab = Schwab (1976); Wooldridge = Wooldridge (1960).

30–60% of the logged areas (Smith and Wass 1980); on flat terrain or over snow cover, however, even tractor skidding may cause negligible disturbances (Bockheim et al. 1975; Klock 1975). These findings indicate that soil disturbance will be minimized when the harvesting system is well matched to particular site characteristics.

Internal changes in soil structure also take place after logging, as tree roots die, sediment fills soil pores, and compaction occurs. The role of large subsurface pathways in the rapid transmission of water has been shown by Cheng et al. (1975), de Vries and Chow (1978), and Hetherington (1988). The collapse or blockage of these "macropores" forces water to flow over the surface, which may accelerate erosion.

Roads and landings have relatively impermeable surfaces, and water runs off them rapidly. Ditches along roads not only collect surface runoff, they can intercept subsurface flow and bring it onto the surface (Megahan 1972). The effects of roads alone on basin hydrology have not received much study, but there is some evidence that roads can accelerate storm runoff and cause higher peak flows in small basins (Harr et al. 1975, 1979; Harr 1979).

Soil properties on upper slopes are remote from the concerns of most managers of fish habitat. Nevertheless, soil disturbances there usually speed up water movement; if disturbances are extensive, the size of peak flows will increase. Only the maintenance of intact surface and subsurface soil structure can assure "normal" hydrologic behavior. Stream and upland managers, loggers, forest hydrologists, soil scientists, and terrain specialists should consult broadly with one another to avoid introducing long-lasting and undesirable hydrologic changes when trees are harvested anywhere in a watershed.

Summary of water balance influences.—Timber management activities can affect streamflow by altering the water balance or by affecting the rate at which water moves from hillsides to stream channels. The more severe an alteration of the hydrologic cycle is, the greater the effect on streamflows, and hence on fish habitats, will be.

Changes in flow condition depend on many factors. The expected effects of soil disturbance on flow dynamics are illustrated in Figure 6.4. Another aid for analyzing the net effect of timber harvesting is the "water resources evaluation of non-point silvicultural sources" (WRENSS: U.S. Forest Service 1980a). Discussions by Isaacson (1977) and Toews and Gluns (1986) also are helpful in this regard.

Beyond the semiquantitative modeling techniques that must be calibrated to the characteristics of a specific watershed, the following broad generalizations usually apply.

• Harvesting activities such as roadbuilding, falling, yarding, and burning can affect watershed hydrology and streamflow much more than can other management activities such as planting and thinning.

• Clear-cutting causes increased snow deposition in the openings and advances the timing and rate of snowmelt. The effect lasts several decades until stand aerodynamics approach those of the surrounding forest. Snowmelt can be accelerated by the large wind-borne energy inputs of warm rain falling on snow.

• Harvested areas contain wetter soils than unlogged areas during periods of evapotranspiration and hence higher groundwater levels and more potential late-summer runoff. The effect lasts 3–5 years until new root systems occupy the soil.

• Road systems, skid trails, and landings accelerate slope runoff, concentrate drainage below them, and can increase soil water content.

• Hydrologic models such as WRENSS help predict the net effect of a harvesting pattern and sequence on runoff, but each basin must be analyzed to ensure that the most important hydrologic processes are understood.

Influences on Water Quality

The principal water quality variables that may be influenced by timber harvesting are temperature, suspended sediment, dissolved oxygen, and nutrients. Elsewhere in this volume, forest chemicals are discussed by Norris et al. (1991), the important role of the riparian zone in controlling energy inputs (temperature

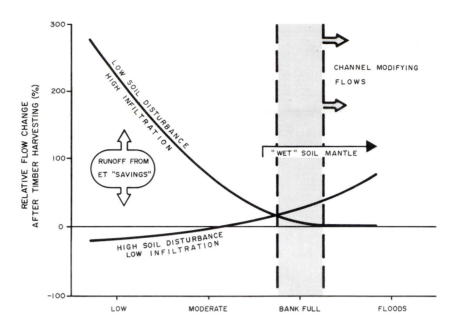

FIGURE 6.4.—Alterations in relative flow after forest harvesting as functions of flow condition when soil disturbances have been small or large. When flow is low, as it may be in late summer, and timber clearance has caused only slight disturbance to the soils, precipitation falling on the soil will infiltrate normally but less will be lost to evapotranspiration (ET) than previously, leaving more water for a sustained augmentation of flow. If soils have been compacted and otherwise disturbed, little rainfall will infiltrate and recharge soil water; most will run off on the surface, causing a transitory peak in flow, and sustained flow will not benefit from an ET "savings." At higher flows, which reflect wetter soil mantles in the watershed, the ET savings become a smaller proportion of the total water budget, so clear-cutting has less relative effect on flow when soil structure remains intact; compacted soils, however, deliver increasing amounts of surface runoff.

and nutrients) is treated by Murphy and Meehan (1991), and the interaction between water quality and fish response is covered by Hicks et al. (1991).

Temperature.—Solar energy is the largest component of energy available to warm stream water in summer. When streamside vegetation is removed, summer water temperatures usually increase in direct proportion to the increase in sunlight that reaches the water surface. Water has a high heat capacity, so a stream's volume, depth, and turbulence affect the actual temperature at any point in the water column. Forest harvesting can cause mean monthly maximum stream temperatures to increase as much as 8°C and mean annual maxima to rise 15°C (Brown and Krygier 1970), but specific stream and watershed conditions cause wide variation in the processes affecting temperature increases (see Beschta et al. 1987 for a comprehensive review).

Figure 6.5 suggests that smaller streams have a greater potential for increases in temperature from streamside harvesting than do larger streams, because a greater proportion of their surface areas will be newly exposed to the sun. However, they may be shaded by smaller trees or deciduous vegetation. Planned openings along

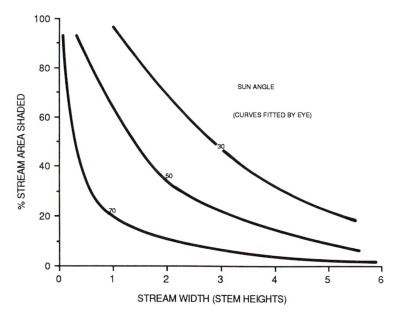

FIGURE 6.5.—Percentage of stream area shaded as functions of stream width and latitude or season. Stream width is indicated as multiples of the height of the prevailing riparian vegetation. Latitude or season is indexed by the noon angle of the sun above the horizontal.

cold coastal streams might enhance fish productivity if other habitat requirements were maintained. In this as in other habitat manipulations, however, caution is required because modest changes in water temperature can change the time required for salmonid eggs to develop and hatch (Holtby 1988a). In northern areas, removal of over-stream coniferous vegetation may lower winter stream temperatures because a net outward energy flow may result, causing slower egg development, deeper surface ice, and bottom-ice formation on gravels. Further, if logging leads to a higher groundwater table in the valley bottom, this will influence the thermal regime of flows in winter (Hetherington 1988)—or, indeed, in any season. Only a careful analysis of the energy balance, including groundwater influences, can indicate the likely direction and magnitude of changes in water temperature that forest harvesting will cause. Techniques are available for predicting changes in a stream's heat budget and consequent changes in water temperature (e.g., Brown 1980; Beschta et al. 1987).

Suspended sediment.—Forest harvesting and silviculture can influence suspended sediment concentrations in a variety of ways, all related to the erosion and sedimentation processes discussed earlier. Most streams carry some sediment, and the amount varies seasonally, but we are most concerned with forest management activities that substantially change the magnitude, timing, or duration of sediment transport and overwhelm the ability of salmonids to cope with or avoid the resulting stress.

Poorly designed roads and skid-trail systems are persistent sources of sediment, but so are open slopes whose soils have been exposed by yarding activities, mass movements, scarification, or intense fire. In cold climates, removal of insulating vegetation promotes formation of ice lenses in and frost heaving of soils, facilitating soil movement during spring thaws (Slaney et al. 1977).

Few studies have identified the component of suspended stream sediments originating from harvesting activity alone (without road influence). Some have illustrated that careful, well-planned logging can take place without appreciable sediment production (Packer 1967), whereas others have documented very high sediment levels (Reinhart et al. 1963) as a result of unplanned activity. Furniss et al. (1991) discuss in more detail the very important role that roads have in sediment production.

We cannot overemphasize the importance of maintaining the integrity of the riparian zone during harvest operations. In addition to disturbing surface soil, activities near the stream bank may destabilize channel margins, releasing sands that settle in and clog the streambed gravels (Scrivener 1988a).

Dissolved oxygen.—Concentrations of dissolved oxygen in intergravel spaces may be reduced if fine organic debris accumulates on and in the streambed. The high chemical and biological oxygen demands of such debris and the bacteria on it may persist for long periods until the bottom material is removed by high flows. Logging and skidding near or across small streams obscured by snow are particularly likely to contribute fine organic debris to watercourses during spring runoffs.

Clogging of surface gravels by fine inorganic sediments can restrict intergravel flow enough to lower dissolved oxygen concentrations. This problem usually occurs only when large or persistent volumes of sediment emanate from active road systems, mass soil movements, bank slumps, or destabilized upstream channels (Scrivener and Brownlee 1989).

During extremely low flows, dissolved oxygen concentrations decline in streams (Bustard 1986). Turbulent exchange of gases with the air decreases. Fish and other respiring organisms—including those associated with organic debris—become concentrated in a few channels and in pools that are nearly or completely isolated. If channels are aggraded and pools shallow, the reservoir of dissolved oxygen is small. In summer, high temperatures both accelerate respiration and lower the solubility of oxygen. In winter, ice cover may prevent diffusion of oxygen from air to water. Harvest activities that impose large oxygen demands on streams exacerbate the normal stresses that low flows place on fish.

Nutrients.—Concentrations of inorganic nutrients (e.g., N, P, K, Ca) in streams may increase after logging, but usually by moderate amounts and for short periods (Fredriksen 1971; Scrivener 1982). Likewise, 5- to 10-fold increases in nutrient releases after slash burning have shown rapid returns to earlier levels. The mobilization of nutrients is tempered by their adsorption onto soil particles and by their uptake by microorganisms that decompose stream detritus (Murphy and Meehan 1991).

Streams in which algal production is limited by a particular nutrient (e.g., phosphorus) may have major algal blooms in response to minor increases of that nutrient, if temperature and flow conditions permit. These blooms can harm salmonid production if their remnants settle into interstitial gravel space. For this reason, forest fertilizers, like pesticides, should not be applied within buffer strips along streams.

Effects of Harvests on Erosion and Sedimentation

Forest harvest activities can influence both upland erosional processes and the way that forest streams process sediment in their channels. The degree of influence varies with geology, climate, vegetation, dominant geomorphic processes, and land uses (H. W. Anderson 1971). The episodic climatic history of western basins over hundreds or thousands of years also makes time an important consideration in the analysis of forestry practices (Benda et al. 1987).

Sediments entering stream channels can affect channel shape and form, stream substrates, the structure of fish habitats, and the structure and abundance of fish populations. In the following discussion, we assume that the goal of forest managers is to maintain streams in their "normal" configurations by minimizing changes in the amount of sediment entering and passing through the systems. Although natural stream processes vary substantially from year to year, and streams change inexorably with time, stream reaches retain characteristic properties over much longer times than those encompassed by forest management cycles. It is against those basic properties that the effects of harvest practices are measured.

Changes in Erosional Processes

Swanston (1991) discusses in this volume how sediment originates either from surface erosion of exposed mineral soil or from mass movements such as landslides, debris torrents, slumps, and earthflows. Furniss et al. (1991) add to the discussion of road-related sediment production.

Surface erosion.—The potential for surface erosion is directly related to the amount of bare compacted soil exposed to rainfall and runoff. Hence, road surfaces, landings, skid trails, ditches, and disturbed clear-cut areas can contribute large quantities of fine sediments to stream channels. Not all hillside sediment reaches the stream channel, but roads and ditches form important pathways. For example, gravel-surfaced logging roads increased sediment production by 40% when they were heavily used by logging trucks (Reid and Dunne 1984). In the Clearwater River basin of Washington, the amount of material less than 2 mm in diameter that washed off roads equalled the amount produced by landslides and has contributed to poor gravel quality for spawning coho salmon.

The quality of management planning strongly influences sediment production from forest-harvesting activity, as illustrated by the classic study of Reinhart et al. (1963) on the Fernow Experimental Watershed, West Virginia. Sediment production varied over 3 orders of magnitude according to the degree of planning and care with which the skidder logging was conducted.

As a general rule, surface erosion results from the exposure of mineral soil, and, as we discussed under soil structure above, it is minimized by the use of yarding systems that are well matched to the terrain and soil types. Packer (1967) reviewed several additional examples and concluded that the best erosion control practices are to avoid operations in very wet seasons, to maintain vegetative buffer zones below open slopes, to skid over snow, and to ensure prompt revegetation.

Silvicultural activities that require scarifying the ground or burning can increase sediment production if buffer strips are not left between treated areas and stream channels. Even when burns do not expose mineral soil, a water-repellent layer can form and reduce the ability of water to infiltrate into the soil (Krammes and DeBano 1965; Bockheim et al. 1973), increasing the runoff available for surface erosion.

An indirect effect of burning is loss of the insulating layer of organic matter. In northern latitudes where soils freeze or permafrost occurs, modifying the freeze–thaw relationship can have serious and long-lasting effects on soil structure and sediment production.

Mass movements.—Mass movement of soil is the predominant erosional process in steep high-rainfall forest lands of Oregon, Washington, British Columbia, and Alaska. The frequency of mass erosion events in forested watersheds is strongly linked to the type and intensity of land treatment in the basin (Rood 1984). Although most mass movements are associated with roads and their drainage systems, many originate on open slopes after logging has raised soil water tables and decreased root strengths (O'Loughlin 1972).

The increase in mass soil movement due to clear-cutting varies widely, ranging from 2–4 times in Oregon and Washington (Ice 1985), to 31 times in the Queen Charlotte Islands of British Columbia (Rood 1984). An increase of up to 6.6 times found by Howes (1987) in the southern Coast Mountains of British Columbia is probably closer to the norm. Although this is much lower than the increases associated with roads, the greater total area of clear-cuts may balance the net result on a weighted-area basis (Swanson and Dyrness 1975).

Much can be done to identify slopes susceptible to mass movements through the use of aerial photography and engineering analyses (Swanson et al. 1987). Howes (1987) developed a procedure—based on terrain mapping and slide occurrence—for quantitatively predicting landslide susceptibility after harvesting. It is usually impossible to harvest unstable hillsides without increasing mass movements, however, except perhaps when careful selective logging with helicopter yarding can be done.

When soils are mass-wasted into stream channels, their effects on salmonid habitats depend on the sediment-processing capability of the stream. They might be beneficial if they bring stable rubble and woody debris complexes to "sediment-poor" channels (Everest and Meehan 1981b). Many mass movements bring soil to higher-gradient reaches, however, and the sediment is carried downstream to a deposition zone where it severely impairs the stream's ability to support fish rearing and spawning.

Remedial measures are available to correct surface erosion problems, but they are costly and far from perfect. Correcting the effects of accelerated mass movements may require tens or hundreds of years, because it involves replacement of stable root systems and the creation of new soil. Measures to accelerate revegetation in severely disturbed areas should include planting deciduous trees, shrubs, and grasses; hydroseeding; and mechanically stabilizing gully systems (Megahan 1974; Heede 1976; Swanston 1976; Carr 1985).

Changes in Sediment Processing by Forest Streams

Sediment transport in forest streams involves the detachment and entrainment of sediment particles, their transport, and their deposition. The process repeats whenever flow velocities are high enough to move the stream's available material.

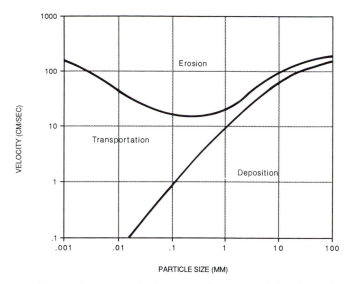

FIGURE 6.6.—Effects of water velocity on sediment particle sizes that are eroded, transported, and deposited in streams. The upper curve indicates the minimum velocities that erode particles of various sizes. Particles of 0.1–1 mm in diameter are the easiest to erode; smaller particles pack more tightly and are bonded by molecular forces, and the mass of larger ones makes them harder to move. The lower curve indicates the minimum velocities that keep particles moving once they already are in motion.

Forest harvesting directly affects these processes when it increases (or decreases) the supply of sediment, when it alters the peak flow or the frequency of high flows, and when it changes the structure of the channel by removing the supply of large woody debris that forms sediment storage sites (Megahan 1982). Bank erosion and lateral channel migration also contribute sediments if protective vegetation and living root systems are removed (Scrivener 1988a).

When additional fine sediments are placed in transport, the intrusion or infiltration of some of the particles into relatively clean or porous surface layers of streambed gravels occurs (Beschta and Jackson 1979). If the source persists, increased amounts may settle deeper into the streambed (Scrivener 1988a) and have longer-lasting effects on egg and fry survival (Hartman et al. 1987).

If the resupply of small sediments from upstream sources is reduced, such as below a debris jam, the gravels become more coarse. In the case of drastic losses of sediment supply, such as below a dam or road sediment trap, downcutting of the channel can occur (Church and Kellerhals 1978).

In streams with gravel beds, most bedload transport takes place during the few ''channel-modifying'' flow days of each year (see Figure 6.6). Analyses of the hydrologic effects of harvesting on sediment movement and channel change in these streams must focus on whether or not the frequency of such flows will be increased or decreased by the proposed harvest pattern.

Effects of Harvests on Channel Forms and Geomorphic Processes

The fluvial environment is part of a larger watershed ecosystem that includes the floodplain, living vegetation and root systems, and organic debris in and adjacent to the channel. Fish habitats result from a complex interaction among water, sediment, and channel structure. Forest management can affect all of these components, as well as the hydrologic and sediment transport processes discussed above.

Integrating Hydrology, Sediment, and Channel Structure

To anticipate the effects of forest management on fish habitats, one must project changes in the hydrologic and sediment processes against the structural framework of the channel. No single technique exists for this very complex task, although component models have been attempted (e.g., Simons et al. 1982; Sullivan et al. 1987). Descriptive studies, such as the Carnation Creek watershed study in British Columbia (Hartman et al. 1987; C. D. Harris 1988), have shown the results of integrated changes, but quantitative prediction remains difficult because of wide variability in forest streams and a general lack of data. Nevertheless, some important interactions among geomorphic processes are understood, and at least the qualitative magnitude and direction of harvesting effects can be anticipated. For example, streams in which structural elements such as embedded logs have been removed have lost stored sediment to downstream reaches and have generally degraded. When there are fewer "steps" in the stream's profile, more energy is released to move sediment, resulting in a simpler, higher-gradient channel with poorer salmonid habitat. Bisson et al. (1987) extensively reviewed the hydrologic role of large woody debris in channels.

Channel environments are very broadly of two types: alluvial channels, whose form is controlled by a balance between flow regime and the sediments of the valley bottom; and bedrock-controlled channels, whose form is dictated by external structure (bedrock). In both types of channel, large woody debris and tree roots can be secondary controlling structures.

Forest harvesting can affect alluvial systems by weakening channel banks, removing the source of large woody debris, altering the frequency of channel-modifying flows, and changing sediment supply. Unlike bedrock-controlled channels, the alluvial system must change its form in response to geomorphic changes until a new balance between aggradation and degradation has been achieved (Leopold et al. 1964). In alluvial channels, both the removal of bank vegetation and increased sediment supply cause channels to become wider and shallower with fewer pools and more riffles.

Channels with more structural control, such as bedrock in the streambed or banks, large tree root systems in the banks, or armor layers (large rocks), are more stable with respect to fluctuations in flow and sediment supply, and maintain narrower and deeper channels. Even very stable channels can be radically modified, however, by the catastrophic effect of debris torrents.

Off-channel fish habitats in the floodplain such as side and flood channels, ponds, and swamps also can be strongly influenced by forest harvesting. Even in large rivers such as the Willamette River in Oregon, the loss of debris jams and related multiple floodplain channels has vastly reduced channel and shoreline area (Sedell and Froggatt 1984; Figure 6.7).

A special case of side channels occurs in glacial systems, where the clear-water sections fed by groundwater or valley-wall runoff provide the only nonturbid

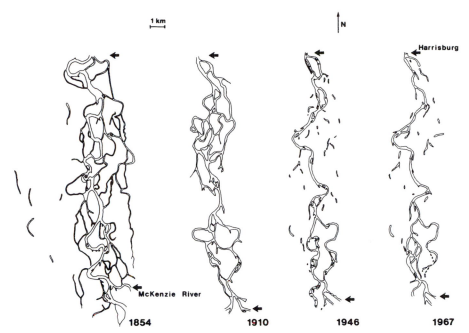

FIGURE 6.7.—Changes in the Willamette River channel, 1854–1967. Arrows show the locations of Harrisburg (top) and the McKenzie River tributary (bottom) in each panel.

habitat in the reach. These habitats are extensively used by rearing chinook salmon fry, and may be important for other species.

Geomorphic processes act over both time and space. If watershed erosion increases, for example, the "new" sediments may persist for long periods as they move through the system under the influence of different streamflows and form alluvial fans, bars, low terraces, sediment wedges behind stable woody debris, or even the streambank or floodplain itself (Hogan 1986). Hence, modifications to a stream system introduced in the early road-building phases of forest harvesting may have to be dealt with decades later when planning begins for the harvest of second-growth timber.

The interactions of hydraulic force, sediment, and channel structure result in geomorphic forms and features that, to a salmonid, are its habitat. We can interpret the hydraulic geometry of stream channels within the framework of fish habitat preferences (Sullivan 1986), and it is useful to focus on these habitat elements as a means of clarifying forest management influences on streams.

Channel Forms and Fish Habitat

Biologists describe stream habitats in terms such as pools, riffles, spawning gravel, obstructions, and side channels, and many classifications are available (e.g., Bisson et al. 1982; Helm 1985). These terms are also geomorphic entities, derived from the processes described above, and they are selectively influenced by different harvesting activities. We will briefly discuss these five habitat elements in the context of the geomorphic processes that control them.

Pools.—Pools are the result of local scour or impoundment induced by structural controls in the channel or streambank. Pools are areas of high water velocity during peak flows, but at low flow their depth creates a depositional environment for fine sediment. Hence, if timber harvesting increases the supply of fine sediments, these sediments settle preferentially in pools, which become less useful to fish. Similarly, if the structural element causing the pool to exist (such as a log or tree root) is removed, the pool will disappear after the next flood flow. Pools are thus very susceptible to falling and yarding operations that influence the availability of large woody debris in or near the channel margins.

Riffles.—Riffles are bars (sediment deposits) with water flowing over them. Because riffles represent the first material deposited after high flows, they usually contain larger particles (gravel, cobbles, and boulders) than are found elsewhere in the stream. Aggrading streams have more depositional areas, and hence have more riffles. Riffles are food-producing areas, but offer few habitats to small fish. Harvesting activities that increase sediment supplies increase the extent and number of riffles. Removal of instream woody structure steepens the stream gradient and hence increases the average size of particles in the substrate.

Spawning gravel.—Spawning gravel is the sorted product of bed scour and redeposition from which sand and finer material has been removed and transported downstream. The maintenance of good spawning gravel requires that the stream's normal sediment supply contain relatively low amounts of fine material, and that flows be sufficiently high to "sort" out the fines that do accumulate. These conditions are often associated with the hydraulic transition zones between pools and riffles; the more transition zones, the more spawning gravels there will be. Hence, harvesting activities that maximize the number of pool-forming structural elements and minimize the influx of fine sediments will favor the maintenance of spawning gravel.

Obstructions.—Obstructions, or barriers to fish migration, are more often associated with road engineering than with timber harvest alone. Culverts or bridges, for example, can cause water velocities to be greater than the swimming ability of small fish (Dane 1978a; Bjornn and Reiser 1991). Excessive debris accumulation, if plugged by sediment, can also block fish passage. Channel aggradation worsens the problem at low flows because water may move entirely below the surface, preventing fish from passing the affected reach. Natural barriers often reflect regional geologic history—resistant rock strata, volcanic intrusions, faults, former sea levels—and may control the distribution of anadromous species over a broad region.

Side channels.—Side channels occur in the stream's margin, or where water is forced out of the channel into the floodplain. Side channels are alternative channel locations, and will remain stable only if their structural controls (usually tree root systems) remain intact. They are vulnerable to timber harvesting in the riparian zone unless harvesting is done with the greatest of care, and they can easily be isolated by dyking or dredging for flood protection, or by road construction without adequate culverts. Side channels have a direct hydrologic relationship to runoff from the valley walls and to the valley groundwater table, and hence may be influenced by many forest management activities.

Summary of Harvesting Influences on Channels

Four major timber management effects can modify a stream's geomorphic process and forms.

• Substantial increases in peak flows or the frequency of channel-modifying flows from increased snowmelt or rain-on-snow events can increase bed scour or accelerate bank erosion. Quantitative assessments of channel stability (Pfankuch 1975) and an analysis of flows at which normal channel changes begin will help determine whether flow increases may be important.

• Substantial increases in sediment supply from mass movements or surface erosion, bank destabilization, or instream storage losses can cause aggradation, pool filling, and a reduction in gravel quality (Madej 1982). Assessments of initial habitat condition (Binns and Eiserman 1979; Bisson et al. 1982; de Leeuw 1982) and estimates of the natural variability in sediment regime (Swanson et al. 1982b) will assist in determining whether sediment-supply increases will be meaningful.

• Streambank destabilization from vegetation removal, physical breakdown, or channel aggradation adds to sediment supply and generally results in a loss of the channel structures that confine flow and promote the habitat diversity required by fish populations (Forward [Harris] 1984; Scrivener 1988a).

• Loss of stable instream woody debris by direct removal, debris torrents, or gradual attrition as streamside forests are converted to managed stands of smaller trees will contribute to loss of sediment storage sites, fewer and shallower scour pools, and less effective cover for rearing fish.

Cumulative Effects of Forest Harvesting

In earlier sections, we described how hydrologic, sediment, and channel processes can be changed by timber-harvesting activities, and hence can affect salmonid habitats. These processes operate over varying time scales, ranging from a few hours for coastal streamflow response to decades or centuries for geomorphic channel change and hill-slope evolution. They are also distributed spatially over the landscape, progressively influencing more land area as timber management extends within watersheds and across regions. The consideration of how harvesting influences the landscape and fish habitats through space and time is the subject of this section.

Identifying Cumulative Effects

Observing and identifying cumulative effects of timber management on biophysical processes or fish habitats are difficult, not only because of technical complexity but also because few research efforts have been sustained or focused over the necessary time periods. Nevertheless, some studies now help demonstrate cumulative effects of logging on streams, beginning with the Wagon Wheel Gap (Colorado) snow accumulation and melt experiment, started in 1910 (Holscher 1967), and carrying through to the Carnation Creek watershed study (Hartman 1988), which began in 1972.

In addition to long-term watershed studies, several specific research techniques exist to provide information about cumulative effects. These include time-series analysis of historical aerial photography, tree ring and similar vegetative dating techniques, and standard geologic techniques applied to recent sediment deposits. Systematic review of historical media and file reports has helped define management treatments and effects on Pacific Northwest river systems (Sedell and Froggatt 1984).

Finally, synoptic survey designs such as those of the Fish/Forestry Interaction Program in the Queen Charlotte Islands (Poulin 1984) can address cumulative effects by simultaneously examining many watersheds in various stages of forest-harvesting development. A synoptic survey design has been proposed for a major new research initiative by the Pacific Biological Station of the Canada Department of Fisheries and Oceans (I. Williams, personal communication).

Management actions to deal with cumulative effects suffer from constraints other than lack of information. The costs of dealing with cumulative effects often are large and must be borne by agencies or jurisdictions that may be reluctant to act because of poor short-term benefit:cost ratios. The question of future accountability for historical effects on public or private fisheries resources is increasingly important as management responsibility shifts to or from the private sector. The long-term effects of changes in physical processes on fish habitats are also confounded by various intensities of use by commercial and sport fisheries, and by urban and industrial development.

Despite these qualifications, the previous discussions of processes linking timber harvest and silviculture to salmonid habitats suggest five main categories of cumulative effects:

- changes in timing or magnitude of small or large runoff events;
- changes in the stability of stream banks;
- changes in the supply of sediment to channels;
- changes in sediment storage and structure in channels, especially those involving large woody debris; and
- changes in energy relationships involving water temperature, snowmelt, and freezing.

The time frame of these changes, especially in the context of normal forest management planning, defines their "cumulative" nature. The persistence of and recovery from changes in the stream ecosystem form a useful analytical framework for examining typical cases of cumulative effects.

Persistence and Recovery

Although change is a normal feature of stream ecosystems, the amount of change tends to vary within limits that are characteristic of a given stream when flow regime, sediment supply, and channel structure are not perturbed. Biological systems have analogous properties, both in individuals and in populations (i.e., homeostasis).

Geologists have also discovered that some rivers have historically undergone episodes of major sedimentation and erosion associated with hundred- or thousand-year events (Benda et al. 1987) and recent climate changes may have profound effects on channel equilibrium. However, we will consider cumulative effects in the time scale of forest-harvesting activity.

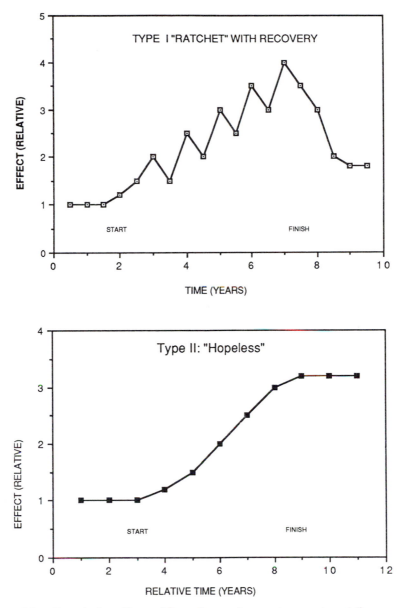

FIGURE 6.8.—Cumulative effects of forest harvesting on streams: type 1 (incremental but reversible changes) and type 2 (irreversible changes).

Foresters and other land managers purposefully impose changes on the ecosystem. We will examine four cases that illustrate different degrees of persistence and recovery. For convenience, they can be classified into two general types, those from which some degree of recovery is possible (type 1) and those from which it is not (type 2). Figure 6.8 graphically illustrates the two types.

Type-1 cumulative effect: incremental change.—Type-1 situations involve management-induced effects that individually are not overwhelming, but that, if compounded, will continue to force the stream into new configurations to the detriment of fish habitat. Type-1 cumulative effects can be corrected if necessary management actions are taken.

The history of forest harvesting in the South Fork Salmon River, Idaho (Platts and Megahan 1975), illustrates a case in which successful recovery occurred. An analysis of this system's history by Sullivan et al. (1987) identified accelerated sedimentation caused by logging and road construction as the source of sediments that gradually inundated pools and degraded gravel quality for spawning fish.

A 12-year moratorium on logging activity, together with watershed rehabilitation measures, allowed the stream to export the fine material; gravel quality was restored and pools were reestablished. The stream was able to recover because sediment input was controlled and because the riparian vegetation remained intact, preserving the structural framework required for normal pool formation and gravel-sorting processes.

Another case of incremental degradation is illustrated by Carnation Creek, British Columbia. In this experimental basin, treatments involving riparian-zone timber removal over a 5-year period, compounded by an upstream debris torrent, have destabilized extensive sections of stream bank and channel (C. D. Harris 1988). In these sections, the channel has widened and established side channels through the adjacent floodplain (Powell 1988). Gravel quality in lower sections of the stream has progressively deteriorated and shows no signs of recovery (Scrivener and Brownlee 1982, 1989).

Recovery in Carnation Creek may be possible if stabilizing riparian vegetation is reestablished, large woody debris is reintroduced to the channel, and sufficient time is allowed to flush accumulated fines from the stream gravels. Time required for recovery will depend on the extent of purposive management actions.

Type-2 cumulative effect: irreversible change.—Type-2 cumulative effects involve changes to the basic watershed processes from which recovery is not possible because of very long time requirements, permanent shifts in social and economic objectives that preclude the required management action, or both.

Sedell and Froggatt (1984) documented the history of the Willamette River from 1854 to 1967. To facilitate transportation and log driving, the river was gradually cleaned of log jams, debris, and streamside trees. Most side channels were logged and cut off, resulting in a much-simplified channel (Figure 6.7) that has vastly reduced shoreline and off-channel habitats. These habitats will never be recovered due to the necessities of navigation and alternative uses of the floodplain land. In some large rivers, however—such as the lower Fraser River, British Columbia— habitat creation to offset industrial alienation may be possible.

A second case of type-2 cumulative effects is illustrated by old-growth timber harvesting adjacent to medium-size or large rivers that depend on very large woody debris. Rivers such as the Yakoun in the Queen Charlotte Islands, British Columbia, depend on spruce log debris 1–3 m in diameter for channel structure and bank stability (de Leeuw 1988). As a result of their loss, the channel is widening and redistributing stored gravel through processes similar to those in Carnation Creek.

Current forest management practices in the Queen Charlotte Islands call for a managed second-growth stand of 80- to 120-year-old trees, so a permanent shift in the size distribution of available large woody debris seems inevitable. This condition is replicated throughout the Pacific Northwest as industrial forests are converted from old-growth to managed stands. Its reversal will depend on implementing a rotation age of 300 or more years for riparian stands. Other resource values (e.g., wildlife and recreation) may contribute to the feasibility of this option in some areas.

These examples clearly show that forest-harvesting activity can have lasting and cumulative effects on fish habitat. Whether the effects can be overcome depends partly on the degree to which stream processes are distorted but more importantly, on the management time scale within which action can be taken. The next section discusses management options to minimize undesirable and maximize desirable effects on salmonid habitat.

Conclusions and Management Options

Management options for ensuring productive fish habitat have evolved considerably over the last 10–20 years as we have learned more about how stream and forest ecosystems function. In this section, we briefly examine the evolution of some successful logging guidelines and then some new directions that may be available for habitat management over the next few decades.

Evolution of Logging Guidelines

In the 1950s and 1960s, planning for fish habitat management took place, if at all, on the streambank, with a biologist and a forester examining the site and using experience and persuasion to arrive at an acceptable management plan. Decisions were usually made with the information at hand for that site, and supported by the policies of the agency with controlling jurisdiction. Much was assumed about what was good or bad, and stream "cleaning" was very popular. Many wheels, both round and square, were reinvented at each "on-site" inspection.

During the 1970s, fisheries agencies became increasingly involved in forest harvest planning and assessment, and began to consolidate and codify approaches to habitat management under various regulatory bodies for forest practices. This had the advantage of encouraging consistency, but the disadvantage of inflexibility with respect to differences among sites and processes. The early "P" or protection clauses used in British Columbia are good examples of guidelines that became inflexible rules (Brownlee and Morrison 1983).

Early guidelines tended to focus on practices that influenced water quality because research on large woody debris and channel geomorphology was not well established. There was considerable reliance on the mitigating influence of the streamside "buffer zone" of arbitrary width (e.g., 10 chains), without reference to the biophysical processes it was influencing. Stream classes, when used (Oregon, Washington), were based on relatively simple criteria such as species "significance" or stream width (e.g., 1 m, 10 m).

During this era, numerous guidelines were developed that specialized in regionally limited procedures for particular forest practices. For example, Packer and Christensen's (1964) classic handbook on how to retard the surface transport of sediment on interior slopes still has application, and many jurisdictions (e.g., Toews and Wilford 1978; Harr 1981) proposed total cut limitations (percentage of watershed) to minimize runoff impacts.

However well intentioned, guidelines tended to become rules and even were incorporated into law in many states. Yet, as we have seen in this chapter, the quality and care with which logging is carried out can have much more bearing on fish habitat quality than what is specified in a planning document. In the 1980s, this knowledge was explicitly recognized in the development of the British Columbia Coastal Fishery/Forestry Guidelines (B.C. Ministry of Forests et al. 1988). In this document, state-of-the-art guidelines are presented as possible means to achieve various defined levels of habitat protection, which, in turn, are related to a stream reach's fishery value. However, the opportunity to devise better ways of meeting these levels of protection is left open to the initiative of the industries and agencies involved. This management philosophy is consistent with two important factors in guideline evolution today: the increasing "privatization" of public resource management responsibilities, and the increasing use of detailed site information and models instead of generalized guidelines.

New Directions

The challenge of resource managers today is both to understand the watershed processes that are important for a given decision and to have enough site information about that watershed to apply the knowledge. This book contributes to the first objective and suggests important types of data that should be gathered, but neither will be of much value without a management framework in which they can be used.

Two important ingredients are necessary to take advantage of *both* knowledge and data. The first is a cooperative attitude between agencies and industry, predicated on commitment from the most senior political levels to the integrated and sustainable management of resources. The second is the development of a technical information infrastructure that makes possible the sharing of knowledge and information *in the planning and decision-making environment*. Both the political and the technical support legs must be in place to move beyond the "spearchucking" days of the not-too-distant past.

Several extensions of current forestry and fisheries management policies have been suggested in previous sections. We list here some that we feel may contribute to the new directions we are seeking.

• *Long rotations.* Large trees have been proven necessary for the maintenance of channel integrity and productivity in most forest streams (Kaufmann 1987). They also contribute to many nonfisheries values. Yet rotation ages of more than 120 years (and much less on high-site land) seem absent from harvesting plans, despite their technical and economic feasibility. Urgent reevaluation of management strategies for remnant old-growth and older second-growth forests seems warranted.

• *Clear-cut stability modeling.* Distributed small-patch cuts have important advantages in some ecosystems, especially where snowpack manipulation is a priority. However, their universal application as a magical panacea, as with "leave strips" (strips of uncut trees between patches) is inappropriate in unstable or windthrow-prone terrain where road construction and edge effects should be minimized. In either situation, stability modeling would provide important management direction, and is almost universally lacking in normal harvest planning.

• *Privatization.*   Some policy analysts (e.g., Pearse 1988) have suggested that the private sector (forest industry) should be given an increased role in the management of fish habitats in exchange for options on the forest resource. This approach offers savings of public management moneys in appropriate jurisdictions, but will be effective only if desired habitat and fishery values can be identified (Platts 1974; Paustian et al. 1983) and an effective performance audit is supported.

• *Regional index streams.*   Very little stream assessment occurs after timber is harvested. Yet the postlogging condition of habitats is the best indicator of adequate harvesting practices. Index streams, considered typical of a regional situation, could be monitored as a check on policy similar to the ambient water quality monitoring of many states and provinces, and the index survey streams of the U.S. Geological Survey. When carried out over several decades (as, for example, in Carnation Creek), these assessments would focus discussion on processes and practices amenable (or not) to change. Without such assessments, most discussions about cumulative effects will remain academic.

• *Accelerated habitat restoration and enhancement.*   In addition to maintaining existing stream habitats, managers need to identify opportunities to restore degraded streams to productive capacity. In most streams this means recreating geomorphic structures and sediment-storage opportunities through techniques such as placing logs or boulders, augmenting off-channel habitats, restoring riparian vegetation, and rebuilding fisheries stocks. A combination of restoration and enhancement measures may be necessary. For detailed examples see Canada Department of Fisheries and Oceans and B.C. Ministry of the Environment (1980) and Bustard (1984).

We conclude this section on management options, as we began the chapter, by suggesting that both timber and fish can be successfully managed in a watershed if timber and fishery managers communicate their needs and coordinate their activities. The technical knowledge base is more than sufficient if the necessary policies and attitudes are in place to support its use.

Chapter 7

Forest Chemicals

L. A. Norris, H. W. Lorz, and S. V. Gregory

Forest chemicals are used to protect or enhance a wide array of forest resources. Their use may have adverse effects on anadromous fish or their habitats. Forest managers, regulatory officials, and the interested public believe strongly that if forest chemicals are used, they must yield significant benefits without imposing unreasonably adverse environmental effects. We review and summarize what is known about the interaction between forest chemicals and salmonid fishes (particularly anadromous populations) and their habitats. Our objective is to provide the reader with a scientific basis for making informed, technically sound decisions about the use of these important management tools with respect to salmonids and their habitats.

Use of Chemicals in the Forest

The three major categories of forest chemicals are pesticides,[1] fertilizers, and fire retardants. Many chemicals are used in both agriculture and forestry, but the magnitude, intensity, and patterns of use are markedly different (Table 7.1). The common, chemical, and trade names of forest chemicals used in this chapter are listed in Table 7.2.

Pesticides

Pesticides are defined for regulatory purposes as agents used to prevent, destroy, repel, or mitigate pests. The term pesticide includes many specific chemical substances, which can be grouped according to the type of pest they are intended to control: herbicides, insecticides, fungicides, rodenticides, piscicides, and animal repellents. Although many pesticides are registered by the U.S. Environmental Protection Agency for use in agriculture, fewer than 10 have substantial use in forestry. Forestry uses account for less than 1% of the total pesticides used in the USA.

---

[1]This publication reports research with pesticides. It does not contain recommendations for their use, nor does it imply that the uses discussed here have been registered. All uses of pesticides must be registered by appropriate state and federal agencies before they can be recommended. The use of trade, firm, or corporation names in this publication is for the information and convenience of the reader. Such use does not constitute an official endorsement or approval by the U.S. Department of Agriculture of any product or service to the exclusion of others that may be suitable.

Influences of Forest and Rangeland Management on Salmonid Fishes and Their Habitats
American Fisheries Society Special Publication 19:207–296, 1991

TABLE 7.1.—Comparative annual use of chemicals in agriculture and forestry.

Chemical	Agriculture	Forestry
Pesticides, 1980 (10^3 kg)[a]		
Insecticides	138,924	71[b]
Herbicides	202,030	169[b]
Fungicides	22,700	9[b]
Fertilizers, 1978 (10^3 tonnes)[c]		
Nitrogen	9,636	55
Phosphorus	2,273	5

[a]Agricultural data from Table 3, Pesticide Industry Sales and Usage, 1980 market estimates, U.S. Environmental Protection Agency, Washington, D.C., September 1980; forestry data are only for U.S. Forest Service, National Forest System land, from Table E1, Pesticide-Use Advisory Memorandum 284 (2150 Pesticide-Use Management and Coordination, March 12, 1981), U.S. Forest Service, Washington, D.C.
[b]U.S. Forest Service, National Forest System land only.
[c]Bengtson (1979).

Before fiscal year (FY) 1987 (fiscal years of the U.S. government extend from October 1 of the previous year to September 30 of the year designated), herbicides and insecticides accounted for more than 80% of U.S. Forest Service applications, fumigants and fungicides accounting for most of the rest (Table 7.3). More recently, however (FY 1987, 1989), fumigants and fungicides have accounted for 20% to nearly 50% of total pesticide use; most of these chemicals are used on tree nurseries. The total amount of pesticides used has varied from 137,000 kg (FY 1989) to 502,000 kg (FY 1983). The ratio of herbicide to insecticide applications has changed annually according to the needs for large-scale insect control and to court-imposed restrictions (which have been applied to herbicides since FY 1984). These figures underestimate the total use of pesticides in forestry because they do not include pesticides applied by other U.S. agencies or by state or private forest management groups.

Tables 7.4 and 7.5 give the herbicides and insecticides used on national forests and on other lands through federal assistance programs coordinated by the U.S. Forest Service. Picloram, alone or in combination with other chemicals, and 2,4-D accounted for about 70% of the herbicides applied in FY 1979–1981, but their use had declined to about 18% in 1989, probably because of a court-ordered ban on herbicides in Pacific northwestern states and of a U.S. Forest Service ban on aerial applications of herbicides nationwide. Uses of hexazinone, triclopyr, and glyphosate have increased as their registration has been granted and as experience with these chemicals has expanded. These three chemicals accounted for more than 75% of all herbicides used in FY 1987–1989.

Malathion and carbaryl accounted for nearly all the silvicultural insecticides used in FY 1979–1985, although the use of each has varied widely (Table 7.5). Since then, use of azinphos-methyl, in particular, has increased. *Bacillus thuringiensis*, a bacterial insecticide, is being used increasingly (Table 7.5) to control gypsy moth *Lymantria dispar* and western spruce budworm *Choristoneura* sp. Typical application rates of some forest chemicals are shown in Table 7.6.

Text continues on page 215

TABLE 7.2.—Common, chemical, and trade names of chemicals referred to in text and tables.

Common name	Chemical name	Trade name used in text
Fertilizer	Urea	None
Fire retardants	None	Fire-Trol 100
		Fire-Trol 931L
		Fire-Trol 934L
		Phos-Chek
		Phos-Chek XAR
		Phos-Chek 202R
		Phos-Chek 259R
Herbicides		
2,4-D	2,4-dichlorophenoxyacetic acid (and various esters and salts)	None
2,4,5-T	2,4,5-trichlorophenoxyacetic acid	None
Amitrole	3-amino-1,2,4-triazole	Amitrole-T
Atrazine	2-chloro-4-ethylamino-6-isopropyl-amino-s-triazine	None
Dalapon	2,2-dichloropropionic acid	None
Dicamba	3,6-dichloro-o-anisic acid	None
Dinoseb	2-sec-butyl-4,6-dinitrophenol	None
DSMA	Disodium methanearsonate	None
Fosamine ammonium	Ammonium ethylcarbamoylphosphonate	Krenite
Glyphosate	N-phosphonomethylglycine	Roundup
Hexazinone	3-cyclohexyl-6-(dimethylamino)-1-methyl-1,3,5-triazine-2,4(1H,3H)-dione	Velpar
MSMA	Monosodium methanearsonic acid	None
Picloram	4-amino-3,5,6-trichloropicolinic acid (and various esters and salts)	Tordon 22K Tordon 101 (also contains 2,4-D)
SDMA	Sodium dimethyl arsonate	None
Silvex	2-(2,4,5-trichlorophenoxy)propionic acid	None
Triclopyr	[(3,5,6-trichloro-2-pyridinyl)oxy] acetic acid	Garlon
Insecticides		
Acephate	0,S-dimethyl acetylphosphoramidothioate	Orthene
Azinphos-methyl	0,0-dimethyl-S-[(4-oxo-1,2,3-benzotriazine-3-(4H)-yl) methyl]phosphorodithioate	Guthion
B.t.	Bacillus thuringiensis	None
Carbaryl	1-naphthyl-N-methylcarbamate	Sevin Sevin-4-Oil
Carbofuran	2,3-dihydro-2,2-dimethyl-7-benzofuranyl methylcarbamate	Furadan
Chlordecone	Decachloro-octahydro-1,3,4-metheno-2H-cyclobuta(cd)pentalene-2-one	Kepone
DDT	Dichlorodiphenyltrichloroethane	None
Malathion	0,0-dimethyl-S-(1,2-dicarbethyoxyethyl)phosphorodithioate	None
Methoxychlor	2,2-bis(p-methoxyphenyl)-1,1,1-trichloroethane	None
NPV	Nuclear polyhedrosis virus	None

TABLE 7.3.—Pesticide applications by the U.S. Forest Service during six fiscal years in the period 1979–1989.[a] Dashes mean that no use was reported; empty cells mean data are unavailable.

Pesticide	Hectares	Kilograms (%)	Hectares	Kilograms (%)
	Fiscal year 1989		**Fiscal year 1987**	
Insecticides	67,296	3,702 (2.7)	255,953	106,763 (38.9)
Herbicides	48,597	65,748 (48.0)	60,458	101,484 (37.0)
Fumigants, fungicides	561	67,358 (49.2)	589	64,010 (23.3)
Repellants	10	16 (<0.1)	6,337	1,395 (0.5)
Rodenticides	23,585	154 (0.1)	23,187	689 (0.3)
Wood preservatives	—	—	—	—
Piscicides, predacides	16,766	11 (<0.1)	13,977	29 (<0.1)
Algicides	—	—	—	—
Behavioral chemicals	—	—	—	—
Total	156,815	136,989 (100)	360,501	274,370 (100)
	Fiscal year 1985		**Fiscal year 1983**	
Insecticides[b]	336,398	180,820 (51.5)	199,861	224,767 (44.8)
Herbicides[c]	61,200	126,113 (35.9)	99,174	238,894 (47.6)
Fumigants, fungicides	916	40,782 (11.6)	1,349	34,806 (6.9)
Repellants	6,108	1,984 (0.6)	11,237	1,940 (0.4)
Rodenticides	29,219	1,301 (0.4)	23,349	1,365 (0.3)
Wood preservatives	—	—	—	—
Piscicides, predacides		36 (<0.1)	12,230	135 (<0.1)
Algicides	—	—	7	29 (<0.1)
Behavioral chemicals	—	—	—	—
Total	433,841	351,036 (100)	347,207	501,936 (100)
	Fiscal year 1981		**Fiscal year 1979**	
Insecticides[b]	20,102	14,331 (6.3)	110,247	78,471 (23.2)
Herbicides[c]	79,742	172,741 (76.0)	74,483	213,725 (63.2)
Fumigants, fungicides	1,464	38,720 (17.0)	540	36,861 (10.9)
Repellants	2,517	580 (0.2)	3,845	4,144 (1.2)
Rodenticides	20,857	712 (0.3)	18,179	4,112 (1.2)
Wood preservatives		116 (<0.1)	—	—
Piscicides, predacides	37	13 (<0.1)	97	415 (0.1)
Algicides	3	160 (<0.1)	22	185 (<0.1)
Behavioral chemicals	—	—	919	8 (<0.1)
Total	124,722	227,373 (100)	208,332	337,921 (100)

[a]Fiscal years of the U.S. government begin on October 1 of the previous year and extend to September 30 of the year designated. Data sources are Pesticide-Use Advisory memoranda (2150 Pesticide-Use Management and Coordination) of the U.S. Forest Service, Washington, D.C.; 1989, Memorandum 450 (May 30, 1990); 1987, Memorandum 429 (July 7, 1988); 1985, Memorandum 388 (April 15, 1986); 1983, Memorandum 355 (May 18, 1984); 1981, Memorandum 316 (April 5, 1982); 1979, Memorandum 246 (June 5, 1980).

[b]Proportions of insecticide weights applied from aircraft: 97% in 1985, 96% in 1983, 29% in 1981, 87% in 1979.

[c]Proportions of herbicide weights applied from aircraft: 0% in 1985, 31% in 1983, 30% in 1981, 26% in 1979.

TABLE 7.4.—Herbicide applications by the U.S. Forest Service during six fiscal years in the period 1979–1989. Dashes mean that no use was reported or that use amounted to less than 0.1% of the total weight of herbicides applied. See Table 7.3, footnote a, for data sources.

Herbicide	Hectares	Kilograms (%)	Hectares	Kilograms (%)
	Fiscal year 1989		**Fiscal year 1987**	
Hexazinone	8,670	16,611 (28.6)	23,191	46,233 (47.9)
2,4-D + picloram	4,604	4,012 (6.9)	5,170	4,955 (5.1)
2,4-D	2,115	3,045 (5.2)	4,100	8,333 (8.6)
Glyphosate	3,194	5,456 (9.4)	4,966	6,101 (6.3)
Picloram	3,180	1,238 (2.1)	4,022	2,317 (2.4)
Triclopyr	17,172	22,276 (38.4)	10,987	17,894 (18.6)
2,4-D +2,4-DP	18	42 (<0.1)	53	654 (0.7)
2,4-D + dicamba	1,061	2,479 (4.3)	1,483	3,641 (3.8)
Fosamine ammonium	228	1,743 (3.0)	212	2,056 (2.1)
Dicamba	815	330 (0.6)	916	1,106 (1.2)
2,4-D[a]	90	93 (0.2)	991	1,721 (1.8)
MSMA	63	200 (0.4)	65	229 (0.2)
Atrazine	224	372 (0.6)	39	192 (0.2)
Simazine	2	10 (<0.1)	105	258 (0.3)
Dalapon	—	—	—	—
Ammonium sulfamate	25	102 (0.2)	212	748 (0.8)
Amitrole	—	—	2	5 (<0.1)
Sodium metaborate + sodium chlorate	—	—	—	—
Mineral spirits	3	75 (0.1)	—	—
Total	41,464	58,084 (100)	56,514	96,443 (100)
	Fiscal year 1985		**Fiscal year 1983**	
Hexazinone	21,226	44,195 (36.6)	14,515	30,756 (13.3)
2,4-D + picloram	10,454	16,445 (13.6)	14,031	22,544 (9.7)
2,4-D	6,815	16,128 (13.4)	28,852	73,975 (31.9)
Glyphosate	7,146	12,338 (10.2)	13,010	25,734 (11.1)
Picloram	3,638	11,480 (9.5)	9,308	11,635 (5.0)
Triclopyr	5,694	9,715 (8.0)	3,387	6,244 (2.7)
2,4-D + 2,4-DP	472	2,377 (2.0)	309	2,674 (1.2)
2,4-D + dicamba	901	1,986 (1.6)	800	1,995 (0.9)
Fosamine ammonium	205	1,793 (1.5)	484	3,697 (1.6)
Dicamba	1,030	1,370 (1.1)	1,741	2,822 (1.2)
2,4-D[a]	428	1,272 (1.1)	148	90 (<0.1)
MSMA	312	714 (0.6)	50	144 (<0.1)
Atrazine	215	249 (0.2)	5,217	21,327 (9.2)
Simazine	67	296 (0.2)	869	4,250 (1.8)
Dalapon	98	235 (0.2)	3,339	22,495 (9.7)
Ammonium sulfamate	12	96 (<0.1)	36	849 (0.4)
Amitrole	64	110 (<0.1)	291	881 (0.4)
Sodium metaborate + sodium chlorate	—	—	—	—
Mineral spirits	—	—	—	—
Total	58,777	120,799 (100)	96,387	232,112 (100)

TABLE 7.4.—Continued.

Herbicide	Hectares	Kilograms (%)	Hectares	Kilograms (%)
	Fiscal year 1981		**Fiscal year 1979**	
Hexazinone	1,841	2,942 (1.8)	155	381 (0.2)
2,4-D + picloram	27,988	40,435 (24.7)	23,068	61,374 (29.7)
2,4-D	29,376	65,986 (40.2)	29,724	84,061 (40.6)
Glyphosate	5,054	7,993 (4.9)	1,484	2,649 (1.3)
Picloram	6,147	15,296 (9.3)	6,416	11,316 (5.5)
Triclopyr	—	—	—	—
2,4-D + 2,4-DP	462	1,896 (1.2)	1,276	4,058 (2.0)
2,4-D + dicamba	652	1,552 (0.9)	2,522	6,791 (3.3)
Fosamine ammonium	689	3,036 (1.9)	789	3,601 (1.7)
Dicamba	1,703	2,171 (1.3)	429	637 (0.3)
2,4-D[a]	—	—	—	—
MSMA	380	280 (0.2)	1,440	8,439 (4.1)
Atrazine	2,415	9,854 (6.0)	2,144	8,580 (4.0)
Simazine	345	3,314 (2.0)	1,739	4,503 (2.2)
Dalapon	1,735	5,758 (3.5)	1,716	4,813 (2.3)
Ammonium sulfamate	105	1,361 (0.8)	182	1,588 (0.8)
Amitrole	399	1,058 (0.6)	356	776 (0.4)
Sodium metaborate + sodium chlorate	6	1,093 (0.7)	4	360 (0.2)
Mineral spirits	—	—	36	2,994 (1.4)
Total	79,297	164,025 (100)	73,480	206,921 (100)

[a]Applied in combinations not otherwise listed.

TABLE 7.5.—Insecticides most commonly applied by the U.S. Forest Service during six fiscal years in the period 1979–1989. Dashes mean that no use was reported or that use amounted to less than 0.1% of the total weight of insecticides applied; empty cells mean data are unavailable. See Table 7.3, footnote a, for data sources.

Insecticide	Hectares[a]	Kilograms (%)	Hectares[a]	Kilograms (%)
	Fiscal year 1989		**Fiscal year 1987**	
Malathion	448	251 (8.4)	3,026	149 (2.1)
Carbaryl	2,337	1,958 (65.5)	55	4,911[b] (68.8)
Azinphos-methyl[c]	168	557 (18.6)	279	1,437 (20.1)
Lindane	116	84 (2.8)	12	194 (2.7)
Carbofuran[c]		23 (0.8)		92 (1.3)
Diazanon[d]	62	103 (3.4)	101	91 (1.3)
Acephate	—	14 (0.5)	424	263 (3.7)
Ethylene dibromide[e]	—	—	—	—
Toxaphene[f]	—	—	—	—
Tetrachlorvinphos[f]	—	—	—	—
Bacillus thuringiensis	53,878	2,144,266[g]	75,453	2,441,686[g]
Total	57,009	2,990 (100)[h]	79,350	7,137 (100)[h]
	Fiscal year 1985		**Fiscal year 1983**	
Malathion	241,626	164,781 (91.6)	231	337 (0.2)
Carbaryl	10,220	9,005 (5.0)	188,711	213,205 (95.4)
Azinphos-methyl[c]	478	4,446 (2.5)	36	4,167 (1.9)
Lindane		1,293 (0.7)		327 (0.1)
Carbofuran[c]	9	173 (<0.1)	8	3,321 (1.5)
Diazinon[d]		130 (<0.1)	68	88 (<0.1)
Acephate	—	—	293	293 (0.1)
Ethylene dibromide[e]	—	—		1,740 (0.8)
Toxaphene[f]	—	—		18 (<0.1)
Tetrachlorvinphos[f]	—	—	9	30 (<0.1)
Bacillus thuringiensis	69,898	1,174,998[g]	5,955	78,798[g]
Total	322,231	179,828 (100)[h]	195,311	223,526 (100)[h]
	Fiscal year 1981		**Fiscal year 1979**	
Malathion	3,855	2,202 (19.3)	78,253	42,416 (54.7)
Carbaryl	2,017	2,051 (18.0)	20,711	22,910 (29.6)
Azinphos-methyl[c]		2,917 (25.6)		1,961 (2.5)
Lindane		74 (0.6)	150	140 (0.2)
Carbofuran[c]		2,500 (21.9)		2,481 (3.2)
Diazinon[d]		73 (0.6)	41	56 (<0.1)
Acephate	1,220	1,026 (9.0)	9,470	5,310 (6.9)
Ethylene dibromide[e]		347 (3.0)		1,144 (1.5)
Toxaphene[f]		218 (1.9)		1,041 (1.3)
Tetrachlorvinphos[f]	—	—	13	31 (<0.1)
Bacillus thuringiensis	—	—	—	—
Total	7,092	11,408 (100)	108,638	77,490 (100)

[a]Not all applications were per hectare. For control of seed and cone insects, for example, the pesticide-use memoranda give values as number of trees treated.

[b]The majority was applied to 12,593 individual trees.

[c]Control of seed and cone insects in seed production areas.

[d]Control of insects in forest tree nurseries.

[e]Control of bark beetles on cut logs.

[f]Control of ticks and lice on cattle.

[g]Billion international units (BIU), not kilograms.

[h]Total does not include *Bacillus thuringiensis* use.

TABLE 7.6.—Typical application rates of some forest chemicals.

Chemical	kg/hectare[a]	Method
Herbicides		
2,4-D	1.12–4.48	
Picloram	≤1.12–5.0	
Hexazinone	0.55–3.36	Broadcast
	1.12–2.24	Basal treatment, stem injection
Atrazine	≤4.48	
Triclopyr	0.28–10.0	
MSMA	4.4–288	
Fosamine ammonium	3.36–6.72	
Glyphosate	<4.48	
Dalapon	0.46–7.6[b]	Ground[b]
	5.6–9.6[b]	Aerial[b]
Insecticides		
Malathion	0.8	Aerial
Carbaryl	0.5–2.24	Agriculture
	<1.12	Forestry
Acephate	1.5	
Fertilizers		
Urea-N	168–224[c]	

[a]Active ingredient.
[b]U.S. Forest Service (1984).
[c]Moore and Norris (1974).

TABLE 7.7.—Fire retardant use in the USA.[a]

Year	Quantity used (L)	User group
1956	87,000	All users
1961	28,400,000	All users
1966	22,500,000	U.S. Forest Service
1966	12,200,000	Calif. Division Forestry
1966	3,800,000	Bureau Land Management
1970	64,400,000	All users
1977[b]	56,669,902	U.S. Forest Service
1978[b]	24,371,221	U.S. Forest Service
1979[b]	54,795,771	U.S. Forest Service
1980[b]	39,348,023	U.S. Forest Service
1981[b]	44,712,371	U.S. Forest Service

[a]G. E. Cargill, U.S. Forest Service, Washington, D.C., personal communications, December 14, 1980, and September 21, 1982 (memorandums with attachments).

[b]Fiscal year: October 1 of the previous year through September 30 of the year designated. About 70% of this use is in Oregon, Washington, and California.

Fertilizers

Fertilizers are applied annually to only a small portion of commercial forest land (Table 7.1). Several private and public land-management groups, however, have been applying forest fertilizers for over 20 years, particularly in the northwestern USA where nitrogen deficiencies occur and, to a much lesser degree, in the southeastern states where phosphorus deficiencies may occur. Between 1965 and 1975, about 300,000 hectares of Douglas-fir forests were fertilized in western Oregon and Washington (Moore 1975b). Allen (1987) estimated that by 1986, more than 1 million hectares of Douglas-fir would have been fertilized. Bengtson (1979) and Allen (1987) wrote excellent articles on the use of fertilizers in American forestry.

Fire Retardants

The use of chemical fire retardants increased steadily after they were introduced in the 1930s and varied between 24 and 65 million liters during the 1970s and early 1980s (Table 7.7). Douglas (1974) and Norris et al.[2] summarized most of the literature through the mid-1970s on both the use and environmental effects of chemical fire retardants. Borate salts were the first chemical fire retardants to be widely used. They were effective, long-lasting retardants, but were also potent soil sterilants that retarded establishment and regrowth of vegetation. Bentonite clay suspensions in water have also been used, but they are not as effective as other materials. The chemical fire retardants in common use today are composed primarily of ammonium phosphate or ammonium sulfate and small amounts of several other chemicals such as dyes, wetting agents, thickeners, corrosion inhibitors, and bactericides.

Relation of Chemical Use to Salmonid Habitats

The quality of the water that forested watersheds yield reflects human activities and natural processes. Forest lands are only one-third of the total area of the USA, but they receive more than half of the total precipitation and yield more than three-fourths of the total streamflow. Forested watersheds in the USA on the average receive more than 114 cm of precipitation and yield more than 51 cm of runoff annually, more than seven times the average amounts from other lands (Storey 1965). Clearly, the possibility that chemical use in forest management may alter water quality, or some other aspect of fish habitat, deserves careful consideration.

The chemicals used in forestry may have direct or indirect effects or no effect on salmonids. Direct effects require that the organism and the chemical come in physical contact. Once in contact, the chemical must be taken up by the organism and moved to the site of biochemical action where the chemical must be present in an active form at a concentration high enough to cause a biological effect

---

[2]Unpublished report, "The behavior and impact of chemical fire retardants in forest streams," by L. A. Norris, C. L. Hawkes, W. L. Webb, D. G. Moore, W. B. Bollen, and E. Holcombe. U.S. Forest Service, Pacific Northwest Research Station, Forestry Sciences Laboratory, Corvallis, Oregon, 1978.

A DIRECT CHEMICAL EFFECT REQUIRES:
1. DIRECT PHYSICAL CONTACT WITH THE CHEMICAL.
2. UPTAKE BY THE ORGANISM.
3. MOVEMENT TO THE BIOCHEMICAL
SITE OF ACTION.
4. RESIDENCE AT THE SITE OF ACTION IN
SUFFICIENT QUANTITY AND IN A TOXIC
FORM TO CAUSE AN EFFECT.

FIGURE 7.1.—A direct chemical effect on an organism requires a chain of events.

(Figure 7.1). Direct chemical effects can be evaluated by using traditional concepts of toxicology and dose–response relationships.

Indirect effects result from chemically induced modification of the habitat. Examples of indirect effects are insecticide-induced decreases in the biomass of terrestrial or aquatic insects that result in a decrease in the supply of food for salmonids, and reductions in cover, shade, and sources of food from riparian vegetation as a result of herbicide deposition in a streamside zone.

Direct Chemical Effects

One of the hazards of using chemicals in the forest is the risk of direct adverse toxic effects on nontarget organisms. The two factors that determine the degree of risk are the toxicity of the chemical and the likelihood that nontarget organisms will be exposed to toxic doses. Toxicity alone does not make a chemical hazardous; exposure to a toxic dose must also occur. Therefore, an adequate risk analysis requires equal consideration of both the likelihood of exposure and the toxicity of the chemical (Norris 1971b; Sanders 1979; U.S. Forest Service 1984).

Toxicity

Acute toxicity is the short-term response of organisms to one or a few relatively large doses of chemical administered over a short period of time. Chronic toxicity is the slow or delayed response of organisms to continuous or repeated, relatively small doses of chemical administered over a long period of time. The kind of response (acute or chronic) depends on the magnitude of the dose and the duration of exposure.

Exposure in the Aquatic Environment

Aquatic organisms may come in direct contact with a chemical in water, sediment, or food. The rate and method of application and behavior of the chemical in the environment determine both the level and the length of time any particular chemical will be in one or more of these three compartments.

Chemicals in water.—Chemicals may enter water by one or more of the following routes: direct application, drift, mobilization in ephemeral stream channels, overland flow, and leaching. Each route of entry results in a different level and duration of entry and, therefore, a different magnitude and duration of exposure. The degree to which any particular route of entry operates depends on the nature of the application, characteristics of the chemical, and characteristics of the area treated.

Many forest chemicals are aerially applied from aircraft (Table 7.3, footnotes b and c), although a large proportion of herbicides is applied by ground-based equipment such as hand-held nozzles fed from either high- or low-pressure pumping systems, backpack sprayers, air-blast sprayers, or direct stem-injection equipment; occasionally, pelletized chemical may be scattered by hand. Aerial applications in or near aquatic zones present the greatest probability of introducing chemicals into the aquatic environment by either direct application or drift. Aerial applications away from aquatic zones do not offer any greater opportunity for chemical entry into water than any other type of application. Chemicals that are applied in or near aquatic zones with ground-based equipment can also enter streams by direct application and drift.

Direct application and drift are physical processes that are largely independent of the chemical properties of the material being applied. The principal variables are vertical and horizontal distance between the points of application and the exposed waters, physical characteristics of the material being applied (droplet or pellet size and characteristics of the carrier), atmospheric conditions (wind speed and direction, relative humidity, and temperature), and type of application equipment and its operating characteristics. The concepts, principles, and practice of aerial pesticide application were presented in a series of five papers (by Maksymiuk, Jasumback, McComb, and Witt) in the proceedings of a pesticide applicators' training course (Capizzi and Witt 1971), the proceedings of a workshop on behavior and assessment of pesticide spray application (Roberts 1976), and a U.S. Department of Agriculture (1976) handbook.

Direct application is the route most likely to introduce significant quantities of chemicals into surface waters. It has the potential to produce the highest concentrations and, therefore, cause the most pronounced acute toxic effects. The duration of entry and the subsequent duration of exposure, however, will be brief–a few minutes to a few days (Norris and Moore 1971; Norris 1978). Concentrations that result depend on the rate of application and the stream's ratio of surface area to volume. The persistence of the chemical in surface water in the application zone depends on the length of the stream treated, the velocity of streamflow, and the hydrologic characteristics of the stream channel. The concentration of introduced chemicals normally decreases rapidly with downstream movement because of dilution and the interaction of the chemical with various physical and biological components of the stream system (Norris and Montgomery 1975).

Drift from nearby spray areas is similar to direct application except that peak concentrations are lower and the probability that stream organisms will be affected is reduced. Accidental drift of chemical from nearby spray areas to stream surfaces is a likely means of chemical entry into surface waters, but one that can be minimized through careful selection of chemical formulations, carriers, and equipment, and attention to atmospheric and operating conditions.

Small and ephemeral stream channels are difficult to see from the air and may be sprayed along with the rest of the area. The problems may be more acute during aerial applications because ground applications usually provide greater opportunity for avoiding these areas. Residues remaining in ephemeral stream channels are available for mobilization by the expanding stream system (described by Hewlett and Hibbert 1967) that develops during heavy precipitation. This process probably accounts for increases in chemicals occasionally observed in streams during the first storms after application (Norris 1967; Norris et al. 1982, 1984).

Overland flow occurs infrequently on most forest lands because the infiltration capacity of the forest floor and soil is usually far greater than rates of precipitation (Rothacher and Lopushinsky 1974). Bare and heavily compacted soil may yield surface runoff, but these areas are not widespread and would seldom be treated with forest chemicals.

Leaching of chemicals through the soil profile is a process of major public concern, but it is the least likely to occur in forest environments. Most chemicals used in forestry are relatively immobile in soil. Intense leaching can move chemicals a few centimeters to 1 m in depth, but these distances are short in comparison to distances between treated areas and streams (Norris 1971a). Most forest chemicals do not persist long enough for significant leaching to occur.

The various routes of chemical entry into streams result in widely different degrees of exposure to aquatic organisms. Direct application and drift are likely to result in the highest concentrations of chemicals in water, but persistence is brief. Mobilization in ephemeral stream channels and overland flow are associated with periods of substantial precipitation; therefore, the concentrations in the water will be considerably less than those resulting from direct applications, although the duration of exposure may be slightly longer. Leaching (if it occurs) can introduce only small amounts of chemical into the stream, although the process could be prolonged.

The degree to which any of these routes of entry is involved depends on the properties of both the chemical and the environment. Properties of the chemical (such as vapor pressure or solubility in water) and the properties of the environment (such as temperature, moisture, and soil characteristics) interact to produce the particular behavior (movement, persistence, and fate) we observe in the environment (Figure 7.2). This behavior largely determines the route of entry of chemicals into forest streams.

Chemicals on sediment.—Stream sediments may be contaminated with forest chemicals by deposition of soils carrying adsorbed chemicals from the land or by adsorption of chemicals from the water (Barnett et al. 1967).

Persistence of the chemical is the predominant factor affecting its presence in the soil. This characteristic will be discussed in more detail in a later section. In general, however, nearly all chemicals are applied between March and October, and surface erosion occurs most frequently during intense winter storms from late November through February. Thus, appreciable quantities of a particular chemical must persist for 1–9 months for harmful amounts to be present in the soil at the time the first winter erosion is likely to occur. Erosion is often accelerated by forest management, but the principal sources of sediment are road construction, road failure, landslides, and streambank erosion (Rice et al. 1972). Chemicals are seldom applied in close temporal and spatial proximity to these erosion events. We believe significant movement of chemical residues to streams by this process is unlikely. The incidence of surface erosion from forest lands near salmonid habitats is discussed in detail by Chamberlin et al. (1991, this volume).

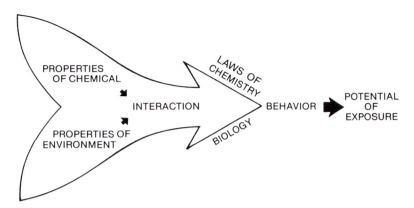

FIGURE 7.2.—The properties of the chemical interact with the properties of the environment in a manner directed by the laws of nature to produce the movement, persistence, and fate of the chemical—which determine the level and duration of an organism's exposure.

Chemicals may be adsorbed from water by sediments already in the stream. Chemicals may bond to sediments by chemical or physical means (or both) according to the physicochemical properties of both chemical and sediment. The adsorption process was reviewed in a series of symposium papers edited by Weber and Matijevic (1968). The adsorption characteristics of forest chemicals are discussed in a later section of this chapter.

Norris (1969) and Norris et al. (1982, 1984) believed that the discharge of pesticides in stream water during periods of heavy precipitation represents the mobilization of chemicals in ephemeral stream channels, though their research did not distinguish between pesticides in solution and those adsorbed on sediments carried in the streamflow.

Chemicals in the food chain.—Chemicals may be in or on the food of salmonids if the food substance is sprayed directly (for instance, if terrestrial insects that are sprayed fall into the water), or if food substances adsorb or bioaccumulate the chemical from the water. Residues in food from direct spraying are likely to occur primarily during or shortly after application. Few data are available on this process.

Bioaccumulation is the uptake by an organism of a chemical from its environment (for example, the uptake by fish, via the gills, of DDT from the water). Kenaga (1975, 1980a, 1980b) and Geyer et al. (1980) provided good reviews and substantial data on bioaccumulation of organic chemicals, including many pesticides. The physicochemical properties of the compound and the organism are the predominant factors that determine the extent of bioaccumulation. The most important properties are the amount of fat in the organism and the ratio of fat solubility to water solubility of the chemical.

Bioaccumulation resulting in concentrations of chemical in an organism that are 100,000 times the concentration of the chemical in the water have been noted. The highest values occur in organisms with a high fat content that are exposed to chemicals with a high ratio of fat to water solubilities. Pertinent examples are DDT or TCDD (tetrachlorodibenzodioxin) in fish. Chemicals that are highly water

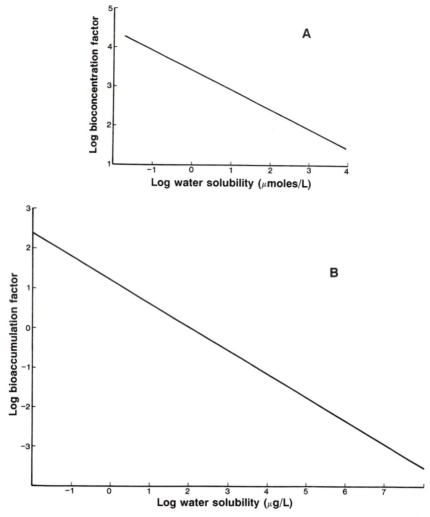

FIGURE 7.3.—Relations of the water solubility of chemicals to their bioaccumulation.
(A) Aqueous solubilities and bioconcentration factors of organic chemicals in rainbow trout. $\log_{10}$ (bioconcentration factor) = $3.41 - 0.508 \log_{10}$ (water solubility); $r^2 = 0.93$. The bioconcentration factor is the concentration of a chemical in fish divided by its concentration in water. (From Figure 2 of Chiou et al. 1977.)
(B) Aqueous solubilities and bioaccumulation factors of organic chemicals in adipose tissues of rats. $\log_{10}$ (bioaccumulation factor) = $1.20 - 0.56 \log_{10}$ (water solubility); $r^2 = 0.64$. The bioaccumulation factor is the concentration of a chemical in adipose tissue divided by its concentration in the diet. (From Figure 1 of Geyer et al. 1980.)

soluble, like picloram or glyphosate, show little tendency to bioaccumulate. The relation of water solubility to bioaccumulation is illustrated in Figure 7.3, and data for specific chemicals are given in Table 7.8. Bioconcentration factors greater than 1,000 indicate a need for precise risk analysis, whereas values less than 100 do not warrant experimental verification (Kenaga 1980b).

TABLE 7.8.—Water solubilities of forest chemicals and measured bioconcentration factors (BCF = concentration in organisms/concentration in exposure medium).

Chemical[a]	Solubility in water (mg/L)	Test organism[b]	Exposure, E (mg/kg or mg/L) or application, A (kg/hectare)	Duration	Amount detected (mg/kg)	BCF	Source[c]
Herbicides							
2,4-D		*Scenedesmus* (alga)	E 0.022	8 h		2.2	1
		Fish[d]	E 2.5	4–14 d	<0.005		6
		Gastropod	E 0.0002–0.05		0		9
Acid	900					13	3
DES	300,000						
Esters	<500						
MP		Fish[d]	E 2.5	4–14 d	0.031–0.122		6
GR		Mussels	A 1.2		0.38–0.70		8
GR		Fish	A 1.2		<0.04		8
BOE		Bluegill	E 3.0	8 d	<0.05		7
Picloram	430					20	3
Hexazinone	33,000						10
Atrazine	33					86	3
		Annelids				3.5	4
		Mayfly				480	4
Triclopyr	430					20	3
MSMA	250,000						
Fosamine	1,790,000						
Glyphosate	12,000					3	3
		Catfish	E 10.0	14 d		0.55	5
		Bass	E 10.0	14 d		0.12	5
		Trout	E 10.0	14 d		0.11	5
		Trout					
		Fillet	E 2.0		80	40	2
		Eggs	E 2.0		60	30	2
		Midge	E 2.0		0		2
Dalapon	800,000					0.4	3
Dinoseb	50					68	3
Insecticides							
DDT	0.002					22,500	3
Malathion	145					37	3
Carbaryl	40					77	3
Azinphos-m	29						
Carbofuran	415					21	3
Acephate	650,000					0.3	3
Fertilizers							
Urea	1,000,000					0.5	3

[a]BOE = butoxyethyl ester; DES = diethylamine salt; GR = granules; MP = metabolic products; azinphos-m = azinphos-methyl; fosamine = fosamine ammonium.

[b]Bass = largemouth bass; catfish = channel catfish; mayfly = nymphs; midge = larvae; trout = rainbow trout.

[c]1 = Boehm and Mueller (1976); 2 = Folmar et al. (1979); 3 = Kenaga (1980b); 4 = Lynch et al. (1982); 5 = Sacher (1978); 6 = Schultz (1973); 7 = Sigmon (1979); 8 = Smith and Isom (1967); 9 = Streit (1979); 10 = U.S. Forest Service (1984).

[d]Three species.

Approaches to Risk Analysis

Several specific risk analysis methods have been used for aquatic species. Most have used a specified fraction (expressed as a decimal) of the LC50 (or similar measure of response) as an estimate of the no-toxic-effect exposure level (U.S. Environmental Protection Agency 1973b, 1976). The LC50 is the chemical concentration lethal to half the test organisms, and the specified fraction of it is called the ''no-observable-effect level,'' or NOEL. When only acute exposures and survival were the primary interest, the estimates of NOEL ranged from 0.1 to 0.05 of the LC50 (Sprague 1971). For compounds that are more persistent in the environment or for estimates of chronic exposures, estimates of the NOEL have ranged from 0.1 to 0.01 of the LC50 (Sprague 1971). These methods were popular because the concepts were easy to understand and apply. The methods relied, however, on an assumption that exposure was continuous at the specified level for a long period (usually 96 h or more). This rationale is perhaps acceptable for large streams receiving a steady input of pollutants or for a specific pollutant point source, but it does not work well for forest streams, in which the concentration of pollutant changes rapidly.

A more refined and realistic method has been published (U.S. Environmental Protection Agency 1980). It requires substantial data that define no-effect levels for a variety of aquatic species. In addition, the method provides procedures that give both an instantaneous maximum permissible concentration and a 24-h average permissible concentration. This procedure is a considerable improvement over earlier methods because it recognizes and allows for variable levels of exposure. It is hampered, however, by a paucity of well-defined no-effect data bases for many compounds. For the purposes of risk assessment in this chapter, we have selected an approach that combines these two approaches. We have used fractional LC50 values as the basis for estimating no-effect concentration values and integrals of the time-concentration curves of pollutants as measured in forest streams to estimate exposure. This approach is described more specifically in a later section on risk analysis. The next section (the behavior and toxicity of commonly used forest chemicals) provides the data on toxicity and exposure that we use in a later section (risk analysis) to relate toxicity to exposure and thereby derive estimates of the margin of safety.

Behavior and Toxicity of Commonly Used Forest Chemicals

The behavior (movement, persistence, and fate) of a chemical in the environment determines, in large measure, the likelihood and the nature of the exposure organisms will receive. Leonard et al. (1976) intensively reviewed this subject for many pesticides. Although their emphasis was on agriculture, many of the concepts and some of the data are relevant in forestry. Malik and Vanden Born (1986) reviewed herbicides as used in Canada.

In this section, we review what is known about the physicochemical properties, movement and persistence in soil, entry and fate in forest waters, bioaccumulation, and toxicity to aquatic species of 10 herbicides, 5 chemical insecticides, 2 biological insecticides, urea fertilizer, and the ammonium-based fire retardants. These specific materials were selected for review because they are (or are likely to be) the most widely used materials in their class in forestry in the USA. To the degree possible, we have relied most heavily on field studies in the northwestern USA and laboratory studies involving species common (or representative of species that are common) in northwestern USA forest ecosystems. In many cases, however, it has been necessary to go beyond these in order to fill critical data gaps or to reinforce other data.

The common and scientific names of invertebrates mentioned in this chapter are in Table 7.9. Information on rates and methods of application and carriers for pesticides are in the "Pacific Northwest Weed Control Handbook" (William et al. 1987), the "Pacific Northwest Insect Control Handbook" (Capizzi et al. 1987), "Pesticide Uses for Forestry,"[3] and "Pesticide Background Statement" (U.S. Forest Service 1984).

Herbicides: 2,4-D

The herbicide 2,4-D is one member of a large family of phenoxy herbicides that have been reviewed by the National Research Council of Canada (1978) and Norris (1981). For many years the most extensively used herbicide in forestry, 2,4-D is formulated as water-soluble amine salts for direct stem injection or as esters that are usually dissolved in diesel oil or emulsified in water for aerial or ground application to foliage or bark. More specific information on the use of this herbicide was reviewed by National Forest Products Association,[3] U.S. Forest Service (1984), and Newton (1987).

Behavior in the environment.—The physicochemical properties of the acid, salt, and ester forms of 2,4-D are pertinent because the herbicide may be in the environment in any of these forms. It is usually applied as the ester, but it is rapidly hydrolized under most circumstances to either the acid or the salt form, depending on the pH of the environment (Paris et al. 1975; National Research Council of Canada 1978; Norris 1981).

The water solubility of 2,4-D in various forms is shown in Table 7.8. Many 2,4-D esters are available; those commonly used in forestry are low in water solubility (<500 mg/L) but are very soluble in organic solvents and oils. The acid and salt forms of 2,4-D have negligible vapor pressure, which means they are not very volatile. The vapor pressure of esters varies from 10^{-2} mm Hg (high-volatile esters) to 10^{-6} mm Hg (low-volatile esters).

The methyl, ethyl, propyl, isopropyl, butyl, and amyl esters are called high-volatile esters. They are not used in forestry. Propylene glycol butyl ether (PGBE), isooctyl, butoxyethyl, 2-ethyl hexyl, and propylene glycol esters (and others of similar properties) are called low-volatile esters and are commonly used in forestry. The physicochemical properties of 2,4-D were reviewed in more detail by House et al.,[4] National Research Council of Canada (1978), U.S. Forest Service (1984), and Weed Science Society of America (1989).

---

[3]Unpublished report, "Pesticide uses for forestry," prepared by National Forest Products Association, Washington, D.C., 1980.

[4]Unpublished final report, "Assessment of ecological effects of extensive or repeated use of herbicides," by W. G. House, L. H. Goodson, H. M. Gadberry, and K. W. Dockter. Advanced Research Project Agency, Department of Defense, Midwest Research Institute Project 3103-B, Contract DAHC 15-68-C-0119, Kansas City, Missouri, 1967.

TABLE 7.9.—Common and scientific names of invertebrates referred to in text and tables.

Common name	Scientific name
Phylum Arthropoda	
	ORDER Amphipoda
Scuds, amphipods	*Gammarus fasciatus* Say
	Gammarus lacustris Sars
	Gammarus pseudolimnaeus Bousfield
	ORDER Cladocera
Daphnids, water fleas	*Daphnia magna* Straus
	Daphnia pulex Leydig
	ORDER Decapoda
Crayfishes	*Orconectes nais* (Faxon)
	Procambarus clarki (Girard)
Glass shrimp	*Palaemonetes kadiakensis* Rathbun
	ORDER Diptera
Crane fly	*Tipula* sp.
Phanton midge	*Chaoborus* sp.
Midges	*Chironomus tenans* (Fabricius)
	Chironomus plumosus (Linnaeus)
	ORDER Ephemeroptera
Mayflies	*Hexagenia bilineata* (Say)
	Baetis sp.
	ORDER Isopoda
Sowbugs, isopods	*Asellus brevicaudus* Forbes
	Asellus hilgendorffii
	ORDER Megaloptera
Dobsonfly	*Nigronia* sp.
	ORDER Odonata
Dragonfly	*Macromia* sp.
Damselfly	*Ischnura venticalis* (Say)
	ORDER Ostracoda
Seed shrimp	*Cypridopsis vidua* (Müller)
	ORDER Plecoptera
Stoneflies	*Pteronarcys californica* Newport
	Pteronarcys dorsata Say
	Pteronarcella badia (Hagen)
	Isoperla sp.
	Skwala sp.
	ORDER Trichoptera
Caddisflies	*Hydropsyche* sp.
	Limnephilus sp.
Phylum Mollusca	
	ORDER Gastropoda
Snails	*Helisoma campanulata* (Say)
	Stagnicola emarginata (Say)

In soil, 2,4-D persists for only short periods (Table 7.10). Research reviewed by House et al.[4] indicates microbial decomposition is the predominant cause of 2,4-D disappearance from soil. Environmental factors that favor rapid microbial metabolism also favor the disappearance of 2,4-D from forest floor and soil. More recent research reviewed by National Research Council of Canada (1978), Norris (1981), and U.S. Forest Service (1984) supports these conclusions.

Soil organic matter adsorbs 2,4-D extensively (Norris 1970b), which tends to reduce the herbicide's mobility in soil. In light, sandy soils with a high pH, however, it may show substantial mobility.[4] Forest soils are usually high in organic matter and low in pH, which inhibits the mobility of 2,4-D. In field studies, 2,4-D residues are not normally found deeper than 20 or 30 cm even after prolonged periods of heavy precipitation (Altom and Stritzke 1972; Plumb et al. 1977; Stewart and Gaul 1977; Norris et al. 1982).

Norris (1981) reviewed the entry and fate of 2,4-D (and the other phenoxy herbicides) in forest waters. He concluded that direct application and drift to surface waters are the processes most likely to produce the highest residue levels, but that persistence is brief. Mobilization of residues from ephemeral stream channels may also introduce 2,4-D to forest stream systems, but the concentrations are not likely to exceed the concentration resulting from direct application or drift.

Norris (1967) reported maximum stream concentrations of 2,4-D ranging from 0.001 to 0.13 mg/L during and shortly after application (Table 7.11). The time required to return to nondetectable levels (<0.001 mg/L) varied with the nature of the area and the maximum concentration observed. Times ranging from less than 1 h to more than 168 h have been noted, but they are usually less than 2 d. Application to marshy areas can lead to higher than normal levels of stream contamination; in one instance, 2,4-D concentrations approaching 0.9 mg/L were found in water flowing from a marshy area. In other areas, long-term outflow of 2,4-D was not noted. Once the initial stream concentration declined to nondetectable levels, no 2,4-D residues were found during subsequent periods of heavy precipitation the first fall after application (Norris 1967, 1968). Norris (1969) and Norris et al. (1982) reported that heavy precipitation will mobilize any surface residues of 2,4-D that are present in ephemeral stream channels.

Few quantitative studies of 2,4-D discharge from whole watersheds have been conducted. In two separate studies, Norris et al. (1982) and Suffling et al. (1974) found that less than 0.02% of the 2,4-D applied to a watershed appeared in streamflow.

When operational applications of 2,4-D have been monitored, the results have largely agreed with research findings. The U.S. Forest Service[5] summarized data on phenoxy herbicides in streams after 304 applications in northwestern forests over 4 years; 84% of the applications resulted in no detectable stream contamination, and only 1% led to herbicide concentrations exceeding 0.01 mg/L.

Few field data are available on 2,4-D levels in sediments or aquatic species in forest streams. The fate of 2,4-D in forest streams has not been determined, but we believe downstream movement, adsorption, and degradation (processes observed in other aquatic systems) all occur. Streit (1979) reported that concentrations of 2,4-D on aquatic sediments were no greater than in the water. Results of some other studies are summarized in Table 7.10. Nesbitt and Watson (1980a,

---

[5]Memorandum, "Summary of phenoxy herbicides in water," (2150, Pesticide-Use Management), from F. J. Kopechky to the Chief, U.S. Department of Agriculture, Forest Service, June 23, 1980.

Text continues on page 229

TABLE 7.10.—Persistence of forest chemicals in soil and water.

Chemical[a]	Substrate[b]	Initial amount in soil or water (mg/kg, mg/L, or kg/hectare*)	Time interval[c]	% remaining	Time to non-detection[c]	Source[d]
Herbicides						
2,4-D	Forest floor (L)		10–20 d	50		25–27
	Oak forest (L)		30 d	0		1
	Forest (F)		31 d	10		40
	Chaparral (F)		15 d	60		30
Picloram	Hardwood forest (NC)	5.0	4 w	50	~28 w	23
Hexazinone	Agricultural (S)		<6 m	50		
	Blueberry fields (NS)	2.0–4.0*	1 y	<5		16
	Loam forest soil (S)		<4 w	50		
	Clay forest soil (S)		6 w	50		
Hexazinone P	Sandy forest soil (S)		14 w	50		
Atrazine	Soil		5 d	33		4
	Agricultural soil		1 y	<10		5
Triclopyr	Soil (WV)	4.4–18	14–16 d	50	28 d	20
	Hill pasture (OR)	3.4, 10.1*	75–81 d	50		28
MSMA	Water		5 d	10–50		42
Fosamine	Greenhouse		10 d	50		14
	DE, IL, FL (F)		7 d	50		14
Glyphosate	Foliage and litter		10–27 d	50		24
	Soil		29–40 d	50		24
	Soil		28 d	55		35,36
	Static water		12 d	50		34
	Soil "A"		32 d	60		22
	Soil "B"		32 d	90.5		22
	Soil "C"		32 d	97		22
Dalapon			<30 d	0		3
Dinoseb	Warm, moist soils		3–5 w	0		18
Insecticides						
Malathion	Sterile, nonsterile soils		24 h	10–50		19
		8.6*	6 m	0		32
	River water		7 d	20	28 d	9
	pH = 7; 37°C (L)		1.3 d	50		10
	pH = 7; 20°C (L)		11 d	50		10
	pH = 6.1		160 d	50		10,19
	Natural aqueous system		230 h	<10		19
	Fresh water		11 d	50		41
	Saline water		<2 d	50		41
Carbaryl	Soil	3.36–30.2*	8 d	50		39
	Soil		1.5–6 m	50		13

TABLE 7.10.—Continued.

Chemical[a]	Substrate[b]	Initial amount in soil or water (mg/kg, mg/L, or kg/hectare*)	Time interval[c]	% remaining	Time to non-detection[c]	Source[d]
	River water	0.01	7 d	5	14 d	9
	Farm pond (water)	6.7*			2 d	33
	Sediment				4 d	6
	Brooks and streams	0.84*	23–28 h	50		37
Azinphos-m	Ponds, pH 7.2–8	1.0	2 d	50	14 d	21
	Muck soils (FL)		1 m	<50		2
	Clay soils (LA)		3 m	>50		2
	Clay soils (KN)		2–3 m	50		2
	Silty clay loam		105 d	1		15
Carbofuran	Loam, sandy soils with oats		14 d	10–40		11
	Soil		46–117 d	50		7
	Sterile, unsterile soils[e]		3–50 w	50		12
Acephate	Soils (PA); 0.56	5.5	20 d	0.5		8
	kg/hectare applied	5.5	70 d	<0.4		8
	Open forest floor (PNW)		10 d	<10		38
	Semiopen or		10 d	<30	30 d	38
	densely covered area	0.1			6 w	31
B.t.	Foliage, cool, cloudy		3.9 d	50		29
	Foliage, hot, sunny		7.7 d	50		29
	White pine		1 d	20		17
	White pine		14 d	1		17
	White pine		28 d	<0.1		17

[a]Azinphos-m = azinphos-methy; *B.t.* = *Bacillus thuringiensis*; fosamine = fosamine ammonium; P = pellets.

[b]DE = Delaware; F = field study; FL = Florida; KN = Kansas; IL = Illinois; L = laboratory study; LA = Louisiana; NC = North Carolina; NS = Nova Scotia; OR = Oregon; PA = Pennsylvania; PNW = Pacific Northwest; S = southeastern USA; WV = West Virginia.

[c]d = day; m = month; w = week; y = year.

[d]1 = Altom and Stritzke (1972); 2 = Anderson et al. (1974); 3 = Ashton (1982); 4 = Axe et al. (1969); 5 = Birk and Roadhouse (1964); 6 = California Department of Fish and Game (1963, unpublished; see text footnote 9); 7 = Caro et al. (1973); 8 = Devine (1975); 9 = Eichelberger and Lichtenberg (1971); 10 = Freed et al. (1979); 11 = Fuhremann and Lichtenstein (1980); 12 = Getzin (1973); 13 = Goring et al. (1975); 14 = Han (1979b); 15 = Iwata et al. (1977); 16 = Jensen and Kimball (1987); 17 = Kearby et al. (1972); 18 = Klingman and Ashton (1975); 19 = Konrad et al. (1969); 20 = McKellar et al. (1982); 21 = Meyer (1965); 22 = Moshier and Penner (1978); 23 = Neary et al. (1985); 24 = Newton et al. (1984); 25 = Norris (1966); 26 = Norris (1970a); 27 = Norris and Greiner (1967); 28 = Norris et al. (1987); 29 = Pinnock et al. (1971); 30 = Plumb et al. (1977); 31 = Rabeni and Gibbs (1977, unpublished, U.S. Forest Service Report NA-FR-7, Broomall, Pennsylvania), 32 = Roberts et al. (1962); 33 = Romine and Bussian (1971, unpublished; see text footnote 8); 34 = Sacher (1978); 35 = Sprankle et al. (1975a); 36 = Sprankle et al. (1975b); 37 = Stanley and Trial (1980); 38 = Szeto et al. (1978); 39 = Union Carbide (1968); 40 = U.S. Forest Service (1977b); 41 = Walker (1978); 42 = Woolson et al. (1976).

[e]Losses were 7–10 times faster in alkaline soils (pH 7.9) than in acid or neutral soils (pH 4.3–6.5).

TABLE 7.11.—Peak concentrations of forest chemicals in soils, lakes, and streams after application.

Chemical[a] and system[b]	Application rate (kg/hectare)	Concentration (mg/L or mg/kg*)		Time interval[c]	Time to non-detection	Source[d]
		Peak	Subsequent			
Herbicides						
2,4-D	2.24	0.001–0.13			1–168 h[e]	17
Marsh	2.24	0.09				17,18
2,4-D BE						
Built pond	23.0					1
Water		3.0	1.0	85 d		
			0.2	180 d		
Sediment		8.0*	4.0*	13+ d		
			0.4–0.6*	82–182 d		
Aquatic plants		206*		7 d		
		8*		82 d	182 d	
2,4-D AS						
Reservoir		3.6	0	13 d		7
Picloram						
Runoff		0.078				19
Runoff		0.038				23
Ephemeral stream	2.8	0.32		157 d	915 d	9
Stream	0.37					3
Hexazinone						
Stream (GA)	1.68	0.044		3–4 m		11
Forest (GA)	1.68					14
Litter		0.177*	<0.01*	60+ d		
Soil		0.108*	<0.01*	90 d		
Ephemeral stream		0.514		3 d		
Perennial stream		0.442		3 d		
Atrazine						
Stream	3.0	0.42	0.02	17 d		16
Built ponds						10
Water		0.50	0.05	14 d		
			0.005	56 d		
Sediments		0.50*	0.9*	4 d		
		0.50*	0.25*	56 d		
Triclopyr						
Pasture (OR)	3.34	0.095*				20
Glyphosate						
Water	3.3	0.27	0.09	5.5 h		15
			<0.01	3 d		
Dalapon						
Field irrigation water		0.023–3.65	<0.01	Sev h		5
Insecticides						
Malathion						
Streams	0.91					24
Unbuffered		0.037–0.042				
Buffered		0–0.017				
Carbaryl						
Streams and ponds (E)		0–0.03				24
Streams, unbuffered (PNW)		0.005–0.011		48 h		24
Water	0.84	0.026–0.042				8
Brooks with buffer	0.84	0.001–0.008				22
Rivers with buffer	0.84	0.000–0.002				22
Streams, unbuffered	0.84	0.016				22

TABLE 7.11.—Continued.

Chemical[a] and system[b]	Application rate (kg/hectare)	Concentration (mg/L or mg/kg*)		Time interval[c]	Time to non-detection	Source[d]
		Peak	Subsequent			
Ponds	0.84					6
Water		0.254			100–400 d	
Sediment		<0.01–5.0*[f]				
Acephate						
Streams		0.003–0.961				4
Streams	0.56	0.113–0.135	0.013–0.065	1 d		21
Pond sediment and fish				14 d		2
		Fertilizers				
Urea	224					
Urea-N						
Forest stream (OR)		0.39	0.39	48 h		12
Dollar Cr (WA)		44.4				13
NH_4^+-N						
Forest stream (OR)		<0.10				12
Tahuya Cr (WA)		1.4				13
NO_3^+-N						
Forest stream (OR)		0.168		72 h		12
Elochoman R (WA)		4.0				13

[a] 2,4-D BE = 2,4-D butoxyethanol ester; 2,4-D AS = 2,4-D amine salt + ester.

[b] E = eastern USA; Cr = Creek; GA = Georgia; PNW = Pacific Northwest; OR = Oregon; R = River; WA = Washington; buffer = wooded riparian strip.

[c] d = day; h = hours; m = months; sev h = several hours. Intervals are times from application to measurement of peak or subsequent concentration, whichever is the last measurement indicated.

[d] 1 = Birmingham and Colman (1985); 2 = Bocsor and O'Connor (1975); 3 = Davis et al. (1968); 4 = Flavell et al. (1977); 5 = Frank et al. (1970); 6 = Gibbs et al. (1984); 7 = Hoeppel and Westerdahl (1983); 8 = Hulbert (1978); 9 = Johnsen (1980); 10 = Maier-Bode (1972); 11 = Mayack et al. (1982); 12 = Moore (1970); 13 = Moore (1975b); 14 = Neary et al. (1983); 15 = Newton et al. (1984); 16 = M. Newton (Oregon State University, personal communication, 1967); 17 = Norris (1967); 18 = Norris (1968); 19 = Norris (1969); 20 = Norris et al. (1987); 21 = Rabeni and Stanley (1979); 22 = Stanley and Trial (1980); 23 = Suffling et al. (1974); 24 = Tracy et al. (1977).

[e] Normally less than 48 h.

[f] One extreme case: 23.8 mg/kg peak concentration, 16 months to nondetection.

1980b) found that the number of live bacteria, nitrogen and phosphorus concentrations, sediment levels, and temperature all affected the persistence of 2,4-D in an Australian river.

Bioaccumulation is most likely to occur when organisms are exposed to persistent chemicals that have low water solubility and high lipid solubility. 2,4-D does not meet these criteria to the same degree that the chlorinated hydrocarbon insecticides do. Organisms exposed to phenoxy herbicides take up some of the chemical, but generally the bioaccumulation factor is low and the residence time is brief once exposure ceases (Table 7.8).

As part of a widespread survey of the Swedish environment for phenoxy herbicides, Erne (1975) reported only 3% of 330 samples of muscles from healthy fish (several species from 120 locations) contained detectable residues of 2,4-D (residues ranged from 0.05 to 1.5 mg/kg). Sanborn (1974) did not detect unmetabolized 2,4-D in the components of a model aquatic–terrestrial ecosystem. Schultz and Whitney (1974) reported 2,4-D residues that ranged from undetectable to 0.162 mg/kg in a variety of fish species; about 80% of samples did not contain detectable residues. Rodgers and Stalling (1972) noted that 2,4-D and its metabolites were rapidly eliminated from fish after exposure ceased. In Georgia, Hoeppel and Westerdahl (1983) found no 2,4-D in most samples of game fish after amine and ester formulations of 2,4-D were applied to a reservoir, although residues up to a maximum of 0.007 mg/kg were found in 18 of 20 gizzard shad. No residues were found 13 d after application.

Extensive data from Ellgehausen et al. (1980) support these findings. The lack of bioaccumulation evident in these results is consistent with the physicochemical properties of the herbicide.

Toxicity.—The toxicity of 2,4-D herbicides to fish varies; 96-h LC50s range from less than 1 to more than 400 mg/L, depending on formulation (National Research Council of Canada 1978). Most studies have incorporated static bioassays to determine lethal concentrations of the compounds, so their field applicability is somewhat limited. The test animals used in most studies have been bluegills, a species generally considered less sensitive than salmonids.

The 2,4-D dimethylamine (DMA) herbicides have relatively low toxicity to fish. Folmar (1976) reported a 96-h LC50 for rainbow trout of 100 mg/L, but he noted avoidance reactions at concentrations well below the 96-h LC50 value. Davis and Hughes (1963) and Hughes and Davis (1963) found considerable variation in the toxicity of different 2,4-D formulations to bluegills and even in the toxicity of a single formulation. The researchers believed these inconsistencies could be attributed to the different batch lots of chemical. The alkanolamine salt and the dimethylamine formulations were the least toxic formulations to bluegills; the isopropyl ester and butyl ester (not used in forestry) were the most toxic (Table 7.12). Davis and Hardcastle (1959) found differences in LC50 values for 2,4-D and other herbicides when waters from two different sources were used in toxicity tests. Results from other authors are summarized in Table 7.12.

Sublethal effects of PGBE esters of 2,4-D have been demonstrated for fish (Cope 1966). Spawning of bluegills was delayed 2 weeks in ponds treated with 5 and 10 mg/L of the herbicide. Hiltibran (1967) observed that fertilized eggs of green sunfish developed normally when exposed to 1 mg/L of the PGBE ester of 2,4-D under static water conditions. Bluegills, green sunfish, lake chubsuckers, and smallmouth bass fry, however, appeared to be more susceptible to the herbicide; they failed to survive the 8-d duration of the test.

Cope et al. (1970) observed bioconcentration of the PGBE ester of 2,4-D in fish tissues 1–3 d after treatment. No detectable residues of the herbicide were found after 4 d in bluegills exposed to a 10-mg/L concentration of the PGBE ester, but histological and biochemical changes were observed in bluegills exposed to this ester at and above 5 mg/L in ponds in Oklahoma (Cope et al. 1970). The pathology included depletions of liver glycogen, globular deposits in the blood vessels, and stasis and engorgement of the brain circulatory system.

Much of the work on fish toxicity of the phenoxy herbicides has concerned the PGBE esters of 2,4-D or 2,4,5-T, but little has been done on mixtures of these compounds. Matida et al. (1975) noted no appreciable change in a stream community when a mixture of 2,4-D and 2,4,5-T as the butoxyethanol esters (commercially called "Brush Killer") was aerially spread over 9.5 hectares of forest at rates of 4.05 kg 2,4-D and 1.95 kg 2,4,5-T (active ingredient) per hectare. The authors were unable to detect the chemical in the stream during the 48-h observation period after spraying. Similarly, fishes (cherry salmon and dace

Text continues on page 235

TABLE 7.12.—Median lethal concentrations (LC50s) and no-observed-effect concentrations (NOEC) of forest chemicals for fish and invertebrates.

Chemical[a] and test species[b]	LC50 (mg/L)[c]			96-h NOEC (mg/L)	Exposure (mg/L)[c]	% mortality[d]	Source[e]
	24 h	48 h	96 h				
Herbicides							
2,4-D AS							
Bluegill		800					6,19
2,4-D B, PGBE, BE							
Fish			<4.0				41
2,4-D BE							
Amphipod[f]	1.4						37
2,4-D IP							
Bluegill		0.8					6,19
2,4-D B							
Salmon				1.0	>1.0	~100	32
Bluegill		1.3					6,19
2,4-D SS							
Bluegill			66.0				41
2,4-D IO							
Salmon				1.0	1.5	Sig	32
Bluegill			160.0				41
Amphipod[f]	6.8						37
2,4-D Na borate							
Bluegill			90.0				41
2,4-D acid							
Salmon				50.0	<50.0	0[g]	32
2,4-D DM							
Coho salmon Y					200	0	25
Rainbow trout			100				10
Bluegill		166					6,19
2,4-D PGBE							
Coho salmon Fr					1.0 (96 h)[h]	26.7	32
Coho salmon Fi				<1.0			32
Cutthroat trout A				0.03	0.06, 0.124		47
Cutthroat trout Fr			0.06–1.0				45
Rainbow trout		1.1					5
Bluegill		2.1					19
Longnose killifish E		4.5					3
Amphipod[f]	2.1						37
2,4-D + 2,4,5-T							
Cherry salmon			0.6				29
Dace			1.3				29
isopod			1.6				29
2,4-D + 2,4,5-T PGBE							
Coho salmon Y					≤0.8 S	0	27
					0.21 F	0	27
Picloram							
Daphnia sp.				1.0			14
Daphnia sp.					380 (24 h)	0	26
Daphnia sp.					530 (24 h)	95	26
Stonefly N[i]	120	48					36
Picloram T							
Lake trout				<0.035			44
Amphipod[j]		0.027					20
Stonefly[k]		0.048					20

Table 7.12.—Continued.

Chemical[a] and test species[b]	LC50 (mg/L)[c]			96-H NOEC (mg/L)	Exposure (mg/L)[c]	% mortality[d]	Source[e]
	24 h	48 h	96 h				
Tordon 22K							
Coho salmon Y	17.5						25
Brook trout			91	69			22
Brown trout			52	22			22
Rainbow trout			58	22			22
Black bullhead			91	69			22
Bluegill			5.4				22
Fathead minnow			29	22			22
Green sunfish			91	39			22
Emerald shiner			30				22
Tordon 101							
Rainbow trout	20.0						25
Hexazinone							
Daphnia sp.			20–50				40
Fiddler crab			>1,000				40
Atrazine							
Coho salmon Y					15 (144 h)	25	25
Brook trout			6.3(4.1–9.7) F				28
Bluegill			6.0–8.0 F				28,42
					0.213	0	28
Fathead minnow			15 F				28
					0.095	0	28
Chubsucker, green sunfish, bluegill					10 (8 d)	NE	18
Triclopyr TE							
Rainbow trout, bluegill			>100				20
Shrimp			895				13
Crabs			>1,000				13
Daphnia magna		1,170					12
Oysters		56–87					13
Triclopyr BE							
Rainbow trout			0.74				7
Bluegill			0.87				7
Triclopyr U							
Rainbow trout			117				7
Bluegill			148				7
Fathead minnow			245 S				30
			120 F				30
MSMA							
Channel catfish Fi					10 (48 h)	<10	31
Amphipod[j]					100 (96 h)	0	35
Fosamine							
Coho salmon Y					200	0	25
Fosamine P							
Rainbow trout, fathead minnow			670				8
Glyphosate R							
Fathead minnow			2.3				11
Channel catfish			13				11
Amphipod[l]			43				11
Glyphosate T							
Rainbow trout			140				11
Glyphosate S							
Rainbow trout			2				11

TABLE 7.12.—Continued.

Chemical[a] and test species[b]	LC50 (mg/L)[c]			96-H NOEC (mg/L)	Exposure (mg/L)[c]	% mortality[d]	Source[e]
	24 h	48 h	96 h				
Dalapon							
Coho salmon			310[m]				2
Bluegill, fathead minnow		>310[n]	290[m]				38
Largemouth bass					1,000 (48 h) S	0	2
					1,000 (48 h) F	100	2
Grass carp			>30,000			0	39
Harlequin fish[o]		44					1
Emerald shiner					3,000 (72 h) S	0	23
Dinoseb							
Coho salmon Y	0.19[p]				0.06 (6 d)	93 (6 d)	25
	0.19[p]				0.06 (6 d)	100 (16 d)	25
	0.19[p]				0.04 (16 d)	94 (16 d)	25
Cutthroat trout			0.41–1.35				44
Lake trout			0.032–1.4				44
Dinoseb T							
Rainbow trout	0.30[q]						24
	0.073[r]						24
Blacknose dace	0.24[q]						24
Dinoseb BAD							
Redside shiner	0.16[s]						24
	0.24[t]						24
			Insecticides				
Malathion							
Chinook salmon			0.023				21
Coho salmon			0.101–0.17				20,27
Cutthroat trout			0.28				20
Rainbow trout			0.20				20,27
Lake trout			0.076				20
Brown trout			0.101–0.20				20,27
Fathead minnow			8.65–23				15,20,34
Walleye			0.064				20
Yellow perch			0.263				20
Bluegill			0.09–0.103				16,20,34
					0.066 (15 d)	100	9
					0.028 (54 d)	100	9
Black bullhead			12.9				20
Daphnia sp. I1	0.001–0.0018						20
Asellus sp. M			3.0				20
Amphipod[j]			0.00076				20
Isoperla sp. Y1			0.00069				20
Limnephilus sp. J			0.0013				20
Carbaryl							
Coho salmon[u]			0.764–4.34				20,21,27
Cutthroat trout			6.7–7.1				20,46
Rainbow trout[u]			1.35–1.95				21,27
Fathead minnow[u]			6.7–14.6				17,20,27
Yellow perch			5.1				20
Bluegill[u]			5.3–6.76				17,20,27
			39[v]				20
Daphnia pulex I1			0.064				20
Asellus sp. M			0.28				20
Amphipod[j] M			0.026				20
Stonefly[k] Y2			0.0048				36

Table 7.12.—Continued.

Chemical[a] and test species[b]	LC50 (mg/L)[c] 24 h	LC50 (mg/L)[c] 48 h	LC50 (mg/L)[c] 96 h	96-H NOEC (mg/L)	Exposure (mg/L)[c]	% mortality[d]	Source[e]
Azinphos-methyl							
Coho salmon[u]			0.0042–0.017				20,21,27
Rainbow trout[u]			0.0014–0.0043				20,21,27
Fathead minnow[u]			0.0093–0.235				17,20,27
Yellow perch			0.04[w]				20
			0.0024[x]				20
Bluegill[u]			0.0052–0.022				17,20,27
Largemouth bass[u]			0.0048–0.005				20,27
Asellus sp. M			0.021				20
Amphipod[j] M			0.00015				20
Stonefly[k] Y2			0.0019				20
Carbofuran							
Salmonids			0.164–0.560				20
Fathead minnow			0.872				20
Sheepshead minnow			0.386				33
Yellow perch			0.147				20
Acephate							
Rainbow trout			1,000				43
Goldfish			9,550				4
Plecoptera			9.5				20
Diptera L			1,000				20
Acephate T (94%)							
Rainbow trout			1,100				20
Acephate SP							
Rainbow trout			730				20
Fire retardants							
Phos-Chek							
Coho salmon			160–320				20
Rainbow trout			160–320				20
Amphipod			40–52				20
Phos-Chek 202							
Salmonids			650				20
Fathead minnow			840				20
Phos-Chek 259							
Salmonids			300				20
Bluegill			350				20

[a]AS = Alkanolamine salt; B = butyl ester; BAD = secondary butyl dinitrophenol + secondary amylbutyl dinitrophenol; BE = butoxyethanol ester; DM = dimethylamine; fosamine = fosamine ammonium; IP = isopropyl ester; IO = isooctyl ester; P = product; PGBE = propylene glycol butyl ether ester; R = Roundup; S = surfactant; SP = soluble product; SS = sodium salt; T = technical grade; TE = triethylamine salt; U = unformulated.

[b]A = alevins; E = estuarine; Fi = fingerlings; Fr = fry; I1 = first instar; J = juvenile; L = larvae; M = mature; N = nymph; Y = yearling; Y1 = first year; Y2 = second year.

[c]F = flow-through (continuous-flow) system; S = static (no-flow) system.

[d]NE = no effect; sig = significant.

[e]1 = Alabaster (1969); 2 = Bond et al. (1960); 3 = Butler (1965); 4 = Chevron (1976, Orthene technical information); 5 = Cope (1966); 6 = Davis and Hughes (1963); 7 = Dow Chemical Company (1983); 8 = Du Pont de Nemours Company (1979, unpublished); 9 = Eaton (1970); 10 = Folmar (1976); 11 = Folmar et al. (1979); 12 = Gersich et al. (1984); 13 = Ghassemi et al. (1982); 14 = Hardy (1966); 15 = Henderson and Pickering (1958); 16 = Henderson et al. (1959); 17 = Henderson et al. (1960); 18 = Hiltibran (1967); 19 = Hughes and Davis (1963); 20 = Johnson and Finley (1980); 21 = Katz (1961); 22 = Kenaga (1969); 23 = Lawrence (1962); 24 = Lipschuetz and Cooper (1961); 25 = Lorz et al. (1979); 26 = Lynn (1965); 27 = Macek and McAllister (1970); 28 = Macek et al. (1976); 29 = Matida et al. (1976); 30 = Mayes et al. (1984); 31 = McCorkle et al. (1977); 32 = Meehan et al. (1974); 33 = Parrish et al. (1977); 34 = Pickering et al. (1962); 35 = Sanders (1970); 36 = Sanders and Cope (1968); 37 = Sanders (1969); 38 = Surber and Pickering (1962); 39 = Tooby et al. (1980); 40 = U.S. Environmental Protection Agency (1982); 41 = Walker (1964a); 42 = Walker (1964b); 43 =

Table 7.12.—Continued.

Willcox and Coffey (1977, U.S. Forest Service, Pennsylvania, unpublished); 44 = Woodward (1976); 45 = D. F. Woodward (1977, U.S. Fish and Wildlife Service, personal communication); 46 = Woodward and Mauck (1980); 47 = Woodward and Mayer (1978).

[f]*Gammarus lacustris.*
[g]Except for pink salmon fry.
[h]Water hardness ranged from 10.0 to 33.6 mg/L as Ca and Mg.
[i]*Pteronarcys californica.*
[j]*Gammarus fasciatus.*
[k]*Pteronarcys* sp.
[l]*Gammarus pseudolimnaeus.*
[m]96-h median tolerance limit.
[n]48-h median tolerance limit.
[o]*Rasbora heteromorpha.*
[p]At 10°C and pH 7.
[q]At pH 8.0.
[r]At pH 6.9.
[s]Water hardness 18 mg/L; pH 7.6.
[t]Water hardness 105 mg/L; pH 8.2.
[u]Various stages or weights.
[v]Carbaryl contained in an oil dispersion, 49% active ingredient.
[w]At 7°C.
[x]Ar 22°C.

[genus not identified] fingerlings) showed no mortality or abnormal behavior, and the standing crop of invertebrates appeared to be unchanged. In a later laboratory study, Matida et al. (1976) found that a mixture of 2,4-D and 2,4,5-T produced toxic effects on aquatic isopods (*Asellus hilgendorffii*), cherry salmon fry, and dace fingerlings (Table 7.12). Exposures of cherry salmon fingerlings to "Brush Killer" at concentrations of 0.47 and 0.62 mg/L for 96 h caused histological changes of liver parenchyma, which the authors considered a nonspecific response to a toxic agent.

Sanders (1969) studied the effect of several 2,4-D formulations on the amphipod *Gammarus lacustris*. The butoxyethanol ester was most toxic, followed by the PGBE ester and the isooctyl ester (6.8 mg/L). The dimethylamine salt was not toxic at 100 mg/L (96 h). In a later study, Sanders (1970) showed the variable toxicity of several 2,4-D formulations to various crustaceans. The PGBE esters were generally most toxic, followed by the butoxyethyl ester formulations. The least toxic was 2,4-D-dimethylamine (DMA). Crayfish were less sensitive in this test than *Daphnia* sp., seed shrimp, glass shrimp, scuds (amphipods), and sowbugs (isopods). Schultz and Harman (1974) published an excellent review of the literature on the use of 2,4-D in fisheries as it relates to toxicity, residues, and effects on organisms. Johnson and Finley (1980) summarized the results of studies (1965–1978) at the U.S. Fish and Wildlife Service's laboratory in Columbia, Missouri, providing a useful table of acute toxicity values for various formulations of 2,4-D applied to a variety of invertebrate and fish species.

Herbicides: Picloram

Picloram is a broad-spectrum herbicide used for control of a wide variety of woody annual and perennial broadleaf weeds. It is available in both salt and ester formulations, but the most common forms used in forestry are potassium and amine salts. It is often applied in combination with 2,4-D (Weed Science Society of America 1989). Picloram may be applied as pellets or, more commonly, as a diluted spray mixture. Picloram may also be used in stem-injection treatments. National Forest Products Association (see footnote 3), U.S. Forest Service (1984), and Newton (1987) reviewed uses of picloram in forestry.

Behavior in the environment.—Amine and potassium salts of picloram are highly water-soluble and have negligible vapor pressure ($<10^{-6}$ mm Hg). The physicochemical properties of picloram were reviewed in detail by the National Research Council of Canada (1974) and the Weed Science Society of America (1989).

Picloram is both persistent and mobile in soil. These characteristics were reviewed in detail by House et al. (see footnote 4), Goring and Hamaker (1971), and National Research Council of Canada (1974). Norris (1970a, 1970b) noted, however, that picloram is adsorbed by organic matter and is degraded by microbial action. In forest soils, which characteristically have high organic matter and low pH, picloram is substantially less mobile and persistent than in agricultural soils.

Movement of the herbicide in soils is governed by the net water flow; maximum losses occur under warm, humid conditions, after heavy rainfall, and in light soils that are low in organic content. The leaching of picloram by rainfall is one of the major factors governing its dissipation under field conditions (National Research Council of Canada 1974). Leached picloram may be transported to aquatic ecosystems. Residues in surface runoff have reached 2 mg/L after applications of 1.1 kg/hectare (National Research Council of Canada 1974). Studies have indicated, however, that usually only small proportions ($<5\%$) of the picloram applied to a watershed are transported in surface runoff.

Norris et al. (1976) determined the persistence and leaching of both picloram and 2,4-D at several sites on power transmission line rights-of-way in Oregon and Washington. Study sites ranged from zones of low to zones of high temperature and rainfall. Both herbicides showed a rapid decline in concentration after application. Biologically significant residues were seldom present more than 12 months after application and no leaching of herbicide below the 30-cm soil horizon was detected (relatively little herbicide was detected below 15 cm). When a layer of decaying forest litter was present, nearly all the herbicide was found in this layer. At another site, Norris et al. (1982) reported that picloram and 2,4-D disappeared from the soil within 29 months without significant leaching. An extensive monitoring effort for picloram and 2,4-D in forest streams flowing across powerline rights-of-way treated with these herbicides failed to show measurable levels of chemicals in streams. In several cases, intensive sampling was done with automatic equipment for periods exceeding 6 months after application (Norris et al. 1976).

Where soil compaction has occurred or where ephemeral streams have been treated, surface residues of picloram may occasionally be mobilized. Some of the peak concentrations are summarized in Table 7.11. Mayeux et al. (1984) studied picloram discharge from an 8-hectare watershed (Bermuda grass pasture, Texas) treated in its entirety at 1.12 kg/hectare in late April and again a year later. The maximum amount of picloram in storm-generated runoff the first year was 38 mg/m^2. The storm occurred 46 d after application. In the second year, six storm runoffs occurred 20–48 d after application; again, the highest concentration occurred in the first (250 mg/m^2). The concentration of herbicide decreased 50 to more than 90% with travel downstream. Of the total amount of picloram applied to the watershed, 1.2% and 6% were recovered in streamflow in the first and second years, respectively. When picloram was intentionally added to flowing water in the study area, 73% remained in the water at 90 m, 16% at 1,170 m, and 0.13% at 5,400 m downstream from the point of addition. Norris et al. (1982) found a similar pattern on a hill pasture site in Oregon.

In these studies, the concentrations were highest with the first runoff events and decreased rapidly. At one site, 0.35% of the picloram applied to a 7-hectare watershed was discharged in stream water in the 7 months between the time of application and the time the last sample containing herbicide was collected. All herbicide discharge occurred during the first storms after application that were sufficient to generate streamflow. Suffling et al. (1974) found about 0.22% of the picloram applied to a Great Lakes forest opening (a powerline right-of-way) was contained in runoff water during the first year after application.

Only negligible residues of picloram occur in streams in treated areas; apparently the herbicide is rapidly diluted (Haas et al. 1971). Field plots adjacent to a small stream were treated with picloram (1.1 kg/hectare), and water samples were collected 0, 0.8, and 1.6 km downstream from the plots after each rain for 5 months after application. Picloram was detected (0.029 mg/L) in stream samples only during the first substantial runoff. No residues were found in subsequent samples (Haas et al. 1971).

Picloram contamination in lakes has not been reported, but levels in farm ponds adjacent to plots treated with 1.1 kg/hectare picloram reached 1 mg/L (National Research Council of Canada 1974). Dissipation of the herbicide in ponds appears to be rapid. One study found an initial decline of 14–18% of the picloram per day, then a decline of less than 1%/d 15 weeks after application (Haas et al. 1971). Residues of picloram (148 µg/kg) in pond sediments immediately after application were only twice that in the water, according to Kenaga (1973, as cited in National Research Council of Canada 1974); after 75 d, 7 µg/kg was detected in the pond sediments and 0.1 µg/kg picloram in the water. Dennis et al. (1977) measured picloram residues in water and sediment from ponds and streams after extensive use of the herbicide for control of woody vegetation on pastures in West Virginia. Picloram residues reached higher levels in pond water (up to 0.437 mg/L) than in streams (up to 0.011 mg/L), although the levels generally decreased with both time and distance from the treated area. Generally, residues were higher in the water than in the sediment in both ponds and streams. No picloram was detected in stream sediments whatever the concentrations in water.

Johnsen and Warskow (1980) injected picloram and 2,4-D into a small stream (discharge, 0.036 m^3/s) for 50 min to achieve a concentration of 6.26 mg/L picloram. The highest concentration outside the treatment zone was 2.4 mg/L at the first sampling station, 0.4 km downstream. Peak concentrations at other downstream locations were 0.94 mg/L at 0.8 km; 0.32 mg/L at 1.6 km; 0.014 mg/L at 3.2 km; and 0.001 mg/L at 6.4 km. The herbicide was not detected after 2 d. Stream water, originally containing 1,280 mg picloram/L, contained only 0.544 mg/L (a 57% reduction) after exposure to direct sunlight for 8.8 h.

The physicochemical properties of picloram are not compatible with extensive bioaccumulation. The high water solubility of picloram and its low lipid solubility suggest it will be rapidly excreted by organisms as exposure decreases. Residue analyses indicate that picloram is not bioconcentrated by aquatic invertebrates or other food-chain organisms (National Research Council of Canada 1974). *Daphnia* sp. exposed to 1 mg/L of the potassium salt of picloram had whole-body residues of the herbicides equal to that present in the water (Hardy 1966). Bioconcentration of picloram (acid) was not evident in mosquitofish exposed to 1 mg/L for 18 d (Youngson and Meikle 1972, as cited in National Research Council of Canada 1974). The concentration factor for these fish on a wet-weight, whole-body basis was only 0.02. The 18-d exposure to picloram was adequate to achieve a steady-state level of accumulation in the mosquitofish. Kenaga (1980a) reported a bioconcentration factor of 31 for organisms in a flowing-water system compared to a factor of 0.02 in a static system.

Toxicity.—The toxicity of picloram to fish is influenced by its formulation and the quality of the water (Sergeant et al. 1970; Woodward 1976). Technical-grade picloram (active ingredient, 90%) was more toxic under alkaline conditions (Woodward 1976) than under nonalkaline conditions. Increasing the pH from 6.5 to 8.5 increased the toxicity to cutthroat trout and lake trout by a factor of 2. Increasing temperature led to an increase in toxicity, but increasing hardness did not (Woodward 1976).

The acute toxicity of picloram varies considerably with the formulation and with fish species. The isooctyl ester of picloram appears to be the most toxic commercial formulation (Kenaga 1969; Sergeant et al. 1970; National Research Council of Canada 1974). The LC50s reported for this formulation are about 1 mg/L for sensitive species. Tordon 22K (potassium salt) is considerably less toxic to several fish species (Table 7.12).

Green sunfish exposed to the 99% analytical-grade picloram (1.2 mg/L) were not affected, but the technical grade or the 22% commercial formulation of picloram (for up to 1 h) caused immobilization but not death (Sergeant et al. 1970). Recovery of normal swimming response followed transfer of the fish to clean pond water. Two subsequent exposures to the herbicide shortened the recovery times; after a fourth exposure, however, many of the fish failed to recover. Analytical grade picloram did not affect swimming behavior of green sunfish. Sergeant et al. (1970) suggested that technical grade and commercial formulations of picloram might contain a toxic impurity.

Based on available information, chronic picloram toxicity to fish is not cumulative in terms of lethality (National Research Council of Canada 1974; Woodward 1976). Long-term exposures, however, affect fish development and growth (Woodward 1976) and swimming response and liver histopathology (Sergeant et al. 1970). Most deaths occurred during yolk absorption, which took 4–5 d longer in picloram-treated fish.

Lorz et al. (1979) estimated the 24-h LC50 of Tordon 22K and Tordon 101 (a 4:1 mixture of 2,4-D:picloram) as 17.5 and 20 mg/L, respectively, for yearling coho salmon. When the survivors were challenged with seawater, some of the groups that had received the lowest herbicide concentration suffered mortalities as much as 70%. Reasons for the deaths in seawater after low herbicide exposure are unknown. When coho salmon yearlings were exposed for 96 and 360 h to Tordon 101 and then released into a small coastal stream, their downstream movement was generally inhibited except for the groups receiving the lowest concentration

Aerial application of herbicide to control grass in a logged area recently replanted with forest seedlings.

(0.3 mg/L). In well-planned spray operations in forestry, similar concentrations (those that might cause inhibition of migration) are unlikely to occur in streams.

Herbicides: Hexazinone

Hexazinone is a relatively new forestry herbicide used selectively for site preparation and release of conifers for uninhibited growth and nonselectively for control of weeds and woody plants. The level of use has increased sharply from 2,994 kg in 1980 to 46,233 kg in 1987, when it was the most extensively used herbicide. The most common trade name is Velpar. U.S. Forest Service (1984) reviewed the uses of hexazinone in forestry.

Behavior in the environment.—In its pure form, hexazinone has a relatively low vapor pressure (6.4×10^{-5} mm Hg at 86°C, which extrapolates to 2×10^{-7} mm Hg at 25°C). Thus the potential for hexazinone to volatilize into the atmosphere is quite small. It is highly soluble in water (3.3 g/100 g water), but is substantially more soluble in a wide array of organic solvents (U.S. Forest Service 1984).

In soil, hexazinone is dissipated by photodegradation, biodegradation, and leaching. Loss from soil by volatilization is minimal, but hexazinone apparently is subject to photodegradation while the residues are confined to the soil surface. The half-lives of hexazinone in field trials are summarized in Table 7.10. Biodegradation occurs in soil under aerobic conditions, but not under anaerobic conditions. Based on studies involving radioactive herbicide, it is apparent that microbial activity, particularly fungal activity, plays a prominent role in the biological dissipation of hexazinone from soil.

Hexazinone is quite mobile. It is readily leached in laboratory soil studies and field studies in southern forests confirm its mobility (U.S. Forest Service 1984). In Nova Scotia soils, detectable residues were found down to 45 cm, the lowest depth sampled; however, except in a sand soil, most of the recovered residues were in the top 15-cm layer (Jensen and Kimball 1987).

Neary et al. (1983) studied the off-site movement of hexazinone in four 1-hectare watersheds in the upper piedmont of Georgia after application at 1.68 kg active ingredient/hectare (10% active ingredient pellets) in April (Table 7.11). Their results show that both decomposition and leaching reduced concentrations in the forest floor and soil. By 90 d after application, however, the residue level in litter had increased to 3.42 mg/kg as foliage from treated plants fell to the forest floor. These added residues had not entered the soil when the 90-d measurements were made, but likely did so later.

Three days after hexazinone was applied to a Georgia forest, residues appeared in both storm-generated flow from ephemeral streams and baseflow in the nearest perennial stream (Neary et al. 1983; Table 7.11). All subsequent measurements were much lower, averaging 0.033 mg/L for 26 storms that produced runoff during 13 months. Flow from five of the last seven storms did not contain detectable residues. Hexazinone appeared in base flow in pulses 90–110 d after application; the peak concentration was 0.023 mg/L and subsequent pulse levels were 0.01 mg/L or less. Overall, 0.53% of the hexazinone applied was discharged from the four 1-hectare Georgia watersheds; 71% of the discharge occurred during the first storm. The amount of hexazinone discharged was 34.9% of the amount that fell directly into ephemeral stream channels. Nearly all was discharged in the dissolved phase.

Hexazinone degrades rapidly in water exposed to sunlight, and its degradation in natural waters is not greatly reduced in the presence of suspended sediments. In dark laboratory conditions, degradation was quite slow, although the test waters may not have contained many microbes. Decomposition is 4–7 times faster in natural water than in distilled water exposed to sunlight (Rhodes 1980; U.S. Forest Service 1984), indicating that photodegradation is only one means by which hexazinone decomposes.

Hexazinone is rapidly metabolized by animals and excreted in urine or eliminated in feces. It does not tend to bioaccumulate and the clearance rate from tissues of exposed animals is rapid once exposure ceases. Bluegills exposed to hexazinone for 4 weeks at concentrations up to 1.0 mg/L had hexazinone residues that reached maximum values of 2.1 mg/kg in the carcass and 6.7 mg/kg in the viscera. After 2 weeks in clean water, no hexazinone was detected in the fish (Rhodes 1980). Animals pretreated with hexazinone clear themselves of residues from subsequent hexazinone exposures more rapidly than animals not pretreated. This indicates some adaptation to more rapid metabolism and excretion as the result of the pretreatment (Rhodes and Jewell 1980). These results indicate little potential for bioaccumulation.

Toxicity.—Hexazinone in its various formulations (soluble powder, pellets, dry flowable and liquid end-use products) is practically nontoxic to aquatic invertebrates (U.S. Environmental Protection Agency 1982); LC50s or no-effect levels for invertebrates and microorganisms are above 10 mg/L (Table 7.12). Over a period of 8 months following application (16.8 kg/hectare) of hexazinone pellets to a forested watershed, there were no major alterations in the composition or diversity of aquatic invertebrate species and no changes in the community composition of small terrestrial arthropods (Mayack et al. 1982).

Available data indicate that hexazinone is only slightly toxic to fish. The LC50s were greater than 100 mg/L in all studies reported (U.S. Forest Service 1984).

At least some aquatic plants are vulnerable to hexazinone. Algal growth, for example, was inhibited by concentrations as low as 0.5 mg/L (U.S. Environmental Protection Agency 1982).

Herbicides: Atrazine

Atrazine is one of a large group of compounds called triazine herbicides. It is widely used, at rates up to 4.48 kg/hectare, as a selective herbicide for control of broadleaf and grassy weeds in both agriculture and forestry. At higher rates of application, it can be used for nonselective control of vegetation on noncroplands. National Forest Products Association (see footnote 3), U.S. Forest Service (1984), and Newton (1987) reviewed the use of atrazine in forestry. An extensive review of the triazine herbicides is included in a special volume of "Residue Reviews" (Gunther and Gunther 1970).

Behavior in the environment.—Atrazine has fairly low solubility in water (33 mg/L) but substantial solubility in several organic solvents (chloroform, 52,000 mg/L; methanol, 18,000 mg/L; diethyl ether, 12,000 mg/L). Although its vapor pressure is low (3×10^{-7} mm Hg), it is reported to evaporate from both vegetation and soil surfaces (Kearney et al. 1964; Burt 1974).

At normal rates of application, most of the atrazine disappears within a year of application (Table 7.10). Birk and Roadhouse (1964) reported 90% loss of atrazine from agricultural soils within 1 year. In the same study, they found that 85% of the atrazine was in the top 2.5-cm layer of soil and 5.7% was in the 2.5–5.0-cm soil layer after 21 cm of rain had fallen. Marriage et al. (1975) reported no significant accumulation of atrazine even after annual applications of 4.5 kg/hectare in nine consecutive years. Measurable residues of atrazine were confined to the upper 15 cm of the soil profile, and most of them were in the 0–5-cm soil layer.

Atrazine losses in runoff water and soil sediment have been measured on agricultural lands. Hall et al. (1972) reported atrazine losses in runoff ranging from 0.01 to 5.0% of the applied atrazine within the first season after application. About 90% of the loss occurred within the first month after application. The magnitude, frequency, and intensity of precipitation largely determined the amount of atrazine in runoff. Runoff of water in this study ranged from 17 to 68% of the incident precipitation, resulting in loss of as much as 10,000 kg soil/hectare (silty clay loam soil, 14% slope). In two small (2.3- and 1.4-hectare) agricultural watersheds in Georgia, 0.2 and 1.9% of the atrazine applied were recovered in storm-generated runoff during the first 90 d after application (1.45 and 4.03 kg/hectare). The first runoff events were 6 and 24 d after application. Most of the atrazine recovered (83 and 99%) was in solution (Leonard et al. 1979).

Frank and Sirons (1979) monitored streams in 11 agricultural watersheds (average size, 4,279 hectares) for atrazine in both water and sediment. The herbicide or its metabolites were found in 80% of the streams; the mean concentration was 0.0014 mg/L and the peak concentration did not exceed 0.032 mg/L. About 62% of the atrazine discharge was associated with storm runoff, 21% was in baseflow, and an additional 22% resulted from chemical spills. Atrazine was detected in 4 of 10 sets of stream-bottom sediment samples at concentrations up to 20 mg/kg.

Smith et al. (1975) analyzed water samples from irrigation ditches and basins that had been sprayed with atrazine when the ditches were dry. After the ditches had been filled twice, no residues of atrazine were detected in the water. These results indicate mobilization of atrazine in ephemeral stream channels is most likely to be restricted to the first few significant storms after application. Weidner (1974) noted significant degradation of atrazine in groundwater, although the rate of degradation was slower than would be expected for the same herbicide in soil.

In a model stream ecosystem that received atrazine (0.25 mg/L) for 30 d followed by a 60-d depuration phase four times in one year, Lynch et al. (1982) found no significant accumulation of the herbicide. Residues greater than 0.1 mg/kg were found in only a few samples of substrate, and these showed no discernible pattern relative to treatment or depuration phases. Bioaccumulation factors during the treatment phase ranged from 3.5 in annelids to 480 in mayfly nymphs. Residues declined to pretreatment levels within a few days during the depuration phase. The authors noted that the sensitivity of detection was limited by the low level of initial uptake of the atrazine; however, the results are consistent with other reports of atrazine persistence in biota. Based on its physicochemical properties, atrazine would be expected to show little tendency for bioaccumulation. Boehm and Mueller (1976) noted that increasing the water solubility of the herbicide resulted in a decrease in the absolute level of the herbicide in algae. The accumulation factor was 31.8. After contaminated algae were transferred into an atrazine-free medium, the herbicide was rapidly desorbed except for about 10% of the residue that apparently was bound irreversibly to cell structures. Streit (1979) reported concentration factors ranging from less than 1 to 8 in some body parts of a stream gastropod exposed to 0.5 mg atrazine/L for 24 h. Paris et al. (1975) reported no measurable adsorption of atrazine by dense populations of microorganisms in aquatic cultures. Ellgehausen et al. (1980) studied the bioaccumulation, depuration, and bioconcentration of atrazine by algae, daphnids, and catfish. They reported bioaccumulation factors of about 90, 1, and 5, respectively; depuration halftimes of 0.03 h, 9.5 h, and 1.5 d; and biomagnification factors of less than 10. The intensive study reported by these authors indicates that no significant bioaccumulation of atrazine will occur in aquatic environments in the forest. A mollusk accumulated atrazine to a level 3–4 times greater than the concentration in water (0.05 mg/L) during a 72-h exposure period. Most of the accumulation occurred in the first 12 h. Similar results were obtained with whitefish. Water rather than food appeared to be the major source of the herbicide for these animals (Gunkel and Streit 1980).

Douglass et al. (1969) found a peak concentration of 0.03 mg atrazine/L in stream water shortly after application (4 kg/hectare) and during the first periods of heavy precipitation. After this time, residues did not exceed 0.010 mg/L (the minimum quantifiable concentration). In a second application (3.36 kg 2,4-D plus 5 kg atrazine per hectare), an unsprayed 3-m buffer strip was left adjacent to the stream. No residues of either herbicide were detected in the water. Streit (1979) found that atrazine concentrations were about 40 times higher on sediments than in water in one test, although the concentration on the sediment seemed independent of the organic matter content over a range from 2.3 to 31.9%.

Toxicity.—Laboratory and field tests have indicated that atrazine is moderately toxic to fish compared with other herbicides. Macek et al. (1976) investigated the effects of atrazine on survival, growth, and reproduction of three species of fish (Table 7.12). Parental survival, egg production, and hatchability of brook trout appeared to be unaffected by exposure to 0.72 mg/L (Macek et al. 1976). Survival and growth of brook trout fry, however, were significantly reduced after 90 d of exposure to 0.72, 0.45, and 0.24 mg atrazine/L. Analysis of muscle tissue from bluegills, fathead minnows, and brook trout indicated that these fish did not bioconcentrate detectable amounts of atrazine after prolonged exposure (Macek et al. 1976).

Walker (1964a) observed no fish mortality after application of 2.0–6.0 mg atrazine/L to ponds infested by aquatic weeds. He suggested, however, that atrazine could affect fish in ways other than direct toxicity. A reduction in bottom fauna was observed immediately after application. Among the most sensitive were mayflies, caddisflies, leeches (Hirudinea), and gastropods (*Musculium* sp.). Studies by Macek et al. (1976) on the chronic toxicity of atrazine to selected aquatic invertebrates indicated that morphological development of progeny is particularly sensitive. Exposure of two successive generations of chironomids to 0.23 mg atrazine/L resulted in reduced hatching success, larval mortality, developmental retardation, and a reduction in the percentage of pupating larvae and emerging adults. Continuous exposure to 0.25 mg atrazine/L significantly reduced production of *Daphnia magna*. Development to the seventh instar of the F_1 generation of gammarids exposed to 0.14 mg atrazine/L was reduced 25% below that of animals exposed to lower concentrations and of controls.

Herbicides: Triclopyr

Triclopyr is marketed in two principal formulations: Garlon 3A, a triethylamine salt; and Garlon 4, the butoxyethyl ester. These formulations have increased substantially in use in recent years—to more than 22,000 kg in 1989 (Table 7.4)—and are most widely used for site preparation and conifer release. Rates of application range from 0.28 to 10 kg/hectare. Most aerial applications do not exceed 3.36 kg/hectare, but ground application rates may average higher; rates to more than 7 kg/hectare have been reported (U.S. Forest Service 1984).

Behavior in the environment.—Triclopyr is only moderately soluble in water (430 mg/L at 25°C), but is highly soluble in a wide array of organic solvents. Specific information on vapor pressure is lacking but, based on their structures, the amine salt and the acid form are likely to have quite low vapor pressures. The vapor pressure of the ester is likely to be higher, but is probably less than 1×10^{-4} mm Hg at 25°C. The acid form resists hydrolysis, but the ester form rapidly hydrolyzes to the acid, which then is converted to a salt at normal environmental pH (U.S. Forest Service 1984; Weed Science Society of America 1989).

Triclopyr dissipates relatively rapidly in soil, apparently by microbial activity; however, triclopyr photodegrades in water and may also in soil. The average half-life in soil is reported to be 30 d, but the half-life can be affected by soil type and other environmental conditions such as moisture, nutrients, and temperature (Table 7.10). In Sweden, triclopyr residues were reported to last more than 2 years in some cases. The reason for this unusually long persistence is not known (Torstensson and Stark 1982).

Aerial application of herbicide to control competing shrubs in a recently forested area.

Triclopyr has the potential to leach in soil, but this is minimized by its rapid dissipation by microbial and photochemical means. In soils of increasing organic matter content, mobility is decreased and dissipation is enhanced. The leaching of triclopyr and its two primary metabolites (trichloropyridinol and trichloromethoxy pyridine) was studied in six soils around the USA; only small amounts were found in the 15–30-cm and the 30–46-cm portions of the soil profile (Ghassemi et al. 1982). In a laboratory study, Choon et al. (1986) applied triclopyr as the acid or ethylene glycol butyl ether ester to packed columns of loam soil collected after duff removal from a cedar–hemlock forest in western British Columbia. Water was added at a rate of 2.5 cm every other day. After 54 d, 65% of the original amount of herbicide added to the columns was recovered as triclopyr (5%) or two metabolites (95%). Residues were found only in the top 10 cm of the column. No residues were detected in the leachate, indicating little leaching under these test conditions. The authors concluded there is little likelihood that triclopyr will leach from forest application sites into water.

There have been few studies of triclopyr entry to water in forest settings. McKellar et al. (1982) monitored triclopyr residues in streams flowing from small West Virginia watersheds that had been treated at 11.2 kg/hectare. Triclopyr concentrations in water samples collected about 61 m downstream ranged from nondetectable to 0.02 mg/L. In an Oregon hill pasture stream, Norris et al. (1987) found the maximum concentration of triclopyr to be 0.095 mg/L within 1 h after the entire 1.74-hectare watershed had been sprayed (3.34 kg/hectare). The intermittent stream was dry during the summer months, but when fall rains recharged the stream, maximum concentrations of 0.015 mg/L were found during the first storm that generated streamflow (6 months after application). The last detectable residue occurred 4 d later. Altogether, 0.003% of the herbicide applied to this watershed was discharged in streamflow.

Photodegradation is a major reason for the disappearance of triclopyr from water; a half-life as short as 10 h has been reported (Weed Science Society of America 1989). The long-term persistence of triclopyr in water does not appear to be a significant problem in forest environments of the northwestern USA.

Toxicity.—There are not many data on the toxicity of triclopyr to invertebrates, microorganisms, or fishes; much of the available data was generated by Dow Chemical Company for its registration of the triethylamine salt (Garlon 3A). These data indicate that the triethylamine salt of triclopyr is only slightly toxic or practically nontoxic to organisms tested. Garlon 4, the butoxyethyl ester of triclopyr, is highly toxic to both rainbow trout and bluegills, whereas unformulated triclopyr is only slightly toxic to both species (Table 7.12).

Herbicides: MSMA

MSMA is a pentavalent organic arsenical herbicide. In forestry, its principal use has been stem injection for precommercial thinning and to aid in control of certain bark beetles. These uses provide only limited opportunity for MSMA to enter the aquatic environment. National Forest Products Association (see footnote 3), U.S. Forest Service (1984), and Newton (1987) reviewed the use of MSMA in forestry. Norris reported the results of a major study of the behavior and impact of organic arsenical herbicides in the forest environment.

Behavior in the environment.—The water solubility of MSMA is 25 g/100 g of water at 20°C. Although it has very little vapor pressure, MSMA may be altered by microbial action to derivatives of arsine that are volatile. The behavior of MSMA in the environment was reviewed by Ray (1975). In soils, MSMA reacts with iron, aluminum, calcium, and magnesium to form compounds of low solubility. Wauchope (1975) reported that organic arsenicals are intensively adsorbed by soils with high contents of clay, iron, and aluminum oxide. The phytotoxicity of MSMA is rapidly dissipated in soil, probably through a strong interaction between the herbicide and soil particles. Some microbial degradation of MSMA has been reported; an arsenate was the product of the metabolism (Von Endt et al. 1968). Robinson (1975) measured arsenic residues in soils over a 5-year period after annual applications of MSMA at rates ranging from 4.4 to 288 kg/hectare. Elemental arsenic did not increase in any plot receiving MSMA at rates less than 36 kg/hectare. The mechanisms of loss in these studies were not determined.

Dickens and Hiltbold (1967) conducted column leaching studies in which, after 20 successive 2.5-cm increments of water were added to a loam sand, about half of the applied MSMA remained in the surface 2.5 cm of soil and none was leached below 15 cm. Using columns of forest-floor material and soil from ponderosa pine, Douglas-fir, and mixed-fir forest types, Norris[6] determined that MSMA was rapidly leached through the forest-floor material, but was not leached in the three forest soils, by 86.4 cm of water applied over a 20-d period. In tests with 2.54 cm of undisturbed forest-floor material, as little as 2.5 cm of water delivered over an 8-d period was sufficient to move about half of the surface-applied MSMA through that material. These results indicate that MSMA deposited on the forest floor will readily move through it to the soil—even with small amounts of precipitation. Once reaching the soil, however, MSMA is rapidly immobilized.[6]

Norris et al. (1983) observed a decline with time in the arsenic concentration in the forest floor under stands that had been precommercially thinned with MSMA. The fate of arsenic in the forest floor was not determined, but the small increases in soil residues indicated some movement from forest floor to soil.

Norris[6] looked for arsenic in four streams flowing from areas that had been precommercially thinned with MSMA. Samples were collected at various intervals after treatment; special emphasis was given to storm periods when runoff might occur and to the spring runoff. Only five samples contained detectable quantities of arsenic; four of these were at the minimum level of detection, and the fifth sample was from an upstream site presumably containing water that had not passed through areas previously thinned with MSMA. The results of this study indicate that careful application of MSMA in thinning programs poses little or no threat of increased arsenic levels in aquatic systems.

Woolson et al. (1976) determined the distribution and persistence of MSMA in two aquatic model ecosystems (Table 7.10). One system contained sandy loam soil as the sediment and was stocked with channel catfish and crayfish *Procambarus clarki*; the second system contained sediment, algae, daphnids, mosquitofish, and crayfish. Channel catfish showed little tendency to bioaccumulate arsenic from MSMA (the bioaccumulation factor was 4 and showed substantial reduction in bioaccumulation level after 14 d in fresh water. Crayfish showed higher levels of accumulation (bioaccumulation factors of 80–480) but also a 50% decrease in arsenic concentration after 18 d in fresh water. The second experiment was conducted similarly, and different results were obtained. Mosquitofish had bioaccumulation ratios of about 100, but crayfish showed bioaccumulation ratios of less than 10. Daphnids and algae had bioaccumulation factors of 5 and 34, respectively. Although MSMA does show a slight tendency for bioaccumulation, the limited probability that it will be present in aquatic systems in the forest reduces the importance of this characteristic.

Toxicity.—Few data are available on the toxicity of MSMA to fish. The 96-h LC50 ranges from 12 to more than 100 mg/L, depending on species, test conditions, and the amount of active ingredient in the formulation tested (Midwest Research Institute 1975; Johnson and Finley 1980). Additional toxicity data for MSMA are shown in Table 7.12. Spehar et al. (1980) conducted experiments on the comparative toxicity of arsenic compounds and their accumulation in invertebrates and fish. These investigators noted that a concentration of 1 mg arsenic/L as arsenic III was lethal to amphipods within 1 week. The same concentration of arsenic supplied as arsenic V, disodium methanearsonate (DSMA), or sodium dimethyl arsonate (SDMA) did not significantly decrease the survival of amphi-

---

[6]Unpublished report, "The behavior and impact of organic arsenical herbicides in the forest: final report on cooperative studies," by L. A. Norris, U.S. Forest Service, Pacific Northwest Research Station, Forestry Sciences Laboratory, Corvallis, Oregon, 1974.

Backpack application of herbicide to control competing vegetation in a young forest plantation.

pods (*Gammarus pseudolimnaeus*) and *Daphnia magna* after 2 weeks of exposure or of stoneflies, snails, and rainbow trout after 28 d.

Herbicides: Fosamine Ammonium

Fosamine ammonium is a new herbicide that is expected to be increasingly used in forestry. It is registered for control of a wide variety of woody vegetation. It is usually applied as a foliar spray either by aerial or ground equipment during the 2 months before fall coloration. National Forest Products Association (see footnote 3), U.S. Forest Service (1984), and Newton (1987) discussed the use of fosamine ammonium in more detail.

Behavior in the environment.—Fosamine ammonium is highly soluble in water (179 g/100 g at 25°C) but substantially less so in nonpolar organic solvents (0.02 g in 100 g *n*-hexane at 25°C). It has little vapor pressure (4×10^{-6} mm Hg at 25°C).

Fosamine ammonium is not persistent in soils; laboratory studies indicate that soil microorganisms rapidly decompose it (Han 1979a; Table 7.10). Fosamine ammonium showed only limited mobility in column leaching studies. After 56 cm of leaching water had been applied, 60–80% of the herbicide was contained in the top 10 cm of the soil column. After 1 year and 165 cm of rain in the field, 93% of the chemical present was in the top 10 cm of soil. Thus, fosamine ammonium is readily bound by soil particles and, despite its high water solubility, has little tendency to leach. The probability of ground-water contamination or movement of fosamine ammonium to streams by leaching is negligible.

Field data on stream contamination with fosamine ammonium are lacking, but because direct application and drift are probably the principal routes by which the chemical enters streams, the data base for 2,4-D is probably applicable. Fosamine ammonium decomposes in water. In laboratory tests at pH 5, fosamine ammonium was completely degraded in 2 weeks; the compound was quite stable in water closer to pH 7, however (Han 1979a). A strong interaction of fosamine ammonium with soil suggests it is likely to be adsorbed on suspended or bottom sediments where it enters the forest streams. Stream-bottom sediments lose fosamine in 3 months or less.[7]

Specific information on the bioaccumulation of fosamine ammonium is limited; as with other pesticides of high water solubility, however, the probability of bioaccumulation is not great. Laboratory tests have demonstrated that fosamine ammonium is not bioaccumulated. Concentrations of the herbicide in fish tissues were similar to those in water (Newton and Norgren 1977). Residues in channel catfish exposed to a 1.1-mg/L concentration of ^{14}C-carbonyl-labeled fosamine ammonium in water for 4 weeks reached a plateau in 2–3 weeks and indicated an accumulation factor of less than 1. In a separate experiment, channel catfish were placed for 4 weeks in a tank containing soil treated with ^{14}C-fosamine ammonium (15 mg/L); the system had been aged for 30 d before it was flooded and fish were exposed to the chemical. The residue levels in this group of channel catfish also reached a plateau in 2–3 weeks with an accumulation factor of less than 1. After the 4-week exposures in both experiments, the fish were transferred to fresh water for 2-week depuration periods, during which residue levels dropped 50–90%. No effects on the fish were observed during these experiments (Han 1979b). In rats, fosamine ammonium was rapidly excreted and only 0.05% of the chemical remained in the body beyond 72 h (Chrzanowski et al. 1979).

Toxicity.—McLeay and Gordon (1980) conducted partial life-cycle studies of coho salmon (egg through smolt) and rainbow trout (egg through fingerling) to assess the toxicity of Krenite (the commercial formulation of fosamine ammonium) on early life stages of fish. For both fish species, the alevin was the stage most sensitive to fosamine ammonium; 96-h LC50s (postexposure mortality was included) were 618 mg/L (coho salmon) and 367 mg/L (rainbow trout). Eggs and embryos generally were very tolerant of Krenite. Swim-up fry and young fingerlings of both species had tolerances between those of eggs and alevins. Yearling coho salmon presmolts were slightly more tolerant than coho salmon fingerlings—96-h LC50s were 7,014 and 5,361 mg/L, respectively—and coho salmon smolts were slightly more sensitive to the herbicide than presmolts. Although all tested life stages suffered some mortality after 96-h exposures to fosamine ammonium, no groups surviving previous exposure to the chemical showed any latent effects throughout the observation period in fresh water. Four-day LC50 values for swim-up fry varied 12-fold when the diluent waters varied in pH, hardness, and alkalinity; toxicity increased with increases in these variables. Overall, the acute toxicity of fosamine ammonium to salmonid fish was

---

[7]Unpublished data of J. Harrod, Biochemicals Department, E. I. du Pont de Nemours and Company, 1007 Market Street, Wilmington, Delaware, 1979.

2–4 orders of magnitude less than those of the brush-control herbicides 2,4-D, 2,4,5-T, silvex, picloram, amitrole, and glyphosate.

Herbicides: Glyphosate

Glyphosate is a relatively new herbicide that is expected to be used increasingly in forestry. It is proving useful for both site preparation and release treatments at rates of application up to 4.48 kg/hectare. National Forest Products Association (see footnote 3) and Newton (1981) discussed the use of glyphosate in more detail; Chykaliuk et al. (1981) published an extensive bibliography on this chemical.

Behavior in the environment.—Glyphosate is highly soluble in water (12,000 mg/L at 25°C) but much less so in organic solvents. It has negligible vapor pressure.

In general, glyphosate is very immobile in soil, being rapidly adsorbed by soil particles, and subject to some degree of microbial degradation. Sprankle et al. (1975a, 1975b) showed that glyphosate was rapidly inactivated in soil, apparently by physical adsorption processes because autoclaving the soil did not stop the inactivation. Addition of phosphate to the soil altered the availability of the glyphosate (Hance 1976). The initial binding of glyphosate to soil was reversible, phosphate ions competing for binding sites. Thus, the initial rapid inactivation of glyphosate in soil probably results from rapid adsorption rather than degradation, although some microbial degradation of the herbicide also occurs (Sprankle et al. 1975a, 1975b). The authors also showed, by thin-layer chromatography, that glyphosate is immobile in soil.

Moshier and Penner (1978) reported that the decomposition of glyphosate differed substantially among soils (Table 7.10). Rueppel et al. (1977) also found that the degree of glyphosate decomposition varied among soil types, ranging from 5 to 50% in 28 d. In two of three soils examined, 90% of the chemical was dissipated in less than 12 weeks. Aminomethylphosphonic acid (AMPA) was the only significant soil metabolite of glyphosate, and it degraded 16–35% in 60 d in various soils. The authors classified the chemical as immobile in soil, based on leaching experiments. These findings on the behavior of glyphosate in soil are consistent with the research reported by Torstensson and Aamisepp (1977) and Hance (1976).

Newton et al. (1984) conducted a thorough study of glyphosate in a forest ecosystem after it was aerially applied (3.3 kg/hectare) to an 8-hectare area in the Oregon Coast Range. The study site contained two beaver ponds and a small (50 L/min) perennial stream. No buffer strips existed and the ponds and stream received direct application of herbicide. Glyphosate residues, and in many cases metabolites, were measured for 55 d after application at various depths in the canopy, on foliage, and in litter, soil, stream water, sediments, and wildlife (Tables 7.10, 7.11). Glyphosate and AMPA reached maximum concentrations of about 0.5 and 0.1 mg/L about 15 d after application. After 55 d, AMPA was no longer detectable, but glyphosate remained at about 0.1 mg/L. None of the fish collected during the 55-d study had detectable residue levels of glyphosate or AMPA (<0.05 mg/kg) despite detectable levels of glyphosate in water for at least 3 d and in the sediment for 55 d.

Glyphosate was applied to an agricultural watershed at rates of 1.10, 3.36, and 8.96 kg/hectare, and runoff from natural rainfall after treatments in early spring was measured and analyzed to define concentration and transport (Edwards et al. 1980). The highest concentration (5.2 mg/L) was found in runoff occurring 1 d after treatment at the highest rate. Glyphosate (0.004 mg/L) was detected in runoff from this watershed up to 4 months after treatment. For the lower rates of application, maximum concentration of the herbicide in runoff was 0.094 mg/L for events occurring 9–10 d after application, and decreased to 0.002 mg/L within 2 months of treatment. The maximum amount transported by runoff was 1.85% of the amount applied, most of which occurred during a single storm on the day after application of the highest rate of glyphosate. In each of the 3 study years, herbicide transported in the first runoff event after treatment accounted for 99% of the total herbicide runoff on one watershed. Glyphosate residues in the upper 2.5 cm of treated soil decreased logarithmically with time; they persisted several weeks longer than they did in the runoff water.

Most of the data on the fate of glyphosate in water come from canals in which glyphosate was used to control weeds on banks. Comes et al. (1976) looked for both glyphosate and its principal metabolite in the first flow of water through two canals after applications of 5.6 kg/hectare to the banks when the canals were dry. Some of the herbicide was applied to surfaces of the canal that would be below the normal waterline. No glyphosate or metabolite was detected in the first flow of water through the canals. Soil samples collected the day before the canals were filled (about 23 weeks after treatment) contained 0.35 mg glyphosate and 0.78 mg metabolite per kilogram in the 0–10-cm layer. When glyphosate was added to flowing canal water (sufficient to achieve 150 μg/L), about 30% of the herbicide was lost in 1.6 km of travel. Thereafter, the rate of disappearance diminished; about 58% was present 8 and 14 km downstream from the introduction sites in two study canals, which implies interaction between the concentration and the mechanism of loss. Rueppel et al. (1977) reported that less than 0.02% of applied glyphosate was removed by runoff from soil after artificial rain was applied at the rate of 1.9 cm/h 1, 3, and 7 d after application of chemical.

Relatively little has been done on the bioaccumulation of glyphosate, primarily because its physicochemical properties are such that bioaccumulation is not expected to be substantial. Studies of fish metabolism demonstrated that glyphosate has a very low bioaccumulation factor (Table 7.8). No residues of glyphosate or its primary metabolite (AMPA) were detected in the fillets or eggs of rainbow trout exposed to the isopropylamine salt (Folmar et al. 1979).

Toxicity.—Folmar et al. (1979) determined the acute toxicities to four aquatic invertebrates and four species of fish of glyphosate, the isopropylamine salt of glyphosate, the formulated herbicide Roundup, and the Roundup surfactant. Technical-grade glyphosate, the active ingredient in Roundup, was less toxic than Roundup or the surfactant (Table 7.12). Roundup was more toxic to rainbow trout and bluegills at higher test temperatures, and was more toxic at pH 7.5 than at pH 6.5. Eyed eggs of rainbow trout were the most resistant life stage, and sensitivity increased as the fish entered the sac-fry and swim-up stages. Rainbow trout did not avoid concentrations of the isopropylamine salt up to 10.0 mg/L; mayfly nymphs avoided Roundup at concentrations of 10 mg/L, but not at 1.0 mg/L.

In a simulated aerial application of Roundup to a forested area, Hildebrand et al. (1980) found no detectable effects on *Daphnia magna* in a forest pond after applications of 2.2, 22, and 220 kg/hectare.

Herbicides: Dalapon

Dalapon is usually formulated as the sodium and magnesium salts. In forestry it is used primarily for site preparation, conifer release, right-of-way maintenance, and grass control.

Behavior in the environment.—Dalapon and its salts are highly soluble in water (800,000 mg/L), but have little solubility in organic solvents. The acid form is relatively volatile, but dalapon is expected to exist as a salt at normal environmental acidities. The sodium and magnesium salts are not volatile; thus, volatilization of this material is unlikely in the field.

Kenaga (1974) and Foy (1975) extensively reviewed the behavior of dalapon in soil. Dalapon is highly mobile in soil because it has little affinity for soil particles in clay and clay loam soils; in muck soils, however, 20% of the dalapon may be adsorbed (Foy 1975). Laboratory studies indicate that leaching from soils should occur readily. In field tests reviewed by Kenaga (1974), however, dalapon did not leach through the soil as expected, indicating that microbial degradation may occur more rapidly than leaching. Numerous studies have indicated that dalapon is subject to microbial degradation; field persistences of less than 1 month have been commonly noted (Ashton 1982). Both dalapon and its salts undergo hydrolysis in soil, but the rates are relatively slow compared to the microbial degradation rate.

Site-specific data are not available for dalapon that may enter forest water as the result of forest vegetation management. The pattern of entry into forest streams is expected to be similar to that for 2,4-D. Dalapon will not likely adsorb strongly or extensively on sediments in aquatic systems. The primary means of inactivation in water will be microbial action, as in soil. One of the important uses of dalapon is for the control of vegetation on ditch banks. As a consequence of this use, dalapon is likely to appear in water near applications of this type. Folmar (1976, 1978) indicated that the expected dalapon concentration in water from ditch bank applications would be 0.2 mg/L.

As a result of its high water solubility and low solubility in organic solvents, dalapon shows virtually no tendency for bioaccumulation. Mammals excreted dalapon rapidly via urine (Kenaga 1974).

Toxicity.—Dalapon is only slightly toxic to fish and amphibians (Table 7.12). Fish toxicity studies of dalapon and its sodium salt formulation were reviewed by Kenaga (1974), who had access to Dow Chemical Company documentation.

Herbicides: Dinoseb

Dinoseb is a contact-action herbicide available in two forms: free phenol and amine or ammonium salt of the phenol. It was registered for use in forestry as a desiccant before lands are burned for forest-site preparation (Oregon only), but all uses are currently suspended, pending hearings by EPA. The likelihood of continued registration in forestry is remote. We include it in this chapter because of its high toxicity to aquatic species and the potential for its use in areas of important anadromous fish habitat in other countries.

Behavior in the environment.—The phenol form of dinoseb has substantial vapor pressure (0.01 mm Hg at 78°C) and is soluble to 52 mg/L in water, 23.4% in ethyl alcohol, and 8.7% in diesel fuel at 25°C (Melnikov 1971). The salt forms are highly soluble in water and have substantially less vapor pressure. Interconversion between the salt and free phenol forms is expected, depending on the pH of the medium and the presence of other ions.

Dinoseb can volatilize from soil. Hollingsworth and Ennis (1953) showed that this process depends on ambient temperature, moisture content of the soil, and the formulation applied. Volatilization was attributed to water-vapor distillation by Barrons et al. (1953) and did not occur at soil pH above 8.

The residual life of dinoseb is 3–5 weeks in warm, moist soils. Carryover from one season to the next is not expected (Klingman and Ashton 1975). Dinoseb is not tightly adsorbed on most agricultural soils and it can leach in many sandy soils; Davis and Selman (1954) reported that the phenol form moved less than 2 cm with 5 cm of rain in any soil they tested. The amine salt, however, leached 3.8 cm in sandy loam, 6.3 cm in clay loam, and 8.9 cm in loam after the same amount of rain. Upchurch and Mason (1962) reported that dinoseb interacted strongly with soil organic matter. Dinoseb was almost completely adsorbed at pH 2.3. In zones of moderate temperature and rainfall, and at normal rates of application, dinoseb should not be leached from the top 30 cm of the acid forest soils of the northwestern USA in the first year after application. Substantial decomposition by microbial action takes place within the first year after application. Phytotoxic levels may remain in soil from 2 weeks to 6 months, depending on the environment in which it is used.

We found no published information on the levels or persistence of dinoseb in stream water. We assume 2,4-D is a reasonable model for dinoseb because direct application and drift are probably the main routes of entry into streams.

Data on dinoseb bioaccumulation are lacking. In the phenol form, bioaccumulation during periods of exposure should be expected. In the salt form, this behavior will be less pronounced. Lorz et al. (1979) found measurable residues of dinoseb in a few coho salmon exposed to 0.02 mg dinoseb/L for 384 h. Most fish sampled, however, did not contain detectable residues. In tests with fathead minnows, Call et al. (1984) reported a whole-body concentration factor for dinoseb of 1.4 (although if based on total radioactive carbon, the value would be about 60). When placed in clean water, fathead minnows eliminated 67% of the dinoseb in 24 h and 95% in 14 d. Rainbow trout injected with dinoseb eliminated 90% in 24 h (50% was dinoseb and the balance was in the form of metabolites).

Toxicity.—Dinoseb is more toxic to humans, animals, and fish than are most herbicides. The acute and chronic effects of dinoseb on cutthroat trout and lake trout were investigated by Woodward (1976), who found that the toxicity of a given exposure was greatly influenced by water quality. Decreasing the pH of the water increased the dinoseb toxicity to fish. Similar findings were reported by Lipschuetz and Cooper (1961) for technical grade dinoseb. Decreasing the pH from 8.0 to 6.9 increased the toxicity of dinoseb to rainbow trout by a factor of 5. High temperature and water hardness also enhance the toxicity of dinoseb to fish, but to a lesser extent than pH (Webb as cited by Lipschuetz and Cooper 1961; Woodward 1976).

Woodward (1976) observed no cumulative mortality of lake trout and cutthroat trout chronically exposed (8–12 d) to dinoseb. Prolonged exposures of 0.005–0.010 mg dinoseb/L, however, affected yolk absorption time and fry growth. Yolk

Coho salmon fingerlings in a static bioassay to determine the acute toxicity of a forest chemical.

absorption time increased by 6–9 d over that of the controls, and fry growth was reduced at all concentrations of dinoseb tested.

Lorz et al. (1979) calculated the 24-h LC50 of dinoseb to be 0.19 mg/L for yearling coho salmon under static conditions at 10°C and pH 7.0 (Table 7.12). When survivors of this bioassay were challenged with seawater, no mortalities occurred. In a flowing-water system, the toxicity of dinoseb appeared to be greater. Releasing dinoseb-exposed coho salmon and monitoring their downstream movement showed that groups exposed to 0.040 and 0.060 mg/L for 48 h were less migratory than the controls. Yearling coho salmon exposed to 0.100 mg/L for 114 h showed extensive necrosis of the liver, kidney, and gill lamellae; however, fish exposed to 0.040 and 0.060 mg/L showed only minor degenerative changes.

Insecticides: Malathion

Malathion is an organophosphate insecticide that is extensively used in both agriculture and forestry. It has been available for use since 1959. Information on the use and effect of malathion in the forest is in two environmental impact statements (U.S. Forest Service 1977b; U.S. Animal and Plant Health Inspection Service 1980). The most recent uses of malathion on lands managed by the U.S. Forest Service have been for control of western spruce budworm and grasshoppers on western forests and ranges.

Behavior in the environment.—Various aspects of the behavior of malathion in the environment are cited in several chapters of Haque and Freed (1975). Malathion has a vapor pressure of 4×10^{-5} mm Hg (30°C) and a water solubility of 145 mg/L. It is soluble in most organic solvents, but is of limited solubility in petroleum oils.

Malathion disappears rapidly from soil, even at high application rates, probably by both chemical and biological means (Table 7.10). Both the persistence and mobility of malathion were determined at terrestrial wastewater disposal sites where the chemicals were applied (0.1 mg/L) in the secondary effluent from a two-stage trickling filter for 15 weeks. Malathion was never present in excess of 0.002 mg/kg in the soil and 0.001 mg/L in the soil water. These results indicate malathion will neither accumulate in soil nor translocate in soil waters under the types of conditions tested (Jenkins et al. 1978).

Tracy et al. (1977) detected low or no malathion concentrations in stream water 48 h after applications of the insecticide for spruce budworm control in Washington in 1976 (Table 7.11). No residues were found in fish or benthic organisms from these streams.

Eichelberger and Lichtenberg (1971) determined the persistence of malathion in river water (Table 7.10). In a soil-free, aqueous system that had been inoculated with a soil extract, malathion disappeared in two phases; a relatively slow phase accounted for about 30% disappearance in 180 h, and a more rapid phase accounted for more than 50% disappearance in the next 60 h. Degradation in the aquatic system would have represented both chemical degradation (the slow phase) and microbial degradation (the rapid phase). Walker (1978) reported that malathion was the shortest lived of the insecticides tested in both fresh and salt water (Table 7.10).

Malathion is expected to show little bioaccumulation. Kenaga (1980a, 1980b) predicted a bioconcentration factor of 37. Paris et al. (1975) found no measurable adsorption of malathion by dense populations of microorganisms. The high water solubility and the low fat solubility of malathion will result in its rapid excretion or elimination from organisms that have accumulated it. Residues of malathion have been found in milk collected from cattle 5 h after they were sprayed at rates several times the normal rate used in aerial applications in forestry. Only trace amounts were found 3 d after treatment. The rapid disappearance of the insecticide from milk was attributed to its rapid excretion by the animal. The short persistence of malathion in the aquatic environment also limits its bioaccumulation.

Toxicity.—Hoffman (1957), Stavinoha et al. (1966), and Livingston (1977) all noted that organophosphate insecticides generally are short-lived in the environment, do not significantly bioaccumulate or biomagnify, and have a relatively uniform and well-understood effect on a variety of organisms. The "safe" concentrations of organophosphate insecticides have been estimated through acute toxicity studies and determinations of environmental persistence (Benson 1969). Although acute toxicities of these compounds to aquatic organisms are generally lower than those of the organochlorines, they vary widely (Tarzwell 1959; Pickering et al. 1962; Macek and McAllister 1970; Johnson and Finley 1980).

Toxic effects on various species have been associated with synergistic or antagonistic effects of the parent compounds and hydrolysis products. Numerous studies have shown that cholinesterase activity is the primary locus of organo-phosphate attack. Symptoms of acute toxicity vary from species to species, however, and diverse formulations have different acute effects.

Eaton (1970) conducted a study of chronic malathion toxicity to bluegills similar to the study by Mount and Stephan (1967b) on the fathead minnow (Table 7.12). Reproduction and early fry survival were unaffected by the 7.4-µg/L concentration that crippled adult fish after exposure for several months.

Mulla and Mian (1981) and Mulla et al. (1981) synthesized and interpreted much of the available information on the effect of malathion and parathion on nontarget flora and fauna in aquatic ecosystems, as well as on the persistence and distribution of these chemicals in aquatic habitats. Malathion had low toxicity to several mollusks, but was considerably more toxic to crustaceans (water fleas, amphipods, shrimp, and juvenile crabs). Immature nontarget insects, such as caddisflies, stoneflies, and mayflies, were highly sensitive. Malathion exhibited differential toxicity to various fish species; some species showed a substantial degree of tolerance.

Although malathion is a widely used organophosphate insecticide that enters surface waters in various ways, interpretation of residue concentrations is difficult because of the toxicity of a "persistent" metabolite (malaoxon) that is not easily identified in tissues. Cook et al. (1976) suggested alternative methods of analysis, including analysis for malathion monoacid in the gut and measurement of brain acetylcholinesterase activity, because the parent compound is rapidly absorbed and altered by fish. Bender (1969) found that two hydrolysis byproducts of malathion, which showed a pronounced synergistic effect with malathion, were more toxic to fathead minnows than the parent compound. Bender and Westman (1976) found that malathion could damage eastern mudminnows through either acute or chronic toxicity at concentrations of 0.09–0.24 mg/L (the LC50s of malathion and its principal hydrolysis products). Desi et al. (1976) found that although malathion was only slightly toxic to guppies, it was highly toxic to invertebrates such as *Daphnia magna* (LC50, 0.003 mg/L) and to juvenile forms of various species. They found that malathion affects aquatic organisms different-ly and, by exerting stress on "sophisticated functions" and exhausting the adaptability of such organisms, it is "not an entirely harmless agent for the environment." Table 7.12 summarizes some of the available data on malathion's acute toxicity to important invertebrate and fish species.

Johnson and Finley (1980) noted that 0.3-g lake trout fry were twice as sensitive to malathion as 45-g fingerlings. An increase in temperature from 7 to 29°C caused a 4-fold increase in toxicity to bluegills. Variations in water hardness did not appreciably alter the toxicity to fish or invertebrates. Salmonids exposed to malathion concentrations of 0.120–0.300 mg/L showed 70–80% inhibition of acetylcholinesterase (AChE), and activity indexes were reduced by 50–70% of those of unexposed fish. Goldfish exposed to sublethal levels showed a signifi-cantly reduced avoidance response at levels below that causing a reduced AChE activity. Exposures of rainbow trout to sublethal levels of malathion for 1 h caused severe damage to gill tissues and minor nonspecific liver lesions. Ponds given four semimonthly treatments up to 0.02 mg/L during May through July produced no discernible effects on resident bluegills or channel catfish. Popula-tions of aquatic insects, however, were significantly depressed by high but not by

Laboratory facility for flow-through, chronic toxicity tests with fish and other aquatic species.

low treatment rates. These data indicate that use of malathion needs careful planning because some species- and habitat-specific reactions to this pesticide can cause adverse effects.

Insecticides: Carbaryl

Carbaryl is a broad-spectrum, relatively nonpersistent carbamate insecticide that has been used for nearly 30 years to suppress various types of insect infestations. Registered for use against many insects, its principal use in agriculture is at rates of 0.5–2.24 kg/hectare, active ingredient, often in repeated spray treatments. In forestry, it is used to control defoliating insects (U.S. Forest Service 1977b). Forest application rates of more than 1.12 kg/hectare are uncommon. In fiscal year 1980, most of the carbaryl used in U.S. Forest Service programs was aerially applied for grasshopper control on western forest and range lands. Mount and Oehme (1981) published an extensive literature review on the chemistry, toxicity, metabolism, environmental degradation, and persistence of carbaryl.

Behavior in the environment.—Carbaryl is soluble in most polar organic solvents and to about 0.01% in water. In the soil, carbaryl is attacked by soil microbes and is not expected to leach significantly from the upper soil surfaces. Bollag and Liu (1971) isolated several microorganisms capable of metabolizing carbaryl in soil. A half-life of about 12 d was noted in several of their systems. Carbaryl was detected in soil and the forest floor for 64 and 128 d, respectively, after application (Willcox 1972). Other values for persistence of carbaryl are presented in Table 7.10.

LaFleur (1976) studied carbaryl movement and loss in the soil profile and its accumulation in underground water over 16 months. Rainfall during the study was 182 cm. The upper 1 m of soil contained about 6% of the applied carbaryl 16 months after application. None was found in the 10–20-cm layer after the fourth month. Loss of carbaryl with time in the upper 1 m of soil depended on concentration, and the half-life was less than 1 month. In underlying groundwater, carbaryl appeared within 2 months after application and persisted through the eighth month. The maximum groundwater concentration was 0.3 μM/L at the end of the second month.

No carbaryl was detected in the field plot or in soil water at a land wastewater disposal site that received carbaryl (0.1 mg/L in water) over a 15-week period (Jenkins et al. 1978). The authors concluded that carbaryl does not accumulate or translocate under the field conditions of this test. Haque and Freed (1974) predicted that carbaryl will leach less than 20 cm in a soil profile that receives an annual rainfall over 150 cm.

Caro et al. (1974) reported that 95% of the carbaryl in an agricultural soil had disappeared within 135 d. Of the 4 kg of carbaryl applied, 5.8 g were recovered during the first year in runoff water and sediment. Over 90% of this loss occurred in association with a single rainfall 19 d after application. About 75% of the seasonal loss was contained in water and 25% in sediment.

Paris et al. (1975) indicated that carbaryl is degraded both chemically and biologically; the rate of biological degradation was proportional to the density of microorganisms. Chemical degradation predominated in their study. The persistence of carbaryl in water appears to be brief. If carbaryl is applied over open water, such as small brooks or ponds, initial deposits of 1 mg/L or less in water about 10 cm deep may be expected to degrade completely or disappear in 1 or 2 d (Lichtenstein et al. 1966).[8,9]

Karinen et al. (1967) reported that the concentration of carbaryl in estuarine water decreased 50% in 38 d. When mud was present, more than 90% loss occurred in 10 d. The carbaryl was adsorbed where decomposition continued at a slower rate. The principal metabolite of carbaryl, 1-napthal, was less persistent. Carbaryl applied to a tidal mud flat (11.2 kg/hectare) disappeared rapidly. The initial residue level of 10.7 mg/kg decreased rapidly the first day when tidal flow removed carbaryl, and the 1-napthal metabolite was not adsorbed on mud. The level in the top 2.5 cm of mud decreased from 3.8 mg/kg 1 d after treatment to 0.1 mg/kg by day 42.

Several authors have measured peak concentrations of carbaryl in water in connection with spraying for control of the spruce budworm (Table 7.11). The rate constant (0.028 h^{-1}) reported by Stanley and Trial (1980) for carbaryl disappearance in streams was similar to the decay constants determined in the laboratory for carbaryl in river water (0.017 h^{-1}) and pond water (0.028 h^{-1}) (Eichelberger

---

[8]Unpublished report, "The degradation of carbaryl after surface application to a farm pond," Project Report 111A13, by R. R. Romine and R. A. Bussian, Union Carbide Corporation, Salinas, California, 1971.

[9]Unpublished report, "An investigation into the effect on fish of Sevin (carbaryl) used in rice culture," Pittman-Robertson Project W-52-R, prepared by Resource Agency, Wildlife Investigations Laboratory, California Department of Fish and Game, Sacramento, 1963.

and Lichtenberg 1971; Kanazawa 1975). Marancik[10] noted that Atlantic salmon, brook trout, and slimy sculpins did not contain detectable residues of carbaryl 24, 48, or 168 h after aerial application of 1.12 kg/hectare to forests in the eastern USA.

Bernhardt et al. (1978) conducted an intensive study of carbaryl in six streams in Washington; peak concentrations of 0.005, 0.013, 0.014, 0.020, 0.029, and 0.121 mg/L were observed. Residues typically declined from peak levels within a few hours after application. Residue levels were much lower in downstream locations. In Squilchuck Creek, the stream that received the greatest exposure, residues of 100–120 mg/kg were measured in benthic organisms, 131–152 mg/kg in cutthroat trout, and 32–335 mg/kg in sediment. Residues were not found in these ecological components at most other locations and, with the exception of sediment, were not found 30 d after application in Squilchuck Creek.

Kenaga (1980b) predicted a bioaccumulation factor of 77 for carbaryl. In a model aquatic ecosystem, Kanazawa et al. (1975) reported higher values. They found bioaccumulation factors of 2,000–4,000 for algae and duckweed, but values of only 1,000–5,000 for snails, catfish, and crayfish. The sediment in the system was the major repository for the chemical. The data suggest that carbaryl was tightly bound to soil particles and humic substances. *Daphnia* sp., which are extremely sensitive to carbaryl, were unaffected when placed in clean water that had been in contact with the sediments from this test for 3 d.

In a similar system, Sanborn (1974) did not detect any unmetabolized carbaryl in several components (including algae) of the ecosystem, although several metabolic products were prominent. Paris et al. (1975) found no measurable adsorption of carbaryl by microorganisms. Exposures of channel catfish for 28 d to ^{14}C-carbaryl in the diet (2.8 mg/kg) or by bath (0.25 mg/L) produced whole-body residues of 9 and 11 µg/kg, respectively. Within 28 d, 78% of these residues were eliminated by the fish exposed via the diet, but only 11% were eliminated by fish exposed to carbaryl baths (Johnson and Finley 1980). Korn (1973) found that channel catfish did not accumulate carbaryl because they metabolize or excrete the compound. Marancik,[10] citing Tompkins (1975), reported that pumpkinseeds exposed to the commercial product Sevin at 5 mg/L for 2 h accumulated 12.6 mg carbaryl/kg in the tissue by the end of the exposure period, but eliminated 99.8% within 24 h after exposure ended. These data suggest that carbaryl bioaccumulation is limited and that its persistence is brief.

Toxicity.—Table 7.12 summarizes the toxicity of carbaryl to several invertebrate and fish species. Courtemanch and Gibbs (1980) noted short- and long-term effects of carbaryl sprayings on stream invertebrates. The initial postspray response was an increase in drift, and the benthos showed significant declines among Plecoptera, Ephemeroptera, and Trichoptera. Plecopterans did not repopulate any treated stream by 60 d after treatment. These findings are similar to those of Burdick et al. (1960), who reported a reduced standing crop of total stream invertebrates after forest spraying with Sevin. The long-term effect of the

---

[10]Unpublished report, "Effect of insecticides used for spruce budworm control in 1975 on fish," pages 11–34 in "1975 Cooperative Pilot Control Project of Dylox, Matacil, and Sumithion: forest spruce budworm control in Maine," by J. Marancik, U.S. Forest Service, State and Private Forestry, Northeastern Area, Upper Darby, Pennsylvania, 1976.

chemical was most apparent on plecopterans, especially in streams treated for 2 consecutive years.

Following the aerial application of carbaryl (0.84 kg/hectare) for control of spruce budworm in Maine, Gibbs et al. (1984) observed woodland ponds for 30 months. The most severe and persistent effects were on amphipods; *Hyallela azteca* and *Crangonyx richmondensis* were reduced to near 0/m² and they failed to recolonize in some of the ponds 30 months after treatment. Numbers of immature Ephemeroptera and Trichoptera were reduced immediately following spray application but this effect did not persist throughout the season or into the following year. Numbers of immature Odonata were reduced following treatment and remained low during the following year. Chironomids did not appear to be affected either as immatures or emerging adults.

Stewart et al. (1967) studied the acute effects of carbaryl and its hydrolytic product 1-naphthal on various marine species. They found that carbaryl was more toxic to larval and adult crustaceans than to larval and adult mollusks and juvenile fishes. Carbaryl was more toxic than 1-naphthal. Carlson (1972) found that long-term exposure of fathead minnows to carbaryl at a concentration of 0.68 mg/L caused adverse effects on survival and spawning.

The teratogenic effects of carbaryl and malathion on developing medaka embryos exposed in static tests were investigated by Solomon (1978) and Solomon and Weis (1979). The primary site of action of these insecticides was the circulatory system. Significant increases in circulatory anomalies were produced at concentrations of 5 mg carbaryl and 20 mg malathion per liter.

Woodward and Mauck (1980) found that stonefly naiads and amphipods were considerably more sensitive than cutthroat trout to carbaryl and thus would show the greatest responses after forest spraying that caused stream contamination. Johnson and Finley (1980) provided the following notes on carbaryl tests conducted at the Columbia (Missouri) Fisheries Research Laboratory of the U.S. Fish and Wildlife Service.

> Little or no alteration in toxicity resulted when temperatures were increased from 10°C to 21°C for daphnids or from 7°C to 17°C for cutthroat trout and Atlantic salmon. Conversely, toxicity to brook trout and yellow perch was significantly increased (4- to 11-fold) by similar temperature increases. Increases in the pH of test solutions from 6.5 to 8.5 decreased toxicity to stoneflies by one-half. However, alkaline test solutions (pH 8.5-9.0) were 1.4–11.4 times more toxic to trout, salmon, and yellow perch than were test solutions with lower pH (6.5–7.5). Variations in hardness (12–300 mg/L) did not appreciably alter toxicity to scuds, trout, or yellow perch. Test solutions aged for 3 weeks were less toxic to stonefly naiads, yet more toxic to cutthroat trout.

Insecticides: Azinphos-Methyl

Azinphos-methyl is an organophosphate insecticide registered for use on a wide variety of plants to control many insect pests. It has been available since it was first registered for use on cotton in 1954; its most extensive use in forestry is in ground applications to control seed and cone insects in seed production areas. Because of this pattern of use, the chemical is unlikely to enter aquatic systems and contaminate aquatic organisms.

Coho salmon fingerlings from a test of chronic chemical toxicity. The top fish, a control, was unaffected. The middle and bottom fish show the effects of increasing toxicant concentration on growth.

Behavior in the environment.—A comprehensive review of the use and behavior of azinphos-methyl in American agriculture was made by Anderson et al. (1974). Inferences about forestry uses can be drawn from the agricultural experience. Azinphos-methyl is soluble to 29 mg/L in water (25°C) and is readily soluble in most organic solvents (except aliphatics).

The Chemagro Division of BayChem Corporation conducted soil persistence studies of azinphos-methyl (Anderson et al. 1974; Table 7.10). The average half-life of the compound was reported to be about 3 months, although it varied substantially in different soil types and in different geographic locations. Haque and Freed (1974) estimated that azinphos-methyl would leach less than 20 cm in soils receiving 150 cm of rainfall. Results of these tests suggest that the persistence of azinphos-methyl and its mobility are not sufficient to result in either buildup of the compound in the soil or its transfer into groundwater.

We did not find any published reports of azinphos-methyl in forest waters. There are unconfirmed reports of azinphos-methyl in surface and subsurface water draining from seed orchards on sandy soil in the southeastern USA. Its predominant pattern of use in forestry minimizes the likelihood that this insecticide will enter forest surface waters in western North America.

Meyer (1965) reported that the half-life of azinphos-methyl would be about 2 d in the aquatic environment (Table 7.10). Flint et al.[11] reported a half-life of 1.2 d in an outdoor pond. The degradation was more rapid where both sunlight and microorganisms were active than in indoor tests. Liang and Lichtenstein (1972) showed that azinphos-methyl is subject to photodecomposition in aquatic systems. These tests suggest that the decomposition of azinphos-methyl in an aquatic environment is relatively rapid and that accumulation is not to be expected.

Azinphos-methyl should show little potential for bioaccumulation. Dairy cattle appear to excrete it rapidly (Everett et al. 1966; Loeffler et al. 1966). No residues were found in milk 1–2 d after treated feed was withdrawn.

Toxicity.—Several researchers have studied the toxicity of azinphos-methyl to invertebrates and fishes (Henderson et al. 1960; Katz 1961; Macek and McAllister 1970; Johnson and Finley 1980; Table 7.12). It is 2–10 times more toxic than malathion.

Johnson and Finley (1980) noted that variations in test temperatures from 2°C to 18°C for rainbow trout and 12°C to 22°C for bluegills produced no change in toxicity of azinphos-methyl at the lower temperatures and a 2-fold increase at the higher temperatures; yellow perch became substantially more susceptible with an increase in temperature (Table 7.12). Variations in water hardness from 12 to 300 mg/L produced no change in toxicity to scuds or fish. Alkaline solutions (pH 8.5–9.0) were slightly less toxic to fish than more acidic solutions (pH 6.5–7.5). Aqueous degradation from 1 to 3 weeks produced a 1.3- to 2-fold increase in 96-h LC50s for Atlantic salmon and yellow perch. Atlantic salmon eggs were highly tolerant of the chemical (11-d LC50 > 50 mg/L). The susceptibility of yolk-sac fry equaled that of fingerlings. Time-independent LC50s (TILC50) were 0.00023, 0.00029, and 0.00032 mg/L for Atlantic salmon, bluegills, and yellow perch, respectively. The TILC50 is a statistical estimate of the toxicant concentration at which 50% of the test population would be expected to survive in a long-term exposure. Cumulative toxicity indexes varied from 10.9 to 20.5, indicating a moderate to high degree of cumulative action (for an organophosphate). The cumulative toxicity index is the numerical ratio of the 96-h LC50 to the TILC50 for a chemical. This ratio can serve as an estimate of the cumulative action of a toxicant. For example, a ratio of 2:1 suggests little cumulative action. Adelman et al. (1976) found that 0.00051 mg azinphos-methyl/L, but not 0.00033 mg/L, drastically reduced egg production by fathead minnows, but caused no other apparent adverse effects.

Insecticides: Carbofuran

Carbofuran is a broad-spectrum carbamate insecticide. It has major registrations for a wide variety of soil and foliar insect pests in numerous agricultural crops. It is used in forestry to control seed and cone insects in nurseries and seed orchards and as a root dip at time of planting (see footnote 3).

---

[11]Unpublished report, "Soil runoff, leaching, and adsorption and water stability studies with Guthion," Report 28936, by D. R. Flint, D. D. Church, H. R. Shaw, and J. Armour, Chemagro Corporation, Kansas City, Missouri, 1970.

Behavior in the environment.—Carbofuran is soluble to 700 mg/L in water (25°C) and has a vapor pressure of 2×10^{-5} mm Hg (33°C). The moderately low vapor pressure suggests low volatility from soil. Tu and Miles (1976) classed carbofuran as "slightly volatile" (the least volatile group) in soil at 20°C. Carbofuran, like the other carbamate insecticides, disappears rapidly from soil (Table 7.10). Goring et al. (1975) included carbofuran in the group of pesticides that is "moderately persistent in soil" (half-lives of 1.5–6 months). Sanborn (1974) did not detect a bioaccumulation of carbofuran in a multicomponent model ecosystem, although each component gave evidence that carbofuran became tightly bound and underwent substantial degradation. Additional specific data on this chemical are lacking, but carbofuran is expected to behave similarly to other carbamate insecticides.

We did not find any published reports of carbofuran in forest waters. There are unconfirmed reports of carbofuran in surface and subsurface water draining from seed orchards on sandy soils in the southeastern USA. The way it is used in forestry minimizes the likelihood that carbofuran will enter forest surface waters in the western USA.

Toxicity.—Data on carbofuran toxicity are limited. It is considerably more toxic than the other carbamate insecticides such as carbaryl. Johnson and Finley (1980) summarized the work carried out at the National Fish Research Laboratory, Columbia, Missouri (Table 7.12). Adult sheepshead minnows exposed to concentrations of 0.049 mg/L or more showed significantly greater mortality than control fish during a 131-d study (Parrish et al. 1977). Hatching success of eggs spawned by fish exposed to 0.049 mg/L was significantly less than that of eggs of unexposed fish. Mortality of fry hatched from eggs spawned by fish exposed to 0.23 and 0.049 mg/L was significantly greater than control fry mortality. Davey et al. (1976) noted that carbofuran was the least toxic of five rice-field pesticides to mosquitofish and green sunfish. Klaassen and Kadoum (1979) found that carbofuran was present in the water and mud of a farm pond only immediately after application of 0.025 mg/L, but observed no adverse effects.

Insecticides: Acephate

Acephate is a moderately persistent, organophosphate insecticide. It is used to control defoliating insects on several agricultural crops. In forestry, it is used to control seed and cone insects in seed orchards and the western spruce budworm in forest stands, where it is applied at a rate of 1.5 kg/hectare (see footnote 3).

Behavior in the environment.—Willcox and Coffey[12] summarized the behavior and the toxicity of acephate. It is degraded in soil by microbial action. Chevron[13] reported that, in soils from nine locations across the USA, acephate had a half-life ranging from 0.5 to 13 d when the soil was fortified to 1 or 10 mg/kg. The longest persistence was in a highly organic muck soil; in the other eight soils, the half-life ranged from 0.5 to 4 d. Other persistence values are shown in Table 7.10.

---

[12]Unpublished report, "Environmental impact of acephate insecticide (Orthene)," by H. Willcox III and T. Coffey, Jr., U. S. Forest Service, State and Private Forestry, Forest Insect and Disease Management, Northeastern Area, Upper Darby, Pennsylvania, 1977.

[13]Unpublished report, "The impact of Orthene on the environment," prepared by Chevron Chemical Company, Richmond, California, 1973.

In laboratory studies, acephate (freshly added) was readily leached in soil. Aged soil residues were much less mobile. The short persistence of acephate in biologically active soils is believed to minimize the likelihood of significant movement to groundwater. According to Chevron, acephate is hydrolyzed slowly in water (half-life at 21°C: 55 d at pH 5.0, 46 d at pH 7.0, and 16 d at pH 9.0). In tests conducted to determine if acephate would be moved by runoff water, residues were found in both runoff water and associated soil particles. Sediments and submerged vegetation also adsorb acephate, but the residue levels decline rapidly.

Flavell et al. (1977) summarized the aquatic data collected during pilot-scale applications of acephate to control the western spruce budworm in three 405-hectare blocks in Montana in 1976 (Table 7.11). Concentrations decreased rapidly, typically to 10% of initial values in 2–6 h. Residues averaged 0.065 mg/kg (range, 0.026–0.139 mg/kg) in fish and 0.036 mg/kg (0.0–0.107 mg/kg) in insects.

Sanborn (1974) reported that acephate did not accumulate in algae, clams, crabs, *Daphnia* sp., *Elodea* sp., mosquitofish, or snails in a model ecosystem that had both terrestrial and aquatic components. The acephate was applied at a rate of 1.12 kg/hectare to the terrestrial portion of the system. The data also indicated more than 95% decomposition of acephate in the system in 33 d.

Bluegills were continuously exposed to 1.0- or 0.01-mg/L concentrations of ^{14}C-labeled acephate for 35 d, and tissue samples were analyzed periodically to determine the rate and extent of ^{14}C-residue accumulation. After the exposure period, the fish were transferred to untreated water for 14 d.[14] The maximum tissue concentration of labeled residues in the edible portion was about 10 times the concentration in water. Upon transfer to uncontaminated water, fish exposed at both levels eliminated more than 50% of the residues in the edible flesh within 3 d. These data indicate a low potential for bioaccumulation.

Toxicity.—The effects on stream fishes and invertebrates of an operational acephate spraying to suppress spruce budworm were investigated by Rabeni and Stanley (1979). Acephate reached its maximum concentration of 0.14 mg/L in North Brook and 0.113 mg/L in South Brook, Maine, within 1 h of spraying, and residues remained in stream water for at least 2 d. The authors concluded that acephate caused relatively minor, short-term perturbations to the stream ecosystem: drift of macroinvertebrates increased, the standing crop of most invertebrates remained unchanged, brain acetylcholinesterase activity was depressed in suckers but not in trout or salmon, and brook trout altered their diet but their growth was not affected. The authors drew these conclusions because the effects observed were either transitory or were not adverse. If the streams were adversely affected by spray drift, it was not detected by the methods used.

Willcox and Coffey (see footnote 12) summarized the pertinent literature on environmental effects of acephate insecticide. Acephate has an extremely low toxicity to fish (Table 7.12); although it is more toxic to invertebrates, no effects on Plecoptera or Ephemeroptera in a Pennsylvania stream and pond were recognized after a treatment of 0.56 kg (active ingredient)/hectare.

---

[14]Unpublished report, "Exposure of fish to ^{14}C-labelled Orthene: accumulation, distribution and elimination of residues," by B. O. Sleight, Bionomics Incorporated, Wareham, Massachusetts, 1972.

Woodward and Mauck (1980) suggested that acephate would be the most acceptable of five forest insecticides tested from the standpoint of its effects on nontarget aquatic organisms. It was nontoxic to cutthroat trout, and the lowest concentration toxic to aquatic invertebrates was much higher than the concentrations that could be expected in water after a spraying operation.

Insecticides: Bacillus thuringiensis

Bacillus thuringiensis (*B.t.*) is a naturally occurring bacterial insecticide first registered in the USA in 1961. It has found broad usage in agriculture and forestry and for mosquito control. It is currently registered for terrestrial food and nonfood crops, greenhouse food crops, forestry, and indoor uses.

Behavior in the environment.—Most of the environmental studies with *B.t.* have focused on the persistence of the material as it affects efficacy. On foliage and probably the surface soil, *B.t.* is rapidly inactivated by sunlight. The rate of inactivation varies from test to test; factors such as humidity, rainfall, and plant species are influential (Table 7.10).

Spores of *B.t.* germinated, grew, and sporulated in soil of neutral pH to which alfalfa or casein had been added. The number of viable spores increased 100-fold. In more acid soils, the spores germinated but the vegetative cells did not survive. It appears *B.t.* spores can remain viable for a long time in soil, and that the organism can compete successfully under conditions favoring the bacillus component of the microbial populations (Saleh et al. 1970; Petras and Casida 1985).

Field and laboratory studies have also examined the persistence of *B.t.* in water. Following aerial application of *B.t.* in eastern Canada to help control eastern spruce budworm, *B.t.* was recovered from rivers and public water distribution systems. Laboratory tests indicate that *B.t.* can survive for extended periods of time in both fresh and marine water at 20°C. The field tests did not reveal detectable quantities of the organism in oysters or clams, even though the water tested positive (Menon and De Mestral 1985).

Bacillus thuringiensis is ubiquitous in the natural environment. For this reason, and because toxicity tests show virtually no effect on most other organisms, little work has been done on the movement, persistence, and fate of *B.t.* for purposes of estimating exposure variables. The U.S. Environmental Protection Agency has no data on the environmental fate of *B.t.* but does not require them, probably because this material is not toxic to most nontarget species (U.S. Environmental Protection Agency 1988).

Toxicity.—Few toxic effects have been reported in studies of aquatic species exposed to *B.t.* A static bioassay with Dipel, a formulated product containing 3.2% *B.t.* variety *kurstaki*, suggested possible toxicity to mussels and brine shrimp. The LC50 for brine shrimp was 85 mg/L, but it was uncertain whether the deaths were caused by the microbe or other factors.

Toxicity studies on *B.t.* variety *israeliensis* were conducted by ToxiGenics for Abbott Laboratories. Rainbow trout and bluegills were subjected in static bioassays to concentrations of 300–370 mg/L (rainbow trout) and 300–600 mg/L (bluegills). One rainbow trout died between 72 and 96 h after exposure to 370 mg/L. Five of 30 bluegills subjected to 300 mg/L died within 96 h, as did 7 of 30 bluegills subjected to 600 mg/L. The LC50s were not calculated by ToxiGenics

(Study 410-0561 and Study 410-0563, Attachments 17 and 18 in U.S. Environmental Protection Agency 1988).

Insecticides: Nuclear Polyhedrosis Virus

Nuclear polyhedrosis virus (NPV) is a biological insecticide. Its use in forestry has been developed specifically for the control of several insects, including European pine sawfly *Neodiprion sertifer*, spruce budworm, and Douglas-fir tussock moth *Orgyia pseudotsugata*. The active ingredient is a nuclear polyhedrosis virus whose infection particles or virons are randomly occluded in an orthagonal crystalline matrix called polyhedral inclusion bodies, or PIBs. The dosage rate of NPV is usually expressed in PIBs per unit area (hectare or acre). A specific NPV is produced for each target organism. For instance, the NPV for the Douglas-fir tussock moth is isolated from millions of tussock moth larvae that have been infected with the virus under closely controlled conditions. The virus is purified, stored, and (when needed) formulated into a material that can be easily applied to the forest.

Behavior in the environment.—Little attention has been given to the movement, persistence, and fate of NPV in forest environments. Active NPV introduced into the forest floor undergoes little vertical movement in the soil, but remains active for at least 11 years. The NPV produced from early instars of insect hosts, however, appears to be largely inactivated before it reaches the forest floor (Thompson and Scott 1979). Jaques (1969) found that the abundance of NPV developed for cabbage looper *Trichoplusia ni* had not decreased significantly 231 weeks after it was applied to the soil, but little virus was detected at depths greater than 7.5 cm; this suggests that the viruses are unlikely to move into groundwater.

Exposure data developed in the traditional way are meaningless because NPV is part of the normal environment. Naturally occurring NPV can persist for up to 41 years after an epizootic of the disease. Concentrations typically are low (<45 PIB/cm^3), but they are sufficient in sheltered locations to infect tussock moth larvae (Thompson et al. 1981). Laboratory tests have shown that NPV is virtually nontoxic and nonpathogenic to mammals, birds, fish, and other nontarget organisms, indicating the highly specific action of this biological insecticide.

Toxicity.—Bluegills and rainbow trout showed no adverse effects when exposed to high doses of PIB. Freshwater crayfish showed no adverse effects when similarly exposed (MicroGeneSystem 1985).

Buckner et al. (1975) conducted an extensive study of the effects of NPV on a wide array of nontarget organisms in the forest. In this study, NPV was applied (247.5×10^9 PIB/hectare) to 160 hectares of forest on Manitoulin Island, Ontario, to control eastern spruce budworm. The area was surveyed for effects on songbirds, small mammals, honey bees, and many aquatic species. No immediate or short-term effects on any of these organisms were found.

Fertilizers

Nitrogen (N), as urea, is the element most commonly applied as a forest fertilizer in the northwestern USA. Application rates vary, but are usually 168–224 kg urea-N/hectare (Moore and Norris 1974). Bengtson (1979) reviewed the use of fertilizers in forestry.

Aerial application of urea fertilizer.

Behavior in the environment.—Urea is highly soluble in water and is readily moved from surface deposits into the forest floor and soil. Hydrolysis to ammonium ion is usually complete in 2 weeks. Ammonium ions may be adsorbed by humic substances, held as exchangeable cations, incorporated by soil micro-organisms, or taken up by forest vegetation. In addition, there is evidence for ammonia volatilization, which can be appreciable in some cases (Derome 1979, 1980; Marshall and DeBell 1980). Usually, the nitrogen is quickly distributed through the biomass and is cycled within the forest ecosystem (Moore and Norris 1974). Pang and McCullough (1982) monitored nutrient distribution in the forest floor and in soil over a 31-month period after urea fertilizer was applied (448 kg N/hectare) to a Douglas-fir forest. The increase in nutrient concentration (sampled with tension lysimeters) was greatest in the forest floor; concentrations up to 200 mg N/L persisted 5 months later, compared to 0.5 mg/L in untreated stands. There was no appreciable difference in nutrient levels between the forest floor and 10- and 30-cm soil depths in the fertilized stand. When the forest was thinned as well as fertilized, however, the concentration of nitrogen was about the same in the forest floor but increased to 80–100 mg/L at 10- and 30-cm depths in the soil. This illustrates the importance of vegetation density in the capture and cycling of nitrogen added to forest ecosystems.

Fertilizer nitrogen enters aquatic environments by the same routes described for pesticides. The highest concentrations of urea result from direct application to stream surfaces. Urea transformation products are mobilized in ephemeral stream channels and move through subsurface drainage networks to perennial streams.

Forest soils filter out plant nutrients very efficiently, but increased levels of

TABLE 7.13.—Nitrogen lost from treated watershed 2 during the first year after application of 224 kg urea-N/hectare and from untreated watershed 4 during the same period, South Umpqua Experimental Forest, Oregon. (From Moore 1971.)

Loss locus or statistic	Urea-N	NH_3-N	NO_3-N	Total
Absolute loss (kg/hectare)				
Watershed 2 (treated)	0.65	0.28	27.09	28.02
Watershed 4 (untreated)	0.02	0.06	2.07	2.15
Net loss (2 − 4)	0.63	0.22	25.02	25.87
Proportional loss				
Percent of total	2.44	0.85	96.71	100.00

various nitrogen species have been measured in several forest stream systems in the northwestern USA. In one of the more intensive efforts, Moore (1970) measured the amounts and forms of nitrogen entering streams during and after aerial application of 224 kg urea-N/hectare to 68 hectares of a southwestern Oregon forest (Table 7.11). Only 0.01% of the nitrogen applied to the watershed was found in streams up to 15 weeks after application. Over the next 24 weeks during the summer and fall, precipitation and hence streamflows were low and essentially no applied nitrogen was lost. November storms brought the soil moisture back to maximum storage capacity, and stream concentrations of nitrate-N reached a second peak of 0.177 mg/L in December. Both streamflow and nitrate-N levels remained high through December and January, during which time 23.8 kg of applied nitrogen were lost. This 2-month washout accounted for 92% of the total amount of fertilizer nitrogen lost during the first year—25.9 kg (Table 7.13). Over the same period, the total amount of soluble inorganic nitrogen lost from the 49-hectare control wastershed was 2.15 kg. Stream data on soluble organic nitrogen, total phosphorus, silica, and exchangeable cations (sodium, potassium, calcium, magnesium, iron, manganese, and aluminum) indicate that nitrogen fertilization did not accelerate losses of native soil nitrogen and other plant nutrients.

Similar data were reported by Moore (1975a, 1975b) for several other monitoring studies conducted throughout the Douglas-fir region. In one study, the concentrations of nitrogen after forest fertilization were determined in 29 streams in the northwestern USA and Alaska (Moore 1975b). The most extreme values from that study are shown in Table 7.11. Increases in the concentration of urea-N ranged from very low to a high of 44.4 mg/L. These increases resulted almost entirely from direct applications to surface water, and the peak concentrations reached were directly proportional to the amount of open surface water in the treated units. The high peak concentrations of urea-N measured in Dollar Creek were associated with the spring runoff of snowmelt.

The peak concentrations of urea-N did not persist for more than a few hours. Concentrations characteristically reached a peak the day of application and then decreased rapidly. Within 3–5 d after application, urea-N in the streams returned to pretreatment concentrations.

Increases in ammonium-N levels also resulted from direct applications of urea fertilizer to open water. Urea is readily hydrolyzed to ammonium-N in the stream system. Urea applied to the forest floor and to soil surfaces does not reach streams because it hydrolyzes rapidly to ammonium carbonate and is then held on cation-exchange sites in the soil and the forest floor like any other ammonium salt.

Peak concentrations of nitrate-N in streams after forest fertilization ranged from no increase in Spencer Creek to a maximum of 4.00 mg/L in a tributary stream of the Elochoman River. The concentration of nitrate-N in stream samples usually reaches a peak 2–4 d after spring applications of fertilizer. Concentrations then decrease, but may remain above background levels for 6–8 weeks. Losses of applied nitrogen are very small because the maximum concentrations of nitrate-N are generally less than 1 mg/L, and streamflow rapidly decreases with the onset of the dry summer season. About half of the applied nitrogen entering the stream during the first 30 d is from direct application and is measured as urea- and ammonium-N. The other half enters as nitrate. In the early fertilization projects, stream buffer strips were either very narrow or not used, and estimated total losses were 2–3% of the applied nitrogen. In later projects, however, direct application to open surface water was minimized by buffer strips along the main streams and tributaries, and measured losses were less than 0.5%.

When monitoring studies have continued through the first winter after fertilization, additional peaks in the concentration of nitrate-N have been measured. These peaks usually coincide with intense winter storms, and the concentration drops sharply between storms. Maximum concentrations measured were low and tended to decrease with each successive storm (Moore 1971).

Patterns of nitrate-N loss to streams after early fall applications of fertilizer (September, October) are similar to those after spring applications. Peak concentrations measured during winter storms may not be as high, however, because shorter periods of warm weather mean less nitrogen is converted to nitrate. The initial peak in nitrate-N concentration after a fall fertilization occurs in November and December. Subsequent peaks during winter storms are similar to those in streams draining untreated areas. Additional losses as nitrate-N may occur the next winter, however.

Hetherington (1985) reported that peak nitrogen concentrations in two small streams were 14 mg/L as urea, 1.9 mg/L as ammonia, and 9.3 mg/L as nitrate within the first 60 d after an early-September application. These values are consistent with the range of concentrations reported by Moore (1975b). However, the total amounts of nitrogen discharged from the study watersheds (228 hectares, 46% fertilized with urea at 224 kg N/hectare; and 78 hectares, 80% fertilized) were 5.9% and 14.5%, respectively, of the amounts applied, values that are substantially higher than the losses of about 1% summarized by Moore (1975b). From 53 to 61% of the discharge occurred in November, the third month after application; 92–98% of the nitrogen was discharged as nitrate. Hetherington concluded that fertilization did not lower water quality below drinking water standards or endanger fish, but he cautioned against direct applications of fertilizer to stream channels, open water, or swampy areas.

Toxicity.—Ammonia is one of the toxic breakdown products of fertilizers. U.S. Environmental Protection Agency (1976) summarized its toxic characteristics as follows.

> Ammonia is a pungent, colorless, gaseous, alkaline compound of nitrogen and hydrogen that is highly soluble in water. It is a biologically active

compound present in most waters as a normal biological degradation product of nitrogenous organic matter. It may also reach ground and surface waters through discharge of industrial wastes containing ammonia as a byproduct, or wastes from industrial processes using "ammonia water."

When ammonia dissolves in water, some of the ammonia reacts with the water to form ammonium ions. A chemical equilibrium is established which contains un-ionized ammonia (NH_3), ionized ammonia (NH_4^+), and hydroxide ions (OH^-). . . . The toxicity of ammonia is very much dependent upon pH as well as the concentration of total ammonia. Other factors also affect the concentration of NH_3 in water solutions, the most important of which are temperature and ionic strength.

In most natural waters, the pH range is such that the NH_4^+ fraction of ammonia predominates; however, in highly alkaline waters, the NH_3 fraction can reach toxic levels. Many laboratory experiments of relatively short duration have demonstrated that the lethal concentrations for a variety of fish species are in the range of 0.2 to 2.0 mg/l NH_3 with trout being the most sensitive and carp the most resistant. Although coarse fish such as carp survive longer in toxic solutions than do salmonids, the difference in sensitivity among fish species to prolonged exposure is probably small. . . . The lowest lethal concentration reported for salmonids is 0.2 mg/l NH_3 for rainbow trout . . . (Liebmann, 1960). The concentration for Atlantic salmon smolts . . . (Herbert and Shurben, 1965) and for rainbow trout (Ball, 1967) was found to be only slightly higher. Although a concentration of NH_3 below 0.2 mg/l may not kill a significant proportion of a fish population, such concentration may still exert an adverse physiological or histopathological effect (Lloyd and Orr, 1969, Smith and Piper, 1975). . . . Burrows (1964) found progressive gill hyperplasia in fingerling chinook salmon . . . during a 6-week exposure to a total ammonia concentration (expressed as NH_4) of 0.3 mg/l (0.002 mg/L NH_3), which was the lowest concentration applied.

Another breakdown product of fertilizers is nitrate. The U.S. Environmental Protection Agency (1976) has established a recommended standard for nitrate but not a mandatory one because nitrate has long been considered almost nontoxic to fish. Westin (1974) reported a 96-h medium tolerance limit (TLm) of 5,800 mg nitrate/L for chinook salmon fingerlings and 6,000 mg/L for rainbow trout fingerlings. Few data are available on other life stages, but Kincheloe et al. (1979) found that sodium nitrate was mildly toxic to the early life stages of several salmonids. Coho salmon eggs and fry were resistant to nitrate toxicity. Eggs and fry of chinook salmon, rainbow trout, steelhead, and Lahontan cutthroat trout exhibited mortalities during exposure to nitrate concentrations as low as 5 mg/L. A complication was that eggs were infested with the fungus *Saprolegnia* sp. The authors believed that nitrate levels of 10 mg/L (2 mg nitrate-N/L) in surface waters of low total hardness would limit survival of some salmonid fish populations because of impaired reproductive success.

Ammonium fertilizers have also been used to increase the productivity of fish ponds (Swingle 1947; Boyd and Sowles 1978). These fertilizers can lower the alkalinity of water (Hunt and Boyd 1981), so fertilized ponds may have to be limed to neutralize the acidity.

Stay et al. (1979) studied the effects of fertilizing a second-growth Douglas-fir forest with 224 kg urea-N/hectare. Although they found sharp increases of urea in a stream during fertilization because of direct application, all nitrogen forms

Aerial application of fertilizer to enhance the growth of young seedlings planted in a recently harvested area.

returned to near background levels shortly afterward. A 2-month rainbow trout bioassay showed no deaths that could be attributed to byproducts or contaminants of urea. Changes in benthic and drifting invertebrates could not be related to the fertilization project.

Fire Retardants

Modern chemical fire retardants are complex mixtures. The most abundant constituent (responsible for the fire-retarding action) is diammonium phosphate (Phos-Chek products), ammonium sulfate (Fire-Trol 100), or ammonium polyphosphate (other Fire-Trol products). Numerous other constituents are in the formulations applied in the field, however (Tables 7.14, 7.15). The behavior and impact of chemical fire retardants have not been extensively studied. Douglas (1974) reviewed this topic, Van Meter and Hardy (1975) conducted an initial stimulation study of retardant distribution in streams, and C. W. George reviewed the literature on retardant toxicity to aquatics (see footnote 2).

The principal toxic ingredient of the chemical fire retardants currently in use is believed to be an ammonium salt (in the form of un-ionized ammonia, NH_3; see footnote 2). One analysis, however, suggested that photolysis of the ferrocyanide in several Fire-Trol retardant formulations may yield sufficient cyanide to be the primary toxicant in these products.[15]

Behavior in the environment.—The behavior of ammonium and ammonia in the environment was described in the previous section on urea fertilizer. Fire-Trol

---

[15]Unpublished draft environmental assessment report, "Toxicity and environmental effects of fire retardant chemicals," prepared by U.S. Forest Service, Pacific Northwest Region, Portland, Oregon, 1979.

TABLE 7.14.—Typical composition of some chemical fire retardants.[a] Empty cells mean information is unavailable.

Retardant and constituent	Empirical formula	% by weight in dry powder or liquid concentration	mg/L in mixed retardant
Phos-Chek XAR,[b] Monsanto			
Diammonium phosphate	$(NH_4)_2HPO_4$	85–90	$1.02–1.08 \times 10^5$
Modified polysaccharide		5–10	6,000–12,000
Iron oxide	Fe_2O_3	0–1	0–1,200
Corrosion inhibitors: soluble salt of			
Silicofluoride	SiF_6^{-2}	0.25–0.58	300–700
Thiosulfate	S_2O_3	0.01–5	1,200–6,000
2-Mercapto-benzothiazole	$C_6H_4SCSH:N$	0.0005–2	600–2,400
Flow conditioner (insoluble)		2–4	2,400–4,800
Phos-Chek 259R (0.14 kg/L), Monsanto			
Diammonium phosphate	$(NH_4)_2HPO_4$	92	111,000
Modified polysaccharide		2.5	3,000
Iron oxide	Fe_2O_3	0.75	902
Corrosion inhibitors: soluble salt of			
Silicofluoride	SiF_6^{-2}	1.47	1,768
Thiosulfate	S_2O_3	0.71	854
2-Mercapto-benzothiazole	$C_6H_4SCSH:N$	0.20	241
Flow conditioner (insoluble)		2.0	2,405
Phos-Chek 259R (0.19 kg/L), Monsanto			
Diammonium phosphate	$(NH_4)_2HPO_4$	92	148,000
Modified polysaccharide		2.5	4,024
Iron oxide	Fe_2O_3	0.75	1,207
Corrosion inhibitors: soluble salt of			
Silicofluoride	SiF_6^{-2}	1.47	2,366
Thisosulfate	S_2O_3	0.71	1,143
2-Mercapto-benzothiazole	$C_6H_4SCSH:N$	0.20	322
Flow conditioner (insoluble)		2.0	3,219
Fire-Trol 100,[c] Chemonics			
Ammonium sulfate	$(NH_4)_2SO_4$	62	169,000
Attapulgite clay		36	90,000
Iron oxide	Fe_2O_3	1	2,500
Corrosion inhibitors: soluble salt of			
Dichromate	CrO_7^{-2}	1	2,500
Fire-Trol 931L,[d] Chemonics			
Ammonium polyphosphate (10-34-0)		93	249,000
Attapulgite clay		4	10,700
Iron oxide	Fe_2O_3	1–2	2,600–5,400
Corrosion inhibitors: Sodium ferrocyanide	$Na_4Fe(CN)_6$	1–2	2,600–5,400
A dye[e]		—	—
Fire-Trol 934L, Chemonics			
Ammonium polyphosphate (10-34-0)		97.5–98	258,000
Sodium ferrocyanide	$Na_4Fe(CN)_6$	1.5	3,900
Surfactant and water[e]			

[a]From Chemical Economics Handbook, January 1978, Menlo Park, California, Phosphorus Products, page L.

[b]U.S. Patent 3,024,100 (March 6, 1962), Corrosion-Inhibited Liquid Fertilizer Compositions, granted to Langguth and Seifter and assigned to Monsanto Chemical Company. U.S. Patent 3,342,749 (September 19, 1967). Corrosion-Inhibited Phosphate Solutions, granted to Handleman, Groves, and Langguth and assigned to Monsanto Company.

[c]U.S. Patent 3,196,108 (July 20, 1965), Fire Supressing Composition for Aerial Application, granted to Nelson and assigned to Arizona Agrochemical Corporation (now Chemical Industries).

[d]U.S. Patent 3,960,735 (June 1, 1976), Corrosion-Inhibited Polyphosphate Compositions, granted to Lacey and assigned to Early California Industries, Inc.

[e]The formulation and concentration of these compounds were furnished by Chemonics and are not included because of their proprietary natures.

TABLE 7.15.—Concentration of specific ions in some chemical fire retardants (estimated from data in Table 7.14).[a]

Retardant and specific ion	Formula	mg/L in mixed retardant
Phos-Chek XA, Monsanto		
Ammonium + ammonia[b]	NH_3	26,300–27,900
Phosphate	PO_4^{-3}	73,000–77,700
Silicofluoride	SiF_6^{-2}	300–700
Thiosulfate	$S_2O_3^{-2}$	1,200–6,000
Mercaptobenzothiazole (MBT)	$C_7H_5NS_2$	600–2,400
Phos-Chek 259R (0.14 kg/L), Monsanto		
Ammonium + ammonia[b]	NH_3	28,600
Phosphate	PO_4^{-3}	79,800
Silicofluoride	SiF_6^{-2}	1,768
Thiosulfate	$S_2O_3^{-2}$	854
Mercaptobenzothiazole (MBT)	$C_7H_5NS_2$	241
Phos-Chek 259R (0.19 kg/L), Monsanto		
Ammonium + ammonia[b]	NH_3	40,140
Phosphate	PO_4^{-3}	112,000
Silicofluoride	SiF_6^{-2}	2,366
Thiosulfate	$S_2O_3^{-2}$	1,143
Mercaptobenzothiazole (MBT)	$C_7H_5NS_2$	322
Fire-Trol 100, Chemonics		
Ammonium + ammonia[b]	NH_3	43,600
Sulfate	SO_4^{-2}	122,900
Dichromate	$Cr_2O_7^{-2}$	2,500
Fire-Trol 931L, Chemonics		
Ammonium + ammonia[b]	NH_3	30,300
Phosphate	PO_4^{-3}	113,300
Ferrocyanide	$Fe(CN)_6^{-4}$	1,800–3,800
Fire-Trol 934L, Chemonics		
Ammonium + ammonia[b]	NH_3	31,370
Phosphate	PO_4^{-3}	117,000
Ferrocyanide	$Fe(CN)_6^{-4}$	2,720

[a]From Table 2, "Draft fire retardant environmental assessment," U.S. Forest Service, Pacific Northwest Region, Portland, Oregon, undated.
[b]The distribution of N between the ammonium and the ammonia forms is both temperature and pH dependent. See unpublished report, "The behavior and impact of chemical fire retardants in forest streams," by Norris, Hawkes, Webb, Moore, Bollen, and Holcombe, U.S. Forest Service, Pacific Northwest Forest and Range Experiment Station, Forestry Sciences Laboratory, Corvallis, Oregon, 1978.

931L and 934L are ammonium-based fire retardants, but they contain ferrocyanide as a corrosion inhibitor. According to Burdick and Lipschuetz (1950, quoting Baudisch and Bass 1922), ferrocyanide solutions "are decomposable to some extent under the influence of light" (sunlight). The product of photolysis is cyanide:

$$Fe(CN)_6^{-4} \rightarrow Fe(CN)_5^{-3} + CN^-.$$

The CN^- then reacts with water:

$$CN^- + H_2O \rightleftharpoons HCN + OH^-;$$

the equilibrium reaction is strongly pH dependent. The CN^- ion is relatively low in toxicity to aquatic species but HCN is quite toxic (analogous to the difference between NH_4^+ and NH_3). At pH 9.3, about half the cyanide is HCN and half CN^- (D'amore and Bellorno 1958). The environmental significance of this reaction was brought to light by a fish kill in New York in 1948. The fish kill extended over 19.3 km of river and was associated with an industrial discharge of ferrocyanides and ferricyanides (Burdick and Lipschuetz 1950). Investigators showed that the ferrocyanide and ferricyanide concentrations were below those generally accepted as lethal.

Studies of ferrocyanide conversion to cyanide were carried out by Burdick and Lipschuetz (1950) in open vessels exposed to sunlight during May and October. Initial potassium ferrocyanide concentrations ranged from 1 to 100 mg/L, and exposure time was 1–5 h. Results were inconsistent, which was attributed to varying light intensity and temperature. The highest percentage conversions to cyanide—up to 25%—occurred at the low initial concentrations of potassium ferrocyanide (1–5 mg/L).

In a more closely controlled experiment with 1-, 2-, and 3-mg/L concentrations of potassium ferrocyanide, the conversions ranged from 10 to 15% in 1 h, after which cyanide values decreased. The decrease was attributed to loss of HCN and recombination of reaction products. In any event, although the percentage conversions of potassium ferrocyanide to cyanide vary, the maximum value is about 25%.

The amount of sodium ferrocyanide that could reach surface water can be calculated, given the following assumptions:

• fire-retardant mixtures contain up to 5,400 mg $Na_4Fe(CN)_6$/L (equivalent to 3,800 mg $Fe(CN)_6^{-4}$/L);

• an air drop covers an area 75 m by 20 m and the rate of deposition is 2 L/m^2;

• a stream 3 m wide and 0.2 m deep runs through the middle and along the long axis of the drop zone; and

• retardant mixes instantaneously in the stream.

Based on these assumptions, the instantaneous stream concentration of $Fe(CN)_6^{-4}$ (before it is diluted by normal flow) would be 38 mg/L. If 25% of the ferrocyanide were photolyzed to cyanide and 90% of the cyanide occurred as HCN, the instantaneous HCN concentration would be more than 8 mg/L.

With time, HCN disappears from water, as indicated by the reports of Burdick and Lipschuetz (1950) and Doudoroff (1956). Although their studies were in the laboratory, we expect the same phenomenon in natural streams, especially where continual mixing allows HCN to be released at the interface of air with water.

The cyanide ion readily forms complexes with many metals, particularly heavy metals in the "d" block of the periodic table. Such metals typically are more abundant in lowland streams than upland forest waters. Reports of cyanide degradation in water are lacking; however, degradation occurs in activated sludges and in nonsterile soil. In nonsterile soil, the carbon of CN^- is oxidized to carbonate and the N goes to NH_3.

In summary, if sodium ferrocyanide from fire retardants is deposited in streams, some cyanide will be produced through photolysis. The concentration will depend on the amount of ferrocyanide deposited in the stream, the light intensity after deposition, and the volume of the stream. The CN^- will not pose a long-term hazard because it volatilizes, becomes diluted, and forms complexes with metals.

Norris et al. (see footnote 2) conducted an extensive study of the entry, behavior, and likely effects of an ammonium-based fire retardant in forest streams in Oregon, Idaho, and California; the results of this study are summarized below.

The retardant was applied across streams at four western locations. Direct application of retardant to the surface of the stream produced detectable changes in water chemistry for distances as far as 1,000 m downstream. The changes were of short duration and not important, either toxicologically or with respect to eutrophication downstream. The rate of application was low, however, and only a single application was made on each stream. (The effects of rate of application, vegetation density in the streamside zone, and other factors on retardant levels in streams were examined in simulation studies, described later in this section.)

The stream chemistry studies showed that direct application to the stream surface was the primary source of retardant components in streams. Once these initial residues left the stream reach, only minor amounts of retardant entered from the streamside zone. Relatively narrow, untreated strips in the streamside zone virtually eliminated movement of retardant from the land to the stream, but the edge of the treated area was only 3 m from the stream at several points.

The principal chemicals that were elevated in the stream within the first 24 h after application were ammonium-nitrogen and total phosphorus. Ammonia is potentially toxic to aquatic species and phosphorus may contribute to downstream eutrophication. After 24 h, nitrate and soluble organic nitrogen were the primary retardant components in the stream. These are transformation products of the diammonium phosphate in the retardant mixture. Both chemicals are low in toxicity and are natural components of aquatic ecosystems.

Leaching studies showed that use of fire retardant next to streams can cause nitrogen to enter the streams in measurable quantities and in a form toxic to fish. The probability that toxic levels will occur is low, however, and can be further minimized if ammonium-based fire retardants are not used on shallow, rocky, poorly developed soils on steep slopes that drain directly into stream channels.

The computerized simulation studies used a combination of real and generated data (1) to develop methods for predicting the amount (concentration) of retardant in streams at the time it is directly applied to stream surfaces, (2) to develop methods for describing the dispersal of retardant in a stream, and (3) to integrate these techniques with data on retardant toxicity to evaluate the effects of various types of retardant application on fish mortality. These simulations suggested that (1) direct application of retardant to streams is likely to cause fish mortality, and that (2) the magnitude of the mortality and the distance over which it occurs vary with characteristics of the application, the site, and the streamflow.

Characteristics of the application (for a constant pattern of distribution) include orientation of the line of flight to the stream, size of each load dropped, number of loads dropped, and the timing and placement of subsequent loads relative to the first load. For instance, a much smaller zone of mortality results when the flight path is perpendicular to a stream than when it is centered on the stream's axis. If the rate of application is doubled over the same area, the zone of mortality increases by a factor of 10 or more. We did not simulate the effects of multiple loads or of the timing and placement of subsequent loads on the mortality zone, but we believe that the effects of sequential loads are at least additive. Where the rate of application increases, substantial increases in the length of the mortality zone occur. The characteristics of the application can be controlled by the fire-control officer and the applicator to minimize effects on the stream.

Characteristics of the site include the width and depth of the stream and the density of overstream vegetation (leaf-area index). The simulation suggested that narrow, deep streams have a much shorter mortality zone than shallow, wide streams (for equivalent flow properties). The more dense the vegetation canopy over the stream, the less chemical will fall into the stream and the shorter will be the mortality zone. The characteristics of the site can be recognized and allowed for by the manager and the applicator, thus minimizing chemical entry into the stream.

Characteristics of streamflow determine the degree and speed with which retardant is mixed and diluted as it travels downstream. For streams of roughly equal gradient (steepness), the simulations showed that a stream with a smooth, straight channel is likely to have a longer mortality zone than one with many pools and riffles. Pools and riffles cause the peak of retardant concentration to spread out, thus reducing the magnitude of exposure. The other streamflow characteristic of importance is the increase in stream discharge with distance downstream because of groundwater inflows and contributions from side streams. Increased stream discharge dilutes the retardant. Managers can recognize streamflow characteristics and take them into consideration when planning fire-control strategies to minimize stream impacts.

Toxicity.—Douglas (1974) stated that retardants appear to have their greatest ecological impact on aquatic ecosystems. Numerous fish kills have been reported but few have been documented (see footnote 2). The few studies on the effects of fire retardants on fish populations showed varying results, mainly because of the multitude of conditions that may be encountered. Blahm (1978) demonstrated that commercial fire retardants were toxic to juvenile coho salmon and rainbow trout and attributed the mortality to ammonia in the retardants; increasing the pH of diluent water from 7 to 8 increased the toxicity. McKee and Wolf (1971) noted that ammonia concentrations as low as 0.3 mg/L were lethal to trout fry and 75 mg/L was extremely lethal to mature trout. Un-ionized ammonia (NH_3) has been reported to be the component of retardants likely to be toxic to fish and other organisms. The concentration of free NH_3 in any of the retardant–water mixtures depends on the amount of NH_4^+ contained in the retardant and the pH of the mixture. Blahm et al.[16] found that two species of juvenile salmonids exposed to four commercial fire retardants had 96-h TLms of 120–940 mg/L.

Johnson and Finley (1980) found that warmwater fish species were less sensitive than salmonids to two Phos-Chek fire-retardant formulations (Table 7.12). Yolk-sac fry of coho salmon and rainbow trout were more sensitive than fingerlings.

The toxicological effects of sodium ferrocyanide, a corrosion inhibitor used in some retardant mixtures, may not have been adequately assessed (sodium ferrocyanide is presently used in Fire-Trol 931-L and 934-L). Doudoroff (1976) stressed that the suitability of cyanide-polluted waters for aquatic life has to be

---

[16]Unpublished report, "Effect of chemical fire retardants on the survival of juvenile salmonids," by T. H. Blahm, W. C. Marshall, and G. R. Snyder, Bureau of Land Management, Contract 53500-CT2-85(N), National Marine Fisheries Service, Environmental Field Station, Prescott, Oregon, 1972.

Aerial application of chemical fire retardant.

expressed as a concentration of free cyanide or molecular HCN, not of total cyanide. Free cyanide concentrations from 0.05 to 0.01 mg/L as CN have proved fatal to many sensitive fishes (Jones 1964), and levels above 0.2 mg/L are rapidly fatal for most species of fish. A level as low as 0.01 mg/L is known to have a pronounced, rapid, and lasting effect on the swimming ability of salmonid fishes (U.S. Environmental Protection Agency 1973b). Blahm (1978) performed comparative evaluations of toxicity for different retardants and concluded that Phos-Chek formulations were more toxic to salmonid fishes than were Fire-Trol compounds. The higher toxicity was believed to be a function of pH and ammonia toxicity; Phos-Chek formulations are more basic than Fire-Trol compounds. Blahm's relative toxicity values for the two compounds are valid only if Fire-Trol 931 is mixed at a 4:1 ratio for field application. When applied as 3:1 or 2:1 mixtures, Fire-Trol 931 may have a higher ammonium toxicity than Phos-Chek compounds. Additional tests are warranted because Fire-Trol 931 and 934 might be more toxic to aquatic life than other approved retardants, especially on sunny days.

Risk Assessment

Risk Assessment at the Organism Level

The toxicological risk of forest chemicals to anadromous fish may be manifested through direct action on the fish themselves or indirect action on fish food organisms. One means of expressing toxic risks is the margin of safety, i.e., the ratio of the "no-effect" level (concentration) to the actual exposure concentration. The no-effect level is the highest concentration that causes no mortality of test animals in acute toxicity tests. When the exposure level is equal to the no-effect level, the margin of safety is 1.0. Margins of safety less than 1.0 indicate the exposure level is greater than the no-effect level and suggest that a direct toxic effect is likely. The larger the margin of safety, the less likely toxic effects will occur.

What constitutes an adequate margin of safety is a matter of judgement. For many pharmaceuticals, caffeine, alcohol, and other materials many humans encounter daily, the margins of safety are as low as 1.5–15, and margins of safety of less than 100 are common. Margins of safety of about 100 are commonly used in setting pesticide tolerances in food and feed. When the species likely to be exposed are extremely valuable or rare, a much larger margin of safety may be appropriate. These margins of safety usually reflect an assumption that long-term chronic exposure will occur. Some margin of safety is necessary because (1) the toxicity testing done thus far may not have identified the "lowest" no-effect level, (2) toxicity-testing conditions usually differ from field conditions, and (3) individuals in the population differ in susceptibility.

Forest chemicals have been investigated mostly for their acute lethal effects; sublethal effects, however, may occur at lower exposures than those that are lethal. Potential sublethal effects of forest chemicals on salmonids include effects on growth, behavior, reproduction, resistance to stress, migration, biochemistry, and physiology. Picloram, 2,4-D, and DDT can reduce fish growth in the field and laboratory (Warner and Fenderson 1962; Cope et al. 1970; Woodward 1976). Several types of behavior (e.g., learning, swimming, temperature preference, predator avoidance) may be altered by exposure to pesticides (Ogilvie and Anderson 1965; Warner et al. 1966; J. M. Anderson 1968, 1971; Anderson and Peterson 1969; Hatfield and Anderson 1972; Hatfield and Johansen 1972; Symons 1973, 1977). Both DDT and 2,4-D can lower the reproductive success of fish (Macek 1968; Wilbur and Whitney 1973). Lorz et al. (1979) showed that diquat and picloram inhibited migration by coho salmon smolts in coastal Oregon streams. Many studies have demonstrated biochemical or physiological changes in fish exposed to pesticides (Weiss and Gakstatter 1964; Grant and Mehrle 1970; Wildish et al. 1971; Hiltibran 1972a, 1972b). One of the best-documented biochemical effects of a forest chemical is the inhibition of acetylcholinesterase activity by organophosphate pesticides (Williams and Sova 1966). Scientists are aware of many potential sublethal effects of forest chemicals; however, data on sublethal effects are scarce and a large portion of the available information pertains to organochlorines, particularly DDT. The no-effect levels for sublethal effects of forest chemicals are likely to be much lower than for acute or chronic toxicities. Our lack of knowledge prevents risk assessment of forest chemicals for sublethal effects and forces us to use margins of safety; increased research on sublethal effects may allow us to better evaluate the potential effects of forest chemicals on salmonids.

Organisms can exhibit numerous kinds of responses when exposed to toxic chemicals. Changes in survival, growth, reproductive success, and behavior are probably the most important of these, but the bulk of the aquatic toxicology literature reports only survival during short-term acute exposures to toxicants. Although this deficiency in the data base is obvious, short-term acute exposures predominate in forest aquatic systems, if exposure occurs at all. Thus, we can use toxicity data on survival of fish (or other more sensitive organisms) to approximate a no-effect level for short-term exposure.

We selected the concentration of 0.1(96-h LC50), or 10% of the 96-h LC50, as the no-effect level for survival after brief acute exposures to peak concentrations of a forest chemical. This value is a little more conservative than the 0.1(48-h LC50) tentatively suggested by the Aquatic Life Advisory Committee (1955). Some have treated this application factor almost as an immutable constant, but others have attacked it as an oversimplification. Tarzwell (1966) pointed out that 10% of the toxic units, or 0.1(toxic units), is a concentration that has been used successfully for the safe disposal of some wastes when firm information was lacking. Sprague (1971) argued that no single value could be expected to fit all types of pollution. In his review of sublethal and "safe" concentrations, Sprague (1971) noted that several application factors had been proposed but "generally speaking, recommendations for maximum levels are 0.1 or 0.05 toxic units for non-persistent pollutants, and 0.1 or 0.01 toxic units for persistent chemicals and pesticides, mostly the lower figure." The U.S. Environmental Protection Agency (1973b) also recommended the use of application factors not exceeding 10% of the 96-h LC50, when materials are nonpersistent or have noncumulative effects, to estimate "safe" concentrations of toxic wastes discharged into receiving streams, unless specific application factors have been determined for a given material.

Relatively few data are available on the no-effect level for other types of responses, particularly for prolonged exposure to the chemicals we have discussed in this chapter. The U.S. Environmental Protection Agency (1973b) recommended that no toxicant concentration should exceed 5% of the 96-h LC50 at any time or place, and that the 24-h average concentration of persistent or cumulative-action toxicants should not exceed 1% of the 96-h LC50.

Allison (1977) and Larson et al. (1978) investigated the relation of toxicant exposure duration, concentration, and periodicity to toxicity, reproduction, and growth. These studies, in which exposure units were used in conjunction with established toxicity data, may allow us to identify a "safe" level and thereby assess the environmental impacts of variable-level, short-term pesticide exposures on the aquatic environment.

Risk assessment for acute toxicity.—Numerous acute exposure values can be used to calculate margins of safety. We used both the single highest instantaneous field concentration we found in surveying the literature and a peak concentration of 0.02 mg/L (Table 7.16), which we believe is the maximum likely to occur if minimum buffer strips are used along streams and lakes and some direct application to surface water occurs. We used these values with 10% of the 96-h LC50 to calculate the margin of safety for acute exposures (Table 7.17). These calculations yield conservative estimates of the margin of safety because the instantaneous peak concentration in the field does not persist for the 96-h period used in toxicity tests and current "best management practices" in the use of forest chemicals will not produce exposure levels that approach the peak concentrations listed in Tables 7.16 and 7.17.

Risk assessment for chronic toxicity.—We calculated the margin of safety for chronic exposures using (1) integrals of concentration–time curves for chemicals in forest streams as estimates of exposure in the field and (2) integrals of concentration–time curves for exposures equal to 1% of the 96-h LC50 as estimates of no-effect exposure levels in toxicity tests. This concept is based on

TABLE 7.16.—Integral of concentration–time curves for 48 h for several pesticides and for 192 h for urea in forest streams after aerial application.[a]

Chemical	Actual peak concentration (mg/L)	Integral for actual peak concentration ([mg/L]h)	Integral for assumed peak concentration of 0.02 mg/L for pesticides and 7.02 mg/L[b] for urea ([mg/L]h)
2,4-D	0.014	0.116	0.167
Amitrole	0.110	0.498	0.091
Dicamba	0.037	0.310	0.167
Malathion	0.040	0.074	0.037
Carbaryl	0.121	0.343	0.057
Acephate	0.471	1.708	0.072
Urea[c]	1.389	38.2	193
Urea[d]	0.700	19.4	195

[a]Based on Figure 7.4.
[b]Mean peak concentration of 28 fertilizer-monitoring projects summarized by Moore (1975b).
[c]Based on Figure 7.4G.
[d]Based on Figure 7.4H.

the use of exposure units, i.e., the integral of duration and level of exposure, as developed by Allison (1977) and Larson et al. (1978).

The use of 0.01(96-h LC50) as the no-observed-effect concentration for chronic exposure (NOEC) is based on (a) the findings of Kenaga (1982), who calculated the acute:chronic no-effect levels for 135 compounds and found 93% of these values expressed as their log was 1.4 or less, and (b) the recent analysis by Slooff et al. (1986) who regressed 164 data pairs of $\log_{10}$(NOEC) versus $\log_{10}$(50%-effect concentration, L[E]C50) in standard acute toxicity tests. Slooff et al. (1986) found $\log_{10}$(NOEC) = -1.28 + $0.95\log_{10}$(L[E]C50); r = 0.89. This equation yields L[E]C50:NOEC ratios with logs of about 1.3, suggesting the actual NOEC value is closer to 0.05(96-h LC50) than to the 0.01(96-h LC50) value we used in our calculations. Thus, our estimates of margins of safety for no-chronic-effect levels are conservative, erring on the side of safety.

Numerous data exist on the concentration of herbicides in forest streams. In an effort to find one that would be representative, we normalized the concentration data for three herbicides and shifted the time scale slightly to show the peak concentration (100%) at 3 h after application (Figure 7.4A–C). The data for both amitrole-T in Wildcat Creek and 2,4-D in Preacher Creek show an increase in concentration as a result of rain (approximately 0.7 cm at Wildcat Creek and 0.6 cm at Preacher Creek on the first day after application). The areas under the curves were measured to give a time–concentration expression ([mg/L]h) of contamination for the first 48 h after application; we used both the actual peak concentration observed and the assumed instantaneous peak concentration of 0.02 mg/L (Table 7.16). The latter value is our estimate of the maximum contamination level likely to result if minimum buffer strips are used and some direct application to surface water occurs (see the related discussion in the section

Text continues on page 282

TABLE 7.17.—Estimated margins of safety for survival of salmon, trout, and other sensitive aquatic species to "short-term" exposure to selected forest chemicals. LC50 is median lethal concentration in laboratory studies; NOEC is no-observed-effect concentration (10% of the LC50)[a]; NOEE is no-observed-effect exposure (integration of time and concentration)[b]; HOC is highest observed concentration (field applications)[c]; STE is short-term exposure integrated over time and concentration (field applications; peak concentration assumed to be 0.02 mg/L).[d]

Formulation and test species	96-h or 48-h* LC50 (mg/L)	NOEC (mg/L)[a]	Margin of safety $\left(\dfrac{NOEC}{HOC}\right)$	$\left(\dfrac{NOEC}{0.02}\right)$[e]	48-h field exposures NOEE ([mg/L]h)[e]	Margin of safety $\left(\dfrac{NOEE}{STE}\right)$
Herbicides						
2,4-D: HOC = 0.84 mg/L; STE = 0.334 (mg/L)h[f]						
Dimethylamine						
Rainbow trout	100	10	11.9	500	48	144
Daphnia sp.	4	0.4	0.5	20	1.92	5.7
Glass shrimp	0.15	0.015	<0.1	0.7	0.072	0.2
Butyl ester						
Cutthroat trout	0.9	0.09	0.1	4.5	0.432	1.3
Pteronarcella sp.	1.5	0.15	0.2	7.5	0.72	2.2
PGBE ester						
Cutthroat trout	1.0	0.1	0.1	5	0.480	1.4
Daphnia sp.	1.2*	0.12	0.1	6	0.576	1.7
Glass shrimp	0.4	0.04	<0.1	2	0.192	0.6
Picloram: HOC = 2.0 mg/L; STE = 0.083 (mg/L)h[g]						
Technical						
Cutthroat trout	3.5	0.35	0.2	17	1.68	20
Pteronarcys sp.	0.048	0.0048	<0.1	0.2	0.023	0.3
Potassium salt						
Cutthroat trout	1.5	0.15	<0.1	7.5	0.72	8.7
Tordon 101[h]						
Rainbow trout	8.6	0.86	0.4	43	4.13	50
Hexazinone: HOC = 0.044 mg/L; STE = 0.5 (mg/L)h[i]						
Rainbow trout	322	32.2	727	1,600	153	306
Bluegill	952	95.2	2,114	4,600	442	884
Daphnia sp.	20	2	45	100	9.6	19
Fiddler crab	>1,000	>100	>2,272	>5,000	>480	>960
Atrazine: HOC = 0.42 mg/L; STE = 0.668 (mg/L)h[j]						
Chironomous tenans	0.72*	0.072	0.2	3.6	3.46	5.2
Daphnia sp.	6.9*	0.69	1.6	34	3.31	5.0
Bluegill	6.7*	0.67	1.6	34	3.22	4.8
Brook trout	4.9*	0.49	1.2	24	2.35	3.5
Triclopyr: HOC = 0.095 mg/L; STE = 0.5 (mg/L)h[i]						
Butoxyethyl ester (Garlon 4)						
Rainbow trout	0.74	0.074	0.8	3.7	0.35	0.7
Bluegill	0.87	0.087	0.9	4.3	0.42	0.8
Triethylamine salt (Garlon 3A)						
Rainbow trout	552	55.2	579	2,750	264	528
Bluegill	891	89.1	937	4,450	427	854
Triethylamine salt						
Fathead minnow	120	12	126	600	57.6	115
Formulation unknown						
Rainbow trout	117	11.7	125	600	57.6	115
Bluegill	148	14.8	158	750	72	144

TABLE 7.17.—Continued.

Formulation and test species	96-h or 48-h* LC50 (mg/L)	NOEC (mg/L)[a]	Margin of safety $\left(\dfrac{NOEC}{HOC}\right)$	Margin of safety $\left(\dfrac{NOEC}{0.02}\right)$[e]	48-h field exposures NOEE ([mg/L]h)[b]	Margin of safety $\left(\dfrac{NOEE}{STE}\right)$
MSMA: HOC = 0.01 mg/L; STE = ?[k]						
Liquid formulation						
Cutthroat trout	100	10	1,000	500	48	l
Gammarus fasciatus	100	10	1,000	500	48	l
Bluegill	12	1.2	120	60	5.76	l
Plus surfactant						
Bluegill	49	4.9	490	245	23	l
Fosamine ammonium: HOC = ?[m]; STE = 0.668 (mg/L)h[j]						
Coho salmon, fingerling	5,361	536	l	>10,000	2,573	3,852
Rainbow trout, yolk-sac fry	528	52.8	l	2,640	253	379
Glyphosate: HOC = 2.6 mg/L; STE = 0.668 (mg/L)h[j]						
Technical						
Rainbow trout	130	13.0	5	650	62.4	93
Liquid formulation						
Rainbow trout, fingerling	8.3	0.83	0.3	41	3.98	6.0
Rainbow trout, swim-up fry	2.4	0.24	<.1	12	1.15	1.7
Daphnia sp.	3	0.3	0.1	15	1.44	2.2
Dalapon: HOC = 3.65 mg/L; STE = 1.4 (mg/L)h[n]						
Rainbow trout	>100	>10	3	500	48	34
Bluegill	115	11.5	3	600	57.6	41
Dinoseb: HOC = ?[m]; STE = 0.334 (mg/L)h[g]						
Cutthroat trout	0.041	0.004	l	0.2	0.019	<0.1
Insecticides						
Malathion: HOC = 0.042 mg/L; STE = 0.037 (mg/L)h[o]						
Daphnia sp.	0.001*	0.0001	<0.1	<0.1	0.0005	<0.1
Pteronarcys sp.	0.01	0.001	<0.1	<0.1	0.0048	0.1
Coho salmon	0.17	0.017	0.4	0.8	0.082	2.2
Carbaryl: HOC = 0.121 mg/L; STE = 0.057 (mg/L)h[o]						
Daphnia sp.	0.006*	0.0006	<0.1	<0.1	0.0029	<0.1
Pteronarcys sp.	0.0017	0.00017	<0.1	<0.1	0.0008	<0.1
Coho salmon	4.34	0.434	3.6	22	2.08	36
Azinphos-methyl: HOC = ?[m]; STE = ?[k]						
Gammarus fasciatus	0.15	0.015	l	0.7	0.072	l
Pteronarcys sp.	0.0019	0.00019	l	<0.1	0.0009	l
Coho salmon	0.006	0.0006	l	<0.1	0.003	l
Carbofuran: HOC = ?[m]; STE = ?[k]						
Coho salmon	0.530	0.053	l	2.6	0.25	l
Rainbow trout	0.380	0.038	l	1.9	0.18	l
Acephate: HOC = 0.961 mg/L; STE = 0.072 (mg/L)h[o]						
Pteronarcella sp.	9.5	0.95	1.0	47	4.56	63.3
Cutthroat trout	100	10	10	500	48	667
Rainbow trout	1,100	110	114	5,500	528	7,333

TABLE 7.17.—Continued.

Formulation and test species	96-h or 48-h* LC50 (mg/L)	NOEC (mg/L)[a]	Margin of safety $\left(\dfrac{NOEC}{HOC}\right)$	$\left(\dfrac{NOEC}{0.02}\right)^e$	48-h field exposures NOEE ([mg/L]h)[b]	Margin of safety $\left(\dfrac{NOEE}{STE}\right)$
Fertilizer						
Urea: HOC = 44.4 mg/L; STE = 193.0 (mg/L)h[o]						
Ammonia: HOC = 0.014 mg/L[p]; STE = 0.83 (mg/L)h[q]						
Coho salmon	0.2	0.02	1.4	1	0.096	0.1
Fire retardant						
Ammonia: HOC = 1.30 mg/L[r]; STE = ?[s]						
Coho salmon	0.2	0.02	<0.1	1	0.096	[l]

[a]0.1(LC50), or 10% of the 96-h or 48-h LC50, is assumed to be the no-effects concentration for survival during short-term acute exposures.

[b]The no-effects exposure is the integral of the 0.01(LC50) curve over 48 h.

[c]The highest observed concentration is the single highest instantaneous concentration reported in the literature for field applications. Some values have been adjusted to reflect registered rates of application in forestry.

[d]Short-term exposures are 48-h integrals of the time–concentration curves in Figure 7.4 for assumed peak concentrations of 0.02 mg/L (see also Table 7.16). Based on operational monitoring, 0.02 mg/L is the maximum instantaneous concentration likely to result during field applications. It is assumed that streams in treated areas have minimum buffer strips and that there is some direct application of chemical to stream surfaces.

[e]Margin of safety for assumed peak concentrations of 0.02 mg/L for pesticides, 7.02 mg/L for urea fertilizer (0.02 mg/L for the ammonia component), and 130 mg/L for fire retardant (0.02 mg/L for the ammonia component).

[f]From Table 7.16, adjusted to a 2.24-kg/hectare application rate (based on data for 2,4-D, Figure 7.4A) and a peak concentration of 0.02 mg/L.

[g]From Table 7.16, adjusted to a 0.56-kg/hectare application rate (based on data for 2,4-D, Figure 7.4A) and a peak concentration of 0.02 mg/L.

[h]Tordon 101 is a 4:1 mixture of 2,4-D and picloram. The risk-assessment calculations were made with exposure data for picloram only, See 2,4-D for relevant data on 2,4-D.

[i]From Table 7.16, adjusted to a 3.36-kg/hectare application rate (based on data for 2,4-D, Figure 7.4A) and a peak concentration of 0.02 mg/L.

[j]From Table 7.16, adjusted to a 4.48-kg/hectare application rate (based on data for 2,4-D, Figure 7.4A) and a peak concentration of 0.02 mg/L.

[k]Data not available. Normal use is not expected to result in stream contamination.

[l]Margin of safety not calculated because no value for exposure is available.

[m]Data not available.

[n]From Table 7.16, adjusted to a 9.6-kg/hectare application rate (based on data for 2,4-D, Figure 7.4A) and a peak concentration of 0.02 mg/L.

[o]From Table 7.16, for an assumed peak concentration of 0.02 mg/L except for urea, which is based on an assumed concentration of 7.02 mg/L.

[p]From Table 7.13; assumes 1% un-ionized ammonia (25°C, pH 7.5).

[q]Based on the proportion of $(NH_3 + NH_4^+)$ to urea, Table 7.13, and 1% un-ionized ammonia (25°C, pH 7.5).

[r]Assumes 1% ammonia in 130-mg/L retardant in stream water, from Norris et al. (1978).

[s]No estimate because of high variability in patterns of retardant use. Applications directly into streams will produce levels of ammonia >1 mg/L.

"Chemicals in water," and U.S. Animal and Plant Health Inspection Service 1980).

The results showed reasonably good agreement among the herbicides: 0.167 (mg/L)h for 2,4-D, 0.091 (mg/L)h for amitrole, and 0.167 (mg/L)h for dicamba (Table 7.16). Based on this analysis, we decided to use the 48-h time–concentration expression of exposure of 0.167 (mg/L)h derived from the 2,4-D data from Preacher Creek (Figure 7.4A), adjusted for rate of application for all the aerially applied herbicides in Table 7.17. MSMA was excluded because it usually is not applied aerially, and the limited monitoring for MSMA has not shown measurable residues in forest streams. Use of the 2,4-D data for the other herbicides is reasonable because we believe the predominant processes of entry are drift, direct application to the stream surface, and mobilization in ephemeral stream channels shortly after application. These processes are largely mechanical and should not vary greatly among the aerially applied herbicides discussed in this chapter.

Data for the concentrations of malathion, carbaryl, acephate, and urea (from fertilizer) in streams at various times after application were plotted, and the areas under the curves were integrated in the same way as for the herbicides (Figures 7.4D–H; Table 7.16). The normal uses of azinphos-methyl and carbofuran—for control of seed and cone insects—will not result in contamination of forest streams.

The no-effect level for survival from chronic exposure to each chemical is expressed as the integral (over 48 h) of the time–concentration curve equivalent to 0.01(96-h LC50) for that chemical. These values are expressed as (mg/L)h for 48 h, just as the exposure data from field studies are expressed. For example, the 96-h LC50 of carbaryl for coho salmon is 4.34 mg/L and 0.01(96-h LC50) is 0.0434 mg/L. Because the exposure level is constant over the 48-h period we are interested in, the integral of the time–concentration curve is 0.0434 mg/L × 48 h = 2.08 (mg/L)h. The ratio of the no-effect exposure integral to the field exposure integral is the margin of safety (Table 7.17).

We believe the margins of safety calculated for chronic exposure are conservative because the toxicity data are based on continuous exposure at the specified level, although we know from field data that peak exposures are quite transitory. For instance, if we were to extend the period of evaluation from 48 h to 30 d, the no-effect exposure integral would increase 15 times, but the field-exposure integral would not change because no further exposure occurs. Thus, the margin of safety would increase 15 times.

Risk Assessment at the Ecosystem Level

Assessments of risk to individual organisms rest on a reasonably adequate data base, but they focus on individual organisms and do not take into account time, space, or the basic resiliency of ecosystems. For instance, our assessment for carbaryl indicates coho salmon will not be directly affected, but some individual invertebrates may be killed in a segment of a stream shortly after aerial application. It fails to recognize that some other individuals will survive (by avoidance or by greater individual tolerance for the chemical) and that repopulation of the affected portion of the stream will occur (by migration from unaffected areas or by hatching). In addition, it fails to recognize that the affected area is likely to be small because of efforts to avoid direct application to streams and because most treatments do not cover large, contiguous areas (some large insect control projects may be an exception). The same area is not likely to be affected repeatedly because, over the course of any one timber rotation, more than three applications to the same area are rare and the time between repeat applications will usually be more than 1 year. As a consequence, we believe that the risk

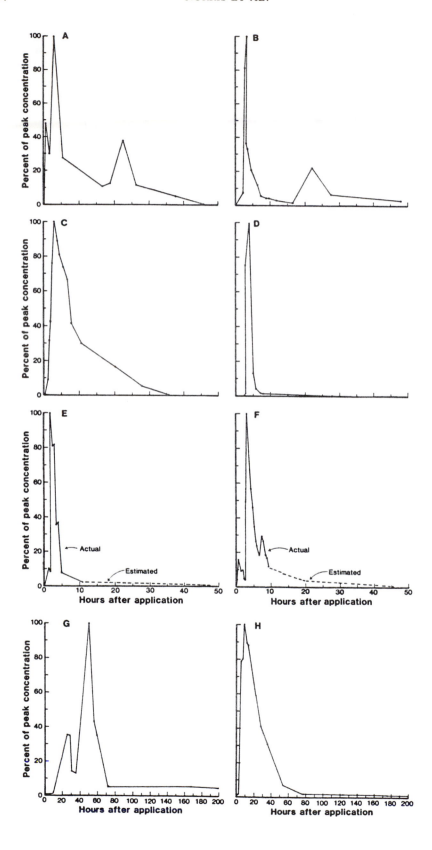

assessments in Table 7.17 are conservative; the true margins of safety for salmonids from exposure to forest chemicals on the large watershed or ecosystem scales are greater than we have calculated.

Indirect Effects of Forest Chemicals

Toxic effects of forest chemicals on aquatic organisms have been investigated for several decades and are an integral component of environmental risk assessment. The intended uses of insecticides, herbicides, fertilizers, and fire retardants alter the structure and biological processes of both terrestrial and aquatic ecosystems, and these indirect effects of forest chemicals may have more profound influences on communities of fish and other aquatic organisms than direct lethal or sublethal toxic effects. Ecological effects of forest chemicals must be assessed from an ecosystem perspective rather than from the more simple perspective of direct toxicity, either lethal or sublethal, to an organism (Barnthouse et al. 1986).

Alteration of terrestrial vegetation and invertebrate communities may change both allochthonous inputs into streams and environmental factors such as light, temperature, water quality, sediment composition, and geomorphology. All of these factors are components of anadromous fish habitat as discussed by Bjornn and Reiser (1991, this volume) and Murphy and Meehan (1991, this volume). Land

---

←

FIGURE 7.4.—Concentrations of chemicals in forest streams at different times after aerial application. Concentration is expressed as a percentage of the peak concentration. Time intervals are 5 h in panels A–F and 10 h in panels G and H.

(A) 2,4-D in Preacher Creek, Oregon, with a partial buffer strip of streamside vegetation. Actual peak concentration was 0.0139 mg/L after an aerial application of 2,4-D at 1.12 kg/hectare. (From Table 10 of Fredriksen et al. 1975.)

(B) Amitrole in Wildcat Creek, Oregon, with no stream buffer. Actual peak concentration was 0.110 mg/L after an aerial application of amitrole at 2.24 kg/hectare. (From Table 10 of Fredriksen et al. 1975.)

(C) Dicamba in Farmer Creek, Oregon, with no stream buffer. Actual peak concentration was 0.037 mg/L after an aerial application of dicamba at 1.12 kg/hectare. (From Figure 2 of Norris and Montgomery 1975.)

(D) Malathion in Hansel Creek, Washington, with no stream buffer. Actual peak concentration was 0.040 mg/L after an aerial application. (From Figure 2 of Tracy et al. 1977.)

(E) Carbaryl in Squilchuck Creek, Washington, with no stream buffer. Actual peak concentration was 0.121 mg/L after aerial an application at 1.12 kg/hectare. (From Figure 7 of Bernhardt et al. 1978.) Note projection of the estimated concentration curve beyond 11 h.

(F) Acephate in Cabin Creek, Montana, with no stream buffer. Actual peak concentration was 0.471 mg/L after an aerial application at 1.12 kg/hectare. (From Table 12 of Flavell et al. 1977.) Note projection of the estimated concentration curve beyond 9.25 h.

(G) Urea in Coyote Creek, Oregon, with no stream buffer. Actual peak concentration was 1.39 mg/L after an aerial application of 224 kg N/hectare (as urea). (From Table 1 of Moore 1975b; and personal communication, D. G. Moore, U.S. Forest Service.) Note the time scale is not the same as in panels A–F.

(H) Urea in Trapper Creek, Washington, with 60-m stream buffer. Actual peak concentration was 0.7 mg/L after aerial application of 224 kg N/hectare (as urea). (From Figure 2 of Moore 1975a.) Note the time scale is not the same as in panels A–F.

managers must be aware of potential indirect effects of forest chemicals on patterns and processes of stream ecosystems.

Herbicides

The following discussion of indirect effects of forest herbicides focuses on alteration of riparian vegetation adjacent to streams, rivers, and lakes. General aquatic processes that may be affected by terrestrial use of herbicides have been investigated extensively (Swanson et al. 1982a; Triska et al. 1982); documented studies of indirect effects of forest chemicals on aquatic systems are rare. Indirect effects of herbicides on aquatic communities have been observed when, for example, aquatic plants were killed and subsequent shifts occurred in other components of stream ecosystems (Haven 1963; Smith and Isom 1967). Most such observations have followed direct applications of herbicide for aquatic weed control. In reviews of secondary effects of pesticides in aquatic systems, Hurlbert (1975) and Newbold (1975) considered mortality to aquatic plants to be the only indirect effect of herbicides. Concentrations of herbicides in surface waters after forest applications are much lower (<0.1 mg/L) than those needed to control aquatic weeds (>2 mg/L) (Norris and Moore 1971, 1976; National Research Council of Canada 1978; Norris 1978), so forest herbicides are unlikely to cause indirect effects due to the death of aquatic vegetation in streams, except in unusual circumstances.

Herbicides may alter natural patterns of plant succession along streams. Herbicide application is intended to control nonconiferous trees and shrubs so that growth and development of commercial conifer species will be accelerated during the first few decades after timber harvest. Plant succession after a disturbance generally goes through three stages: an herbaceous stage, generally lasting less than 5 years; a shrub stage, roughly lasting from the 5th year through the 15th year; and a tree-dominated stage, which begins after about 10–15 years (Dyrness 1973; Franklin and Dyrness 1973; Swanson et al. 1982a). In western North America, tree communities in the early stages of succession are often dominated by deciduous trees such as alder, bigleaf maple, or vine maple. Large shrubs such as rhododendron, ceanothus, and salmonberry are also major components of plant communities during this time. Between 20 and 60 years after cutting, coniferous species begin to dominate the tree communities.

In timber management, herbicides are often applied during the first decade after logging to control nonconiferous trees and shrubs. In essence, natural patterns of succession are altered because development and duration of early successional stages of trees and shrubs are reduced. Dominance of terrestrial vegetation is changed from herbs, shrubs, or hardwoods to conifers. This change in plant communities has many implications for stream communities in logged watersheds because deciduous vegetation differs greatly from coniferous vegetation in form, growth habitats, timing of litterfall, and quality of organic matter produced. Herbicide applications in the northwestern USA may have other long-term ecological implications because several pioneer species such as red alder and ceanothus are nitrogen fixers, and terrestrial plant production in this region is generally nitrogen limited. Therefore, reduction of pioneer communities may alter the nitrogen dynamics in watersheds, but few relevant data from herbicide-treated areas are available (Tarrant and Trappe 1971).

Control of terrestrial vegetation may alter physical characteristics of the stream environment such as streamflow, temperature, and light intensity. Immediately after reduction of nonconiferous plant biomass by herbicides, streamflow may increase because of reduced evapotranspiration (Hibbert 1967). Cutting of forests is known to cause increases in both base flow and peak discharge (Hewlett and Hibbert 1961; Hornbeck et al. 1970; Harr 1977). Similar responses have been observed in watersheds treated with herbicides on rangelands (Ingebo 1971) and in northeastern forests (Mrazik et al. 1980). Herbicides are generally applied after watersheds have been logged, so they are not the primary cause of increased streamflow; rather, they may extend the period of increased streamflow after deforestation. Increased base flow may be beneficial to many stream organisms, but increased peak flows may be detrimental. Reduction of streamside vegetation increases the amount of solar radiation that reaches the stream channel, which can raise summer water temperatures under many conditions of flow, gradient, and geomorphology (Brown 1969).

When the vegetative structure of watersheds is altered, streambanks may lose stability and hillslopes may erode more. The degree to which the vegetation and the rooting systems are altered by logging determines the extent of sedimentation and channel modification, but the sedimentation rates in deforested watersheds are frequently more than double those in forested watersheds (Swanston and Swanson 1976). To the extent that herbicide applications retard vegetative recovery in a watershed, they may extend the period of increased sedimentation, but there are no published studies on this matter. The detrimental effects of sedimentation and channel degradation on the structure and function of stream ecosystems are documented elsewhere in this volume.

In sufficient concentrations, herbicides may directly affect aquatic primary producers (plants); indirect effects of herbicide applications may also alter primary producers in streams. If increases in solar radiation result from alteration of streamside vegetation, aquatic primary production may be stimulated (McIntire and Phinney 1965; Hansmann 1969; Gregory 1980). Such responses have been observed after control of riparian vegetation by herbicides in rangelands of the southwestern USA (Smith et al. 1975). Temperature increases may also elevate rates of gross primary production in streams (McIntire 1966). Conversely, sedimentation from terrestrial systems influenced by herbicides may cover benthic algal communities, scour algal cells from substrate surfaces, or otherwise reduce standing crops of primary producers (Cordone and Pennoyer 1960; Chapman 1963; Nuttall 1972).

Primary production in streams may be stimulated by increased nutrient concentrations. Herbicide application has been followed by increased nitrogen inputs to streams (Sollins et al. 1981). Nitrogen concentrations in stream water increased after herbicide treatment of a watershed in New Hampshire (Likens et al. 1970); however, the herbicide application rate there was much greater than commonly used in forestry (Likens et al. 1970). Primary production in most northwestern U.S. streams is nitrogen limited (Thut and Haydu 1971; Gregory 1980), and increases in dissolved nitrogen released by herbicide treatments may stimulate stream productivity.

Aquatic invertebrates may be affected by physical changes that result from herbicide application. Any increase in sedimentation could scour or otherwise degrade their habitats (Cummins and Lauff 1969; Burns 1972; Brusven and Prather 1974; Cederholm and Lestelle 1974). Temperature increases may stimulate the growth and production of aquatic insects if the increases are slight; if stream temperatures exceed a species' optimum, however, the effect will be negative.

Alteration of terrestrial vegetation by herbicides may influence communities of aquatic invertebrates. The initial increase in deciduous leaf fall into streams after herbicide application temporarily increases the food supply of aquatic invertebrates. In addition, the nitrogen content of this leaf material is greater than that of leaves that go through normal abscission (Jensen 1929; Sollins et al. 1981). Aquatic invertebrates attain faster growth and higher production on leaf material with high nitrogen content (Russell-Hunter 1970; Sedell et al. 1975). The duration of enhancement is short, however, because the conversion of deciduous riparian vegetation to conifers reduces the quality of food for detritus-feeding invertebrates.

The production of grazing insects could increase if aquatic primary production is stimulated after herbicide treatment. Grazers in streams are often food limited (McIntire and Colby 1978); therefore, increases in their food supply enhances their production. This enhancement of grazing invertebrates is gradually diminished as the developing coniferous stands shade the streams.

Aquatic predators, both invertebrate and vertebrate, could benefit from the enhancement of lower trophic levels. If production of grazing, collecting, and shredding invertebrates is increased as previously described, production of aquatic predators would also increase. Production of predators in streams in logged watersheds sometimes is greater than it is in forested sections (Aho 1976; Erman et al. 1977; Hall et al. 1978; Murphy 1979; Murphy et al. 1981; Hawkins et al. 1983). If herbicide treatment prolongs the stage of opened canopy after logging, this period of increased production could be extended. Release of the conifers may shorten the deciduous successional phase, however, and this phase may well be more productive for the stream biota. Enhanced production of aquatic biota must, therefore, be viewed in the context of the normal patterns of ecosystem development.

Fish populations, especially salmonids, could also be detrimentally affected by herbicides. Salmonids prefer cold, clear streams; therefore, increased temperature and sedimentation from herbicide use may adversely affect them. Sedimentation may reduce egg and fry survival (Neave 1947; Phillips 1964; Koski 1966; Bjornn[17]) and the quality of rearing habitat (Everest and Chapman 1972; Bjornn et al. 1974). Salmonids also require cover; streamside vegetation provides a major portion of this feature (Lewis 1969; Hunt 1978). Reduction of streamside vegetation by forest herbicides would, therefore, adversely affect salmonid populations.

Thus, herbicides may indirectly affect stream ecosystems either positively or negatively. The degree of effect is a function of the extent, level, patterns, and timing of applications. Evaluations of potential effects of herbicides on stream ecosystems must take all these factors into account.

---

[17]Unpublished annual completion report, "Embryo survival and emergence studies," by T. C. Bjornn, Project F-49-R-6, Job 6, Salmon-Steelhead Investigations, Embryo Survival and Emergence Studies, Idaho Fish and Game Department, Boise, 1969.

Insecticides

Application of forest insecticides can indirectly influence stream ecosystems, primarily by the mortality of terrestrial or aquatic insects it causes. These insects have relatively short life cycles (often 1 year or less), so their communities can be expected to recover in less than 5 years. For this reason, indirect effects of forest insecticides on stream ecosystems are of shorter duration than those of herbicides, though they may be more dramatic.

Insecticides may directly kill stream invertebrates or induce catastrophic drift of invertebrates out of treatment areas. Early studies of the effects of DDT on aquatic organisms noted that invertebrate drift increased immediately after spraying, invertebrate densities were reduced, and the composition of invertebrate communities in streams was altered for up to 4 years (Filteau 1959; Ide 1967). Experimental applications of permethrin, a synthetic pyrethroid, along streams in Canadian forests resulted in decreased abundances of aquatic invertebrates for 3–16 months (Kreutzweiser 1982; Kingsbury 1983). The reductions were attributed to both catastrophic drift that lasted for 3–12 h and invertebrate mortality (piles of dead invertebrates were observed on the stream bottoms). Invertebrate abundances in the stream were depressed for up to 2 km downstream from the application areas. Similar responses were observed when the carbamate insecticide aminocarb was applied near an Ontario trout stream (Holmes and Kingsbury 1982). Such alterations of abundance and community structure of aquatic insects can, in turn, change the abundances and community dynamics of the predators that feed on them.

Benthic algal communities in streams are frequently controlled by grazing invertebrates. The mortality of these aquatic invertebrates from insecticides may release the primary producers and result in higher standing crops. In streams in which insecticides were released directly, either intentionally or accidentally, standing crops of primary producers have increased 2- to 20-fold (Barnley and Prentice 1958; Hynes 1961; Binns 1967; Chutter 1970). Similar responses have been observed in streams when watersheds were treated with DDT to control forest insects (Adams et al. 1949; Morgan and Kremer 1952; Webb and MacDonald 1958; Filteau 1959; Ide 1967). Benthic algal communities are reduced as soon as invertebrate communities recover (Chutter 1970).

Insecticides usually cause direct mortality of stream invertebrates as a result of toxicity. Those invertebrates that are resistant or have short generations may actually increase in number or size because of decreased competition, decreased predation, or increased algal food supply. In a Canadian stream that was inadvertently contaminated with gamma-BHC, populations of oligochaetes and midges increased (Hynes 1961). This increase was attributed to mortality of predators. An increase in small chironomids was observed after aerial application of DDT to forests in New Brunswick (Ide 1967). A decrease in predatory insects was also observed in this stream. A similar pattern of changes in invertebrate community structure was observed in streams within watersheds treated with carbaryl for control of spruce budworm (Courtemanch and Gibbs 1980).

Recolonization of streams affected by insecticides is dominated initially by invertebrates with short life cycles. Aquatic insects with life cycles of 1 year or more require several years to return to pretreatment population levels (Ide 1967), and their full recovery may be further delayed by competition with established short-lived species. Predators tend to have longer life cycles than other types of invertebrates, so full recovery of invertebrate communities may require 5–10 years. Nevertheless, invertebrate predators sometimes increase after application of forest insecticides. For example, populations of dobsonfly larvae (*Nigronia* sp.) increased in streams flowing through Connecticut watersheds that were treated for spruce budworm (Hitchcock 1965). Other populations of predacious insects, such as plecopterans, decreased during this period.

Insecticide use can not only kill aquatic insects and increase the rate of insect drift (Crouter and Vernon 1959; Ide 1967; Kreutzweiser 1982), it is likely to greatly increase the number of terrestrial insects that fall on stream surfaces (Warner and Fenderson 1962; Kreutzweiser 1982). These insects are ingested by drift-feeding fish such as trout and salmon and may induce a secondary toxic effect on the fish. If the toxic effect is slight (or nonexistent), the sudden increase in food may cause a brief acceleration of predator growth. Such an enhancement of food supply is brief at best, however; a more frequent response is an overall reduction in invertebrate prey and a decline in predator growth. For example, the diets of brook trout and slimy sculpins reflected changes in both abundance and community structure of aquatic insects after a synthetic pyrethroid was applied to a forest (Kruetzweiser and Kingsbury 1982). As insect communities recovered, food consumption by fish returned to previous quantities and composition; after 16 months, condition factors of fish in treated and untreated areas were similar. Growth rates of 1- and 2-year-old Atlantic salmon parr decreased immediately after deposition of the same synthetic pyrethroid in another stream, but increased in late summer to the extent that fish in treated and untreated areas achieved the same size by summer's end (Kingsbury 1983). Over the long term, decreased populations of aquatic insects will most likely result in decreased growth and production of fish populations. Recovery of fish populations is determined, therefore, by recovery of invertebrate communities.

Microbial pathogens are being considered increasingly for control of forest insect pests because of their specificity for target organisms and low toxicity to other organisms. Polyhedral viruses have been used in forests to control insect pests and appear to be safer than chemical insecticides (Pimentel 1980), but there have been few, if any, studies of indirect effects of viruses in aquatic ecosystems. Specific strains of the bacterium *Bacillus thuringiensis* (*B.t.*) have been used for the control of Lepidoptera and Diptera in forest environments. Aquatic Lepidoptera are relatively rare, but caddisflies, a major component of most stream ecosystems, are closely related and might be more susceptible than most other aquatic insects. Aquatic Diptera are exceedingly common; the most common dipteran pests for which *B.t.* is applied are mosquitoes and blackflies, both aquatic insects. Application of *B.t.* for control of aquatic insects alters the aquatic community structure and so influences other aquatic organisms, and assessment of the need for such control projects must consider these potential effects. Although the potential exists for effects on nontarget organisms, little evidence has been found for such responses (Buckner et al. 1974; Ali 1981; Burges 1982). The high degree of specificity of *B.t.* for target organisms makes it unlikely that indirect effects will be substantial.

Fertilizers

Some forests in the northwestern USA are fertilized for several decades after logging. Urea, the most common fertilizer, is quickly converted to ammonium or nitrate in the soil, so nitrogen can enter streams in all three forms. Most of the urea that enters streams does so within the first 48 h after application (Moore 1975a, 1975b). After that, nitrogen enters streams primarily as nitrate. Fertilization generally increases the nitrogen content of stream water by 50 mg/L or less, and these nitrogen pulses last for about 1 year (Fredriksen et al. 1975; Moore 1975a, 1975b).

As previously described, streams in the northwestern USA are commonly nitrogen limited, and primary production in such streams may be enhanced by fertilization (Thut and Haydu 1971; Stockner and Shortreed 1976; Gregory 1980). Nutrient stimulation of primary production occurs only with sufficient light intensity (Gregory 1980), but trees in most fertilized watersheds are less than 40 years old, so unless old-growth buffer strips had been left along streams, shading should not inhibit stream productivity.

Increased primary production can result in greater production of consumers. Greater insect and trout production in open streams has been observed in many studies (Albrecht and Tesch 1961; Albrecht 1968; LeCren 1969; Mills 1969; Hall et al. 1978; Murphy et al. 1981; Hawkins et al. 1983) and attributed to greater primary production. Fertilization could, therefore, indirectly enhance production of trout and salmon. This increase would be limited to less than 5 years at best, but would be extended by repeated application of fertilizer at 5- or 10-year intervals.

Fire Retardants

Chemical fire retardants such as ammonium sulfate, ammonium polyphosphate, or diammonium phosphate are used extensively in the northwestern USA for the suppression and control of forest fires. Fires often start on ridgetops, away from streams. As fires develop, they may sweep across streams and rivers, so direct entry of fire retardants into streams is possible.

Application of fire retardants usually increases the concentrations of ammonia in stream waters (see footnote 2). These concentrations may range from 0.01 to 100 mg N/L. As already discussed, such nitrogen increases can stimulate primary and secondary production in streams. Increased production of aquatic biota could be precluded if toxic effects occurred. Potential indirect effects of retardants on the mortality of invertebrates or fish are the same as those previously described for insecticides—if concentrations in streams are sufficiently high. In an experimental release of a fire retardant containing diammonium phosphate, no significant positive or negative effects on benthic invertebrates or fish were observed (see footnote 2). The pulsed nature of the introduction may have prevented the stimulatory effect that might result when a large area is treated and the release time of nitrogen to the stream is longer. Most fire-retardant drops occur in watersheds well drained by streams, but if retardants are used in or around basins with oligotrophic lakes, bogs, or swamps, their aquatic effects may be prolonged and exaggerated.

If fire retardants are not used and fires are allowed to burn, this too has implications for aquatic environments. Fire is a natural reset mechanism in northwestern forests and a fundamental driver of terrestrial plant succession. Human logging practices have duplicated many of the results of fire by converting much forest land to a pioneer stage of succession. These effects were reviewed by Norris et al. (see footnote 2) and Swanston (1991, this volume). Briefly, potential effects of fire on salmonid habitat may include decreased input of leaves and needles, increased input of wood, increased sedimentation, increased streamflow, increased solar radiation at the water surface, increased stream temperature, and increased nutrient inputs. The previous discussions of the effects of herbicides and fertilizers have dealt with these factors, and the potential indirect effects described would apply to watersheds that have been burned. If the hazards of fire retardants are to be assessed accurately, indirect effects of fire retardants must be weighed against those that would result if fire were not controlled.

General Perspectives on Indirect Effects of Forest Chemicals

Forest chemicals have great potential for indirectly altering aquatic communities and salmonid habitat. Such changes must be examined within the context of all land-use practices. Forest chemicals are seldom used on watersheds that have not been previously altered; therefore, impacts of forest chemicals on fish habitats must be considered in relation to previous or simultaneous effects of other forestry and land-use practices.

Herbicides modify the natural patterns of terrestrial plant succession on logged watersheds so that the duration of early deciduous-dominated stages is reduced and coniferous vegetation develops more rapidly. The following features of aquatic systems are influenced by the alteration of terrestrial succession: allochthonous organic inputs; tree and shrub canopy over streams; stream chemistry; and sedimentation rates. These factors are major fundamental determinants of the structure and function of stream ecosystems and are affected by logging with or without the use of herbicides. The basic effects of herbicides are to extend the early stages of watershed recovery, to minimize intermediate stages, and to accelerate development of coniferous stages. Potential indirect effects of herbicides on aquatic ecosystems must be viewed within this successional framework.

Fertilizers are applied to logged watersheds to stimulate production of vegetation. Nutrient inputs to streams from application of fertilizer may influence aquatic communities, particularly through stimulation of primary producers; however, these aquatic communities will have already been altered by the effects of logging. Fertilizers may indeed enhance many of the stimulatory effects of logging on aquatic primary producers. In coniferous forests, fertilizers are usually applied after the conifer canopy has closed to avoid stimulating growth of competing species and to allow greater utilization by conifers. Fertilization at 5-year intervals could gradually increase nitrogen concentrations in forest streams at base flow.

Fire retardants, unlike other forest chemicals, are generally applied while watersheds are being acutely modified. Fire has many effects on salmonid habitats, as reviewed by Swanston (1991). The indirect effects of fire retardant are generally limited to stimulation of primary production, and even that effect is greatly influenced by the extent to which the fire itself reduces the vegetation canopy over streams.

Insecticides are applied more frequently than other forest chemicals to watersheds that are least influenced by human activities. Even so, the effects of insecticides on aquatic systems must be viewed in relation to the effects of not using them and of allowing insect damage to forests. Insect-related effects are much less severe than the effects associated with logging or fire, but still must be incorporated into decision-making processes.

In assessing potential indirect effects of forest chemicals on salmonid habitats, land managers must consider the influence of protective measures (particularly buffer strips) on aquatic systems. Frequently, corridors along streams or around lakes are left unsprayed and the terrestrial communities and processes within these "spray buffer strips" may be practically identical to similar areas in untreated watersheds. Effects of chemical spraying must be transferred through such zones and become greatly diminished in the process. In clearcut watersheds where buffer strips of uncut vegetation are left, the additional use of spray buffer strips would be even more effective in reducing indirect effects of forest chemicals on aquatic communities. If buffer strips of uncut vegetation and no-spray zones are used in watershed management, many of the indirect effects of forest chemicals on stream ecosystems described in this chapter would not occur.

Indirect effects of forest chemicals on salmonids and aquatic ecosystems must be evaluated on appropriate temporal and spatial scales. Most biological processes in streams exhibit strong seasonal patterns, and the responses of aquatic organisms are closely related to the timing of application of a forest chemical. For example, summer is a period of low streamflow and winter is a period of high streamflow in many streams of the northwestern USA. Application of fertilizer to a watershed has a potentially greater effect on aquatic primary production in summer, when discharge is low and solar radiation is high, than in winter, when discharge is high and solar radiation is low. Location within a basin also influences the ecological responses to chemicals. The abundance and distribution of aquatic organisms change from headwaters downstream to large rivers (Vannote et al. 1980). Streams are connected within a drainage, and application of chemicals at one point may influence downstream communities. The terrestrial adults of many aquatic insects disperse upstream to lay their eggs, and effects of forest chemicals at one point in a drainage may influence insect recruitment to upstream reaches. Salmonids may spawn in one area of a basin, but the fry may rear in either upstream or downstream reaches and tributaries. The complex patterns of biological processes through time and the distribution of communities throughout a basin must be considered when the potential indirect effects of forest chemicals on salmonids and other aquatic organisms are evaluated.

Forest chemicals are major tools in forest management. Risks of chemical use must be evaluated, however. Direct toxic effects of chemicals on aquatic organisms are major concerns, and forest chemicals may have indirect effects on aquatic ecosystems at concentrations much lower than those observed to cause mortality. Potential effects of forest chemicals must be evaluated on the basis of four factors:

- changes in aquatic communities directly caused by forest chemicals;
- subsequent changes in other communities of aquatic organisms;
- alteration of terrestrial systems that influence aquatic ecosystems; and

• effects on patterns of recovery in watersheds that have already been altered by logging or fire.

Although few studies of indirect effects of forest chemicals on salmonid habitats are available to land managers, the perspectives presented in this chapter will provide a basis for evaluating potential indirect effects and designing management systems to minimize them.

Research Needs

The greater the amount and quality of information available on any subject, the more certain a decision maker can be of reaching correct conclusions about it. This truism prompts scientists to prepare lengthy lists of research needs, many items of which are repetitions of earlier lists. All research needs are not equally important. We have attempted to identify gaps in knowledge that cause the greatest uncertainty in the information presented earlier in this chapter. We believe that these specific gaps are discrete and small enough to be filled by a single scientist with supporting staff. No one area will require major long-term grants or funding programs, although in aggregate, the solutions of these problems will require substantial effort. We present the list of research needs in the order the subjects appeared in the chapter.

Behavior of Chemicals in the Environment

• *Quantify the influence of buffer strips on concentrations of forest chemicals in streams.* Research and practice have demonstrated that buffer strips reduce the entry of chemicals into forest streams, but the degrees of protection provided by strips of different widths have not been quantified. Some relatively simple experiments are needed to show the degree of improvement that can be achieved with buffer strips of various widths.

• *Determine the patterns of entry of atrazine, fosamine ammonium, glyphosate, triclopyr, and hexazinone herbicides, as well as fire retardants, into western forest streams under actual conditions of use.* Most of the research and monitoring of the entry of chemicals into streams, particularly in connection with operational applications, were done when phenoxy herbicides were the predominant forest chemicals. Consequently, few data are available on other forest chemicals. The lack of data is particularly acute for the chemicals listed above.

• *Determine more precisely the fates of all forest chemicals in forest streams.* Almost no data are available on the distribution of chemicals among the various parts of western forest stream systems. The data used in this chapter are mostly from laboratory studies or from intentional applications of chemicals to ponds or slow-moving streams for aquatic weed control. Extensive work in this area is not needed, only enough to establish the degree to which concepts developed in other types of aquatic systems fit the systems used by salmonids.

Toxicity of Chemicals to Aquatic Species

• *Determine the toxicity characteristics of the combinations of forest chemicals that are likely to be applied together.* Studies on the effects of combinations of chemicals (for example, picloram and 2,4-D) have generally been restricted to plants. Similar work with sensitive aquatic vertebrates and invertebrates is required to assess adequately the effects of combined chemicals.

• *Characterize the interaction between concentration and exposure duration for forest chemicals with respect to the more sensitive aquatic species.* Most toxicity tests hold the concentration of chemical constant for a specified period (such as 24, 48, or 96 h) and evaluate organism response soon afterward. In the field, aquatic organisms typically are exposed to concentrations of chemical that increase to a peak within a few hours after aerial application and then decrease rapidly to much lower levels in a few hours. Calibrations need to be established that will permit use of the extensive constant-exposure toxicity data base for evaluations of field exposures. In this chapter, we used an integral of the time–concentration curve, but this approach has not been fully validated.

• *Determine if the results of classical 96-h exposure tests with forest chemicals are adequate predictors of the long-term well-being of aquatic organisms.* Nearly all the toxicity testing on aquatic organisms has incorporated short-term exposures and only short-term observations of effects. Research is needed to determine if long-term latent effects result from short-term exposures. Tests with a few chemicals and a few key species may be sufficient to establish this point. With a few notable exceptions, we do not believe that latent effects will develop from short-term exposures to most toxicants.

Indirect Effects of Forest Chemicals

• *Quantify indirect effects of forest chemicals on aquatic organisms under field conditions. Determine sublethal effects of forest chemicals on aquatic organisms.* Indirect and sublethal effects may result from very low chemical concentrations; both laboratory and (especially) field research on these subjects are needed before safe use of forest chemicals can be assured. Indirect effects on aquatic ecosystems most probably involve several types of aquatic organisms; such effects, therefore, would be much more complex and subtle than direct toxic effects. Research must be tightly focused, appropriately located, and properly timed to permit the observation of changes in aquatic communities.

Conclusions

The use of forest chemicals can result in both direct and indirect effects on salmonids and their habitats. Direct toxic effects are those resulting from the exposure of fish to a chemical in water, food, or sediment. The potential for direct effects can be estimated based on knowledge of the toxicity characteristics of the chemical and its movement, persistence, and fate in the environment.

The most important process by which chemicals enter streams is direct application, but drift from nearby treatment areas or units is also important. Mobilization of residues in ephemeral stream channels during the first storms after application is sometimes important. All three processes can be influenced by forest managers. Selection and orientation of spray units to avoid streams, and attention to the details of application to avoid drift, will minimize chemical entry into streams and thereby reduce the likelihood of direct toxic effects on stream organisms.

The margin of safety (no-effect level/exposure level) is a good index of the probability that use of a specific forest chemical will directly affect salmonids. The larger the margin of safety, the less likely direct effects will occur. Margins of safety less than 1.0 indicate direct effects are likely to occur. We calculated margins of safety for fish, based on the maximum acute and short-term chronic exposures likely to occur in operational uses of these chemicals (Table 7.17). These margins of safety will be 5–10 times greater when streams do not occur in areas to be treated, when buffer strips are used along streams, and when full attention is given to the details of application to prevent drift and direct application to surface water.

Indirect effects are manifested through chemically induced changes in the densities and community organization of aquatic and terrestrial plants and insects. These effects may include alteration of nutrient, sediment, and temperature characteristics of the water and changes in cover, food, or some other environmental characteristic important to the well-being of salmonid fishes. These changes have not been as thoroughly studied as the direct effects, but may be the most likely to occur.

Chapter 8

Road Construction and Maintenance

M. J. Furniss, T. D. Roelofs, and C. S. Yee

Forest and rangeland roads can cause serious degradation of salmonid habitats in streams. Numerous studies during the past 25 years have documented the changes that occur in streams as a result of forest and rangeland roads and related effects. Once the mechanisms of these changes are understood, it is possible to design roads that have less harmful effects on stream channels and their biota.

Only recently have steps been taken to minimize the negative effects of roads on streams. In the past, the primary considerations in road planning, construction, and maintenance have been traffic levels and economics, and little concern was expressed for the environmental influences of roads (Gardner 1979).

It should be recognized that only rarely can roads be built that have no negative effects on streams. Roads modify natural drainage networks and accelerate erosion processes. These changes can alter physical processes in streams, leading to changes in streamflow regimes, sediment transport and storage, channel bank and bed configurations, substrate composition, and stability of slopes adjacent to streams. These changes can have important biological consequences, and they can affect all stream ecosystem components. Salmonids require stream habitats that provide food, shelter, spawning substrate, suitable water quality, and access for migration upstream and downstream during their life cycles. Roads can cause direct or indirect changes in streams that affect each of these habitat components.

Many studies have shown how roads affect the physical environment of streams, and how the physical environment of streams affects fish. This research permits the diagnosis of problems and the design of engineering solutions to reduce negative effects.

Effects of Roads on Streams

Roads can affect streams directly by accelerating erosion and sediment loadings, by altering channel morphology, and by changing the runoff characteristics of watersheds. These processes interact to cause secondary changes in channel morphology. All of these changes affect fish habitats.

Accelerated Erosion Rates

Construction of a road network can lead to greatly accelerated erosion rates in a watershed (Haupt 1959; Swanson and Dyrness 1975; Swanston and Swanson 1976; Beschta 1978; Gardner 1979; Reid and Dunne 1984). Increased sedimenta-

Influences of Forest and Rangeland Management on Salmonid Fishes and Their Habitats
American Fisheries Society Special Publication 19:297–323, 1991

tion in streams following road construction can be dramatic and long-lasting. The sediment contribution per unit area from roads is often much greater than that from all other land management activities combined, including log skidding and yarding (Gibbons and Salo 1973).

Sediment entering streams is delivered chiefly by mass soil movements and surface erosion processes (Swanston 1991, this volume). Failure of stream crossings, diversions of streams by roads, washout of road fills, and accelerated scour at culvert outlets are also important sources of sedimentation in streams within roaded watersheds.

Mass soil movement.—Where forest and rangelands occur on steep terrain, mass soil movement is often the primary mode of erosion and sediment delivery to streams from roads. Four types of mass movement common to western forest lands are described by Swanston (1991): slumps and earthflows, debris avalanches, debris flows, and debris torrents. These processes are differentiated on the basis of speed of travel and shape of the failure surface. Forest and rangeland roads can increase the incidence and severity of each type of mass movement. Several studies in the western Cascade Range in Oregon showed that mass soil movements associated with roads are 30 to more than 300 times greater than in undisturbed forests (Sidle et al. 1985) (Table 8.1).

Construction of roads can increase the frequency of slope failures from several to hundreds of times, depending on such variables as soil type, slope steepness, bedrock type and structure, and presence of subsurface water. Road location is the most important factor because it affects how much all of these variables will contribute to surface failure (H. W. Anderson 1971; Larse 1971; Swanston 1971; Swanston and Swanson 1976; Lyons and Beschta 1983). Mass soil movements triggered by roads can continue for decades after the roads are built.

The most common causes of road-related mass movements are improper placement and construction of road fills, inadequate road maintenance, insufficient culvert sizes, very steep hillslope gradient, placement or sidecast of excess materials, poor road location, removal of slope support by undercutting, and alteration of slope drainage by interception and concentration of surface and subsurface water (Wolf 1982).

Surface erosion.—Surface erosion from roadbed surfaces, drainage ditches, and cut-and-fill surfaces can severely affect streams below the right-of-way (Burns 1970; Brown and Krygier 1971; Larse 1971; Gibbons and Salo 1973; Weaver et al. 1987). In a study on the Clearwater River in Washington, Cederholm et al. (1981) found that the percentage of fine sediment in spawning gravels increased above natural levels when more than 2.5% of basin area was covered by roads. The chief variables in surface erosion are the inherent erodibility of the soil, slope steepness, surface runoff, slope length, and ground cover.

Surface erosion can be the major source of sediment delivered to streams in sensitive terrain, such as areas with soils derived from granite and from highly fractured sedimentary rocks. Surface erosion and piecemeal mass movement from landslide surfaces can prolong sediment delivery to streams after initial landslide events. Such chronic secondary erosion could be as damaging to stream biota as catastrophic or episodic sediment inputs from mass-movement events, because the particles will be finer and they will be delivered over longer time periods.

TABLE 8.1.—Comparative rates of soil mass movement with various land uses, based on landslide inventories over relatively long time periods. (From Sidle et al. 1985.)

Area (source[a])	Land use	Years of record	Number of landslides	Mass erosion	
				Annual rate (m^3/hectare)	Multiple of undisturbed land
H. J. Andrews	Forest	25	32	0.87	1.0
Forest, Oregon	Clear-cuts	25	36	2.45	2.8
Cascade Range:	Roads	25	71	26.19	30
unstable zone					
(1)					
Oregon Cascade	Forest	25	7	0.45	1.0
Range: Alder	Clear-cuts	15	18	1.17	2.6
Creek (2)	Roads	15	75	155.65	346
Oregon Cascade	Forest	34	19	0.37	1.0
Range: Blue	Clear-cuts	22	30	3.22	8.7
River (3)	Roads	25	69	16.3	44
Oregon Coast	Forest	15		0.19	1.0
Range: Mapleton	Clear-cuts	15		0.7	3.7
area (4)					
Oregon Coast	Forest	15	34	0.28	1.0
Range: Mapleton	Clear-cuts	10	186	1.13	4.0
area, soil type	Roads	15	41	34.91	125
47 (5)					
Oregon Coast	Forest	15	42	0.32	1.0
Range: Mapleton	Clear-cuts	10	317	0.62	1.9
area, slideprone	Roads	15	89	15.85	50
soils (5)					
Olympic Peninsula,	Forest	84	25	0.7	1.0
Washington (6)	Clear-cuts	6	0	0	0
	Roads	6	83	117.74	168
Coastal southwest	Forest	32	29	0.11	1.0
British Columbia	Clear-cuts	32	18	0.25	2.3
(7)	Roads	32	11	2.83	26
Idaho Batholith:	Forest			0.07[b]	1.0
Pine Creek	Burned[c]	2	9	1.38	20
burn (8)	Roads[d]	2	9	13.15	188
North Westland,	Forest			1.0[e]	1.0
New Zealand (9)	Clear-cut[f]	3	25	11.8	11.8
	Clear-cut[g]	3	72	40.4	40.4
	Roads[h]	3	32	267	267

[a]Sources: (1) Swanson and Dyrness (1975); (2) Morrison (1975); (3) Marion (1981); (4) Ketcheson and Froelich (1978); (5) Swanson et al. (1977); (6) Fiksdal (1974); (7) O'Loughlin (1972); (8) Gray and Megahan (1981); (9) O'Loughlin and Pearce (1976).

[b]Estimated from Zena Creek data (Megahan and Kidd 1972).

[c]Includes some clear-cut areas.

[d]Assumed that 6% of land area was in the road right-of-way.

[e]Estimated.

[f]Gravel substrate.

[g]Sandstone substrate.

[h]Calculations based on 4% of land area occupied by roads and 25% of observed landslides directly related to roads.

Surface erosion from road networks is usually reduced through time by natural revegetation (Beschta 1978), and it can be controlled by mulching, reseeding, and mechanical slope protection (Dyrness 1970; Megahan 1974; U.S. Environmental Protection Agency 1975; Carr 1980; Carr and Ballard 1980). Reid and Dunne (1984) found that sediment yield from roadbeds increased greatly with the amount of truck traffic. Sediment loss from road surfaces is partially a function of the surface composition and road maintenance.

Other sources.—Other erosional processes can cause accelerated erosion and sediment delivery to streams. Failure of road fills is common in steep terrain, particularly on low-standard roads where road fill is not compacted or woody material is incorporated into the fill.

Where flow restrictions such as culverts are placed in stream channels, the scouring power of streamflow is increased. This can lead to increased channel scour, streambank erosion, and undermining of the crossing structure and fill.

Failure of stream crossings can be a major source of increased sediment loading of streams. When stream crossings fail, they often do so catastrophically, causing extensive local scour and deposition and additional erosion downstream. Stream-crossing failures that divert streamflow onto nonstream areas are particularly damaging and persistent (Weaver et al. 1987).

Alterations in Channel Morphology

A stream adjusts its geometry to accommodate the water and sediment it carries. When the amount of water or sediment a stream must carry increases, channel geometry must change to accommodate the increase. When channel geometry is artificially changed, such as by a stream crossing, a stream will adjust by altering its geometry upstream or downstream of the change. The nature of the adjustment depends on the original geometry and composition of the channel, how these are changed, and the ability of the channel to reshape itself. Channel adjustments that occur, in order of smallest to largest energy requirements, are changes in channel bed form, channel bed armor, channel width, channel pattern (alignment), and longitudinal profile (Heede 1980).

Hagans et al. (1986) demonstrated that road construction and inadequate maintenance lead to substantial increases in stream-channel drainage densities and channel dimensions. Adjustments can occur quickly, but often continue over many years. The adjustments usually are detrimental to fish habitat. Therefore, road crossings that modify and restrict channel geometry least, such as bridges or low-water crossings, are likely to have the least adverse effects on fish habitat.

Channel morphology is also sensitive to indirect changes resulting from other effects that roads may have on streams. Increases in sediment loading and peak flows cause changes in channel morphology that can be detrimental to fish habitat.

Other Effects of Roads on Streams

Although sedimentation and stream-channel changes are the primary negative effects of roads on streams, roads can adversely affect streams in other ways. These include changes in rainfall–runoff relationships, hillslope drainage, potential for chemical contamination, the amount and type of organic debris in stream channels, and human access to streams and fish populations.

Roads can change the stream hydrograph and affect sediment deposition in streams. Harr et al. (1975) reported an increase in peak flows following road construction. King and Tennyson (1984) found that the hydrologic behaviors of small forested watersheds were altered when as little as 3.9% of the watershed was occupied by roads.

Hauge et al. (1979) discussed several ways that roads can affect hillslope drainage, including changes in infiltration rates, interception and diversion of subsurface flow, changes in the watershed area of small streams, changes in the time distribution of water yield to channels, and changes in the fine (micro) details of drainage. These changes combine to cause a rerouting of hillside drainage that can lead to changes in erosion and the hydrologic behavior of small streams.

Chemicals used to suppress dust, stabilize or deice road surfaces, and fertilize or control roadside vegetation can enter streams directly or can be transported by runoff water or on sediment. Little is known about the effects of these chemicals on stream biota. Furthermore, a chemical-spill hazard exists wherever roads are near streams or road drainage enters streams.

Organic debris from construction clearing and landslides caused by roads can enter and block streams. These materials can cause additional erosion and alteration of channel morphology, and can form migration barriers. However, they can also provide important cover and channel diversity for juvenile fish. Removal of large organic debris at stream crossings can eliminate important components of fish habitat.

Roads allow easier human access to streams, facilitating both legal and illegal fishing. They also give access to biologists for fish habitat and population assessment, and for habitat restoration and enhancement projects. In some cases a road can be a positive contribution to a fisheries management program for a stream, provided the road is located, designed, constructed, and maintained to protect fish and fish habitats.

Effects of Roads on Salmonid Habitats

The habitat requirements of salmonids are reviewed by Bjornn and Reiser (1991, this volume). The particular habitat requirements for each salmonid species vary with the season and life cycle of the fish. All salmonids require access to spawning areas, appropriate substrates for reproduction (including substrates that can support egg incubation, alevin development, and fry emergence), and suitable water quality. Species that rear in streams for months to years before they enter the ocean also require food organisms and shelter or cover. Physical alterations in sediment loading, channel morphology, substrate composition, riparian conditions, and other road-related changes can adversely affect all freshwater stages of these fish: migration, spawning, incubation, emergence, and rearing.

Migration

Improperly designed roads can prevent or interfere with upstream migration of both adult and juvenile salmonids in several ways. Macroinvertebrate movements can also be impaired or prevented by road-related changes to stream channels (Pearce and Watson 1983). Culverts pose the most common migration barriers associated with road networks. Hydraulic characteristics and culvert configuration can impede or prevent fish passage (discussed in detail later in this chapter). Extreme sedimentation from roads can cause streamflow to become subsurface or too shallow for upstream fish movement. Likewise, stream-crossing structures can impede gravel movement in streams, leading to bed aggradation and subsurface flows that block migration. Large landslides or debris avalanches can form temporary dams that prevent fish passage (Pearce and Watson 1983). In very cold climates, large ice buildups at culverts can create barriers to migration.

Spawning

Adult salmonids have exacting habitat requirements for spawning, including requirements for substrate sizes, water depth, and velocity (Bjornn and Reiser 1991). The abundance and quality of spawning substrate can be severely affected by sedimentation. Fine sediment can be deposited in gravel interstices, even in fast-moving streams, because of the lower water velocities within the gravels. If the amount of fine material in the gravel matrix is too great, the gravels may become so cemented or indurated that fish are unable to excavate a redd.

In low-velocity stream reaches, an excess of fine sediment can completely cover suitable spawning gravel, rendering the reach useless for spawning. Excessive sediment loading of streams can also result in channel braiding, increased width:depth ratios, increased incidence and severity of bank erosion, reduced pool volume and frequency, and increased subsurface flow. These changes can result in a reduction in quality and quantity of available spawning habitat.

Gravel extraction for road construction may directly remove suitable spawning substrate. In some cases, gravel removal creates additional spawning areas, but such gravels often are hydraulically unstable. This can attract spawners to gravels that will not stay in place long enough to successfully incubate embryos.

Incubation

Successful incubation of salmonids in stream gravels depends on intragravel water flow to provide oxygen and to remove carbon dioxide and other waste metabolites (Bams 1969). If the gravel interstices are filled with fine sediments, intragravel water flow and gas exchange are reduced and egg development is slowed or halted. Fry emergence is likewise hampered by excessive fine sediments that can trap fry in the gravel (Phillips et al. 1975).

The gravels of redds must be stable throughout the incubation period. Developing embryos can be destroyed by gravel scour resulting from peak flows. Increases in peak flows and sedimentation can increase the incidence of redd destruction by scouring.

Juvenile Rearing

Increased sediment in streams can adversely affect juvenile salmonids in several ways. Most of the food items in the diets of juveniles are macroinvertebrates living in the stream. Large amounts of fine sediment reduce or eliminate much of the suitable substrate for producing macroinvertebrates, thereby limiting the food available to juvenile fish (Cordone and Kelley 1961).

Excessive sediment delivery to streams can modify the stream channel configuration, decreasing the depth and number of pools and reducing the physical space available for rearing fish. These changes can also lead to reduced survival of juvenile fish by filling interstitial spaces in the boulder and large cobble substrates where fish reside over the winter.

Riparian vegetation provides important components of rearing habitat, including shade (which often maintains cool water temperatures), food supply, channel stability, and channel structure. Road construction near streams often removes riparian vegetation directly. Mass soil movements and channel changes resulting from roads can also eliminate or damage riparian vegetation. The essential role of large woody riparian debris in salmonid streams was reviewed by Bisson et al. (1987).

Everest et al. (1987a) reviewed the effects of fine sediment on fish habitats and fish production. They demonstrated that the effects of fine sediment on salmonids are complex and depend on many interacting factors, including species and race of fish, duration of freshwater rearing, spawning escapement within a stream system, presence of other fish species, availability of spawning and rearing habitats, stream gradient, channel morphology, sequence of flow events, basin lithology, and history of land use.

How to Prevent or Minimize Damage

The basic strategy to prevent or minimize damage from roads is to understand the physical and biotic conditions that could be affected. Then, planning should ensure that roads are designed, constructed, and maintained to reduce the risks of erosion; that the risk of eroded material entering streams is low; that disturbances to channel morphology will be reduced or eliminated; that the alteration of hillslope drainage patterns will be minimized; and that fish will be able to migrate past stream crossings.

Four general principles should be considered to control erosion resulting from roads.

- Know what the erosional processes are, how roads can affect these processes, and the appropriate measures to prevent or control changes in erosional patterns.

- Avoid building roads in areas with high erosion hazards to the greatest extent possible. Minor changes in location can often prevent major problems. This is usually the single most important consideration in preventing degradation of fish habitat.

- It is almost always less expensive and more effective to design and build roads so that erosion is prevented or minimized than to control sediment once it is mobilized. Remedial measures for major erosional events usually are much more costly than preventing the events in the first place.

- Minimize the effects of roads on streams by keeping road disturbances as far from streams as possible, and by providing buffers of undisturbed land between roads and streams.

Planning and Reconnaissance

Larse (1971) pointed out that the most important steps that can be taken to minimize the impacts of roads on streams usually occur during planning, recon-

FIGURE 8.1.—Roads built near watercourses often have severe adverse effects on fish habitats. Sediments eroded from exposed and disturbed ground by rain, runoff, or streamflow move directly into stream habitats.

naissance, and route selection rather than during or after construction. Many problems can be eliminated or reduced by including on the planning team specialists such as geologists, soil scientists, hydrologists, and biologists, along with engineers. Key environmental problems and constraints are easily overlooked when routes are located and roads are designed by one person.

The following guidelines will help reduce adverse effects of roads on streams.

• Conduct long-range transportation planning for large areas to ensure that roads will serve future needs. This will result in less total road distance, roads built to appropriate standards, reduced costs of development, and fewer effects on streams.

• Use adaptable road standards to avoid sensitive areas. The prevailing planning philosophy should be to *fit the road to the landscape*. Rigid design standards, especially when limits on grade are inflexible, can severely restrict options for location, and often result in roads that pass through areas with high erosion hazards. Short grades of 14–22% can be practical for low-volume roads, and they can make it possible to avoid landslides or other sensitive areas.

FIGURE 8.2.—Steep slopes close to waterways are high-risk locations for roads because they usually are the most erosion-prone areas in a watershed. Sediments eroded here are readily delivered to fish habitats.

- Avoid midslope locations in favor of higher, flatter areas. Ridgetop roads usually have the least effect on streams.
- Locate ridgetop roads to avoid headwalls at the source of tributary drainages. Headwall areas also are very prone to landslides (Weaver et al. 1987).
- Do not locate roads within the inner valley gorge (the oversteepened slopes adjacent to streams). These areas have the highest incidence of landsliding of any portion of an upland watershed (Wolfe 1982) (Figures 8.1, 8.2).
- Avoid slopes that show signs of excessive wetness, such as springs or water-loving vegetation.
- Avoid slopes where sidecast material could enter streams, or plan to end-haul excess material.
- Avoid slopes where large cuts and fills would be required.
- Locate roads to minimize roadway drainage area and to avoid modifying the natural drainage areas of small streams.
- Locate valley-bottom roads to provide a buffer strip of natural vegetation between the road and stream.
- Locate roads to take advantage of natural log-landing areas, such as flatter, higher, drier, and more stable terrain with good access to the timber to be removed. Good landing locations can also reduce the amount of necessary roading.
- Minimize the number of stream crossings consistent with the above considerations.

FIGURE 8.3.—A low-impact road fitted to the landscape with a narrow roadbed, narrow clearing limits, small cuts and fills, and outslope drainage. There is no inboard ditch to concentrate the erosive power of running water.

• Locate stream crossings to minimize channel changes and the amount of excavation or fill needed at the crossing.

Design

The following guidelines for road design will help minimize adverse effects on salmonid habitats.

• Use the minimum design standards practical with respect to road width, radius, and gradient (Figure 8.3).
• Minimize excavation with a balanced earthwork design wherever possible. Bench or terrace and drain natural slopes to provide a sound foundation for embankments.
• Design cut slopes to be as steep as practical. Some sloughing and bank failure is usually an acceptable trade-off for the reduced initial excavation required.
• Determine the type and extent of fish habitat before selecting criteria for drainage structure design. Bridges and arch culverts are preferred for streams with migratory fish. Where culverts are used, the gradient should be less than 1%, the culvert should be placed at or below the original streambed elevation, and

FIGURE 8.4.—Stream crossings pose the greatest risk to fish habitats of any road feature. When culverts are plugged by debris or overtopped by high flows, road damage, channel realignment, and severe sedimentation often result. The capacity of the culvert shown here was exceeded during a heavy storm, and a large slug of sediment was rapidly delivered to fish habitats downstream. Water was not diverted down the road, however. Roads should be constructed so they will not divert streams; where existing roads have the potential to do so, creation of a simple dip or "failure point" will prevent the catastrophic effects that can result from a diversion.

water depth and velocity at both low and high flows should be integrated into the design (discussed in detail later in this chapter).

• Control scouring at culvert outlets with energy dissipators such as heavy rock riprap, weirs, or gabions, consistent with fish passage considerations.

• Design drainage structures to accommodate peak streamflow based on at least a 50-year-interval flood (100-year flood for large permanent bridges and major culverts), and give consideration to the possibility that bed load and debris will restrict the flow capacity of the structure. The risk of failure can be calculated by

$$F = 1 - (1 - 1/t)^n;$$

F is the chance of failure during the design life, t is the flood recurrence interval, and n is the design life of the road or structure. For example, a culvert sized for a 50-year flood has a 33% chance of failure during a 20-year design life. Campbell and Sidle (1984) described methods for predicting peak flows and sizing culverts for small watersheds. Keep in mind that, whatever the design life, any crossing structure has a virtually 100% chance of failing over its installation life if it is not removed after the road is abandoned.

• At stream crossings, avoid channel-width changes and protect embankments with riprap, masonry headwalls, or other retaining structures. Align culverts with the natural course and gradient of the stream. Debris that floats during high

FIGURE 8.5.—If road drainage becomes concentrated, it must be discharged into places that can handle the flow without accelerated erosion. When the natural drainage of small streams is changed and concentrated flow is discharged into nondrainage areas, severe gullying and landslides can result.

streamflow can plug or restrict flow at culverts, causing severe changes in road embankments, streambanks, or channels (Figure 8.4). Trash racks can reduce culvert plugging, but can easily become barriers to fish passage. Avoid the need for trash racks by designing culverts to pass debris downstream.

• Wherever possible, disperse drainage rather than concentrating it, except in streams. Always strive to keep water flowing where it would naturally flow.

• Avoid the discharge of large amounts of concentrated runoff onto non-drainage areas (Figure 8.5).

• Do not change natural drainage areas by means of culvert or waterbar placement.

• Surface forest and rangeland roads wherever practical to control erosion and to maintain the surface drainage configuration under expected traffic conditions. Design road surfaces to remain stable and erosion-resistant during the wettest period of use. Control access on roads intended for dry-season use only.

• Use outslope drainage wherever feasible to disperse runoff. This results in the least potential for erosion and does not require as wide a road (no ditchline).

Generally, outslope drainage works well where sideslopes are greater than 20% and grades are less than about 12%, and where surface configuration can be maintained. Insloping with frequent cross-drainage is appropriate on roads with steeper grades. Cross-drainage on outsloped roads should be considered as a backup to outsloping, which can become ineffective under some traffic and surfacing conditions.

• Where inslope-and-ditch drainage is used, relieve the ditchline of drainage at frequent intervals onto areas that will not erode excessively or cause sediment to enter streams. Special care must be taken to avoid discharging drainage onto areas prone to gullying, slumping, or landsliding. Ditches along steep grades and in sensitive areas should be lined with rock to control ditchline erosion.

• When discharging drainage onto a long, erodible fill, use a discharge pipe or flume to convey the drainage to the bottom of the fill. Place energy dissipators at the outlet.

• Provide for vegetative or mechanical stabilization in areas where cut-and-fill erosion will cause sediment delivery to streams. Several publications describe erosion-control measures for cut-and-fill surfaces (Patric 1976; Carr 1980; Carr and Ballard 1980; Rothwell 1983; Swift 1986).

• Keep approaches to streams as close to right angles as possible to minimize streamside disturbances.

• Develop a specific plan for stream-crossing construction that addresses stream diversion, disturbance limits, equipment limitations, erosion control, and the operational time period when disturbances caused by construction can be most easily limited.

• Where necessary, use retaining walls with properly designed drainage to reduce excavation, contain bank material, and prevent stream encroachment.

• Design and construct stream crossings so that they will not divert streamflow out of the channel and down the road alignment if the culvert should fail or plug with debris (Figure 8.6) (Weaver et al. 1987).

• Field-check the designs before the plan drawings are complete to make certain that the design fits the terrain, that drainage needs have been met, that all critical slope conditions have been identified, and that appropriate solutions have been designed for all problem areas.

Construction

A challenge to the road builder is to construct the designed facility with the least possible disturbance of the right-of-way and without damage to or contamination of the adjacent landscape and streams. Poor construction practices can lead to severe erosion problems, toxic spills, and other water-quality problems. The following construction practices will help reduce adverse effects on salmonid habitats.

• Schedule construction during noncritical times for the local fish populations. Consult a fisheries biologist for this information. For example, avoid construction when eggs or alevins are in the gravels downstream, and do not restrict or block streamflow when adult fish are migrating upstream.

• Ensure that erosion-control measures are completed prior to rainy weather, even if construction is incomplete.

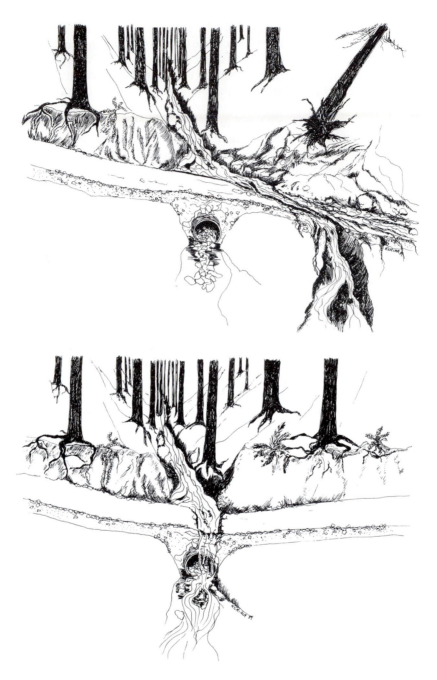

FIGURE 8.6.—Stream crossings can be considered dams that are designed to fail. The risk of failure is substantial for most crossings, so *how* they fail is of critical importance. In the upper sketch, the crossing has failed and the road grade has diverted the stream down the road, resulting in severe erosion and downstream sedimentation; such damage to aquatic habitats can persist for many years once begun. Stream diversions are easy to prevent, however, as illustrated by the lower sketch, in which the road grade was such that a crossing failure only caused the loss of some road fill.

FIGURE 8.7.—Incorporation of woody debris into road fill and sidecast material inevitably leads to mass failure and surface erosion.

• Remove earth material and debris from streambanks so they cannot enter the stream later.

• Locate fuel storage areas well away from streams, and construct dikes to contain the largest possible spill. Leaks of motor oil and hydraulic fluids from heavy equipment should be monitored and controlled to prevent water contamination.

• Restrict gravel-removal operations to areas above the high-water level of the design flood. Coordinate gravel removal with a fisheries biologist. Sometimes beneficial changes can be made, but only when the fluvial system is understood and great care is taken.

• Locate and construct water withdrawal points to prevent streambank degradation and sedimentation.

• Locate road-building camps away from streams and manage wastes properly.

• Use spill-control planning and practice to keep construction toxicants out of streams.

• Do not incorporate woody or vegetative material into road fills (Figure 8.7).

Maintenance

Regular maintenance is required to keep roads in good condition and to identify and correct problems promptly. Preventive maintenance should be practiced on *all* roads, not just actively used roads. Maintenance requirements should be considered during planning and design. The higher initial costs of designing and constructing roads that weather well can be amortized by lower maintenance costs. The following practices will help reduce the adverse effects of road deterioration on salmonid habitats.

• Do not leave berms along the outboard edge of roads, unless an outboard berm was specifically designed to be a part of the road and low-energy drainage is provided for. The creation of outboard berms during road grading is a common mistake, and frequently turns low-impact roads into high-impact, chronic sediment producers.

• Grade and shape roads to conserve existing surface material. Road grading and shaping should maintain, not destroy, the design drainage of the road, unless modification is necessary to improve drainage problems that were not anticipated during the design phase.

• Inspect ditches and culverts frequently, and clean them out when necessary. Do not over-clean them, however, because excessive cleaning of ditches causes unnecessary sedimentation.

• When blading and shaping roads, do not sidecast excess material onto the fill. Periodic sidecasting can prevent fill stabilization and promote erosion.

• Do not use herbicides where they might contaminate streams, such as on areas near streams or in ditchlines that discharge into streams.

• Apply oil, other dust-abatement additives, and stabilization chemicals so they do not enter streams. Subsequent transport of these substances into water courses should be evaluated (Norris et al. 1991, this volume).

• Promptly remove debris that obstructs drainage systems.

• Close unsurfaced roads during the wet season, particularly those that can directly contribute sediment to streams.

• Close and reclaim unneeded roads. They should be put into shape to be stable and drain properly without maintenance. This usually requires earthwork for removing culverts or "dishing out" crossings that have high diversion potentials, and shaping the road for long-term stability (Figure 8.8; Eubanks 1980; Weaver et al. 1987). Where high-value fisheries are at risk from abandoned roads, more extensive obliteration and reclamation of roads should be considered.

Roads and Fish Migration

Forest and rangeland roads frequently cross streams. All crossings must be engineered to allow the efficient passage of water under the road. When the streams support fish, a means for their passage must be incorporated as well.

In western streams, anadromous salmonids migrate upstream and downstream during their life cycles, usually over long distances. Many resident salmonids and other fish also move extensively upstream and downstream to seek food, shelter, better water quality, and spawning areas.

Road crossings can be barriers to migration, usually because of outfall barriers, excessive water velocity, insufficient water depth in culverts, disorienting turbulent flow patterns, lack of resting pools below culverts, or a combination of these conditions (Figure 8.9).

The incorporation of fish-passage facilities at stream crossings should be based on assessments of the life-cycle requirements of fish species, of habitat quality, and of the accessibility of sites to fish. Natural barriers downstream or immediately upstream from the site may eliminate the need to provide fish-passage facilities. Usually, a knowledgeable fisheries biologist must be consulted to assess the habitat.

FIGURE 8.8.—When a road is abandoned, most future erosion can be prevented if roads are backfilled, stream crossings are removed, stream channels are reconstructed to stable configurations, and all bare surfaces are revegetated. Severe erosion is almost inevitable if stream crossings are left in place along abandoned roads.

Typical stream crossings involve bridges or culverts. Bridges are preferred because they usually cause less modification of stream channels than do culverts, and they are often the best way to assure fish passage. Building bridges on low-volume forest and rangeland roads is often uneconomical, however, and less-costly culverts are used. Culverts are by far the most common type of crossing device and the most likely to cause barriers to fish migration.

Low-water crossings are sometimes used where transportation requirements are seasonal and stream channel and slope configurations are suitable. Low-water crossings with concrete sills or grade-control structures can be barriers during low-flow conditions, but this can be easily mitigated in design. Low-water crossings are preferable to culverts for fish passage because high-flow migration is unimpaired and low-water migration is easy to provide for.

Consideration of fish passage during planning and design of road stream crossings can greatly reduce or eliminate the barrier effects that crossing structures can have. In many situations, structures must be designed with fish passage as the primary engineering requirement.

Where culverts are deemed necessary for stream crossings, the road designer should be aware of factors that affect the fish, and of the choices among crossing locations and structures. Close coordination between fishery biologists and engineers is critical, especially during planning stages.

The first consideration is whether or not the stream to be crossed is used by migrating fish. If not, the design problem is reduced to one of adequate discharge capacity. If the stream is used by fish that migrate at any time during their life cycles, the designer must know which species use the stream, when they migrate,

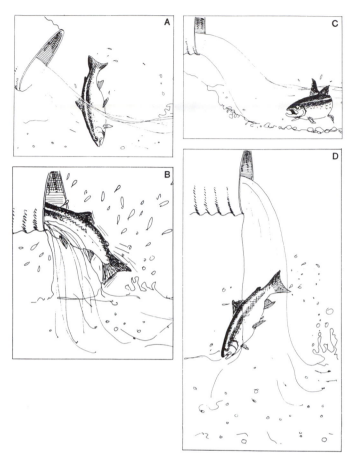

FIGURE 8.9.—Culvert conditions that block fish passage: (A) water velocity too great; (B) water depth in culvert too shallow; (C) no resting pool below culvert; (D) jump too high. (After Evans and Johnston 1980.)

and what their swimming capabilities are. Facilities for fish passage must be based on the swimming abilities of the least-capable migrating fish in the stream, not the champion swimmers.

For fish to overcome obstacles in their migration, the following conditions are necessary.

• A resting–jumping pool must be present immediately below the obstacle. This allows the fish to conserve energy and build up swimming speed to overcome the obstacle.

• Individual jumps must not be too high. For adult trout, a single vertical jump should be no higher than 0.3 m, and individual jumps in series should be 0.15 m high or less. A good working assumption is that adult salmon and steelhead can negotiate single jumps of 0.6–0.9 m or a series of 0.3-m-high jumps.

• Water depth through the culvert must be adequate for swimming. A minimum water depth of 0.15 m for trout and 0.3 m for salmon and steelhead is necessary.

Swimming speeds of young anadromous fish

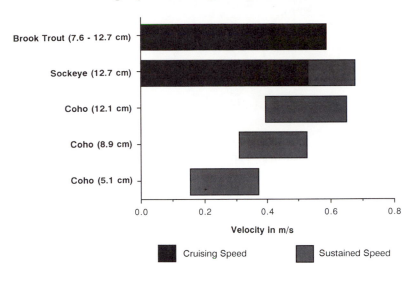

Swimming speeds of adult anadromous fish

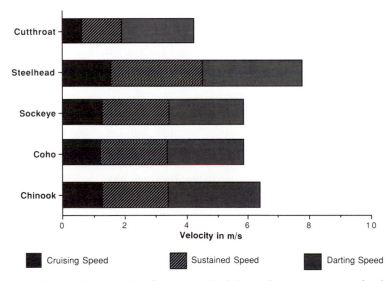

FIGURE 8.10.—Swimming speeds of young and adult anadromous trout and salmon.

• The water velocity in the culvert must not exceed the maximum sustained swimming ability of the migrating species for which passage is designed. Figure 8.10 shows the swimming speeds of adult and juvenile anadromous fish.

• Resting areas must be provided en route wherever the swimming distance through a difficult obstacle exceeds 15–30 m.

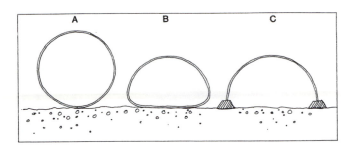

FIGURE 8.11.—Types of metal culverts used on western forest and rangeland roads: (A) corrugated-round; (B) corrugated pipe-arch; (C) structural plate-arch with concrete footings.

• A resting pool at the upstream end of a difficult obstacle is necessary so that exhausted fish are not swept downstream.

The choice of crossing location is very important in terms of both sedimentation effects and fish passage. For fish passage, preferred locations are those that do not cause large increases in velocity and have no abrupt changes in gradient or alignment of the channel. Reaches with uniform alignment, good bank stability, and uniform gentle gradients are the easiest to cross with provisions for fish passage.

Types of Culverts

Three types of metal culverts are commonly used for western forest and rangeland roads. They are classified by shape and are either standard corrugated-round, standard corrugated pipe-arch, or structural plate-arch (Figure 8.11). The first two may be prefabricated, as is usual for the smaller sizes (up to 1.5 m in diameter), or they may be of multiplate design. Structural plate-arch culverts are always of multiplate design because they are so large and are usually fabricated on site.

The structural plate-arch set in concrete footings (Figure 8.11C) is the most desirable culvert type for fish because the natural streambed is left mostly unchanged. Little narrowing of the flow occurs at either end of the culvert and there is no significant change in water velocity. Where concrete footings are not practical, split, wide-flanged, buried steel footings have been used successfully in their place. Many fisheries biologists believe that the structural plate-arch is the only acceptable culvert type where fish passage is required (Evans and Johnston 1980).

Pipe-arch culverts (Figure 8.11B) are less desirable than the structural plate-arch, but they can usually be installed to allow fish passage. Fabricated in smaller sizes, they can be used in smaller, lower fills where structural steel arches would not fit. Wherever pipe arches are used, the gradient must be kept below 1% to minimize water velocities. During periods of low flow, the water in culverts with this shape can be spread so thinly across the bottom that fish passage is impossible. Baffles may be needed to increase the flow depth through the pipe arch (baffle systems are discussed in detail later).

Although the standard corrugated-round culvert (Figure 8.11A) is the type most commonly used in western forest and rangeland roads, it is the least desirable for

FIGURE 8.12.—Culverts installed above the grade of a stream can be a barrier to upstream fish migration. The culvert shown here is impassable to salmon and steelhead.

fish passage. The width constriction from stream channel to culvert is usually severe and the gradient of the pipe must be at or near 0% to keep water velocities within an acceptable range for fish passage. This type of culvert is also the most likely to be installed with its outfall above the tailwater elevation, producing an outfall barrier (Figure 8.12). Elevated outfalls must be avoided or mitigated.

Culvert crossings have been installed in thousands of streams with little or no thought to their effects on fish populations. A single poorly installed culvert can eliminate the fish population of an entire stream system. Poor culvert design and location can still be ranked among the most devastating problems for fish habitats on western forests and rangelands.

Following are some important considerations for culvert installation.

• Installation of round culverts should be avoided where fish passage is necessary. Install either open-arch culverts or bridges, especially if culverts longer than 30 m are required or where the stream gradient is steep (>2%).

• The two most important considerations for fish passage through culverts are maximum acceptable water velocity and minimum acceptable water depth for the migrating species.

• The diameter of culverts must be adequate to pass maximum flows and the expected debris. Washing out of culverts and their earth fills damages the road and is a source of sedimentation. Channel-bank stability upstream and downstream of culverts should be provided for. Road crossings alter the hydraulics of streams above and below the crossing for considerable distances, sometimes making banks more susceptible to erosion. Severe erosion can alter the configuration of the stream and crossing, and can eliminate the design components that provide for fish passage.

• A single large culvert is better than several small ones because it is less likely to become plugged and it carries water at lower velocities.

• The entire length of round culverts should be placed slightly below normal stream grade, at a slope near 0%, to reduce fish passage problems.

• Any structure for fish passage must function through the range of flows during which fish migration occurs. Streams used by salmonids fluctuate widely and have occasional high peak flows. An acceptable practice in culvert design has been to not require conditions suitable for fish passage during the 5% of the year when the flows are the greatest (Evans and Johnston 1980). Fish do not normally migrate during peak flows, so little or no disruption of migration occurs. This practice often results in substantial savings in construction costs. The objective should be to ensure fish passage during all but the highest flows.

• Installations that would require baffling for fish passage should be avoided; a bridge, a low-water crossing, a pipe-arch culvert, a larger culvert, a reduced gradient, or another solution should be used instead. Baffles normally require additional maintenance and occasionally cause debris accumulations. Baffles are sometimes necessary when high water velocities are unavoidable or when fish-passage problems must be corrected at existing culverts.

• Where culverts are installed in stream sections with steep gradients, it is important to create or improve resting pools, cover, and bank protection along the stream above and below the culvert. Maintaining a stable stream bottom through the culvert-influenced area is essential.

Water Velocity in Culverts

The swimming abilities of salmonids increase with the size of the fish. Hence, the species and life history stages that must navigate the culvert determine the allowable maximum water velocity. The swimming abilities of salmonids are not adequately defined, but general information has recently become available. Figure 8.10 shows maximum, sustained, and average swimming velocities for common salmonids in the west.

Metsker (1970) pointed out that the culvert velocity a fish can overcome varies not only with fish size but also with the distance between resting pools above and below the culvert. The Oregon State Game Commission (1971) recommended maximum water velocities of 2.4 m/s for adult salmon and steelhead and 1.2 m/s for trout. The recommended velocities in Oregon, however, were for round culverts up to 30.5 m long. Water velocities in longer culverts should not exceed 1.8 m/s for adult salmon and steelhead or 0.9 m/s for trout.

To aid road designers in estimating the water velocities through culverts, both the Oregon State Game Commission (1971) and the U.S. Forest Service (Evans and Johnston 1980) have produced velocity curves based on Manning's equation for open-channel flow (Chow 1959). The Oregon State Game Commission curves are only for round culverts that range in diameter from 0.6 to 2.1 m. Gradients range from 0.25 to 5.0%. Figure 8.13 is an example of the Oregon velocity curves for a 1.8-m culvert. Fish passage through culverts normally occurs between a minimum depth of 7.6 cm and a maximum depth of two-thirds the pipe diameter; the Oregon curves cover only these depths.

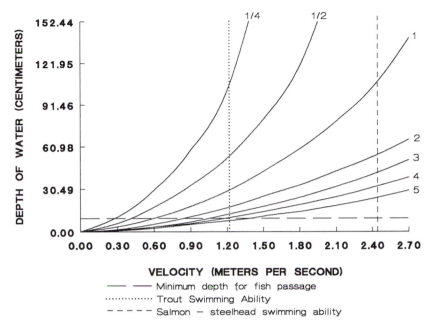

FIGURE 8.13.—Depth–velocity curves (Oregon State Game Commission 1971) for water flowing through a round, 1.8-m-diameter culvert. Curves represent gradients of 0.25, 0.5, . . ., 5%.

The U.S. Forest Service velocity curves are more detailed and comprehensive than the Oregon curves. Velocity curves are provided for round culverts (0.9–3.0 m), for concrete box culverts (0.7–3.0 m), and for corrugated metal pipe-arches (2.1 × 1.5 m to 5.1 × 3.1 m, span × rise). The U.S. Forest Service curves yield both velocity and depth of flow for any given discharge, culvert gradient, and diameter. Figure 8.14 illustrates the format of the U.S. Forest Service curves for a metal pipe-arch.

Salmonid spawning streams in the west are often mountain streams with steep gradients. Even culverts placed on the same grade as the original streambed may carry water at velocities greater than migrating fish can overcome. To control velocity in such situations, installation of baffles may be necessary. For new stream crossings, adequate water depth for fish passage should be integral to the structure design, and should not rely on baffles. Where existing crossings block migration because of inadequate water depth, baffles can be used to increase depth.

Culvert baffles are structures that impede water flow to produce pockets of lower-velocity flow in the culvert, where fish can rest momentarily, or that increase the overall depth of the flow. Impeding water flow in culverts is contrary to the primary engineering purpose of the culvert, which is to efficiently pass water under the road. The biologist and the engineer must work together to solve both problems simultaneously.

Many different baffle designs are available; little is known about their hydraulic principles, however, and additional applied research in this area is necessary. The best information on baffle design can be found in a Washington Department of Fisheries report by McKinley and Webb (1956). The principles in this report are

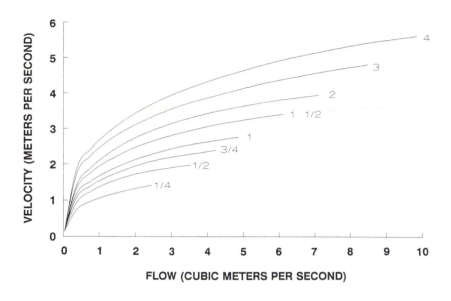

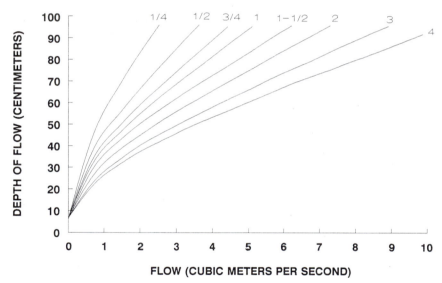

FIGURE 8.14.—Velocity–flow and depth–flow curves (U.S. Forest Service) for water flowing through a 2.1-m × 1.6-m metal pipe-arch. Curves represent gradients of 0.25, 0.5, . . ., 4%. (After Evans and Johnston 1980.)

sufficiently sound to be used as present guidelines, pending results of further research.

A few general principles apply to the use of baffles in culverts.

• Wherever possible, fish passage problems should be solved without baffles, preferably through use of bridges, low-water crossings, arch culverts, or round

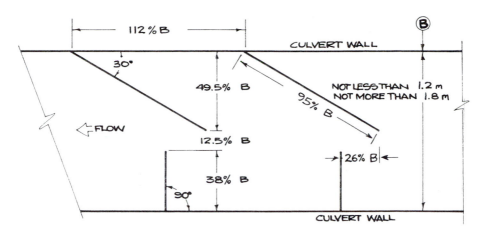

FIGURE 8.15.—Baffle design recommended by the U.S. Forest Service for culverts. Dimensions are scaled (as percentages) to culvert width (B), which can range from 1.2 to 1.8 m. (After Evans and Johnston 1980.)

culverts of adequate size and configuration. Culverts should be installed at or below streambed level such that water velocity is low.

• If higher velocities, extensive distance, or inadequate depth are unavoidable in a round- or box-culvert installation, baffles will be necessary. Baffles and the quieter waters they create allow fish to swim in short spurts through high-velocity water and to enter rest areas parallel to the higher-velocity flow.

• A large, single culvert provides better fish passage than do several smaller ones. Where multiple units are required in parallel, only one must be baffled to pass fish. Selection of the culvert for baffling is based on the route most likely to attract fish. At such installations, low flows should be diverted through the baffled culvert only.

• Large culverts, particularly the box type, can be divided so that baffles are placed in one side only.

• The baffle design illustrated in Figure 8.15 is recommended for use by the California Region of the U.S. Forest Service for solving excessive velocity problems (Evans and Johnston 1980). This design is adaptable to installations of various sizes; dimensions are given as percentages of the total width of the baffled section. Baffles should be at least 0.3 m high and 12.7–15.2 cm wide.

• Passage of water through the culvert will be somewhat impaired by baffle structures. Most culvert designs incorporate large safety factors, so the pipe diameter is considerably larger than is needed for the discharge conditions. Although the actual impairment of discharge capacity due to baffles is relatively small, a larger pipe may be necessary or a lesser safety factor must be tolerated.

• Construction materials for baffles may be wood, metal, or concrete, depending on the local situation. Concrete baffles can be precast and drilled or grouted into place. Metal baffles are usually bolted onto the culvert floor through metal plates, which give added strength.

FIGURE 8.16.—Series of low-head dams that prevent a road culvert from being an outflow barrier to upstream fish migration.

- Most baffle designs work best when water flow just overtops the baffle elements. With greater water depth, baffle effectiveness is inversely proportional to the depth of water over them (Gebhards and Fisher 1972).
- Solving fish-passage problems during design and construction of new crossings is substantially less expensive than modifying existing culverts.

Culvert Outfall Barriers

Culverts can be insurmountable barriers to migrating fish when the outlet of the culvert is so far above the tailwater that fish cannot enter the pipe. This condition is termed an outfall barrier (Figures 8.9D, 8.12). When new culverts are to be installed on streams with migrating fish, every attempt should be made to avoid constructing outfall barriers. Putting a new culvert outlet below the tailwater elevation is sometimes not possible, and many existing culverts form outfall barriers.

One way to correct an outfall barrier is to provide for one or a series of low-head dams below the culvert outfall (Figure 8.16). These dams may be nothing more than hand-placed rock "reefs," wire-basket gabions filled with local rock, or concrete sills. These downstream dams raise the tailwater elevation and flood the culvert. Access by fish is not only enhanced, but water velocity in the culvert is decreased. The downstream dams should not create outfall barriers themselves and should therefore be limited to about 0.3 m in height.

For dams of greater heights, there must be a pass-through notch in the center. Because the back-flooding decreases velocity and hence discharge, a culvert of larger diameter may be necessary to handle peak flows when downstream dams are used. Furthermore, it may be necessary to armor the downstream sides of the low-head dams to prevent scouring by the cataracts formed.

In some streams, the range of flows is so great that it is impossible not to have the culvert outlet above the tailwater at some time. Also, where severe fluctuations in flow require large culverts, fish passage may be impeded during low flows because of shallow flow over the broad culvert bottom. In such cases, stacked- or multiple-culvert installations can be used to provide fish passage. Placing the stacked culverts at different elevations assures adequate discharge capacity as well as fish passage over a wider range of flows.

Structures for Debris Control

The use of debris-control structures, such as trash or debris racks, is growing in western forest and rangelands due to the high cost of failed crossings. Trash racks, however, are detrimental to fish passage. The same freshets that often bring debris downstream are those in which many fish can move up to spawning areas. Although the protected culvert may not be a velocity or outfall barrier, a debris-laden trash rack can be impassable to fish. Debris-catching structures on streams used by migrating fish should therefore be avoided, and crossings should be designed to transmit debris downstream.

To compensate for the loss of culvert protection from a debris-catching structure, the culvert should be large enough to allow debris to pass through it. Passing debris through the culvert is a valid alternative to intercepting it above the inlet, and should not be overlooked. Of course, increasing the culvert diameter adds to its cost and sometimes may be impractical. On the other hand, when debris can be passed through the structure without clogging it, maintenance costs will be lower than when debris is intercepted and must be removed.

Summary

Forest and rangeland roads can have substantial adverse effects on salmonid habitats. These effects can be greatly reduced if the protection of fish habitat is integrated into the planning, design, construction, and maintenance of roads. The guidelines presented in this chapter for erosion control and for preventing or correcting fish migration barriers can be used by interdisciplinary teams of engineers, biologists, and earth scientists to plan and manage forest roads to maintain fish runs and habitats.

Chapter 9

Water Transportation and Storage of Logs

J. R. Sedell, F. N. Leone, and W. S. Duval

Transportation is one of the major problems facing the entrepreneur in the lumber industry. Bryant (1913) hypothesized that the "transportation of forest products to mill or market represents 75% or more of the total delivered cost of raw material, exclusive of stumpage value." Log transportation and stumpage acquisition and value are still the two major costs before the mill processes. Logs have always been considered a heavy, bulky, and cheap commodity that could not stand expensive transportation charges. Those successful in the lumber industry had to become specialists in transporting logs over the long distances that separated the primary producer from the consuming market. Indeed, the transportation of logs is still one of the central pivots around which success or failure of a lumbering operation revolves.

In the past, transporting the logs inexpensively was the industry's biggest concern. Only in the last decade has the concern for aquatic or coastal marine environments been a main consideration. In earlier days, river navigation and sawmill waste resulted in environmental changes that are still detectable. Present environmental concerns over log handling in coastal waters are well documented for intertidal areas but less so for subtidal environments.

Environmental effects of water transportation of logs in western North America can be divided into those caused by the historical driving of logs in rivers and streams and those due to the current dumping, rafting, and storage of logs in rivers and estuaries. The historical perspective focuses on habitat losses and the volumes of logs transported by water, both fresh water and marine. Many changes in stream-channel structure and evidence of habitat simplification still exist today, nearly 100 years after river-driving activities have ceased. The current perspectives on British Columbia and southeastern Alaska, as well as on a few locations in Oregon and Washington, draw extensively on excellent summaries, reviews, and task-force reports from both Canada (Duval et al. 1980) and the USA (Hansen et al. 1971).

The objectives of this chapter are to review and describe historical log transportation in rivers, which was extensive in the western USA and eastern British Columbia; to provide perspectives on the volume of logs transported and areal extent of the estuarine and river habitats allocated to log transfer and storage; and to describe the environmental effects of log transfer and storage that relate to fish habitats.

Influences of Forest and Rangeland Management on Salmonid Fishes and Their Habitats
American Fisheries Society Special Publication 19:325–368, 1991

Historical Log Transportation

Numerous books have described the history of the timber industry, and many articles have glorified log drives on rivers. However, one book (Rector 1953) stands out for its descriptions of the role that water transportation played in the early days of the timber industry. Extensive reports produced from research undertaken for the State Lands Division of Oregon document the extent of navigation for each of Oregon's major river basins (J. E. Farnell, Oregon Division of State Lands, Salem, personal communication). Each of 23 basin studies was issued as a navigability report that records the extent, duration, and dependence on water of log transportation.

The first sawmills on the west coast of North America, established between 1840 and 1870, were supplied with logs from trees that had grown at the edge of bays or large rivers. The trees were felled directly or rolled into the water, and the logs were then floated to the mills (Cox 1974). By the early 1880s, the best timber within 3.2 km of the entire shoreline of Hood Canal, Washington, had been cut (Buchanan 1936). The same was true of most other readily accessible areas. Loggers constantly sought out streams along which the timber had not yet been cut. If a stream was large enough to float logs, it was soon in use. In 1883, a newspaper (*The West Shore*) announced that in Columbia County, Oregon, every "stream of any size has been cleared of obstructions, so that logs can be run down them in the high water season." By the end of the 1880s the same was true of almost any county along the lower Columbia River, around Puget Sound, or along the "lumber coast" (Cox 1974). The centers of the timber industry reflected this dependence on water (Figure 9.1).

Historically, the lumber industry in the northwestern USA had its markets in San Francisco, San Diego, and the Pacific Rim countries. The industry depended on markets reached by sea. Thus, mills were located at seaports or along the lower Columbia River (Cox 1974). Many of these lumber centers had disappeared by the turn of the century. The big lumber centers today are still usually located where they can service markets by both rail and sea.

Commerce Clause and Navigable Streams

From the earliest days, efforts to improve streams have encountered legal difficulties. To keep mill owners and farmers from blocking the rivers with dams and other obstructions, a stream had to be declared navigable. In Michigan, Wisconsin, and Minnesota, the courts decided that a stream that could float a saw log was a "public highway" and that saw logs had just as much right to be on the rivers as rafts, barges, and steamboats. Navigable streams were not to be blocked by bridges, piers, fences, or duck ponds. At the same time, lumbermen were not to build storage and splash dams without special legislative permission (Rector 1953).

The U.S. government transferred ownership of the beds of the navigable waterways to a state when it entered the Union. To ascertain which riverbeds were transferable, the U.S. Supreme Court defined a navigable river as follows:

> Those rivers must be regarded as public navigable rivers in law which are navigable in fact. And they are navigable in fact when they are used, or

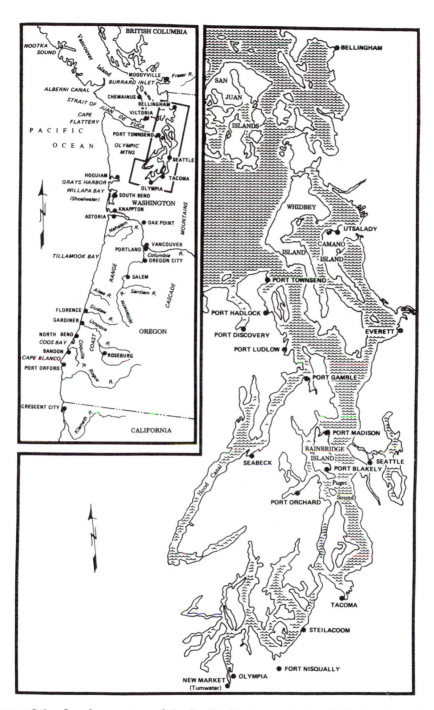

FIGURE 9.1.—Lumber centers of the Pacific Northwest before 1900. The Puget Sound area, boxed in the small-scale map, also is shown at an expanded scale. (From Cox 1974.)

susceptible of being used, in their ordinary condition, as highways for commerce, over which trade and travel are or may be conducted in the customary modes of trade and travel on water. (The Daniel Ball 1870.)

Washington, Oregon, and California all must, in general, comply with this definition of navigable waters.

In Washington, any stream capable of successfully floating logs was considered a floatable stream, and the logger had a right to use its waters to float logs toward the mill or market. Even though a stream was completely incapable of such log floating during the dry season, its waters were public if natural freshets provided enough water to float logs. If the stream was reasonably capable of navigation by boats or canoes and commerce was carried on, the state owned the streambed. If the stream was floatable but not navigable in the usual commercial sense, the adjoining landowner or owners owned the bed of the stream. In both instances, the waters were public and the public could use them. The state had exclusive control of these so-called floatable waters. The U.S. government had overriding control of truly navigable waters, although the states had jurisdiction. Streams too small to float timber were considered private, and loggers probably would not use such streams unless they owned them. Thus, the logger had no right over the objections of the riparian owner to put in roll dams to cause backwaters or splash dams to create artificial freshets. The boom and driving companies were able to obtain the right to drive a floatable stream because they were quasipublic corporations (Bridges 1910). As such, they had the power of eminent domain and could run their splash dams by condemning the property and paying in advance to every landholder adjoining the stream. Even though litigation frequently resulted, most streams in western Oregon and Washington were used for log drives.

Log Drives and River Modifications

Log driving is the process of transporting logs by floating them in loose aggregations in water; the motive power is supplied by the natural or flushed streamflow. At first, all timber within easy access of the stream was cut and floated down the adjacent river. If timber was too far away to be profitably hauled by oxen to the mill or stream, the logger moved to another location. Gradually, loggers had to go greater distances for timber, which introduced the use of river landings, log yards, log driving, rafting, towing, and booming (Rector 1949). Still later, the more distant timber required the use of splash dams and sluiceways, expensive stream alterations, canals, tramways, trestles, log chutes and slides, trucks, and railroads for log transport, floating, and driving.

As more logs were needed, artificial freshets were created by splash dams. A splash dam was a device for turning tiny streams into torrents large enough to float logs. It was built of log cribbing and sometimes was many meters in height and width. When it accumulated a large head of water, the water was released. Logs that had been dumped into the pond behind the dam, together with others collected along the watercourse below the dam, were quickly sluiced downstream to where they could be handled by conventional means.

Streams of all sizes had to be "improved" before a log drive could begin. Two principal forms of stream improvement were used (Brown 1936). (1) Sloughs, swamps, low meadows, and banks along wider parts of the streams were blocked off with log cribbing to keep the logs and water in the main stream channel. (2) Boulders, large rocks, leaning trees, sunken logs, or obstructions of any kind in the main bed during periods of low flow were blasted out or otherwise removed. Obstructions or accumulations of debris, such as floating trees, brush, and rocks, often caused serious and expensive log jams during the driving seasons. Small, low-gradient streams often were substantially widened during log driving by frequent flushings of the stream from splash dams and by the impacts of logs along the streambank. Excellent historical accounts of activities to clear river obstructions and methods of stream improvement were provided through interviews with pioneers, county and state court records, and reports of the U.S. Army Corps of Engineers (e.g., 1937).

By 1900, over 130 incorporated river and stream-improvement companies were operating in Washington. Use of major splash dams in western Washington and western Oregon was common practice and very extensive. Over 150 major dams existed in coastal Washington rivers, and over 160 splash dams were used on coastal streams and Columbia River tributaries in Oregon. On many smaller tributaries, temporary dams were used seasonally, but no records of these were kept. Many of these dams formed barriers to fish migration (Wendler and Deschamps 1955), but the long-term damage to fish habitats was probably caused by stream alterations made before drives and the scouring, channel widening, and displacement of main-channel gravels that occurred during the drive.

Small streams were seriously affected by logging of western redcedar, which occurred many years before clear-cut harvest. Because redcedar was used for shingles and not just for lumber like Douglas-fir, it could be cut up into small bolts (<1-m lengths) and driven down very small streams. "By taking out shingle bolts from inaccessible localities far from the mills and driving them down streams impossible for logs, it is possible to utilize overmature cedar that would deteriorate before general logging on the tract was possible" (West Coast Lumberman 1914). Much of the best and most plentiful cedar timber occurred along streams in Puget Sound and in rich, moist, coastal valleys, and it was exploited more rapidly than Douglas-fir. Even for driving cedar bolts, small streams had to be cleared of fallen trees, big boulders, and vegetation rooted in the channels. Streams were maintained clear of obstructions until the cedar logging in the drainage was completed.

To maintain unimpeded navigation of logs and commercial barges, snag boats operated on Puget Sound streams from 1890 to 1978. During this period, about 3,000 snags per year were removed from 322 km of the Skagit, Nooksack, Snohomish, Stillaguamish, and Duwamish rivers. In 1890, Coquille County, Oregon, authorized a public snagging operation on the Coquille River system that continued until the early 1970s.

Clearing of streams and rivers for passage of boats and logs has reduced the interaction of the stream system with its flood-plain vegetation. Draining, ditching, and diking of valley bottoms and lowlands has also reduced terrestrial–aquatic interaction. Flood-control levees have reduced or eliminated complex sloughs and side channels, which are valuable rearing areas for salmonids (Sedell et al. 1980).

River improvements and log drives on coastal Oregon and Washington rivers and rivers on the west side of Puget Sound strongly affected the estuaries. When large, natural debris dams were cleared out of the lower Nooksack River, Washington, in the mid-1880s, the resulting flush of channel sediments filled more than a kilometer's stretch of Bellingham Bay (U.S. Congress 1892). Sediments released during cleanup activities and transported by the Siletz River filled Siletz Bay between 1905 and 1923 (Rea 1975). River snagging caused sediments to be displaced from main channels and deposited in the bays below. All coastal Oregon and Washington rivers reflect alterations resulting from "improvements" required for log drives.

Along the arid west-central coast of California, rivers and streams also supported log drives. In western Nevada from 1853 to 1914, over 64 sawmills operated on sections that are now relatively treeless. Millions of cubic meters of timber were driven down the Truckee, Carson, and Walker river systems for lumber, firewood, and other uses related to the development of the silver mines around Virginia City (Timberman 1941). Many of the mining and smelting activities in Arizona, Montana, Utah, and Colorado in the late 1880s depended on stream transportation of logs. The transcontinental railroads required large and continual supplies of railroad ties, which were not preserved with creosote in those days. The demand was met by logging watersheds adjacent to the railways and driving the logs down streams that intersected the line (Brown 1936).

The rivers in the more arid parts of the USA also had to be improved before log drives could begin. Marble Creek on the St. Joe River in Idaho is one example. Blake (1971) described the numerous debris jams that had been there for many years. In a 29-km stretch ending at Homestead Creek, over 1,180 m^3 (500,000 board feet) of good timber were recovered from the stream channel. An additional large amount of wood was used to fuel the steam donkey's trip up the canyon to Homestead Creek. Blake described the fishing in these creeks as exceptional, but noted that the once-numerous larger fish were no longer present after the log drives.

In Alaska and western British Columbia, log drives were not common in the history of logging or stream degradation. Log drives in the Yukon, Chena, and Tenana rivers and their tributaries have been well documented; in particular, they supplied timber during the gold rush in the early 1900s. Tributaries of the Fraser River, British Columbia, were driven extensively from 1910 to 1946. A log drive in 1965 on the Stellako River was the only one ever studied from a fish habitat point of view (International Pacific Salmon Fisheries Commission 1966).

All of these rivers had to be altered in one way or another. Blasting boulders and pulling debris and snags was usually all that was required on the larger streams. Throughout western North America, the story was the same: sloughs and backwaters were closed off, pools were filled, and pools above rapids were lowered by blasting. The gradients of the streams were evened out and habitat complexity was lost.

Ironically, "river improvement" attitudes from the log-driving days have been common in fisheries management until recently. Debris-jam removal and snagging for navigation and fisheries reasons have resulted in the long-term loss of fish habitat along thousands of kilometers of streams in the western USA (Sedell et al. 1982; Sedell and Luchessa 1982). Salvage logging and snagging at the lower ends of rivers in Oregon, Washington, and Alaska continue on a large scale today. The salvage results in loss of habitat complexity essential for both spawning and rearing of salmonids. Many philosophies carried over from the log transportation and navigation days need to be overcome if we are to have an effective plan for protecting salmonid habitats.

Historical Review of Effects of Log Handling on Salmonid Populations

Scouring and Flow Manipulations

During early development of logging along the Pacific coast of the USA, log driving in many streams that had insufficient flow required periodic releases of water from splash dams. These surges of water and logs eroded streambeds, gouged banks, straightened river channels, and prevented fish from spawning. Eggs previously deposited were subject to heavy losses from the scouring and silting associated with water releases and from the dewatering that occurred when the splash dams were closed. In addition, rearing areas for salmon and trout were largely destroyed.

Over 150 splash dams were installed in the Gray's Harbor–Willapa Bay area of southwestern Washington alone (Sedell and Luchessa 1982). The effects of these operations on salmon runs were described by Wendler and Deschamps (1955) as follows.

> The actual splashing of a dam affected fish in several ways. If fish were spawning, the sluiced logs and tremendously increased flows would drive them off their nests. On the day prior to the splashing of one of the large Stockwell dams on the Humptulips River, an observer had noted a large number of steelhead below the apron of the dam. After splashing, no fish were seen, nor were any seen the following day.
>
> Besides harming the fish, splashing often adversely affected the stream environment. Moving logs gouged furrows in the gravel, and the suddenly increased flows scoured or moved the gravel bars, leaving only barren bedrock or heavy boulders. New stream channels were constantly being created and the existing ones changed. If the sudden influx of logs into the stream below the dam caused a log jam, as often happened, dynamite or black powder was used to clear the obstruction. In those days the policy seems to have been that if two boxes of powder would suffice, four were used. On some areas below dams in the lower Humptulips region, an average of five boxes of powder a day were used to break up log jams. Great numbers of salmon and steelhead trout were reportedly killed by these blasts.
>
> Dam operators have stated that fish runs reaching the dams were reduced within 3 to 4 years after the initial construction, and they recognized that splashing deleteriously affected spawning below the structure. When splashing was done because of economic conditions and flow was normal below the dams, operators claimed that spawning was more successful as evidenced by increased runs in the next cycle.

The streambed was gouged by logs even though flows provided by splash dams presumably were adequate for log transport. In addition to damage from periodic surges of water, the logs themselves appear to have contributed to streambed damage and the reported decline in salmon runs.

Similar logging practices were employed in western Oregon on all coastal streams. The Coquille River had 10 logging dams and innumerable log jams were created by logging debris. "Splash dams in the Coos and Coquille systems, built for the purpose of sluicing logs down the rivers, blocked the salmon runs and eliminated the productivity of the streams above them. This practice has also resulted in the sluicing of the gravel and destruction of the spawning area below the splash dams" (Gharrett and Hodges 1950). A study of the effects of logging on coho salmon production in the Coquille River showed a significant relation between production of lumber in Coos County (in which most of the Coquille River lies) and the catch of coho salmon 6 years later; high lumber production was generally followed by a decrease in the catch (McKernan et al. 1950). This relation did not exist in an adjacent county where logging was less extensive.

The history of sockeye salmon runs to Lower Adams River, tributary to the Fraser River in British Columbia, provides an exceptional example of the effects of log driving on salmon. A typical splash dam operated at the upper end of the river sent surges of water and logs over spawning grounds used by large numbers of sockeye salmon. The operation of this dam was of great concern to the local fishery manager, who tried (unsuccessfully) to avoid the adverse effects of sudden releases of water (Shotton 1926). Thompson (1945) concluded that manipulation of river flow by the dam had adversely affected the Adams River sockeye salmon run and most likely had caused the decline in this run that was observed after 1913, though the damage caused by water surges could not be distinguished from that caused by log gouging. Subsequent increases in the sockeye salmon population were attributed to the return to more normal flow conditions in 1922. The dam ceased to be used in the late 1920s and was removed by the International Pacific Salmon Fisheries Commission in 1945. In their survey of the Lower Adams River in 1940, however, Bell and Jackson (1941) noted extensive and persistent alterations of the stream that had resulted from splashing; the stream was recovering only slowly.

Most splash dams were temporary, and were abandoned after timber in the immediate vicinity had been removed. Of the 139 dams reported in Washington, 53 washed or rotted out, and 44 were later removed at the expense of the fishery agencies (Wendler and Deschamps 1955).

In its 1955 brief to the Sloan Commission on Forestry, the Canada Department of Fisheries (Whitmore 1955) summed up the effects of log driving and concluded that driving in shallow rivers had caused extensive damage in the past and still remained a threat to the salmon fishery. In addition to the destruction caused by gouging of gravel spawning bars and resultant channel erosion, construction of so-called "river improvements" created further dangers to salmon spawning and incubation by disrupting the normal flow regime of the river. "Stranded logs may divert water flow from gravel bars, resulting in drying out of deposited spawn, or diversion of normal water flows from potential spawning areas" (Larkin et al. 1959).

The modern method of transporting logs from the forests to mills or shipping points is by trucks that use public or private roads. As a consequence, log driving is no longer common. No log drives are occurring in the rivers of Washington or Oregon, nor in any California streams used by salmonids for spawning. The Clearwater River in Idaho was used for log driving until the late 1960s, but little spawning by steelhead and spring chinook salmon takes place in affected parts of the river.

Bark Losses and Deposits

Much of the bark on logs is knocked off during a drive by contact with the streambed or bank and other logs. About one third of the bark was removed from logs driven down the Stellako River (International Pacific Salmon Fisheries Commission 1966). Vladykov (1959) reported that about 40% of the bark was removed during pulpwood drives in Quebec, and several tonnes of bark were deposited in some rivers each year. Because of this deposition, spawning areas may be reduced and rich food-production areas may be completely smothered. McCrimmon (1954) concluded that bark deposits not only reduce spawning area, but also destroy the shelter for salmon fry, making them more vulnerable to predators.

In northern British Columbia, logging was carried on during the winter when the ground was frozen and roads remained passable. Where water transport was to be used, logs were stored until the waterways were open. Although bark was more securely attached to these winter-cut trees than to trees cut in summer, it became waterlogged and easily removed if the logs were stored in water. When dislodged, the bark sank to the bottom, as observed on both the Nadina and Stellako rivers (International Pacific Salmon Fisheries Commission 1966).

River Modifications

Rarely can logs be driven down a river that is not "improved" in some way to prevent permanent stranding or jamming at difficult spots. Even in a large river such as the Fraser near Quesnel, British Columbia, booms had to be constructed to direct logs away from certain areas (International Pacific Salmon Fisheries Commission 1966). In the Quesnel River, projecting rocks have been removed to prevent log jams, and some side channels have been closed to prevent loss of logs in shallow water. This practice was common on all rivers in Oregon and Washington from the 1860s to the 1920s. In Washington, over 300 river- and stream-improvement companies were registered from 1898 to 1948, over 75% of them between 1898 and 1920. In the Stellako River, a new channel was made near the lower end of the river, diverting flow from the original channel. This not only destroyed spawning grounds along 200–300 m of river below the diversion, it changed the hydraulic structure and reduced the amount of suitable spawning ground for about 500 m upstream from the new channel. The new channel was never productive of fish (International Pacific Salmon Fisheries Commission 1966).

The Canada Department of Fisheries (1964) reported that channeling on the Kitsumgallum River, British Columbia, did not stabilize the river bed because as the flow was directed from one place, it scoured others. During log driving on this river (now discontinued), the logging company continually made requests for further river improvements and, in some instances, had to repair or rebuild previous work. Despite construction to facilitate log driving, stranding of logs remained a major problem. The salvage of stranded logs is an inevitable feature of river log driving. Salvage may require river boats and personnel, dynamite to break up jams, or bulldozers to push logs back into the river. Such operations break down the river banks, gouge the stream bed, and otherwise disturb (often lethally) fish and their eggs.

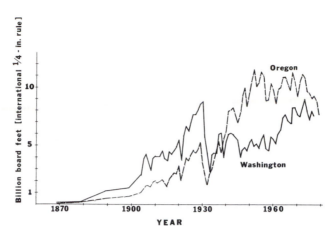

FIGURE 9.2.—Lumber production in Oregon and Washington, 1869–1980.

Intensity of Log Rafting and Forest Operations: Regional Differences

The history of development of the timber industry in western North America reflects geographical patterns. Shipping and cargo mills led to the development and persistence of processing centers located to accommodate railways and seaports. The interiors of British Columbia, Washington, Oregon, Idaho, Montana, and northern California developed with the railroads and the mining industry. The problems and phasing of log handling in fresh water are different from those in salt water.

The freshwater problems are largely historical. Although the extent and pervasive effect of log transportation on western rivers is impressive, physical alterations do not exist entirely as a result of log handling. They persist because of log-salvage policies for road and bridge protection, and flood and debris control, as well as because of current management guidelines for fish habitats.

New laws and better enforcement of them have considerably reduced the degradation of water quality. Economic factors have played a large part by forcing the continual closing and consolidation of wood-processing facilities. McHugh et al. (1964) reported that Oregon had about 4,860 hectares of log ponds and 800 hectares of sloughs or canals used as log-storage sites in the early 1960s, Washington had about 1,620 hectares of log ponds and 600 hectares of storage sloughs, northern California had about 1,620 hectares of such storage areas, and Idaho had 400 hectares. The size of the ponds varied from less than 1 to over 160 hectares in surface area and from 1 to 9 m in depth. These figures are probably half as large now because of mill closures and dry-land sorting and processing. Figure 9.2 illustrates lumber production during the last century for Oregon and Washington, the major timber-producing states in the western USA. The use of water for log storage and transportation in the western USA reflects the same trends that were seen in Washington during its peak transfer production in the late 1920s.

Historical Intensity of Log Rafting in Western North America

Oregon.—Oregon's major rivers, the Columbia and Willamette, and its estuaries have been used intensively from the beginning of timber production to the present for log handling and transportation. Marriage (1958), J. W. Johnson (1972), Oregon Division of State Lands (1973), and Percy et al. (1974) provided excellent summaries of key characteristics of Oregon estuaries derived from detailed map analyses and surveys and from zoning and state land-use records. Percy et al. (1974) identified and tabulated 21 Oregon estuarine areas ranging from about 53 to 3,800 hectares in surface area (to the inland extent of tidal action) and draining areas of between 35 and 13,000 km².

Log-processing and -shipping centers in Oregon are located in nine major areas where aquatic environments are affected: Coos Bay, Umpqua River mouth, Siuslaw Bay, Yaquina Bay, Tillamook Bay, Youngs Bay, the Columbia River estuary, the Columbia River between its mouth and Bonneville Dam (Portland), and the Willamette River around Oregon City. Of the current 16.5 million m³ (7 billion board feet) of timber annually transported to mills, 25% are towed in these areas. Log-transport activity throughout the state has fluctuated over the years, sometimes substantially, in response to many events that influenced timber production, including forest fires, timber demand, mill openings and closures, changes in timber management strategies, environmental regulation, construction and housing starts, and relocation of major lumber centers. Different areas, however, experienced different periods of peak activity according to the factors influencing timber production at that time. The Columbia and Willamette river basins have supported log traffic from before 1890 and experienced peaks during World War II, but timber transport in the other major river basins did not reach heights of activity until the late 1950s and early 1960s. The mid to late 1970s saw a significant increase in logging activity in most major coastal waterways as a result of a national housing boom.

During World War II, over 2.3 million m³ (1 billion board feet) of timber were transported annually from the Willamette basin down the Willamette River, through the Oregon City Locks, to Portland and Columbia River sawmills. This activity ceased, however, as processing centers moved closer to the supply of logs (Cornwall 1941).

Washington.—In Washington, the Columbia River, Puget Sound, and Grays Harbor are the principal areas affected by log handling. Simenstad et al. (1982) identified 96 coastal and inland estuaries in 14 regions of the state. Estuaries within these regions are structurally, hydrologically, and biologically diverse, and range downward in size from drowned river valleys, which form the major estuaries (for example, Grays Harbor and Skagit Bay–Port Susan), to the numerous small stream-channel estuaries characteristic of Puget Sound and the Strait of Juan de Fuca, as well as southeastern Alaska and much of British Columbia. One region, the island archipelago of northern Puget Sound, has no major estuaries, but is greatly influenced by freshwater outflow from the Fraser (British Columbia) and Skagit rivers.

Like most west coast estuaries, Washington's have undergone extensive changes since the area was first settled. The natural estuarine environments have been affected both directly and indirectly, the latter via log drives, urbanization, and diking in their watersheds. Currently, the U.S. Army Corps of Engineers removes 2.3 million m³ of sediments annually from Washington estuaries as part of maintenance dredging operations, nearly half of this from Grays Harbor (cited by Simenstad et al. 1982). Although changes in most west coast estuaries have not been quantified, Bortleson et al. (1980) reported changes in 11 major estuaries of Puget Sound. Such estuaries as the Duwamish and Puyallup river deltas have lost essentially all their original wetland habitat. Although most smaller, less-urbanized estuaries in both Oregon and Washington escaped such devastation, most now have road causeways or dikes that usually have altered the natural estuarine hydraulics. Thus, assigning a cause to a biological impact is extremely difficult. Quantitative information relating changes in estuarine habitats to changes in populations of salmonids and other estuarine fishes is distinctly lacking (Dorcey et al. 1978; Simenstad et al. 1982).

Washington's primary timber transport waterways include the Cowlitz, Lewis, and Chehalis rivers and Tacoma and Grays harbors. These areas closely reflect periods of timber activity for the entire state, and have themselves been responsible for the transport and storage of 2.3–5.9 million m³ (1–2.5 billion board feet) annually during several periods over the years. As with Oregon, Washington's peak periods of timber transport activity corresponded to the many factors influencing timber production cycles, including diminishing old-growth stands and the initiation of second-growth harvesting. Peaks in river–harbor transport activity depended on the particular system and associated factors that influenced regional timber production; overall, however, peaks in timber transport activity occurred after 1910 and into the mid-1930s, during the late 1940s to early 1950s, in the early to mid-1960s, and again during the mid-1970s.

In the early days, 100% of the logs were transported by water. Grogan (1924) estimated that 60% of the logs that supplied the sawmills on Puget Sound and the Columbia River were transported either all or most of the way from the woods to the mill by water (representing about 12 million m³ or about 5 billion board feet). Towing distances were between 160 and 320 km and the rafts were flat, not bundled; hence, many logs were lost, although in those days only prime Douglas-fir and western redcedar were used.

British Columbia.—The coastal harvest of British Columbia timber is greater than 30 million m³ (12 billion board feet) annually (Edgell et al. 1983). The most economical means of transporting logs from the forests to the mills is by marine waterways, large interior lakes, and the Fraser River system. Cottel (1977), Boyd (1979), and Edgell et al. (1983) estimated that about 90% of the coastal timber harvest is placed in the water during part of its transportation to processing areas. Boyd (1979) documented regional differences in production, species harvested, and modes of log transport within the coastal British Columbia forest industry during 1978.

Alaska.—Alaska totally depends on water to move logs to four major processing centers: Wrangell, Petersburg, Sitka, and Ketchikan. The number of estuaries counted in Alaska has ranged between 1,000 and 22,000, depending on how "estuary" is defined; the large glacial bays (fjords), each with numerous tributaries, and the many large and small islands make the delimitation of estuaries quite arbitrary (Faris and Vaughan 1985). In any case, Alaska's total estuarine area exceeds even that of British Columbia. Almost 650,000 km² of estuarine area, 47%

of which is less than 18 m deep, abut the Tongass National Forest (Faris and Vaughan 1985).

Alaska was a relatively late starter as a timber producer; the primary mills in Ketchikan and Sitka opened in the mid to late 1950s. Both production and log transport activity are less than in several other timber-producing jurisdictions in northwestern North America. The mills of Ketchikan and Sitka collectively handle 700,000 to more than 1.1 million m^3 (300–500 million board feet) of timber per year; Ketchikan receives more than 60% of this total. The largest harvests so far occurred in the mid 1960s to mid 1970s. The total Alaska timber harvest peaked at more than 1.3 million m^3 (570 million board feet) in 1970 and probably will not exceed 1.7–2.1 million m^3 (750–900 million board feet) per year during the best of times.

Idaho and Montana.—Large numbers of logs have been and continue to be rafted down the St. Joe River to Coeur d'Alene Lake, Idaho, then across the lake and down the Spokane River into Washington. Log volumes peaked in the 1920s and since then have been sustained at an annual rafted volume of about 236,000 m^3 (about 100 million board feet). Lakes and rivers that received the transported logs in the past are Flathead Lake in Montana, and Coeur d'Alene Lake, St. Joe River, Pend Oreille River between Priest River and Ione, and Priest River in Idaho. Peak activity for all but Flathead Lake was in the 1920s. Flathead Lake mills served the mines and railroads from 1905 to 1920.

California.—California's waterways have carried logs for two centuries. Many streams in the redwood forests of Santa Cruz, Del Norte, Mendocino, and Humboldt counties experienced many log drives. The Sacramento River floated millions of cubic meters to mills located along its length. The records are almost nonexistent for volumes of logs handled in California estuaries. The principal estuaries used were San Francisco Bay, Los Angeles Harbor, and San Diego Harbor; they received hundreds of millions of cubic meters of logs shipped from Oregon and Washington. Humboldt Bay was too shallow to maintain a great volume of log rafts in its waters, although some logs still are rafted near the mills

TABLE 9.1.—Location and average size of coastal British Columbia log-handling leases.[a] (From FERIC 1980.)

Location	Area (hectares)	Portion of total leases (percent)	Average area (hectares)
Lake[b]	197.8	2.2	12.4
River[c]	1,200.2	13.4	6.3
Estuary	954.6	10.7	25.1
Intertidal	2,259.1	25.2	15.5
Deep water	2,997.0	33.5	14.5
River–estuary	50.9	0.6	25.5
Estuary–intertidal	164.3	1.8	16.4
Intertidal–deep water	1,083.5	12.1	22.6
Other combinations	48.8	0.5	12.2
Total	8,956.2	100.0	

[a]Based on a questionnaire survey of 187 companies with 943 leases; the response rate by the British Columbia coastal forest industry was 66%.

[b]Pitt and Harrison lakes.

[c]Fraser River constitutes 98% of this use.

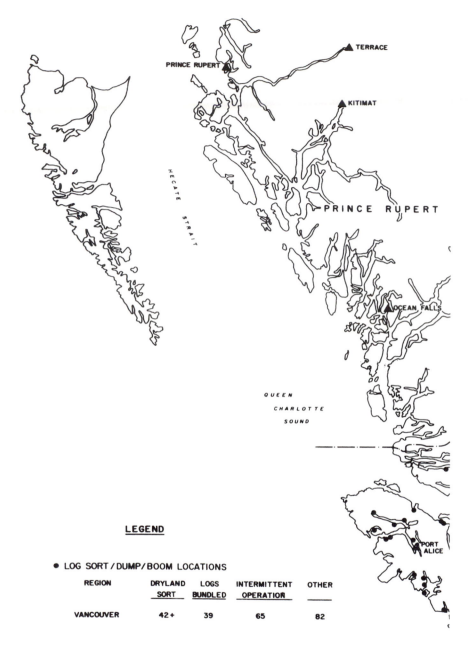

LEGEND

● LOG SORT / DUMP / BOOM LOCATIONS

REGION	DRYLAND SORT	LOGS BUNDLED	INTERMITTENT OPERATION	OTHER
VANCOUVER	42 +	39	65	82

▲ PROCESSING CENTRES

REGION	SAWMILLS	PULP / PAPEP MILLS	PANELBOARD MILLS	SHINGLE / SHAKE MILLS	TREATMENT PLANTS
VANCOUVER	68	10	14	22	3
PR. RUPERT (COAST)	7	3	–	–	–
TOTAL	75	13	14	22	3

FIGURE 9.3.—Modern locations of log sorting, dumping, booming, and processing along the south coast of British Columbia. (From Ainscough 1979.)

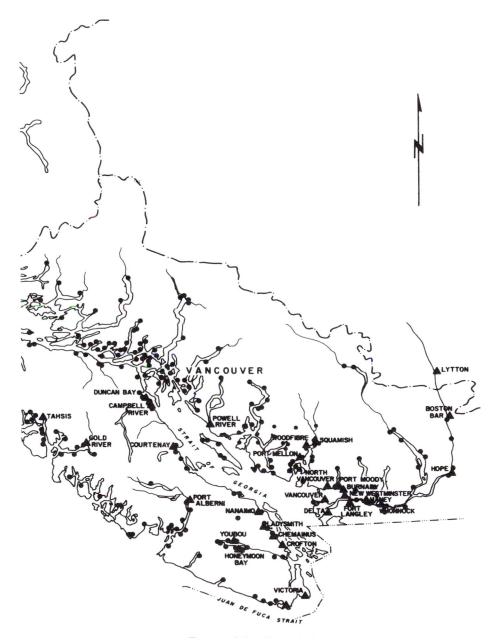

FIGURE 9.3.—Extended.

TABLE 9.2.—Major uses of coastal British Columbia log-handling leases.[a] (From FERIC 1980.)

Use	Area (hectares)	Portion of area (percent)
Log dumping	204.2	2.3
Barge dumping	132.6	1.5
Barge loading	205.6	2.3
Log sorting and booming	1,312.0	14.6
Log bundling	86.0	1.0
Log storage	5,696.1	63.6
No present use	796.4	8.9
Other	522.9	5.8
Total	8,955.8	100.0

[a]Based on a questionnaire survey of 187 companies with 943 leases (66% response).

there. Most of California's bays are not located in timber country or are too small and rocky to handle much log transportation.

Extent of Leased Log-Storage Acreages

Leased log-storage acreages in Oregon total 794 hectares. Of these, 41% are in coastal estuaries and most of the rest are along the Columbia and Willamette rivers. In Washington, 943 hectares are leased for log handling, of which 85% are in estuaries.

In 1981, British Columbia had 950 coastal lease areas and reserves occupying about 11,000 hectares (Wilson 1981, cited in Edgell et al. 1983). A survey by FERIC (1980) the previous year indicated a slightly smaller total lease area; the majority of sites were in coastal rivers, intertidal areas, and deep-water environments. Log-handling sites in estuaries tend to be larger than other leased areas because most log-processing sites are located there (Table 9.1). Ainscough (1979) documented the locations of major log-sorting, -dumping, -booming, and -processing sites along the south coast of British Columbia (Figure 9.3).

The FERIC survey indicated that the greatest proportion of log-handling water leases in coastal British Columbia were used for log storage; relatively minor areas were used for dumping and, to a lesser extent, sorting (Table 9.2). This information has been considered representative of present Canadian coastal practices. In a comprehensive report of British Columbia log-handling practices and coastal zone management, Edgell et al. (1983) showed that 64% of coastal water lease areas were reserved for log storage. They also found that of 27,000 km of British Columbia coastline (including 950 km north of the 49th parallel), only a very small proportion could feasibly be used for log-handling operations; of those areas leased, 47% were shallow intertidal areas, estuaries, and bays. Along its inside waters, 33–57% of British Columbia's log-handling lease areas are centered in estuaries. Edgell et al. (1983) noted the ever-increasing demand for suitable log storage areas, projected to increase 20% by the year 2000, which will compound current shortage problems. Of further significance, southern Vancouver Island and the lower British Columbia mainland, which combined produce only 22% of the coastal timber harvest, handle more than 70% of coastal timber processing (Boyd 1979).

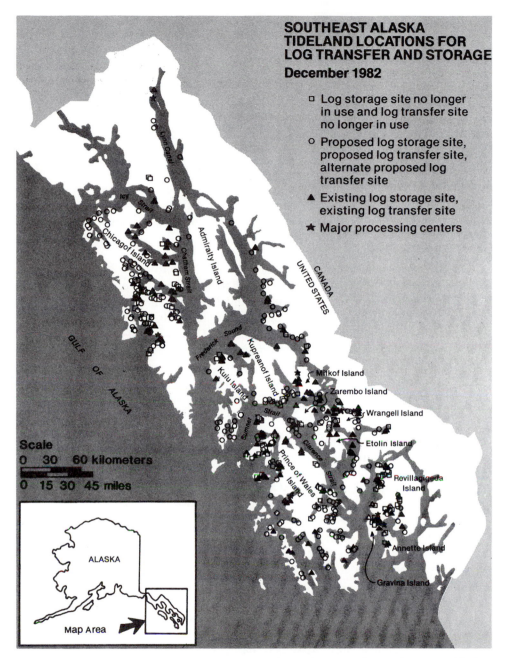

FIGURE 9.4.—Tideland locations for log transfer and storage in southeastern Alaska, 1982. (From Faris and Vaughan 1985.)

Alaska has 430 hectares under lease, representing 89 log-transfer sites and 49 log-storage sites. Another 228 sites are proposed for log-transfer facilities and 12 sites are proposed for log storage (Faris and Vaughan 1985). Faris and Vaughn (1985) mapped processing plants; abandoned, new, and proposed dump sites; and abandoned, currently occupied, and proposed storage sites (Figure 9.4). They

TABLE 9.3.—Comparison by state and province of log-handling leases, area affected, and board feet of logs transported.

State or province	Number of sites leased	Number of hectares leased	Estimated board feet of logs transported or stored (millions)
Southeastern Alaska	81	430	400
British Columbia	943	8,956	6,030
Washington	154	943	4,000
Oregon	100	794	3,500

estimated that 0.01% of the total estuarine area was affected by bark accumulation adjacent to the log-transfer facilities and projected that a worst case for the future would represent 0.04% of the estuarine total. Volumes of logs are not great in Alaska when compared with log-handling activity in British Columbia, Washington, and Oregon (Table 9.3).

When the activity per hectare leased is compared to total estuary available, log handling, although occupying sensitive intertidal zones, impinges on less than 0.001% of the estuary area available. Guidelines are in effect to minimize the effects by limiting site location. Log transportation directly affects estuaries in British Columbia much more than in Alaska, Washington, and Oregon (Table 9.3). British Columbia has also spent more money and time analyzing and researching the problem than has any other jurisdiction.

Major Phases of Coastal Log Handling: British Columbia and Southeast Alaska

In both southeastern Alaska and western British Columbia, geography and lack of roads have required the use of coastal marine and riverine waters for log storage and transportation. Log-handling and -storage facilities that require water are log-transfer sites for individual timber sales, log-raft formation and storage areas near timber sales, winter log-raft storage areas, and storage and sorting areas near the mills.

The major phases of log handling were reviewed in detail by Boyd (1979), Duval et al. (1980), and FERIC (1980) for British Columbia and by Beil (1974) and Forest Engineering Incorporated (1982) for southeastern Alaska. The different methods used, as well as the economics of alternative methods of dumping, sorting, booming, and transporting, are fully discussed in these reviews.

Logs are transported from the land–water transfer site or "dump" to sorting and booming grounds. They are then towed in rafts to storage areas or transported on barges to dumping sites. At sites of barge dumps or central sorting sites, logs are sorted, boomed, and stored. They are then towed to mill storage sites and finally to the processing facility.

Many combinations of methods have been and can be applied to the four major log-handling processes: dumping, booming, storage, and transport.

Dumping.—Dumping is the process of introducing cut timber into the water for sorting, booming, and transport. Dumping is generally done at a landing constructed along a watered bank at a site adjacent to major harvest areas, but it also is done from previously loaded barges on the water. Methods of dumping include use of stationary vertical-hoist systems such as A-frames, ginpoles, and parbuckles; cranes; mobile equipment such as Caterpillar tractors, skidders, and front-end loaders; slide ramps; cable carriages; and self-tipping barges.

Booming.—Historically, many kinds of rafts and booms have been used. The two basic types currently used are flat rafts and bundle booms. Flat rafts consist of logs stored and towed loose inside a series of channel boomsticks. These rafts cover about 0.4 hectare. In Canada, the rafts are divided into sections of about 21 × 21 m; each section holds 35–238 m^3 (15–101 thousand board feet). Rafts of up to 30 sections are common. Bundle booms comprise logs that are bundled loosely with wire or metal bands. Bundles range from 7 to 106 m^3 (3–45 thousand board feet) and usually draw 1.5–2.5 m of water. The bundles are stored and rafted like the flat rafts. A raft of bundles contains a log volume of 707–1,416 m^3 (300 to 600 thousand board feet). Fewer logs are lost from bundles than from flat rafts, and bundles make the sorting process more economical and efficient.

Storage.—Marine storage of logs can occur in intertidal, shallow, or deep water. Logs are often stored near freshwater inflows to reduce infestations of the marine molluskan shipworms *Teredo navalis* and *Bankia setacea*, although the degree of protection this technique affords depends on salinity, currents, storage time, and season. The most efficient means of reducing shipworm damage is to keep storage times short. Storage areas differ in size. Larger areas generally are needed if logs have to be stored for extended periods; conversely, proximity to harvest sites may dictate use of small areas. Average storage leases in British Columbia range from 200 to 400 hectares (Edgell et al. 1983).

Transport.—Logs are moved directly on the water as flat rafts, from which log loss is high and which are limited to calm inside waters, and as bundles, which retain logs better than flat rafts and which are less limited by weather in exposed areas. Barging is a common method of transportation in British Columbia because barges can be operated year-round in exposed areas and because high volumes of logs pass through only a few sites. These barges can be self-dumping, self-loading, or both, and the logs can be barged either loose or in bundles. Barge-mounted cranes capable of handling 22 bundles of 79,830 kg each have been developed and should reduce the barging and dumping of loose logs.

The principal activities that may affect the marine environment are limited by economic and operational requirements to lands that are adjacent to water and that have acceptable combinations of geophysical and morphological features. Duval et al. (1980) summarized the typical locations and required conditions for each phase of log handling. These conditions are indicated in Table 9.4.

Effects of Log Handling on Estuarine Biotic Communities

The interaction of forestry practices and fishery resources has generated increasing discussion and debate since the early 1970s. Much of the discussion has centered on lotic freshwater systems and their responses to timber harvest strategies, but concern also has grown over the highly sensitive and productive estuarine environments that are used extensively for handling and storing of logs. As a result of intensified research efforts over the years, forest management guidelines and regulations that help protect the environmental integrity of

TABLE 9.4.—Typical conditions for log handling on British Columbia coastal waters and adjacent land.

Log-handling phase	Minimum depth of water (m)			Estuaries		
	0–4.5	4.6–7.5	Over 7.5	Muddy shore, 0–20% slope	Mud to gravel, 20–40% slope	Rocky shore, 40–80% slope (deep water)
Skidding (not common)						
Skidding onto beach	X				X	
Yarding into water						X
Tractor pushing					X	
Dumping						
Lift and lower bundles	X	X		X		X
Lift and lower loose logs		X		X		X
Parbuckle onto log, skids bundles		X		X	X	X
Parbuckle onto log, skids loose logs	X	X		X	X	X
Mobile loader over skids bundles		X			X	X
Mobile loader on gravel ramp, loose logs	X	X			X	
Helicopter drop			X			X
Sorting in water						
Loose logs		X			X	
Loose logs to make bundles		X			X	
Bundles			X		X	
Booming						
Bundle booms		X				
Flat rafts		X				
Bag booms		X				
Storage						
Bundle booms		X				
Flat rafts	X	X				
Bag booms	X	X				
Dry-land sort					X	
Barge loading and dumping						
Loose logs					X	
Bundles					X	
Transporting						
Bag booms	X	X		X	X	X
Flat booms	X	X		X	X	X
Bundle booms		X		X	X	X
Barges					X	X
Retrieval						
Flat raft		X			X	X
Bundle boom		X		X	X	X

freshwater stream systems are now in place. Management policies are still being formulated for the estuarine environment. Estuaries provide unique environments at the junctions of fresh and salt water, and support numerous forms of life. Estuaries are very important for salmonids and other anadromous fishes; adults use them as staging areas for upstream spawning migrations and juveniles and smolts use them as rearing areas. Because estuaries are so essential to these and many other species, the effects of particular estuarine disturbances on species and

TABLE 9.4.—Extended.

Log-handling phase	Bays and sheltered reaches			Exposed shoreline	
	Tidal marshes, muddy shore, 10% slope	Gravel shore, 10–40% slope	Rocky shore, 40–60% slope (deep water)	Gravel, 10–20% slope	Rocky, 20–50% slope (deep water)
Skidding (not common)					
Skidding onto beach		X		X	
Yarding into water			X		
Tractor pushing		X		X	X
Dumping					
Lift and lower bundles		X			
Lift and lower loose logs		X			
Parbuckle onto log, skids bundles	X	X	X		
Parbuckle onto log, skids loose logs	X	X	X		
Mobile loader over skids bundles	X	X	X	X	X
Mobile loader on gravel ramp, loose logs		X		X	
Helicopter drop			X		X
Sorting in water					
Loose logs	X	X			
Loose logs to make bundles		X			
Bundles					
Booming					
Bundle booms	X	X			
Flat rafts	X	X			
Bag booms	X	X			
Storage					
Bundle booms	X	X			
Flat rafts	X	X			
Bag booms	X	X			
Dry-land sort		X			
Barge loading and dumping					
Loose logs		X			
Bundles		X			
Transporting					
Bag booms	X	X	X		
Flat booms	X	X	X		
Bundle booms		X	X		X
Barges		X	X	X	
Retrieval					
Flat raft	X	X	X		
Bundle boom		X	X		

communities must be better understood. Log handling and storage cause both physical and chemical disturbances. Most foreshore areas are leased for log-handling operations because these operations require sheltered areas as well as proximity to mill centers and adequate inflows of fresh water for discouraging wood-boring shipworms (Edgell et al. 1983). Consequently, log handling is generally sited in biologically sensitive environments.

As summarized earlier in this chapter, water transportation and storage of logs have been practiced for more than 100 years in western North America, and many north Pacific estuaries are still used for these purposes today. Thus, one must take into account the duration of timber-related disturbances and consider their possible cumulative effects. We point out, however, that large woody debris is an important ecological feature of freshwater and estuarine systems even in the absence of logging, so the effects of current log-handling activities are not necessarily all negative.

The transportation and storage of logs along aquatic systems generates, as previously noted, two distinct modes of disturbance: physical and chemical. Both modes create direct as well as indirect effects on fish habitat and abundance, and these various influences may interact to produce synergistic effects. These processes and their outcomes must be viewed independently as mitigating management strategies are developed.

The spatial extents and degrees of log-handling impact are directly related to the flushing characteristics of waters near handling sites, the methods of handling logs, and the intensity of use in each area. With these general principles in mind, we next consider the specific effects that log-handling operations have on aquatic systems. Tables 9.5–9.7 summarize our discussion. We hope these tables also will serve as a management tool to identify causes and effects and to guide research and mitigation efforts.

Physical Disturbances

Physical disturbances resulting from log-handling operations (dumping, sorting, storage, and transport) include substrate disturbances in areas where logs contact the bottom or log-moving machinery is used in shallow areas; deposition and subsequent dispersion of whole logs, bark, wood debris, and other debris (for example, bundling bands) associated with log handling; disruption of the water column; and reductions in wave action and light penetration. The magnitude and spatial extent of these disturbances differ among types and volumes of log-handling activity, water depths, site morphologies and substrates, species and ages of logs handled, seasons, and prevailing currents and circulation patterns. Because log sorting, booming, and storage frequently occur in conjunction with dumping, it may be difficult to distinguish the separate effects of these activities. Quantitative information about these physical disturbances is limited and primarily addresses log-storage operations.

Biotic communities are affected by scouring of both hard and soft substrates, compaction of soft substrates, shading and other alterations in the light environment, deposition of bark and wood debris, and physical disturbances of the water column (Conlan 1975; Bell and Kallman 1976b). Although several authors have discussed the effects of various phases of log handling on plants, no quantitative data and only a limited amount of observational information are available describing these effects. Despite this shortage of published information, damage to emergent vegetation in particular is clearly evident in many coastal areas used for log handling (Duval et al. 1980). Studies relating the effects of log handling to benthic invertebrates in coastal environments have been conducted in southeastern Alaska (Pease 1974), British Columbia (Conlan 1977; Conlan and Ellis 1979; Sibert and Harpham 1979), and Washington and Oregon (Schaumburg 1973; Smith

TABLE 9.5.—Summary of log-handling effects on aquatic plant communities.

Evaluation	Effect			
	Compaction or scouring of soft substrates	Scouring or abrasion of hard substrates	Accumulation of wood and bark debris	Changes in light quality and intensity
Major source of effect	Log dumping in shallow areas and intertidal log storage; propeller wash in shallow areas	Log dumping in shallow areas; stranding of lost logs in intertidal environments	Log dumping and sorting; minimal contribution by log storage	Log dumping related to increases in water turbidity; shading by rafted logs; presence of highly colored leachates
Positive effects and modes of action	None	None	Increased habitat for some macrophytes in areas with scattered debris; use of dissolved organic compounds in leachates by heterotrophic forms. Direct and indirect action	None
Negative effects and modes of action	Physical damage and uprooting of eelgrass and emergent vegetation; potential decreased primary production by benthic microalgae. Direct action	Physical damage to intertidal algae. Direct action	Decreased species diversity and abundance of benthic microalgae and macrophytes. Direct action.	Decreased primary production by autotrophic species; potential changes in species composition in benthic forms under rafted logs. Indirect action.
Degree of effect	Insignificant to minor	Insignificant	Insignificant to moderate	Insignificant to minor
Factors influencing degree of effect	Presence of extensive eelgrass meadows would increase potential for effects; intertidal log storage in estuaries would also increase effects	Increased effects from intertidal log storage; reduced algal and epibenthic invertebrate forms	Effect assessment hampered by data deficiencies; effects would be greatest in estuarine areas where plant communities provide habitat and food for invertebrates, fish, and birds	Shading by extensive log storage in estuaries would increase potential for light-related effects; also depends on time of year

1977; Zegers 1978); reviews of available literature describing effects of log handling on invertebrates were provided by Conlan (1975, 1977), Hansen et al. (1971), and Smith (1977).

Substrate disturbances.—Substrate disturbances may occur during log dumping, sorting, storage, and transport, though generally only when these activities occur in shallow intertidal waters. The effects of sediment scouring and compaction at dumps have not been documented because at shallow sites where such

TABLE 9.6.—Summary of log-handling effects on benthic and intertidal invertebrates.

Evaluation	Effect			
	Bottom scouring	Sediment compaction	Accumulation of wood and bark debris; lowered oxygen levels; toxic accumulations of H_2S and log leachates	Physical changes in sediment and bottom composition
Major source of effect	Free-fall dumping in shallow waters (including barge dumping); tug wash in shallow estuaries	Free-fall dumping in shallow waters and intertidal log storage	Free-fall dumping; water sorting; log storage is generally a minor contributor	Free-fall dumping and water sorting; flat-rafting may contribute to log sinkers
Positive effects and modes of action	None	Possible increase in abundance of some species of mobile epifauna such as harpacticoids. Indirect action	None	Increased abundance of epifauna where scattered bark and debris provide additional habitat and attachment sites (woodboring species, amphipods, shrimp, prawns, crabs, tunicates, nonburrowing anemones). Indirect action
Negative effects and modes of action	Crushing of epifaunal and infaunal species; habitat disturbance. Direct action	Destruction of habitat and crushing of suspension-feeding fauna (bivalves, polychaetes); decrease of infauna and sedentary species of epifauna. Direct and indirect action	Mortality of epifauna and infauna; potential sublethal effects resulting in altered secondary production. Direct action	Infauna—decreased biomass, elimination of suspension feeders (bivalves and polychaetes); lower species diversity. Epifauna—reduced abundance when bark and debris have decomposed to soft, flocculent consistency. Indirect action
Degree of effect	Insignificant to minor	Insignificant to moderate (moderate when site used 10 years)	Insignificant to moderate	Minor to moderate
Factors influencing degree of effect	Dumping or other activities causing scouring in important areas, such as estuaries or commercial and recreational shellfish-harvesting areas, would lead to minor effect	Large storage areas in important estuaries or commercial and recreational shellfish-harvesting areas; duration of use of log-handling area	Few reported instances; lack of information for benthic environments; dumping and sorting in important estuaries or commercial and recreational shellfish-harvesting areas may increase effects	Extent of debris coverage; importance of area; important estuary or commercial and recreational shellfish-harvesting area

TABLE 9.7.—Summary of log-handling effects on fish.

Evaluation	Effect		
	Bottom compaction and scouring	Accumulation of wood and bark debris and floating material	Physical disturbance to water column and bottom
Major source of effect	Free-fall dumping; water sorting; intertidal log storage	Log storage and bark and wood debris accumulations at dump and water-sorting areas	Free-fall dumping; water-sorting in shallows; intertidal log storage
Positive effects and modes of action	None	Increased abundance of some fish-food organisms; possible attraction of some species to log raft or debris habitats. Indirect action	None
Negative effects and modes of action	Loss of aquatic plants for Pacific herring spawning; loss of invertebrate food organisms. Indirect action	Toxicity or sublethal effects from log leachates and low dissolved oxygen; loss of fish-food organisms in areas of heavy debris accumulation. Direct action	Disturbance to fish present; destruction of Pacific herring and smelt spawning. Direct action
Degree of effect	Insignificant to moderate (potential)	Insignificant	Insignificant to minor
Factors influencing degree of effect	Importance of spawning area and areal extent of disturbance determine site-specific effect (no documentation of effects on fish populations)	Toxicity-related effects may increase with decrease in salinity and decrease in degree of tidal flushing (no documented instance of toxicity to fish in the field)	Fish use depends on time of year and is restricted to some areas (no documented evidence of effect)

disturbances are likely, large accumulations of bark and wood debris simultaneously distort the bottom ecology. Parbuckle dumps and any form of skidding are likely to cause the greatest amount of scour and compaction, "lift and lower" and helicopter dumps the least. Because terrestrial log dumps remain in a single location while logging goes on in a particular area, substrate disturbances are likely to be localized except where widespread accumulation of bark requires periodic dredging of larger areas. Barge dumps could cause major substrate disturbances in shallow water, but most barge dump sites must be in areas deep enough to allow passage of large tugs, so the direct effects of this activity on bottom sediments are probably small.

Dumps of bundled logs are more likely to disturb substrates than dumps of loose logs because bundles sink deeper before floating. The proportions of logs that are dumped loose or in bundles differ markedly by region. For all of coastal British Columbia, about 69% of the cut is bundled before dumping (FERIC 1980). In southeastern Alaska, over 99% of the timber cut is dumped as bundles (Faris and Vaughan 1985).

Faunas are expected to be depleted in the relatively small areas where logs come in contact with the bottom during dumping. Among species that could be affected are clams, crabs, oysters, sedentary polychaetes, and many other animals that depend on macrophytes that may be eliminated such as eelgrass (*Zostera marina*).

Several authors have observed or suggested effects on plant communities resulting from the scouring or compaction of substrates by rafted logs. Bell and Kallman (1976c) reported that logs stored in the Nanaimo River estuary had adverse effects on eelgrass meadows as well as on the macrobenthic and microbenthic algae, but did not provide details regarding the type and extent of this damage. Physical disturbances to substrates may also result when lost logs become stranded along shorelines and on beaches and when log dozers create propeller wash during sorting operations. Narver (1972b) and Trethewey (1974) suggested that either propeller wash or dragged logs had gouged the substrate in and near the larger eelgrass beds in the Nanaimo estuary. Tug propeller wash during transport of flat rafts and bundle booms in the Nanaimo River estuary has scoured substrates to depths ranging from 0.5 to 1.5 m, although scoured areas gradually fill in with sediments transported by the river (Fish Habitat and Log Management Task Force 1980). The grounding of bundle booms during towing in this estuary contributes to additional scouring and the accumulation of inorganic debris (rafting cable and bundle fasteners), which causes (among other effects) windrowing of oysters and washout of clams (Duval. et al. 1980). Naiman and Sibert (1979) reported that scouring of sediments in the Nanaimo estuary had severely limited benthic primary production, but provided no quantitative data to support their view. Other studies of log storage in the Cowichan, Chemainus, Campbell, Squamish, and Kitimat River estuaries, British Columbia, have indicated similar results (Levings and McDaniel 1976; Bell and Kallman 1976a, 1976b; E.V.S. Consultants Ltd. and F.L.C. Reed and Associates 1978).

The morphologies and growth patterns of aquatic plants affect the likelihood that they will be removed by substrate disturbances. Perennial plants that can regenerate from roots or holdfasts have a better chance of surviving after disturbance than those that require a portion of blade or frond for regeneration. Annuals will not reestablish themselves in a given year if they are removed by substrate compaction or scouring before their reproductive period. Eelgrass is a very common inhabitant of soft, muddy substrates in coastal British Columbia waters, substrates that also support several species of red, green, and dwarf brown algae in some areas (Scagel 1971; Ranwell 1972). Abrasion of eelgrass and emergent vascular plants by logs in these soft substrates probably fragments or uproots them. Although quantitative data are lacking, extensive damage to emergent vegetation fringing intertidal log-storage areas has been noted by several authors. Recovery of eelgrass in areas previously used for log handling was indicated during a study by Pease (1974), and emergent vegetation may similarly recolonize disturbed habitats.

Physical disturbance to substrates at log-storage sites has only been documented in intertidal storage areas where log booms or bundles "ground" during low tide. In scuba surveys conducted by Ellis (1973) under floating log rafts in Hanus Bay, Alaska, no distinguishable differences were observed in the character of substrates from those in control areas. Pease (1974), however, reported that in an intertidal log-storage area, portions of the bottom contained large depressions and were compacted to the consistency of sandstone by the action of log bundles grounding at low tide. Similar observations have been made in the estuaries of the Squamish and Snohomish rivers in Washington (Levings and McDaniel 1976; Smith 1977) and the Nanaimo River (Sibert and Harpham 1979). In the Squamish estuary, sediments on beaches were abrased and scoured by logs that came to rest at low tide, and further disrupted when logs were towed on and off the beach. Sibert and Harpham (1979) examined the substrate under an intertidal log-storage area in the Nanaimo River estuary where both flat raft and bundle booms were present. The bottom was grooved, up to 15 cm deep, parallel to the stored logs. They also noted that movement of bundle booms by tugs contributed to substrate scouring and subsequent release of hydrogen sulfide. Smith (1977) also reported the presence of troughs and ridges caused by grounding of logs in the Snohomish River estuary. Bundle booms, because of their greater draft, are more likely to disturb intertidal substrates than other types of storage, although bundling also minimizes disturbances resulting from log sinkage. Some operators, however, locate storage facilities in sheltered areas with sufficient water depths to prevent grounding of bundles or flat rafts at all times.

Plant communities on both rocky and soft substrates may be damaged as a result of such activities. At Bath Island, Georgia Strait, loose logs removed all algae from flat table rocks but generally not from vertical faces or crevices in the rock (Duval et al. 1980). In an attempt to simulate and assess the long-term effects of log abrasion on an algal community, DeWreede (cited by Duval et al. 1980) removed *Lithothrix* sp., a coralline alga, from a portion of intertidal substrate, and found that the area was subsequently recolonized by a filamentous red alga *Rhodomela larix*. In a similar study, Dayton (1971) reported that log abrasion removed intertidal algae from several sites in the San Juan Islands, Washington, and this subsequently affected the species composition of intertidal invertebrate communities. In such disturbed areas, changes in abundance of invertebrates, species composition of invertebrate communities, or both have been significant and measurable.

Data describing the effects of disturbance on intertidal invertebrates by the accumulation of lost logs is limited (Dayton 1971), although both positive and negative influences are likely. When salvage operations are undertaken to recover lost logs, physical effects on shoreline areas are relatively short term and small. When stranded logs are left in rocky areas, however, they may crush organisms, particularly if they shift repeatedly to different areas on subsequent tidal cycles. On gradually sloping shorelines where most log accumulations occur (Waelti and MacLeod 1971), substrate compaction may affect the infauna (animals living within the substrate) in the same way as log grounding affects it in intertidal storage areas. Sediment compaction caused by the repeated grounding of log booms during low tides may prevent substrate use by larger suspension feeders such as clams and result in a shift to predominately infaunal detritus feeders; sometimes the whole benthic infauna is crushed and eliminated (Pease 1974; Smith 1977; Zegers 1978; Sibert and Harpham 1979). For example, at Buckley Bay on Vancouver Island, Conlan and Ellis (1979) reported that populations of clams and oysters were reduced in areas of intertidal log storage as a result of sediment compaction. Studies in southeastern Alaska (Pease 1974) and in Washington (Smith 1977) also indicate significant decreases in the abundance of benthic epifauna (animals living on the substrate or on other organisms) at intertidal storage sites where sediment compaction had occurred over prolonged periods. Zegers (1978) found 88–95% reductions in the total number of benthic organisms on areas of Coos Bay, Oregon, subject to log grounding.

In contrast, Sibert and Harpham (1979) observed no adverse effects of intertidal log storage on benthic epifauna in the Nanaimo River estuary. They found a greater density of epibenthic harpacticoid copepods (an important prey species of some juvenile salmon) under intertidal log booms, but reported no consistent trends in harpacticoid densities relative to the intertidal storage of flat rafts or bundles. Although measurements of infaunal abundance were not undertaken during their study, Sibert and Harpham (1979) did suggest that infaunal habitat was probably reduced by sediment compaction.

Some intertidal organisms may benefit from log-debris accumulation in the intertidal zone. For example, the amphipod *Anisogammarus confervicolus* and the isopod *Exosphaeroma oregonensis* are extremely abundant within and adjacent to decomposing logs and wood debris in the mud flats of the Squamish River estuary, Washington (Levings and McDaniel 1976), although deeper areas in the substrate characterized by high concentrations of hydrogen sulfide are devoid of macrofauna (Duval et al. 1980). Increased habitat associated with log debris is likely to be most beneficial to those organisms inhabiting the upper portions of the intertidal zone characterized by "old drift" (Waelti and MacLeod 1971). In an extensive comparative study of epibenthic invertebrates in a log-storage site and a natural marsh off the Fraser River estuary, British Columbia, Levy et al. (1982) found distinct habitat-specific differences in the distribution and abundance of certain resident species, although a total negative effect associated with the disturbed site was not observed.

Bark and wood debris accumulations.—The deposition of bark and wood debris at log dumps has been examined or discussed by several authors, including Ellis (1973), Schaumburg and Walker (1973), Pease (1974), Conlan (1975, 1977), B.C. Ministry of the Environment (1976), and Schultz and Berg (1976). The subject of most intensive investigation has been the abundance and distribution of wood debris under log-storage areas. Most studies have shown that bark accumulation in areas used for log storage is considerably less than in areas used for log dumping, although water circulation patterns also influence the degree of bark accumulation (Pease 1974; Sibert and Harpham 1979).

In a scuba survey of four log-dump sites in coastal Alaska, three of which had been abandoned for two or more years, divers observed considerable variability in depth of bark and wood deposits between sites (Ellis 1973). One inactive dump site had only scattered deposits in bottom depressions up to 10 m deep; another had accumulations of debris several meters thick and apparently anaerobic. Debris accumulations were noted at water depths up to 23 m at two log dumps, and the effects of dumping were evident within a 45-m radius around the center of one site. Sibert and Harpham (1979) reported that accumulations of bark and other debris under log booms were localized and relatively small. They further noted that sediment particle size was smaller and organic content was higher in sediment samples collected under log booms than in control samples. These trends supported the earlier findings of Schaumburg and Walker (1973) at a log-storage site in the Yaquina River estuary, Oregon.

Sinking rates and dispersion of debris from log dumping are also related to bark particle size. In experiments conducted on Douglas-fir bark, Schaumburg (1973) reported that smaller pieces of bark sank first, and that 10, 47, and 75% of the bark had sunk after 1, 30, and 60 d. Water currents near dump sites can move bark both while it floats and after it sinks.

In an extensive examination of eight log dump sites in southeastern Alaska, five of which had been abandoned, Pease (1974) reported that bark deposition was at least partially related to the period of activity of the dump site, the volume of logs handled, or both. One site that had been active for 10 years had bark deposits 60–90 cm deep, but only 5–8 cm of bark were found at a dump that had been active for only 1 year. Ellis (1973) found a similar correlation between the depth of bark deposition and the period of use at other southeastern Alaska dump sites. Pease (1974) also noted that the area of substrate covered by bark differed between active and abandoned sites. At the oldest active dumping sites (7–10 years), the bark-covered area extended at least 60 m from the point where log bundles were introduced into the water. At the sites that had been abandoned for 1–11 years, this radius was reduced to about 15–23 m. Scattered patches of white powder were observed attached to the bark at many dump sites. Pease suggested that this material was either magnesium or calcium sulfide. Bark deposits may trap silt particles transported from adjacent areas or introduced into the water column with the logs. Silt accumulations in bark deposits have been documented by Ellis (1973) and Pease (1974).

In a study of 32 log-transfer facilities in southeastern Alaska, Schultz and Berg (1976) calculated that for 31 sites, the areas covered by bark ranged from 0 to 3.7 hectares. Recalculating these data, Faris and Vaughan (1985) obtained an average of about 0.8 hectares of bark accumulation for the 31 sites, with a mode of 0.4 hectares. At 13 sites, no measurable accumulation of bark or debris was found around the site; presumably, the material had been carried to deeper waters or covered by sediments, or had decayed. Faris and Vaughan concluded that conditions varied too much among the log-transfer locations to generalize about where and how much bark and debris would accumulate. In an earlier study of three active dump sites in southeastern Alaska, Ellis (1970) found that water currents affected the extent of bark deposition; although these sites had been used for 12 years, no bark and wood debris had accumulated. It has been suggested that bundling logs before dumping them results in less bark loss (Hansen et al. 1971; B.C. Ministry of the Environment 1976; Conlan 1977), although bark loosened during preparation and handling of the bundles may remain within the bundle and be deposited in areas where bundles are broken.

Conlan (1977) studied an active and an abandoned dump site at Mill Bay, British Columbia, and reported bark debris deposits of about 1 km^2 for each site, with heaviest accumulations (>15 cm) closest to the dumps. Considerable deposits persisted at the site that had been abandoned for 20 years, supporting observations of Ellis (1973) and Pease (1974) that dispersal of debris was slow from areas with poor water circulation. In none of these studies were currents measured directly, however; poor circulation was inferred from the remaining deposits. Earlier, Hansen et al. (1971) had found that bark debris was still evident in a coastal Oregon lake after 30–40 years.

TABLE 9.8.—Incremental percentages of bark dislodged during logging, unloading, and raft transport; ND = no data. (From Schaumburg 1973.)

Species	During logging	During unloading	During raft transport	During unloading and transport
Douglas-fir	18.2	16.8	4.9	21.7
Ponderosa pine	5.7	ND	ND	6.2

Schaumburg (1973) studied the effects of species of log handled on the amount of bark loss; 17% of Douglas-fir bark was lost during dumping of loose logs, but only 6% of ponderosa pine bark, which is more tightly bound (Table 9.8). Schaumburg also examined the effect of dumping method on bark loss by Douglas-fir; losses averaged 17% for slide-ramp (parbuckle) and 7% for A-frame hoist (lift and lower) methods. Robinson-Wilson and Jackson (1986) examined the relation between bark loss and the method of transfer of bundled logs at five transfer sites in southeast Alaska. Bark loss was directly correlated with the velocity of the bundle just before it entered the water. If bark accumulation at transfer sites poses potential problems, cranes or low-angle slides with rails should be used because they result in the least bark loss.

Logs lost during handling activities are another considerable source of wood debris accumulations. These logs frequently remain afloat and subsequently become stranded along shorelines. The volume of natural debris (as well as of logging debris that does not result from handling) has not been well documented. In southeastern Alaska, most woody debris is natural (Beil 1974; Forest Engineering Incorporated 1982), but up to 90% of the woody debris on some British Columbia beaches has cut ends, indicating it originates from logging or construction. Waelti and MacLeod (1971) estimated that 680,000 m³ of logs were lost annually in the coastal Vancouver Forest Region, and the Council of Forest Industries (1974, 1980) estimated that gross log losses throughout British Columbia, including sinkage, but excluding recoveries by the British Columbia Log Spill Recovery Association, amounted to 827,000 m³. About 40% of these latter losses were eventually recovered by log-salvage permittees and others, another 35% (chiefly western hemlock) sank, and the remaining 25% were lost to beaches or open seas.

Evans (1977) noted that the greatest proportion (about 70%) of wood debris in Georgia Strait resulted from log-handling losses (Table 9.9). Western hemlock was always the primary species lost, particularly among the smaller logs. Recent moves by some companies to increase dry-land sorting, water bundling, or both have greatly reduced flat rafting and associated log losses. The Council of Forest Industries (1974) estimated log losses by species and log size for each of four basic handling methods; overall, barging and flat rafting of loose logs produced the highest loss rates (Table 9.10). Waelti and MacLeod (1971) reported that gently sloping beaches accumulate the most log debris; rocky, steep shorelines trap relatively few logs. They further classified beach debris into three "age-groups": transient material lying below average high tide, which may be naturally removed within one change of the tide; material lying above the average high tide ("new drift"), which is subject to dislocation and drift to another area during extreme tides; and "old drift" deposited permanently above and behind normal high-tide

TABLE 9.9.—Sources and volumes of logs and debris in Georgia Strait. (From Evans 1977.)

Source	Volume of logs and debris (m^3)
Log transport and storage	297,000
Mills on Burrard Inlet and Fraser River	42,000–85,000
Howe Sound sorting	6,000–11,000

lines by extreme tides and wind. New drift makes up most of the beach wood, and old drift typically is at least partially decomposed.

Most of the effects of log-handling on benthic and intertidal invertebrates have been attributed to the accumulation of bark, wood, and other debris at transfer and storage areas, where they lie on top of and within the sediments. The extent of these physical changes depends on the amount of tidal flushing in the log-handling area, the methods used to dump, sort, and store logs, and the length of time the area has been used for log handling.

Studies of bark-deposit effects on plant communities are lacking, but a report by E.V.S. Consultants Ltd. and F.L.C. Reed and Associates (1978) showed that intertidal areas with heavy debris accumulation in the Campbell River estuary had fewer species of benthic plants than elsewhere and depletion of oxygen within the sediments; no adverse effects of log handling were observed in subtidal regions. Duval et al. (1980) summarized several reports that also suggested bark accumulations may result in decreased abundance of benthic micro- and macroalgae, although again, quantitative supporting data were lacking.

Pease (1974) examined algae and eelgrass communities at several abandoned and active log-dumping or storage sites in southeastern Alaska. Plants were sparse at two dump sites that had been in operation for 10 years, but at two other sites in use for only 1 year, green algae (Chlorophyta) and eelgrass were described as "abundant." Pease (1974) found no consistent trends in rates of algal or eelgrass recolonization at abandoned log-storage and dumping sites.

The most thorough examination of the physical effects of bark and debris accumulation on benthic infaunal organisms was made by Conlan (1977) at Mill Bay, British Columbia. In this study, the physical effects of debris were clearly separated from the concurrent effects of chemical changes in the environment. The sandy bottoms in control areas with no debris had a wide diversity of organisms, including suspension-feeding bivalves and polychaetes. In areas with

TABLE 9.10.—Estimated log losses for each of four basic handling methods. (From Council of Forest Industries 1974.)

Log-handling method	Coastal production in 1974 (%)	Percent lost
Dry-land sorting and bundling, direct trucking to mills, or both	20	0.33
Water-bundling before towing to mills	23	1.7
Dumping, sorting, and flat rafting to mills	35	3.2
Barging of loose logs, dumping, and flat rafting to mills	22	6.1

debris accumulation, (1) suspension-feeding organisms were eliminated, (2) dominant benthic species were fewer and invertebrate biomass was less than in control areas, and (3) numbers of wood-boring bivalves (*Bankia* sp.) and isopods (*Limnoria* sp.) were greater than in control areas. These effects were particularly evident where depth of debris exceeded 1 cm. Areas that had been abandoned for 17 years or more showed little recovery in normal community structure and abundance. Conlan's results were generally consistent with those of earlier investigations of benthic infauna at active and abandoned log-handling areas (Pease 1974; Conlan and Ellis 1979) and demonstrated that, although the changes to infauna are not necessarily pronounced, they are measurable. Jackson (1986) found that macroinfauna densities and biomasses were lower in areas covered with bark, regardless of differences in depths between 3 and 6 and 7 and 10 m. Deposit feeders were less affected by bark deposits than suspension feeders. Additionally, considerable differences in species abundance were observed between depths at control sites, whereas sites affected by bark deposition showed no differences by depth except in the biomass of some species.

In general, the accumulation of bark and wood debris has had some, but not much, adverse effect on epibenthic communities. In areas with thick, soft deposits of decomposing bark but no sunken logs, Ellis (1973) found fewer epibenthic species (such as crabs) and attached forms (including anemones and tunicates). Pease (1974) reported similar adverse effects on both microalgae and eelgrass resulting from heavy bark accumulation and poor tidal flushing. Sometimes, light accumulations of debris may benefit some macroalgae (kelps) by providing more suitable substrates. At sites where scattered bark and sunken-log debris provided additional habitat, Ellis (1973), McDaniel (1973), Pease (1974), and Conlan and Ellis (1979) all reported increased abundances of epibenthic fauna, particularly amphipods, *Munida* sp., shrimp, crabs, anemones, and tunicates. However, in a comparative study of production by the amphipod *Eogammarus confervicolus* in three habitat types within the Squamish River estuary, British Columbia—a log-debris area, an embankment along a *Carex lyngbyei* marsh, and a *Fucus distichus* algal community—Stanhope and Levings (1985) found the highest mortality and lowest production in areas of accumulated wood debris, although they suggested that these areas may continue to provide sufficient food reserves for juvenile salmonids.

The evidence to date, therefore, suggests that suspension-feeding infaunal organisms are adversely affected by the physical changes associated with accumulation of bark and wood debris, whereas epibenthic organisms remain generally unaffected or sometimes may benefit from increased habitat. The epifauna seems to be adversely affected only where decomposition of bark debris creates a soft, flocculent substrate (Conlan 1977). O'Clair and Freese (1985) reported on a series of laboratory experiments with female Dungeness crabs (*Cancer magister*) exposed to bark debris from benthic deposits at log-transfer facilities in southeast Alaska. Feeding rates were higher in a clean sand control than in treatment sections with bark deposits. Bark deposits from a transfer site that had been inactive for 17 years caused higher mortality of Dungeness crabs relative to control animals, but fresh bark deposits did not. The percentage of eggs extruded was significantly lower in two of the four bark treatments than in the controls. Fecundities of Dungeness crabs on bark deposits at six log-transfer sites were reported to be only 44% of those of crabs found in the control sites. In addition, egg mortality was twice as great at log-transfer sites than at control sites and appeared directly related to an increase in the density of the parasitic worm *Carcinonemerges errans*. Densities and sizes of Dungeness crabs were greater in control sites than in sites with bark, where there was a greater incidence of lost leg segments.

Light attenuation.—Many reports that discussed the effects of log handling on marine plant communities suggested that stored, floating logs create shade and that log dumping and sorting in shallow water increase turbidity. Although these types of disturbances undoubtedly occur, neither light intensity, spectral composition, nor water turbidity has been measured near log-handling sites, and adverse effects of these changes on plants have largely been inferred. Rates of primary production and standing stocks of plant communities affected by various aspects of log handling also have not been determined.

The effects of changes in light regimes probably vary among plant species and with seasonal differences in the light requirements of those species. Greatest effects likely are caused by shade under rafted logs. Decreased light intensity may reduce rates of primary production and growth, and may eventually lead to the loss of benthic microalgae and macrophytes from these areas. Free-floating plants (phytoplankton) would not be substantially affected by shading because they would not remain long in environments with reduced light. Reductions in plant community structure and abundance may affect various invertebrates that rely on these plants.

Particulate matter such as silt and fine bark debris may enter the water column as a result of log handling and raise the turbidity. When present in sufficient quantities, suspended particulates not only reduce light intensities, they also change the spectral composition of light by differentially scattering short-wavelength radiation (<500 nm). Both types of change cause decreases in the rates of photosynthesis and plant growth, but they are probably extremely localized and of minor concern for log-handling operations in coastal marine environments.

Chemical Disturbances

The major chemical consequences of log handling are increased biochemical oxygen demand (BOD), production of hydrogen sulfide (H_2S) and ammonia (NH_4) during the decomposition of bark and woody debris, and release of soluble organic compounds (leachates) from logs. When present in sufficient quantities, leachates also exert an oxygen demand on and impart a yellow to brown color to the water. The decomposition of bark and wood debris in water proceeds in two phases: a relatively rapid process mediated by heterotrophic bacteria, followed by a slower one requiring lignin-decomposing fungi; the fungi are common in terrestrial ecosystems but not in marine environments. Decomposition in this slower phase, however, is often augmented by boring organisms such as *Bankia setacea* (feathery shipworm) and *Limnoria lignorum*, which give the fungi access to the interior of wood. The decomposition of bark and wood requires oxygen, and this process can locally deplete dissolved oxygen concentrations if there is no movement of water to impart fresh oxygen supplies. Anaerobic conditions are most likely to develop on the bottom, where currents typically are slowest. Currents greater than 0.01 m/s, however, prevent the biochemical oxygen demand of wood debris from having a notable effect on dissolved oxygen concentrations (Pease 1974). Such currents usually occur in the water columns of tidally influenced bodies.

To date, the chemical effects of log-handling on plant communities have not been examined, although both positive and negative effects are possible. Some authors have suggested that the chemical effects of bark and wood accumulations on benthic organisms are minor. Schaumburg (1973) and Pease (1974) reported that the BOD of these materials is low enough that oxygen levels in waters within or above the substrates are generally unaffected, or at least are not substantially changed from those normally associated with marine sediments. Similarly, the opportunity for dilution available in most log-handling areas usually prevents the accumulation of H_2S or wood leachates in the water column. Exceptions have been documented in poorly flushed areas where extensive debris has accumulated on the substrate. The potential, however, for chemical effects on benthic invertebrates in these areas is relatively high. A study by FERIC (1980) indicated that 4,208 hectares (47%) of log-handling lease sites examined in British Columbia were located in areas with negligible tidal currents. The BOD in such areas becomes a measurable and significant feature of the water–sediment interface, where circulation of oxygenated interstitial water may be reduced and bark deposits may accumulate.

The oxygen uptake of benthic bark deposits has been measured by McKeown et al. (1968), Schaumburg (1973), and Pease (1974). These authors reported daily oxygen demands of 0.2–4.4 g O_2/m^2. Schaumburg (1973) found that the oxygen demand of bark deposits in coastal Oregon waters increased with both the concentration of organic solids in the deposits and the surface area of the log debris. He also indicated that oxygen demand was not related to the depth of bark deposits. Ponce (1974) also demonstrated a relation between oxygen demand and particle-size distribution and surface area of log debris. McKeown et al. (1968) indicated that mixing or water turbulence above the substrate increases the oxygen demand of benthic bark deposits by accelerating decomposition. Daily uptake ranged from 0.2 to 0.8 g O_2/m^2 under stagnant conditions, but water movement above the deposits increased the demand to 2.7 g O_2/m^2. Gentle scouring of the benthic bark deposits further raised the daily oxygen demand to 4.4 g O_2/m^2.

Pease (1974) reported on one log-dump site in southeastern Alaska where low oxygen and high concentrations of H_2S and wood leachates were associated with a virtual absence of benthic fauna. Ellis (1973) also reported that epibenthic organisms were less abundant in log-handling areas where thick layers of decomposing bark and wood debris were deposited. The latter study, however, was based only on divers' observations; as a result, the effects of low oxygen and high H_2S concentrations could not be distinguished from the concurrent physical changes in sediment composition. Conlan (1975) stated that quantitative information was lacking on the accumulation of leachates or H_2S in interstitial or intertidal environments near log-handling sites. Both of these environments are directly affected by the decomposition of bark and wood deposits and may have limited flushing potential. Sublethal or lethal chemical effects on plants would likely be restricted to benthic species in the immediate vicinity of these deposits and to both pelagic and benthic species near recently immersed logs still releasing leachates. Although H_2S is toxic to some species of fish (McKee and Wolf 1971), marine benthic infauna are normally exposed to H_2S produced by decomposition in the sediments and are unlikely to be greatly affected by the additional H_2S associated with decomposition of bark and wood debris. On the other hand, some epifauna and pelagic invertebrates (for example, zooplankton) could be adversely affected by H_2S that may accumulate in the water column of poorly flushed areas. However, no data are available on the toxicity of H_2S to epibenthic and pelagic marine invertebrates.

With the exception of beaches exposed to a strong surf, marine sediments are generally anaerobic and chemically reducing beneath a relatively thin oxidized layer (Fenchel and Riedl 1970). Consequently, degradation of wood and bark deposits in estuarine and marine sediments is primarily by means of sulfate reduction. This bacterially mediated process results in production of H_2S, various organic compounds, and carbon monoxide (CO). Hydrogen sulfide reacts with soluble iron in interstitial waters to form ferrous sulfide (FeS), although phosphate also competes with sulfides for available iron in interstitial waters. Pyrite, formed from FeS, decreases the total sulfide capacity and increases the probability of free sulfide formation (Bella 1975). The tendency for the leached extracts from bark and wood to exhaust the iron in surface sediments is evident from the high concentrations of free H_2S present in benthic wood deposits (Pease 1974). Within undisturbed sediments, the FeS content increases as available organics are decomposed, inhibiting free sulfide production as long as it remains below the sulfide capacity. Physical disturbance or flushing of the sediment with aerobic waters oxidizes the FeS and releases the sulfide. As a result, the sediments undergo a series of cycles in which the FeS increases during periods of physical stability and rapidly decreases during sediment disturbance. Studies by Vigers and Hoos (1977) and Sibert and Harpham (1979) documented such processes in the Campbell and Nanaimo river estuaries of British Columbia as a result of tugboat-propeller wash from log-handling operations. At all log-handling sites, free sulfide inevitably forms if associated organic deposits are excessive and exceed the available iron capacity. Conlan (1975), however, cited only one instance when resultant H_2S concentrations reached toxic levels, which occurred when organic matter was buried under beach gravel (Hansen et al. 1971). Other laboratory studies with fish have shown that acute lethal concentrations of H_2S have ranged from 0.8 to 7.0 mg/L depending on test species and pH (U.S. Environmental Protection Agency 1971).

Substantial amounts of soluble organic compounds are released by logs stored in water as well as by submerged bark deposits (Conlan 1975). The character of these leachates depends on the tree species, but they generally include tannins, resins, oils, fats, terpenes, flavanoids, quinones, carbohydrates, glycosides, and alkaloids (Wise 1959). The tannin, flavanoid, resin, and quinone components are primarily responsible for the yellow to brown color associated with leachates, and each of these components contributes differently to oxygen demand (Schaumburg 1973). Some 60–80% of the chemicals leached from wood are volatile (Schaumburg 1973). Leaching is faster in salt water than in fresh water. In stable flowing water, the leaching process is nearly constant for at least 30 d (Hansen et al. 1971), but the leaching rate increases with the flushing rate and (when flushing rates are low) it decreases as the concentration of organics in the surrounding water builds up. The leaching rate also varies with the species and age of wood, the residence time of the wood or bark in water, and temperature (Atkinson 1971; Gove and Gellman 1971). Gove and Gellman (1971) noted that the greatest proportion of leachate was released from the cut ends of logs and the bark. Although in-place leaching rates may be quite different, Pease (1974) ranked tree species according to their leaching rates (from highest to lowest) as follows: western redcedar, Alaska-cedar, western hemlock, and Sitka spruce. Schaumburg (1973) reported a decrease in the BOD of Douglas-fir leachates from 0.46 to 0.07 g O_2/m^2 daily after 25–30 d.

Of further concern is the potential for colored, light-attenuating leachates to reduce autotrophic production, although log leachates may have positive influences as well. Some constituents of wood leachates, such as glucose, may stimulate growth by plant species capable of heterotrophic uptake. This uptake, however, is not likely to be important for benthic microalgae adapted to low light and already relying primarily on heterotrophic production.

Schaumburg (1973) believed that the potential toxicity of log leachates to marine animals is negligible because of the tendency for lignin constituents to precipitate with divalent cations in seawater. Nevertheless, accumulation of leachates in freshwater or slightly brackish log-handling areas (such as the tidal portions of rivers) is of concern, primarily because of the effects of plicatic acid on the pH of these poorly buffered waters (Peters 1974). Furthermore, laboratory studies of marine and freshwater invertebrates by Buchanan et al. (1976) and Peters et al. (1976), respectively, indicate that log leachates can have toxic effects that vary with the species of tree and the species and life stage of invertebrate. Pease (1974) conducted similar studies both in the laboratory and in the field, recording the highest leachate concentrations observed in nature: 280–320 mg/L in a poorly flushed Alaskan log-storage site. These concentrations were about five times the threshold concentrations for acute toxicity to pink salmon fry determined in the laboratory. No bioassays were conducted at the log-storage site to determine if the receiving waters were actually toxic to benthic fauna, however.

Consequences of Log Handling and Storage Operations for Fish

Having described the primary physical and chemical effects of log-handling and storage on estuarine and intertidal biotic communities, we turn now to particular consideration of fish. Fish species that may inhabit the areas most frequently used for log handling (estuaries, sheltered bays, and inlets) include the anadromous salmonid species (Pacific salmon, cutthroat and rainbow trout, Dolly Varden), marine smelts (surf smelts, capelin, longfin smelt, eulachon), Pacific herring, various rockfishes, and bottom-dwelling species. Some of these species have commercial and recreational importance, and many of them are important prey for marine mammals and aquatic birds. The life history phases of these fishes that are most likely to be affected by log handling include rearing (all species), migration (salmonids, smelts), and spawning and incubation (smelts, herring); the timing of these phases for some important fish species in Pacific Northwest coastal waters is presented in Table 9.11.

The direct effects of log handling on fish have not been quantitatively assessed except by Levy et al. (1982). The following sections therefore describe probable effects of log handling, based on observations of other communities such as

TABLE 9.11.—Life history phases of some important fish species in British Columbia coastal waters.

Species	Activity	J	F	M	A	M	J	J	A	S	O	N	D
Salmonids	Fry and smolts, estuary residence[a]	━	━	━	━	━	━	━	━	━	━		
	Adults, migration staging	━	━	━	━	━	━	━	━	━	━	━	
Pacific herring	Spawning activity		━	━			━	━					
	Rearing activity				━	━	━	━					
Surf smelt	Spawning and incubation	━	━	━	━	━	━	━	━	━	━	━	━
	Residence	━	━	━	━	━	━	━	━	━	━	━	━
Capelin	Spawning and incubation									━	━		
Longfin smelt	Adult migration										━	━	━
	Residence	━	━	━	━	━	━	━	━	━	━		
Eulachon	Adult migration and recovery				━	━							

[a]Information on timing from Hart (1973).

benthic invertebrates, and on indirect evidence of effects cited in the few references available on this topic.

Direct effects.—The most comprehensive study of fish densities, growth, and feeding behavior was conducted in the Fraser River estuary, British Columbia, (Levy et al. 1982). Within the north arm of the estuary, a pristine marsh was compared with a marsh with extensive log-storage booms. Levy et al. (1982) found salmonid densities to be similar in both areas, and they concluded that juvenile salmon did not avoid booms of stored logs in this well-flushed estuary. They also found that chinook salmon fry in the log-storage area were substantially larger than in the pristine marsh site. The size of chum salmon fry did not differ between log-storage and pristine marshes.

Juvenile salmon in two adjacent intertidal areas of the Fraser River estuary—the Point Grey log-storage area and the Musqueam Marsh—displayed major dietary differences (Levy et al. 1982). A dietary shift in the log-storage area appeared to be caused by a decrease in estuarine insects, because marsh plants were absent there, and by a greater availability of fish larvae and the mysid *Neomysis mercedis*. Levy et al. (1982) concluded that "in spite of the drastic physical impact of intertidal log storage at Point Grey there was no strong negative effect on fish utilization of the area. There were no decreases in fish abundance or fish growth that could be attributed to the presence of stored log booms." Because the Point Grey log-storage area is well flushed, the authors suggested that research is needed to test the hypothesis that fish also do not avoid log booms in poorly flushed areas.

Potential direct effects of log handling on fish may result from physical disturbances associated with transfer and sorting activities. For example, bark accumulations may suffocate incubating eggs of nonsalmonid species or interfere with other uses of habitats by fish. Chemical effects may be exerted by leachates released from stored logs and by oxygen demand of decomposing wood and bark debris at log dumps and, to a lesser extent, log-storage sites. No information on the importance of these direct disturbances to fish populations is available, however.

Large numbers of juvenile salmon rear in many rivers, estuaries, and coastal areas, and adults aggregate there during spawning migrations to natal streams (Neave 1966; Scott and Crossman 1973; Stasko et al. 1973; Levy et al. 1979). Anadromous cutthroat trout, Dolly Varden, and steelhead may use some of these coastal environments throughout the year (Scott and Crossman 1973). Other species, including smelts and herrings, may concentrate in estuaries, inlets, and bays during their spawning and migration periods (Table 9.11). Only the surf smelt, capelin, and Pacific herring spawn and deposit eggs in marine environments potentially used for log handling, however (Hart 1973). Quantitative assessment is impossible because direct effects of log handling on fish have not been studied. Log-transfer and -sorting activities, however, are unlikely to interfere substantially and directly with fish outside the relatively small area where the disturbances occur, and fish would probably avoid such areas. Nevertheless, log dumping, tugboat propeller wash during sorting, and intertidal log storage may destroy some of the incubating eggs of smelt and herring. Other fish, including shallow-water rockfish and bottom-dwelling species, are widely distributed in coastal British Columbia, southeastern Alaska, and Puget Sound waters. The areas used for log handling represent only a minor portion of their available habitat. Note, however, that no data are available to describe the site-specific effects of log handling on the limited, unique habitats for some fish resources and the potential for disproportionate effects of these activities on fisheries productivity.

The potential chemical effects of log leachates on fish have been examined in several laboratory bioassays and in limited field studies, including those of Schaumburg (1973) and Pease (1974). In laboratory experiments, log leachates were toxic to fish and also raised the biochemical oxygen demand in the water. The toxicity of leachates is significantly lower in sea- and brackish-water environments than in fresh water, however. Both Schaumburg (1973) and Pease (1974) concluded that the large volume of water available for dilution usually prevents either accumulation of leachates to toxic concentrations or reduction in oxygen concentration that could adversely affect fish. Any increase in leachate concentration that could be toxic would usually be temporary and extremely localized. Of 13 active or inactive log-dumping and storage areas examined by Pease (1974) in southeastern Alaska, only one had leachate and oxygen concentrations that could adversely affect fish. No information is available, however, on the frequency of this type of occurrence in British Columbia. The high proportion (47%) of coastal British Columbia log-handling sites reported to have negligible tidal flushing (27% have depths less than 3 m: FERIC 1980) suggests that direct chemical effects of this type may occur in some areas.

Indirect effects.—Alterations in fish habitat or in the abundance of fish prey may indirectly affect fish populations either positively or negatively. For example, many intertidal or estuarine log-handling sites in British Columbia support communities of eelgrass or rockweed or both, which are common substrates for deposition of Pacific herring spawn (Outram and Humphreys 1974; Patterson 1975). Several authors have suggested that the abundance of aquatic flora has been dramatically reduced in some intertidal areas used for log storage through shading (B.C. Ministry of the Environment 1976; Waldichuk 1979), grounding of rafts with resultant scouring and compaction of sediments (Pease 1974; Sibert and

Harpham 1979; Waldichuk 1979), and uprooting of plants by tugboat activity (Sibert 1978). These effects may be responsible for elimination of herring spawn deposition in Ladysmith Harbor near Dunsmuir Island (Patterson 1975) and in the Mamquam Channel area of the Squamish River estuary (Hoos and Vold 1975). No evidence suggests, however, that the population of Pacific herring has declined as a result. Healey (1978) suggested that intertidal log storage has resulted in the destruction of some juvenile salmon rearing habitat in the central and western portions of the Nanaimo River estuary, although quantitative data to substantiate his hypothesis are apparently lacking.

Declines in the abundance of benthic epifauna and infauna, which may be important fish food, have been reported in some areas where bark and wood debris accumulate or where intertidal log storage occurs (Ellis 1973; Pease 1974; Conlan and Ellis 1979); fish populations using these nearshore environments could be indirectly affected. Conversely, some prey organisms may become more abundant in areas of scattered log debris and bark. For example, Levings (1973) noted large populations of amphipods (*Anisogammarus pugettensis*) in association with a dense diatom–chlorophyte community among older logs stored in the Squamish River estuary. Goodman and Vroom (1972) reported that salmonids using this area preyed on these amphipods. Similar indirect positive effects of log handling have been recorded in the Kitimat River estuary, British Columbia (H. Paish and Associates Ltd. 1974; Higgins and Schouwenberg 1976). Conlan (1977) also reported that the abundance of amphipod species is either increased or unaffected by log storage.

Herrmann (1979) calculated the effects of log-rafting sites on benthic invertebrates and fish production in all of Coos Bay, Oregon. He estimated that the summer benthic invertebrate biomasses were 2,050 kg (dry weight) on 85 hectares of intertidal log-storage areas, 64,370 kg in the upper bay, and 257,000 kg on all of the Coos Bay tideflats. He further estimated that the 2,050 kg of benthos in the storage areas could support production of about 1,370 kg (live weight) of fish tissue—about 0.6% of fish production estimated for the entire Coos Bay tidal area.

Although some authors have inferred that compaction of sediments under intertidal log booms has contributed to a decrease in benthic amphipods and copepods that are major prey of juvenile salmon (Healey 1978; Waldichuk 1979), this relation has not been satisfactorily demonstrated. Sibert (1978) and Sibert and Harpham (1979) reported that although larger infaunal species disappeared from log-storage areas of the Naniamo River estuary, the total abundance of major meiofaunal taxa, nematodes, and harpacticoid copepods (important prey of juvenile chum salmon) could not be related to the presence of log booms.

Some observations further suggest that some fish species, including prey species of marine mammals, may be attracted to areas where wood and bark debris increase the abundance of food sources. Ellis (1973) found Pacific sand lances, blennies, sculpins, and yellowfin sole in areas of undecayed bark and debris under log-storage areas in Hanus Bay, Alaska. Schultz and Berg (1976) also reported fish species such as Pacific cod, shiner perch, rockfishes, and searcher in association with submerged logs, branches, and benthic deposits in southeastern Alaska.

Such evidence suggests that log-handling operations may not be responsible for substantial reductions in fish habitat and fish-food organisms. One frustrating aspect of our concern for the environment is the lack of research data to support decisions. With the exceptions of Coos Bay and the Nanaimo River estuary on southeastern Vancouver Island, no comprehensive ecological study of log-rafting and -storage effects on a total estuary has been conducted. Intertidal habitats have been well documented near mill sites in Oregon, Washington, and British Columbia. Leachate toxicity and BOD problems, although well documented in the laboratory, have not been documented in the field. Environmental concerns related to log transportation in southeastern Alaska are poorly based in fact; a well-organized study of the estuarine ecosystem should be conducted on both benthic and epibenthic organisms.

Summary

The assessment of effects of log handling and storage on biotic communities is hampered by the lack of quantitative information on plant communities, chemical stresses, and community interrelationships. Another problem is the difficulty of distinguishing between the effects of two or more concurrent forms of disturbance. The degree of disturbance is largely determined by the spatial extent of a log-handling operation and its location with respect to potentially sensitive areas such as estuaries.

Physical and chemical perturbations are the two primary disturbances associated with log-handling operations. Physical disturbances include substrate scouring and compaction, modification of sediment composition, accumulation of wood and bark debris, alteration of light levels, disruption of the water column, and increases in turbidity. Chemical disturbances include changes in water quality, decomposition of wood debris deposits, leaching of potentially toxic chemicals from wood, and deoxygenation of water and substrate.

Log-dumping and -sorting activities and the storage of logs in sensitive intertidal areas are considered the most detrimental aspects of log handling to biotic communities. Such operations have destroyed benthic habitats and crushed benthic organisms, altered the composition and abundance of benthic infaunas, disturbed substrates for eelgrass and emergent plants, reduced levels of light needed by primary producers, and diminished water quality through leachate activity and wood-debris accumulations. Tables 9.5 and 9.6 summarize these effects on plant and invertebrate communities. Although it appears that most effects are detrimental to aquatic environments (particularly estuarine environments), there are some positive influences as well. These include increased habitat complexity for some benthic organisms that is provided by light accumulations of wood debris and the potential for enhanced heterotrophic production by those plants that can metabolize chemicals leached from wood.

Log-handling and -storage activities can have either direct or indirect effects on fish habitat and abundance, as summarized in Table 9.7. The extent of log-handling and -storage operations throughout the northwestern USA and western Canada must be determined so we can better understand their effects on the fishery resource. Many of the alleged negative effects of log handling on fish are speculative, based on few observations and fewer quantitative studies. The degree of harm to the fish resources of coastal British Columbia and southeastern Alaska probably ranges from insignificant to minor. The greatest potential detriment is destruction of Pacific herring spawning areas. Some observations suggest that fish may receive positive indirect benefits from log-handling operations in the form of more abundant invertebrate prey in areas where log debris accumulates.

The degree to which local environments and fish populations are affected by log-handling and -storage operations depends in large part on the size of the disturbed area, local flushing characteristics, and water depth. A study of log-handling leases in coastal British Columbia waters by FERIC (1980) indicated that 27% of them (totaling 2,400 hectares) were less than 3 m deep, and that the potential for damage to nearshore plant communities was highest in these areas. Primary production by benthic microalgae could also be reduced in such areas, subsequently affecting secondary production by invertebrate grazers. It can be seen, therefore, that such effects on a local environment generally have deleterious consequences for more than one species. Once the biotic community structure is so altered, organisms at higher trophic levels (fish) will likely be affected as well.

Information Gaps and Research Recommendations

Much information is available on certain aspects of log handling and storage. Most studies have concentrated on bark loss, benthic habitat alteration, benthic organisms, leachates, and grounding effects from dumping and stray logs. This information has been used to help establish corrective regulations and policies. Most fisheries biologists, ecologists, environmentalists, and conservationists, as well as much of the public, would answer yes to the question: "Is log transfer and storage detrimental to the estuary and salmonid species?" Most believe that estuaries are essential for survival of anadromous salmonid stocks in western North America and that any disturbance to the estuary is detrimental, no matter how small the area affected.

Although data show that only a small fraction of the total available estuarine area might be affected by log-handling operations, there is good reason to locate these operations on the least damageable portion of each estuary. We are only just beginning to understand the role that certain areas of the estuary play in salmon production. Even though a large proportion of the original marshlands and intertidal areas have been lost in California, Oregon, Washington, and British Columbia, it is impossible to say how this has affected salmon runs. We do not know whether the amount of intertidal and marsh area is approaching some lower limit critical to the survival of the present salmon production. Further, all along the Pacific coast, from California to central Alaska, major investments are being made to enhance salmon runs, and we do not know whether the intertidal estuaries and marshes are adequate to support the increased numbers. Clearly, the consequences of allowing estuarine areas to be destroyed are highly uncertain, and valuable salmon runs could be put in jeopardy. This uncertainty about the adequacy of estuarine areas for salmonids is likely to persist in the immediate future, despite the best research efforts. The estuarine and marsh areas and the salmon runs associated with them are complex, and the life cycles of salmonids that use estuaries both as juveniles and as adults can last four or more years.

These characteristics make the research task difficult, lengthy, and costly. Currently, our technology and organization of research is poorly developed to meet the challenge.

Planning for log transportation, whether by floating or land-to-barge systems, as well as for other competing developments, must consider this continuing uncertainty. Guidelines for ecological impact assessment must be designed so that the information reflects what can reasonably be developed in a short time and does not falsely imply that effects on salmon can be measured in a short time.

From our review of the literature, the evidence is inconclusive about the importance that small areas of the size affected by log transfer and storage have for the overall production and population success of bivalves, crabs, or salmonids. Log-transfer sites and estuarine ecosystems vary greatly and, with the present status of knowledge, great caution must be used when evidence from one estuary is applied to another.

Information gaps exist; for example, knowledge is inadequate on the availability and the quality of alternative habitats for salmonids and other species. Such information is essential if one is to evaluate the importance of present and proposed log-transfer and -storage sites to the species of interest. Would organisms—fish, for example—congregate in the remaining transfer site in an estuary or would they occupy other estuarine or coastal habitats? In those alternative habitats, would fish have comparable survival rates, or would their survival be poorer? The same questions need to be answered for crabs, clams, and oysters.

Dry-land alternatives to freshwater or marine log transfer and storage may permanently damage both upland and shoreline habitats. Facilities that allow logs to be transferred to and from barges without touching the water may require permanent structures that displace nearshore marine habitat with pilings and rock fill. Onshore storage and handling of logs, although protecting the marine habitat, can permanently change the shoreline and present a different set of bark disposal problems (Forest Engineering Incorporated 1982).

Marine birds and mammals use log rafts as feeding and resting stations; birds use them as nesting areas. Older rafts in fresh water with brush growing on them also may be used by terrestrial birds and waterfowl for nesting. Both the birds and mammals are vital components of the ecosystem; the relations between these organisms and log rafts—and the consequences of raft removal—should be studied.

Except for cursory observations, the importance of log rafts as habitat or protective cover for fish has not been well documented. We need to determine whether storage and dumping areas provide substantial habitat for fish, or if certain species avoid the rafts because of leachates or other factors. Studies could be limited to determining whether fish abundance and distribution are influenced by the rafts and dumping activities. Emphasis should be placed on sloughs and backwater areas where leachate concentrations are expected to be greatest.

When sunken logs are retrieved, the benthic habitat is disturbed. Maintenance dredging of log-dumping areas and the disturbance of bottom sediments by tugs and other log-handling vessels may cause similar effects. The significance of such disruptions has not been documented or quantified. Because the potential for such negative effects as resuspension of toxic materials or damage to benthic habitat should be weighed against the positive result of retrieving salvageable logs, an examination should be made of the extent of area affected by retrieval operations, maintenance dredging, and activities of vessels in log-handling areas.

In general, less emphasis should be placed on studying effects that have already been described because regulations are in effect or are being developed to alleviate them. Both positive and negative effects not previously studied should be given more emphasis, particularly relative to the entire ecosystem. Research priority should be given to areas of poor water circulation because effects of log handling are greatest in these areas.

Recommended Practices

The following protective measures, based on a Task Force Report on Log Storage and Rafting in Public Waters (Hansen et al. 1971; approved by the Pacific Northwest Pollution Control Council), were designed to minimize the effects of log handling on the aquatic environment and remain applicable today.

• Dry-land handling and sorting is preferred to water handling and sorting, although the location of dry-land facilities should not be in fisheries-sensitive zones such as estuaries, salt marshes, herring spawning areas, or shellfish beds.
• The free-fall, violent dumping of logs into water should be prohibited, because this is the major cause and point source of loose bark and other log debris.
• Easy-let-down devices should be used to place logs in the water, thereby reducing bark separation and generation of other wood debris.
• Control of bark and wood debris, including proper collection and disposal methods, should be used at log dumps, raft-building areas, and mill-side handling zones for both floating and sinking particles.
• Log dumps should not be located in rapidly flowing waters or other zones where control of bark and debris cannot be effective.
• Accumulations of bark and other debris on the land and docks around dump sites should be kept out of the water.
• Whenever possible, logs should not be dumped, stored, or rafted where grounding, particularly on sensitive habitats, will occur.
• Where water depths permit the floating of bundled logs, logs should be secured in bundles on land before being placed in the water. Bundles should not be broken again except on land or at the mill.
• The inventory of logs in water for any purpose should be kept to the lowest possible number for the shortest possible time.

Additional site-specific measures can be applied to a particular operation to ensure protection of aquatic habitats (Toews and Brownlee 1981), depending on the specific resources present and the details of the operation. A technical assessment of a log-handling proposal might therefore include the following considerations.

• Site sensitivity and uniqueness: (a) resource values present (e.g., shellfish, herring spawn, emergent vegetation, salmonid rearing); (b) physical characteristics of site (e.g., substrate, depth, currents, tidal flushing).

• Details of proposal: (a) dumping, sorting, and transport methods; (b) log volumes and inventory, seasonal log flow; (c) duration of operation (usually related to upland logging); (d) positive debris-control measures (recovery and disposal of both floating and sinking debris).

• Potential effects based on the above considerations for both proposed and alternative sites (alternative sites may include those on dry land).

Chapter 10

Processing Mills

R. N. Thut and D. C. Schmiege

Many pulp and paper mills in North America are located on tidal estuaries or rivers flowing into marine or estuarine waters. Resident and anadromous salmonids can come into contact with mill effluents during at least part of their life cycles. Whether or not the effluents affect the fish depends on several factors. The most important of these are the level of treatment provided by the mill and dilution by the receiving water.

Considerable technological progress in the past decades has reduced the harmful effects of pulp and paper mill effluents. Modern mills that meet federal and local requirements for pollution abatement differ substantially from the mills that operated 20 or 30 years ago. At present, virtually all mills in the USA and many mills in Canada practice primary and secondary treatment. There are in-mill process modifications that can also reduce pollutant levels. This approach has been emphasized in other parts of the world.

In reviewing the substantial literature on the environmental effects of pulp and paper mill effluents, studies of untreated or primary-treated effluent must be distinguished from studies of secondary-treated effluent. Most of the older literature (pre-1970) and most of the European literature consider untreated or primary-treated effluents and consequently are of limited usefulness in making an assessment of most North American facilities. A well-operated biological treatment system can substantially reduce the concentrations of pulp and paper mill pollutants. For example, biochemical oxygen demand (BOD) is generally reduced by 85–95% and resin acid concentrations are often reduced by 70% or more.

Pulp and paper mills are large users of water. A mill of average size could use and discharge 100,000 m^3/d, equivalent to the domestic discharge by cities with a population of over a hundred thousand. Consequently, these mills are almost always located on rivers of large size or on estuaries or marine waters where tidal flushing can afford an adequate degree of dilution.

Pulp and paper mill effluents are complex, containing many kinds of organic and inorganic compounds. They can cause several kinds of environmental effects if the concentrations exceed the appropriate biological thresholds. Effects on salmonids and other fish may be either direct or indirect. The direct effect most studied is toxicity, either lethal or sublethal. The fish can also be affected indirectly through the food web. The environmental effects can be inhibitory or stimulatory. For example, algae can be stimulated by the nutrients in an effluent but inhibited by toxicants or color.

Influences of Forest and Rangeland Management on Salmonid Fishes and Their Habitats
American Fisheries Society Special Publication 19:369–387, 1991

This chapter addresses each of the major pollutant categories and the environmental effects attributable to each, then examines field studies in the vicinity of pulp and paper mills. Such studies can provide an assessment of the integrated effect of the various pollutant categories.

Conventional Pollutants

There is a group of pollutants whose discharge is subject to guidelines promulgated by the U.S. Environmental Protection Agency (EPA). For the pulp and paper industry, the most important of these conventional pollutants are BOD and total suspended solids (TSS). These are specifically regulated because large quantities of BOD and suspended solids are discharged by mills and problems were caused in some localities before the implementation of the guidelines. Regulatory agencies in other countries also emphasize BOD and TSS control.

Treatment of pulp mill effluents is largely directed to removing conventional pollutants and is characterized as primary or secondary. Primary treatment involves the removal of suspended solids from an effluent by gravity. This can be accomplished in a simple quiescent settling basin or it can be accelerated by various mechanical or chemical techniques. In secondary treatment, organic constituents are broken down by bacteria and other microorganisms. This is accomplished in aerated basins or in similar, but faster-acting, systems called activated sludge reactors.

Biochemical oxygen demand is a measure of the readily degraded organic constituents in an effluent or water sample (generally over a period of 5 d). The primary effect of excessive BOD in a receiving water is low dissolved oxygen concentration. Almost all pulp and paper mills in the USA are now required to meet or exceed the EPA standards. Those few mills not required to meet the standards discharge into marine waters where high dilution reduces the likelihood of any environmental impact. If the BOD in a discharge is at guideline levels but still causes the dissolved oxygen in the receiving water to fall below a state's water quality standard, the amount of BOD permitted is decreased to assure the standard is not violated. This quantity is determined by waste load allocation modeling for projected worst-case conditions (i.e., low flow and high temperature). Most regulatory authorities require or are in the process of requiring every discharger of BOD to conform with this policy. The net result will be to maintain dissolved oxygen concentrations at or above state standards at virtually every time and place.

Before primary treatment was practiced, discharge of suspended solids, primarily cellulose fibers, was a significant problem at some locations. Fibers occasionally settled to form large deposits; sometimes they became entangled in fishing nets. With primary and secondary treatment, the fibers are removed, but biosolids are discharged. Biosolids are those bacteria (or bacterial remains) that account for BOD reduction in biological treatment systems. They are small (generally less than 5 μm) and up to 40% protein (Costa et al. 1979; Stengle et al. 1979). Depending on the process used to produce the paper, the suspended solids may also contain clay or other inert coating materials (Zanella et al. 1978).

Because of their small size, biosolids are essentially nonsettleable. When biosolids were tagged with ^{14}C, 95% of the total remained in suspension in a slow-flowing stream (Costa et al. 1980). At typical levels of dilution (50:1 to 100:1), biosolids affect turbidity only slightly. In most receiving waters, the increase in turbidity caused by a pulp-mill discharge would be 1 NTU (nephelometric turbidity unit) or less (Lee et al. 1978).

In the receiving environment, most biosolids are biodegraded, but some enter directly into the food chain leading to fish. In the ^{14}C study by Costa et al. (1980), biosolids appeared in the guts of filter-feeding caddisfly (Trichoptera) and black fly (Simuliidae) larvae. In a laboratory experiment by Zanella et al. (1978), *Daphnia* sp. survived and reproduced on a diet made up solely of biosolids; caddisfly larvae ate the biosolids but needed supplementary food types to survive. Even at very high concentrations of biosolids (>5,000 mg/L), salmonids can survive in a 96-h bioassay. Growth studies of up to 12 d showed no significant effect on salmonids at the highest biosolid concentration tested, 20 mg/L (Costa et al. 1979).

Bark and Wood Debris

Bark and other woody debris can enter the aquatic environment from log handling and log processing. Particles of bark and wood come mainly from hydraulic barkers and from transfer operations between ships and shore facilities. Log-transfer sites often contain heavy accumulations of bark and other woody debris (Schaumburg 1973). Many facilities now have settling and skimming devices to control the escape of such material and have replaced hydraulic barkers with mechanical barkers. Bark can also slough off logs during raft transport and storage (Sedell et al. 1991, this volume).

Bark and wood debris can cause long-term effects on the aquatic environment. As these materials settle and begin to cover the bottom, the benthic fauna can be killed or forced to move. Fish that normally feed on or near the bottom may also find the area unattractive and move elsewhere. As the organic materials decompose, the dissolved oxygen may be exhausted and hydrogen sulfide may be produced. Although these conditions do not occur often, they can be a matter of concern in inlets and other restricted locations that are poorly flushed.

Farther upstream, bark accumulations may contaminate salmon spawning grounds (Servizi et al. 1968). The oxygen demand of bark is great enough and of long enough duration that eggs can be killed. Fine bark particles can also clog the gravel, causing egg mortality. Servizi et al. (1968) estimated bark concentrations of 4% and more were likely to increase egg-to-fry mortality because of oxygen depletion. Fry emergence could be retarded at bark concentrations as low as 1%.

Leachates from logs and other wood debris in or near the water can affect the aquatic environment. The leachates contain wood sugars and other biodegradable materials that can exert a biochemical oxygen demand. Even though bark leachates contain toxicants, leachates from logs in natural waters have little toxic effect (Schaumburg 1973).

In a study of wood-room effluents (where logs are processed before they are sawed or chipped), Howard and Leach (1973) found that leachates from softwood species tended to be more toxic than leachates from hardwood species. Extracts of Sitka spruce bark were toxic to pink salmon fry, shrimp *Pandalus borealis*, and larval Dungeness crab *Cancer magister* (Buchanan et al. 1976). Toxic effects on salmon fry were observed as soon as 3 h after exposure to both western hemlock and spruce bark extracts. Spruce bark extracts were about half as toxic to the fry as those from hemlock. In contrast, hemlock extracts had little effect on the invertebrates tested but spruce extracts were consistently toxic to them.

Extracts from western redcedar, in particular a group of chemicals called tropolones, are also toxic. In a study of western redcedar extracts (Peters et al. 1976), coho salmon fry were the most sensitive of the organisms or life stages tested and the invertebrates were among the least. The authors concluded that leachates from cedar debris in landfills or cedar log decks could be an environmental concern.

Color

One readily apparent characteristic of pulp and paper mill effluents, particularly those from bleached paper mills, is an often intense brown color. The compounds responsible for the color are derived from the lignin in the wood (Dugal et al. 1976) and are related to the compounds causing color in swamps and bogs. These color compounds are relatively stable and degrade slowly in both biological treatment systems and receiving waters.

In addition to aesthetic degradation, color substances are likely to affect photosynthesis by aquatic plants. This is a complex issue because plant production can be inhibited by toxicants as well as by color and stimulated by nutrients in the effluent. Attempts have been made to distinguish these factors in the laboratory or in controlled chambers in the field and to determine thresholds of color effect (e.g., Soniassy et al. 1977; Howard et al. 1979). Results have been inconsistent and additional field or modeling studies in this area are warranted.

The color compounds of pulp and paper mill effluents strongly absorb wavelengths between 400 and 500 nm (Stockner and Cliff 1976). This part of the spectrum is important to aquatic plants for photosynthesis. It coincides with one of two absorbance peaks for chlorophyll *a* and most peaks for the accessory pigments.

Phytoplankton production measured by Stockner and Cliff (1976) near the marine discharge of a bleached kraft mill in British Columbia was reduced to a tenth of that measured at a control station. The effects were much less at a greater distance from the outfall and at other mills that discharged to better-flushed receiving waters. In spite of this decrease in production, the standing crop of phytoplankton (as measured by numbers and chlorophyll *a*) was not affected in the vicinity of the outfall. Stockner and Cliff concluded that this demonstrated the significance of light and the absence of a toxic effect. The phytoplankton became metabolically inactive while in the effluent plume but returned to normal activity once they were dispersed out of the plume.

Algae have some ability to adapt to high levels of color caused by pulp and paper mill effluents. Three species of marine phytoplankton adapted to and exhibited normal growth in relatively high concentrations of mill effluent. Stockner and Costella (1976), who conducted this experiment, concluded phytoplankton in eutrophic marine waters would not be seriously affected if untreated kraft and newsprint effluents did not constitute more than 30–40% of the receiving water.

Nutrients

Elevated concentrations of nitrogen and phosphorus can be found in treated pulp and paper mill effluents. The prevalent forms are generally ammonia, orthophosphate, and particulate nitrogen and phosphorus. The primary source of these nutrients is the wood used as the raw material. Nitrogen and phosphorus are added to some secondary treatment systems to enhance the removal of BOD.

At low effluent concentrations (at which inhibition due to high color or toxicants would not be a factor), algal growth can be enhanced by these nutrients in an effluent (Stockner and Costella 1976). Similarly, algal bioassay results often show growth inhibition at high effluent concentrations and stimulation at low concentrations. Walsh et al. (1982) found increasing production of the alga *Skeletonema costatum* at concentrations of pulp mill effluent up to about 25% and a marked decline at greater concentrations.

Algal enhancement by effluent nutrients is most likely in shallow streams, where the effects of color on light attenuation are slight. In experimental, continuous-flow troughs simulating shallow streams, the rate of attached algae accumulation increased with each increment of secondary-treated bleached kraft mill effluent from 0.5 to 25% (Bothwell and Stockner 1980).

Either nitrogen or phosphorus can be the primary agent causing algal enhancement, depending on background water quality. In flowing waters, the concentrations of nutrients at which maximum growth occurs can be very low. Growth rates of attached algae in the Thompson River, British Columbia, saturated at orthophosphate concentrations less than 1 µg/L and algal biomass reached maximum levels at 5–25 µg/L. Reductions in point-source loading of phosphorus to this system would have to be very thorough in order to achieve significant reductions in algal growth (Bothwell 1987).

Toxicity

It has been known at least since Ebeling's (1931) work in Sweden that effluents from pulp and paper mills may be toxic to fish and other aquatic animals. Effluents from kraft, sulfite, and other types of mills are complex mixtures. The toxicity of mill effluents can result from the combined activity of several chemicals, some of which have not yet been identified.

The difficulty of separating effects of chemical toxicity from effects of BOD, and the inability to identify chemical constituents of effluents responsible for toxicity, have complicated studies in the past. However, the development and testing of reproducible bioassay procedures and extraordinary advances in analytical chemistry have changed the situation. Simple, accurate, and sensitive biological assessments are now possible (Walden 1976). Laboratory bioassays have been used to predict toxicity under conditions found in natural ecosystems.

Toxic Constituents

Several hundred organic compounds have been identified from pulp mill effluents. The most common are simple sugars, acids, and aldehydes that contribute to BOD but have little effect on toxicity. Acute lethal toxicity can generally be attributed to the resin and fatty acids. As an example, Leach and

Thakore (1973) attributed over 80% of the total acute toxicity of a pulping effluent to three resin acids and most of the remainder to fatty acids. Chlorinated compounds, particularly chlorinated phenolics, and resin acids are often implicated when sublethal effects occur.

The lethal thresholds for these compounds are in the low parts-per-million range. The 96-h LC50 (the concentration lethal to half the test organisms in 96 h) ranges from 0.4 to 1.7 mg/L for resin acids, from 1.5 to 8.2 mg/L for fatty acids, and from 0.2 to 2.8 mg/L for chlorinated phenolics (McLeay et al. 1986). Sublethal thresholds for the resin acids and chlorinated phenolics are much lower, usually below 0.1 mg/L (McLeay et al. 1986) and sometimes below 0.01 mg/L (Tana 1988).

In an EPA study of 48 U.S. pulp mills (Dellinger 1980), the total concentration of the four major resin acid types in treated effluent ranged from 0 to 1.46 mg/L (weighted mean, 0.19 mg/L) and the total concentration of fatty acids ranged from 0.01 to 0.73 mg/L (weighted mean, 0.10 mg/L). Only two chlorinated phenolics were monitored in that study; most of the values were zero and no pulp mill category had values exceeding 0.004 mg/L. Other studies have detected higher levels of chlorinated phenolics in treated effluents. In a study of nine Canadian mills, the mean concentration of total chlorinated phenolics was 0.19 mg/L and the range was 0.06 to 0.32 mg/L (Kovacs et al. 1984).

Although the chlorinated phenolics have attracted the most attention, there are many other chlorinated compounds in treated pulp mill effluents. The most prevalent of these are the chlorinated acetic acids and chloroform (Lindstrom and Mohamed 1988). However, the toxicity thresholds for these compounds are orders of magnitude higher than for the chlorinated phenolics. Of the chlorinated organics specifically identified and studied, the types of functional groups and the degree of chlorine substitution appear to be the key determinants of toxicity (Voss et al. 1980; Kuivasniemi et al. 1985).

Measures of total organic chlorine (or an alternative test, adsorbable organic halide) in effluent have yielded values in the range of about 10 mg/L (Lindstrom and Mohamed 1988) to 30 mg/L (Bryant et al. 1987). Much of this chlorine (80–85%) is attached to polymeric lignin material with a molecular weight greater than 1,000. In this form, chlorine is not expected to be biologically active. However, little is known about its eventual fate in the receiving environment. Eriksson et al. (1985) demonstrated this high-molecular-weight material slowly decomposed to products that included various chlorinated phenolics. If the material settles, dechlorination is also possible. In the sediment at the bottom of a treatment lagoon, virtually complete dechlorination occurs due to a combination of aerobic and anaerobic microbial action (Bryant et al. 1987).

Analyses of pulp mill effluents have been conducted for the EPA list of priority pollutants. Concentrations of these pollutants are almost always low or below the detection limit (Turoski et al. 1983). The EPA regulates the discharge of priority pollutants via their BAT (best available technology) guidelines. Discharges of zinc and pentachlorophenol are regulated in this manner, but the use and discharge of these chemicals by the industry have been virtually eliminated through process changes and chemical substitution.

Recently, it has been discovered that 2,3,7,8-tetrachlorodibenzo-p-dioxin (TCDD) and 2,3,7,8-tetrachlorodibenzofuran (TCDF) are found in the effluents from some bleached-pulp facilities. The reason for the discovery at this time was not a change in bleaching practices, but greatly improved analytical capabilities. Concentrations in the low parts per trillion (pptr, 10^{-12}) and parts per quadrillion (ppq, 10^{-15}) can be detected in solid and liquid matrices, respectively. Results from only a few mills are available. In a cooperative study of five mills conducted by the EPA and the pulp and paper industry, the concentrations of TCDD ranged from nondetectable (at 3 ppq) to 120 ppq and the concentrations of TCDF ranged from nondetectable (at 7 ppq) to 2,180 ppq (Amendola et al. 1989). Because TCDD and TCDF are very hydrophobic, these compounds are largely adsorbed to the suspended solids in the effluent. Although their concentrations are very low, TCDD and TCDF are highly toxic to fish, and lethal and sublethal thresholds in pure solution occur in this same general concentration range. For example, the 56-d LC50 of TCDD for rainbow trout has been estimated at 46 ppq (46 pg/L: Mehrle et al. 1988). These toxicants also have a high propensity to bioaccumulate. Resident fish downstream from bleached pulp mills had body TCDD concentrations ranging from nondetectable (5 pptr) to 85 pptr (85 ng/kg: Amendola et al. 1989). In order to determine how representative these few values are and to fully assess the significance of the discharge of TCDD and TCDF, all of the bleached pulp mills in the USA and Canada are presently being studied. Studies to identify causative factors and in-mill or end-of-pipe solutions are also underway.

Three excellent reviews recently summarized what is known about the chemistry of toxic substances and other environmentally important pulp and paper mill pollutants. The in-mill origin and derivation of organic pollutants, particularly chlorinated compounds, was the primary topic addressed by Kringstad and Lindstrom (1984). Walden et al. (1986) discussed the biological impact and environmental fate of the key toxic groups in pulp and paper mill effluents. McLeay et al. (1986) provided a comprehensive review of both the chemical basis of toxicity and the laboratory and field studies that addressed toxic effects.

Toxicity Removal

Secondary treatment is an effective means of removing many of the toxicants from pulp mill waste streams. On the average, about 70% of the total resin acids and 90% of the total fatty acids are removed by secondary treatment (Dellinger 1980), and the net result of these reductions is an effluent that is not generally lethal to fish or other aquatic life. In salmonid and other fish bioassays, survival is usually 100% in undiluted effluent. Exceptions to this can be caused by spills within the mill or by treatment system malfunctions (Fisher 1982). In reviewing the literature on toxicity, it is important to distinguish between those bioassays conducted on secondary-treated effluents and those conducted on untreated or primary-treated effluents.

Secondary treatment is less effective on chlorinated compounds. From 20 to 40% of the total organic chlorine is removed (Bryant et al. 1987; Lindstrom and Mohamed 1988). Removal of the smaller, more biologically active compounds is somewhat more effective. About 35–40% of the chlorinated phenolics and 55–95% of the chlorinated acetic acids were removed in aerated lagoons studied by Lindstrom and Mohamed (1988). As a consequence of these lower removal efficiencies, secondary treatment is less effective in reducing sublethal toxicity than in reducing acute lethal toxicity.

Several kinds of treatment systems are used to process effluents. Aerated lagoons and extended activated sludge treatment have a history of effective toxicity removal, provided nutrients, oxygen, mixing, and pH are maintained at appropriate levels. High-rate (shorter-term) activated sludge treatment systems are also effective, but they must be managed more carefully to avoid toxicity shocks. Toxicity reductions of 90% are possible with these high-rate systems (Mueller et al. 1977). When treatment systems do fail, the most likely causes are liquor spills, pH variations, and thermal shocks (Walden and Howard 1974). Any change to a treatment system can affect its removal efficiency. Cooler temperatures in fall and winter can temporarily reduce removal efficiency until the microorganisms become adapted. The start-up of a mill (after a shutdown for maintenance or holidays) is also a critical time requiring careful management by the operator.

Lethal Toxicity

There is a substantial data base on the acute toxicity of pulp mill effluents. Many mills in North America are required to conduct periodic bioassays. Generally, the bioassays are 96 h in duration and use a fish species of local importance.

Several factors can affect bioassay results and recognition of this provides some insight into the effect of effluents in receiving waters. McLeay et al. (1979b) used 10 different fresh waters for dilution in a series of acute toxicity bioassays with rainbow trout and coho salmon. The toxicity of a bleached kraft mill effluent differed widely when bioassays were conducted at the normal pH of each dilution water. Bioassay values varied 3.5-fold; this was attributed primarily to pH effects, and secondarily to differences in concentrations of ionizable inorganic constituents. In general, acute toxicity was less at higher pH (up to pH 8.5–9.5). The toxicity of kraft mill effluent was identical in fresh and salt water if the pH was held at the same value (McLeay et al. 1979a). This observation is consistent with the earlier finding that inorganic constituents are of secondary importance in determining the toxicity of pulp and paper mill effluent in a receiving water.

Howard and Walden (1965) studied the toxicity of kraft process effluent streams to guppies and sockeye salmon in fresh water at neutral pH. As much as 75% of the mortality reported by previous authors was caused by an imbalance in pH. Fish were capable of acclimating to increasing concentrations of effluents in a few days. Test fish exposed to gradually increasing concentrations of effluent could survive at concentrations considerably higher than the values demonstrated as lethal in standard bioassays. Length of exposure, other stressors on the fish, pH and temperature of the water, age of the test fish, and many other factors can significantly affect the concentration thresholds necessary to cause fish mortality.

Although most acute bioassay tests are conducted for 96 h, studies of long-term survival have also been conducted. Juvenile coho salmon were exposed to secondary-treated bleached kraft mill effluent by McLeay and Brown (1979). The coho salmon survived for 95 d in 27% effluent and for 200 d in 5%; these were the highest concentrations tested.

On the Pacific coast, bioassays are most often conducted on salmonids, usually rainbow trout or coho salmon. As a group, the salmonids are more sensitive than most other fish species routinely used in bioassays (e.g., fathead minnow, golden shiner, bluegill). Invertebrate bioassays are being used more frequently to assess industrial discharges. The EPA has recently developed a bioassay method using the cladoceran *Ceriodaphnia dubia* to determine chronic effects. This test has appeared as a condition in some recent discharge permits. The oyster larvae bioassay and sediment bioassays with amphipods have been used to assess environmental impacts in marine or estuarine waters. Cladocerans are less sensitive than salmonids (Nikunen 1983) and oyster larvae are more sensitive (Woelke et al. 1972) when these tests are applied to pulp and paper mill effluents.

Sublethal Toxicity

Several types of sublethal tests have been conducted on pulp and paper mill effluents, including histological, physiological, behavioral, growth, and reproductive assessments of organisms exposed for periods ranging from a few hours to almost a full year. Several species of fish and invertebrates have been tested, although most of the work appears to have been done with salmonids. In these bioassays, the range of results is broad. Effect thresholds for effluents have been identified from less than 1 to 100%.

In Table 10.1, bioassay results for Pacific coast salmonids and invertebrates exposed to bleached kraft mill effluents (the most common mill type) are summarized. The most sensitive indicators of stress appear to be blood chemistry, fish behavior (attraction), and oyster larvae development; effect thresholds occur at concentrations of about 1% or less for either treated or untreated effluents. The thresholds for tests that integrate the effects of several factors are somewhat higher. For example, effects on salmonid growth occur over a concentration range of about 5 to 10% or more. In general, treated effluents have higher thresholds of effect than untreated effluents.

Several metabolic functions in fish have been studied in relation to short- and long-term exposure to pulp and paper mill effluents. Liver glycogen decreased and plasma glucose and lactate increased in juvenile coho salmon exposed to secondary-treated pulp mill effluent for 30–200 d; effects were noted at concentrations as low as 5% (McLeay and Brown 1979). In another study, reductions in liver glycogen could be induced by 30-d exposures to mixtures of resin acids and chlorinated phenolics (Oikari et al. 1984), suggesting that these pollutants could be the responsible agent in pulp mill effluents.

Pollution-induced stress can cause changes in red and white blood cell counts in fish. The white blood cell count decreased in rainbow trout and juvenile coho salmon exposed for 24 h to concentrations of primary-treated bleached kraft mill effluent at median threshold levels of about 4 and 7%, respectively. With secondary treatment, similar effects were not noted at concentrations of 90% (the highest concentration tested; McLeay and Gordon 1977). Similar results were found for both treated and untreated bleached sulfite mill effluents. Effect thresholds were 2–6% for untreated effluents and 56–72% for treated effluents (Fisher 1982). Other kinds of effluent had effect thresholds that were much lower. The thresholds for treated and untreated effluents from the chemimechanical pulping of spruce were 2 and 5%, respectively. The treatment system in this case was a high-rate reactor that is generally less effective at removing toxicants (Fisher 1982). Longer-term (300-d) exposures of rainbow trout to treated bleached kraft mill effluents produced no change in white blood cell count at concentrations up to 5% (the highest tested). Small changes in red blood cell count (both positive

TABLE 10.1.—Summary of sublethal effect thresholds for Pacific coast salmonids and invertebrates exposed to bleached kraft mill effluents. (Adapted from McLeay et al. 1986.)

Sublethal test response	Effluent treatment	Median effective concentration[a]
Salmonids		
Elevated blood chemistry	Untreated or primary	0.6%
	Secondary	<5%
Decreased blood cell count	Untreated or primary	3% to <12%
	Secondary	>90%
Increased cough frequency	Untreated or primary	11–20%
Temperature tolerance	Untreated or primary	5–8%
	Secondary	>25%
Swimming performance	Untreated or primary	8% to >14%
	Secondary	65–100%
Avoidance	Untreated or primary	<2.5–28%
	Secondary	32%
Attraction	Untreated or primary	0.1%
	Secondary	0.5–1%
Decreased growth of early life stages	Untreated or primary	3% to <25%
	Secondary	10%
Abnormal development of early life stages	Secondary	32%
Long-term survival	Untreated or primary	6% to >25%
	Secondary	1% to 91%
Invertebrates		
Oyster larvae development	Untreated or primary	1.8%
	Secondary	1.3%
Amphipod behavior	Untreated or primary	20%

[a] Percent of the test water that was effluent.

and negative) occurred in these effluents at concentrations above 1% (National Council of the Paper Industry for Air and Stream Improvement 1984). Similar changes in blood cell count were induced in fish by exposure to mixtures of resin acids (Oikari et al. 1984).

Respiratory effects have also been observed. Increased cough frequency has been noted for rainbow trout and sockeye salmon exposed to untreated bleached kraft mill effluent (Walden et al. 1970; Davis 1973), but there was no such response to secondary-treated bleached kraft mill effluent (Howard and Walden 1974). Other respiratory effects (e.g., reduced arterial oxygen tension and increased oxygen uptake rate) have been measured in fish exposed to untreated effluents and to pulp mill effluent components such as chlorinated phenolics and resin acids (Davis 1973; Nikinmaa and Oikari 1982). Similar studies of treated effluents are not available. Dehydroabietic acid (one of the more common resin acids) caused damage to the fine-ridged structure of gill lamellae of rainbow trout during 12- to 96-h exposures to concentrations as low as 70 μg/L (Howard and Monteith 1977).

The effects on the circulatory and respiratory systems described above could also account for the observed effects on swimming stamina. The swimming stamina of juvenile coho salmon was impaired at median concentrations of 8%

primary-treated bleached kraft mill effluent (McLeay and Howard 1977). With laboratory-simulated, secondary-treated bleached kraft mill effluent, the concentration threshold at which swimming stamina was affected was much higher, between 40 and 100%, depending on the level of treatment (Howard 1975).

Juvenile chinook salmon demonstrated an avoidance reaction to untreated kraft mill effluent at concentrations as low as 2.5% (Jones et al. 1956). Coho salmon appeared to be less sensitive. Thresholds for avoidance response were in the range of 14–28% for untreated bleached kraft mill effluent (Jones et al. 1956; Gordon and McLeay 1978). Avoidance of treated bleached kraft mill effluent by rainbow trout and coho salmon did not occur until concentrations reached or exceeded 32%. At very low concentrations, fish may be attracted to the effluent (Gordon and McLeay 1978). In laboratory tests of avoidance and preference, the color of the effluent may attract fish by providing the perception (to the fish) of greater cover.

Exposure to pulp mill effluents can also affect the ability of fish to withstand other stressors in the environment. The tolerance by coho salmon and rainbow trout of high temperatures or low dissolved oxygen concentrations can be affected by primary-treated effluents at concentrations of 5 to 8%. The threshold for secondary-treated effluents, however, is 25% or greater (Howard and Walden 1974; McLeay and Howard 1977; McLeay and Gordon 1978).

Other studies have examined the effects of pulp mill effluents on growth, reproduction, and production. These measures have the advantage of integrating the effects of several physiological and behavioral components. Many of these studies have been conducted in experimental channels, either indoors or outdoors.

Rainbow trout were exposed to treated bleached kraft mill effluent for almost a full year during each of 4 years in an experimental channel facility in Idaho (National Council of the Paper Industry for Air and Stream Improvement 1982, 1983, 1984, 1985). Effluent concentrations ranging from 1.3 to 5.1% had no substantial effect on fish production. Supplemental evaluation of histopathology and in-gravel incubation of eggs and larvae indicated no difference between control fish and fish exposed to the effluent. Water quality factors such as color (light attenuation) and nutrients played an important role in determining stream community response to effluent addition. At the lower effluent concentrations, inorganic nutrient stimulation of algal growth occurred. At the higher concentrations, light attenuation was a factor, but the organic nutrients stimulated heterotrophic production. Consequently, in spite of lower algal production, the invertebrate biomass was 25% greater in the treatment streams. At the higher effluent concentrations tested, rainbow trout production was increased by about 20%. Together with the increase in invertebrate biomass, there was a decrease in diversity; the Shannon–Weiner diversity index declined from 1.6 to 1.2 at the highest effluent concentration tested. Snails and clams were most abundant in the treatment streams and midge larvae were most abundant in the control streams.

Bioaccumulation

Some of the pollutants found in pulp and paper mill effluents can bioaccumulate in fish and other animal tissues. The route of entry can be through the water directly or via the food chain. The two most studied groups of mill effluent chemicals have been the resin acids and the chlorinated organics. The amount of these substances that accumulates in tissues is a function of the particular chemical species, the particular organism, the particular organ, and several environmental factors.

In several laboratory studies, fish have been exposed to known concentrations of pulp mill effluents or effluent constituents and the bioconcentration factor (BCF) has been determined. The BCF is the ratio of the concentration of a chemical in an organism to the concentration in the test solution or environment. For the resin acids, both sockeye salmon and rainbow trout have been studied (Kruzynski 1979; Oikari et al. 1982). The liver, brain, kidney, and plasma had the highest concentrations of resin acids with BCFs of 100 to 1,000. The muscle tissue and whole body samples had BCFs of only 10. One of the more important groups of chlorinated organics in pulp and paper mill effluents, the chlorinated phenolics, generally had similar BCFs. These chlorinated organics are found at the highest concentrations in fatty or liver tissue. The degree of bioaccumulation is related to the number of chlorine atoms on the organic molecule (Hattula et al. 1981). Two of the most common chlorinated organics in pulp and paper mill effluents are the chlorinated catechols and guaiacols. The guaiacols have much higher BCFs. The catechols have a more polar molecular structure than the guaiacols and apparently are more readily cleared from fish tissues (Landner et al. 1977). The chlorinated organics are quickly cleared if the fish are transferred to clean water (Landner et al. 1977; Renberg et al. 1980). Renberg et al. (1980) determined that about 75% of the accumulated chlorinated organics were cleared after 1 d in clean water and were below the limits of detection after 2 weeks. Consequently, a fish migrating through an area influenced by a mill discharge would eventually clear itself of these compounds. On the other hand, a resident fish would retain this chemical burden until it moved to another area.

Several field studies of bioaccumulation in the vicinity of pulp mill discharges have yielded results consistent with the laboratory studies (Oikari et al. 1980; Paasivirta et al. 1981; Voss and Yunker 1983). Resin acids and chlorinated phenolics have been found in fish tissues, and the higher concentrations occurred in fish captured nearer the discharge. Bioaccumulation of pulp mill pollutants in the food chain has been demonstrated in the laboratory by Seppovaara and Hattula (1977) and in the field by Paasivirta et al. (1980); the latter investigators tested phyto- and zooplankton, mollusks, and two fish species. Chlorinated phenolics were found in the tissues of these organisms, and higher concentrations of some compounds occurred in the fish. These results suggest that biomagnification through the food chain did occur. The concentration of these compounds in tissues is a function of the degree to which the effluent is diluted. In a study of two bleached kraft mills on the British Columbia coast, high dilution rates of the primary-treated effluents occurred (Voss and Yunker 1983). The concentrations of chlorinated phenolics were low or below the detection limit in fish muscle tissue and in several shellfish. Only liver tissue from chum salmon had significant concentrations; liver tissue from rockfish had concentrations below the detection limit.

Among effluent components that bioaccumulate in fish tissues, some cause taste and odor problems. Four groups of compounds (phenols, volatile hydrocarbons, resin acids, and reduced sulfur compounds) were identified as the major tainting contributors in a kraft mill effluent (Naishe and Brouzes 1980). Terpenes and their derivatives (Berg 1983), chlorinated organic acids, and neutral compounds (Paasivirta et al. 1983) have also been implicated.

The most striking characteristic of the tainting phenomenon is the very low threshold at which it can occur. For salmonids in kraft mill effluent, the tainting thresholds range from 0.2 to 3% (Shumway and Chadwick 1971; Whittle and Flood 1977; Gordon et al. 1980).

Tainting propensity is somewhat reduced by secondary treatment. Bleached kraft mill effluent impaired the flavor of rainbow trout flesh when concentrations were between 0.2 and 0.8% for untreated effluent and between 2.0 and 2.9% for treated effluent (Gordon et al. 1980). The off-flavors in fish flesh are reversible; if fish are transferred to clean water, the flavor returns to normal in a matter of days.

Field Studies

The most effective way to assess the impact of pulp and paper mill discharges on the environment is often through field studies. These studies are usually designed to compare the situation before and after an event, such as the construction of a mill or the implementation of an improved treatment method, or upstream and downstream from a discharge point. Almost invariably, however, there are factors that confound the investigator. In upstream–downstream studies, the substrate, current velocity, and other important variables are never exactly the same from place to place. Before–after studies encounter the problem of temporal variability (a problem that is particularly acute with anadromous salmonids). Consequently, the level of resolution with which pollutional effects can be discerned is rather coarse; only fairly substantial biological effects can be distinguished.

The environmental impact of a discharge depends on several factors, the most important of which is dilution via river flow or tidal displacement. Generally, the rivers and estuaries in western North America afford substantially greater dilution than is available in other parts of the continent. Under low-flow conditions, dilutions (at complete mix and near the outfall) of 50:1 to 100:1 are fairly common. Depending on the rate at which the effluent completely mixes, the concentration of effluent near the discharge will be considerably higher. The impact of an effluent is also affected by background water quality, including the presence of other industrial or municipal discharges.

Several field measures have been used to determine the effect of pulp and paper mill discharges. Ellis (1977) compared the efficacy for pulp mill discharges (using British Columbia data) of 20 field measurement techniques. He concluded that about two-thirds of the techniques provided "conclusive" evidence on the effects of the pulp mill discharges. Tests rejected included quantification of subtidal epibenthos and fixed algae, quantitative intertidal surveys, and zooplankton and phytoplankton counts. For a field investigation, a range of tests was recommended. The biological recommendations included quantification of subtidal infauna, installation of settling plates for macroorganisms, conduct of qualitative intertidal surveys, and determination of oyster condition factor.

Plume dispersion studies, for which a tracer such as rhodamine dye or some naturally occurring substance is placed in the effluent, are useful adjuncts to field surveys (Thut et al. 1980). Used in conjunction with effluent chemistry and bioassays, they can provide accurate assessments of ecological effects in specific parts of the receiving water. In addition, plume dispersion data allow more informed chemical and biological field sampling designs. Of the 11 mill effluents studied in this manner by Thut et al. (1980), 4 imposed statistically significant changes below their discharges in dissolved oxygen, 8 in color, and 3 in nutrients. Changes were not detected in pH, total suspended solids, and turbidity at any of the mills.

Effluents from pulp and paper mills can both stimulate and inhibit production. The remaining organic matter and the phosphorus and nitrogen in the effluents can increase the production of bacteria and algae. Total invertebrate production may respond accordingly. Invertebrate species composition can change, which may or may not affect the production of the higher life forms that feed on them. Fish populations can be affected directly by effluents (their response being death, debilitation, or avoidance) or indirectly via the food chain. Visible fish kills below pulp and paper mills are rare. Willard (1983) documented 14 such incidents in the USA from 1977 to 1981. Most of the fish kills could be associated with in-mill spills rather than with normal operations.

A substantial number of pulp and paper mill field surveys have been reported in the literature. This review emphasizes those conducted on rivers or marine waters in western North America. Many of these studies were conducted in the 1960s and 1970s before laboratory analyses of sublethal effects had been done or had received wide circulation. In the field studies, organisms were counted or weighed before and after an event or above and below a facility. If done well, such studies tell a resource manager if the size or species makeup of an aquatic community has been affected. However, it is not always clear from such studies what chemical or physiological mechanism is responsible for an observed effect.

In Sweden, Sodergren (1987) attempted to apply bioassay technology to receiving-water studies. In addition to laboratory bioassays and field surveys, several biochemical and histological tests were applied to fish captured in the vicinity of a pulp mill. The most intensively studied area was near a bleached kraft mill on the Baltic Sea. Fish and invertebrates, as well as water and sediment samples, were collected at several distances from the mill out to about 10 km, where the untreated effluent was diluted by more than 1,000:1. European perch, used as the test animals, were less abundant within 4 km of the mill discharge; perch larvae and fry were almost abundant at the outermost station. Gradients in several morphological and biochemical indices for field-caught fish were correlated with distance from the discharge, and there were some statistically significant deviations from normal even at the 10-km station. Levels of extractable organic chlorine in the fish and sediments also showed a gradient with distance from the mill. The authors concluded that lowered perch density and recruitment in the vicinity of the discharge were manifestations of the morphological and physiological disturbances caused by the mill effluent (Larsson et al. 1988). Bengtsson (1988) arrived at similar conclusions in a study of skeletal abnormalities in the fourhorn sculpin.

Although the European perch in Sodergren's (1987) Swedish study were adversely affected by the mill discharge, other fish species were affected differently. All fish were less abundant within 1.5 km of the discharge; however, eutrophication caused by the effluent resulted in a zone of high fish density 1.5–4 km from the discharge. The most abundant fish in this area were the ruffe and the roach (Neuman and Karas 1988). Differential responses by algae and mollusks were also observed (Sodergren 1987).

These studies have received considerable attention because of the very low effect thresholds noted for many of the biochemical and physiological tests. Effects were noted at effluent concentrations of 0.1% or less. These thresholds are much lower than those determined in almost all prior laboratory studies and model ecosystem studies. There are several explanations or possible explanations. The effluents were untreated. As noted earlier, secondary treatment reduces sublethal toxicity. In general, Swedish mills tend to be more efficient than North American mills in their use of water. Consequently, the effluents are somewhat more concentrated. In addition, the Baltic Sea has several other northern European pollution sources. Even background or control stations in the Baltic Sea probably have elevated levels of some pollutants. These could be reacting and interacting with the pulp mill effluents to give a magnified effect. In any event, studies in North America, following the example of the Swedish study, are clearly warranted.

Although the number of field studies conducted in western North America is limited, they do illustrate certain points. Studies of mills without secondary treatment often reveal environmental disturbances in the vicinity of the facilities.

Oysters and other invertebrates in Stuart Channel, British Columbia, were affected by the discharge of an untreated effluent from a bleached kraft, mechanical pulping, and newsprint facility (Nelson 1979). A commercial oyster fishery had been present there for many years; however, within 6 years after mill operations began, the quality of the fishery had deteriorated to the point where the oysters could not be marketed. The condition of the oysters was lowest near the outfall and became progressively better as samples were collected farther away (Davis et al. 1976). The number and diversity of other invertebrates were also lower near the discharge. At intermediate distances, however, the abundances of a polychaete worm and two species of amphipods were greater. Initially, the poor condition of the oysters was thought to be due to elevated zinc levels in the effluent. However, subsequent reductions in the amount of zinc discharged did not have a positive effect on oyster condition and the problem is now believed to be due to another contaminant from the mill (Ellis et al. 1981).

The effect of an untreated bleached kraft mill effluent on Howe Sound near Port Mellon, British Columbia, has been documented. Live-box studies within 350 m of the outfall demonstrated occasional acute lethal toxicity to Pacific herring and juvenile chinook, coho, and chum salmon (Birtwell and Harbo 1980). Vertically oriented avoidance–preference chambers placed near the outfall showed that juvenile salmon avoided the top 1 m of the water column (where the effluent had stratified). At more distant stations, the salmon preferred the upper layer (Birtwell 1977). In part due to the deposition of fiber, diversity and total numbers of subtidal benthic invertebrates were lower within 0.4 km of the outfall. The intertidal fauna was affected at greater distances; total numbers were lower up to 2 km from the outfall (Nelson 1979).

Studies have been conducted before and after the implementation of secondary treatment or other modifications that significantly reduce pollutant levels. A long series of studies has been conducted on Neroutsos Inlet on the west coast of Vancouver Island, British Columbia, where a sulfite mill has been operating since 1917. Since 1977, spent sulfite liquor has been collected and incinerated, and the effluent BOD has decreased about 70% as a result (Corbett et al. 1978). The improved effluent quality accounted for an increase in dissolved oxygen concentration of about 2 mg/L throughout the inlet. Previously, the dissolved oxygen concentrations had been less than 3 mg/L at times (Cross and Ellis 1981). Before the modification, live-box studies of juvenile coho and sockeye salmon demonstrated acute lethal toxicity near the outfall and, periodically, as far away as 4.7 km (Davis et al. 1978). Fewer outmigrant chum salmon were found within 2 km of the outfall. In in situ avoidance–preference chambers, juvenile chum salmon avoided the top 1 m (where the effluent was stratified) up to 10 km away. In unaffected areas, the salmon tended to prefer the uppermost layer. The avoidance was thought to be due to lower pH and dissolved oxygen (McGreer and Vigers 1980). After the modification, the zone of pulp mill influence substantially decreased. Fish in live boxes as close as 0.5 km from the outfall survived (Tokar et al. 1982) and the avoidance response was less pronounced (Cross and Ellis 1981). Plankton production and intertidal flora and fauna also improved, but the numbers and diversity of the organisms studied (gammarid amphipods, epifauna on kelp) were still greater farther from the outfall. The populations were depressed within a 4-km radius from the discharge point (Cross and Ellis 1981).

The Everett Harbor and Port Gardner areas of Puget Sound receive the effluents from several municipal and industrial discharges. At one time, two sulfite mills were the major volume sources of discharge in the area; the untreated wastes from these two mills were combined and dispersed through a deep-water diffuser. This discharge apparently had no effect on the numbers of English sole, the most important commercial fish species in the area (English 1967). Several life stages were investigated and observations were made on the incidence of parasites and disease. Over the years, treatment (or effluent dispersion) was improved or permanent closures occurred that significantly reduced pollutants entering the harbor. The BOD resulting from the pulp mills declined by 97% between 1974 and 1981. Studies were begun to determine the environmental effects of these major reductions in pulp mill pollutants (Clark 1986). In situ bioassays were conducted at six stations. At two stations, the water remained acutely lethal to four species of juvenile salmon, in one case apparently because of sulfides resulting from wood-chip sludge deposits, in the other because of the nearby bleached waste water discharge. Toxicity declined at one station near the former point of discharge of the pulp mill, which had ceased operations. As pollution declined, the invertebrate populations near one of the remaining discharges changed. Certain bivalves (e.g., *Nucula bellotii*) appeared for the first time and the numbers of two others (*Macoma carlottensis* and *M. elimata*) substantially increased. The numbers of gammarid amphipods declined, however. The investigators could not state with certainty that these changes resulted from closure of the pulp mill or from longer-term natural changes (Kisker 1986). Trend analysis showed significant declines in spent sulfite liquor concentrations and significant increases (although of small magnitude) in dissolved oxygen and pH. No trend in benthic species diversity could be shown (Determan 1986).

Even with secondary treatment, environmental problems can occur below a pulp mill if the receiving water is inadequately flushed or provides little dilution, or if the treatment system is substandard. The effects of a newsprint bleached kraft pulp mill at the head of Alberni Inlet in British Columbia have been studied for over 20 years (Parker et al. 1972). The secondary-treated effluent, when discharged into the inlet, is confined largely to the upper layer of a salinity-stratified system. Dissolved oxygen concentrations in the lower layer have reached very low levels (5% of saturation) because effluent color attenuates light, thereby affecting photosynthesis. As a consequence, the numbers of salmonids are much higher in the surface layer even though the effluent is found there. Within this surface layer, salmonid numbers close to the discharge point are not significantly different from those farther away (Birtwell et al. 1983). In situ, vertically oriented avoidance–preference chambers have shown that juvenile chinook salmon avoid the lower layer (Birtwell 1978; Birtwell and Harbo 1980). When juvenile chinook salmon were placed in this lower layer (at 4 m) in live boxes, mortality was 83%; mortality was 25% in the surface layer. No such differences were found within the surface layer as a function of distance from the outfall. This inlet is the migration route for sockeye, chinook, coho, and chum salmon. No evidence was found that salmon runs had declined as a result of the pulp mill (Parker et al. 1972). The number and diversity of benthic invertebrates increased with increasing distance from the outfall. Nelson (1979) postulated that light attenuation and fiber deposits may have contributed to the lower invertebrate numbers and diversity closer to the outfall.

The secondary-treated effluent of a bleached kraft mill had a significant effect on the benthic community of the Kootenay River in British Columbia (Derkson and Lashmar 1981). Fewer pollution-sensitive invertebrates (such as mayfly and stonefly nymphs) were found below the mill than above. In addition, increases in periphyton standing crop and changes in algal species were found below the mill. The treatment system at this mill has since been improved.

Both freshwater and estuarine benthic communities were monitored near a treated unbleached kraft mill on the Kitimat River in British Columbia (Derkson 1981). The effluent was a considerable portion of the total river flow (up to 5% in the worst case). The freshwater benthic community was somewhat affected; however, the estuarine benthic community farther downstream did not substantially change after the mill began operations.

Grays Harbor, an estuary in Washington, was the subject of a joint agency–industry study in 1974 (Washington State Department of Ecology 1975). Two sulfite mills and a paper mill discharged treated effluents into the estuary along with several other municipal and industrial discharges. Several kinds of bioassays were conducted on downstream-migrating salmon between May and July. One test period included a holiday shutdown of the mills. Continuous-flow bioassays conducted on a barge revealed higher mortality of chinook salmon late in the test period (18%) than early in the test period (5%). During the shutdown, mortality was 5%. No mortalities occurred among the other species tested (coho salmon, steelhead, and cutthroat trout). Downstream-migrating coho and chinook salmon were studied in live-boxes. Mortality of chinook salmon late in the study period was 30% higher than in the shutdown period. Swimming stamina of chinook salmon also declined late in the study period. The investigators concluded that the pulp mill effluents probably had some effect on the chinook salmon (either directly or from lower dissolved oxygen), but other natural factors (higher temperature, lower salinity, and some *Vibrio* infections in the test fish) helped to exacerbate the problem.

Receiving-water studies in the vicinity of some mills have shown little or no environmental impact. Often this can be associated with high river flow or tidal flushing or to high-quality effluents that meet or exceed current standards. The Sacramento River above and below the discharge of a bleached kraft mill was studied from 2 years before to 16 years after the mill began operating (Zanella and Weber 1981). During the 18 years, treatment changed from only primary to activated sludge to aerated stabilization basins. After the basins were installed, the final effluent demonstrated low and infrequent toxicity (as determined by acute lethal fish and sublethal fish egg bioassays). Benthic surveys were conducted during the 18 years at 12 stations above and below the mill. No significant changes in number of taxa or total number of invertebrates were detected during the study or when stations were compared with one another.

A 140-km stretch of the lower Columbia River was studied by Young et al. (1981). Within this stretch, six pulp and paper mills discharge secondarily treated effluent. Other industrial and municipal discharges occur as well. The water quality of this part of the river was generally high. Occasionally, dissolved oxygen concentrations fell below the water quality standard, but these did not appear to be related to any specific discharge. Based on mass balance calculations, the effect of the mill discharges on water quality at low flow was estimated. Of the variables measured, calculations showed that ultimate BOD (1-mg/L increase), color (1- to 4-unit increase), and copper and zinc (0.5-μg/L increase) would be affected. Nitrogen, phosphorus, iron, manganese, and mercury would not be affected. Phytoplankton analyses indicated the presence of a healthy, moderately productive assemblage that indicated no shift to eutrophic conditions. Coliform bacteria were below the applicable water-quality standards.

A study of the effect of three bleached kraft mills on the upper Fraser River began in 1963; data were collected for 3 years before and 5 years after the mills became operational (Stone et al. 1974). Benthic invertebrates were collected above and below the mills, and the specimens were categorized as pollution-sensitive, pollution-tolerant, or intermediate. The benthic fauna had a fairly low productivity and showed considerable natural variation. No apparent changes in the proportions of the three categories were attributed to the pulp mills. Nutrients in the effluent caused an increase in population densities, but the pollution-sensitive species were still present.

Summary and Conclusions

Pulp and paper mills discharge some of the largest volumes of effluent among all the industries. Consequently, the potential exists for considerable environmental impact. Most pulp mills in North America now practice both primary and secondary treatment. Much of the older literature and much of the European literature report the environmental effects of untreated effluents; the information is of limited value for assessments of modern North American facilities.

Twenty years ago, most of the concern about pulp mill effluents was centered on low dissolved oxygen caused by BOD discharges and accumulations of settleable solids such as wood fibers. With a few exceptions, these difficulties have been largely obviated; however, if effluent concentrations exceed the appropriate thresholds, other environmental effects of consequence can arise.

Algae, at the base of the food web, can be either stimulated or inhibited by pulp mill effluents. Nitrogen, phosphorus, and other nutrients in effluents have caused increased algal production in some flowing-water systems. Color, toxicants, or both have been responsible for reductions in phytoplankton production in estuarine and marine systems.

Instances of acute lethal toxicity of treated effluents to fish or invertebrates are rare and can usually be traced to accidental spills or to some other operational malfunction. Recently, several kinds of sublethal tests have been applied to pulp mill effluents. Thresholds of effect have been identified for both treated and untreated effluents. Although treatment generally reduces sublethal toxicity, effects can still be found at treated effluent concentrations ranging from less than 1 to 100%. The significance of these sublethal effects is a function of instream waste concentration, duration of exposure, and the nature of the biochemical, physiological, or behavioral effect being measured.

Field measures of the environmental effects of pulp mill discharges have yielded a wide range of results. Untreated effluents or primary-treated effluents often cause reductions in the population size or the general health of important species. Biochemical and physiological effects have been noted that may translate into reduced reproduction or growth. Secondary-treated effluents have lesser effects. In some field studies, no measurable biological effect could be discerned. However, even secondary-treated effluents of high quality can cause an environmental effect if dilution is poor or if some other special circumstance occurs (e.g., stratification of the effluent). Population numbers of indigenous species may be reduced, organic or inorganic enrichment may occur, and more tolerant plant or animal species may proliferate.

Chapter 11

Livestock Grazing

W. S. Platts

Public range and forest lands are managed for multiple uses. The quality of this management influences the quality of the riparian environments of streams and, consequently, the productivity of stream fisheries. Behnke (1977) believed that the best opportunity for increasing populations of resident fish species in western North America is to improve riparian habitats that have been adversely modified by livestock grazing. I agree with his statement and believe that anadromous fish habitats could also be improved. Many streams in the west are in their present degraded condition partly because many small annual effects have accumulated to become major detriments to fisheries; western streams reflect a century of these cumulative effects. Today's land managers not only must administer their own grazing programs properly, but they must also correct the mistakes of the past.

The range environment includes 485.6 million hectares in the USA. Sixty-nine percent of this rangeland was grazed by livestock in 1970, furnishing 213 million animal unit months of forage (the forage required to sustain one cow for 1 month). Much of this rangeland has become depleted of natural and desirable vegetation, adversely affecting runoff and altering sediment recruitment and transport to and within streams. Even though livestock use on western ranges has passed the 100-year mark, the importance of grazing effects on aquatic resources is just beginning to be understood (Figure 11.1). Research has not fully identified these problems, described their magnitude, or provided methods for their solution. Consequently, resource managers have insufficient information to help them correct problems as they become apparent.

This chapter discusses rangeland history, condition, and management as they relate to fishery needs and productivity. Rangeland grazing strategies are evaluated and interpreted to assist fishery and range specialists in their efforts towards better rangeland management.

Grazing History

Before the immigration of Europeans into North America, natural ecosystems existed in which wild ungulates usually grazed within the carrying capacity of the range. If forage produced by a given range suddenly became scarce or nonexistent, wild grazing animals either moved to more favorable ranges or perished, bringing populations into balance with range capacity.

The early settlers recognized that the vast rangelands could be used for livestock production, and increased grazing soon altered or eradicated natural

389

FIGURE 11.1.—Fish and cattle share parts of the same ecosystem.

vegetation on much of our rangeland (Alderfer and Robinson 1947; Lusby et al. 1971; Sartz and Tolsted 1974; Behnke 1983). Livestock are attracted to the riparian areas (areas that border aquatic zones and show an influence of water that is not normally found in adjacent uplands), and these habitats soon became overused.

As the livestock industry grew through the 19th century and well into the 20th, the number of animals increased far beyond the carrying capacity of the available range. Serious concern about overgrazing of National Forest lands developed in the late 1920s, but little attempt was made to control grazing and detrimental effects continued to occur. By 1930, ranges were in poor condition and the U.S. Forest Service's Grazing Service (predecessor of the U.S. Bureau of Land Management) and the U.S. Soil Conservation Service were created. One of their chief responsibilities was range rehabilitation. Nevertheless, the situation had become so critical by the mid-1930s that Congress enacted the Taylor Grazing Act in 1934 to reverse the trend on public rangeland and help stabilize the livestock industry.

Where the ranges were heavily stocked and livestock were confined within barriers, the vegetation changed. Livestock trampled and compacted the soil, and the high-quality, fibrous-rooted plants gradually gave way to shallow-rooted annual species or taprooted perennials that could grow in areas with lowered water tables. As soil compacted and favorable ground cover diminished, infiltration of water into deep soils lessened and surface runoff increased (Johnston 1962; Tromble et al. 1974; Heady 1975; Stoddart et al. 1975; Hibbert 1976; Winegar 1977). Accelerating erosion seriously affected terrestrial and aquatic productivity. Rich topsoil was lost by the erosive action of wind and water, and the quality of streams receiving the eroded material was reduced. Fine sediment smothered the spawning and rearing habitats of fish. Many riparian habitats were converted from trees, to brush, to herbaceous grasses, and finally to bare soil.

By the mid-1960s, management by allotment (designated areas that fit the needs of the livestock operator to successfully graze animals) had become an accepted practice on pubic lands, and remains so today. Public awareness of environmental quality—including that of rangelands—brought into clearer focus the original goals of the Taylor Grazing Act. New approaches to range management were being considered during this period, such as those described by Johnson (1965) and Hormay (1970) who demonstrated that rest rotation grazing (rotation of nongrazing periods among pastures) can improve upland range. Livestock-grazing studies still focused on effects on forage and physical characteristics of watersheds; influences of grazing on aquatic ecosystems were still largely ignored.

In the 1970s, the importance of riparian vegetation to wildlife was becoming apparent (Patton 1977). Fishery biologists, however, were not well informed about grazing problems, and their contribution to the understanding of land management during this period was insignificant. Today, decision makers and fishery biologists see the need for better management of streamside areas, and scientists are undertaking studies of the interactions between livestock management and fish needs. These trends are encouraging and will lead to better management of livestock and fish habitat.

As the U.S. Forest Service, the U.S. Bureau of Land Management, the U.S. Soil Conservation Service, and private range owners instituted improved grazing practices, the ranges began to improve. Busby (1979) stated that range conditions today are far better than they were in the early 1900s. Platts (1981b) contended, however, that studies leading to this conclusion were based mainly on data collected from the drier upland ranges and usually did not take into account the still-deteriorated riparian areas. Riparian areas may have recovered some since 1930, but not nearly to the extent that overall range has improved. The main reason is that not enough emphasis was placed on riparian management; insufficient expertise (such as that of experienced fishery biologists, range conservationists, and watershed specialists) was available to identify habitat deterioration and to provide solutions, and people have only recently become concerned about riparian and fishery needs.

McGowan (1977) and Platts (1975, 1978, 1979a, 1981c) expressed doubts that present grazing strategies can solve the problem of grazing effects on riparian habitats. Sheep can convert forage to red meat without direct, significant effects on the riparian habitat (Figure 11.2), but they have been replaced by cattle on many grazing allotments. Cattle prefer to graze streamside environments; consequently, riparian areas now may be receiving heavier use than in the past.

Current Situation

Forums, seminars, symposia, workshops, and town hall sessions have been held throughout the USA to determine the current situation in riparian management. After a review of the publications from these meetings (Townsend and Smith 1977; Cope 1979; King 1980; Menke 1983; Warner and Hendrix 1984; Johnson et al. 1985), I conclude that riparian habitats on grazed lands are degraded; solutions to land-use problems causing the degradation are not easily

FIGURE 11.2.—Sheep grazing a high-elevation meadow.

found; the problems are most likely to be solved through an interdisciplinary approach; enough experience and knowledge exists to begin correcting the problems; and more research is needed to develop better understanding and provide solutions.

New Congressional acts, such as the Forest and Rangeland Renewable Resources Planning Act of 1974, call for increased demands on rangeland for the production of domestic livestock. With an expanding human population, the demand for red meat production may well increase in coming decades and more pressure will be placed on public ranges. Similar demands will also be placed on the production of fish for recreation and food. With stream riparian environments in need of improvement and with pressure to produce more forage, land managers are caught in the middle and forced to rely on grazing strategies that cannot maximize goals for production of both livestock and fish.

Because we do not completely understand cause and effect in livestock grazing and fisheries, controversy exists over what effects grazing has on streams and streamside environments. Some scientists maintain grazing causes no detrimental effects and others believe it does. The Council for Agricultural Science and Technology (1974) stated that livestock grazing is being managed and integrated with other uses of federal lands and that no evidence has been found that well-managed grazing by domestic livestock is not compatible with a high-quality environment. Hayes (1978) concluded that a rest rotation grazing system in the meadows studied did not significantly accelerate stream-channel movement. Kimball and Savage (1977) concluded that unrestricted livestock grazing can be detrimental to riparian zones because of streambank trampling and overuse of streamside vegetation but that, under intensive livestock management, aquatic ecosystems can be restored or maintained at a lower cost than would be required to install artificial stream-improvement structures. Gifford (1975) discussed some beneficial effects of range-improvement practices on runoff and erosion. The literature well demonstrates, however, that improper livestock grazing degrades streams and their riparian environments (Meehan and Platts 1978). The solution, therefore, is to determine how best to manage streamsides so that forage can be used and the fishery protected.

Because scientists still differ in their interpretation of the effects of grazing strategies on streams and riparian habitats, resource management is complicated. These disagreements must be resolved, because additional pressure is being applied to land managers to increase the production of all resources. Projected needs call for an additional 28.3 million hectares of range within the next 25 years to meet the demands for red meat (Council for Agricultural Science and Technology 1974), but the area of grazing land is continually being reduced by agricultural conversion, urbanization, and other land uses. The increasing demands for energy development, recreation, and high-quality water will all conflict with the demand for red meat unless management can be made more effective.

The solution to the livestock–fishery issue is certainly not to argue whether livestock grazing degrades riparian and aquatic systems, but to identify and develop grazing strategies that are compatible with fish habitat productivity. In an extensive literature review, Meehan and Platts (1978) were unable to identify any widely used grazing strategy compatible with the environmental needs of aquatic ecosystems. The task of modifying existing grazing strategies or developing new ones will be difficult. The problem becomes more complex when range-management practices other than grazing alter streams and streamside environments. These practices include fertilization of lands; irrigation; drainage of wetlands; brush, forb, and pest control; debris disposal; mechanical treatment of soil; seeding; prescribed burning; water supply development; fencing; and timber thinning.

Effects of Grazing on the Environment

Livestock grazing can affect the riparian environment by changing, reducing, or eliminating vegetation, and by actually eliminating riparian areas through channel widening, channel aggrading, or lowering of the water table (Figure 11.3). Riparian zones are often grazed more heavily than upland zones because they have flatter terrain, water, shade, and more succulent vegetation (Holscher and Woolford 1953; Armour 1977; Duff 1983; Platts and Nelson 1985c). Streams modified by improper livestock grazing are wider and shallower than they would have been normally (Duff 1983; Marcuson 1977; Platts 1979a; Van Velson 1979; U.S. Bureau of Land Management 1974; Platts et al. 1985a). Generally, in grazed areas, stream channels contain more fine sediment, streambanks are more unstable, banks are less undercut, and summer water temperatures are higher than is the case for streams in ungrazed areas; therefore, salmonid populations are reduced (Armour 1977; Benke and Zarn 1976; Platts 1983).

FIGURE 11.3.—A heavily grazed stream reach with very unstable banks.

Effects of land use on aquatic systems are often difficult to detect because aquatic systems themselves are dynamic and hence naturally variable. Annual stresses may be so small that they go unnoticed until major problems occur, or conditions may be poor for so long that they are accepted as natural. Over time, accumulated small changes may be the most harmful to fisheries because these changes are difficult to detect with our present methods. Consequently, short-term management objectives do not adequately allow these effects to be detected, evaluated, or corrected. Whether a stream has suffered a catastrophic event, such as a flood that ripped out the channel and riparian vegetation, or has suffered through a long period of accumulated small degrading events, such as the gradual loss of its riparian vegetation, the end result for the fish may be similar.

Land managers and scientists have experienced frustration in dealing with complex range-management problems and the necessity of making decisions based on limited data (Miller 1972). The Natural Resources Defense Council in a 1973 lawsuit questioned the adequacy of a U.S. Bureau of Land Management (BLM) environmental impact statement, "Livestock Grazing Management of National Resource Lands," for protection of the environment. In the 1974 settlement of that suit, the BLM agreed to complete more than 200 separate environmental impact statements for livestock grazing on public lands in the western USA. This task has proven to be extremely difficult because data bases with sound interpretations have not been available to help in the planning and analysis stages.

Leopold (1975) said that livestock grazing may have cumulative ecological ill effects on productivity of both lands and waters. He admitted this hypothesis was intuitive, with few supporting facts, and pleaded for studies to clear up the issue. During the same period, the BLM reported that riparian and aquatic habitats were being damaged on BLM lands by improper livestock grazing (U.S. Bureau of Land Management 1974).

The Council for Agricultural Science and Technology (1974) assigned a national interdisciplinary team of 18 scientists to evaluate a court-requested environmental impact statement on range management on selected BLM lands. The team concluded that it would be futile for the BLM to predict future responses of other resources (fish, wildlife, recreation, water, and timber) to grazing management without a strong record of trends in range condition. In addition, the report said that many of the scientific declarations in the impact statement about adverse effects on grazing were made without substantiating data. The report implied that many disciplines make far-reaching, conclusive statements without background research to substantiate them. Nevertheless, Behnke and Zarn (1976) identified livestock grazing as the greatest threat to the integrity of trout stream habitat in the western USA. Saltzman (1977) stated that overgrazing and irrigation are the most serious and least understood ecological problems in the western states. Gallizioli (1977) reported that the single most important range-management problem limiting fish and wildlife benefits in Arizona was overgrazing by livestock. Bakke (1977) observed that loss of trout and salmon habitats from overgrazing has long been a frustrating problem in Oregon.

Importance of Streamside Vegetation

Most geologic processes that give shape to landforms, and in turn to streams, are measured in millions of years. The surrounding soils developed in thousands of years, and most soils are of no more than Holocene age. Plant associations around streams, however, can often be measured in only tens or hundreds of years. These plant associations, especially under human influence, are continually being modified, but because they respond to changes in management practices, the opportunity exists to convert present associations to more beneficial ones for fish. The response time of these rehabilitative changes depends on climatic conditions and soil fertility. Instant rehabilitation would be a foolish expectation; however, the vegetation component of certain streamside habitat types does respond more quickly to improved management practices than do other components such as bank morphology (Platts 1981a, 1981c, 1983). This response, in turn, speeds up the rehabilitation of other stream components, thus giving the land manager a tool with which to develop better streams. Because the vegetative component of certain riparian habitats can be manipulated quickly, immediate benefits to the fisheries often are less costly and much easier to obtain through vegetation rehabilitation than through channel changes or modifications.

Cover

The importance of cover to fish is well documented by the many studies that show a decline in salmonid abundance as stream cover is reduced (Boussu 1954) and an increase as cover is added (Hunt 1969, 1976; Hanson 1977). Binns and Eisermann (1979) found that cover was a highly significant determinant of fish biomass in Wyoming streams; as cover increased, fish populations increased. The

FIGURE 11.4.—A Great Basin stream with a narrow corridor of riparian habitat.

often narrow fringe of bordering riparian vegetation is essential for building and maintaining the steam structure necessary for productive aquatic habitats (Figure 11.4). This vegetation not only provides cover but buffers the stream from incoming sediments and other pollutants.

Trees, brush, grasses, and forbs each play an important role in building and maintaining productive streams. Trees provide shade and streambank stability because of their large size and massive root systems (Figure 11.5). As trees mature and fall into or across streams, they not only create high-quality pools and riffles, but their large mass also helps to control the slope and stability of the channel. In many aquatic habitats, if it were not for the constant entry of large organic debris (trees) into the streams, the channel would degrade and soon flow on bedrock, leaving insufficient spawning gravels and few high-quality rearing pools for fish (Platts et al. 1985a). Tree fall, or artificial addition of large organic debris, is therefore important and often essential for maintaining stream stability.

Brush not only protects the streambank from water erosion, its low overhanging height adds cover that is used by fish. Brush, like trees, builds stability in streambanks through its root systems and litterfall (Figure 11.6). Grasses form the vegetative mats and sod banks that reduce surface erosion and mass wasting of streambanks. Streamside vegetation needs to be vigorous and dense and to have enough species diversity that it can form layers over the ground. Each vegetative type plays an important role in forming and protecting the aquatic habitat (Platts 1983). Grasses and grass-like plants, especially the sod-forming types, help build and bind bank materials and reduce erosion. As well-sodded banks gradually erode, they create the undercuts so important as hiding places for salmonids. In

FIGURE 11.5.—A Great Basin stream with thick forested riparian habitat.

other situations, the root systems of grasses and other plants trap sediment to help rebuild damaged banks. All of these vegetative constituents of healthy streambanks can be damaged by improper grazing practices.

Streambank Stability

Natural surface erosion and mass wasting of streambanks occur over prolonged periods but usually in equilibrium with bank rebuilding processes. During the past century, we have upset this equilibrium by destroying the banks much faster than they can be rebuilt.

During floods, water moving at high velocity transports large amounts of sediment within streams. As it rises up and then over its banks, it flattens flexible streamside vegetation such as willows and grasses into mats that hug the streambank and adjacent ground. These mats reduce the water velocity along the stream edge, causing sediments to settle out and become part of the bank (Figure 11.7). Such deposition of sediments into the vegetative mats contributes nutrients to the bank soils and increases plant production and vigor. A compact mass of streambank vegetation can contribute substantially to the acquisition of sediments needed to build and maintain productive streambanks.

Streams of the intermountain and Pacific regions of North America are often icebound in the winter. When winter "chinooks" (spring thaws) arrive, the ice breaks up and starts to drift. The ice often forms shifting dams that force stream water from its channel. Where streamside vegetation is insufficient and protective mats are absent, the banks erode; grazing, by depleting vegetation, can accelerate this erosion (Platts 1981c).

FIGURE 11.6.—A Rocky Mountain stream with heavy willow-covered riparian habitat.

When animals graze directly on streambanks, mass erosion from trampling, hoof slide, and streambank collapse causes soil to move directly into the stream. The only way the streambank can remain in equilibrium is to trap enough sediment to rebuild itself. Because streams meander, some banks are subjected to more erosive force from water than are others; the centrifugal force of the water hitting the concave bank (the outside bank of the curve) causes velocity to increase, which in turn increases friction on the bank. All concave banks should be well vegetated with deeply rooted plants.

Stream Temperature Control

Streamside vegetation shades the stream and therefore influences water temperature. Summer stream temperature has probably increased in western streams over the past century as streamside vegetation has been reduced (Platts and Nelson 1989). This increase could partially explain the gradual shift from salmonids to nongame fish in many western streams. Nongame fish are generally more tolerant of higher water temperatures. In western North America, streams that have lost their riparian vegetation or have had a change in riparian plant forms (e.g., from brush to grass) are often too warm in the summer to support salmonid populations. Streams can also be too cold for successful trout survival. If winter temperature falls low enough, anchor ice can form on the bottom of the stream. Streams with little or no vegetative canopy are very susceptible to the formation of anchor ice.

Riparian vegetation intercepts and reduces the intensity of solar radiation and reduces back-radiation during cold months. It provides daytime cover in the form of shade, especially along the margins of a stream. Shaded streamside areas are preferred habitats of juvenile salmonids.

FIGURE 11.7.—A Rocky Mountain stream with heavily sodded banks.

The ability of plants to control stream temperature varies with their morphology. Grass crowns provide modest overhanging cover but grasses are too short to keep much solar radiation from reaching the water, except along very small streams (stream orders 1 and 2). The larger the stream, the higher the streamside vegetation must be to effectively intercept the sun's rays over water. On sixth- and seventh-order streams, only trees provide effective shading. On still larger streams, vegetation has little moderating effect on stream temperature. In small to medium-size streams (stream orders 3–5) brush is sufficient to moderate water temperature but grasses and forbs have little effect. Claire and Storch (1983) found that willow cover in an ungrazed area within a livestock exclosure provided 75% more shade to the stream than was found in the adjacent grazed area where willows were less abundant.

Production of Fish Prey

Streamside vegetation provides habitat for terrestrial insects, which are important food for salmonids and other fish species. This vegetation also directly provides organic material to the stream, which makes up about 50% of the stream's nutrient energy supply for the food chain (Cummins 1974). Removal of streamside vegetation can therefore affect the diet of fish by reducing production of both terrestrial and aquatic insects (Chapman and Demory 1963). Because soils in some watersheds, especially those of granitic parent material, provide insufficient nutrients to the stream, riparian vegetation assumes a major role in the production of fish food by providing habitat for terrestrial insects that fall directly into the stream. Detritus from incoming terrestrial plants is a principal source of

TABLE 11.1.—Summary of studies, and the conclusions drawn from them, of the responses of riparian habitats and fish populations to livestock grazing.

Author	Riparian condition			Fish populations		
	Improved	No change	Degraded	Increased	No change	Decreased
Berry and Goebel (1978)			X			X
Chapman and Knudsen (1980)			X			X
Claire and Storch (1983)			X			X
Dahlem (1979)			X	a		
Duff (1983)			X			X
Gunderson (1968)			X			X
Keller et al. (1979)			X			X
Kennedy (1977)			X			X
Lorz (1974)			X			X
Marcuson (1977)			X			X
Platts (1978)			X			X
Platts (1981a)			X			X
Platts (1981b)	X				X	
Platts (1981c)			X		X	
Platts et al. (1983)			X			X
Platts and Nelson (1985a)			X		X	
Starostka (1979)			X		X	
Storch (1979)			X			X
Van Velson (1979)			X			X
Winegar (1977)			X	a		
Winget and Reichert (1976)			X			X

[a] Fish populations not studied.

food for aquatic invertebrates that eventually become food for fish (Minshall 1967).

Effects of Grazing on Fish Habitats and Populations

The general consensus among investigators, as reported in the literature, is that improper livestock grazing degrades riparian and aquatic habitats, resulting in decreased production of salmonids. Twenty of the 21 studies summarized in Table 11.1 showed that stream and riparian habitats had been degraded by livestock grazing, and that these habitats improved when grazing was prohibited. These studies have biases in study design (discussed later) that could affect conclusions, but habitat studies are on more solid ground then are fish-response studies. Platts (1981b) was the only author who found that conditions may have improved with grazing, and this was on a well-managed sheep allotment (permitted grazing area) on which pastures were rested periodically and animals were herded to protect the riparian areas. Duff (1983) found that riparian vegetation biomass increased 63% in an exclosure (a fenced area from which livestock were excluded) along Big Creek, Utah, during 4 years of rest. Marcuson (1977) found that ungrazed sections of Rock Creek, Montana, had 82% more vegetative cover per unit of stream length than did grazed areas. Van Velson (1979) found remarkable increases in the amount of riparian vegetation adjacent to Otter Creek, Nebraska, once cattle grazing was eliminated.

In a study on Rock Creek, Montana, Gunderson (1968) reported that brown trout biomass was 31% greater per unit area in a stream reach flowing through an ungrazed section than in a reach flowing through an adjacent grazed section. Marcuson (1977), in a follow-up study, found brown trout biomass was 3.4 times greater per unit stream area in the ungrazed section than in the grazed section. These studies were confounded by other variables, however, as field studies almost always are. After a major flood in the stream, the grazed section was channelized and cleared of vegetation by the U.S. Army Corps of Engineers. Also, the grazed section, but not the ungrazed section, had been burned in the 1930s. Thus, it is difficult to attribute smaller fish biomasses solely to grazing.

Storch (1979) found that, after 10 years of rest from livestock grazing inside an exclosure along Camp Creek, Oregon, game fish made up 77% of the stream's fish population; in the grazed areas outside the exclosure, however, only 24% of the stream's population was game fish. Storch failed to show that the two areas were closely comparable to begin with or that the differences reported could not occur naturally, so his conclusions can be debated. They strongly suggest, however, that grazing was a possible detrimental factor.

Van Velson (1979) blamed heavy livestock grazing along Otter Creek, Nebraska, for the elimination of trout spawning runs in the stream. He stated that large spawning runs composed of catchable-size trout entered Otter Creek before grazing, and that, after grazing began, runs soon became insignificant. Later, when livestock were excluded from the upper 3.2 km of stream, rainbow trout spawning runs again developed. A confounding factor is that, with cessation of livestock grazing, the Nebraska Game and Parks Commission began to stock fingerling rainbow trout in the stream. Furthermore, no fish population data are available for the period before grazing was prohibited. No case can be made for or against grazing from this example.

Starostka (1979), studying Sevenmile Creek, Utah, found that trout numbers per unit stream area in an ungrazed 3.2-km section of land were about the same as in adjacent grazed sections. The exclosure had been constructed in 1961 but was no longer functioning by 1970, and the area had been returned to grazing. In 1974, the exclosure was refurbished and grazing was eliminated, but no changes in fish populations could be detected. This study contains the same problem as most studies—no pregrazing data were available—so its results are ambiguous.

Platts (1981a) found that fish density in Horton Creek, Idaho, was 10.9 times higher in a lightly grazed or ungrazed meadow than it was along an adjacent heavily grazed section. The grazed portion of the meadow had been heavily and continuously grazed by sheep for 80 years; the lightly or ungrazed meadow had been rested during most or all of this period. It cannot be proven that the two stream reaches were similar prior to livestock grazing, and the evidence for a grazing effect is circumstantial to this extent.

Platts (1981b) studied a sheep-grazing strategy of rest rotation with seasonal preference (i.e., pastures were used that would be least affected by grazing) along Frenchman Creek, Idaho, and concluded that sheep grazing was having no detrimental effect on the fish population. Again, Platts had no pregrazing information to compare. His conclusions were based on results obtained by comparing fish populations in creek sections adjacent to grazed and ungrazed pastures; the fish population and the stream riparian habitat in the area grazed by sheep were in good condition.

Figure 11.8.—A high-elevation meadow being grazed with a three-pasture, rest rotation strategy.

Platts (1981b) studied a three-pasture, rest rotation cattle-grazing system established during 1979 in a previously ungrazed drainage of the South Fork Salmon River, Idaho (Figure 11.8). He compared the results of the treatment with pregrazing information and two controls, and concluded that the first cycle of the rest rotation system had no effect on the fish population. As this study progresses through additional grazing cycles, however, the fish population may change.

Chapman and Knudsen (1980) compared pairs of grazed and ungrazed stream riparian sections in the Puget Sound area of Washington and found that, although livestock-altered reaches contained less total cutthroat trout biomass, young-of-the-year trout biomass was higher. No pregrazing data were available for comparison, so the possibility that the results might have been the same without grazing cannot be proved.

Duff (1983) found that trout numbers within an ungrazed exclosure on Big Creek, Utah, were 3.6 times greater than those within a downstream grazed area. An upstream grazed area that was influenced by beaver dams, however, had 1.5 times as many trout as the ungrazed exclosure. Again, as in most studies, the author gave no supporting data to establish whether the areas were similar before treatments were applied. Also, the addition of 17 instream habitat structures inside and outside the exclosure in 1970, the construction of 26 more structures within the exclosure in 1971, and an annual fish-stocking program may have biased the study conclusions relating to fish populations.

Keller et al. (1979) studied the effects of exclosures on Summit Creek, Idaho. Below the headwater spring source, 3.2 km of the stream were fenced to exclude cattle, and the authors reported a remarkable recovery in aquatic habitat conditions. A high variation in fish population estimates precluded statistically valid appraisals of what happened to the fish population. Also, the closer the fish were to the spring source, the higher were their population densities; this trend could cause confusion. Again, the sites selected for comparison had no pretreatment information to determine whether or not they were truly comparable.

The weight of evidence from these studies as a group is that fish abundances and biomasses decline in the presence of grazing. Nevertheless, each study separately was flawed to a greater or lesser degree and its results were compromised accordingly. Future research must be designed to eliminate the biases and ambiguities that have plagued work to date.

Livestock-Grazing Strategies and Fisheries Compatibility

Livestock-grazing strategies have been developed to increase forage production and vigor, to increase plant and litter cover, to encourage more favorable plant species composition for forage needs, and to decrease soil erosion. These objectives should also benefit fisheries, but little research has been done to determine if these objectives are being met in stream riparian systems and if they are of benefit to fishery resources. Published evaluations of grazing strategies as they would relate to fishery productivity are lacking (Meehan and Platts 1978).

Holechek (1983) pointed out that grazing strategies have become a major focus of range research and management, yet analysis of the conditions under which individual grazing strategies give the best results is lacking. Holechek also found little difference in cattle performance and diet quality between the different grazing strategies (e.g., continuous season-long use versus rest rotation). This lack of effect can reduce the economic incentive for managers and users to change from a poor riparian grazing strategy to one more beneficial to fisheries. Therefore, fishery needs and benefits from improved grazing strategies must be displayed.

Developing Grazing Strategy

Gifford and Hawkins (1976) showed that no developed grazing strategy reported in the literature consistently or significantly increases plant and litter covers on watersheds. Additionally, grazing strategies appear to affect plant species differentially: where one plant species increases in density, another may decrease, and the net result may be a decrease in watershed protection. Manipulation of plant species density has much application in stream riparian management. This density change has negatively affected many streams in the western USA, where once abundant plant canopy cover has been lost.

Range management strategies have historically combined the different vegetation communities under one management prescription. This management scheme is still commonly used and has caused serious fisheries problems because of the natural attraction of livestock to stream riparian zones. Rangeland researchers and managers have had difficulty developing grazing strategies that prevent livestock concentration in riparian zones. Holechek (1983) partly addressed this point when he stated that any grazing strategy, if it is to work, must be tailored to fit the needs of the vegetation, terrain, and class or kind of livestock in addition to those of the particular ranching operation. Fisheries specialists must also include streambanks, stream channels, water quality, and streamside vegetation in this list of needs.

Only preliminary evaluations of grazing strategies, as they relate to fisheries needs, are currently available (Table 11.2). Research is proceeding slowly, but fisheries specialists must recognize that management decisions cannot and will not wait for the perfect research answer. Managers must make decisions daily, using the best information and interpretation available.

Options for Specialized Grazing Strategies

Seven major options—alone or in combination—should be considered as methods are developed to build fishery compatibility into grazing strategies:

- rest from grazing;
- control of livestock numbers;
- control of livestock distribution;
- control of timing of forage use;
- control of kind and class of livestock;
- control of forage use; and
- artificial rehabilitation of stream riparian ecosystems.

When a successful grazing strategy is being planned, several possible effects on stream and riparian systems should be considered.

Effects on streambanks.—Following are some effects of grazing on streambanks:

- shear of streambank soils by hoof or head action (Figure 11.9);
- water and wind erosion of exposed streambanks and channel soils because of loss of vegetative cover;
- caving-in of streambanks from animal pressure;
- elimination of streambank vegetation; and
- reduction of streambank undercuts.

Effects on the water column.—Grazing practices can affect the water column in the following ways:

- withdrawal of streamflow to irrigate pasture lands;
- drainage of wet meadows or lowering of the water table;
- return of water from irrigated pasture lands;
- changes in magnitude and timing of nutrients entering the stream;
- increases in solar radiation on the stream;
- increases in fecal coliform bacteria;
- decreases in canopy cover;
- changes in water column form;
- changes in timing and magnitude of streamflow; and
- increases in stream width and decreases in stream depth, including reduction of streamshore depth (the depth where the water surface meets the channel or streambank; Figure 11.10).

Effects on the channel.—Effects of grazing on the stream channel include changes in channel form, and increase in sediment transport and deposition rates.

TABLE 11.2.—Evaluation and rating of grazing strategies based on the author's personal observations, as related to stream riparian habitats.

Strategy	Level at which riparian vegetation is commonly used	Control of animal distribution (allotment)	Stream-bank stability	Brushy species condition	Seasonal plant regrowth	Stream riparian rehabilitation potential	Rating[a]
Continuous season-long use (cattle)	Heavy	Poor	Poor	Poor	Poor	Poor	1
Holding (sheep or cattle)	Heavy	Excellent	Poor	Poor	Fair	Poor	1
Short-duration, high-intensity (cattle)	Heavy	Excellent	Poor	Poor	Poor	Poor	1
Three-herd, four-pasture (cattle)	Heavy to moderate	Good	Poor	Poor	Poor	Poor	2
Holistic (cattle or sheep)	Heavy to light	Good	Poor to good	Poor	Good	Poor to excellent	2–9
Deferred (cattle)	Heavy to moderate	Fair	Poor	Poor	Fair	Fair	3
Seasonal suitability (cattle)	Heavy	Good	Poor	Poor	Fair	Fair	3
Deferred rotation (cattle)	Heavy to moderate	Good	Fair	Fair	Fair	Fair	4
Stuttered deferred rotation (cattle)	Heavy to moderate	Good	Fair	Fair	Fair	Fair	4
Winter (sheep or cattle)	Heavy to moderate	Fair	Good	Fair	Fair to good	Good	5
Rest rotation (cattle)	Heavy to moderate	Good	Fair to good	Fair	Fair to good	Fair	5
Double rest rotation (cattle)	Moderate	Good	Good	Fair	Good	Good	6
Seasonal riparian preference (cattle or sheep)	Moderate to light	Good	Good	Good	Fair	Fair	6
Riparian pasture (cattle or sheep)	As prescribed	Good	Good	Good	Good	Good	8
Corridor fencing (cattle)	None	Excellent	Good to excellent	Excellent	Good to excellent	Excellent	9
Rest rotation with seasonal preference (sheep)	Light	Good	Good to excellent	Good to excellent	Good	Excellent	9
Rest or closure (cattle or sheep)	None	Excellent	Excellent	Excellent	Excellent	Excellent	10

[a]Strategies are rated on a scale of 1 (poorly compatible with fishery needs) to 10 (highly compatible).

FIGURE 11.9.—Shear damage to streambanks.

Effects on riparian vegetation.—Grazing can affect riparian vegetation in several ways:

- changes in species composition of vegetation (e.g., brush to grass to forbs);
- drainage of wet meadows or lowering of the water table;
- reductions of streambank vegetation;
- decreases in plant vigor;
- mechanical or herbicide clearing of brushy vegetation from streambanks;
- changes in timing and amounts of organic energy leaving the riparian zone;
- decreases in canopy cover;
- elimination of riparian areas; and
- reductions of vegetation hanging over and into the water column.

Grazing Strategy Evaluation

Specialists have progressed slowly in evaluating grazing strategies with respect to fishery needs, and our understanding today is rudimentary. It requires time to obtain the information needed to reach sound conclusions, but managers must make decisions day by day using the best information and interpretation available. Managers do not have the luxury of waiting years for researchers to gather all possible data and produce a definitive solution. The fishery specialist must recognize the current limits of our understanding but still be prepared to apply the best information available to decision making today.

This section summarizes my interpretation of the ability of some current grazing strategies to meet fisheries needs (Table 11.2). This interpretation is based on information in the literature and, to a great extent, on my personal experience.

FIGURE 11.10.—A northern Rocky Mountain meadow stream widened by livestock grazing.

Future research will refine and correct the weaknesses in these interpretations. Evaluation of the grazing strategies is based on the stocking rates and grazing intensities commonly used on today's allotments. My information and experiences have been gained mainly in the northern Rocky Mountains and the Great Basin, but they should be applicable in other areas. Range specialists and land managers might evaluate some of these strategies differently, but this is not a problem; one of the purposes of this chapter is to outline a starting point from which future refinements can be developed.

My descriptions of the commonly used grazing strategies are summaries of publications by Gifford and Hawkins (1976) and Holechek (1983). Their work was also used to identify problems and benefits associated with the strategies. Discussions of corridor fencing, riparian pasture, rest, rest rotation, double rest rotation, and seasonal preference as related to fisheries needs are based on reports of Platts (1981a, 1981b, 1984), and Platts and Nelson (1985a, 1985b, 1985c, 1985d). Definitions of grazing strategies also appear in Platts (1989).

On the following pages, I describe and evaluate each grazing strategy in terms of fishery productivity, particularly with respect to problems, benefits, and compatibility with fishery needs. I also rate each grazing strategy on a range of 1 to 10, 1 having little or no fishery compatibility and 10 being completely compatible with fishery needs.

Continuous Season-Long Use (Cattle)

Definition.—Continuous season-long use, as the name implies, means that cattle graze a particular pasture throughout the grazing season year after year.

FIGURE 11.11.—A sheep-holding-strategy pasture in the northern Rocky Mountains.

Problems.—Livestock congregate and linger on streambank areas because of the convenience of forage, water, terrain, and cover. Preferred plants and riparian areas receive excessive use even under light stocking rates. Continuous regrowth of riparian vegetation keeps cattle on streambanks during the complete grazing season. Livestock exhibit maximum forage selectivity and put great stress on streambank vegetation.

Benefits.—Operating costs are kept to a minimum. Minimum fencing is required. Livestock disturbance from gathering, trailing, and changing pastures is low. Sudden changes in forage types and quality are not required.

Compatibility.—This strategy is seldom compatible with fisheries under commonly used grazing intensities and seasons of use because too much pressure is exerted on riparian plants and streambanks; it could be one of the poorest grazing strategies presently being used.

Rating.—(1).

Holding (Sheep or Cattle)

Definition.—Holding strategies call for animals to be kept in an area for short-term, interim grazing until other areas become available. Examples are holding on lower-elevation meadows until higher-elevation areas are ready for grazing, and holding on areas until transportation to another area can be arranged (Figure 11.11).

Problems.—Problems are usually the same as with continuous season-long use.

Benefits.—Benefits are usually the same as with continuous season-long use.

Compatibility.—This strategy is usually not compatible with fisheries because season of use and proper use receive little consideration. When sheep are forced to concentrate on stream riparian areas, they adversely affect these environments much the way cattle would.

Rating.—(1).

Short-Duration, High-Intensity (Cattle)

Definition.—Short-duration, high-intensity grazing usually requires many pastures. Sometimes these are laid out in a "wagon-wheel" arrangement in which water and livestock-handling facilities are at the hub of the grazing area and individual pastures are arrayed like areas between spokes in a wheel. Each paddock or pasture is used for a short period of intensive grazing by animals stocked at a high density, then left unused for a longer period.

Problems.—Adequate season-long precipitation is required for plants to regrow in each pasture. Too much grazing and mechanical pressure is placed on brushy species, and resulting damage may be severe. Intensive grazing is used during periods when streambanks have high moisture content and are susceptible to mechanical damage. Initial expense to develop the pastures is high.

Benefits.—Animals can be distributed to make even use of pastures. The strategy has been successful on flat upland grasslands. Stocking rates can often be substantially higher than continuous season-long grazing can support.

Compatibility.—Compatibility varies considerably, depending on soil moisture, and it can place livestock in the riparian stream habitat over intervals covering the complete grazing season. High grazing intensities can be detrimental to brushy species. Cattle are on streambanks during periods when banks are susceptible to shear and erosion.

Rating.—(1).

Three-Herd, Four-Pasture (Cattle)

Definition.—Under three-herd, four-pasture plans, each of four pastures is grazed continuously for 12 months and then rested for 4 months. By the end of a 4-year cycle, the period of nonuse in each pasture has occurred during each quarter of the year.

Problems.—Livestock graze streambank vegetation during all periods of the year. Early grazing can cause streambank shear; late grazing can eliminate the vegetative mat needed to buffer the erosive forces of high water and floods. Constant grazing pressure is kept on brushy species during the year of continuous grazing.

Benefits.—Higher plant production can be obtained on uplands, if sufficient precipitation occurs during the entire year, than on drier sites. The strategy has been effective on upland ranges where plants grow throughout the year. Periods of pasture rest allow plant regrowth, resulting in increased plant vigor.

Compatibility.—This strategy is somewhat incompatible with fisheries because livestock graze streambank vegetation during susceptible shear periods and, during most years, the animals eliminate the vegetative mats needed to protect streambanks from erosion. The 4-month period of nonuse allows some rehabilitation.

Rating.—(2).

Holistic (Cattle or Sheep)

Definition.—Difficult to define, the holistic strategy is partly in the mind of the beholder. It is usually characterized by heavy stocking and frequent movement of animals according to the growth cycle of the plants. The timing of grazing and rest are supposedly keyed to environmental conditions and needs.

Problems.—The user has difficulty determining forage use, forage timing, and animal movements. Livestock are used to churn the soil, break up the surface soil capping, trample ground litter, and disturb soils to increase soil porosity. In the process, however, streambank stability and form are degraded. The strategy resembles and often mimics short-duration, high-intensity grazing but requires more intensive training and more management time than that strategy.

Benefits.—Upland range condition is improved by the increase in soil porosity.

Compatibility.—This strategy is somewhat incompatible with fisheries because hoof-churning of soils can damage streambanks and high-intensity grazing could damage brushy species and retard development of stream canopies.

Rating.—(2).

Deferred (Cattle)

Definition.—Deferred grazing means use of a pasture is delayed until the more important forage plants develop mature seeds or gain needed regrowth.

Problems.—A considerable amount of fencing and cattle movement are required. Deferred late-season grazing can remove the vegetative mat needed to protect streambanks from ice and water scouring. If grazing deferrals are accompanied by higher-than-usual stocking rates during the period of pasture use, streambank shear can result.

Benefits.—Periods of nonuse provide reasonable opportunities for preferred grazing plants to improve vigor and grazing areas to improve cover. This results in good animal distribution over the entire grazing area. The strategy is especially beneficial where considerable differences exist among palatabilities of plants and conveniences of grazing. Plants are allowed to gain the necessary growth to set seed and maintain root structure.

Compatibility.—This strategy is more compatible with fisheries than strategies discussed previously because the vegetation is allowed recovery periods that could improve its capacity to protect streambanks from erosion. Animal stocking still needs to be matched to the capacity of the riparian habitat.

Rating.—(3).

Seasonal Suitability (Cattle)

Definition.—Under seasonal suitability strategies, the range or allotment is partitioned into pastures based on vegetative types or condition classes. The pasture that is best nutritionally is used for each season of the year. This strategy is sometimes called the "best-pasture" system.

Problems.—Fencing costs and the need to move animals from pasture to pasture are high. The riparian habitat could be the one selected as the "best pasture" during periods when streambank damage occurs most readily. This strategy does not account for the needs to decrease streambank erosion and protect brushy species.

Benefits.—The strategy could be programmed or modified to give relief to pastures containing riparian habitats. The strategy provides some deferment from grazing during selected periods of the grazing season.

Compatibility.—This strategy is moderately compatible with fisheries because selected periods of nonuse allow degraded streambanks and riparian vegetation some time to recover. Because each pasture is grazed every year, however, this programmed nonuse may not be adequate. Riparian areas would probably receive heavy grazing under the "best-pasture" principle.

Rating.—(3).

Deferred Rotation (Cattle)

Definition.—In a deferred rotation plan, at least one pasture is left ungrazed during part of the grazing season and this deferment is rotated among pastures in succeeding years. This strategy is commonly used to graze one pasture during the early part of the grazing season and the remaining pastures later in the season. The following year, the sequence is usually reversed.

Problems.—Deferred rotation grazing requires substantial amounts of fencing and shifting of herds. Every other year, livestock graze streambanks early when riparian areas may be susceptible to shear damage. In alternate years, grazing is late when plant regrowth may be needed to protect streambanks from ice and flood scour.

Benefits.—Vegetation has the opportunity to store carbohydrates and set seed every other year. Better control of animal distribution is provided, resulting in more uniform use of all herb species.

Compatibility.—This system is somewhat compatible with fisheries because nonuse occurs during some critical periods and thus plant cover increases. Over a 2-year period, however, each pasture is grazed over the complete grazing season, so streambanks might shear and vegetative mats might be eliminated.

Rating.—(4).

Stuttered Deferred Rotation (Cattle)

Definition.—With stuttered as well as standard deferred rotation, one pasture is deferred for part of the plant growth period and this period is rotated among pastures in succeeding years. Whereas the standard strategy is to graze one pasture early one year and another pasture late and then to reverse the pattern the following year, the stutter sequence calls for using one pasture early and a second pasture late for two years in a row and then reversing the timing for the next two years; thus, 4 years are required to complete the cycle.

Problems.—The problems are the same as with deferred rotation.

Benefits.—Benefits are similar to those of deferred rotation except the two successive years of early grazing and two of late grazing can give brushy species some relief, especially during the back-to-back late-grazing sequences. Early in the grazing season, brushy species are often underused because cattle prefer more succulent vegetation, and they can get a good start on growth. During late-fall grazing, livestock tend to take only 1 year's growth from brushy plants, and the 4-year stutter cycle preserves more plant growth than the standard 2-year cycle.

Compatibility.—Stuttered deferred rotation is somewhat more compatible with fisheries than ordinary deferred rotation to the extent that sturdier brush can develop in riparian areas to stabilize streambanks.

Rating.—(4).

Winter (Sheep or Cattle)

Definition.—A winter **grazing** strategy restricts use of a pasture to periods when streambanks are mainly frozen and plants are in the dormant stage; snowfall must be light enough that livestock can reach the forage.

Problems.—This strategy is only successful when air temperatures are cold enough to freeze and toughen streambanks, snowfall is light enough to make grazing feasible, and the range is not grazed at other times of the year. The regional climate may not provide these required conditions each year. The streambank vegetative mat, needed to prevent soil erosion from winter and spring floods, may not be adequate to stop erosion during certain climatic conditions.

Benefits.—Supplemental winter feeding can be reduced or eliminated. Grazing does not occur during plant growth. Frozen streambanks are at their toughest stage. Streambank shear is minimized. Seeds ripen every year. Carbohydrates have returned to the root system.

Compatibility.—This strategy is fairly compatible with fisheries because frozen streambanks usually hold up well under cold-season grazing. Plants are in the dormant stage and nutrients are stored mainly in the roots. Plant vigor is sustained or enhanced because plants are protected during the growing season. However, overstocking of winter ranges can lead to degradation of brushy species.

Rating.—(5).

Rest Rotation (Cattle)

Definition.—In rest rotation schemes, one pasture receives at least 1 year of complete rest during the grazing cycle (Figure 11.12). The period of rest is rotated among (usually three) pastures over the cycle.

Problems.—Benefits to fish habitat that accrue during the year of rest from grazing may be nullified by the higher forage use that occurs on the grazed pastures. Over the period of one grazing cycle, livestock will have grazed the streambanks during all seasons of use. In 1 year during each 3-year grazing cycle, the streambank vegetative mat is grazed off and the cover necessary to buffer erosion from floods and ice is removed. In 1 year during each 3-year grazing cycle, streambanks are grazed when soil moisture is high (usually in spring) and shear damage can result. The livestock operators must move animals from pasture to pasture. Livestock numbers may have to be reduced to prevent excessive forage use in the remaining grazed pastures.

Benefits.—The long rest period allows plants and streambanks to recover from past damage. In 2 of every 3 years of each grazing cycle, the vegetative mat is left on the streambanks to buffer future erosion; in two of every 3 years, livestock do not graze streambanks during periods of high shear potential.

Compatibility.—This strategy is fairly compatible with fisheries because the year of complete rest allows streambanks and riparian vegetation the opportunity to recover from any stress received during the past 2 years of concentrated grazing. Riparian areas that have a high natural recovery rate can do so during this rest period, but those with lower recovery rates may continue to degrade.

Rating.—(5).

FIGURE 11.12.—A grazed (left) and a rested (right) pasture within a three-pasture rest rotation grazing scheme.

Double Rest Rotation (Cattle)

Definition.—Double rest rotation strategies allow the pasture with the highest riparian stream benefits twice as much rest as it would receive during a standard rest rotation cycle. This pasture is rested 2 years, then grazed late the third year, then rested 2 years and grazed late the following year; thus, 6 years are required to complete the cycle.

Problems.—Problems are about the same as those associated with a standard rest rotation strategy.

Benefits.—This strategy is more beneficial than common rest rotation because the stream riparian habitat has 2 years to recover from past damages.

Compatibility.—Fishery compatibility is somewhat better than that of standard rest rotation because the riparian habitat receives two successive years of complete rest. This gives the stream twice the normal amount of time to recover from any previous degradation. Brushy species also have 2 years to set short growth before grazing again occurs.

Rating.—(6).

Seasonal Riparian Preference (Cattle or Sheep)

Definition.—Under seasonal preference strategies, the pasture containing the highest riparian stream benefits or in need of the most rehabilitation is grazed only during that period of the grazing season when the least environmental damage will occur.

Problems.—Streambanks can still receive some shear stress, and late-season grazing can reduce the vegetative mat. The preference requirements can cause overgrazing in other pastures. Additional pastures that may be needed require more fencing and movement of animals. Determining seasonal preference is difficult because seasonal climatic conditions vary from year to year.

Benefits.—Streambanks can be grazed during the time when they are most stable and when brushy species would be used least.

Compatibility.—Under intensive management, this strategy can be more compatible with fishery needs than other strategies, but managers must have a good data base or experience to determine the preferred period of use.

Rating.—(6).

Riparian Pasture (Cattle or Sheep)

Definition.—The stream riparian zone, or high-value portions of it, can be designated as one pasture. The timing of forage use in the riparian pasture is then programmed to meet the manager's objectives for the riparian zone.

Problems.—Additional fencing and maintenance are required to delineate a riparian pasture. Unless stocking is closely managed for the whole allotment, use of a riparian pasture can cause imbalances in animal distribution and forage use in the remaining pastures during certain parts of the season. Reduction in forage use within the riparian pasture may be necessary to meet environmental objectives. Livestock must be moved fairly often.

Benefits.—Forage use and timing can be programmed to meet the ability of the stream riparian habitat to maintain itself productively. A much simpler grazing strategy can be used in the surrounding upland pastures. As the riparian vegetation regains its vigor and productivity, available forage for livestock use often can be increased.

Compatibility.—Compatibility of this strategy with fisheries is good because, within the riparian pasture, the stream riparian habitat is managed for optimum benefits. If the uplands are improperly grazed, however, off-site stress can still affect the riparian pasture and the stream.

Rating.—(8).

Corridor Fencing (Cattle)

Definition.—The entire riparian corridor, or any required portion thereof, is fenced for complete rest or to control desired grazing methods (Figure 11.13).

Problems.—Extensive fencing, which increases costs and can interfere with animal distribution in the uplands, is required. Forage for livestock use can be eliminated. The livestock industry opposes this method.

Benefits.—Riparian habitats can be rehabilitated. Simpler upland strategies can be used to meet grazing targets. Animal distribution within the stream riparian habitat can be controlled. The riparian zone may be increased in size, possibly providing more riparian-type forage outside the fenced corridor.

Compatibility.—Compatibility of this strategy with fisheries is good because it allows riparian rehabilitation and maintains stream riparian habitats, but stress from improperly managed uplands can still affect the stream.

Rating.—(8).

FIGURE 11.13.—A Utah stream with corridor fencing protection on the left and grazing on the right.

Rest Rotation with Seasonal Preference (Sheep)

Definition.—The seasonal rest rotation strategy for sheep is the same as rest rotation for cattle, except that, through herding, riparian habitats are grazed at selected times of least impact.

Problems.—The livestock operator must move sheep into different pastures to meet seasonal requirements.

Benefits.—The long rest period gives plants and streambanks the opportunity to recover from past damage. Because sheep are herded, riparian habitats can be grazed with proper timing and intensity.

Compatibility.—Fishery compatibility is good because, with proper herding and animal stocking rates, grazing can be programmed to meet the needs of both the riparian and upland habitats. Sheep are grazers that usually prefer slopes and upland areas; therefore, they tend to graze streambanks less than cattle do. This strategy can be very successful without significant damage to fish habitats.

Rating.—(8).

Rest (Cattle or Sheep)

Definition.—The allotment or selected pastures are rested (ungrazed) until riparian stream habitats improve to meet stated goals.

Problems.—All forage use by livestock is eliminated. Livestock managers would be hit hard financially. This strategy is usually not acceptable politically, socially, or economically.

Benefits.—Riparian stream habitats immediately move towards their potential productivity, and products resulting from this increased potential increase in value. Degraded allotments, pastures, and stream riparian habitats can regain productivity in the shortest time and then can be placed under suitable grazing strategies.

Compatibility.—This strategy is entirely compatible with fisheries because, in time, all stream riparian habitats would return to their optimum productivity and would regain their natural potential to provide fishery resources.

Rating.—(10).

Large Storms in Grazed Watersheds

Researchers and managers have long been interested in the effects of large floods on riparian and stream habitats (Gregory and Madew 1982; Lyons and Beschta 1983), but little information has related large storms to livestock. In 1983 and 1984, runoff was intensive in large areas of the USA, bringing marginal to dramatic changes in stream riparian habitats. Many studies showed that flood damage was small where streamside vegetation was abundant (Platts et al. 1985a).

The ability of floods to damage channel morphology, and thus fish and riparian habitats, depends chiefly on the resistance of material to fluvial entrainment and the physical destruction of streambanks. These two factors can be controlled, to some extent, by the types of land use and management in the riparian zone. If streambank vegetation is reduced, a stream usually responds to floods by adjusting its channel width. Physical destruction of the streambank delivers sediments to an over-widening channel. The initial response of channels to these increased sediments is to reduce bedform roughness (Heede 1980; Jackson and Beschta 1984), usually by filling pools with sediments. Subsequent adjustments may include changes in width, depth, meander pattern, or longitudinal profile. When these adjustments take place, fish populations usually decline.

Three western streams in livestock-grazed watersheds were studied from 1978 through 1984 by Platts et al. (1985a) to determine changes in fish habitats. During this period, broad areas of the western USA experienced some of the lowest and highest stream flows on record. The study streams were in Nevada (Chimney and Gance creeks) on the northern fringe of the Basin and Range physiographic province, and in Utah (Big Creek) on the fringe of the middle Rocky Mountain physiographic province. Historically, the watersheds of all three streams have been heavily grazed by livestock. Storm flows in Chimney Creek had magnitudes expected only once every 500 years. Gance Creek, during 1983 and 1984, exceeded 14 times its mean annual discharge peak. Big Creek probably exceeded all past 40-year flow records during the study period.

Chimney Creek

In past years, the shore of Chimney Creek was heavily dominated by aspen forest. Evidence of this aspen forest still exists in the abundant, decomposing aspen logs in the Chimney Creek channel. The drastic decrease in number of standing aspens probably occurred because beavers cut the large mature trees, heavy cattle grazing prevented regrowth of aspen, and many trees were affected by disease and blowdown.

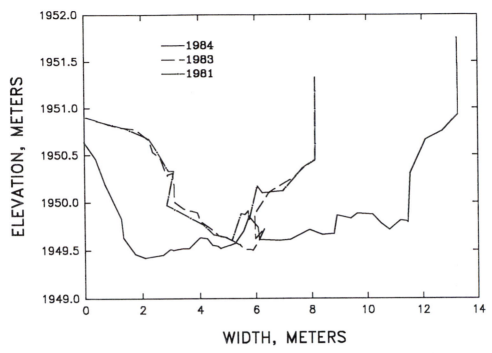

FIGURE 11.14.—Cross sections of Chimney Creek, Nevada, 1981–1984.

The large aspen limbs and logs that held the Chimney Creek channel together decreased in volume and decomposed so they no longer held the acquired alluvium underlying the channel. Consequently, the large floods that occurred during the study period scoured alluvial materials, accelerated erosion of streambanks, and left a broader, flatter channel than existed previously (Figure 11.14).

Gance Creek

The major floods in Gance Creek primarily deepened the channel (Figure 11.15). Some cross sections showed lateral change, but the streambank vegetation dominated by trees allowed the creek to resist most pressures for lateral movement. Had Gance Creek still retained the beaver dams that helped control its flow in the 1950s and 1960s, it would probably have been less affected by the high flows. The only changes that might have been caused by the high flows would have been reductions in channel gravels (as happened in Chimney Creek), increases in stream width (due primarily to higher summer flows), and reductions in vegetative overhang.

Big Creek

One area of Big Creek had been rested (ungrazed) for about 10 years and showed dramatic rehabilitation whereas the other area had been heavily grazed up to the time of the study. Stream width increased dramatically, by about 40%, between 1982 and 1984 (1983 and 1984 were flood years) in the grazed reaches. The improved riparian bank conditions in the ungrazed area contained the excess streamflow, and stream width increased only slightly there. In the grazed area,

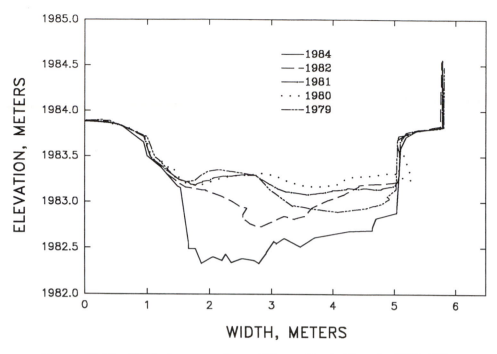

FIGURE 11.15.—Typical cross sections of Gance Creek, Nevada, 1979–1984.

extensive lateral movement and redeposition of bedload sediments occurred, except only bank cutting (no deposition) occurred immediately downstream from the ungrazed site.

Streambank angle—the greater the angle, the more the bank is outsloped and the less its value as fish habitat—increased only slightly in the grazed sites, but the banks were already outsloped. From 1982 to 1984, bank angle in the ungrazed site decreased by 27%, to 75°. The large decrease in bank angle also corresponded with a 72% increase in bank undercut, a move toward better salmonid habitat.

The habitat rating (a vegetative classification by form) decreased dramatically in the grazed sites because of the large increase in newly eroded sediments that dominated the streambank structure and the increase in exposed banks created by lateral movements and bank scour. Streambanks were greatly altered in the grazed area after the 1983–1984 floods but changed little in the ungrazed section, demonstrating the ability of improved riparian areas to resist damage from unusual runoff events.

Conclusions

The main conclusion to be drawn from these studies is if streams are to maintain their productivity when subjected to large storms, they must be in basins with good watershed conditions and they must be surrounded by productive riparian vegetation that stabilizes the streambanks.

Rehabilitation

Human activities—especially heavy grazing of livestock—have altered many riparian habitats on rangelands. Because certain riparian features, particularly vegetation, respond quickly to changes in management, they can usually be restored. The time required depends on climate, soil fertility, groundwater table, intensity of rehabilitation measures, and surrounding land use. Rehabilitation of riparian vegetation can reduce stream width, increase depth, lower summer water temperatures, reduce anchor-ice buildup in winter, increase forage-fish populations, and increase populations of desired fish. Reeves et al. (1991, this volume) provide a detailed discussion of stream-habitat enhancement techniques, some of which can be applied to streams affected by livestock grazing.

Fencing Riparian Areas

Research usually shows that riparian areas quickly improve when they are fenced to exclude grazing (Duff 1980, 1983), but stream morphology improves slowly and fish populations may or may not be improved (Platts 1981b). The usual goal of riparian fencing is the improvement of fish populations, but resulting increases in fish numbers, sizes, and biomass have not been documented adequately. Size and location of exclosures and the length of stream requiring protection need to be determined before actual fishery improvement has a good chance to occur.

Costs.—According to Platts and Wagstaff (1984), four-wire fence costs about US\$3,728/km of stream, if fencing is on both sides. To fence all of the 24,135 km of fishable streams on U.S. Bureau of Land Management lands would cost \$90 million. About 7.5 animal unit months/km would be removed from grazing, and annual maintenance costs would run from \$37 to \$124/km of stream. If fishery benefits alone are to equal fencing costs, fishing use would have to increase an average of 29 angler-days/km annually. Everest and Summers (1982) stated that the annual number of angler trips per kilometer of U.S. Forest Service streams averaged 8.4; therefore, benefits on many stream reaches would not equal fencing costs. Benefits other than fishing (wildlife, higher water quality, esthetics, stable streambanks, less sediment movement) are also to be gained from improvements in riparian ecosystems. Based on the literature and the author's knowledge of past studies, these other benefits have not been adequately evaluated.

Results of fencing.—Platts (1981a) reported that streambanks were trampled and eroded away from the original channel along a reach of Horton Creek, Idaho, heavily grazed by sheep. This stream reach was four times wider and only one-fifth as deep as an adjacent fenced stream reach whose riparian zone was ungrazed to lightly grazed. Undercut banks were rare in the grazed area and water depth along the bank was only one-thirteenth that in the fenced, protected area. Fish numbers were 7.6-fold and biomass was 10.9-fold greater per unit area in the fenced areas than in the heavily grazed areas.

Platts et al. (1983) compared a continuously grazed area on Tabor Creek, Nevada, with an adjacent area that had been rested 5 years. Once grazing ceased, streambanks rebuilt rapidly and stream width was significantly less inside than outside the rested exclosure. Bank undercuts in the ungrazed reach averaged

FIGURE 11.16.—A Utah stream fenced to protect the stream riparian habitat. The left pasture was being grazed, the right one rested.

about twice those in the grazed reach; however, the differences were not significant.

On Big Creek, Utah, a reach of stream within an exclosure subjected to light or no grazing since 1974 was compared with an adjacent, heavily grazed reach (Platts and Nelson 1985b). The stream was significantly narrower and deeper, had more bank undercut, and had less bank angle in the ungrazed area than in the grazed area (Figure 11.16). Keller et al. (1979) reported similar changes in a rested, fenced exclosure on Summit Creek, Idaho.

Investigators who have examined riparian habitats that have been fenced or protected from grazing have reported enhancements (summarized by Platts and Wagstaff 1984). Duff (1980) reported that riparian habitats grazed throughout the season remained in poor condition, whereas adjacent ungrazed riparian habitats attained good condition within 4 years. After a decade of fenced protection, an Oregon stream received 75% more shade from alder and willow cover than when it had been grazed (Claire and Storch 1983). Keller et al. (1979) found that fencing markedly reduced grazing damage to the riparian area of Summit Creek, Idaho. Studies reported in the literature demonstrate that degraded riparian habitats can be rehabilitated or enhanced if protected from domestic livestock grazing. Research, however, has not provided methods other than fencing for accomplishing this goal. Current improved management practices (e.g., rest rotation and deferred grazing) where grazing had been heavy have not always been effective.

Streambank Rehabilitation

Streambanks are transition zones between terrestrial and aquatic environments. The amount of rehabilitation needed by grazed streambanks often is great. Gunderson (1968) reported that the amount of brush overhanging a Montana stream was 76% greater along banks not subjected to domestic livestock grazing than along an adjacent grazed area. Similarly, Patterson (1976) reported 60% more overhanging vegetation, 60% more vegetative biomass, and five-times taller vegetation along California streams that had been rip-rapped and planted with vegetation than along untreated, channelized reaches. Streams with dead juniper trees laid on the banks had 66–73% lower flow velocity than streams without junipers. Keller et al. (1979) recorded more cover on ungrazed banks of an Idaho stream than on grazed banks, and Platts (1981c) found three times as much cover on streambanks lightly grazed by sheep than on banks heavily grazed by sheep. Intensive grazing also resulted in less bank stability, greater bank angle, and streambank retreat.

Banks of small streams provide the habitat edges necessary to maintain high populations of salmonid fishes. Adult salmonids are attracted to this habitat interface because stable, well-vegetated banks provide cover, control water velocities and temperatures, and supply terrestrial foods. The condition of the banks often governs the depths and water velocities in which fish must live.

Research has demonstrated that streambanks can be rehabilitated and enhanced through fencing and protection from grazing. Little research has been done, however, on rehabilitation of banks by construction of channel structures when land uses such as grazing are continued. Duff (1983) showed that instream structures improved pool quality in Big Creek, Utah, where there was no grazing, but structures along adjacent areas of grazed banks soon failed and could not be maintained. Platts and Nelson (1985b) found that even structures placed along ungrazed areas were ineffective because they functioned as fine sediment traps and fish populations did not respond to the artificially changed conditions. Additional research needs to be done on artificial bank enhancement under current land-use practices.

Water-Column Rehabilitation

Stream width normally decreases when domestic livestock are removed or grazing is eliminated from the surrounding area (Gunderson 1968; Keller et al. 1979; Platts 1981c; Platts and Nelson 1985b). Width reduction has ranged from small (10%) to large (400%) in various studies. Platts (1981b) observed reduced water velocities in reaches of a stream in areas subjected to heavy grazing; Gunderson (1968) reported that water surface area increased and water depth decreased in streams passing through grazed areas. These trends should reverse during rehabilitation. Water depth has been found to be slightly (10–33%) to markedly (500%) greater in sections of stream in ungrazed areas than in sections in grazed areas (Gunderson 1968; Keller et al. 1979; Platts 1981b). Heede (1977) found that Alkali Creek, Colorado, changed from an ephemeral to a perennial stream after watershed rehabilitation that included gully plugs and some structures.

Research Needs

Studies of physicochemical and biological aspects of the interrelation between livestock grazing and aquatic habitat are needed to give resource managers quantitative, objective data for land-use planning. The effects that livestock have on water quality, stream channel morphology, streambed conditions, and the riparian zone must be learned in detail.

Biologists who attempt to evaluate the effects for different systems of livestock grazing must develop methods to detect, within required limits, natural variation in streamside vegetation, streambank and stream channel conditions, and standing crops and community structures of fish. The combined influences of geology, climate, soil, vegetation, and water runoff often create unstable stream conditions even without livestock grazing. Most aquatic sites have been modified by land uses for a long time, and recognizing what is and what is not "natural" variation is difficult.

Advanced grazing systems have been implemented to enhance the welfare of ranges and production of livestock. Resource managers need to know how these grazing systems influence other resources, including populations of anadromous and resident salmonids.

The broad research needs encompass a wide area: inventory, assessment, and classification; ecosystem dynamics; autecology and physiology of tree species; effects of land-management practices; social and economic problems; and alternative modes of riparian management.

Fishery biologists are confronted with the problem of determining how different types of grazing systems affect the various aquatic components and how changes in these components affect fish health and survival. Fishery research needs are thus reduced to seeking answers to the following questions.

- Which of the existing grazing systems are most compatible with the fishery resource?
- What innovations are needed to make livestock grazing more compatible with fishery needs?
- Is one grazing strategy best suited for riparian areas?
- What is required and how long does it take for a stream altered by livestock grazing to return to natural conditions?
- What techniques are available or should be developed to reduce the recovery time for degraded streams?
- How much can fish production be increased by improvement of or protection from livestock grazing of streamside areas?
- If streams should be protected by fences, what type of stream and how much of each stream should be fenced?
- How much vegetative canopy is needed on streambanks to prevent unacceptable fluctuations in water temperature?
- What are the first indicators that a stream is beginning to deteriorate or to improve from management of livestock?
- How much forage use can the different vegetative and streambank types support without unacceptable changes?
- Is livestock grazing less damaging at some times of the year than at others?

Once these questions are answered, strategies for range management can be improved. In the future, streams should be as productive as possible in grazed areas, and the first step is an effective research program to provide answers to the questions posed above.

Summary

Historical management practices have allowed streamside environments to deteriorate. Decision makers now generally accept the need to improve the management of these streamside areas. In addition, scientists are now studying livestock–fishery interactions and developing good data banks. Before progress can be made in improving the management of riparian areas, however, riparian environments must first be accepted as discrete management units and receive specialized, site-specific consideration. Ordinary allotment management, based primarily on the needs of livestock, originated in the early 1960s and will no longer suffice unless the allotments are further broken down into their respective habitat types.

Livestock grazing can affect all components of the aquatic system. Grazing can affect the streamside environment by changing, reducing, or eliminating vegetation bordering the stream. Channel morphology can be changed by accrual of sediment, alteration of channel substrate, disruption of the relation of pools to riffles, and widening of the channel. The water column can be affected by increasing water temperature, nutrients, and suspended sediment, and by changes in the timing and volume of streamflow. Livestock can trample streambanks, causing banks to slough off, creating false or retreating banks, and accelerating bank erosion.

Documenting and evaluating effects of these alterations are difficult because natural events can produce similar alterations and effects (see Swanston 1991, this volume). Fishery biologists must determine how different grazing systems affect the various aquatic components and how changes in these components affect fish health and survival. Whether a stream suffers from a catastrophic, debilitating event or from an accumulation of lesser events (such as those resulting from livestock grazing) over a longer period of time, the result for fishes can be the same, and recovery may take years.

Improved livestock management will result in more stable streambanks and stream channels; reduction of soil erosion and, consequently, reduced stream sedimentation; improvement of streamside vegetative cover; improved water quality; increased riparian forage; and increased fish production. Improvement of streamside vegetation will also increase the abundance and diversity of terrestrial wildlife. Proper management of livestock will increase resource values and, in turn, economic benefits to all users. A short-term loss of forage for livestock may occur when overused and degraded riparian communities are put under proper management, but increased forage production should ultimately be a result of improved resource management.

Chapter 12

Mining

R. L. Nelson, M. L. McHenry, and W. S. Platts

Mining has been an important activity in the USA and Canada since the two countries were settled. Vast mineral resources are located in the western states and provinces. Because minerals are important to industry and to quality of life, the U.S. Congress passed the U.S. Mining Laws Act in 1872, granting top land-use priority to mineral extraction on all public lands not specifically withdrawn from mineral development. As a result, some 300 million hectares, or 68% of all public lands, are open to mining (Sheridan 1977). Because only 0.12% of the land surface in the USA is presently being mined (Starnes 1983), the effects of extraction on the land surface may appear superficially to be localized. Localized degradations, however, can be transferred throughout a watershed and affect other resources.

The appropriateness of granting top priority to mining on public lands is being questioned increasingly as the public becomes more environmentally aware. Although neither the Multiple-Use Sustained Yield Act of 1960 (Public Law 86-517) nor the Federal Land Policy and Management Act of 1976 (PL 94-579) specifically countermand the authority of the U.S. Mining Laws Act, they do reflect a growing public desire to reduce the negative effects associated with consumptive land uses and to attain balanced use of public resources.

The mining industry recognizes the probability that mining has degraded the quality of America's surface waters more than any other component of the environment (Cummins and Given 1973a). Mining operations have historically affected both recreational and commercial fisheries. Between 1961 and 1975, for example, a conservatively estimated 10 million fish were killed by mining-related water pollution in the USA (U.S. Environment Protection Agency 1979).

In western North America, fisheries represent a renewable resource of considerable economic importance. In the four Pacific coast states of Alaska, Washington, Oregon, and California, for example, the aggregate annual commercial salmon catch averaged 76,676,000 fish between 1976 and 1980, and attained a gross dockside value of US$438.2 million in 1981. The average annual wholesale market value of finished products from these fish has been estimated at about $1 billion. Recreational values are more difficult to assess, but they may be as high as $83 million annually in Washington, Oregon, and California alone (Huppert et al. 1985). Consequently, impairment of salmonid production by degradation of aquatic environments is a potentially serious economic threat, as well as an affront to our esthetic sensibilities.

Influences of Forest and Rangeland Management on Salmonid Fishes and Their Habitats
American Fisheries Society Special Publication 19:425–457, 1991

Congress first addressed concern over mining-induced deterioration of water quality with the Water Pollution Control Act amendments of 1972 (PL 92-500). These amendments contain provisions for regulating effluent discharge, and these have been used to support requirements of the Surface Mining Control and Reclamation Act (SMCRA) of 1977 (PL 95-87) that mining operations on public lands recognize other resource values. The SMCRA states that mining activities must be performed so as to "minimize disturbances and adverse impacts of the operation on fish, wildlife and related environmental values, and achieve enhancement of such resources where practicable."

In this chapter, we review mining practices and their effects on aquatic resources in general, and examine how such disturbances may affect salmonid populations in particular.

Survey of Mining Practices

Recoverable minerals occur in the earth's crust from the surface to thousands of meters below ground, and in a variety of geological settings. Mining engineers have developed an array of extraction techniques that can be tailored to the precise situation in which a deposit lies. The two broad categories of mining operations are surface mining and underground mining (Cummins and Given 1973a). Surface mining comprises all forms of open mines, including strip mines, open-pit mines, quarries, and alluvia that can be dredged or hydraulically mined. Underground mining includes operations beneath the earth's surface in a system of tunnels and shafts in which minerals are extracted by physical or chemical means. Occasionally, certain mineral deposits can be most effectively recovered by a combination of these practices, such as underground mining of placer deposits or underground quarrying.

Surface Mining

Surface mining alters the landscape by removing terrestrial vegetation and organic topsoil, thereby exposing large areas of land surface to erosion. Surface mining is suitable for the extraction of ore deposits lying on or near the surface. These surficial deposits include clays, coal, lignite, phosphate, and gypsum, as well as alluvial deposits containing uranium, gold, and a variety of other ores typically found in low concentrations. Once the ore deposit is exposed, it is usually removed with heavy equipment.

Nonalluvial deposits.—The two principal forms of nonalluvial ore extraction are strip mining and open-pit mining. Both types of operation disturb aquatic habitats if they block or redirect surface flows, accelerate sediment delivery to streams and lakes, or disrupt groundwater flows.

Strip mining is the most basic type of surface mining, generally used to remove coal and other minerals lying near the surface. Strip mining either creates a long, continuous excavation bordered by one or two parallel waste piles ("contour mining") or it generates an alternating series of parallel excavations and waste piles covering a broad area ("area mining") (U.S. Environmental Protection Agency 1973a). In addition, "auger mining," drilling horizontally into the deposit, may be used near completion of an operation to recover some material isolated behind the mine's highwall (U.S. Environmental Protection Agency 1973a). Water quality problems associated with strip mining include acidification, sedimentation, and physical disruption of entire aquifers.

Open-pit mining is used to recover both metallic and nonmetallic ores, particularly (in western North America) copper, gold, molybdenum, and phosphate. It is especially suitable when the mineral deposits are concentrated (Spaulding and Ogden 1968). As the land surface is excavated, minerals are recovered from the sides of the pit on terraces whose size is determined by the type of excavating machinery (U.S. Forest Service 1977a). These mines can be enormous, producing as much as 272,727 tonnes of ore and waste per day (Cummins and Given 1973a). Quarrying, a smaller-scale but similar operation, is used to extract nonmineral materials such as limestone, sand, and gravel.

Recently, a new form of open-pit mining has gained popularity in the western USA. Known as heap leaching, the process is used to extract gold from low-grade ore deposits. Ore extracted from a pit is crushed and shaped into "pads" over which a dilute solution of sodium cyanide (NaCN) is sprayed. The cyanide solution percolates through the pad to bond with the gold and drain into catch basins. Further processing, usually flotation, allows the gold to be recovered.

Water pollution associated with open-pit mining typically concerns acidification caused by the oxidation of iron-containing waste products, which then are carried with runoff into local drainages. Heap leaching also can introduce sodium cyanide, a highly toxic substance, into local streams.

Alluvial deposits.—Alluvial ore frequently occurs as deposits of discrete grains called "placers," the extraction of which is generically known as "placer mining." Extraction of placer deposits requires direct disturbance of aquatic habitats. Two historically common types of placer mining are dredging and hydraulic mining.

Placers are frequently dredged, a process of digging unconsolidated alluvial deposits from beneath standing water or saturated soils adjacent to watercourses. Dredging is used to extract minerals such as gold and rare earths that are heavier than surrounding materials.

Dredges are of two types: large bucket-line dredges and smaller, less efficient dragline dredges. Both are floating processing plants that extract the ore-bearing material from the substrate, separate the ore from the mixture by gravity within a stream of flowing water, and stack the waste or tailings away from the dredging area. Dredges are extremely efficient at moving the unconsolidated materials of alluvial deposits. Bucket-line dredges (Figure 12.1), for example, can dig as deeply as 46 m and move as much as 686,544 m^3 of material in 1 month (Cummins and Given 1973b).

Dredging usually disturbs the lake- or streambed itself, and spoils are spread over the land surface; restoration to original appearances may be impossible because the material takes up 20% more space after dredging (U.S. Forest Service 1977a). Dredged areas may also degrade aquatic habitats by contributing large amounts of sediment to local drainages.

Hydraulic mining consists of spraying jets of water under high pressure onto ore-bearing alluvial gravels that form the banks of modern streams. This method erodes soil quickly to produce unconsolidated mixtures of gravel and ore that can then be pumped to processing stations. Hydraulic mining radically alters the land surface and can deposit large quantities of sediment in nearby streams. Environ-

FIGURE 12.1.—Bucket-line dredge used to extract rare earths from placer deposits in Bear Valley, Idaho, in the 1950s. The conveyer belt at right lifts stream or lake deposits into the central housing where the heavy ore-bearing materials settle out in a water stream. Wastes are deposited on the shoreline via the chute at left.

mental concerns have led to legislation that has nearly eliminated hydraulic mining, but it was used extensively by early western gold miners, and is still used in some coastal areas to remove sand and in western gold and coal extraction operations. Environmental impacts of early hydraulic-mining operations continue to be felt in many western areas (Figure 12.2).

Underground Mining

Many types of underground mines are used to extract minerals. The most common underground mines are "shaft" or "slope" mines, which have vertical or inclined entryways, and "adit" mines, used to recover ores via horizontal entry tunnels (also called "drift mines" when coal is the target). Minerals are generally extracted mechanically, often with heavy equipment, from the walls of underground tunnels.

Some deposits, such as those of sulfur, copper, uranium, and salt, may be recovered from underground deposits by a process called "solution mining." In this procedure, a chemical solvent is pumped underground through a borehole. The solvent reacts with the metal being mined and the resulting ore-bearing solution is then pumped to the surface for recovery.

Regardless of the process employed, mining and its waste products alter the landscape (Figure 12.3). The type of mineral to be mined influences not only the extraction method, but also the processing techniques, thereby influencing environmental impacts. Metalliferous deposits, for example, generally contain a high proportion of waste relative to ore; the reverse is generally true of nonmetallic deposits. Such differences affect the amount of processing (for example, concentration procedures) needed at the mine site (Cummins and Given 1973a), and thus the magnitude of potential environmental effects. Mining also has secondary effects, including construction of access roads and generation of chemical as well as solid wastes, that contribute to long-term environmental impacts before, during, and after mining operations.

FIGURE 12.2.—Historic photograph of hydraulic mining in action. The water jet washes poorly consolidated bank materials into a slurry that can be processed for its mineral content.

Effects of Mining on Fish and Fish Habitats

Acid Waste

Pollution of streams by acid mine drainage is generally considered to be the most serious water pollution aspect of mining operations. Cummins and Given (1973a) estimated that 1.6–1.8 million tonnes of sulfuric acid (H_2SO_4) have been transported annually from mine sites. Although frequently associated with eastern coal mining, acid drainage is not limited to the east, nor is it limited to coal mining; it can occur anywhere that pyrite (FeS_2) occurs. Pyrite readily oxidizes in water to form sulfuric acid when it is exposed to atmospheric oxygen (Figure 12.4). Anaerobic generation of sulfuric acid may also occur primarily through the oxidation of pyrite by ferric iron, or it may be facilitated by the anaerobic bacterium *Ferrobacillus ferroxidans*, which influences the rate of pyrite oxidation by mediating ferrous iron oxidation (Stumm and Morgan 1970). Much mineral recovery in the western USA occurs in granitic deposits that contain pyrite, and acid drainage in these operations can be a serious problem. In addition, a variety of other metallic sulfides, including chalcopyrite ($CuFeS_2$), sphalerite (ZnS), galena (PbS), and greenockite (CdS) undergo similar acid-generating processes (Fuller et al. 1978). Effluent waters under such conditions may have low pH (2.0–4.5), which is directly toxic to most forms of aquatic life (Hill 1974), is conducive to the mobilization of toxic metals (Fuller et al. 1978), and is instrumental in forming ferric hydroxide ($FeOH_3$), the noxious precipitate commonly called "yellow boy." Sources of acidic effluent include discharge from

FIGURE 12.3.—Aerial view of the stibnite mine in central Idaho showing massive alteration of the landscape.

underground mining operations, surface runoff over tailings piles, and leakage from settling ponds.

The optimal pH range for fish has been reported to be from 6.5 to 8.7, or nearly neutral to slightly alkaline (U.S. Environmental Protection Agency 1976). Fish can survive at pH values outside this range for limited periods, but any pH below 6.0 is generally regarded as unfavorable (Spaulding and Ogden 1968). Toxic effects of low pH on individual fish include direct mortality, reduced growth rate, reproductive failure, skeletal deformities, and increased uptake of heavy metals (Haines 1981). Low pH also causes system-wide effects such as elimination of sensitive species and proliferation of tolerant species; reductions in density, biomass, and diversity in aquatic systems; increasing degrees of abnormal behavior by affected organisms; and reproductive, emergence, and rearing failure.

Declines in salmonid populations that are caused by discharges of acidic mine effluent often result from failure to recruit young age-classes (Nelson 1982). Studies have shown that early developmental stages of fish are more sensitive than later stages to low pH (McKim 1977; Brungs et al. 1978), and several studies on salmonids have documented considerable susceptibility to low pH during the alevin stage (Kwain 1975; Menendez 1976; Daye and Garside 1980). Trojnar (1977) showed that brook trout eggs hatched when pH was as low as 4.0, but that fry survival increased (to >60%) when pH was 4.6–5.0. Peterson et al. (1980a, 1980b) demonstrated that hatching of Atlantic salmon failed at pH 5.0 because the embryos' choriolytic enzyme activity was disrupted. Nelson (1982) described reduced hatching success, growth rate, development of pigmentation, ossification, and heart rate at a pH of 4.3, and showed that these effects were offset

Aerobic oxidation:

1. $2FeS_2 + 7O_2 + 2H_2O <===> 2Fe^{+2} + 4SO_4^{-2} + 4H^+$
2. $4Fe^{+2} + O_2 + 4H^+ <===> 4Fe^{+3} + 2H_2O$
3. $Fe^{+3} + 3H_2O <===> Fe(OH)_3 + 3H^+$

Anaerobic oxidation:

1. $FeS_2 + 14Fe^{+3} + 8H_2O <===> 15Fe^{+2} = 2SO_4^{-2} + 16H^+$

FIGURE 12.4.—Pathways of aerobic and anaerobic oxidation reported for pyrite in sulfuric acid mine effluent. (Adapted from Stumm and Morgan 1970; Olem and Unz 1980; Starnes 1985.)

somewhat by large environmental concentrations of calcium (Ca^{+2}). Weiner et al. (1986) also showed that gametogenesis, particularly spermatogenesis, seemed to be impaired in adult rainbow trout in water of pH 5.5, that hatching failure occurred below pH 4.5, and that yolk-sac fry were lethargic at pH levels of 5.0 and 5.5. In addition, reduced recruitment could result from altered behavior by spawning adults, as suggested in a study by Johnson and Webster (1977) that demonstrated an avoidance reaction of brook trout in water of pH below 5.0.

Direct mortality of fish from low pH has been attributed to two principal factors: alteration of ionic and respiratory exchanges, and increased environmental concentrations of toxic metals (Haines 1981). Gill damage occurs at low pH levels (McKenna and Duerr 1976; Daye 1981), as do changes in ion exchange through the gills (Brungs et al. 1978). Specifically, changes in membrane permeability may allow displacement of sodium ions (Na^+) in the blood by hydrogen ions (H^+) (Kerstetter et al. 1970; Packer and Dunson 1970; Fromm 1980). Acid interference with sodium transport varies among types of acid at similar pH levels, and the rate of sodium loss—not necessarily just the magnitude of loss—is inversely related to survival time under acidic conditions (Packer and Dunson 1972). Acidic mine effluent seems to be less toxic than sulfuric acid alone, perhaps because of the presence of metals including zinc, magnesium, manganese, and iron (Packer and Dunson 1972). Aluminum, however, has been implicated as an important determinant of acid toxicity to fish. Haines (1981), discussing acid precipitation studies by Cronan and Schofield (1979), Baker and Schofield (1980), Herrmann and Baron (1980), Leivestad et al. (1980), Muniz and Leivestad (1980), and Schofield and Trojnar (1980), stated that mortality of brook trout and brown trout at low pH is greater when aluminum is present than when it is absent. Causes of reduced oxygen consumption at low pH are unclear, but they may include mechanical impairment of the gills, altered permeability of gill membranes to dissolved oxygen (O_2), and reduced affinity of blood for O_2 at low blood pH (Packer and Dunson 1972).

Just as life-history stage influences a fish's ability to tolerate acidic conditions, genetic factors also play a role. Brook trout seem to be generally more tolerant of low pH levels than other species commonly found in waters affected by acid mine drainage, but variations are also found among individual strains (Swarts et al.

1978). Some studies have suggested that time of exposure to various nonlethal pH levels may encourage acclimation to acidic conditions. Trojnar (1977) demonstrated better survival of trout fry that were incubated in and emerged at pH 4.6–5.0 than when emergence at pH 4.0 followed incubation at pH 8.1. Studies of embryonic, juvenile, and adult brook trout of several strains by Swarts et al. (1978), however, did not support the concept of acclimation, though they did suggest that wild fish withstood acidity better than fish raised in a hatchery. Falk and Dunson (1977) reported that the resistance of brook trout to pH 3.15 and 5.0 varied distinctly among seasons but that the fish showed no definite tendency for acclimation.

Results of several studies suggest at least the potential for acclimation to moderately acidic conditions, however. Vaala and Mitchell (1970), for example, demonstrated an increase in blood hemoglobin, hematocrit, and peripheral red cell count in brook trout when water pH was reduced from neutral to 3.5 over a 4-d period. They reasoned that this change occurred to compensate for reduced blood oxygen tension brought about by reduced oxygen diffusion efficiency across gill membranes, apparently the beginnings of an acclimation response to reduced pH. In addition, McWilliams (1980) showed that brown trout acclimated to water of pH 6.0 for 6 weeks before being exposed to water of pH 4.0 maintained a more balanced sodium metabolism than did nonacclimated fish.

Several research efforts have demonstrated that acidification can also reduce or eliminate aquatic invertebrate populations, a chief source of food for fish. Katz (1969), who found no viable fishery in waters with a pH at or below 3.5, noted that the invertebrate community was dominated by chironomids (midges) and a species of *Sialis* (alderflies), which are considered indicative of poor water quality. He found no members of the desirable fish food such as caddisflies (Trichoptera), mayflies (Ephemeroptera), or stoneflies (Plecoptera). In Coal Creek, Colorado, Reiser et al. (1982) found significantly fewer invertebrate taxa and reduced numbers of organisms immediately below an abandoned gold and silver mine, which had produced effluents in the pH range of 3.0–4.0 for 30–40 years, compared to stream reaches above the outflow. Because a treatment facility had just been installed and only treated effluent was entering Coal Creek at the time of the survey, the authors attributed the depauperate invertebrate fauna to the heavy coating of "yellow boy" and sediments on the stream bottom. In a historic gold-mining area of Shasta County, California, Fuller et al. (1978) found very low benthic invertebrate diversity in two portions of streams with very low pH (2.4–4.0). In all sites where pH was below 4.0, acid-tolerant chironomids made up the bulk, by number, of the invertebrate community, reaching 98.9% of all organisms at a pH of 2.4. At and above pH 4.0, diversity increased as did the number of occupied trophic levels. In a benthic invertebrate study conducted on waters receiving acid drainage from coal mining operations, Roback and Richardson (1969) also showed that ephemeropterans, plecopterans, and trichopterans were most sensitive to the acid discharge, though a caddisfly of the genus *Ptilostomus* apparently tolerated pH levels as low as 3.0. Where silty substrates occurred in conjunction with low pH, Roback and Richardson also found chironomids and *Sialis* sp. in abundance.

In addition to the direct lethality and the problems associated with yellow boy deposition that it causes, acidity also enhances the toxicity to fish of metallic pollutants that are generated by mining activities.

Toxic Metals

Metals are naturally present in varying concentrations (referred to as the "background" level) in all surface waters, and many are required by fish in trace quantities for proper physiological function. Mining, however, may cause concentrations of dissolved metals to exceed background levels, particularly in situations involving acid mine discharge (Finlayson and Ashuckian 1979; Phillips 1985). Mining may introduce toxic metals into streams through acid-stimulated mobilization of metal ions from metalliferous minerals like chalcopyrite, sphalerite, galena, and greenockite (Fuller et al. 1978), particularly if discharge occurs through waste piles. Duaime et al. (1985) estimated that loadings from an abandoned mine on Silver Bow Creek, Montana, were up to 13.6 kg Cu/d for copper and 1.6–145.5 kg Zn/d for zinc. The chief metals released to streams by mining operations are arsenic (As), cadmium (Cd), chromium (Cr), cobalt (Co), copper (Cu), iron (Fe), lead (Pb), manganese (Mn), mercury (Hg), nickel (Ni), and zinc (Zn). These substances may produce toxic effects alone, in combination, or synergistically, or they may behave antagonistically to reduce toxicity.

Contamination by metals may affect large areas. Johns and Moore (1985) discovered enrichment of copper and zinc 4–10 times background levels 560 km away from the major source of contamination in the Clark Fork River, Montana. In Idaho, mining at the Blackbird Mine, site of one of the largest cobalt deposits in the world, effectively eliminated spawning by chinook salmon in Panther Creek, a tributary of the Salmon River. Mining for cobalt and copper began in the drainage in the 1890s, reached its peak during the 1940s and 1950s in response to military needs, and has continued at some level until the present (Chertudi 1986). Several occurrences detrimental to aquatic habitats have been noted in the Panther Creek drainage, including disposal of tailings in tributaries (1930s), failure of settling ponds (1940s), deposition of up to 1.7 tonnes of waste rock in headwaters areas (1950s), and adit construction leading to drainage problems (1960s). Acidic drainage (with pH levels as low as 2.75) has washed a variety of heavy metals into the drainage, only to be deposited as precipitates on the streambed when the effluent was diluted by streamwater of higher pH (Chertudi 1986). Panther Creek historically supported spawning runs of up to 2,000 adult salmon, but runs began to decline in the 1940s and dropped to zero by 1963, and reduction in runs was closely correlated with the level of mining activity in the drainage (Reiser 1986). Acid mine drainage and copper loadings of 41–147 kg/d are the major water quality problems persisting in the Panther Creek drainage.

Many independent studies have demonstrated the high toxicity of artificially elevated metal concentrations to fish (Cairns and Scheier 1957; Lloyd 1960, 1961a, 1961b; Tarzwell and Henderson 1960; Lloyd and Herbert 1962; Mount and Stephan 1967a). In general, mortality is usually attributed to high metal concentrations, but continuous exposure to sublethal levels may produce such chronic effects as behavioral changes and reproductive failure (Chapman 1973); both effects ultimately determine species survival in the affected habitat.

Toxicity of specific metals to fish can be difficult to determine; it varies with species, age, and developmental stage (Lloyd 1960). In addition, the physico-chemical properties of water affect the toxic properties of metals. This is especially true of hardness, expressed as milligrams of calcium carbonate ($CaCO_3$) per liter, which is inversely proportional to the toxicity of many metals (Hale 1977; Wilson et al. 1981). Water temperature, pH, and dissolved oxygen all influence toxicity (Doudoroff and Katz 1953). In addition, the toxicities of various metals determined by laboratory studies frequently have been inconsistent (Table 12.1). Doudoroff and Katz (1953) attributed these differences to variations in experimental design and water quality. Although imprecise, such studies may be used in conjunction with governmental water quality guidelines to estimate tolerance ranges for mineral extraction and mine-reclamation operations, as in Table 12.2. It should be remembered, however, that the values reported in bioassay studies are based on acute (short-term) exposures that cause rapid mortality. The effects of sublethal doses of toxic metals may be as great, but are not yet completely understood.

Arsenic.—Arsenic is not technically a metal, but is classified as a transitory element or metalloid (that is, metallic in appearance, and possessing some properties of a metal). Elemental arsenic is insoluble in water but many arsenates, particularly arsenic trioxide (As_2O_3), are highly soluble; arsenic compounds therefore occur naturally in trace amounts in many western streams and lakes (McKee and Wolf 1971). In surveys of 130 stations in the western USA, Kopp and Kroner (1967) found arsenic concentrations ranging from 5.0 to 336 µg/L. Mining, milling, and smelting of ore containing arsenic can pollute surface waters as the metalloid leaches from tailings ponds and waste piles; later, arsenic can be mobilized in acid drainage from abandoned mines.

Arsenic, though not biologically accumulated, is toxic to fishes and poses a hazard to salmonids in areas of deposition. McKee and Wolf (1971) recommended limits of 1.0 mg As/L in water occupied by aquatic biota. In a study of acute toxicity, Hale (1977) reported a 96-h median lethal concentration (LC50) of 10.8 mg/L. Nichols et al. (1984) reported significant chronic effects on coho salmon from much lower concentrations; a 6-month exposure to 300 µg As_2O_3/L delayed the normal increase in plasma thyroxine and caused a transitory reduction in gill sodium–potassium ATPase activity. Treated coho salmon exhibited less success in seaward migration than control fish, although the arsenic exposure caused no apparent direct effects on growth and survival.

Animals at lower trophic levels appear to be more resistant to arsenic. Arsenic concentrations of 3.0–14.0 and 10.0–20.0 mg/L were reported as nontoxic to mayfly and dragonfly nymphs, respectively (Rudolfs et al. 1950).

Cadmium.—Cadmium occurs naturally as a sulfide salt, commonly in associa-tion with zinc and lead ores. Accumulation of cadmium in soils near mines and smeltering operations may result in high local concentrations in nearby waters (Hale 1977). Rice and Ray (1985) found that cadmium concentrations of 5.0 µg/L were present in riparian soils of the Clark Fork River, Montana; an estimated 70% of the cadmium originated from upstream tailing sources and 30% was attributable to airborne deposition from smelting operations.

Cadmium may be highly toxic to biotas in low-alkalinity waters. The carbonate and hydroxide forms of cadmium are insoluble; at high pH values, therefore,

TABLE 12.1.—Reported toxicities of metals in soft water (<45 mg/L as $CaCO_3$).

Substance	Species	Reported toxicity		Source
		Method[a]	Concentration	
Aluminum (Al)	Brook trout	LC50	3.6–4.0 mg/L	Decker and Menendez (1974)
Arsenic (As)	Rainbow trout	LC50	10.8 mg/L	Hale (1977)
Cadmium (Cd)	Rainbow trout	LC50	6.6 μg/L	Hale (1977)
	Brook trout	MATC	1.7–3.4 μg/L	Benoit et al. (1976)
Chromium (Cr)	Rainbow trout	LC50	24.1 mg/L	Hale (1977)
	Rainbow trout	LC50	69.0 mg/L	Benoit (1976)
	Rainbow trout	MATC	0.2–0.35 mg/L	Benoit (1976)
	Brook trout	LC50	59.0 mg/L	Benoit (1976)
	Brook trout	MATC	0.2–0.35 mg/L	Benoit (1976)
Copper (Cu)	Coho salmon	LC50	46.0 μg/L	Chapman and Stevens (1978)
	Rainbow trout	LC50	253.0 μg/L	Hale (1977)
	Rainbow trout	LC50	125.0 μg/L	Wilson (1972)
	Rainbow trout	LC50	57.0 μg/L	Chapman and Stevens (1978)
	Rainbow trout	ILL	37.0 μg/L	Sprague and Ramsay (1965)
	Atlantic salmon	ILL	32.0 μg/L	Sprague and Ramsay (1965)
	Atlantic salmon	ILL	0.52 mg/L	Sprague (1964)
	Brook trout	MATC	9.5–17.4 μg/L	McKim and Benoit (1971)
Copper–zinc	Atlantic salmon	TU	1.0 mg/L	Sprague and Ramsay (1965)
Iron (Fe)	Brook trout	LC50	1.75 mg/L	Decker and Menendez (1974)
Lead (Pb)	Rainbow trout	LC50	8.0 mg/L	Hale (1977)
	Rainbow trout (eggs)	MATC	4.1–7.6 μg/L	Davies et al. (1976)
Mercury (Hg)	Rainbow trout	LC50	33.0 mg/L	Hale (1977)
Nickel (Ni)	Rainbow trout	LC50	35.5 mg/L	Hale (1977)
Uranium (U)	Brook trout	LC50	2.8 mg/L	Parkhurst et al. (1984)
Zinc (Zn)	Coho salmon	LC50	905.0 μg/L	Chapman and Stevens (1978)
	Rainbow trout	LC50	1,755 μg/L	Chapman and Stevens (1978)
	Rainbow trout	LC50	0.18–0.39 mg/L	Finlayson and Ashuckian (1979)
	Rainbow trout	ILL	560 μg/L	Sprague and Ramsay (1965)
	Atlantic salmon	ILL	0.092 mg/L	Sprague (1964)
	Atlantic salmon	ILL	0.15–1.0 mg/L	Zitko and Carson (1977)
	Atlantic salmon	ILL	420 μg/L	Sprague and Ramsay (1965)
	Brook trout	MATC	534–1,360 μg/L	Holcombe et al. (1979)

[a] LC50 = lethal concentration for 50% of test organisms; MATC = maximum acceptable toxic concentration; ILL = incipient lethal level; TU = toxic units.

cadmium is precipitated, reducing its toxicity to fishes (McKee and Wolf 1971). Chapman and Stevens (1978) found that cadmium-induced mortality of adult salmonids was slow in onset, but 50% mortality occurred after more than a week when coho salmon were exposed to 3.7 and steelhead to 5.2 μg Cd/L. Benoit et al. (1976) exposed three generations of brook trout to concentrations of cadmium ranging from 0.06 to 6.4 μg/L over a 3-year period and reported significant mortality of first- and second-generation spawning males at 3.4 μg/L. This concentration also significantly retarded the growth of second- and third-generation offspring. For water quality standards, Wilson et al. (1981) recommend that

TABLE 12.2.—Summary of water quality criteria (LOEL = lowest observed effect level[a]) for metals commonly found in mining-polluted waters. NA = not available. (U.S. Environmental Protection Agency 1986.)

Metal	Acute criterion (LOEL, μg/L)	Chronic criterion (LOEL, μg/L)	Potential use	
			Consumption of fish and water (μg/L)	Consumption of fish only (μg/L)
Antimony	9,000	1,600	146	45,000
Arsenic	360	190	NA	NA
Beryllium	130	5.3	6.8	117
Cadmium	3.9	1.1	10.0	NA
Chromium				
Hexavalent	16	11	50	NA
Trivalent	1,700[b]	210[b]	170,000	3,433,000
Copper	18[b]	12[b]	NA	NA
Cyanide	22	5.2	200	NA
Iron	NA	1,000	300	NA
Lead	82[b]	3.2[b]	50	NA
Manganese	NA	NA	50	100
Mercury	2.4	0.012	0.144	0.146
Nickel	1,800[b]	96[b]	13.4	100
Selenium	260	35	10	NA
Silver	4.1[b]	0.12[b]	50	NA
Zinc	320[b]	47[b]	NA	NA

[a]Lowest observed effect levels are not regulatory, but reflect the latest scientific knowledge about the effects and behavior of pollutants in receiving waters.
[b]Hardness dependent (100 μg/L used as criterion).

cadmium concentrations in waters occupied by salmonids should not exceed 0.4 μg/L.

Fish exposed to cadmium become hyperactive, then suffer respiratory distress and paralysis. Cearly and Coleman (1974) suggested that the toxic effect of cadmium on the nervous system is consistent with the metal's inhibition of the enzyme cholinesterase, resulting in paralysis of the respiratory center.

Fish exposed to cadmium accumulate the greatest concentrations of the metal in gills, kidney, liver, and testes; tissue residues apparently reach equilibrium with cadmium concentrations in water (Kumada et al. 1973; Eaton 1974). Kumada et al. (1973) noted that rainbow trout exposed to cadmium for 30 weeks and then transferred to clean water for 10 weeks lost some accumulated cadmium from gill tissues but retained high concentrations in kidney and liver tissues. Wilson et al. (1981), who studied heavy metal concentrations in the trout of a California stream contaminated by acid mine wastes, also found that cadmium concentrations in livers (but not in flesh) were closely correlated with environmental concentrations. The long-term physiological effects of such accumulations are unknown, however.

Chromium.—Chromium, although a relatively abundant metal, is rarely found in natural waters; however, it may be present in waters disturbed by mining activity, particularly in trivalent or hexavalent forms (Hale 1977). Few studies have addressed the toxic effects of chromium on fishes. Olson and Foster (1956) showed that survival of chinook salmon and rainbow trout was adversely affected by a chromium concentration of 0.20 mg/L. Benoit (1976) reported that exposure of rainbow trout fry to 0.34 mg Cr/L for 8 months significantly increased mortality; no effect on egg hatchability and survival was found. Chronic toxicity values for brook and rainbow trout have been reported as 2.61 mg/L, although growth is affected at lower concentrations (U.S. Environmental Protection Agency 1986).

Effects of chromium vary among aquatic invertebrates. Reported acute toxicities have ranged from 23.1 μg/L for a species of cladoceran to 1.87 g/L for a species of trichopteran (U.S. Environmental Protection Agency 1986).

Copper.—Copper is relatively insoluble in natural waters but becomes more soluble as pH declines, so it may be introduced into streams via acid mine drainage. Kopp and Kroner (1967) found soluble copper in 74% of over 1,500 surface water samples collected in the USA; the average concentration was 15.0 μg/L. McKee and Wolf (1971) recommended an allowable maximum copper concentration of 0.02 mg/L in waters inhabited by fish, but this concentration is often exceeded. Phillips (1985) measured copper concentrations of 0.3 mg/L in the Clark Fork River, Montana. Copper concentrations of 90 mg/L were measured by Fuller et al. (1978) in West Squaw Creek, California.

Copper-induced mortality of fishes occurs when insoluble copper–protein compounds form on gill surfaces; these cause sloughing of gill epithelia, and the fish eventually suffocate (Wilson et al. 1981). Mortality of fish by copper poisoning has been reported at various concentrations. Hale (1977) reported that the LC50 for 2-month rainbow trout was 253 μg Cu/L. Chapman and Stevens (1978) found that the LC50 values for adult coho salmon and steelhead were 46.0 and 57.0 μg Cu/L, respectively. Sprague (1964) stated that Atlantic salmon were killed at copper concentrations of 52 μg/L. The discrepancies in copper bioassays are generally attributable to differences in water hardness. Lloyd and Herbert (1962), Sprague and Ramsay (1965), Chapman and Stevens (1978), and Wilson et al. (1981) reported that copper toxicity decreases as calcium carbonate concentration and alkalinity increase.

Fish exposed to low concentrations of copper may also be affected. Wilson et al. (1981) found that copper did not accumulate in muscle tissue of trout in the upper Sacramento River basin, California, but did accumulate in liver tissue by as much as 1,200%. The authors concluded that continued heavy metal pollution in the system represented a threat to native fish populations. McKim and Benoit (1971) exposed all developmental stages of brook trout to copper concentrations ranging from 1.9 to 32.5 μg/L. Copper concentrations greater than 17.4 μg/L adversely affected growth and survival of alevins and juvenile fish, and the highest concentration (32.5 μg/L) reduced the hatchability of embryos. Concentrations below 17.4 μg/L had no apparent effect on any life stage of brook trout.

Fish exposed to copper may react behaviorally. In laboratory tests, Sprague (1964) found that Atlantic salmon avoided copper at a concentration of 2 μg/L. McKim and Benoit (1971) noted that juvenile fish raised in low copper concentrations were lethargic and took feed poorly. Drummond et al. (1973) found behavioral changes in brook trout at concentrations as low as 5 μg/L.

Iron.—Iron is the earth's fourth most abundant element by weight and occurs naturally in a variety of forms. Oxidation of ferrous minerals in iron-containing ores is a primary source of environmental acids (Figure 12.4). The toxicity of iron to fishes increases significantly as the pH decreases (Decker and Menendez 1974). For example, Decker and Menendez (1974) reported that the median lethal iron dose (LD50) for brook trout was 1.75 mg/L at pH 7.0 and 0.48 mg/L at pH 6.0. Ellis (1940) stated that iron concentrations above 2.0 mg/L are indicators of acid pollution, but the toxic effects of iron on aquatic organisms are not well understood. Iron mobilized in acidic mine drainages precipitates as nearly insoluble ferric hydroxide (yellow boy) when it reaches more alkaline natural waters. Mitsch and Letterman (1979) found that deposition of yellow boy on the streambed of Ben's Creek, Pennsylvania, was as great as 3.0 g/m^2 daily downstream from the effluent discharge of an abandoned mine. The oxide and hydroxide precipitates are the forms of iron most lethal to aquatic animals because they coat gills and cause suffocation (Van Duijn 1967). Lewis (1960) reported that heavy precipitates of iron hydroxide killed trout eggs, primarily by forming an exchange barrier to oxygen. In contrast, exposure to 0.75–12.0 mg/L of lime-neutralized (pH-neutral) suspended iron had no effect on the hatching success of brook trout and coho salmon (Smith and Sykora 1976). In the same study, however, survival of coho salmon alevins declined in 6.0 and 12.0 mg Fe/L of water. Safe limits of suspended iron were reported as 0.97–1.27 mg/L for coho salmon and 7.5–12.5 mg/L for brook trout (U.S. Environmental Protection Agency 1986).

Lead.—Lead occurs naturally as the mineral galena and its solubility in water is inversely proportional to water hardness (Davies et al. 1976). Hale (1977) reported that the aqueous solubility of lead ranges from 500 µg/L in soft water (<100 mg/L as $CaCO_3$) to 3.0 µg/L in hard water. Water quality specialists recommend that safe lead concentrations in water should not exceed 0.03 mg/L (Ray 1978). McKee and Wolf (1971) recommended that the lead content of surface water be restricted to less than 0.1 mg/L. Lead is one of the most toxic elements known; however, research into the effects of lead on aquatic life is relatively recent.

Lead-induced mortality of fishes is similar to that of iron. In water containing lead salts, a suffocating film of coagulated mucus forms over the body and gills (Carpenter 1930). Effects of chronic exposure of fishes to high lead levels have been reported by Davies et al. (1976) and Hale (1977). Long-term exposure to low concentrations of lead may also be harmful to fish. Holcombe et al. (1976) found that when three generations of brook trout were exposed to lead concentrations ranging from 0.001 to 0.5 mg/L, second- and third-generation trout developed spinal deformities (scoliosis). Davies et al. (1976) reported that rainbow trout exposed to aqueous solutions of lead suffered from blackening of the tail, scoliosis, caudal atrophy, and caudal fin erosion; the authors further theorized that the observed physical manifestations of lead toxicity were attributable to direct neurological damage. Toxicity of lead is inversely related to oxygen concentration; Lloyd (1961a) showed that lead toxicity to rainbow trout increases with a reduction in dissolved oxygen concentration.

Ray (1978) speculated that fishes take up lead with their food. Czarneki (1985) found that among all fish species in the Big River, Missouri, a stream contaminated by severe erosion of tailing piles, benthic fishes had the highest muscle tissue concentrations (1.3 µg/kg) of lead. Czarneki concluded (in contrast to Ray's theory) that these fishes had the highest concentrations because they were most in contact with the source of lead (stream sediments).

Lead accumulates in organisms, particularly in liver and kidney tissues. Pagenkopf and Newman (1974) observed mean lead concentrations of 4.2 mg/kg in livers of trout raised in river water containing about 3 µg Pb/L. Ray (1978) calculated a concentration factor of 4,700 times for livers of Atlantic salmon raised in the Miramichi River, New Brunswick. Whether or not residual lead in fishes causes any physiological or biological damage is not known at present, however.

Mercury.—Mercury is recovered from cinnabar (HgS) deposits, but it is also found in lesser amounts in association with western coal deposits (Chadwick et al. 1975). Mercury has no biological value and is highly toxic to animal life. Mercury is a cumulative systemic toxin (Hale 1977). Organomercury compounds are up to 31 times more toxic than elemental mercury (U.S. Environmental Protection Agency 1986), and methyl-mercury is generally recognized as the most toxic and readily accumulated form of mercury (Clarkson 1973). Many microorganisms that commonly occur in natural waters can convert inorganic mercury to methyl-mercury, which they then may release to the water. Doudoroff (1957) found that mercury concentrations of 0.004–0.02 mg/L were toxic to several freshwater fish species. Toxicity of mercury to rainbow trout has been estimated at 33.0 μg/L (Hale 1977). Human poisonings resulting from the consumption of fishes contaminated by mercury, particularly marine species, have been reported often (National Academy of Sciences 1979).

Mercury finds its way into the bodies of fishes by way of diet or direct absorption from the water. Phillips et al. (1980) found that mercury concentration in fishes from the Tongue River, Montana, increased with both size and age. The authors further stated that the rate of mercury accumulation was faster in piscivorous species than in planktivores. Phillips and Buhler (1978) found that rainbow trout assimilated 10–12% of the methyl-mercury passing over their gills, indicating that at least some mercury is absorbed from the water.

Although economically recoverable deposits of cinnabar are limited in the western USA, mercury's association with western coal deposits may have consequences for fisheries. Fish reared in water decanted from a western coal mine accumulated significant amounts of the metal (Phillips and Gregory 1980). Mercury is also used to extract goal and silver during refining processes, and much of this mercury has been improperly discarded and deposited in natural stream systems. In Nevada's Carson River drainage, site of the famed Comstock lode, 200,000 flasks (6.75×10^6 kg) of mercury were estimated by Cooper and Vigg (1984) to have been used in placer processing during the 30-year period 1869–1899; only 0.5% of this mercury was ever recovered. Cooper and Vigg also reported mercury contaminations ranging from 0.11 to 3.95 mg/kg in muscle tissues of dead fish recovered from the Carson River drainage.

Zinc.—Zinc is usually found in nature as a sulfide, often associated with sulfides of lead, copper, cadmium, and iron (Hale 1977). The toxicity of zinc to aquatic animals, like the toxicity of other metals, is modified by environmental variables such as water hardness, dissolved oxygen, pH, and temperature (McKee and Wolf 1971).

Zinc concentrations apparently have to be fairly high to significantly affect aquatic populations (Table 12.1). Chapman (1978) found that growth of sockeye salmon was stimulated at concentrations of 242 μg Zn/L. Holcombe et al. (1979) found that exposure of three generations of brook trout to concentrations of zinc ranging from 2.6 to 534.0 μg/L had no significant effect on survival, growth, and reproductive success. When embryos and larvae were raised in water with high zinc concentrations (1,368 μg/L), however, significant reductions in survival were found. Holcombe et al. (1979) attributed the reduction in embryo survival to diminished capacity of the chorion to resist rupture. Exposure to 0.8 mg Zn/L for 72 h was toxic to rainbow trout, causing acid–base disturbances in blood and net loss of plasma ions through gill tissue (Spry and Wood 1985). Zinc pollution may impair physiological functions in fishes. Zitko and Carson (1977) found that Atlantic salmon were most sensitive to zinc during the parr—smolt transformation, and studies by Lorz and McPherson (1977) support their finding.

Antagonism and synergism of metals.—Although pure metal solutions prepared for toxicity tests can kill fishes, the toxic actions of metals in nature are often modified by processes referred to as antagonism and synergism. Antagonistic metal reactions, which reduce the toxicity of metals primarily through precipitation (Doudoroff and Katz 1953), result in solutions that are much less toxic than simple metal solutions. For example, calcium, a common component of natural waters, markedly counteracts the toxic effects of copper, lead, magnesium, potassium, sodium, and zinc (Doudoroff and Katz 1953).

Conversely, combinations of highly toxic metals such as zinc and copper are highly synergistic; that is, their joint effect is greater than the sum of their separate effects. Sprague and Ramsay (1965) found that lethal concentrations of copper–zinc solutions act two to three times faster on fish than do the metals singly. (Lloyd 1960, however, had reported simple additive effects of copper–zinc solutions.) Finlayson and Verrue (1980), working with chinook salmon, reported 83-d LC50 values for 1:3, 1:6, and 1:11 stock-solution ratios of copper to zinc as 44 μg Cu and 160 μg Zn/L, 27 μg Cu and 206 μg Zn/L, and 17 μg Cu and 253 μg Zn/L, respectively. Cadmium also is known to act synergistically. Hublou et al. (1954) reported that cadmium concentrations of 0.03 mg/L in combination with 0.15 mg Zn/L induced mortality of salmon fry.

Radioactive Contamination

About 90% of the USA's recoverable uranium reserves occur in the west (Moore and Mills 1977), primarily in Arizona, New Mexico, Nevada, Utah, and Montana. Exploration for and recovery of these resources may be expected to increase if demand for nuclear power generation once again increases. Extraction of uranium and other less-valuable, naturally radioactive minerals produces a variety of toxic threats.

Uranium and its isotopes are metallic substances similar to other potentially hazardous heavy metals. Uranium ore occurs chiefly in sandstone deposits, and it is recovered principally by open-pit or underground techniques. Solution mining may be used to leach the highly soluble uranium salts from marginal deposits or nearly depleted mines (Woodmansee 1975). Of these recovery techniques, open-pit operations probably pose the most environmental hazard from radioactivity because of the large amount of waste generated in removal of the overburden (Yamamoto 1982). Uranium mine tailings retain approximately 85% of the initial radioactivity of the source ore, about 90% of which is contributed by ^{238}uranium, the rest by the isotopes ^{230}thorium, ^{226}radium, and ^{210}lead (Bryant et al. 1979). Fresh liquid tailings ponds associated with uranium recovery may be neutral to alkaline in pH, but seepage and runoff from abandoned solid tailings can be very acidic (Bryant et al. 1979). In addition, some uranium may be extracted from the parent ore by treatment with sulfuric acid (Vinot and Larpent 1984) and fresh tailings may be treated with barium chloride to co-precipitate barium, radium, and sulfate in lagoons (Bryant et al. 1979). Consequently, the effects of uranium extraction on fishery resources may include heavy metal toxicity, acidification, and radioactivity, alone or in combination.

Toxicity.—The toxicity of uranium to fish has been poorly evaluated, but is known to be related to water hardness and length of exposure. The chemical toxicity of uranium also varies with the development stage of the fish. Tarzwell and Henderson (1960) determined that uranium from uranyl sulfate ($UO_2SO_4 \cdot 3H_2O$) had 96-h LC50 values with fathead minnows as low as 2.8 mg/L in soft water (2 mg/L as $CaCO_3$) and as high as 135 mg/L in hard water (400 mg/L as $CaCO_3$). Brook trout studies by Parkhurst et al. (1984) indicated a static 96-h uranium LC50 of 5.5 mg/L in soft water (35 mg/L as $CaCO_3$) and 23 mg/L in hard water (208 mg/L as $CaCO_3$). These figures are somewhat misleading, however, in that uranium concentration had a threshold effect: all brook trout survived for 96 h in uranium concentrations below 3.9 mg/L and 16.4 mg/L for soft and hard water, respectively, but none survived at higher concentrations. In this same study, flowing-water tests with hard (184 mg/L as $CaCO_3$), alkaline (146 mg/L) water indicated a 48-h LC50 of 59 mg U/L; flowing water with less than 10 mg U/L had no significant effect on egg-hatching success or fry survival and growth.

Bioaccumulation of radionuclides.—Specific effects of radioactivity itself on the survival of salmonids are even more obscure. Concern often centers around human consumption of contaminated fish or contact with radioactive waste piles and tailings ponds. Of particular interest is bioaccumulation of radionuclides in fish themselves, as well as in other components of the aquatic food chain. Bioaccumulation of various radionuclides varies among species and with attributes of the environment, but few definitive data are currently available.

Uranium, although potentially toxic, is a relatively weak emitter of radiation and is probably a much less serious radiation hazard than [226]radium (Justyn and Lusk 1976). Radium apparently acts as a nutrient analog of calcium in some biological processes (Whicker and Schultz 1982) and environmental [226]Ra may be accumulated by fish as part of their normal calcium metabolism. Rope and Whicker (1985) found that the [226]Ra concentration in the bones of brook trout and rainbow trout taken from settling ponds near a Wyoming uranium mine was significantly higher than the concentration in skin and fins, where it was significantly higher than in flesh. This bioaccumulation appeared to be greater where ambient calcium concentrations were lower (that is, as water became softer); however, although the [226]Ra concentrations in the settling ponds ranged from 67 to 333 times greater than in uncontaminated water, Rope and Whicker (1985) concluded that human consumption of fish from the ponds posed little health hazard. Poston (1982) exposed juvenile rainbow trout to solutions of 1.0×10^{-3} µg [228+232]thorium, 1.1×10^{-3} µg [232]uranium, or 1.0 µg [238]uranium per milliliter and found insignificant net bioaccumulation above these background levels following 27-d uptake and 25-d depuration periods for thorium and 35-d uptake and 25-d depuration periods for uranium.

Acidity caused by oxidation of pyrite associated with uranium deposits is known to increase the solubility of wastes containing [228]Th and [210]Pb. On the other hand, treatment of some tailings with barium chloride effectively reduced the amount of available ^{226}Ra; however, this procedure creates potentially toxic situations for *Daphnia pulex* and rainbow trout (Bryant et al. 1979).

Work by Jenkins (1969) suggests that some Pacific salmon may concentrate ambient radionuclides. This study concerned bioaccumulation of contaminants from atmospheric fallout rather than from mine wastes, but indicated that chum salmon roe had a ^{226}Ra concentration factor of 1,200 and that chinook salmon from Alaska concentrated sufficient radioactivity to pose a potential health threat to people consuming the fish. Thus, accumulation of radiation by salmon in natal streams affected by uranium mining or milling, followed by additional accumulation from ocean waters as adults, could lead to serious contamination of Pacific Northwest salmon stocks.

Not only fish accumulated radiation from the water. Work by Blevins et al. (1985) demonstrated extensive accumulation of alpha and beta radiation in pondweed *Potamogeton tenuifoleus*—concentration factors were 10,000 and 7,000, respectively—downstream from a uranium processing facility in Tennessee. Accumulation of radiation in aquatic vegetation and stream sediments may serve as a reservoir of radioactivity available to the entire aquatic food chain and, ultimately, to fish and the people who eat them.

Miscellaneous radionuclides.—A variety of minor radionuclides are also mined for various industrial applications. Most important to salmonid habitats are the radioactive rare earths, often called "black sands" or "radioactive blacks." These minerals are generally scarce, but may occur as concentrated lenses in alluvial deposits, where they can be dredged. In addition, ^{232}Th, a closely related element useful in uranium breeding for nuclear power generation (Kauffman and Baber 1956; Poston 1982), is frequently associated with rare earth deposits (Kauffman and Baber 1956).

With the possible exception of thorium, mining for rare earths is not likely to pose a widespread environmental threat because their industrial use is fairly limited, although sometimes strategic. Columbium, for example, is very rare but useful in producing heat-resistant steel alloys suitable for jet engines; tantalum is extremely resistant to corrosive agents (Kauffman and Baber 1956). Dredging operations to recover black sands may be locally damaging, however, and attempts to recover thorium may increase as uranium reserves are consumed. One major example of rare earth mining occurred in Bear Valley, Idaho, where as much as 99% of the columbium and tantalum used in the USA during the late 1950s was produced (Anonymous 1958). Two bucket-line dredges were used; the larger dredge could dig down to 16.8 m below the water and had a 3.7-m draft. Together, the two dredges could move 198.1–226.4 m^3 of alluvial material daily (Anonymous 1958). Despite attempts by the dredging operators to limit environmental disruptions, they could not prevent excessive accumulations of fine sediments in the streambed that were still affecting anadromous and resident salmonids nearly 20 years later (Chaney 1981; Platts and Nelson 1986).

Sediment Production

Sediment accrues in streams naturally and is a normal component of salmonid habitat. Major disruption of the system occurs when sediment delivery substantially exceeds the natural level and the amounts of sediment deposited (Platts and Megahan 1975) (Figure 12.5) and the turbidity become excessive. Deposition of

FIGURE 12.5.—Highly erodible tailings piles at the Blackbird cobalt mine in central Idaho.

excessive fine sediment on the stream bottom eliminates habitat for aquatic insects; reduces density, biomass, number, and diversity of aquatic insects; reduces the permeability of spawning gravels; and blocks the interchange of subsurface and surface waters (Vaux 1962; McNeil 1964; Cooper 1965; Koski 1966).

Mining can be a significant source of bedload sediment and can cause suspended solids to enter aquatic ecosystems. Glancy (1973) found annual sediment yields of 218–2,670 tonnes/km^2 from mined areas; undisturbed areas yielded only 21–326 tonnes/km^2. The recovery of a stream affected by manganese strip-mining operations was monitored by Cumming and Hill (1971); turbidity was elevated over background levels for 6 years. Branson and Batch (1971) concluded that the most damaging pollutant in a strip mine area was sediment from eroding spoil banks. Research in Kentucky indicated that sediment yields from forested areas increased 1,000 times as a result of strip mining (Musser 1963).

In Idaho, sediment deposition in Bear Valley Creek, a major tributary of the Middle Fork of the Salmon River, reached very high and destructive levels as a result of dredging for rare earths. During the mining operations, Bear Valley Creek was routed away from its natural channel, which was subsequently dredged. As a result, 2.3 km of original stream channel were filled with tailings piles. After mining ceased, Bear Valley Creek breached the system of dikes and levees that kept it contained, and returned to its original channel. In the process, the stream cut through 2–5 m of tailings and deposited 500,000 m^3 of sediment downstream. These sediments have covered valuable spawning and rearing areas for spring chinook salmon and steelhead; chinook salmon redds counted in Bear

Valley Creek have declined from over 1,000/year in the 1950s to less than 70/year in the 1980s (Konopacky et al. 1985). This area is currently being rehabilitated by the Shoshone-Bannock tribe in conjunction with the Bonneville Power Administration.

Elsewhere in Idaho, Spaulding and Ogden (1968) estimated that hydraulic mining for gold in the Boise River Basin produced 116,500 tonnes of silt in 18 months. Dredging in the Salmon River, Idaho, produced enough silt to cover 20.9 km of stream bottom with 0.16 cm of silt every 10 d, and this reduced salmon spawning by 25% (Spaulding and Ogden 1968). Platts et al. (1979a) found that the average substrate particle size above a cobalt mine was 22.4 mm, but directly below the mine sediment size was reduced to 0.22 mm. Clearly, erosion of surface-mined lands and mine spoils represents one of the greatest threats to salmonid habitats in the western USA.

Elevated levels of suspended sediment may have both acute and sublethal effects on salmonids. Noggle (1978) reported that suspended sediment concentrations of 1,200 mg/L caused direct mortality of underyearling salmonids; reduced growth and feeding activity has been reported at concentrations as low as 300 mg/L (Noggle 1978; Sigler et al. 1984). McLeay et al. (1984) tested the responses of wild Arctic grayling in the laboratory to sediment obtained from a Yukon gold dredging operation. They reported that underyearling fish could withstand long-term exposure (6 months) to suspended sediment concentrations up to 1,000 mg/L, but that a variety of sublethal effects (for example, impaired feeding activity, decreased scope for activity, reduced growth, downstream displacement, and decreased resistance to other environmental stressors) occurred at concentrations as low as 100 mg/L. Later, McLeay et al. (1987) showed that Arctic grayling could tolerate short-term (4-d) exposures to suspended sediment concentrations as high as 250 g/L at 15°C, but that tolerance was reduced at 5°C. Sigler et al. (1984) reported downstream displacement of salmonids in response to concentrations of suspended sediment greater than 100 g/L, which raises the possibility that mined-land disturbances can have the same effect. The specific effects of suspended sediment on the aquatic biota, particularly various life stages of the salmonids, are discussed in detail by Bjornn and Reiser (1991, this volume).

Toxic heavy metals leached from mine spoils and eroded into stream courses can precipitate on bedload sediment particles and remain in the aquatic environment to be released later (Funk et al. 1975). Sediments may also contain nutrients such as nitrogen and phosphorus. Excessive nutrients can lead to blooms of algal species that may kill fish by depleting dissolved oxygen when they die.

Other Water Quality Issues

So far, we have considered the effects on fisheries of only large-scale mining operations. Recreational mining with small, portable suction dredges may also have localized but important consequences. The popularity of suction dredges for recreational, as well as profit-generating, pursuits has paralleled recent surges in gold prices; indeed, the amount of recreational dredging is directly proportional to gold prices. Thomas (1985) reported that small suction dredges reduced the abundance of aquatic insects within the dredged area in a Montana stream. Griffith and Andrews (1981) found that entrainment of cutthroat trout eggs in a small suction dredge caused 100% mortality of uneyed stages, and 35% mortality among eyed stages. The authors also reported that the mortality of rainbow trout sac fry entrained in the same dredge reached 83%. These results strongly suggest that suction dredging is harmful to salmonids in early life stages.

The effects of recreational dredging on stream substrates are less well researched. A standard 7.6-cm-diameter intake dredge is rated by manufacturers to move 3.1 m^3 of stream substrate hourly. Thomas (1985) reported that dredging caused localized increases in suspended sediments, downstream deposition of fine sediments, and filling of pools. Furthermore, digging deep holes, which is often necessary to reach gold deposits, resulted in unstable piles of gravel. Such deposits can be transported downstream, filling in pool habitats. Therefore, the effects of large local concentrations of dredges on fish habitat may be severe. Additional habitat damage may occur if the streambanks are worked (a practice illegal in some states).

Activities associated with mining operations, such as road building, may be as damaging as the mining itself. Road building on forested watersheds can cause mass soil movement and surface erosion, resulting in soil creep, slumping, earthflows, and debris avalanches (Roelofs et al. 1991, this volume), and effectively nullifying efforts to construct environmentally well-planned mines. Although the effects of forest roads are well documented in this volume, a few statistics will help to explain the potential magnitude of the problem. On the Olympic Peninsula of Washington, construction of 0.7 km of forest road resulted in 83 landslides that moved 11,825 m^3/km^2 of soils annually. Morrison (1975) found that forest roads produced 344 times more eroded material than was found in undisturbed watersheds.

Several products associated with mineral exploration are reported to be toxic to fish. Drilling fluids, which lubricate drills, seal the walls of the drill hole, and flush the cuttings from the hole, are colloidal suspensions of clay in water, to which a variety of chemicals are added. Large quantities of these substances are sometimes used; Sprague and Logan (1979) estimated that drilling to a depth of 3,700 m requires at least 1,700 m^3 of fluid. Sprague and Logan (1979) also tested the toxicity to rainbow trout of 21 commonly used drilling fluids, and found that paraformaldehyde and capryl alcohol were toxic at concentrations less than 100 mg/L; organic compounds of bentonite and barite were least toxic.

Chemicals used in the processing and recovery of metalliferous deposits may also be toxic. Webb et al. (1976) reported that the flotation reagents sodium ethyl and potassium amyl xanthate were highly toxic to brook trout; LC50s were in the range of 30–50 µg/L. In the same study xylenol (cresylic acid) was toxic to brook trout at 3.2–5.6 mg/L. Hawley (1972) tested the toxicity of cresylic acid to chinook, coho, and pink salmon and found that critical concentrations were as low as 1.65 mg/L.

Cyanide (HCN), an extremely toxic chemical, is extensively used to extract gold, particularly in heap-leaching operations. Cyanide rarely occurs freely in nature, but when used in mining operations it often forms complexes with such metals as copper, nickel, and iron. These complexes are often less toxic than free cyanide, but dissociation to release free cyanide can occur (Caruso 1975). The chemistry of cyanide is very complex; a more thorough discussion can be found in reports by Caruso (1975) and Doudoroff (1976).

In heap-leaching operations, cyanide solutions are sprayed on the pads and contained in settling ponds, from where they might contaminate groundwater (via percolation) and surface waters (via groundwater recharge and leakage and overflow from ponds). The latter occurred in 1986 on a tributary of Wolf Creek, California, when a large snowstorm was followed by warm weather and rain. In this spill, a 5–20-mg/L solution of free cyanide was released in the tributary at a rate of about 0.022 m^3/s, and free cyanide in the tributary ranged from 20 to 30 mg/L. No cyanide was detected in Wolf Creek 2.4 km downstream, and no biotic effects were reported (Anonymous 1986).

Cyanide achieves its toxicity by interfering with oxygen transport into organisms. Lethal concentrations are reached at about 10 mg/L, and a variety of sublethal effects have been reported at lower concentrations. Koenst et al. (1977) found that brook trout egg production was reduced by 50% at concentrations of 0.027 mg HCN/L. Cyanide also inhibits the swimming ability of fish (Broderious 1970), and histopathological effects after a 9-d exposure to HCN concentrations of 0.01–0.03 mg/L were reported in rainbow trout by Dixon and Leduc (1981). Fortunately, however, cyanide is not environmentally persistent, and it degrades naturally to less toxic compounds by a variety of volatilization, oxidation, photodecomposition, and biodegradation mechanisms (Schmidt et al. 1981).

Mined-Land Hydrology

Because surface mining operations involve drastic alteration of vegetation, soils, and subsurface materials, accompanying changes in surface and subsurface hydrology can be anticipated. Whether these effects will be transitory or long-term depends on the reclamation techniques used (Starnes 1983). The hydrologic character of surface-mined lands is determined by several variables, including precipitation, solar input, slope steepness, vegetation types and composition, and characteristics of the spoils or overburden.

In general, surface mining results in higher streamflow and stormflow runoff (Sullivan 1967; Collier et al. 1970; Touysinhthiphonexay and Gardner 1984), primarily because compaction of mine spoils, reduction of vegetative cover, and complete loss of organic topsoils impair the infiltration of water into the ground. Rainfall on undisturbed watersheds is readily absorbed by forest soils and transferred downward, even during periods of intense rainfall. When vegetation and soils are stripped, however, infiltration and runoff patterns are likely to be modified. Merz and Finn (1951) reported infiltration rates of 43.2 cm/h on graded spoil banks and 452.1 cm/h on adjacent undisturbed soils. Grandt and Lang (1958) measured infiltrations of 2.3 cm/h on graded soil and 13.2 cm/h on ungraded ridges. When the infiltration capacity of soils is reduced, overland and channel flows result. Overland flows run directly to streams, leading to high peak stream discharges and short lag times between precipitation and streamflow increases (Sawyer and Crowl 1968; Minnear and Tschantz 1974; Baker 1977). The increases in streamflow, particularly in stormflow, place hydrological stresses on the ability of a particular stream channel to transport the additional flows. Schumm (1973) found an extrinsic threshold that changes the balance between stressive and resistive forces in stream channels. When the channel's threshold for resistance to erosion is exceeded, typically because of shear stress applied by increased peak

FIGURE 12.6.—Unnatural forced meander pattern that remains after gold dredging in Crooked River in northern Idaho.

discharge, channel size is increased to transport the additional flow. Touysinhthiphonexay and Gardner (1984) found that the response of 29 first-order streams to mining in small central Pennsylvania watersheds was enlarged channel size through erosion and increased size of eroded colluvial blocks; these effects were more pronounced in smaller basins. Slope steepness also reinforces these effects, because the mean velocity of overland flow is related directly to the slope (U.S. Forest Service 1980c). Any increase in overland flow, particularly over disturbed lands, increases the amount of sediment entering stream courses. Erosion of mine spoils and tailings, which typically contain a variety of toxic metals, may severely affect the aquatic biota of receiving waters draining these spoils.

Drastic physical changes in stream courses may be anticipated during placer and dredge mining. Many valuable metals are found in alluvial material associated with stream courses. Recovery of these materials requires dredging streams, floodplains, and meadow soils, often to depths of 35 m or more. Waste material, which may occupy as much as 20% more volume after it is dredged, is difficult to dispose of and is often deposited adjacent to streams, forming extremely unstable streambanks. Western gold mining during the past century has severely affected fishery resources by such techniques. At Crooked River, Idaho, dredging for gold caused total destruction of meadow and riparian vegetation, as well as loss of topsoils, resulting in a channel that changes from unnatural forced meanders to straight channels of high gradient (Figure 12.6).

In arid regions of the western USA, mining may significantly affect limited water supplies. Processing, milling, and refining of mine products require massive amounts of water. Lewis and Burraychak (1979) estimated that refining 907 kg of copper ore requires 380,000 L of water. Lindskov and Kimball (1984) estimated that a proposed oil shale industry that would extract 400,000 barrels of oil annually from the Uinta basin of Utah, Colorado, and Wyoming would require $8.6 \times 10^7 \, m^3$ of water per year. Furthermore, because water would be obtained from adjacent aquifers of poor water quality, salinity of the Colorado River at Hoover Dam would be expected to increase by 4–6 mg/L. Greater effects on water quality and fishery resources could be expected if surface water sources were used.

Abandoned Mines

Cessation of mining operations does not necessarily mean the end of environmental degradation; abandoned or "orphan" mines may present a long-term water pollution hazard unless the site is properly reclaimed. Acid pollution from abandoned mines has persisted 100 years after mining ceased (Cummins and Given 1973a). Sudden failures of dikes or dams on tailings ponds may release large volumes of toxic waste into natural waters.

Environmental problems left by abandoned mines continue to affect other resource values throughout the western USA. Several studies have shown persistent acidification below abandoned mines. Brown and Johnston (1976) showed that high acidity continued to destroy aquatic life downstream from an open-pit mine in Montana that had been closed in the 1950s. In addition, a steady supply of acidic spoil continued to erode into the adjacent Stillwater River because high soil acidity prevented recolonization by native vegetation. Platts et al. (1979a) showed that stream acidity continued to be higher downstream from the Blackbird Mine, Idaho, than upstream from the mine after mining had ceased. Concentrations of a variety of toxic contaminants in the water column were higher below than above the effluent discharge, and were exceedingly high at some sampling stations; concentrations reached 208 mg Co, 1,385 mg Cu, 245 mg Fe, and 37 mg Mn per liter, and pH was as low as 2.2. Fuller et al. (1978) reported that effluent discharging from the abandoned Balakala Mine in northern California was highly toxic (pH 2.0; 800 mg Fe, 5.2 mg Mg, 0.9 mg Cd, 170 mg Cu, and 180 mg Zn per liter). Dredge mining on Bear Valley Creek in south-central Idaho disrupted a considerable area of alluvial meadow in the 1950s, and salmonid spawning downstream still is reduced because of sediments transported from the dredged area (Chaney 1981; Konopacky et al. 1985; Platts and Nelson 1986). Conversely, Prokopovich and Nitzberg (1982) reported that dredge mining in the American River, California, may have actually improved spawning conditions for anadromous salmonids by physically removing most of the natural fine sediments from the substrates.

In the past, mine operators did not consider the possible effects that orphaned mines might have on aquatic ecosystems. Mine cleanup and reclamation of the land were not issues. Problems of legal responsibility are still evident. On private land, the landowner assumes responsibility for any problem resulting from the condition of the land at the time title is taken; on federal land, however, abandoned claims are passed to the government, which has little recourse against the claim holder, particularly if the operation was small. Recent state reclamation laws, which generally require the payment of a reclamation bond based on the amount of ore removed from the ground, help assure that proper reclamation will be carried out. Some states such as Utah and Arizona, however, have yet to enact this type of legislation.

Orphan mines also present reclamation problems. Most unreclaimed abandoned mines began operations before passage of the 1977 Surface Mining Control and Reclamation Act, and these mines typically were developed with little thought to postmining effects and reclamation. Consequently, no premining reclamation practices such as stockpiling of topsoil or development of a reclamation plan were undertaken. This lack of planning increases the cost of reclamation and reduces the likelihood that land management agencies will be able to reclaim the many abandoned mines that continue to degrade other resource values. Low pH in mine spoils reduces natural revegetation (Farmer et al. 1976; Butterfield and Tueller 1980). Highly acidic soil conditions, as well as high concentrations of heavy metals in soils within the rooting zone of plants, hinder reclamation efforts (Johnston et al. 1975). Verma and Felix (1977) discussed efforts to reclaim abandoned mine sites in Arizona that present continuing water pollution problems, but pointed out that treating all abandoned mine spoils in the Lynx Creek watershed is not economical because of their great numbers and land status. The persistent watershed degradation from many abandoned mines indicates a need to raise reclamation priorities if high-quality salmonid habitat is to be created and maintained.

Mined-Land Reclamation

Reclamation of mined areas has recently emerged as an integral part of mining operations. The deleterious effects of mining on esthetic values, as well as on fisheries, wildlife, and water resources, and the persistence of these effects once mineral extraction has been completed prompted the U.S. Congress, in 1977, to enact the Surface Mining Control and Reclamation Act (SMCRA) to supplement existing state regulations. This federal law requires restoration of mined land to premining condition and prohibits mining where mandated restoration would not be possible. Consequently, spoils can no longer be treated simply as an unpleasant byproduct of mineral recovery important only to those directly affected; rather, their ultimate disposition must be planned in advance. Because provisions of SMCRA also specifically call for the restoration and, if possible, enhancement of fish and wildlife habitats, which coincide with requirements of both the Multiple-Use Sustained Yield and Federal Land Policy and Management Acts, we suggest that both rehabilitation and enhancement of fishery resources affected by mining should be part of the planning and reclamation processes. To some extent, they have been included because of the need to improve water quality by allowing pollutants to settle (Spaulding and Ogden 1968), chiefly to produce standing water for recreation and esthetics. The emphasis on standing water is illustrated by the U.S. Fish and Wildlife Service's guide to enhancing fish and wildlife values on abandoned mine sites (Nawrot et al. 1982); it scarcely mentions running water fisheries or riparian habitats. We believe that riparian- and stream-enhancement techniques currently being developed should be integrated with traditional mined-land reclamation techniques where fluvial salmonid habitats have been affected by mines.

In nonalluvial surface mining, most attention will be paid to reestablishing nearly natural terrestrial conditions and preventing deterioration of nearby waterways. Planning of new operations should include both stockpiling of topsoil for later reclamation and measures to prevent inputs of mining-generated solids and toxic materials into nearby streams; planning for stream enhancement should also be considered at this time. Alluvial operations require even greater stream and riparian rehabilitation, and the need for predevelopment planning is obvious. The U.S. Forest Service recommends saving topsoil for reclamation instead of trying to reclaim land with unsurfaced spoils alone; it also recommends that stockpiles be designed and located to limit erosion and contamination of local waterways (U.S. Forest Service 1979). Some input of debris into streams may also be controlled by silt fences constructed along the riparian corridor of affected streams, as the Bonneville Power Administration and Shoshone-Bannock Tribe have built for their reclamation–enhancement project on Bear Valley Creek, Idaho. Although nonalluvial mining may not require rehabilitation of resources directly related to watersheds, incidental destruction of riparian vegetation by road construction, stripping of foodplains or wooded draws, and alteration of local hydrology may occur (Young 1983), in which case methods for riparian recovery must be considered as well.

Prevention of direct effects on streams during large-scale dredging is much more complicated, so planning for future rehabilitation and enhancement of the streams assumes even more importance in such projects. Piles of boulders and rubble alongside waterways allow little capacity for spontaneous recovery, and unsophisticated rehabilitation procedures may fail miserably. When dredging for rare earths in Bear Valley, Idaho, was completed, for example, dredge piles were covered with topsoil and reseeded with a mixture of grasses. This reclamation was thought to be so thorough that "in a few years it will never be evident that the area has been dredged" (Anonymous 1958). After 30 years, however, the dredging is still very evident. Dredging operations may also create highly unnatural channel morphology requiring intensive rehabilitation. An excellent example is provided by the Crooked River, Idaho (Figure 12.6), where channelization devegetated banks and straightened reaches (Petrosky and Holubetz 1985).

Toxic Effluents

Several techniques have been used to neutralize the acidity of mine effluents. Reiser et al. (1982) reported considerable improvement in water quality and recovery of aquatic biota after "flocculation–coagulation" treatment of effluent to a stream that had been severely degraded by acid mine drainage. Acidic water can be treated with hydrated lime or limestone to raise pH (Pearson and McDonnell 1975; Wilmoth 1977). Limestone is also used to neutralize acidity in piles of mine tailings to aid revegetation. Starnes et al. (1978) reported some incidental amelioration of acidity in stream waters because of erosion and deposition of lime-treated tailings. Fuller et al. (1978), drawing on information in Hill (1968), suggested treating acidic effluents from abandoned mines near Mt. Shasta, California, with lime to reduce pH and coprecipitate ferric hydroxide and dissolved metals. Use of iron-oxidizing bacteria in rotating disk contactors to precipitate ferric hydroxide has also been described (Olem and Unz 1980). Precipitation of ferric hydroxide in lagoons before effluents are released into

TABLE 12.3.—Brief, nontechnical summary of reclamation procedures used to treat mining-related water quality problems.

Method	Chemical action	Practical considerations
Lime neutralization	Hydrated lime is added to wastewater in a mixing tank to raise pH to 9.0, then aerated; heavy metals precipitate as hydroxides and can be removed by clarification	A low-cost and easily applied procedure that neutralizes acidity and produces low metal concentrations in wastewater. Sludge disposal can be a problem
Limestone neutralization	Limestone ($CaCO_3$) raises pH and causes precipitation of metal ions as hydroxides	Can effectively raise pH (neutralize acidity) but the metal hydroxides are not easily recovered
Sulfide precipitation	Lime neutralization followed by addition of a sulfide compound to further reduce the solubility of heavy metals	Useful where high water quality must be maintained. Sulfides reduce dissolved oxygen in wastewater and sludge disposal can be a problem
Reverse osmosis	Water is forced through a semipermeable membrane that retains metal ions	Produces high-quality effluent but requires acid neutralization before filtration
Electrochemical precipitation	Electric current is applied across consumable iron electrodes to produce ferrous (Fe^{+2}) ions. Ferrous ions coprecipitate other metals	Inflowing water must have its acidity neutralized first. Sludge disposal can be a problem
Biological treatment	Microorganisms (usually bacteria) are used to remove metals	Only partially effective. Does nothing to raise pH

stream waters can help prevent accumulation of yellow boy on stream substrates. Some of these procedures are summarized in Table 12.3.

Hydrologic Considerations

Lands denuded by mining need to be stabilized as quickly as possible to limit erosion and transport of sediments and toxic materials into nearby waterways. Surface mining frequently produces not only land denuded of vegetation, but also steeper and longer slope topography and soils that are less stable because they have been physically disturbed (Fisher and Deutsch 1983). Bare soils have lower hydraulic resistance than soils with dense sod cover (Manning's *n* values are as low as 0.02 and as high as 0.4, respectively). Bare spoils may produce double the overland water flow and 10 times more sediment than spoils covered by topsoil alone (U.S. Forest Service 1980c). The first step in reclaiming nonalluvial mining disturbances is to restore the land's original contour, as well as to stabilize and develop settling ponds, strip-mine ponds, water-filled pits, and stock dams for other uses. In alluvial areas where dredging has altered channel structure and left unconsolidated alluvial material, construction of a stabilized channel suited to the normal hydrologic regime is desirable.

Various mathematical models have been developed to determine how best to reshape mine spoils for controlling sediment discharge to nearby streams. Smith and Woolhiser (1978) discussed simulation models that incorporate climatic factors, watershed characteristics, surface topographies, soil erodibility, and treatment costs to predict potential sediment discharges from reclaimed spoils. Khanbilvardi et al. (1983) tested a mathematical soil erosion model on a reclaimed strip mine in Pennsylvania and found they could predict actual erosion and deposition within 25% after several small storms; the model allowed predictions for specific portions of the watershed. Such predictive ability is valuable in limiting erodibility of reclaimed lands and for discovering sources of excessive sediment production.

Reconstruction of stable stream channels has yet to receive the attention it deserves, but increasing interest in the value of riparian areas may encourage additional study. Doubt (1965) stated that stable channel designs must incorporate channel capacity, channel geometry, and streambed and bank stability. Ideally, the rehabilitated channel will imitate a natural channel, and natural channels are clearly not static. When they designed a stable channel for coarse alluvium, Jackson and Van Haveren (1984), drawing on work by Andrews (1982) and Jackson and Beschta (1982), assumed that streams have mobile bed conditions and exhibit fluctuations in geometry about a relatively stable, long-term mean. They designed a trapezoidal channel with banks outsloped at an angle of 20° and a broad floodplain sloped away from the stream at an angle of 2%; the latter angle allows the floodplain to contain overflow during flooding and to control lateral migration of the channel. A similar design is being applied on a large scale to Bear Valley Creek, Idaho, in an area severely altered by dredge mining (James M. Montgomery, Consulting Engineers 1985). Streams in low-gradient valleys typically form meander patterns that can be recreated in some form as part of the reclamation process. Hasfurther (1985) discussed the use of meander parameters (wavelength, sinuosity, radius of curvature, and meander-belt width), which are determined by a basin's hydrologic characteristics and an associated Fourier analysis, to help design stabilized channels for stream reclamation.

Revegetation

Seedbed preparation.—Surface mining destroys the natural characteristics of the mined area's soil resource, which cannot be fully reconstructed. Mining spoils generally are poor media in which to reestablish plant communities (Fisher and Deutsch 1983). Spoils generated in strip-mining western coal, for example, are typically low in acid, extremely fine-textured, and high in montmorillonitic clay. Spent shale from some western oil-shale operations consists of fine silt that is highly saline and devoid of plant nutrients (U.S. Department of Agriculture 1980). Conversely, spoils left by uranium mining are frequently highly acidic (Thornburg 1982), and natural topsoils in the area may be poorly developed because of the geoclimate common to western regions containing uranium reserves (Yamamoto 1982). Revegetation efforts must be suited to the sites.

Saving topsoil preserves the natural growing medium for plants that will be used to revegetate the spoils, along with some of the natural biota including mycorrhizae. Carrying topsoil preservation a step further, Fisher and Deutsch (1983) recommended separately stockpiling the topsoil (A horizon and upper portion of the B horizon) and the subsoil (remainder of the B and, sometimes, the C horizons) for covering spoils during reclamation. Sometimes, however, stockpiling may not be cost-effective, because it may be the single most expensive operation in mine reclamation (Richardson and Farmer 1983). An alternative means of producing a substitute from overburden is offered by Anaconda Corporation's experience in revegetating uranium spoils in New Mexico (Reynolds et al. 1978). Several studies have demonstrated that, if necessary (as with orphan mines), revegetation can be achieved without replacement of topsoils, although some physical and chemical treatment may be needed (Murray and Moffett 1977; Reynolds et al. 1978; Aldon 1984; Butterfield and Tueller 1980).

In general, techniques for establishing plants on mined lands are not much different from those used to revegetate ranges and pastures (Thornburg 1982). Characteristics of the material to be revegetated should be analyzed to determine pH, salinity, fertility, and concentrations of potentially toxic materials, all of which may have been done before mining if top soil was set aside during removal of the overburden (U.S. Forest Service 1979). Attempts to revegetate tailings ponds also requires knowledge of the local water regime, water chemistry, and light penetration (Olson 1981). For streamside areas, additional considerations may be required, such as incidence of flooding and streambank stability. Anderson and Ohmart (1985) discussed a variety of factors that influence riparian restoration, including tillage needs, soil density, weeds, and irrigation. Clay (1981) discussed techniques for preparing entrenched meadow streams so water tables will rise to support meadow vegetation. Packer et al. (1982) provided useful models for estimating revegetation potential that incorporate information on local climates and soils as well as on proposed revegetation treatments.

If necessary, toxic materials should be buried at least deep enough that they will not be taken up by plants or discharged into waterways (U.S. Environmental Protection Agency 1973a; Thornburg 1982)—unless contamination is so great that spoils should be treated like mill tailings (Yamamoto 1982). Plants take up near-surface contaminants. Moffett and Tellier (1977) demonstrated uptake of uranium and [226]radium by grasses growing on uranium mine tailings in Ontario, although they deemed the radium concentration factor of 0.03 too low to indicate active concentration of the isotope. Fourwing saltbush—commonly used for revegetation in the west—concentrates selenium (which commonly occurs in the same sedimentary deposits that contain uranium: Moore and Mills 1977) to toxic levels if soil selenium exceeds 2 μg/g (Booth 1985). Required depth of burial varies with the characteristics of the plants to be grown on the reclaimed spoils; most range species produce roots in the top 30 cm of soil, but some drought-adapted species may extend their roots below 2.7 m (Munshower 1983). Burial depths are sometimes specified by state law.

Seedbeds should be adequately prepared to support plant growth. Preparation may include fertilization, neutralization, and mulching (Thornburg 1982), as well as tilling. Proper tillage helps aerate the soil, promotes mixing of fertilizers and mulches, roughens the surface to reduce erosion, and encourages water infiltration (U.S. Forest Service 1979). Primary (deep) tilling techniques typically include ripping, disking, chisel plowing, and stubble mulch tilling; secondary (shallow) methods include disk harrowing, roller harrowing and packing, and tooth harrowing (U.S. Forest Service 1979). Norem and Day (1985) reported better grass production on reclaimed open-pit copper mine spoils (both those covered with topsoil and those uncovered) in Arizona when a spike-tooth chain drag was used for final seedbed preparation than when a sheepfoot roller was used followed by mulching with wheat straw. Characteristics of the seedbed material are important, however, and mulching may be neither necessary nor desirable if good soil is available; Ferguson and Frischknecht (1985) showed that effectiveness of seedbed preparation (harrowing, cultipacking, or gouging) varied with soil type. Riparian zones are typically inaccessible to the heavy equipment used in revegetation, however, and much work must be performed manually. For streamsides subject to variable flows, bank stabilization (discussed later) may also be required to create an adequate seedbed (Monsen 1983; Platts et al. 1987).

Fertilizer may be required to compensate for naturally poor or absent topsoil or for alkalinity (sodicity) or acidity of the seedbed. Lime, limestone, or similar basic materials are frequently used to correct acidity (U.S. Forest Service 1979), and the amount of lime required may even be estimated where pyrite oxidation is continually changing soil pH (Murray and Moffett 1977). Sodicity may be corrected by excessive irrigation or by chemical treatments that include calcium salts, sulfur, or sulfuric acid (U.S. Forest Service 1979). Little is known about the soil chemistry of tailings ponds (Olson 1981), and revegetation requires favorable water and soil chemistry; soil chemistry of such ponds appears to be a fruitful area for reclamation research. Platts et al. (1987) provided information on treatment of streamside areas to rehabilitate degraded riparian vegetation; in general, however, treatments must be tailored to specific characteristics of each site.

Seeding and transplantation.—Seeding of terrestrial sites can be accomplished by drilling or broadcasting. Thornburg (1982) recommended drilling on suitable sites. Broadcast seeding appears to give a better plant distribution (Day and Ludeke 1973), but drilling is generally considered a superior technique because it puts the seed in the ground at the proper depth and allows control of seeding rate and soil compaction simultaneously (U.S. Forest Service 1979). Although topographic irregularities may complicate planting in riparian areas, traditional techniques usually can be used. Monsen (1983) and Platts et al. (1987) described techniques for seeding riparian areas.

Transplanting is also used, sometimes in combination with seeding (U.S. Forest Service 1979), to establish vegetation on disturbed sites, particularly to establish woody species (Thornburg 1982). Transplant stock includes containerized seedlings, bare-root stock, cuttings, wildlings, and plugs. Trees and shrubs may be established successfully in developing grass stands (Bjugstad 1984); Monsen and Plummer (1978) provided some guidelines for reducing competition and establishing the woody species. Because of the importance of woody and sod-forming species for salmonids and for maintaining healthy aquatic ecosystems (Platts 1983), these techniques should prove useful in rehabilitating streamside areas that have been damaged by mining. Eckert (1983), Monsen (1983), and Platts et al. (1985b, 1987) discussed the use of woody transplants, cuttings, and containerized and bare-root stock in rehabilitating disturbed streams. McCluskey et al. (1983) described techniques for planting willows to improve riparian habitat. Platts et al. (1987) discussed transplanting sod-forming sedges (*Carex* sp.) to help restore streambanks, and Ratliff (1985) reported successful use of sedge plugs in gravel areas, which could be applied to degraded streams.

Seeding often needs to be done quickly to prevent erosion of topsoil. Time of planting may not be optimal when the spoils are ready, so fast-growing, temporary grasses may be planted to provide interim protection (U.S. Forest Service 1979). Two-phase planting (Jones et al. 1975; Murray and Moffett 1977) may provide rapid stabilization and may help prepare the spoils for more productive and permanent vegetative cover.

Species selection.—Selection of plant species for reclamation depends on the ultimate goals of revegetation and the characteristics of the planting site. Revegetation to produce agricultural crops, for example, will require a different prescription than revegetation to recreate near-natural conditions. Some exotic species may be better adapted to the growing conditions on disturbed sites, or for other reasons may establish themselves more quickly than native species. Aldon and Pase (1981) surveyed the adaptability of several exotic and native plants to mine spoils in New Mexico, and Nicholas and McGinnies (1982) evaluated the forage production of several native and exotic grasses and legumes on Colorado mine spoils with and without topsoil. Many other studies have dealt with these considerations (for example, Day and Ludeke 1973, 1981; Brown and Johnston 1976; Murray and Moffett 1977; Reynolds et al. 1978; Butterfield and Tueller 1980; Richardson and Farmer 1982; Severson and Gough 1983; Weiler and Gould 1983; Booth 1985; Norem and Day 1985). Thornburg (1982) provided a detailed list of plant materials available for revegetating disturbed areas, as well as discussions of their suitability for particular uses.

Revegetation of riparian areas in the western USA is a relatively young field, and many details of plant culture and species assemblages have yet to be elucidated. In a study in northeastern Nevada, Platts et al. (1985b) described using a mixture of grasses and woody species, including willow, woods rose, red-osier dogwood, and quaking aspen, to revegetate an unstable riparian area. Early indications from this study are that woods rose planted early in the spring does well in the Great Basin where the water table may recede quickly, and need not be planted in mesic positions; that containerized aspen seedlings planted in mesic positions (for example, near springs) should survive; and that large bare-root aspens are difficult to establish even in mesic positions. Eckert (1983) reported successful revegetation of streambanks and dam faces in Nevada with golden willow and Siberian peashrub and moderate success with common bladdersenna, all nonnative species. Monsen (1983) compiled lists of species suitable for revegetating riparian areas, with notes on areas of adaptation and how to produce transplant materials; Platts et al. (1987) provided lists of willows, sedges, grasses, and forbs suitable for use in riparian areas, along with notes on their tolerances of environmental conditions, growth rates, transplant capabilities, and habitat adaptations.

Streambank Stabilization and Stream Enhancement

Reclamation of streams degraded by mining must include rehabilitation and enhancement of fish habitats. We have already made reference to several contemporary efforts to reclaim salmonid habitats damaged by mining (James M. Montgomery, Consulting Engineers 1985; Petrosky and Holubetz 1985; Platts et al. 1985b). This aspect of the influence of land-use practices on salmonid habitat, however, is presented in greater detail by Reeves et al. (1991, this volume).

Summary

Mineral extraction, whether it be by surface or underground mining in their diverse forms, affects salmonids and their habitats in many ways. Increasing public awareness of the value of aquatic resources has led to legislation designed to protect, restore, or enhance areas that have been or will be mined. This positive trend has also led to a growing body of knowledge about the specific effects of mining-related pollutants on salmon and trout and the mechanisms by which habitat degradation may be reversed.

Some of the adverse effects of mining on salmonid habitats are obvious. Placer mining converts natural streams to channels between barren rubble piles; hydraulic mining erodes hillsides and deposits the eroded material into nearby streams. Road building and removal of surface vegetation may also contribute to direct streambed disturbances and sediment influxes.

Other influences, however, may be less obvious and much more insidious. One of the principal and most persistent results of mining is acid mine drainage. Both orphaned and currently operated mines may contribute acidic drainage to nearby waters. Acid production can occur in coal deposits by the generation of sulphuric acid or through the action of oxidizing bacteria on pyrite, a common component of the granitic material in which many western ore deposits occur. The consequences of acid drainage are many and they are expressed in a variety of ways. If pH levels are sufficiently low, fish populations may be reduced directly through fish kills or less directly through reduction in the viability of individuals, their gametes, or their progeny. Aquatic invertebrates, an important source of food for many salmonids, may also be affected by acid drainage; they may be directly poisoned or their habitats may be degraded by deposition of ferric hydroxide. In addition, the toxicity of many metallic poisons is increased at low pH levels.

Tailings piles and settling ponds also may contribute pollutants. Cyanide, a highly toxic chemical that is often used to recover gold, has sometimes entered streams through failure of settling ponds. Acid drainage through tailings piles contributes metallic pollutants to nearby waterways. Many metals (including arsenic, cadmium, chromium, copper, iron, and uranium) that are either the object of mining or are associated with extraction of other minerals are highly toxic to fish, and their toxicity may be greatly influenced by pH. In many cases, metallic compounds are relatively insoluble in natural waters that are of nearly neutral pH, but become increasingly soluble as acidity increases, thereby increasing the concentration of toxic metal ions.

The effects of mining on aquatic resources do not necessarily end when the operations end. Many old and abandoned mines continue to release pollutants into nearby streams and many dredged areas continue to provide poor aquatic and riparian habitats for salmon and trout. Acidity may be neutralized simply by adding lime or limestone, or more sophisticated treatments may be used to help remove metals. In many cases, reworking the land surface is required to restore it to nearly its original topography and to protect and restore habitats for fish and wildlife. Federal legislation, specifically the Surface Mining Control and Reclamation Act in the USA, and complementary state statutes have been enacted not only to insure this process, but also to make the reclamation process part of overall mine planning.

In many ways, reclamation of mined lands parallels other forms of reclamation used after various land-use practices. The techniques associated with both reforestation after logging and range rehabilitation are applicable. In order to protect, restore, and enhance aquatic resource values, much of the current effort being expended in the growing fields of riparian and fisheries rehabilitation and stream repair technologies should be applied where mining degradation has occurred. These are relatively new fields of study that are enjoying rapid growth in research and development as the links between aquatic, riparian, and terrestrial ecosystems become better understood.

Conclusions

Extraction of minerals in western North America has affected fishery resources tremendously, and it continues to degrade salmonid habitat in many areas. Mining is economically necessary and has national strategic implications; however, the spirit of multiple-use management shows that people value a variety of resource uses, and that destruction of these other resources will not be tolerated. Minerals can be extracted without destroying the viability of competing values, or mined lands can be restored to provide them. Where mine spoils exist and where abandoned operations continue to pollute waterways and damage downstream fishery potentials, mitigation techniques are available.

Realistically, federal, state and provincial, and local governments can help prevent the deterioration of fisheries and promote restorative efforts where degradation has occurred. State and local governments are taking an increasingly active role in controlling irresponsible mining operations. The Surface Mining Control and Reclamation Act requires mined sites to be restored to their premining character, and proposes enhancement of fish and wildlife values, if possible. Most western states require operators to draw up a mining plan that details potential environmental damage from the operation, and reclamation performance bonds must be posted. Detailed federal and state water quality standards have been established to protect aquatic ecosystems. These procedures are designed to reduce immediate impacts and to prevent persistent fishery damages; they represent steps in the right direction.

Several factors limit the ability of governmental agencies to effectively protect water resources, however. Funding limitations restrict all aspects of the protection and mitigation process: basic research into the responses of aquatic organisms to water pollutants and into the effects of land use on fish habitats; personnel to coordinate the various agencies as well as to oversee mine operations; and enforcement of regulations. Management of public goods, particularly those with many competing uses, requires public support; funding for environmental protection must be adequate or protection will not occur.

Chapter 13

Recreation

R. N. Clark and D. R. Gibbons

Salmonids have received a great deal of attention, both culturally and economically, over a long period of time. Salmon support a large commercial fishing industry; salmon, trout, and char support valuable sport fisheries. Anadromous salmonids still occur throughout much of their original range, but their numbers in some locations have been greatly reduced by overfishing, habitat degradation, and natural climatic changes. Nevertheless, many millions of adult anadromous fish are still produced in the waters of the western USA and Canada. The distribution of the major species of salmonids, as well as their life histories, are presented earlier in this volume by Meehan and Bjornn (1991). National Forest lands in the western USA alone have over 69,200 km of streams that produce anadromous salmonids (U.S. Forest Service 1982). On National Forest lands in southeastern Alaska, anadromous salmonids are found in over 4,850 streams, with a total length exceeding 48,270 km, and in 48,560 hectares of lakes (Everest and Summers 1982). This production is fished commercially, for subsistence, and for sport. On National Forests alone, nearly 2 million visitor-days annually are related to fishing (Sport Fishing Institute 1982).

Alaska, by having more than 36 times as much freshwater habitat per resident as any other western state, has the greatest potential for fish production and angling. Washington, Oregon, and Idaho will have trouble maintaining their present fish production because the construction of hydroelectric dams on the Columbia River has eliminated half of the potential spawning habitat of anadromous salmonids (Rettig 1981). The 1980 Northwest Power Act is an attempt to return anadromous fish stocks to predam levels by providing for the improvement of anadromous fish habitats and the successful migration of smolts and adult fish. California is the only western state that has an excessive demand for sport fishing, and it has the least of its original fishing habitat accessible. California is the most populous state, and has plans for many new water development projects. The percentage of Californians who fish for recreation will probably decline in the years to come because losses of aquatic habitats needed to produce anadromous salmonids will initially increase fishing pressure and eventually lead to angler dissatisfaction.

The freshwater habitats used by salmonids, both resident and anadromous forms, are generally in the same aquatic–riparian ecosystems in which productive timber stands and wildlife habitats are found. Important recreational opportunities are also located in these same areas.

Influences of Forest and Rangeland Management on Salmonid Fishes and Their Habitats
American Fisheries Society Special Publication 19:459–481, 1991

In this chapter, we discuss current knowledge of the relation of recreational use to salmonid fishes and their habitats; describe an approach for integrating the recreational and fishery systems; identify links among recreation, salmonid fisheries, and other forest resource systems (for example, timber, wildlife, and forage); establish a basis for evaluating effects both of alternative recreation management options on salmonids and of alternative fisheries management strategies on recreation; and outline research needed to improve understanding of recreation and fisheries interactions. The main emphasis is on how recreational use and management directly affect fish habitats, but we also briefly discuss the implications of fishery management for recreational opportunities and use. Although we recognize the many positive ways in which the general public and specific interest groups can be involved to protect and enhance fish habitat, this topic is beyond the scope of this chapter and we refer the reader to Brouha (1991, this volume) for a discussion of this subject.

The information and conclusions presented in this chapter are based on empirical evidence about recreational use and its relation to fish habitats; existing concepts, theories, and frameworks for relating recreation influences to fish habitats; and judgments based on current knowledge and experience. Continuing professional debate, management experience, and formal research will determine how well the assumptions we make and the conclusions we draw fit real conditions.

Multiresource Systems Perspective

The relation between recreation and anadromous fish is inherently complex, representing an interaction among people, various resources, and the uses of those resources. For example, not only may recreational use directly affect fish and their habitats, but other resource uses (such as timber harvesting and road building) may affect recreational use, which may in turn lead to additional effects. Consequently, to understand how recreation and anadromous fisheries are related requires a multiresource approach. Recreation specialists can use this perspective to avoid or solve conflicts and to identify and use positive opportunities. Some of the basic parts of this complex system are described below.

The basic social and biological communities present in most areas (Figure 13.1A) cannot exist without influencing or being influenced by the others (Figure 13.1B). Most management and research activities have focused on either people, fish, or trees, but most of the controversies and problems in resource management are found in the areas of overlap. We know the least about where the various physical and biological systems overlap—and interact. This simple idea is expanded (Figure 13.2) to separate the two basic fisheries components (habitat and fish) and recreation, which includes settings ("people habitat"), recreational activities, and recreational experiences. Recreation may affect both fish habitats and fish populations (Figure 13.2A). Some fish habitat management programs may affect recreational use as well, either positively or negatively. Other resource uses, such as logging, may have a negative or positive influence on certain types of recreational opportunities and may subsequently affect the fisheries system.

A specific example of this complex relationship is shown in Figure 13.2B. Roads built for logging may directly cause increased sedimentation, which adversely

A. Components

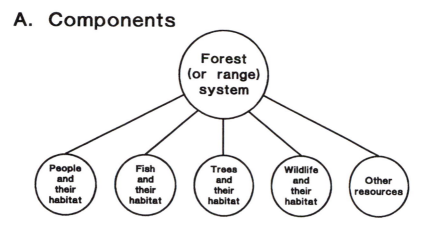

B. Interactions

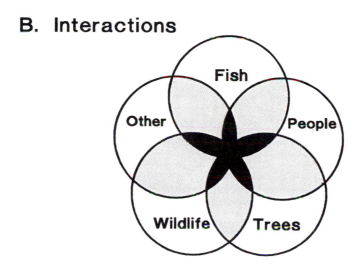

FIGURE 13.1.—Resource components and interactions in a forest resource system.

affects fish survival. Roads also provide access for recreationists that may lead to changing patterns of use in an area (desirable to some people, undesirable to others). Changed or increased use may have either detrimental effects on the fish populations (reduction in stock below optimum) or on fish habitats (loss of vegetation, increased sedimentation), or positive effects on fish populations (harvest limited to reproductive surplus). When other resource uses are introduced, the interactions become even more complex and difficult to sort out.

The system we are examining is not simple and is beyond the domain of one discipline (C. L. Smith 1980). We will use the general relations briefly presented here to organize current knowledge about recreational effects on salmonids.

A. The fishery

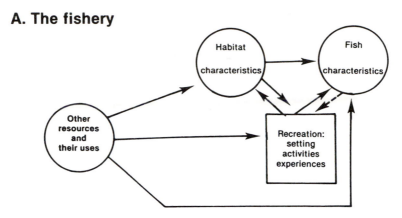

B. Interrelations

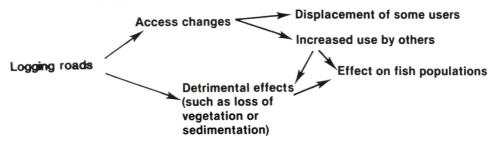

FIGURE 13.2.—Interactions of an anadromous fishery and recreation.

The Recreational System

In this section, we describe recreational characteristics that provide a background for evaluating recreational effects on the fishery. We believe that a general understanding of recreation will help in the evaluation and prediction of potential effects on fish habitats.

Since the 1950s, research has addressed recreation in general as well as specific activities such as fishing. We will identify some basic conclusions and principles from those studies on interactions between recreation and salmonids. All recreational activities (fishing and nonfishing) occurring in areas that support anadromous fish will be considered.

What We Know About Outdoor Recreation

In both the formal and popular literature related to outdoor recreation, terms such as motives, satisfactions, and experiences are commonly used, sometimes ambiguously. The definitions used in this chapter are as follows.

Motives are the underlying reasons for engaging in a recreational pursuit (for example, health, relaxation, and strengthening of family ties).
Preferences are the favored alternatives for activities, experiences, or setting attributes.

Expectations are conditions presumed to be encountered during recreation (expectations are based on knowledge and experience).

Opportunities are chances for recreation, consisting of settings, activities, experiences, and satisfactions.

Settings are the combinations of social, managerial, and natural features that give recreational value to a place.

Activities (uses) are various ways that people behave in their leisure time.

Experiences are the products resulting from participation in a recreational activity or set of activities in a particular setting.

Satisfactions are the enjoyments that people derive from participation in various recreational pursuits.

The following generalizations suggest how people relate to recreational opportunities and areas that may sustain a salmonid fishery.

Recreationists' preferences and motives span a range of settings.—People use particular locations for different reasons. Water, whether in lakes, streams, or oceans, is an important consideration in recreational choices (Lucas 1964; Lime 1971; Clark et al. 1984; Clark and Downing 1985). Forests, fish, and wildlife also play a key role for many people.

A variety of preferences may be related to users' choices to use areas considered to be habitat for salmonids, and managers should not presuppose what a particular recreation user finds desirable about specific recreational sites. Anglers will, of course, prefer the presence of fish; however, other attributes— such as a place to camp, parking for vehicles or boats, or a place for family and friends to get together—may be important enough to take precedence over fishing.

Recreational activities are diverse.—Recreationists can take part in a wide variety of activities; for example, hiking, camping, boating, hunting, and off-road vehicle use can all take place in areas where salmonids are present. In common among such activities are the base resources used, the number of people using them, and the type of management provided. Just because a stream has an abundant salmonid population does not mean fishing will necessarily be the primary use of the area. The river (or lake) may be important to all users, but the fish may be critical for only some of them.

When recreational effects on the fisheries are studied, all activities in the areas influencing fish habitats (riparian and related uplands, as well as the aquatic areas) must be considered. Whether a person is standing on a bank for the purpose of fishing or taking photos makes little difference. Important considerations related to all recreational activities are where they take place in relation to fish habitat (upland, on bank, in water); when they occur (seasons, stage of fish's life cycle); the duration of the activity; the number of people in an area (intensity of use); and how widespread the use is over an area (extent of use).

The same activity may take on different styles.—People can participate in the same recreational activity in a variety of ways and in places that range from city parks to wilderness. An activity such as hiking is basically the same in all areas, but the motives for engaging in the activity, the style of participation, and the resulting experiences can differ dramatically from one area to another.

Fishing is a good example. Bryan (1976) described four types of anglers: *occasional anglers*, who have novice ability and interest in the sport and for whom any fish will do as long as the challenge is not too difficult; *generalists*, who focus on catching numbers of fish by any means or tackle; *tackle–species specialists*, who specialize in method (for example, fly-fishing) and species (for example, steelhead) and who place importance on the skill and the esthetic quality of the experience, as opposed to just catching and keeping fish; and *method–species–setting specialists*, who specialize in method, species, and setting (spring or meadow streams), who are preoccupied with skill and overall quality of experience, and who tend to center much of their lives around leisure activities. As anglers move from the "occasional angler" to the "method–species–setting specialist" class, they become more particular as to species, technique, tackle preferences, and setting requirements. Two different philosophies of fishery management can be used to meet these varied demands: managing the indigenous salmonid populations as part of the natural ecosystem, in which harvest is limited to the reproductive surplus; or intensive stocking of hatchery fish to build up the fishery.

Activities cannot be equated with motives for recreation or resulting experiences.—Recreation researchers have concluded that people can have different motives for engaging in the same activity (such as fishing). Motives may include nature appreciation, interaction with other people, challenge, and relaxation, as well as catching fish. But catching fish (or shooting game) is not necessarily related to satisfaction and enjoyment (Potter et al. 1973; Hendee et al. 1977; Brown 1982). This knowledge is relevant when attempts are made to change patterns of recreational use. Changing these patterns by managing the fishery (increasing or decreasing stocking, changing species composition) will affect only people whose primary motive is catching fish (Carpenter and Bowlus 1976).

Salmonid habitats can be more effectively managed when the motives of those using them are known. If nonfishing recreational values are the major reason for visiting an area, the fish take on secondary importance. When fishing is a trophy or subsistence activity, the taking of fish is the primary concern. Understanding of various motives for visiting specific areas and for fishing will allow managers to develop strategies consistent with users' values.

Access is an important influence on recreational choices and the location and amount of recreational use.—Access plays a critical role in either facilitating or hindering recreational use. Roads facilitate recreational preferences for people preferring some form of motorized access. Road access will hinder recreational opportunities that are not compatible (necessary or desired) with roads. Road construction and use may have major detrimental effects on salmonid habitats (Gibbons and Salo 1973; Furniss et al. 1991, this volume). Yet, decisions made about roads—needs, location, and type—are not usually made with recreational objectives in mind. Later in this chapter we will discuss considerations for identifying and evaluating both positive and negative implications of access management alternatives.

Most people take recreational trips in areas near their communities.—Some studies demonstrate that people take most of their recreational trips in areas around their residential communities (Clark et al. 1982). A "home range" exists that is based on type of access and time of travel. Other recreationists are migratory (tourists) and visit other sites well beyond their home ranges where most outings occur (Clark 1987, 1988). Residents and tourists may or may not be attracted to the same types of areas. When the effects of recreation are considered, it is important to think in terms of specific populations rather than some vague, ill-defined public. By understanding the relation between recreational users and available recreational opportunities, resource managers can better predict the consequences of their policies and actions on both populations. Some changes by management may have significant effects on patterns of recreational use in areas considered as salmonid habitat.

Managers and recreationists disagree about the importance of recreational effects.—Studies show that resource managers are more sensitive to the effects of recreation than are recreationists (Clark et al. 1971; Clark and Stankey 1979a; Downing and Clark 1979; Lucas 1979). One explanation for the difference is that managers are likely to have a longer and more intense experience with the effects of recreation than are most users and may be more sensitive to resource changes.

Managers should recognize that such disparities exist and attempt to accommodate user perspectives and educate users concerning the problems that may be created by recreational activities. Each group must understand how the other relates to resource changes before any effective controls can be developed and carried out.

People need good information to make choices in keeping with their preferences.—When considering opportunities for outdoor recreation, people choose the setting, the activities, and the kinds of experiences to seek. Recreationists who have information describing the range of possible recreation settings will be in the best position to make recreational choices in keeping with their desires (Clark and Stankey 1979b).

Recreationists are more likely to be satisfied with a particular trip or activity when what they encounter is consistent with pretrip expectations (Roggenbuck and Schreyer 1977; Clark and Stankey 1979a). A high degree of satisfaction can also occur when recreationists are able and willing to modify their plans whenever expectations are not met.

The Recreation Opportunity Spectrum

The recreation opportunity spectrum (ROS) is a framework that helps to clarify relations among recreational settings, activities, and experiences (Brown et al. 1978; Clark and Stankey 1979b; Buist and Hoots 1982; Clark 1982). The assumption underlying the ROS is that quality is best assured by providing diverse opportunities. The ROS recognizes that opportunities sought by recreationists range from easily accessible, highly developed areas with modern conveniences to undeveloped areas in remote locations. Within each of the general types of settings, a variety of activities, such as fishing, camping, and hiking, are possible.

A recreation opportunity setting is defined by the combination of social, physical, biological, and managerial conditions that give perceived value to a place. It is distinguished by varying conditions ranging from modern to primitive. The ROS includes six factors that influence recreational behavior and have significance to management. A more detailed description of these six factors may be found in Clark and Stankey (1979b), but briefly they are

• access into and within the area and the degree of difficulty associated with access and the permitted means of conveyance;

• the extent to which other nonrecreation resource uses (such as timber harvest, commercial fishery management, and mining) are compatible (from the user's perspective) with various outdoor recreational activities;

• onsite management—the extent, visibility, and complexity of modification, including the use of exotic vegetation, landscaping, traffic barriers, and facilities (tables, toilets, water supplies);

• social interaction—the relative intensity of use per unit area, including the amount of intergroup contact and the space requirements associated with different opportunities;

• level of regimentation—the nature, extent, and degree of control over recreational use exercised by management; and

• amount and degree of visitor effects acceptable in different opportunities (as perceived by users).

A recreation setting is created by specific combinations of these factors in a particular place. Alternative combinations lead to different opportunity settings ranging from modern-urban to primitive, providing many options to recreationists. An example of how these factors can be combined to create a range of settings is shown in Figure 13.3. Each of these factors is characterized by a range of conditions. For example, access ranges from areas where mechanical access on wide, paved highways is appropriate to areas without trails where only foot travel is permitted. Similarly, social interaction varies from high-density use (where it is appropriate and expected, such as in some urban parks and modern campgrounds) to places of maximum solitude. The appropriateness of these conditions varies along the spectrum. Well-developed roads and large numbers of people with frequent contact between parties are not appropriate in wilderness, although they can be in places like beaches, near an urban area, or in highly developed campgrounds.

Recreation settings are also composed of natural features in addition to the six ROS factors described above. Land-form types, vegetation, scenery, water (lakes and streams), wildlife, and fish are all important elements of recreation environments; they influence where people go and the kinds of activities that are possible. As Cheek et al. (1976) suggested, the nature of participation in recreational activities depends on the place in which it occurs. No intrinsic quality of these other natural features suggests the appropriate type of recreation opportunity setting, however. Any of the ROS classes are as possible and appropriate in mountainous areas as they are in desert settings. Greatest diversity would be assured if the full spectrum of opportunity types (modern-urban to primitive) could be found across the range of environmental settings.

The ROS assists resource planning and management by helping to integrate and coordinate recreation with other resource uses and management activities. The ROS can be applied to all kinds of land-use planning and resource management and is not only for recreation managers. Many of the factors defining recreational opportunity settings (access and use of other resources, for example) are traditionally the responsibility of other disciplines and functions (such as timber management and engineering). Coordination between different areas is necessary to ensure that appropriate management objectives are stated (and achieved) and to

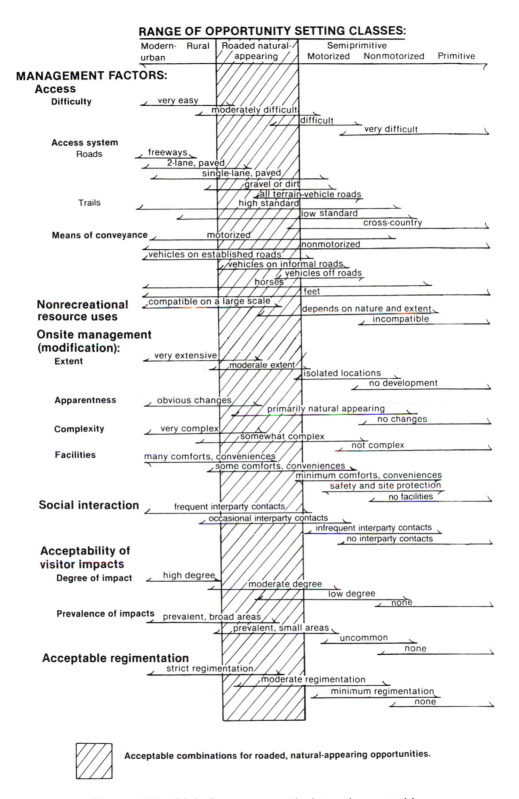

FIGURE 13.3.—Links between recreationists and opportunities.

TABLE 13.1.—Importance of recreational activities to anadromous fish and fish habitats: 0 = no effect likely; (X) = possible minor effect; X = possible major effect.

Zone of influence	Effects on fish populations	Effects on habitat
Marine		
Coastal (open ocean)	(X)	0
Estuarine	(X)	0
Freshwater		
Streams	X	X
Lakes	X	(X)

help point out potential conflicts and compatibilities among resources (Brown et al. 1978; Clark and Stankey 1979b).

The ROS helps planners and managers explicitly state their assumptions, their management objectives, and the presumed consequences of management alternatives for recreational opportunities. The ROS will not make decisions; it does allow planners and managers to test assumptions, and it provides the possible consequences of various options. Stating management objectives (for example, what to provide, how, where, when, and for whom) helps in successfully using the ROS. Specific ways to use the ROS to evaluate recreational effects on anadromous fisheries are described later in this chapter.

Interrelations between Recreation and Anadromous Fish

Any fish population or its habitat can be affected by recreationists if the usage is intensive enough. The intensity threshold varies with fish species, size and specific characteristics of the water body, the number and timing of recreationists, the type of recreation activity, and the degree to which use is concentrated in time and space. Recreation can directly affect fish in four basic zones—coastal–marine, estuarine, riparian–stream, and lake (Table 13.1).

Direct Effects on Fish

In all of these zones, direct recreational effects on fish occur primarily through fishing. Adult salmonids are the primary targets of anglers. Fishing, depending on the available fish population and the intensity of fishing, may have either minor or major adverse influences on the fish. Hooking, even if the fish are released, can result in injuries and diseases that may lead to death. Handling hooked fish before releasing them also contributes to mortality. The combination of effects on the fish from harvesting or hooking and releasing can influence the size and species composition of populations.

Effects on Fish Habitat

The ways in which recreation may influence elements making up the stream and lake habitats of salmonids are summarized in Table 13.2. Recreation is considered in two ways: the factors defining the recreational setting (habitat), and the recreational activities taking place. We have attempted to isolate recreational components that appear related to elements of fish habitat. The habitat require-

TABLE 13.2.—Effects from recreational activities by zones of influence: 1 = primary effect; 2 = secondary effect.

Activity	Upland vegetation			Riparian vegetation			
	Overstory	Understory	Soils	Overstory	Understory	Soils	Aquatic
Hiking	2	1	1	2	1	1	2
Horses	2	1	1	1	1	1	2
Vehicles							
On roads			2	2	2	2	2
Off roads	1	1	1	1	1	1	1
Camping	1	1	2	1	1	1	1
Fishing				2	1	2	1
Boating				2	1	1	1
Waterplay							
Swimming				2	2	2	1
Temporary dams				2	2	2	1
Removing debris				2	2	2	1
Bathing, dishwashing				2	2	2	1

ments of salmonids are complex, but are condensed here into four principal components—cover, food, space, and spawning area. These four habitat components are associated with migration, spawning, incubation, rearing, and the habitat zones of influence (Table 13.3).

The literature, our professional experience and judgment, and common sense suggest that certain combinations of recreational factors defining settings, coupled with specific activities, may affect salmonid habitat. Whether or not the possible effects we identify are important cannot be readily determined. Resource managers will have to evaluate the consequences of encouraging or discouraging individual recreational uses on a local basis.

Little documentation exists regarding specific effects of recreation on salmonid habitat. Some research, briefly summarized here, has been conducted on the effects of recreation on soils and vegetation in general and along streams in particular. We also speculate about how recreation can affect other environmental factors listed in Table 13.3, and the implications such changes have for salmonids in various stages of their life cycle.

Recreational use can affect salmonid habitats in the following ways:

- upland changes in soils and vegetation that may affect runoff and erosion;
- riparian changes that influence erosion, cover, food sources, and water quality; and
- instream changes that affect stream morphology, water quality, streamflow, substrate, and debris.

Upland soils and vegetation.—Changes in vegetation from recreational activities in upland and riparian areas appear to be generally similar in type but not magnitude to effects of livestock grazing (see Platts 1991, this volume, for a discussion of the effects of livestock grazing). Cole (1979) discussed problems in studying recreational effects on vegetation and concluded that most change results from initial light use. Continued or increased recreational use at sites may have little additional effect.

TABLE 13.3.—Relations of zones of influence to the freshwater habitat requirements and life cycles of anadromous salmonids: 0 = no relation anticipated; 1 = primary relationship; 2 = secondary relationship.

Feature	Habitat requirement				Life cycle phase			
	Cover	Food	Space	Spawning substrate	Migration	Spawning	Incubation	Rearing
Upland zone								
Vegetation								
Overstory	0	0	0	2	0	0	0	0
Understory	0	0	0	2	0	0	0	0
Soils	0	0	0	2	0	1	1	0
Riparian zone								
Vegetation								
Overstory	1	1	2	0	0	0	0	1
Understory	1	1	0	0	0	0	0	1
Soils	2	0	2	1	0	1	1	2
Aquatic zone								
Vegetation	1	1	0	0	2	0	0	1
Streamflow	2	2	1	1	1	1	1	1
Channel morphology								
Riffles	2	1	2	1	0	1	1	2
Pools	1	1	1	0	2	0	0	1
Water quality								
Suspended sediment	2	1	0	0	2	0	0	1
Bedload sediment	1	1	1	1	0	1	1	1
Temperature	0	1	0	1	1	1	1	1
Dissolved oxygen	0	2	2	0	2	1	1	1
Bacteria	0	2	0	0	0	0	2	2
Chemicals	0	1	0	0	2	1	1	1
Barriers	2	2	2	0	1	2	0	2
Debris	1	2	0	0	1	2	0	1

Settergren's (1977) review identified six possible effects on soils of recreation along rivers: compaction; root exposure; destruction of the soil profile through loss of vegetation; reduction in organic matter; increased bulk density; and decreased soil moisture. He concluded (in agreement with Cole) that the greatest compaction occurs immediately after an area is opened for use, after which the soil tends to stabilize. As soil compaction and vegetation loss occur, erosion may accelerate. This can decrease the depth of soil profiles and expose roots.

Landform patterns in upland and riparian areas may also be affected by recreational use. Hiking and use of off-road vehicles or horses may create ruts and trails that gather runoff, leading to increased erosion. Whether such changes will occur, or to what extent, depends on local soils, vegetation, topographic conditions, and the proximity of the damage to riparian areas.

Settergren's (1977) review also described five types of vegetation changes: mortality of overstory; loss of tree vigor; mechanical injury; root kill; and loss of ground cover. Recreational activities can cause direct physical or mechanical injury and indirect physiological and morphological changes by affecting the soil. Settergren concluded that mechanical injury is common, increasing the likelihood of disease and possible subsequent mortality. Decline in tree vigor is sometimes associated with soil degradation, and reduced ground cover (both total amount and number of species) is one of the first signs of recreational use. Settergren believed that a shift towards fewer, more tolerant species may occur when vegetation is adversely affected by recreational uses.

The consequences of these changes for the quality of fish habitat are uncertain. Vegetation loss may lead to soil loss, compaction, or both; increased sedimentation; and reduced fish spawning habitat. No research has been specifically conducted to establish whether, or under what conditions, such results might occur.

Riparian habitat.—The U.S. Forest Service defines a riparian ecosystem as "a transition between the aquatic ecosystem and the adjacent terrestrial ecosystem [that] is identified by soil characteristics and distinctive vegetation communities that require free or unbound water." For minimum management purposes, riparian boundaries are defined as "the land and vegetation extending at least 100 feet measured horizontally from the edges of all perennial streams, lakes, and other bodies of water" (U.S. Forest Service 1980b).

When potential effects from recreational activities are evaluated, local conditions affecting the size of the riparian area must be considered. Substantial differences in the recreational use and its effects can occur in areas where the actual riparian area is 90 m rather than 2 m wide. In general, greatest disruptions are likely to occur within 5 m of the stream. Thus, our definition of the riparian zone is the area of land and vegetation that provides a transition between the aquatic and terrestrial environments and directly influences the stream.

In the riparian zone, recreational activities (as well as management actions that support them) may alter habitat elements important to salmonid populations. Recreational use of the riparian zone does not always greatly disrupt fish habitat, however. Both the size and importance of effects must be taken into account in evaluating whether intolerable effects have occurred.

Streamside vegetation directly influences the quality of salmonid habitat. Overstory riparian vegetation directly affects cover, food, and streambank stability, as does the understory, but it also provides shade, resulting in increased rearing space and the cool waters that favor salmonid growth. Riparian vegetation provides shade and an insulating canopy that ameliorates water temperatures during both summer and winter. It also acts as a filter to prevent addition of sediment, and its roots provide streambank stability and cover for rearing fish. Riparian vegetation directly influences the food chain of a stream ecosystem by providing organic detritus and terrestrial insects, and by controlling aquatic productivity that depends on solar radiation. A more complete discussion of the relation of riparian vegetation to fish habitat can be found in Murphy and Meehan (1991, this volume).

Understory vegetation in the riparian area can be reduced or removed when recreational activities occur along the edge of rivers and lakes, depending on the intensity and type of activity. Loss of understory vegetation directly affects the rearing habitat of fish by reducing hiding cover, food production, and streambank stability. How quickly bank loss occurs and how much of the shoreline will be affected depends on the type of recreational activity taking place and its frequency. The addition of sediment directly affects spawning gravels, and the loss of undercut banks has a negative effect on rearing areas.

Aquatic Habitat.—A variety of characteristics are associated with the aquatic environment. Those that are critical to salmonid habitat and that are susceptible to recreation effects are described here.

• *Vegetation.* Anadromous fish habitat is affected when the sedimentation rate or volume of streamflow is changed by either indirect recreational activities or removal of the aquatic vegetation. These effects may be temporary or permanent, depending on the type and duration of the activity. Loss of vegetation can affect fish production by removing cover and reducing available food.

• *Streamflow.* Reduction in streamflow as a result of diversions or dam construction is a common problem that can be directly detrimental to both spawning and rearing habitats. Reduced streamflow can impede or block both downstream fish movements and upstream adult migrations, increase water temperatures, and reduce available rearing and spawning habitats.

• *Channel morphology—riffles.* The depth and flow of water over and through riffles defines the quality of spawning habitat for the various species of salmonids. Activities such as swimming, boating, and instream use of off-road vehicles can affect riffle quality. Swimming-hole construction or enlargement and streamflow concentration for boat passage can disturb habitats and fish. If the quality of riffle areas decreases, production of usable food for fish will also decrease.

• *Channel morphology—pools.* Pools are used by salmonids for rearing and for resting during migration. Pools can also be used by recreationists for swimming, boating, suction dredge mining, bathing, and other activities. A change in pool character (depth, width, debris) generally results in a decline in salmonid populations. Pool character is affected most often by a change in the quantity of cover (logs, limbs, rocks, and undercut banks).

• *Suspended sediment.* The concentration of suspended sediment above which fish resources are damaged and below which they are unaffected is not sharply defined (Gibbons 1982). Sediment can be produced from almost any recreational activity in uplands and transported to instream locations. Sediment can also affect angling time and success. Phillips (1971) stated that fishing success declines when suspended sediment exceeds 25 mg/L and may cease when concentrations are greater than 100 mg/L. Recent studies concerning the effects of sedimentation on rearing fish have indicated seasonal differences ranging from 1,500 mg/L to over 30,000 mg/L before damage occurs (Noggle 1978). Thus, the intermittent additions of suspended sediment generally affect recreational angling and not necessarily the fish.

• *Bedload sediment.* Excessive amounts of fine sediment deposited in streams can reduce aquatic insect populations and diversity, available living space for fish, and survival of incubating embryos. Recreational activities can add sediment to streams directly by trampling of streambanks and secondarily by affecting upland soils. Through the use of riparian management strips, streambank stability can be improved, and upland sediments can be prevented from entering the stream channel.

• *Temperature.* Water temperature is a major determinant of salmonid production. Riparian vegetation directly influences water temperature by providing shade in summer and an insulating effect in winter; recreational activities can remove this riparian vegetation.

• *Dissolved oxygen*. Adequate dissolved oxygen is important to salmonids during all phases of their life cycle. The amount of dissolved oxygen is normally near saturation; recreational activities can, however, decrease these amounts by adding organic waste to slow-moving water. In general, the effects of recreation on dissolved oxygen levels are likely to be minor. Other effects would become critical before recreational activities would reduce dissolved oxygen to dangerously low levels.

• *Fecal coliform bacteria*. Water pollution resulting from animal (including human) wastes is generally determined by the numbers and kinds of bacteria present, particularly fecal coliform types. Proper siting and treating of human waste and of waste from pack and riding stock can prevent stream contamination from these sources. Additions of fecal coliform bacteria by bathers and swimmers should be minor.

• *Chemicals*. Bathing and dish-washing soaps, herbicides, and insecticides are the principal recreational contaminators of water. Chemicals sprayed at campsites to control vegetation and insects can enter the water systems. Even low concentrations can drastically affect fish spawning and rearing success. Chemical additions to streams should not occur as a regular result of recreational activities. Norris et al. (1991, this volume) thoroughly discuss these chemical effects.

• *Barriers*. Stream barriers can provide both valuable rearing habitat and migration blocks to anadromous fish. The probability that recreational pursuits will create barriers to fish migration is slight, but they can be critical if they occur.

• *Debris*. Large woody debris is an important habitat component of a healthy salmonid stream. Swimmers, boaters, anglers, and others sometimes remove debris. Removal of large quantities can result in as much as an 80% reduction in anadromous fish populations (Elliott and Hubartt 1978), but such removal would rarely be a result of recreation. Debris removal by recreationists is primarily localized and should have minor effects on the total fish population of any stream. However, fish habitat restoration activities of angler groups can benefit fishes.

Evaluating the Effects of Recreation

Recreational effects likely differ by region, river type, vegetation and soil conditions, season, and the nature and extent of recreational use. Evaluation of these effects is largely judgmental; seldom are definitive answers available to allow accurate prediction.

Some of the patterns of recreational use that should be considered in these evaluations are temporal variation (daily, weekly, seasonal), intensity of use (concentrated, dispersed use), spatial distribution (upland, riparian; on or in water). Several questions need to be addressed. Do use and resulting effects coincide with areas of key fish production? Is the effect serious enough to create a change in habitat components? Will the change be quick or slow to occur? Will it be a long-term or a short-term change? Are cumulative effects likely? Are the recreational uses and any resulting effects concentrated in only a small portion of the stream, or are they widely dispersed? Answers to these and other related

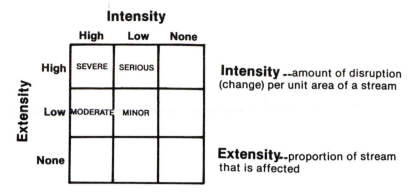

FIGURE 13.4.—Effects of existing or potential recreational use along portions of a stream.

questions will help determine whether any action will be required to prevent or ameliorate further changes in fish habitat conditions.

Some general observations about recreational use and its relation to salmonid habitat follow.

• Recreational use is not uniform in its distribution over either time or space. Some physical features such as water draw and concentrate use.
• The amount of use is not necessarily directly related to the effects on the area. Sometimes the practices of the individual or party in an area are more important than the number of people (Aitcheson et al. 1977).
• Most of the change in vegetation results from initial light use (Cole 1979).
• Anglers can affect upland and riparian habitats in addition to directly affecting fish populations because they often spend time in other recreational activities, such as sightseeing, walking, and camping, in areas near the lakes or streams in which they fish.

An example guide for judging the severity of effects from recreational use is shown in Figure 13.4. We believe that by considering both the intensity and extensity of effects, actual or potential effects can be ranked. To use such a framework will require that specific criteria be developed for defining "light," "moderate," and "severe" effects.

After the severity of the possible recreation effects is determined, the manager has several options. When the effects exceed acceptable limits as defined by management objectives, the manager can:

• do nothing, thereby accepting the consequences of the use or uses in question;
• mitigate the effects by limiting or eliminating use in critical areas through regulations or by changing the site design;
• redefine overall recreational objectives for all or part of the area, and reexamine fishery values and fish management programs in this light; or
• use a combination of the second and third alternatives.

Managerial decisions will require judgments about the consequences and feasibility (biological, social, and political) of each alternative. Information about the size of the effect on fish habitats and the importance of the change for various resource uses, including recreation, will be helpful in making judgments.

Effects of Management on Recreation

Resource management decisions may affect recreation in a variety of ways. When possible effects of existing and potential recreational uses on fish habitat are evaluated, the influences of these actions must also be considered. Here we focus on the effects of recreation management and fishery management. In particular, planners and managers must be alert for possible effects outside of the recreation system itself (such as road construction) that may cause a chain reaction, ultimately changing the nature of recreational opportunities and future activities.

Recreation Management

Certain decisions and actions of recreation managers may have implications for one or more aspects of fish habitat. The recreation opportunity spectrum (ROS) described earlier provides a framework for evaluating management actions. Two basic types of actions are designation of ROS classes and management of ROS factors. Examples of both of these are briefly described below.

ROS class designation.—Defining an ROS class in an area will not affect fish habitat until the area is used recreationally. Defining and managing ROS classes, however, may set in motion a chain of events that will affect the fishery. After classes are designated, management standards will be determined that are consistent with recreation goals. Presuming this all occurs according to plan, we can draw some general conclusions about the relation between ROS classes and fish habitat. The two extreme ROS classes (modern-urban and primitive) are used here for illustration.

The *modern-urban* class is characterized by concentrated use, many facilities, paved roads, and diverse nonprimitive activities. Locating a modern-urban setting such as a developed campground on or near fish habitats can have major implications. Locally, substantial loss of vegetation, soil compaction, loss of streambank stability, and even some changes in the stream channel can occur. Water quality may be affected when sanitation facilities are near streams or when insecticides or herbicides are used to control insects or brush. Use of horses or vehicles along or in streams may accelerate deterioration of banks and substrate.

At the other end of the spectrum, the *primitive* class is characterized by light (dispersed) use, lack of most comfort and safety facilities, and primitive means of transportation (foot or horse). Effects on fish habitat can range from none or minor, where use in infrequent (although as Cole 1979 pointed out, initial light use may account for most of the effect on soils and vegetation), to substantial, where use is more concentrated such as along trails or at popular campsites. Anticipating and precluding use in certain areas is generally easier than controlling use after a problem has occurred. Careful selection of sites for roads, trails, camps, and other facilities can influence use patterns (Beardsley and Wagar 1971; Settergren 1977). Campsites usually should be located away from riparian areas or in areas of least disruption (Kuska 1977). It is better to encourage fishery uses along lakes than along stream banks because lake shores are the less likely to be disturbed by recreational activities.

ROS management factors.—Management of ROS factors (access, other resource uses, etc.) has important effects on recreation. Whether the factors that define the ROS are managed to influence recreational use or for some other purpose, recreational use can be affected in nature and extent in specific areas (Figure 13.3). Because the ROS focuses on specific features of the physical, social, and managerial setting, it simplifies analysis of how proposed management actions will alter the nature of a specific recreational opportunity. Several examples are described here.

• *Access* decisions will have major implications for the nature and extent of recreational use and subsequent effects on fish habitat. The location and design of roads and trails will in large part determine the patterns and amounts of use. Roads can be provided specifically for recreation or for other resource uses. Recreational use often increases dramatically when roads are open for public use regardless of their original purpose. Increased road use in sensitive locations may result in unacceptable effects on fish production. If road and trail routes are at some distance from the water, effects on fish habitats will be minimized. Habitat disruptions are likely where stream crossings occur, and they will be exacerbated according to the nature and extent of resulting recreational activities. As the distance from access points increases on salmonid streams, recreation density (including anglers) decreases. The design and location of roads and trails near rivers will influence the probability and distribution of recreational use and the resulting resource effects. A road immediately adjacent to a river is more likely to have detrimental effects on the fishery than is a road built farther away (Figure 13.5). The mode of access—foot, horse, vehicle—may also have different effects. Clark and Stankey (1979a) indicated that managers can control the type of access to anadromous fish streams and the means of conveyance allowed. Both access elements can vary along the spectrum from easy to extremely difficult. Design and management standards are important in defining the range of access. Often, topography and the type of vegetation define the range of possible access. Thus, managers are able to use a combination of natural features, design and maintenance standards, and regulations to control the amount of access into any area. New roads or facilities should be designed and constructed to minimize disturbance. A review of road-construction practices for the protection of salmonid habitats is presented by Furniss et al. (1991). Unanticipated effects are less likely to occur when all of the resources are considered during planning.

• *Other resource uses* in an area will influence the type of recreation that occurs. Timber management activities, for example, can have major effects on recreational use. Conversion of a roadless natural area to one with a road changes the recreational setting. Roadless areas receive little use, and that use is dispersed over broad areas. Roads and clearings, particularly those near water, provide opportunities for concentrated use. As changes are made, redistribution of use likely will occur (Figure 13.3). When roads are located near riparian areas, recreational activities have an increased effect on fish habitat. Where temporary or long-term logging camps are located (such as in British Columbia and southeastern Alaska), recreational use will increase in nearby areas. The decision

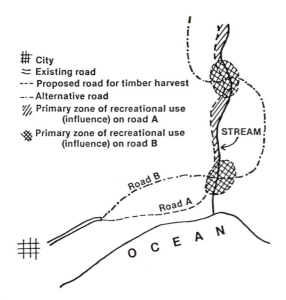

City
≃ Existing road
--- Proposed road for timber harvest
–·– Alternative road
/// Primary zone of recreational use (influence) on road A
❋ Primary zone of recreational use (influence) on road B

FIGURE 13.5.—Potential effects of alternative road locations on recreational use.

to develop an area for timber harvest has the obvious consequence of changing the amount and obtrusiveness of nonrecreational resource uses, but logging also may improve access to an area. Improved access can lead to higher use and greater demand for facilities. Many of these changes can be anticipated by management. The ROS provides management with a simple, graphic way of portraying these anticipated outcomes and evaluating whether they are appropriate or desirable.

• *Onsite modifications* provided for recreation—boat-launching facilities, docks, restrooms, tables, fireplaces, shelters, etc.—can substantially affect the distribution of recreational uses. Some people will find these conveniences disruptive, and they will look for less-developed places. People desiring such conveniences will congregate there.

• *Other management actions*, such as the spraying of herbicides or insecticides, may also have some consequences for fish habitat. Removal of dangerous trees in areas of intense recreation can lead to loss of overhead and instream cover and to increased soil and bank instability, which can reduce food sources, cover, and shade for fish.

Fisheries Management

Fishery managers can affect recreation by habitat manipulation, chemical treatment, biological manipulation, and regulatory action. Various specific actions under each of these categories include the following.

• *Habitat manipulation*: installing fish ladders, planting riparian vegetation, removing instream debris, adding instream woody debris and boulders, modifying barriers (removing beaver dams, blasting falls), creating pools (blasting), adding spawning gravel, removing fine sediment, creating spawning channels, building weirs and dams. Habitat manipulation projects may either decrease or increase recreational use. When roads are necessary for project access and left open for public use, they can increase use as described earlier. While the project is underway, recreational activities occurring near the project might be disrupted. Structures that result from projects may also have some effect on recreational activities. Regulations in most of the western USA usually prohibit fishing, but not other activities, near such structures. The sight of structures may cause some people to go elsewhere along the stream, which may expand the area affected by recreational use. On the other hand, the presence of fish enhancement structures may be an attraction for some people. Creation of pools, with their potential for swimming, bathing, and fishing, may attract people to an otherwise undesirable site.

• *Chemical treatments*: fertilizing lakes, eradicating fish (for example, with rotenone), controlling plants. Chemical treatments are most often used for lakes, although streams are occasionally treated. For example, in the California Golden Trout Wilderness, brown trout are being eradicated so that the less competitive species—the golden trout—can repopulate its native habitats. This type of action may also affect recreational use.

• *Biological manipulation*: stocking from hatcheries ("put-and-take" stocking or to build up populations), installing instream incubation boxes, removing unwanted fish populations (predators or competitors), introducing exotic species. Biological manipulation also may result in permanent structures, such as migration barriers, that can affect recreation. Artificial production can play an important role in moderating changes in the environment, but for many anglers it is a less desirable alternative than the natural production of salmonids. Furthermore, stocking influences only where and how much fishing occurs and has little significance for other recreational activities.

• *Regulatory actions*: setting bag limits, setting size limits, setting license quotas (rationing), limiting seasons, regulating gear, limiting access (boat-launching facilities). Regulatory actions are generally limited to effects on fishing, with the exception of such actions as controlling access and building boat-launching facilities.

Managing Recreation to Protect Fish

Managers have a variety of options to manage recreation in key areas of salmonid habitats. Some of these options have been described earlier in this chapter. Several additional opportunities are briefly covered below.

Recreation Activity Management

Managing activities directly is often advisable when adverse effects from recreation occur or are expected to occur. Regulating and prohibiting certain activities in key areas may help solve problems if users understand and agree with the rationale behind the restriction (Clark et al. 1971). Managers cannot control the adverse effects from recreation merely by regulating fishing because some people using the area may not fish and would not be affected by actions such as creel limits and gear restrictions. A clear understanding of the nature, location, and extent of all recreation activities is a prerequisite to effective management.

Education and Involvement of Recreationists

Educating users might help prevent or control problems. If recreationists are aware of how they may influence the fishery, they are more likely to avoid practices endangering fish habitat. Recreational anglers and other groups can have positive influences on fish habitat through their stream rehabilitation activities. Some negative effects of recreation and other management practices are beginning to be partly, if not totally, offset by the habitat restoration activities of organized anglers. Placement of habitat structures in streams by such groups as Oregon Trout, Northwest Steelheaders, and Trout Unlimited is growing. In addition to this direct habitat improvement, a growing awareness of the need for habitat maintenance is resulting from an improved conservation ethic.

Resting Recreation Sites

Allowing sites in key fish habitat areas to rest may reduce the effects of recreational use. Such a policy may spread the effects over a broader area, however (Cole 1979); most of the changes in vegetation result from initial light use and not from continuous and increased recreation. Furthermore, recovery from detrimental effects may take many years or may never occur if users do not comply with the restriction (Cole and Ranz 1983). Other alternatives should be seriously considered before this approach is adopted.

Problems can be solved more effectively if a variety of strategies is used. Preventing a problem through planning is easier than controlling one after it occurs (Magill 1977). Defining clear integrated management objectives in advance of any action is a prerequisite for effective solutions (Roggenbuck and Schreyer 1977; Brown 1979; Clark and Stankey 1979b). Management without such objectives can only be reactive. Objectives based on perception are appropriate if assumptions are made explicit (Thomas 1979; Clark 1982). Coordination among resource uses is critical, and recreational objectives must be integrated with the management objectives for fish and other resources.

Summary and Conclusions

The riparian zone tends to be more important from a recreation standpoint than are other areas. People are drawn to water and, as a consequence, may engage in activities there that adversely affect fish production. Riparian areas are managed for a variety of human values, and this management affects the nature and extent of recreational uses. We have described various ways in which recreational uses and salmonid habitats are interrelated. Empirical knowledge about these interactions is scarce; hence, the conclusions we make in this chapter must be regarded as tentative.

Given current knowledge, we believe recreation will usually have minor negative effects on fish habitats. Any recreational use of upland and riparian areas will have some effects, but they are likely to be minor compared to the influence of roads, logging, livestock grazing, and mining. The biggest recreational effect is likely to be harvesting of fish populations, not destruction of habitats. The effects of recreational activities on salmonids throughout North America are so variable, however, that they must be evaluated locally. Managers should pay particular attention to vegetative changes along long reaches of important rivers. Healthy vegetation appears to play a critical role in fish habitat productivity and is one of the first habitat components affected by recreational use.

Establishing management objectives before the start of any on-site action is essential to effective recreation management. Making explicit decisions will help managers anticipate influences from all uses, including recreation. A clear understanding of the rationale behind options will help in the application of those options. Identifying problems and issues and setting management objectives have often been overlooked in resource management planning (Stankey 1980). Defining limits of acceptable change to fish habitat will simplify monitoring and evaluating changes that occur (Stankey et al. 1985). To aid in this task, Bjornn et al. (1980), Gibbons (1982), and Heller et al. (1983) discussed methods for determining risks to salmonid habitat as a result of management activities.

Recreation is interdependent with other resource uses; if the nature and extent of effects from recreational use are to be understood, these links must be examined. Planners and managers responsible for anadromous fish habitat must have a method for analyzing management actions and their consequences and must incorporate such analyses in making multiresource decisions.

Fisheries managers must be careful that their actions do not detract from recreational opportunities and use. A balance between user and resource must maintain the natural capacity of the stream to produce wild fish, must retain management options for the future, must answer diverse and often competing demands for recreation (including fishing), must consider the relative success of stocked and wild fish, and must preserve esthetic values that are part of the recreational experience. We should beware of using projections of historical trends as a sole basis for planning because this can lead to managing for an intensive fishery and to dependence on artificial production. Consideration of all users equally will provide the means for the continuation and use of recreational resources. Managers must understand the demands for fishing, for catching fish, and for maintaining fish habitat in the context of the total recreational experience an area can provide.

We have shown how little documentation exists about the interrelations between recreational uses and salmonids and their habitats. Some of the topics that warrant further study are summarized below.

Aitcheson et al. (1977), Kuska (1977), and Clark and Lucas (1978) pointed out the need for objective baseline information on the supply and use of rivers for a variety of recreational pursuits. In addition, site conditions must be documented to provide a basis for monitoring and evaluating recreational effects on fish habitat. An adequate data base will assist specific studies of both the social and biological systems. Baseline information is needed for regions, watersheds, and specific sites.

For individual river systems, we need to determine the importance of effects from various kinds of recreational uses on components of fish habitats. How these effects differ by river and ecosystem types should also be evaluated. Studies to determine the effects of intensive versus dispersed recreation should be conducted through an experimental design that evaluates alternative recreational-use patterns for micro- and macrosites. Strategies to reduce or ameliorate unacceptable effects should be tested.

Studies are also required to separate the effects of recreational use from those associated with roads, logging, grazing, and mining. Determining the conditions under which various uses interact to affect the habitat of anadromous fish requires multifunctional, multisystems research.

Chapter 14

Responses of Salmonids to Habitat Changes

B. J. Hicks, J. D. Hall, P. A. Bisson, and J. R. Sedell

Streams in western North America provide spawning and rearing habitats for several species of salmon and trout that are of substantial economic importance in the region. Timber that grows on lands through which these streams flow is also economically important, and its harvest can substantially change habitat conditions and aquatic production in salmonid streams. Undisturbed forests, the streams that flow through them, and the salmonid communities in these streams have intrinsic scientific, genetic, and cultural values in addition to their economic importances. The complex relations between salmonids and their physical environment, and the changes in these relations brought about by timber harvest, have been investigated extensively (see the bibliography by Macdonald et al. 1988). However, in spite of considerable evidence of profound changes in channel morphology and in light, temperature, and flow regimes associated with timber harvests, much uncertainty exists about the responses of salmonids to these changes.

Responses of salmonid populations to changes in their freshwater environment brought about by forest-management activities are similar in many respects to those caused by other land-management activities such as mining (Nelson et al. 1991, this volume) and livestock grazing (Platts 1991, this volume). For example, fine sediment potentially has the same biological effect in streams whether it results from mining effluent, streambank erosion in grazed pasture lands, or road construction and clear-cut logging (Lloyd et al. 1987). The severity of its effect, however, depends on particle size and concentration, which in turn are related to sediment source. Changes in stream productivity caused by increased nutrient loading can similarly result from mining, livestock grazing, or forest management. Removal of riparian vegetation by any management activity changes the light and temperature regimes of a stream, leading to changes in primary and secondary production, in emergence times of salmonid fry, and in summer and winter survival of juvenile salmonids. There are also similarities between effects of natural catastrophic events, such as volcanic eruptions, and those of timber harvest (Sedell and Dahm 1984; Martin et al. 1986; Bisson et al. 1988).

Despite substantial research by federal, state, and provincial agencies, universities, and the timber industry (Salo and Cundy 1987), effects of forest practices on salmonids are still not well known. Less information is available on effects of livestock grazing and mining on salmonids (Rinne 1988; Nelson et al. 1991). We

Influences of Forest and Rangeland Management on Salmonid Fishes and Their Habitats
American Fisheries Society Special Publication 19:483–518, 1991

have thus chosen to focus our evaluation on the effects of timber harvest. Many of our conclusions, however, should be applicable to habitat changes caused by any management activity.

We consider the effects of logging on salmonids and their freshwater habitats in several ways. We first describe the effects of logging and other aspects of forest management on isolated parts of salmonid life cycles. Then we discuss integrated effects of forest practices on stream-dwelling salmonid populations. We also attempt to elucidate patterns of regional variation in the response of fish populations and to evaluate management practices that best protect fish habitat.

Responses to Specific Components of Habitat Change

In this section we examine the evidence that specific types of environmental change associated with logging practices have influenced short-term survival and growth of salmon and trout. Categories of environmental change commonly attributed to timber harvest activities, and their generalized consequences for salmonids, are shown in Table 14.1. The data supporting the generalizations in Table 14.1 were drawn from a variety of studies; some studies were process-specific and some examined the integrated effects of logging within a drainage. Furthermore, some of the studies were short-term comparisons of logged and unlogged basins whereas others were longer-term comparisons of a particular basin before and after logging. Duration of postlogging assessments has varied from 1 year to over a decade. For some types of habitat change, short-term studies have been sufficient to determine the responses of salmonid populations. For other types of change (e.g., the rate of recruitment of large woody debris), short-term studies have been inadequate to evaluate population response, and multisite comparisons of specific habitat change have been weakened by confounding factors. We considered these limitations as we reviewed each of the possible types of habitat change associated with timber harvest.

TABLE 14.1.—Influences of timber harvest on physical characteristics of stream environments, potential changes in habitat quality, and resultant consequences for salmonid growth and survival.

Forest practice	Potential change in physical stream environment	Potential change in quality of salmonid habitat	Potential consequences for salmonid growth and survival
Timber harvest from streamside areas	Increased incident solar radiation	Increased stream temperature; higher light levels; increased autotrophic production	Reduced growth efficiency; increased susceptibility to disease; increased food production; changes in growth rate and age at smolting
	Decreased supply of large woody debris	Reduced cover; loss of pool habitat; reduced protection from peak flows; reduced storage of gravel and organic matter; loss of hydraulic complexity	Increased vulnerability to predation; lower winter survival; reduced carrying capacity; less spawning gravel; reduced food production; loss of species diversity

TABLE 14.1.—Continued.

Forest practice	Potential change in physical stream environment	Potential change in quality of salmonid habitat	Potential consequences for salmonid growth and survival
	Addition of logging slash (needles, bark, branches)	Short-term increase in dissolved oxygen demand; increased amount of fine particulate organic matter; increased cover	Reduced spawning success; short-term increase in food production; increased survival of juveniles
	Erosion of streambanks	Loss of cover along edge of channel; increased stream width, reduced depth	Increased vulnerability to predation; increased carrying capacity for age-0 fish, but reduced carrying capacity for age-1 and older fish
		Increased fine sediment in spawning gravels and food production areas	Reduced spawning success; reduced food supply
Timber harvest from hillslopes; forest roads	Altered streamflow regime	Short-term increase in streamflows during summer	Short-term increase in survival
		Increased severity of some peak flow events	Embryo mortality caused by bed-load movement
	Accelerated surface erosion and mass wasting	Increased fine sediment in stream gravels	Reduced spawning success; reduced food abundance; loss of winter hiding space
		Increased supply of coarse sediment	Increased or decreased rearing capacity
		Increased frequency of debris torrents; loss of instream cover in the torrent track; improved cover in some debris jams	Blockage to migrations; reduced survival in the torrent track; improved winter habitat in some torrent deposits
	Increased nutrient runoff	Elevated nutrient levels in streams	Increased food production
	Increased number of road crossings	Physical obstructions in stream channel; input of fine sediment from road surfaces	Restriction of upstream movement; reduced feeding efficiency
Scarification and slash burning (preparation of soil for reforestation)	Increased nutrient runoff	Short-term elevation of nutrient levels in streams	Temporary increase in food production
	Inputs of fine inorganic and organic matter	Increased fine sediment in spawning gravels and food production areas; short-term increase in dissolved oxygen demand	Reduced spawning success

Changes in Stream Temperature and Light Regime

Changes in stream temperature and light regime after logging can have both positive and negative consequences for salmonid production. As a result, the effects of changes in temperature and light on salmonids are difficult to predict. Removal of streamside vegetation allows more solar radiation to reach the stream surface, increasing water temperature and light available for photosynthesis (Brown and Krygier 1970). In small streams (first to third order), increased daily temperature fluctuations also result from opening the vegetative canopy (Meehan 1970; Beschta et al. 1987; Bisson et al. 1988). The interpretation of much of the early research on temperature changes induced by logging was that these alterations were predominantly harmful to salmonids (Lantz 1971). Recent evidence has suggested that, under certain conditions, temperature and light increases can be beneficial.

Beschta et al. (1987) summarized studies of stream temperature changes associated with canopy removal over small streams in Pacific coastal drainages. They found a latitudinal gradient in increase of daily maximum temperature in summer that ranged from only a few degrees Celsius in Alaska to more than 10°C in Oregon. In the first 5 years following the 1980 eruption of Mount St. Helens, Washington, which virtually devegetated the watersheds of many Toutle River tributaries, Martin et al. (1986) and Bisson et al. (1988) measured peak midsummer stream temperatures of 29.5°C and diel variations as great as 17.0°C.

Although large changes in thermal and light regimes after timber harvest have been observed during summer, winter temperatures do not appear to be strongly affected by canopy removal, although even minor changes can have important consequences for streams when water temperatures are low. In general, forest canopy removal results in increased winter temperatures in low-elevation coastal drainages (Beschta et al. 1987). In northern latitudes and at higher elevations, a reduction in winter stream temperatures may occur due to loss of insulation from the surrounding forest coupled with increased radiative cooling of the stream. Where winter temperatures are lowered, ice forms more rapidly and the possibility of winter freeze-up increases. Such conditions may reduce habitat quality if anchor ice formation is extensive or if ice jams occur and then release ice flows to scour the streambed (Needham and Jones 1959). In contrast, slight postlogging increases in late-winter water temperature were found in Carnation Creek, a coastal stream on Vancouver Island, British Columbia (Hartman et al. 1987; Holtby 1988b). These temperature increases led to accelerated development of coho salmon embryos in the gravel and earlier emergence of juveniles in the spring. Earlier emergence resulted in a prolonged growing season for the young salmon, but increased the risk of their downstream displacement during late-winter freshets. Many changes in salmonid growth and survival resulted from the stream temperature increases in this watershed (Figure 14.1).

Among the potential benefits of elevated light and temperature during summer are increased primary and secondary production, which may lead to greater availability of food for fish. Solar radiation is an important factor limiting algal growth in forested streams (Hansmann and Phinney 1973; Stockner and Shortreed 1978; Gregory 1980; Gregory et al. 1987). Shifts in periphyton composition in response to elevated temperatures have been observed in laboratory streams

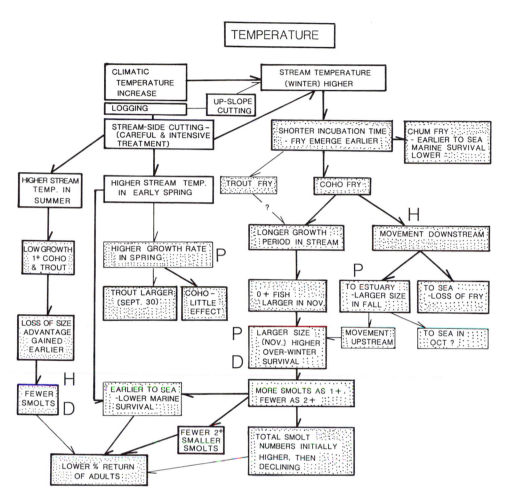

FIGURE 14.1.—Effects of logging on temperature-dependent processes at Carnation Creek, British Columbia, and the effects of temperature changes on fish populations. (From Hartman 1988.) The letter D, H, or P indicates the existence of an interaction with woody debris, stream hydrology, or production-related processes. Firmly established conclusions and cause-and-effect relations are indicated by heavy lines. Effects on fish are indicated by stippling.

(Phinney and McIntire 1965; Bisson and Davis 1976). Typically, well-lit warm streams are dominated by filamentous green algae instead of the epilithic diatoms that predominate in heavily shaded streams. After logging, increases in filamentous green algae promote the abundance of grazer invertebrates as the stream shifts from allochthonous to autochthonous carbon sources. Streams in clear-cut drainages often produce more baetid mayflies, grazing caddisflies, and orthocladiid midges than do streams in forested watersheds (Hawkins et al. 1982). These groups are often more likely to enter the drift and thus become potential food items for salmonids (Gregory et al. 1987). Wilzbach et al. (1986) found that cutthroat trout captured drifting prey more efficiently in open areas than in adjacent old-growth forest, where light intensities were reduced by canopy shading. In some streams, increased food availability can mitigate those detrimental habitat changes associated with removal of riparian vegetation, including high summer temperatures (Bisson et al. 1988).

The importance of autochthonous production to salmonid populations in clear-cut watersheds of the western USA has been suggested by several studies (Murphy and Hall 1981; Hawkins et al. 1983; Bisson and Sedell 1984; Bilby and Bisson 1987). In a whole-river enrichment study on Vancouver Island, British Columbia, stimulation of algal growth by inorganic nutrient addition resulted in greater benefits to salmonids than did stimulation of heterotrophic production through addition of cereal grains (Slaney et al. 1986; Perrin et al. 1987). Bilby and Bisson (1989) also found that summer production of juvenile coho salmon was more directly related to the amount of organic matter produced by autochthonous sources (algal photosynthesis) than to organic matter produced by allochthonous carbon sources (terrestrial litter inputs and fluvial transport), regardless of whether the stream flowed through a clear-cut or an old-growth forest.

Potentially negative effects on salmonids of logging-related changes in summer temperature were reviewed by Beschta et al. (1987). These include temperature elevation beyond the range preferred for rearing, inhibition of upstream migration of adults, increased susceptibility to disease, reduced metabolic efficiency with which salmonids convert food intake to growth, and shifts of the competitive advantage of salmonid over nonsalmonid species. Of these five categories of effects, the last is least understood. Reeves et al. (1987) found that stream temperature influenced the outcome of competitive interactions between redside shiners and juvenile steelhead. The shiners were more active and competitively dominant at warm temperatures whereas steelhead were dominant at cool temperatures. The authors hypothesized that a long-term increase in stream temperature could allow redside shiners to displace steelhead from reaches where steelhead formerly enjoyed a competitive advantage. From the perspective of basin-wide temperature, the most important role of tributaries may be to provide cool water downstream. Positive effects of canopy removal in tributaries may be more than offset by reduced cooling influence in main-stem habitats.

Decreased Supply of Large Woody Debris

Among the most important long-term effects of forest management on fish habitat in western North America have been changes in the distribution and abundance of large woody debris in streams. These changes have extended from small headwater streams to the estuaries of major rivers (Sedell and Luchessa 1982; Maser et al. 1988). Overall trends have included reduction in the frequency of pieces of large, stable debris in streams of all sizes; concentration of debris in large but infrequent accumulations; and loss of important sources of new woody material for stream channels (Bisson et al. 1987). As noted elsewhere in this volume (see Reeves et al. and Sedell et al.), these trends have been accelerated by stream channelization and by debris removal for navigation (Sedell and Luchessa 1982), for upstream fish migration (Narver 1971), and for reduction of property damage during floods (Rothacher and Glazebrook 1968).

Large woody debris plays an important role in controlling stream channel morphology (Keller and Swanson 1979; Lisle 1986b; Sullivan et al. 1987), in

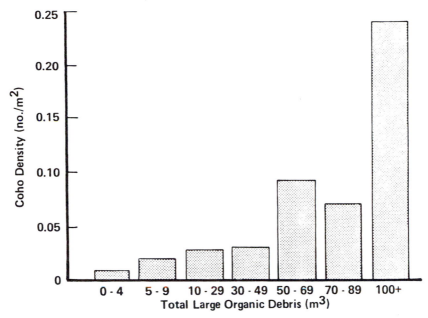

FIGURE 14.2.—Relationship between abundance of woody debris and density of juvenile coho salmon during winter in southeastern Alaska. (From Murphy et al. 1984a.)

regulating the storage and routing of sediment and particulate organic matter (Swanson et al. 1976; Swanson and Lienkaemper 1978; Naiman and Sedell 1979; Bilby 1981; Megahan 1982; Bilby and Ward 1989), and in creating and maintaining fish habitat (Bryant 1983; Lisle 1986a; Murphy et al. 1986; Bisson et al. 1987). The abundance of salmonids is often closely linked to the abundance of woody debris (Figure 14.2), particularly during winter (Bustard and Narver 1975b; Tschaplinski and Hartman 1983; Murphy et al. 1986; Hartman and Brown 1987). Large woody debris creates a diversity of hydraulic gradients that increases microhabitat complexity (Forward 1984), which in turn supports the coexistence of multispecies salmonid communities (Figure 14.3).

Prior to the development of extensive road networks, large streams and rivers were used to float logs downstream to mills. Widespread reaches of rivers were cleared of snags to permit navigation and to prevent logs from accumulating in large jams during transport (Sedell and Luchessa 1982; Sedell et al. 1991, this volume). Channel clearance accompanied timber harvest in the lower portions of river basins. As logging progressed upstream and the streams became too small to transport logs effectively, splash dams were built to store logs and water until sufficient head had accumulated to allow the logs to be sluiced downstream to a larger river. Splash dams were numerous in coastal watersheds (Wendler and Deschamps 1955; Sedell and Luchessa 1982). The long-term effect of channel clearance and splash damming was to remove vast quantities of woody debris from medium- and large-sized streams, a condition from which many rivers have apparently not recovered after 50 to 100 years (Sedell et al. 1991). Little is known about the effects of snag removal and splash damming on salmonid populations, partly because these practices are not frequently used today. It is likely, however,

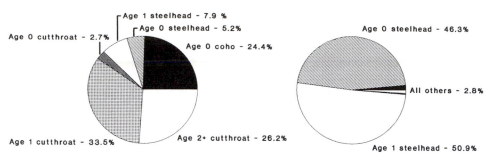

Beaver Creek

Age 1 steelhead - 7.9 %
Age 0 steelhead - 5.2%
Age 0 cutthroat - 2.7%
Age 0 coho - 24.4%

Age 1 cutthroat - 33.5%
Age 2+ cutthroat - 26.2%

Thrash Creek

Age 0 steelhead - 46.3%
All others - 2.8%
Age 1 steelhead - 50.9%

74.0% Pools
26.0% Riffles
Total Biomass = 3.28 g/m^2

22.2% Pools
77.8% Riffles
Total Biomass = 3.00 g/m^2

FIGURE 14.3.—Comparison of salmonid communities in two Washington streams with similar fish biomasses: Beaver Creek, a debris-rich stream in the Nisqually River system, and Thrash Creek, a debris-poor stream in the Chehalis River system. (P. A. Bisson, Weyerhaeuser Corporation, unpublished; reproduced in part from Sullivan et al. 1987.)

that species making extensive use of larger stream channels (e.g., chinook and chum salmon) were greatly affected.

Beginning in the early 1970s, forest practice rules in some western states required removal of slash (limbs and tops) from streams immediately after timber harvest. In many cases, stream cleaning also removed large pieces of merchantable prelogging debris from the channel. Recent case studies have assessed the immediate effects of debris removal on salmonid populations. Almost without exception, removal of large woody debris has resulted in loss of important habitat features and a decline in salmonid population abundance (Bryant 1980; Toews and Moore 1982a; Lestelle and Cederholm 1984; Dolloff 1986; Elliott 1986). Debris removal caused a decline in channel stability and a corresponding reduction in the quality and quantity of pools and cover. Bisson and Sedell (1984) observed enlarged riffles and a reduction in the number of pools in cleaned stream channels in Washington. The increased frequency of riffles favored underyearling steelhead and cutthroat trout, which preferred riffle habitat, but caused a decrease in the relative proportions of coho salmon and older age classes of steelhead and cutthroat trout, which preferred pools.

Removal of nearly all large trees from riparian zones during logging has also caused a long-term reduction in the recruitment of new large woody debris to stream channels, leading to a reduction in the quality of fish habitat. There may be a short-term increase in the debris load caused by entry of slash during harvesting and yarding, but this small unstable debris is often floated downstream within a few years, to be trapped in a few widely spaced debris jams (Bryant 1980). If the debris load of a channel is not replenished by large-scale inputs such as extensive blowdowns or debris avalanches, the second-growth riparian zone becomes the principal source of new woody debris. In young forest stands, inputs of debris large enough to be stable in streams with channel widths greater than about 15 m remain low for at least the first 60 years of riparian forest regrowth (Grette 1985; Long 1987). Many streams in second-growth forests have become progressively debris-impoverished following logging to the edge of the channel. Young riparian stands do not produce sufficient debris of the proper size and quality to replace material lost when channels are cleaned and large preharvest debris gradually decays (Sedell et al. 1984; Andrus et al. 1988). The effect on fish habitat has been a decrease in channel complexity, in number and volume of pools, in quality of cover, and in capacity of streams to store and process organic matter.

Some debris jams formed after logging or after a logging-related debris flow have blocked upstream fish migration. The improper design, construction, or maintenance of culverts on forest roads can also prevent or hinder upstream movements (Toews and Brownlee 1981; Furniss et al. 1991, this volume). To date, the relative importance of natural barriers, logging-related debris jams, and impassable culverts in limiting upstream movements of salmonids has not been assessed in any basin-wide survey. With the exception of dams on large rivers, we have little information on the extent to which fish-passage problems occurring in an entire drainage system have limited salmonid production.

Reduced Dissolved Oxygen Concentration

The introduction of fine logging slash, leaves, and needles into streams as a result of timber harvest can increase biochemical oxygen demand at critical times of low flows and high temperatures. In one small coastal Oregon drainage that was logged to the stream edge, dissolved oxygen concentrations of surface water decreased following timber harvest to below levels acceptable for salmonid survival and growth (Hall and Lantz 1969; Moring 1975a). Accumulation of fine organic matter from logging debris, in combination with increased stream temperature, was responsible for the decrease in dissolved oxygen. However, apart from short-lived effects in small streams in areas that naturally experience high summer insolation, there is no evidence of a major effect of logging on salmonids from low dissolved oxygen concentrations in surface water.

Of more importance than the usually transient decreases in dissolved oxygen in surface water are postlogging reductions in intragravel oxygen levels. These reductions may be caused by increased oxygen demand from fine organic matter introduced into the gravel matrix or by reduced interchange of surface and intragravel water. Several field studies have demonstrated reductions in oxygen concentration in redds following logging (e.g., Ringler and Hall 1975). However, increased intragravel sediment, decreased permeability, and decreased velocity of intragravel water often coincide with reduced levels of dissolved oxygen. Hence, the importance of reduced oxygen levels as a primary cause of mortality of embryos and alevins in gravel is difficult to assess.

It is rare for oxygen deprivation to directly kill many embryos and alevins in stream gravels after logging, but emergent juveniles that have incubated in oxygen-poor gravels may have reduced viability, and this may be an important factor in the regulation of salmonid populations. In an extensive review of the effects of intragravel oxygen on salmonid embryos and alevins, Chapman (1988) concluded that any reduction in dissolved oxygen below saturation may cause salmonids to be smaller than normal at emergence. Smaller juveniles are at a competitive disadvantage and likely have reduced fitness within the population (Mason 1969).

Altered Streamflow

The pattern of a stream's discharge affects the water depths and velocities that stream-dwelling salmonids will encounter, the amount of habitat available at different times of the year, and, to some extent, stream temperatures. Changes in streamflow caused by timber harvest are discussed in detail by Chamberlin et al. (1991, this volume). The effect of timber harvest on streamflow varies with logging method, soil permeability, season, and climate. Vegetation influences streamflow by intercepting precipitation and transpiring water (Bosch and Hewlett 1982). Removal of timber reduces transpiration and interception, and summer low flows and early fall peak flows usually increase as a result (Harr et al. 1975; Harr 1983). Of particular concern in western North America are increased peak flows that result from rainfall on snow following clear-cut logging in the transient snow zone (Harr 1986).

Streamflow does not always increase following logging. The presence of a well-developed coniferous forest can result in greater streamflows than occur after timber harvest. In coastal watersheds or at high elevations, fog drip can augment streamflow. This effect, caused by interception of wind-blown fog by tall trees, is most influential in summer (Harr 1982). In addition, increases in streamflow that result from timber harvest are generally short-lived within a timber harvest rotation; streamflow returns toward preharvest conditions as vegetation regrows (Harr 1983). Summer flows 10 years or more after logging may actually be lower than preharvest summer flows (Hicks et al., in press).

The effects on salmonids of changes in streamflow have not been documented separately from other effects of logging. To what extent the ameliorating effect of short-term increases in summer flows may be counterbalanced by increased severity of floods in other seasons is not known. In large basins, timber harvest activities are usually dispersed in space and over time. The result is that logging in large basins causes proportionately smaller changes in streamflow than it does in small basins (Duncan 1986).

Increased Fine Sediment

Fine sediment can enter streams during and after timber harvest as a result of road construction, timber harvest, and yarding activities (Everest et al. 1987a). Mass soil movements following road construction and timber harvest produce fine sediment, but the amount of fine sediment washing from the unpaved surfaces of actively used logging roads can equal that produced by landslides (Reid and Dunne 1984). Fine sediment that settles in streams or moves in suspension can reduce salmonid viability. Determination of the effects that deposited fine sediments have on salmonids is complicated by the variability in responses among salmonid species and by the adaptability of salmonids to ambient sediment levels (Everest et al. 1987a). Fine sediment deposited in spawning gravel can reduce interstitial water flow, leading to depressed dissolved oxygen concentrations, and can physically trap emerging fry in the gravel (Koski 1966; Meehan and Swanston 1977; Everest et al. 1987a). Survival of coho salmon in natural and simulated redds is related to the proportion of fine particles in the gravel (Figure 14.4).

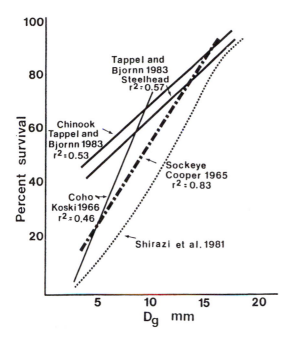

FIGURE 14.4.—Survival to emergence in relation to geometric mean particle size (D_g) for natural coho salmon redds (Koski 1966), and for other salmonids in laboratory gravels (Cooper 1965; Tappel and Bjornn 1983). The composite model of Shirazi et al. (1981) is plotted in the same D_g range (3–17 mm). (Entire figure from Chapman 1988.)

Salmonid survival apparently was affected when timber harvest increased the amount of fine sediment in spawning gravels of some Alaska streams (Smedley 1968; Smedley et al. 1970); in some cases, however, the amount of sediment in gravels returned to prelogging conditions within 5 years (McNeil and Ahnell 1964; Sheridan and McNeil 1968; Sheridan et al. 1984). Studies in coastal drainages of the Olympic Peninsula, Washington, have addressed the effects on spawning success of sediment from landslides and logging road surfaces (Cederholm and Salo 1979; Cederholm et al. 1981; Cederholm et al. 1982; Cederholm and Reid 1987). The concentration of intragravel fine sediment in spawning riffles was positively correlated with mass soil movements and the extent of roading within watersheds. The effects of sedimentation on salmonid spawning success were estimated by monitoring the survival of embryos and alevins in natural redds (Tagart 1976) and in experimental redds containing a mixture of gravel meant to simulate conditions in Clearwater River tributaries. Based on these studies, Cederholm et al. (1981) believed that accelerated erosion caused by landslides and logging roads led to a significant reduction in emergence of coho salmon fry. Coupled with high rates of ocean harvest and resultant low spawner densities, the reduced survival to emergence was thought to have resulted in lower smolt yields from the Clearwater River basin. Studies in British Columbia (Scrivener and Brownlee 1989), Oregon (Hall et al. 1987), and Idaho (Stowell et al. 1983) have also shown declines in survival to emergence or in salmonid abundance associated with sediment increases after logging.

Some studies showed temporary increases in sedimentation related to logging, although subsequent effects on salmonids have been difficult to document. Female salmon clean gravel as they construct redds, which may be one reason that effects of fine sediment in gravel are often less than predicted (Everest et al. 1987a). Chapman (1988) reviewed the laboratory evidence for the effect of fine sediment on salmonid reproduction. He found that laboratory studies had generally failed to reproduce conditions in the egg pocket of the redd and therefore did not yield accurate predictions of survival in natural streams. He concluded, however, that increases of fine sediment did reduce survival to emergence.

In addition to directly affecting salmonid survival, fine sediment in deposits or in suspension can reduce primary production and invertebrate abundance and thus can affect the availability of food within a stream (Cordone and Kelley 1961; Lloyd et al. 1987). In northern California, diversity of invertebrates was lower in streams passing through clear-cut areas with no buffers or only narrow buffers than it was in streams in unlogged watersheds. However, the densities of invertebrates were higher in the clear-cut areas or not significantly different from those in unlogged watersheds (Newbold et al. 1980; Erman and Mahoney 1983). The effect on fish production of this change in invertebrate community structure was not investigated. The detrimental effects of large amounts of fine sediment are generally accepted, but precise thresholds of fine sediment concentrations that result in damage to benthic invertebrates are difficult to establish (Chapman and McLeod 1987).

Increases in suspended sediment can affect salmonids in several ways. Suspended sediment can alter behavior and feeding efficiency. Fish may avoid high concentrations of suspended sediment (Bisson and Bilby 1982; Sigler et al. 1984); at lower concentrations, fish may cease feeding (Noggle 1978; Sigler et al. 1984) and their social behavior may be disrupted (Berg and Northcote 1985). In nearly all cases, suspended sediment concentrations resulting from timber harvest are not sufficient to cause significant abrasion of the skin or gills of salmonids (Everest et al. 1987a; Bjornn and Reiser 1991, this volume), although temporary spikes of suspended sediment from landslides may approach lethal thresholds.

Increased Coarse Sediment

Channel morphology changes when timber harvesting increases the rate at which coarse sediment is delivered to streams. Increased frequencies of landslides and other mass wasting events can cause channels to aggrade where the gradient and other aspects of valley topography permit gravel deposition. Stream reaches that are aggraded with coarse sediments typically become wider, shallower, and more prone to lateral movement and bank erosion (Sullivan et al. 1987). More water passes through deposited gravels, reducing surface flow. Total riffle area increases but pool area decreases, and other types of habitat may be lost (Everest et al. 1987a).

Habitat alteration caused by debris torrents has been well documented in the Queen Charlotte Islands, British Columbia. In stream sections affected by debris torrents, average pool depth was reduced by 20–24%, and pool area was reduced by 38–45%. Cover associated with large woody debris was reduced by 57%, and undercut bank cover was reduced by 76%. Riffle area increased by 47–57%, and stream channel width increased by 48–77% (Tripp and Poulin 1986b). The amount of landsliding was directly related to the proportion of the basin area logged (Tripp and Poulin 1986b). The effect of logging was to increase landsliding frequency by 34 times in this geologically unstable terrain (Rood 1984). The frequency of debris torrents increased by about 40 times in logged areas compared to unlogged areas, and increased by 76 times in roaded areas compared to unlogged areas without roads (Rood 1984). A combination of logging and landsliding reduced the salmonid cover attributable to large woody debris by 58%. Reaches with landsliding had reduced width:depth ratios and less surface flow (Tripp and Poulin 1986b).

In erosion-prone areas of the Oregon Coast Range, logging roads caused rates of debris avalanche erosion that were 26–350 times greater than in adjacent forested areas. Rates were 2.2–22 times greater in clear-cut areas than in unharvested forest. When these rates were adjusted for the smaller area that was occupied by roads compared to that in clear-cuts, forest roads accounted for 77% of the total accelerated debris avalanche erosion (Swanson et al. 1981). In one stream in this area with little cover from boulders or large woody debris, debris torrents added new structure to the channel, temporarily enhancing the abundance of coho salmon (Everest and Meehan 1981a).

Altered Nutrient Supply

Stream concentrations of plant nutrients and other dissolved ions increase for a few years following logging (Brown et al. 1973; Scrivener 1982, 1988b). When accompanied by increased light, these nutrient additions often result in increased algal growth (Gregory et al. 1987). However, the effects of nutrient increases on invertebrate and salmonid populations have not been thoroughly studied.

Bisson et al. (1976) studied the effects of adding nitrate-nitrogen to model stream channels in southwestern Washington. They observed a temporary increase in the biomass of benthic invertebrates and in the production of stocked rainbow trout. After 2 years of continuous nutrient additions, however, no significant differences were found in either invertebrate biomass or trout production between enriched and unenriched streams. Slaney et al. (1986) added both nitrogen and phosphorus to the Keogh River on the east coast of Vancouver Island, British Columbia, after which steelhead grew faster and smolted when younger but larger. Steelhead smolt output also increased to as much as twice the preenrichment level (P. A. Slaney, Fisheries Branch, British Columbia Ministry of the Environment, personal communication), but it is not yet clear if the size of the returning adult run has increased.

Studies indicate that nutrient increases (mostly nitrate) are limited to the first decade after logging; that primary production is stimulated in the presence of increased light and nutrient concentrations; that watersheds dominated by volcanic rock are more likely to show enhanced autotrophic production after logging than watersheds dominated by sedimentary or metamorphic rock; that herbivorous invertebrates will most likely benefit from increased algal growth; and that salmonid production may or may not be enhanced during periods of increased nutrient concentration (Gregory et al. 1987).

Responses of Salmonid Populations to Forest Management

Thus far we have reviewed evidence that the growth or survival of salmonids at various life stages changes in response to changes in individual components of the habitat. It is also important to know the combined effect on salmonid populations of all the changes that occur in the course of normal forest management. In this section, we review results of several long- and short-term studies designed to measure response of salmonid populations to timber harvest. We have included

TABLE 14.2.—Physical characteristics and salmonid species at sites where combined effects of timber harvest on salmonid population abundance have been measured.

Location[a]	Latitude (°N)	Watershed area (km²)		Discharge (m³/s)	
		Mean	Range	Minimum	Maximum
(1) Southeastern AK	56–57			0.01–0.38	
(2) Queen Charlotte Islands, BC	52–53	8.2	0.5–47.5		
(3) Carnation Creek, Vancouver Island, BC	49	10		0.03	63
(4) Coast and Cascade ranges, WA	46–48	8.3	1–30		
(5) Coast Range, OR	45		0.8–3.0	0.0006–0.0085	1.4–5.7
(6) Coast Range, OR	44–45		5.1–23.7		
(7) Mack Creek, Cascade Range, OR	44	8.3		0.05–0.45	8–11
(8) Cascade Range, OR	44		0.3–17.9		
(9) Cascade Range, OR	44		4.0–8.2	0.02–0.09	
(10) Cascade Range, OR	44		5.4–6.8		
(11) Northern Coast Range, CA	39–42		4.3–25.1	0.002–0.014	0.26–1.42
(12) Northern Coast Range, CA	41		7.3–8.1		

[a]AK = Alaska; BC = British Columbia; CA = California; OR = Oregon; WA = Washington.

[b]1 = chum salmon; 2 = coho salmon; 3 = cutthroat trout (resident or anadromous); 4 = rainbow trout or steelhead; 5 = Dolly Varden.

[c]1 = Aho (1976); 2 = Bisson and Sedell (1984); 3 = Burns (1972); 4 = Chamberlin (1988); 5 = Hall et al. (1987); 6 = Hartman (1982); 7 = Hartman and Scrivener (1990); 8 = Hawkins et al. (1983); 9 = Heifetz et al. (1986); 10 = Johnson et al. (1986); 11 = Koski et al. (1984); 12 = Moring (1975a); 13 = Moring (1975b); 14 = Moring and Lantz (1975); 15 = Murphy and Hall (1981); 16 = Murphy et al. (1981); 17 = Murphy et al. (1986); 18 = Poulin (in press); 19 = Tripp and Poulin (1986a); 20 = Tripp and Poulin (1986b); 21 = Tripp and Poulin (in press).

[d]Species not identified by site.

studies in which quantitative estimates have been made of the abundance of salmonids and their habitats. In conjunction with our evaluation, we recommend management practices that protect fish populations and their habitats from harmful effects. The studies that meet our criteria, their locations, and descriptions of the watersheds involved are listed in Table 14.2. We excluded studies limited to specific parts of salmonid life history, such as studies of embryo survival in gravel infiltrated by fine sediment.

Role of Streamside Management Zones

One of the major developments in forest management in relation to fisheries over the past 25 years has been increased protection of streamside vegetation

TABLE 14.2.—Extended.

Location[a]	Channel gradient (%)	Surface water temperature (°C)		Species[b]	Reference[c]
		Winter	Summer		
(1)	0.1–3.0	1.2–4.8	13–17	2,3,4,5	9,10,11,17
(2)	0.9–10.0 (mean, 4.2)			2,4,5	18,19,20,21
(3)	0.2 (lower section)	1	18	1,2,3,4	4,6,7
(4)	1–8			2,3,4	2
(5)	1.4–2.5	5–12.2	14.4–29.5	2,3,4	5,12,13,14
(6)	0.3–2.0		22	2,3,4[d]	8
(7)	10		14.4–17.0 (at high elevation)	3	1
(8)	1–13			3	15
(9)	1–10		<21	3,4	16
(10)	1–10		15.5–18.5	3,4[d]	8
(11)	3–5		13.9–25.3	2,3,4	3
(12)	8.0–18.0		22	2,3,4[d]	8

during timber harvest. The gradual development of streamside management concepts has come about partly because of the studies we review and partly because more has been learned about the ecological structure and function of riparian zones (Swanson et al. 1982a; Gregory et al. in press).

The importance of streamside management as a tool to protect fishery values has been demonstrated in several studies that have compared fish habitat and salmonid populations in streams that were and were not given riparian protection during timber harvests. The evidence shows that streamside management zones minimize damage to habitat and effectively maintain the integrity of fish populations. This evidence is generally consistent over a wide span of time and space.

Alsea Watershed.—In the Alsea Watershed Study on the Oregon coast, fish populations and stream habitats were much less altered in a watershed that was patch-cut with intact streamside zones than in one that was completely clear-cut to both streambanks (Hall and Lantz 1969; Moring and Lantz 1975; Hall et al. 1987). This long-term evaluation of the influence of timber harvest on streams and their salmonid populations was established in 1958. It extended for 15 years and compared an unlogged control watershed with one that was completely clear-cut and another that was patch-cut with buffer zones left along the main channel.

Changes in physical habitat were extreme in the clear-cut basin. Only minor changes occurred in the patch-cut basin. Among the changes in the clear-cut stream was a large increase in summer stream temperature (Brown and Krygier 1970). A substantial reduction in dissolved oxygen occurred in surface water during the summer of logging, owing to accumulation of fine debris in the stream channel (Hall and Lantz 1969). During the first winter after logging, suspended sediment in the clear-cut stream increased about fivefold above the prelogging concentrations (Beschta 1978). Suspended sediment levels returned nearly to normal by the end of the 7-year postlogging phase of the study. There were increases in concentration and changes in vertical distribution of fine sediment in spawning gravels in the clear-cut watershed (Moring 1975a; Ringler and Hall 1988). As a consequence, gravel permeability in the clear-cut stream was substantially reduced below that in the patch-cut stream (Moring 1982). There were two episodes of short-term increase in suspended sediment in the patch-cut watershed caused by debris avalanches associated with roads, but these increases persisted for only 1 year. The avalanches occurred high in the watershed and formed settling basins that trapped most of the material from the hillslope. Thus they did not influence channel structure in the lower reaches inhabited by anadromous salmonids.

The two dominant salmonid species, coho salmon and cutthroat trout, responded differently to these habitat changes. Response of the coho salmon populations was difficult to assess. Smolt production in all three watersheds decreased after logging, as measured by the size of the normal smolt migration from February through May. However, owing to a progressive decline in numbers of smolts produced in the control watershed over the period of the study, and to substantial year-to-year variation in smolt abundance, the significance of the reductions was uncertain. The only change in abundance or behavior of smolt-sized coho salmon that could be attributed to timber harvest was a substantially earlier migration from the clear-cut watershed for the first 4 years after logging. A high proportion (average, 41%) of the total numbers of smolt-sized salmon migrated from November through January in those 4 years. The fate of these early downstream migrants could not be determined, but they were presumed to have suffered above-average mortality.

Another source of salmon production in these watersheds was affected by logging. Numbers of migrant fry that left headwater streams soon after emergence from the gravel declined to less than half the prelogging value in the clear-cut watershed (Hall et al. 1987) but changed little in the other two basins (Figure 14.5). The most likely cause of this reduced migration was the impaired gravel permeability, which could have substantially lowered survival from egg deposition to emergence (Hall et al. 1987).

Cutthroat trout resident in the clear-cut basin during late summer decreased to about one-third of their prelogging abundance immediately following logging (Figure 14.6). Their numbers remained near that low level for the entire postlogging study period (Moring and Lantz 1975). Abundance of cutthroat trout did not change in the patch-cut or control streams.

By its completion in 1973, the Alsea Watershed Study had established the value of riparian zone protection during logging as a means of maintaining productive

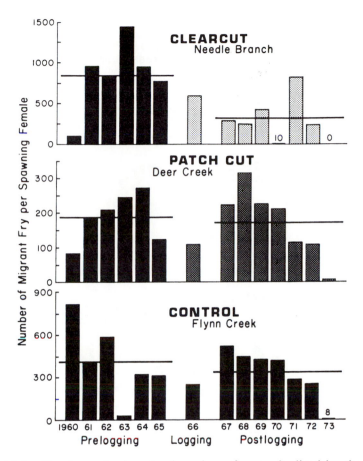

FIGURE 14.5.—Numbers of migrant coho salmon fry standardized by the number of spawning females that produced them in each stream of the Alsea Watershed Study, Oregon Coast Range. Horizontal lines are means of pre- and postlogging periods. (From Hall et al. 1987.)

fish habitat. Management practices and forest practice rules gradually began to incorporate greater protection for streamsides zones.

Carnation Creek.—The value of protecting the streamside zone was also demonstrated in the most comprehensive study of its kind to date, at Carnation Creek, British Columbia (see Poulin and Scrivener 1988 for an annotated bibliography). The watershed, on the west coast of Vancouver Island, has a cool, maritime climate. The study began in 1970 with a 5-year prelogging phase; it continued through a 6-year logging phase and a 5-year postlogging evaluation. Some monitoring continues, although the major research effort has been completed.

The study design involved three streamside harvest treatments, each applied to a different part of the same main-stem channel. In the lowest part of the basin, an unlogged buffer strip, varying in width from 1 to 70 m, was left along the stream. The next section upstream received a "careful treatment," in which all streamside trees were felled but were not yarded into or across the stream. Farthest

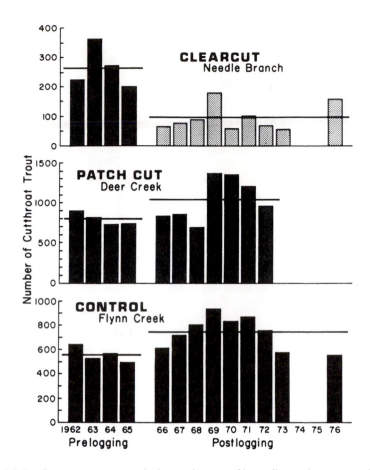

FIGURE 14.6.—Late-summer population estimates of juvenile cutthroat trout in the three streams of the Alsea Watershed Study, Oregon Coast Range. Horizontal lines are means of pre- and postlogging periods. (From Hall et al. 1987.)

upstream, in an "intensive-treatment" section, timber was felled into the stream and yarded from it (Hartman and Scrivener 1990). It was difficult to assess the effects of these treatments on salmonid populations because timber was harvested progressively and a variety of treatments was applied to the same channel. In several instances, downstream transport of material derived from a more severe upstream treatment influenced physical processes, habitat quality, and fish populations in the lower sections where treatment had been more conservative. Nonetheless, much useful information and several management recommendations have come from the study (e.g., Toews and Brownlee 1981; Hartman 1988).

Several physical changes in the stream were related to the intensity of streamside treatment. Owing to removal of streamside vegetation from a substantial length of the main channel and of its tributaries, stream temperature increased in all months, the mean increase ranging from 0.7°C in December to 3.2°C in August. In contrast to other Pacific coast streams, in which autotrophic production increased notably when the canopy was opened, periphyton abundance in Carnation Creek was low before logging and did not increase after logging

(Shortreed and Stockner 1983). The failure of primary production to respond to increased light levels was attributed to a low level of phosphorus. The volume and stability of large woody debris decreased in the two sections without a buffer strip, but did not change consistently in the section with a buffer strip. Streambank erosion and stream widening were significantly greater upstream from the buffered section than within it; stream width increased nearly 2 m in the careful-treatment section between 1979 and 1985 but only about 0.1 m in the protected reach (Hartman and Scrivener 1990). Bank erosion and scour and redeposition of stream substrates were the primary causes of an increase in fine sediment in spawning gravels. The major source of fine sediment appeared to be the two sections without a buffer strip, especially an area affected by a debris torrent (Hartman and Scrivener 1990). The fraction of the bed composed of small gravel and sand increased from about 29% before logging to about 38% in 1985–1986 (5 years after the end of logging), an increase of about 30% above baseline (Scrivener and Brownlee 1989). Levels of suspended sediment were low and variable, and did not appear to increase significantly after logging.

Increased fine sediment in spawning gravel was accompanied by a reduction in estimated survival of chum salmon to emergence, from 22% before logging to 12% after (Scrivener and Brownlee 1989). Holtby and Scrivener (1989) predicted that this increased mortality, combined with an earlier migration of emergent fry to the estuary in response to increased stream temperature, would adversely affect future numbers of adult chum salmon returning to spawn. Adult returns were estimated to have been reduced by 25% as a result of logging, and year-to-year variation in abundance increased.

The number of steelhead smolts leaving Carnation Creek declined dramatically following the start of logging (Figure 14.7A), possibly because of reduced winter habitat for age-1 fish. Comparison of steelhead smolt production and adult numbers in Carnation Creek with numbers in adjacent rivers suggests that the changes were not part of a coast-wide trend, but rather the result of logging-related changes (Hartman and Scrivener 1990). Cutthroat trout smolts did not change in abundance following logging (Figure 14.7A). The size of smolts of both cutthroat trout and steelhead fluctuated substantially over the period of the study, but showed no clear change as a result of logging (Figure 14.7B).

Coho salmon in Carnation Creek, like chum salmon, experienced a reduction in estimated survival to emergence as a result of increased fine sediment in spawning gravel caused by logging (Scrivener and Brownlee 1989). Average survival of coho salmon was 29% before logging but 16% after logging. The extended consequences of increased early mortality were difficult to interpret, however, because subsequent survival to spawning was influenced by other logging-related changes in the watershed as well as by climatic, biological, and fishery dynamics during the oceanic phase of the life cycle. Higher stream temperatures after logging caused juvenile coho salmon to emerge earlier and to grow faster during their first summer, resulting in larger sizes of both age-1 and age-2 smolts (Figure 14.8B). Winter survival from age 0 to age 1 in the main channel should have been reduced by decreases in the amount and stability of large woody debris (Tschaplinski and Hartman 1983). Because age-0 fish were larger in autumn, however, and because they made extensive use of a well-developed floodplain rearing area during winter, overwinter survival actually increased and a larger proportion of smolts went to

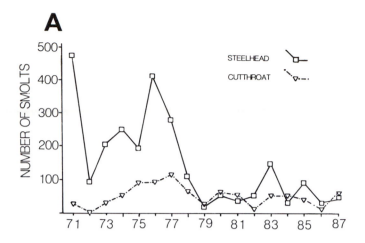

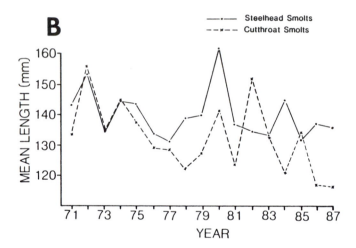

FIGURE 14.7.—Numbers (A) and size (B) of steelhead and cutthroat trout smolts leaving Carnation Creek from 1971 to 1987. Logging occurred between 1975 and 1981. (From Hartman and Scrivener 1990.)

sea at age 1 than was the case prior to logging. Consequently, total numbers of emigrants increased (Figure 14.8A). Nevertheless, the survival of smolts at sea probably declined because their spring migration took place an average of 2 weeks earlier than it did before logging (Holtby 1988b). The net result of logging was estimated to be a 6% reduction in returns of adult coho salmon and greater year-to-year variation in the number of returning spawners (Holtby and Scrivener 1989).

Changes in abundance of fish populations in Carnation Creek have been difficult to attribute to specific streamside treatments because there was only a single fish trap at the outlet of the watershed, and most of the assessment was based on overall changes in populations of the entire basin. In addition, there was no unlogged control watershed. These limitations were largely overcome by means of

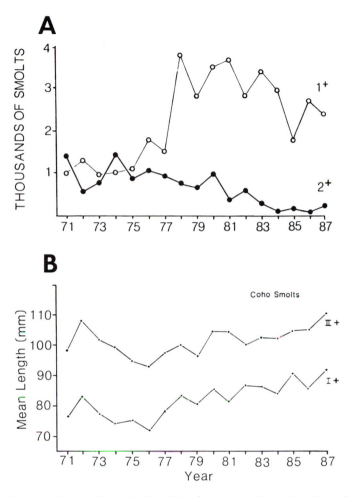

FIGURE 14.8.—Numbers (A) and size (B) of age-1 and age-2 coho salmon smolts migrating from Carnation Creek from 1971 to 1987. Logging occurred between 1975 and 1981. (From Hartman and Scrivener 1990.)

an elaborate series of linked regression models that accounted for the effects of logging, climate, and fishing (Holtby 1988b; Holtby and Scrivener 1989). This integrated approach to understanding the effects of logging on a salmonid population identified five distinct changes in the life history of coho salmon that were related to year-round temperature increases. These changes were (1) accelerated embryo development and earlier alevin emergence; (2) larger size at the end of summer, resulting from increased length of the growing season; (3) greater overwinter survival due to larger size; (4) more and larger age-1 coho salmon smolts and fewer age-2 smolts; and (5) earlier seaward migration of smolts in the spring. This analysis, which considered all life-history phases, illustrates the detail needed to understand the complex effects on salmonids of logging-related changes in streams. These efforts stand out as the most comprehensive attempt to place logging impacts within the context of the entire life cycle of an anadromous salmonid population.

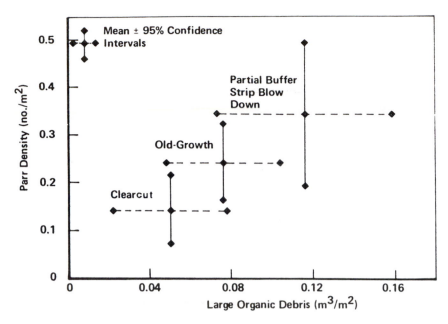

FIGURE 14.9.—Relationship between abundance of woody debris and density of coho salmon parr during winter in southeastern Alaska. Buffer-strip sites had experienced partial windthrow and had more debris than did old-growth sites. (From Murphy et al. 1984a.)

Southeastern Alaska.—Streamside management zones were shown to be effective in maintaining habitat and salmonid populations in a postlogging study of 18 streams in southeastern Alaska. Responses of coho salmon, Dolly Varden, and cutthroat trout populations to two treatments—clear-cutting to the stream edge (1–12 years previously) and clear-cutting with a buffer zone (3–10 years previously)—were assessed for 1 year (Murphy et al. 1986). Some buffer strips had experienced windthrow or had been selectively logged. In summer, coho salmon fry were more abundant in clear-cut and buffered reaches with partially open canopies than in old-growth reaches, apparently because increased primary production led to increased food availability. In winter, parr densities were positively correlated with the amounts of large woody debris present in streams (Figure 14.9). Juvenile salmonids depended on pools with cover created by large woody debris and on the protection provided by undercut banks (Heifetz et al. 1986). As a result, parr were less abundant in clear-cut reaches, where most of the large debris had been removed, than they were in old-growth and buffered reaches, where debris remained. Thus the increased abundance of coho salmon during their first summer was believed to have been more than offset by declines associated with loss of winter habitat (Koski et al. 1984). The net result was lower abundances of parr in, and lower predicted smolt outputs from, clear-cut reaches compared with sites with buffer strips or in old-growth forest (Murphy et al. 1986). Steelhead fry and parr responded like coho salmon (Johnson et al. 1986).

Northern California.—Logging in the north Coast Range of California was compatible with natural production of anadromous fish when adequate attention was given to stream protection (Burns 1972). Four streams were studied for one summer before, during, and after logging (3 years total). The two streams in watersheds that were carefully logged with protection of streamside vegetation showed minimal changes in habitat characteristics and in salmonid populations.

Cascade Mountains.—In some locations, lack of a streamside management zone has not appeared to be detrimental to production of salmonids in the years immediately following logging. Frequently, short-term production has even been enhanced by removal of all streamside vegetation. This was particularly true for small clear-cuts along high-gradient stream reaches where sediment and temperature changes were minimal (Gregory et al. 1987). A trend towards short-term enhancement of cutthroat trout populations in streams in the western Cascades of Oregon and Washington was shown by initial comparisons of logged and unlogged streams (Aho 1976; Hall et al. 1978; Murphy and Hall 1981; Bisson and Sedell 1984). Comparisons of 24 stream reaches in the Oregon Cascades showed that biomass of cutthroat trout was highest in clear-cut, intermediate in old-growth, and lowest in second-growth forests (Murphy and Hall 1981). The different responses of trout to logging in the Cascades and in the Oregon Coast Range (Alsea Watershed Study) led to further attempts to determine the underlying mechanisms. Paired logged and unlogged sites were compared in the Oregon Cascades and in the Oregon and California Coast Ranges (Murphy et al. 1981; Hawkins et al. 1983). The results of these studies, which included both high- and low-gradient streams, were generally consistent with the earlier work in the Cascades. Trout populations were higher in most of the recently logged sites than in the shaded forest sites.

Increased food abundance seemed to be the primary basis for increased growth and biomass of the trout populations in these streams. Opening of the canopy allowed greater primary production, which led to greater abundances of invertebrates in both the benthos and the drift (Hawkins et al. 1982; Wilzbach et al. 1986). In addition, trout were able to forage more effectively in the open sites; efficiency of prey capture was directly related to the amount of sunlight reaching the stream surface (Wilzbach et al. 1986). The conclusion from most of these studies was that greater food availability compensated for any negative effects of increased sedimentation and other habitat changes, at least in the first 10–15 years after logging. There were some indications that the return of heavy shade to the streams after 15 years was associated with a decrease in trout abundance to levels below those found in old-growth forests. This could be a particular problem in low-gradient sites, where sediment accumulation is greatest (Murphy and Hall 1981; Murphy et al. 1981).

Timber harvesting along streams where streamside management zones are not provided, particularly when accompanied by removal of large woody debris from the channel and banks, often leads to substantial modification of channel structure (Sullivan et al. 1987). Such alterations may lead to changes in the relative abundance and age structure of salmonid species in these streams. Shifts in species and age composition were noted when populations of cutthroat trout, steelhead, and coho salmon were compared at 25 logged and unlogged sites in southwestern Washington (Bisson and Sedell 1984). The 12 logged sites had been clear-cut from 1 to 11 years prior to the survey. No protection had been provided in the streamside zones of the logged watersheds, and woody debris had been removed from the channels. Habitat changes associated with timber harvest and debris removal included decreases in pool area and volume and increases in riffle length. Where paired comparisons could be made in the same drainage basin, the biomass of all salmonids combined averaged 1.5 times greater in logged than in unlogged sites (Bisson and Sedell 1984). In most logged streams, the proportion of age-0 steelhead and age-0 cutthroat trout increased, but the proportion of age-0 coho salmon and age-1 and age-2 cutthroat trout decreased.

Bilby and Bisson (1987) studied the factors controlling the summer residency and production of age-0 hatchery-raised coho salmon in the upper Deschutes River, Washington, a relatively cool area at 1,200 m elevation. These fish were stocked at high density (up to $6/m^2$) in paired old-growth and clear-cut watersheds. Production in the clear-cut watershed ranged from 1.2 to 2.6 times greater than production in the old-growth watershed over 2 years. Proportionately more fish remained in the old-growth site, which possessed better physical rearing habitat than did the clear-cut site. However, summer mortality in the old-growth site was significantly greater than in the clear-cut site, and growth rates were lower in the old-growth site. The number of coho salmon remaining in the two streams at the end of summer was not significantly different, but fish in the clear-cut site weighed about 20% more than fish in the old-growth site. Bilby and Bisson (1987) concluded that summer production was most strongly influenced by trophic conditions (the clear-cut site having more available food), whereas volitional residency was most strongly influenced by habitat quality (the old-growth site having better rearing habitats).

Benefits of streamside management zones.—The benefits of opening the canopy when timber is harvested to the stream edge may be offset by reduced diversity of fish species or increased annual variation in production. In the long term (over the length of a timber harvest rotation), most evidence indicates that careful streamside treatment is a better strategy than clear-cutting to the stream edge. Originally, the primary purpose of streamside management zones was control of stream temperatures. Recent timber harvest policies and forest practice rules have acknowledged the additional role of such zones in protecting channel stability and in providing future sources of large woody debris. We now recognize many more functions of the riparian zone (Gregory et al., in press). Future management efforts need to be directed toward prescription of the appropriate sizes and densities of trees in streamside management zones so that these zones accomplish all desired functions (Steinblums et al. 1984; Bisson et al. 1987).

In summary, intact streamside management zones have the following benefits:

• maintenance of stable streambanks, with overhanging cover and undercut banks.
• protection for stable large wood in the channel.
• provision for a continuing source of large wood for the future.
• maintenance of stable streambed and stream channel, minimizing increased sedimentation.
• prevention of substantial modification of stream temperature.

Effects of Roads and Hillslope Timber Harvest

Valuable as it may be, protection of streamside zones alone is not necessarily sufficient to insure maintenance of productive stream ecosystems in watersheds where timber is harvested. Particularly in steep terrain, debris avalanches and related mass movements of soil, timber, and debris from hillslopes may adversely affect salmonid habitats. Increased frequency of debris torrents resulting from road building and logging has been implicated as a major cause of degradation of fish habitat in some areas with steep slopes, unstable soils, and predisposing climate.

One series of studies has documented the effect of landslides on salmonids and their habitats in small streams on the Queen Charlotte Islands, British Columbia. Salmonid habitats were surveyed in 44 streams with known logging histories (Tripp and Poulin 1986b). Stream reaches studied included those in logged basins with debris torrents, those in logged basins without debris torrents, and those in unlogged basins without torrents. Methods of stream rehabilitation, effects of different cutting patterns, and alternative harvest methods to reduce mass soil movement were studied.

As part of the same study, salmonid abundance was investigated in 29 streams, and smolt migration was assessed in seven of these (Tripp and Poulin 1986b). Densities of juvenile coho salmon in late summer were almost as high in streams affected by debris torrents as they were in logged streams without torrents. The amount of cover present in summer was similar in both groups of streams but the type of cover differed greatly between groups. The cover in streams unaffected by debris torrents was predominantly rootwads, small and large woody debris, undercut banks, and deep water. In streams affected by debris torrents, cover was formed by rocks, boulders, and associated turbulence at the water surface.

Winter survival following logging was substantially lower in streams with debris torrents than in those without torrents, and was related to the type of cover in the two groups of streams. Winter cover was less abundant and less diverse, and pieces of large woody debris were less numerous, in streams affected by debris torrents than in unaffected streams. The amount of pool habitat regarded as good for overwintering juvenile salmonids, especially coho salmon, was reduced by an average of 79% in affected streams compared to unaffected ones, and the amount of cover suitable for overwintering was reduced by 75%. Correspondingly in these logged areas, overwinter survival of coho salmon averaged 1.8% in stream reaches affected by debris torrents compared to 24.5% in unaffected streams. Smolt yield averaged 0.02 fish per lineal meter in affected streams but 0.24 fish/m in unaffected streams, a 12-fold difference. Smolt yield from streams in unlogged areas unaffected by torrents was not measured, but was estimated to be 1.1–1.4 fish/m based on results from a stream in which habitat had been improved with channel structures (Tripp and Poulin, in press). Among western North American streams that flow through unlogged forests and have less than 10 km of their lengths accessible to anadromous salmonids, the average smolt yield is 1.4/m (Marshall and Britton 1980; Holtby and Hartman 1982).

Channel morphology in Queen Charlotte Island streams was profoundly influenced by logging-associated debris torrents. We can speculate on the species-specific effects of changes in stream reaches affected by debris torrents. Reduced average pool depth and area, reduced cover, and increased riffle area and channel width (Tripp and Poulin 1986b) would decrease habitat suitability for pool-dwelling species such as coho salmon. Comparison of hydraulic conditions in two Queen Charlotte Island streams, one in a logged and the other in an unlogged area, led Hogan and Church (1989) to conclude that there indeed was a decrease in rearing area for coho salmon at higher discharges in the logged area. Habitat suitability for species such as juvenile steelhead, which can occupy shallow-water habitats (Everest and Chapman 1972; Hicks 1990), might increase following logging. However, surface water flow decreased after mass wasting, owing to percolation through gravel in riffles and side channels (Tripp and Poulin 1986b), reducing the quality of these channel units as fish habitat. Riffle habitat quality was similarly reduced in Carnation Creek following logging (G. Hartman, Canada Department of Fisheries and Oceans, personal communication). The dramatically increased occurrence of mass wasting in logged basins, and especially in logged and roaded basins, indicates that channel widening, reduced area and quality of pools, and reduced surface flow might be a widespread result of logging in similar geoclimatic regions.

Timber harvest and road construction on unstable slopes, combined with several years of above-average rainfall, damaged spawning areas in the South Fork Salmon River, Idaho (Platts and Megahan 1975). Fine gravel and sand (<4.7 mm) from weathered granite entered stream channels as a result of accelerated surface erosion and landslides, increasing river bedload by 3.5 times and practically destroying the spawning potential of the main river. A moratorium was placed on logging and road construction on National Forest lands in the watershed in 1965, vegetation was planted, and roads were stabilized, after which surface and landslide erosion declined dramatically. The proportion of fine sediments in spawning areas decreased progressively in four monitored areas from a range of 45 to more than 80% in 1966 to 12–26% in 1974, and the particle-size distribution returned to near optimum for spawning of chinook salmon (Platts and Megahan 1975). The response of fish runs to improved spawning conditions was difficult to evaluate owing to problems of fish passage at numerous downstream hydroelectric dams in the Snake and Columbia river basins.

In this section, we have identified logging-induced changes in the rate of erosional processes as potentially damaging to salmonid populations. These harmful changes can be ameliorated by reduced road building and by careful design, placement, and construction of the forest roads that are built (Furniss et al. 1991). Lands especially susceptible to erosion should be excluded from logging. Exclusion of headwall areas from timber harvest, because of their high risk of landslides, has been used experimentally in the Oregon Coast Range (Swanson and Roach 1987).

Geoclimatic Trends in Salmonid Response

Geology, geomorphology, and climate control hillslope angles, soil depth, and resistance of bedrock to weathering. However, at the time scales considered in most studies of logging effects on salmonid populations (1–15 years), the geomorphic surface of a basin controls erosion rates (Gregory et al., in press).

Geomorphology and Geology

Hillslope angles, soil depth, and resistance of bedrock to weathering determine the susceptibility of hillslopes to failure, the geomorphic structure and stability of stream channels, and the hydrologic and nutrient regimes. In the Queen Charlotte

Islands, steep slopes, high rainfall, and erosive soils were responsible for the increased mass wasting that followed logging and damaged salmonid populations (Gimbarzevsky 1988; Poulin, in press).

The geomorphic configuration of a stream and its valley can influence salmonid population dynamics (Sullivan et al. 1987). Many of the juvenile coho salmon in Carnation Creek overwintered in the floodplain of the lower stream, which contained a network of sloughs, beaver ponds, and abandoned meander channels (Tschaplinski and Hartman 1983; Brown 1987). Winter survival and growth of coho salmon in these slack-water areas far exceeded those of coho salmon overwintering in the main stem (T. G. Brown 1985).

Geology has also been used to explain local differences in stream channel morphology and salmonid populations (Sullivan et al. 1987). In the Oregon Coast Range, cutthroat trout and steelhead predominated in watersheds underlain by basalt, whereas coho salmon predominated in streams cut through sandstone (Hicks 1990). Streams in sandstone valleys had lower gradients and a greater proportion of their lengths consisted of pools compared with streams of the same size in basalt areas, which were dominated by riffles.

Boulders can create stable stream structure and diverse habitat in the absence of large woody debris, and boulder-rich streams can continue to support good populations of salmonids if debris is lost (Osborn 1981; Hicks 1990). Complex geologic factors such as resistance of bedrock, amount of fracturing, and distance from source control the size distribution of substrate elements (e.g., Hack 1957; Dietrich and Dunne 1978), which partly determines channel geometry and habitat quality (Hicks 1990).

Differences in watershed geology influence nutrient availability, and these differences have helped explain some of the responses of fish populations to logging. In southeastern Alaska, periphyton, benthos, and coho salmon fry were abundant in both old-growth and clear-cut portions of watersheds rich in limestone. Little periphyton and few coho salmon were found in logged reaches in watersheds dominated by igneous rock (Murphy et al. 1986). Other studies also have related nutrient concentrations and biological productivity to watershed geology (Thut and Haydu 1971; Swanston et al. 1977; Gregory et al. 1987). Nitrogen is often the primary limiting nutrient in watersheds dominated by volcanic parent material, whereas streams draining glacial deposits or granitic bedrock are more often phosphorus-limited.

Geography and Climate

Studies of logging effects show some influences of latitude and climate. Mean annual precipitation, surface water temperature, and snowfall vary with latitude, altitude, and distance from the coast (Geraghty et al. 1973). As maximum surface water temperatures increase from north to south, thermal loading as a result of clear-cutting increases (Brown 1969, 1970; Beschta 1984). This effect is superimposed on higher ambient surface water temperatures in more southern and inland areas (Beschta et al. 1987).

We speculate that seasonally related effects of logging on salmonid production are more severe in the southern portions of the species' ranges than in the north. Summer streamflows are lower in the south than in the north. Higher water temperatures and lower surface flows associated with logging, combined with higher ambient summer temperatures, may reduce food and space resources, which will intensify competition (Allen 1969) and limit survival of salmonids in summer.

Large woody debris mediates winter survival of salmonids throughout western North America, but the mechanism appears to differ between the northern and southern portions of their ranges. Protection from the high velocities of winter peak flows is the main role of woody debris in areas with winter floods (Chamberlin et al. 1991). In the north, where winter is a period of low flow, the maintenance of pool depth by scour around woody debris is important in preventing stream freezing.

Our attempt to evaluate trends in response of populations from west to east, from the Cascades to the Rocky Mountains and eastward, was hampered by a lack of data. There have been several coordinated studies, including those of the Slim–Tumuch watershed in British Columbia, the Tri-Creeks system in Alberta, and the Nashwaak basin in New Brunswick (Macdonald et al. 1988), and several isolated investigations (e.g., Platts and Megahan 1975; Welch et al. 1977; Grant et al. 1986; Lanka et al. 1987), but little has been published on the response of salmonid populations to timber harvest in these more easterly areas.

Climate also influences the occurrence and rate of mass wasting, which is the predominant means by which large amounts of soil, rock, and organic material are delivered to streams (Everest et al. 1987a). Antecedent weather conditions and storm intensity were more important than geology in determining the susceptibility of different bedrock types to erosion in the Queen Charlotte Islands (Poulin, in press). Bedrock type, however, influenced the slope of valley walls, which in turn influenced the extent of mass wasting (Gimbarzevsky 1983, 1988). The effects of mass wasting on winter fish survival in logged streams affected by debris torrents were thought to be so severe that too few adults might return to sustain a population of coho salmon in the future (Tripp and Poulin 1986b).

Geomorphologic and geologic variables have been used successfully to explain salmonid abundance in logging-related studies (Ziemer 1973; Swanston et al. 1977; Heller et al. 1983; Lanka et al. 1987). However, no two studies have identified the same set of variables as being important. This shows that we have some understanding of the link between geology, geomorphology, and fish abundance that can be useful locally to predict the effects of timber harvest, but that we still have no models that apply over a wide area.

Limits of Present Knowledge

Uncertainties remain about the effects of forest practices on salmonid populations, demonstrating the limits of our present knowledge. Nevertheless, there appear to be some unifying links among studies of the integrated salmonid response to logging. An increase in solar radiation reaching a stream after removal of streamside vegetation usually enhances production of algae and invertebrates. The net effect is often greater salmonid production within the first 20 years after timber harvest. At least some of the benefit of increased summer production can be lost by reduced winter survival. Reduction in winter survival can result from loss of habitat structure caused by reduced amounts and stability of large woody debris and by increased amounts of coarse sediment. Differing habitat requirements of salmonid species such as coho salmon and steelhead (Hartman 1965) result in varied responses to logging-related changes in channel morphology (Reeves and Everest, in press). Reductions in habitat complexity and pool depth truncate the diversity of species and age-classes, favoring single species and age-classes. Increases in riffle area increase the suitability of habitat for steelhead, if streamflows are sufficient to maintain adequate water depth.

Incongruous Time Scales

In our opinion, one explanation for the incomplete state of knowledge lies in the very different time scales characteristic of management practices, natural processes, and evaluative studies. The period of a single rotation in timber harvest in western North America is 45–100 years. The natural processes that influence stream productivity and that may mitigate changes caused by timber harvest operate over a variety of time scales ranging from months to centuries. Yet almost all of the studies evaluating the effects of forest management on stream habitat and salmonid populations have encompassed less than 5 years. Nearly all have concentrated on changes immediately following timber harvest.

Of the few studies at the population level carried out to date, only the Carnation Creek and the Alsea Watershed studies extended for 15 years or more, and even that length of time is inadequate for full evaluation of logging effects. Some population studies (e.g., Murphy and Hall 1981) dealt with streams whose watersheds had been logged as many as 30–40 years earlier, but none of the studies was capable of monitoring the effects of environmental disturbance over the length of a rotation. The need for long-term evaluation is further illustrated by observations from the Carnation Creek study. Had the study terminated in the first few years after logging, the eventual impact on the coho salmon population would not have been detected (Hartman et al. 1987). Studies of salmonid populations in Great Britain (Egglishaw and Shackley 1985; Elliott 1985) also show the need for long-term research. These studies monitored anadromous salmonid populations in watersheds that had not experienced recent disturbance, yet Elliott (1985) noted that even 18 years of data on population abundance, streamflow, and water quality had failed to provide a clear indication of the environmental factors that limit production.

Short-term studies cause a biased perspective of habitat change. Some change that is most apparent persists for only a few years. Undue concern may be raised over a condition that is transient in the time scale of forest succession. Increased levels of suspended and deposited sediment could be considered an example of this sort (Everest et al. 1987a). In contrast, some effects that are beneficial or neutral in the short term can be followed by negative effects over the longer term. The short-term increase in productivity that accompanies higher light levels after canopy removal from some streams is an example. As the canopy closes during forest succession, the overall production of salmonids may drop below that of unlogged watersheds and remain there for many years (Gregory et al. 1987). Speed of canopy closure following removal of streamside vegetation depends on the local environment. Return of insolation at the stream surface to preharvest or lower levels as streamside vegetation regrows may be rapid in some locations such as the Oregon Coast Range, but the canopy may remain open for many years in an environment where plant growth is slow (Summers 1983).

A decrease in the supply of large woody debris is another change in habitat that may not occur for many years. Recent studies in Oregon have indicated that many existing stable pieces of large woody debris entered streams years ago. Heimann (1988) found that in watersheds logged without a buffer strip, preharvest debris continued to be the predominant wood in streams 140 years after timber harvest, but the total amounts of debris were only about 30% of preharvest levels. Unless adequate provision is made to supply streams with large pieces of wood into the future, the quality of fish habitat may decline severely. Decomposition times of some tree species are so long (e.g., >100 years for western redcedar: Swanson et al. 1976) that there may be a lag time of many years before the shortfall is apparent.

Two problems confound the clear separation of logging effects from those caused by other environmental changes and by fishery management activities. The first problem is that most studies of logging effects have used present-day habitats and fish populations as the baseline for comparison with postlogging conditions. As a consequence, logging-related reductions of salmonid populations that may have occurred over the past 100 years or more have gone undetected. In many areas, present-day levels of wild salmonid stocks are only small fractions of historical abundances. There has been little study of long-term (100 years or more) change in habitat of the sort undertaken by Sedell and Luchessa (1982) and Sedell and Froggatt (1984). Among the causes of habitat loss have been channel scour during log drives, removal of debris to improve navigation, logging of riparian conifers, and salvage of large wood from stream channels.

The second problem is that the effects of logging are difficult to separate from the effects of other activities, such as power generation, irrigation, grazing practices, and fishery management (Pella and Myren 1974). Overfishing and loss of productive spawning and rearing habitat (e.g., Chapman 1986) have occurred concurrently with logging. In particular, excessive ocean harvests, especially of coho and chinook salmon, have often resulted in inadequate returns of wild fish to spawn. The low level of spawning has complicated assessment of the natural productive potential of streams (Cederholm et al. 1981). These conditions combined have made it extremely difficult to separate logging effects on fish populations from the effects of other natural and cultural influences within the time scales of evaluative studies.

Climatic Variation

A further difficulty in tracking logging-related habitat disturbances over time is introduced by long-term fluctuations in climate or the effect of a single event of very large magnitude. Large floods occurring periodically have disproportionate influences on channel morphology. Unusually severe storms occurred in the northwestern USA in 1949, 1955, 1964, and 1972. These intense storms caused high discharges, bed-load movements, landslides and associated debris torrents, and erosion of streambanks and floodplain terraces, all of which resulted in substantial, widespread changes in stream habitats. To some extent, timber harvest has intensified the effects of such floods on stream habitats (Anderson et al. 1976), and evidence of the resulting channel changes may persist for decades or more (Swanson et al. 1987). Frissell and Hirai (1989) described a complex interaction between land-management practices and long-term changes in the timing of storms that appears to have contributed to reductions in spawning success of chinook salmon in coastal streams of southern Oregon. Less apparent physically, but perhaps no less important biologically, are severe droughts such as those that occurred in the 1930s. Another unusual climatic event that can exert a strong influence on population abundance is an oceanic El Niño (Bottom et al. 1986; Johnson 1988).

In the evaluation of logging-related habitat changes and their effects on fish populations, disturbance regimes imposed by management should be compared to natural disturbances in both frequency and amplitude. Salmonid populations in western North America have evolved in a landscape where they experienced severe environmental stresses, including forest fires, floods, mass soil and ice movements, debris torrents, glaciation, and volcanism. Through evolutionary processes, salmonids have developed life history strategies enabling them to withstand considerable environmental variation and unpredictability. Salmon and trout accomodate exploitation and other stresses, at least in the short-term, through compensatory responses at one or more life stages. However, some effects of timber harvest may be more severe than similar natural perturbations, resulting in mortality beyond the range of compensation. For example, the abundance of large woody debris has been more substantially reduced by logging and associated salvage and stream-cleaning activities than by wildfire or volcanism (Sedell and Dahm 1984).

A major consequence of all these sources of variability in the natural environment is the large natural variation—both temporal and spatial—in the abundance of salmonids (Burns 1971; Lichatowich and Cramer 1979; Hall and Knight 1981; Cederholm et al. 1981; Platts and McHenry 1988). This variation is often large enough to obscure changes caused by timber harvest or other land management activities (Pella and Myren 1974; Platts and Nelson 1988).

Spatial Scales

Incongruence of spatial scale, as well as of temporal scale, has hindered interpretation of many studies. Bisson (in press) compared typical variations in western Washington salmonid populations in space and time on the basis of both standing stocks and smolt yields. He concluded that the smaller the scale, the greater the variability among sites. That is, differences in population abundance and smolt production tended to be greatest among limited stream reaches, whereas differences in smolt yield for whole basins tended to be proportionately smaller. Because most studies of timber harvest have focused on stream reaches or small watersheds, they have taken place at a spatial scale often characterized by relatively great variability, thus making logging-related changes more difficult to separate from natural variation.

Focus on individual stream reaches has also limited the accuracy of many studies. The study designs used have underestimated sampling error and have not addressed the comparative importance of different parts of a basin (Hankin 1984, 1986). Reach analysis does not effectively assess cumulative effects that may accrue from a multitude of small disturbances within a large watershed, or downstream changes that result from a single type of disturbance repeated over time. The criticism applies most strongly to short-term postharvest evaluations, but the limitation also occurs in watershed-level studies.

There may be problems of scale in extrapolating work in relatively small basins to larger watersheds. For instance, debris torrents that remove channel structure from steep, lower-order drainages can add structure to higher-order, lower-gradient reaches downstream (Benda 1985b). In addition, larger main-stem reaches have been shown to rear proportionately more fish on a basin-wide scale than the combined lower-order tributaries, despite high fish densities in headwater streams (Dambacher, in press; J. R. Sedell, U.S. Forest Service, unpublished). Though main-stem production in some systems is now low, its historic role may have been greater before channel complexity was lost (Sedell and Froggatt 1984).

There are several reasons why studies have been concentrated in small basins. First, isolation of the effects of timber harvest from other activities requires working within watershed boundaries where logging is the only management influence. The mosaic of patterns of land use and other influences found in large basins therefore usually limits the size of study basins to small watersheds. Logging of large basins also occurs over too long a period to allow evaluation of its effects, because only a small proportion of the watershed area is normally harvested at any one time. Secondly, small streams have often been selected for study because they could be sampled easily, rather than because of their significance to total basin production. This is particularly true for the siting of facilities for counting salmonid smolts and adults. Maintaining effective fish traps during high streamflows is a major constraint on the size of stream that can be effectively monitored. Recent development of small, portable, floating smolt traps (McLemore et al. 1989) should provide the ability to monitor much larger systems than has been possible in the past.

Suggestions for Future Studies

We suggest three principal approaches for evaluation of the influences of logging on salmonids: (1) substitution of space for time by extensive evaluation of many watersheds in a short period, (2) long-term studies before and after logging, and (3) innovations in design that could improve data collection efficiency or strengthen the inferences drawn from data. In earlier analyses, Hall et al. (1978) and Hall and Knight (1981) suggested that studies of the effects of logging could be grouped in a two-way classification. The basis for grouping is (1) whether the studies are before-and-after comparisons or posttreatment evaluations of timber harvest, and (2) whether detailed studies are carried out on one or few streams (intensive) or shorter surveys are conducted on many streams (extensive). This classification results in four categories, the advantages and disadvantages of which are listed in Table 14.3. There is no single optimum study design, but Hall and Knight (1981) favored the extensive posttreatment survey, especially when it is combined with carefully designed process-oriented studies. Given the substantial work done since that time, and a recent further evaluation of study design (Grant et al. 1986), we have reviewed those conclusions.

Extensive posttreatment analysis, especially when coupled with pairing of treatment and control streams or watersheds, is an attractive and relatively inexpensive method of analysis. In certain circumstances, it appears to have been effective (e.g., Murphy and Hall 1981; Bisson and Sedell 1984; Murphy et al.

TABLE 14.3.—Summary of advantages and disadvantages of the four major approaches to watershed stream analysis. (From Hall and Knight 1981.)

Advantages	Disadvantages
(A) Intensive before-after (5–7 years before treatment, 5–7 years after)	
Possible to assess year-to-year variation and place size of effects in context of that variation	No replication; results must be viewed as a case study
	Results not necessarily applicable elsewhere (areas of different soils, geology, fish species, etc.)
Can assess short-term rate of recovery (about 5 years)	Results influenced by changes in weather
No assumptions required about initial conditions	Final results and management recommendations require exceptionally long time to complete—15 years or more after initial planning stage
Possible to monitor effects over whole watersheds (provided substantial investment in facilities such as flow and sediment sampling weirs, fish traps)	Difficult to maintain intensity of investigation and continuity of investigators over such a long period
	Considerable coordination required; must rely on outside agencies or firms to complete logging as scheduled
Long time frame provides format for extensive process studies	
(B) Extensive before–after (1–2 years before treatment, 1–2 years after)	
Provides broader geographical perspective than (A)	Little opportunity to observe year-to-year variation
	Able to assess only immediate results, which may not be representative of longer time sequence
Larger number of streams lessens danger of bias by extreme case	Treatment influenced by unusual weather
Increased generality of results allows some extrapolation to other areas	Must rely on coordinated efforts (see A above)
Relatively short time to achieve results (3–4 years from planning stage)	
(C) Intensive posttreatment (one watershed, paired sites; several years after treatment)	
Shorter time for results than (A)	Provides no separate control stream; requires assumption that upstream control reach was similar to treated area prior to treatment
Moderate ability to assess year-to-year variation	"Control" most logically must be located upstream of treatment; strong downstream trend in any variable would confound analysis
Provides opportunity for moderate level of effort on process studies	Provides no spatial perspective; results of limited application elsewhere
(D) Extensive posttreatment (e.g., 10–30 watersheds); all observations made in 1–2 years (time after treatment variable)	
Wide spatial perspective allows extrapolation to other areas	No data available on pretreatment conditions, forcing assumption that control and treatment sites were the same before treatment
Long temporal perspective is possible; recovery can be assessed for as many years as past logging has occurred	Control predominantly upstream
	Total cost and sampling effort concentrated in short period; requires extensive planning
Provides ability to assess interaction of physical setting and treatment effects (e.g., effects of sediment input at different stream gradients)	Not as effective as (A) in assessing whole watershed effects
Requires least time of the four designs to complete (as little as 2 years)	Harvest methods used in early logging may not be comparable to those used later
Probably most economical of the four approaches per unit of information	

1986). In a test of this study design in some streams in eastern Canada, Grant et al. (1986) concluded that the basic structure of the design was valid, although they detected no clear changes in salmonid biomass in response to timber harvest. However, comparison of paired sites close together along the same stream channel is less appropriate for assessing the effects of whole watershed disturbances than for assessing the effects of localized disturbances. Further consideration has led us to conclude that stream-reach comparisons, a feature of most extensive survey designs, should be broadened to a larger watershed perspective. Recent development of basin-wide sampling designs for both habitat characteristics and fish populations (Hankin and Reeves 1988) should allow more effective assessment of habitat changes in entire basins.

Some studies, particularly earlier ones, did not examine certain key habitat variables that we now know to be important. Recent advances in the classification and quantitative description of stream habitats (Bisson et al. 1982; Frissell et al. 1986; Grant 1986; Sullivan et al. 1987), along with recognition of the important role of large woody debris (Sedell et al. 1984, 1988), have improved our ability to describe deleterious changes in habitat quality. Nonetheless, our present understanding seems inadequate to predict changes in fish populations by analysis of habitat changes alone. Understanding often seems inhibited by a tendency to focus on a limited subset of habitat variables, such that insufficient consideration is given to potential limiting factors (Everest and Sedell 1984; Chapman and McLeod 1987; Everest et al. 1987a; Bisson, in press).

Research effort has not been applied equally to all species. There has been a strong bias towards studies of coho salmon, cutthroat trout, and steelhead (Table 14.2). Chinook salmon in particular have been much less studied relative to their distribution and abundance, probably because most studies have focused on small watersheds. There has been some emphasis on pink and chum salmon in Alaska and British Columbia, but little of the work has been focused on responses at the population level.

We suggest that more emphasis is needed on long-term analysis of logging impacts. This recommendation is based on several related observations. The successful and insightful analyses that have come from the Carnation Creek study could not have resulted from a shorter-term study. The evaluation of long-term ecological studies by Strayer et al. (1986) highlighted the advantages and contributions of such studies and provided a good perspective on the value of extended monitoring. Increased support from the U.S. National Science Foundation for research on long-term ecological reserves reflects a recognition by the scientific community of the value of such work. Finally, analysis of long-term trends in habitat condition (Sedell and Luchessa 1982; Sedell and Froggatt 1984) has convinced us that gaining an accurate perspective on change in habitat may require a very long time.

One innovative study design was suggested by an historical analysis of habitat condition prior to large-scale timber harvest and salvage of downed timber in the Breitenbush River in western Oregon (J. R. Sedell, U.S. Forest Service, unpublished). The original data forms from a survey of the river system conducted in 1937 by the U.S. Bureau of Fisheries were recovered. The survey was repeated in 1986 and showed a loss of more than 70% of pool habitat over the past 50 years. The river had changed to a single channel without debris jams and did not match its earlier description as "a mass of channels criss-crossed with downed logs and debris." The early surveys did not include quantitative assessment of fish populations, however. In a related attempt to evaluate the cumulative effects of timber harvest on channel structure, Grant (1988) used aerial photographs spanning the years from 1959 to 1979 to discern increases in stream channel width in the same reach of the Breitenbush River. Lyons and Beschta (1983) also used analysis of aerial photographs to measure changes in channel width in the Willamette River drainage in the Oregon Cascade Range over the same time period. They found major increases in channel width associated with timber harvest and road building. If it were possible to couple such analyses with models relating habitat quality to population abundance (see Fausch et al. 1988), a much clearer picture of the long-term effects of logging might emerge. We suspect that there are many such early surveys containing valuable information that have since been misplaced, forgotten, or otherwise ignored. If properly interpreted, these archived surveys could be used to provide a valuable baseline against which present-day conditions could be compared.

Conclusions

One conclusion that cannot be avoided from the studies relating salmonid populations to timber harvest activities is that fish habitats have been simplified over time and that this process of simplification continues. In this respect, agriculture, mining, grazing, and urbanization have the same net negative effects on habitat diversity and population abundances of major fish groups. The phenomenon is world-wide and is well documented for agricultural lands (Karr et al. 1983) and urbanized areas (Leidy 1984; Leidy and Fiedler 1985). Habitat degradation by simplification is one of the most important limits on the diversity of fish communities (Karr and Schlosser 1978). Highly diverse fish communities have been documented in association with stable channels, instream cover from boulders, living streamside trees, and downed trees in channels (Karr and Schlosser 1978; Welcomme 1985).

Our understanding of the changes in stream habitat and salmonid populations brought about by timber harvest has improved, but our knowledge remains limited. Certain changes in stream habitats caused by logging—increased temperature and fine sediment, for example—appear to be less detrimental and more transient than originally perceived. Others—such as loss of large woody debris and changes in channel morphology and stability—were not forseen as problems earlier but have contributed to significant habitat degradation in the long term.

We are concerned that logging impacts will become more severe as timber harvest moves to progressively less stable landforms and as the area of managed forest increases. As timber is harvested from the accessible and gentle terrain, logging occurs on steeper and less stable slopes, as it has in the Queen Charlotte Islands, for example. The results there and from other areas of steep terrain in western North America argue for intensified efforts to develop hazard-assessment techniques that will predict the potential disturbances to fish habitat from mass erosion and debris torrents. Some progress in this direction has been made (Benda 1985b; Swanson et al. 1987).

There is still much to learn before we can predict with confidence the effects of a particular logging operation on salmon and trout populations or prescribe management activities that will provide optimum habitat protection. However, a much wider array of analytical tools is now available. Several useful management guidelines and procedures for translating research findings into management practices have recently been produced (e.g., Toews and Brownlee 1981; Bryant 1983; E. R. Brown 1985; B.C. Ministry of Forests et al. 1988; Hartman 1988; Bilby and Wasserman 1989).

Finally, we emphasize that our review of 30 or more years of research on forestry and fisheries interactions has yielded several general principles that should be considered when logging operations are planned and implemented. Some of the most important of these follow.

• Protection of streamside zones by leaving streamside vegetation intact will help maintain the integrity of channels and preserve important terrestrial–aquatic interactions.

• Productivity of streams for salmonid populations tends to be enhanced under conditions of moderate temperatures, low to moderate sediment levels, high light levels, adequate nutrients, an abundance of cover, and a diversity of habitat and substrate types.

• Productive floodplain and side-channel habitats should be protected.

• Streams should be protected against frequent and extreme episodes of bed-load movement or sediment deposition through careful streamside management and through proper planning and engineering of roads and timber harvest systems.

• Management of streamside zones should include provisions for long-term recruitment of large woody debris into stream channels and for protection of existing stable large woody debris.

• The geology, geomorphology, and climate of a watershed mediate the response of fish populations to timber harvest. Site-specific management recommendations must consider regional landforms and climatic variation.

No single research approach will provide all the answers to the many complex questions that remain. We advocate a combination of short-term extensive studies over broad geographic regions and long-term intensive studies that emphasize critical terrestrial–aquatic interactions at the watershed scale. We further suggest that future long-term studies involve both biologists and foresters at the planning stage so that various logging treatments can be experimentally evaluated in a sound scientific manner. This process will also help to reduce the perceived conflict between forest and fishery management that has all too often hindered progress. We note that two of the most successful research efforts, the Alsea Watershed Study in Oregon and the Carnation Creek study in British Columbia, used such an approach. Coordinated experiments that are thoughtfully designed can speed solution of many of the remaining problems, resulting in our improved ability to intelligently manage all the resources of forested watersheds.

Chapter 15

Rehabilitating and Modifying Stream Habitats

G. H. Reeves, J. D. Hall, T. D. Roelofs,
T. L. Hickman, and C. O. Baker

Techniques for rehabilitating and modifying habitats have been used for over 50 years in fishery management, but they have been applied to a relatively small degree in the management of western North American salmonids, particularly anadromous stocks. Increased rates of harvest and other threats to the survival of many wild populations of salmon and trout call for intensified fishery management. Intensified logging, grazing, irrigation, agriculture, and urbanization have diminished the quality and quantity of habitats available to wild salmonid stocks. In principle, rehabilitation and modification of habitats are attractive means to restore the abundance of these salmonids.

A recently renewed interest in habitat management has been accompanied by several review articles, symposia, and bibliographies (e.g., Parkinson and Slaney 1975; Maughan et al. 1978; Canada Department of Fisheries and Oceans and B.C. Ministry of the Environment 1980; Hassler 1981, 1984; Hall and Baker 1982; Reeves and Roelofs 1982; Gore 1985; Platts and Rinne 1985; Wesche 1985; Miller et al. 1986; Duff et al. 1988). In this chapter we focus more directly on anadromous fish habitats in the forested regions of western North America, but we have also included techniques used for resident and anadromous salmonids in streams throughout the continent. We present a general review and evaluation of past efforts in habitat management, both successful and unsuccessful. We also review current practices in western North America, outline successful techniques, and include specific recommendations on implementation.

One purpose of this review is to make practical information available to field managers wishing to rehabilitate damaged habitats or to enhance habitats that are naturally low in productive capacity. Our task was made more difficult by the scarcity of written documentation of past work. Too many projects have not been evaluated at all, or if any review has been undertaken, it has not been made generally available. As a result, we were forced to rely heavily on personal communications and may have missed some important developments. Even when reports on manipulation of stream habitat were completed, many of the studies did not provide accurate assessments of the outcome. In addition, a bias no doubt exists in the published record because of administrative or editorial decisions

Influences of Forest and Rangeland Management on Salmonid Fishes and Their Habitats
American Fisheries Society Special Publication 19:519–557, 1991

against publication of inconclusive or unfavorable results. We hope that one outcome of our review will be increased awareness of the need to evaluate and document all projects—even those that are unsuccessful. Valuable lessons often can be learned from apparent failure.

Another purpose of this review is to inject a note of caution about adopting a process that sometimes, it seems to us, moves too quickly. Large programs of stream rehabilitation have been implemented before many of the techniques have been evaluated and proven. In the past 10 years, many millions of dollars have been spent on stream habitat management in western North America. We find little documented evidence of increased abundances of salmonids associated with these massive expenditures. Funds for construction and maintenance of facilities and structures are increasingly available, but too often these projects do not include adequate funding for evaluation (and in some cases, for initial project planning). Managers must insist on evidence of effectiveness. Without such evaluation, potentially valuable management techniques may lose public support and become liabilities rather than assets.

As the science of wildlife management developed, manipulation of habitat was the last technique recognized as an important tool for managers (Leopold 1933). The same has generally been true in fisheries. The first large-scale habitat management in streams began during the 1930s in Michigan (Hubbs et al. 1932). Abetted in part by the availability of labor from the U.S. Civilian Conservation Corps during the years of great economic depression, many projects followed (e.g., Davis 1934; Tarzwell 1935, 1937; Fearnow 1941). The apparent success of these efforts in midwestern and eastern North America was followed by several projects west of the Rocky Mountains (e.g., Burghduff 1934; Madsen 1938; Tarzwell 1938). Many evaluations of Pacific coast efforts concluded that failure was more common than success (Ehlers 1956; Richard 1963; Calhoun 1966). Rehabilitation and modification continued at a substantial pace in the midwestern USA nevertheless (Shetter et al. 1949; Hale 1969; Hunt 1969, 1976), and several manuals for habitat improvement were produced by state and federal agencies (Davis 1935; U.S. Forest Service 1952; White and Brynildson 1967; U.S. Bureau of Land Management 1968; Payne and Copes 1986). Over the years, modifications gradually made techniques more applicable in streams prone to freshets.

Some of the early enthusiasm for stream improvement was probably misguided, in that project planners failed to account for factors that limited trout production in a particular stream. Initial stream improvement efforts often included the use of poorly engineered gabions and weirs that did not withstand dynamic stream forces. For these reasons and others, some fishery biologists took a pessimistic view of the potential of stream "improvement" (e.g., Mullan 1962; Richards 1964; Calhoun 1966). Nonetheless, several well-designed research studies since 1932 have shown that the quality of habitat is an important determinant of salmonid biomass and production. Although nearly all this work has been done on nonmigratory populations, many conclusions can be related to anadromous species. The research effort has taken two related approaches: quantitative evaluation of changes in habitat, and assessment of salmonid populations before and after habitat modification.

Habitat Modifications for Salmonid Populations

Case Studies

One early, well-documented study evaluated the effects of deflectors in a small brook trout stream in Michigan (Shetter et al. 1949). The deflectors caused an increase in the number, size, and depth of pools. Survival and stock size of young brook trout increased, leading to a significant improvement in catch rate and total catch. Angling effort increased 64%, and anglers' catch increased 141% in total weight and 46% in weight caught per hour.

A study of cover manipulation in a Montana trout stream showed significant responses of rainbow and brook trout to the treatments (Boussu 1954). Inventories before and after habitat manipulation showed that trout abundances increased more than three times after brush cover was added to about 5% of the stream area. Removal of brush cover from about 10% of the stream surface area caused about a 40% reduction in trout biomass. Removal of undercut bank cover that provided shelter over less than 2% of the stream area reduced trout abundance by one-third.

The best-documented study of habitat manipulation was undertaken on a brook trout stream in Wisconsin (Hunt 1971). A 1.7-km section of Lawrence Creek was altered in 1964 by addition of structures to provide bank cover and deflect currents. As a result, stream surface area was reduced by 50%, average water depth increased 60%, the number of pools increased 52%, and the length of streambank with permanent overhanging cover increased 416%. These changes in the physical habitat greatly increased overwinter survival and biomass of the trout population. A large increase in angler effort resulted in an even greater increase in total catch. Average harvest during 1965–1967 was nearly three times the preimprovement average (Hunt 1971). The response of the trout population to habitat development continued through the period 1968–1970, when the total trout biomass increased to 2.8 times the preimprovement value (Hunt 1976).

Several other evaluations of habitat improvement projects have been made in eastern North America and many have shown a positive response by trout populations. The results of many of these evaluations conducted through 1975 are summarized in Table 15.1. The Wisconsin Department of Natural Resources has been particularly active in habitat development of trout streams, and that agency has recently released an exemplary evaluation of 45 projects conducted between 1953 and 1985 (Hunt 1988).

Habitat Evaluation

Additional evidence of the importance of habitat quality to salmonid abundance has come from analyses (usually through correlation techniques) of trout abundance in relation to specific habitat characteristics. Studies by Lewis (1969), Stewart (1970), Wesche (1976), and Wesche et al. (1987) showed that cover in some form was the habitat characteristic most closely associated with abundance of brook, brown, and rainbow trout. More complex combinations of habitat variables have been included in multiple-regression analyses that provided statistically significant predictors of abundance for juvenile steelhead and cutthroat trout in Oregon (Nickelson et al. 1979), for four species of trout in Wyoming

TABLE 15.1.—Management evaluations of habitat modification in midwestern and eastern North America by measurements of resident trout abundance over several years. (Adapted from White 1975a.)[a]

Stream; wild trout species: reference	Primary management	Schedule of population inventories	Effects on trout populations and angling yield[b]
Lawrence Creek, Wisconsin; brook trout: Hunt (1971)	Bank-cover deflectors in 1.7 km of stream (compared with 1.4-km control)	3 years before, 3 years after management	141% rise in age-2+ biomass from better overwinter survival; 156% more fish over 20 cm in April; 200% greater anglers' catch
Big Roche-a-Cri Creek, Wisconsin; brook and a few brown trout: White (1972, 1975b)	Bank-cover deflectors in 6 km of stream (compared with 5 km of interspersed control areas); cattle fenced out; beaver dams removed	3 years before, 2 years during, 5 years after management	200% rise in numbers of age-2+ fish (3 pre- versus 3 postmanagement years of similar flow regime) in the 3-km section of most intensive alteration; greatest effect was improvement of drought (low-water) abundances of fish; 36% increase in catch per angler-hour
West Branch Split Rock River, Minnesota; brook trout: Hale (1969)	Deflectors, bank covers, low dams in 1.6 km of stream (compared with 1.6-km control area)	3 years before, 3 years after management	9-fold increase in numbers of age-0 fish; 2-fold increase in numbers of age-1+ fish; angler success increased from 0.58 to 0.89 fish/ angler-hour in managed area, decreased in control area
Hayes Brook, Prince Edward Island; brook trout: Saunders and Smith (1962)	Low dams, deflectors, cover of poles and brush in 0.4 km of stream (no control area)	5 years before, 1 year after management	Number of age-1+ fish in year after construction was highest on record, nearly double the previous 5-year average
Hunt Creek, Michigan; brook trout: Shetter et al. (1949)	Deflectors in 0.5 km of stream (no control area)	1 year before, 3 years after (creel census 3 years before, 5 years after) management	35% increase in catch per angler hour; little change in standing crop
Pigeon River, Michigan; brook and brown trout: Latta (1972)	Deflectors in 2 km of stream (compared with 2-km control)	5 years before, 5 years after management, then 5 years after dismantling	Trout abundance in managed section (in terms of fall population plus anglers' catch in previous summer) was originally lower than in control but increased to equality after management, then decreased when devices were intentionally dismantled
Kinnikinnic River, Wisconsin; brook and brown trout; Frankenberger (1968)	Rock deflectors, rock revetments, fences along 2.2 km of stream (compared with an unmanaged control)	5 years before, 3 years after management	400–500% rise in numbers of brook trout over 14 cm and 150–200% rise in numbers of brown trout over 14 cm; populations in control area remained essentially static

Table 15.1.—Continued.

Stream; wild trout species: reference	Primary management	Schedule of population inventories	Effects on trout populations and angling yield
Bohemian Valley Creek, Wisconsin; brown trout: Frankenberger and Fassbender (1967)	Floodwater detention dams, rock deflectors, rock revetments, low dams, fencing in 4.3 km of stream (compared with 1.2-km control)	6 years before, 4 years after management	Originally negligible brown trout abundance (sometimes fewer than 5/km) increased to about 250/km
McKenzie Creek, Wisconsin; brown trout: Lowry (1971)	Deflectors, bank covers, brush covers, low dams in 5 km of stream (compared with 0.6-km control)	2 years before, 6 years after management	10–15% increase in total biomass (25% increase for age-1+, 100% increase for age-2+ fish); inconclusive changes in numbers of fish larger than 15 cm
Black Earth Creek, Wisconsin; brown trout: White (1975a)	Fencing, dam removal, few deflectors, bank revetments in 8 km of stream (control: Mt. Vernon Creek)	3 years during, 5 years after management	3-fold increases in age-0 fish, total biomass, and anglers' catch per hour of wild trout; 5-fold increase in spring (preangling) numbers of fish larger than 15 cm
Mt. Vernon Creek, Wisconsin; brown trout: White (1975a)	Unmanaged control for Black Earth Creek (adjoining drainage basin); dam removed	Concurrent with Black Earth Creek	Relatively minor increases in age-0 fish, total biomass, and anglers' catch per hour of wild trout; 2-fold increase in spring numbers of fish larger than 15 cm, attributable to hydrologic events

[a]Table was prepared for publication and referenced in White (1975a) but omitted from publication by editorial error (R. J. White, Montana State University, personal communication).

[b]A + sign means "the given age and older"; for example, age-2+ fish means age-2 and older fish.

(Binns and Eiserman 1979), and for three trout species in Ontario (Bowlby and Roff 1986). Fausch et al. (1988) provided an excellent review and evaluation of models that use habitat characteristics to predict standing crops of stream fishes.

Appropriate Habitat Modifications

The quality and quantity of physical habitat influence the abundance of salmonid populations, but an important question remains: can habitat be modified cost-effectively in a configuration that will withstand the dynamic forces of streams? Recent work has focused on the importance of hydraulics, hydrology, and geomorphology in the design of stream habitat structures (e.g., Klingeman 1984; Beschta and Platts 1986; Orsborn and Anderson 1986; Rosgen and Fittante 1986); consequently, we have become more optimistic about the chances that habitat modification for salmonids will succeed in western North America.

A fundamental concept of habitat management—that fish production is limited by discrete factors—deserves emphasis here (Everest and Sedell 1984; Reeves et

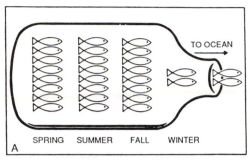

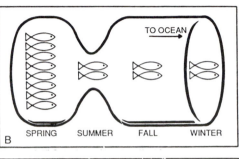

FIGURE 15.1.—Examples of limiting factor "bottlenecks" that occur (A) during the winter, just before salmon smolts migrate to the ocean, and (B) during summer, early in the life of young salmon. Attempts to increase fish abundance before a limiting factor acts on the population, such as by augmenting the food supply (C), usually fail (Mason 1976). (Adapted from Hall and Field-Dodgson 1981.)

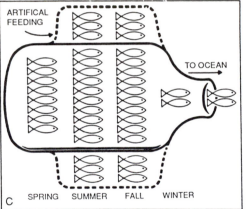

al. 1989; Bisson, in press). Care must be taken to identify aspects of habitat that limit production, and attention must be focused on improving those elements. The timing of life history events is also an important consideration. Increasing the quantity or quality of some aspect of habitat that limits the abundance of fry will generally be of little use if a critical shortage of cover or some other resource occurs at a later stage in the life cycle. A crude, but useful, analogy of a limiting factor to a bottleneck is shown in Figure 15.1. Note that the neck is not necessarily at the end of the bottle; a critical limitation can occur well before fish migrate to the ocean, for example (Figure 15.1B), or after they have reached the ocean.

An example that illustrates the futility of enhancing numbers of fish before the final limiting factor comes into play was provided by an experiment in a British Columbia stream that supports coho salmon (Mason 1976). In that system, most young coho salmon go to sea as smolts after 1 year of stream rearing. Artificial feeding of underyearlings during one summer greatly reduced emigration and increased the growth rate of remaining residents. As a result, biomass at the end of summer was 6–7 times that observed in stream sections where fish were not fed. The number of smolts estimated to have left the system in the following spring, however, was within the range expected from natural production (Figure 15.1C). In this stream, the ultimate limitation to smolt production appeared to be some aspect of winter habitat.

The idea that a single limiting factor "bottleneck" controls production is obviously an oversimplification of complex ecological processes. In the context of a total system, the search for a single factor can be misleading. Not only may the ultimate limitation vary from year to year, it may be composed of interacting elements; when one is improved, others may take over. Such an interaction may account for the failure of some of the well-intentioned attempts at habitat improvement. Nonetheless, the general concept of limiting factors requires more attention in future habitat improvement work.

Watershed Protection

The most successful method of habitat rehabilitation has been watershed protection. Hynes (1975) effectively made the case that a stream and its valley are an inseparable ecological unit. A stream rehabilitation program will be effective only if the watershed is concurrently protected.

The goal of resource managers should be to maintain the integrity of a stream system and its streamside zones (Everest et al. 1987a). All of the habitat modification techniques discussed in the following pages, whether they pertain to spawning, rearing, or some other habitat, have had variable successes. These methods cannot be relied upon to mitigate poor management practices. The importance of preventing habitat degradation now, instead of being forced to rebuild habitats in the future because of today's management practices, cannot be overemphasized. Protection of habitat is by far the most effective stream rehabilitation and enhancement technique.

The first specific method of habitat rehabilitation discussed later in this chapter is cleaning gravel. Gravel cleaning usually provides only temporary benefits unless the source of sedimentation is identified and measures are taken to reduce it. Often, the most effective rehabilitation measure for excessive instream sediment is improved watershed protection.

An example of the success of such a protection program comes from the South Fork Salmon River in Idaho (Platts and Megahan 1975). Four years of above-average rainfall followed logging activity and road construction on steep, unstable slopes. The river channel became choked with sediment from accelerated surface erosion and landslides. The resulting 3.5-fold increase in river bed load practically destroyed the spawning potential of the main river. As a result, the U.S. Forest Service declared a moratorium on logging and road construction on National Forest lands in the watershed of the South Fork Salmon River in 1965. Watershed rehabilitation began that year and included planting vegetation and stabilizing roads. Throughout the program, sediment concentrations in the river channel were monitored.

After the moratorium was declared, sediment sources for the river were reduced substantially because of dramatic reductions in surface and landslide erosion. From 1966 to 1974, the percentage of fine sediments (<4.7 mm) in the spawning areas decreased progressively. Concentrations in four monitored areas decreased from an average of about 55% in 1966 (range, 45 to >80%) to about 21% in 1974 (range, 12–26%). When sediment input decreased, the energy of the river gradually moved the accumulated fine sediments downstream. The particle-size distribution in the South Fork Salmon River was near optimum for spawning of chinook salmon in 1974 (Platts and Megahan 1975). Further improvement in the condition of fish habitat led to a cautious lifting of the moratorium on logging and road construction in 1978; close monitoring of the river continued (Megahan et al. 1980).

In the following evaluation we treat rehabilitation and modification methods under two headings: spawning habitat (which includes its quality, quantity, and accessibility) and rearing habitat. These two categories are integral constituents of the salmonid environment, and effects on both spawning and rearing habitats must be considered when any rehabilitation and modification work is planned.

Spawning Habitat

The decline of wild salmonids west of the Rocky Mountains has been partly attributed to declines in the quantity and quality of spawning habitat. Salmonids require good spawning habitat to reproduce successfully (Bjornn and Reiser 1991, this volume). The loss of spawning habitat is most often associated with human activities, the effects of which may vary. Dams may restrict the recruitment of new gravels to traditional spawning areas (Reisenbichler 1989). Gravel quality decreases when sedimentation increases because of timber harvesting, road construction, livestock grazing, mining, or other activities. Wickett (1958), Cordone and Kelley (1961), and McNeil and Ahnell (1964) associated reductions in spawning success of various salmonids in certain situations with increased amounts of fine sediments within gravels. Everest et al. (1987a) thoroughly reviewed the effects of fine sediments on the spawning success of salmonids and pointed out that the effect varies with the species and the physical nature of the stream, among other things.

Several innovative approaches have been used to improve spawning habitats in the Pacific Northwest. The most successful techniques have been removal of fine sediments from existing spawning gravels, creation of new spawning areas, and provision of access to suitable but previously inaccessible areas.

Gravel Restoration

Cleaning gravel.—Salmonids disturb gravels when they dig redds, which allows fine sediments to wash away (Everest et al. 1987a). The mitigating effect that redd digging has on increased sedimentation from human activities is not well understood, but rehabilitation efforts have attempted to supplement or duplicate spawning action.

An early development in restoration of spawning habitat was the design and testing of a self-propelled amphibious vehicle for cleaning fine sediment from spawning gravel. Known as the "riffle sifter," the machine was designed to remove sediment by action of high-pressure underwater jets (Outdoor California 1968). A suction pump forced sediment-laden water through a nozzle onto nearby streambanks. The riffle sifter was greeted with great enthusiasm, and early field tests in Alaska and northern California appeared promising (Meehan 1971). In the end, however, the machine had many mechanical problems and was abandoned as an expensive failure.

Researchers at Washington State University modified the riffle sifter, now called "Gravel Gertie," using hydraulic jets to flush fine materials from depths of 15–30 cm in the substrate and to spray the concentrated silt onto the streambank (Mih 1978; Mih and Bailey 1981). Personnel of the Washington Department of Fisheries and the Washington Department of Wildlife have successfully used Gravel Gertie in particular circumstances in western Washington. Only channels with spring sources or side channels are cleaned. These areas are protected from high flow scour and have had spawning gravels introduced into them. Efforts to remove fines in main-stem channels have been less successful because streambeds have consisted of large, uneven, angular substrates. In some instances, the stream was immediately recontaminated as the silt slurry washed from the banks back into the channel (D. Allen, Washington Department of Fisheries, personal communication).

Bulldozers have been used to clean spawning gravels (Reeves and Roelofs 1982), but their use has declined in recent years. Initial reports were apparently overly optimistic; upstream sediments sometimes caused degradation of downstream gravels. This technique has helped to rehabilitate some degraded spawning gravels, however. The percentage of fine sediment in spawning areas along the Stillaguamish River, Washington, was reduced from 19.0 to 8.7%, although use of the areas by spawning fish did not increase significantly after the gravels were cleaned (Heiser 1972). West (1984) reported that spawning by chinook salmon increased in the Scott River in northern California after gravels were cleaned with a bulldozer. Nevertheless, bulldozers should be used to clean spawning gravels only after all the potential effects of the action, both in the immediate area and downstream, have been considered.

Less complicated means of gravel cleaning also can be effective. Mundie and Mounce (1978) reported the successful use of a portable pump and fire hose to clean gravel in a small channel. Crews turned over gravel with shovels to remove silt and debris that accumulated after beavers constructed a dam on a small Alaskan creek; the dam was then broken, producing a freshet that removed the released material (D. C. Nelson, Alaska Department of Fish and Game, personal communication). A 4-fold increase in survival of sockeye salmon from egg to fry was recorded in the following spawning season. This cleaning was done for only 1 year, as a special case. Similar work was done in a small Washington stream with a portable pump and fire hose, but there sediment was not successfully removed (D. Allen, personal communication). As with the use of bulldozers to release fine sediment, caution should be employed when this procedure is used so that other areas are not degraded.

Placing gravel.—Bed-load materials are naturally transported from headwaters to lower river areas and then flushed from the system. Source inputs determine the replenishment of moved particles, and the size distribution of particles changes as sediment moves through the system (Hack 1957). These processes can be disrupted by dam construction, debris jam formation, extreme hydrologic events, and other disturbances. In some systems, gravel recruitment from natural sources is limited or a stream lacks the hydraulic environments and physical structures needed to accumulate well-sorted deposits of gravel. Fishery managers have tried to solve these problems in several ways.

When the natural source of gravel is limited, gravel may be added to streams. Gravel placement is a promising means of rehabilitating streams dredged during gold mining. In 1961, the Oregon State Game Commission replaced over 10,000 m³ of gravel and rock that had been dredged from 5.4 km of Clear Creek in northeastern Oregon (West et al. 1965a). Rock sills were used to help stabilize the introduced gravels. The number of chinook salmon spawning in Clear Creek increased more than 5-fold after the addition of gravel; the average number of redds in the area was 24 during the 3 years before improvement and 137 during the 3 years after. Although channel morphology and gravel accumulations have changed considerably since gravel placement, some gravel deposits continue to provide spawning sites for salmon (E. W. Claire, Oregon Department of Fish and Wildlife, personal communication).

Before 1972, adequate spawning gravel was lacking in Perkins Creek, Washington (Gerke 1973). Wooden weirs were installed to catch introduced graded gravel and establish an optimum gradient for spawning chum salmon. Holes were drilled in the weirs to allow passage of intragravel water. Spawner density was twice as high in areas where gravel had been introduced than in unimproved areas, and fry output from the stream increased (Gerke 1974). This approach has limited capability and should be used only when degradation is severe and natural gravel recruitment is poor. Introduced material should be of appropriate sizes for the species present. Repeated introductions of gravel may be required.

Wilson (1976) stated, "One problem that has occurred with stabilization, and to a lesser extent with some of the gravel replacement projects, is stabilization of gravel during the first year's high flows. The mechanical disturbance of the streambed during construction and the change of gradient cause the streambed materials to establish a new equilibrium within the physical constraints of the stream. Spawners seem to sense this instability and tend to avoid an improved area the first year after it is in use." Gravel introduced into a stream is usually cleaned and washed free of fine sediment (Anderson and Cameron 1980). In natural situations, some small particles may bind the gravel, helping retain and stabilize the larger material. Platts et al. (1979b) found that spring and summer chinook salmon in the Salmon River drainage of Idaho consistently built redds in areas where the particle size of most of the sediments was less than 19 mm.

Developing spawning areas.—Spawning areas have been improved in regions where spawning habitat was lacking or extreme flow conditions reduced the egg-to-fry survival rate (Althauser 1985). Such improvements are restricted to areas that have adequate groundwater flow for oxygenating eggs and removing metabolic wastes from the gravel. Such areas are generally limited to existing side channels in the floodplain of a river system. Spawning areas have been constructed or improved by removing silt and sand, introducing gravel of a specific size (usually 1–5 cm in diameter), excavating the stream bottom, and augmenting flow by diverting surface water (Althauser 1985). Species targeted generally are those with the fewest requirements for rearing habitat, such as chum salmon. The

Canada Department of Fisheries and Oceans has such a program to develop new spawning areas for chum salmon in southern British Columbia. Groundwater flow is enhanced in former flood channels now isolated from the main river. Assessment of fry production from these areas indicates that the technique has promise (Lister et al. 1980). A groundwater tributary of the Chilkat River near Haines, Alaska, used by chum salmon as spawning habitat, was enhanced for coho salmon spawning and rearing (Bachen 1984) by the techniques developed in British Columbia (Lister et al. 1980). The stream was deepened, spawning gravel was added, and a 1.5% gradient was developed. Streamflow increased as a result of the channel manipulations, and the upper end of the channel, which previously experienced dewatering, maintained water levels adequate for both spawning and rearing. Stream temperatures increased an average of 4°C.

Another successful manipulation of spawning areas occurred in the East Fork of the Satsop River in western Washington (King and Young 1986). Five groundwater-fed side channels either were excavated with a bulldozer, had existing gravel cleaned, or received up to 46 cm of added gravel. Over 1 million chum salmon fry and 100,000 coho salmon fry were produced in the cleaned channels in 1985.

Recommendations.—All of the methods reviewed for gravel restoration have limited applications. As discussed by Everest et al. (1987a), it is difficult to isolate the biological effects of fine sediment as a factor that limits salmonid populations. If fine sediments are found to limit salmonid populations, the most effective control is to stop the input source.

When gravel is added to streams because natural sources are inadequate, managers must be prepared to add more gravel periodically. Additions can be minimized if catchment structures are included as part of the project design.

Development of spawning areas can be an effective method of enhancing wild populations if construction requirements can be met. Such areas represent a compromise between wild and hatchery propagation. They preserve the natural pairing of adults while increasing the number of spawning pairs that can be accommodated and increasing the rate of survival to emergence.

Gravel Catchment

Gabions.—In streams with adequate movement of the gravel bed load, spawning area may be limited if structures that can catch and hold the gravel are lacking. Catchment devices have been used with some success to provide additional spawning gravels. Gabions—rectangular wire-mesh baskets filled with rock—have been most commonly used, but they have been successful only recently. Problems have been structural instability, failure to retain material of adequate size, and blockage of upstream fish movements at low flows. The first attempts to use gabions to collect and retain spawning gravels met with limited or no success.

Several attempts to create spawning habitat with gabions have been made along Oregon coastal streams, particularly where bedrock forms a substantial portion of the substrate (Fessler 1970; Garrison 1971a, 1971b; Magill 1971). These structures were placed perpendicular to the flow in a large river and failed to slow the rate at which introduced materials were carried downstream or to accumulate adequate replacement gravel. Ultimately these projects were abandoned.

Recent modifications in the design and placement of gabions have led to

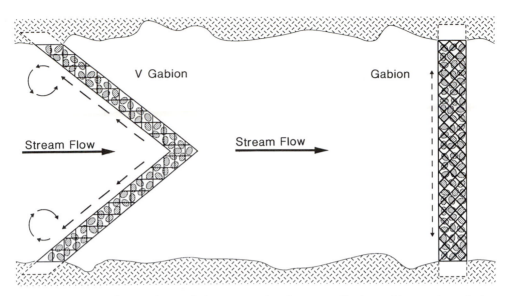

FIGURE 15.2.—Comparison of the conventional, perpendicular gabion weir and the V-shaped gabion. In the conventional design, water deflects to the side, washing around the end and weakening the structure. In the V-shaped design, flow is concentrated to the center of the structure, and deflected flows form back eddies. (After J. W. Anderson et al. 1984.)

important improvements. The Coos Bay (Oregon) District of the U.S. Bureau of Land Management has installed V-shaped structures (Anderson and Cameron 1980), rather than placing the gabion across the stream perpendicular to the flow (Figure 15.2). The ends of the V-shaped gabion structure are toed 1–1.5 m into the banks and riprapped to prevent flows from washing around the ends. Sections are cabled together and the entire structure is cabled to large trees or rocks near the banks (J. W. Anderson et al. 1984). With a 1% slope from bank to midstream, these V-shaped structures dissipate the energy of flowing water, reduce the chances of wash-out, and create pools better than do structures perpendicular to the flow. The gabion weirs are placed in series; the upstream structure dissipates the energy of the water by creating a drop, and the downstream weir accumulates and retains gravel. Best results have been obtained when the bottom of the upstream weir was level with the top of the downstream structure (Figure 15.3). When weirs are placed at the same elevation, gravel deposition occurs only in a small area near the downstream structure. When the downstream weir is too low,

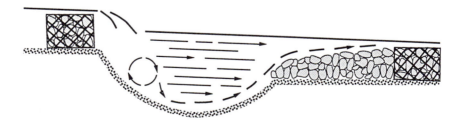

FIGURE 15.3.—Best spawning conditions develop when the top of the downstream gabion is about level with the bottom of the upstream gabion.

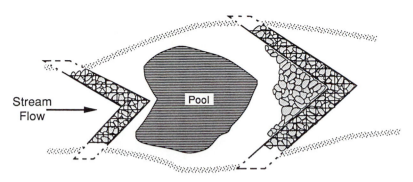

FIGURE 15.4.—Series of gabions, showing the function of individual weirs. The upstream structure is placed just upstream from where the channel widens. The downstream gabion is located upstream from the natural channel constriction. The upstream gabion dissipates the energy of the flowing water; gravel accumulates and is retained behind the lower structure. (After J. W. Anderson et al. 1984.)

an inadequate pool forms below the upstream structure, and gravel eventually fills in the pool. Placement of an upstream structure at a point where the stream begins to widen improves chances of success by further dissipating the energy of the water; a downstream gabion situated immediately above a natural channel constriction, where water begins to pick up energy again, is especially likely to accumulate gravel (Figure 15.4). Gabions should not be placed on sharp bends because this aggravates bank cutting and gravel scouring (Wilson 1976). V-shaped gabions have worked best on gradients less than 1.5%, but they have also been used on steeper gradients with some success. Further testing of different designs has confirmed the superiority of the V-shaped structures (J. W. Anderson et al. 1984).

Production of pink and chum salmon in Puget Sound streams often was limited by the amount of available spawning gravel and by flows that shifted and scoured streambed materials. An experimental program began in the late 1960s to enhance spawning habitats in a few of these streams (Gerke 1973). Early work included the use of log weirs, rubber tires, and large rocks, but gabion weirs most effectively stabilized and retained gravel. Because of their flexibility, gabion baskets did not crack, shift, or break if the substrate settled (Gerke 1974). Structures like those in Figure 15.5 have been the most stable and long-lived. A standard basket—0.3 m high by 1.5 m wide by the desired length—was set in the substrate and filled so that the top was level with the streambed to form a base and splash apron. A basket 0.3 m high by 1 m wide by the desired length then was wired to the upstream half of the apron so that the downstream portion of the lower basket prevented undercutting and thus increased stability. A slot 1.45 m wide and 0.13 m deep was constructed in the center of the upper basket to ensure fish passage at low flows (Gerke 1973). Sharp, angular quarry rock was the best fill material, forming the most stable structures. Rounded, river-run material tended to shift more readily, reducing a structure's stability. Similar results were reported by Engels (1975) in Oregon. When gabions were incorrectly constructed or located, dams (similar in structure to the weirs but with a large opening in the center) were built immediately downstream to create pools that facilitated passage of fish upstream. Ends of the gabions were toed 1–1.5 m into each bank and riprapped

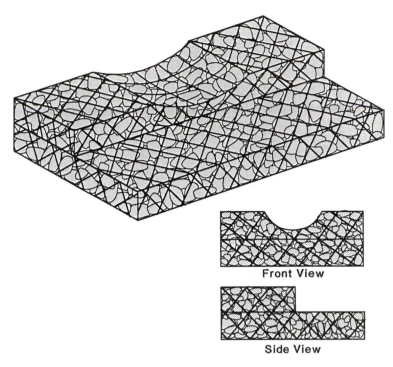

Front View

Side View

FIGURE 15.5.—Two-tiered gabion weir used to accumulate and stabilize spawning gravel. Note notch in center to allow fish to pass at low flows. (D. A. Wilson, Washington Department of Fisheries, personal communication.)

with rock there and upstream to prevent bank erosion and washout. Riprapping must not constrict the natural channel.

Gabions are built at intervals to obtain the optimum gradient for the desired species, usually 0.2–0.3% for pink and chum salmon (D. A. Wilson, Washington Department of Fisheries, personal communication). Experience has shown that structures with single 0.3-m-high baskets built in series, one for each 0.3-m drop in stream elevation, are more stable than higher baskets spaced at greater intervals. For example, if 0.6 m is the height required, two 0.3-m-high baskets will be more stable than a single 0.6-m-high basket.

The ability of gabions to increase spawning and summer rearing habitats for salmonids was documented by House and Boehne (1985, 1986). Two or more gabion structures were placed in a V-configuration spanning the channel in some coastal Oregon streams. Close monitoring of pre- and posttreatment salmonid populations showed increases in salmonid spawning and juvenile rearing in the treatment areas. The absence of large woody debris on Tobe Creek was determined to limit spawning and rearing habitat for salmonids. After gabions were installed, the complexity of habitat increased, as did the biomass of juvenile salmonids. Similar work was done on East Fork Lobster Creek, which had been radically altered by logging, stream cleaning, and flooding. Gabions were built, salmonid spawning increased near them, and densities of summer-rearing salmonids increased during the next 6 years.

After a debris torrent scoured large woody debris from Sachs Creek, Queen Charlotte Islands, British Columbia, tandem V-shaped gabion structures were installed to improve spawning habitat for pink salmon (Klassen and Northcote 1986). In high-gradient (>3%) areas, gabions were unstable and trapped little gravel. In low-gradient (1%) areas, gabions stabilized after the first winter and effectively trapped spawning gravel. The gabions appeared to improve rearing habitat by increasing pool area and cover; intragravel conditions also improved significantly. Survival of pink salmon eggs did not differ between gabion and reference sites in the first winter after construction, but Klassen and Northcote (1988) suggested that future egg survival may be enhanced because gravel should be more stable near the gabions than in the natural streambed.

Gabion construction has evolved primarily by trial and error, and gabion use has become more successful as more efficient designs have been developed (Engels 1975; Klingeman 1984). The longevity of gabions depends on the experience of the biologists, hydrologists, geomorphologists, engineers, and construction crews who design and build the structures, as well as on the stability of the watershed. Gabions have been used most successfully to stabilize spawning gravels when hillslope erosion has been controlled and stream channels have been stabilized (Overton 1984). Concerns over initial cost, esthetics, and maintenance cost, however, have led stream managers to favor the use of more natural materials over wire gabions. In our opinion, gabions should be considered only when natural materials are not available or are not suitable for catching gravel.

Rock and log sills.—In 1972, the Oregon Fish Commission built a series of rock sills on lower Anvil Creek, a major chinook salmon spawning tributary of the coastal Elk River (Bender 1978). Large boulders were bulldozed together across the stream channel so that silt and debris could lodge among them to form pools and collect spawning gravels. The structures failed when high flows scoured underlying materials (R. Bender, Oregon Department of Fish and Wildlife, personal communication). The following year, five log sills (Figure 15.6) were constructed by the Oregon Fish Commission, at a total cost of US$1,800, to replace the rock structures (Bender 1978). Large logs were set partially into the streambed and extended into the banks, where they were anchored with riprap. Support posts were angled into the streambed (parallel to the flow) and nailed to the logs. Gravel was bulldozed behind each structure and sloped to the top. Cyclone fencing was overlaid on the posts and attached to both posts and logs for stability. Gravel accumulated behind the structures during the first winter and was readily used by spawning chinook salmon and steelhead. Emerging fry move almost immediately into Elk River and estuarine nursery areas, so little rearing habitat is required in Anvil Creek. This situation and the pristine condition of the watershed have probably been largely responsible for the success of the project (R. Bender, personal communication).

Attempts to create spawning habitat with rock sills have not been as promising, however. In 1984, 21 cross-channel boulder–rock sills were constructed to capture and retain spawning gravels in Fish Creek, a tributary of the Clackamas River in western Oregon (Everest et al. 1985). A 10- to 15-year-interval storm altered the position of some of the sills, and the design objectives were only partially met. The size of the boulders compared to the size of the channel was the major determinant of stability; the larger the boulders, the more stable the structure. In

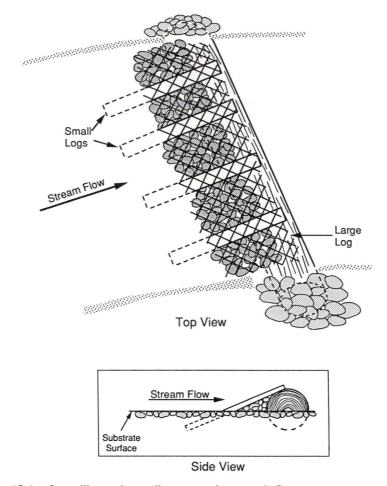

Top View

Side View

FIGURE 15.6.—Log sills used to collect spawning gravel. Support posts are attached to the main log and anchored in the substrate. Gravel is placed on top of the log and sloped upstream. Cyclone fencing is then laid over and attached to the log and support posts. (R. Bender, Oregon Department of Fish and Wildlife, personal communication.)

smaller channels, cross-channel structures withstood the storm flow and continued to capture and retain gravel.

Personnel of the U.S. Bureau of Land Management have designed and built cedar-board structures (Figure 15.7) on small Oregon streams to accumulate gravel and to provide holding areas for steelhead adults and rearing pools for juveniles (J. W. Anderson et al. 1984). These structures, placed in a series, have been successful. A main support log is laid across the stream and anchored into the banks. An open-ended "V" is formed by attaching two more supports to the first log and angling one into each bank. Shakes (made of readily available cedar) 2–2.5 cm thick are secured to the side supports and slanted down into the streambed. They incline to slightly above winter flow levels so that most of the water flows to the center to make better pools. Additional shakes are set at right angles to the main support (paralleling the stream banks) between the side

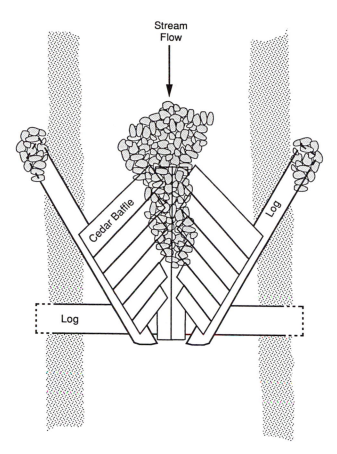

FIGURE 15.7.—Cedar-board structures designed to accumulate spawning gravels and create holding pools in small streams. (J. W. Anderson, U.S. Bureau of Land Management, personal communication.)

supports. The downstream edge of an upstream shake should overlap the upstream edge of a downstream shake to prevent displacement of shakes by high flows. Construction and installation is inexpensive and quick because most necessary materials can be found near the sites.

Recommendations.—Several techniques can be used to slow the movement of gravels through a watershed. To determine whether gabions and log or rock sills will catch and retain bedload, a few steps should be followed. The physical structure of the stream mainly determines how appropriate an artificial structure will be. Hydrologists and geomorphologists can help with this evaluation. For example, a stream with a gradient of less than 1.5% and with sufficient bedload transport to provide spawning material, but with no structures to catch and hold the material, would be a candidate for V-shaped gabion construction. Biological aspects such as target species and life history phase must be considered. An hydraulic engineer should be consulted to help insure that the structures will withstand streamflow dynamics. Any habitat manipulation proposal should specify procedures for pre- and postconstruction studies so resulting physical and biological changes can be evaluated.

Access Improvement

Access improvement—including removal of debris and log jams, construction of fishways, and installation of culverts—probably has been the most common type of project undertaken to enhance habitats for anadromous salmonids. Few of these efforts have been well evaluated, and some have not even been documented. This has hindered our review of access improvement.

Stream clearing.—Historically, streams and rivers in the Pacific Northwest contained large amounts of wood and boulders. Settlers cleared large woody debris from many areas to open channels for navigation and transportation of goods and materials (Sedell et al. 1982). As a result, the physical structure of streams has been dramatically altered in many instances (Sedell and Luchessa 1982; Sedell and Frogatt 1984). The historical impact of debris removal on fish populations has not been well documented because the importance of large woody debris to stream fish has been recognized only within the past decade or so.

Removal of jams considered blocks to fish migration was a major effort of management agencies from 1950 to the late 1960s. One of the earliest documented efforts to remove debris jams was reported by Merrell (1951). About 170 jams were removed from 43 km of the Clatskanie River system in Oregon. Stream clearance and access development were also an integral part of projects to improve coastal streams in Oregon during the early 1960s (Summers and Neubauer 1965). More than a dozen fishways were installed or repaired and more than 50 log jams were removed.

Extensive stream clearance has also been undertaken in California. During the late 1950s and into the 1960s, a program to remove old log jams was carried out by the California Department of Fish and Game on nearly every major coastal river system that supported anadromous fish, from the Oregon border south to Santa Cruz. This effort was very extensive and expensive, but very few of the submitted reports were published. An exception was the work on the Noyo River, where nearly 60 km of stream were cleared of log jams, partial barriers, and debris that threatened to form future jams (Holman and Evans 1964).

Log debris jams have also received attention elsewhere along the Pacific coast. Roppel (1978) listed 88 major stream clearance projects conducted in Alaska by the U.S. Forest Service and the Alaska Department of Fish and Game between 1952 and 1978. Saltzman (1964) reported on major efforts to clear debris in the Siuslaw River basin in western Oregon. The Oregon Fish Commission identified numerous log jams in many of the headwater tributaries of the coastal Alsea and Nestucca rivers and rivers entering Tillamook Bay during the late 1940s and early 1950s. Some of these jams were over 500 m long and up to 10 m deep, and many of them were completely removed during the mid-1950s. Another intensive effort to clear tributaries of the Alsea River was undertaken by the Bureau of Land Management in the early 1970s (House and Boehne 1987b). The extent of debris jam removal is vastly underestimated because many efforts, particularly those undertaken before 1950, were never reported.

Surprisingly little effort has been made to evaluate the effects of these stream clearance projects on the anadromous fish populations they were designed to enhance or on the quality of habitat downstream from the removal area (House and Boehne 1987a). Large amounts of fine sediment are usually stored behind debris jams, and complete removal of the jam allows that material to be transported downstream. Removal of one particularly large jam in the Oregon Coast Range released over 5,000 m^3 of sediment to the stream channel below (Beschta 1979). Lestelle and Cederholm (1984) documented the removal of about 70% of the natural debris from a small tributary in the Clearwater River drainage, Washington. Cutthroat trout populations and the number of pools decreased the following winter. Within a year, however, fish numbers returned to pretreatment levels and pools formed by large woody debris were essentially restored to their original abundance. The authors attributed this recovery to the recruitment of new debris into the stream channel from banks and hillslopes.

In a study of seven removal sites in western Oregon, Baker (1979) found that the principal short-term effects were the release of sediment and debris trapped behind the jam and destruction of existing habitat within the jam. Sometimes these negative results can be offset by greatly increased habitat use by anadromous fish above the jam, but the trade-offs are often hard to evaluate. Baker's work suggested that increased emphasis should be placed on partial removal of debris jams.

Alteration or removal of debris jams should be approached with caution. Debris jams provide cover for juvenile fish (Bustard and Narver 1975a) and can provide many other benefits to fish habitats (Hall and Baker 1975). Once established, they may be important stabilizing features within streams, providing slope breaks along the longitudinal profile that are needed for the establishment of pools (Bilby 1984). Sheridan (1969) recommended consideration of the following factors before a debris accumulation or jam is removed.

• Does the jam seriously impede migration of desired fish? (Evaluations must be made at both low and high flows; what is impassable at low flows may be passable at higher flows.)
• Does the debris remove suitable spawning areas from production?
• What will be the effect on stream gradient and general stream configuration if the debris is removed?

Consideration also should be given to the potential effect of debris jam removal on resident fish populations above the barrier. The quantity and quality of rearing habitat being blocked should be taken into account. Barriers should be removed as soon as possible, before they trap sediment and more debris.

Once a debris jam has become established in the stream and is found to impede the migration of anadromous salmonids, partial removal is usually best (Baker 1979). A channel allowing water flow should be formed, following the natural stream course as closely as possible. U.S. Forest Service personnel in Oregon opened areas to coho salmon on Cedar Creek and Peach Creek by partial removal methods. Using paint, they marked debris to be removed, then closely supervised the contract workers to make necessary adjustments in the removal plan as the jams were exposed (D. B. Hohler, U.S. Forest Service, personal communication). Experienced fishery biologists and hydrologists should participate in actual operations to ensure that not too much debris is removed. J. W. Anderson (U.S.

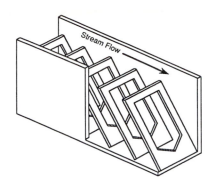

FIGURE 15.8.—Commonly used variation of the Denil fishway. (After Orsborn 1986.)

Bureau of Land Management, personal communication) has suggested placing gabions or other suitable structures downstream in a stable channel area (not in the immediate removal area) to retain potential spawning gravel released by debris jam removal. Downcutting of the streambed is unpredictable in disturbed areas, and freshets could scour the bottom down to bedrock.

Fishways.—Fishways are another means of providing access to areas blocked by natural or artificial barriers. The history, description, and specifications of individual fish passage facilities have been the subject of numerous publications. Among the devices used to pass fish up- and downstream are fish ladders, locks, tramways, and trolleys. Clay (1961) and Bell (1986) are good references for fishways, fish screens, and spawning channels. Orsborn (1986) summarized current fish-ladder designs, the history and design of fishways, and the energy requirements of various species of fish. He also presented an analysis of barriers to migration.

Of the various fish passage facilities, one general type—the Denil fishway—has particular significance to fishery managers. Denil fishways are steep flumes with baffles or deflectors on the sides, the bottom, or both. The baffles force flowing water to deflect back upon itself, thus reducing its velocity. Use of these structures in west coast streams was limited until the 1950s, when Ziemer (1962, 1965) began using them experimentally. Ziemer tested several modifications for flow velocity, fish passage, species preference for various gradients, and hydraulic characteristics. His tests resulted in a portable device known as the "Alaskan steeppass," an aluminum fishway of 2.8-m sections that can be assembled in various lengths to provide relatively steep passage over obstructions (Figure 15.8).

As with most other enhancement structures, development of the Alaskan steeppass was marked by initial failures. With careful planning by experienced fishery biologists and engineers, however, the device has been used to open new areas to anadromous salmonids. Sweet (1975) listed over 20 steeppass projects in Alaska. The largest facility was built on Kodiak Island to establish new runs of salmon in previously inaccessible Frazer Lake (Blackett 1979). Eggs and fry of sockeye salmon from nearby stocks were planted in the lake's tributaries beginning in 1951. Adult fish returning to the lake from 1956 through 1961 were backpacked over the 10-m-high barrier falls. In 1962 a 4-step steeppass, 70 m long, was built to allow returning fish to swim past the falls. By 1978, the run had increased to 142,000 fish (Blackett 1979), and the steeppass had to be modified to accommodate the run. A thorough evaluation indicated that these structural modifications were successful (Blackett 1987); in 1985, more than 485,800 sockeye salmon ascended the fishway. Similar successes on Kodiak and Afognak islands have been reported (Blackett 1985).

Steeppass facilities in Alaska that initially failed to pass fish upstream did so after they were modified. The Ketchikan Creek fishway was constructed in 1965, but passed only 300–400 pink salmon annually over a falls. It was rebuilt in 1977 and passed 10,000 fish (Roppel 1978). Low flows limited upstream movement through the Gretchen Creek steeppass on Afognak Island. A 12.2-m concrete-faced gabion deflector was constructed above the steeppass to raise and divert water through it, allowing fish to move upstream at all flows (McDaniel 1978). Such a diversion also reduces mortality of outmigrant fry.

Fishery engineers in the U.S. Forest Service have established criteria for building steeppasses for access into the short, steep drainages found in much of southeastern Alaska. The physical habitat requirements of the salmonids under consideration must be met. When an area is opened to coho salmon, for example, both spawning gravels and suitable rearing habitat must be available. Coho salmon will ascend steeppass runs exceeding a length of 13 m and a slope of 35% between resting pools, but the design for chum salmon is generally limited to 6- to 7-m runs at 20–30% slopes. The Alaskan steeppass operates most effectively when the entrance is nearly submerged and located at the uppermost area currently accessible to fish (D. J. Kanen, U.S. Forest Service, personal communication).

Laddering of barriers has also been used in many access projects farther south. Narver (1976) recorded 28 fishways in British Columbia. Of 20 fishways built in British Columbia between 1954 and 1978, only two did not justify their costs (Canada Fisheries and Marine Service 1978). Oregon had fish passage facilities at 56 natural and 79 artificial obstructions, not including those at dams on the main Columbia River (Narver 1976). Few reports, however, have evaluated the performance of these smaller facilities.

Culverts.—Improperly installed culverts create access problems for both adult and juvenile fish. Fish passage can be impeded by excessive water velocity or inadequate water depth in and below a culvert, excessive height of the culvert entrance above the stream, and lack of adequate resting pools in the approach to a culvert. Reviews of culvert types and fish-passage problems associated with each type were published by the U.S. Forest Service (1977c) and Dane (1978a, 1978b). An annotated bibliography of reports dealing with fish passage at road crossings was prepared by Anderson and Bryant (1980). Most culvert designs or culvert modifications have emphasized the upstream passage of adult salmonids,

FIGURE 15.9.—Use of weirs to help fish reach the level of a poorly installed culvert. (Anderson 1973b.)

but movements of juveniles must also be considered (Skeesick 1970; Everest 1973).

Replacement may be the best remedy when a culvert hinders or blocks upstream access. Furniss et al. (1991, this volume) discuss problems associated with improper placement of culverts and criteria for their replacement. In southeastern Alaska, an enlarged culvert (with a diameter 30–45 cm larger than necessary to carry a once-in-25-year storm flow) is partially buried 15–30 cm into the streambed (U.S. Forest Service 1977c). This reduces the slope of the culvert and allows bedload sediments to accumulate in it. Bedload deposition decreases the water velocity in the pipe and provides an irregular texture, creating dart-and-rest areas for small fish. A plunge pool (such as is formed by a gabion or piling) is often created at the culvert outlet, increasing the end area of the channel and dissipating the energy of the flowing water as it runs into the slow-moving water in the pool.

Log and gabion weirs sometimes have been installed to alleviate passage problems resulting from poor culvert installation (Figure 15.9; Anderson 1973b; Evans and Johnston 1980). Series of self-scouring log structures installed in eastern Oregon streams allowed anadromous fish to move through previously impassable culverts (Claire 1978b). An unforeseen benefit from these structures was deposition of gravel behind the logs, where resident salmonids have spawned. Also, the pools created by these structures contained up to five times more fish than did adjacent areas without structures.

Baffles have been placed in culverts to facilitate fish passage. They produce pockets of low water velocity where fish can rest (U.S. Forest Service 1977c; Katopodis et al. 1978). Furniss et al. (1991) discuss various baffle types that can be used.

Other methods of access improvement.—Falls have been blasted to create jump pools that allow fish better access to upstream areas. Sweet (1975) listed 10 such projects in Alaska. Similar efforts undoubtedly have been made elsewhere, but documentation and evaluation are lacking. Falls should not be modified without consideration of the same potential consequences described previously for barrier removal projects. Esthetics should be included in project evaluation.

Boulders can be placed to create pools. This method was used to provide steelhead access into previously inaccessible steep-gradient tributaries of the Smith River in western Oregon (J. J. Cameron, U.S. Bureau of Land Management, personal communication). Fish moved into the streams during the first spawning season after completion. The boulders reduce the velocity of water entering a culvert on one stream; they also trap gravel and provide resting pools for migrating salmonids. Concurrent installation of cedar-board structures on another stream in the drainage contributed to the success of the project.

Recommendations.—The unique biological and engineering requirements of each access project, as well as insufficient evaluation of past efforts, make general guidelines for developing access projects difficult. Initial efforts have often failed and modification or replacement of facilities has been required to allow fish passage. A fishery biologist must help with the planning of access projects to ensure that biological requirements of fish populations are considered in the project design.

Some important procedures (modified from U.S. Forest Service 1977c) for planning access improvement projects follow.

• Make certain all planned structures or barrier removals are evaluated by a fishery biologist early in the planning process.

• Determine if fish passage is required and for what species; make a stream survey if necessary.

• Determine periods of the year when fish passage is required.

• With assistance from a forest hydrologist, define the maximum and minimum flows for which fish passage should be provided. Data can be obtained from U.S. Geological Survey (USGS) records or from precipitation records and converted to discharge from charts. Procedures are available from the USGS for estimating discharge in ungaged streams from regional relations between precipitation and drainage area.

• Supply the above information in writing to a forest engineer with a request for an opportunity to review and approve plans.

• Review the type, size, and slope of structure recommended by the engineer to meet flood requirements.

• Have the proposal examined jointly by the biologist and the engineer to determine if adequate fish passage is provided. If fish passage will be impeded, develop alternative designs.

• When a suitable design for fish passage has been agreed upon, have the engineer double-check that adequate provisions for flood flow requirements have been made.

• Have the biologist indicate in writing to the engineer that the proposed design plan meets fisheries requirements.

• Have the engineer and the biologist review and approve preliminary design drawings as related to fish passage.

• Submit written recommendations for any special considerations for soil-erosion control, esthetics, and effects on resident fish populations at the site during and after construction, as determined jointly by the biologist and the engineer.

Further Considerations for Spawning Habitat Manipulation

Several factors should be considered before projects to improve spawning habitat are undertaken. Best results are obtained in stable watersheds where erosion and runoff problems are minimal. Stable drainage conditions have contributed substantially to much of the successful work discussed in this section. The history of an area's use by adult and juvenile fish must be evaluated. Streams in which runs have been reduced have shown the best response to enhancement efforts. In some areas where stocks are absent, fish may be introduced after habitat rehabilitation or enhancement. Accessibility for necessary equipment also must be taken into account.

Possible adverse effects on fish and other aquatic organisms should be considered in planning and implementing spawning habitat enhancement and rehabilitation projects. Instream work, such as gravel cleaning, gravel placement, and gabion or riprap placement, causes temporary increases in suspended solids and turbidity downstream. These suspended materials can reduce benthic invertebrate populations and fish spawning success in lower sections (Dames and Moore, Inc. 1978). Areas disturbed by project activities, however, are repopulated quickly by invertebrates and algae from unaffected regions upstream (Meehan 1971). Environmental impacts of projects to improve spawning habitat in Washington have been minimized by confining the work to a period when little fish activity occurs (Dames and Moore, Inc. 1978). These Washington streams were used mostly by pink and chum salmon. It will be more difficult to avoid some initial adverse effects in areas inhabited year-round by salmonids.

Even when projects for the enhancement of spawning habitat are carefully planned and conducted, results are not always predictable. For example, construction of three artificial spawning channels in streams feeding Babine Lake, British Columbia, led to an increase in the number of sockeye salmon smolts leaving the lake (McDonald and Hume 1984). Adult returns showed a corresponding increase in odd-numbered years, but production targets have not been met in even-numbered years. Fishery biologists are managing for the odd-year fisheries until they determine what factors are affecting the even-year fisheries. Careful monitoring of pre- and postenhancement conditions to determine which techniques are successful will allow adjustments to present management methods and will guide future research.

Habitats for juvenile salmonids can be lost or reduced when on-site materials are used to improve or create spawning habitats. For example, the original sills constructed in Fish Creek, Oregon, were made of boulders collected from the edges of the stream channel (Everest et al. 1985). Subsequent evaluation indicated that removal of those boulders had reduced overwintering habitat for young-of-the-year steelhead. Boulder habitat manipulations since that time have been with quarried rock only. Hamilton (1983) reported similar problems when bank boulders were used to build deflectors on Nooning Creek in northern California. Removal of the boulders from the banks may have contributed to bank erosion and habitat degradation.

Hogan (1987) found that gravel in undisturbed stream channels is stored in numerous small sites rather than in the fewer, large pockets found in perturbed systems. The smaller pockets tended to be more stable. Attempts to capture gravels should therefore be directed towards creating several small pockets of gravel rather than a few large areas.

The literature and many of the people we interviewed have pessimistic views of projects for improving spawning habitat, especially those using gabions. A reluctance to attempt any type of project is evident for fear of failure from catastrophic natural events, or because of limitations of the structures and techniques. Techniques applied successfully in one area may not be directly applicable in others. Principles derived from these efforts, however, can be modified to meet specific requirements by using careful assessment of hydrologic conditions, creative thinking, and the work of others in trial-and-error experiments.

To accurately assess projects to improve spawning habitats, the use of an area by spawning adults both before and after habitat manipulation must be determined. Progress beyond our current knowledge will be slow until fishery managers regularly document successes and failures.

Rearing Habitat

Justification for Enhancing Rearing Habitat

Concern has been raised that instream enhancement projects merely redistribute fish and do not increase the carrying capacity of a stream. However, the territorial behavior of juvenile salmonids (Chapman 1962a; Hartman 1965; Everest and Chapman 1972) may ensure that all suitable habitat in an area is occupied. Less dominant fish are forced to emigrate to less desirable areas. If an area that previously contained few or no fish is "enhanced" and becomes used, fish will still occupy the unenhanced habitat. Rather than being forced from a system in search of suitable living space, some "nomads" (Chapman 1962a) may remain in the area and either establish territories in the improved sections or use the areas formerly occupied by the more dominant fish that have been attracted to the new habitat. An increase in the amount of suitable habitat (for example, cover) should increase the numbers of fish and thus could increase fish production in a stream.

Most of the early work on developing rearing habitat was done in the eastern USA, where augmentations of bank cover and pool area significantly increased the abundance and harvest of legal-sized brook trout (Shetter et al. 1949; Hunt 1976). Tarzwell (1938), however, observed that most eastern techniques were not directly transferable to west coast streams. Highly variable flow regimes, including frequent floods and droughts, made many structures unsuitable or unstable. As a result, fishery biologists have had to develop innovative techniques for rehabilitating or enhancing rearing habitats in western North America.

Placing Boulders

Placing boulders in streams has been one of the most common techniques used to create rearing habitat. Madsen (1938) and Tarzwell (1938) both found that boulder placement was one of the few enhancement procedures available. Later efforts involving boulder placement occurred in California trout streams (Calhoun 1964, 1966). Follow-up photographs clearly showed that large boulders could withstand major storm flows and continue to provide desirable habitat. Since then, several studies have emphasized the association between rock cover and abundance of salmonids (Hartman 1965; Chapman and Bjornn 1969; Everest and Chapman 1972; Narver 1976), and a few additional efforts have been made to place boulders to enhance habitats. In Idaho streams, Bjornn (1971) found that the introduction of large rock into small headwaters near spawning areas increased the carrying capacity for, and slowed the downstream movement of, presmolt chinook salmon and steelhead over winter. In sections of the Tracadie River, New Brunswick, where large angular rock (up to 1.2 m in diameter) had been placed, the number of juvenile Atlantic salmon increased dramatically—in some instances, from no fish present to 25–50 fish/100 m^2 (Redmond 1975). Boulders placed in Redcap Creek, a Klamath River tributary in northern California, increased both numbers and biomass of age-1 steelhead over 300% above those of control sections (Brock 1986). Ward and Slaney (1979, 1981) found that boulder groups were more successful and cost-effective than gabions and rock deflectors in creating rearing habitat in the upper Keogh River, British Columbia.

Placing boulders in streams in eastern Oregon has created rearing habitat. On the South Fork of the John Day River in Oregon, boulders 0.45–1.1 m in diameter were placed with a front-end loader in areas that contained no salmonids (Claire 1978c). The boulders were arranged in patterns similar to those occurring naturally in areas with salmonids, and additional rocks were placed in open stream areas and near overhanging trees. Cutbanks were riprapped, and rock deflectors were placed where current deflection was needed. Juvenile salmonids were subsequently found in the improved area. A highway realignment along Beech Creek, Oregon, resulted in numerous channel changes and deep cuts through bedrock. Boulders placed in steep areas reduced water velocities and created pools and gravel bars used by spawning and rearing steelhead (Claire 1978c).

In an attempt to increase complexity in the system, boulders and wing deflectors were placed in the thalweg (deepest part of the channel) and in edge habitat of Hurdygurdy Creek in northern California (Moreau 1984). The stream had lost much of its roughness due to a 100-year storm flow in 1964. After 2 years, the structures were functioning as designed and providing spawning and rearing habitats for salmonids (Figure 15.10). Similar results were achieved with boulder groups and wing deflectors on the Salmon River in northern California (West 1984).

Hamilton (1983) evaluated the effectiveness of boulder deflectors as creators of rearing habitat in ten 22-m-long reaches in a northern California stream. Within 1 year, only 15% of the structures were intact and fish populations were unchanged. The failures occurred, Hamilton concluded, because the stream's hydrologic forces were not considered when the structures were designed, and because the remaining structures provided poor cover. In the planning and conduct of

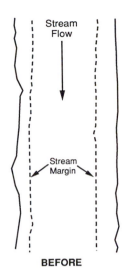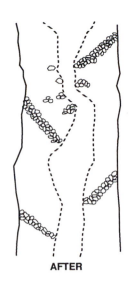

Stream
Flow

Stream
Margin

BEFORE

AFTER

FIGURE 15.10.—Use of boulders to alter stream channel and increase spawning and rearing habitat. (After Moreau 1984.)

enhancement projects, emphasis should be placed on integrated watershed management, careful planning and design of structures, and evaluation of project effectiveness as expressed by the response of fish populations (Hamilton 1983).

Fontaine (1988) evaluated the ability of several types of rock and log structures to improve habitat for juvenile steelhead in a major tributary of the North Umpqua River, Oregon. One important finding was that fish responded differently to the structures from season to season. During summer, the most effective structures were located near the thalweg. During winter, boulder and rubble structures placed in zones of slow water attracted the largest concentrations of juvenile steelhead. This work also demonstrated an improved system of anchoring instream structures: a cartridge-dispensed, polyester resin was used to quickly bond cables into holes drilled in bedrock or large boulders (Fontaine and Merritt 1988).

The substrate on which rocks and boulders are placed must be stable enough to prevent the large rocks from being undercut and buried (Klingeman 1984). Boulders should be taken from beyond the bankfull channel width to prevent loss of refuge areas during storms (Everest et al. 1985). Hydrologists and geomorphologists should help plan projects to ensure their success. Although boulder placement may be one of the more worthwhile enhancement techniques on the western coast of North America, potential problems should not be overlooked. For example, an overabundance of newly placed boulders might prevent streams from flushing sediments adequately, and excessive erosion could result if new boulders caused streams to change their meander patterns.

Rock-Drop Structures

The pool–riffle sequence is regarded as the basic unit of the stream environment (Mundie 1974). Alteration of this pattern can adversely affect fish populations (Whitney and Bailey 1959; Johnson 1964; Elser 1968). Rock-drop structures (Figure 15.11) were constructed to control stream gradient and to form rearing and holding pools for steelhead in Fifteen-mile Creek, Oregon (Newton 1978). The

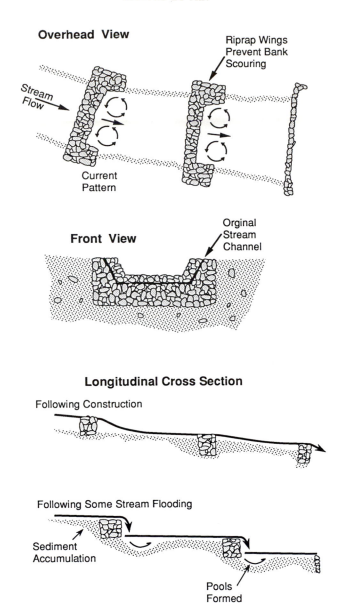

Overhead View

Riprap Wings
Prevent Bank
Scouring

Stream
Flow

Current
Pattern

Orginal
Stream
Channel

Front View

Longitudinal Cross Section

Following Construction

Following Some Stream Flooding

Sediment
Accumulation

Pools
Formed

FIGURE 15.11.—Rock-drop structures used to form rearing and holding pools. (After Newton 1978.)

stream had been straightened and channelized following 100-year floods in 1964 and 1974. A series of trenches was excavated with a backhoe across the channel and into the banks. The trenches were filled with angular riprap rock to a height of 0.45 m above the streambed. Pools formed above the structures and filled with gravel and silt during the first winter, and new pools scoured out below each structure. The only adult steelhead observed in the stream during the first spring after installation were in the newly created pools. Steelhead redds were also observed near the rock-drop structures. Juveniles have used the pools for rearing; interstices in the structures also provide escape cover.

Another benefit of these structures has been to control channel and streambed erosion. Arranged in tandem, they reduce flow velocity and dissipate much of the erosive force of water as it plunges over the structure (J. A. Newton, Oregon Department of Fish and Wildlife, personal communication). During the winter of 1977, streamflows attained levels of 1 m over the structures with no appreciable streambank erosion or destabilization.

Large Woody Debris

Large woody debris is an important component of fish habitat (Koski et al. 1984; Sedell and Swanson 1984; Sedell et al. 1984; Bisson et al. 1987; House and Boehne 1987a), and its function as a physical determinant of stream dynamics has been well documented (Swanson et al. 1976; Bryant 1983; Bilby 1984; Beschta and Platts 1986; Lienkaemper and Swanson 1987). A dramatic change has taken place in the physical structure of rivers in North America since the arrival of European settlers (Sedell and Luchessa 1982). Splash dams and intensive debris snagging to open navigational channels, combined with slash removal from streams, have greatly altered salmonid habitats. The effects that losses of large woody debris have on fish populations are just beginning to be understood (Bisson and Sedell 1984; Hicks et al. 1991, this volume).

Recent studies have shown the effects of debris removal on populations of rearing juvenile salmonids. Two second-order streams in southeastern Alaska, in watersheds that had been clear-cut 10 years earlier, were selectively cleaned to preserve existing channel structure; only small or unstable pieces of debris were removed (Dolloff 1986). Subsequent declines were observed in the abundance of both coho salmon and Dolly Varden. Elliott (1986) conducted a similar experiment in southeastern Alaska to determine the effect of removing logging debris on rearing Dolly Varden; he found a progressive loss of larger fish and a decreased mean size of individuals after debris was removed.

In systems where large woody debris is lacking, large conifers have been blasted into streams with dynamite (Boehne and Wolfe 1986). Initial results of adding large debris to Fish Creek, Oregon, have been mixed; high flows removed some pieces of debris from the active channel (Everest et al. 1986), but more trees were added and cabled in place, and results appear promising (Figure 15.12; Everest et al. 1987b). In southeastern Alaska, trees were added to Kennel Creek and the root masses were left on the bank to anchor the downed logs. Estimates of juvenile coho salmon and Dolly Varden populations were made before and after insertion of the debris; initial results indicate the new wood has provided cover and protection from high flows (W. Lorenz, U.S. Forest Service, personal communication).

Tripp (1986) reported an extensive evaluation of the use of large woody debris to rehabilitate habitat structure in a stream on the Queen Charlotte Islands, British Columbia. Two major debris torrents had severely degraded habitat in the stream, leaving cobble-bedded riffles, few pools, and little cover. Placement of debris in an experimental reach was followed in the first winter by substantial increases in pool number, pool area, and habitat complexity. Overwinter survival and smolt output of juvenile coho salmon were several times greater in the rehabilitated section of

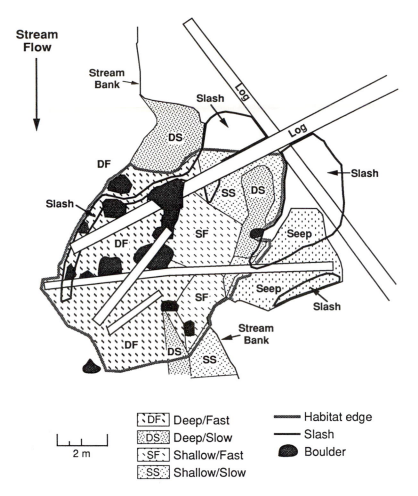

FIGURE 15.12.—Large woody debris added to streams increases both channel complexity and summer and winter habitats. (After Everest et al. 1987b.)

the stream than in a control reach. Subsequent debris torrents in the next 3 years reduced the effectiveness of the structures, leading the author to suggest ideas for further study and preliminary guidelines for the use of debris in streams affected by torrents.

Kaufmann (1987) studied the relation between the amount of habitat with low-velocity flow and discharge in undisturbed channels with naturally occurring woody debris and in channels with boulder berms constructed for enhancement purposes. As discharge increased, the area of low-velocity flow in the channel with boulder berms remained the same, but it increased in channels with woody debris (Figure 15.13).

Long-term management of fish habitats requires management of the riparian zone. A concise summary of the concept and influence of the riparian zone was presented by Swanson et al. (1982a). In terms of the large woody debris needed, fish habitat requirements extend beyond the bank into the "riparian area of influence" (Sedell et al. 1989). Fishery and forestry managers must expand their traditional thinking and begin to manage the wood in the riparian zone to provide both present and future sources of large debris (Figure 15.14). Rainville et al. (1985) presented a model with management prescriptions for the riparian zone. The model maximizes recruitment of wood to a stream by setting a standard for thinning stands in the riparian zone. Rainville et al. also recommended opening 4–5% of the streambank length per decade, provided that lengths of the openings do not exceed 180 m.

Rearing Pools

Some of the earliest efforts to develop pools in western streams occurred in the Sierra Nevada of California, where various structures were built. Forty-one structures built on the East Fork of the Kaweah River during the 1930s were evaluated 18 years later by Ehlers (1956). Although most of the other structures had failed, 9 of 15 log dams had survived; 6 were operating properly and providing added trout habitat. Flows as high as 70 m³/s, about 500 times base flow, were estimated to have occurred since construction.

Small log and rock step dams were constructed to provide additional trout habitat in the headwaters of Sagehen Creek, California, in 1957. No trout were present in this area, so brook trout taken from lower Sagehen Creek were introduced to the newly formed pools. The trout survived and grew well, establishing a self-sustaining population (Gard 1961a). After 12 years, the area was resurveyed; 6 of the 14 original dams were in good to excellent condition and the trout population had persisted (Gard 1972). The technique was believed to be a cost-effective way to enhance headwater populations. In one Montana trout stream, however, step dams had very short useful lives, the majority lasting only about 1 year (Lund 1976).

The importance of pools as summer rearing habitats for juvenile coho salmon has stimulated several efforts to create new pools in the Oregon Coast Range. Pools are scarce during low summer flows in many coastal streams that have bedrock substrates. Personnel of the U.S. Bureau of Land Management used dynamite to blast a test pool in a sandstone bedrock section of Vincent Creek, Oregon (Anderson 1973a). Initial results appeared favorable, and 12 additional pools were created in 1974. The comprehensive follow-up report produced by Anderson and Miyajima (1975) is an exemplary model for project evaluation. Diagrams of techniques and recommendations for improvement accompany an evaluation of fish populations before and after the project.

Although only one sample was obtained in the year before construction and two in the year after, some of the changes observed were large enough to be statistically significant. Numbers of juvenile coho salmon in the new pools of Vincent Creek were 10 times greater than they were in comparable areas before blasting (Anderson and Miyajima 1975). Coho salmon in the newly formed pools were significantly longer than those found in the control areas before construction, but fish in the control riffle were also larger than before. No change was found in cutthroat trout abundance, but those in the new pools averaged 8 cm larger than fish in control areas. These larger fish have provided recreation for anglers, but they may also have become predators on juvenile coho salmon (J. W. Anderson, U.S. Bureau of Land Management, personal communication). The

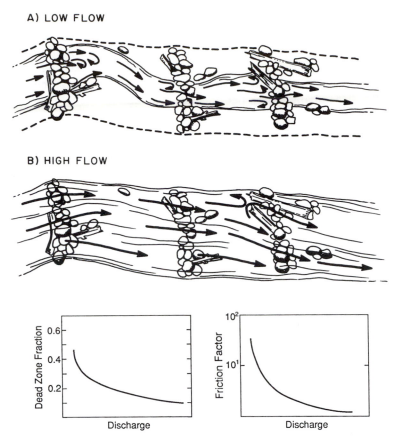

FIGURE 15.13.—Changes in the dead zone fraction and in flow resistance over a range of discharges in a simple, boulder-berm channel (above) compared to those in a channel with large woody debris (facing page). (After Kaufmann 1987.)

data were too limited to assess changes in other fish species (speckled dace, redside shiner, and age-0 steelhead).

These pools also may have provided thermal refuges during summer low flows. Water temperatures at the bottom of one pool were 2.2°C cooler than peak temperatures in an adjacent riffle. Also, temperatures were above 22°C for a much shorter period each day in the pool than in the riffle (Anderson and Miyajima 1975). Unanticipated benefits from the newly formed pools included heightened production of crayfish, which are increasingly sought for sport and food in some coastal areas of Oregon. Another benefit has been the occasional deposition of gravel at the tail of a pool, which has been used by steelhead for spawning.

The Oregon Department of Fish and Wildlife created 15 pools with dynamite on six tributaries of the Siuslaw River (Hutchison 1973). No significant changes in fish populations have been observed, but a few cutthroat trout have been found in pools where none had occurred before. One explanation for the failure of coho salmon to respond may be the very low numbers of adult fish that are able to spawn in the gravel-limited system.

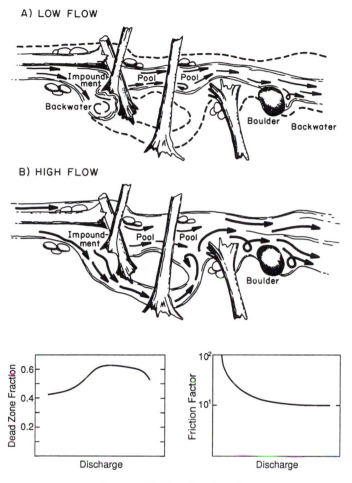

A) LOW FLOW

B) HIGH FLOW

FIGURE 15.13.—Continued.

In a nearby area, however, results of pool blasting appeared more favorable. In 1978, U.S. Forest Service personnel blasted seven pools in Cedar Creek, a tributary to the Siuslaw River; in 1979, they enlarged five natural pools in a tributary of the Smith River. The pools have been self-cleaning, as planned. Those on Cedar Creek in particular have stimulated a substantial increase in numbers of juvenile coho salmon rearing in an area that was predominantly bedrock. Evaluation of the project suggested the value of varying the size and configuration of the pools; small pools created with just a few sticks of dynamite may have more potential as rearing habitat than previously appreciated. Eight years after construction, the pools in both streams were still functioning; 2 of the 12 pools have filled with gravel, but these are now used for spawning by chinook salmon (D. A. Heller, U.S. Forest Service, personal communication).

Blasting of pools to enhance rearing habitat has been restricted to streams with a substrate of solid bedrock and low ability to store bedload within their channels. The technique has been only somewhat successful. Efforts to create pools in

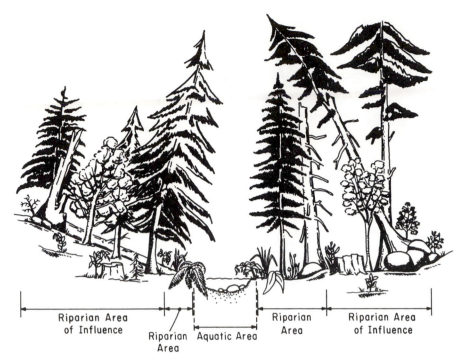

FIGURE 15.14.—Long-term management of fish habitat includes management of the riparian area of influence. (Sedell et al. 1989.)

streams with more typical rubble–cobble substrates probably would be unsuccessful because the pools would fill rapidly unless they were designed to ensure hydraulic scouring.

Winter Habitat

Evidence increasingly points to the importance of winter habitat as a limit on production of salmonid smolts in some stream systems. Intermittent side pools, back channels, and other areas of relatively still water that become inundated during high flows provide valuable winter habitat for juvenile salmonids, particularly in coastal areas (Bustard and Narver 1975a, 1975b; Kralik and Sowerwine 1977; Tschaplinski and Hartman 1983; Hartman and Brown 1987). In Carnation Creek, British Columbia, overwinter survival of juvenile coho salmon that moved into a side-channel tributary in the fall averaged 74% for four winters. Comparable survival of fish remaining in the main channel was 23% (Narver 1978). In southeastern Alaska, most wintering salmonids stay in deep pools with woody cover (Heifetz et al. 1986). In another southeastern Alaska study, two streams that were selectively cleaned of woody debris showed a decline in juvenile salmonid production. Age-1 and older coho salmon and Dolly Varden were most affected by the loss of overwintering habitat (Dolloff 1986).

Studies on winter growth and survival of fish in natural spring ponds on the Olympic Peninsula of Washington suggest that increasing the area of lowland ponds adjacent to salmonid streams has great potential for enhancing abundance of coho salmon (Peterson 1982a, 1982b). Many juvenile salmon that had reared in streams during spring and summer moved into these springs ponds during fall and winter. Fish in the ponds survived and grew better than those overwintering in tributary streams.

As part of enhancement efforts on Fish Creek, Oregon, an off-channel pond was developed (Everest et al. 1986). The pond has been highly successful, representing less than 1% of the basin's habitat but contributing 50% of the coho salmon smolts 3 years after construction (Everest et al. 1987b). Overwinter survival of coho salmon exceeds 50% in the pond but is less than 30% in other areas.

Augmenting Streamflow

Augmenting low summer flows by building small check dams on headwater lakes has been an effective and inexpensive way to enhance habitats for resident trout in the Sierra Nevada of California (Burghduff 1934; Cronemiller and Fraser 1954; Cronemiller 1955). Application of this technique to anadromous fish has been limited, however. Several studies have shown a strong positive association of streamflow with natural production of coho salmon (Smoker 1955; Mathews and Olson 1980; Scarnecchia 1981); thus, increasing production of anadromous salmonids by supplementing low summer streamflow with water stored upstream might be possible. One such project on a 28-hectare lake on Vancouver Island, British Columbia, provides an additional 0.04–0.06 m^3/s of flow downstream during the dry summer (Canada Department of Fisheries and Oceans and B.C. Ministry of the Environment 1980). Before any large-scale development of this kind goes forward, it will be important to insure that limits on carrying capacity in winter will not negate benefits gained during the summer and fall.

A more promising approach is to augment flow in intermittent streams supporting anadromous fish. At least one such attempt has been made in a steelhead stream in eastern Oregon (West et al. 1965b). Subterranean weirs, constructed with plastic sheeting placed in trenches, brought groundwater to the surface and maintained surface flow for short distances above and below some of the structures, where the channel had previously been dry. The scheme was considered expensive and impractical, however, because of the large number of structures required and the damage sustained during spring runoff (Claire 1978a).

Building dams may not be the only means of augmenting streamflow. An unexpected increase in low flow occurred when a heavily grazed section of stream riparian habitat in eastern Oregon was fenced to exclude livestock (Winegar 1977). A 4-km section was fenced in 1966, and 5.6 km of stream channel were added to the exclosure in 1974. In spite of the significant increase in riparian vegetation, summer low flow has increased. In addition, the stream no longer consistently freezes solid during winter (Winegar 1978). Although the cause of the increased flow is not certain, removal of the cattle reduced streamside soil compaction, apparently resulting in increased infiltration and greater groundwater recharge (H. H. Winegar, Oregon Department of Fish and Wildlife, personal communication).

Adding Nutrients

Some evidence (reviewed by Hall and Knight 1981) suggests that stream chemistry influences the abundance and growth of juvenile salmonids. A few attempts have been made to increase biological production in streams by adding nutrients. Stockner and Shortreed (1978) and Gregory (1980) showed measurable responses of attached algae to nutrient addition in small-scale experiments in British Columbia and Oregon. An experiment in British Columbia showed a response of stream invertebrates to the addition of cereal grain and soybeans (Mundie et al. 1983). An earlier fertilization experiment by Huntsman (1948) in an eastern Canada stream showed a small increase in the abundance of juvenile Atlantic salmon and associated fish species, as well as some increase in invertebrate numbers.

One large-scale fertilization experiment in British Columbia had as an objective the increased production of anadromous salmonids. In a pilot study during 1981, personnel of the Fisheries Branch of the Ministry of the Environment added inorganic phosphorus (P) and nitrogen (N) to two sections of the Keogh River, a nutrient-poor system on northeastern Vancouver Island. Rolled barley was added to one additional section. In the sections where inorganic nutrients were added, positive response of attached algae was followed by substantial increases in growth of juvenile coho salmon and steelhead (Perrin et al. 1987). In the section where grain was added, salmonid growth increased, but less so than in the sections fertilized with inorganic nutrients. Based on those results, an enrichment experiment was carried out in the entire river from 1984 through 1987. From May through September each year, approximately 13 tonnes of inorganic fertilizer (N and P) were added to 29 km of the Keogh River (average flow during the fertilization period was 1.2–2.5 m^3/s). Downstream trapping allowed assessment of any change in output of smolts.

The primary influence on steelhead was an increase in growth rate and a consequent reduction of 1 year in the predominant age of smolting (Slaney et al. 1986). Total smolt output increased substantially. For the years when smolts had been fully affected by fertilization, their abundance was approximately double the previous average level of 6,000 (P. A. Slaney, Fisheries Branch, B.C. Ministry of the Environment, personal communication). Juvenile coho salmon also appeared to benefit from the fertilization, but evaluation of a change in smolt production was more difficult for this species. Analysis of the results of the Keogh River project continues. In the meantime, fertilization work is beginning in two other British Columbia rivers, including the Nechako River with a flow of approximately 55 m^3/s.

Based on these results, further experimental work on nutrient addition to streams seems warranted. Though requiring continual nutrient inputs, this nonstructural approach to enhancement is more easily reversible than most structural work if it proves to be ineffective or undesirable. This advantage, coupled with the recent finding by Bilby and Bisson (1989) that production of juvenile coho salmon can depend more on production of algae than on contributions of allochthonous organic material from litterfall, further supports the continued study of nutrient addition as a means to increase production of anadromous salmonids in watersheds of naturally low fertility.

Considerations in Planning and Evaluating Habitat Modifications

In the approximately 10 years since we began our review of habitat modification, activity in this field has exploded. Annual expenditures of many millions of dollars are now being made for habitat modification. With this increase in emphasis and activity, planning, coordination, and evaluating must be stepped up as well. We offer the following guidance for planning and evaluating this work.

Improved methods of evaluation are a primary need. These methods must be accompanied by a greater commitment to evaluation by the program managers and biologists who implement projects. Expenditures of such magnitude require responsible accountability, a feature that has been woefully inadequate in many enhancement programs. Attempts have been made recently to develop strategic plans for evaluation (Everest et al., in press), but none so far have successfully made the necessary compromise between coverage and cost. Providing intensive evaluation of every enhancement project is unwise; the cost of such evaluation will probably exceed the cost of the enhancement program. Selected programs should be intensively evaluated to determine their success.

For the purpose of extrapolating results to programs or basins that have not been intensively evaluated, development of a system of watershed classification should be a priority. Here again, some proposals have been made recently (Frissell et al. 1986; Rosgen and Fittante 1986), but nothing has progressed to the point of providing practical guidelines for on-the-ground sampling.

Another important component of planning is a watershed-wide perspective, which allows projects to be sited within basins and subbasins in a way that provides adequate dispersion of appropriate habitats throughout the basin (Everest and Sedell 1984). With the number of federal, state, and provincial agencies, Indian tribes, and other groups doing enhancement work in some large drainages (especially in the Columbia River basin), achieving this goal will require substantial coordination.

Physical scientists should participate more in planning and evaluating enhancement programs. Stream hydraulics, hydrology, and geomorphology must be carefully evaluated before any instream work is undertaken (Apmann and Otis 1965; Heede 1980; Klingeman 1984; Orsborn and Anderson 1986). Early recognition of the importance of this point by Mackin (1948) seems worthy of emphasis.

> In connection with control of rivers by men, a safe general implication is that the engineer who alters natural equilibrium relations by diversion or damming or channel-improvement measures will often find that he has a bull by the tail and is unable to let go—as he continues to correct or suppress undesirable phases of the chain reaction of the stream to the initial "stress" he will necessarily place increasing emphasis on study of the genetic aspects of the equilibrium in order that he may work *with* rivers, rather than merely *on* them. It is certain that the long-term response of streams to the operations of the present generation of engineers will provide much employment for future generations of engineers and lawyers.

A broad ecological perspective is necessary in planning. Habitat improvement sometimes may be based on the desires of anglers rather than on requirements of the fish (Hunt 1978). Also, habitat-improvement projects are often directed at only one species of fish, generally the "preferred" fish in a region. All fish species and stocks present should be considered or adverse side effects may result. Narver (1976) presented an excellent example. In British Columbia, enhancement of a sockeye salmon run was so successful that increased commercial harvesting of sockeye salmon threatened to deplete other stocks of fish that migrate along with them, including the valuable steelhead. Anderson (1984) found that creating habitat for coho salmon resulted in a decline in available habitat for other species and in the number of steelhead.

A related concern is raised by proposals to increase access into a basin for anadromous species. When a barrier to anadromous fish is removed, how might resident fish populations above the barrier be affected? How will fish passage structures such as ladders or steeppasses affect esthetic values? "Improvement" projects may create unanticipated side effects, both favorable and unfavorable. Stream-improvement plans should be evaluated not only in terms of the proposed benefit, but also with thought to potential adverse effects. The failure to adequately consider this need early in the planning process can result in substantial frustration and unneeded expenditures.

Another requirement for improved effectiveness of enhancement projects is greater concern for analysis of limiting factors in project planning. As we discussed earlier, this analysis is complex and difficult, but it must be attempted. When habitat improvement projects are planned, seasonal and age-specific habitat requirements of target species should be evaluated. Habitat requirements for an individual species may change significantly during the year, particularly between summer and winter (Chapman 1966; Bustard and Narver 1975a, 1975b; Narver 1976; Bjornn and Reiser 1991). Preferred habitats may also change as fish grow (Mundie 1974; Bustard and Narver 1975a). For example, habitat improvement may be directed at increasing spawning potential, but any increase in production of fry will be negated if rearing habitat or winter cover is not available. In one instance, for example, an attempt was made to increase the quantity of summer habitat for juvenile steelhead in Fish Creek, Oregon (Everest et al. 1985, 1986). The means chosen was to rearrange instream boulders to form berms that increased pool volume in summer. This procedure led to a reduction in winter habitat and thus failed to meet design objectives.

Biologists have often been concerned more with mitigating past problems than with preventing future ones. Several problems in aquatic habitats are associated entirely with processes and management activities well upslope from stream channels, such as the relation between log-debris jams and debris torrents caused by land management activities. In some unstable headwater streams, habitat protection can be accomplished only by controlling timber-harvesting activities and using specific yarding systems and debris-management policies. Although few fishery biologists have experience in related fields such as forestry, soils, and geology, most are associated with personnel who have expertise in these disciplines. Protection of salmonid habitat must be an interdisciplinary activity. As Hynes (1975) stated, "We must . . . not divorce the stream from its valley." We must recognize riparian disturbances and hillslope processes as integral parts of habitat management. Intelligent management of all resources within a basin is the key to maintaining stream systems that have productive habitats (Richards 1964).

Conclusions

The history of habitat rehabilitation and enhancement for stream-dwelling salmonids has been a mixture of failure and success. When adequate documentation has been available, learning from failure has been possible and techniques and approaches have improved. We believe that sufficient background and experience are now accumulating to guide consideration of these techniques as part of fishery management. Future success of habitat restoration will depend on the ability and willingness of current practitioners to continually update their methods and to incorporate new information as it becomes available.

Most fishery managers agree that rehabilitation and modification projects should be evaluated whenever possible. In the past, limited funds and personnel often precluded pre- and postproject evaluation. Managers were required to improve or restore a certain amount of habitat, and they were unable to give adequate consideration to planning and follow-up. We emphasize that proper evaluation of projects is an integral part of any rehabilitation program, and future work should include appropriate evaluations.

Since our earlier reviews on this subject (Hall and Baker 1982; Reeves and Roelofs 1982), a substantially greater dialogue has occurred on the question of identifying limiting factors, and some useful guidelines have been produced (Everest and Sedell 1984; Reeves et al. 1989; Bisson, in press). The discussion remains contentious, however, as might be expected given its complexity, and much more analysis and evaluation are required. One possible guideline that comes from our evaluation is the observation that results of habitat enhancement seem best when premanipulation conditions were the worst.

From an ecological perspective, the techniques of habitat management discussed are often soundly based. They are ideally suited to the goal of maintaining such natural wild stocks as still exist and preserving genetic variability where possible. In the face of increasing concern about the effects of large-scale hatchery production on the genetic constitution of wild stocks, this rationale may be one of the strongest arguments for emphasis on improving quality and quantity of stream habitats.

We conclude by emphasizing what well may be the most important point in this entire review—that habitat rehabilitation must never be viewed as a substitute for habitat protection. This point has often been made (e.g., Narver 1973; Power 1973), but it deserves frequent reinforcement. Communication between fishery managers and foresters is an essential element of habitat protection (e.g., Toews and Brownlee 1981). Habitat management can now be cost-effective and, as we learn more, it should become more so. In almost every instance, however, preventing initial habitat degradation is more economical of total resources than repairing it, and some damage simply is not reversible. Past mistakes require efforts to rehabilitate many streams, but our efforts in habitat management must continue to put an equally strong priority on protection of watershed and stream resources.

Chapter 16

Economic Considerations in Managing Salmonid Habitats

D. D. Huppert and R. D. Fight

The several species of Pacific salmon, Atlantic salmon, trouts, and chars support diverse and widespread fisheries in North America. Salmonid fisheries create substantial economic benefits and are responsible for extensive economic impacts in fishing communities. To obtain the greatest possible benefits from salmonid fisheries, resource managers must tackle some difficult challenges. This chapter highlights the economic dimensions of salmonid fisheries and describes some economic aspects of salmonid resource management. It also provides an introduction to concepts and procedures for measuring the economic values. The discussion proceeds through three main topics: description of economic activity and economic impacts; measurement of economic benefits and costs from salmonid fisheries; and an economic approach to salmonid habitat management.

Economic assessment of resource policy is commonly cast in a benefit–cost framework. This is one means of organizing and summarizing quantitative information about the pros and cons of alternative resource decisions. The benefit–cost approach is reflected in various official government guidelines for project evaluation and regulatory impact analysis. Examples include the U.S. Water Resources Council's (1983) Principles, the President's Executive Order 12291, and the U.S. Forest Service's (1987) Resource Pricing and Valuation Guidelines.

Resource managers frequently need to deal with two distinct economic consequences of management decisions: the size of net economic benefits created, and the distribution of these benefits among regions and resource user groups. The net economic benefit is, ideally, a comprehensive measure of all economic values flowing from the resource management regime minus the associated costs. Economic efficiency analysis is associated with maximizing these net economic benefits. This is the usual domain of benefit–cost analysis.

Most practical management actions benefit some people while harming others; benefits and costs are not uniformly spread among the population. When particular user groups or regional economies are strongly affected, resource managers will want to know about the distribution of net benefits. That information will permit adjustment of management actions to promote income and employment in particular regimes or to achieve a more equitable distribution of benefits.

Influences of Forest and Rangeland Management on Salmonid Fishes and Their Habitats
American Fisheries Society Special Publication 19:559–585, 1991

TABLE 16.1.—Average annual north Pacific commercial salmon catches (tonnes), 1981–1984. (Source: Food and Agriculture Organization 1988.)

Country	Sockeye salmon	Chum salmon	Pink salmon	Coho salmon	Chinook salmon	Total
USSR	4,339	16,063	71,621	3,961	1,551	97,535
Japan	4,376	125,594	12,914	9,450[a]	938	153,272
Canada	19,532	8,832	23,757	9,243	6,772	68,136
USA	109,561	43,564	107,540	20,470	12,679	293,814
Total	137,808	194,053	215,832	43,124	21,940	612,757

[a]Includes Japanese catch of cherry (masu) salmon.

Economic values derived from fishing must be examined in relation to the economic values of other, sometimes incompatible, uses. Because the natural habitat of salmonids, including the waters and surrounding lands, serves competing uses, a benefit–cost approach to resource management must gauge the value of fisheries relative to nonfishery activities such as timber harvesting, cattle grazing, flood control, hydropower, and farming. Because the information requirements are massive, it is a forbidding task to include all these alternative values in a single analysis. However, even when available information is inadequate to support accurate estimation of all economic benefits, it is useful to examine many resource management problems from a benefit–cost perspective.

Noneconomic objectives often cause managers to modify or overrule the economic criteria in decisions. These objectives serve needs not directly connected to the economic well-being of today's human population. They include, for example, preservation of genetic diversity or endangered species, compliance with legal or political requirements, and favors for particular social groups. Nevertheless, economic considerations, such as net economic benefits and economic impacts, encompass some of the major factors used in evaluating resource management regimes, and they heavily influence resource policy formation.

Economic Dimensions of Salmonid Fisheries

Commercial Fisheries

Commercial salmon harvests by all nations bordering the north Pacific Ocean have averaged over 600,000 tonnes in recent years (Table 16.1). The USA ranks highest in volume landed, followed in order by Japan, the USSR, and Canada. In the decade following the declaration of the 200-nautical-mile Exclusive Economic Zone (EEZ), Japanese high-seas salmon catches have dropped by 80%, from almost 80,000 tonnes in 1972–1976 to about 16,000 tonnes in 1982–1985 (Nasaka 1988). Over the same period, U.S. fisheries off Alaska increased by 440%, largely due to record runs of sockeye and pink salmon.

Commercial salmon fisheries are segmented by geographic location and fishing gear employed. Table 16.2 shows catches by the more important gear types. Commercial fishing by purse seine and gill net is widespread in Alaska, the Strait of Georgia, Puget Sound, and the Columbia River. Because international agreements prohibit salmon fishing with nets in the ocean off the continental USA, commercial trolling dominates the ocean fishery off California, Oregon, and

TABLE 16.2.—Estimated number of commercial fishing units and employment in North American Pacific salmon fisheries.

State or province	Number of vessels by gear			Number of crew (including captain)
	Troll gear	Gill net	Purse seine	
Alaska[a]	2,598	7,798	1,372	25,296
British Columbia[b]	1,695	2,234	521	9,616
Washington	650[c]	3,151[d]	445[d]	7,926[d]
Oregon	2,053[c]	718[e]	0	4,085[e]
California	2,562[c]	0	0	5,124[e]
Total	9,558	13,901	2,338	52,047

[a]Ben Muse, Alaska Commercial Fisheries Entry Commission, personal communication of 1988 data.

[b]Michelle James, Canada Department of Fisheries and Oceans, personal communication of 1988 data.

[c]Pacific Fishery Management Council (1989): numbers of troll vessels in Washington, Oregon, and California in 1988.

[d]Natural Resources Consultants (1986): numbers of purse seine and gill net vessels in Washington in 1985, and crew per vessel for troll, gill-net, and purse-seine vessels.

[e]U.S. National Marine Fisheries Service (1980): number of gill-net vessels in Oregon and crew per vessel for Oregon and California.

Washington. Historically, some species of salmon were captured in rivers by traps, "fish wheels," and dip nets during spawning runs (Netboy 1980). These fishing techniques were effective and inexpensive relative to ocean fishing, but are now largely prohibited except in Alaska's Yukon River.

The 25,000 commercial Pacific salmon fishing operations employ about 52,000 fishermen at least part-time in the USA and Canada. Many of these fishing vessels are commercially fished only during peak salmon seasons. Others engage in a variety of commercial marine fisheries during the remainder of the year (e.g., fisheries for Dungeness crab *Cancer magister*, albacore, or groundfish). Recreational fisheries for salmon also support many commercial businesses. For example, in Washington, Oregon, and California, about 760 party-boat and charter-boat operators derive at least some of their total business income from salmon anglers.

By comparison, the average monthly employment in logging was about 22,000 in Oregon and Washington in 1987. Because employment in logging is seasonal, the average monthly employment is substantially less than the total number of people employed in logging at some time during the year. The average monthly employment in the broader timber industry (which includes logging, sawmills, veneer and plywood mills, and pulp and paper mills) in California, Oregon, and Washington was 239,000 in 1987. In Alaska, where the salmon fishery is a major activity that employs about 25,000 people in the harvesting sector alone, the forest industry employs around 3,000 people on a monthly average and generates about $700 million in wholesale value of forest products.

For the USA and Canada combined, the dollar value of salmon sales by fishermen (i.e., ex-vessel value) has grown from about $270 million in the early 1970s to around $500 million in the mid-1980s (Figure 16.1). The wholesale value of finished salmon products (mostly canned pack, cured, and fresh or frozen fillets

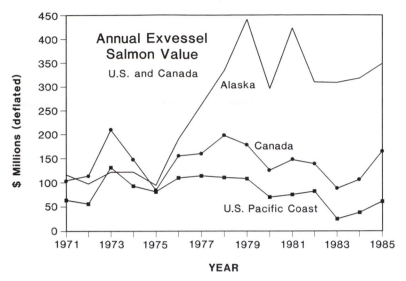

FIGURE 16.1.—Ex-vessel revenues received by U.S. and Canadian salmon fishermen during 1971–1985.

and steaks) in 1985 was $754 million in Alaska, $350 million (U.S. dollar equivalent) in British Columbia, and $143 million among the contiguous Pacific coast states. Among all U.S. commercial fisheries in 1987, the salmon fishery was the first in ex-vessel value and third in total volume. Among renewable resource industries in general, however, the fishery is not a leading economic activity. For example, the estimated wholesale value of timber products produced in Alaska, Washington, Oregon, and California combined was about $12.7 billion in 1987.

Artificial salmon production, including hatchery-raised salmon released to the open sea (popularly called salmon "ranching") and penned or caged fish (called salmon "farming"), has grown rapidly in importance during the past decade. Japanese production of ranched chum salmon, for example, rose from about 2 million adult fish in 1960 to a peak of about 50 million fish (weighing about 168,000 tonnes) in the early 1980s. Production of farmed Atlantic salmon expanded from 11,800 tonnes in 1981 to 98,000 tonnes in 1988. Norway is the leading producer of Atlantic salmon, but several other nations are increasing their participation in farming and ranching of salmon. Production of artificially propagated salmon is expected to double by the year 2000 (Lannan 1988). If this product becomes a close substitute for salmon captured in traditional ways, the market price of fresh and frozen salmon could be depressed, and ocean harvests of wild stocks would decline in importance. At this time, it is unclear if the farmed salmon will ultimately take the market from ocean harvests or if the two products will find separate market niches, each with steady or increasing demand (Johnston 1988).

Recreational Fisheries

Recreational salmonid fishing is more widespread than commercial salmonid fishing in North America, and it involves more people overall. Sport harvests of Pacific salmon nearly doubled from an average of 546,000 fish per year in

TABLE 16.3.—Salmon sportfishing trips and expenditures in the north-western USA. Economic values are in US$.

State	Estimated number of angler trips	Estimated expenditure per trip	Total estimated expenditures per year
Alaska[a]	689,600	$76.78	$ 52,947,488
California[b]	143,800	$49.90	$ 7,175,620
Idaho[c]	13,000	$43.23	$ 561,990
Oregon[d]	233,500	$49.15	$ 11,476,525
Washington[e]	1,505,200	$59.57	$ 89,664,764
Total or mean	2,585,100	$62.60	$161,826,387

[a]Total expenditures equals salmon fishing expenditure for the southcentral region, from Jones and Stokes Associates (1987, page 4-2), scaled up by factor of 1.39 for the Alaska total, based on the proportion of Alaska recreational salmon harvest that occurs in the southcentral region (Mills 1986, page 22). The number of trips was estimated by dividing total expenditures by the per-trip expenditure.

[b]Average number of ocean angler trips, 1981–1985, from Pacific Fishery Management Council (1988); expenditure per salmon angler trip was calculated from data in Thomson and Huppert (1987).

[c]Number of salmon fishing days in 1986, from Pacific Marine Fisheries Commission (1988, page 23); the average cost per angler-day for steelhead fishing (primary-purpose trips) is from Donnelly et al. (1985, page 8).

[d]Average number of ocean trips, 1981–1985, from Pacific Fishery Management Council (1988); expenditure per trip is the average for private and charter boat trips from Carter and Radtke (1988).

[e]Average for 1982–1985, from ICF Technology, Inc. (1988, page 20).

1950–1954 to over 1 million fish per year in 1976–1985. Total number of angler trips per year was about 2.6 million in the mid-1980s (Table 16.3). Although it takes far fewer fish than the commercial fishery, the sport fishery harvests a substantial portion of coho and chinook salmon, and it takes almost all of the steelhead. As shown in Table 16.3, annual expenditures by Pacific salmon anglers on gear, travel, and other fishing-related expenses was about $162 million.

The number of U.S. freshwater and saltwater sport fishermen more than doubled between 1955 and 1985 (Table 16.4). Over the same period, days fished increased from less than 400 million to nearly 1 billion. In 1985, about 40% of the 42 million freshwater anglers in the USA fished for salmon, steelhead, or trout in fresh water at least part of the time, and salmonid species were sought on about 12% of the days fished in 1985 (Table 16.5). If expenditures per day for salmonid fishing equals the average for all fishing, the salmonid recreational trips account for about 12% of the more than $19 billion spent on sport fishing in 1985.

Concept of Economic Impacts

Regional economic impact analysis attempts to predict changes in personal income, economic output, and employment caused by the expansion or contraction of a specific economic activity. An initial change, such as the opening of a new industrial plant or a new national park, directly impacts the regional economy by providing new employment and regional income. This initial effect sets off a series of additional regional economic impacts. The new industry purchases supplies, equipment, and services from other sectors, which expand to support the new industry. The increased income paid to the local work force and

TABLE 16.4.—Freshwater and saltwater fishing in the USA, 1955–1985. (Source: U.S. Fish and Wildlife Service 1982, 1988.)

Sector	1955	1960	1965	1970	1975	1980	1985
Participation, thousands of anglers							
Total[a]	20,813	25,323	28,348	33,158	41,299	41,873	46,357
Freshwater	18,420	21,677	23,962	29,363	36,599	37,081	39,823
Saltwater	4,557	6,292	8,305	9,460	13,738	13,332	13,709
Fishing effort, thousands of days							
Total[b]	397,447	465,769	522,759	706,187	1,058,075	1,001,637	976,564
Freshwater	338,826	385,167	426,922	592,494	890,576	840,607	827,944
Saltwater	58,621	80,602	95,837	113,694	167,499	160,678	155,172
Aggregate expenditures, thousands of U.S. dollars (deflated; 1985 = 100)							
Total[b,c]	7,142,161	9,104,102	9,139,661	12,586,029	21,846,052	23,461,049	28,145,527
Freshwater	5,317,946	6,985,489	6,641,272	9,477,633	16,114,312	18,767,651	19,382,971
Saltwater	1,824,215	2,118,609	2,498,402	3,108,396	5,731,740	4,693,398	7,242,874
Expenditure per day (US$)							
All Fishing	17.97	19.55	17.48	17.82	20.65	23.42	28.82
Freshwater	15.70	18.14	15.56	16.00	18.09	22.33	23.57
Saltwater	31.12	26.28	26.07	27.34	34.22	29.21	46.68

[a]Saltwater and freshwater fishermen do not add to total fishermen because some anglers fished both types of water.

[b]Detail does not always add to total because of multiple responses.

[c]Dollar values are corrected for inflation according to the gross national product price deflator, base 1985.

landowners fuels an expansion of consumer demand for goods and services from retail and wholesale dealers. The economic expansion may cause immigration of labor and firms to the region and increased employment of previously unemployed regional labor.

The regional economic impact is expressed in three successive stages: a "direct impact," which is the increased regional economic output, income, and employment occurring in the expanding sector; an "indirect impact," which is the expansion of industries associated with or supporting the sector that started the expansion; and an "induced impact," which is the broader expansion of all local businesses induced by the demand for consumer goods. The ratio of direct plus indirect impact to direct impact is called a type-I impact multiplier. The ratio of total direct, indirect, and induced impact to direct impact is a type-II impact multiplier. If the direct income per dollar of expenditure by consumers (called the direct income coefficient) is known, the type-I or type-II regional impact can be computed by the shortcut of multiplying the direct change in expenditure times the direct income coefficient times the income multiplier.

For example, a new fishery that generates $1 million dollars of new sales may directly employ 20 people and pay out $500,000 in local wages, rents, and profits. The remaining $500,000 is paid to suppliers, stockholders, and others living outside the region. The increased regional income of $500,000 is a direct income impact. Indirect expansion of ancillary businesses may add 10 more employees and other $250 thousand to local income. Induced expansion of local retail and wholesale outlets could add another 5 employees and $100 thousand to income. In this example, the type-I income multiplier (i.e., the direct plus indirect income

TABLE 16.5.—Number of U.S. freshwater anglers (16 years old or older), days fished, and expenditures by type of fish sought, 1985. (Source: U.S. Fish and Wildlife Service 1988.)

Type of fishing	Number of fishermen (1,000s)	Number of days fished (1,000s)	Estimated expenditures[a] (US$1,000s)
Exclusive of Great Lakes			
All species[b]	38,433	785,855	17,795,427
Trout	11,317	159,255	1,629,350
Salmon	1,170	15,562	159,216
Steelhead	850	12,981	132,810
Great Lakes			
All species[b]	3,766	46,417	1,560,107
Lake trout	910	9,481	126,704
Other trout	511	6,730	89,939
Salmon	1,425	12,490	166,916
Steelhead	555	7,826	104,586
Total freshwater			
All species[b]	42,199	832,272	19,355,534
Trout	11,828	165,985	1,719,289
Lake trout	910	9,481	126,704
Salmon	2,595	28,052	326,132
Steelhead	1,405	20,807	237,396

[a]Expenditures by species sought are estimated by allocation of total national expenditures proportionally among trips for various species.

[b]All species does not equal sum of individual species because many trips are not exclusively associated with a single species.

divided by direct income) is 750/500 = 1.5. The type-II income multiplier (the ratio of total income impact to direct income) is 850/500 = 1.7.

The size of the impact multiplier varies among regions and economic sectors. It depends on the extent to which the regional economy is an integrated, independent unit. To the extent that the firms and consumers must purchase supplies from outside the region, the dollars being spent "leak out" of the local economy, and do not induce increased regional economic activity. The degree of "leakage" thus determines the size of the total impacts. Total income impacts experienced per dollar of sales will generally be lower in a tourism-based economy (in which nearly everything sold to residents and tourists is imported from outside) than in a large, integrated economy. Stated differently, impact multipliers are larger when the local economy accounts for a larger fraction of the total value added to products sold. Retail sales, for example, represent only a small portion of total value added. To account for a large portion of value added, the regional economy must have basic industries producing raw materials and manufactured goods.

Sample impact calculation.—To determine the amount of interindustry purchases, direct payments to households (i.e., direct income coefficient), and income "leakages" due to imported goods, the analyst needs a complete table of regional economic accounts. Most economic impact analysts use an input–output (I–O) model to serve this purpose. The basis for the I–O model is a matrix of intersectoral transactions showing how a dollar of final sales in each economic

TABLE 16.6.—Clatsop County (Oregon) income coefficients for commercial fisheries based upon the U.S. Forest Service's IMPLAN model. (Source: Carter and Radtke 1988, page 151, as modified by H. Radtke, personal communication.)

Salmon harvester expenditure category	Personal income coefficients[a]			
	Direct	Indirect	Induced	Total
Repair work	0.3016	0.0694	0.1401	0.5111
Gear replacement	0.2934	0.0414	0.2885	0.6233
Fuel and oil	0.3601	0.0524	0.3035	0.7160
Ice and bait	0.5015	0.0877	0.3173	0.9065
Food and supplies	0.2842	0.0627	0.2603	0.6072
Transportation	0.4198	0.0512	0.1909	0.6619
Dues and fees	0.3072	0.0483	0.2377	0.5932
Miscellaneous	0.6560	0.0852	0.5044	1.2456
Wages, salaries, profit	1.000	0.3716	0.2512	1.6228

[a]Each income coefficient equals the amount of personal income in Clatsop County associated with one dollar of sales in the sector identified by the row heading. Direct income is essentially the amount of salary, wages, and other income in the sector per dollar of sales. Indirect income represents analogous income payments in other sectors of Clatsop County due to purchases by the row sector per dollar of sales. The induced income coefficient represents income generated throughout the county due to increased expenditures associated with increased personal income.

sector is distributed: purchases from other sectors in the region; payments for labor, rents, and interest to local lenders; and payments to suppliers, lenders, and owners outside the region. Basic accounting convention requires that, in each sector, the total receipts from sales equal the sum of payments to workers, interest on loans, earning retained by owners, rents paid for land and buildings, and purchases from local and out-of-region suppliers (including nontangible purchases for insurance, freight, etc.). Put differently, the market value of outputs must equal the payments for all inputs. This is the accounting standard that makes the total national income equal the value of net national product. The I–O matrix for a region simply shows the sources of receipts for each output sector and the destinations of all payments to each input sector.

The I–O table for a region can be developed from detailed surveys of local businesses, or it can be constructed from national I–O coefficients, which are readily available. If national coefficients are used, we assume that underlying production technology is unchanging across regions. If a farmed trout worth $1.00 requires $0.30 of feed on a national average, then 30% of trout sales value is consumed in feed costs everywhere. Total sales for each sector in the region, which can be derived from special surveys of businesses in the region, are needed to complete a regional I–O model based on national coefficients. One I–O model used for county-level impact analyses is the U.S. Forest Service's IMPLAN model (Siverts et al. 1983).

An example of an IMPLAN-based income impact analysis, taken from Carter and Radtke (1988), is summarized in Tables 16.6 and 16.7. Based on survey information from Clatsop County, Oregon, it was determined that the nine sectors represented by rows in Table 16.6 account for all expenditures by the salmon fishing industry. For each row sector in the table, the direct income coefficients are dollars of income payments made per dollar spent in each sector in the county.

TABLE 16.7.—Calculation of total income impact associated with the landing of a commercially caught chinook salmon in Clatsop County, Oregon, at a price of US$23.31. (Based on Carter and Radtke 1988.)

Salmon harvester expenditure category	Percent of expenditure in category	Dollars spent in category per fish	Income impact per fish
Repair work	4.10	$ 0.9557	$ 0.490
Gear replacement	6.84	$ 1.594	$ 0.996
Fuel and oil	10.26	$ 2.392	$ 1.712
Ice and bait	1.03	$ 0.2401	$ 0.217
Food and supplies	5.13	$ 1.196	$ 0.726
Transportation	2.52	$ 0.5874	$ 0.388
Dues and fees	0.68	$ 0.1585	$ 0.095
Miscellaneous	2.52	$ 0.5874	$ 0.730
Wages, salaries, profit	66.92[a]	$15.60	$25.307
Total	100.00	$23.31	$30.66

[a]Assumes fixed costs (interest, depreciation, insurance, etc.) are not increased if an additional chinook salmon is landed.

For instance, each dollar of boat repair work causes a $0.3016 direct income impact, a $0.0694 indirect impact, a $0.1401 induced impact, and a $0.5111 total county impact. This implies a type-I income multiplier of (0.3016 + 0.0694)/0.3016 = 1.23, and a type-II multiplier of (0.3016 + 0.0694 + 0.1401)/0.3016 = 1.69 for salmon vessel repair services. Note that the total county impact of a $1.00 expenditure is less than $1.00 for most sectors, indicating substantial spending on products imported from outside the county. Also, the direct coefficient of "wages, salaries, and profits" equals 1.0, because all payments to labor and profits are taken as direct contributions to county income.

To compute income impacts from the harvest of an additional chinook salmon, each of the sectoral income coefficients in Table 16.6 would be multiplied by the amount fishing firms spend on each expenditure category per fish. The total impact equals the sum of these products across categories. In Table 16.7, the typical costs of a salmon troller, expressed as percent of fish sales (column 1), are multiplied by the fish price ($23.31) to obtain expenditures per fish by category (column 2). Multiplying the expenditure per fish in each category by the corresponding total income coefficients from Table 16.6 yields the income impact per fish (column 3) in each category. Summation of the income impacts across categories yields the estimated total county income impact of $30.66 per chinook salmon landed. This represents the added county income associated with landing and exporting one additional chinook salmon, if the average costs in each category remain constant.

Impacts versus fishery benefits.—Users of economic impact analyses need to be aware of certain limitations and common errors. First, because regional impact models are often concerned primarily with a small region or community, there is a tendency to focus on the in-region impact and to disregard the possible compensating effects elsewhere. For example, if the total allowable harvest of salmon is fixed, an increased catch in one county necessarily means a decrease in other counties. Overall, the positive impacts will be approximately balanced by negative impacts. The I–O impact analysis can predict the amount of income that will be redistributed among counties. Only increased fish abundance may generate a real increase in total fishery-related income.

Similar considerations apply to impacts associated with recreational fishing. An expansion of recreational fishing in one locale may attract anglers and expenditures from elsewhere. Thus, expansion in one region will be mainly at the expense of reduced expenditures in another region. In aggregate, therefore, a new recreational facility mainly shifts income and employment among neighboring regions. From a national perspective, the impacts generally wash out; they do not reflect a net increase in income or employment.

Second, economic impacts calculated from I–O models are only as accurate as the estimate of the initial change that sets off the sequence of impacts. To project whether a new reservoir, an improved fish-stocking program, or increased availability of fish will attract additional boaters and fishermen to a community, the analyst needs a regional recreational demand model of the type described in the following section. That model will predict shifts in recreational activity. If the shift in recreational activity in accurately predicted, the associated impact analysis may provide useful planning advice to the affected communities. It is not correct simply to assume that every fishery enhancement will attract more fishermen, who will spend more money on recreation.

Similarly, the economic impact of an increase in commercial harvest will depend crucially on the character of the initial change. An increase in fishing activity associated with an allocation of harvest quota will have a different economic effect from an increased harvest due to enhanced fish abundance. The allocation will not affect the fishing costs in various expenditure categories, whereas an enhanced stock should decrease average costs per fish. These two contrasting mechanisms will generate different economic impacts.

Third, changes in regional output, income, and employment do not measure the economic *benefits* associated with the commercial fishery or recreation. Instead, they represent accounting measures of transactions and income payments. To determine whether a fishery generates net benefits, we need to estimate the project's economic value to consumers or sportsmen and subtract the cost of building and operating the project. This net benefit would represent the project's value to the economy at large. Economic impact analyses do not address the question of whether values generated exceed costs of particular policies, projects, or enhancements.

A full explanation of the input–output approach to impact analysis is beyond the scope of this chapter. Interested readers are referred to textbooks such as Miernyk (1965). More extensive explanations of impact analysis applied to fisheries are available in Scott (1984), Radtke (1984), and Radtke et al. (1987).

Summary

This section has shown that North American salmonid fisheries are extremely widespread, diverse, and economically significant. Salmonids provide employment and income to thousands of commercial fishermen and shoreside workers. Salmon and steelhead are extremely popular target species among recreational fishermen in Alaska and the Pacific Northwest, and trout fishing occupies an important place in the freshwater recreational fishery. All this suggests that salmonids are a resource worthy of substantial consideration in resource management decisions.

Concept and Measurement of Economic Value

Estimating the monetary value of diverse products and services flowing from the resource is an important step in assessing the economic benefits of any fishery, fish stock, or conservation program. Two major categories of value are associated with fish stocks. The first category, "use value," is the value associated with catching, consuming, or otherwise directly using the fish. The use value obviously includes the value of commercial products and recreational fishing. Use values are frequently reflected in market prices or the amounts that individuals pay to obtain access to a resource. For nonmarket goods, like fish stocks in most water bodies, economists must estimate use values using models that are described below.

The second category, "existence value," is the value that people place on simply knowing that something exists or is preserved for future generations. For example, many people express a willingness to incur costs to preserve the Grand Canyon or the giant sequoias even though they themselves may never visit these natural wonders. Randall and Stoll (1983) noted that all objects conceivably have existence value, but that existence value probably will be of most importance for unique or irreplaceable natural assets. Although existence value is infrequently measured, it may turn out to be an important component of value for some unique or endangered salmonid stocks.

In dealing with any resource value, it is important to distinguish between total and marginal values. The total economic value of a recreational fishing site, for example, is expressed as an "all-or-nothing" site value—that is, the value of having the existing site versus not having the site at all. In other cases, we may be interested in the value of additional fishing trips or the value of improved fishing conditions at the site. Incremental changes or enhancements to the fishing site entail "marginal values," rather than an all-or-nothing site value. The increased value of fishing at a site due to a small fish stock enhancement is a marginal value. Similarly for commercial fishing, the value of an additional tonne of salmon harvested is marginal.

The following discussion outlines the concepts and measurement techniques for use values, emphasizing the special problems and techniques appropriate to fisheries applications. Existence values are so rarely estimated that only a short review of existence value information is provided.

Concept of Use Value

The use value component of economic value can be separated into value to consumers (recreational fishermen and buyers of commercial fishery products) and value to producers (those harvesting fish or supplying services to fishermen). Values derived from both commercial products and recreational activities are based on a common underlying economic concept.

Economic value measures for consumers.—For consumers, the value of a quantity of product can be expressed as either "willingness to pay" (WTP) or "willingness to accept compensation" (WTA), depending upon whether we are considering adding to or subtracting from existing entitlements. The WTP value is

FIGURE 16.2.—Typical de-
mand curve showing the relation
between the quantity that consumers demand and the price
they pay. When quantity Q1 is
sold for price P1, area A represents consumer surplus, the
amount consumers would be
willing to pay above the amount
they actually pay. When quantity
Q2 is sold for price P2, consumer
surplus is the sum of areas A, B,
and C.

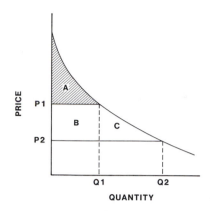

equivalent to the maximum reduction is spendable income a person is willing to incur to obtain a desired commodity or to engage in a desired activity (i.e., the price one is willing to pay). The WTA value is the minimum increase in income a person would accept in order to give up something (i.e., the minimum compensation that is acceptable). If the person is giving up an owned object or resource, the WTA value may also be termed the "willingness to sell." When the quantity being valued is small relative to total supply, and if it is not critical to the consumer, the WTP and WTA values would be about equal.

For most commodities that are supplied in competitive markets, the amount that people actually pay is determined by a market price. The amount actually paid for commodities (i.e., the price times quantity purchased) is generally less than the total amount consumers would be willing to pay rather than go without the commodity. That is, the total value (the "all-or-nothing" value) is greater than the sales revenue generated in the market. For example, people cannot survive without water, yet the amount people spend for water service is frequently a very minor fraction of the household budget. When WTP exceeds the amount consumers actually have to pay for a commodity, the excess of WTP over and above actual payment is called the "consumer surplus." This is a measure of the net value gained by consumers in the purchase of the commodity.

Economic benefits enjoyed by consumers are reflected in the market demand curve, an example of which is depicted in Figure 16.2. The demand curve indicates the quantity (e.g., cases of canned pink salmon, or thousands of fishing trips) that consumers will purchase as a function of price charged. If people allocate their incomes among purchases in order to maximize their well-being, consumers will purchase more of a product when prices are low and less when prices are high, giving the demand curve a negative slope. The price corresponding to any particular quantity supplied (the demand price) is a measure of the *marginal use value* at that quantity. This is equivalent to the consumer's WTP for one additional unit of the product.

Any large change in quantity supplied to the market will induce a change in price. Reduced supply will induce higher prices; as price rises, reflecting increased marginal value to consumers, quantity demanded falls. If price becomes really high, demand may be choked off entirely. The total consumer WTP for the quantity sold (i.e., the all-or-nothing value) is approximated by the area under the demand curve. In Figure 16.2, the quantity Q1 is demanded at price P1. If the quantity supplied were smaller than Q1, the price consumers would pay (their marginal WTP) rises. If we add up the marginal WTPs for sequentially greater quantities from 0 through Q1, we get a total value for Q1. This total WTP is depicted in Figure 16.2 as area A plus the sales revenue, Q1 × P1.

The "consumer surplus" is the amount consumers are willing to pay over and above the amount they actually pay. Because consumers actually pay Q1 × P1, the consumer surplus is equal to area A. Consumer surplus is a measure of how much better off the consumer is when given the opportunity to purchase at the price offered. By similar reasoning, the increase in consumer's surplus associated with an increase in quantity from Q1 to Q2, accompanied by a price decrease from P1 to P2, is represented by the sum of areas B and C in Figure 16.2. Thus, consumer benefits associated with increased quantities of fish products can be expressed as a dollar amount estimated from market demand curves.

Benefits for producers.—Producers, like consumers, may enjoy a "surplus." The producer surplus is the excess of sales revenue over the costs of production; costs include payments to labor, management, normal return on capital invested, and payments for other raw material inputs. This surplus has two components: profits earned by firms in the industry, and resource rents paid to owners of fixed resources. These two terms, profits and rents, are used rather loosely and ambiguously in everyday language. In economics, they have more specific meanings.

In common usage, "profit" is often applied to many sources of earnings. Economic profit refers to any monetary returns over and above the normal return on investment. Thus, the profit must reflect returns in excess of the usual rewards for labor, risk-taking, skillful management, etc.; in competitive industries, economic profit occurs in special situations, and usually for short periods of time. For example, a new marina or an enhanced fish stock may attract increased angling activity to a lake. Initially, the expended demand for goods and services will generate profits, through increased prices and expanded sales volumes, for local firms supplying anglers.

In theory and often in practice, competition and free entry to an industry will stimulate entry and exit of firms until prospective economic profits by new entrants are approximately zero. This defines a competitive equilibrium for the industry. In the example of the lake fishery, as new firms are attracted to the lake and established firms expand in competition for business, the prices and market shares of the original firms will fall, ultimately reducing their economic profits. Even in a competitive equilibrium, some firms will be more profitable and successful than others due to extraordinary skill, good management, or luck. The greater-than-normal profits earned by more successful firms represent a real producer surplus value. In general, this surplus value is small relative to total sales revenue. Really large commercial profits can usually be sustained only through barriers to entry to the industry or through noncompetitive industry practices.

As used in common parlance, payments for "rent" include a combination of various categories of cost. For instance, the monthly rent on an apartment covers return on investment in buildings and land, interest on loans, labor payments for upkeep and repair, and possibly even heat and electricity. In economics, we are careful to categorize these components as labor income, interest income, return to

FIGURE 16.3.—Simple bioeconomic model of a single-species fishery. MSY is maximum sustainable yield, produced by effort E at cost D and yielding revenue C. Fishery yield and revenues decline when effort increases beyond E; when effort reaches A, revenue = costs = B. Maximum net economic value (F − G) is produced by effort H.

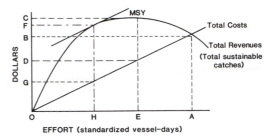

management, raw materials cost, and land rent. The "economic rent" includes only the value of using the fixed, nonrenewable land resource. The rental value of land depends crucially upon its location and physical features. Because these are largely a "gift of nature," the rental payments to the land owner represent, from a social standpoint, a surplus value. Similarly, fish stocks, forests, and other natural assets may generate rents that represent a surplus economic value contributed by nature.

Returning to the example of an enhanced lake fishery, some landowners may control a limited number of favorable locations for launching ramps and marinas. These owners will be able to charge higher rents for these locations once the local recreational fishing business expands. This increased rent reflects a more permanent flow of net economic value than does the transitory profit enjoyed by local firms immediately following the business expansion.

In summary, the three categories of use value to be included in the "net economic benefit" are consumer surplus, producer's economic profits, and resource rents.

Measurement of Use Values

Commercial and recreational use of salmonids and their habitats present special problems for economic assessment. Due to competition when there is open (unrestricted) access to fisheries, commercial fishing firms are typically not very profitable, and the rental value of the underlying resources is not captured by the public "owner" of the fish stocks under most fishery management systems. Nevertheless, many observers claim that a substantial economic value is reflected in the commercial fishing income generated in communities where alternative occupations are scarce. Outdoor recreation is a nonmarket good, which means that, with few exceptions, it is not offered for sale at a price in competitive markets. This raises the problem of measuring benefits without recourse to commercial transactions data concerning the thing being valued. Special analytical techniques for estimating nonmarket values for commercial and recreational fishing are briefly described below.

Measuring benefits of commercial fisheries.—A simple economic model of commercial fishing, based on the sustained yield concept, is depicted in Figure 16.3. Fishing effort is a measure of commercial fishing "inputs" (i.e., labor, fuel, capital invested in fishing vessels). In the simplest model, costs of fishing are assumed to be proportional to level of fishing effort, making the total cost curve in Figure 16.3 a straight line with slope equal to the cost per unit effort. It is also assumed that fishing effort is proportional to the fishing mortality rate (i.e., the rate at which fish are killed by fishing). As fishing mortality rate grows, the sustained yield initially rises, but eventually reaches a maximum sustainable yield (MSY), and then falls as the fish population is depleted. The rise and fall of the sustained yield curve is a biological phenomenon associated with reproductive success, somatic growth, and survival, all of which may vary with density of adult fish (Crutchfield and Pontecorvo 1969, chapter 2.)

The total sales revenue curve for the fishery is just the sustained yield multiplied by ex-vessel price. If the fishery being examined is small, the variation in harvest volume would not appreciably affect the market price and there would be no consumer surplus associated with this fishery. For a small fishery, therefore, the net economic value equals total sales revenue minus total fishing cost. In Figure 16.3, the maximum net economic value is achieved at effort level H. This economic optimum entails a lower level of fishing effort than needed to achieve MSY. If the fish stock were controlled by a resource owner, the net value per year would equal the owner's potential resource rent for the stock.

This simple economic model (Figure 16.3) illustrates the problem of competitive, commercial fishing when there is open access to the resource. As noted earlier, commercial fishermen, who are attracted to a fishery by prospective profits, will expand fishing effort until the costs and revenues are equal. The "competitive equilibrium" fishing effort occurs at A, where the total revenue and total cost curves intersect. To prevent the fish stock from being depleted below the MSY level, management agencies often control annual harvests through catch quotas, closed seasons, size limits, and gear limitations. This approach to management maintains spawning stocks and annual yields by limiting fishing effort to level "E," but it does not reduce the fishing fleet capacity nor does it assure significant net economic returns in the fishery. Excessive investments in fishing capacity permit the commercial fishery to take the allowable harvest in relatively short seasons, and this raises the cost per unit of effort above the level depicted by the total cost curve in Figure 16.3. To achieve a competitive equilibrium in the commercial fishery, with traditional quota regulations and short seasons, requires that the slope of the cost curve (i.e., cost per unit effort) be raised until it intersects the yield curve at the MSY.

It is important to note that net economic value is a definable, usable concept for devising fishery management strategy. To achieve maximum economic value, however, one must abandon open-access fishing. As discussed extensively elsewhere (Rettig and Ginter 1978; Pearse 1982), a limited-access system may limit the number of fishing firms permitted into the fishery, in which case it is called a license limitation system, or it may issue a number of quantitative harvest rights to fisherman. The quantitative rights are called individual tradeable quotas in New Zealand's groundfish fishery, and enterprise quotas in the Canadian Atlantic offshore fishery. An alternative to limiting access through public regulation is the establishment of private, enforceable rights to the fish in situ. Property rights to salmonids are traditional in certain parts of Great Britain and in Iceland.

The extensive experience in Alaska, British Columbia, and the other Pacific coast states indicates that salmon license limitation fails to completely discourage excessive investment in fishing capacity. Nevertheless, some substantial net economic value may be generated under license limitation. This value should be reflected in the prices now prevailing for salmon fishing permits in Alaska and elsewhere. Between 1975 and 1984, the average price paid for salmon permits in Alaska rose from $5,488 to $51,276. As noted by Karpoff (1983), price increases correlate strongly with increases in profitability of the fishery. Theoretically, the price reflects the prospective purchaser's estimate of discounted future profits in the fishery. It is clear that license limitation is responsible for some increase in rents earned. Nevertheless, many fisheries economists (e.g., Pearse 1982) have concluded that an individual tradeable quota system would be more effective in achieving economic efficiency in commercial harvesting.

Given the economic inefficiency of open-access fisheries, the economic evaluation of increments to salmonid stocks for commercial fisheries is a difficult problem. If one accepts the theory of open-access fisheries, no significant economic rents are associated with commercial fishing. On the other hand, all North American commercial Pacific salmon fisheries are restricted by license limitation systems. To the extent that the license limitation restrains excess investment in harvest capacity associated with open competition for fish, some resource rents may be generated. Because the resource owner does not collect the rent earned, however, rents will not be accounted for in a straightforward manner. Economic rents will appear as economic profits earned by commercial harvesters. Where licenses are bought and sold in competitive markets, however, the license prices will reflect the expected level of profits.

Few empirical studies of commercial fisheries provide real guidance on actual levels of economic profits and resource rents. Obviously, given reliable data on costs and sales revenues, one could estimate economic profits by subtracting costs from market value of fish harvested. Another pragmatic approach adopts the assumption that producer surplus equals a fixed fraction of ex-vessel revenue. Rettig and McCarl (1984), for example, concluded that net economic value from commercial Pacific salmon fishing would fall somewhere between 50 and 90% of gross ex-vessel value. The logic behind this approach has two parts. First, because the existing fleet can harvest additional fish with no additional capital investment, only the variable costs of fishing (fuel, labor, consumable supplies, repairs) will increase as the harvest expands. As a fraction of ex-vessel revenues, variable costs average about 50%. Second, if the fishermen have no alternative employment opportunities, the crew payments are not real costs (i.e., the full payment is an economic surplus), and could be counted as part of the producer surplus. Crew remuneration in Pacific salmon fisheries averages about 40% of ex-vessel sales. Subtracting labor payments from variable costs, therefore, leaves only about 10% of the ex-vessel revenue as costs.

The logic of the "50 to 90% of gross" estimate of net economic value is valid only where the method's assumptions are literally true, particularly where increased fishing capacity will not follow an increase in harvest quota and where complete unemployment is the only alternative to fishing for crew members. Even when numbers of vessels are restricted by license limitation programs, however, vessel owners tend to overinvest in fishing capacity by increasing the speed and capability of their vessels. This implies that, over the longer term, increased catches will attract some increased investment in harvest capacity. Also, it has not been demonstrated that commercial crews generally have no alternative employment opportunities, especially over the long term. Consequently, the use of this short-cut approach to estimating producer surplus is warranted only when valuation is applied to very short-term incremental harvests by fishing fleets in remote communities with high unemployment rates. To estimate economic values in all other cases, one must engage in the necessary and arduous collection and analysis of fishing costs and market prices.

Measuring recreational fishing values.—Like other forms of outdoor recreation, sportfishing is not sold like a commodity, and it does not have a price per se. Information necessary for estimating the benefits of sportfishing, or of enhanced sport-fish stocks, requires special surveys and careful analysis. The measurement of recreational fishing values is based on the demand for fishing, which can be estimated either by indirect methods, such as the travel cost method, or by a direct method like the contingent valuation method. Economic valuation methods were described in detail by McConnell (1985) and Walsh (1986).

Although angler expenditures per fishing trip superficially resemble a price for fishing, angler expenditures are not an accurate guide to the economic value of recreational fishing. Anglers are often "buying" more than just fishing on fishing trips, and the expenditures reflect costs associated with vacation travel and complementary activities (like sight-seeing and visiting friends or relatives) in addition to the cost of fishing. Furthermore, because catching fish is only one of several factors contributing to an enjoyable fishing experience (e.g., boating and enjoying the outdoors with friends may also be important), even expenditures strictly for fishing do not measure the value of fish to anglers. Finally, except when expenditures represent economic rents paid to resource owners (e.g., payment for access to the fish stock), they are a measure of costs, not net economic values.

Travel cost method.—Although anglers do not pay a price for fishing trips, we can estimate economic values by using angler responses to the variable costs incurred in traveling to and fishing at a given site. This procedure is considered an *indirect* valuation method, because the travel cost data do not themselves measure the value. Instead, the angler's behavior in response to changing travel costs permits estimation of the demand for fishing. Again referencing Figure 16.2, we may replace price by travel cost per trip for a particular site. Quantity is the number of times per season (or year) that the angler goes fishing. With lower costs per trip, anglers go fishing more often, implying a downward-sloping demand curve for fishing. The travel cost method (TCM) approach to estimating recreational demand infers a demand curve for a fishing site from observed differences in participation rates due to differences in distance to the site and associated travel costs.

In its simplest form, the TCM demand curve is estimated by regression analysis from survey data on numbers of anglers fishing a given site from various distances away. For example, Brown et al. (1980) estimated the following demand curve for ocean salmon fishing off Oregon:

$$\log_e (\text{TCAP}_i) = -2.508 - 0.01875 \text{ TC}_i + 0.06931 \text{ INC}_i - 0.001224 \text{ INC}_i^2;$$

$$R^2 = 0.6607;$$

TCAP_i is number of fishing trips per capita from distance zone i; TC_i is travel cost from the residence zone to the fishing site, and INC_i is average income of anglers in the zone. The equation shows that participation in ocean salmon angling falls

FIGURE 16.4.—A shift in the demand curve from D1 to D2 without a change in price P increases the consumer surplus by an amount equal to the area OCS.

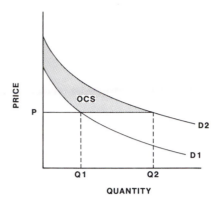

with increasing travel cost and increases with income. This is similar to consumer demand for marketed commodities. The consumer surplus for angling is equal to the area under the demand curve minus the costs incurred. The travel costs vary across distance zones. To estimate the economic value of ocean salmon fishing in Oregon, we multiply the number of anglers by the consumer surplus per angler in each zone, and sum the products across zones. The result is an all-or-nothing value for the fishing site, equivalent to the total area under a demand curve for fishing salmon in the ocean off Oregon.

A demand curve in semilogarithmic form (as in the equation above) has the special property that consumer surplus per angler is simply calculated by dividing the trips taken per angler by the absolute value of the inverse of the travel cost coefficient. This means that the consumer surplus per angler trip equals the absolute value of the inverse of the travel cost coefficient. For the Oregon salmon fishing equation, the consumer surplus is $53.33 (equal to 1/0.01875) per angler trip. The total consumer surplus associated with all salmon angling off Oregon during the period studied by Brown et al. (1980) was $13.1 million.

The simple TCM demand equation provides an estimate of average value per day and supports the calculation of total consumer surplus for a fishing site, but it does not estimate marginal values associated with enhancement of fish stocks. Yet these marginal values are often of most relevance to a benefit–cost analysis of stock management or habitat preservation. An increase in fish availability at a given fishing site, for example, will make fishing at that site more desirable. The resulting increase in demand is depicted in Figure 16.4 as a rightward shift in the demand curve; more fishing trips will be taken at each price level. The benefit associated with this shift is the increased consumer surplus, labelled OCS in Figure 16.4. To estimate the degree to which increased fish catch shifts the curve, a TCM model can be estimated from data collected over a variety of fishing sites with different catch rates, or over a period of time at one site with varying catch rate. The site- or time-specific catch rate becomes an additional variable in the estimated demand curve. Regional, multiple-site travel cost models have been developed in recent years to fill this need.

An important example was presented by Loomis (1988), who reported a multiple-site TCM demand model for ocean salmon sportfishing in Washington and Oregon, freshwater salmon sportfishing in Oregon, and freshwater steelhead fishing in Oregon. For example, the estimated equation for Washington ocean salmon fishing is

$$\log_e(\text{TCAP}_{ij}) = -4.283 - 0.791(\log_e D_{ij}) + 0.404(\log_e \text{OSC}_j) - 0.06(\log_e \text{SUB}_j);$$
$$R^2 = 0.508;$$

TCAP_{ij} is trips per capita from origin i to site j, D_{ij} is travel distance from origin i to site j, OSC_j is ocean sport catch at site j, and SUB_j is an index of the quality of substitute sites. Because the equation reveals how trip-taking behavior responds to variation in catch at specific sites, it can be used to estimate the marginal value (i.e., increased angler consumer surplus) associated with an increased salmon catch. Loomis (1988) calculated marginal values per salmon ranging from $21.43 at Illwaco, Washington, to $64.61 at Tillamook, Oregon.

Samples and Bishop (1985) developed a multiple-site demand model for Lake Michigan anglers fishing for trout and salmon, using angler data collected in 1978. To determine the marginal value of increased angler success, they used a two-step approach. The first step involved estimating travel-cost demand equations for 11 fishing sites having different angler catch rates, and calculating the consumer surplus values associated with each site. The second step involved estimating the relationship between angler site values and angler catch rate. This latter relationship permitted the computation of marginal values per additional fish caught, given the average level of angler catch rate of 0.47 fish per trip. For Lake Michigan, Samples and Bishop (1985) estimated that an additional fish landed would be worth $10.44 in 1985 dollars (converted from 1978 dollars by application of the gross national product price deflator).

Contingent valuation method.—The contingent valuation method (CVM) is based on direct expression of consumer surplus for hypothetical changes in natural resources. That is, the CVM calculates values contingent upon some hypothetical change. Whereas users of the TCM interpret data collected from observed recreational behavior, users of the CVM generate new data by asking individuals directly about their values or about hypothetical behavior under changed situations. Use of CVM requires skill in designing questionnaires that accurately elicit respondents' willingness to pay for gains, or willingness to accept compensation for losses.

For example, Donnelly et al. (1985) dealt with steelhead fishing in Idaho by iterative questioning of anglers to find the most that they would pay in increased costs per fishing trip before they would abandon steelhead fishing. The resulting consumer surplus estimates varied among fishing sites between $19.00 and $50.98 per fishing trip, and averaged $31.45. Donnelly et al. also estimated TCM values for steelhead fishing, obtaining an average value of $27.87 per trip. Thus, the two techniques can generate similar values in some instances.

In another survey, Thomson and Huppert (1987) asked saltwater salmon and striped bass anglers in central California to indicate the largest amount they would be willing to contribute annually to a fish enhancement fund if the enhancement effort would double angler catch rates. The average response was $41.06 per year, and the total estimated willingness to pay (WTP) in the survey region for the enhancement was $9.8 million. Similarly, the willingness to accept compensation (WTA) for a decrease of 50% in angler catch averaged $81.77 per angler, and the estimated total WTA for losses by central California anglers was $20.7 million.

TABLE 16.8.—Estimates of recreational salmon and steelhead fishing values (US$).

Source	Recreational fishery	Method[a]	Unit valued[a]	Value in $1985[b]
Brown and Shalloof (1986)	Oregon			
	Freshwater salmon	TCM	CS/trip	22.75
	Steelhead	TCM	CS/trip	31.02
	Ocean salmon	TCM	CS/trip	59.97
	Washington ocean salmon	TCM	CS/trip	61.00
Crutchfield and Schelle (1978)	Washington	CVM	WTA/day	62.55
	Ocean salmon and steelhead	CVM	WTP/day	28.15
Charbonneau and Hay (1978)	USA	CVM	WTP/day	96.06
	Freshwater salmon	TCM	CS/day	118.67
Sorg and Loomis (1986)	Idaho steelhead	TCM	CS/trip	31.13
			CS/day	15.96
		CVM	WTP/trip	35.13
			WTP/day	22.66

[a]Values based on a travel cost demand curve (TCM) are assumed to represent estimates of consumer surplus (CS). Values from a contingent value method (CVM) are explicitly either willingness to pay (WTP) or willingness to accept compensation (WTA), depending upon the wording of the questions. Units of measurement are per fishing day or per fishing trip.
[b]Values are adjusted to 1985 dollars according to the gross national product price deflator.

The WTA is expected to be larger than the WTP, but the difference between these two value estimates is surprisingly large. Nevertheless, this example shows that CVM can directly value resource changes without the use of a recreational fishing demand model.

This short review provides only cursory guidance on design and use of the CVM and TCM. Each method has its strengths and weaknesses. For example, economic values from travel cost demand models are strongly influenced by estimates of cost associated with time spent in travel and in fishing. The time cost component is not estimated with great precision in most recreational studies. Also, when recreational trips are not solely for the purpose of fishing, the travel cost method requires some arbitrary decisions about allocation of fixed trip costs among trip activities. Nevertheless, its reliance on data regarding actual behavior of anglers, and actual costs incurred, lends credence to the TCM approach.

Contingent valuation surveys are subject to various sources of error associated with biased responses, inappropriate wording of questions, and respondent refusal to "play the game." When implemented with skill, however, either the TCM or the CVM can reliably estimate economic use values for nonmarketed resources. For valuing large hypothetical changes beyond the experience of current resource users, for valuing public goods (like clean air or preservation of a species), or for estimating "existence values" for unique resources, the TCM is not applicable. In these cases, one has to rely on CVM. The best general, advanced references on the CVM are Cummings et al. (1986) and Mitchell and Carson (1989).

Typical recreational values.—Tables 16.8 and 16.9 summarize some recent recreational value estimates. Table 16.8 displays salmon and steelhead fishing values per day of fishing or per fishing trip. Table 16.9 includes freshwater fishing for trouts and other coldwater species. Using CVM questions included in a 1980

TABLE 16.9.—Economic value estimates for coldwater or trout fishing (US$).

Source	Recreational fishery	Method[a]	Unit valued[a]	Value in $1985[b]
Sorg and Loomis (1986)	Idaho coldwater	TCM	CS/trip	47.95
			CS/day	28.54
		CVM	WTP/trip	25.15
			WTP/day	15.91
Charbonneau and Hay (1978)	U.S. trout fishing	CVM	WTP/day	35.56
Brown and Hay (1987)	U.S. trout fishing in			
	Alaska	CVM	WTP/day	36.55
	California	CVM	WTP/day	20.89
	Colorado	CVM	WTP/day	16.97
	Idaho	CVM	WTP/day	13.06
	Maine	CVM	WTP/day	11.75
	Montana	CVM	WTP/day	15.67
	New York	CVM	WTP/day	11.75
	Texas	CVM	WTP/day	31.33
	Wisconsin	CVM	WTP/day	11.75

[a]Values based on a travel cost demand (TCM) curve are assumed to represent estimates of consumer surplus (CS). Values from a contingent value method (CVM) are explicitly willingness to pay (WTP). Units of measurement are per fishing day or per fishing trip.

[b]Values adjusted to 1985 dollars according to the gross national product price deflator.

survey of fishing, hunting, and wildlife-associated recreation, Brown and Hay (1987) estimated average net economic values per day and per season for trout fishing in each state. The trout fishing value per day varied from $28 in Alaska to $7 in Ohio, New Hampshire, and Vermont. That effort did not yield marginal values per fish caught. The wide range of values in Table 16.8 is due partly to variations in research methodology, and partly to variation in the quality of recreational fishing being studied. Some of the factors that make recreational fishing a heterogeneous commodity among fishing sites are accessibility, scenery, congestion, and catch rates. Consequently, there can be no generally applicable values for recreational fishing. Each site must be assessed either by a special study of that site or by analogy to similar fishing sites.

A major difference between recreational and commercial commodities is that commercial goods are generally distributed widely, resulting in uniform prices among geographically disparate markets, whereas outdoor recreation, by its very nature, cannot be delivered to consumers. Anglers have to go to the fishing site and produce, as it were, their own recreation. Because the price of frozen salmon fillets varies only slightly among cities due to shipping costs, the average price is a good approximation of the marginal value to consumers, regardless of where the fish are landed or finally consumed. In contrast, because travel costs will be higher for anglers living further from fishing sites, location of fishing sites relative to metropolitan areas will have a significant influence on the total economic benefits derived from the fishing site. Consequently, an average economic value per angler at one site may not be applicable to fisheries and anglers in other circumstances.

Existence Values

As noted earlier, existence values are probably most significant for unique and rare natural resources. If substantial amounts of all salmonid species are widely available, we would not expect large existence values to be associated with the incremental changes in salmonid stocks frequently evaluated by benefit–cost analysis. Nevertheless, various subspecies, local stocks, or seasonal runs of fish that are severely depressed may have important existence value components. Also, when entire river systems are at risk due to, for example, droughts, destruction of critical habitat, or hydropower developments, existence values may become a significant issue.

Only a contingent value approach can be used to determine existence values. In one of the few studies of existence value for salmonid species, Meyer (1978) summarized a survey of households in British Columbia that inquired about the existence value of salmon and steelhead in the Fraser river. The mean value per household associated with preserving anadromous salmonids in the lower mainland area was $225 per year. This was slightly higher than the average recreation value of $182 per household. Extrapolated over all households in the area, a total existence value of about $92 million was estimated. Apparently, preservation of anadromous salmonid runs has great value to British Columbia residents. It is unclear how much this value changes, if at all, with the size of the fish runs.

One might expect significant existence values to enter a benefit–cost study of rare, threatened, or severely depressed species, such as the golden trout in the southern Sierra Nevada mountains or the winter run of chinook salmon in the upper Sacramento River, California, but surveys to measure these values have not been conducted. Hence, salmonid existence value remains an intriguing but seldom-addressed component of economic valuation.

Net Present Value

In addition to value associated with current use and existence of fish, we are concerned with values that will accrue in the future. To evaluate a long-term project, a benefit–cost analyst develops a schedule of expected future expenses and benefits. Future values are compared to current values through discounting over time, that is, by multiplying the value i years in the future by a discount factor, $1/(1 + r)^i$. The discount rate, r, is similar to an interest rate. The higher the discount rate is, the lower will be the current value of the future benefit. The time stream of benefits and costs is consolidated in a single measure called "net present value" (NPV):

$$\text{NPV} = \sum_{i=1}^{T} (B_i - C_i)/(1 + r)^i;$$

T is the "time horizon" (i.e., the number of years over which prospective benefits and costs occur), and B_i and C_i are the estimated benefits and costs accruing in year i. The benefits are measured by consumer surplus, producer surplus, and resource rent. Selecting projects based on NPV is economic decision-making for efficiency.

Controversy over discounting hinges on the argument that it unfairly burdens future generations by depleting resources. However, the use of discounting is mainly for efficiency. Capital invested yields a positive rate of return in other sectors. Efficient allocation of capital requires resource-based projects to yield a competitive rate of return. In an extensive review of this subject, Lind et al. (1982, page 448) concluded that a discount rate of 3.0 to 4.6% seems most appropriate. The net discounted value criterion assures that public projects are economically efficient.

Management of Salmonid Fisheries and Habitats

To include concerns about salmonid fisheries in a comprehensive assessment of forest and rangeland management practices requires information on economic and other benefits from the fisheries, costs of foregone production in the timber and grazing sectors, and public costs of land management activities including those involving salmonid habitat maintenance and enhancement. A benefit–cost approach to the design of management programs will key upon the overall difference between the value of enhanced fisheries and costs in timber and livestock production and public costs of management. This is, of course, just a generalized economic efficiency criterion.

Some of the benefits, especially those from ocean and river fisheries, depend upon the regulations of national and state fishery management agencies, which are largely outside the purview of land management agencies. An introduction to the biological concepts and objectives prevalent in management of anadromous fisheries is provided below.

Benefits derived from freshwater fisheries are frequently more directly controlled by forest and rangeland managers. In most freshwater fisheries, commercial harvest is of little importance. If each land area with its fish stocks, forests, and rangelands is to be treated as a multiple-use resource, one needs to assess both the costs of imposing restrictive practices on land users and the benefits accruing from fishery preservation and enhancement. This approach highlights the economic trade-off between fisheries and other uses. Similarly, camping and backpacking may be incompatible with some forest uses. Even different classes of recreational use (such as wilderness camping and developed motor home camping) cannot use a given area simultaneously without conflict. Hence, it is widely recognized that optimal use of forest lands requires balance among competing uses.

The broadest conclusion from economics is that the marginal value of each permitted use should be equal to or greater than the marginal value of all other uses. Any increase in timber cutting would have a net economic value at least as large as the potential net value of fishing, camping, or other uses foregone due to the additional cutting. It is easy to see why this kind of balance is optimal. If the fish or camping opportunities lost due to timber operations on a particular plot are worth more than the timber products, it would be better not to cut the timber. On the other hand, where the timber value is greater than the fishery or recreational value, timber harvesting should be permitted. This concept of economic balance does not imply that all management areas should be divided up among all uses. It suggests a means of defining a best mix of uses.

Salmonid Biological Concepts and Objectives

Each distinct group of anadromous fish spawning in a specific river or river system is treated as a separate "stock." The sustainable yield of each stock depends upon such factors as extent and quality of spawning gravel, streamflow

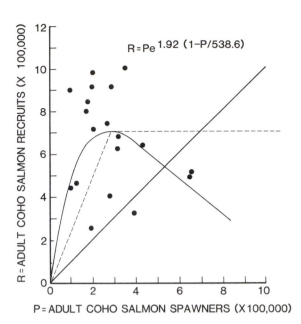

FIGURE 16.5.—Spawner–recruit curve (continuous curved line) for Oregon coastal coho salmon. Recruits are adult fish returning to streams 3 years after they had been produced by the spawners. The curve has been fitted to 19 data points representing 22 years of fish counts. The solid diagonal line indicates 1:1 replacement. (From Oregon Department of Fish and Wildlife 1982.)

(quantity and seasonal profile), dissolved nutrients, and food supply for fry, smolts, and juveniles. Additional factors include mortality during downstream migration, ocean survival, and mortality during upstream migration. Because managers of ocean and river fisheries control only the quantity and timing of harvests during the ocean-feeding stage and spawning migration of the fish, population models developed for fishery management purposes tend to assume a given size and quality of the freshwater habitat.

Management objectives and regulations for naturally spawning salmon are derived from a "spawner–recruit" model, as illustrated in Figure 16.5. For this biological model, it is assumed that the number of mature adults migrating back to each stream of origin (recruitment) depends upon the size of the prior spawning population (brood stock). This example pertains to coho salmon stocks spawning in Oregon coastal streams (Oregon Department of Fish and Wildlife 1982). It is typical of models for other species and stocks. On the horizontal axis is number of spawners, in this case an estimate of adult coho salmon reaching spawning sites in Oregon streams. The vertical axis plots number of adult fish recruited to the fishery 3 years later.

The fitted curve predicts the recruitment that will result from any given spawning stock. The diagonal line from the origin is the replacement line. Recruits in excess of the replacement level may be harvested without reducing this year's spawning stock below that of the brood year. Thus, for any given spawning stock size, the sustainable yield is the difference between recruitment and replacement. Maximum recruitment occurs at the peak of the spawner-recruit curve (maximum recruitment of 704,000 coho salmon occurs at a spawning stock of 281,000 fish). Maximum sustainable yield (MSY) occurs where the difference between recruitment and replacement is greatest (MSY is approximately 468,000 fish at a spawning stock of 197,000 fish). Salmon managers commonly adopt the objective of maintaining a spawning stock just sufficient to achieve MSY on average.

Because this requires regulating the fishery to permit escapement of a target number of spawners to the spawning grounds, it is called a "fixed escapement" policy.

The wide scatter of points about the fitted curve is clear indication that the annual predictions of recruitment will be fairly inaccurate. Managers frequently must adapt fishery catch regulations to compensate for over- and under-fishing in relation to the escapement objective. The wide variety of adaptive management approaches will not be described in detail here, but the interested reader may want to consult Walters (1986). The important point is that biological feedback mechanisms create a natural limitation on sustainable catch; these mechanisms, however, contain a high degree of annual variability.

This simplified version of fish stock dynamics shows that fishery regulation and habitat management have complementary roles. When stocks are low due to insufficient escapement, habitat enhancement has relatively little effect on stock size; reduced fishing is needed to increase stock size. When escapement is kept at high levels, additional restrictions on fishing are not called for; habitat enhancement is the way to increase stocks and associated fishery benefits. Some stocks are habitat-limited while others are limited by fishing mortality. Where harvest of mixed stocks occurs, both habitat enhancement and harvest regulation may be needed simultaneously.

A final consideration is that of hatcheries, which are essentially a substitute for the natural spawning habitat. Many salmon hatcheries, which release fish directly into rivers to supplement naturally produced stocks, were constructed as mitigation for salmon spawning grounds that were destroyed or made inaccessible by dams. The fish produced by freshwater trout hatcheries are frequently released into lakes and rivers to enhance the fishable yield to meet recreational fishing demand. The analysis of hatchery operations is beyond the scope of this chapter, but we note that there are negative as well as positive biological consequences from release of hatchery fish into natural ecosystems. First, the hatchery fish may compete with and reduce populations of naturally occurring stocks of the same or different species. Second, the reliance of hatcheries on relatively small gene pools tends to reduce the genetic diversity of wild fish stocks as a whole. Thus, although salmonid hatcheries can substantially increase the annual fish harvest, they may introduce some worrisome long-term effects as well.

Trade-offs between Forestry and Fishery Values

To quantify the economic consequences of alternative management plans requires substantial information on biophysical linkages between land management practices and the economic benefits of land use. Such a comprehensive approach has great appeal, but is seldom accomplished. Interdisciplinary teams of researchers must work together to assess bioeconomic effects of resource management practices. In two case studies, Loomis (1988, 1989) demonstrated a practical approach to assessing the effects of timber harvest strategy on fishing values in the Siuslaw National Forest of Oregon and in the Porcupine–Hyalite wilderness study area of the Gallatin National Forest in Montana.

Loomis' (1988) Siuslaw National Forest model links specific incremental effects of logging activity to economic benefits from salmon fishing. The analysis builds up the causal linkages by combining a habitat model—relating watershed characteristics to carrying capacity of fish habitat—with the fish habitat index model developed by Heller et al. (1983). The fish habitat index model involves several equations that were developed from information gathered in the Siuslaw National Forest. For example, a watershed conditions index is specified as a function of sediment increase, temperature increase, debris index, and debris torrent index. Each of the variables in the watershed conditions index equation is affected by logging and is a critical factor in determining habitat quality for several life stages of both salmon and steelhead. In addition to the watershed conditions index, there is an equation for natural habitat quality, and an equation that relates fish production to fish habitat quality.

Loomis (1988) used the biophysical model to generate impacts of five timber-harvesting alternatives, each of which was characterized by amount of timber harvested, acres of forest managed for timber, number of catchable salmon, and number of catchable steelhead. Commercial fishing value was calculated as catch times ex-vessel price, and consumer surpluses from recreational fishing were calculated as marginal values derived from the multisite recreational demand model described earlier. Timber values were derived from the relevant U.S. Forest Service plans. If logging continues as currently planned, total fishery losses over a 30-year time span are calculated to be $1.55 million. If all logging ceased, the net gain to fishery values would be $1.67 million. However, due to the high value of timber from the forest, the loss in timber value under the minimal logging alternative would exceed the value of enhanced fishing.

In the Porcupine–Hyalite wilderness study (Loomis 1989), two alternatives were considered. The first was to establish wilderness protection for 58,682 hectares in the area; the second was to leave 28,329 hectares in "near natural condition," allow intensive grazing on 8,642 hectares, and harvest timber on about 14,569 hectares of private forest land. The principal effect of timber harvesting and associated road construction on fisheries in this area is through increased sedimentation of trout streams, resulting in lower standing stocks of trout and reduced angler catch rates. Loomis estimated the value of recreational fishing in the area using travel cost demand equations, and determined the effect of reduced catch on economic values in a manner similar to that used in the Suislaw study. In this area of the Gallatin National Forest, the timber harvest value is less than the value of fishing that would be lost under the logging alternative, which could justify selection of the no-logging alternative.

These examples show that the combination of biological, physical, and economic models can support analyses that will help land managers make decisions about the best mix of resource activities to permit in multiple-use areas.

Problems of Implementation

Economic considerations discussed in this chapter should contribute to improved management policy for salmonid habitats. Although economics has a great deal to say regarding policy, it is clear that economic criteria, like biological criteria, do not dominate policy formulation. There is an important element of political decision making in public resource management, and this assures that divergent views and interests influence policies and regulations. In addition, the translation of the best general concepts of economics into specific rules is often difficult and fraught with uncertainty. This is frequently due to inadequate economic research and data collection by resource management agencies.

In fishery management, for example, uncertainties in biological assessments of potential yields require most practical management decisions to be based on "order-of-magnitude" estimates of sustainable yield. In the economic realm, harvesting costs depend on management strategies in the fishery as well as on market prices of fuel and other inputs used in fishing. Fish prices are subject to a wide variety of influences beyond the scope of any fishery or river system. These and similar considerations in the land management realm dictate that economic considerations be taken as general guidelines only, and that continued effort be made to refine the quantitative results from benefit–cost studies. Despite empirical shortcomings, however, the principles of economic efficiency as manifested in the benefit–cost framework are exceedingly useful organizing concepts for resource management.

Principles for managing salmonid habitat are complex and numerous, particularly in the case of anadromous salmonids that move from freshwater streams through sensitive estuarine habitats to oceanic feeding grounds and back to the stream of origin. Political units do not easily deal with fish having such a life cycle; individual states and nations often control only one portion of a fish population's full habitat. Regional Fishery Management Councils in the USA, for example, have management responsibility in the 200-nautical mile Fishery Conservation Zone, while individual states have substantial discretion in nearshore and inland waters. As a further example, chinook salmon from the Columbia River system migrate to the ocean off southeast Alaska and British Columbia, thus crossing international, federal, state, and provincial zones as well as treaty areas where Native American tribes exercise management authority. Interregional and international negotiations are necessary for overall management of these fish runs. The interweaving of responsibilities and authorities makes it difficult to translate simple economic efficiency propositions into management rules, because values, costs, and objectives vary among various regions and governmental bodies.

One consequence of institutional complexity is that the real choice of policy guidelines for freshwater habitat management is severely limited. Legal authorities of federal and state agencies are often circumscribed by compromises necessary to satisfy international agreements. Legislatures rarely give management agencies sufficient discretionary power to implement some of the more economically attractive management methods (such as landings royalties or creation of private property rights to instream habitat). Given the limited menu of possible management approaches, the economic objectives that can be adopted in practice are limited also.

As land and water management practices become more aligned with multiple-use concepts, however, the basic economic consideration—efficient utilization of available natural habitats through balancing of marginal net economic values among alternative uses—will become more feasible.

Chapter 17

Fish Habitat Planning

P. Brouha

As noted in the introductory chapter of this volume (Meehan 1991b), two means of protecting or enhancing natural stocks of salmonids are available to resource managers: limiting the number of fish caught; and maintaining and managing adequate habitat. Harvest management planning has been the focus of state, provincial, and federal fishery management agencies acting individually and jointly through such regional bodies as fishery management councils, established in the USA under authority of the Magnuson Fishery Conservation and Management Act of 1976, and the Great Lakes Fishery Commission. Although this allocation process is critical to successful fishery resource management, it is beyond the scope of this book. In this chapter, fishery resource planning is approached from the perspective of maintaining and managing adequate habitat, a facet that has been addressed by private landowners, states, provinces, and federal land-management and resource-development agencies.

Streams flow through public and private lands that have diverse histories of management and use. Although most public land-management agencies recognize the concept of multiple benefits, many private lands are managed to meet the owner's single-use objectives. In many cases, management practices or land uses have extensively altered fish habitats on forests and rangelands. While acknowledging that most fishes survive quite well under a wide range of natural perturbations, Platts and Rinne (1985) emphasized that "the best fishery habitat management practice available today, is to maintain these unaltered aquatic habitats in their natural condition." They went on to caution that management agencies should carry out enhancement efforts only on degraded streams in which fish habitats will not return to natural states in a reasonable period even when deleterious practices are suspended. Aquatic habitat management planning to maintain public fishery resources must consistently address a combination of habitat protection, rehabilitation, and enhancement measures throughout the public and private lands that affect streams. Establishing standardized habitat protection criteria, inventory methods, and planning procedures that satisfy the needs of all owners should improve understanding of available options and ultimately should result in better protection of fish habitats.

Federal, state, and provincial agencies that manage lands and other natural resources are being confronted by increasing numbers of conflicts among resource users and increasingly complex issues of environment quality. They have been

Influences of Forest and Rangeland Management on Salmonid Fishes and Their Habitats
American Fisheries Society Special Publication 19:587–597, 1991

forced to turn to planning to clarify their intentions, to define courses of action, to measure progress, and to evaluate and document results.

Crowe (1983) defined planning as "an integrated system of management that includes all activities leading to the development and implementation of goals, program objectives, operational strategies, and progress evaluation." He developed this definition by posing four benchmark questions as the basis of a planned management approach:

- Where are we?
- Where do we want to be?
- How will we get there?
- Did we make it?

Four federal, two provincial, and six state land- and resource-management agencies surveyed have adopted planning procedures based on answering these four questions. All these procedures require consideration of fisheries in the context of multiple uses that affect a forest or rangeland natural resource base.

The Planning Process

An Example: U.S. Forest Service Procedures

The planning procedures used by the U.S. Forest Service exemplify a comprehensive process for land and resource management. The other agencies surveyed follow these steps or have functional equivalents of them in one form or another.

The Forest Service's planning process, which has evolved over time in consultation with interested states and other federal agencies, has 10 steps (Brouha 1982; U.S. Office of the Federal Register 1982): (1) identify issues, concerns, and opportunities; (2) develop process and decision criteria; (3) collect data; (4) analyze the management situation; (5) formulate alternatives; (6) estimate effects of alternatives; (7) evaluate alternatives; (8) select final plan; (9) implement the plan; and (10) monitor and evaluate results. Steps (1–4) address the question "Where are we?" Steps (5–7) address "Where do we want to be?" Steps (8) and (9) address "How will we get there?" Step (10) addresses "Did we make it?"

(1) Identify issues, concerns, and opportunities.—Before goals and objectives are established, planners must ask the public and resource managers what issues the plan needs to address. Planners should determine the long-range resource concerns of managers as well as the public's shorter-term reactions to present issues, and they should document opportunities to improve the productivity or use of the resource base. The public issues are often symptoms of problems that resource managers can address once realistic objectives are identified. For example, anglers may be concerned about the small average size and reduced number of cutthroat trout caught during raft trips down a Montana river, and they ask why there are not more and bigger fish. Resource managers may then define objectives related to the regulation of land use, road access, and harvest to provide higher-quality fishing experiences along the river.

From this step of the process should come a clear understanding of what is perceived to be wrong with a resource or its use and an indication of what goals and objectives may be needed to achieve desired resource benefits. In addition, the effect of managing one resource on the management of another (timber versus fish, for example) should become clear as managers identify conflicts.

During this process, the concerns of informed resource managers may be submerged in and overwhelmed by more visible public issues. Instead of focusing issues and pointing the way toward solutions, managerial insights may become lost in overly broad issue statements unless a public constituency becomes aware of them and presses for their recognition. Fishery and other resource managers are well advised to educate their constituents to ensure their concerns are known and supported by their publics. If the public is not educated as draft multiple-use plans are published, the lack of objectives important to an interest group may trigger adverse reactions that require a "final" plan to be redone.

(2) Develop criteria.—The two types of planning criteria are process and decision criteria. Process criteria are the standards that govern planning actions. They are the ground rules set by laws, agency policy and direction, and the goals and objectives in higher-level or long-range plans. They are also based on recommendations from resource managers and the public concerning resource use and development opportunities, and on the technical, financial, and political constraints on various management alternatives. Fishery resource management prescriptions, environmental standards, and economic analysis guidelines are examples of process criteria.

Decision criteria are categories of resource outputs or benefits used to evaluate and select a preferred alternative. Decision criteria for fisheries include population levels of certain species, projected fishery resource use, and fish habitat quality standards to be achieved by specified time periods. Decision criteria can also be used to determine data collection needs, to establish monitoring requirements, and to guide formulation of management alternatives. An example of such a criterion is one that would restrict the fine sediment content of spawning gravels to less than 20%; this restriction would direct and constrain consideration of management approaches.

If process and decision criteria have been properly developed, designated plan reviewers should be able to evaluate the specific procedures that will be used to protect, maintain, or enhance fish habitat. They should also be able to ascertain what improvement activities are scheduled, whether or not these activities are mitigation for other planned developments, and what effect the total planned program will have on desired fish species and on recreational, subsistence, and commercial use of those species.

(3) Collect data.—Having defined the goals and objectives that the plan will address—based on the issues and opportunities identified in step (1)—and the procedures for attaining them—based on the process criteria established in step (2)—land and water managers, biologists, and the rest of the planning team should then design a procedure to collect, compile, and display data that will provide a basis for meeting the goals and objectives. For example, if the productivity of riparian and aquatic habitats is an issue, productivity must be defined and measured. If a certain catch rate and size of trout is a recreational angling goal, the present catch rate and size must be determined.

The key point is to ensure that an appropriate data base is created and clearly displayed to address the defined issues and concerns, to permit evaluation of alternatives, and to demonstrate management opportunities. At a minimum, present and desired habitat capabilities for fish management indicator species should be defined along with present and projected resource use. In many instances, adequate inventory data are not available from federal, state, or provincial agencies. Limitations of data must be clearly stated. When critically needed data are not available, the plan should address collection of these data as a first priority.

(4) Analyze the management situation.—Analysis of the management situation should allow the fishery resource manager to present, for each selected management indicator species, (a) population numbers ranging from minimum viable levels, through present populations, to an approximation of maximum potential; (b) an approximation of present and projected future demand for the fishery resource; (c) an analysis of imbalance between supply and demand; and (d) the opportunities, costs, and changes in management needed to increase supply where demand exceeds it. For example, a low-gradient stream whose riparian area is subject to livestock grazing has a potential standing crop of 1,233 legally catchable trout per hectare of which 40% or 494 could be harvested annually. The present standing crop is 370 catchable trout/hectare and the minimum viable catchable population is 74/hectare. The annual harvestable surplus is presently 148 catchable trout/hectare affected by grazing, but the demand is projected to increase to 395 catchable trout/hectare yearly, which would require a standing crop of 988 catchable trout/hectare. How can the manager increase the standing crop from 370 to 988/hectare? Present grazing strategies must be modified to permit recovery of bank stability, overhead shade, and cover. In addition, fine sediments in stream spawning gravels must be reduced to less than 20% of total substrate volume. What will be the trade-offs with other resource production to achieve this recovery? Grazing effects will have to be reduced by modifying the numbers of livestock and the periods of grazing in riparian areas along those streams. As a result, 12 animal unit months/hectare will be lost each year during the next decade. Thus the trade-off between fish and livestock production can be assessed. Proper livestock management to permit natural recovery is the preferred management alternative, but where additional improvements in stream habitat are required to increase production of catchable trout, the cost per fish and the expected increase in number of fishing days can be calculated. With such information, the reviewer and the planning team can evaluate opportunity costs and tradeoffs.

(5) Formulate alternatives.—Among the management alternatives presented, the planning team must develop those that address a reasonable range of possible outputs for each fish species or species group of interest in relation to the defined planning issues, concerns, and opportunities. The alternatives should establish a framework of various intensity levels for an active goal-oriented fishery management program. Projected public benefits (e.g., weight of fish landed, number of angler-days supported) must be defined along with management standards and guidelines and the expected habitat conditions.

The planning team and reviewers are responsible for providing an alternative that maximizes (or optimizes) fish outputs in the multiple-use framework of the plan. When interjurisdictional management of fish populations is necessary, the objectives of other agencies should be considered. A discussion should be included of how fishery objectives will be achieved (e.g., changes in management for other resources, investments in habitat improvement, control of access for recreational use).

(6) Estimate effects of alternatives.—Fishery outputs from each alternative program should be compared to maximum potentials and minimum viable populations. Comparative costs and benefits should be displayed for each alternative. The physical, biological, economic, and social effects of implementing each alternative should be displayed.

(7) Evaluate alternatives.—The evaluation step shows the necessity for having established quantified and measurable fish habitat characteristics and population objectives.

Alternatives should be evaluated against the established decision criteria. The importance of establishing decision criteria prior to formulating alternatives cannot be overemphasized. These criteria become the only measures by which alternatives can be evaluated.

(8) Select final plan.—In the rationale and documentation that support the final selection of a management alternative, the public benefits and consequences for fishery resources of that alternative should be compared to the benefits and consequences of other alternatives.

The rationale should clearly present how the fishery resources will be harmed or improved by the selected alternative as compared to other alternatives. This level of specificity should address all components affecting fishery resources. The public has the right to question whether a sound basis for resource management exists, and documentation of the decision process must allow the public to understand how each decision was reached.

(9) Implement the plan.—Whether or not the selected alternative provides a framework for developing an active fish management program, the reviewers need to stay involved to ensure that land and water managers are meeting stated goals and objectives. The direction should be reflected in annual program proposals, budget allocations, and completed projects that meet the plan objectives. Other resource development should be occurring in conformance to standards.

(10) Monitor and evaluate results.—If desired resource outputs and public benefits, as well as management standards and guidelines, are sufficiently quantified in the plan to allow measurement, the design of a monitoring plan is relatively straightforward. The question to ask is, "Is the contract being carried out?"

A well-designed procedural tool should be developed to assess whether outputs and effects are being produced in conformance to standards and guidelines at the agreed-upon rate. The first level of monitoring is to determine if activities are occurring as planned. The second level is to assess if desired results are being achieved. To assess results, the monitoring plan must be sensitive enough to detect changes in indicator fish populations and in the quality of their habitats relative to baseline conditions established in the inventory data base. Planners must recognize that below a certain magnitude, induced changes in habitats and fish populations may not be statistically detectable by the best available monitoring methodology. If monitoring techniques can only detect a change of 20% or greater, or if the cost of monitoring smaller changes is excessive, this situation should be taken into account and avoided during the formulation and evaluation of alternatives. Monitoring and evaluation criteria should include a protocol that establishes the limits of success and failure beyond which management activities (and perhaps objectives) will be modified. For example, the absence of detectable change in a fish population over 3 years would trigger a reevaluation of management strategies.

It is advisable to develop an annual report that details monitoring results, outputs, and benefits for various resources; management budgets for each resource; and the adjustments made to planned objectives, along with the rationale for those adjustments. This annual report should allow internal reviewers and the public to understand the status of planned resource management as well as the progress toward planned objectives. Review of the annual report by outside resource specialists should be encouraged.

These 10 basic planning steps provide a comprehensive procedural framework for fishery resource planning in forest and rangeland ecosystems. The planning process is designed to bring about true multiple-resource management. A planning process is one thing; changing years of tradition and developed political alliances in an agency is quite another. As each year passes, however, multiple-use agencies are giving more consideration to fishery resources and their uses. Fisheries have been enfranchised in the integrated planning framework despite minimal planning direction in many instances. Public interest in, and controversy over, each land- and resource-management plan will ensure that the planned changes are carried out.

It is very difficult to stay productively involved throughout an agency's planning effort, which has exceeded 8 years in some cases. It is time consuming to comment on each step and perseverance is required. Agency personnel and management direction often change several times during the development of a plan. Most plans involve resource managers and planners who are going through the process for the first time and may lack the knowledge of what options are available at each step in the planning process. Maintaining effective communication and trust in such a working framework is not easy. The most successful resource managers, planners, and members of public interest groups have followed four general guidelines:

- they have entered the process as early as possible;
- they have continually interacted with plan formulators;
- they have not held false expectations that they will prevail over every issue or concern;
- they have documented comments in writing as they progressed through the process.

Having arrived at the end of the process, interested outside individuals, groups, or agencies may still be dissatisfied with the final plan. In such cases, a final remedial, agency-sponsored step usually is available: an administrative appeal to the agency director to stay plan implementation pending resolution of the issue. This step sometimes has assured consideration when previous efforts have failed. If satisfaction still is not obtained, one may seek a judicial court injunction if planning inadequacies have occurred and can be documented.

Other Fishery Planning

Although the U.S. Forest Service planning procedures were presented as an example, the agency's fisheries planning has not proceeded in a vacuum. Other agencies with joint jurisdiction over fisheries have worked with fishery interest groups to develop plans at the same time. Examples of such activity include the Trinity River basin fish and wildlife management program of the Trinity River Fish and Wildlife Restoration Task Force; the fish and wildlife program of the Northwest Power Planning Council; and the cooperative fisheries enhancement plans of Alaska, their regional aquaculture associations, and the U.S. Forest Service.

Trinity River Basin Fish and Wildlife Restoration Task Force.—The Trinity basin task force was created as a result of the construction of the Trinity River Division (Clair Engle Dam) of the Central Valley Project started in California in 1963. The project substantially reduced the streamflow of the Trinity River; pools and spawning gravels became filled with sediment and rearing habitat for fish was reduced. The Trinity River Task Force was reactivated in 1974 to develop a long-term management program for the basin. The Task Force, representing 13 federal, state, and local government groups, was charged with restoring full natural steelhead and salmon production in the undammed portion of the Trinity River; hatchery-produced fish were to be used to compensate for spawning and rearing habitats lost as a result of Clair Engle Dam. The Task Force was also to recommend measures to manage fishery harvests and to restore the watershed. In 1976 funding was obtained from the U.S. Congress to begin an interim action program and to develop a long-term management program for the basin. Studies and planning efforts, which followed procedures functionally equivalent to those detailed above, took 6 years; in March 1982, the long-term program was published, detailing 11 major actions with a cost of US$33 million. In 1984, the first major action—establishing and authorizing funding for a field organization—was accomplished. Personnel have now been selected and habitat restoration work, begun during the interim action phase, has continued under their guidance.

Northwest Power Planning Council.—The Northwest Power Planning Council was created by the Pacific Northwest Electric Power Planning and Conservation Act in 1980. The Act resulted from a legislative compromise between power users and fisheries interests who were outraged by the depletion of anadromous fish runs in the Columbia River that had resulted from hydroelectric development. Its purpose was to require the Bonneville Power Administration to conform with a regional power-planning and conservation plan to be developed by the Council. Further, it directed the Council to develop a program to protect, mitigate, and enhance fish and wildlife resources (including related spawning grounds and habitat) of the Columbia River and its tributaries. Finally, the Act required the federal water-management agencies to give fish and wildlife "equitable treatment" during project operations for other purposes. The Council—composed of representatives from Idaho, Montana, Oregon, and Washington—is funded by the users of Columbia basin hydroelectric power through the Bonneville Power Administration. In 1981, the Council began protecting, mitigating, and enhancing fish and wildlife. The Council's recommendations formed the basis of the program, which was published in draft form in September 1982 after extensive public involvement and consultation by Council staff with technical advisory committees. The final program was adopted in November 1982, amended in October 1984, and amended again in February 1987.

Alaska cooperative fisheries enhancement plans.—The Alaska cooperative plans are a result of direction provided in Section 507(a) of the Alaska National Interest Lands Conservation Act of 1980, complemented by state legislation enacted in 1977 and codified under Title 16, Fish and Game, Alaska Statutes. Cooperative fisheries enhancement planning in Alaska is a process that integrates regional comprehensive plans for salmon and other fisheries into forest plans and their implementation (R. Dewey, U.S. Forest Service, personal communication). Through the planning process, the comprehensive salmon plans provide data, fisheries rehabilitation and enhancement recommendations, and fisheries demand information for the national forests. The cooperative planning process, through coordination with the Alaska Department of Fish and Game and user groups such as the regional aquaculture associations, provides National Forest managers with fisheries enhancement recommendations that best meet long-term harvest objectives (year 2000) of the comprehensive salmon plans. Recommendations are evaluated for compatibility with other objectives and incorporated through forest planning and requirements of the National Environmental Policy Act of 1969. National Forest fisheries enhancement projects are compiled and scheduled in 5-year action plans and then implemented through regular budgets of the Forest Service and its cooperators. Project monitoring, evaluating, and reporting are an integral part of National Forest cooperative fisheries planning and are to be accomplished through shared responsibility between the Forest Service and its cooperators.

As can be seen from these three examples, the planning procedures of other agencies can be (and in fact have been) readily integrated with the 10-step process detailed above. Stronger plans result if information from complementary plans can be included by reference.

Other U.S. Federal Agency Planning

U.S. Fish and Wildlife Service (FWS).—The FWS has 428 national wildlife refuges (L. Starnes, FWS, personal communication). Covering more than 36 million hectares, they are located in 49 states and 5 trust territories. The smallest, on Mille Lacs Lake in Minnesota, covers less than 0.4 hectare; the largest spreads across nearly 8 million hectares of Alaska's Yukon River delta. The refuges include 4.9 million hectares of aquatic habitat, of which about 1.8 million have substantial fishery potentials.

As the name implies, refuges were created to protect wildlife. The first was established in 1903 by Theodore Roosevelt on Pelican Island, Florida, to protect egrets, herons, and other birds then under heavy commercial hunting pressure. Today's refuges are located in mountains, deserts, forests, and grasslands, and on seashores and lakes. The majority of these refuges protect migratory birds such as ducks and geese but many have been established for other purposes such as protecting habitats of sea turtles and endangered fish species.

Nearly 27 million people annually visit national wildlife refuges. Publicity about refuges typically concentrates on their waterfowl viewing or hunting, but the greatest single public use of refuges is for fishing (31% of all public use). Anglers fished 19.6 million hours on refuges in 1985.

To achieve multiple-use management and to accommodate competing priorities (e.g., wetland, waterfowl, and fishery resources), the FWS has a refuge master-planning process. Refuge master planning allows the capacities of individual refuges and the refuge system to be evaluated.

All master planning employs a three-phase process to structure decision making and to determine long-range planning direction. This process begins with a comprehensive inventory of existing resource conditions. An analysis then is made of the capacities of these resources to support desired future uses. The process concludes with allotments of land use based on a synthesis of the analyzed data with proposed planning objectives and estimated trends of resource use in the present and future. Alternative ways of arranging land uses are compared; the most effective alternative becomes the master plan. A management plan addressing fisheries is one of many that make up the refuge master plan. Along with all other management plans, it must be oriented to achieve the refuge objectives established within the refuge master plan.

In 1982, the FWS began a program to optimize fishery values on national wildlife refuges (insofar as fisheries would not conflict with the other objectives of each refuge). Of 428 refuges, 210 are open to sport fishing. Of these 210 refuges, 74 were identified in 1982 as having adequate plans, and 136 needed fishery-management plans. Since 1982, 76 plans have been developed, and the FWS is working to complete the remaining 60.

Progressive fishery management on national wildlife refuges can have dramatic results. For example, fishery management at the Valentine National Wildlife Refuge in Nebraska once was restricted to removal of common carp. Carp control was attempted, at considerable expense, because these fish roil the bottom muds; suspended mud reduces penetration of sunlight, which decreases growth of the aquatic plants on which waterfowl depend. Refuge practice changed from physical removal of the pest to stocking of predator fish species (largemouth bass and northern pike). Since then, the population of common carp has been kept within acceptable limits, waterfowl populations have improved, and the stocked predators have provided one of Nebraska's premier fisheries.

Bureau of Land Management (BLM).—Nearly 13.5 million hectares in 11 western states and Alaska are administered by BLM (M. Crouse, BLM, personal communication). These public lands are primarily rangelands but also include 1.8 million hectares of commercial forests and 7.3 million hectares classified as woodlands. The BLM manages a major aquatic resource that includes 6.1 million hectares of riparian habitat and 135,266 km of perennial streams, many of which support trout, salmon, and other sport fishes as well as many nongame, threatened, and endangered species.

Laws that regulate the uses of public lands require BLM to manage not only fish and wildlife habitats, but also energy resources, minerals, timber production, livestock grazing, recreation, wilderness, and other competing uses. The Federal Lands Policy and Management Act of 1976 and the National Environmental Policy Act established a planning process by which these competing uses are identified, analyzed, and balanced under the principles of multiple use and sustained yield. To allocate resources and select appropriate uses for the public lands within a resource area (a subunit of a BLM district), BLM managers prepare resource-management plans.

The process used by BLM to prepare resource-management plans is identical to that described for Forest Service planning, except in the way the plans are implemented (step 9). The BLM has added one additional step to the process by requiring that certain program staffs, including fish and wildlife management, forestry, and livestock-grazing management personnel, prepare detailed site-specific activity plans.

Activity plans related to fish and wildlife management are called habitat-management plans. The following activities related to fish and wildlife habitats are usually deferred until habitat-management plans have been prepared: detailed actions needed to manage specific priority species or habitats in a geographic area much smaller than the resource area; specific funding and personnel needs for implementing high-priority habitat-management efforts; identification of specific habitat improvement locations and projects needed to improve or maintain high-priority habitats; and detailed descriptions of studies and analyses needed to evaluate habitat-management prescriptions. State fish and game agencies are strongly encouraged to participate in preparing and implementing habitat-management plans, and consultation is required with other federal and state agencies and local governments where their lands are adjacent to the habitat-management area. Currently, BLM has 80 new and partially implemented plans related to fish, aquatic, and riparian habitats.

In addition to the preparation of habitat plans, fisheries-related management objectives are included in other activity plans for management of livestock grazing (allotment-management plans) and forestry (timber-management plans).

Future Planning and Program Development

The success of planning by any agency is critically linked to the identification of all interested groups and to the proper scoping of planning actions. Establishing closer ties to all user groups (consumptive and nonconsumptive) can be an important benefit of planning that gives an agency the opportunity to meet the users' needs. For fisheries, it is vital to integrate planned resource objectives with the needs of recreational, subsistence, and commercial fishing groups. These users must see the planning alternatives as opportunities to satisfy their desires in a particular planning area. Such a perception will ensure their support for a plan and its implementation.

Coalitions of groups interested in using and conserving fishery resources have only recently begun to rally to support the fisheries plans and programs of U.S. land-management and -development agencies. Fishery programs of the U.S. Forest Service, Soil Conservation Service, and Bureau of Land Management have been small and almost invisible in the larger "multiple-use" strategies that traditionally have focused on commodity production. Development agencies, including the Bonneville Power Administration, Bureau of Reclamation, U.S. Army Corps of Engineers, and Federal Energy Regulatory Commission, generally have not considered fishery resources except in grudging terms of mitigation for resource damage caused by projects they were involved in. Fishery interest groups have focused on stopping agency activities they consider detrimental to fishery resources. As a result, fisheries programs of these agencies have emphasized mitigation and conflict resolution, rather than restoration and enhancement of the fish habitats over which they have jurisdiction.

The traditional U.S. fishery-management agencies (National Marine Fisheries Service and U.S. Fish and Wildlife Service), along with the Environmental Protection Agency and state fishery resource agencies, have often been enlisted by fishery interest groups as they battled to stop resource-damaging activities by the land management and development agencies. The interagency distrust engendered by these battles—at times approaching outright animosity and disdain—has resulted in less restoration and enhancement of fishery resources than if the politics of cooperation had been practiced. The development and management agencies have responded to "attacks" on their plans by closing the door to effective public and interagency participation in their planning processes. As a result, published alternatives have not met user needs, and criticism has been heavy and prolonged.

In developing a strategy for identification and scoping of planning actions by interest groups, an agency must define who cares about what happens to the fishery resources in the planning area. In general, recreational and commercial fishermen, outfitters and guides, and people in the supporting services and production sectors of their economies care. The subsistence users and the people who appreciate seeing fish or knowing about their existence and life cycles care. The organizations used by these groups to express their political desires must be included in the planning process. The ability of the planning process to meet these users' needs must be defined and realized to the extent possible. At the completion of a plan, interest groups must be enlisted to promote funding of those portions of the plan that meet their needs. In response to this political support, the responsible agency must clearly present its record of meeting planned objectives in periodic status reports to the interest groups. Planning of fisheries programs and development of support strategies, based on highlighting benefits to interested users, must be followed at each level in an agency hierarchy if it is to be successful. In this way, fisheries plans can be transformed into reality instead of gathering dust as they lie forgotten on a disappointed resource manager's bookshelf!

Chapter 18

Managing Salmonid Habitats

J. L. Kershner, H. L. Forsgren, and W. R. Meehan

The nature and quality of stream habitats are linked to those of adjacent terrestrial environments, a principle documented throughout this book. A stream cannot be sustained and managed as a viable place for fish without an understanding of the ways in which watershed dynamics affect the stream itself. The overall goal for fish habitats should be to manage the physical and biological functions of watershed areas—uplands, floodplains, riparian zones, and channels—to assure that some dynamic equilibrium is maintained. Fish habitat managers often have to consult with geologists, soil scientists, hydrologists, and other specialists to achieve this goal.

Evaluation of fish habitat dynamics requires several important decisions. One is to determine the appropriate spatial scale of assessments. The watershed or drainage basin is a logical land unit for planning purposes because it represents the area in which streams are most directly influenced by processes occurring around them (Swanston 1991, this volume). The relevant watershed size varies greatly with the project under consideration and with the species of principal interest; a resident population can be studied within a small subbasin, for example, but an anadromous stock can range over an entire drainage basin. When the spatial scale is large, subbasins may have to be studied to determine local effects on populations; the local results then must be aggregated to estimate cumulative effects for the entire basin.

The appropriate temporal scales for assessments also must be chosen. Seasonal habitat characteristics influence the distribution and abundance of aquatic organisms, and year-to-year variation can be an important long-term consideration. If the evaluation period is too short, misguided management may result. If it is too long, money is wasted.

Selection of biological criteria is the most obvious prerequisite of habitat evaluation, but it is rarely straightforward. Traditional management has focused on "management indicator species"—species of commercial importance or species whose habitat requirements are judged to best represent those of coexisting species. This focus is required of the U.S. Forest Service by the National Forest Management Act of 1976, but the use of a single indicator species or population index as an unvalidated surrogate for others is risky, as Landres et al. (1988) pointed out. Evaluation of functional guilds—groups of species that have similar habitat requirements and that presumably compete with one another (Hawkins and MacMahon 1989)—overcomes some of the risks associated with

599

single indicator species, though it must be assumed that guild members will respond similarly to environmental change (Verner 1984). This approach still is limited because habitat conditions for species outside the guild may not be represented. Community assessments provide the greatest insights into habitat function, but they are complex and costly. Finally, life stage as well as species or assemblage must be considered, for young and mature animals may use entirely different habitats, or they may use the same general habitat entirely differently.

Ideally, evaluations and management of habitat function should be coextensive in space and time with the life histories of the species involved, though the ideal is often compromised by limitations of knowledge, personnel, and money. Whether compromised or not, watershed management to sustain high-quality aquatic habitats is a complex and difficult task. It can only be accomplished by careful program planning and a clear and precise definition of program goals and objectives.

Goals and Objectives

Fisheries managers must have clear, long-term goals supported by measurable objectives in order to effectively manage habitats. In the following sections, we use "program" as the collective term for all activities undertaken in support of goals, and "project" to mean the activities undertaken to achieve objectives.

• *Goals* describe the ultimate state that a program is designed to achieve; goals, therefore, should be realistic and achievable. A goal may comprise either a single aim, such as to rehabilitate a coho salmon run to a specified previous level, or several purposes, such as to sustain an average harvest of X adult trout by Y anglers per month along a stream flowing through a grazing allotment that should support Z animal units per month. Goals usually have measurable components, but they can be essentially qualitative: "reforestation of the bottomland with native hardwoods" is an example.

• *Objectives* describe the discrete projects needed to achieve a stated goal. These projects may be undertaken sequentially or, in some cases, simultaneously; the timing of individual projects—and the number of them—depends on the nature of the overall goal. Objectives should always be measurable and quantifiable.

Goals (and hence objectives) must be set early in a planning process. They are most likely to be achieved, however, if they are based on prior assessments of the ecological capability of the resource, the legal and institutional requirements placed on the managers, and the social and economic expectations of the resource users. Generally, the current capability is a snapshot in time and reflects only one within a range of possible conditions.

Habitat Management Framework

Program Planning

Planning and implementing programs to protect, restore, and enhance salmonid habitats generally require the skills of several disciplines. Among the people who may be required for a program are fishery biologists, entomologists, geologists,

Strategies for Setting Goals and Objectives

Determine range of conditions
(Historic   Current   Expected)

Develop habitat goals and objectives*

Monitor goals and objectives

Assess effectiveness of current goals and objectives

Adapt goals and objectives with new information

Begin process again

*Within a framework of constraints--legal, social, political, financial.

FIGURE 18.1.—Procedural strategy to establish goals and objectives for salmonid habitats.

geomorphologists, hydrologists, engineers, chemists, soil scientists, silviculturists, timber and range managers, contracting officers, equipment operators, and procurement agents. Natural stream channels are so complex and watershed processes are so dynamic and episodic that "cookbook" treatments will rarely be useful. Programs and projects must be tailored to meet existing and desired conditions and to accommodate the goals and objectives of all interested user groups; hence, each operation must be uniquely planned and implemented.

In addition to professionals of the relevant disciplines, it is important to include all user and land-ownership groups in the planning process from its beginning. Failure to do so may lead to recriminations and even lawsuits that can hamper or stop a program later.

Planning is an iterative process (Figure 18.1). Once a need is identified, it is useful to draft preliminary goals and objectives for meeting that need. This draft provides an organizational framework for collecting background information on the subject in the form of field surveys and literature searches. With this information in hand, the goals and objectives can be refined. Likely constraints of funding, existing laws, and sociopolitical attitudes can be factored into a further refinement. Inclusion of user groups in the process may provoke yet another draft before implementation of the plan begins. As each objective is met, the plan should be reexamined and (if necessary) modified in light of project results to date. When the goal is finally achieved, the plan and its evolution should be studied

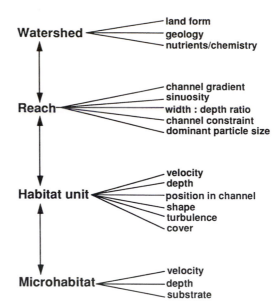

FIGURE 18.2.—Representative hierarchy for designing salmonid habitat inventories.

once more for the lessons the process can offer to future programs. The process never really ends.

Resource Surveys

Historical information such as resource surveys, descriptive narratives, and aerial or ground photographs often provide excellent baseline information on resources that are at various levels of exploitation. Such surveys often provide insights into potential future conditions as well. Many stream alterations that occurred 50–100 years ago still affect stream and watershed processes today, such as in the Willamette River, Oregon, and other western watersheds that were radically altered by logging, river log drives, and tie hacking (Sedell and Luchessa 1982; Schmal and Wesche 1989). Documentation of resource condition over time has contributed to an understanding of recovery rates.

Inventories of current geological conditions, soil types, vegetation, and other resources provide information on existing habitats and the processes likely to influence them. In aquatic systems, hierarchical inventories are useful for describing existing stream conditions (Figure 18.2). They allow descriptions of conditions at large scales such as watersheds (Strahler 1957), at intermediate scales such as stream reaches (Rosgen 1985; Grant et al. 1990) and individual habitat units (Bisson et al. 1982; Helm 1985), and at small scales within habitat units (Bovee 1982). The physical information gathered should be detailed enough to document the conditions of interest to biologists. For example, a simple descriptive survey of a previously unsampled watershed may just summarize the areas or volumes of pools and riffles within the watershed, whereas an evaluation of sedimentation caused by roads may include measures of residual pool depths and a detailed substrate analysis for each habitat. Because aquatic environments form a continuum, inventories should be performed throughout the basin of interest. Subsampling habitat types and characteristics in representative reaches or by various transect methods may give decidedly biased results (Hankin and Reeves 1988; Kershner and Snider, in press).

Describing the distribution of aquatic organisms within a basin allows biologists to gain insights into the relationships between physical conditions and assemblages of organisms in streams. Several authors have described relationships between habitat characteristics and use of habitats by fish. Bisson et al. (1982) and Bisson and Sedell (1984), for example, found that coho salmon, steelhead, and cutthroat trout used distinctly different habitats at different life stages. Sullivan (1986) observed similar relationships in Washington streams. The principle here is that physical conditions within channels influence the distribution and abundance of salmonids. By understanding the functional relationships between habitat and fish, one can gain an understanding of the physical factors limiting salmonid production. Again, the amount of effort dedicated to population surveys will be determined by the questions asked. More detailed questions involving complex relationships may require more sampling effort. We recommend that basin-level inventories of fish be made in order to estimate population abundance and distribution (Hankin and Reeves 1988).

To determine what factor or factors are limiting production, it may be necessary to sample throughout the year or at least during more than one season (Reeves et al. 1989). Conditions that occur during one particular season may have a profound effect on the overall survival and success of fish in a system. For example, it is often assumed that the amount of available habitat during summer low flows limits salmonid populations, but winter constraints on habitat use may be the primary limiting factor (Chisholm et al. 1987; McMahon and Hartman 1989).

Goals and Objectives

Once the range of possible resource conditions has been established, some idea of realistic goals and objectives can be obtained. Habitat conditions may range from optimal to unacceptable for salmonid production. In any case, managers should identify a set of minimum conditions that will clearly protect the long-term habitat capability for salmonids. This set of conditions may not constitute the management goal, but it sets the threshold for aggressive changes in habitat management or improvement. Habitat conditions vary through time and space in natural systems, and goals and objectives need to be flexible enough to accommodate this variability. By understanding the continuum that exists, managers can develop realistic expectations of habitat condition.

As mentioned earlier, interested public groups as well as biologists and other specialists should be involved in determining long-term habitat goals. Various user groups are interested in the future of salmonids. Knowing the expectations of these groups may be as important in setting goals as knowing the range of habitat conditions. As with most resource issues, expectations vary considerably among user groups. Commercial fishermen, for example, may favor habitat goals that optimize anadromous fish production, whereas timber managers may want to balance anadromous fish production with timber goals. In any case, overlaying the range of habitat conditions with the range of consumer expectations will reveal an array of resource alternatives that can guide the formulation of resource goals and later management decisions.

Monitoring and Validation

Monitoring provides essential feedback to managers on whether goals and objectives are actually being met. In addition, monitoring helps us understand the ecological foundations of our programs, and ultimately helps to improve the quality of management activities. The type of monitoring needed depends on the complexity of resource issues, the risks involved if goals and objectives are not met, and the questions to be answered. Legal constraints also may affect the design of monitoring plans.

Generally, goals and objectives can be monitored at three different levels (Solomon 1989). Ranging from simple to more complex, these are implementation monitoring, effectiveness monitoring, and validation monitoring (program validation).

Implementation monitoring.—Implementation monitoring, the most simple and straightforward type of monitoring, answers the question "Were the prescribed activities for an objective implemented correctly on the ground?" For example, an objective for stream temperature in an area to be logged may state that summer water temperatures should not exceed 20°C after timber harvest. To achieve this objective, we decide that all trees within 30 m of the stream must be left undamaged to provide shade. Our implementation monitoring could be as simple as a field check after harvest to determine if the stipulated riparian buffer strip actually was left and if the trees are undamaged. Because failure to leave the buffer could compromise or negate our temperature objective, however, the project area should be checked periodically during timber harvest, so that noncompliance can be identified and corrected before the consequences become too severe. If the basin is large, we may have to devise a statistically sound random-sampling program so we can put confidence limits on the estimates of buffer width and tree damage. Generally, implementation monitoring can be conducted by either fisheries or nonfisheries staff.

Effectiveness monitoring.—The purpose of effectiveness monitoring is to determine if an objective was actually achieved by the activities undertaken. In terms of the previous example, in which we required timber harvesters to leave a 30-m-wide buffer strip of trees along a stream so water temperatures would not exceed 20°C, effectiveness monitoring answers the question "Did stream temperatures actually stay at 20°C and below?" If the answer is "Yes," based on afternoon temperature measurements made throughout the warmest season, the objective has been met and we might assume the practice was effective. If the answer is "No," the practice must be reexamined. A field survey may show that the existing trees cast a highly variable amount of shade, suggesting that canopy closure standards might have been more effective than buffer width in meeting our temperature objective. To evaluate this possibility, it may be necessary to generate a quantitatively testable hypothesis and to consult a statistician for help with framing alternative questions that can be answered with appropriate precision and accuracy.

Effectiveness monitoring also is used to judge whether or not goals have been met. Suppose our overall program goal is to prevent salmonid biomass from declining in a stream when the watershed is partially logged. The program encompasses several projects, the objective of one being to keep water temperature within limits favorable to salmonids that use the stream. When all the objectives have been met, the measure of goal success will be the quantity of salmonids still in the stream relative to the quantity there before logging began. If the goal had been formulated in terms of species and age-class distributions, these details would be accommodated in the monitoring plan. Again, the sampling procedure should be statistically rigorous and justifiable.

Validation monitoring (program validation).—Knowledge is never complete, and many goals and objectives are necessarily based on untested hypotheses and informed judgment. Whenever possible, the hypotheses and judgments associated with a project should be tested and validated, for the lessons that can be learned will improve the formulation of future goals and objectives.

Validation work is needed in two general circumstances. The more obvious one arises when a goal or objective cannot be met for reasons other than poor project execution. In the example previously described, failure of a riparian buffer zone to control water temperature within acceptable limits would mean that the benefits of streamside shade were less than anticipated; we would want to know why our previous expectations were flawed and what other approaches to temperature control would be more reliable.

The other need for validation arises when a goal or objective is met (or seems to be) but we are uncertain why. Suppose stream temperatures did stay below 20°C when a riparian buffer strip was preserved. Without additional information, we could not be sure that the temperature control was due to the streamside vegetation or to some other factor, such as hidden springs, that would keep the water cool even in the absence of a buffer strip. If we wrongly attribute benefits to a management technique, we soon will apply the technique wrongly, at considerable cost in money (to someone) and in management credibility.

Validation needs can become apparent at any time during a project, but they should receive particular attention during the final project review. Identifying the need for validation is a responsibility of managers, who also should participate in the planning of validation studies. Much of the design and execution of validation work, however, is the proper domain of research.

Woody debris management provides an example of how such research has changed management objectives. As recently as the 1960s, streams were regularly cleared of debris to provide passage for salmonids and to stabilize stream banks. Research into the historic role of woody debris strongly suggested that debris is an essential part of healthy streams (Sedell and Luchessa 1982; Sedell and Froggatt 1984; Bisson et al. 1987). This inference has since been confirmed by surveys and experimental manipulations of debris in streams. These results led to fundamental changes in management policies, goals, and objectives with respect to large woody debris, which is now understood to have a major role in maintaining salmonid habitat quality.

Validation studies thus are essential for examining the foundations of habitat protection and enhancement, and they play an important role as a feedback mechanism in our strategies for setting goals and objectives (Figure 18.1). This type of work, conducted primarily by fishery researchers, is founded in hypothesis testing, and it requires strong statistical designs.

Application of Monitoring and Validation

The monitoring of objectives is designed to provide insights into the effects of a management activity on habitat characteristics and ultimately on fish production. Several factors should be considered when a monitoring plan is developed.

Any management-induced change has an element of risk, and sometimes the risk is high. For instance, if a habitat objective is to place woody debris structures in a stream above a small hydroelectric dam, managers must consider the risk that debris will be dislodged during high flows, move downstream, and block penstock intakes or lodge in a spillway. It may be necessary to analyze expected project benefits in relation to the costs of project failure, of extra anchoring effort to keep the structures in place, and of the intensive effectiveness monitoring required to track debris movement and to manage or minimize the risk. In contrast, if the debris structures are to be placed in a remote watershed where there is no risk to downstream facilities, a simple, inexpensive plan for implementation monitoring may be all that is needed.

In all cases, the risk associated with a management activity must be weighed against the cost of monitoring the activity. Monitoring budgets are always limited, so a decision to proceed with the activity, to adopt an alternative technique, or to abandon the habitat objective altogether requires professional judgement.

Professional judgement is required of all fishery biologists. In some cases, the judgement will be backed by considerable scientific fact and the results of inventory or monitoring projects. In others, the biologist will be asked to render opinions with little information. It is always desirable to have as much information as possible before making a decision, but complete information often is not available. Experience in other similar situations and a knowledge of the literature pertinent to the topic may be reasonably substituted for scientific data. Even with locally gathered information, biologists have to interpret results and speculate on the outcomes. Biologists must be willing to render opinions and provide as much interpretation as possible. The "need more data" response is valid in some cases, but in others it impedes good management decisions.

Conclusions

The management of salmonid habitats is a dynamic process involving not only the habitats themselves, but social and economic considerations as well. Successful implementation of any fish habitat management program depends on clearly defined goals and objectives. Formulation of goals and objectives, in turn, depends on an understanding of habitat and population dynamics, of the expectations held by other natural resource users, of the concerns voiced by land owners who may be affected, and of public values. It is important to recognize the role of change and adaptation in management processes. Environmental, social, and economic conditions are constantly changing, and successful guidelines for fish habitat management must adapt to these changes. Although the management approach described in this chapter provides a foundation for, and encourages, quantitative planning and evaluation, the use of professional judgement and risk assessment will continue to be an important part of fish habitat management. The value of salmonids and the precarious situation faced by many stocks demand that management decisions be made even in the absence of complete quantitative information. Professional judgement then must be employed and the underlying rationale and assumptions fully described.

References

Adams, A. K. 1954. Some physico-chemical effects of beaver dams upon Michigan trout streams in the Watersmeet area. Doctoral dissertation. University of Michigan, Ann Arbor.

Adams, B. L., W. S. Zaugg, and L. R. McLain. 1973. Temperature effect on parr–smolt transformation in steelhead trout (*Salmo gairdneri*) as measured by gill sodium–potassium stimulated adenosine triphosphatase. Comparative Biochemistry and Physiology A, Comparative Physiology 44:1333–1339.

Adams, L., M. G. Hanavan, N. W. Hosley, and D. W. Johnston. 1949. The effects on fish, birds and mammals of DDT used in the control of forest insects in Idaho and Wyoming. Journal of Wildlife Management 13:245–254.

Adelman, I. R., L. L. Smith, Jr., and G. D. Siesennop. 1976. Chronic toxicity of Guthion to the fathead minnow (*Pimephales promelas* Rafinesque). Bulletin of Environmental Contamination and Toxicology 15:726–733.

Aho, R. S. 1976. A population study of the cutthroat trout in an unshaded and shaded section of stream. Master's thesis. Oregon State University, Corvallis.

Ainscough, G. 1979. The dragons and the St. Georges of the coastal forest. Pages 77–103 *in* A. H. J. Dorsey, editor. Coastal resources in the future of British Columbia. University of British Columbia, Westwater Research Centre, Vancouver.

Aitchison, S. W., S. W. Carothers, and R. R. Johnson. 1977. Some ecological considerations associated with river recreation management. Pages 222–225 *in* Proceedings, river recreation management and research symposium. U.S. Forest Service General Technical Report NC-28.

Alabaster, J. S. 1969. Survival of fish in 164 herbicides, insecticides, fungicides, wetting agents and miscellaneous substances. International Pest Control 11(2):29–35.

Alabaster, J. S., D. W. M. Herbert, and J. Hemens. 1957. The survival of rainbow trout (*Salmo gairdnerii* Richardson) and perch (*Perca fluviatilis* L.) at various concentrations of dissolved oxygen and carbon dioxide. Annals of Applied Biology 45:177–188.

Alabaster, J. S., D. G. Shurben, and M. J. Mallett. 1979. The survival of smolts of salmon *Salmo salar* L. at low concentrations of dissolved oxygen. Journal of Fish Biology 15:1–8.

Albrecht, M. 1968. Die Wirkung des Lichtes auf die quantitativ Verteilung der Fauna im Fliessgewasser. Limnologica 6:71–82.

Albrecht, M.-L., and F. W. Tesch. 1961. Das Wachstum der Bachforelle (*Salmo trutta fario* L.) in der Polenz in Abhängigkeit von verschiedenen Umweltbedingungen. Zeitschrift für Fischerei und deren Hilfswissenschaften, New Series 10:253–273.

Alderdice, D. F., and F. P. J. Velsen. 1978. Relation between temperature and incubation time for eggs of chinook salmon (*Oncorhynchus tshawytscha*). Journal of the Fisheries Research Board of Canada 35:69–75.

Alderdice, D. F., W. P. Wickett, and J. R. Brett. 1958. Some effects of temporary exposure to low dissolved oxygen levels on Pacific salmon eggs. Journal of the Fisheries Research Board of Canada 15:229–250.

Alderfer, R. B., and R. R. Robinson. 1947. Runoff from pastures in relation to grazing intensity and soil compaction. Journal of the American Society of Agronomy 39:948–958.

Aldon, E. F. 1984. Broadcast seeded western wheatgrass successfully spreads on mine spoil. Reclamation and Revegetation Research 3:167–170.

Aldon, E. F., and C. P. Pase. 1981. Plant species adaptability on mine spoils in the Southwest: a case study. U.S. Forest Service Research Note RM-398.

607

Ali, A. 1981. *Bacillus thuringiensis* serovar. *israelensis* (ABG-6108) against chironomids and some nontarget aquatic invertebrates. Journal of Invertebrate Pathology 38:264–272.

Allan, J. D. 1981. Determinants of diet of brook trout (*Salvelinus fontinalis*) in a mountain stream. Canadian Journal of Fisheries and Aquatic Sciences 38:184–192.

Allan, J. D. 1982. The effects of reduction in trout density on the invertebrate community of a mountain stream. Ecology 63:1444–1455.

Allan, J. D. 1983. Food consumption by trout and stoneflies in a Rocky Mountain stream, with comparison to prey standing crop. Pages 371–390 *in* T. D. Fontaine III and S. M. Bartell, editors. Dynamics of lotic ecosystems. Ann Arbor Science, Ann Arbor, Michigan.

Allen, H. L. 1987. Forest fertilizers. Journal of Forestry 85:37–46.

Allen, K. R. 1940. Studies on the biology of the early stages of the salmon (*Salmo salar*). 2. Feeding habits. Journal of Animal Ecology 10:47–76.

Allen, K. R. 1969. Limitations on production in salmonid populations in streams. Pages 1–18 *in* Northcote (1969b).

Allen, M. A. 1986. Population dynamics of juvenile steelhead trout in relation to density and habitat characteristics. Master's thesis. Humboldt State University, Arcata, California.

Alley, N. F., and B. Thomson. 1978. Aspects of environmental geology, parts of Graham Island, Queen Charlotte Islands. Ministry of the Environment, Bulletin 2, Victoria, British Columbia.

Allison, D. T. 1977. Use of exposure units for estimating aquatic toxicity of organophosphate pesticides. U.S. Environmental Protection Agency, Ecological Research Series EPA-600/3-77-077.

Althauser, D. R. 1985. Groundwater-fed spawning channel development in the Pacific Northwest. Master's thesis. University of Washington, Seattle.

Altom, J. D., and J. F. Stritzke. 1972. Persistence of brush control herbicides in a blackjack and post oak soil. Proceedings of the Southern Weed Science Society 25:302. (Abstract.)

Amendola, G., D. Barna, R. Blosser, L. LaFleur, A. McBride, F. Thomas, T. Tiernan, and R. Whittemore. 1989. The occurrence and fate of PCDDs and PCDFs in five bleached kraft pulp and paper mills. Chemosphere 18:1181–1188.

American Society of Civil Engineers. 1949. Hydrology handbook. American Society of Civil Engineers, Manuals of Engineering Practice 28, New York.

Anderson, B. W., and R. D. Ohmart. 1985. Riparian revegetation as a mitigating process in stream and river restoration. Pages 41–79 *in* Gore (1985).

Anderson, C. A., J. C. Cavagnol, C. J. Cohen, A. D. Cohick, R. T. Evans, L. J. Everett, J. Hensel, R. P. Honeycutt, E. R. Levy, W. W. Loeffler, D. L. Nelson, T. Parr, T. B. Waggoner, and J. W. Young. 1974. Guthion (azinphosmethyl): organophosphorus insecticide. Residue Reviews 51:123–180.

Anderson, H. W. 1967. Snow accumulation as related to meteorological, topographic, and forest variables in central Sierra Nevada, California. International Association of Scientific Hydrology Publication 76:215–224.

Anderson, H. W. 1971. Relative contributions of sediment from source areas, and transport processes. Pages 55–63 *in* Krygier and Hall (1971).

Anderson, H. W. 1976. Fire effects on water supply, floods, and sedimentation. Proceedings, Tall Timbers Fire Ecology Conference 15:249–260.

Anderson, H. W., M. D. Hoover, and K. G. Reinhart. 1976. Forests and water: effects of forest management on floods, sedimentation, and water supply. U.S. Forest Service General Technical Report PSW-18.

Anderson, J. M. 1968. Effect of sublethal DDT on the lateral line of brook trout, *Salvelinus fontinalis*. Journal of the Fisheries Research Board of Canada 25:2677–2682.

Anderson, J. M. 1971. Assessment of the effects of pollutants on physiology and behaviour. Proceedings of the Royal Society of London, B, Biological Sciences 177:307–320.

Anderson, J. M., and M. R. Peterson. 1969. DDT: sublethal effects on brook trout nervous system. Science (Washington, D.C.) 164:440–441.

Anderson, J. W. 1973a. Evaluation of excavated fish rearing pool in Vincent Creek. U.S. Bureau of Land Management Technical Note, Coos Bay, Oregon.

Anderson, J. W. 1973b. Gold Creek fish passage structure. U.S. Bureau of Land Management, Technical Note 6, Coos Bay, Oregon.

Anderson, J. W. 1984. A method for monitoring and evaluating salmonid habitat carrying capacity of natural and enhanced Oregon coastal streams. Proceedings of the Annual Conference Western Association of Fish and Wildlife Agencies 64:288–296.

Anderson, J. W., and J. J. Cameron. 1980. The use of gabions to improve aquatic habitat. U.S. Bureau of Land Management, Technical Note 342, Coos Bay, Oregon.

Anderson, J. W., and L. Miyajima. 1975. Analysis of the Vincent Creek fish rearing pool project. U.S. Bureau of Land Management, Technical Note 274, Coos Bay, Oregon.

Anderson, J. W., R. A. Ruediger, and W. F. Hudson, Jr. 1984. Design, placement and fish use of instream structures in southwestern Oregon. Pages 165–180 in Hassler (1984).

Anderson, L., and M. Bryant. 1980. Fish passage at road crossings: an annotated bibliography. U.S. Forest Service General Technical Report PNW-117.

Anderson, N. H., and K. W. Cummins. 1979. Influences of diet on the life histories of aquatic insects. Journal of the Fisheries Research Board of Canada 36:335–342.

Anderson, N. H., and J. R. Sedell. 1979. Detritus processing by macroinvertebrates in stream ecosystems. Annual Review of Entomology 24:351–377.

Anderson, N. H., J. R. Sedell, L. M. Roberts, and F. J. Triska. 1978. The role of aquatic invertebrates in processing of wood debris in coniferous forest streams. American Midland Naturalist 100:64–82.

Anderson, N. H., R. J. Steedman, and T. Dudley. 1984. Patterns of exploitation by stream invertebrates of wood debris (xylophagy). Internationale Vereinigung für theoretische und angewandte Limnologie Verhandlungen 22:1847–1852.

Andrews, E. D. 1982. Bank stability and channel width adjustment, East Fork River, Wyoming. Water Resources Research 18:1184–1192.

Andrus, C. W., B. A. Long, and H. A. Froehlich. 1988. Woody debris and its contribution to pool formation in a coastal stream 50 years after logging. Canadian Journal of Fisheries and Aquatic Sciences 45:2080–2086.

Andrusak, H., and T. G. Northcote. 1971. Segregation between adult cutthroat trout (Salmo clarki) and Dolly Varden (Salvelinus malma) in small coastal British Columbia lakes. Journal of the Fisheries Research Board of Canada 28:1259–1268.

Anonymous. 1958. Idaho placer is source of 99 percent of U.S. columbium–tantalum output. Mining World 20(1):38–43, 62.

Anonymous. 1986. Cyanide spills at heap leaching practices in the western United States and their impacts. Heap and Dump Leaching News 3:14–17.

Apmann, R. P., and M. B. Otis. 1965. Sedimentation and stream improvement. New York Fish and Game Journal 12:117–126.

Aquatic Life Advisory Committee. 1955. Aquatic life water quality criteria. Sewage and Industrial Wastes 27:321–331.

Armantrout, N. B., editor. 1982. Acquisition and utilization of aquatic habitat inventory information symposium. American Fisheries Society, Western Division, Bethesda, Maryland.

Armour, C. L. 1977. Effects of deteriorated range streams on trout. U.S. Bureau of Land Management, Boise, Idaho.

Armstrong, R. H. 1970. Age, food and migration of Dolly Varden smolts in southeastern Alaska. Journal of the Fisheries Research Board of Canada 27:991–1004.

Armstrong, R. H. 1974. Migration of anadromous Dolly Varden (Salvelinus malma) in southeastern Alaska. Journal of the Fisheries Research Board of Canada 31:435–444.

Armstrong, R. H. 1984. Migration of anadromous Dolly Varden charr in southeastern Alaska—a manager's nightmare. Pages 559–570 in L. Johnson and B. Burns, editors. Biology of the Arctic charr: proceedings, international symposium on Arctic charr. University of Manitoba Press, Winnipeg.

Armstrong, R. H., and J. E. Morrow. 1980. The Dolly Varden charr, Salvelinus malma. Pages 99–140 in Balon (1980a).

Arnold, D. E. 1971. Ingestion, assimilation, survival, and reproduction by *Daphnia pulex* fed seven species of blue-green algae. Limnology and Oceanography 16:906–920.

Aro, K. V., and M. P. Shepard. 1967. Pacific salmon in Canada. International North Pacific Fisheries Commission Bulletin 23:225–272.

Ashton, F. M. 1982. Persistence and biodegradation of herbicides. Pages 117–131 *in* F. Matsumura and C. R. K. Murti, editors. Biodegradation of pesticides. Plenum Press, New York.

Atkinson, C. E., J. H. Rose, and T. O. Duncan. 1967. Pacific salmon in the United States. International North Pacific Fisheries Commission Bulletin 23:43–223.

Atkinson, S. W. 1971. BOD [biochemical oxygen demand] and toxicity of log leachates. Master's thesis. Oregon State University, Corvallis.

Averett, R. C., and F. A. Espinosa, Jr. 1968. Site selection and time of spawning by two groups of kokanee in Odell Lake, Oregon. Journal of Wildlife Management 32:76–81.

Axe, J. A., A. C. Mathers, and A. F. Wiese. 1969. Disappearance of atrazine, propazine and trifluralin from soil and water. Proceedings of the Southern Weed Science Society 22:367. (Abstract.)

Bachen, B. A. 1984. Development of salmonid spawning and rearing habitat with groundwater-fed channels. Pages 51–62 *in* Hassler (1984).

Bachman, R. A. 1984. Foraging behavior of free-ranging wild and hatchery brown trout in a stream. Transactions of the American Fisheries Society 113:1–32.

Baggerman, B. 1960. Factors in the diadromous migrations of fish. Symposia of the Zoological Society of London 1:33–60.

Bailey, J. E. 1966. Effects of salinity on intertidal pink salmon survival. Pages 12–15 *in* W. L. Sheridan, editor. Proceedings, 1966 Northeast Pacific pink salmon workshop. Alaska Department of Fish and Game, Informational Leaflet 87, Juneau.

Bailey, J. E., and D. R. Evans. 1971. The low-temperature threshold for pink salmon eggs in relation to a proposed hydroelectric installation. U.S. National Marine Fisheries Service Fishery Bulletin 69:587–593.

Bailey, R. G. 1971. Landslide hazards related to land use planning in Teton National Forest, northwest Wyoming. U.S. Forest Service, Intermountain Region, Ogden, Utah.

Baker, C. O. 1979. The impacts of logjam removal on fish populations and stream habitat in western Oregon. Master's thesis. Oregon State University, Corvallis.

Baker, J. P., and C. L. Schofield. 1980. Aluminum toxicity to fish as related to acid precipitation and Adirondack surface water quality. Pages 292–293 *in* Drablos and Tollan (1980).

Baker, V. R. 1977. Stream–channel response to floods, with examples from central Texas. Geological Society of America Bulletin 88:1057–1071.

Bakkala, R. G. 1970. Synopsis of biological data on the chum salmon, *Oncorhynchus keta* (Walbaum) 1792. U.S. Fish and Wildlife Service Circular 315.

Bakke, B. M. 1977. Grazing is destroying our fish. Trout Unlimited, Action Line (July), Portland, Oregon.

Baldes, R. J., and R. E. Vincent. 1969. Physical parameters of microhabitats occupied by brown trout in an experimental flume. Transactions of the American Fisheries Society 98:230–238.

Baldridge, J. E., and D. Amos. 1982. A technique for determining fish habitat suitability criteria: a comparison between habitat utilization and availability. Pages 251–258 *in* Armantrout (1982).

Ball, I. R. 1967. The relative susceptibilities of some species of fresh-water fish to poisons—1. Ammonia. Water Research 1:767–775.

Balon, E. K. 1968. Notes to the origin and evolution of trouts and salmons with special reference to the Danubian trout. Vestnik Ceskoslovenske Spolecnosti Zoologicke 32:1–21.

Balon, E. K., editor. 1980a. Charrs: salmonid fishes of the genus *Salvelinus*. Dr. W. Junk, The Hague, Netherlands.

Balon, E. K. 1980b. Early ontogeny of the lake charr, *Salvelinus (Cristivomer) namaycush*. Pages 485–562 *in* Balon (1980a).

Bams, R. A. 1969. Adaptations of sockeye salmon associated with incubation in stream gravels. Pages 71–87 *in* Northcote (1969b).

Bams, R. A. 1970. Evaluation of a revised hatchery method tested on pink and chum salmon fry. Journal of the Fisheries Research Board of Canada 27:1429–1452.

Barnett, A. P., E. W. Hauser, A. W. White, and J. H. Holladay. 1967. Loss of 2,4-D in washoff from cultivated fallow land. Weeds 15:133–137.

Barnley, G. R., and M. A. Prentice. 1958. *Simulium neavei* in Uganda. East Africa Medical Journal 35:475.

Barnthouse, L. W., R. O. O'Neill, S. M. Bartell, and G. W. Suter II. 1986. Population and ecosystem theory in ecological risk assessment. ASTM (American Society for Testing and Materials) Special Technical Publication 921:82–96.

Barrons, K. C., G. E. Lynn, and J. D. Eastman. 1953. Experiments on the reduction of high temperature injury to cotton from DNOSBP. Proceedings of the Southern Weed Control Conference 6:33–37.

Baudisch, O., and L. W. Bass. 1922. Eisen als licht-chemischer Katalysator. 1. Uber die Zersetzung von Ferrocyankalium im Tageslicht. Chemische Berichte 55:2698–2706. (Not seen; cited in Burdick and Lipschuetz 1950.)

Baxter, G. 1961. River utilization and the preservation of migratory fish life. Proceedings of the Institution of Civil Engineers 18:225–244.

B.C. (British Columbia) Ministry of Forests, B.C. Ministry of the Environment, Federal Department of Fisheries and Oceans, and Council of Forest Industries. 1988. Coastal fisheries–forestry guidelines, 2nd edition. A joint publication by these agencies, Victoria and Vancouver, British Columbia.

B.C. (British Columbia) Ministry of the Environment. 1976. Ladysmith Harbour, a guide for environmental management of foreshore resources. British Columbia Lands Service, Land Management Branch, Victoria.

Beacham, T. D., and C. B. Murray. 1985. Effects of female size, egg size, and water temperature on developmental biology of chum salmon (*Oncorhynchus keta*) from the Nitinat River, British Columbia. Canadian Journal of Fisheries and Aquatic Sciences 42:1755–1765.

Beacham, T. D., and P. Starr. 1982. Population biology of chum salmon, *Oncorhynchus keta*, from the Fraser River, British Columbia. U.S. National Marine Fisheries Service Fishery Bulletin 80:813–825.

Beamish, F. W. H. 1964. Respiration of fishes with special emphasis on standard oxygen consumption: 2. Influence of weight and temperature on respiration of several species. Canadian Journal of Zoology 42:177–188.

Beardsley, W. G., and J. A. Wagar. 1971. Vegetation management on a forested recreation site. Journal of Forestry 69:728–731.

Becker, C. D., and R. G. Genoway. 1979. Evaluation of the critical thermal maximum for determining thermal tolerance of freshwater fish. Environmental Biology of Fishes 4:245–256.

Becker, C. D., and D. A. Neitzel. 1985. Assessment of intergravel conditions influencing egg and alevin survival during salmonid redd dewatering. Environmental Biology of Fishes 12:33–46.

Becker, C. D., D. A. Neitzel, and D. W. Carlile. 1986. Survival data for dewatered rainbow trout (*Salmo gairdneri* Rich.) eggs and alevins. Journal of Applied Ichthyology 2:102–110.

Becker, C. D., D. A. Neitzel, and D. H. Fickeisen. 1982. Effects of dewatering on chinook salmon redds: tolerance of four developmental phases to daily dewaterings. Transactions of the American Fisheries Society 111:624–637.

Beckett, D. C., C. R. Bingham, and L. G. Sanders. 1983. Benthic macroinvertebrates of selected habitats of the lower Mississippi River. Journal of Freshwater Ecology 2:247–261.

Behnke, R. J. 1966. Relationships of the far eastern trout, *Salmo mykiss* Walbaum. Copeia 1966:346–348.

Behnke, R. J. 1977. Fish faunal changes associated with land-use and water development. Great Plains–Rocky Mountain Geological Journal 6(2):133–136.

Behnke, R. J. 1983. Impact of livestock grazing on stream fisheries: problems and solutions. Pages 170–173 in Menke (1983).

Behnke, R. J. 1988. Phylogeny and classification of cutthroat trout. American Fisheries Society Symposium 4:1–7.

Behnke, R. J., and R. L. Wallace. 1986. A systematic review of the cutthroat trout, Salmo clarki Richardson, a polytypic species. Pages 1–27 in Griffith (1986a).

Behnke, R. J., and M. Zarn. 1976. Biology and management of threatened and endangered western trouts. U.S. Forest Service General Technical Report RM-28.

Beil, K. E. 1974. The economics of rafting vs. barging as means of transporting logs in southeast Alaska waters. International Forestry Consultants, Seattle.

Beland, K. F., R. M. Jordan, and A. L. Meister. 1982. Water depth and velocity preferences of spawning Atlantic salmon in Maine rivers. North American Journal of Fisheries Management 2:11–13.

Bell, L. M., and R. J. Kallman. 1976a. The Cowichan–Chemanus River estuaries: status of environmental knowledge to 1975. Canada Fisheries and Marine Service, Special Estuary Series 4, Vancouver.

Bell, L. M., and R. J. Kallman. 1976b. The Kitimat River estuary: status of environmental knowledge to 1976. Canada Fisheries and Marine Service, Special Estuary Series 6, Vancouver.

Bell, L. M., and R. J. Kallman. 1976c. The Nanaimo River estuary: status of environmental knowledge to 1976. Canada Fisheries and Marine Service, Special Estuary Series 5, Vancouver.

Bell, M. C. 1986. Fisheries handbook of engineering requirements and biological criteria. U.S. Army Corps of Engineers, Office of the Chief of Engineers, Fish Passage Development and Evaluation Program, Portland, Oregon.

Bell, M. C., and R. I. Jackson. 1941. Adams River Dam. International Pacific Salmon Fisheries Commission unpublished report, on file, Vancouver, British Columbia.

Bella, D. A. 1975. Tidal flats in estuarine water quality analysis. U.S. Environmental Protection Agency Ecological Research Series EPA 660/3-75-025.

Benda, L. E. 1985a. Behavior and effect of debris flows on streams in the Oregon Coast Range. Pages 153–163 in D. S. Bowles, editor. Delineation of landslides, flash floods, and debris flow hazards in Utah. Utah State University, Utah Water Research Laboratory General Series UWRL/G-85/03, Logan.

Benda, L. E. 1985b. Delineation of channels susceptible to debris flows and debris floods. Pages 195–201 in Proceedings, international symposium on erosion, debris flow, and disaster prevention. Erosion Control Engineering Society, Sabo, Japan.

Benda, L. E., F. H. Everest, and J. R. Sedell. 1987. Influences of forest management on channel environments in the Oregon Coast Range. Pages 40–46 in R. O. Blosser, editor. Proceedings, managing Oregon's riparian zones for timber, fish and wildlife symposium. National Council of the Paper Industry for Air and Stream Improvement, Technical Bulletin 514, New York.

Bender, M. E. 1969. The toxicity of the hydrolysis and breakdown products of malathion to the fathead minnow (Pimephales promelas Rafinesque). Water Research 3:571–582.

Bender, M. E., and J. R. Westman. 1976. The toxicity of malathion and its hydrolysis products to the eastern mudminnow, Umbra pygmaea (DeKay). Chesapeake Science 17:125–128.

Bender, R. 1978. Log sills. Page 7 in Proceedings, fish habitat improvement workshop, Ochoco Ranger Station. Oregon Department of Fish and Wildlife, Portland.

Bengtson, G. W. 1979. Forest fertilization in the United States: progress and outlook. Journal of Forestry 77:222–229.

Bengtsson, B. E. 1988. Effects of pulp mill effluents on skeletal parameters in fish—a progress report. Water Science and Technology 20(2):87–94.

Benoit, D. A. 1976. Toxic effects of hexavalent chromium on brook trout (Salvelinus fontinalis) and rainbow trout (Salmo gairdneri). Water Research 10:497–500.

Benoit, D. A., E. N. Leonard, G. M. Christensen, and J. T. Fiandt. 1976. Toxic effects of cadmium on three generations of brook trout (*Salvelinus fontinalis*). Transactions of the American Fisheries Society 105:550–560.

Benson, N. G. 1953. The importance of ground water to trout populations in the Pigeon River, Michigan. Transactions of the North American Wildlife Conference 18:269–281.

Benson, W. R. 1969. The chemistry of pesticides. Annals of the New York Academy of Sciences 160:7–29.

Berg, L., and T. G. Northcote. 1985. Changes in territorial, gill-flaring, and feeding behavior in juvenile coho salmon (*Oncorhynchus kisutch*) following short-term pulses of suspended sediment. Canadian Journal of Fisheries and Aquatic Sciences 42:1410–1417.

Berg, N. 1983. Chemical and sensory analysis of off-flavours in fish from polluted rivers in Norway. Water Science and Technology 15(6–7):59–65.

Berg, O. K., and B. Jonsson. 1989. Migratory patterns of anadromous Atlantic salmon, brown trout and Arctic charr from the Vardnes River in northern Norway. Pages 106–115 *in* Brannon and Jonsson (1989).

Berndt, H. W. 1965. Snow accumulation and disappearance in lodgepole pine clearcut blocks in Wyoming. Journal of Forestry 63:88–91.

Bernhardt, J., J. Praveza, and H. Tracy. 1978. Aquatic monitoring of the 1977 spruce budworm Sevin-4-oil aerial spray project in Washington State. Washington Department of Ecology Technical Report 78-4, Olympia.

Berris, S. N. 1984. Comparative snow accumulation and melt during rainfall in forest and clearcut. Master's thesis. Oregon State University, Corvallis.

Berris, S. N., and R. D. Harr. 1987. Comparative snow accumulation and melt during rainfall in forested and clear-cut plots in the western Cascades of Oregon. Water Resources Research 23:135–142.

Berry, C. R., Jr., and P. J. Goebel. 1978. The use of livestock enclosures as a fishery management tool. Encyclia: the Journal of the Utah Academy of Sciences, Arts, and Letters 55:97. (Abstract.)

Beschta, R. L. 1978. Long-term patterns of sediment production following road construction and logging in the Oregon Coast Range. Water Resources Research 14:1011–1016.

Beschta, R. L. 1979. Debris removal and its effects on sedimentation in an Oregon Coast Range stream. Northwest Science 53:71–77.

Beschta, R. L. 1984. TEMP-84: A computer model for predicting stream temperatures resulting from the management of streamside vegetation. U.S. Forest Service, Watershed Systems Development Group, Report WSDG-AD-00009, Fort Collins, Colorado.

Beschta, R. L., R. E. Bilby, G. W. Brown, L. B. Holtby, and T. D. Hofstra. 1987. Stream temperature and aquatic habitat: fisheries and forestry interactions. Pages 191–232 *in* Salo and Cundy (1987).

Beschta, R. L., and W. L. Jackson. 1979. The intrusion of fine sediments into a stable gravel bed. Journal of the Fisheries Research Board of Canada 36:204–210.

Beschta, R. L., and W. S. Platts. 1986. Morphological features of small streams: significance and function. Water Resources Bulletin 22:369–379.

Bethlahmy, N. 1974. More streamflow after a bark beetle epidemic. Journal of Hydrology (Amsterdam) 23:185–189.

Bilby, R. E. 1981. Role of organic debris dams in regulating the export of dissolved and particulate matter from a forested watershed. Ecology 62:1234–1243.

Bilby, R. E. 1984. Removal of woody debris may affect stream channel stability. Journal of Forestry 82:609–613.

Bilby, R. E., and P. A. Bisson. 1987. Emigration and production of hatchery coho salmon (*Oncorhynchus kisutch*) stocked in streams draining an old-growth and a clear-cut watershed. Canadian Journal of Fisheries and Aquatic Sciences 44:1397–1407.

Bilby, R. E., and P. A. Bisson. 1989. Relative importance of allochthonous vs. authochthonous carbon sources as factors limiting coho salmon production in streams.

Pages 123–135 *in* B. G. Shepherd, rapporteur. Proceedings, 1988 Northeast Pacific chinook and coho salmon workshop. American Fisheries Society, North Pacific International Chapter. (Available from the B.C. Ministry of Environment, Penticton.)

Bilby, R. E., and G. E. Likens. 1979. Effect of hydrologic fluctuations on the transport of fine particulate organic carbon in a small stream. Limnology and Oceanography 24:69–75.

Bilby, R. E., and G. E. Likens. 1980. Importance of organic debris dams in the structure and function of stream ecosystems. Ecology 61:1107–1113.

Bilby, R. E., and J. W. Ward. 1989. Changes in characteristics and function of woody debris with increasing size of streams in western Washington. Transactions of the American Fisheries Society 118:368–378.

Bilby, R. E., and L. J. Wasserman. 1989. Forest practices and riparian management in Washington state: data based regulation development. Pages 87–94 *in* R. E. Gresswell, B. A. Barton, and J. L. Kershner, editors. Practical approaches to riparian resource management: an educational workshop. U.S. Bureau of Land Management, BLM-MT-PP-89-001-4351, Billings, Montana.

Bilton, H. T., D. F. Alderdice, and J. T. Schnute. 1982. Influence of time and size at release of juvenile coho salmon (*Oncorhynchus kisutch*) on returns at maturity. Canadian Journal of Fisheries and Aquatic Sciences 39:426–447.

Binns, N. A. 1967. Effects of rotenone treatment on the fauna of the Green River, Wyoming. Wyoming Game and Fish Commission, Fisheries Research Bulletin 1, Cheyenne.

Binns, N. A., and F. M. Eiserman. 1979. Quantification of fluvial trout habitat in Wyoming. Transactions of the American Fisheries Society 108:215–228.

Birk, L. A., and F. E. B. Roadhouse. 1964. Penetration of and persistence in soil of the herbicide atrazine. Canadian Journal of Plant Science 44:21–27.

Birmingham, B. C., and B. Colman. 1985. Persistence and fate of 2,4-D butoxyethanol ester in artificial ponds. Journal of Environmental Quality 14:100–104.

Birtwell, I. K. 1977. A field technique for studying the avoidance of fish to pollutants. Pages 69–86 *in* Proceedings, 3rd aquatic toxicity workshop. Canada Environmental Protection Service, Technical Report EPS-5-AR-77-1, Halifax, Nova Scotia.

Birtwell, I. K. 1978. Studies on the relationship between juvenile chinook salmon and water quality in the industrialized estuary of the Somass River. Canada Fisheries and Marine Service Technical Report 759:57–78.

Birtwell, I. K., and R. M. Harbo. 1980. Pulp mill impact studies at Port Alberni and Port Mellon, B.C. Transactions of the Technical Section of the Canadian Pulp and Paper Association 6:85–89.

Birtwell, I. K., S. Nelles, and R. M. Harbo. 1983. A brief investigation of fish in the surface waters of the Somass River Estuary, Port Alberni, British Columbia. Canadian Manuscript Report of Fisheries and Aquatic Sciences 1744.

Bishop, D. M., and M. E. Stevens. 1964. Landslides on logged areas in southeast Alaska. U.S. Forest Service Research Paper NOR-1.

Bisson, P. A. In press. Importance of identification of limiting factors in an evaluation program. *In* Proceedings, fish habitat enhancement and evaluation workshop. Bonneville Power Administration, Portland, Oregon.

Bisson, P. A., and R. E. Bilby. 1982. Avoidance of suspended sediment by juvenile coho salmon. North American Journal of Fisheries Management 2:371–374.

Bisson, P. A., R. E. Bilby, M. D. Bryant, C. A. Dolloff, G. B. Grette, R. A. House, M. L. Murphy, K. V. Koski, and J. R. Sedell. 1987. Large woody debris in forested streams in the Pacific Northwest: past, present, and future. Pages 143–190 *in* Salo and Cundy (1987).

Bisson, P. A., and G. E. Davis. 1976. Production of juvenile chinook salmon, *Oncorhynchus tshawytscha*, in a heated model stream. U.S. National Marine Fisheries Service Fishery Bulletin 74:763–774.

Bisson, P. A., R. B. Herrmann, and R. N. Thut. 1976. Trout production in fertilizer nitrogen enriched experimental streams. Weyerhaeuser Company, Interim Report, Project Number 040-5086, Tacoma, Washington.

Bisson, P. A., J. L. Nielsen, R. A. Palmason, and L. E. Grove. 1982. A system of naming habitat types in small streams, with examples of habitat utilization by salmonids during low streamflow. Pages 62–73 *in* Armantrout (1982).

Bisson, P. A., J. L. Nielsen, and J. W. Ward. 1988. Summer production of coho salmon stocked in Mount St. Helens streams 3–6 years after the 1980 eruption. Transactions of the American Fisheries Society 117:322–335.

Bisson, P. A., and J. R. Sedell. 1984. Salmonid populations in streams in clearcut vs. old-growth forests of western Washington. Pages 121–129 *in* Meehan et al. (1984).

Bjornn, T. C. 1957. A survey of the fishery resources of Priest and Upper Priest lakes and their tributaries, Idaho. Master's thesis. University of Idaho, Moscow.

Bjornn, T. C. 1961. Harvest, age structure, and growth of game fish populations from Priest and Upper Priest lakes. Transactions of the American Fisheries Society 90:27–31.

Bjornn, T. C. 1968. Survival and emergence of trout and salmon fry in various gravel–sand mixtures. Pages 80–88 *in* Logging and salmon: proceedings of a forum. American Institute of Fishery Research Biologists, Alaska District, Juneau.

Bjornn, T. C. 1971. Trout and salmon movements in two Idaho streams as related to temperature, food, stream flow, cover, and population density. Transactions of the American Fisheries Society 100:423–438.

Bjornn, T. C. 1978. Survival, production, and yield of trout and chinook salmon in the Lemhi River, Idaho. University of Idaho, College of Forestry, Wildlife and Range Sciences Bulletin 27, Moscow.

Bjornn, T. C., M. A. Brusven, M. Molnau, F. J. Watts, R. L. Wallace, D. R. Neilson, M. F. Sandine, and L. C. Stuehrenberg. 1974. Sediment in streams and its effects on aquatic life. University of Idaho, Water Resource Research Institute, Technical Completion Report, Project B-025-IDA, Moscow.

Bjornn, T. C., M. A. Brusven, M. P. Molnau, J. H. Milligan, R. A. Klamt, E. Chacho, and C. Schaye. 1977. Transport of granitic sediment in streams and its effects on insects and fish. University of Idaho, Forest, Wildlife and Range Experiment Station Bulletin 17, Moscow.

Bjornn, T. C., D. C. Burns, A. W. Collotzi, H. W. Newhouse, and W. S. Platts. 1980. A method for predicting fish response to sediment yields: a working draft. U.S. Forest Service, Intermountain and Northern Regions, Wildlife Management, Ogden, Utah, and Missoula, Montana.

Bjornn, T. C., D. R. Craddock, and D. R. Corley. 1968. Migration and survival of Redfish Lake, Idaho, sockeye salmon, *Oncorhynchus nerka*. Transactions of the American Fisheries Society 97:360–373.

Bjornn, T. C., and G. A. Liknes. 1986. Life history, status, and management of westslope cutthroat trout. Pages 57–71 *in* Griffith (1986a).

Bjornn, T. C., and J. Mallet. 1964. Movements of planted and wild trout in an Idaho river system. Transactions of the American Fisheries Society 93:70–76.

Bjornn, T. C., and C. F. Morrill. 1972. Migration response of juvenile chinook salmon to substrates and temperatures. University of Idaho, Water Resources Research Institute, Research Technical Completion Report, Project A-038-IDA, Moscow.

Bjornn, T. C., and D. W. Reiser. 1991. Habitat requirements of salmonids in streams. American Fisheries Society Special Publication 19:83–138.

Bjugstad, A. J. 1984. Establishment of trees and shrubs on lands disturbed by mining in the West. Pages 434–438 *in* Proceedings, new forests for a changing world. Society of American Foresters, Washington, D.C.

Blackett, R. F. 1968. Spawning behavior, fecundity, and early life history of anadromous Dolly Varden, *Salvelinus malma* (Walbaum), in southeastern Alaska. Alaska Department of Fish and Game, Research Report 6, Juneau.

Blackett, R. F. 1979. Establishment of sockeye (*Oncorhynchus nerka*) and chinook (*O. tshawytscha*) salmon runs at Frazer Lake, Kodiak Island, Alaska. Journal of the Fisheries Research Board of Canada 36:1265–1277.

Blackett, R. F. 1985. Annual area report, FRED Division, Kodiak. Alaska Department of

Fish and Game, Division of Fisheries Rehabilitation, Enchancement, and Development, Kodiak.

Blackett, R. F. 1987. Development and performance of an Alaska steeppass fishway for sockeye salmon (*Oncorhynchus nerka*). Canadian Journal of Fisheries and Aquatic Sciences 44:66–76.

Blahm, T. H. 1978. Toxicity of chemical fire retardants to juvenile coho salmon and rainbow trout. Doctoral dissertation. Dissertation Abstracts International 39:4115B.

Blake, O. W. 1971. Timber down the hill. (Privately published.) Available from Oregon State University Library, Corvallis.

Blevins, R. D., J. C. Schreiber, and O. C. Pancorbo. 1985. Gross alpha and beta radioactivities associated with aquatic environments of upper-east Tennessee impacted by industrial and mining activities. Archives of Environmental Contamination and Toxicology 14:83–88.

Bley, P. W., and J. R. Moring. 1988. Freshwater and ocean survival of Atlantic salmon and steelhead: a synopsis. U.S. Fish and Wildlife Service Biological Report 88(9).

Bockheim, J. G., T. M. Ballard, and R. P. Willington. 1975. Soil disturbance associated with timber harvesting in southwestern British Columbia. Canadian Journal of Forest Research 5:285–290.

Bockheim, J. G., T. M. Ballard, R. P. Willington, and J. L. Larson. 1973. Impact of clearcutting on soils and watersheds, southwestern British Columbia. Canadian Forestry Service, Pacific Forest Research Center Contract Report, on file, Victoria, British Columbia.

Bocsor, J. G., and T. F. O'Connor. 1975. Impact on the aquatic ecosystem. Pages 29–47 *in* Environmental impact study of aerially applied Orthene on a forest and aquatic ecosystem. State University of New York, Lake Ontario Environmental Laboratory Report 174, Oswego.

Boehm, H.-H., and H. Mueller. 1976. Model studies on the accumulation of herbicides by microalgae. Naturwissenschaften 63:296.

Boehne, P. L., and R. A. House. 1983. Stream ordering: a tool for land managers to classify western Oregon streams. U.S. Bureau of Land Management, Technical Note OR-3, Portland, Oregon.

Boehne, P. L., and J. R. Wolfe, Jr. 1986. Use of explosives to add large organic debris to streams. North American Journal of Fisheries Management 6:599–600.

Bollag, J.-M., and S.-Y. Liu. 1971. Degradation of Sevin by soil microorganisms. Soil Biology and Biochemistry 3:337–345.

Bond, C. E., R. H. Lewis, and J. L. Fryer. 1960. Toxicity of various herbicidal materials to fishes. Pages 96–101 *in* C. M. Tarzwell, compiler. Biological problems in water pollution: transactions of the 1959 seminar. Robert A. Taft Sanitary Engineering Center, Technical Report W60–3, Cincinnati, Ohio.

Booth, D. T. 1985. The role of fourwing saltbush in mined land reclamation: a viewpoint. Journal of Range Management 38:562–565.

Bortleson, G. C., M. J. Chrzastowski, and A. K. Helgerson. 1980. Historical changes of shoreline and wetland at eleven major deltas in the Puget Sound region, Washington. U.S. Geological Survey Hydrologic Investigations Atlas HA-617.

Bosch, J. M., and J. D. Hewlett. 1982. A review of catchment experiments to determine the effect of vegetation changes on water yield and evapotranspiration. Journal of Hydrology (Amsterdam) 55:3–23.

Bothwell, M. L. 1987. Phosphorus control of algal production in the Thompson River, British Columbia. Environment Canada, National Hydrology Research Institute Scientific Series, Contribution 87002, Saskatoon, Saskatchewan.

Bothwell, M. L., and J. G. Stockner. 1980. Influence of secondarily treated kraft mill effluent on the accumulation rate of attached algae in experimental continuous-flow troughs. Canadian Journal of Fisheries and Aquatic Sciences 37:248–254.

Bottom, D. L., T. E. Nickelson, and S. L. Johnson. 1986. Research and development of Oregon's coastal salmon stocks. Oregon Department of Fish and Wildlife, Job Final Report, Fish Research Project AFC-127, Portland.

Boussu, M. F. 1954. Relationship between trout populations and cover on a small stream. Journal of Wildlife Management 18:229–239.

Bovee, K. D. 1978. Probability-of-use criteria for the family Salmonidae. U.S. Fish and Wildlife Service, FWS/OBS-78–07.

Bovee, K. D. 1982. A guide to stream habitat analysis using the instream flow incremental methodology. U.S. Fish and Wildlife Service, FWS/OBS-82/26.

Bovee, K. D. 1986. Development and evaluation of habitat suitability criteria for use in the instream flow incremental methodology. U.S. Fish and Wildlife Service, Biological Report 86(7).

Bovee, K. D., and T. Cochnauer. 1977. Development and evaluation of weighted criteria, probability-of-use curves for instream flow assessments. U.S. Fish and Wildlife Service, FWS/OBS-77–63.

Bovee, K. D., and R. Milhous. 1978. Hydraulic simulation in instream flow studies: theory and techniques. U.S. Fish and Wildlife Service, FWS/OBS-78/33.

Bowlby, J. N., and J. C. Roff. 1986. Trout biomass and habitat relationships in southern Ontario streams. Transactions of the American Fisheries Society 115:503–514.

Boyd, C. E. 1970. Amino acid, protein, and caloric content of vascular aquatic macrophytes. Ecology 51:902–906.

Boyd, C. E., and J. W. Sowles. 1978. Nitrogen fertilization of ponds. Transactions of the American Fisheries Society 107:737–741.

Boyd, K. G. 1979. Water transport of wood: B.C. coast. Pulp and Paper Canada 80(11):28–34.

Brannon, E., and B. Jonsson, editors. 1989. Proceedings, 1987 salmonid migration and distribution symposium. University of Washington, Seattle, and Norwegian Institute for Nature Research, Trondheim.

Brannon, E. L. 1965. The influence of physical factors on the development and weight of sockeye salmon embryos and alevins. International Pacific Salmon Fisheries Commission Progress Report 12.

Brannon, E. L., and E. O. Salo, editors. 1982. Proceedings, salmon and trout migratory behavior symposium. University of Washington, College of Fisheries, Seattle.

Branson, B. A., and D. L. Batch. 1971. Effects of strip mining on small stream fishes in east-central Kentucky. Proceedings of the Biological Society of Washington 84(59):507–517.

Brett, J. R. 1952. Temperature tolerance in young Pacific salmon, genus *Oncorhynchus*. Journal of the Fisheries Research Board of Canada 9:265–323.

Brett, J. R. 1964. The respiratory metabolism and swimming performance of young sockeye salmon. Journal of the Fisheries Research Board of Canada 21:1183–1226.

Brett, J. R. 1967. Swimming performance of sockeye salmon (*Oncorhynchus nerka*) in relation to fatigue time and temperature. Journal of the Fisheries Research Board of Canada 24:1731–1741.

Brett, J. R., and D. F. Alderdice. 1958. The resistance of cultured young chum and sockeye salmon to temperatures below 0°C. Journal of the Fisheries Research Board of Canada 15:805–813.

Brett, J. R., and J. M. Blackburn. 1981. Oxygen requirements for growth of young coho (*Oncorhynchus kisutch*) and sockeye (*O. nerka*) salmon at 15°C. Canadian Journal of Fisheries and Aquatic Sciences 38:399–404.

Brett, J. R., M. Hollands, and D. R. Alderdice. 1958. The effect of temperature on the cruising speed of young sockeye and coho salmon. Journal of the Fisheries Research Board of Canada 15:587–605.

Brett, J. R., J. E. Shelbourn, and C. T. Shoop. 1969. Growth rate and body composition of fingerling sockeye salmon, *Oncorhynchus nerka*, in relation to temperature and ration size. Journal of the Fisheries Research Board of Canada 26:2362–2394.

Bridges, J. B. 1910. Definition of the law governing the use of driving streams. Pages 50–51 *in* Proceedings, 2nd annual session of the Pacific Logging Congress. The Timberman, Portland, Oregon.

Briggs, J. C. 1953. The behavior and reproduction of salmonid fishes in a small coastal stream. California Department of Fish and Game Fish Bulletin 94.

Brock, W. A. 1986. Enhancement of rearing habitat for juvenile steelhead trout (*Salmo gairdneri*) by boulder placement in a tributary to the Klamath River. Master's thesis. Humboldt State University, Arcata, California.

Broderius, S. J. 1970. Determination of molecular hydrocyanic acid in water and studies of the chemistry and toxicity to fish of the nickelcyanide complex. Master's thesis. Oregon State University, Corvallis.

Brouha, P. 1982. The forest planning game: changing the score. Fisheries 7(5):11–13.

Brouha, P. 1991. Fish habitat planning. American Fisheries Society Special Publication 19:587–597.

Brown, E. R., editor. 1985. Management of wildlife and fish habitats in forests of western Oregon and Washington. U.S. Forest Service, Pacific Northwest Region, Publication R6-F&WL-192-1985, Portland, Oregon.

Brown, G. 1979. Alternate transportation systems for reducing natural resources impact. Pages 257–262 *in* Ittner et al. (1979).

Brown, G., Jr., and M. J. Hay. 1987. Net economic recreation values for deer and waterfowl hunting and trout fishing, 1980. U.S. Fish and Wildlife Service, Division of Policy and Directives, Management Working Paper 23.

Brown, G. W. 1969. Predicting temperatures of small streams. Water Resources Research 5:68–75.

Brown, G. W. 1970. Predicting the effect of clearcutting on stream temperature. Journal of Soil and Water Conservation 25:11–13.

Brown, G. W. 1980. Forestry and water quality. Oregon State University Book Stores, Inc., Corvallis.

Brown, G. W., A. R. Gahler, and R. B. Marston. 1973. Nutrient losses after clear-cut logging and slash burning in the Oregon Coast Range. Water Resources Research 9:1450–1453.

Brown, G. W., and J. T. Krygier. 1970. Effects of clear-cutting on stream temperature. Water Resources Research 6:1133–1139.

Brown, G. W., and J. T. Krygier. 1971. Clear-cut logging and sediment production in the Oregon Coast Range. Water Resources Research 7:1189–1198.

Brown, N. C. 1936. Logging-transportation. Wiley, New York.

Brown, P. J. 1982. Recreation opportunity spectrum with implications for wildlife-oriented recreation. Transactions of the North American Wildlife and Natural Resources Conference 47:705–711.

Brown, P. J., B. L. Driver, and C. McConnell. 1978. The opportunity spectrum concept and behavioral information in outdoor recreation resource supply inventories: background and application. U.S. Forest Service General Technical Report RM-55:73–84.

Brown, R. W., and R. S. Johnston. 1976. Revegetation of an alpine mine disturbance: Beartooth Plateau, Montana. U.S. Forest Service Research Note INT-206.

Brown, T. G. 1985. The role of abandoned stream channels as over-wintering habitat for juvenile salmonids. Master's thesis. University of British Columbia, Vancouver.

Brown, T. G. 1987. Characterization of salmonid over-wintering habitat within seasonally flooded land on the Carnation Creek flood-plain. British Columbia Ministry of Forests and Lands, Land Management Report 44, Victoria.

Brown, W. G., and F. M. Shalloof. 1986. Recommended values for Columbia River salmon and steelhead for current fishery management decisions. Oregon State University, Department of Agricultural and Resource Economics, Corvallis.

Brown, W. G., C. Sorhus, and K. C. Gibbs. 1980. Estimated expenditures by sport anglers and net economic values of salmon and steelhead for specified fisheries in the Pacific Northwest. Report prepared for Pacific Northwest Regional Commission, Contract 10790006. Oregon State University, Department of Agricultural and Resource Economics, Corvallis.

Brownlee, M. J., and D. C. Morrison. 1983. A preliminary examination of the content, application and administration of the stream protection clauses ("P" clauses) on Vancouver Island. Canadian Industry Report of Fisheries and Aquatic Sciences 143:31–73.

Brungs, W. A., R. W. Carlson, W. B. Horning II, J. H. McCormick, R. L. Spehar, and J. D. Yount. 1978. Effects of pollution on freshwater fish. Journal of the Water Pollution Control Federation 50(6):1582–1637.

Brusven, M. A., W. R. Meehan, and J. F. Ward. 1986. Summer use of simulated undercut banks by juvenile chinook salmon in an artificial Idaho channel. North American Journal of Fisheries Management 6:32–37.

Brusven, M. A., and K. V. Prather. 1974. Influence of stream sediments on distribution of macrobenthos. Journal of the Entomological Society of British Columbia 71:25–32.

Bryan, H. 1976. The sociology of fishing: a review and critique. Pages 83–92 in Proceedings, marine recreational fisheries symposium. Sport Fishing Institute, Washington, D.C.

Bryant, C. W., G. L. Amy, and B. C. Alleman. 1987. Organic halide and organic carbon distribution and removal in a pulp and paper wastewater lagoon. Journal of the Water Pollution Control Federation 59:890–896.

Bryant, D. N., D. B. Cohen, and R. W. Durham. 1979. Leachability of radioactive constituents from uranium mine tailings: status report. Canada Environmental Protection Service, Technology Development Report EPS 4-WP-79-4, Burlington, Ontario.

Bryant, M. D. 1980. Evolution of large, organic debris after timber harvest: Maybeso Creek, 1949 to 1978. U.S. Forest Service General Technical Report PNW-101.

Bryant, M. D. 1983. The role and management of woody debris in West Coast salmonid nursery streams. North American Journal of Fisheries Management 3:322–330.

Bryant, M. D. 1984. The role of beaver dams as coho salmon habitat in southeast Alaska streams. Pages 183–192 in J. M. Walton and D. B. Houston, editors. Proceedings, Olympic wild fish conference. Peninsula College, Fisheries Technology Program, Port Angeles, Washington.

Bryant, M. D. 1985. Changes 30 years after logging in large woody debris, and its use by salmonids. Pages 329–334 in Johnson et al. (1985).

Bryant, R. C. 1913. Logging: the principles and general methods of operation in the United States. Wiley, New York.

Buchanan, D. V., P. S. Tate, and J. R. Moring. 1976. Acute toxicities of spruce and hemlock bark extracts to some estuarine organisms in southeastern Alaska. Journal of the Fisheries Research Board of Canada 33:1188–1192.

Buchanan, I. L. 1936. Lumbering and logging in the Puget Sound region in territorial days. Pacific Northwest Quarterly 27:34–53.

Buckley, B. M., and F. J. Triska. 1978. Presence and ecological role of nitrogen-fixing bacteria associated with wood decay in streams. Internationale Vereinigung für theoretische und angewandte Limnologie Verhandlungen 20:1333–1339.

Buckner, C. H., B. B. McLeod, and P. D. Kingsbury. 1975. The effect of an experimental application of nuclear polyhedrosis virus on selected forest fauna. Canadian Forestry Service, Chemical Control Research Institute, Information Report CC-X-101.

Buckner, C. H., B. B. McLeod, P. D. Kingsbury, K. L. Mortensen, and D. G. H. Ray. 1974. Impact of aerial treatment on non-target organisms, Algonquin Park, Ontario and Spruce Woods, Manitoba. Pages F1–F72 in Evaluation of commercial preparations of Bacillus thuringiensis with and without chitinase against spruce budworm. Canadian Forestry Service, Chemical Control Research Institute, Information Report CC-X-59.

Bugert, R. M. 1985. Microhabitat selection of juvenile salmonids in response to stream cover alteration and predation. Master's thesis. University of Idaho, Moscow.

Buist, L. J., and T. A. Hoots. 1982. Recreation opportunity spectrum approach to resource planning. Journal of Forestry 80:84–86.

Bulkley, R. V. 1967. Fecundity of steelhead trout, Salmo gairdneri, from Alsea River, Oregon. Journal of the Fisheries Research Board of Canada 24:917–926.

Burck, W. A., and P. E. Reimers. 1978. Temporal and spatial distribution of fall chinook salmon spawning in Elk River. Oregon Department of Fish and Wildlife, Information Report Series, Fisheries 78-3, Portland.

Burdick, G. E., H. J. Dean, and E. J. Harris. 1960. The effect of Sevin upon the aquatic environment. New York Fish and Game Journal 7:14–25.

Burdick, G. E., and M. Lipschuetz. 1950. Toxicity of ferro- and ferricyanide solutions to fish, and determination of the cause of mortality. Transactions of the American Fisheries Society 78:192–202.

Burger, C. V., R. L. Wilmot, and D. B. Wangaard. 1985. Comparison of spawning areas and times for two runs of chinook salmon (*Oncorhynchus tshawytscha*) in the Kenai River, Alaska. Canadian Journal of Fisheries and Aquatic Sciences 42:693–700.

Burges, H. D. 1982. Control of insects by bacteria. Parasitology 84:79–117.

Burghduff, A. E. 1934. Stream improvement. California Fish and Game 20:113–118.

Burner, C. J. 1951. Characteristics of spawning nests of Columbia River salmon. U.S. Fish and Wildlife Service Fishery Bulletin 52(61):97–110.

Burns, J. W. 1970. Spawning bed sedimentation studies in northern California streams. California Fish and Game 56:253–270.

Burns, J. W. 1971. The carrying capacity for juvenile salmonids in some northern California streams. California Fish and Game 57:44–57.

Burns, J. W. 1972. Some effects of logging and associated road construction on northern California streams. Transactions of the American Fisheries Society 101:1–17.

Burrows, R. E. 1964. Effects of accumulated excretory products on hatchery-reared salmonids. U.S. Fish and Wildlife Service, Bureau of Sport Fisheries and Wildlife Research Report 66.

Burt, G. W. 1974. Volatility of atrazine from plant, soil, and glass surfaces. Journal of Environmental Quality 3:114–117.

Burton, T. M., R. M. Stanford, and J. W. Allan. 1985. Acidification effects on stream biota and organic matter processing. Canadian Journal of Fisheries and Aquatic Sciences 42:669–675.

Busby, F. E. 1979. Riparian and stream ecosystems, livestock grazing, and multiple-use management. Pages 6–12 in Cope (1979).

Busch, D. E., and S. G. Fisher. 1981. Metabolism of a desert stream. Freshwater Biology 11:301–307.

Bustard, D. R. 1984. Queen Charlotte Islands stream rehabilitation studies: a review of potential techniques. British Columbia Ministry of Forests, Land Management Report 28, Victoria.

Bustard, D. R. 1986. Some differences between coastal and interior streams and the implications to juvenile fish production. Canadian Technical Report of Fisheries and Aquatic Sciences 1483:117–126.

Bustard, D. R., and D. W. Narver. 1975a. Aspects of the winter ecology of juvenile coho salmon (*Oncorhynchus kisutch*) and steelhead trout (*Salmo gairdneri*). Journal of the Fisheries Research Board of Canada 32:667–680.

Bustard, D. R., and D. W. Narver. 1975b. Preferences of juvenile coho salmon (*Oncorhynchus kisutch*) and cutthroat trout (*Salmo clarki*) relative to simulated alteration of winter habitat. Journal of the Fisheries Research Board of Canada 32:681–687.

Butler, P. A. 1965. Effects of herbicides on estuarine fauna. Proceedings of the Southern Weed Conference 18:576–580.

Butler, R. L., and V. M. Hawthorne. 1968. The reactions of dominant trout to changes in overhead artificial cover. Transactions of the American Fisheries Society 97:37–41.

Butterfield, R. I., and P. T. Tueller. 1980. Revegetation potential of acid mine wastes in northeastern California. Reclamation Review 3:21–31.

Cairns, J., and A. Scheier. 1957. The effects of temperature and hardness of water upon the toxicity of zinc to the common bluegill (*Lepomis macrochirus*). Notulae Naturae (Philadelphia) 299:1–12.

Calhoun, A. 1964. *Homo* vs. *Salmo*. Proceedings of the Annual Conference Western Association of Game and Fish Commissioners 43:243–245.

Calhoun, A. 1966. Habitat protection and improvement. Pages 40–48 in A. Calhoun, editor. Inland fisheries management. California Department of Fish and Game, Sacramento.

Call, D. J., L. T. Brooke, R. J. Kent, S. H. Poirier, M. L. Knuth, P. J. Shubat, and E. J.

Slick. 1984. Toxicity, uptake, and elimination of the herbicides alachlor and dinoseb in freshwater fish. Journal of Environmental Quality 13:493–498.

Campbell, A. J., and R. C. Sidle. 1984. Prediction of peak flows on small watersheds in Oregon for use in culvert design. Water Resources Bulletin 20:9–14.

Canada Department of Fisheries. 1964. Fisheries problems associated with the development of logging plans within the Morice River drainage system. Vancouver, British Columbia.

Canada Department of Fisheries and Oceans and B.C. Ministry of the Environment. 1980. Stream enhancement guide. Vancouver, British Columbia.

Canada Fisheries and Marine Service. 1978. The salmonid enhancement program. Department of Fisheries and the Environment, Vancouver, British Columbia.

Capizzi, J., C. Baird, and A. Antonelli, compilers and editors. 1987. Pacific Northwest insect control handbook. Oregon State University, Corvallis.

Capizzi, J., and J. M. Witt, editors. 1971. Pesticides, pest control and safety on forest and range lands. Oregon State University, Corvallis.

Carl, L. M. 1984. Chinook salmon (*Oncorhynchus tshawytscha*) density, growth, mortality, and movement in two Lake Michigan tributaries. Canadian Journal of Zoology 62:65–71.

Carlson, A. R. 1972. Effects of long-term exposure to carbaryl (Sevin) on survival, growth, and reproduction of the fathead minnow (*Pimephales promelas*). Journal of the Fisheries Research Board of Canada 29:583–587.

Carlson, C. E., and L. L. Bahls, editors. 1985. Proceedings, Clark Fork River symposium. Montana Academy of Sciences and Montana College of Mineral Science and Technology, Butte.

Caro, J. H., H. P. Freeman, D. E. Glotfelty, B. C. Turner, and W. M. Edwards. 1973. Dissipation of soil-incorporated carbofuran in the field. Journal of Agricultural and Food Chemistry 21:1010–1015.

Caro, J. H., H. P. Freeman, and B. C. Turner. 1974. Persistence in soil and losses in runoff of soil-incorporated carbaryl in a small watershed. Journal of Agricultural and Food Chemistry 22:860–863.

Carpenter, K. E. 1930. Further researches on the action of metallic salts on fishes. Journal of Experimental Zoology 56:407–422.

Carpenter, M. R., and D. R. Bowlus. 1976. Attitudes toward fishing and fisheries management of users in Desolation Wilderness, California. California Fish and Game 62:168–178.

Carr, W. W. 1980. A handbook for forest roadside surface erosion control in British Columbia. British Columbia Ministry of Forests, Land Management Report 4, Victoria.

Carr, W. W. 1985. Watershed rehabilitation options for disturbed slopes on the Queen Charlotte Islands. British Columbia Ministry of Forests, Land Management Report 36, Victoria.

Carr, W. W., and T. M. Ballard. 1980. Hydroseeding forest roadsides in British Columbia for erosion control. Journal of Soil and Water Conservation 35:33–35.

Carson, K. A. 1985. A model of salmonid egg respiration. Master's thesis. Colorado State University, Fort Collins.

Carter, C., and H. Radtke. 1988. Coastal community impacts of the recreational–commercial allocation of salmon in the ocean fisheries. Pages 139–154 *in* McNeil (1988).

Caruso, S. C. 1975. The chemistry of cyanide compounds and their behavior in the aquatic environment. Carnegie–Mellon Institute of Research, Chicago.

Cavender, T. M. 1978. Taxonomy and distribution of the bull trout, *Salvelinus confluentus* (Suckley), from the American Northwest. California Fish and Game 64:139–174.

Cearley, J. E., and R. L. Coleman. 1974. Cadmium toxicity and bioconcentration in largemouth bass and bluegill. Bulletin of Environmental Contamination and Toxicology 11:146–151.

Cederholm, C. J., and L. C. Lestelle. 1974. Observations on the effects of landslide siltation on salmon and trout resources of the Clearwater River, Jefferson County,

Washington, 1972–73. University of Washington, Fisheries Research Institute, FRI-UW-7404, Seattle.

Cederholm, C. J., and N. P. Peterson. 1985. The retention of coho salmon (*Oncorhynchus kisutch*) carcasses by organic debris in small streams. Canadian Journal of Fisheries and Aquatic Sciences 42:1222–1225.

Cederholm, C. J., and L. M. Reid. 1987. Impact of forest management on coho salmon (*Oncorhynchus kisutch*) populations of the Clearwater River, Washington: a project summary. Pages 373–398 *in* Salo and Cundy (1987).

Cederholm, C. J., L. M. Reid, B. G. Edie, and E. O. Salo. 1982. Effects of forest road erosion on salmonid spawning gravel composition and populations of the Clearwater River, Washington. Pages 1–17 *in* K. A. Hashagen, editor. Habitat disturbance and recovery: proceedings of a symposium. California Trout Inc., San Francisco.

Cederholm, C. J., L. M. Reid, and E. O. Salo. 1981. Cumulative effects of logging road sediment on salmonid populations in the Clearwater River, Jefferson County, Washington. Pages 38–74 *in* Proceedings, conference on salmon spawning gravel: a renewable resource in the Pacific Northwest? Washington State University, Water Research Center Report 39, Pullman.

Cederholm, C. J., and E. O. Salo. 1979. The effects of logging road landslide siltation on the salmon and trout spawning gravels of Stequaleho Creek and the Clearwater River basin, Jefferson County, Washington, 1972–1978. University of Washington, Fisheries Research Institute, FRI-UW-7915, Seattle.

Cederholm, C. J., and W. J. Scarlett. 1982. Seasonal immigrations of juvenile salmonids into four small tributaries of the Clearwater River, Washington, 1977–1981. Pages 98–110 *in* Brannon and Salo (1982).

Chadwick, E. M. P. 1982. Stock-recruitment relationship for Atlantic salmon (*Salmo salar*) in Newfoundland rivers. Canadian Journal of Fisheries and Aquatic Sciences 39:1496–1501.

Chadwick, R. A., R. C. Rice, C. M. Bennett, and R. A. Woodruff. 1975. Sulfur and trace elements in the Rosebud and McKay coal seams, Colstrip field, Montana. Pages 167–175 *in* Energy resources of Montana. Proceedings, 22nd annual meeting of the Montana Geological Society, Billings.

Chamberlin, T. W., editor. 1988. Proceedings of the workshop: applying 15 years of Carnation Creek results. Pacific Biological Station, Carnation Creek Steering Committee, Nanaimo, British Columbia.

Chamberlin, T. W., R. D. Harr, and F. H. Everest. 1991. Timber harvesting, silviculture, and watershed processes. American Fisheries Society Special Publication 19: 181–205.

Chaney, E. 1981. Investigative report on the proposed withdrawal from entry, location and patent under the mining laws of approximately 17,500 acres in central Idaho's Bear Valley and Marsh Creek drainages tributary to the Middle Fork of the Salmon River. U.S. Fish and Wildlife Service, Division of Ecological Services, Boise, Idaho.

Chapman, D. W. 1962a. Aggressive behavior in juvenile coho salmon as a cause of emigration. Journal of the Fisheries Research Board of Canada 19:1047–1080.

Chapman, D. W. 1962b. Effects of logging upon fish resources of the West Coast. Journal of Forestry 60:533–537.

Chapman, D. W. 1963. Physical and biological effects of forest practices upon stream ecology. Pages 321–330 *in* Proceedings, forest watershed management symposium. Society of American Foresters and Oregon State University, School of Forestry, Corvallis.

Chapman, D. W. 1965. Net production of juvenile coho salmon in three Oregon streams. Transactions of the American Fisheries Society 94:40–52.

Chapman, D. W. 1966. Food and space as regulators of salmonid populations in streams. American Naturalist 100:345–357.

Chapman, D. W. 1986. Salmon and steelhead abundance in the Columbia River in the nineteenth century. Transactions of the American Fisheries Society 115:662–670.

Chapman, D. W. 1988. Critical review of variables used to define effects of fines in redds of large salmonids. Transactions of the American Fisheries Society 117:1–21.

Chapman, D. W., and T. C. Bjornn. 1969. Distribution of salmonids in streams, with special reference to food and feeding. Pages 153–176 *in* Northcote (1969b).

Chapman, D. W., and R. L. Demory. 1963. Seasonal changes in the food ingested by aquatic insect larvae and nymphs in two Oregon streams. Ecology 44:140–146.

Chapman, D. W., and E. Knudsen. 1980. Channelization and livestock impacts on salmonid habitat and biomass in western Washington. Transactions of the American Fisheries Society 109:357–363.

Chapman, D. W., and K. P. McLeod. 1987. Development of criteria for fine sediment in the northern Rockies ecoregion. U.S. Environmental Protection Agency EPA 910/9-87-162.

Chapman, D. W., D. E. Weitkamp, T. L. Welsh, and T. H. Schadt. 1982. Effects of minimum flow regimes on fall chinook spawning at Vernita Bar, 1978–82. Final report to Grant County Public Utility District 2, prepared by Parametrix, Inc., Bellevue, Washington, and Don Chapman Consultants, Inc., McCall, Idaho.

Chapman, G. 1973. Effect of heavy metals on fish. Pages 141–162 *in* Heavy metals in the environment. Oregon State University, Water Resources Research Institute, Report SEMN-WR-D16.73, Corvallis.

Chapman, G. A. 1978. Toxicities of cadmium, copper, and zinc to four juvenile stages of chinook salmon and steelhead. Transactions of the American Fisheries Society 107:841–847.

Chapman, G. A., and D. G. Stevens. 1978. Acutely lethal levels of cadmium, copper, and zinc to adult male coho salmon and steelhead. Transactions of the American Fisheries Society 107:837–840.

Charbonneau, J. J., and M. J. Hay. 1978. Determinants and economic values of hunting and fishing. Transactions of the North American Wildlife and Natural Resources Conference 43:391–403.

Charlon, N., B. Barbier, and L. Bonnet. 1970. Thermal resistance of rainbow trout, *Salmo gairdneri* Richardson, to abrupt temperature variation. Annals of Hydrobiology 1:73–89.

Cheek, N. H., D. R. Field, and R. J. Burdge. 1976. Leisure and recreation places. Ann Arbor Science, Ann Arbor, Michigan.

Cheng, J. D., T. A. Black, J. de Vries, R. P. Willington, and B. C. Goodell. 1975. The evaluation of initial changes in peak steamflow following logging of a watershed on the west coast of Canada. International Association of Hydrological Sciences Publication 117:475–486.

Chertudi, C. 1986. Blackbird Mine: past and present. Idaho Clean Water 1986:8–9.

Chevalier, B., and C. Carson. 1985. Modeling the transfer of oxygen between the stream and stream substrate: with application to the survival rates of salmonid embryos. Colorado State University, Department of Agricultural and Chemical Engineering, ARS Project 5602-20813-008A, Fort Collins.

Chevalier, B., and V. G. Murphy. 1985. Intragravel dissolved-oxygen model. Colorado State University, Department of Agricultural and Chemical Engineering, ARS CWU 5402-20810-004-01S, Fort Collins.

Chiou, C. T., V. H. Freed, D. W. Schmedding, and R. L. Kohnert. 1977. Partition coefficient and bioaccumulation of selected organic chemicals. Environmental Science and Technology 11:475–478.

Chisholm, I. M., W. A. Hubert, and T. A. Wesche. 1987. Winter stream conditions and use of habitat by brook trout in high-elevation Wyoming streams. Transactions of the American Fisheries Society 116:176–184.

Choon, H. L., P. C. Oloffs, and S. Y. Szeto. 1986. Persistence, degradation, and movement of triclopyr and its ethylene glycol butyl ether ester in a forest soil. Journal of Agricultural and Food Chemistry 34:1075–1079.

Chow, V. T. 1959. Open-channel hydraulics. McGraw-Hill, New York.

Christner, J., and R. D. Harr. 1982. Peak streamflows from the transient snow zone, Western Cascades, Oregon. Pages 27–38 *in* Proceedings, 50th western snow conference. Colorado State University Press, Fort Collins.

Chrzanowski, R. L., J. C-Y. Han, and C. L. McIntosh. 1979. Metabolism of [^{14}C]fosamine ammonium in the rat. Journal of Agricultural and Food Chemistry 27:550–554.

Church, M. 1983. Concepts of sediment transfer and transport on the Queen Charlotte Islands. British Columbia Ministry of Forests, Fish–Forestry Interaction Program Working Paper 4/83, Vancouver.

Church, M., and R. Kellerhals. 1978. On the statistics of grain size variation along a gravel river. Canadian Journal of Earth Sciences 15:1151–1160.

Churchill, J. E. 1980. Beaver are killing our trout streams. Trout 21 (4):22–25.

Chutter, F. M. 1970. Hydrobiological studies in the catchment of Vaal Dam, South Africa. Part 1. River zonation and the benthic fauna. Internationale Revue der gesamten Hydrobiologie 55:445–494.

Chykaliuk, P. B., J. R. Abernathy, and J. R. Gipson. 1981. Bibliography of glyphosate. Texas A & M University, Texas Agricultural Experiment Station, College Station.

Claire, E. 1978a. Flow recovery. Page 9 in Proceedings, fish habitat improvement workshop, Ochoco Ranger Station. Oregon Department of Fish and Wildlife, Portland.

Claire, E. 1978b. Log sills. Page 7 in Proceedings, fish habitat improvement workshop, Ochoco Ranger Station. Oregon Department of Fish and Wildlife, Portland.

Claire, E. 1978c. Rock work. Pages 2–3 in Proceedings, fish habitat improvement workshop, Ochoco Ranger Station. Oregon Department of Fish and Wildlife, Portland.

Claire, E. W., and R. L. Storch. 1983. Streamside management and livestock grazing in the Blue Mountains of Oregon: a case study. Pages 111–128 in Menke (1983).

Clark, D. K. 1986. Ecological baseline and monitoring project final report. Part 1: livebox bioassay studies in Port Gardner, Washington. Washington State Department of Ecology, Olympia.

Clark, R. N. 1982. Promises and pitfalls of the ROS in resource management. Australian Parks and Recreation (May):9–13.

Clark, R. N. 1987. Recreation management: a question of integration. Western Wildlands 13:20–23.

Clark, R. N. 1988. Enhancing recreation opportunities in silvicultural planning. U.S. Forest Service General Technical Report INT-243:61–69.

Clark, R. N., and K. B. Downing. 1985. Why here and not there: the conditional nature of recreation choice. U.S. Forest Service General Technical Report INT-184:61–70.

Clark, R. N., J. C. Hendee, and F. L. Campbell. 1971. Values, behavior, and conflict in modern camping culture. Journal of Leisure Research 3:143–159.

Clark, R. N., D. R. Johnson, and D. R. Field. 1982. The Alaska public survey—a comprehensive assessment of recreational values and use patterns and natural resource management. Minnesota Agricultural Experiment Station Miscellaneous Publication 18:115–119.

Clark, R. N., R. W. Koch, M. L. Hogans, H. H. Christensen, and J. C. Hendee. 1984. The value of roaded, multiple-use areas as recreation sites in three National Forests of the Pacific Northwest. U.S. Forest Service Research Paper PNW-319.

Clark, R. N., and R. C. Lucas. 1978. The forest ecosystem of southeast Alaska: 10. Outdoor recreation and scenic resources. U.S. Forest Service General Technical Report PNW-66.

Clark, R. N., and G. H. Stankey. 1979a. Determining the acceptability of recreational impacts: an application of the outdoor recreation opportunity spectrum. Pages 32–42 in Ittner et al. (1979).

Clark, R. N., and G. H. Stankey. 1979b. The recreation opportunity spectrum: a framework for planning, management, and research. U.S. Forest Service General Technical Report PNW-98.

Clarkson, T. W. 1973. The pharmacodynamics of mercury and its compounds with emphasis on the short-chain alkylmercurials. Pages 332–354 in D. R. Buhler, editor. Mercury in the western environment. Oregon State University Continuing Education Publications, Corvallis.

Clay, C. H. 1961. Design of fishways and other fish facilities. Canada Department of Fisheries, Ottawa.

Clay, D. H. 1981. High mountain meadow restoration. Pages 477–479 *in* Proceedings, California riparian systems conference. University of California, Davis.

Cloern, J. E. 1976. The survival of coho salmon (*Oncorhynchus kisutch*) eggs in two Wisconsin tributaries of Lake Michigan. American Midland Naturalist 96:451–461.

Coble, D. W. 1961. Influence of water exchange and dissolved oxygen in redds on survival of steelhead trout embryos. Transactions of the American Fisheries Society 90:469–474.

Cole, D. N. 1979. Reducing the impact of hikers on vegetation: an application of analytical research methods. Pages 71–78 *in* Ittner et al. (1979).

Cole, D. N., and B. Ranz. 1983. Temporary campsite closures in the Selway–Bitterroot Wilderness. Journal of Forestry 81:729–732.

Colinvaux, P. A. 1973. Introduction to ecology. Wiley, New York.

Collier, C. R., R. J. Pickering, and J. J. Musser, editors. 1970. Influences of strip mining on the hydrologic environment of parts of Beaver Creek basin, Kentucky, 1955–66. U.S. Geological Survey Professional Paper 427-C.

Collings, M. R. 1972. A methodology for determining instream flow requirements for fish. Pages 72–86 *in* Proceedings, instream flow methodology workshop. Washington State Water Program, Olympia.

Collings, M. R. 1974. Generalization of spawning and rearing discharges for several Pacific salmon species in western Washington. U.S. Geological Survey Open File Report, Tacoma, Washington.

Colman, S. M. 1973. The history of mass movement processes in the Redwood Creek Basin, Humboldt County, California. Master's thesis. Pennsylvania State University, University Park.

Combs, B. D. 1965. Effect of temperature on the development of salmon eggs. Progressive Fish-Culturist 27:134–137.

Combs, B. D., and R. E. Burrows. 1957. Threshold temperatures for the normal development of chinook salmon eggs. Progressive Fish-Culturist 19:3–6.

Comes, R. D., V. F. Bruns, and A. D. Kelley. 1976. Residues and persistence of glyphosate in irrigation water. Weed Science 24:47–50.

Conder, A. L., and T. C. Annear. 1987. Test of weighted usable area estimates derived from a PHABSIM model for instream flow studies on trout streams. North American Journal of Fisheries Management 7:339–350.

Conlan, K. E. 1975. The biological effects of log dumping and storage in southern British Columbia: Report 2. Literature review and Master's thesis progress report (unpublished). On file, University of Victoria, Victoria, British Columbia.

Conlan, K. E. 1977. The effects of wood deposition from coastal log handling operation on the benthos of a shallow sand bed in Saanich Inlet, British Columbia. Master's thesis. University of Victoria, Victoria, British Columbia.

Conlan, K. E., and D. V. Ellis. 1979. Effects of wood waste on sand-bed benthos. Marine Pollution Bulletin 10:262–267.

Cook, G. H., J. C. Moore, and D. L. Coppage. 1976. The relationship of malathion and its metabolites [sic] to fish poisoning. Bulletin of Environmental Contamination and Toxicology 16:283–290.

Cooper, A. C. 1965. The effect of transported stream sediments on the survival of sockeye and pink salmon eggs and alevin. International Pacific Salmon Fisheries Commission Bulletin 18.

Cooper, J. J., and S. Vigg. 1984. Extreme mercury concentrations of a striped bass, *Morone saxatilis*, with a known residence time in Lahontan Reservoir, Nevada. California Fish and Game 70:190–192.

Cope, O. B. 1957. The choice of spawning sites by cutthroat trout. Proceedings of the Utah Academy of Sciences, Arts, and Letters 34:73–79.

Cope, O. B. 1966. Contamination of the freshwater ecosystem by pesticides. Journal of Applied Ecology 3 (Supplement):33–44.

Cope, O. B., editor. 1979. Proceedings, grazing and riparian–stream ecosystems forum. Trout Unlimited, Vienna, Virginia.

Cope, O. B., E. M. Wood, and G. H. Wallen. 1970. Some chronic effects of 2,4-D on the bluegill (*Lepomis macrochirus*). Transactions of the American Fisheries Society 99:1–12.

Corbett, P. G., J. P. Campbell, and S. H. Olsen. 1978. Environmental improvement at Neroutsos Inlet, B.C. Volume 2: water quality and biological studies in Neroutsos Inlet, B.C. Rayonier Canada, Port Alice, British Columbia.

Cordone, A. J., and D. W. Kelley. 1961. The influences of inorganic sediment on the aquatic life of streams. California Fish and Game 47:189–228.

Cordone, A. J., and S. Pennoyer. 1960. Notes on silt pollution in the Truckee River drainage. California Department of Fish and Game, Inland Fisheries Administrative Report 60-14, Sacramento.

Corley, D. R., and L. A. Burmeister. 1979. Fishery habitat survey of the South Fork Salmon River—1979. U.S. Forest Service, Boise, Idaho.

Cornwall, G. F. 1941. The Willamette basin: river log traffic booming. The Timberman 42(10):11–16.

Costa, H. S., J. J. McKeown, and R. O. Blosser. 1979. Studies on characterization, fate, and impact of residual solids of biological treatment origin. TAPPI 62(10):41–46.

Costa, H. S., J. J. McKeown, and D. L. Borton. 1980. Fate of suspended biological solids discharged to receiving waters. Journal of the Water Pollution Control Federation 52:2432–2441.

Cottel, P., editor. 1977. Coastal log handling and transportation. University of British Columbia, Association of British Columbia Professional Foresters, Faculties of Forestry and Continuing Education, Vancouver.

Council for Agricultural Science and Technology (CAST). 1974. Livestock grazing on federal lands in the 11 western states. Journal of Range Management 27:174–181.

Council of Forest Industries. 1974. Report of the task force on log losses. Vancouver, British Columbia.

Council of Forest Industries. 1980. Report of the task force on log losses—1980 update. Vancouver, British Columbia.

Courtemanch, D. L., and K. E. Gibbs. 1980. Short- and long-term effects of forest spraying of carbaryl (Sevin-4-oil) on stream invertebrates. Canadian Entomologist 112:271–276.

Cox, T. R. 1974. Mills and markets: a history of the Pacific Coast lumber industry to 1900. University of Washington Press, Seattle.

Cramer, F. K. 1940. Notes on the natural spawning of cutthroat trout (*Salmo clarkii clarkii*) in Oregon. Proceedings of the 6th Pacific Science Congress 3:335–339.

Cramer, S. P., T. D. Satterwaite, R. B. Boyce, and B. P. McPherson. 1985. Lost Creek Dam fisheries evaluation, phase I completion report. Volume 1: impacts of Lost Creek Dam on the biology of anadromous salmonids in the Rogue River. Submitted to U.S. Army Corps of Engineers, Portland District, Portland, Oregon. Oregon Department of Fish and Wildlife, Research and Development Section, Corvallis.

Cronan, C. S., and C. L. Schofield. 1979. Aluminum leaching response to acid precipitation: effects on high-elevation watersheds in the Northeast. Science (Washington, D.C.) 204:304–306.

Crone, R. A., and C. E. Bond. 1976. Life history of coho salmon, *Oncorhynchus kisutch*, in Sashin Creek, southeastern Alaska. U.S. National Marine Fisheries Service Fishery Bulletin 74:897–923.

Cronemiller, F. P. 1955. Making new trout streams in the Sierra Nevada. Pages 583–586 *in* The yearbook of agriculture, 1955: water. U.S. Department of Agriculture, Washington, D.C.

Cronemiller, F. P., and J. Fraser. 1954. Stretching our Sierra trout streams. Outdoor California 15(4):3–7.

Cross, S. F., and D. V. Ellis. 1981. Environmental recovery in a marine ecosystem impacted by a sulfite process pulp mill. Journal of the Water Pollution Control Federation 53:1339–1346.

Crouse, M. R., C. A. Callahan, K. W. Malueg, and S. E. Dominguez. 1981. Effects of fine sediments on growth of juvenile coho salmon in laboratory streams. Transactions of the American Fisheries Society 110:281–286.

Crouter, R. A., and E. H. Vernon. 1959. Effects of black-headed budworm control on salmon and trout in British Columbia. Canadian Fish Culturist 24:23–40.

Crowe, D. M. 1983. Comprehensive planning for wildlife resources. Wyoming Game and Fish Department, Cheyenne.

Crutchfield, J. A., and G. Pontecorvo. 1969. The Pacific salmon fisheries: a study of irrational conservation. Johns Hopkins University Press, Baltimore.

Crutchfield, J. A., and K. Schelle. 1978. An economic analysis of Washington ocean recreational salmon fishing with particular emphasis on the role played by the charter vessel industry. Report to the Pacific Fishery Management Council, NOAA/NMFS grant 04-7-158-44024. Portland, Oregon.

Culp, J. M., and R. W. Davies. 1983. An assessment of the effects of streambank clear-cutting on macroinvertebrate communities in a managed watershed. Canadian Technical Report of Fisheries and Aquatic Sciences 1208.

Cumming, K. B., and D. M. Hill. 1971. Stream faunal recovery after manganese strip mining reclamation. U.S. Environmental Protection Agency, Water Pollution Control Research Series 18050-DO14.

Cummings, R. G., D. S. Brookshire, and W. D. Schulze, editors. 1986. Valuing environmental goods: an assessment of the contingent valuation method. Rowman and Allanheld, Totowa, New Jersey.

Cummins, A. B., and I. A. Given. 1973a. SME mining engineering handbook, volume 1. Society of Mining Engineers of American Institute of Mining, Metallurgical, and Petroleum Engineers, Inc., New York.

Cummins, A. B., and I. A. Given. 1973b. SME mining engineering handbook, volume 2. Society of Mining Engineers of American Institute of Mining, Metallurgical, and Petroleum Engineers, Inc., New York.

Cummins, K. W. 1973. Trophic relations of aquatic insects. Annual Review of Entomology 18:183–206.

Cummins, K. W. 1974. Structure and function of stream ecosystems. BioScience 24:631–641.

Cummins, K. W., M. J. Klug, R. G. Wetzel, R. C. Petersen, K. F. Suberkropp, B. A. Manny, J. C. Wuycheck, and F. O. Howard. 1972. Organic enrichment with leaf leachate in experimental lotic ecosystems. BioScience 22:719–722.

Cummins, K. W., and G. H. Lauff. 1969. The influence of substrate particle size on the microdistribution of stream macrobenthos. Hydrobiologia 34:145–181.

Cummins, K. W., R. C. Petersen, F. O. Howard, J. C. Wuycheck, and V. I. Holt. 1973. The utilization of leaf litter by stream detritivores. Ecology 54:336–345.

Cunjak, R. A., and G. Power. 1986. Winter habitat utilization by stream resident brook trout (*Salvelinus fontinalis*) and brown trout (*Salmo trutta*). Canadian Journal of Fisheries and Aquatic Sciences 43:1970–1981.

Czarneki, J. M. 1985. Accumulation of lead in fish from Missouri streams impacted by lead mining. Bulletin of Environmental Contamination and Toxicology 34:736–745.

Dadswell, M. J., R. J. Klauda, C. M. Moffitt, R. L. Saunders, R. A. Rulifson, and J. E. Cooper, editors. 1987. Common strategies of anadromous and catadromous fishes. American Fisheries Society Symposium 1.

Dahlberg, M. L., D. L. Shumway, and P. Doudoroff. 1968. Influence of dissolved oxygen and carbon dioxide on swimming performance of largemouth bass and coho salmon. Journal of the Fisheries Research Board of Canada 25:49–70.

Dahlem, E. A. 1979. The Mahogany Creek watershed—with and without grazing. Pages 31–34 in Cope (1979).

Dahm, C. N. 1981. Pathways and mechanisms for removal of dissolved organic carbon from leaf leachate in streams. Canadian Journal of Fisheries and Aquatic Sciences 38:68–76.

Dahm, C. N. 1984. Uptake of dissolved organic carbon in mountain streams. Internationale

Vereinigung für theoretische und angewandte Limnologie Verhandlungen 22: 1842–1846.

Dambacher, J. In press. Rearing ecology of juvenile steelhead (*Oncorhynchus mykiss*), and habitat analysis of Steamboat Creek basin, Oregon. Master's thesis. Oregon State University, Corvallis.

Dames and Moore, Inc. 1978. Streambed improvement program. Washington Department of Fisheries Draft Environmental Impact Statement, Olympia.

D'amore, G., and A. Bellorno. 1958. Photolysis of solutions of potassium ferrocyanide. Atti della Societa Peloritana di Scienze Fisiche, Matematiche e Naturali 5:449–457.

Dance, K. W., H. B. N. Hynes, and N. K. Kaushik. 1979. Seasonal drift of solid organic matter in two adjacent streams. Archiv für Hydrobiologie 87:139–151.

Dane, B. G. 1978a. Culvert guidelines: recommendations for the design and installation of culverts in British Columbia to avoid conflict with anadromous fish. Canada Fisheries and Marine Service Technical Report 811.

Dane, B. G. 1978b. A review and resolution of fish passage problems at culvert sites in British Columbia. Canada Fisheries and Marine Service Technical Report 810.

Daniel Ball, The. 1870. 10 Wall 557, 563. U.S. Supreme Court, Washington, D.C.

Davey, R. B., M. V. Meisch, and F. L. Carter. 1976. Toxicity of five ricefield pesticides to the mosquitofish, *Gambusia affinis*, and green sunfish, *Lepomis cyanellus*, under laboratory and field conditions in Arkansas. Environmental Entomology 5:1053–1056.

Davies, P. H., J. P. Goettl, Jr., J. R. Sinley, and N. F. Smith. 1976. Acute and chronic toxicity of lead to rainbow trout *Salmo gairdneri*, in hard and soft water. Water Research 10:199–206.

Davis, E. A., P. A. Ingebo, and C. P. Pase. 1968. Effect of a watershed treatment with picloram on water quality. U.S. Forest Service Research Note RM-100.

Davis, F. L., and F. L. Selman. 1954. Effects of water upon the movement of dinitro weed killers in soils. Weeds 3:11–20.

Davis, G. E., J. Foster, C. E. Warren, and P. Doudoroff. 1963. The influence of oxygen concentration on the swimming performance of juvenile Pacific salmon at various temperatures. Transactions of the American Fisheries Society 92:111–124.

Davis, H. S. 1934. The purpose and value of stream improvement. Transactions of the American Fisheries Society 64:63–67.

Davis, H. S. 1935. Methods for the improvement of streams. U.S. Bureau of Fisheries Memorandum I-133, Washington, D.C.

Davis, J. C. 1973. Sublethal effects of bleached kraft pulp mill effluent on respiration and circulation in sockeye salmon (*Oncorhynchus nerka*). Journal of the Fisheries Research Board of Canada 30:369–377.

Davis, J. C. 1975. Minimal dissolved oxygen requirements of aquatic life with emphasis on Canadian species: a review. Journal of the Fisheries Research Board of Canada 32:2295–2332.

Davis, J. C., I. G. Shand, G. Christie, and G. Kosakoski. 1978. Biological and oceanographic observations in the Neroutsos Inlet area with emphasis on the effect of sulfite pulp mill waste on Pacific salmon. Canada Fisheries and Marine Service Manuscript Report 1447.

Davis, J. C., I. G. Shand, and B. J. Mason. 1976. Biological and oceanographic studies at a kraft pulp and paper mill outfall at Crofton, B.C. Canada Fisheries and Marine Service Technical Report 652.

Davis, J. T., and W. S. Hardcastle. 1959. Biological assay of herbicides for fish toxicity. Weeds 7:397–404.

Davis, J. T., and J. S. Hughes. 1963. Further observations on the toxicity of commercial herbicides to bluegill sunfish. Proceedings of the Southern Weed Conference 16:337–340.

Dawson, F. H. 1980. The origin, composition and downstream transport of plant material in a small chalk stream. Freshwater Biology 10:419–435.

Day, A. D., and K. L. Ludeke. 1973. Stabilizing copper mine tailing disposal berms with giant bermudagrass. Journal of Environmental Quality 2:314–315.

Day, A. D., and K. L. Ludeke. 1981. Revegetation of copper tailings ponds in the southwestern U.S.A. with annual grasses. Desert Plants 3(4):210–212.

Day, F. 1887. British and Irish salmonidae. Williams and Norgate, London.

Daye, P. G. 1981. The impact of acid precipitation on the physiology and toxicology of fish. International Atlantic Salmon Foundation Special Publication Series 10:29–36.

Daye, P. G., and E. T. Garside. 1980. Structural alterations in embryos and alevins of the Atlantic salmon, *Salmo salar* L., induced by continuous or short-term exposure to acidic levels of pH. Canadian Journal of Zoology 58:27–43.

Dayton, P. K. 1971. Competition, disturbance, and community organization: the provision and subsequent utilization of space in a rocky intertidal community. Ecological Monographs 41:351–389.

Debano, L. F., S. M. Savage, and D. A. Hamilton. 1976. The transfer of heat and hydrophobic substances during burning. Soil Science Society of America Journal 40:779–782.

Decker, C., and R. Menendez. 1974. Acute toxicity of iron and aluminum to brook trout. Proceedings of the West Virginia Academy of Science 46:159–167.

deGraaf, D. A., and L. H. Bain. 1986. Habitat use by and preferences of juvenile Atlantic salmon in two Newfoundland rivers. Transactions of the American Fisheries Society 115:671–681.

de Leeuw, A. D. 1982. A British Columbia stream habitat and fish population inventory system. Pages 32–40 *in* Armantrout (1982).

de Leeuw, A. D. 1988. Commentary on cumulative effects. Pages 40–41 *in* Chamberlin (1988).

Dellinger, R. W. 1980. Development document for effluent limitations. Guidelines and standards for the pulp, paper and paperboard and the builders' paper and board mills. U.S. Environmental Protection Agency Report EPA-440/1-80/025-b.

Dempson, J. B., and A. H. Kristofferson. 1987. Spatial and temporal aspects of the ocean migration of anadromous Arctic char. Pages 340–357 *in* Dadswell et al. (1987).

Dennis, D. S., W. H. Gillespie, R. A. Maxey, and R. Shaw. 1977. Accumulation and persistence of picloram (*Tordon 10K*) in surface water and bottom sediments in West Virginia. Archives of Environmental Contamination and Toxicology 6:421–433.

Derkson, G. 1981. Environmental review of the Eurocan pulp mill at Kitimat, British Columbia. Canada Environmental Protection Service, Pacific Region, Regional Program Report 81-27, Vancouver.

Derkson, G., and M. Lashmar. 1981. Environmental review of the Crestbrook pulp mill at Skookumchuk, British Columbia. Canada Environmental Protection Service, Pacific Region, Regional Program Report 81–24, Vancouver.

Derome, J. R. M. 1979. Urea hydrolysis and ammonia volatilization from urea pellets spread on top of the litter layer. Metsantutkimuslaitoksen Julkaisuja 97(2):1–22.

Derome, J. R. M. 1980. Urea hydrolysis and ammonia volatilization from the humus layer: laboratory study. Metsantutkimuslaitoksen Julkaisuja 98(6):1–23.

Desi, I., G. Dura, L. Gonczi, Z. Kneffel, A. Strohmayer, and Z. Szabo. 1976. Toxicity of malathion to mammals, aquatic organisms and tissue culture cells. Archives of Environmental Contamination and Toxicology 3:410–425.

Determan, T. A. 1986. Ecological baseline and monitoring project. Part 4: the effects of pulp mill load reductions on water quality in Port Gardner, Washington. Washington State Department of Ecology, Olympia.

Devine, J. M. 1975. Persistence of Orthene residues in the forest and aquatic environment. Pages 48–82 *in* Environmental impact study of aerially applied Orthene on a forest and aquatic ecosystem. State University of New York, Lake Ontario Environmental Laboratory Report 174, Oswego.

de Vries, J., and T. L. Chow. 1978. Hydrologic behavior of a forested mountain soil in coastal British Columbia. Water Resources Research 14:935–942.

Dickens, R., and A. E. Hiltbold. 1967. Movement and persistence of methanearsonates in soil. Weeds 15:299–304.

Dietrich, W. E., and T. Dunne. 1978. Sediment budget for a small catchment in mountainous terrain. Zeitschrift für Geomorphologie, Supplementband 29:191–206.

Dill, L. M., R. C. Ydenberg, and A. H. G. Fraser. 1981. Food abundance and territory size in juvenile coho salmon (*Oncorhynchus kisutch*). Canadian Journal of Zoology 59:1801–1809.

Dixon, D. G., and G. Leduc. 1981. Chronic cyanide poisoning of rainbow trout and its effects on growth, respiration, and liver histopathology. Archives of Environmental Contamination and Toxicology 10:117–131.

Dolloff, C. A. 1983. The relationships of wood debris to juvenile salmonid production and microhabitat selection in small southeast Alaska streams. Doctoral dissertation. Montana State University, Bozeman.

Dolloff, C. A. 1986. Effects of stream cleaning on juvenile coho salmon and Dolly Varden in southeast Alaska. Transactions of the American Fisheries Society 115:743–755.

Donnelly, D. M., J. B. Loomis, C. F. Sorg, and L. J. Nelson. 1985. Net economic value of recreational steelhead fishing in Idaho. U.S. Forest Service Resource Bulletin RM-9.

Dorcey, A. H. J., T. G. Northcote, and D. V. Ward. 1978. Are the Fraser marshes essential to salmon? University of British Columbia, Westwater Research Centre Lecture Series 1, Vancouver.

Doubt, P. D. 1965. Design of stable channels in erodible materials. U.S. Department of Agriculture Miscellaneous Publication 970:373–376.

Doudoroff, P. 1956. Some experiments on the toxicity of complex cyanides to fish. Sewage and Industrial Wastes 28:1020–1040.

Doudoroff, P. 1957. Water quality requirements of fishes and effects of toxic substances. Pages 403–430 *in* M. E. Brown, editor. The physiology of fishes, volume 2. Academic Press, New York.

Doudoroff, P. 1976. Toxicity to fish of cyanides and related compounds: a review. U.S. Environmental Protection Agency EPA-600/3-76-038.

Doudoroff, P., and M. Katz. 1953. Critical review of literature on the toxicity of industrial wastes and their components to fish. II. The metals, as salts. Sewage and Industrial Wastes 25:802–839.

Doudoroff, P., and C. E. Warren. 1965. Environmental requirements of fishes and wildlife: dissolved oxygen requirements of fishes. Oregon Agricultural Experiment Station Special Report 141.

Douglas, G. W. 1974. Ecological impact of chemical fire retardants: a review. Canadian Forestry Service, Northern Forest Research Centre Information Report NOR-X-109.

Douglass, J. E., D. R. Cochrane, G. W. Bailey, J. I. Teasley, and D. W. Hill. 1969. Low herbicide concentration found in streamflow after a grass cover is killed. U.S. Forest Service Research Note SE-108.

Dow Chemical Company. 1983. Technical information on triclopyr, the active ingredient of Garlon herbicides. Dow Chemical Company, Agricultural Products Department Technical Data Sheets 137-859-483, Midland, Michigan.

Downing, K., and R. N. Clark. 1979. Users' and managers' perceptions of dispersed recreation impacts: a focus on roaded forest lands. Pages 18–23 *in* Proceedings, recreational impact on wildlands conference. U.S. Forest Service, Pacific Northwest Region, and U.S. National Park Service, Portland, Oregon.

Drablos, D., and A. Tollan, editors. 1980. Proceedings, international conference on the ecological impact of acid precipitation. Acid Precipitation—Effects on Forest and Fish Project, Aas, Norway.

Drummond, R. A., W. A. Spoor, and G. F. Olson. 1973. Some short-term indicators of sublethal effects of copper on brook trout, *Salvelinus fontinalis*. Journal of the Fisheries Research Board of Canada 30:698–701.

Duaime, T., J. Sonderegger, and M. Zaluski. 1985. Hydrogeology of the Colorado tailings area. Pages 4–21 *in* Carlson and Bahls (1985).

Duff, D. 1980. Construction and operating efficiency of various stream habitat improvement structures in Utah. Pages 153–158 *in* M. E. Seehorn, coordinator. Proceedings, trout stream habitat improvement workshop. U.S. Forest Service, Atlanta, Georgia.

Duff, D. A. 1983. Livestock grazing impacts on aquatic habitat in Big Creek, Utah. Pages 129–142 *in* Menke (1983).

Duff, D. A., N. Banks, E. Sparks, W. E. Stone, and R. J. Poehlmann. 1988. Indexed bibliography on stream habitat improvement (4th revision). U.S. Forest Service, Intermountain Region, Ogden, Utah.

Dugal, H. S., M. A. Buchanan, E. E. Dickey, and J. W. Swanson. 1976. Color characterization of kraft linerboard decker effluent. Paperi ja Puu (Paper and Timber) 58:211–225.

Duncan, S. H. 1986. Peak stream discharge during thirty years of sustained yield timber management in two fifth order watersheds in Washington State. Northwest Science 60:258–264.

Duncan, W. F. A., and M. A. Brusven. 1985a. Energy dynamics of three low-order southeast Alaska streams: allochthonous processes. Journal of Freshwater Ecology 3:233–248.

Duncan, W. F. A., and M. A. Brusven. 1985b. Energy dynamics of three low-order southeast Alaskan streams: autochthonous production. Journal of Freshwater Ecology 3:155–166.

Dunford, E. G., and C. H. Niederhof. 1944. Influence of aspen, young lodgepole pine, and open grassland types upon factors affecting water yield. Journal of Forestry 42:673–677.

Durbin, A. G., S. W. Nixon, and C. A. Oviatt. 1979. Effects of the spawning migration of the alewife, *Alosa pseudoharengus*, on freshwater ecosystems. Ecology 60:8–17.

Duval, W. S., ESL Environmental Sciences Ltd., and F. F. Slaney and Company Ltd. 1980. A review of the impacts of log handling on coastal marine environments and resources. Prepared for Council of Forest Industries–Government Estuary, Foreshore, and Water Log Handling and Transportation Study, Vancouver, British Columbia.

D. W. Kelley and Associates. 1982. Ecological investigations on the Tucannon River, Washington. U.S. Soil Conservation Service, SCS-AS-1, Spokane, Washington.

Dwyer, W. P. 1987. Effect of lowering water temperature on hatching time and survival of lake trout eggs. Progressive Fish-Culturist 49:175–176.

Dwyer, W. P., and R. G. Piper. 1987. Atlantic salmon growth efficiency as affected by temperature. Progressive Fish-Culturist 49:57–59.

Dwyer, W. P., R. G. Piper, and C. E. Smith. 1983. Brook trout growth efficiency as affected by temperature. Progressive Fish-Culturist 45:161–163.

Dyrness, C. T. 1965. Surface soil condition following tractor and high-lead logging in the Oregon Cascades. Journal of Forestry 63:272–275.

Dyrness, C. T. 1967a. Mass soil movements in the H. J. Andrews Experimental Forest. U.S. Forest Service Research Paper PNW-42.

Dyrness, C. T. 1967b. Soil surface conditions following skyline logging. U.S. Forest Service Research Note PNW-55.

Dyrness, C. T. 1969. Hydrologic properties of soils on three small watersheds in the western Cascades of Oregon. U.S. Forest Service Research Note PNW-111.

Dyrness, C. T. 1970. Stabilization of newly constructed road backslopes by mulch and grass–legume treatments. U.S. Forest Service Research Note PNW-123.

Dyrness, C. T. 1973. Early stages of plant succession following logging and burning in the western Cascades of Oregon. Ecology 54:57–69.

Dyrness, C. T., and C. T. Youngberg. 1957. The effect of logging and slash-burning on soil structure. Soil Science Society of America Proceedings 21:444–447.

EA Engineering, Science, and Technology, Inc. 1986. Instream flow methodologies. Electric Power Research Institute, Research Project 2194-2, Final Report, Lafayette, California.

Eaton, J. G. 1970. Chronic malathion toxicity to the bluegill (*Lepomis macrochirus* Rafinesque). Water Research 4:673–684.

Eaton, J. G. 1974. Chronic cadmium toxicity to the bluegill (*Lepomis macrochirus* Rafinesque). Transactions of the American Fisheries Society 103:729–735.

Ebel, W. J. 1970. Supersaturation of nitrogen in the Columbia River and its effect on salmon and steelhead trout. U.S. Fish and Wildlife Service Fishery Bulletin 68:1–11.

Ebel, W. J., and H. L. Raymond. 1976. Effect of atmospheric gas supersaturation on salmon and steelhead trout of the Snake and Columbia rivers. Marine Fisheries Review 38(7):1–14.

Ebeling, G. 1931. Recent results of the chemical investigation of the effect of waste waters from cellulose plants on fish. Vom Wasser 5:192–200.

Eckert, R. E., Jr. 1983. Methods for improving mountain meadow communities. U.S. Forest Service General Technical Report INT-157:67–75.

Edgell, M., C. R. Ross, and W. M. Ross. 1983. Marine log transportation and handling systems in British Columbia: impacts on coastal zone management. Journal of Coastal Zone Management 2 (1–2):41–69.

Edmundson, E., F. E. Everest, and D. W. Chapman. 1968. Permanence of station in juvenile chinook salmon and steelhead trout. Journal of the Fisheries Research Board of Canada 25:1453–1464.

Edwards, W. M., G. B. Triplett, Jr., and R. M. Kramer. 1980. A watershed study of glyphosate transport in runoff. Journal of Environmental Quality 9:661–665.

Egglishaw, H. J., and P. E. Shackley. 1985. Factors governing the production of juvenile Atlantic salmon in Scottish streams. Journal of Fish Biology 27 (Supplement A):27–33.

Ehlers, R. 1956. An evaluation of stream improvement devices constructed eighteen years ago. California Fish and Game 42:203–217.

Eichelberger, J. W., and J. J. Lichtenberg. 1971. Persistence of pesticides in river water. Environmental Science and Technology 5:541–544.

Eiserman, F., G. Dern, and J. Doyle. 1975. Cold water stream handbook for Wyoming. U.S. Soil Conservation Service, Cheyenne, Wyoming.

Ellgehausen, H., J. A. Guth, and H. O. Esser. 1980. Factors determining the bioaccumulation potential of pesticides in the individual compartments of aquatic food chains. Ecotoxicology and Environmental Safety 4:134–157.

Elliott, J. M. 1973. The food of brown and rainbow trout (*Salmo trutta* and *S. gairdneri*) in relation to the abundance of drifting invertebrates in a mountain stream. Oecologia (Berlin) 12:329–347.

Elliott, J. M. 1985. Population dynamics of migratory trout, *Salmo trutta*, in a Lake District stream, 1966–83, and their implications for fisheries management. Journal of Fish Biology 27 (Supplement A):35–43.

Elliott, S., and D. Hubartt. 1978. Study of land use activities and their relationship to sport fishing resources in Alaska. Alaska Department of Fish and Game, Juneau.

Elliott, S. T. 1986. Reduction of a Dolly Varden population and macrobenthos after removal of logging debris. Transactions of the American Fisheries Society 115:392–400.

Ellis, D. V. 1977. Pollution control regulations and monitoring technology: a review of research and development from the pulp and paper industry. Progress in Water Technology 9:673–682.

Ellis, D. V., P. Gee, and S. Cross. 1981. Recovery from zinc contamination in a stock of Pacific oysters. Water Pollution Research Journal of Canada 15:303–310.

Ellis, M. W. 1940. Water conditions affecting aquatic life in Elephant Butte Reservoir. U.S. Department of the Interior Bulletin 34.

Ellis, R. J. 1970. Preliminary reconnaissance of some log rafting and dumping areas in southeast Alaska, and their relationship to marine fauna. U.S. National Marine Fisheries Service [Bureau of Commerical Fisheries], Auke Bay, Alaska.

Ellis, R. J. 1973. Preliminary biological survey of log-rafting and dumping areas in southeastern Alaska. Marine Fisheries Review 35(5–6):19–22.

Elser, A. A. 1968. Fish populations of a trout stream in relation to major habitat zones and channel alterations. Transactions of the American Fisheries Society 97:389–397.

Elson, P. F. 1962. Predator–prey relationships between fish-eating birds and Atlantic salmon (with a supplement on fundamentals of merganser control). Fisheries Research Board of Canada Bulletin 133.

Elwood, J. W., and D. J. Nelson. 1972. Periphyton production and grazing rates in a stream measured with a ^{32}P material balance method. Oikos 23:295–303.

Elwood, J. W., J. D. Newbold, A. F. Trimble, and R. W. Stark. 1981. The limiting role of phosphorus in a woodland stream ecosystem: effects of P enrichment on leaf decomposition and primary producers. Ecology 62:146–158.

Engels, J. D. 1975. Use of gabions in stream habitat improvement. U.S. Bureau of Land Management, Eugene, Oregon.

English, T. S. 1967. Preliminary assessment of the English sole in Port Gardner, Washington. Journal of the Water Pollution Control Federation 39(8):1337–1350.

Eriksson, K.-E., M.-C. Kolar, P. O. Ljungquist, and K. P. Kringstad. 1985. Studies on microbial and chemical conversions of chlorolignins. Environmental Science and Technology 19:1219–1224.

Erman, D. C., and D. Mahoney. 1983. Recovery after logging in streams with and without bufferstrips in northern California. University of California, Water Resources Center, Contribution 186, Davis.

Erman, D. C., J. D. Newbold, and K. B. Roby. 1977. Evaluation of streamside bufferstrips for protecting aquatic organisms. University of California, Water Resources Center Contribution 165, Davis.

Erne, K. 1975. Phenoxy herbicide residues in Swedish fish and wildlife. Pages 192–195 in F. Coulston and F. Korte, editors. Environmental quality and safety. Volume 3 (Supplement): pesticides. Third International Congress of Pesticide Chemistry, Georg Thieme, Stuttgart, Germany.

Eschmeyer, P. H. 1964. The lake trout (*Salvelinus namaycush*). U.S. Fish and Wildlife Service Fishery Leaflet 555.

Eubanks, S. T. 1980. Full-restoration method for closing spur roads. Journal of Forestry 78:644–645.

Evans, R. S. 1977. Water born debris control in the lower Straight of Georgia. Pages 141–146 in P. Cottell, editor. Coastal log handling and transportation. Association of British Columbia Professional Foresters, University of British Columbia, Faculties of Forestry and Continuing Education, Vancouver.

Evans, W. A., and B. Johnston. 1980. Fish migration and fish passage: a practical guide to solving fish passage problems. U.S. Forest Service, EM-7100-2, Washington, D.C.

Everest, F. H. 1969. Habitat selection and spatial interaction of juvenile chinook salmon and steelhead trout in two Idaho streams. Doctoral dissertation. University of Idaho, Moscow.

Everest, F. H. 1973. Ecology and management of summer steelhead in the Rogue River. Oregon State Game Commission, Fishery Research Report 7, Corvallis.

Everest, F. H., R. L. Beschta, J. C. Scrivener, K. V. Koski, J. R. Sedell, and C. J. Cederholm. 1987a. Fine sediment and salmonid production: a paradox. Pages 98–142 in Salo and Cundy (1987).

Everest, F. H., and D. W. Chapman. 1972. Habitat selection and spatial interaction by juvenile chinook salmon and steelhead trout in two Idaho streams. Journal of the Fisheries Research Board of Canada 29:91–100.

Everest, F. H., and W. R. Meehan. 1981a. Forest management and anadromous fish habitat productivity. Transactions of the North American Wildlife and Natural Resources Conference 46:521–530.

Everest, F. H., and W. R. Meehan. 1981b. Some effects of debris torrents on habitat of anadromous salmonids. National Council of the Paper Industry for Air and Stream Improvement, Technical Bulletin 353:23–30, New York.

Everest, F. H., G. H. Reeves, J. R. Sedell, D. B. Hohler, and T. Cain. 1987b. The effects of habitat enhancement on steelhead trout and coho salmon smolt production, habitat utilization, and habitat availability in Fish Creek, Oregon, 1983–86. 1986

Annual Report, Bonneville Power Administration, Division of Fish and Wildlife, Project 84-11, Portland, Oregon.

Everest, F. H., G. H. Reeves, J. R. Sedell, J. Wolfe, D. Hohler, and D. A Heller. 1986. Abundance, behavior, and habitat utilization by coho salmon and steelhead trout in Fish Creek, Oregon, as influenced by habitat enchancement. 1985 Annual Report, Bonneville Power Administration, Division of Fish and Wildlife, Project 84-11, Portland, Oregon.

Everest, F. H., and J. R. Sedell. 1984. Evaluating effectiveness of stream enhancement projects. Pages 246–256 in Hassler (1984).

Everest, F. H., J. R. Sedell, G. H. Reeves, and M. D. Bryant. In press. Planning and evaluating habitat projects for anadromous salmonids. American Fisheries Society Symposium 10.

Everest, F. H., J. R. Sedell, G. H. Reeves, and J. Wolfe. 1985. Fisheries enhancement in the Fish Creek basin—an evaluation of in-channel and off-channel projects, 1984. 1984 Annual Report, Bonneville Power Administration, Division of Fish and Wildlife, Project 84-11, Portland, Oregon.

Everest, F. H., and P. B. Summers. 1982. The sport fishing resource of the National Forests—its extent, recreational use, and value. U.S. Forest Service, Washington, D.C.

Everett, L. J., C. A. Anderson, and D. MacDougall. 1966. Nature and extent of Guthion residues in milk and tissues resulting from treated forage. Journal of Agricultural and Food Chemistry 14:47–53.

E.V.S. Consultants Ltd. and F.L.C. Reed and Associates. 1978. A study of the biological impacts and economics of primary forest industries in the Campbell River estuary. Report prepared for Elk River Timber Company and Raven Lumber Ltd., North Vancouver, British Columbia.

Falk, D. L., and W. A. Dunson. 1977. The effects of season and acute sub-lethal exposure on survival times of brook trout at low pH. Water Research 11:13–15.

Faris, T. L., and K. D. Vaughan. 1985. Log transfer and storage facilities in southeast Alaska: a review. U.S. Forest Service General Technical Report PNW-174.

Farmer, E. E., B. Z. Richardson, and R. W. Brown. 1976. Revegetation of acid mining wastes in central Idaho. U.S. Forest Service Research Paper INT-178.

Fast, D. E., and Q. J. Stober. 1984. Intragravel behavior of salmonid alevins in response to environmental changes. University of Washington, Fisheries Research Institute, Project Completion Report FRI-UW-84-14, Seattle.

Fausch, K. D. 1984. Profitable stream positions for salmonids: relating specific growth rate to net energy gain. Canadian Journal of Zoology 62:441–451.

Fausch, K. D., C. L. Hawkes, and M. G. Parsons. 1988. Models that predict standing crop of stream fish from habitat variables: 1950–85. U.S. Forest Service General Technical Report PNW-213.

Fausch, K. D., and R. J. White. 1981. Competition between brook trout (Salvelinus fontinalis) and brown trout (Salmo trutta) for positions in a Michigan stream. Canadian Journal of Fisheries and Aquatic Sciences 38:1220–1227.

Fausch, K. D., and R. J. White. 1986. Competition among juveniles of coho salmon, brook trout, and brown trout in a laboratory stream, and implications for Great Lakes tributaries. Transactions of the American Fisheries Society 115:363–381.

Fearnow, T. C. 1941. An appraisal of stream improvement programs of the national forests of Northeastern states. Transactions of the North American Wildlife Conference 6:161–168.

Fenchel, T. M, and R. J. Riedl. 1970. The sulfide system: a new biotic community underneath the oxidized layer of marine sand bottoms. Marine Biology 7:255–268.

Ferguson, R. B., and N. C. Frischknecht. 1985. Reclamation on Utah's Emery and Alton coal fields: techniques and plant materials. U.S. Forest Service Research Paper INT-335.

FERIC (Forest Engineering Research Institute of Canada, Western Division). 1980. Compilation and summary of the results of the Council of Forest Industries questionnaire on logging use of foreshore leases on the coast of British Columbia. Council of Forest Industries, Vancouver.

Fessler, J., R. Aho, G. Concannon, J. Zakel, and B. Cates. 1977. Population characteristics and life history of wild Deschutes River chinook salmon. Oregon Department of Fish and Wildlife Completion Report, Project F-88-R-6, Portland.

Fessler, J. L. 1970. Spawning area development for fall chinook salmon. Pages 16–17 *in* H. J. Rayner, H. J. Campbell, and W. C. Lightfoot, editors. Progress in game and sportfish research 1963–1970. Oregon State Game Commission, Research Division Report, Portland.

Fiksdal, A. J. 1974. A landslide survey of the Stequaleho Creek Watershed. University of Washington, Fisheries Research Institute, Supplement to Final Report FRI-UW-7404, Seattle.

Filteau, G. 1959. Effets des vaporisations aériennes au DDT sur les insects aquatiques. Naturaliste Canadien 86(517):113–128.

Finlayson, B. J., and S. H. Ashuckian. 1979. Safe zinc and copper levels from the Spring Creek drainage for steelhead trout in the upper Sacramento River, California. California Fish and Game 65:80–99.

Finlayson, B. J., and K. M. Verrue. 1980. Estimated safe zinc and copper levels for chinook salmon, *Oncorhynchus tshawytscha*, in the upper Sacramento River, California. California Fish and Game 66:68–82.

Fish Habitat and Log Management Task Force. 1980. Nanaimo Estuary, Fish Habitat and Log Management Task Force summary report. Canada Department of Fisheries and Oceans, Vancouver.

Fisher, J. N. 1982. Employing acute and subacute toxicity measurements in on-site biomonitoring studies. TAPPI 65(11):89–91.

Fisher, S., and P. Deutsch. 1983. The soil resource: its importance in the West and its role in coal development and reclamation. Pages 845–984 *in* D. Books, technical editor. Coal development: collected papers: Papers presented at coal development workshops in Grand Junction, Colorado, and Casper, Wyoming. Volume 2. U.S. Bureau of Land Management, Washington, D.C.

Fisher, S. G., and G. E. Likens. 1972. Stream ecosystem: organic energy budget. BioScience 22:33–35.

Fisher, S. G., and G. E. Likens. 1973. Energy flow in Bear Brook, New Hampshire: an integrative approach to stream ecosystem metabolism. Ecological Monographs 43:421–439.

Flavell, T. H., S. Tunnock, and H. E. Meyers. 1977. A pilot project evaluating trichlorfon and acephate for managing western spruce budworm: Helena National Forest, Montana—1976. U.S. Forest Service, State and Private Forestry Report 77-16, Missoula, Montana.

Florsheim, J. L. 1985. Fluvial requirements of gravel bar formation in northwestern California. Master's thesis. Humboldt State University, Arcata, California.

Foerster, R. E. 1968. The sockeye salmon, *Oncorhynchus nerka*. Fisheries Research Board of Canada Bulletin 162.

Folmar, L. C. 1976. Overt avoidance reaction of rainbow trout fry to nine herbicides. Bulletin of Environmental Contamination and Toxicology 15:509–514.

Folmar, L. C. 1978. Avoidance chamber responses of mayfly nymphs exposed to eight herbicides. Bulletin of Environmental Contamination and Toxicology 19:312–318.

Folmar, L. C., H. O. Sanders, and A. M. Julin. 1979. Toxicity of the herbicide glyphosate and several of its formulations to fish and aquatic invertebrates. Archives of Environmental Contamination and Toxicology 8:269–278.

Fontaine, B. L. 1988. An evaluation of the effectiveness of instream structures for steelhead trout rearing habitat in the Steamboat Creek basin. Master's thesis. Oregon State University, Corvallis.

Fontaine, B. L., and T. D. Merritt. 1988. An anchoring system for fish habitat structures: field technique, evaluation, and application. U.S. Forest Service Research Note PNW-481.

Food and Agriculture Organization of the United Nations (FAO). 1988. Yearbook of fishery statistics, 1986, volume 62. FAO Fisheries Series.

Forest Engineering Incorporated. 1982. Evaluation of alternative log handling and transportation systems for southeast Alaska: Phase 1. A comparison of the rafting and barging of logs in southeast Alaska. U.S. Forest Service, Alaska Region, Juneau.

Forward [Harris], C. D. 1984. Organic debris complexity and its effect on small scale distribution and abundance of coho (*Oncorhynchus kisutch*) fry populations in Carnation Creek, British Columbia. Bachelor's thesis. University of British Columbia, Vancouver.

Foy, C. I. 1975. The chlorinated aliphatic acids. Pages 399–452 *in* P. C. Kearney and D. D. Kaufman, editors. Herbicides: chemistry, degradation and mode of action, volume 1, 2nd edition. Marcel Dekker, New York.

Fraley, J. J., and B. B. Shepard. 1989. Life history, ecology and population status of migratory bull trout (*Salvelinus confluentus*) in the Flathead Lake and River system, Montana. Northwest Science 63:133–143.

Frank, P. A., R. J. Demint, and R. D. Comes. 1970. Herbicides in irrigation water following canal-bank treatment for weed control. Weed Science 18:687–691.

Frank, R., and G. J. Sirons. 1979. Atrazine: its use in corn production and its loss to stream waters in southern Ontario, 1975–1977. Science of the Total Environment 12:223–239.

Frankenberger, L. 1968. Effects of habitat management on trout in a portion of the Kinnikinnic River, St. Croix County, Wisconsin. Wisconsin Department of Natural Resources, Bureau of Fish Management, Report 22, Madison.

Frankenberger, L., and R. Fassbender. 1967. Evaluation of the effects of the habitat management program and the watershed planning program on the brown trout fishery in Bohemian Valley Creek, La Crosse County, Wisconsin. Wisconsin Department of Natural Resources, Bureau of Fish Management, Report 16, Madison.

Franklin, J. F., and C. T. Dyrness. 1973. Natural vegetation of Oregon and Washington. U.S. Forest Service General Technical Report PNW-8.

Frantz, T. C., and A. J. Cordone. 1970. Food of lake trout in Lake Tahoe. California Fish and Game 56:21–35.

Fraser, F. J. 1969. Population density effects on survival and growth of juvenile coho salmon and steelhead trout in experimental streams. Pages 253–268 *in* Northcote (1969b).

Fraser, J. M. 1981. Comparative survival and growth of planted wild, hybrid, and domestic strains of brook trout (*Salvelinus fontinalis*) in Ontario lakes. Canadian Journal of Fisheries and Aquatic Sciences 38:1672–1684.

Fredriksen, R. L. 1971. Comparative chemical water quality—natural and disturbed streams following logging and slash burning. Pages 125–137 *in* Krygier and Hall (1971).

Fredriksen, R. L. 1973. Impact of forest management on stream water quality in western Oregon. Pages 37–50 *in* M. H. Mater, editor. Pollution abatement and control in the forest products industry, 1971–72. Forest Products Research Society, Madison, Wisconsin.

Fredriksen, R. L., D. G. Moore, and L. A. Norris. 1975. The impact of timber harvest, fertilization, and herbicide treatment on streamwater quality in western Oregon and Washington. Pages 283–313 *in* B. Bernier and C. H. Winget, editors. Forest soils and forest land management. Proceedings, 4th North American forest soils conference. Les Presses de l'Université Laval, Quebec.

Freed, V. H., C. T. Chiou, and D. W. Schmedding. 1979. Degradation of selected organophosphate pesticides in water and soil. Journal of Agricultural and Food Chemistry 27:706–708.

French, R., H. Bilton, M. Osako, and A. Hartt. 1976. Distribution and origin of sockeye salmon (*Oncorhynchus nerka*) in offshore waters of the North Pacific Ocean. International North Pacific Fisheries Commission Bulletin 34.

Fried, S. M., J. D. McCleave, and G. W. LaBar. 1978. Seaward migration of hatchery-reared Atlantic salmon, *Salmo salar*, smolts in the Penobscot River estuary, Maine: riverine movements. Journal of the Fisheries Research Board of Canada 35:76–78.

Frissell, C. A., and T. Hirai. 1989. Life history patterns, habitat change, and productivity of fall chinook stocks of southwest Oregon. Pages 85–94 *in* B. G. Shepherd, rapporteur. Proceedings, 1988 northeast Pacific chinook and coho salmon workshop. American Fisheries Society, North Pacific International Chapter. (Available from the B.C. Ministry of Environment, Penticton.)

Frissell, C. A., W. J. Liss, C. E. Warren, and M. D. Hurley. 1986. A hierarchical framework for stream habitat classification: viewing streams in a watershed context. Environmental Management 10:199–214.

Froehlich, H. A. 1973. Natural and man-caused slash in headwater streams. Loggers Handbook 33:15–17, 66, 68, 70, 82, 84, 86. Pacific Logging Congress, Portland, Oregon.

Fromm, P. O. 1980. A review of some physiological and toxicological responses of freshwater fish to acid stress. Environmental Biology of Fishes 5:79–93.

Fry, F. E. J. 1947. Effects of the environment on animal activity. Publications of the Ontario Fisheries Research Laboratory 68. University of Toronto Press, Toronto, Ontario.

Fuhremann, T. W., and E. P. Lichtenstein. 1980. A comparative study of the persistence, movement, and metabolism of six carbon-14 insecticides in soils and plants. Journal of Agricultural and Food Chemistry 28:446–452.

Fuller, R. H., J. M. Shay, R. F. Ferreira, and R. J. Hoffman. 1978. An evaluation of problems arising from acid mine drainage in the vicinity of Shasta Lake, Shasta County, California. U.S. Geological Survey, Water-Resources Investigations 78-32.

Fuller, R. L., and R. J. Mackay. 1981. Effects of food quality on the growth of three *Hydropsyche* species (Trichoptera: Hydropsychidae). Canadian Journal of Zoology 59:1133–1140.

Funk, W. H., F. W. Rabe, R. Filby, G. Bailey, P. Bennett, K. Shah, J. C. Sheppard, N. Savage, S. B. Bauer, A. Bourg, G. Bannon, G. Edwards, D. Anderson, P. Syms, J. Rothert, and A. Seamster. 1975. An integrated study on the impact of metallic trace element pollution in the Coeur d'Alene–Spokane Rivers and Lake drainage system. Washington State University–University of Idaho Joint Project, Completion Report to U.S. Office of Water Research and Technology, Project C-4145. Washington State University, Pullman.

Furniss, M. J., T. D. Roelofs, and C. S. Yee. 1991. Road construction and maintenance. American Fisheries Society Special Publication 19:297–323.

Gallizioli, S. 1977. Statement on improving fish and wildlife benefits in range management. Pages 90–96 *in* J. F. Townsend and R. J. Smith, editors. Proceedings, improving fish and wildlife benefits in range management seminar. U.S. Fish and Wildlife Service, FWS/OBS/77-1.

Gangmark, H. A., and R. G. Bakkala. 1960. A comparative study of unstable and stable (artificial channel) spawning streams for incubating king salmon at Mill Creek. California Fish and Game 46:151–164.

Gard, R. 1961a. Creation of trout habitat by constructing small dams. Journal of Wildlife Management 25:384–390.

Gard, R. 1961b. Effects of beaver on trout in Sagehen Creek, California. Journal of Wildlife Management 25:221–242.

Gard, R. 1972. Persistence of headwater check dams in a trout stream. Journal of Wildlife Management 36:1363–1367.

Gardner, R. B. 1979. Some environmental and economic effects of alternative forest road designs. Transactions of the American Society of Agricultural Engineers 22:63–68.

Garrels, R. M. 1951. A textbook of geology. Harper and Brothers, New York.

Garrison, R. L. 1971a. Fall chinook rehabilitation on the Alsea River. Pages 33–38 *in* Oregon State Game Commission, Annual Progress Report, Project AFS-57-1, Portland.

Garrison, R. L. 1971b. Spawning area development for fall chinook and subsequent survival from egg deposition to seaward migration. Oregon State Game Commission, Job Final Report, Project AFS-27-1, Portland.

Garside, E. T. 1973. Ultimate upper lethal temperature of Atlantic salmon *Salmo salar* L. Canadian Journal of Zoology 51:898–900.

Garstka, W. U., L. D. Love, B. C. Goodell, and F. A. Bertle. 1958. Factors affecting snowmelt and streamflow: a report on the 1946–53 cooperative snow investigations at the Fraser Experimental Forest, Fraser, Colorado. U.S. Bureau of Reclamation and U.S. Forest Service. U.S. Government Printing Office, Washington, D.C.

Gary, H. L., and G. B. Coltharp. 1967. Snow accumulation and disappearance by aspect and vegetation type in the Santa Fe Basin, New Mexico. U.S. Forest Service Research Note RM-93.

Gebhards, S., and J. Fisher. 1972. Fish passage and culvert installations. Idaho Fish and Game Department, Boise.

Geraghty, J. J., D. W. Miller, F. Van Der Leeden, and F. W. Troise. 1973. Water atlas of the United States. Water Information Center, Inc., Port Washington, New York.

Gerke, R. J. 1973. Spawning ground improvement study. Washington Department of Fisheries, Project Completion Report, Project AFC-59-2, Olympia.

Gerke, R. J. 1974. Salmon spawning habitat improvement study. Washington Department of Fisheries, Project Progress Report, Project 1-93-D, Olympia.

Gersich, F. M., C. G. Mendoza, D. M. Hopkins, and K. M. Bodner. 1984. Acute and chronic toxicity of triclopyr triethylamine salt to *Daphnia magna* Straus. Bulletin of Environmental Contamination and Toxicology 32:497–502.

Gerstung, E. R. 1986. The status and management of the Lahontan cutthroat trout, *Salmo clarki henshawi*. Pages 81–101 *in* Griffith (1986a).

Getzin, L. W. 1973. Persistence and degradation of carbofuran in soil. Environmental Entomology 2:461–467.

Geyer, H., A. G. Kraus, and W. Klein. 1980. Relationship between water solubility and bioaccumulation potential of organic chemicals in rats. Chemosphere 9:277–291.

Gharrett, J. T., and J. I. Hodges. 1950. Salmon fisheries of the coastal rivers of Oregon south of the Columbia. Oregon Fish Commission, Contribution 13, Portland.

Ghassemi, M., P. Painter, M. Powers, N. B. Akesson, and M. Dellarco. 1982. Estimating drift and exposure due to aerial application of insecticides in forests. Environmental Science and Technology 16:510–514.

Gibbons, D. R. 1982. A streamside management plan for the protection of salmonid habitat in southeast Alaska. Doctoral dissertation. University of Washington, Seattle.

Gibbons, D. R., and E. O. Salo. 1973. An annotated bibliography of the effects of logging on fish of the western United States and Canada. U.S. Forest Service General Technical Report PNW-10.

Gibbs, K. E., T. M. Mingo, and D. L. Courtemanch. 1984. Persistence of carbaryl (Sevin-4-oil) in woodland ponds and its effects on pond macroinvertebrates following forest spraying. Canadian Entomologist 116:203–213.

Gibson, R. J. 1978. The behavior of juvenile Atlantic salmon (*Salmo salar*) and brook trout (*Salvelinus fontinalis*) with regard to temperature and to water velocity. Transactions of the American Fisheries Society 107:703–712.

Gifford, G. 1975. Beneficial and detrimental effects of range improvement practices on runoff and erosion. Pages 216–274 *in* Proceedings, watershed management symposium. American Society of Civil Engineers, Irrigation and Drainage Division, Logan, Utah.

Gifford, G. F., and R. H. Hawkins. 1976. Grazing systems and watershed management: a look at the record. Journal of Soil and Water Conservation 31:281–283.

Giger, R. D. 1972. Ecology and management of coastal cutthroat trout in Oregon. Oregon State Game Commission, Research Division, Fishery Research Report 6, Portland.

Giger, R. D. 1973. Streamflow requirements of salmonids. Oregon Wildlife Commission, Job Final Report, Project AFS-62-1, Portland.

Gilfilian, R. E., W. L. Kline, T. E. Osterkamp, and C. S. Benson. 1973. Ice formation in a small Alaskan stream. International Association of Hydrological Sciences Publication 107:505–513.

Gimbarzevsky, P. 1983. Regional overview of mass wasting on the Queen Charlotte Islands. British Columbia Ministry of Forests, and British Columbia Ministry of the Environment, Fish–Forestry Interaction Program Working Paper 3/83, Victoria.

Gimbarzevsky, P. 1988. Mass wasting on the Queen Charlotte Islands: a regional inventory. British Columbia Ministry of Forests and Lands, Land Management Report 29, Victoria.

Glancy, P. A. 1973. A reconnaissance of streamflow and fluvial sediment transport, Incline Village Area, Lake Tahoe, Nevada. Nevada Division of Water Resources, Water Resources Information Series, Second Progress Report, 1971, Carson City.

Glova, G. J. 1984. Management implications of the distribution and diet of sympatric populations of juvenile coho salmon and coastal cutthroat trout in small streams in British Columbia, Canada. Progressive Fish-Culturist 46:269–277.

Glova, G. J. 1986. Interaction for food and space between experimental populations of juvenile coho salmon (*Oncorhynchus kisutch*) and coastal cutthroat trout (*Salmo clarki*) in a laboratory stream. Hydrobiologia 132:155–168.

Godin, J.-G. J. 1982. Migrations of salmonid fishes during early life history phases: daily and annual timing. Pages 22–50 *in* Brannon and Salo (1982).

Golding, D. L. 1987. Changes in streamflow peaks following timber harvest of a coastal British Columbia watershed. International Association of Hydrological Sciences Publication 167:509–517.

Goodman, D., and P. R. Vroom. 1972. Investigations into fish utilization of the inner estuary of the Squamish River. Environment Canada, Fisheries Service, Vancouver.

Gordon, D. J., and H. R. MacCrimmon. 1982. Juvenile salmonid production in a Lake Erie nursery stream. Journal of Fish Biology 21:455–473.

Gordon, M. R., and D. J. McLeay. 1978. Avoidance reactions of salmonids to pulpmill effluents. Canada Environmental Protection Service, CPAR Project Report 688-1, Ottawa.

Gordon, M. R., J. C. Mueller, and C. C. Walden. 1980. Effect of biotreatment on fish tainting propensity of bleached kraft whole mill effluent. Transactions of the Technical Section of the Canadian Pulp and Paper Association 6:2–8.

Gore, J. A., editor. 1985. The restoration of rivers and streams: theories and experience. Butterworth, Stoneham, Massachusetts.

Goring, C. A. I., and J. W. Hamaker. 1971. The degradation and movement of picloram in soil and water. Down to Earth 27(1):12–15.

Goring, C. A. I., D. A. Laskowski, J. W. Hamaker, and R. W. Meikle. 1975. Principles of pesticide degradation in soil. Pages 135–172 *in* R. Haque and V. H. Freed, editors. Environmental dynamics of pesticides. Plenum, New York.

Gove, G. W., and I. Gellman. 1971. Paper and allied products. [In a review of 1970 literature of wastewater and water pollution control.] Journal of the Water Pollution Control Federation 43:956–983.

Graham, J. M. 1949. Some effects of temperature and oxygen pressure on the metabolism and activity of the speckled trout, *Salvelinus fontinalis*. Canadian Journal of Research 27:270–288.

Grandt, A. F., and A. L. Lang. 1958. Reclaiming Illinois strip coal land with legumes and grasses. University of Illinois, Agricultural Experiment Station Bulletin 628, Champaign.

Grant, B. F., and P. M. Mehrle. 1970. Chronic endrin poisoning in goldfish, *Carassius auratus*. Journal of the Fisheries Research Board of Canada 27:2225–2232.

Grant, G. 1988. The RAPID technique: a new method for evaluating downstream effects of forest practices on riparian zones. U.S. Forest Service General Technical Report PNW-220.

Grant, G. E. 1986. Downstream effects of timber harvest activities on the channel and valley floor morphology of western Cascade streams. Doctoral dissertation. Johns Hopkins University, Baltimore, Maryland.

Grant, G. E., F. J. Swanson, and M. G. Wolman. 1990. Pattern and origin of stepped-bed morphology in high-gradient streams, Western Cascades, Oregon. Geological Society of America Bulletin 102:340–352.

Grant, J. W. A., J. Englert, and B. F. Bietz. 1986. Application of a method for assessing the impact of watershed practices: effects of logging on salmonid standing crops. North American Journal of Fisheries Management 6:24–31.

Gray, D. H., and W. F. Megahan. 1981. Forest vegetation removal and slope stability in the Idaho Batholith. U.S. Forest Service Research Paper INT-271.

Gray, J. R. A., and J. M. Edington. 1969. Effect of woodland clearance on stream temperature. Journal of the Fisheries Research Board of Canada 26:399–403.

Greacen, E. L., and R. Sands. 1980. Compaction of forest soils: a review. Australian Journal of Soil Research 18:163–189.

Gregory, K. J., and J. R. Madew. 1982. Land use changes, flood frequency and channel adjustment. Pages 757–781 in R. D. Hey, J. C. Bathurst, and C. R. Thorne, editors. Gravel-bed rivers. Wiley, New York.

Gregory, S. V. 1978. Phosphorus dynamics on organic and inorganic substrates in streams. Internationale Vereinigung für theoretische und angewandte Limnologie Verhandlungen 20:1340–1346.

Gregory, S. V. 1980. Effects of light, nutrients, and grazing on periphyton communities in streams. Doctoral dissertation. Oregon State University, Corvallis.

Gregory, S. V. 1983. Plant–herbivore interactions in stream systems. Pages 157–189 in J. R. Barnes and G. W. Minshall, editors. Stream ecology: application and testing of general ecological theory. Plenum, New York.

Gregory, S. V., G. A. Lamberti, D. C. Erman, K. V. Koski, M. L. Murphy, and J. R. Sedell. 1987. Influence of forest practices on aquatic production. Pages 233–255 in Salo and Cundy (1987).

Gregory, S. V., F. J. Swanson, and W. A. McKee. In press. An ecosystem perspective of riparian zones. BioScience.

Gresswell, R. E., and J. D. Varley. 1986. Effects of a century of human influence on the cutthroat trout of Yellowstone Lake. Pages 36–46 in Griffith (1986a).

Grette, G. B. 1985. The role of large organic debris in juvenile salmonid rearing habitat in small streams. Master's thesis. University of Washington, Seattle.

Grier, C. C. 1975. Wildfire effects on nutrient distribution and leaching in a coniferous ecosystem. Canadian Journal of Forest Research 5:599–607.

Griffin, D. R. 1955. Bird navigation. Pages 154–197 in A. Wolfson, editor. Recent studies in avian biology. University of Illinois Press, Urbana.

Griffith, J. S., editor. 1986a. The ecology and management of interior stocks of cutthroat trout. Special Publication of the American Fisheries Society, Western Division, Idaho State University, Pocatello.

Griffith, J. S. 1986b. Interactions of cutthroat trout with other fishes. Pages 102–108 in Griffith (1986a).

Griffith, J. S., and D. A. Andrews. 1981. Effects of a small suction dredge on fishes and aquatic invertebrates in Idaho streams. North American Journal of Fisheries Management 1:21–28.

Griffith, J. S., Jr. 1972. Comparative behavior and habitat utilization of brook trout (Salvelinus fontinalis) and cutthroat trout (Salmo clarki) in small streams in northern Idaho. Journal of the Fisheries Research Board of Canada 29:265–273.

Griffith, J. S., Jr. 1974. Utilization of invertebrate drift by brook trout (Salvelinus fontinalis) and cutthroat trout (Salmo clarki) in small streams in Idaho. Transactions of the American Fisheries Society 103:440–447.

Grogan, W. W. 1924. Water transportation of logs in the Northwest. University of Washington Forest Club Quarterly 3(2):24–27.

Groot, C. 1982. Modifications on a theme—a perspective on migratory behavior of Pacific salmon. Pages 1–21 in Brannon and Salo (1982).

Gross, M. R. 1987. Evolution of diadromy in fishes. Pages 14–25 in Dadswell et al. (1987).

Gross, M. R., R. M. Coleman, and R. M. McDowall. 1988. Aquatic productivity and the evolution of diadromous fish migration. Science (Washington, D.C.) 239:1291–1293.

Gudjonsson, S. 1989. Migration of anadromous Arctic charr, (Salvelinus alpinus L.), in a glacier river, River Blanda, North Iceland. Pages 116–123 *in* Brannon and Jonsson (1989).

Gunderson, D. R. 1968. Floodplain use related to stream morphology and fish populations. Journal of Wildlife Management 32:507–514.

Gunkel, G., and B. Streit. 1980. Mechanisms of bioaccumulation of a herbicide (atrazine, s-triazine) in a freshwater mollusc (*Ancylus fluviatilis* Mull.) and a fish (*Coregonus fera* Jurine). Water Research 14:1573–1584.

Gunther, F. A., and J. D. Gunther. 1970. The triazine herbicides. Residue Reviews 32:1–413.

Gurtz, M. E., J. R. Webster, and J. B. Wallace. 1980. Seston dynamics in southern Appalachian streams: effects of clear-cutting. Canadian Journal of Fisheries and Aquatic Sciences 37:624–631.

Gyselman, E. C. 1984. The seasonal movements of anadromous Arctic charr at Nauyuk Lake, Northwest Territories, Canada. Pages 575–578 *in* L. Johnson and B. Burns, editors. Biology of the Arctic charr: proceedings of the international symposium on Arctic charr. University of Manitoba Press, Winnipeg.

Haas, R. H., C. J. Scifres, M. G. Merkle, R. R. Hahn, and G. O. Hoffman. 1971. Occurrence and persistence of picloram in grassland water sources. Weed Research 11:54–62.

Hack, J. T. 1957. Studies of longitudinal stream profiles in Virginia and Maryland. U.S. Geological Survey Professional Paper 294-B:45–97.

Hagans, D. K., W. E. Weaver, and M. A. Madej. 1986. Long term on-site and off-site effects of logging and erosion in the Redwood Creek basin, northern California. National Council of the Paper Industry for Air and Stream Improvement, Technical Bulletin 490:38–66, New York.

Hahn, P. K. J. 1977. Effects of fluctuating and constant temperatures on behavior of steelhead trout (*Salmo gairdneri*). Doctoral dissertation. University of Idaho, Moscow.

Haines, T. A. 1981. Acidic precipitation and its consequences for aquatic ecosystems: a review. Transactions of the American Fisheries Society 110:669–707.

Hale, J. G. 1969. An evaluation of trout stream habitat improvement in a north shore tributary of Lake Superior. Minnesota Fisheries Investigations 5:37–50.

Hale, J. G. 1977. Toxicity of metal mining wastes. Bulletin of Environmental Contamination and Toxicology 17:66–73.

Hall, J. D., and C. O. Baker. 1975. Biological impacts of organic debris in Pacific Northwest streams. 13 pages *in* Logging debris in streams, notes for a workshop. Oregon State University, School of Forestry, Corvallis.

Hall, J. D., and C. O. Baker. 1982. Rehabilitating and enhancing steam habitat: 1. Review and evaluation. U.S. Forest Service General Technical Report PNW-138.

Hall, J. D., G. W. Brown, and R. L. Lantz. 1987. The Alsea watershed study: a retrospective. Pages 399–416 *in* Salo and Cundy (1987).

Hall, J. D., and M. S. Field-Dodgson. 1981. Improvement of spawning and rearing habitat for salmon. Pages 21–28 *in* C. L. Hopkins, compiler. Proceedings, salmon symposium. New Zealand Ministry of Agriculture and Fisheries, Fisheries Research Division, Occasional Publication 30, Wellington.

Hall, J. D., and N. J. Knight. 1981. Natural variation in abundance of salmonid populations in streams and its implications for design of impact studies. U.S. Environmental Protection Agency EPA-600/S3-81-021.

Hall, J. D., and R. L. Lantz. 1969. Effects of logging on the habitat of coho salmon and cutthroat trout in coastal streams. Pages 355–375 *in* Northcote (1969b).

Hall, J. D., M. L. Murphy, and R. S. Aho. 1978. An improved design for assessing impacts of watershed practices on small streams. Internationale Vereinigung für theoretische und angewandte Limnologie Verhandlungen 20:1359–1365.

Hall, J. K., M. Pawlus, and E. R. Higgins. 1972. Losses of atrazine in runoff water and soil sediment. Journal of Environmental Quality 1:172–176.

Hall, R. J., G. E. Likens, S. B. Fiance, and G. R. Hendrey. 1980. Experimental acidification of a stream in the Hubbard Brook Experimental Forest, New Hampshire. Ecology 61:976–989.

Hallock, R. J., R. F. Elwell, and D. H. Fry, Jr. 1970. Migrations of adult king salmon *Oncorhynchus tshawytscha* in the San Joaquin Delta as demonstrated by the use of sonic tags. California Department of Fish and Game, Fish Bulletin 151.

Hamilton, J. B. 1983. Performance of rock deflectors for rearing habitat improvement on a tributary of the Mattole River, Northern California. Master's thesis. Humboldt State University, Arcata, California.

Han, J. C-Y. 1979a. Residue studies with [^{14}C]fosamine ammonium in channel catfish. Journal of Toxicology and Environmental Health 5:957–963.

Han, J. C-Y. 1979b. Stability of [^{14}C]fosamine ammonium in water and soils. Journal of Agricultural and Food Chemistry 27:564–571.

Hance, R. J. 1976. Adsorption of glyphosate by soils. Pesticide Science 7:363–366.

Hankin, D. G. 1984. Multistage sampling designs in fisheries research: applications in small streams. Canadian Journal of Fisheries and Aquatic Sciences 41:1575–1591.

Hankin, D. G. 1986. Sampling designs for estimating the total number of fish in small streams. U.S. Forest Service Research Paper PNW-360.

Hankin, D. G., and G. H. Reeves. 1988. Estimating total fish abundance and total habitat area in small streams based on visual estimation methods. Canadian Journal of Fisheries and Aquatic Sciences 45:834–844.

Hanley, T. A. 1987. Physical and chemical response of understory vegetation to deer use in southeastern Alaska. Canadian Journal of Forest Research 17:195–199.

Hanley, T. A., and R. D. Taber. 1980. Selective plant species inhibition by elk and deer in three conifer communities in western Washington. Forest Science 26:97–107.

Hansen, E. A. 1975. Some effects of groundwater on brown trout redds. Transactions of the American Fisheries Society 104:100–110.

Hansen, G., G. Carter, W. Towne, and G. O'Neal. 1971. Log storage and rafting in public waters: Pacific Northwest Pollution Control Council, a task force report. U.S. Environmental Protection Agency, Seattle, Washington.

Hansmann, E. W. 1969. The effects of logging on periphyton communities of coastal streams. Doctoral dissertation. Oregon State University, Corvallis.

Hansmann, E. W., and H. K. Phinney. 1973. Effects of logging on periphyton in coastal streams of Oregon. Ecology 54:194–199.

Hanson, D. L. 1977. Habitat selection and spatial interaction in allopatric and sympatric populations of cutthroat and steelhead trout. Doctoral dissertation. University of Idaho, Moscow.

Haque, R., and V. H. Freed. 1974. Behavior of pesticides in the environment: "environmental chemodynamics." Residue Reviews 52:89–116.

Haque, R., and V. H. Freed, editors. 1975. Environmental dynamics of pesticides. Plenum, New York.

Hardy, C. J. 1963. An examination of eleven stranded redds of brown trout (*Salmo trutta*), excavated in the Selwyn River during July and August, 1960. New Zealand Journal of Science 6:107–119.

Hardy, J. L. 1966. Effect of Tordon herbicides on aquatic chain organisms. Down to Earth 22(2):11–13.

Hargrave, B. T. 1972. Aerobic decomposition of sediment and detritus as a function of particle surface area and organic content. Limnology and Oceanography 17:583–596.

Hargrave, B. T. 1976. The central role of invertebrate faeces in sediment decomposition. Pages 301–321 *in* J. M. Anderson and A. Macfadyen, editors. The role of terrestrial and aquatic organisms in decomposition processes. Blackwell Scientific Publications, Oxford, UK.

Harmon, M. E., J. F. Franklin, F. J. Swanson, P. Sollins, S. V. Gregory, J. D. Lattin, N. H. Anderson, S. P. Cline, N. G. Aumen, J. R. Sedell, G. W. Lienkaemper, K. Cromack, Jr., and K. W. Cummins. 1986. Ecology of coarse woody debris in temperate ecosystems. Advances in Ecological Research 15:133–302.

Harr, R. D. 1976. Hydrology of small forest streams in western Oregon. U.S. Forest Service General Technical Report PNW-55.

Harr, R. D. 1977. Water flux in soil and subsoil on a steep forested slope. Journal of Hydrology 33:37–58.

Harr, R. D. 1979. Effects of timber harvest on streamflow in the rain-dominated portion of the Pacific Northwest. Pages 2–45 *in* Proceedings, scheduling timber harvest for hydrologic concerns workshop. U.S. Forest Service, Pacific Northwest Region, Portland, Oregon.

Harr, R. D. 1981. Scheduling timber harvest to protect watershed values. Pages 269–280 *in* D. M. Baumgartner, editor. Proceedings, interior west watershed management symposium. Washington State University, Pullman.

Harr, R. D. 1982. Fog drip in the Bull Run Municipal Watershed, Oregon. Water Resources Bulletin 18:785–789.

Harr, R. D. 1983. Potential for augmenting water yield through forest practices in western Washington and western Oregon. Water Resources Bulletin 19:383–393.

Harr, R. D. 1986. Effects of clearcutting on rain-on-snow runoff in western Oregon: a new look at old studies. Water Resources Research 22:1095–1100.

Harr, R. D., R. L. Fredriksen, and J. Rothacher. 1979. Changes in streamflow following timber harvest in southwestern Oregon. U.S. Forest Service Research Paper PNW-249.

Harr, R. D., W. C. Harper, J. T. Krygier, and F. S. Hsieh. 1975. Changes in storm hydrographs after road building and clear-cutting in the Oregon Coast Range. Water Resources Research 11:436–444.

Harr, R. D., and F. M. McCorison. 1979. Initial effects of clearcut logging on size and timing of peak flows in a small watershed in western Oregon. Water Resources Research 15:90–94.

Harris, C. D. 1988. A summary of the effects of streamside logging treatments on organic debris in Carnation Creek. Pages 26–30 *in* Chamberlin (1988).

Harris, C. K. 1988. Recent changes in the pattern of catch of North American salmonids by the Japanese high seas salmon fisheries. Pages 41–66 *in* McNeil (1988).

Hart, D. D. 1985. Grazing insects mediate algal interactions in a stream benthic community. Oikos 44:40–46.

Hart, G. 1963. Snow and frost conditions in New Hampshire, under hardwoods and pines and in the open. Journal of Forestry 61:287–289.

Hart, J. L. 1973. Pacific fishes of Canada. Fisheries Research Board of Canada Bulletin 180.

Hartman, G., J. C. Scrivener, L. B. Holtby, and L. Powell. 1987. Some effects of different streamside treatments on physical conditions and fish population processes in Carnation Creek, a coastal rain forest stream in British Columbia. Pages 330–372 *in* Salo and Cundy (1987).

Hartman, G. F. 1963. Observations on behavior of juvenile brown trout in a stream aquarium during winter and spring. Journal of the Fisheries Research Board of Canada 20:769–787.

Hartman, G. F. 1965. The role of behavior in the ecology and interaction of underyearling coho salmon (*Oncorhynchus kisutch*) and steelhead trout (*Salmo gairdneri*). Journal of the Fisheries Research Board of Canada 22:1035–1081.

Hartman, G. F. 1969. Reproductive biology of the Gerrard stock rainbow trout. Pages 53–67 *in* Northcote (1969b).

Hartman, G. F., editor. 1982. Proceedings of the Carnation Creek workshop: a ten-year review. Pacific Biological Station, Nanaimo, British Columbia.

Hartman, G. F. 1988. Carnation Creek, 15 years of fisheries–forestry work, bridges from research to management. Pages 189–204 *in* Chamberlin (1988).

Hartman, G. F., B. C. Andersen, and J. C. Scrivener. 1982. Seaward movement of coho salmon (*Oncorhynchus kisutch*) fry in Carnation Creek, an unstable coastal stream in British Columbia. Canadian Journal of Fisheries and Aquatic Sciences 39:588–597.

Hartman, G. F., and T. G. Brown. 1987. Use of small, temporary, floodplain tributaries by juvenile salmonids in a west coast rain-forest drainage basin, Carnation Creek, British Columbia. Canadian Journal of Fisheries and Aquatic Sciences 44:262–270.

Hartman, G. F., and C. A. Gill. 1968. Distributions of juvenile steelhead and cutthroat trout (*Salmo gairdneri* and *S. clarki clarki*) within streams in southwestern British Columbia. Journal of the Fisheries Research Board of Canada 25:33–48.

Hartman, G. F., and J. C. Scrivener. 1990. Impacts of forest practices on a coastal stream ecosystem, Carnation Creek, British Columbia. Canadian Bulletin of Fisheries and Aquatic Sciences 223.

Hartman, W. L., W. R. Heard, and B. Drucker. 1967. Migratory behavior of sockeye salmon fry and smolts. Journal of the Fisheries Research Board of Canada 24:2069–2099.

Hasfurther, V. R. 1985. The use of meander parameters in restoring hydrologic balance to reclaimed stream beds. Pages 21–40 *in* Gore (1985).

Hasler, A. D., and J. E. Larsen. 1955. The homing salmon. Scientific American (August):3–6.

Hasler, A. D., A. T. Scholz, and R. M. Horrall. 1978. Olfactory imprinting and homing in salmon. American Scientist 66:347–355.

Hassler, T. J., editor. 1981. Proceedings, symposium on propagation, enchancement, and rehabilitation of anadromous salmonid populations and habitat in the Pacific Northwest. California Cooperative Fishery Research Unit, Humboldt State University, Arcata.

Hassler, T. J., editor. 1984. Proceedings, Pacific Northwest stream habitat management workshop. California Cooperative Fishery Research Unit, Humboldt State University, Arcata.

Hatfield, C. T., and J. M. Anderson. 1972. Effects of two insecticides on the vulnerability of Atlantic salmon (*Salmo salar*) parr to brook trout (*Salvelinus fontinalis*) predation. Journal of the Fisheries Research Board of Canada 29:27–29.

Hatfield, C. T., and P. H. Johansen. 1972. Effects of four insecticides on the ability of Atlantic salmon parr (*Salmo salar*) to learn and retain a simple conditioned response. Journal of the Fisheries Research Board of Canada 29:315–321.

Hattula, M. L., V.-M. Wasenius, H. Reunanen, and A. U. Arstila. 1981. Acute toxicity of some chlorinated phenols, catechols and cresols to trout. Bulletin of Environmental Contamination and Toxicology 26:295–298.

Hauge, C. J., M. J. Furniss, and F. D. Euphrat. 1979. Soil erosion in California's Coast Forest District. California Geology (June):120–129.

Haupt, H. F. 1959. Road and slope characteristics affecting sediment movement from logging roads. Journal of Forestry 57:329–332.

Haupt, H. F. 1979. Effects of timber cutting and revegetation on snow accumulation and melt in north Idaho. U.S. Forest Service Research Paper INT-224.

Hausle, D. A., and D. W. Coble. 1976. Influence of sand in redds on survival and emergence of brook trout (*Salvelinus fontinalis*). Transactions of the American Fisheries Society 105:57–63.

Haven, D. 1963. Mass treatment with 2,4-D of milfoil in tidal creeks in Virginia. Proceedings of the Southern Weed Conference 16:345–350.

Hawke, S. P. 1978. Stranded redds of chinook salmon in the Mathias River, South Island, New Zealand. New Zealand Journal of Marine and Freshwater Research 12:167–171.

Hawkins, A. D. 1989. Factors affecting the timing of entry and upstream movement of Atlantic salmon in the Aberdeenshire Dee. Pages 101–105 *in* Brannon and Jonsson (1989).

Hawkins, C. P., and J. A. MacMahon. 1989. Guilds: the multiple meanings of a concept. Annual Review of Entomology 34:423–451.

Hawkins, C. P., M. L. Murphy, and N. H. Anderson. 1982. Effects of canopy, substrate composition, and gradient on the structure of macroinvertebrate communities in Cascade Range streams of Oregon. Ecology 63:1840–1856.

Hawkins, C. P., M. L. Murphy, N. H. Anderson, and M. A. Wilzbach. 1983. Density of fish and salamanders in relation to riparian canopy and physical habitat in streams of the northwestern United States. Canadian Journal of Fisheries and Aquatic Sciences 40:1173–1185.

Hawkins, C. P., and J. R. Sedell. 1981. Longitudinal and seasonal changes in functional organization of macroinvertebrate communities in four Oregon streams. Ecology 62:387–397.

Hawley, J. R. 1972. Use, characteristics, and toxicity of mine–mill reagents in the province of Ontario. Ministry of the Environment, Toronto.

Hayes, F. A. 1978. Streambank stability and meadow condition in relation to livestock grazing in mountain meadows of central Idaho. Master's thesis. University of Idaho, Moscow.

Hayes, F. R., I. R. Wilmot, and D. A. Livingstone. 1951. The oxygen consumption of the salmon egg in relation to development and activity. Journal of Experimental Zoology 116:377–395.

Hazzard, A. S. 1932. Some phases of the life history of the eastern brook trout, *Salvelinus fontinalis* Mitchill. Transactions of the American Fisheries Society 62:344–350.

Heady, H. F. 1975. Rangeland management. McGraw-Hill, New York.

Healey, M. C. 1978. Utilization of the intertidal area of the Nanaimo estuary by juvenile salmon. Mimeographed file report, Department of Fisheries and Oceans, Pacific Biological Station, Nanaimo, British Columbia.

Healey, M. C. 1980. The ecology of juvenile salmon in Georgia Strait, British Columbia. Pages 203–205 *in* W. J. McNeil and D. C. Himsworth, editors. Salmonid ecosystems of the North Pacific. Oregon State University Press, Corvallis.

Healey, M. C. 1983. Coastwide distribution and ocean migration patterns of stream- and ocean-type chinook salmon, *Oncorhynchus tshawytscha*. Canadian Field-Naturalist 97:427–433.

Healey, M. C., and C. Groot. 1987. Marine migration and orientation of ocean-type chinook and sockeye salmon. Pages 298–312 *in* Dadswell et al. (1987).

Heard, W. R. 1978. Probable case of streambed overseeding—1967 pink salmon, *Oncorhynchus gorbuscha*, spawners and survival of their progeny in Sashin Creek, southeastern Alaska. U.S. National Marine Fisheries Service Fishery Bulletin 76:569–582.

Heede, B. H. 1976. Gully development and control: the status of our knowledge. U.S. Forest Service Research Paper RM-169.

Heede, B. H. 1977. Case study of a watershed rehabilitation project: Alkali Creek, Colorado. U.S. Forest Service Research Paper RM-189.

Heede, B. H. 1980. Stream dynamics: an overview for land managers. U.S. Forest Service General Technical Report RM-72.

Heggberget, T. G. 1988. Timing of spawning in Norwegian Atlantic salmon (*Salmo salar*). Canadian Journal of Fisheries and Aquatic Sciences 45:845–849.

Heifetz, J., M. L. Murphy, and K. V. Koski. 1986. Effects of logging on winter habitat of juvenile salmonids in Alaskan streams. North American Journal of Fisheries Management 6:52–58.

Heimann, D. C. 1988. Recruitment trends and physical characteristics of coarse woody debris in Oregon Coast Range streams. Master's thesis. Oregon State University, Corvallis.

Heiser, D. W. 1972. Spawning ground improvement—gravel loosening, 1971–1972. Washington State Department of Fisheries Progress Report, Olympia.

Helle, J. H. 1966. Behavior of displaced adult pink salmon. Transactions of the American Fisheries Society 95:188–195.

Helle, J. H. 1984. Age and size at maturity of some populations of chum salmon in North America. Pages 126–143 *in* P. A. Moiseev, editor. Proceedings, Pacific salmon biology conference, 1978. Pacific Scientific Institute of Fisheries and Oceanography (TINRO), Vladivostok, USSR.

Heller, D. A., J. R. Maxwell, and M. Parsons. 1983. Modeling the effects of forest management on salmonid habitat. U.S. Forest Service, Siuslaw National Forest, Corvallis, Oregon.

Helm, W. T., editor. 1985. Aquatic habitat inventory: glossary and standard methods. American Fisheries Society, Western Division, Bethesda, Maryland.

Heming, T. A. 1982. Effects of temperature on utilization of yolk by chinook salmon (*Oncorhynchus tshawytscha*) eggs and alevins. Canadian Journal of Fisheries and Aquatic Sciences 39:184–190.

Hemphill, N., and S. D. Cooper. 1984. Differences in the community structure of stream pools containing or lacking trout. Internationale Vereinigung für theoretische und angewandte Limnologie Verhandlungen 22:1858–1861.

Hendee, J. C., R. N. Clark, and T. E. Dailey. 1977. Fishing and other recreation behavior at high-mountain lakes in Washington State. U.S. Forest Service Research Note PNW-304.

Henderson, C., and Q. H. Pickering. 1958. Toxicity of organic phosphorus insecticides to fish. Transactions of the American Fisheries Society 87:39–51.

Henderson, C., Q. H. Pickering, and C. M. Tarzwell. 1959. Relative toxicity of ten chlorinated hydrocarbon insecticides to four species of fish. Transactions of the American Fisheries Society 88:23–32.

Henderson, C., Q. H. Pickering, and C. M. Tarzwell. 1960. The toxicity of organic phosphorus and chlorinated hydrocarbon insecticides to fish. U.S. Public Health Service Technical Report W60–3.

Herbert, D. W. M., and D. S. Shurben. 1965. The susceptibility of salmonid fish to poisons under estuarine conditions—2. Ammonium chloride. International Journal of Air and Water Pollution 9:89–91.

Herrmann, R., and J. Baron. 1980. Aluminum mobilization in acid stream environments, Great Smoky Mountains National Park, U.S.A. Pages 218–219 *in* Drablos and Tollan (1980).

Herrmann, R. B. 1979. Intertidal log raft storage impacts in Coos Bay, Oregon. Weyerhaeuser Company, Research and Development Technical Report, Project 042-4403-01, Federal Way, Washington.

Herrmann, R. B., C. E. Warren, and P. Doudoroff. 1962. Influence of oxygen concentration on the growth of juvenile coho salmon. Transactions of the American Fisheries Society 91:155–167.

Hetherington, E. D. 1985. Streamflow nitrogen loss following forest fertilization in a southern Vancouver Island watershed. Canadian Journal of Forest Research 15:34–41.

Hetherington, E. D. 1988. Hydrology and logging in the Carnation Creek watershed—What have we learned? Pages 11–15 *in* Chamberlin (1988).

Hewlett, J. D. 1967. A hydrologic response map for the state of Georgia. Water Resources Bulletin 3(3):4–20.

Hewlett, J. D., and A. R. Hibbert. 1961. Increases in water yield after several types of forest cutting. Bulletin of the International Association of Scientific Hydrology 6:5–17.

Hewlett, J. D., and A. R. Hibbert. 1967. Factors affecting the response of small watersheds to precipitation in humid areas. Pages 275–290 *in* Sopper and Lull (1967).

Hewlett, J. D., and W. L. Nutter. 1970. The varying source area of streamflow from upland basins. Pages 65–68 *in* Proceedings, interdisciplinary aspects of watershed management symposium. American Society of Civil Engineers, New York.

Hibbert, A. R. 1967. Forest treatment effects on water yield. Pages 527–543 *in* Sopper and Lull (1967).

Hibbert, A. R. 1976. Percolation and streamflows in range and forest lands. Pages 61–72 *in* H. F. Heady, D. J. Falkenborg, and J. P. Riley, editors. Proceedings, 5th workshop on watershed management on range and forest lands. United States–Australian Rangelands Panel. Utah State University, Utah Research Laboratory, Logan.

Hicks, B. J. 1990. The influence of geology and timber harvest on channel morphology and salmonid populations in Oregon Coast Range streams. Doctoral dissertation. Oregon State University, Corvallis.

Hicks, B. J., J. D. Hall, P. A. Bisson, and J. R. Sedell. 1991. Responses of salmonids to habitat changes. American Fisheries Society Special Publication 19:483–518.

Hicks, B. J., R. D. Harr, and R. L. Beschta. In press. Long-term changes in streamflow following logging and implications in western Oregon. Water Resources Bulletin.

Higgins, R. J., and W. J. Schouwenberg. 1976. Biological surveys in the Kitimat River estuary during 1974 and 1975. Canada Fisheries and Marine Service, Vancouver.

Hildebrand, L. D., D. S. Sullivan, and T. P. Sullivan. 1980. Effects of Roundup herbicide on populations of *Daphnia magna* in a forest pond. Bulletin of Environmental Contamination and Toxicology 25:353–357.

Hill, R. D. 1968. Mine drainage treatment—state of the art and research needs. U.S. Federal Water Pollution Control Administration, Mine Drainage Control Activities BCR68-150, Cincinnati, Ohio.

Hill, R. D. 1974. Mining impacts on trout habitat. Pages 45–57 *in* Proceedings, trout habitat research and management symposium. Appalachian Consortium Press, Boone, North Carolina.

Hillman, T. W., J. S. Griffith, and W. S. Platts. 1987. Summer and winter habitat selection by juvenile chinook salmon in a highly sedimented Idaho stream. Transactions of the American Fisheries Society 116:185–195.

Hiltibran, R. C. 1967. Effects of some herbicides on fertilized fish eggs and fry. Transactions of the American Fisheries Society 96:414–416.

Hiltibran, R. C. 1972a. Effects of the chlorogroups of phenoxy compounds on the oxidative phosphorylation. Transactions of the Illinois State Academy of Science 65(3–4):81–85.

Hiltibran, R. C. 1972b. The hydrolysis of adenosine triphosphate by bluegill liver mitochondria in the presence of 2,4,5-T and silvex derivatives. Transactions of the Illinois State Academy of Science 65(1–2):51–57.

Hitchcock, S. W. 1965. Field and laboratory studies of DDT and aquatic insects. Connecticut Storrs Agricultural Experiment Station Bulletin 668.

Hjulstrom, F. 1935. Studies of the morphological activity of rivers as illustrated by the River Fyris. Bulletin of the Geological Institutions of the University of Uppsala 25:221–527.

Hoar, W. S. 1976. Smolt transformation: evolution, behavior, and physiology. Journal of the Fisheries Research Board of Canada 33:1234–1252.

Hobbie, J. E., and G. E. Likens. 1973. Output of phosphorus, dissolved organic carbon, and fine particulate carbon from Hubbard Brook watersheds. Limnology and Oceanography 18:734–742.

Hobbs, D. F. 1937. Natural reproduction of quinnat salmon, brown and rainbow trout in certain New Zealand waters. New Zealand Marine Department Fisheries Bulletin 6.

Hoeppel, R. E., and H. E. Westerdahl. 1983. Dissipation of 2,4-D DMA and BEE from water, mud, and fish at Lake Seminole, Georgia. Water Resources Bulletin 19:197–204.

Hoffman, R. A. 1957. Toxicity of three phosphorus insecticides to cold water game fish. Mosquito News 17:213.

Hogan, D. L. 1986. Channel morphology of unlogged, logged, and debris torrented streams in the Queen Charlotte Islands. British Columbia Ministry of Forests and Lands, Land Management Report 49, Victoria.

Hogan, D. L. 1987. The influence of large organic debris on channel recovery in the Queen Charlotte Islands, British Columbia, Canada. International Association of Hydrological Sciences Publication 165:343–353.

Hogan, D. L., and M. Church. 1989. Hydraulic geometry in small, coastal streams: progress toward quantification of salmonid habitat. Canadian Journal of Fisheries and Aquatic Sciences 46:844–852.

Holcombe, G. W., D. A. Benoit, and E. N. Leonard. 1979. Long-term effects of zinc exposures on brook trout (*Salvelinus fontinalis*). Transactions of the American Fisheries Society 108:76–87.

Holcombe, G. W., D. A. Benoit, E. N. Leonard, and J. M. McKim. 1976. Long- term effects of lead exposure on three generations of brook trout (*Salvelinus fontinalis*). Journal of the Fisheries Research Board of Canada 33:1731–1741.

Holechek, J. L. 1983. Considerations concerning grazing systems. Rangelands 5:208–211.

Hollingsworth, E. B., and W. B. Ennis, Jr. 1953. Some studies on the vapor action of certain dinitro compounds upon young cotton plants. Proceedings of the Southern Weed Control Conference 6:23–31.

Holman, G., and W. A. Evans. 1964. Stream clearance project—completion report, Noyo River, Mendocino County. California Department of Fish and Game, Inland Fisheries Administrative Report 64–10, Sacramento.

Holmes, S. B., and P. D. Kingsbury. 1982. Comparative effects of three Matacil® field formulations on stream benthos and fish. Canadian Forestry Service, Forest Pest Management Institute Information Report FPM-X-55.

Holscher, C., and E. Woolford. 1953. Forage utilization by cattle in the northern Great Plains Range. U.S. Department of Agriculture Circular 918.

Holscher, C. E. 1967. Forest hydrology research in the United States. Pages 99–103 in Sopper and Lull (1967).

Holtby, L. B. 1988a. The effects of logging on the coho salmon of Carnation Creek, British Columbia. Pages 159–174 in Chamberlin (1988).

Holtby, L. B. 1988b. Effects of logging on stream temperatures in Carnation Creek, British Columbia, and associated impacts on the coho salmon (*Oncorhynchus kisutch*). Canadian Journal of Fisheries and Aquatic Sciences 45:502–515.

Holtby, L. B., and G. F. Hartman. 1982. The population dynamics of coho salmon (*Oncorhynchus kisutch*) in a west coast rain forest stream subjected to logging. Pages 308–347 in Hartman (1982).

Holtby, L. B., and J. C. Scrivener. 1989. Observed and simulated effects of climatic variability, clear-cut logging, and fishing on the numbers of chum salmon (*Oncorhynchus keta*) and coho salmon (*O. kisutch*) returning to Carnation Creek, British Columbia. Canadian Special Publication of Fisheries and Aquatic Sciences 105:62–81.

Hooper, D. R. 1973. Evaluation of the effects of flows on trout stream ecology. Pacific Gas and Electric Company, Department of Engineering Research, Emeryville, California.

Hoos, L. M., and C. L. Vold. 1975. The Squamish River estuary; status of environmental knowledge to 1974. Environment Canada, Special Estuary Series 2, Vancouver.

Hoover, M. D., and C. R. Hursh. 1943. Influence of topography and soil-depth on runoff from forest land. American Geophysical Union Transactions 24:693–698.

Hormay, A. L. 1970. Principles of rest-rotation grazing and multiple-use land management. U.S. Forest Service Training Text 4(2200), Washington, D.C.

Hornbeck, J. W., R. S. Pierce, and C. A. Federer. 1970. Streamflow changes after forest clearing in New England. Water Resources Research 6:1124–1132.

Hourston, W. R., and D. MacKinnon. 1957. Use of an artificial spawning channel by salmon. Transactions of the American Fisheries Society 86:220–230.

House, R. A., and P. L. Boehne. 1985. Evaluation of instream enhancement structures for salmonid spawning and rearing in a coastal Oregon stream. North American Journal of Fisheries Management 5:283–295.

House, R. A., and P. L. Boehne. 1986. Effects of instream structures on salmonid habitat and populations in Tobe Creek, Oregon. North American Journal of Fisheries Management 6:38–46.

House, R. A., and P. L. Boehne. 1987a. The effect of stream cleaning on salmonid habitat and populations in a coastal Oregon drainage. Western Journal of Applied Forestry 2:84–87.

House, R. A., and P. L. Boehne. 1987b. Upper Lobster Creek habitat and fish use analysis report. U.S. Bureau of Land Management, Salem, Oregon.

Howard, T., J. Malick, and C. Walden. 1979. Effluent color and algal impact. Pulp and Paper Canada 80(9):100–104.

Howard, T. E. 1975. Swimming performance of juvenile coho salmon (*Oncorhynchus kisutch*) exposed to bleached kraft pulpmill effluent. Journal of the Fisheries Research Board of Canada 32:789–793.

Howard, T. E., and J. M. Leach. 1973. Identification and treatment of toxic materials in pulp and paper woodroom effluents. Canadian Forestry Service, CPAR Project Report 148-1, Ottawa.

Howard, T. E., and D. D. Monteith. 1977. Site of action of chemicals from pulp mill effluent that are toxic to fish. Canada Environmental Protection Service, CPAR Report Number 488-1, Ottawa.

Howard, T. E., and C. C. Walden. 1965. Pollution and toxicity characteristics of kraft pulp mill effluents. TAPPI 48(3):136–141.

Howard, T. E., and C. C. Walden. 1974. Measuring stress in fish exposed to pulp mill effluents. TAPPI 57(2):133–135.

Howes, D. E. 1987. A method for predicting terrain susceptible to landslides following forest harvesting: a case study from the southern Coast Mountains of British Columbia. Pages 143–154 *in* R. H. Swanson, P. Y. Bernier, and P. D. Woodward, editors. Forest hydrology and watershed management. International Association of Hydrological Sciences Publication 167.

H. Paish and Associates Ltd. 1974. A biological assessment of the Kitimat. Report prepared for District of Kitimat, British Columbia. Vancouver.

Hubbs, C. L., J. R. Greeley, and C. M. Tarzwell. 1932. Methods for the improvement of Michigan trout streams. Michigan Department of Conservation, Institute for Fisheries Research Bulletin 1.

Hublou, W. F., J. W. Wood, and E. R. Jeffries. 1954. The toxicity of zinc or cadmium for chinook salmon. Fish Commission of Oregon Research Briefs 5(1):8–14.

Hughes, J. S., and J. T. Davis. 1963. Variations in toxicity to bluegill sunfish of phenoxy herbicides. Weeds 11:50–53.

Hughes, R. M., and G. E. Davis. 1986. Production of coexisting juvenile coho salmon and steelhead trout in heated model stream communities. ASTM (American Society for Testing and Materials) Special Technical Publication 920:322–337.

Hulbert, P. J. 1978. Mattawamkaeg River studies: 2. Effects of Sevin insecticide on fish and invertebrates in 1976. University of Maine, Migratory Fish Research Institute, Orono.

Hunt, D., and C. E. Boyd. 1981. Alkalinity losses from ammonium fertilizers used in fish ponds. Transactions of the American Fisheries Society 110:81–85.

Hunt, R. L. 1969. Effects of habitat alteration on production, standing crops and yield of brook trout in Lawrence Creek, Wisconsin. Pages 281–312 *in* Northcote (1969b).

Hunt, R. L. 1971. Responses of a brook trout population to habitat development in Lawrence Creek. Wisconsin Department of Natural Resources Technical Bulletin 48.

Hunt, R. L. 1974. Annual production by brook trout in Lawrence Creek during eleven successive years. Wisconsin Department of Natural Resources Technical Bulletin 82.

Hunt, R. L. 1976. A long-term evaluation of trout habitat development and its relation to improving management-related research. Transactions of the American Fisheries Society 105:361–364.

Hunt, R. L. 1978. Instream enhancement of trout habitat. Pages 19–27 *in* K. Hashagen, editor. Proceedings, national wild trout management symposium. California Trout, Inc., San Francisco.

Hunt, R. L. 1979. Removal of woody streambank vegetation to improve trout habitat. Wisconsin Department of Natural Resources Technical Bulletin 115.

Hunt, R. L. 1988. A compendium of 45 trout stream habitat development evaluations in Wisconsin during 1953–1985. Wisconsin Department of Natural Resources Technical Bulletin 162.

Hunter, J. G. 1976. Arctic char and hydroelectric power in the Sylvia Grinnell River. Fisheries Research Board of Canada Manuscript Report Series 1376.

Hunter, J. W. 1973. A discussion of game fish in the State of Washington as related to water requirements. Report by the Washington State Department of Game, Fishery Management Division, to the Washington State Department of Ecology, Olympia.

Huntington, C. W. 1985. Deschutes River spawning gravel study. Buell and Associates,

Inc., Final Report for Bonneville Power Administration Project 83–423, Portland, Oregon.

Huntsman, A. G. 1948. Fertility and fertilization of streams. Journal of the Fisheries Research Board of Canada 7:248–253.

Huppert, D. D., R. D. Fight, and F. H. Everest. 1985. Economic considerations. U.S. Forest Service General Technical Report PNW-181.

Hurlbert, S. H. 1975. Secondary effects of pesticides on aquatic ecosystems. Residue Reviews 57:81–148.

Hutchison, J. 1973. Use of dynamite to create fish rearing pools in Siuslaw River tributaries. Oregon State Game Commission, Portland.

Hynes, H. B. N. 1961. The effect of sheep-dip containing the insecticide BHC on the fauna of a small stream, including *Simulium* and its predators. Annals of Tropical Medicine and Parasitology 55:192–196.

Hynes, H. B. N. 1970. The ecology of running waters. University of Toronto Press, Toronto.

Hynes, H. B. N. 1975. The stream and its valley. Internationale Vereinigung für theoretische und angewandte Limnologie Verhandlungen 19:1–15.

Ice, G. W. 1985. Catalog of landslide inventories for the northwest. National Council of the Paper Industry for Air and Stream Improvement, Technical Bulletin 456, New York.

ICF Technology, Inc. 1988. Economic impacts and net economic values associated with non-Indian salmon and sturgeon fisheries: a report to the State of Washington Department of Community Development, Redmond.

Ide, F. P. 1967. Effects of forest spraying with DDT on aquatic insects of salmon streams in New Brunswick. Journal of the Fisheries Research Board of Canada 24:769–805.

IEC Beak. 1984. Natural propagation and habitat improvement. Volume 2B. Washington: Similkameen River habitat inventory. Bonneville Power Administration, Final Report, Project 83-477, Portland, Oregon.

Ikeda, H. 1975. On the bed configuration in alluvial channels: their types and condition of formation with reference to bars. Geographical Review of Japan 48:712–730.

Ingebo, P. A. 1971. Suppression of channel-side chaparral cover increases streamflow. Journal of Soil and Water Conservation 26:79–81.

International North Pacific Fisheries Commission. 1982. Statistical yearbook. INPFC, Vancouver.

International Pacific Salmon Fisheries Commission. 1966. Effects of log driving on the salmon and trout populations in the Stellako River. IPSFC, Progress Report 14, Vancouver.

Irvine, J. R. 1978. The Gerrard rainbow trout of Kootenay Lake, British Columbia—a discussion of their life history with management, research and enhancement recommendations. British Columbia Fish and Wildlife Branch, Fisheries Management Report 72, Victoria.

Irving, J. S., and T. C. Bjornn. 1984. Effects of substrate size composition on survival of kokanee salmon and cutthroat and rainbow trout embryos. University of Idaho, Cooperative Fishery Research Unit, Technical Report 84-6, Moscow.

Irving, R. B. 1955. Ecology of the cutthroat trout in Henrys Lake, Idaho. Transactions of the American Fisheries Society 84:275–296.

Isaacson, J. A. 1977. A computer model for determining water yield from forest activities: IPNF*LIB.H20Y 1977 version. U.S. Forest Service, Idaho Panhandle National Forest, Coeur d'Alene.

Ittner, R., D. R. Potter, J. K. Agee, and S. Anschell, editors. 1979. Proceedings, recreational impact on wildlands conference. U.S. Forest Service, Pacific Northwest Region, and U.S. National Park Service, Portland, Oregon.

Iwamoto, R. N., E. O. Salo, M. A. Madej, and R. L. McComas. 1978. Sediment and water quality: a review of the literature including a suggested approach for water quality criteria. U.S. Environmental Protection Agency EPA 910/9-78-048.

Iwata, Y., W. E. Westlake, J. H. Barkley, G. E. Carman, and F. A. Gunther. 1977. Behavior of phenthoate (Cidial) deposits and residues on and in grapefruits, lemons and lemon leaves, oranges and orange leaves, and in the soil beneath orange trees. Journal of Agricultural and Food Chemistry 25:362–368.

Jackson, R. G. 1986. Effects of bark accumulation on benthic infauna at a log transfer facility in southeast Alaska. Marine Pollution Bulletin 17:258–262.

Jackson, W. L., and R. L. Beschta. 1982. A model of two-phase bedload transport in an Oregon Coast Range stream. Earth Surface Processes and Landforms 7:517–527.

Jackson, W. L., and R. L. Beschta. 1984. Influences of increased sand delivery on the morphology of sand and gravel channels. Water Resources Bulletin 20:527–533.

Jackson, W. L., and B. P. Van Haveren. 1984. Design for a stable channel in coarse alluvium for riparian zone restoration. Water Resources Bulletin 20:695–703.

Jacoby, J. M. 1985. Grazing effects on periphyton by *Theodoxus fluviatilis* (Gastropoda) in a lowland stream. Journal of Freshwater Ecology 3:265–274.

Jaeggi, M. N. R. 1984. Formation and effects of alternate bars. Journal of Hydrological Engineering 110:142–156.

James M. Montgomery, Consulting Engineers. 1985. Bear Valley Creek, Idaho, fish habitat enhancement project preferred alternative report. James M. Montgomery, Consulting Engineers, Inc., Boise, Idaho.

Jaques, R. P. 1969. Leaching of the nuclear-polyhedrosis virus of *Trichoplusia ni* from soil. Journal of Invertebrate Pathology 13:256–263.

Jenkins, C. E. 1969. Radionuclide distribution in Pacific salmon. Health Physics 17:507–512.

Jenkins, D., S. A. Klein, M.-S. Yang, R. J. Wagenet, and J. W. Biggar. 1978. The accumulation, translocation and degradation of biocides at land wastewater disposal sites: the fate of malathion, carbaryl, diazinon and 2,4-D butoxyethyl ester. Water Research 12:713–723.

Jenkins, T. M., Jr., C. R. Feldmeth, and G. V. Elliott. 1970. Feeding of rainbow trout (*Salmo gairdneri*) in relation to abundance of drifting invertebrates in a mountain stream. Journal of the Fisheries Research Board of Canada 27:2356–2361.

Jensen, A. J., and B. O. Johnsen. 1986. Different adaption strategies of Atlantic salmon (*Salmo salar*) populations to extreme climates with special reference to some cold Norwegian rivers. Canadian Journal of Fisheries and Aquatic Sciences 43:980–984.

Jensen, H. L. 1929. On the influence of the carbon:nitrogen ratios of organic material on the mineralisation of nitrogen. Journal of Agricultural Science 19:71–82.

Jensen, K. I. N., and E. R. Kimball. 1987. Persistence and degradation of the herbicide hexazinone in soils of lowbush blueberry fields in Nova Scotia, Canada. Bulletin of Environmental Contamination and Toxicology 38:232–239.

Johns, C., and J. Moore. 1985. Copper, zinc and arsenic in bottom sediments of Clark Fork River reservoirs: preliminary findings. Pages 74–88 *in* Carlson and Bahls (1985).

Johnsen, T. N., Jr. 1980. Picloram in water and soil from a semiarid pinyon–juniper watershed. Journal of Environmental Quality 9:601–605.

Johnsen, T. N., Jr., and W. L. Warskow. 1980. Picloram dissipation in a small southwestern stream. Weed Science 28:612–615.

Johnson, D. W., and D. A. Webster. 1977. Avoidance of low pH in selection of spawning sites by brook trout (*Salvelinus fontinalis*). Journal of the Fisheries Research Board of Canada 34:2215–2218.

Johnson, H. E. 1963. Observations on the life history and movement of cutthroat trout, *Salmo clarki*, in Flathead River drainage, Montana. Proceedings of the Montana Academy of Sciences 23:96–110.

Johnson, J. H., and E. Z. Johnson. 1981. Feeding periodicity and diel variation in diet composition of subyearling coho salmon, *Oncorhynchus kisutch*, and steelhead, *Salmo gairdneri*, in a small stream during summer. U.S. National Marine Fisheries Service Fishery Bulletin 79:370–376.

Johnson, J. H., and N. H. Ringler. 1980. Diets of juvenile coho salmon (*Oncorhynchus kisutch*) and steelhead trout (*Salmo gairdneri*) relative to prey availability. Canadian Journal of Zoology 58:553–558.

Johnson, J. W. 1972. Tidal inlets on the California, Oregon, and Washington coasts. University of California, Hydraulic Engineering Laboratory, HEL 24-12, Berkeley.

Johnson, L. 1972. Keller Lake: characteristics of a culturally unstressed salmonid community. Journal of the Fisheries Research Board of Canada 29:731–740.

Johnson, L. 1980. The Arctic charr, *Salvelinus alpinus*. Pages 15–98 *in* Balon (1980a).

Johnson, R. L. 1964. Southwest Montana fishery study—stream channel alteration survey—Shields River. Montana Fish and Game Department, Project Completion Report, Project F-9-12, Helena.

Johnson, R. L., P. E. Giguere, and E. P. Pister. 1966. A progress report on the Pleasant Valley spawning channel. California Department of Fish and Game, Administrative Report 66-4, Sacramento.

Johnson, R. R., C. D. Ziebell, D. R. Patton, P. F. Ffolliott, and R. H. Hamre, technical coordinators. 1985. Riparian ecosystems and their management: reconciling conflicting uses. U.S. Forest Service General Technical Report RM-120.

Johnson, S. L. 1988. The effects of the 1983 El Niño on Oregon's coho (*Oncorhynchus kisutch*) and chinook (*O. tshawytscha*) salmon. Fisheries Research 6:105–123.

Johnson, S. W., J. Heifetz, and K. V. Koski. 1986. Effects of logging on the abundance and seasonal distribution of juvenile steelhead in some southeastern Alaska streams. North American Journal of Fisheries Management 6:532–537.

Johnson, T. H. 1977. Catch-and-release and trophy-fish angling regulations in the management of cutthroat trout populations and fisheries in northern Idaho streams. Master's thesis. University of Idaho, Moscow.

Johnson, W. M. 1965. Rotation, rest-rotation, and season-long grazing on a mountain range in Wyoming. U.S. Forest Service Research Paper RM-14.

Johnson, W. W., and M. T. Finley. 1980. Handbook of acute toxicity of chemicals to fish and aquatic invertebrates. U.S. Fish and Wildlife Service Resource Publication 137.

Johnston, A. 1962. Effects of grazing intensity and cover on the water-intake rate of fescue grassland. Journal of Range Management 15:79–82.

Johnston, J. M. 1982. Life histories of anadromous cutthroat with emphasis on migratory behaviour. Pages 123–127 *in* Brannon and Salo (1982).

Johnston, R. S. 1988. The market for salmon. Pages 155–164 *in* McNeil (1988).

Johnston, R. W., R. W. Brown, and J. Cravens. 1975. Acid mine rehabilitation problems at elevation. Pages 66–79 *in* Proceedings, watershed management symposium. American Society of Civil Engineers, Irrigation and Drainage Division, Logan, Utah.

Jones and Stokes Associates. 1987. Southcentral Alaska sport fishing economic study. A report to the Alaska Department of Fish and Game. Sacramento, California.

Jones, B. F., C. E. Warren, C. E. Bond, and P. Doudoroff. 1956. Avoidance reactions of salmonid fishes to pulp mill effluents. Sewage and Industrial Wastes 28:1403–1413.

Jones, J. N., Jr., W. H. Armiger, and O. L. Bennett. 1975. A two-step system for revegetation of surface mine spoils. Journal of Environmental Quality 4:233–235.

Jones, J. R. E. 1964. Fish and river pollution. Butterworths, London.

Jones, J. W. 1959. The salmon. Collins, London.

Jonsson, B. 1985. Life history patterns of freshwater resident and sea-run migrant brown trout in Norway. Transactions of the American Fisheries Society 114:182–194.

Jonsson, B., and J. Ruud-Hansen. 1985. Water temperature as the primary influence on timing of seaward migrations of Atlantic salmon (*Salmo salar*) smolts. Canadian Journal of Fisheries and Aquatic Sciences 42:593–595.

Jordan, D. S., D. W. Evermann, and H. W. Clark. 1930. Checklist of fishes and fishlike vertebrates of North and Middle America north of the northern boundary of Venezuela and Colombia. Report of the U.S. Fisheries Commission for 1928, Part 2.

Jungwirth, M., and H. Winkler. 1984. The temperature dependence of embryonic development of grayling (*Thymallus thymallus*), Danube salmon (*Hucho hucho*), Arctic char (*Salvelinus alpinus*) and brown trout (*Salmo trutta fario*). Aquaculture 38:315–327.

Justyn, J., and S. Lusk. 1976. Evaluation of natural radionuclide contamination of fishes in streams affected by uranium ore mining and milling. Zoologicke Listy 25(3):265–274.

Kalleberg, H. 1958. Observations in a stream tank of territoriality and competition in juvenile salmon and trout (*Salmo salar* L. and *S. trutta* L.). Institute of Freshwater Research Drottningholm Report 39:55–98.

Kanazawa, J. 1975. Uptake and excretion of organophosphorus and carbamate insecticides by fresh water fish, *Motsugo pseudorasbora parva*. Bulletin of Environmental Contamination and Toxicology 14:346–352.

Kanazawa, J., A. R. Isensee, and P. C. Kearney. 1975. Distribution of carbaryl and 3,5-xylyl methylcarbamate in an aquatic model ecosystem. Journal of Agricultural and Food Chemistry 23:760–763.

Kane, D. L., and C. W. Slaughter. 1973. Seasonal regime and hydrological significance of stream icings in central Alaska. International Association of Hydrological Sciences Publication 107:528–540.

Kapuscinski, A. R. D., and J. E. Lannan. 1983. On density of chum salmon (*Oncorhynchus keta*) eggs in shallow matrix substrate incubators. Canadian Journal of Fisheries and Aquatic Sciences 40:185–191.

Karinen, J. F., J. G. Lamberton, N. E. Stewart, and L. C. Terriere. 1967. Persistence of carbaryl in the marine estuarine environment: chemical and biological stability in aquarium systems. Journal of Agricultural and Food Chemistry 15:148–156.

Karpoff, J. M. 1983. Limited entry permit prices. Alaska Commercial Fisheries Entry Commission, Report 83-6, Juneau.

Karr, J. R., and I. J. Schlosser. 1978. Water resources and the land–water interface. Science (Washington, D.C.) 201:229–234.

Karr, J. R., L. A. Toth, and G. D. Garman. 1983. Habitat preservation for midwest stream fishes: principles and guidelines. U.S. Environmental Protection Agency, EPA-600/3-83-006, Corvallis, Oregon.

Katopodis, C., P. R. Robinson, and B. G. Sutherland. 1978. A study of model and prototype culvert baffling for fish passage. Canada Fisheries and Marine Service Technical Report 828.

Kattelmann, R. C. 1982. Water yield improvement in the Sierra Nevada snow zone: 1912–1982. Pages 39–48 *in* B. A. Shafer, editor. Proceedings, western snow conference. Colorado State University, Fort Collins.

Kattelmann, R. C. 1987. Water releases from forested snowpacks during rainfall. International Association of Hydrological Sciences Publication 167:265–272.

Katz, M. 1961. Acute toxicity of some organic insecticides to three species of salmonids and to the threespine stickleback. Transactions of the American Fisheries Society 90:264–268.

Katz, M. 1969. The biological and ecological effects of acid mine drainage, with particular emphasis to the waters of the Appalachian region. Appendix F *in* Impact of mine drainage on recreation and stream ecology. Appalachian Region Commission, Washington, D.C.

Kauffman, A. J., Jr., and K. D. Baber. 1956. Potential of heavy-mineral-bearing alluvial deposits in the Pacific Northwest. U.S. Bureau of Mines Information Circular 7767.

Kaufmann, P. R. 1987. Channel morphology and hydraulic characteristics of torrent-impacted forest streams in the Oregon Coast Range, USA. Doctoral dissertation. Oregon State University, Corvallis.

Kaushik, N. K., and H. B. N. Hynes. 1971. The fate of the dead leaves that fall into streams. Archiv für Hydrobiologie 68:465–515.

Kearby, W. H., D. L. Hostetter, and C. M. Ignoffo. 1972. Laboratory and field evaluation of *Bacillus thuringiensis* for control of the bagworm. Journal of Economic Entomology 65:477–480.

Kearney, P. C., T. J. Sheets, and J. W. Smith. 1964. Volatility of seven s-triazines. Weeds 12:83–87.

Keller, C., L. Anderson, and P. Tappel. 1979. Fish habitat changes in Summit Creek, Idaho, after fencing the riparian area. Pages 46–52 *in* Cope (1979).

Keller, E. A., and F. J. Swanson. 1979. Effects of large organic material on channel form and fluvial processes. Earth Surface Processes 4:361–380.

Keller, E. A., and T. Tally. 1979. Effects of large organic debris on channel form and fluvial processes in the coastal redwood environment. Pages 169–197 *in* D. D. Rhodes and

G. P. Williams, editors. Adjustments of the fluvial system. Kendall/Hunt, Dubuque, Iowa.

Kelsey, H. M. 1978. Earthflows in Franciscan melange, Van Duzen River basin, California. Geology 6:361–364.

Kenaga, E. E. 1969. Tordon herbicides—evaluation of safety to fish and birds. Down to Earth 25(1):5–9.

Kenaga, E. E. 1974. Toxicological and residue data useful in the environmental safety evaluation of dalapon. Residue Reviews 53:109–151.

Kenaga, E. E. 1975. Partitioning and uptake of pesticides in biological systems. Pages 217–273 in R. Haque and V. H. Freed, editors. Environmental dynamics of pesticides. Plenum, New York.

Kenaga, E. E. 1980a. Correlation of bioconcentration factors of chemicals in aquatic and terrestrial organisms with their physical and chemical properties. Environmental Science and Technology 14:553–556.

Kenaga, E. E. 1980b. Predicted bioconcentration factors and soil sorption coefficients of pesticides and other chemicals. Ecotoxicology and Environmental Safety 4:26–38.

Kenaga, E. E. 1982. Predictability of chronic toxicity from acute toxicity of chemicals in fish and aquatic invertebrates. Environmental Toxicology and Chemistry 1:347–358.

Kennedy, C. E. 1977. Wildlife conflicts in riparian management: water. U.S. Forest Service General Technical Report RM-43:52–58.

Kershner, J. L., and W. M. Snider. In press. Importance of a habitat level classification system to design instream flow studies. In P. J. Boon, P. Armitage, and P. Calow, editors. The conservation and management of rivers. Wiley, New York.

Kerstetter, T. H., L. B. Kirschner, and D. D. Rafuse. 1970. On the mechanisms of sodium ion transport by the irrigated gills of rainbow trout (Salmo gairdneri). Journal of General Physiology 56:342–359.

Ketcheson, G. L., and H. A. Froehlich. 1978. Hydrology factors and environmental impacts of mass soil movements in the Oregon Coast Range. Report by the Water Resources Research Institute, Oregon State University, Corvallis.

Khanbilvardi, R. M., A. S. Rogowski, and A. C. Miller. 1983. Predicting erosion and deposition on a stripmined and reclaimed area. Water Resources Bulletin 19:585–593.

Kimball, J., and F. Savage. 1977. Diamond Fork aquatic and range habitat improvement. U.S. Forest Service, Uinta National Forest, Provo, Utah.

Kincheloe, J. W., G. A. Wedemeyer, and D. L. Koch. 1979. Tolerance of developing salmonid eggs and fry to nitrate exposure. Bulletin of Environmental Contamination and Toxicology 23:575–578.

King, D., and R. Young. 1986. An evaluation of four groundwater-fed side channels of the East Fork Satsop River—Spring 1985 outmigrants. Washington Department of Fisheries Technical Report 90.

King, J. G., and L. C. Tennyson. 1984. Alteration of streamflow characteristics following road construction in north central Idaho. Water Resources Research 20:1159–1163.

King, W., editor. 1980. Proceedings, wild trout II symposium. Trout Unlimited and Federation of Fly Fishermen, Vienna, Virginia.

Kingsbury, P. D. 1983. Permethrin in New Brunswick salmon nursery streams. Canadian Forestry Service, Forest Pest Management Institute Report FPM-X-52.

Kisker, D. S. 1986. Ecological baseline and monitoring project final report (Part 3): Distribution and abundance of benthic macrofauna adjacent to a sulfite pulp mill discharge pipeline in Port Gardner, Washington, 1974 through 1976. University of Washington, Department of Oceanography, Seattle.

Klaassen, H. E., and A. M. Kadoum. 1979. Distribution and retention of atrazine and carbofuran in farm pond ecosystems. Archives of Environmental Contamination and Toxicology 8:345–353.

Klassen, H. D., and T. G. Northcote. 1986. Stream bed configuration and stability following gabion weir placement to enhance salmonid production in a logged watershed subject to debris torrents. Canadian Journal of Forest Research 16:197–203.

Klassen, H. D., and T. G. Northcote. 1988. Use of gabion weirs to improve spawning habitat for pink salmon in a small logged watershed. North American Journal of Fisheries Management 8:36–44.

Klingeman, P. C. 1984. Evaluating hydrologic needs for design of stream habitat modification structures. Pages 191–213 *in* Hassler (1984).

Klingman, G. C., and F. M. Ashton. 1975. Weed science: principles and practices. Wiley, New York.

Klock, G. O. 1975. Impact of five postfire salvage logging systems on soils and vegetation. Journal of Soil and Water Conservation 30:78–81.

Klock, G. O., and J. D. Helvey. 1976a. Debris flows following wildfire in north central Washington. Pages 91–98 *in* Proceedings, 3rd federal interagency sedimentation conference. Volume 1: sediment yield and sources. Water Resources Council Sedimentation Committee and U.S. Government Printing Office, Washington, D.C.

Klock, G. O., and J. D. Helvey. 1976b. Soil-water trends following wildfire on the Entiat Experimental Forest. Proceedings, Tall Timbers Fire Ecology Conference 15:193–200.

Klotz, R. L. 1985. Factors controlling phosphorus limitation in stream sediments. Limnology and Oceanography 30:543–553.

Klotz, R. L., and E. A. Matson. 1978. Dissolved organic carbon fluxes in the Shetucket River of eastern Connecticut, U.S.A. Freshwater Biology 8:347–355.

Koenst, W. M., L. L. Smith, Jr., and S. J. Broderius. 1977. Effect of chronic exposure of brook trout to sublethal concentrations of hydrogen cyanide. Environmental Science and Technology 11:883–887.

Konopacky, R. C. 1984. Sedimentation and productivity in a salmonid stream. Doctoral dissertation. University of Idaho, Moscow.

Konopacky, R. C., E. C. Bowles, and P. J. Cenera. 1985. Salmon River habitat enhancement. Annual report, 1984. U.S. Department of Energy, Contract DE-A179–84BP14383. Bonneville Power Administration, Portland, Oregon.

Konrad, J. G., G. Chesters, and D. E. Armstrong. 1969. Soil degradation of malathion, a phosphorodithioate insecticide. Soil Science Society of America Proceedings 33:259–262.

Kopp, J. F., and R. C. Kroner. 1967. Trace metals in the waters of the United States. U.S. Federal Water Pollution Control Administration, Cincinnati, Ohio.

Korn, S. 1973. The uptake and persistence of carbaryl in channel catfish. Transactions of the American Fisheries Society 102:137–139.

Koski, K. V. 1966. The survival of coho salmon (*Oncorhynchus kisutch*) from egg deposition to emergence in three Oregon coastal streams. Master's thesis. Oregon State University, Corvallis.

Koski, K. V. 1975. The survival and fitness of two stocks of chum salmon (*Oncorhynchus keta*) from egg deposition to emergence in a controlled-stream environment at Big Beef Creek. Doctoral dissertation. University of Washington, Seattle.

Koski, K. V. 1981. The survival and quality of two stocks of chum salmon (*Oncorhynchus keta*) from egg deposition to emergence. Rapports et Procès-Verbaux des Réunions, Conseil International pour l'Exploration de la Mer 178:330–333.

Koski, K. V., J. Heifetz, S. Johnson, M. Murphy, and J. Thedinga. 1984. Evaluation of buffer strips for protection of salmonid rearing habitat and implications for enhancement. Pages 138–155 *in* Hassler (1984).

Koski, K. V., and D. A. Kirchofer. 1984. A stream ecosystem in an old-growth forest in southeast Alaska. Part IV: Food of juvenile coho salmon, *Oncorhynchus kisutch* in relation to abundance of drift and benthos. Pages 81–87 *in* Meehan et al. (1984).

Kovacs, T. G., R. H. Voss, and A. Wong. 1984. Chlorinated phenolics of bleached kraft mill origin: an olfactory evaluation. Water Research 18:911–916.

Kraft, M. E. 1968. The effects of controlled dewatering on a trout stream. Master's thesis. Montana State University, Bozeman.

Kraft, M. E. 1972. Effects of controlled flow reduction on a trout stream. Journal of the Fisheries Research Board of Canada 29:1405–1411.

Kralik, N. J., and J. E. Sowerwine. 1977. The role of two northern California intermittent streams in the life history of anadromous salmonids. Joint Master's thesis. Humboldt State University, Arcata, California.

Krammes, J. S., and L. F. DeBano. 1965. Soil wettability: a neglected factor in watershed management. Water Resources Research 1:283–286.

Kreutzweiser, D. P. 1982. The effects of permethrin on the invertebrate fauna of a Quebec forest. Canadian Forestry Service, Forest Pest Management Institute Information Report FPM-X-50.

Kreutzweiser, D. P., and P. D. Kingsbury. 1982. Recovery of stream benthos and its utilization by native fish following high dosage permethrin applications. Canadian Forestry Service, Forest Pest Management Institute Information Report FPM-X-59.

Kringstad, K. P., and K. Lindstrom. 1984. Spent liquors from pulp bleaching. Environmental Science and Technology 18:236A–248A.

Krueger, S. W. 1981. Freshwater habitat relationships, pink salmon (*Oncorhynchus gorbuscha*). Alaska Department of Fish and Game, Habitat Division, Anchorage.

Kruzynski, G. M. 1979. Some effects of dehydroabietic acid on hydromineral balance and other physiological parameters in juvenile sockeye salmon. Doctoral dissertation. University of British Columbia, Vancouver.

Krygier, J. T., and J. D. Hall, directors. 1971. Proceedings, forest land uses and stream environment symposium. Continuing Education Publications, Oregon State University, Corvallis.

Kuivasniemi, K., V. Eloranta, and J. Knuutinen. 1985. Acute toxicity of some chlorinated phenolic compounds to *Selenastrum capricornutum* and phytoplankton. Archives of Environmental Contamination and Toxicology 14:43–49.

Kumada, H., S. Kimura, M. Yokote, and Y. Matida. 1973. Acute and chronic toxicity and retention of cadmium in freshwater organisms. Bulletin of the Freshwater Fisheries Research Laboratory (Tokyo) 22:157–165.

Kuska, J. J. 1977. Biological approach to river planning and management. U.S. Forest Service General Technical Report NC-28:296–303.

Kwain, W. 1975. Effects of temperature on development and survival of rainbow trout, *Salmo gairdneri*, in acid waters. Journal of the Fisheries Research Board of Canada 32:493–497.

Kwain, W. 1982. Spawning behavior and early life history of pink salmon (*Oncorhynchus gorbuscha*) in the Great Lakes. Canadian Journal of Fisheries and Aquatic Sciences 39:1353–1360.

Kwain, W. 1987. Biology of pink salmon in the North American Great Lakes. Pages 57–65 *in* Dadswell et al. (1987).

Kwain, W., and E. Thomas. 1984. The first evidence of spring spawning by chinook salmon in Lake Superior. North American Journal of Fisheries Management 4:227–228.

Ladle, M., J. A. B. Bass, and W. R. Jenkins. 1972. Studies on production and food consumption by the larval Simuliidae (Diptera) of a chalk stream. Hydrobiologia 39:429–448.

LaFleur, K. S. 1976. Movement of carbaryl through Congaree soil into ground water. Journal of Environmental Quality 5:91–92.

Lamberti, G. A., and V. H. Resh. 1983. Stream periphyton and insect herbivores: an experimental study of grazing by a caddisfly population. Ecology 64:1124–1135.

Landner, L., K. Lindstrom, M. Karlsson, J. Nordin, and L. Sorensen. 1977. Bioaccumulation in fish of chlorinated phenols from kraft pulp mill bleachery effluents. Bulletin of Environmental Contamination and Toxicology 18:663–673.

Landres, P. B., J. Verner, and J. W. Thomas. 1988. Ecological uses of vertebrate indicator species: a critique. Conservation Biology 2:316–328.

Lanka, R. P., W. A. Hubert, and T. A. Wesche. 1987. Relations of geomorphology to stream habitat and trout standing stock in small Rocky Mountain streams. Transactions of the American Fisheries Society 116:21–28.

Lannan, J. E. 1988. Contemporary trends in world salmon production and management policy. Pages 7–12 *in* McNeil (1988).

Lantz, R. L. 1971. Influence of water temperature on fish survival, growth and behavior. Pages 182–193 *in* Krygier and Hall (1971).

Larkin, P. A., and graduate students. 1959. The effects on fresh water fisheries of man-made activities in British Columbia. Canadian Fish Culturist 25:27–59.

Larse, R. W. 1971. Prevention and control of erosion and stream sedimentation from forest roads. Pages 76–83 *in* Krygier and Hall (1971).

Larson, G. L., C. E. Warren, F. E. Hutchins, L. P. Lamperti, D. A. Schlesinger, and W. K. Seim. 1978. Toxicity of residual chlorine compounds to aquatic organisms. U.S. Environmental Protection Agency EPA-600/3-78-023.

Larson, K. R., and R. C. Sidle. 1981. Erosion and sedimentation data catalog of the Pacific Northwest (September 1980). U.S. Forest Service, Pacific Northwest Region Report R6-WM-050-1981, Portland, Oregon.

Larsson, A., T. Andersson, L. Forlin, and J. Hardig. 1988. Physiological disturbances in fish exposed to bleached kraft mill effluents. Water Science and Technology 20(2):67–76.

Latta, W. C. 1972. The effects of stream improvement upon the angler's catch and standing crop of trout in the Pigeon River, Otsego County, Michigan. Michigan Department of Natural Resources, Research and Development Report 265, Lansing.

Lawrence, J. M. 1962. Aquatic herbicide data. U.S. Department of Agriculture, Agriculture Handbook 231.

Leach, J. M., and A. N. Thakore. 1973. Identification of the constituents of kraft pulping effluent that are toxic to juvenile coho salmon (*Oncorhynchus kisutch*). Journal of the Fisheries Research Board of Canada 30:479–484.

Leaf, C. F., and G. E. Brink. 1973. Hydrologic simulation model of Colorado subalpine forest. U.S. Forest Service Research Paper RM-107.

LeCren, E. D. 1969. Estimates of fish populations and production in small streams in England. Pages 269–280 *in* Northcote (1969b).

Lee, E., J. Mueller, and C. Walden. 1978. Non-settleable suspended solids: their impact on receiving waters. Pulp and Paper Canada 79(10):39–42, 45.

Lee, R. M., and J. N. Rinne. 1980. Critical thermal maxima of five trout species in the southwestern United States. Transactions of the American Fisheries Society 109:632–635.

Leider, S. A., M. W. Chilcote, and J. J. Loch. 1986. Movement and survival of presmolt steelhead in a tributary and the main stem of a Washington river. North American Journal of Fisheries Management 6:526–531.

Leidy, R. A. 1984. Distribution and ecology of stream fishes in the San Francisco Bay drainage. Hilgardia 52(8):1–175.

Leidy, R. A., and P. L. Fiedler. 1985. Human disturbance and patterns of fish species diversity in the San Francisco Bay drainage, California. Biological Conservation 33:247–267.

Leivestad, H., I. P. Muniz, and B. O. Rosseland. 1980. Acid stress in trout from a dilute mountain stream. Pages 318–319 *in* Drablos and Tollan (1980).

Leonard, R. A., G. W. Bailey, and R. R. Swank, Jr. 1976. Transport, detoxification, fate, and effects of pesticides in soil and water environments. Pages 48–78 *in* Land application of waste materials. Soil Conservation Society of America, Ankeny, Iowa.

Leonard, R. A., G. W. Langdale, and W. G. Fleming. 1979. Herbicide runoff from upland Piedmont watersheds—data and implications for modeling pesticide transport. Journal of Environmental Quality 8:223–229.

Leopold, A. 1933. Game management. Charles Scribner's Sons, New York.

Leopold, A. S. 1975. Ecosystem deterioration under multiple use. Pages 96–98 *in* W. King, editor. Proceedings, wild trout management symposium. Trout Unlimited, Vienna, Virginia.

Leopold, L. B., M. G. Wolman, and J. P. Miller. 1964. Fluvial processes in geomorphology. Freeman, San Francisco.

Lestelle, L. C., and C. J. Cederholm. 1984. Short-term effects of organic debris removal on resident cutthroat trout. Pages 131–140 *in* Meehan et al. (1984).

Levings, C. D. 1973. Intertidal benthos, especially *Anisogammarus confervicolus* (Crustracea, Amphipoda), in a disrupted B.C. estuary. On file at West Vancouver

Laboratory, Canada Department of Fisheries and Oceans, West Vancouver, British Columbia.

Levings, C. D., and N. McDaniel. 1976. Industrial disruption of invertebrate communities on beaches in Howe Sound. Canada Fisheries and Marine Service Technical Report 663.

Levy, D. A., T. G. Northcote, and R. M. Barr. 1982. Effects of estuarine log storage on juvenile salmon. University of British Columbia, Westwater Research Centre Technical Report 26, Vancouver.

Levy, D. A., T. G. Northcote, and G. J. Birch. 1979. Juvenile salmon utilization of tidal channels in the Fraser River estuary. University of British Columbia, Westwater Research Centre Technical Report 23, Vancouver.

Lewis, M. A., and R. Burraychak. 1979. Impact of copper mining on a desert intermittent stream in central Arizona: a summary. Arizona–Nevada Academy of Science 14:22–29.

Lewis, S. L. 1969. Physical factors influencing fish populations in pools of a trout stream. Transactions of the American Fisheries Society 98:14–19.

Lewis, W. M. 1960. Suitability of well water with a high iron content for warm-water fish culture. Progressive Fish-Culturist 22:79–80.

Lewynsky, V. A. 1986. Evaluation of special angling regulations in the Coeur d'Alene River trout fishery. Master's thesis. University of Idaho, Moscow.

Liang, T. T., and E. P. Lichtenstein. 1972. Effect of light, temperature, and pH on the degradation of azinphosmethyl. Journal of Economic Entomology 65:315–321.

Liaw, W. K., and H. R. MacCrimmon. 1977. Assessment of particulate organic matter in river water. Internationale Revue der gesamten Hydrobiologie 62:445–463.

Lichatowich, J., and S. Cramer. 1979. Parameter selection and sample sizes in studies of anadromous salmonids. Oregon Department of Fish and Wildlife, Fish Division, Research and Development Section Information Report Series Fisheries 80-1, Portland.

Lichtenstein, E. P., K. R. Schulz, R. F. Skrentny, and Y. Tsukano. 1966. Toxicity and fate of insecticide residues in water. Archives of Environmental Health 12:199–212.

Liebmann, H. 1960. Handbuch der Frischwasser- und Abwasser-Biologie, volume 2. R. Oldenbourg, Munich, Germany.

Lienkaemper, G. W., and F. J. Swanson. 1987. Dynamics of large woody debris in streams in old-growth Douglas-fir forests. Canadian Journal of Forest Research 17:150–156.

Likens, G. E., F. H. Bormann, N. M. Johnson, D. W. Fisher, and R. S. Pierce. 1970. Effects of forest cutting and herbicide treatment on nutrient budgets in the Hubbard Brook watershed-ecosystem. Ecological Monographs 40:23–47.

Lillehammer, A. 1973. An investigation of the food of one-to-four-month-old salmon fry (*Salmo salar*) in the River Suldalslagen, West Norway. Norwegian Journal of Zoology 21:17–24.

Lime, D. W. 1971. Factors influencing campground use in the Superior National Forest of Minnesota. U.S. Forest Service Research Paper NC-60.

Lind, R. C., K. J. Arrow, G. R. Corey, P. Dasgupta, A. K. Sen, T. Stauffer, J. E. Stiglitz, J. A. Stockfisch, and R. Wilson. 1982. Discounting for time and risk in energy policy. Johns Hopkins University Press, Baltimore, Maryland.

Lindroth, A. 1942. Sauerstoffverbrauch der Fische. 2. Verschiedene Entwicklungs- und Altersstadien vom Lachs und Hecht. Zeitschrift für vergleichende Physiologie 29:583–594.

Lindsey, C. C. 1964. Problems in zoogeography of the lake trout, *Salvelinus namaycush*. Journal of the Fisheries Research Board of Canada 21:977–994.

Lindsey, C. C., T. G. Northcote, and G. F. Hartman. 1959. Homing of rainbow trout to inlet and outlet spawning streams at Loon Lake, British Columbia. Journal of the Fisheries Research Board of Canada 16:695–719.

Lindskov, K. L., and B. A. Kimball. 1984. Water resources and potential hydrologic effects of oil-shale development in the Southeastern Uinta Basin, Utah and Colorado. U.S. Geological Survey Professional Paper 1307.

Lindstrom, K., and M. Mohamed. 1988. Selective removal of chlorinated organics from kraft mill total effluents in aerated lagoons. Nordic Pulp and Paper Research Journal 1:26–33.

Lipschuetz, M., and A. L. Cooper. 1961. Toxicity of 2-secondary-butyl-4,6-dinitrophenol to blacknose dace and rainbow trout. New York Fish and Game Journal 8:110–121.

Lisle, T. E. 1986a. Effects of woody debris on anadromous salmonid habitat, Prince of Wales Island, southeast Alaska. North American Journal of Fisheries Management 6:538–550.

Lisle, T. E. 1986b. Stabilization of a gravel channel by large streamside obstructions and bedrock bends, Jacoby Creek, northwestern California. Geological Society of America Bulletin 97:999–1011.

Lister, D. B., D. E. Marshall, and D. G. Hickey. 1980. Chum salmon survival and production at seven improved groundwater-fed spawning areas. Canadian Manuscript Report of Fisheries and Aquatic Sciences 1595.

Livingston, R. J. 1977. Review of current literature concerning the acute and chronic effects of pesticides on aquatic organisms. CRC Critical Reviews in Environmental Control 7:325–351.

Lloyd, D. S., J. P. Koenings, and J. D. LaPerriere. 1987. Effects of turbidity in fresh waters of Alaska. North American Journal of Fisheries Management 7:18–33.

Lloyd, R. 1960. The toxicity of zinc sulfate to rainbow trout. Annals of Applied Biology 48:84–94.

Lloyd, R. 1961a. Effect of dissolved oxygen concentrations on the toxicity of several poisons to rainbow trout (*Salmo gairdneri* Richardson). Journal of Experimental Biology 38:447–455.

Lloyd, R. 1961b. The toxicity of mixtures of zinc and copper sulfates to rainbow trout (*Salmo gairdnerii* Richardson). Annals of Applied Biology 49:535–538.

Lloyd, R., and D. W. M. Herbert. 1962. The effect of the environment on the toxicity of poisons to fish. Journal of the Institute of Public Health Engineering (July):132–145.

Lloyd, R., and L. D. Orr. 1969. The diuretic response by rainbow trout to sublethal concentrations of ammonia. Water Research 3:335–344.

Loeffler, W. W., Jr., G. W. Trimberger, F. H. Fox, R. L. Ridgeway, D. J. Lisk, and G. G. Gyrisco. 1966. Extent of residues in milk resulting from use of Guthion-treated forage. Journal of Agricultural and Food Chemistry 14:46–47.

Long, B. A. 1987. Recruitment and abundance of large woody debris in an Oregon coastal stream system. Master's thesis. Oregon State University, Corvallis.

Loomis, J. B. 1988. The bioeconomic effects of timber harvesting on recreational and commercial salmon and steelhead fishing: a case study of the Suislaw National Forest. Marine Resource Economics 5:43–60.

Loomis, J. B. 1989. A bioeconomic approach to estimating the economic effects of watershed disturbance on recreational and commerical fisheries. Journal of Soil and Water Conservation 44:83–87.

Lord, R. F. 1933. Type of food taken throughout the year by brook trout in a single Vermont stream with special reference to winter feeding. Transactions of the American Fisheries Society 63:182–197.

Lorz, H., and B. McPherson. 1977. Effects of copper and zinc on smoltification of coho salmon. U.S. Environmental Protection Agency EPA-600/3-77-032.

Lorz, H. W. 1974. Ecology and management of brown trout in Little Deschutes River. Oregon Wildlife Commission Fishery Research Report 8, Portland.

Lorz, H. W., S. W. Glenn, R. H. Williams, C. M. Kunkel, L. A. Norris, and B. R. Loper. 1979. Effects of selected herbicides on smolting of coho salmon. U.S. Environmental Protection Agency, Environmental Research Laboratory, EPA-600/3-79-071, Corvallis, Oregon.

Lorz, H. W., and T. G. Northcote. 1965. Factors affecting stream location, and timing and intensity of entry by spawning kokanee (*Oncorhynchus nerka*) into an inlet of Nicola Lake, British Columbia. Journal of the Fisheries Research Board of Canada 22:665–687.

Lotspeich, F. B. 1980. Watersheds as the basic ecosystem: this conceptual framework provides a basis for a natural classification system. Water Resources Bulletin 16:581–586.

Lotspeich, F. B., and F. H. Everest. 1981. A new method for reporting and interpreting textural composition of spawning gravel. U.S. Forest Service Research Note PNW-369.

Love, L. D. 1955. The effect on stream flow of the killing of spruce and pine by the Engelmann spruce beetle. Transactions of the American Geophysical Union 36:113–118.

Lowry, G. R. 1971. Effect of habitat alteration on brown trout in McKenzie Creek, Wisconsin. Wisconsin Department of Natural Resources, Research Report 70, Madison.

Lucas, K. C. 1960. The Robertson Creek spawning channel. Canadian Fish Culturist 27:3–23.

Lucas, R. C. 1964. Wilderness perception and use: the example of the Boundary Waters Canoe Area. Natural Resources Journal 3:394–411.

Lucas, R. C. 1979. Perceptions of non-motorized recreational impacts: a review of research findings. Pages 24–31 in Ittner et al. (1979).

Lull, H. W. 1959. Soil compaction on forest and range lands. U.S. Forest Service Miscellaneous Publication 768, Washington, D.C.

Lund, J. A. 1976. Evaluation of stream channelization and mitigation on the fishery resources of the St. Regis River, Montana. U.S. Fish and Wildlife Service, FWS/OBS-76/06.

Lusby, G. C., V. H. Reid, and O. D. Knipe. 1971. Effects of grazing on the hydrology and biology of the Badger Wash Basin in western Colorado, 1953–66. U.S. Geological Survey, Water-Supply Paper 1532-D.

Lush, D. L., and H. B. N. Hynes. 1973. The formation of particles in freshwater leachates of dead leaves. Limnology and Oceanography 18:968–977.

Lush, D. L., and H. B. N. Hynes. 1978. The uptake of dissolved organic matter by a small spring stream. Hydrobiologia 60:271–275.

Lutz, H. J., and F. S. Griswold. 1939. The influence of tree roots on soil morphology. American Journal of Science 237:389–400.

Lynch, T. R., H. E. Johnson, and W. J. Adams. 1982. The fate of atrazine and a hexachlorobiphenyl isomer in naturally-derived model stream ecosystems. Environmental Toxicology and Chemistry 1:179–192.

Lynn, G. E. 1965. A review of toxicological information on Tordon herbicides. Down to Earth 20(4):6–8.

Lyons, J. K., and R. L. Beschta. 1983. Land use, floods, and channel changes: Upper Middle Fork Willamette River, Oregon (1936–1980). Water Resources Research 19:463–471.

Mabbott, L. B. 1982. Density and habitat of wild and introduced juvenile steelhead trout in the Lochsa River drainage, Idaho. Master's thesis. University of Idaho, Moscow.

MacCrimmon, H. R., and B. L. Gots. 1986. Laboratory observations on emergent patterns of juvenile rainbow trout, *Salmo gairdneri*, relative to test substrate composition. Pages 63–76 in Miller et al. (1986).

Macdonald, J. S., G. Miller, and R. A. Stewart. 1988. The effects of logging, other forest industries and forest management practices on fish: an initial bibliography. Canadian Technical Report of Fisheries and Aquatic Sciences 1622.

Macek, K. J. 1968. Growth and resistance to stress in brook trout fed sublethal levels of DDT. Journal of the Fisheries Research Board of Canada 25:2443–2451.

Macek, K. J., K. S. Buxton, S. Sauter, S. Gnilka, and J. W. Dean. 1976. Chronic toxicity of atrazine to selected aquatic invertebrates and fishes. U.S. Environmental Protection Agency Ecological Research Series EPA-600/3-76-047.

Macek, K. J., and W. A. McAllister. 1970. Insecticide susceptibility of some common fish family representatives. Transactions of the American Fisheries Society 99:20–27.

Mackin, J. H. 1948. Concept of the graded river. Bulletin of the Geological Society of America 59:463–511.

MacKinnon, D., L. Edgeworth, and R. E. McLaren. 1961. An assessment of Jones Creek spawning channel 1954–1961. Canadian Fish Culturist 30:3–14.

MacLean, J. A., D. O. Evans, N. V. Martin, and R. L. DesJardine. 1981. Survival, growth, spawning distribution, and movements of introduced and native lake trout (*Salvelinus namaycush*) in two inland Ontario Lakes. Canadian Journal of Fisheries and Aquatic Sciences 38:1685–1700.

Madej, M. A. 1982. Sediment transport and channel changes in an aggrading stream in the Puget Lowland, Washington. Pages 97–108 *in* Swanson et al. (1982b).

Madsen, M. J. 1938. A preliminary investigation into the results of stream improvement in the intermountain forest region. Transactions of the North American Wildlife Conference 3:497–503.

Magill, A. R. 1971. Rehabilitation problems. Pages 230–231 *in* Krygier and Hall (1971).

Magill, A. W. 1977. Workshop 5—methods to control negative impacts of recreation use. U.S. Forest Service General Technical Report NC-28:402–404.

Maher, F. P., and P. A. Larkin. 1955. Life history of the steelhead trout of the Chilliwack River, British Columbia. Transactions of the American Fisheries Society 84:27–38.

Maier-Bode, H. 1972. Behavior of herbicides in water, muck and fish after application in fish ponds. Schriftenreihe des Vereins für Wasser-, Boden- und Lufthygiene, Berlin-Dahlem 37:67–75.

Major, R. L., and J. L. Mighell. 1966. Influence of Rocky Reach Dam and the temperature of the Okanogan River on the upstream migration of sockeye salmon. U.S. Fish and Wildlife Service Fishery Bulletin 66:131–147.

Malik, N., and W. H. Vanden Born. 1986. Use of herbicides in forest management. Canadian Forestry Service, Northern Forest Research Center Information Report NOR-X-282.

Mann, K. H. 1975. Patterns of energy flow. Pages 248–263 *in* Whitton (1975).

Marcuson, P. E. 1977. The effect of cattle grazing on brown trout in Rock Creek, Montana. Montana Department of Fish and Game, Special Report, Project F-20-R-21, 11-a, Helena.

Marion, D. A. 1981. Landslide occurrence in the Blue River drainage, Oregon. Master's thesis. Oregon State University, Corvallis.

Marriage, L. D. 1958. The bay clams of Oregon. Fish Commission of Oregon, Educational Bulletin 2, Portland.

Marriage, P. B., W. J. Saidak, and F. G. Von Stryk. 1975. Residues of atrazine, simazine, linuron and diuron after repeated annual applications in a peach orchard. Weed Research 15:373–379.

Marshall, D. E., and E. W. Britton. 1980. Carrying capacity of coho streams. Canada Department of Fisheries and Oceans, Enhancement Services Branch, Vancouver.

Marshall, V. G., and D. S. DeBell. 1980. Comparison of four methods of measuring volatilization losses of nitrogen following urea fertilization of forest soils. Canadian Journal of Soil Science 60:549–563.

Martin, D. J., L. J. Wasserman, and V. H. Dale. 1986. Influence of riparian vegetation on posteruption survival of coho salmon fingerlings on the west-side streams of Mount St. Helens, Washington. North American Journal of Fisheries Management 6:1–8.

Martin, N. V., and C. H. Olver. 1980. The lake charr, *Salvelinus namaycush*. Pages 205–277 *in* Balon (1980a).

Martin, R. M., and A. C. Wertheimer. 1987. Survival of coho salmon (*Oncorhynchus kisutch*) cultured in fresh water and in estuarine pens. Aquaculture 61:181–191

Maser, C., R. F. Tarrant, J. M. Trappe, and J. F. Franklin, technical editors. 1988. From the forest to the sea: a story of fallen trees. U.S. Forest Service General Technical Report PNW-229.

Mason, J. C. 1969. Hypoxial stress prior to emergence and competition among coho salmon fry. Journal of the Fisheries Research Board of Canada 26:63–91.

Mason, J. C. 1976. Response of underyearling coho salmon to supplemental feeding in a natural stream. Journal of Wildlife Management 40:775–788.

Mason, J. C., and D. W. Chapman. 1965. Significance of early emergence, environmental rearing capacity, and behavioral ecology of juvenile coho salmon in stream channels. Journal of the Fisheries Research Board of Canada 22:173–190.

Mathews, S. B., and F. W. Olson. 1980. Factors affecting Puget Sound coho salmon (*Oncorhynchus kisutch*) runs. Canadian Journal of Fisheries and Aquatic Sciences 37:1373–1378.

Mathisen, O. A., and M. Berg. 1968. Growth rates of the char, *Salvelinus alpinus* (L.), in the Vardnes River, Troms, northern Norway. Institute of Freshwater Research, Drottningholm, Report 48:177–186.

Matida, Y., Y. Furuta, H. Kumada, H. Tanaka, M. Yokote, and S. Kimura. 1975. Effects of some herbicides applied in the forest to the freshwater fishes and other aquatic organisms: 1. Survey on the effects of aerially applied sodium chlorate and a mixture of 2,4-D and 2,4,5-T on the stream community. Bulletin of the Freshwater Fisheries Research Laboratory (Tokyo) 25(1):41–53.

Matida, Y., S. Kimura, H. Tanaka, and M. Yokote. 1976. Effects of some herbicides applied in the forest to the freshwater fishes and other aquatic organisms: 3. Experiments on the assessment of acute toxicity of herbicides to aquatic organisms. Bulletin of the Freshwater Fisheries Research Laboratory (Tokyo) 26(2):79–84.

Maughan, O. E., K. L. Nelson, and J. J. Ney. 1978. Evaluation of stream improvement practices in southeastern trout streams. Virginia Water Resources Research Center Bulletin 115, Blacksburg.

Mauser, G. 1972. Abundance and emigration of north Idaho cutthroat trout enclosed within sections of a tributary stream. Master's thesis. University of Idaho, Moscow.

Mayack, D. T., P. B. Bush, D. G. Neary, and J. E. Douglass. 1982. Impact of hexazinone on invertebrates after application to forested watersheds. Archives of Environmental Contamination and Toxicology 11:209–217.

Mayes, M. A., D. C. Dill, K. M. Bodner, and C. G. Mendoza. 1984. Triclopyr triethylamine salt toxicity to life stages of the fathead minnow (*Pimephales promelas* Rafinesque). Bulletin of Environmental Contamination and Toxicology 33:339–347.

Mayeux, H. S., Jr., C. W. Richardson, R. W. Bovey, E. Burnett, M. G. Merkle, and R. E. Meyer. 1984. Dissipation of picloram in storm runoff. Journal of Environmental Quality 13:44–49.

McCleave, J. D. 1967. Homing and orientation of cutthroat trout (*Salmo clarki*) in Yellowstone Lake, with special reference to olfaction and vision. Journal of the Fisheries Research Board of Canada 24:2011–2044.

McCluskey, D. C., J. Brown, D. Bornholdt, D. A. Duff, and A. H. Winward. 1983. Willow planting for riparian habitat improvement. U.S. Bureau of Land Management Technical Note 363.

McConnell, K. E. 1985. The economics of outdoor recreation. Pages 677–722 *in* A. V. Kneese and J. L. Sweeney, editors. Handbook of natural resource and energy economics, volume 2. Elsevier, Amsterdam.

McCorkle, F. M., J. E. Chambers, and J. D. Yarbrough. 1977. Acute toxicities of selected herbicides to fingerling channel catfish, *Ictalurus punctatus*. Bulletin of Environmental Contamination and Toxicology 18:267–270.

McCrimmon, H. R. 1954. Stream studies on planted Atlantic salmon. Journal of the Fisheries Research Board of Canada 11:362–403.

McCuddin, M. E. 1977. Survival of salmon and trout embryos and fry in gravel–sand mixtures. Master's thesis. University of Idaho, Moscow.

McDaniel, N. G. 1973. A survey of the benthic macroinvertebrate fauna and solid pollutants in Howe Sound. Fisheries Research Board of Canada Technical Report 385.

McDaniel, T. 1978. Afognak Island fishpass maintenance and evaluation progress report. Alaska Department of Fish and Game, Fisheries Rehabilitation, Enhancement, and Development Division, Kodiak.

McDonald, J., and J. M. Hume. 1984. Babine Lake sockeye salmon (*Oncorhynchus nerka*) enhancement program: testing some major assumptions. Canadian Journal of Fisheries and Aquatic Sciences 41:70–92.

McDowall, R. M. 1987. The occurrence and distribution of diadromy among fishes. Pages 1–13 *in* Dadswell et al. (1987).

McDowell, W. H., and S. G. Fisher. 1976. Autumnal processing of dissolved organic matter in a small woodland stream ecosystem. Ecology 57:561–569.

McFadden, J. T. 1969. Dynamics and regulation of salmonid populations in streams. Pages 313–329 *in* Northcote (1969b).

McFadden, J. T., and E. L. Cooper. 1962. An ecological comparison of six populations of brown trout (*Salmo trutta*). Transactions of the American Fisheries Society 91:53–62.

McGowan, T. 1977. Statement on improving fish and wildlife benefits in range management. U.S. Fish and Wildlife Service, FWS/OBS-77/1:97–102.

McGreer, E. R., and G. A. Vigers. 1980. The use of in situ preference/avoidance studies with fish in monitoring sulfite mill effluent. Canadian Technical Report of Fisheries and Aquatic Science 975:152–161.

McHugh, R. A., L. S. Miller, and T. E. Olsen. 1964. The ecology and naturalistic control of log pond mosquitoes in the Pacific Northwest. Oregon State Board of Health, Portland.

McIntire, C. D. 1966. Some factors affecting respiration of periphyton communities in lotic environments. Ecology 47:918–930.

McIntire, C. D. 1973. Periphyton dynamics in laboratory streams: a simulation model and its implications. Ecological Monographs 43:399–420.

McIntire, C. D. 1975. Periphyton assemblages in laboratory streams. Pages 403–430 *in* Whitton (1975).

McIntire, C. D., and J. A. Colby. 1978. A hierarchical model of lotic ecosystems. Ecological Monographs 48:167–190.

McIntire, C. D., and H. K. Phinney. 1965. Laboratory studies of periphyton production and community metabolism in lotic environments. Ecological Monographs 35:237–258.

McKee, J. E., and H. W. Wolf. 1971. Water quality criteria, 2nd edition. California Water Resources Control Board Publication 3-A, Sacramento.

McKellar, R. L., O. E. Schubert, B. C. Byrd, L. P. Stevens, and E. J. Norton. 1982. Aerial application of Garlon 3A herbicide to a West Virginia watershed. Down to Earth 38(2):15–19.

McKenna, M. G., and F. Duerr. 1976. Effects of ambient pH on the gills of *Ictalurus melas* Raf. American Zoologist 16:224. (Abstract.)

McKeown, J. J., A. H. Benedict, and G. M. Locke. 1968. Studies on the behavior of benthal deposits of wood origin. Journal of the Water Pollution Control Federation 40(8), Part 2:R333–R353.

McKernan, D. L., D. R. Johnson, and J. I. Hodges. 1950. Some factors influencing the trends of salmon populations in Oregon. Transactions of the North American Wildlife Conference 15:427–449.

McKim, J. M. 1977. Evaluation of tests with early life stages of fish for predicting long-term toxicity. Journal of the Fisheries Research Board of Canada 34:1148–1154.

McKim, J. M., and D. A. Benoit. 1971. Effects of long-term exposures to copper on survival, growth, and reproduction of brook trout (*Salvelinus fontinalis*). Journal of the Fisheries Research Board of Canada 28:655–662.

McKinley, W. R., and R. D. Webb. 1956. A proposed correction of migratory fish problems at box culverts. Washington Department of Fisheries, Fisheries Research Paper 1(4):33–45.

McLeay, D. J., I. K. Birtwell, G. F. Hartman, and G. L. Ennis. 1987. Response of Arctic grayling (*Thymallus arcticus*) to acute and prolonged exposure to Yukon placer mining sediment. Canadian Journal of Fisheries and Aquatic Sciences 44:658–673.

McLeay, D. J., and D. A. Brown. 1979. Stress and chronic effects of untreated and treated bleached kraft pulpmill effluent on the biochemistry and stamina of juvenile coho salmon (*Oncorhynchus kisutch*). Journal of the Fisheries Research Board of Canada 36:1049–1059.

McLeay, D. J., G. L. Ennis, I. K. Birtwell, and G. F. Hartman. 1984. Effects on Arctic grayling (*Thymallus arcticus*) of prolonged exposure to Yukon placer mining sediment: a laboratory study. Canadian Technical Report of Fisheries and Aquatic Sciences 1241.

McLeay, D. J., and M. R. Gordon. 1977. Leucocrit: a simple hematological technique for measuring acute stress in salmonid fish, including stressful concentrations of pulpmill effluent. Journal of the Fisheries Research Board of Canada 34:2164–2175.

McLeay, D. J., and M. R. Gordon. 1978. Effect of seasonal photoperiod on acute toxic responses of juvenile rainbow trout (*Salmo gairdneri*) to pulpmill effluent. Journal of the Fisheries Research Board of Canada 35:1388–1392.

McLeay, D. J., and M. R. Gordon. 1980. Toxicity studies with the brush-control herbicide "Krenite" and salmonid fish. British Columbia Research, Project Report 1-01-305, University of British Columbia, Vancouver.

McLeay, D. J., and T. E. Howard. 1977. Comparison of rapid bioassay procedures for measuring toxic effects of bleached kraft mill effluents to fish. Pages 141–155 *in* Proceedings, 3rd aquatic toxicity workshop. Canada Environmental Protection Service, Technical Report EPS-5-AR-77-1, Halifax, Nova Scotia.

McLeay, D. J., A. B. McKague, and C. C. Walden. 1986. Aquatic toxicity of pulp and paper mill effluent: a review. Project report prepared by D. McLeay and Associates Ltd., West Vancouver, British Columbia, for Environment Canada, Fisheries and Oceans Canada, Canadian Pulp and Paper Association, and Ontario Ministry of the Environment.

McLeay, D. J., C. C. Walden, and J. R. Munro. 1979a. Effect of pH on toxicity of kraft pulp and paper mill effluent to salmonid fish in fresh and seawater. Water Research 13:249–254.

McLeay, D. J., C. C. Walden, and J. R. Munro. 1979b. Influence of dilution water on the toxicity of kraft pulp and paper mill effluent, including mechanisms of effect. Water Research 13:151–158.

McLemore, C. E., F. H. Everest, W. R. Humphreys, and M. F. Solazzi. 1989. A floating trap for sampling downstream migrant fishes. U.S. Forest Service Research Note PNW-490.

McMahon, R. F., R. D. Hunter, and W. D. Russell-Hunter. 1974. Variation in aufwuchs at six freshwater habitats in terms of carbon biomass and of carbon:nitrogen ratio. Hydrobiologia 45:391–404.

McMahon, T. E., and G. F. Hartman. 1989. Influence of cover complexity and current velocity on winter habitat use by juvenile coho salmon (*Oncorhynchus kisutch*). Canadian Journal of Fisheries and Aquatic Sciences 46:1551–1557.

McMullin, S. L. 1979. The food habits and distribution of rainbow and cutthroat trout in Lake Koocanusa, Montana. Master's thesis. University of Idaho, Moscow.

McNeil, W. J. 1964. A method of measuring mortality of pink salmon eggs and larvae. U.S. Fish and Wildlife Service Fishery Bulletin 63:575–588.

McNeil, W. J. 1966a. Distribution of spawning pink salmon in Sashin Creek, southeastern Alaska, and survival of their progeny. U.S. Fish and Wildlife Service Special Scientific Report—Fisheries 538.

McNeil, W. J. 1966b. Effect of the spawning bed environment on reproduction of pink and chum salmon. U.S. Fish and Wildlife Service Fishery Bulletin 65:495–523.

McNeil, W. J. 1968. Migration and distribution of pink salmon spawners in Sashin Creek in 1965, and survival of their progeny. U.S. Fish and Wildlife Service Fishery Bulletin 66:575–586.

McNeil, W. J. 1969. Survival of pink and chum salmon eggs and alevins. Pages 101–117 *in* Northcote (1969b).

McNeil, W. J., editor. 1988. Salmon production, management, and allocation: biological, economic, and policy issues. Proceedings, World Salmonid Conference, 1986. Oregon State University Press, Corvallis.

McNeil, W. J., and W. H. Ahnell. 1964. Success of pink salmon spawning relative to size of spawning bed materials. U.S. Fish and Wildlife Service Special Scientific Report—Fisheries 469.

McPhail, J. D., and C. C. Lindsey. 1970. Freshwater fishes of northwestern Canada and Alaska. Fisheries Research Board of Canada Bulletin 173.

McWilliams, P. G. 1980. Acclimation to an acid medium in the brown trout *Salmo trutta*. Journal of Experimental Biology 88:269–280.

Meehan, W. R. 1970. Some effects of shade cover on stream temperature in southeast Alaska. U.S. Forest Service Research Note PNW-113.

Meehan, W. R. 1971. Effects of gravel cleaning on bottom organisms in three southeast Alaska streams. Progressive Fish-Culturist 33:107–111.

Meehan, W. R. 1974. The forest ecosystem of southeast Alaska: 3. Fish habitats. U.S. Forest Service General Technical Report PNW-15.

Meehan, W. R., editor. 1991a. Influences of forest and rangeland management on salmonid fishes and their habitats. American Fisheries Society Special Publication 19.

Meehan, W. R. 1991b. Introduction and overview. American Fisheries Society Special Publication 19:1–15.

Meehan, W. R., and T. C. Bjornn. 1991. Salmonid distributions and life histories. American Fisheries Society Special Publication 19:47–82.

Meehan, W. R., M. A. Brusven, and J. F. Ward. 1987. Effects of artificial shading on distribution and abundance of juvenile chinook salmon (*Oncorhynchus tshawytscha*). Great Basin Naturalist 47:22–31.

Meehan, W. R., T. R. Merrell, Jr., and T. A. Hanley, editors. 1984. Proceedings, fish and wildlife relationships in old-growth forests symposium. American Institute of Fishery Research Biologists, Asheville, N.C.

Meehan, W. R., L. A. Norris, and H. S. Sears. 1974. Toxicity of various formulations of 2,4-D to salmonids in southeast Alaska. Journal of the Fisheries Research Board of Canada 31:480–485.

Meehan, W. R., and W. S. Platts. 1978. Livestock grazing and the aquatic environment. Journal of Soil and Water Conservation 33:274–278.

Meehan, W. R., F. J. Swanson, and J. R. Sedell. 1977. Influences of riparian vegetation on aquatic ecosystems with particular reference to salmonid fishes and their food supply. U.S. Forest Service General Technical Report RM-43:137–145.

Meehan, W. R., and D. N. Swanston. 1977. Effects of gravel morphology on fine sediment accumulation and survival of incubating salmon eggs. U.S. Forest Service Research Paper PNW-220.

Megahan, W. F. 1972. Subsurface flow interception by a logging road in mountains of central Idaho. Pages 350–356 *in* S. C. Csallany, T. G. McLaughlin, and W. D. Striffler, editors. Proceedings, watersheds in transition symposium. American Water Resources Association, Urbana, Illinois.

Megahan, W. F. 1974. Deep-rooted plants for erosion control on granitic road fills in the Idaho batholith. U.S. Forest Service Research Paper INT-161.

Megahan, W. F. 1982. Channel sediment storage behind obstructions in forested drainage basins draining the granitic bedrock of the Idaho batholith. Pages 114–121 *in* Swanson et al. (1982b).

Megahan, W. F., and W. J. Kidd. 1972. Effects of logging and logging roads on erosion and sediment deposition from steep terrain. Journal of Forestry 70:136–141.

Megahan, W. F., and D. E. Molitor. 1975. Erosional effects of wildfire and logging in Idaho. Pages 423–444 *in* Proceedings, watershed management symposium. American Society of Civil Engineers, Irrigation and Drainage Division, Logan, Utah.

Megahan, W. F., and R. A. Nowlin. 1976. Sediment storage in channels draining small forested watersheds in the mountains of central Idaho. Pages 4-115 to 4-126 *in* Proceedings, 3rd federal inter-agency sedimentation conference. Water Resources Council, Denver, Colorado.

Megahan, W. F., W. S. Platts, and B. Kulesza. 1980. Riverbed improves over time: South Fork Salmon. Pages 380–395 *in* Proceedings, watershed management symposium. American Society of Civil Engineers, New York.

Mehrle, P. M., D. R. Buckler, E. E. Little, L. M. Smith, J. D. Petty, P. H. Peterman, D. L. Stalling, G. M. De Graeve, J. J. Coyle, and W. J. Adams. 1988. Toxicity and bioconcentration of 2,3,7,8-tetrachlorodibenzodioxin and 2,3,7,8-tetrachlorodibenzofuran in rainbow trout. Environmental Toxicology and Chemistry 7:47–62.

Melnikov, N. N. 1971. Chemistry of pesticides. Residue Reviews 36:1–480.

Menendez, R. 1976. Chronic effects of reduced pH on brook trout (*Salvelinus fontinalis*). Journal of the Fisheries Research Board of Canada 33:118–123.

Menke, J. W., editor. 1983. Proceedings, workshop on livestock and wildlife–fisheries relationships in the Great Basin. University of California, Agricultural Sciences Special Publication 3301, Berkeley.

Menon, A. S., and J. De Mestral. 1985. Survival of *Bacillus thuringiensis* var. *kurstaki* in waters. Water, Air and Soil Pollution 25:265–274.

Merrell, T. R. 1951. Stream improvement as conducted in Oregon on the Clatskanie River and tributaries. Fish Commission of Oregon Research Briefs 3(2):41–47.

Merrell, T. R., Jr. 1962. Freshwater survival of pink salmon at Sashin Creek, Alaska. Pages 59–72 *in* N. J. Wilimovsky, editor. Symposium on pink salmon. H. R. MacMillan Lectures in Fisheries, University of British Columbia, Vancouver.

Merritt, R. W., and K. W. Cummins. 1978. An introduction to the aquatic insects of North America. Kendall/Hunt, Dubuque, Iowa.

Merritt, R. W., D. H. Ross, and G. J. Larson. 1982. Influence of stream temperature and seston on the growth and production of overwintering larval black flies (Diptera: Simuliidae). Ecology 63:1322–1331.

Merz, R. W., and R. F. Finn. 1951. Differences in infiltration rates on graded and ungraded strip-mined lands. U.S. Forest Service Research Note CS-65.

Metsker, H. E. 1970. Fish versus culverts: some considerations for resource managers. U.S. Forest Service Engineering Technical Report ETR-7700-5.

Meyer, F. P. 1965. The experimental use of Guthion as a selective fish eradicator. Transactions of the American Fisheries Society 94:203–209.

Meyer, P. A. 1978. Updated estimates for recreation and preservation values associated with the salmon and steelhead of the Fraser River. Environment Canada, Fisheries and Marine Service, Habitat Protection Directorate, Pacific Region, Vancouver, British Columbia.

Michel, B. 1973. Properties and processes of river and lake ice. International Association of Hydrological Sciences Publication 107:454–481.

MicroGeneSystem. 1985. A biological product to control European pine sawfly. Micro-GeneSystem, Inc., West Haven, Connecticut.

Midwest Research Institute. 1975. Substitute chemical program: initial scientific review of MSMA/DSMA. Prepared for U.S. Environmental Protection Agency, EPA-540/1-75-020, Washington, D.C.

Miernyk, W. H. 1965. The elements of input–output analysis. Random House, New York.

Mih, W. C. 1978. A review of restoration of stream gravel for spawning and rearing of salmon species. Fisheries 3(1):16–18.

Mih, W. G., and G. C. Bailey. 1981. The development of a machine for the restoration of stream gravel for spawning and rearing of salmon. Fisheries 6(6):16–20.

Mihursky, J. A., and V. S. Kennedy. 1967. Water temperature criteria to protect aquatic life. American Fisheries Society Special Publication 4:20–32.

Miller, J. G., J. A. Arway, and R. F. Carline, editors. 1986. Proceedings, 5th trout stream habitat improvement workshop. Pennsylvania Fish Commission, Harrisburg.

Miller, J. N. 1972. The nibbling away of the West. Reader's Digest (December):107–111.

Miller, R. B. 1954. Movements of cutthroat trout after different periods of retention upstream and downstream from their homes. Journal of the Fisheries Research Board of Canada 11:550–558.

Miller, R. B. 1957. Permanence and size of home territory in stream dwelling cutthroat trout. Journal of the Fisheries Research Board of Canada 14:687–691.

Miller, R. J., and E. L. Brannon. 1982. The origin and development of life history patterns in Pacific salmonids. Pages 296–309 *in* Brannon and Salo (1982).

Miller, R. R. 1950. Notes on the cutthroat and rainbow trouts with the description of a new species from the Gila River, New Mexico. University of Michigan, Museum of Zoology Occasional Papers 529.

Miller, W. J. 1985. Tucannon River percent fry emergence model. Colorado State University, ARS CWU 5402-20810-004-01S, Fort Collins.

Mills, D. H. 1969. The survival of juvenile Atlantic salmon and brown trout in some Scottish streams. Pages 217–228 *in* Northcote (1969b).

Mills, M. J. 1986. Statewide harvest report, RT-2. Alaska statewide sport fish harvest studies. Alaska Department of Fish and Game, Juneau.

Minnear, R. A., and B. A. Tschantz. 1974. Contour coal mining overburden as solid waste and its impact on environmental quality. Appalachian Resources, Project Report 30, University of Tennessee, Knoxville.

Minshall, G. W. 1967. Role of allochthonous detritus in the trophic structure of a woodland springbrook community. Ecology 48:139–149.

Minshall, G. W. 1978. Autotrophy in stream ecosystems. BioScience 28:767–771.

Minshall, G. W., R. C. Petersen, K. W. Cummins, T. L. Bott, J. R. Sedell, C. E. Cushing, and R. L. Vannote. 1983. Interbiome comparison of stream ecosystem dynamics. Ecological Monographs 53:1–25.

Mitchell, R. C., and R. T. Carson. 1989. Using surveys to value public goods: the contingent valuation method. Published for Resources for the Future, Inc., by Johns Hopkins University Press, Baltimore, Maryland.

Mitsch, W. J., and R. D. Letterman. 1979. Mine drainage impact on water quality and ecosystem energetics in a western Pennsylvania stream. U.S. Fish and Wildlife Service, FWS/OBS-78/81:99–106.

Moffett, D., and M. Tellier. 1977. Uptake of radioisotopes by vegetation growing on uranium tailings. Canadian Journal of Soil Science 57:417–424.

Monan, G. E., J. H. Johnson, and G. F. Esterberg. 1975. Electronic tags and related tracking techniques aid in study of migrating salmon and steelhead trout in the Columbia River basin. Marine Fisheries Review 37(2):9–15.

Monsen, S. B. 1983. Plants for revegetation of riparian sites within the intermountain region. U.S. Forest Service General Technical Report INT-157:83–89.

Monsen, S. B., and A. P. Plummer. 1978. Plants and treatment for revegetation of disturbed sites in the Intermountain area. Pages 155–173 *in* R. A. Wright, editor. The reclamation of disturbed arid lands. University of New Mexico Press, Albuquerque.

Moore, D. G. 1970. Forest fertilization and water quality in the Pacific Northwest. American Society of Agronomy Abstracts 1970:160–161.

Moore, D. G. 1971. Fertilization and water quality. Pages 1–4 *in* Western Forestry and Conservation Association annual meeting, Portland, Oregon.

Moore, D. G. 1975a. Effects of forest fertilization with urea on stream water quality—Quilcene Ranger District, Washington. U.S. Forest Service Research Note PNW-241.

Moore, D. G. 1975b. Impact of forest fertilization on water quality in the Douglas-fir region—a summary of monitoring studies. Pages 209–219 *in* Forestry issues in urban America. Society of American Foresters, Washington, D.C.

Moore, D. G., and L. A. Norris. 1974. Soil processes and introduced chemicals. U.S. Forest Service General Technical Report PNW-24:C1–C33.

Moore, R., and T. Mills. 1977. An environmental guide to western surface mining. Part 2: Impacts, mitigation, and monitoring. U.S. Fish and Wildlife Service, FWS/OBS-78/04.

Moreau, J. K. 1984. Anadromous salmonid habitat enhancement by boulder placement in Hurdygurdy Creek, California. Pages 97–116 *in* Hassler (1984).

Morgan, L. S., and R. W. Kremer. 1952. Some observations of effect on streams from the DDT spraying for hemlock looper. Pennsylvania Forests and Waters 4:138–140.

Moring, J. R. 1975a. The Alsea watershed study: effects of logging on the aquatic resources of three headwater streams of the Alsea River, Oregon. Part 2—Changes in environmental conditions. Oregon Department of Fish and Wildlife, Fishery Research Report 9, Corvallis.

Moring, J. R. 1975b. The Alsea watershed study: effects of logging on the aquatic resources of three headwater streams of the Alsea River, Oregon. Part 3—Discussion and recommendations. Oregon Department of Fish and Wildlife, Fishery Research Report 9, Corvallis.

Moring, J. R. 1982. Decrease in stream gravel permeability after clear-cut logging: an indication of intragravel conditions for developing salmonid eggs and alevins. Hydrobiologia 88:295–298.

Moring, J. R., and R. L. Lantz. 1975. The Alsea watershed study: effects of logging on the aquatic resources of three headwater streams of the Alsea River, Oregon. Part 1—Biological studies. Oregon Department of Fish and Wildlife, Fishery Research Report 9, Corvallis.

Morrison, P. H. 1975. Ecological and geomorphological consequences of mass movements in the Alder Creek watershed and implications for forest land management. Bachelor's thesis. University of Oregon, Eugene.

Moshier, L. J., and D. Penner. 1978. Factors influencing microbial degradation of ^{14}C-glyphosate to $^{14}CO_2$ in soil. Weed Science 26:686–691.

Mosley, M. P. 1981. The influence of organic debris on channel morphology and bedload transport in a New Zealand forest stream. Earth Surface Processes and Landforms 6:571–579.

Mottley, C. McC. 1934. The origin and relations of the rainbow trout. Transactions of the American Fisheries Society 64:323–327.

Mount, D. I., and C. E. Stephan. 1967a. A method for detecting cadmium poisoning in fish. Journal of Wildlife Management 31:168–172.

Mount, D. I., and C. E. Stephan. 1967b. A method for establishing acceptable toxicant limits for fish—malathion and the butoxyethanol ester of 2,4-D. Transactions of the American Fisheries Society 96:185–193.

Mount, M. E., and F. W. Oehme. 1981. Carbaryl: a literature review. Residue Reviews 80:1–64.

Moyle, P. B., and D. M. Baltz. 1985. Microhabitat use by an assemblage of California stream fishes: developing criteria for instream flow determinations. Transactions of the American Fisheries Society 114:695–704.

Mrazik, B. R., D. L. Mader, and W. P. MacConnell. 1980. Integrated watershed management: an alternative for the Northeast. University of Massachusetts, Agricultural Experiment Station Research Bulletin 664, Amherst.

Mueller, J. C., J. M. Leach, and C. C. Walden. 1977. Detoxification of bleached kraft mill effluents—a manageable problem. TAPPI 60(9):135–137.

Mulholland, P. J., J. W. Elwood, J. D. Newbold, J. R. Webster, L. A. Ferren, and R. E. Perkins. 1984. Phosphorus uptake by decomposing leaf detritus: effect of microbial biomass and activity. Internationale Vereinigung für theoretische und angewandte Limnologie Verhandlungen 22:1899–1905.

Mulla, M. S., and L. S. Mian. 1981. Biological and environmental impacts of the insecticides malathion and parathion on nontarget biota in aquatic ecosystems. Residue Reviews 78:101–135.

Mulla, M. S., L. S. Mian, and J. A. Kawecki. 1981. Distribution, transport, and fate of the insecticides malathion and parathion in the environment. Residue Reviews 81:1–172.

Mullan, J. W. 1962. Is stream improvement the answer? West Virginia Conservation 26(6):25–30.

Mundie, J. H. 1969. Ecological implications of the diet of juvenile coho in streams. Pages 135–152 in Northcote (1969b).

Mundie, J. H. 1974. Optimization of the salmonid nursery stream. Journal of the Fisheries Research Board of Canada 31:1827–1837.

Mundie, J. H., S. M. McKinnell, and R. E. Traber. 1983. Responses of stream zoobenthos to enrichment of gravel substrates with cereal grain and soybean. Canadian Journal of Fisheries and Aquatic Sciences 40:1702–1712.

Mundie, J. H., and D. E. Mounce. 1978. Application of stream ecology to raising salmon smolts in high density. Internationale Vereinigung für theoretische und angewandte Limnologie Verhandlungen 20:2013–2018.

Mundie, J. H., and R. E. Traber. 1983. Carrying capacity of an enhanced side-channel for rearing salmonids. Canadian Journal of Fisheries and Aquatic Sciences 40:1320–1322.

Muniz, I. P., and H. Leivestad. 1980. Toxic effects of aluminum on the brown trout, *Salmo trutta*, L. Pages 320–321 *in* Drablos and Tollan (1980).

Munshower, F. F. 1983. Problems in reclamation planning and design. Pages 1287–1307 *in* D. Books, technical editor. Coal development: collected papers: Papers presented at coal development workshops in Grand Junction, Colorado, and Casper, Wyoming, volume 2. U.S. Bureau of Land Management, Washington, D.C.

Munson, B. H., J. H. McCormick, and H. L. Collins. 1980. Influence of thermal challenge on conditioned feeding forays of juvenile rainbow trout. Transactions of the American Fisheries Society 109:116–121.

Murphy, M. L. 1979. Predator assemblages in old-growth and logged sections of small Cascade streams. Master's thesis. Oregon State University, Corvallis.

Murphy, M. L. 1984. Primary production and grazing in freshwater and intertidal reaches of a coastal stream, southeast Alaska. Limnology and Oceanography 29:805–815.

Murphy, M. L., and J. D. Hall. 1981. Varied effects of clear-cut logging on predators and their habitat in small streams of the Cascade Mountains, Oregon. Canadian Journal of Fisheries and Aquatic Sciences 38:137–145.

Murphy, M. L., C. P. Hawkins, and N. H. Anderson. 1981. Effects of canopy modification and accumulated sediment on stream communities. Transactions of the American Fisheries Society 110:469–478.

Murphy, M. L., J. Heifetz, S. W. Johnson, K. V. Koski, and J. F. Thedinga. 1986. Effects of clear-cut logging with and without buffer strips on juvenile salmonids in Alaskan streams. Canadian Journal of Fisheries and Aquatic Sciences 43:1521–1533.

Murphy, M. L., K. V. Koski, J. Heifetz, S. W. Johnson, D. Kirchhofer, and J. F. Thedinga. 1984a. Role of large organic debris as winter habitat for juvenile salmonids in Alaska streams. Proceedings of the Annual Conference Western Association of Fish and Wildlife Agencies 64:251–262.

Murphy, M. L., J. M. Lorenz, J. Heifetz, J. F. Thedinga, K. V. Koski, and S. W. Johnson. 1987. The relationship between stream classification, fish, and habitat in southeast Alaska. U.S. Forest Service, Alaska Region, Wildlife and Habitat Management Note 12, Juneau.

Murphy, M. L., and W. R. Meehan. 1991. Stream ecosystems. American Fisheries Society Special Publication 19:17–46.

Murphy, M. L., J. F. Thedinga, K. V. Koski, and G. B. Grette. 1984b. A stream ecosystem in an old-growth forest in southeast Alaska. Part 5: seasonal changes in habitat utilization by juvenile salmonids. Pages 89–98 *in* Meehan et al. (1984).

Murray, D., and D. Moffett. 1977. Vegetating the uranium mine tailings at Elliot Lake, Ontario. Journal of Soil and Water Conservation 32:171–174.

Musser, J. J. 1963. Description of physical environment and of strip-mining operations in parts of Beaver Creek basin, Kentucky. U.S. Geological Survey, Professional Paper 427-A, Washington, D.C.

Naiman, R. J. 1976. Primary production, standing stock, and export of organic matter in a Mohave Desert thermal stream. Limnology and Oceanography 21:60–73.

Naiman, R. J., and J. R. Sedell. 1979. Characterization of particulate organic matter transported by some Cascade Mountain streams. Journal of the Fisheries Research Board of Canada 36:17–31.

Naiman, R. J., and J. R. Sedell. 1980. Relationships between metabolic parameters and stream order in Oregon. Canadian Journal of Fisheries and Aquatic Sciences 37:834–847.

Naiman, R. J., and J. R. Sibert. 1978. Transport of nutrients and carbon from the Nanaimo River to its estuary. Limnology and Oceanography 23:1183–1193.

Naiman, R. J., and J. R. Sibert. 1979. Detritus and juvenile salmon production in the Nanaimo estuary: 3. importance of detrital carbon to the estuarine ecosystem. Journal of the Fisheries Research Board of Canada 36:504–520.

Naishe, V. A., and R. J. P. Brouzes. 1980. New fish tainting test points to trouble spots. Pulp and Paper Canada 81(10):112–115.

Narver, D. W. 1971. Effects of logging debris on fish production. Pages 100–111 *in* Krygier and Hall (1971).

Narver, D. W. 1972a. A survey of some possible effects of logging on two eastern Vancouver Island streams. Fisheries Research Board of Canada Technical Report 323.

Narver, D. W. 1972b. Waterfowl at the Nanaimo River estuary. Unpublished report on file at Pacific Biological Station, Nanaimo, British Columbia.

Narver, D. W. 1973. Are hatcheries and spawning channels alternatives to stream protection? Fisheries Research Board of Canada Circular 93.

Narver, D. W. 1976. Stream management for West Coast anadromous salmonids. Trout 17(1)(Supplement):7–13.

Narver, D. W. 1978. Ecology of juvenile coho salmon—can we use present knowledge for stream enhancement? Canadian Fisheries and Marine Service Technical Report 759:38–43.

Nasaka, Y. 1988. Salmonid programs and public policy in Japan. Pages 25–32 in W. J. McNeil, editor. Salmon production, management, and allocation: biological, economic, and policy issues. Oregon State University Press, Corvallis.

National Academy of Sciences. 1979. Surface mining of non-coal minerals: a study of mineral mining from the perspective of the Surface Mining Control and Reclamation Act of 1977. NAS, Washington, D.C.

National Council of the Paper Industry for Air and Stream Improvement. 1982. Effects of biologically stabilized bleached kraft mill effluent on cold water stream productivity as determined in experimental streams—1st progress report. NCPIASI, Technical Bulletin 368, New York.

National Council of the Paper Industry for Air and Stream Improvement. 1983. Effects of biologically stabilized bleached kraft mill effluent on cold water stream productivity in experimental streams—2nd progress report. NCPIASI, Technical Bulletin 413, New York.

National Council of the Paper Industry for Air and Stream Improvement. 1984. Effects of biologically treated bleached kraft mill effluent on cold water stream productivity in experimental stream channels—3rd progress report. NCPIASI, Technical Bulletin 445, New York.

National Council of the Paper Industry for Air and Stream Improvement. 1985. Effects of biologically treated bleached kraft mill effluent on cold water stream productivity in experimental stream channels—4th progress report. NCPIASI, Technical Bulletin 474, New York.

National Research Council of Canada. 1974. Picloram: the effects of its use as a herbicide on environmental quality. National Research Council of Canada, NRCC 13684, Ottawa.

National Research Council of Canada. 1978. Phenoxy herbicides—their effects on environmental quality, with accompanying scientific criteria for 2,3,7,8-tetrachlorodibenzo-p-dioxin (TCDD). National Research Council of Canada, NRCC 16075, Ottawa.

Natural Resources Consultants. 1986. Commercial fishing and the State of Washington. NRC, Seattle.

Nawrot, J. R., A. Woolf, and W. D. Klimstra. 1982. A guide for enhancement of fish and wildlife on abandoned mine lands in the eastern United States. U.S. Fish and Wildlife Service, FWS/OBS-80/67.

Neary, D. G., P. B. Bush, and J. E. Douglass. 1983. Off-site movement of hexazinone in stormflow and baseflow from forest watersheds. Weed Science 31:543–551.

Neary, D. G., P. B. Bush, J. E. Douglass, and R. L. Todd. 1985. Picloram movement in an Appalachian hardwood forest watershed. Journal of Environmental Quality 14:585–592.

Neave, F. 1947. Natural propagation of chum salmon in a coastal stream. Fisheries Research Board of Canada, Pacific Coast Station Progress Report 70:20–21, Nanaimo, British Columbia.

Neave, F. 1953. Principles affecting the size of pink and chum salmon populations in British Columbia. Journal of the Fisheries Research Board of Canada 9:450–491.

Neave, F. 1958. The origin and speciation of *Oncorhynchus*. Transactions of the Royal Society of Canada 52:25–39.

Neave, F. 1966. Pink salmon in British Columbia. International North Pacific Fisheries Commission Bulletin 18:71–80.

Neave, F., T. Ishida, and S. Murai. 1967. Pink salmon in offshore waters. International North Pacific Fisheries Commission Bulletin 22:1–39.

Needham, P. R., and A. C. Jones. 1959. Flow, temperature, solar radiation, and ice in relation to activities of fishes in Sagehen Creek, California. Ecology 40:465–474.

Neilson, J. D., and C. E. Banford. 1983. Chinook salmon (*Oncorhynchus tshawytscha*) spawner characteristics in relation to redd physical features. Canadian Journal of Zoology 61:1524–1531.

Neitzel, D. A., and C. D. Becker. 1985. Tolerance of eggs, embryos, and alevins of chinook salmon to temperature changes and reduced humidity in dewatered redds. Transactions of the American Fisheries Society 114:267–273.

Nelson, H. 1979. Pulp mill environmental impact assessment: MacMillan Bloedel Ltd, Alberni Pulp and Paper Division. Canada Environmental Protection Service, Regional Program Report 79-11, Vancouver.

Nelson, J. A. 1982. Physiological observations on developing rainbow trout, *Salmo gairdneri* (Richardson), exposed to low pH and varied calcium ion concentrations. Journal of Fish Biology 20:359–372.

Nelson, R. L., M. L. McHenry, and W. S. Platts. 1991. Mining. American Fisheries Society Special Publication 19:425–457.

Nesbitt, H. J., and J. R. Watson. 1980a. Degradation of the herbicide 2,4-D in river water. 1: Description of study area and survey of rate determining factors. Water Research 14:1683–1688.

Nesbitt, H. J., and J. R. Watson. 1980b. Degradation of the herbicide 2,4-D in river water. 2: The role of suspended sediment, nutrients and water temperature. Water Research 14:1689–1694.

Netboy, A. 1980. The Columbia River salmon and steelhead trout: their fight for survival. University of Washington Press, Seattle.

Neuman, E., and P. Karas. 1988. Effects of pulp mill effluent of a Baltic coastal fish community. Water Science and Technology 20(2):95–106.

Newbold, C. 1975. Herbicides in aquatic systems. Biological Conservation 7:97–118.

Newbold, J. D., D. C. Erman, and K. B. Roby. 1980. Effects of logging on macroinvertebrates in streams with and without buffer strips. Canadian Journal of Fisheries and Aquatic Sciences 37:1076–1085.

Newbold, J. D., P. J. Mulholland, J. W. Elwood, and R. V. O'Neill. 1982. Organic carbon spiralling in stream ecosystems. Oikos 38:266–272.

Newton, J. 1978. Rock work. Pages 3–4 *in* Proceedings, fish habitat improvement workshop, Ochoco Ranger Station. Oregon Department of Fish and Wildlife, Portland.

Newton, M. 1981. Herbicides in forestry. Pages 78–93 *in* R. E. Whitesides, compiler. Oregon weed control handbook. Oregon State University, Corvallis.

Newton, M. 1987. Herbicides in forestry. Pages 105–121 *in* R. D. William, L. C. Burrill, R. Parker, D. G. Swan, S. W. Howard, and D. W. Kidder, compilers. Pacific Northwest weed control handbook. Oregon State University, Corvallis.

Newton, M., K. M. Howard, B. R. Kelpsas, R. Danhaus, C. M. Lottman, and S. Dubelman. 1984. Fate of glyphosate in an Oregon forest ecosystem. Journal of Agricultural and Food Chemistry 32:1144–1151.

Newton, M., and J. A. Norgren. 1977. Silvicultural chemicals and protection of water quality. U.S. Environmental Protection Agency, EPA 910/9-77-036.

Nicholas, J. W. 1978. Life history differences between sympatric populations of rainbow and cutthroat trouts in relation to fisheries management strategy. Pages 181–188 *in* J. R. Moring, editor. Proceedings, wild trout–catchable trout symposium. Oregon Department of Fish and Wildlife, Corvallis.

Nicholas, P. J., and W. J. McGinnies. 1982. An evaluation of 17 grasses and 2 legumes for revegetation of soil and spoil on a coal strip mine. Journal of Range Management 35:288–293.

Nichols, J. W., G. A. Wedemeyer, F. L. Mayer, W. W. Dickhoff, S. V. Gregory, W. T. Yasutake, and S. D. Smith. 1984. Effects of freshwater exposure to arsenic trioxide on the parr-smolt transformation of coho salmon (*Oncorhynchus kisutch*). Environmental Toxicology and Chemistry 3:143–149.

Nickelson, T. E. 1986. Influences of upwelling, ocean temperature, and smolt abundance on marine survival of coho salmon (*Oncorhynchus kisutch*) in the Oregon Production Area. Canadian Journal of Fisheries and Aquatic Sciences 43:527–535.

Nickelson, T. E., W. M. Beidler, and M. J. Willis. 1979. Streamflow requirements of salmonids. Oregon Department of Fish and Wildlife Final Report, Project AFS-62 (Contract 14-0001-78-525), Portland.

Nickelson, T. E., and R. R. Reisenbichler. 1977. Streamflow requirements of salmonids. Oregon Department of Fish and Wildlife, Annual Progress Report, Project AFS-62 (Contract 14-16-0001-4247), Portland.

Nielson, B. G., and L. Lentsch. 1988. Bonneville cutthroat trout in Bear Lake: status and management. American Fisheries Society Symposium 4:128–133.

Nikinmaa, M., and A. Oikari. 1982. Physiological changes in trout (*Salmo gairdneri*) during a short-term exposure to resin acids and during recovery. Toxicology Letters 14:103–110.

Nikunen, E. 1983. The acute toxicity of some Finnish pulp and paper mill effluents and comparison of three measurement methods. Paperi ja Puu (Paper and Timber) 65:726–730.

Nilsson, N.-A. 1967. Interactive segregation between fish species. Pages 295–313 *in* S. D. Gerking. The biological basis of freshwater fish production. Blackwell, Oxford.

Nilsson, N.-A., and T. G. Northcote. 1981. Rainbow trout (*Salmo gairdneri*) and cutthroat trout (*S. clarki*) interactions in coastal British Columbia lakes. Canadian Journal of Fisheries and Aquatic Sciences 38:1228–1246.

Nobel, E. L., and L. J. Lundeen. 1971. Analysis of rehabilitation treatment alternatives for sediment control. Pages 86–96 *in* Krygier and Hall (1971).

Noerenberg, W. H. 1955. Prince William Sound spawning ground survey: 1955. University of Washington, Fisheries Research Institute Circular 81, Seattle.

Noggle, C. C. 1978. Behavioral, physiological and lethal effects of suspended sediments on juvenile salmonids. Master's thesis. University of Washington, Seattle.

Norem, M. A., and A. D. Day. 1985. Managing copper tailing slopes for revegetation in the south-western United States. Reclamation and Revegetation Research 4:83–92.

Norris, L. A. 1966. Degradation of 2,4-D and 2,4,5-T in forest litter. Journal of Forestry 64:475–476.

Norris, L. A. 1967. Chemical brush control and herbicide residues in the forest environment. Pages 103–123 *in* Proceedings, herbicides and vegetation management in forests, ranges, and noncrop lands symposium. Oregon State University, Corvallis.

Norris, L. A. 1968. Stream contamination by herbicides after fall rains on forest land. Pages 33–34 *in* Western Society of Weed Science, Research Progress Report, Boise, Idaho.

Norris, L. A. 1969. Herbicide runoff from forest lands sprayed in summer. Pages 24–26 *in* Western Society of Weed Science, Research Progress Report, Reno, Nevada.

Norris, L. A. 1970a. Degradation of herbicides in the forest floor. Pages 397–411 *in* C. T. Youngberg and C. B. Davey, editors. Tree growth and forest soils. Oregon State University Press, Corvallis.

Norris, L. A. 1970b. The kinetics of adsorption and desorption of 2,4-D, 2,4,5-T, picloram, and amitrole on forest floor material. Pages 103–105 *in* Western Society of Weed Science, Research Progress Report, Sacramento, California.

Norris, L. A. 1971a. The behavior of chemicals in the forest. Pages 90–106 *in* J. Witt and J. Capizzi, editors. Pesticides, pest control and safety on forest and range lands. Continuing Education Publications, Oregon State University, Corvallis.

Norris, L. A. 1971b. Chemical brush control: assessing the hazard. Journal of Forestry 69:715–720.

Norris, L. A. 1978. Toxic materials in forest streams. Pages 43–68 *in* Proceedings, toxic materials in the aquatic environment seminar. Oregon State University, Water Resources Research Institute, Corvallis.

Norris, L. A. 1981. The movement, persistence, and fate of the phenoxy herbicides and TCDD in the forest. Residue Reviews 80:65–135.

Norris, L. A., P. R. Canutt, and J. F. Neuman. 1983. Arsenic in the forest environment after thinning with MSMA and cacodylic acid. Bulletin of Environmental Contamination and Toxicology 30:309–316.

Norris, L. A., and D. Greiner. 1967. The degradation of 2,4-D in forest litter. Bulletin of Environmental Contamination and Toxicology 2:65–74.

Norris, L. A., C. L. Hawkes, W. L. Webb, D. G. Moore, W. B. Bollen, and E. Holcombe. 1978. A report of research on the behavior and impact of chemical fire retardants in forest streams. U.S. Forest Service, Forestry Sciences Laboratory, Corvallis, Oregon.

Norris, L. A., H. W. Lorz, and S. V. Gregory. 1991. Forest chemicals. American Fisheries Society Special Publication 19:207–296.

Norris, L. A., and M. L. Montgomery. 1975. Dicamba residues in streams after forest spraying. Bulletin of Environmental Contamination and Toxicology 13:1–8.

Norris, L. A., M. L. Montgomery, and F. Gross. 1976. The behavior of picloram and 2,4-D in soil on western powerline rights-of-way. Pages 9–10 *in* Abstracts, 1976 meeting of the Weed Science Society of America, Champaign, Illinois.

Norris, L. A., M. L. Montgomery, B. R. Loper, and J. N. Kochenderfer. 1984. Movement and persistence of 2,4,5-trichlorophenoxyacetic acid in a forest watershed in the eastern United States. Environmental Toxicology and Chemistry 3:537–549.

Norris, L. A., M. L. Montgomery, and L. E. Warren. 1987. Triclopyr persistence in western Oregon hill pastures. Bulletin of Environmental Contamination and Toxicology 39:134–141.

Norris, L. A., M. L. Montgomery, L. E. Warren, and W. D. Mosher. 1982. Brush control with herbicides on hill pasture sites in southern Oregon. Journal of Range Management 35:75–80.

Norris, L. A., and D. G. Moore. 1971. The entry and fate of forest chemicals in streams. Pages 138–158 *in* Krygier and Hall (1971).

Norris, L. A., and D. G. Moore. 1976. Forests and rangelands as sources of chemical pollutants. Pages 17–35 *in* Non-point sources of water pollution. Oregon State University, Water Resources Research Institute, Corvallis.

Northcote, T. G. 1969a. Patterns and mechanisms in the lakeward migratory behavior of juvenile trout. Pages 183–204 *in* Northcote (1969b).

Northcote, T. G., editor. 1969b. Symposium on salmon and trout in streams. H. R. MacMillan Lectures in Fisheries, University of British Columbia, Institute of Fisheries, Vancouver.

Nunan, C. P., and D. L. G. Noakes. 1985. Response of rainbow trout (*Salmo gairdneri*) embryos to current flow in simulated substrates. Canadian Journal of Zoology 63:1813–1815.

Nuttall, P. M. 1972. The effects of sand deposition upon the macroinvertebrate fauna of the River Camel, Cornwall. Freshwater Biology 2:181–186.

O'Clair, C. E., and L. Freese. 1985. Responses of Dungeness crabs, *Cancer magister*, exposed to bark debris from benthic deposits at log transfer facilities: survival, feeding and reproduction. Pages 227–230 *in* Proceedings, Dungeness crab biology and management symposium. University of Alaska, Alaska Sea Grant Report 85-3, Fairbanks.

Ogilvie, D. M., and J. M. Anderson. 1965. Effect of DDT on temperature selection by young Atlantic salmon, *Salmo salar*. Journal of the Fisheries Research Board of Canada 22:503–512.

Oikari, A., B. Holmbom, E. Anas, and H. Bister. 1980. Distribution in a recipient lake and bioaccumulation in fish of resin acids from kraft pulp mill waste waters. Paperi ja Puu (Paper and Timber) 62:193–201.

Oikari, A., B. Holmbom, and H. Bister. 1982. Uptake of resin acids into tissues of trout (*Salmo gairdneri* Richardson). Annales Zoologici Fennici 19:61–64.

Oikari, A., T. Nakari, and B. Holmbom. 1984. Sublethal actions of simulated kraft pulp mill effluents (KME) in *Salmo gairdneri*: residues of toxicants and effects on blood and liver. Annales Zoologici Fennici 21:45–53.

Olem, H., and R. F. Unz. 1980. Rotating disc biological treatment of acid mine drainage. U.S. Environmental Protection Agency, Industrial Environmental Research Laboratory, Interagency Energy/Environment Research and Development Program Report EPA-600/7-80-006, Cincinnati, Ohio.

Olin, P. G. 1984. Genetic variability in hatchery and wild populations of coho salmon, *Oncorhynchus kisutch*, in Oregon. Master's thesis. University of California at Davis.

O'Loughlin, C. L. 1972. An investigation of the stability of the steepland forest soils in the Coast Mountains, southwest British Columbia. Doctoral dissertation. University of British Columbia, Vancouver.

O'Loughlin, C. L., and A. J. Pearce. 1976. Influence of Cenozoic geology on mass movement and sediment yield response to forest removal, North Westland, New Zealand. Bulletin of the International Association of Engineering Geology 14:41–46.

Olson, P. A., and R. F. Foster. 1956. Effect of chronic exposure to sodium dichromate on young chinook salmon and rainbow trout. Battelle Pacific Northwest Laboratories, HW-41500:34–47, Portland, Oregon.

Olson, R. A. 1981. Wetland vegetation, environmental factors, and their interaction in strip mine ponds, stockdams, and natural wetlands. U.S. Forest Service General Technical Report RM-85.

Olsson, T. I., and B.-G. Persson. 1986. Effects of gravel size and peat material concentrations on embryo survival and alevin emergence of brown trout, *Salmo trutta* L. Hydrobiologia 135:9–14.

Orcutt, D. R., B. R. Pulliam, and A. Arp. 1968. Characteristics of steelhead trout redds in Idaho streams. Transactions of the American Fisheries Society 97:42–45.

Oregon Department of Fish and Wildlife. 1982. Comprehensive plan for production and management of Oregon's anadromous salmon and trout: Part 2. Coho salmon plan. ODFW, Fish Division, Anadromous Fish Section, Portland.

Oregon Division of State Lands. 1973. Preliminary information for wetlands reports. Salem.

Oregon State Game Commission. 1971. Fish passage through culverts. Special Report, Portland.

Orsborn, J. F. 1986. New concepts in fish ladder design: Part 1, summary. U.S. Department of Energy, Bonneville Power Administration, Division of Fish and Wildlife Final Project Report, Project 82–14, Portland, Oregon.

Orsborn, J. F., and J. W. Anderson. 1986. Stream improvements and fish response: a bio-engineering assessment. Water Resources Bulletin 22:381–388.

Orska, J. 1963. The influence of temperature on the development of meristic characters of the skeleton in Salmonidae. 2. Variations in dorsal and anal fin ray count correlated with temperature during development of *Salmo irideus* Gibb. Translations, Biological Abstracts 47(6): Abstract 28237.

Orth, D. J., and O. E. Maughan. 1982. Evaluation of the incremental methodology for recommending instream flows for fishes. Transactions of the American Fisheries Society 111:413–445.

Osborn, J. G. 1981. The effects of logging on cutthroat trout (*Salmon clarki*) in small headwater streams. Master's thesis. University of Washington, Seattle.

Osterdahl, L. 1969. The smolt run of a small Swedish river. Pages 205–216 *in* Northcote (1969b).

Otto, C. 1981. Food related adaptations in stream living caddisfly larvae feeding on leaves. Oikos 37:117–122.

Outdoor California. 1968. It's new! The "riffle sifter." Outdoor California 29(5):12–13.

Outram, D. N., and R. D. Humphreys. 1974. The Pacific herring in British Columbia waters. Canada Fisheries and Marine Service, Pacific Biological Station Circular 180, Nanaimo, British Columbia.

Overton, C. K. 1984. Evaluation of stream channel enhancement needs. Pages 156–164 in Hassler (1984).

Paasivirta, J., J. Knuutinen, J. Tarhanen, T. Kuokkanen, K. Surma-Aho, R. Paukku, H. Kaariainen, M. Lahtipera/Okasis, and A. Veijanen. 1983. Potential off-flavour compounds from chlorobleaching of pulp and chlorodisinfection of water. Water Science and Technology 15(6–7):97–104.

Paasivirta, J., J. Sarkka, M. Aho, K. Surma-Aho, J. Tarhanen, and A. Roos. 1981. Recent trends of biocides in pikes of the Lake Paijanne. Chemosphere 10:405–414.

Paasivirta, J., J. Sarkka, T. Leskijarvi, and A. Roos. 1980. Transportation and enrichment of chlorinated phenolic compounds in different aquatic food chains. Chemosphere 9:441–456.

Pacific Fishery Management Council. 1988. Review of 1987 ocean salmon fisheries. PFMC, Portland, Oregon.

Pacific Fishery Management Council. 1989. Review of 1988 ocean salmon fisheries. PFMC, Portland, Oregon.

Pacific Marine Fisheries Commission. 1988. Fortieth annual report of the Pacific Marine Fisheries Commission for the year 1987. PMFC, Portland, Oregon.

Packer, P. E. 1967. Forest treatment effects on water quality. Pages 687–699 in Sopper and Lull (1967).

Packer, P. E., and G. F. Christensen. 1964. Guides for controlling sediment from secondary logging roads. U.S. Forest Service, Northern Region, Missoula, Montana.

Packer, P. E., C. E. Jensen, E. L. Noble, and J. A. Marshall. 1982. Models to estimate revegetation potentials of land surface mined for coal in the West. U.S. Forest Service General Technical Report INT-123.

Packer, R. K., and W. A. Dunson. 1970. Effects of low environmental pH on blood pH and sodium balance of brook trout. Journal of Experimental Zoology 174:65–71.

Packer, R. K., and W. A. Dunson. 1972. Anoxia and sodium loss associated with the death of brook trout at low pH. Comparative Biochemistry and Physiology 41:17–26.

Pagenkopf, G. K., and D. R. Newman. 1974. Lead concentrations in native trout. Bulletin of Environmental Contamination and Toxicology 12:70–75.

Palmer, C., and E. Siverts. 1985. IMPLAN analysis guide, version 1.1. U.S. Forest Service, Land Management Planning System Section, Fort Collins, Colorado.

Pang, P. C., and K. McCullough. 1982. Nutrient distribution in forest soil leachates after thinning and fertilizing Douglas-fir forest. Canadian Journal of Soil Science 62:197–208.

Paris, D. F., D. L. Lewis, J. T. Barnett, Jr., and G. L. Baughman. 1975. Microbial degradation and accumulation of pesticides in aquatic systems. U.S. Environmental Protection Agency, EPA-660/3-75-007, Corvallis, Oregon.

Parker, R. R., D. H. Heller, C. R. Horwood, and J. G. Sanderson. 1972. Some facets of the impact of pulp mill effluent on the Alberni Inlet. Pulp and Paper Magazine of Canada 73(10):T289–T299.

Parker, R. R., and W. Kirkness. 1956. King salmon and the ocean troll fishery of southeastern Alaska. Alaska Department of Fisheries Research Report 1, Juneau.

Parkhurst, B. R., R. G. Elder, J. S. Meyer, D. A. Sanchez, R. W. Pennak, and W. T. Waller. 1984. An environmental hazard evaluation of uranium in a Rocky Mountain stream. Environmental Toxicology and Chemistry 3:113–124.

Parkinson, E. A., and P. A. Slaney. 1975. A review of enhancement techniques applicable to anadromous gamefishes. British Columbia Fish and Wildlife Branch, Fisheries Management Report 66, Victoria.

Parrish, P. R., E. E. Dyar, M. A. Lindberg, C. M. Shanika, and J. M. Enos. 1977. Chronic toxicity of methoxychlor, malathion, and carbofuran to sheepshead minnows (*Cyprinodon variegatus*). U.S. Environmental Protection Agency, EPA 600/3-77-059, Washington, D.C.

Parsons, B. G. M., and W. A. Hubert. 1988. Influence of habitat availability on spawning site selection by kokanees in streams. North American Journal of Fisheries Management 8:426–431.

Patric, J. H. 1966. Rainfall interception by mature coniferous forests of southeast Alaska. Journal of Soil and Water Conservation 21:229–231.

Patric, J. H. 1976. Soil erosion in the eastern forest. Journal of Forestry 74:671–677.

Patterson, D. W. 1976. Evaluation of habitats resulting from stream bank protection projects in Siskiyou and Mendocino counties, California. California–Nevada Wildlife Transactions 47:53–59.

Patterson, J. H. 1975. An inventory of the fisheries resources of Ladysmith Harbour. Canada Fisheries and Marine Service, Internal Report Series PAC/1-75-1, Vancouver.

Patton, D. R. 1977. Riparian research needs. U.S. Forest Service General Technical Report RM-43:80–82.

Paustian, S. J., D. Perkinson, D. A. Marion, and P. Hunsicker. 1983. An aquatic value rating procedure for fisheries and water resource management in southeast Alaska. Pages 17–1 to 17–29 in Managing water resources for Alaska's development. Water Resources Association, Alaska Section, Fairbanks.

Pautzke, C. F., and R. C. Meigs. 1941. Studies on the life history of the Puget Sound steelhead trout (Salmo gairdnerii). Transactions of the American Fisheries Society 70:209–220.

Payne, N. F., and F. Copes, technical editors. 1986. Wildlife and fisheries habitat improvement handbook. U.S. Forest Service, Wildlife and Fisheries Administrative Report (unnumbered), Washington, D.C.

Pearce, A. J., and A. Watson. 1983. Medium-term effects of two landsliding episodes on channel storage of sediment. Earth Surface Processes and Landforms 8:29–39.

Pearse, P. H. 1979. Introduction to the symposium on managing fishing effort. Journal of the Fisheries Research Board of Canada 36:711–714.

Pearse, P. H. 1982. Turning the tide: a new policy for Canada's Pacific fisheries. British Columbia Department of Fisheries and Oceans, Commission on Pacific Fisheries Policy Final Report, Vancouver.

Pearse, P. H. 1988. Rising to the challenge: a new policy for Canada's freshwater fisheries. Canadian Wildlife Federation, Ottawa.

Pearson, F. H., and A. J. McDonnell. 1975. Limestone barriers to neutralize acidic streams. Proceedings of the American Society of Chemical Engineers 101(EE3):425–441.

Pearson, L. S., K. R. Conover, and R. E. Sams. 1970. Factors affecting the natural rearing of juvenile coho salmon during the summer low flow season. Oregon Fish Commission, Portland.

Pease, B. C. 1974. Effects of log dumping and rafting on the marine environment of southeast Alaska. U.S Forest Service General Technical Report PNW-22.

Pella, J. J., and R. T. Myren. 1974. Caveats concerning evaluation of effects of logging on salmon production in southeastern Alaska from biological information. Northwest Science 48:132–144.

Percy, K. L., C. Sutterlin, D. A. Bella, and P. C. Klingeman. 1974. Description and information sources for Oregon estuaries, 2nd edition. Oregon State University, Sea Grant College Program, Corvallis.

Perrin, C. J., M. L. Bothwell, and P. A. Slaney. 1987. Experimental enrichment of a coastal stream in British Columbia: effects of organic and inorganic additions on autotrophic periphyton production. Canadian Journal of Fisheries and Aquatic Sciences 44:1247–1256.

Peterman, R. M. 1982. Model of salmon age structure and its use in preseason forecasting and studies of marine survival. Canadian Journal of Fisheries and Aquatic Sciences 39:1444–1452.

Peterman, R. M. 1987. Review of the components of recruitment of Pacific salmon. Pages 417–429 in Dadswell et al. (1987).

Peters, G. B. 1974. The effect of leachate from western red cedar, (Thuja plicata Donn.), on aquatic organisms. Master's thesis. University of Washington, Seattle.

Peters, G. B., H. J. Dawson, B. F. Hrutfiord, and R. R. Whitney. 1976. Aqueous leachate from western red cedar: effects on some aquatic organisms. Journal of the Fisheries Research Board of Canada 33:2703–2709.

Petersen, R. C., and K. W. Cummins. 1974. Leaf processing in a woodland stream. Freshwater Biology 4:343–368.

Peterson, G. R. 1966. The relationship of invertebrate drift abundance to the standing crop of benthic organisms in a small stream. Master's thesis. University of British Columbia, Vancouver.

Peterson, N. P. 1982a. Immigration of juvenile coho salmon (*Oncorhynchus kisutch*) into riverine ponds. Canadian Journal of Fisheries and Aquatic Sciences 39:1308–1310.

Peterson, N. P. 1982b. Population characteristics of juvenile coho salmon (*Oncorhynchus kisutch*) overwintering in riverine ponds. Canadian Journal of Fisheries and Aquatic Sciences 39:1303–1307.

Peterson, R. H., P. G. Daye, and J. L. Metcalfe. 1980a. The effects of low pH on hatching of Atlantic salmon eggs. Pages 328–329 *in* Drablos and Tollan (1980).

Peterson, R. H., P. G. Daye, and J. L. Metcalfe. 1980b. Inhibition of Atlantic salmon (*Salmo salar*) hatching at low pH. Canadian Journal of Fisheries and Aquatic Sciences 37:770–774.

Petras, S. F., and L. E. Casida, Jr. 1985. Survival of *Bacillus thuringiensis* spores in soil. Applied and Environmental Microbiology 50:1496–1501.

Petrosky, C. E., and T. B. Holubetz. 1985. Idaho habitat evaluation for offsite mitigation record: annual report FY 1984. U.S. Department of Energy, Bonneville Power Administration, Division of Fish and Wildlife, Portland, Oregon.

Pfankuch, D. J. 1975. Stream reach inventory and channel stability evaluation. U.S. Forest Service, Northern Region, Missoula, Montana.

Phillips, G. R. 1985. Relationship among fish populations, metal concentrations, and stream discharge in the upper Clark Fork River. Pages 57–73 *in* Carlson and Bahls (1985).

Phillips, G. R., and D. R. Buhler. 1978. The relative contributions of methylmercury from food or water to rainbow trout (*Salmo gairdneri*) in a controlled laboratory environment. Transactions of the American Fisheries Society 107:853–861.

Phillips, G. R., and R. W. Gregory. 1980. The accumulation of selected elements (As, Cu, Hg, Pb, Se, Zn) by northern pike (*Esox lucius*) reared in surface coal mine decant water. Proceedings of the Montana Academy of Sciences 39:44–50.

Phillips, G. R., T. E. Lenhart, and R. W. Gregory. 1980. Relation between trophic position and mercury accumulation among fishes from the Tongue River Reservoir, Montana. Environmental Research 22:73–80.

Phillips, R. W. 1964. The influence of gravel size on survival to emergence of coho salmon and steelhead trout. Pages 90–97 *in* Proceedings, 15th Northwest fish culture conference. Oregon State University, Corvallis.

Phillips, R. W. 1971. Effects of sediment on the gravel environment and fish production. Pages 64–74 *in* Krygier and Hall (1971).

Phillips, R. W., and H. J. Campbell. 1961. The embryonic survival of coho salmon and steelhead trout as influenced by some environmental conditions in gravel beds. Pages 60–73 *in* 14th annual report of the Pacific Marine Fisheries Commission, Portland, Oregon.

Phillips, R. W., R. L. Lantz, E. W. Claire, and J. R. Moring. 1975. Some effects of gravel mixtures on emergence of coho salmon and steelhead trout fry. Transactions of the American Fisheries Society 104:461–466.

Phinney, H. K., and C. D. McIntire. 1965. Effect of temperature on metabolism of periphyton communities developed in laboratory streams. Limnology and Oceanography 10:341–344.

Pickering, Q. H., C. Henderson, and A. E. Lemke. 1962. The toxicity of organic phosphorus insecticides to different species of warmwater fishes. Transactions of the American Fisheries Society 91:175–184.

Pimentel, D. 1980. Environmental risks associated with biological controls. Pages 11–24 *in* B. Lundholm and M. Stackerud, editors. Environmental protection and biological forms of control of pest organisms. Ecological Bulletin 31, Statens naturvetenska-pliga forskningsrd, Stockholm, Sweden.

Pinnock, D. E., R. J. Brand, and J. E. Milstead. 1971. The field persistence of *Bacillus thuringiensis* spores. Journal of Invertebrate Pathology 18:405–411.

Pitlick, J. 1981. Organic debris in tributary stream channels of the Redwood Creek basin. Pages 177–190 *in* R. N. Coats, editor. Proceedings, watershed rehabilitation in Redwood National Park and other Pacific coastal areas symposium. John Muir Institute for Environmental Studies, Napa, California.

Platts, W. S. 1974. Geomorphic and aquatic conditions influencing salmonids and stream classification with application to ecosystem classification. U.S. Department of Agriculture, SEAM (Surface Environment and Mining) Program, Billings, Montana.

Platts, W. S. 1975. The effects of livestock grazing in high mountain meadows on aquatic environments, streamside environments, and fisheries. U.S. Forest Service Research Proposal, Intermountain Forest and Range Experiment Station, Boise, Idaho.

Platts, W. S. 1978. Livestock interactions with fish and aquatic environments: problems in evaluation. Transactions of the North American Wildlife and Natural Resources Conference 43:498–504.

Platts, W. S. 1979a. Livestock grazing and riparian-stream ecosystems—an overview. Pages 39–45 *in* Cope (1979).

Platts, W. S. 1979b. Relationships among stream order, fish populations, and aquatic geomorphology in an Idaho river drainage. Fisheries 4(2):5–9.

Platts, W. S. 1981a. Effects of sheep grazing on a riparian-stream environment. U.S. Forest Service Research Note INT-307.

Platts, W. S. 1981b. Impairment, protection and rehabilitation of Pacific salmonid habitats on sheep and cattle ranges. Pages 82–92 *in* Hassler (1981).

Platts, W. S. 1981c. Sheep and cattle grazing strategies on riparian-stream environments. Pages 251–270 *in* Proceedings, wildlife–livestock relationships symposium. University of Idaho, Forest, Wildlife and Range Experiment Station, Moscow.

Platts, W. S. 1983. Vegetation requirements for fisheries habitats. Pages 184–188 *in* S. B. Monsen and N. Shaw, compilers. Managing intermountain rangelands—improvement of range and wildlife habitats. U.S. Forest Service General Technical Report INT-157.

Platts, W. S. 1984. Compatibility of livestock grazing strategies with riparian-stream systems. Pages 67–74 *in* Proceedings, Pacific Northwest range management short course: range watersheds, riparian zones and economics: interrelationships in management and use. Oregon State University, Corvallis.

Platts, W. S. 1989. Compatibility of livestock grazing strategies with fisheries. Pages 103–110 *in* R. E. Gresswell, B. A. Barton, and J. L. Kershner, editors. Practical approaches to riparian resource management. U.S. Bureau of Land Management, Billings, Montana.

Platts, W. S. 1991. Livestock grazing. American Fisheries Society Special Publication 19:389–423.

Platts, W. S., C. Armour, G. D. Booth, M. Bryant, J. L. Bufford, P. Cuplin, S. Jensen, G. W. Lienkaemper, G. W. Minshall, S. B. Monsen, R. L. Nelson, J. R. Sedell, and J. S. Tuhy. 1987. Methods for evaluating riparian habitats with applications to management. U.S. Forest Service General Technical Report INT-221.

Platts, W. S., K. A. Gebhardt, and W. L. Jackson. 1985a. The effects of large storm events on basin-range riparian stream habitats. Pages 30–34 *in* Johnson et al. (1985).

Platts, W. S., S. B. Martin, and E. R. J. Primbs. 1979a. Water quality in an Idaho stream degraded by acid mine waters. U.S. Forest Service General Technical Report INT-67.

Platts, W. S., and M. L. McHenry. 1988. Density and biomass of trout and char in western streams. U.S. Forest Service General Technical Report INT-241.

Platts, W. S., and W. F. Megahan. 1975. Time trends in riverbed sediment composition in salmon and steelhead spawning areas: South Fork Salmon River, Idaho. Transactions of the North American Wildlife and Natural Resources Conference 40:229–239.

Platts, W. S., and R. L. Nelson. 1985a. Impacts of rest-rotation grazing on stream banks in forested watersheds in Idaho. North American Journal of Fisheries Management 5:547–556.

Platts, W. S., and R. L. Nelson. 1985b. Stream habitat and fisheries response to livestock grazing and instream improvement structures, Big Creek, Utah. Journal of Soil and Water Conservation 40:374–379.

Platts, W. S., and R. L. Nelson. 1985c. Streamside and upland vegetation use by cattle. Rangelands 7:5–7.

Platts, W. S., and R. L. Nelson. 1985d. Will the riparian pasture build good streams? Rangelands 7:7–10.

Platts, W. S., and R. L. Nelson. 1986. Effects of livestock grazing on aquatic and riparian environments and fisheries in high mountain meadows: Bear Valley Creek, Valley County, Idaho. Progress report 2: June 1975 through January 1986. U.S. Forest Service, Intermountain Research Station, Forestry Sciences Laboratory, Boise, Idaho.

Platts, W. S., and R. L. Nelson. 1988. Fluctuations in trout populations and their implications for land-use evaluation. North American Journal of Fisheries Management 8:333–345.

Platts, W. S., and R. L. Nelson. 1989. Stream canopy and its relationship to salmonid biomass in the intermountain West. North American Journal of Fisheries Management 9:446–457.

Platts, W. S., R. L. Nelson, O. Casey, and V. Crispin. 1983. Riparian stream habitat conditions on Tabor Creek, Nevada, under grazed and ungrazed conditions. Proceedings of the Annual Conference Western Association of Fish and Wildlife Agencies 63:162–174.

Platts, W. S., and V. E. Penton. 1980. A new freezing technique for sampling salmonid redds. U.S. Forest Service Research Paper INT-248.

Platts, W. S., and J. N. Rinne. 1985. Riparian and stream enhancement management and research in the Rocky Mountains. North American Journal of Fisheries Management 5:115–125.

Platts, W. S., M. A. Shirazi, and D. H. Lewis. 1979b. Sediment particle sizes used by salmon for spawning with methods for evaluation. U.S. Environmental Protection Agency EPA-600/3-79-043, Corvallis, Oregon.

Platts, W. S., R. J. Torquemada, and R. L. Nelson. 1985b. Livestock–fishery interaction studies: Chimney Creek, Nevada. Progress report 3: 1983–1984. U.S. Forest Service, Intermountain Forest and Range Experiment Station, Forestry Sciences Laboratory, Boise, Idaho.

Platts, W. S., and F. J. Wagstaff. 1984. Fencing to control livestock grazing on riparian habitats along streams: is it a viable alternative? North American Journal of Fisheries Management 4:266–272.

Plumb, T. R., L. A. Norris, and M. L. Montgomery. 1977. Persistence of 2,4-D and 2,4,5-T in chaparral soil and vegetation. Bulletin of Environmental Contamination and Toxicology 17:1–8.

Pollard, R. A. 1955. Measuring seepage through salmon spawning gravel. Journal of the Fisheries Research Board of Canada 12:706–741.

Pollock, R. D. 1969. Tehama–Colusa Canal to serve as spawning channel. Progressive Fish-Culturist 31:123–130.

Ponce, S. L. 1974. The biochemical oxygen demand of finely divided logging debris in stream water. Water Resources Research 10:983–988.

Poston, T. M. 1982. Observations on the bioaccumulation potential of thorium and uranium in rainbow trout (*Salmo gairdneri*). Bulletin of Environmental Contamination and Toxicology 28:682–690.

Potter, D. R., J. C. Hendee, and R. N. Clark. 1973. Hunting satisfaction: game, guns, or nature? Transactions of the North American Wildlife and Natural Resources Conference 38:220–229.

Poulin, V. A. 1984. A research approach to solving fish–forestry interactions in relation to mass wasting in the Queen Charlotte Islands. British Columbia Ministry of Forests, Land Management Report 27, Victoria.

Poulin, V. A. In press. Fish–forestry interaction program: summary. Part 1. Extent and severity of mass wasting on the Queen Charlotte Islands and impact on fish habitat and forest sites. British Columbia Ministry of Forests and Lands, Land Management Report 51, Victoria.

Poulin, V. A., and J. C. Scrivener. 1988. An annotated bibliography of the Carnation Creek fish–forestry project—1970 to 1988. Canadian Technical Report of Fisheries and Aquatic Sciences 1640.

Powell, L. H. 1988. Stream channel morphology changes since logging. Pages 16–25 in Chamberlin (1988).

Power, G. 1973. Salmon management—myths and magic. International Atlantic Salmon Foundation Special Publication Series 4:427–439.

Power, G. 1980. The brook charr, Salvelinus fontinalis. Pages 141–203 in Balon (1980a).

Power, G., M. V. Power, R. Dumas, and A. Gordon. 1987. Marine migrations of Atlantic salmon from rivers in Ungava Bay, Quebec. Pages 364–376 in Dadswell et al. (1987).

Powers, P. D., and J. F. Orsborn. 1985. Analysis of barriers to upstream fish migration: an investigation of the physical and biological conditions affecting fish passage success at culverts and waterfalls. U.S. Department of Energy, Bonneville Power Administration, Project 82–14 Final Report (contract DE-A179-82BP36523), Portland, Oregon.

Pratt, K. L. 1984. Habitat use and species interactions of juvenile cutthroat (Salmo clarki lewisi) and bull trout (Salvelinus confluentus) in the upper Flathead River basin. Master's thesis. University of Idaho, Moscow.

Prokopovich, N. P., and K. A. Nitzberg. 1982. Placer mining and salmon spawning in American River Basin, California. Bulletin of the International Association of Engineering Geology 19:67–76.

Ptolemy, R. A. 1986. Assessment of highway construction impacts and fisheries mitigation in the Coquihalla River near Hope, British Columbia: progress in 1985. Manuscript Report, British Columbia Ministry of Transportation and Highways, British Columbia Ministry of Environment and Parks, Victoria.

Quinn, T. P., and K. Fresh. 1984. Homing and straying in chinook salmon (Oncorhynchus tshawytscha) from Cowlitz River Hatchery, Washington. Canadian Journal of Fisheries and Aquatic Sciences 41:1078–1082.

Rabeni, C. F., and J. G. Stanley. 1979. Operational spraying of acephate to suppress spruce budworm has minor effects on stream fishes and invertebrates. Bulletin of Environmental Contamination and Toxicology 23:327–334.

Radtke, H. 1984. Estimating economic impacts associated with recreational and commercial salmon and steelhead fishing. U.S. National Marine Fisheries Service Technical Memorandum NMFS F/NWR-8:270–285.

Radtke, H., C. M. Dewees, and F. J. Smith. 1987. The fishing industry and Pacific coastal communities: understanding the assessment of economic impacts. University of California, Sea Grant Marine Advisory Publication UCSGMAP-87-1, La Jolla.

Rago, P. J., and C. P. Goodyear. 1987. Recruitment mechanisms of striped bass and Atlantic salmon: comparative liabilities of alternative life histories. Pages 402–416 in Dadswell et al. (1987).

Rainville, R. P., S. C. Rainville, and E. L. Lider. 1985. Riparian silvicultural strategies for fish habitat emphasis. Pages 186–196 in Foresters' future: Leaders or followers? Proceedings, 1985 Society of American Foresters national convention, Society of American Foresters, Bethesda, Maryland.

Raleigh, R. F., W. J. Miller, and P. C. Nelson. 1986. Habitat suitability index models and instream flow suitability curves: chinook salmon. U.S. Fish and Wildlife Service Biological Report 82(10.122).

Randall, A., and J. R. Stoll. 1983. Existence value in a total valuation framework. Pages 265–274 in R. D. Rowe and L. G. Chestnut, editors. Managing air quality and scenic resources at national parks and wilderness areas. Westview Press, Boulder, Colorado.

Randall, R. G., M. C. Healey, and J. B. Dempson. 1987. Variability in length of freshwater residence of salmon, trout, and char. Pages 27–41 in Dadswell et al. (1987).

Ranwell, D. S., editor. 1972. Ecology of salt marshes and sand dunes. Chapman and Hall, London.

Ratliff, R. D. 1985. Rehabilitating gravel areas with short-hair sedge sod plugs and fertilizer. U.S. Forest Service Research Note PSW-371.

Ray, B. 1975. Fate of organic arsenicals in soils and plants. International Pest Control 17(1):9–14.

Ray, S. 1978. Bioaccumulation of lead in Atlantic salmon (*Salmo salar*). Bulletin of Environmental Contamination and Toxicology 19:631–636.

Raymond, H. L. 1988. Effects of hydroelectric development and fisheries enhancement on spring and summer chinook salmon and steelhead in the Columbia River basin. North American Journal of Fisheries Management 8:1–24.

Rea, C. C. 1975. The erosion of Siletz Spit, Oregon. Master's thesis. Oregon State University, Corvallis.

Rector, W. G. 1949. From woods to sawmill: transportation problems in logging. Agricultural History 23:239–244.

Rector, W. G. 1953. Log transportation in the Lake States lumber industry 1840–1918. Arthur H. Clark Company, Glendale, California.

Reddin, D. G., and W. M. Shearer. 1987. Sea-surface temperature and distribution of Atlantic salmon in the northwest Atlantic Ocean. Pages 262–275 *in* Dadswell et al. (1987).

Redmond, M. A. 1975. Natural production. International Atlantic Salmon Foundation Special Publications Series 6:134–135.

Reeves, G. H., and F. H. Everest. In press. Stream type as a predictor of habitat conditions and anadromous salmonid populations in western Oregon streams. *In* Proceedings, fish habitat enhancement and evaluation workshop. U.S. Department of Energy, Bonneville Power Administration, Portland, Oregon.

Reeves, G. H., F. H. Everest, and J. D. Hall. 1987. Interactions between the redside shiner (*Richardsonius balteatus*) and the steelhead trout (*Salmo gairdneri*) in western Oregon: the influence of water temperature. Canadian Journal of Fisheries and Aquatic Sciences 44:1603–1613.

Reeves, G. H., F. H. Everest, and T. E. Nickelson. 1989. Identification of physical habitats limiting the production of coho salmon in western Oregon and Washington. U.S. Forest Service General Technical Report PNW-245.

Reeves, G. H., J. D. Hall, T. D. Roelofs, T. L. Hickman, and C. O. Baker. 1991. Rehabilitating and modifying stream habitats. American Fisheries Society Special Publication 19:519–557.

Reeves, G. H., and T. D. Roelofs. 1982. Rehabilitating and enhancing stream habitat: 2. Field applications. U.S. Forest Service General Technical Report PNW-140.

Regan, C. 1911. The freshwater fishes of the British Isles. Methven, London.

Reger, S. J., and N. R. Kevern. 1981. Benthic macroinvertebrate diversity in three Michigan streams. Journal of Freshwater Ecology 1:179–187.

Reid, K. A. 1952. Effects of beaver on trout waters. Maryland Conservationist 29(4):21–23.

Reid, L. M., and T. Dunne. 1984. Sediment production from forest road surfaces. Water Resources Research 20:1753–1761.

Reingold, M. 1968. Water temperature affects the ripening of adult fall chinoook salmon and steelhead. Progressive Fish-Culturist 30:41–42.

Reinhart, K. G., A. R. Eschner, and G. R. Trimble, Jr. 1963. Effect on streamflow of four forest practices in the mountains of West Virginia. U.S. Forest Service Research Paper NE-1.

Reisenbichler, R. R. 1989. Utility of spawner-recruit relations for evaluating the effect of degraded environment on the abundance of chinook salmon, *Oncorhynchus tshawytscha*. Canadian Special Publication of Fisheries and Aquatic Sciences 105:21–32.

Reiser, D. W. 1986. Habitat rehabilitation, Panther Creek, Idaho. Final Report, Project 84-29, prepared by Bechtel National, Inc., for U.S. Department of Energy, Bonneville Power Administration, Portland, Oregon.

Reiser, D. W., and R. T. Peacock. 1985. A technique for assessing upstream fish passage problems at small-scale hydropower developments. Pages 423–432 *in* F. W. Olson, R. G. White, and R. H. Hamre, editors. Symposium on small hydropower and fisheries. American Fisheries Society, Bethesda, Maryland.

Reiser, D. W., and M. Ramey. 1984. Instream flow investigations associated with the U.S. Borax Quartz Hill molybdenum project, Southeast Alaska. Technical Report prepared by Bechtel Civil and Minerals, Inc., for U.S. Borax and Chemical Corp., Los Angeles.

Reiser, D. W., and M. P. Ramey. 1987. Feasibility plan for the enhancement of the Yankee Fork of the Salmon River, Idaho. Final Report prepared by Bechtel National, Inc., for the Shoshone–Bannock Tribes, Fort Hall, Idaho.

Reiser, D. W., M. W. Vitter, and J. Todd. 1982. Re-establishment of fish and aquatic invertebrate populations in a stream severely impacted by acid mine drainage. Proceedings of the Annual Conference Western Association of Fish and Wildlife Agencies 62:555–563.

Reiser, D. W., and T. A. Wesche. 1977. Determination of physical and hydraulic preferences of brown and brook trout in the selection of spawning locations. Wyoming Water Resources Research Institute, Water Resources Series 64, Laramie.

Reiser, D. W., and R. G. White. 1981a. Effects of flow fluctuation and redd dewatering on salmonid embryo development and fry quality. Idaho Water and Energy Resources Research Institute, Research Technical Completion Report, Contract DE-AC79-79BP10848, Moscow.

Reiser, D. W., and R. G. White. 1981b. Incubation of steelhead trout and spring chinook salmon eggs in a moist environment. Progressive Fish-Culturist 43:131–134.

Reiser, D. W., and R. G. White. 1983. Effects of complete redd dewatering on salmonid egg-hatching success and development of juveniles. Transactions of the American Fisheries Society 112:532–540.

Reiser, D. W., and R. G. White. 1988. Effects of two sediment-size classes on steelhead trout and chinook salmon egg incubation and juvenile quality. North American Journal of Fisheries Management 8:432–437.

Renberg, L., O. Svanberg, B.-E. Bengtsson, and G. Sundstrom. 1980. Chlorinated guaiacols and catechols: Bioaccumulation potential in bleaks (*Alburnus alburnus*, Pisces) and reproductive and toxic effects on the harpacticoid *Nitrocra spinipes* (Crustacea). Chemosphere 9:143–150.

Rettig, R. B. 1981. The economics of natural reproduction. Pages 176–194 *in* Salmon-spawning gravel: a renewable resource in the Pacific Northwest? Washington State University, Water Research Center Report 39, Pullman.

Rettig, R. B., and J. J. C. Ginter, editors. 1978. Limited entry as a fishery management tool. University of Washington Press, Seattle.

Rettig, R. B., and B. A. McCarl. 1984. Potential and actual benefits from commercial fishing activities. Pages 199–214 *in* Making economic information more useful for salmon and steelhead production decisions. U.S. National Marine Fisheries Service Technical Memorandum NMFS F/NWR-8.

Reynolds, J. F., M. C. Cwik, and N. E. Kelley. 1978. Reclamation at Anaconda's open pit uranium mine, New Mexico. Reclamation Review 1:9–17.

Rhodes, R. C. 1980. Studies with ^{14}C-labeled hexazinone in water and bluegill sunfish. Journal of Agricultural and Food Chemistry 28:306–310.

Rhodes, R. C., and R. A. Jewell. 1980. Metabolism of ^{14}C-labeled hexazinone in the rat. Journal of Agricultural and Food Chemistry 28:303–306.

Rice, P. M., and G. J. Ray. 1985. Heavy metal deposits along the upper Clark Fork River. Pages 26–45 *in* Carlson and Bahls (1985).

Rice, R. M., J. S. Rothacher, and W. F. Megahan. 1972. Erosional consequences of timber harvesting: an appraisal. Pages 321–329 *in* S. C. Csallany, T. G. McLaughlin, and W. D. Striffler, editors. Proceedings, watersheds in transition symposium. American Water Resources Association, Urbana, Illinois.

Richard, J. B. 1963. Log stream improvement devices and their effects upon the fish population, South Fork Mokelumne River, Calaveras County, California. California

Department of Fish and Game, Inland Fisheries Administrative Report 63–7, Sacramento.

Richards [Richard], J. 1964. You can't build a trout stream. Outdoor California 25(7):3–4.

Richardson, B. Z., and E. E. Farmer. 1982. Changes in sodium adsorption ratios following revegetation of coal mine spoils in southeastern Montana. U.S. Forest Service Research Paper INT-287.

Richardson, B. Z., and E. E. Farmer. 1983. Revegetation of phosphate mined lands in the Intermountain West. Pages 373–389 *in* D. J. Robertson, editor. Proceedings, reclamation and the phosphate industry symposium. Florida Institute of Phosphate Research, Clearwater Beach, Florida.

Richey, J. E., M. A. Perkins, and C. R. Goldman. 1975. Effects of kokanee salmon (*Oncorhynchus nerka*) decomposition on the ecology of a subalpine stream. Journal of the Fisheries Research Board of Canada 32:817–820.

Riddell, B. E., and W. C. Leggett. 1981. Evidence of an adaptive basis for geographic variation in body morphology and time of downstream migration of juvenile Atlantic salmon (*Salmo salar*). Canadian Journal of Fisheries and Aquatic Sciences 38:308–320.

Rieman, B. E., and B. Bowler. 1980. Kokanee trophic ecology and limnology in Pend Oreille Lake. Idaho Department of Fish and Game Fisheries Bulletin 1, Boise.

Rimmer, D. M., U. Paim, and R. L. Saunders. 1984. Changes in the selection of microhabitat by juvenile Atlantic salmon (*Salmo salar*) at the summer–autumn transition in a small river. Canadian Journal of Fisheries and Aquatic Sciences 41:469–475.

Ringler, N. H. 1970. Effects of logging on the spawning bed environment in two Oregon coastal streams. Master's thesis. Oregon State University, Corvallis.

Ringler, N. H., and J. D. Hall. 1975. Effects of logging on water temperature and dissolved oxygen in spawning beds. Transactions of the American Fisheries Society 104:111–121.

Ringler, N. H., and J. D. Hall. 1988. Vertical distribution of sediment and organic debris in coho salmon (*Oncorhynchus kisutch*) redds in three small Oregon streams. Canadian Journal of Fisheries and Aquatic Sciences 45:742–747.

Rinne, J. N. 1988. Grazing effects on stream habitat and fishes: research design considerations. North American Journal of Fisheries Management 8:240–247.

Roback, S. S., and J. W. Richardson. 1969. The effects of acid mine drainage on aquatic insects. Proceedings of the Academy of Natural Sciences of Philadelphia 121:81–107.

Roberts, J. E., R. D. Chisholm, and L. Koblitsky. 1962. Persistence of insecticides in soil and their effects on cotton in Georgia. Journal of Economic Entomology 55:153–155.

Roberts, R. B., technical coordinator. 1976. Pesticide spray application, behavior, and assessment: workshop proceedings. U.S. Forest Service General Technical Report PSW-15.

Roberts, R. G. 1987. Stream channel morphology: major fluvial disturbances in logged watersheds on the Queen Charlotte Islands. British Columbia Ministry of Forests and Lands, Land Management Report 48, Victoria.

Robertson, O. H., M. A. Krupp, S. F. Thomas, C. B. Favour, S. Hane, and B. C. Wexler. 1961. Hyperadrenocorticism in spawning migratory and nonmigratory rainbow trout (*Salmo gairdnerii*); comparison with Pacific salmon (genus *Oncorhynchus*). General and Comparative Endocrinology 1:473–484.

Robinson, E. L. 1975. Arsenic in soil with five annual applications of MSMA. Weed Science 23:341–343.

Robinson-Wilson, E. F., and R. Jackson. 1986. Wildlife and fisheries habitat management notes: relationship between bark loss and log transfer methods at five log transfer facilities in southeast Alaska. U.S. Forest Service, Alaska Region, Administrative Document 157, Juneau.

Rodgers, C. A., and D. L. Stalling. 1972. Dynamics of an ester of 2,4-D in organs of three fish species. Weed Science 20:101–105.

Roggenbuck, J. W., and R. M. Schreyer. 1977. Relations between river trip motives and perception of crowding, management preference, and experience satisfaction. U.S. Forest Service General Technical Report NC-28:359–364.

Rood, K. M. 1984. An aerial photograph inventory of the frequency and yield of mass wasting on the Queen Charlotte Islands, British Columbia. British Columbia Ministry of Forests, Land Management Report 34, Victoria.

Rope, S. K., and F. W. Whicker. 1985. A field study of Ra accumulation in trout with assessment of radiation dose to man. Health Physics 49:247–257.

Roppel, P. 1978. Existing and currently proposed fisheries rehabilitation and enhancement projects in southeast Alaska. Alaska Department of Fish and Game, Fisheries Rehabilitation, Enhancement, and Development Division, Juneau.

Rosgen, D., and B. L. Fittante. 1986. Fish habitat structures—a selection guide using stream classification. Pages 163–179 in Miller et al. (1986).

Rosgen, D. L. 1985. A stream classification system. U.S. Forest Service General Technical Report RM-120:91–95.

Rothacher, J. 1963. Net precipitation under a Douglas-fir forest. Forest Science 9:423–429.

Rothacher, J. 1965. Snow accumulation and melt in strip cuttings on the west slopes of the Oregon Cascades. U.S. Forest Service Research Note PNW-23.

Rothacher, J. 1971. Regimes of streamflow and their modification by logging. Pages 40–54 in Krygier and Hall (1971).

Rothacher, J., C. T. Dyrness, and R. L. Fredriksen. 1967. Hydrologic and related characteristics of three small watersheds in the Oregon Cascades. U.S. Forest Service, Pacific Northwest Forest and Range Experiment Station, Portland, Oregon.

Rothacher, J. S., and T. B. Glazebrook. 1968. Flood damage in the national forests of Region 6. U.S. Forest Service, Pacific Northwest Forest and Range Experiment Station, Portland, Oregon.

Rothacher, J., and W. Lopushinsky. 1974. Soil stability and water yield and quality. U.S. Forest Service General Technical Report PNW-24:D1–D23.

Rothwell, R. L. 1983. Erosion and sediment control at road–stream crossings. Forestry Chronicle 59:62–66.

Rounsefell, G. A. 1958. Anadromy in North American Salmonidae. U.S. Fish and Wildlife Service Fishery Bulletin 58(131):171–185.

Rowe, P. B., and T. M. Hendrix. 1951. Interception of rain and snow by second-growth ponderosa pine. Transactions of the American Geophysical Union 32:903–908.

Rudolfs, W., G. E. Barnes, G. P. Edwards, H. Heukelekian, H. Hurwitz, C. E. Renn, S. Steinberg, and W. F. Vaughn. 1950. Review of literature on toxic materials affecting sewage treatment processes, streams and B.O.D. determinations. Sewage and Industrial Wastes 22:1157–1168.

Rueppel, M. L., B. B. Brightwell, J. Schaefer, and J. T. Marvel. 1977. Metabolism and degradation of glyphosate in soil and water. Journal of Agricultural and Food Chemistry 25:517–528.

Ruggles, C. P. 1966. Depth and velocity as a factor in stream rearing and production of juvenile coho salmon. Canadian Fish Culturist 38:37–53.

Russell-Hunter, W. D. 1970. Aquatic productivity: an introduction to some basic aspects of biological oceanography and limnology. Macmillan Company, London.

Ruth, R. H. 1967. Silvicultural effects of skyline crane and high-lead yarding. Journal of Forestry 65:251–255.

Ruth, R. H., and R. A. Yoder. 1953. Reducing wind damage in the forests of the Oregon Coast Range. U.S. Forest Service Research Paper PNW-7.

Ruttner, F. 1971. Fundamentals of limnology (Translated from German by D. G. Frey and F. E. J. Fry). University of Toronto Press, Toronto, Ontario.

Ryan, P. M. 1986. Lake use by wild anadromous Atlantic salmon, Salmo salar, as an index of subsequent adult abundance. Canadian Journal of Fisheries and Aquatic Sciences 43:2–11.

Sacher, R. M. 1978. Safety of Roundup® in the aquatic environment. Pages 315–322 in Proceedings, 5th symposium on aquatic weeds. European Weed Research Council, Amsterdam.

Saleh, S. M., R. F. Harris, and O. N. Allen. 1970. Fate of *Bacillus thuringiensis* in soil: effect of soil pH and organic amendment. Canadian Journal of Microbiology 16:677–680.

Salo, E. O., and T. W. Cundy, editors. 1987. Streamside management: forestry and fishery interactions. University of Washington, Institute of Forest Resources Contribution 57, Seattle.

Saltzman, W. O. 1964. A report of the stream clearance activities conducted by the Oregon State Game Commission on the Siuslaw River system. Oregon State Game Commission, Portland.

Saltzman, W. O. 1977. Impact of stream-side use on fisheries. American Fisheries Society Special Publication 10:160–163.

Samples, K. C., and R. C. Bishop. 1985. Estimating the value of variations in anglers' success rates: an application of the multiple-site travel cost method. Marine Resource Economics 2:55–57.

Sams, R. E., and L. S. Pearson. 1963. Methods for determining spawning flows for anadromous salmonids. Oregon Fish Commission, Portland.

Sanborn, J. R. 1974. The fate of select pesticides in the aquatic environment. U.S. Environmental Protection Agency, EPA-660/3-74-025.

Sanders, H. O. 1969. Toxicity of pesticides to the crustacean *Gammarus lacustris*. U.S. Bureau of Sport Fisheries and Wildlife Technical Paper 25.

Sanders, H. O. 1970. Toxicities of some herbicides to six species of freshwater crustaceans. Journal of the Water Pollution Control Federation 42 (Part 1):1544–1550.

Sanders, H. O., and O. B. Cope. 1968. The relative toxicities of several pesticides to naiads of three species of stoneflies. Limnology and Oceanography 13:112–126.

Sanders, W. M., III. 1979. Exposure assessment: a key issue in aquatic toxicology. ASTM (American Society for Testing and Materials) Special Technical Publication 667:271–283.

Sartz, R. S., and D. N. Tolsted. 1974. Effect of grazing on runoff from two small watersheds in southwestern Wisconsin. Water Resources Research 10:354–356.

Sartz, R. S., and G. R. Trimble, Jr. 1956. Snow storage and melt in a northern hardwoods forest. Journal of Forestry 54:499–502.

Saunders, J. W., and M. W. Smith. 1962. Physical alteration of stream habitat to improve brook trout production. Transactions of the American Fisheries Society 91:185–188.

Saunders, R. L., and C. B. Schom. 1985. Importance of the variation in life history parameters of Atlantic salmon (*Salmo salar*). Canadian Journal of Fisheries and Aquatic Sciences 42:615–618.

Sautner, J. S., T. Vining, and T. A. Rundquist. 1984. An evaluation of passage conditions for adult salmon in sloughs and side channels of the middle Susitna River. Alaska Department of Fish and Game, Aquatic Habitat and Instream Flow Investigations Report 3, Chapter 6, Juneau.

Sawyer, L. E., and J. M. Crowl. 1968. Planning and engineering design of surface coal mines: land reclamation. Pages 247–266 *in* E. P. Pfleider, editor. Surface mining. American Institute of Mining, Metallurgical, and Petroleum Engineers, Inc., New York.

Scagel, R. F. 1971. Guide to common seaweeds of British Columbia. British Columbia Provincial Museum, Victoria.

Scarnecchia, D. L. 1981. Effects of streamflow and upwelling on yield of wild coho salmon (*Oncorhynchus kisutch*) in Oregon. Canadian Journal of Fisheries and Aquatic Sciences 38:471–475.

Schaffer, W. M., and P. F. Elson. 1975. The adaptive significance of variations in life history among local populations of Atlantic salmon in North America. Ecology 56:577–590.

Schaumburg, F. D. 1973. The influence of log handling on water quality. U.S. Environmental Protection Agency EPA-R2–73–085.

Schaumburg, F. D., and J. Walker. 1973. The influence of benthic bark deposits on the aquatic community and the quality of natural waters: final research report on Water

Resource Research Institute project. U.S. Department of the Interior, Office of Water Resources Research, Washington, D.C.

Schindler, D. W., H. E. Welch, J. Kalff, G. J. Brunskill, and N. Kritch. 1974. Physical and chemical limnology of Char Lake, Cornwallis Island (75°N Lat.). Journal of the Fisheries Research Board of Canada 31:585–607.

Schmal, R., and T. Wesche. 1989. Historical implications of the railroad crosstie industry on current riparian and stream habitat management in the central Rocky Mountains. Page 189 *in* R. E. Gresswell, B. A. Barton, and J. L. Kershner, editors. Practical approaches to riparian resource management. American Fisheries Society, Montana Chapter, Bethesda, Maryland.

Schmidt, J. W., L. Simovic, and E. Shannon. 1981. Natural degradation of gold mining effluents. Environment Canada, Wastewater Technology Centre, Burlington, Ontario.

Schneider, M. J., and T. J. Connors. 1982. Effects of elevated water temperature on the critical swim speeds of yearling rainbow trout, *Salmo gairdneri*. Journal of Thermal Biology 7:227–230.

Schofield, C. L., and J. R. Trojnar. 1980. Aluminum toxicity to brook trout (*Salvelinus fontinalis*) in acidified waters. Pages 341–366 *in* T. Y. Toribara, M. W. Miller, and P. E. Morrow, editors. Polluted rain. Plenum Press, New York.

Schultz, D. P. 1973. Dynamics of a salt of 2,4-dichlorophenoxyacetic acid in fish, water, and hydrosol. Journal of Agricultural and Food Chemistry 21:186–192.

Schultz, D. P., and P. D. Harman. 1974. A review of the literature on the use of 2,4-D in fisheries. U.S. Fish and Wildlife Service FWS-LR-74-18.

Schultz, D. P., and E. W. Whitney. 1974. Monitoring 2,4-D residues at Loxahatchee National Wildlife Refuge. Pesticides Monitoring Journal 7(3–4):146–152.

Schultz, R. D., and R. J. Berg. 1976. Some effects of log dumping on estuaries. U.S. National Marine Fisheries Service, Alaska Region, Environmental Assessment Division, Juneau.

Schumm, S. A. 1973. Geomorphic thresholds and complex response of drainage systems. Pages 299–310 *in* M. Morisawa, editor. Fluvial geomorphology. State University of New York, Binghamton.

Schwab, J. W. 1976. Soil disturbance associated with steep slope logging in the Quesnel highlands, Cariboo Forest District. Bachelor's thesis. University of British Columbia, Vancouver.

Scott, D. 1958. Ecological studies on the Trichoptera of the River Dean, Cheshire. Archiv für Hydrobiologie 54:340–392.

Scott, M. J. 1984. A fishery manager's guide to understanding secondary economic impact of northwest salmon and steelhead. U.S. National Marine Fisheries Service Technical Memorandum NMFS F/NWR-8:243–269.

Scott, W. B., and E. J. Crossman. 1973. Freshwater fishes of Canada. Fisheries Research Board of Canada Bulletin 184.

Scrivener, J. C. 1982. Logging impacts on the concentration patterns of dissolved ions in Carnation Creek, British Columbia. Pages 64–80 *in* Hartman (1982).

Scrivener, J. C. 1988a. Changes in composition of the streambed between 1973 and 1985 and the impacts on salmonids in Carnation Creek. Pages 59–65 *in* Chamberlin (1988).

Scrivener, J. C. 1988b. Changes in concentration of dissolved ions during 16 years at Carnation Creek, British Columbia. Pages 75–80 *in* Chamberlin (1988).

Scrivener, J. C., and B. C. Andersen. 1984. Logging impacts and some mechanisms that determine the size of spring and summer populations of coho salmon fry (*Oncorhynchus kisutch*) in Carnation Creek, British Columbia. Canadian Journal of Fisheries and Aquatic Sciences 41:1097–1105.

Scrivener, J. C., and M. J. Brownlee. 1982. An analysis of Carnation Creek gravel-quality data, 1973 to 1981. Pages 154–176 *in* Hartman (1982).

Scrivener, J. C., and M. J. Brownlee. 1989. Effects of forest harvesting on spawning gravel and incubation survival of chum (*Oncorhynchus keta*) and coho salmon (*O. kisutch*) in Carnation Creek, British Columbia. Canadian Journal of Fisheries and Aquatic Sciences 46:681–696.

Sedell, J. R., P. A. Bisson, and J. A. June. 1980. Ecology and habitat requirements of fish populations in South Fork Hoh River, Olympic National Park. Pages 47–63 *in* Proceedings, 2nd conference on scientific research in national parks. U.S. National Park Service, NPS/ST-80/02/7, 7.

Sedell, J. R., P. A. Bisson, F. J. Swanson, and S. V. Gregory. 1988. What we know about large trees that fall into streams and rivers. U.S. Forest Service General Technical Report PNW-229:47–81.

Sedell, J. R., and C. N. Dahm. 1984. Catastrophic disturbances to stream ecosystems: volcanism and clear-cut logging. Pages 531–539 *in* M. J. Klug and C. A. Reddy, editors. Current perspectives in microbial ecology. Michigan State University, East Lansing, and American Society for Microbiology, Washington, D.C.

Sedell, J. R., F. H. Everest, and D. R. Gibbons. 1989. Streamside vegetation management for aquatic habitat. Pages 115–125 *in* Proceedings, national silvicultural workshop—silviculture for all resources. U. S. Forest Service, Timber Management, Washington, D.C.

Sedell, J. R., F. H. Everest, and F. J. Swanson. 1982. Fish habitat and streamside management: past and present. Pages 41–52 *in* H. C. Black, editor. Proceedings, technical session on effects of forest practices on fish and wildlife production. Society of American Foresters, Washington, D.C.

Sedell, J. R., and J. L. Froggatt. 1984. Importance of streamside forests to large rivers: the isolation of the Willamette River, Oregon, U.S.A., from its floodplain by snagging and streamside forest removal. Internationale Vereinigung für theoretische und angewandte Limnologie Verhandlungen 22:1828–1834.

Sedell, J. R., F. N. Leone, and W. S. Duval. 1991. Water transportation and storage of logs. American Fisheries Society Special Publication 19:325–368.

Sedell, J. R., and K. J. Luchessa. 1982. Using the historical record as an aid to salmonid habitat enhancement. Pages 210–223 *in* Armantrout (1982).

Sedell, J. R., R. J. Naiman, K. W. Cummins, G. W. Minshall, and R. L. Vannote. 1978. Transport of particulate organic material in streams as a function of physical processes. Internationale Vereinigung für theoretische und angewandte Limnologie Verhandlungen 20:1366–1375.

Sedell, J. R., and F. J. Swanson. 1984. Ecological characteristics of streams in old-growth forests of the Pacific Northwest. Pages 9–16 *in* Meehan et al. (1984).

Sedell, J. R., F. J. Swanson, and S. V. Gregory. 1984. Evaluating fish response to woody debris. Pages 222–245 *in* Hassler (1984).

Sedell, J. R., F. J. Triska, J. D. Hall, N. H. Anderson, and J. H. Lyford. 1974. Sources and fates of organic inputs in coniferous forest streams. Pages 57–69 *in* R. H. Waring and R. L. Edmonds, editors. Integrated research in the coniferous forest biome. University of Washington, Coniferous Forest Biome Bulletin 5, Seattle.

Sedell, J. R., F. J. Triska, and N. S. Triska. 1975. The processing of conifer and hardwood leaves in two coniferous forest streams: 1. Weight loss and associated invertebrates. Internationale Vereinigung für theoretische und angewandte Limnologie Verhandlungen 19:1617–1627.

Sedell, J. R., J. E. Yuska, and R. W. Speaker. 1983. Study of westside fisheries in Olympic National Park, Washington. U.S. National Park Service, Final Report CX-9000-0-E-081.

Seelbach, P. W. 1987. Effect of winter severity on steelhead smolt yield in Michigan: an example of the importance of environmental factors in determining smolt yield. Pages 441–450 *in* Dadswell et al. (1987).

Sekulich, P. T. 1980. The carrying capacity of infertile forest streams for rearing juvenile chinook salmon. Doctoral dissertation. University of Idaho, Moscow.

Seppovaara, O., and T. Hattula. 1977. The accumulation of chlorinated constituents from pre-bleaching effluents in a food chain in water. Paperi ja Puu (Paper and Timber) 59:489–494.

Sergeant, M., D. Blazek, J. H. Elder, C. A. Lembi, and D. J. Morre. 1970. The toxicity of 2,4-D and picloram herbicides to fish. Proceedings of the Indiana Academy of Science 80:114–123.

Servizi, J. A., R. W. Gordon, and D. W. Martens. 1968. Toxicity of two chlorinated catechols, possible components of kraft pulp mill bleach waste. International Pacific Salmon Fisheries Commission Progress Report 17.

Settergren, C. D. 1977. Impacts of river recreation use on streambank soils and vegetation—state-of-the-knowledge. U.S. Forest Service General Technical Report NC-28:55–59.

Severson, R. C., and L. P. Gough. 1983. Boron in mine soils and rehabilitation plant species at selected surface coal mines in western United States. Journal of Environmental Quality 12:142–146.

Sharpe, C. F. S. 1960. Landslides and related phenomena: a study of mass-movements of soil and rock. Pageant Books, Paterson, New Jersey.

Shaw, P. A., and J. A. Maga. 1943. The effect of mining silt on yield of fry from salmon spawning beds. California Fish and Game 29:29–41.

Shepherd, B. G., G. F. Hartman, and W. J. Wilson. 1986a. Relationships between stream and intragravel temperatures in coastal drainages, and some implications for fisheries workers. Canadian Journal of Fisheries and Aquatic Sciences 43:1818–1822.

Shepherd, B. G., J. E. Hillaby, and R. J. Hutton. 1986b. Studies on Pacific salmon (*Oncorhynchus* spp.) in phase I of the salmonid enhancement program. Volume 1: Summary. Canadian Technical Report of Fisheries and Aquatic Sciences 1482.

Sheppard, J. D., and J. H. Johnson. 1985. Probability-of-use for depth, velocity, and substrate by subyearling coho salmon and steelhead in Lake Ontario tributary streams. North American Journal of Fisheries Management 5:277–282.

Sheridan, D. 1977. Hard rock mining on the public land. Council of Environmental Quality. U.S. Government Printing Office, Washington, D.C.

Sheridan, W. L. 1962a. Relation of stream temperatures to timing of pink salmon escapements in Southeast Alaska. Pages 87–102 *in* N. J. Wilimovsky, editor. Symposium on pink salmon. H. R. MacMillan Lectures in Fisheries, University of British Columbia, Vancouver.

Sheridan, W. L. 1962b. Waterflow through a salmon spawning riffle in Southeastern Alaska. U.S. Fish and Wildlife Service Special Scientific Report—Fisheries 407.

Sheridan, W. L. 1969. Benefit/cost aspects of salmon habitat improvement in the Alaska Region. U.S. Forest Service, Alaska Region, Juneau.

Sheridan, W. L., and A. M. Bloom. 1975. Effects of canopy removal on temperatures of some small streams in southeast Alaska. U.S. Forest Service, Alaska Region, Juneau.

Sheridan, W. L., and W. J. McNeil. 1968. Some effects of logging on two salmon streams in Alaska. Journal of Forestry 66:128–133.

Sheridan, W. L., M. P. Perensovich, T. Faris, and K. Koski. 1984. Sediment content of streambed gravels in some pink salmon spawning streams in Alaska. Pages 153–165 *in* Meehan et al. (1984).

Shetter, D. S., O. H. Clark, and A. S. Hazzard. 1949. The effects of deflectors in a section of a Michigan trout stream. Transactions of the American Fisheries Society 76:248–278.

Shirazi, M. A., and W. K. Seim. 1981. Stream system evaluation with emphasis on spawning habitat for salmonids. Water Resources Research 17:592–594.

Shirazi, M. A., W. K. Seim, and D. H. Lewis. 1981. Characterization of spawning gravel and stream system evaluation. Pages 227–278 *in* Proceedings, conference on salmon spawning gravel: a renewable resource in the Pacific Northwest? Washington State University, Water Research Center Report 39, Pullman.

Shirvell, C. S., and R. G. Dungey. 1983. Microhabitats chosen by brown trout for feeding and spawning in rivers. Transactions of the American Fisheries Society 112:355–367.

Short, R. A., and P. E. Maslin. 1977. Processing of leaf litter by a stream detritivore: effect on nutrient availability to collectors. Ecology 58:935–938.

Shortreed, K. S., and J. G. Stockner. 1983. Periphyton biomass and species composition in a coastal rainforest stream in British Columbia: effects of environmental changes caused by logging. Canadian Journal of Fisheries and Aquatic Sciences 40:1887–1895.

Shotton, H. 1926. [Letter to District Inspector A. P. Halloday, 15 November 1926.] On file at Pacific Salmon Commission, Vancouver.

Shumway, D. L., and G. G. Chadwick. 1971. Influence of kraft mill effluent on the flavor of salmon flesh. Water Research 5:997–1003.

Shumway, D. L., C. E. Warren, and P. Doudoroff. 1964. Influence of oxygen concentration and water movement on the growth of steelhead trout and coho salmon embryos. Transactions of the American Fisheries Society 93:342–356.

Sibert, J. R. 1978. Review of salinity, biological productivity and other aspects of habitat on the Nanaimo River delta in relation to intertidal log storage. Canada Department of Fisheries and Oceans, Pacific Biological Station, Nanaimo, British Columbia.

Sibert, J. R., and V. J. Harpham. 1979. Effects of intertidal log storage on the meiofauna and interstitial environment of the Nanaimo River delta. Canada Fisheries and Marine Service Technical Report 883.

Sidle, R. C., A. J. Pearce, and C. L. O'Loughlin. 1985. Hillslope stability and land use. Water Resources Monograph Series 11.

Siedelman, D. L., and P. D. Kissner. 1988. The importance of large organic debris for rearing chinook salmon habitat. Pages 26–30 in W. R. Heard, rapporteur. Report of the 1987 Alaska chinook salmon workshop. U.S. National Marine Fisheries Service, Auke Bay Fisheries Laboratory, Auke Bay, Alaska.

Sigler, J. W., T. C. Bjornn, and F. H. Everest. 1984. Effects of chronic turbidity on density and growth of steelheads and coho salmon. Transactions of the American Fisheries Society 113:142–150.

Sigmon, C. 1979. Oxygen consumption in Lepomis machrochirus exposed to 2,4-D or 2,4,5-T. Bulletin of Environmental Contamination and Toxicology 21:826–830.

Silver, S. J., C. E. Warren, and P. Doudoroff. 1963. Dissolved oxygen requirements of developing steelhead trout and chinook salmon embryos at different water velocities. Transactions of the American Fisheries Society 92:327–343.

Simenstad, C. A., K. L. Fresh, and E. O. Salo. 1982. The role of Puget Sound and Washington coastal estuaries in the life history of Pacific salmon: an unappreciated function. Pages 343–364 in V. S. Kennedy, editor. Estuarine comparisons. Academic Press, New York.

Simons, D. B., R. Li, T. J. Ward, and L. Y. Shiao. 1982. Modeling of water and sediment yields from forested drainage basins. Pages 24–38 in Swanson et al. (1982b).

Sinsabaugh, R. L., III, E. F. Benfield, and A. E. Linkins III. 1981. Cellulase activity associated with the decomposition of leaf litter in a woodland stream. Oikos 36:184–190.

Siverts, E., C. Palmer, and K. Walters. 1983. IMPLAN user's guide. U.S. Forest Service, Fort Collins, Colorado.

Skeesick, D. G. 1970. The fall immigration of juvenile coho salmon into a small tributary. Fish Commission of Oregon Research Reports 2(1):90–95.

Slaney, P. A., T. G. Halsey, and H. A. Smith. 1977. Some effects of forest harvesting on salmonid rearing habitat in two streams in the central interior of British Columbia. British Columbia Ministry of Recreation and Conservation, Fish and Wildlife Branch, Fisheries Management Report 71, Victoria.

Slaney, P. A., C. J. Perrin, and B. R. Ward. 1986. Nutrient concentration as a limitation to steelhead smolt production in the Keogh River. Proceedings of the Annual Conference Western Association of Fish and Wildlife Agencies 66:146–158.

Slooff, W., J. A. M. van Oers, and D. de Zwart. 1986. Margins of uncertainty in ecotoxicological hazard assessment. Environmental Toxicology and Chemistry 5:841–852.

Smedley, S. C. 1968. Progress report of joint stream monitoring by the Alaska Department of Fish and Game and the U.S. Forest Service. Pages 48–61 in Logging and salmon: proceedings of a forum. American Institute of Fishery Research Biologists, Juneau, Alaska.

Smedley, S. C., K. E. Durley, C. C. Larson, D. Bishop, W. L. Sheridan, and F. Stephens.

1970. Effects of land use on salmon production. Alaska Department of Fish and Game, Commercial Fisheries Research and Development Act, Completion Report, Projects 5-8-R and 5-19-R, Juneau.

Smith, A. E., R. Grover, G. S. Emmond, and H. C. Korven. 1975. Persistence and movement of atrazine, bromacil, monuron, and simazine in intermittently-filled irrigation ditches. Canadian Journal of Plant Science 55:809–816.

Smith, A. K. 1973. Development and application of spawning velocity and depth criteria for Oregon salmonids. Transactions of the American Fisheries Society 102:312–316.

Smith, B. H. 1980. Not all beaver are bad; or, an ecosystem approach to stream habitat management, with possible software applications. Pages 32–37 in Proceedings, 15th annual meeting, American Fisheries Society, Colorado–Wyoming Chapter, Fort Collins, Colorado.

Smith, C. E., and R. G. Piper. 1975. Lesions associated with chronic exposure to ammonia. Pages 497–514 in W. E. Ribelin and G. Migaki, editors. The pathology of fishes. University of Wisconsin Press, Madison.

Smith, C. L. 1980. Attitudes about the value of steelhead and salmon angling. Transactions of the American Fisheries Society 109:272–281.

Smith, E. J., and J. L. Sykora. 1976. Early developmental effects of lime-neutralized iron hydroxide suspensions on brook trout and coho salmon. Transactions of the American Fisheries Society 105:308–312.

Smith, G. E., and B. G. Isom. 1967. Investigation of effects of large-scale applications of 2,4-D on aquatic fauna and water quality. Pesticide Monitoring Journal 1:16–21.

Smith, H. A., and P. A. Slaney. 1980. Age, growth, survival and habitat of anadromous Dolly Varden (Salvelinus malma) in the Keogh River, British Columbia. British Columbia Ministry of the Environment, Fish and Wildlife Branch, Fisheries Management Report 76, Victoria.

Smith, J. F. 1977. A baseline study of invertebrates and of the environmental impact of intertidal log rafting on Snohomish River delta. University of Washington, Cooperative Fisheries Research Unit, Seattle.

Smith, J. J., and H. W. Li. 1983. Energetic factors influencing foraging tactics of juvenile steelhead trout, Salmo gairdneri. Pages 173–180 in D. L. G. Noakes, D. G. Lindquist, G. S. Helfman, and J. A. Ward, editors. Predators and prey in fishes. Dr. W. Junk, The Hague, Netherlands.

Smith, J. L. 1974. Hydrology of warm snowpacks and their effects upon water delivery—some new concepts. Pages 76–89 in Advanced concepts and techniques in the study of snow and ice resources. National Academy of Sciences, Washington, D.C.

Smith, J. L., and H. G. Halverson. 1969. Hydrology of snow profiles obtained with the profiling snow gage. Pages 41–48 in Proceedings, western snow conference 37th annual meeting. U.S. Department of Agriculture, Soil Conservation Service, Spokane, Washington.

Smith, O. R. 1941. The spawning habits of cutthroat and eastern brook trouts. Journal of Wildlife Management 5:461–471.

Smith, R. B., and E. F. Wass. 1980. Tree growth on skidroads on steep slopes logged after wildfires in central and southeastern British Columbia. Canadian Forestry Service, Pacific Forest Research Centre, Victoria, British Columbia.

Smith, R. E., and D. A. Woolhiser. 1978. Some applications of hydrologic simulation models for design of surface mine topography. Pages 189–196 in R. A. Wright, editor. The reclamation of disturbed arid lands. Proceedings, annual meeting of the American Association for the Advancement of Science. University of New Mexico Press, Albuquerque.

Smith, S. B. 1969. Reproductive isolation in summer and winter races of steelhead trout. Pages 21–38 in Northcote (1969b).

Smoker, W. A. 1955. Effects of streamflow on silver salmon production in western Washington. Doctoral dissertation. University of Washington, Seattle.

Sodergren, A. 1987. Biological effects of effluents from pulp mills—preliminary results from the Swedish Environment–Cellulose Project. Paperi ja Puu (Paper and Timber) 69:422–426.

Sollins, P., K. Cromack, Jr., F. M. McCorison, R. H. Waring, and R. D. Harr. 1981. Changes in nitrogen cycling at an old-growth Douglas-fir site after disturbance. Journal of Environmental Quality 10:37–42.

Solomon, D. J. 1982. Migration and dispersion of juvenile brown and sea trout. Pages 136–145 in Brannon and Salo (1982).

Solomon, H. M. 1978. The teratogenic effects of the insecticides DDT, carbaryl, malathion and parathion on developing medaka eggs (Oryzias latipes). Doctoral dissertation. Dissertation Abstracts International 39:2176B–2177B.

Solomon, H. M., and J. S. Weis. 1979. Abnormal circulatory development in medaka caused by the insecticides carbaryl, malathion and parathion. Teratology 19:51–62.

Solomon, R. 1989. Implementing nonpoint source control: Should BMPs equal standards? U.S. Forest Service General Technical Report SE-50:155–162.

Soniassy, R. N., J. C. Mueller, and C. Walden. 1977. The effects of BKME color and toxic constituents on algal growth. Pulp and Paper Canada 78(8):T179–T184.

Sopper, W. E., and H. W. Lull, editors. 1967. Forest hydrology: proceedings, forest hydrology seminar. Pergamon Press, New York.

Sorenson, D. L., M. M. McCarthy, E. J. Middlebrooks, and D. B. Porcella. 1977. Suspended and dissolved solids effects on freshwater biota. U.S. Environmental Protection Agency, EPA-600/3-77-042.

Sorg, C. F., and J. B. Loomis. 1986. Economic value of Idaho sport fisheries with an update on valuation techniques. North American Journal of Fisheries Management 6:494–503.

Sowden, T. K., and G. Power. 1985. Prediction of rainbow trout embryo survival in relation to groundwater seepage and particle size of spawning substrates. Transactions of the American Fisheries Society 114:804–812.

Spaulding, W. M., Jr., and R. D. Ogden. 1968. Effects of surface mining on the fish and wildlife resources of the United States. U.S. Fish and Wildlife Service, Bureau of Sport Fisheries and Wildlife Resource Publication 68.

Speaker, R., K. Moore, and S. Gregory. 1984. Analysis of the process of retention of organic matter in stream ecosystems. Internationale Vereinigung für theoretische und angewandte Limnologie Verhandlungen 22:1835–1841.

Spehar, R. L., J. T. Fiandt, R. L. Anderson, and D. L. DeFoe. 1980. Comparative toxicity of arsenic compounds and their accumulation in invertebrates and fish. Archives of Environmental Contamination and Toxicology 9:53–63.

Sport Fishing Institute. 1982. Recreational fishing in the National Forest System. Sport Fishing Institute Bulletin 333.

Sprague, J. B. 1964. Lethal concentrations of copper and zinc for young Atlantic salmon. Journal of the Fisheries Research Board of Canada 21:17–26.

Sprague, J. B. 1971. Measurement of pollutant toxicity to fish—3. Sublethal effects and "safe" concentrations. Water Research 5:245–266.

Sprague, J. B., and W. J. Logan. 1979. Separate and joint toxicity to rainbow trout of substances used in drilling fluids for oil exploration. Environmental Pollution 19:269–281.

Sprague, J. B., and B. A. Ramsay. 1965. Lethal levels of mixed copper–zinc solutions for juvenile salmon. Journal of the Fisheries Research Board of Canada 22:425–432.

Sprankle, P., W. F. Meggitt, and D. Penner. 1975a. Adsorption, mobility, and microbial degradation of glyphosate in the soil. Weed Science 23:229–234.

Sprankle, P., W. F. Meggitt, and D. Penner. 1975b. Rapid inactivation of glyphosate in the soil. Weed Science 23:224–228.

Spry, D. J., and C. M. Wood. 1985. Ion flux rates, acid-base status, and blood gases in rainbow trout, Salmo gairdneri, exposed to toxic zinc in natural soft water. Canadian Journal of Fisheries and Aquatic Sciences 42:1332–1341.

Stalnaker, C. B. 1979. The use of habitat structure preferenda for establishing flow regimes necessary for maintenance of fish habitat. Pages 321–337 in J. V. Ward and J. A. Stanford, editors. The ecology of regulated streams. Plenum Press, New York.

Stalnaker, C. B., and J. L. Arnette. 1976a. Basic stream flow measurements and relationships. Pages 16–34 in C. B. Stalnaker and J. L. Arnette, editors. Methodologies for the determination of stream resource flow requirements: an assessment. U.S. Fish and Wildlife Service, Office of Biological Services, Washington, D.C.

Stalnaker, C. B., and J. L. Arnette. 1976b. Methodologies for determining instream flows for fish and other aquatic life. Pages 89–138 in C. B. Stalnaker and J. L. Arnette, editors. Methodologies for the determination of stream resource flow requirements: an assessment. U.S. Fish and Wildlife Service, Office of Biological Services, Washington, D.C.

Stanhope, M. J., and C. D. Levings. 1985. Growth and production of *Eogammarus confervicolus* (Amphipoda: Anisogammaridae) at a log storage site and in areas of undisturbed habitat within the Squamish estuary, British Columbia. Canadian Journal of Fisheries and Aquatic Sciences 42:1733–1740.

Stankey, G. H. 1980. Integrating wildland recreation research into decision making: pitfalls and promises. Pages 43–56 in Applied research for parks and recreation in the 1980's: Proceedings of a symposium. University of Victoria, Victoria, British Columbia.

Stankey, G. H., D. N. Cole, R. C. Lucas, M. E. Petersen, and S. S. Frissell. 1985. The limits of acceptable change (LAC) system for wilderness planning. U.S. Forest Service General Technical Report INT-176.

Stanley, J. G., and J. G. Trial. 1980. Disappearance constants of carbaryl from streams contaminated by forest spraying. Bulletin of Environmental Contamination and Toxicology 25:771–776.

Starnes, L. B. 1983. Effects of surface mining on aquatic resources in North America. Fisheries 8(6):2–4.

Starnes, L. B. 1985. Aquatic community response to techniques utilized to reclaim eastern U.S. coal surface mine-impacted streams. Pages 193–222 in Gore (1985).

Starnes, L. B., J. B. Maddox, and T. G. Zarger. 1978. Effects of remedial reclamation treatments on terrestrial and aquatic ecosystems—a progress report. U.S. Fish and Wildlife Service, FWS/OBS-78/81:276–286.

Starostka, V. J. 1979. Some effects of rest rotation grazing on the aquatic habitat of Sevenmile Creek, Utah. Proceedings of the Bonneville Chapter of the American Fisheries Society 1985:61–73. Utah Division of Wildlife Resources, Salt Lake City, Utah.

Stasko, A. B., R. M. Horrall, A. D. Hasler, and D. Stasko. 1973. Coastal movements of mature Fraser River pink salmon (*Oncorhynchus gorbuscha*) as revealed by ultrasonic tracking. Journal of the Fisheries Research Board of Canada 30: 1309–1316.

Stavinoha, W. B., J. A. Rieger, Jr., L. C. Ryan, and P. W. Smith. 1966. Effects of chronic poisoning by an organophosphorus cholinesterase inhibitor on acetylcholine and norepinephrine content of the brain. Advances in Chemistry Series 60:79–88.

Stay, F. S., A. Katko, K. W. Malueg, M. R. Crouse, S. E. Dominguez, and R. E. Austin. 1979. Effects of forest fertilization with urea on major biological components of small Cascade streams, Oregon. U.S. Environmental Protection Agency EPA-600/3-79-099.

Stein, R. A. 1977. Selective predation, optimal foraging, and the predator–prey interaction between fish and crayfish. Ecology 58:1237–1253.

Steinblums, I. J., H. A. Froehlich, and J. K. Lyons. 1984. Designing stable buffer strips for stream protection. Journal of Forestry 82:49–52.

Stengle, W. B., C. G. Hollis, and W. K. Phillips. 1979. A characterization of effluent suspended solids. TAPPI 62(7):73–75.

Stephens, E. P. 1956. The uprooting of trees: a forest process. Soil Science Society of America Proceedings 20:113–116.

Stevens, D. G., A. V. Nebeker, and R. J. Baker. 1980. Avoidance responses of salmon and trout to air-supersaturated water. Transactions of the American Fisheries Society 109:751–754.

Steward, C. R., and T. C. Bjornn. 1987. The distribution of chinook salmon juveniles in pools at three discharges. Proceedings of the Annual Conference Western Association of Fish and Wildlife Agencies 67:364–374.

Stewart, D. K. R., and S. O. Gaul. 1977. Persistence of 2,4-D, 2,4,5-T and dicamba in a dykeland soil. Bulletin of Environmental Contamination and Toxicology 18:210–218.

Stewart, N. E., R. E. Millemann, and W. P. Breese. 1967. Acute toxicity of the insecticide Sevin and its hydrolytic product 1-naphthol to some marine organisms. Transactions of the American Fisheries Society 96:25–30.

Stewart, P. A. 1970. Physical factors influencing trout density in a small stream. Doctoral dissertation. Colorado State University, Fort Collins.

Stober, Q. J., S. C. Crumley, D. E. Fast, E. S. Killebrew, R. M. Woodin, G. Engman, and G. Tutmark. 1982. Effects of hydroelectric discharge fluctuation on salmon and steelhead in the Skagit River, Washington. Final Report for City of Seattle, Department of Lighting. University of Washington, Fisheries Research Institute, FRI-UM-8218, Seattle.

Stockner, J. G., and D. D. Cliff. 1976. Effects of pulpmill effluent on phytoplankton production in coastal marine waters of British Columbia. Journal of the Fisheries Research Board of Canada 33:2433–2442.

Stockner, J. G., and A. C. Costella. 1976. Marine phytoplankton growth in high concentrations of pulpmill effluent. Journal of the Fisheries Research Board of Canada 33:2758–2765.

Stockner, J. G., and K. R. S. Shortreed. 1976. Autotrophic production in Carnation Creek, a coastal rainforest stream on Vancouver Island, British Columbia. Journal of the Fisheries Research Board of Canada 33:1553–1563.

Stockner, J. G., and K. R. S. Shortreed. 1978. Enhancement of autotrophic production by nutrient addition in a coastal rainforest stream on Vancouver Island. Journal of the Fisheries Research Board of Canada 35:28–34.

Stoddart, L. A., A. D. Smith, and T. W. Box. 1975. Range management, 3rd edition. McGraw-Hill, New York.

Stone, D., T. C. Griffing, and M. C. Knight. 1974. Biological monitoring of the Fraser River near Prince George, B.C. Pulp and Paper Canada 75 (Convention Issue):T110–T116.

Storch, R. L. 1979. Livestock–streamside management programs in eastern Oregon. Pages 56–59 in Cope (1979).

Storey, H. C. 1965. Watershed management research. Pages 55–64 in Who's responsible for water resources research? Oregon State University, Water Resources Research Institute, Corvallis.

Stout, R. J., and W. H. Taft. 1985. Growth patterns of a chironomid shredder on fresh and senescent tag alder leaves in two Michigan streams. Journal of Freshwater Ecology 3:147–153.

Stowell, R., A. Espinosa, T. C. Bjornn, W. S. Platts, D. C. Burns, and J. S. Irving. 1983. Guide for predicting salmonid response to sediment yields in Idaho Batholith watersheds. U.S. Forest Service, Northern Region, Missoula, Montana, and Intermountain Region, Ogden, Utah.

Strahler, A. N. 1957. Quantitative analysis of watershed geomorphology. Transactions of the American Geophysical Union 38:913–920.

Strayer, D., J. S. Glitzenstein, C. G. Jones, J. Kolasa, G. E. Likens, M. J. McDonnell, G. G. Parker, and S. T. A. Pickett. 1986. Long-term ecological studies: an illustrated account of their design, operation, and importance to ecology. Institute for Ecosystem Studies Occasional Publication 2, New York Botanical Garden, Mary Flagler Cary Arboretum, Millbrook.

Streit, B. 1979. Uptake, accumulation, and release of organic pesticides by benthic invertebrates. 2. Reversible accumulation of lindane, paraquat, and 2,4-D from aquous [sic] solution by invertebrates and detritus. Archiv für Hydrobiologie, Supplementband 55(3–4):349–372.

Stuart, T. A. 1953. Spawning migration, reproduction and young stages of the loch trout (S. trutta L.). Scottish Home Department, Freshwater and Salmon Fisheries Research Report 5, Edinburgh.

Stuart, T. A. 1962. The leaping behaviour of salmon and trout at falls and obstructions.

Department of Agriculture and Fisheries for Scotland, Freshwater and Salmon Fisheries Research Report 28, Edinburgh.

Stuehrenberg, L. C. 1975. The effects of granitic sand on the distribution and abundance of salmonids in Idaho streams. Master's thesis. University of Idaho, Moscow.

Stumm, W., and J. S. Morgan. 1970. Aquatic chemistry: an introduction emphasizing chemical equilibria in natural waters. Wiley-Interscience, New York.

Suberkropp, K., G. L. Godshalk, and M. J. Klug. 1976. Changes in the chemical composition of leaves during processing in a woodland stream. Ecology 57:720–727.

Suberkropp, K., M. J. Klug, and K. W. Cummins. 1975. Community processing of leaf litter in woodland streams. Internationale Vereinigung für theoretische und angewandte Limnologie Verhandlungen 19:1653–1658.

Suffling, R., D. W. Smith, and G. Sirons. 1974. Lateral loss of picloram and 2,4-D from a forest podsol during rainstorms. Weed Research 14:301–304.

Sullivan, G. D. 1967. Current research trends in mined-land conservation and utilization. Mining Engineering 19(3):63–67.

Sullivan, K. 1986. Hydraulics and fish habitat in relation to channel morphology. Doctoral dissertation. Johns Hopkins University, Baltimore, Maryland.

Sullivan, K., T. E. Lisle, C. A. Dolloff, G. E. Grant, and L. M. Reid. 1987. Stream channels: the link between forests and fishes. Pages 39–97 in Salo and Cundy (1987).

Summers, R. P. 1983. Trends in riparian vegetation regrowth following timber harvesting in western Oregon watersheds. Master's thesis. Oregon State University, Corvallis.

Summers, V. C., and E. K. Neubauer. 1965. Closing report for the coastal stream improvement and rehabilitation program. Fish Commission of Oregon, Portland.

Surber, E. W., and Q. H. Pickering. 1962. Acute toxicity of endothal, diquat, hyamine, dalapon, and silvex to fish. Progressive Fish-Culturist 24:164–171.

Sutherland-Brown, A. 1968. Geology of the Queen Charlotte Islands, British Columbia. British Columbia Department of Mines and Petroleum Resources, Bulletin 54, Victoria.

Swanson, C. D., and R. W. Bachmann. 1976. A model of algal exports in some Iowa streams. Ecology 57:1076–1080.

Swanson, F. J. 1980. Geomorphology and ecosystems. Pages 159–170 in R. W. Waring, editor. Forests: fresh perspectives from ecosystem analysis. Proceedings, 40th annual biology colloquium. Oregon State University, Corvallis.

Swanson, F. J. 1981. Fire and geomorphic processes. U.S. Forest Service General Technical Report WO-26:401–420.

Swanson, F. J., L. E. Benda, S. H. Duncan, G. E. Grant, W. F. Megahan, L. M. Reid, and R. R. Ziemer. 1987. Mass failures and other processes of sediment production in Pacific Northwest forest landscapes. Pages 9–38 in Salo and Cundy (1987).

Swanson, F. J., M. D. Bryant, G. W. Lienkaemper, and J. R. Sedell. 1984. Organic debris in small streams, Prince of Wales Island, southeast Alaska. U.S. Forest Service General Technical Report PNW-166.

Swanson, F. J., and C. T. Dyrness. 1975. Impact of clear-cutting and road construction on soil erosion by landslides in the western Cascade Range, Oregon. Geology (Boulder) 3:393–396.

Swanson, F. J., S. V. Gregory, J. R. Sedell, and A. G. Campbell. 1982a. Land–water interactions: the riparian zone. US–IBP (International Biological Program) Synthesis Series 14:267–291.

Swanson, F. J., R. J. Janda, T. Dunne, and D. N. Swanston, technical editors. 1982b. Sediment budgets and routing in forested drainage basins. U.S. Forest Service General Technical Report PNW-141.

Swanson, F. J., and G. W. Lienkaemper. 1978. Physical consequences of large organic debris in Pacific Northwest streams. U.S. Forest Service General Technical Report PNW-69.

Swanson, F. J., G. W. Lienkaemper, and J. R. Sedell. 1976. History, physical effects, and management implications of large organic debris in western Oregon streams. U.S. Forest Service General Technical Report PNW-56.

Swanson, F. J., and C. J. Roach. 1987. Administrative report—Mapleton leave area study. U.S. Forest Service, Pacific Northwest Research Station, Portland, Oregon.

Swanson, F. J., M. M. Swanson, and C. Woods. 1977. Inventory of mass erosion in the Mapleton Ranger District, Siuslaw National Forest. Final Report. U.S. Forest Service, Forestry Sciences Laboratory, Corvallis, Oregon.

Swanson, F. J., M. M. Swanson, and C. Woods. 1981. Analysis of debris avalanche erosion in steep forest lands: an example from Mapleton, Oregon, USA. International Association of Hydrological Sciences Publication 132:67–75.

Swanston, D. N. 1967. Debris avalanching in thin soils derived from bedrock. U.S. Forest Service Research Note PNW-64.

Swanston, D. N. 1969. Mass wasting in coastal Alaska. U.S. Forest Service Research Paper PNW-83.

Swanston, D. N. 1970. Mechanics of debris avalanching in shallow till soils of southeast Alaska. U.S. Forest Service Research Paper PNW-103.

Swanston, D. N. 1971. Principal mass movement processes influenced by roadbuilding, logging and fire. Pages 29–40 in Krygier and Hall (1971).

Swanston, D. N. 1974. Slope stability problems associated with timber harvesting in mountainous regions of the western United States. U.S. Forest Service General Technical Report PNW-21.

Swanston, D. N. 1976. Erosion processes and control methods in North America. Pages 251–275 in Proceedings, 16th IUFRO (Internation Union of Forestry Research Organizations) World Congress, Division I. Norwegian Forest Institute, Aas, Norway.

Swanston, D. N. 1991. Natural processes. American Fisheries Society Special Publication 19:139–179.

Swanston, D. N., G. W. Lienkaemper, R. C. Mersereau, and A. B. Levno. 1988. Effects of timber harvesting on progressive hillslope deformation in southwest Oregon. Bulletin of the Association of Engineering Geologists 25:371–381.

Swanston, D. N., W. R. Meehan, and J. A. McNutt. 1977. A quantitative geomorphic approach to predicting productivity of pink and chum salmon streams in southeast Alaska. U.S. Forest Service Research Paper PNW-227.

Swanston, D. N., and F. J. Swanson. 1976. Timber harvesting, mass erosion, and steepland forest geomorphology in the Pacific Northwest. Pages 199–221 in D. R. Coates, editor. Geomorphology and engineering. Dowden, Hutchinson, and Ross, Stroudsburg, Pennsylvania.

Swarts, F. A., W. A. Dunson, and J. E. Wright. 1978. Genetic and environmental factors involved in increased resistance of brook trout to sulfuric acid solutions and mine acid polluted waters. Transactions of the American Fisheries Society 107:651–677.

Sweet, M. 1975. Fish habitat improvement information for the Alaska Region. U.S. Forest Service, Alaska Region, Juneau.

Swift, D. R. 1965. Effect of temperature on mortality and rate of development of the eggs of the Windermere char (Salvelinus alpinus). Journal of the Fisheries Research Board of Canada 22:913–917.

Swift, L. W., Jr. 1986. Filter strip widths for forest roads in the southern Appalachians. Southern Journal of Applied Forestry 10:27–34.

Swingle, H. S. 1947. Experiments on pond fertilization. Alabama Polytechnic Institute, Agricultural Experiment Station Bulletin 264, Auburn.

Symons, P. E. K. 1968. Increase in aggression and in strength of the social hierarchy among juvenile Atlantic salmon deprived of food. Journal of the Fisheries Research Board of Canada 25:2387–2401.

Symons, P. E. K. 1973. Behavior of young Atlantic salmon (Salmo salar) exposed to or force-fed fenitrothion, an organophosphate insecticide. Journal of the Fisheries Research Board of Canada 30:651–655.

Symons, P. E. K. 1977. Dispersal and toxicology of the insecticide fenitrothion: predicting hazards of forest spraying. Residue Reviews 68:1–36.

Szeto, S. Y., H. R. MacCarthy, P. C. Oloffs, and R. F. Shepherd. 1978. Residues in Douglas-fir needles and forest litter following an aerial application of acephate

(Orthene). Journal of Environmental Science and Health Part B, Pesticides, Food Contaminants, and Agricultural Wastes 13(2):87–103.

Tagart, J. V. 1976. Survival from egg deposition to emergence of coho salmon in the Clearwater River, Jefferson County, Washington. Master's thesis. University of Washington, Seattle.

Tagart, J. V. 1984. Coho salmon survival from egg deposition to fry emergence. Pages 173–181 in J. M. Walton and D. B. Houston, editors. Proceedings of the Olympic wild fish conference. Peninsula College and Olympic National Park, Port Angeles, Washington.

Takagi, K., K. V. Aro, A. C. Hartt, and M. D. Dell. 1981. Distribution and origin of pink salmon (Oncorhynchus gorbuscha) in offshore waters of the North Pacific Ocean. International North Pacific Fisheries Commission Bulletin 40.

Tana, J. J. 1988. Sublethal effects of chlorinated phenols and resin acids on rainbow trout (Salmo gairdneri). Water Science and Technology 20(2):77–85.

Tang, J., M. D. Bryant, and E. L. Brannon. 1987. Effect of temperature extremes on the mortality and development rates of coho salmon embryos and alevins. Progressive Fish-Culturist 49:167–174.

Tappel, P. D., and T. C. Bjornn. 1983. A new method of relating size of spawning gravel to salmonid embryo survival. North American Journal of Fisheries Management 3:123–135.

Tarrant, R. F., and J. M. Trappe. 1971. The role of Alnus in improving the forest environment. Pages 335–348 in T. A. Lie and E. G. Mulder, editors. Biological nitrogen fixation in natural and agricultural habitats. Plant and Soil, special volume. Martinus Nijhoff, The Hague, Netherlands.

Tarzwell, C. M. 1935. Progress in lake and stream improvement. Transactions of the American Game Conference 21:119–134.

Tarzwell, C. M. 1937. Experimental evidence on the value of trout stream improvement in Michigan. Transactions of the American Fisheries Society 66:177–187.

Tarzwell, C. M. 1938. An evaluation of the methods and results of stream improvement in the Southwest. Transactions of the North American Wildlife Conference 3:339–364.

Tarzwell, C. M. 1959. The toxicity of some organic insecticides to fishes. Proceedings of the Annual Conference Southeastern Association of Game and Fish Commissioners 12:233–239.

Tarzwell, C. M. 1966. Water quality requirements for aquatic life. Pages 185–197 in Proceedings, national symposium on quality standards for natural waters. University of Michigan, School of Public Health, Continued Education Series 161, Ann Arbor.

Tarzwell, C. M., and C. Henderson. 1960. Toxicity of less common metals to fishes. Industrial Wastes 5:12.

Tautz, A. F., and C. Groot. 1975. Spawning behavior of chum salmon (Oncorhynchus keta) and rainbow trout (Salmo gairdneri). Journal of the Fisheries Research Board of Canada 32:633–642.

Tchernavin, V. 1939. The origin of salmon (Salmo salar): is its ancestry marine or freshwater? Salmon and Trout Magazine 95:120–140.

Terhune, L. D. B. 1958. The Mark VI groundwater standpipe for measuring seepage through salmon spawning gravel. Journal of the Fisheries Research Board of Canada 15:1027–1063.

Thielke, J. 1985. A logistic regression approach for developing suitability-of-use functions for fish habitat. Pages 32–38 in F. W. Olson, R. G. White, and R. H. Hamre, editors. Symposium on small hydropower and fisheries. American Fisheries Society, Bethesda, Maryland.

Thomas, J. W., technical editor. 1979. Wildlife habitats in managed forests of the Blue Mountains of Oregon and Washington. U.S. Forest Service Agriculture Handbook 553. Published in cooperation with the U.S. Bureau of Land Management and the Wildlife Management Institute, Washington, D.C.

Thomas, V. G. 1985. Experimentally determined impacts of a small, suction gold dredge on a Montana stream. North American Journal of Fisheries Management 5:480–488.

Thompson, C. G., and D. W. Scott. 1979. Production and persistence of the nuclear polyhedrosis virus of the Douglas-fir tussock moth in the forest ecosystem. Journal of Invertebrate Pathology 33:57–65.

Thompson, C. G., D. W. Scott, and B. E. Wickman. 1981. Long-term persistence of the nuclear polyhedrosis virus of Douglas-fir tussock moth, *Orgyia pseudotsugata* (Lepidoptera: Lymantriidae), in forest soil. Environmental Entomology 10:254–255.

Thompson, K. 1972. Determining stream flows for fish life. Pages 31–50 *in* Proceedings, instream flow requirements workshop. Pacific Northwest River Basins Commission, Vancouver, Washington.

Thompson, W. F. 1945. Effect of the obstruction at Hell's Gate on the sockeye salmon of the Fraser River. International Pacific Salmon Fisheries Commission Bulletin 1.

Thomson, C. J., and D. D. Huppert. 1987. Results of the Bay Area sportfish economic study (BASES). U.S. National Marine Fisheries Service, Southwest Fisheries Center Technical Memorandum NMFS-SWFC-78, La Jolla, California.

Thornburg, A. A. 1982. Plant materials for use on surface-mined lands in arid and semiarid regions. U.S. Environmental Protection Agency, EPA-600/7-79-134.

Thorpe, J. E., and K. A. Mitchell. 1981. Stocks of Atlantic salmon (*Salmo salar*) in Britain and Ireland: discreteness and current management. Canadian Journal of Fisheries and Aquatic Sciences 38:1576–1590.

Thurber Consultants Ltd. 1983. Debris torrent and flooding hazards, Highway 99, Howe Sound. Report to British Columbia Ministry of Transportation and Highways, Victoria.

Thut, R. N., and E. P. Haydu. 1971. Effects of forest chemicals on aquatic life. Pages 159–171 *in* Krygier and Hall (1971).

Thut, R. N., R. B. Herrmann, and J. N. Fisher. 1980. Monitoring the treated effluent and receiving waters of pulp and paper mills. TAPPI 63(8):43–46.

Tiedemann, A. R. 1973. Stream chemistry following a forest fire and urea fertilization in north-central Washington. U.S. Forest Service Research Note PNW-203.

Tiedemann, A. R., C. E. Conrad, J. H. Dieterich, J. W. Hornbeck, W. F. Megahan, L. A. Viereck, and D. D. Wade. 1979. Effects of fire on water: a state-of-knowledge review. U.S. Forest Service General Technical Report WO-10.

Timberman. 1941. Queen of them all was Virginia City: history of lumbering in western Nevada. The Timberman 42:11–14, 50–62.

Tippets, W. E., and P. B. Moyle. 1978. Epibenthic feeding by rainbow trout (*Salmo gairdneri*) in the McCloud River, California. Journal of Animal Ecology 47:549–559.

Toews, D. A. A., and M. J. Brownlee. 1981. A handbook for fish habitat protection on forest lands in British Columbia. Canada Department of Fisheries and Oceans, Vancouver.

Toews, D. A. A., and D. R. Gluns. 1986. Snow accumulation and ablation on adjacent forested and clearcut sites in southeastern British Columbia. Pages 101–111 *in* Proceedings, western snow conference 54th annual meeting, Spokane, Washington.

Toews, D. A. A., and M. K. Moore. 1982a. The effects of streamside logging on large organic debris in Carnation Creek. British Columbia Ministry of Forests, Land Management Report 11, Victoria.

Toews, D. A. A., and M. K. Moore. 1982b. The effects of three streamside logging treatments on organic debris and channel morphology of Carnation Creek. Pages 129–153 *in* Hartman (1982).

Toews, D. A. A., and D. Wilford. 1978. Watershed management consideration for operational planning on TFL 39 (Block 6A) Graham Island. Canadian Fisheries and Marine Service Manuscript Report 1473.

Tokar, E. M., J. P. Campbell, and R. Tollefson. 1982. Environmental improvement at Port Alice, B.C. Pulp and Paper Canada 83(5):50–53.

Tooby, T. E., J. Lucey, and B. Stott. 1980. The tolerance of grass carp, *Ctenopharyngodon idella* Val., to aquatic herbicides. Journal of Fish Biology 16:591–597.

Torstensson, L., and J. Stark. 1982. Persistence of triclopyr in forest soils. Twenty-third Swedish Weed Conference. Weeds and Weed Control 2:393–399.

Torstensson, N. T. L., and A. Aamisepp. 1977. Detoxification of glyphosate in soil. Weed Research 17:209–212.

Touysinhthiphonexay, K. C. N., and T. W. Gardner. 1984. Threshold response of small streams to surface coal mining, bituminous coal fields, central Pennsylvania. Earth Surface Processes and Landforms 9:43–58.

Townsend, J. E., and R. J. Smith, editors. 1977. Proceedings, Improving fish and wildlife benefits in range management seminar. U.S. Fish and Wildlife Service, FWS/OBS-77/1.

Tracy, H. B., J. Bernhardt, D. Freeman, and B. Purvis. 1977. A report on aquatic monitoring of the 1976 spruce budworm control project in Washington State. Department of Ecology Technical Report DOE-77-3, Olympia.

Trethewey, D. E. C. 1974. A discussion of the impact of the proposed Nanaimo Harbour development on wildlife. Appendix 2 in Environmental assessment of Nanaimo Port alternatives, Delta, B.C. Canada Department of Environment, Wildlife Service, Vancouver.

Trihey, E. W., and D. L. Wegner. 1981. Field data collection procedures for use with the physical habitat simulation system of the instream flow group. U.S. Fish and Wildlife Service, Cooperative Instream Flow Service Group, Fort Collins, Colorado.

Tripp, D. B. 1986. Using large organic debris to restore fish habitat in debris-torrented streams. British Columbia Ministry of Forests and Lands, Land Management Report 47, Victoria.

Tripp, D. B., and V. A. Poulin. 1986a. The effects of logging and mass wasting on salmonid spawning habitat in streams on the Queen Charlotte Islands. British Columbia Ministry of Forests and Lands, Land Management Report 50, Victoria.

Tripp, D. B., and V. A. Poulin. 1986b. The effects of mass wasting on juvenile fish habitats in streams on the Queen Charlotte Islands. British Columbia Ministry of Forests and Lands, Land Management Report 45, Victoria.

Tripp, D. B., and V. A. Poulin. In press. The effects of logging and mass wasting on juvenile salmonid populations in streams on the Queen Charlotte Islands. British Columbia Ministry of Forests and Lands, Land Management Report, Victoria.

Triska, F. J. 1984. Role of wood debris in modifying channel geomorphology and riparian areas of a large lowland river under pristine conditions: a historical case study. Internationale Vereinigung für theoretische und angewandte Limnologie Verhandlungen 22:1876–1892.

Triska, F. J., and J. R. Sedell. 1975. Accumulation and processing of fine organic debris. 14 pages in Logging debris in streams, notes for a workshop. Oregon State University, School of Forestry, Corvallis.

Triska, F. J., J. R. Sedell, and B. Buckley. 1975. The processing of conifer and hardwood leaves in two coniferous forest streams: II. Biochemical and nutrient changes. Internationale Vereinigung für theoretische und angewandte Limnologie Verhandlungen 19:1628–1639.

Triska, F. J., J. R. Sedell, and S. V. Gregory. 1982. Coniferous forest streams. US–IBP (International Biological Program) Synthesis Series 14:292–332.

Troendle, C. A., and R. M. King. 1985. The effect of timber harvest on the Fool Creek watershed, 30 years later. Water Resources Research 21:1915–1922.

Troendle, C. A., and C. F. Leaf. 1980. Pages III.i–III.173 in An approach to water resources evaluation of non-point silvicultural sources (a procedural handbook). U.S. Environmental Protection Agency EPA-600/8-80-012.

Trojnar, J. R. 1977. Egg hatchability and tolerance of brook trout (Salvelinus fontinalis) fry at low pH. Journal of the Fisheries Research Board of Canada 34:574–579.

Tromble, J. M., K. G. Renard, and A. P. Thatcher. 1974. Infiltration for three rangeland soil–vegetation complexes. Journal of Range Management 27:318–321.

Tschaplinski, P. J. 1988. The use of estuaries as rearing habitats by juvenile coho salmon. Pages 123–142 in Chamberlin (1988).

Tschaplinski, P. J., and G. F. Hartman. 1983. Winter distribution of juvenile coho salmon (Oncorhynchus kisutch) before and after logging in Carnation Creek, British

Columbia, and some implications for overwinter survival. Canadian Journal of Fisheries and Aquatic Sciences 40:452–461.

Tsukamoto, Y. 1966. Raindrops under forest canopies and splash erosion. Bulletin of the Experimental Forests, Tokyo University of Agriculture and Technology 5:65–77.

Tu, C. M., and J. R. W. Miles. 1976. Interactions between insecticides and soil microbes. Residue Reviews 64:17–65.

Turoski, V. E., D. L. Woltman, and B. F. Vincent. 1983. Determination of organic priority pollutants in the paper industry by GC/MS. TAPPI 66(4):89–90.

Union Carbide Corporation. 1968. Technical information on Sevin carbaryl insecticide. Union Carbide Corporation Booklet ICG-0449A, Salinas, California.

University of Pittsburgh. 1972. The effects of strip mining upon navigable waters and their tributaries: discussion and selected bibliography. University of Pittsburgh Graduate Center, Public Works Administration, Pittsburgh, Pennsylvania.

Upchurch, R. P., and D. D. Mason. 1962. The influence of soil organic matter on the phytotoxicity of herbicides. Weeds 10:9–14.

U.S. Animal and Plant Health Inspection Service. 1980. Rangeland grasshopper cooperative management program. Final Environmental Impact Statement. USDA, Washington, D.C.

U.S. Army Corps of Engineers. 1937. Survey of the Willamette River. House Document 544, 75th Congress, 3rd session, Washington, D.C.

U.S. Army Corps of Engineers. 1956. Snow hydrology. U.S. Army Corps of Engineers, Portland, Oregon.

U.S. Bureau of Land Management. 1968. Stream preservation and improvement. Section 6760 in Bureau of Land Management manual. USBLM, Washington, D.C.

U.S. Bureau of Land Management. 1974. The effects of livestock grazing on wildlife, watershed, recreation and other resource values in Nevada. USBLM, Washington, D.C.

U.S. Congress. 1892. Report of the examination of Nooksack River, Washington. House Document 32, 52nd Congress, 2nd session, Washington, D.C.

U.S. Department of Agriculture. 1976. Aerial application of agricultural chemicals. USDA Agriculture Handbook 287.

U.S. Department of Agriculture. 1980. Reclamation and revegetation of land areas disturbed by man: an annotated bibliography of agricultural research, 1972–80. Science and Education Administration, bibliographies and literature of agriculture 8. U.S. Government Printing Office, Washington, D.C.

U.S. Environmental Protection Agency. 1971. Water quality criteria data book: volume 3. Effects of chemicals on aquatic life. Prepared by Battelle Columbus Laboratory, Columbus, Ohio for USEPA, Project 18050, EPA-68-01-0007, Washington, D.C.

U.S. Environmental Protection Agency. 1973a. Processes, procedures, and methods to control pollution from mining activities. EPA-430/9-73-011.

U.S. Environmental Protection Agency. 1973b. Water quality criteria 1972. Prepared by National Academy of Sciences–National Academy of Engineering, for USEPA, EPA-R3-73-033. Washington, D.C.

U.S. Environmental Protection Agency. 1975. Methods of quickly vegetating soils of low productivity: construction activities. USEPA, EPA-440-75-006, Washington, D.C.

U.S. Environmental Protection Agency. 1976. Quality criteria for water. USEPA, EPA-440/9-76-023, Washington, D.C.

U.S. Environmental Protection Agency. 1979. Fish kills caused by pollution: Fifteen-year summary, 1961–1975. USEPA, EPA-440/4-78-011, Washington, D.C.

U.S. Environmental Protection Agency. 1980. Appendix B—Guidelines for deriving water quality criteria for the protection of aquatic life and its uses. Federal Register 45(231):79341–79347.

U.S. Environmental Protection Agency. 1982. Hexazinone (3-cyclohexyl-6-dimethyl-amino-1-methyl-1,3,5-triazine-2,4(1H, 3H)-dione). Pesticide Registration Standards. Office of Pesticides and Toxic Substances, Washington, D.C.

U.S. Environmental Protection Agency. 1986. Quality criteria for water. EPA-440/5-86-001.

U.S. Environmental Protection Agency. 1988. Guidance for the reregistration of pesticide products containing *Bacillus thuringiensis* as the active ingredient. USEPA, Environmental Case 0247, Washington, D.C.

U.S. Fish and Wildlife Service. 1982. 1980 national survey of fishing, hunting, and wildlife-associated recreation. USFWS, Washington, D.C.

U.S. Fish and Wildlife Service. 1988. 1985 national survey of fishing, hunting, and wildlife associated recreation. USFWS, Washington, D.C.

U.S. Forest Service. 1952. Fish stream improvement handbook. USFS, Washington, D.C.

U.S. Forest Service. 1958. Timber resources for America's future. USFS, Forest Resource Report 14, Washington, D.C.

U.S. Forest Service. 1977a. Anatomy of a mine from prospect to production. U.S. Forest Service General Technical Report INT-35.

U.S. Forest Service. 1977b. Final environmental statement, addendum to the final 1976 cooperative western spruce budworm pest management plan. USFS, Pacific Northwest Region, Portland, Oregon.

U.S. Forest Service. 1977c. Fish-culvert roadway drainage guide. USFS, Alaska Region, Juneau.

U.S. Forest Service. 1977d. The nation's renewable resources—an assessment, 1975. USFS, Forest Resource Report 21, Washington, D.C.

U.S. Forest Service. 1979. User guide to soils: mining and reclamation in the West. U.S. Forest Service General Technical Report INT-68.

U.S. Forest Service. 1980a. An approach to water resources evaluation of non-point silvicultural sources (a procedural handbook). Prepared for U.S. Environmental Protection Agency, EPA-600/8-80-012, Washington, D.C.

U.S. Forest Service. 1980b. Section 2526.11 *in* Forest Service manual. USFS, Washington, D.C.

U.S. Forest Service. 1980c. User guide to hydrology: mining and reclamation in the West. U.S. Forest Service General Technical Report INT-74.

U.S. Forest Service. 1982. Enhancing a great resource: anadromous fish habitat. USFS, Pacific Northwest Region, Portland, Oregon.

U.S. Forest Service. 1984. Pesticide background statements. Volume 1. Herbicides. USDA Agriculture Handbook 633.

U.S. Forest Service. 1987. Resource pricing and valuation guidelines for the 1990 RPA Program. Report of the Chief's Technical Coordinating Committee on resource values for the 1990 RPA, Washington, D.C.

U.S. National Marine Fisheries Service. 1980. Fishery statistics of the United States, 1976. Statistical Digest 70.

U.S. Office of the Federal Register. 1982. National Forest System land and resource management planning 47(190). Code of Federal Regulations, Title 36, Part 219. U.S. Government Printing Office, Washington D.C.

U.S. Water Resources Council. 1983. Economic and environmental principles and guidelines for water and related land resources implementation studies. U.S. Government Printing Office, Washington, D.C.

Utter, F. M., F. W. Allendorf, and H. O. Hodgins. 1973. Genetic variability and relationships in Pacific salmon and related trout based on protein variations. Systematic Zoology 22:257–270.

Vaala, S. S., and R. B. Mitchell. 1970. Blood oxygen-tension changes in acid-exposed brook trout. Proceedings of the Pennsylvania Academy of Science 44:41–44.

Van Duijn, C. 1967. Diseases of fishes. Charles C. Thomas, Springfield, Illinois.

Van Hyning, J. M. 1973. Factors affecting the abundance of fall chinook salmon in the Columbia River. Fish Commission of Oregon Research Reports 4(1):1–87.

Van Meter, W. P., and C. E. Hardy. 1975. Predicting effects on fish of fire retardants in streams. U.S. Forest Service Research Paper INT-166.

Vannote, R. L. 1969. Detrital consumers in natural systems. Pages 20–23 *in* The stream ecosystem: an American Association for the Advancement of Science symposium. Michigan State University, Institute of Water Research, Technical Report 7, East Lansing.

Vannote, R. L., G. W. Minshall, K. W. Cummins, J. R. Sedell, and C. E. Cushing. 1980. The river continuum concept. Canadian Journal of Fisheries and Aquatic Sciences 37:130–137.

Van Velson, R. 1979. Effects of livestock grazing upon rainbow trout in Otter Creek, Nebraska. Pages 53–55 *in* Cope (1979).

Van Wyhe, G. L., and J. W. Peck. 1968. A limnological survey of Paxson and Summit lakes in interior Alaska. Alaska Department of Fish and Game Informational Leaflet 124, Juneau.

Vaux, W. G. 1962. Interchange of stream and intragravel water in a salmon spawning riffle. U.S. Fish and Wildlife Service Special Scientific Report—Fisheries 405.

Vaux, W. G. 1968. Intragravel flow and interchange of water in a streambed. U.S. Fish and Wildlife Service Fishery Bulletin 66:479–489.

Velsen, F. P. J. 1987. Temperature and incubation in Pacific salmon and rainbow trout: compilation of data on median hatching time, mortality, and embryonic staging. Canadian Data Report of Fisheries and Aquatic Sciences 626.

Verma, T. R., and E. N. Felix. 1977. Reclamation of orphaned mine sites and their effect on the water quality of the Lynx Creek watershed. Pages 49–59 *in* Hydrology and watershed resources in Arizona and the Southwest, Volume 7. Proceedings, 1977 meetings of the Arizona Section of the American Water Resources Association and the Hydrology Section of the Arizona Academy of Science, Las Vegas, Nevada.

Verner, J. 1984. The guild concept applied to management of bird populations. Environmental Management 8:1–14.

Vernier, J-M. 1969. Chronological table of the embryonic development of rainbow trout. Annales d'Embryologie et de Morphogenese 2:495–520.

Vernon, E. H. 1962. Pink salmon populations of the Fraser River system. Pages 53–58 *in* N. J. Wilimovsky, editor. Symposium on pink salmon. H. R. MacMillan Lectures in Fisheries, University of British Columbia, Institute of Fisheries, Vancouver.

Vigers, G. A., and L. Hoos. 1977. Hotham Sound log dumping, sorting and loading operation: literature review on the effects on oysters. Crown Zellerbach, New Westminster, British Columbia.

Vining, T. J., J. S. Blakely, and G. M. Freeman. 1985. An evaluation of the incubation life-phase of chum salmon in the middle Susitna River, Alaska. Alaska Department of Fish and Game Report 5, Anchorage.

Vinot, H., and J. P. Larpent. 1984. Water pollution by uranium ore treatment works. Hydrobiologia 112:125–129.

Vladykov, V. D. 1959. The effects on fisheries of man-made changes in fresh water in the province of Quebec. Canadian Fish Culturist 25:7–12.

Von Endt, D. W., P. C. Kearney, and D. D. Kaufman. 1968. Degradation of monosodium methanearsonic acid by soil microorganisms. Journal of Agricultural and Food Chemistry 16:17–20.

Voss, R. H., J. T. Wearing, R. D. Mortimer, T. Kovacs, and A. Wong. 1980. Chlorinated organics in kraft bleachery effluents. Paperi ja Puu (Paper and Timber) 62:809–814.

Voss, R. H., and M. B. Yunker. 1983. A study of chlorinated phenolics discharged into kraft mill receiving waters. Project report prepared for the Council of Forest Industries by the Pulp and Paper Research Institute of Canada and Dobrocky Seatech Ltd., Vancouver.

Waananen, A. O., D. D. Harris, and R. C. Williams. 1971. Floods of December 1964 and January 1965 in the far Western states: Part 1. Description. U.S. Geological Survey Water-Supply Paper 1866-A.

Waelti, A. E., and D. I. MacLeod. 1971. British Columbia Forest Service log and debris salvage in the Strait of Georgia. British Columbia Forest Service, Victoria.

Wagner, H. H. 1974. Seawater adaptation independent of photoperiod in steelhead trout (*Salmo gairdneri*). Canadian Journal of Zoology 52:805–812.

Wahle, R. J., E. Chaney, and R. E. Pearson. 1981. Areal distribution of marked Columbia River basin spring chinook salmon recovered in fisheries and at parent hatcheries. U.S. National Marine Fisheries Service Marine Fisheries Review 43(12):1–9.

Wahle, R. J., and R. R. Vreeland. 1978. Bioeconomic contribution of Columbia River hatchery fall chinook salmon, 1961 through 1964 broods, to the Pacific salmon fisheries. U.S. National Marine Fisheries Service Fishery Bulletin 76:179–208.

Walden, C. C. 1976. The toxicity of pulp and paper mill effluents and corresponding measurement procedures. Water Research 10:639–664.

Walden, C. C., and T. E. Howard. 1974. Effluent toxicity removal on the West Coast. Pulp and Paper Canada 75(11):88–92.

Walden, C. C., T. E. Howard, and G. C. Froud. 1970. A quantitative assay of the minimum concentrations of kraft mill effluents which affect fish respiration. Water Research 4:61–68.

Walden, C. C., D. J. McLeay, and A. B. McKague. 1986. Cellulose production processes. Pages 1–34 in O. Hutzinger, editor. The handbook of environmental chemistry, volume 3, part D. Springer-Verlag, Berlin.

Waldichuk, M. 1979. Ecological impact of logs. Marine Pollution Bulletin 10:33–34.

Wales, J. H. 1946. Castle Lake investigation. First phase: interrelationships of four species. California Fish and Game 32:109–143.

Walker, C. R. 1964a. Simazine and other s-triazine compounds as aquatic herbicides in fish habitats. Weeds 12:134–139.

Walker, C. R. 1964b. Toxicological effects of herbicides on the fish environment: part 1. Water and Sewage Works 111:113–116.

Walker, W. W. 1978. Insecticide persistence in natural seawater as affected by salinity, temperature, and sterility. U.S. Environmental Protection Agency, EPA-600/3-78-044.

Walkotten, W. J. 1976. An improved technique for freeze sampling streambed sediments. U.S. Forest Service Research Note PNW-281.

Wallace, J. B., and A. C. Benke. 1984. Quantification of wood habitat in subtropical Coastal Plain streams. Canadian Journal of Fisheries and Aquatic Sciences 41:1643–1652.

Wallace, J. B., J. R. Webster, and W. R. Woodall. 1977. The role of filter feeders in flowing waters. Archiv für Hydrobiologie 79:506–532.

Wallis, J. R., and H. W. Anderson. 1965. An application of multivariate analysis to sediment network design. International Association of Scientific Hydrology Publication 67:357–378.

Wallis, P. M. 1981. The uptake of dissolved organic matter in groundwater by stream sediments—a case study. Pages 97–111 in M. A. Lock and D. D. Williams, editors. Perspectives in running water ecology. Plenum Press, New York.

Walsh, G. E., K. M. Duke, and R. B. Foster. 1982. Algae and crustaceans as indicators of bioactivity of industrial wastes. Water Research 16:879–883.

Walsh, R. G. 1986. Recreation economic decisions: comparing benefits and costs. Venture Publishing, State College, Pennsylvania.

Walter, R. A. 1984. A stream ecosystem in an old-growth forest in southeast Alaska. Part 2: structure and dynamics of the periphyton community. Pages 57–69 in Meehan et al. (1984).

Walters, C. 1986. Adaptive management of renewable resources. Macmillan, New York.

Wangaard, D. B., and C. V. Burger. 1983. Effects of various water temperature regimes on the egg and alevin incubation of Susitna River chum and sockeye salmon. U.S. Fish and Wildlife Service, National Fishery Research Center, Anchorage, Alaska.

Ward, B. R., and P. A. Slaney. 1979. Evaluation of instream enhancement structures for the production of juvenile steelhead trout and coho salmon in the Keogh River: progress 1977 and 1978. British Columbia Ministry of the Environment Fisheries Technical Circular 45, Victoria.

Ward, B. R., and P. A. Slaney. 1981. Further evaluation of structures for the improvement of salmonid rearing habitat in coastal streams of British Columbia. Pages 99–108 in Hassler (1981).

Ward, G. M. 1984. Size distribution and lignin content of fine particulate organic matter (FPOM) from microbially processed leaves in an artificial stream. Internationale Vereinigung für theoretische und angewandte Limnologie Verhandlungen 22:1893–1898.

Ward, G. M., and N. G. Aumen. 1986. Woody debris as a source of fine particulate organic matter in coniferous forest stream ecosystems. Canadian Journal of Fisheries and Aquatic Sciences 43:1635–1642.

Ward, G. M., and K. W. Cummins. 1979. Effects of food quality on growth of a stream detritivore, *Paratendipes albimanus* (Meigen) (Diptera: Chironomidae). Ecology 60:57–64.

Warner, K. 1963. Natural spawning success of landlocked salmon, *Salmo salar*. Transactions of the American Fisheries Society 92:161–164.

Warner, K., and O. C. Fenderson. 1962. Effects of DDT spraying for forest insects on Maine trout streams. Journal of Wildlife Management 26:86–93.

Warner, R. E., and K. M. Hendrix, editors. 1984. Proceedings, California riparian systems workshop: ecology, conservation, and productive management. University of California Press, Berkeley.

Warner, R. E., K. K. Peterson, and L. Borgman. 1966. Behavioural pathology in fish: a quantitative study of sublethal pesticide toxication. Journal of Applied Ecology 3 (Supplement):223–247.

Warren, C. E. 1971. Biology and water pollution control. W. B. Saunders Company, Philadelphia.

Warren, C. E., J. H. Wales, G. E. Davis, and P. Doudoroff. 1964. Trout production in an experimental stream enriched with sucrose. Journal of Wildlife Management 28:617–660.

Washington State Department of Ecology. 1975. Grays Harbor fish toxicity studies, 1974. WSDE, Olympia.

Waters, B. F. 1976. A methodology for evaluating the effects of different streamflows on salmonid habitat. Pages 254–266 *in* J. F. Orsborn and C. H. Allman, editors. Instream flow needs, volume 2. American Fisheries Society, Western Division, Bethesda, Maryland.

Waters, T. F. 1961. Standing crop and drift of stream bottom organisms. Ecology 42:532–537.

Waters, T. F. 1969. The turnover ratio in production ecology of freshwater invertebrates. American Naturalist 103:173–185.

Watts, F. J. 1974. Design of culvert fishways. University of Idaho, Water Resources Research Institute Report, Project A-027–IDA, Moscow.

Wauchope, R. D. 1975. Fixation of arsenical herbicides, phosphate, and arsenate in alluvial soils. Journal of Environmental Quality 4:355–358.

Weaver, W., D. Hagans, and M. A. Madej. 1987. Managing forest roads to control cumulative erosion and sedimentation effects. *In* Proceedings, California watershed management conference. University of California, Wildland Resources Center Report 11, Berkeley.

Webb, F. E., and D. R. MacDonald. 1958. Studies of aerial spraying against the spruce budworm in New Brunswick. 10. Surveys of stream-bottom fauna in some sprayed and unsprayed streams, 1955–1957. Canada Department of Agriculture, Forest Biology Laboratory, Interim Report 1957-3, Fredericton, New Brunswick.

Webb, M., H. Ruber, and G. Leduc. 1976. The toxicity of various mining flotation reagents to rainbow trout (*Salmo gairdneri*). Water Research 10:303–306.

Weber, W. J., Jr., and E. Matijevic. 1968. Adsorption from aqueous solutions. Advances in Chemistry Series 79.

Webster, J. R. 1983. The role of benthic macroinvertebrates in detritus dynamics of streams: a computer simulation. Ecological Monographs 53:383–404.

Webster, J. R., and S. W. Golladay. 1984. Seston transport in streams at Coweeta Hydrologic Laboratory, North Carolina, U.S.A. Internationale Vereinigung für theoretische und angewandte Limnologie Verhandlungen 22:1911–1919.

Weed Science Society of America. 1989. Herbicide handbook, 6th edition. Champaign, Illinois.

Wehrhahn, C. F., and R. Powell. 1987. Electrophoretic variation, regional differences, and gene flow in the coho salmon (*Oncorhynchus kisutch*) of southern British Columbia. Canadian Journal of Fisheries and Aquatic Sciences 44:822–831.

Weidner, C. W. 1974. Degradation in groundwater and mobility of herbicides. Master's thesis. University of Nebraska, Lincoln.

Weiler, G., and W. L. Gould. 1983. Establishment of blue grama and fourwing saltbush on coal mine spoils using saline ground water. Journal of Range Management 36:712–717.

Weiner, G. S., C. B. Schreck, and H. W. Li. 1986. Effects of low pH on reproduction of rainbow trout. Transactions of the American Fisheries Society 115:75–82.

Weiss, C. M., and J. H. Gakstatter. 1964. Detection of pesticides in water by biochemical assay. Journal of the Water Pollution Control Federation 36(2):240–253.

Welch, H. E., P. E. K. Symons, and D. W. Narver. 1977. Some effects of potato farming and forest clearcutting on New Brunswick streams. Canada Fisheries and Marine Service Technical Report 745.

Welcomme, R. L. 1985. River fisheries. Food and Agriculture Organization of the United Nations, Fisheries Technical Paper 262, Rome.

Wells, R. A., and W. J. McNeil. 1970. Effect of quality of the spawning bed on growth and development of pink salmon embryos and alevins. U.S. Fish and Wildlife Service Special Scientic Report—Fisheries 616.

Wendler, H. O., and G. Deschamps. 1955. Logging dams on coastal Washington streams. Washington Department of Fisheries, Fisheries Research Papers 1:27–38.

Wesche, T. A. 1973. Parametric determination of minimum stream flow for trout. University of Wyoming, Water Resources Research Institute, Water Resources Series 37, Laramie.

Wesche, T. A. 1974. Relationship of discharge reductions to available trout habitat for recommending suitable streamflows. University of Wyoming, Water Resources Research Institute, Water Resources Series 53, Laramie.

Wesche, T. A. 1976. Development and application of a trout cover rating system for IFN determinations. Pages 224–234 in J. F. Orsborn and C. H. Allman, editors. Instream flow needs, volume 2. American Fisheries Society, Western Division, Bethesda, Maryland.

Wesche, T. A. 1985. Stream channel modifications and reclamation structures to enhance fish habitat. Pages 103–163 in Gore (1985).

Wesche, T. A., C. M. Goertler, and C. B. Frye. 1985. Importance and valuation of instream and riparian cover in smaller trout streams. Pages 325–328 in Johnson et al. (1985).

Wesche, T. A., C. M. Goertler, and C. B. Frye. 1987. Contribution of riparian vegetation to trout cover in small streams. North American Journal of Fisheries Management 7:151–153.

Wesche, T. A., and P. A. Rechard. 1980. A summary of instream flow methods for fisheries and related research needs. University of Wyoming, Water Resources Research Institute, Eisenhower Consortium Bulletin 9, Laramie.

West Coast Lumberman. 1914. Characteristics and utilization of western red cedar. West Coast Lumberman (February 1) 25(296):34–40.

West, D. C., J. A. Reeher, and J. A. Hewkin. 1965a. Habitat improvement to enhance anadromous fish production. Oregon State Game Commission, Columbia River Fisheries Development Program Closing Report, Clear Creek Project 11, Portland.

West, D. C., J. A. Reeher, and J. A. Hewkin. 1965b. Habitat improvement to enhance anadromous fish production. Oregon State Game Commission, Columbia River Fisheries Development Program Closing Report, Tex Creek Project 10, Portland.

West, J. R. 1984. Enhancement of salmon and steelhead spawning and rearing conditions in the Scott and Salmon rivers, California. Pages 117–127 in Hassler (1984).

Westin, D. T. 1974. Nitrate and nitrite toxicity to salmonid fishes. Progressive Fish-Culturist 36:86–89.

Westlake, D. F. 1975. Macrophytes. Pages 106–128 in Whitton (1975).

Wetzel, R. G. 1975. Primary production. Pages 230–247 in Whitton (1975).

Wetzel, R. G., and B. A. Manny. 1972. Decomposition of dissolved organic carbon and nitrogen compounds from leaves in an experimental hard-water stream. Limnology and Oceanography 17:927–931.

Whicker, F. W., and V. Schultz. 1982. Radioecology: nuclear energy and the environment. CRC Press, Boca Raton, Florida.

White, H. C. 1957. Food and natural history of mergansers on salmon waters in the maritime provinces of Canada. Fisheries Research Board of Canada Bulletin 116.

White, R. G. 1976. Predicted effects of water withdrawal on the fish populations of the Teton River, Idaho. Completion Report to U.S. Bureau of Reclamation. University of Idaho, Forest, Wildlife and Range Experiment Station Contribution 63, Moscow.

White, R. G., J. H. Milligan, A. E. Bingham, R. A. Ruediger, T. S. Vogel, and D. H. Bennett. 1981. Effects of reduced stream discharge on fish and aquatic macroinvertebrate populations. University of Idaho, Water and Energy Resources Research Institute, Research Technical Completion Report, Project B-045-IDA, Moscow.

White, R. J. 1972. Responses of trout populations to habitat change in Big Roche-a-Cri Creek, Wisconsin. Doctoral dissertation. University of Wisconsin, Madison.

White, R. J. 1975a. In-stream management for wild trout. Pages 48–58 in W. King, editor. Proceedings, wild trout management symposium. Trout Unlimited, Vienna, Virginia.

White, R. J. 1975b. Trout population responses to streamflow fluctuation and habitat management in Big Roche-a-Cri Creek, Wisconsin. Internationale Vereinigung für theoretische und angewandte Limnologie Verhandlungen 19:2469–2477.

White, R. J., and O. M. Brynildson. 1967. Guidelines for management of trout stream habitat in Wisconsin. Wisconsin Department of Natural Resources Technical Bulletin 39, Madison.

Whitman, R. P., T. P. Quinn, and E. L. Brannon. 1982. Influence of suspended volcanic ash on homing behavior of adult chinook salmon. Transactions of the American Fisheries Society 111:63–69.

Whitmore, A. J. 1955. Brief on behalf of the Canada Department of Fisheries, presented 28 September by the Chief Supervisor of Fisheries, Pacific Area, regarding certain aspects of the fisheries of British Columbia in relation to the forest resources. Submitted to the Honourable Gordon McG. Sloan, Commissioner, Canada Department of Fisheries, Vancouver.

Whitmore, C. M., C. E. Warren, and P. Doudoroff. 1960. Avoidance reactions of salmonid and centrarchid fishes to low oxygen concentrations. Transactions of the American Fisheries Society 89:17–26.

Whitney, A. N., and J. E. Bailey. 1959. Detrimental effects of highway construction on a Montana stream. Transactions of the American Fisheries Society 88:72–73.

Whittle, D. M., and K. W. Flood. 1977. Assessment of the acute toxicity, growth impairment, and flesh tainting potential of a bleached kraft mill effluent on rainbow trout (Salmo gairdneri). Journal of the Fisheries Research Board of Canada 34:869–878.

Whitton, B. A., editor. 1975. River ecology. University of California Press, Berkeley.

Wickett, W. P. 1954. The oxygen supply to salmon eggs in spawning beds. Journal of the Fisheries Research Board of Canada 11:933–953.

Wickett, W. P. 1958. Review of certain environmental factors affecting the production of pink and chum salmon. Journal of the Fisheries Research Board of Canada 15:1103–1126.

Wickett, W. P. 1962. Environmental variability and reproduction potentials of pink salmon in British Columbia. Pages 73–86 in N. J. Wilimovsky, editor. Symposium on pink salmon. H. R. MacMillan Lectures in Fisheries, University of British Columbia, Institute of Fisheries, Vancouver.

Wilbur, R. L., and E. W. Whitney. 1973. Toxicity of the herbicide Kuron (silvex) to bluegill eggs and fry. Transactions of the Americian Fisheries Society 102:630–633.

Wildish, D. J., W. G. Carson, T. Cunningham, and N. J. Lister. 1971. Toxicological effects of some organophosphate insecticides to Atlantic salmon. Fisheries Research Board of Canada Manuscript Report 1157.

Willard, H. K. 1983. Toxicity production of pulp and paper mill waste water. U.S. Environmental Protection Agency Contract 68–03–3-28.

Willcox, H., III. 1972. Environmental impact study of aerially applied Sevin-4-oil on a forest and aquatic ecosystem. State University of New York, Lake Ontario Environmental Laboratory Progress Report, Oswego, New York.

William, R. D., L. C. Burrill, R. Parker, D. G. Swan, S. W. Howard, and D. W. Kidder, compilers. 1987. Pacific Northwest weed control handbook. Oregon State University, Corvallis.

Williams, A. K., and C. R. Sova. 1966. Acetylcholinesterase levels in brains of fishes from polluted waters. Bulletin of Environmental Contamination and Toxicology 1:198–204.

Williams, D. D. 1981. The first diets of postemergent brook trout (*Salvelinus fontinalis*) and Atlantic salmon (*Salmo salar*) alevins in a Quebec river. Canadian Journal of Fisheries and Aquatic Sciences 38:765–771.

Wilmoth, R. C. 1977. Limestone and lime neutralization of ferrous iron acid mine drainage. U.S. Environmental Protection Agency Technology Series EPA-600/2-77-101, Industrial Environmental Research Laboratory, Cincinnati, Ohio.

Wilson, D., B. Finlayson, and N. Morgan. 1981. Copper, zinc, and cadmium concentrations of resident trout related to acid-mine wastes. California Fish and Game 67:176–186.

Wilson, D. A. 1976. Salmonid spawning habitat improvement study. Washington State Department of Fisheries, Project Completion Report, Project 1-93-D, Olympia.

Wilson, R. C. H. 1972. Prediction of copper toxicity in receiving waters. Journal of the Fisheries Research Board of Canada 29:1500–1502.

Wilson, W. J. 1984. Pink and chum salmon spawning, egg incubation, and outmigration from two streams on Kodiak Island, Alaska. Pages 26–35 *in* K. L. Fresh and S. L. Schroder, rapporteurs. Proceedings of the 1983 Northeast Pacific pink and chum salmon workshop. Washington State Department of Fisheries, Olympia.

Wilzbach, M. A. 1985. Relative roles of food abundance and cover in determining the habitat distribution of stream-dwelling cutthroat trout (*Salmo clarki*). Canadian Journal of Fisheries and Aquatic Sciences 42:1668–1672.

Wilzbach, M. A., K. W. Cummins, and J. D. Hall. 1986. Influence of habitat manipulations on interactions between cutthroat trout and invertebrate drift. Ecology 67:898–911.

Winegar, H. 1978. Fencing. Page 9 *in* Proceedings, fish habitat improvement workshop, Ochoco Ranger Station. Oregon Department of Fish and Wildlife, Portland.

Winegar, H. H. 1977. Camp Creek channel fencing—plant, wildlife, soil, and water response. Rangeman's Journal 4(1):10–12.

Winget, R., and M. Reichert. 1976. Aquatic survey of selected streams with critical habitats on NRL affected by livestock and recreation. U.S. Bureau of Land Management, Utah State Office, Salt Lake City.

Wise, L. E. 1959. The chemical nature and importance of extraneous components of wood. Forest Products Journal 7:124–127.

Witzel, L. D., and H. R. MacCrimmon. 1981. Role of gravel substrate on ova survival and alevin emergence of rainbow trout, *Salmo gairdneri*. Canadian Journal of Zoology 59:629–636.

Witzel, L. D., and H. R. MacCrimmon. 1983. Redd-site selection by brook trout and brown trout in southwestern Ontario streams. Transactions of the American Fisheries Society 112:760–771.

Woelke, C. E., T. Schink, and E. Sanborn. 1972. Effect of biological treatment on the toxicity of three types of pulping wastes to Pacific oyster embryos. U.S. Environmental Protection Agency Contract 68-01-377, Washington Department of Fisheries, Olympia.

Wolfe, M. D. 1982. The relationship between forest management and landsliding in the Klamath Mountains of northwestern California. Earth Resources Monograph 11. U.S. Forest Service, Pacific Southwest Region, San Francisco.

Wood, C. C., B. E. Riddell, and D. T. Rutherford. 1987. Alternative juvenile life histories of sockeye salmon (*Oncorhynchus nerka*) and their contribution to production in the Stikine River, northern British Columbia. Canadian Special Publication of Fisheries and Aquatic Sciences 96:12–24.

Woodmansee, W. C. 1975. Uranium. Pages 1177–1200 *in* A. W. Knoerr, editor. Mineral facts and problems. U.S. Bureau of Mines, Washington, D.C.

Woodward, D. F. 1976. Toxicity of the herbicides dinoseb and picloram to cutthroat (*Salmo clarki*) and lake trout (*Salvelinus namaycush*). Journal of the Fisheries Research Board of Canada 33:1671–1676.

Woodward, D. F., and W. L. Mauck. 1980. Toxicity of five forest insecticides to cutthroat trout and two species of aquatic invertebrates. Bulletin of Environmental Contamination and Toxicology 25:846–853.

Woodward, D. F., and F. L. Mayer, Jr. 1978. Toxicity of three herbicides (butyl, isooctyl, and propylene glycol butyl ether esters of 2,4-D) to cutthroat trout and lake trout. U.S. Fish and Wildlife Service Technical Paper 97.

Wooldridge, D. D. 1960. Watershed disturbance from tractor and skyline crane logging. Journal of Forestry 58:369–372.

Woolson, E. A., A. R. Isensee, and P. C. Kearney. 1976. Distribution and isolation of radioactivity from ^{74}As-arsenate and ^{14}C-methanearsonic acid in an aquatic model ecosystem. Pesticide Biochemistry and Physiology 6:261–269.

Yamamoto, T. 1982. A review of uranium spoil and mill tailings revegetation in the western United States. U.S. Forest Service General Technical Report RM-92.

Young, S. A. 1983. The importance of riparian vegetation communities in Colorado, Montana, Wyoming and North Dakota. Pages 1087–1164 *in* D. Books, technical editor. Coal development: collected papers, volume 2. Papers presented at coal development workshops in Grand Junction, Colorado, and Casper, Wyoming. U.S. Bureau of Land Management, Washington, D.C.

Young, S. A., W. P. Kovalak, and K. A. Del Signore. 1978. Distances travelled by autumn-shed leaves introduced into a woodland stream. American Midland Naturalist 100:217–222.

Young, S. R., S. W. Vincent, and W. G. Hines. 1981. The impact of pulp and paper effluents on the water quality of the lower Columbia River: a case study. Pages 245–260 *in* Proceedings, 1981 environmental conference. TAPPI (Technical Association of the Pulp and Paper Industry) Press, Atlanta.

Zanella, E., J. Conkey, and M. Tesmer. 1978. Nonsettleable solids—characteristics and use by two aquatic food chain organisms. TAPPI 61(10):61–65.

Zanella, E. F., and J. R. Weber, Jr. 1981. Monitoring the ecological impact of kraft mill effluents on the Sacramento River. Pages 1–7 *in* Proceedings, TAPPI (Technical Association of the Pulp and Paper Industry) environmental conference. Institute of Paper Chemistry, Appleton, Wisconsin.

Zegers, P. 1978. The effects of log raft grounding on the benthic invertebrates of the Coos estuary. Oregon Department of Environmental Quality, Portland.

Ziemer, G. L. 1962. Steeppass fishway development. Alaska Department of Fish and Game Informational Leaflet 12, Juneau.

Ziemer, G. L. 1965. Steeppass fishway development. Alaska Department of Fish and Game Informational Leaflet 12 (addenda), Juneau.

Ziemer, G. L. 1973. Quantitative geomorphology of drainage basins related to fish production. Alaska Department of Fish and Game Informational Leaflet 162, Juneau.

Ziemer, R. R., and D. N. Swanston. 1977. Root strength changes after logging in southeast Alaska. U.S. Forest Service Research Note PNW-306.

Zitko, V., and W. G. Carson. 1977. Seasonal and developmental variation in the lethality of zinc to juvenile Atlantic salmon (*Salmo salar*). Journal of the Fisheries Research Board of Canada 34:139–141.

Glossary

Abandoned mine (also orphan mine): Mine that has been deserted and in which further operations are not intended.

Ablation: Disappearance of snow and ice by melting and evaporation.

Absorption: The taking up, assimilation, or incorporation of molecules, ions, or energy into the interior of a solid or liquid. (Compare *adsorption*.)

Acidification (of mine spoils): Oxidation of reduced minerals in mine waste or surfaces of mine shafts by atmospheric oxygen and water to form acids (e.g., formation of sulfuric acid [H_2SO_4] from pyrite [iron sulfide, FeS_2] that is exposed to oxygen and water).

Acid waste: Overburden or mine spoil that has high acidification potential. (See *acidification*.)

Acute toxicity: Toxic or poisonous effect that occurs during or soon after exposure to a toxicant. The term usually refers to a lethal effect (death) or to a major sublethal effect such as greatly altered behavior or physiology. Formal acute toxicity tests establish the concentration of a substance that kills a specified fraction of the test organisms (usually 50%) within a specified time (usually 96 h or less). (Compare *chronic toxicity*.)

Adfluvial: Migrating between lakes and rivers or streams. (Compare *fluvial*.)

Adit mine: Underground mine with horizontal entry tunnels (also called "drift mine" when coal is the target).

Adsorption: Physical adhesion of molecules of gases, liquids, or dissolved substances to the surfaces of solids or liquids with which they are in contact. (Compare *absorption*.)

Aerobic: Living, growing, or occurring only where free oxygen is present. (Compare *anaerobic*.)

Age-class: A group of individuals of a species that have the same age.

Aggradation: Deposition in one place of material eroded from another. Aggradation raises the elevation of streambeds, flood plains, and the bottoms of other water bodies. (Compare *degradation*.)

Alaskan steeppass: Improved Denil fishway for use at remote sites. It consists of aluminum sections light enough to be transported by trail or by air and assembled at the project site. (See *Denil fishway*.)

Alevin (also sac fry or yolk-sac fry): Larval salmonid that has hatched but has not fully absorbed its yolk sac, and generally has not yet emerged from the spawning gravel. Absorption of the yolk sac, the alevin's initial energy source, occurs as the larva develops its mouth, digestive tract, and excretory organs and otherwise prepares to feed on natural prey.

Alkalinity: Measure of the power of a solution to neutralize hydrogen ions (H^+), usually expressed as the equivalent concentration (mg/L) of calcium carbonate ($CaCO_3$).

Influences of Forest and Rangeland Management on Salmonid Fishes and Their Habitats
American Fisheries Society Special Publication 19:709–732, 1991

Allochthonous: Derived from outside a system, such as leaves of terrestrial plants that fall into a stream. (Compare *autochthonous*.)

Allopatric: Not co-occurring in the same area. (Compare *sympatric*.)

All-or-nothing value: Value of having an existing resource or commodity versus not having it at all; total economic value of a good; total consumer's willingness to pay for a good.

Allotment (grazing): Area designated for the use of a prescribed number and kind of livestock under one plan of grazing management.

Alluvial: Deposited by running water.

Alluvium: Material deposited by running water, including the sediments laid down in riverbeds, flood plains, lakes, and estuaries.

Amphidromous: Moving from fresh water to the sea, or vice versa, for nonreproductive purposes such as feeding.

Anadromous: Moving from the sea to fresh water for reproduction.

Anaerobic: Living, growing, or occurring in the absence of free oxygen. (Compare *aerobic*.)

Anchor ice: Ice formed below the surface of a stream—on the streambed or some other surface—when the rest of the water is not frozen.

Animal-unit month (AUM): Amount of feed or forage required by one animal-unit grazing on a pasture for 1 month. An animal-unit is one mature (454-kg) cow or the equivalent of other animals, based on an average daily forage consumption of 12 kg dry matter. An AUM is also defined as the 1-month tenure of one animal-unit.

Annulus: Yearly mark formed on the hard parts (scales, bones, otoliths) of fish, corresponding to a period of slow growth.

Antagonism (chemical): Interaction of chemicals in a mixture to produce a lesser toxic effect than would be expected from the sum of the toxicities of the individual chemicals. (Compare *synergism*.)

Aquifer: A saturated permeable material (often sand, gravel, sandstone, or limestone) that contains or carries groundwater.

Area mining: Technique of mining large areas with alternating series of open pits paralleled by waste piles.

Armoring: Forming an armor layer.

Armor layer: Erosion-resistant layer of relatively large particles on the surface of a streambed. Such layers typically result from removal of finer particles by erosion.

Aufwuchs: Complex assemblage of plants and animals living on the surface of a submerged mineral or organic substrate. It includes diatoms, blue-green algae, protozoa, rotifers, and nematodes.

Auger mining: Drilling horizontally into a deposit.

Autecology: Ecological study of a single organism or a single species.

Autochthonous: Derived from within a system, such as organic matter in a stream resulting from photosynthesis by aquatic plants. (Compare *allochthonous*.)

Autotrophic: Making its own food by photosynthesis or requiring only inorganic chemicals for metabolic synthesis.

Background level: Concentration of an element or compound intrinsic to a system. Perturbations due to mining, pesticide application, or other land-use practices must be detected and measured against background levels.

Backwater pool: Pool formed by an eddy along a channel margin downstream from an obstruction such as a bar, rootwad, or boulder, or by back-flooding upstream from an obstruction; sometimes separated from the channel by sand or gravel bars. Also, a body of water whose stage is controlled by some downstream channel feature, or a cove or flooded depression with access to the main stream.

Balanced earthwork: Earth-moving construction in which cuts and fills have the same magnitude, all excavated material becoming fill.

Bankfull width: Channel width between the tops of the most pronounced banks on either side of a stream reach.

Bar: Ridge-like accumulation of sand, gravel, or other alluvium formed in the channel, along the banks, or at the mouth of a stream where a decrease in water velocity induces deposition. Also, a structure (of alluvium, bedrock, or other material) that obstructs flow and induces deposition.

Barker: Large, mechanically rotated drum in which logs are tumbled to remove bark by abrasion.

Base flow: Portion of stream discharge derived from such natural storage sources as groundwater, large lakes, and swamps situated outside the area of net rainfall that creates local surface runoff; the sustained discharge that does not result from direct runoff or from stream regulation, water diversion, or other human activities.

Basin: See *drainage area*.

Bedform roughness (also bed roughness): Measure of the irregularity of stream-bed materials that contributes resistance to streamflow. Commonly represented by Manning's roughness coefficient.

Bed load: Sediment moving on or near the streambed.

Bed-load sediment: That part of a stream's total sediment load moved along the bottom by running water. (Compare *suspended sediment*.)

Bed roughness: See *bedform roughness*.

Behavior (of a chemical): Movement, persistence, and fate of a chemical in the environment.

Benefit–cost analysis: A project evaluation in which all economic benefits and costs accruing from a project are displayed. Benefits include those of market activities (sale of fish, employment of fishing guides) and of nonmarket values (recreation and existence values). Costs include direct costs associated with purchase of inputs (fuel, plant construction, wages paid, etc.) and opportunity costs associated with loss of alternative uses of scarce resources (e.g., loss of some recreation in logged forests).

Benthos: Animals and plants living on or within the substrate of a water body (freshwater, estuarine, or marine).

Bioaccumulation: Process by which organisms take up and accumulate environmental chemicals directly from their medium or indirectly via their food.

Bioaccumulation factor: Concentration of a chemical in tissue divided by its concentration in the diet.

Bioassay: Use of organisms to assess water quality, often qualitatively; test to determine the relative potency of a chemical (usually a drug or vitamin group) by comparing its effect on living organisms with the effect of a standard preparation or placebo on the same type of organisms.

Bioconcentration factor (BCF): Concentration of a chemical in an organism divided by its concentration in the test solution or environment (e.g., concentration in fish divided by concentration in water).

Biodegradation: Breakdown of chemicals by organisms into smaller constituents. Often refers to the metabolic alteration of toxic chemicals to less- or nontoxic residues.

Bioeconomic model: Mathematical model linking animal population dynamics to economic dynamics. Its main objectives are to show how human exploitation affects fish (or other animal) populations and to investigate the economic consequences of alternative fishing strategies (e.g., open-access competition, regulated fishing effort, limited access).

Biological or biochemical oxygen demand (BOD): Amount of molecular oxygen that can be taken up by nonliving organic matter as it decomposes by aerobic biochemical action.

Biomagnification: Process of concentrating bioaccumulated chemicals to higher and higher concentrations as the chemicals are transferred from one trophic level to the next (plants to herbivores to predators).

Biomass (also standing crop): Summed mass or weight of individuals in one or more species, usually related to a defined area or volume.

Biosolids: Bacteria or their remains in the effluent from a biological treatment system of a pulp and paper mill. They are small (generally less than 5 μm) and up to 40% protein.

Blowdown: See *windthrow*.

Boom: Barrier across a river or around an area of water to prevent floating logs from dispersing.

Boom sticks: Pieces of timber, generally logs, that are linked end to end by chains or cables to contain or guide floating logs.

Boulders: Substrate particles greater than 256 mm in diameter. Often subclassified as small (256–1,024 mm) and large boulders (>1,024 mm).

Braided stream (also channel braiding): Stream that forms an interlacing network of branching and recombining channels separated by branch islands or channel bars.

Broadcast burning: Intentional burning in which fire is induced to spread throughout a specific area.

Bucket-line dredge: Dredge with a series of bucket shovels attached to a large endless belt or wheel, used to extract alluvial deposits.

Buffer strip (also leave strip): Strip of vegetation left intact along a stream or lake during and after logging.

Button-up fry: Salmonid fry that has emerged from the spawning gravel but has not completely absorbed its yolk sac.

Canopy: Branches and leaves above ground or water.

Canopy cover (of a stream): Vegetation projecting over a stream, including crown cover (generally more than 1 m above the water surface) and overhang cover (less than 1 m above the water).

Carrying capacity: Maximum average number or biomass of organisms that can be sustained in a habitat over the long term. Usually refers to a particular species, but can be applied to more than one.

Cascade: Stream segment with a stepped series of drops characterized by exposed rocks and boulders, high gradient, swift current, and much turbulence.

Catchment area: See *drainage area*.

Channel: Natural or artificial waterway of perceptible extent that periodically or continuously contains moving water. It has a definite bed and banks that serve to confine water.

Channel braiding: See *braided stream*.

Chinook (wind): Warm, moist, southwest wind blowing from the sea onto Oregon, Washington, and British Columbia in winter and spring, often causing spring thaws. Also, a warm, dry wind blowing down the east slope of the Rocky Mountains.

Chipping: Use of a chipping machine to reduce large wood pieces to small pieces of generally uniform size.

Choriolytic enzyme: Enzyme that lyses (breaks down) the chorion.

Chorion: Tough outer membrane that surrounds an embryo before it hatches.

Chronic toxicity: Toxic effect caused by long-term exposure to sublethal concentrations of a toxicant; sometimes refers to an effect manifested long after an exposure. (Compare *acute toxicity*.)

Cinnabar: Mercuric sulfide (HgS), the principal ore of mercury.

Clay: Substrate particles generally smaller than 0.004 mm in diameter.

Clear-cut: Area from which all trees have been removed by cutting.

Clear-cutting: Removal of the entire standing crop of trees from an area; in practice, much unsalable material may be left standing.

Coarse sediment: Sediment with particle sizes greater then 2.0 mm, including gravel, cobbles, and boulders. (Compare *fine sediment*.)

Cobble (also rubble): Substrate particles 64–256 mm in diameter. Often subclassified as small (64–128 mm) and large cobble (128–256 mm).

Colluvial material: See *colluvium*.

Colluvies: See *colluvium*.

Colluvium (also colluvial material; colluvies): Loose deposits of soil and rock moved by gravity. Colluvium on or below steep slopes or cliffs often is called talus; piled mine and dredge wastes such as washings, dregs, or offscourings are colluvies.

Concrete frost: Wet soil that has become solidly frozen.

Consumer demand: Quantity of a commodity that consumers will buy at a given price. The relationship between the quantity demanded and the price is a demand curve. Demand normally falls as price rises. Economists estimate demand functions for commercial products by statistically analyzing the quantities sold, price, and other determinants of demand. For a commodity not supplied at a price, the demand concept is still applicable, but the demand curve must be based on indirect information (as in the travel cost method) or consumer surveys (as in the contingent valuation method).

Consumer surplus: Amount that consumers would be willing to pay for a commodity or nonmarket good minus the amount that they actually do pay; the consumers' all-or-nothing value minus the amount spent. It is a component of net economic value.

Contact action herbicide: Herbicide that exerts its primary toxic effect upon contact with plant tissues (such as foliage that intercepts a spray), rather than after translocation to roots or other organs.

Contingent value method (CVM): Method of commodity valuation that relies on interviews to determine consumer values for nonmarket goods. A value is elicited from each respondent after it is explained that enjoyment of the good is contingent upon a payment of some kind. The hypothetical situation under which the payment would be required and the vehicle by which the payment would be made are devised in a realistic way and explained in detail to the respondent.

Contour mining: Surface mining of a horizontal ore deposit exposed on a hill slope; characterized by long excavations bordered by one or two parallel waste piles.

Creep: Slow, continual downslope movement of mineral, rock, and soil particles under the influence of gravity.

Cultipacking: Firming, pulverizing, or breaking clods with a corrugated roller to prepare seedbeds.

Culvert: Buried pipe structure that allows streamflow or road drainage to pass under a road.

Cut and fill: Construction of a road on undulating ground that is partly excavated and partly filled.

Debris avalanche: Rapid landslide of soil, rock, and organic debris along a shallow plane parallel to the slope, usually caused by protracted heavy rains that completely saturate the soil mantle.

Debris torrent: Deluge of water charged with soil, rock, and organic debris down a steep stream channel.

Degradation: Erosional removal of materials from one place to another. Degradation lowers the elevation of streambeds and flood plains. (Compare *aggradation*.)

Deme: See *stock*.

Denil fishway: Fishway that dissipates the water's energy so fish can swim over low barriers without undue stress. A Denil fishway has lateral baffles projecting at an angle from each side of a straight chute and a clear passage up the middle.

Density: Number of organisms or items per unit area or volume.

Depositional areas: Local zones within a stream where the energy of flowing water is reduced and suspended material settles out, accumulating on the streambed. (Compare *scoured areas*.)

Depression storage: Water retained in puddles, ditches, and other depressions in the surface of the ground.

Depuration phase: Period after exposure to a toxicant when an organism lowers its bodily concentration of the chemical via excretion and metabolism.

Detritivore: Animal that consumes decomposing organic particles, deriving nutrition primarily from microbes on the particles.

Detritus: Undissolved organic or inorganic matter resulting from the decomposition of parent material.

Dewatering: Lowering of the water table in stream channel deposits caused by a channel shift or a flow reduction.

Diadromous: Fish that migrate from fresh water to the sea, or vice versa, to feed or breed.

Discharge: Volume of water flowing past a reference point per unit time (usually expressed as m^3/s).

Discount rate: Interest rate used to translate monetary values of benefits and costs occurring in different years into a common unit of comparison, usually a net present value. It usually falls in the range of 2–10%. Key factors that influence calculation of a discount rate for a particular circumstance include the rate of interest consumers pay to exchange future payments for current consumption, the rate of return on private investment, and the costs of public capital expenditures.

Diversity index: Numerical value derived from the number of individuals per taxon (abundance) and the number of taxa present (richness).

Donkey: Portable power unit mounted on skids and equipped with winch drum(s) and cable(s).

Drag line: Earth-moving equipment consisting of a scoop-type bucket suspended and controlled by a steel cable and running line from a crane or derrick; also, any cable or chain that does the actual hauling.

Drainage area (also catchment area; watershed; basin): Total land area draining to any point in a stream, as measured on a map, aerial photo, or other horizontal, two-dimensional projection.

Drainage density: Total length of natural drainage channels in a given area, expressed as kilometers of stream channel per square kilometer of drainage area.

Dredge mining (also dredging): Extraction of unconsolidated alluvial deposits from beneath standing water or from saturated soils adjacent to watercourses.

Dredging: See *dredge mining*.

Drift (invertebrate): Collectively, stream invertebrates (almost wholly the aquatic larval stages of insects) that voluntarily or accidentally leave the substrate to move or float with the current, as well as terrestrial invertebrates that drop into the stream. Also, any detrital material transported in the water current.

Drift feeders: Fish and other predators that forage on invertebrates drifting on the water surface or in the water column.

Drift mine: Underground coal mine with horizontal entry tunnels.

Dry ravel: Tumbling, rolling, and bounding of single particles downslope under the influence of gravity.

Earthflow: Slow downslope movement of weathered rock or soil. Many flows begin as one or more slumps. By a combination of true rheological flow of the clay fraction and slumping and sliding of individual blocks, an earthflow moves downslope with a continuity of motion resembling the flow of a viscous fluid.

Economic benefit: Total of economic values generated from a project. It includes consumer surplus and producer surplus as well as existence values.

Economic efficiency: Production of the largest possible net benefit in the use of a resource. One use is more efficient than another if it produces more total value without increasing the cost, or if it produces the same value at a lower cost.

Economic impact: Most frequently, the income or employment generated in a particular region due to a change in some economic activity. Impacts are often called "secondary benefits" because they represent increases in regional economic activity that benefit local businesses, but they do not correspond to increases in net economic benefits.

Economic profit: Any monetary return over and above the normal return on investment.

Ecosystem: The physical and climatic features and all the living and dead organisms in an area that are interrelated in the transfer of energy and material.

Eddy: Circular current of water, sometimes quite strong, diverging from the main current. It usually forms where the flow passes some obstruction or at the inside of river bends, and often forms backwater pools or pocket water in riffles.

Effluent: Complex fluid waste material such as sewage or industrial refuse that is released into the environment.

Embeddedness: Degree to which large particles (boulders, rubble, gravel) are surrounded or covered by fine sediment, usually measured in classes according to percent coverage.

Emergence (fish): Departure of fry from the incubation gravel into the water column.

End-haul: To move excess excavated material off site for use or disposal, generally with dump trucks.

Endogenous: Produced or occurring within an organism, stream, or other system.

Ephemeral stream: Stream that flows briefly and only in direct response to local precipitation, and whose channel is always above the water table.

Epibenthic: Living on the surface of bottom sediments in a water body.

Epifauna: Animals living on the surface of the substrate.

Epilithic: Living on rocks or other stoney matter.

Epiphyte: Nonparasitic plant that grows on a surface other than soil or sediment, usually on another plant.

Epithelium: Cellular tissue lining or covering an exposed surface.

Epizootic: Disease that affects many animals of one kind at the same time.

Escapement: That portion of an anadromous fish population that escapes the commercial and recreational fisheries and reaches the freshwater spawning grounds.

Estuary: Semi-enclosed body of water that has a free connection with the open ocean and within which seawater is measurably diluted with fresh water derived from land drainage.

Eutrophic: Rich in dissolved nutrients, photosynthetically productive, and often deficient in oxygen during warm periods. (Compare *oligotrophic*.)

Evapotranspiration: Loss of water by evaporation from the soil and transpiration from plants.

Even-year runs: Populations of fish returning to spawning grounds in even-numbered years.

Exclosure: Area from which livestock or other animals are excluded.

Existence value: Economic value that people place on simply knowing that a resource is available, whether or not they expect to ever use it.

Expanding stream system: Stream system that expands during periods of heavy precipitation, as intermittent channels begin to carry water and as the zone of saturated soil in the riparian area extends upslope due to the influx of water from subsurface and overland flow.

Ex-vessel value: Value of fish at first sale by fishermen at the dock, distinguished from wholesale or retail value.

Eyed egg: Fish egg that has developed far enough that the eyes of the embryo are visible through the egg wall.

Fall-run fish: Anadromous fish that return to fresh water in the fall and spawn during fall or early winter.

Fecal coliform bacteria: Aerobic bacteria found in the colon or feces, often used as indicators of fecal contamination of water supplies.

Fecundity: Fertility; the number of live eggs produced by a female fish.

Fill: Verb: local deposition of material eroded or excavated elsewhere, including aggradation of naturally eroded material in streams (compare *scour*), deliberate placing of material in and along streams, and dumping of material to create roadbeds. Noun: the material so deposited.

Fines: See *fine sediment*.

Fine sediment (also *fines*): Sediment with particle sizes of 2.0 mm and less, including sand, silt, and clay. (Compare *coarse sediment*.)

Fingerling: Young fish, usually in its first or second year and generally between 2 and 25 cm long. (Compare *fry*; *parr*.)

Fixed escapement policy: Management policy of allowing escapement of a predetermined target number of spawners to the spawning grounds.

Flocculation: Aggregation, due to molecular charges, of precipitated or suspended materials into small masses called flocculants.

Flood plain: Level lowland bordering a stream onto which the stream spreads at flood stage.

Flotation: Ore-concentrating method applicable to sulfides of lead, zinc, and copper, to some carbonates, and to some silicates. Pulverized ore is mixed with water, and carefully selected oil and air are blown into the mixture to create a froth. The metal-bearing particles are hydrophobic and attach to the oil; the gangue particles (rock, clay, sand, etc.) are hydrophilic and sink to the bottom of the tank. The froth is removed and the ore is recovered from it in highly concentrated form.

Fluvial: Pertaining to streams or rivers, or produced by stream action; also, migrating between main rivers and tributaries. (Compare *adfluvial*.)

Fluvial entrainment: Suspension and transport of solid materials by running water.

Focal point: Location of an organism; for fish, usually the position of the snout. Habitat measurements made at that position (depth, water velocity, etc.) are focal point measurements.

Forage fish: Fish species that as adults are small enough to be prey of larger species; often nongame fish.

Forb: Generally, any herb that is not a grass.

Frass: Debris or excrement produced by insects.

Frazil ice (also slush ice): Fine spicules of ice formed in open channels where the current is too swift for the ice to become attached or to coalesce into a surface sheet. Frazil ice forms in supercooled water when the air temperature is far below freezing (most often below −8°C).

Freshet: See *storm flow*.

Fry: Life stage of trout and salmon between full absorption of the yolk sac and a somewhat arbitrarily defined fingerling or parr stage, which generally is reached by the end of the first summer. (Compare *fingerling*; *parr*.)

Functional groups (ecology): Groups of organisms that obtain energy in similar ways. Autotrophic plants fix energy from sunlight. Fungi and bacteria decompose organic matter. Shredders chew large particles like tree leaves. Scrapers rasp periphyton and microbes from solid substrates. Collectors filter fine particles from the water or gather them from deposits.

Gabion: Wire basket filled with stones, used to stabilize streambanks and improve aquatic habitats.

Galena: Lead sulfide (PbS), the principal ore of lead.

Gametogenesis (also spermatogenesis; oogenesis): Production of gametes (mature haploid sex cells). Sperm are produced by spermatogenesis, eggs by oogenesis.

Gill membrane: Outer cellular layer on gills, where oxygen, carbon dioxide, and many salts are passively or actively transported into or out of a fish.

Gin pole: Simple hoisting device consisting of a block and tackle suspended from near the top of a single pole (mast) that is held vertically or obliquely by guy lines.

Glacial till: Heterogeneous veneer of clay, silt, sand, gravel, and boulders left on the ground by melting glaciers.

Glide: Slow, relatively shallow stream section with water velocities of 10–20 cm/s and little or no surface turbulence. (Compare *rapids; riffle; run*.)

Gradient (topographic slope): Average change in vertical elevation per unit of horizontal distance, usually measured as meters of drop per kilometer of map distance.

Gravel: Substrate particles between 2 and 64 mm in diameter.

Greenockite: Cadmium sulfide (CdS), a rare mineral ore of cadmium.

Groundwater: That part of the subsurface water that is in the zone of saturation, including underground streams.

Guild: Group of organisms that exhibit similar habitat requirements and that respond in a similar way to changes in their environment.

Gully erosion: See *gullying*.

Gullying (also gully erosion): Formation or extention of gullies by surface runoff water.

Half-life: Period required for half the atoms of a radioactive isotope to disintegrate, or for half the molecules of a substance to decompose.

Hardness: Total concentration of calcium and magnesium ions, expressed as the equivalent concentration (mg/L) of calcium carbonate.

Headwall: Steep slope at the head of a valley.

Heap leaching: Mineral extraction technique in which ore is crushed, heaped into large pads, and treated with a chemical (often sodium cyanide for gold). The chemical percolates through the pad, binds the target ore, and drains into a collection facility for processing.

Heavy metals: Metals with specific gravities of 5.0 and higher, including cadmium, chromium, cobalt, copper, gold, lead, nickel, and many others.

Hematocrit: Volume percentage of blood cells and platelets within a sample of whole blood.

Heterotrophic: Requiring complex organic chemicals for metabolic synthesis.

Hexavalent: Able to gain or donate six electrons in a chemical reaction.

High-lead yarding: Method of powered cable logging in which the mainline blocks are fastened high on a spar so logs can be skidded with one end off the ground.

Highwall: Working face of a surface mine or quarry.

Holocene Age: Most recent geological epoch, comprising the 10,000 or so years since the last major continental glaciation.

Homeostasis: Maintenance of an organism's internal stability by coordinated responses of organ systems to compensate for stresses imposed by environmental change.

Hydraulic mining: Use of high-pressure water jets to erode ore-bearing alluvial deposits.

Hydrolysis: Chemical reaction of a compound with the ions of water (H^+ and OH^-) to produce a weak acid, a weak base, or both.

Hydrophobic: Incapable of uniting with or absorbing water.

Hydroseeding: Hydraulic spraying of seed, fertilizer, and mulch onto steep slopes.

Hydrostatic pressure: Pressure exerted at a given point within water at rest, a function of the weight of overlying water.

Hypolimnion: Lowermost, noncirculating layer of cold water in a thermally stratified lake, usually deficient in oxygen.

Infauna: Aquatic animals living within the matrix of bottom sediment.

Instar: An insect or other arthropod that is between molts.

Instream flow incremental methodology (IFIM): Technique to predict the biomass of a fish species or life stage that a stream reach can support at a given flow, given knowledge of the fishes' physical habitat preferences.

Interception (precipitation): Retention of precipitation on vegetation, from which it is subsequently evaporated without reaching the ground.

Intragravel flow: Water moving through the substrate pores of a streambed.

Ion: Atom that has lost (cation, positive charge) or gained (anion, negative charge) one or more valence electrons.

Ion exchange: Reversible exchange of one type of ion with another of like charge at a site on a solid, insoluble medium. Also, exchange of ions across a physiological membrane such that a consistent ionic charge is maintained on either side of the membrane.

Isotopes: Atoms of a chemical element with the same atomic number and chemical properties but with different atomic masses.

Iteroparous: Able to spawn more than one time; reproducing annually, or having more than one brood.

Jack: Young salmon, usually a male, that matures precociously.

Kelt: Atlantic salmon or anadromous trout that is weak and emaciated after spawning.

Kraft pulp: Chemical wood pulp obtained by digesting wood chips at high temperature and pressure in a solution of sodium hydroxide and sodium sulfide.

Lacustrine: Of or having to do with a lake.

Lag deposit: Coarse material remaining on a surface after the finer material has been blown or washed away by wind or water; also, coarse material that is rolled or dragged along the bottom of a stream at a slower rate than the finer material.

Lake-type fish: Fish that rear for a year or more in a lake.

Landing (forestry): Any place where round timber is assembled for further (and commonly different) transport.

Landslide: Any sudden movement of earth and rocks down a steep slope.

Large woody debris (LWD): Any large piece of woody material that intrudes into a stream channel, whose smallest diameter is greater than 10 cm, and whose length is greater than 1 m.

LC50: Concentration of toxicant lethal to 50% of test organisms during a defined time period and under defined conditions.

LD50: Dose of a chemical lethal to 50% of test organisms (rarely used with aquatic organisms because LD50 indicates the quantity of material injected or ingested).

Leachate: Solution of material leached from a solid (e.g., dissolved organic matter leached from fallen leaves).

Leave strip: See *buffer strip*.

Lensing: Thinning-out of a stratum in one or more directions (e.g., the lateral disappearance of a stream).

Lignin: Amorphous, cellulose-like, organic substance that binds cellulose fibers in wood and certain herbs and adds strength and stiffness to cell walls.

Limiting factor: Environmental factor that limits the growth or activities of an organism or that restricts the size of a population or its geographical range.

Littoral zone: Region along the shore.

Log dozer: Bulldozer used to move logs, generally by skidding.

Longitudinal profile: Plot of the elevation versus the length of a stream channel. Elevation is normally the ordinate and length the abscissa.

Lotic: Of or in running water such as a stream or river.

Low-volatile esters: Organic acid herbicides reacted with high-molecular-weight alcohols to form an herbicide of low vapor pressure. Some organic acid herbicides (such as 2,4-D) are usually formulated as esters. Some are highly volatile, such as methyl esters, ethyl esters, and others derived from low-molecular-weight alcohols. These are not used as herbicides in the USA today. Esters formed from high-molecular-weight alcohols such as ethylene glycol, butoxyethyl alcohol, or propyleneglycol butyl ether alcohol are low-volatile esters.

Low-water crossing: Stream crossing where the road is at or near the channel bottom and all streamflow passes over the road. Such crossings are dangerous when streamflows are strong.

Macroalgae: Multicellular algae (green, blue-green, and red algae) having filamentous, sheet, or mat-like morphology.

Macrobenthos: Organisms (e.g., insect larvae) living in or on aquatic substrates and large enough to be seen with the naked eye. (Compare *microbenthos*.)

Macrofauna: Animals large enough to be seen with the naked eye. (Compare *meiofauna; microfauna*.)

Macroinfauna: Animals living within aquatic sediments and large enough to be seen with the naked eye.

Macroinvertebrates: Invertebrates large enough to be seen with the naked eye (e.g., most aquatic insects, snails, and amphipods).

Macrophytes: Plants large enough to be seen with the naked eye.

Macropore: Pore too large to hold water by capillary action.

Main stem: Principal stream or channel of a drainage system.

Management indicator species: A species whose habitat requirements most reflect those of the species community in the habitat of concern, usually used to indicate habitat quality and to predict future conditions.

Manning's *n*: Empirical coefficient for computing stream bottom roughness; used to determine water velocity in stream discharge calculations.

Marginal value: The increase in economic value associated with a small (e.g., one-unit) increase in the quantity of something. The marginal value of most products is reasonably well represented by the market price.

Margin of safety: Ratio of the no-effect exposure integral for a chemical to the field exposure integral.

Mass movement: See *soil mass movement*.

Mass wasting: See *soil mass movement*.

Meiofauna: Animals ranging in size from approximately 0.1 mm to 1 mm that live within sediments; the size class of transition from micro- to macrofauna (see those terms).

Membrane permeability: Measure of an ion's passive transport rate across a membrane. As membrane permeability increases, the transport rate increases, as does the size of ions passed. Membrane permeability is critical in ion exchange.

Mesic: Moderately wet, such as in locations near springs or with moderate rainfall, as opposed to hydric (wet) or xeric (dry).

Metabolism: The suite of chemical reactions in living organisms and cells by which protoplasm is built up from assimilated food, energy is released for vital processes, and waste byproducts are generated.

Metabolite: Any substance produced by or taking part in metabolism.

Metalliferous: Metal-bearing; used in reference to ores and deposits.

Microbenthos: Organisms (e.g., protozoa, nematodes) living on or in aquatic substrates and too small to be seen with the naked eye. (Compare *macrobenthos*.)

Microfauna: Animals too small to be seen with the naked eye. (Compare *macrofauna; meiofauna*.)

Microhabitat: Specific combination of habitat elements in the place occupied by an organism for a specific purpose.

Mine spoils: Overburden and other waste material remaining after an ore has been extracted.

Mycorrhiza: Symbiotic association between a fungus and (usually) the root of a higher plant.

Natal area (also natal stream): Locality of birth.

Natal stream: See *natal area*.

Needle ice: Ice crystals caused by frost heaving in rocks and soils.

Nephelometric turbidity unit (NTU): Measure of the concentration or size of suspended particles (cloudiness) based on the scattering of light transmitted or reflected by the medium.

Net present value (NPV): Discounted value of future net benefits as computed by the formula

$$\text{NPV} = \sum_{i=1}^{T} (B_i - C_i)/(1 + r)^i;$$

T is the number of years over which prospective benefits and costs occur, B_i and C_i are the estimated benefits and costs accruing in year i, and r is the discount rate. The benefits include the consumer surplus, producer surplus, and resource rent.

Nickpoint: Interruption or break of slope, especially a point of abrupt change or inflection in the longitudinal profile of a stream or its valley, resulting from rejuvenation, glacial erosion, or the outcropping of a resistant bed.

Nonpoint-source pollution: Pollution from sources that cannot be defined as discrete points, such as areas of timber harvesting, surface mining, and construction. (Compare *point-source pollution*.)

No-toxic-effect exposure level: Maximum level of exposure that produces no discernible effect on test organisms. This level varies with species, type of test, and environmental conditions.

NTU: See *nephelometric turbidity unit*.

Ocean-type fish: Anadromous fish that shows no indication on its scales or other hard parts of an extended freshwater residence early in its life.

Odd-year run: Population of fish that returns to spawning grounds in odd-numbered years.

Old growth: See *old-growth stand*.

Old-growth forest: See *old-growth stand*.

Old-growth stand (also old growth; old-growth forest): Forest stand dominated by trees reaching natural senescence; the last stage in forest succession.

Oligotrophic: Poor in dissolved nutrients, of low photosynthetic productivity, and rich in dissolved oxygen at all depths. (Compare *eutrophic*.)

Oogenesis: See *gametogenesis*.

Open-access resource: A resource, such as a marine fish stock, that is open to use by all.

Open-pit mine: Large surface mine excavated by machinery, layer by layer, on multiple terrace levels.

Order (stream): See *stream order*.

Organic debris: Debris consisting of plant or animal material.

Orographic: Pertaining to mountains, especially in regard to the precipitation that results when moisture-laden air encounters mountains and is forced to ri° over them.

Orphan mine: See *abandoned mine*.

Osmosis: The tendency of a solvent (such as water) to pass through a meable membrane (such as a living cell wall) into a solution concentration so as to equalize concentrations of solutes on bot membrane.

Ossification: Development and growth of bone.

Overburden (also surface-soil capping): Soil or rock layers deposits and must be removed prior to mining.

Paddock: Enclosed piece of land, such as a pasture

Parbuckle: Rope device that moves a log (or othe° log as a simple movable pulley. Two rope end. The ropes are passed around the lo° and back to their respective anchor hand or winch), the log rolls toward the device acts as a sling. If the ° be rolled up a ramp onto the truck off-loaded from trucks.

Parr: Young salmonid, in the stage between alevin and smolt, that has developed distinctive dark "parr marks" on its sides and is actively feeding in fresh water. (Compare *fingerling; fry*.)

Peak flow: Greatest stream discharge recorded over a specified period of time, usually a year but often a season.

Pelagic: Of or in open waters of lakes or seas.

Penstock: Sluice gate or valve for restraining, deviating, or otherwise regulating a flow (as of water or sewage).

Periphyton: Algae and associated microorganisms growing attached to any submerged surface.

Permafrost: Permanently frozen subsoil.

Permeability: A measure of the rate at which a substrate can pass water, the rate depending on substrate composition and compaction; the apparent velocity per unit of hydraulic gradient, expressed in cm/h.

Pesticide: Chemical used to kill, control, or manage plant or animal pests; includes herbicides, fungicides, insecticides, rodenticides, and piscicides.

pH: A measure of the hydrogen-ion activity in a solution, expressed as the negative $\log_{10}$ of hydrogen ion concentration on a scale of 0 (highly acidic) to 14 (highly basic); a pH of 7 is neutral.

Phenoxy herbicides: Organic acid herbicides that include a phenoxy moiety, usually chlorinated. Examples: 2,4-D; 2,4,5-T.

Photodecomposition: Chemical breakdown of a molecule by means of radiant energy.

Photodegradation: Rapid degradation in water exposed to sunlight.

Photolysis: Chemical decomposition due to the action of light.

Photoperiod: Recurring cycle of light and dark periods. The natural photoperiod is approximately 24 h, and the ratio of light to dark hours slowly changes over the course of a year. In controlled experiments, the photoperiod is usually (but not necessarily) retained at 24 h, and the light:dark ratio is typically constant.

Photosynthesis: Production of organic substances from carbon dioxide and water in the presence of light. Most photosynthesis occurs in green plant cells, where chlorophyll helps transform radiant energy into chemical energy.

Phytoplankton: Small (often microscopic) aquatic plants suspended in water.

Phytotoxicity: Toxicity to plants.

Placer: Fluvial or glacial deposit of gravel or sand containing heavy ore minerals, such as gold or platinum, that have been eroded from bedrock and concentrated as small particles that can be washed out.

Placer mining: Mining of placer deposits by washing, dredging, or hydraulic methods.

Plankton: Small (often microscopic) plants and animals floating, drifting, or weakly swimming in bodies of fresh or salt water.

Plunge pool: Basin scoured out by vertically falling water.

Pocket water: A series of small pools surrounded by swiftly flowing water, usually formed by eddies behind boulders, rubble, or logs, or by potholes in the stream bed.

Point-source pollution: Pollution emanating from a confined, discrete source such

as a pipe, ditch, tunnel, well, or floating craft. (Compare *nonpoint-source pollution.*)

Pool: Portion of a stream with reduced current velocity, often with deeper water than surrounding areas and with a smooth surface.

Pool:riffle ratio: Ratio of the surface area or length of pools to the surface area or length of riffles in a given stream reach, frequently expressed as the relative percentage of each category.

Population: Organisms of the same species that occur in a particular place at a given time. A population may contain several discrete breeding groups or stocks.

Pore-water pressure: Stress transmitted by water that fills the voids between particles of a soil or rock mass; that part of the total normal stress in a saturated soil caused by the presence of interstitial water.

Primary production: Production of organic substances by photosynthesis; the quantity of material so produced per unit time.

Producer surplus: The net value accruing to the producers of a commodity: the amount that the producers are paid minus the amount they would be willing to accept for producing and supplying a quantity of goods. It is a component of net economic value (or economic benefits) on the supply side.

Profit: The return to a producer or supplier that exceeds the normal or expected return: sales revenue minus all labor, materials, rents, and normal rate of return on investment. Profit is a component of producer surplus.

Pulp: Mixture of ground-up, moistened cellulose material, such as wood, from which paper is made.

Quarrying: Extraction of non-ore materials such as limestone, sand, and gravel from open pits (quarries).

Race: See *stock.*

Radionuclides: Atoms that radiate alpha, beta, or gamma particles; radioactive atoms.

Rapids: Stream section with considerable surface agitation, swift current, and drops up to 1 m. Some waves may be present; rocks and boulders may be exposed at all but high flows. (Compare *glide; riffle; run.*)

Reach (also stream reach): Section of stream between two specified points.

Recreation opportunity spectrum (ROS): Conceptual framework designed to clarify relations among recreational settings, activities, and opportunities.

Recruit (fish): Juvenile that has survived long enough to become part of (i.e., recruited into) a population or an exploitable segment of a population.

Redd: Nest made in gravel, consisting of a depression hydraulically dug by a fish for egg deposition (and then filled) and associated gravel mounds.

Reduction (chemical): Increase in the proportion of hydrogen or base-forming elements in a compound, or addition of electrons to an atom. Oxidation is the reverse process.

Regional index streams: Streams considered typical of a region.

Resource rent: Amount paid for the use of a scarce resource over and above the cost of maintaining the resource; the excess of actual payment above the resource owners' minimum willingness to accept compensation. It is an economic surplus counted on the benefits side of a benefit–cost analysis.

Rheological: Pertaining to change in the form and flow of matter, including elastic, viscous, and plastic deformations and flows.

Riffle: Shallow section of a stream or river with rapid current and a surface broken by gravel, rubble, or boulders. (Compare *glide; rapids; run*.)

Rill: One of the first and smallest channels formed by surface erosion; also, a very small brook or trickling stream of water.

Rill erosion: See *rilling*.

Rilling (also rill erosion): Development of numerous minute, closely spaced channels resulting from the uneven erosion of soil by running water.

Riparian area: Area with distinctive soils and vegetation between a stream or other body of water and the adjacent upland. It includes wetlands and those portions of floodplains and valley bottoms that support riparian vegetation.

Riparian vegetation: Vegetation growing on or near the banks of a stream or other body of water in soils that exhibit some wetness characteristics during some portion of the growing season.

Riprap: Layer of large, durable materials (usually rocks; sometimes car bodies, broken concrete, etc.) used to protect a stream bank or lake shore from erosion; may also refer to the materials used.

River continuum: Gradual changes in the biological community of a river as energy sources and physical conditions change from headwaters to lowlands.

River-type fish: Anadromous fish that rear for a year or more in rivers.

Rootwad: Root mass of a tree.

Rotation: The planned number of years between successive cuttings of a forest; livestock grazing strategy in which cattle are moved from one pasture to another during the grazing season.

Rubble: See *cobble*.

Run (fish): A group of fish migrating in a river (most often on a spawning migration) that may comprise one or many stocks.

Run (stream): Swiftly flowing stream reach with little surface agitation and no major flow obstructions. Often appears as a flooded riffle. (Compare *glide; riffle; rapids*.)

Runoff: The part of precipitation and snowmelt that reaches streams (and thence the sea) by flowing over the ground.

Sac fry: See *alevin*.

Salmon farming: Rearing of salmon in pens or cages until harvest.

Salmonids: Fish of the family Salmonidae, including salmon, trout, chars, whitefish, ciscoes, and grayling. In general usage, the term most often refers to salmon, trout, and chars.

Salmon ranching: Early rearing of salmon in pens, cages, or a hatchery, after which the fish are released to the open sea and harvested upon their return to spawn.

Sand: Substrate particles 0.062–2 mm in diameter.

Scoliosis: Lateral curvature of the spinal column.

Scour: Local removal of material from streambeds by flowing water. (Compare *fill*.)

Scoured areas: Local zones within a stream where material is removed from the streambed by flowing water. (Compare *depositional areas*.)

Scour pool: Pool formed by scour when flowing water impinges against and is diverted by a stream bank or channel obstruction (rootwad, woody debris, boulder, bedrock, etc.).

Secchi disk: Black and white disk lowered into the water to measure water transparency; an average is taken of the depth at which the disk disappears when lowered and reappears when raised.

Secondary production: Elaboration of tissue by heterotrophic organisms, minus tissue metabolized; the amount of such tissue produced per unit time, regardless of its fate.

Second growth: See *second-growth stand*.

Second-growth forest: See *second-growth stand*.

Second-growth stand (also second growth; second-growth forest): Forest stand that has come up naturally after some drastic interference such as logging, fire, or insect attack.

Sediment: Fragments of rock, soil, and organic material transported and deposited in beds by wind, water, or other natural phenomena. The term can refer to any size of particles but is often used to indicate only fragments smaller than 6 mm.

Sedimentation: Deposition of material suspended in water or air, usually when the velocity of the transporting medium drops below the level at which the material can be supported.

Sediment loading: The total sediment in a stream system, whether in suspension (suspended load) or on the bottom (bed load).

Sediment wedge: Thick, wedge-shaped deposit of mixed soil, rock, and organic debris injected into a stream channel by debris avalanches and debris flows from adjacent hillslopes.

Sensitive species: Species that can only survive within a narrow range of environmental conditions and whose disappearance from an area is an index of pollution or other environmental change.

Seston: Particulate matter suspended in water.

Shaft mine: Underground mine with vertical or inclined entryways.

Sheet erosion: Initial surface erosion by water running off as sheets, as distinct from channelized erosion in rills and gullies.

Shelterwood cutting: Selective cutting of regenerating plants so as to establish a new tree crop under the protective remnants of a former stand.

Side-cast: Noun: road construction material that is not used for fill and is pushed to or placed on the down-slope side of the road. Such material may travel long distances down slope before coming to rest. Verb: to so move such material.

Sill (geological): Intrusive body of igneous rock that has solidified in horizontal sheets between the bedding planes of stratified rocks.

Silt: Substrate particles 0.004–0.062 mm in diameter.

Silviculture: The tending, harvesting, and replacement of forests, resulting in forests of distinctive form.

Site-specific: Applying only to particular locations; said of effects that vary depending on local conditions.

Skidding: Loose term for hauling logs by sliding or dragging them.

Skyline yarding: Method of powered cable logging in which a heavy cable, the skyline, is stretched between two spars and functions as an overhead track for a load-carrying trolley.

Slash: Woody residue left on the ground after trees are felled, or accumulated there as a result of a storm, fire, or silvicultural treatment.

Slide-ramp: Inclined chute or ramp used to slide logs by gravity, such as down a bank into the water.

Slope mine: Underground coal mine with inclined entryways.

Sluiceway: Artificial channel for water, often having a gate or valve at its head to regulate the flow.

Slump: Sudden downward movement of a block of rock or soil by backward rotation along a broadly concave failure surface.

Slush ice: See *frazil ice*.

Smolt: Juvenile salmonid one or more years old that has undergone physiological changes to cope with a marine environment; the seaward migrant stage of an anadromous salmonid.

Smoltification: Suite of physiological, morphological, biochemical, and behavioral changes, including development of the silvery color of adults and a tolerance for seawater, that take place in salmonid parr as they prepare to migrate downstream and enter the sea.

Sodicity: Sodium content of a solid or liquid.

Soil mass movement (also mass movement; mass wasting): Downslope transport of soil and rocks due to gravitational stress.

Solution mining: Underground mining in which a chemical solvent is pumped underground through a borehole to bind the target mineral; the resulting ore-bearing solution is pumped to the surface for recovery.

Spawner–recruit model: Biological model that relates the number of recruits or mature spawners in one generation to the number of spawners in the previous generation. (See *recruit*.)

Species-specific: Applying only to particular species; said of effects that vary depending on the species in question.

Spermatogenesis: See *gametogenesis*.

Sphalerite: Zinc sulfide (ZnS), the principal ore of zinc.

Spiralling: Recycling of organic matter and nutrients between streambed and water column along a stream course.

Splash dam: Dam built to create a head of water for driving logs.

Spring-run fish: Anadromous fish that return to fresh water in the spring, migrate to spawning areas, and spawn during late summer or early autumn.

Standing crop: See *biomass*.

Static bioassay: Bioassay during which the test solution is not changed during the exposure period.

Stem flow: Precipitation that is temporarily intercepted by trees and other vegetation but eventually runs to the ground along stems.

Stem-injection treatment: Application of herbicide to a tree through a cut in the bark.

Stock (also race; deme): Group of fish that is genetically self-sustaining and isolated geographically or temporally during reproduction.

Storm flow (also freshet): Rapid temporary rise in stream discharge caused by heavy rains or rapid melting of snow or ice.

Stream order: A number from 1 to 6 or higher, ranked from headwaters to river terminus, that designates the relative position of a stream or stream segment in a drainage basin. First-order streams have no discrete tributaries; the junction of two first-order streams produces a second-order stream; the junction of two second-order streams produces a third-order stream; etc.

Stream reach: See *reach*.

Stream-type fish: Fish that rear for a year or more in a stream.

Strip mining: Surface mining that creates either a long, continuous excavation bordered by one or two parallel waste piles to remove a horizontal deposit from a hillside (*contour mining*), or an alternating series of parallel excavations and waste piles to remove a deposit from a broad surface area.

Stumpage: Value of timber as it stands uncut.

Subadult: Stage in which a fish has developed many but not all adult characteristics and is not sexually mature.

Sublethal: Not quite sufficient to cause death.

Sublimation: Vaporization of a solid without an intermediate liquid phase.

Substrate: Mineral or organic material that forms the bed of a stream.

Subyearling (also young of the year; underyearling): A juvenile fish less than 1 year old.

Suitability index curve: Graph that depicts the suitability of a physical habitat variable for a fish species or life stage; often assumed to depict the species' or life stage's relative preference for values of the variable.

Sulfite pulping: Digestion of wood chips in an acidic or neutral solution containing a sulfite salt.

Summer-run fish: Anadromous fish that return to fresh water during June through September, migrate inland toward spawning areas, overwinter in the larger rivers, resume migration in early spring to natal streams, and then spawn.

Supercooled water: Water that remains liquid even though its temperature is below the equilibrium freezing point (0°C).

Supersaturate: To make more highly concentrated than normal saturation at a given temperature.

Surface-soil capping: See *overburden*.

Surface storage: Precipitation retained temporarily in depressions of the ground surface, neither infiltrating nor running off until after a rainfall period.

Suspended sediment: That part of a stream's total sediment load carried in the water column. (Compare *bed-load sediment*.)

Swim-up fry: Salmonid fry beginning to actively swim in search of food.

Sympatric: Co-occurring in the same area. (Compare *allopatric*.)

Synergism (chemical): Interaction of chemicals in a mixture to produce a greater toxic effect than would be expected from the sum of the toxicities of the individual chemicals. (Compare *antagonism*.)

Tailings: Portions of washed or milled ore regarded as too poor to be treated further; often left as tailings piles after mining.

Taxon: Any formal taxonomic unit or category of organisms: subspecies, species, genus, family, order, etc. (Plural: taxa.)

Temperature unit: Unit of water temperature (usually 1°C) prevailing over a defined period of time (usually 1 d), expressed in terms of a reference temperature (usually 0°C). For example, 5°C sustained for 48 h (2 d) and 20°C sustained for 12 h (0.5 d) both represent 10 temperature units (sometimes expressed as degree-days above freezing).

Teratogenic effect: Toxic or mutagenic induction of malformations during embryonic or later development.

Thalweg: Line connecting the deepest parts of a stream channel.

Thermocline: Layer of water between the warmer surface zone and the colder deep zone of a thermally stratified body of water. In the thermocline, temperature decreases rapidly with depth.

Thermomechanical pulping: Conversion of wood chips to fiber by mechanical grinding aided by heat (if aided by chemicals, this is called chemimechanical pulping).

Tie hacking: Cutting railroad ties, usually by hand, out of small timber.

Toxicity test: Controlled laboratory test to determine the toxicity of a chemical to an organism in terms of specific chemical concentrations. An *acute* toxicity test establishes the concentration required to kill a predetermined proportion of test organisms within a relatively short period of time, typically 4 d or less. A *chronic* toxicity test reveals the effects of a sublethal concentration applied throughout part or all of a life cycle. (See *acute toxicity; chronic toxicity*.)

Trace quantity: Very low, barely detectable concentration of an element or compound. Some chemicals that are beneficial nutrients in trace amounts become toxic when bioaccumulated.

Transpiration: Passage of water vapor and other gases from a living body through membranes or pores; usually used to mean loss of water from leaves and other plant surfaces.

Travel cost method (TCM): Method of estimating demand curves for recreational activities based on the relationship between participation levels at a recreational site and travel costs to the site.

Tributary: Stream flowing into a lake or larger stream.

Trophic level: Stage in a food chain or web leading from primary producers (lowest trophic level) through herbivores to primary and secondary carnivores (consumers—highest level). (See *trophic web*.)

Trophic web: Feeding relationships in communities that determine the flow of energy and materials from plants to herbivores, carnivores, and scavengers.

Underyearling: See *subyearling*.

Use value: Value that users place on resource services or commodities (e.g., the value associated with catching, consuming, or otherwise directly using fish). The vast majority of values estimated by economists are use values.

Valley inner gorge: That portion of a montane stream valley where the slopes adjacent to the stream channel are oversteepened (usually greater than 65%), are considerably steeper than slopes above, and are especially prone to landsliding.

Vascular macrophytes: Aquatic plants with specialized conducting tissue systems including xylem and phloem.

Volcaniclastic: Containing volcanic material within clastic rock or sediment. Clastic materials are fragments of preexisting rocks or minerals.

Waterbar: Shallow channel (cross-drain) or raised barrier (packed earth or a thin pole) laid diagonally across the surface of a road to guide water off the road.

Watershed: See *drainage area*.

Water table: Irregular surface of contact between the zone of saturation and the zone of aeration; that surface of a body of unconfined groundwater at which the pressure is equal to that of the atmosphere.

Weighted usable area (WUA): Index of the capacity of a stream reach to support a species or life stage, expressed as an actual or percentage of habitat area available per unit length of stream at a given flow. Also, the total surface area having a certain combination of hydraulic and substrate conditions, multiplied by the probability that fish will use that area at a given flow.

Weir: Notch or depression in a dam or other water barrier through which the flow of water is measured or regulated. Also, a barrier constructed across a stream to divert fish into a trap or to raise the water level or divert water flow.

Wet-mantle peak flow: Highest flow or discharge that results when the soil is almost or completely saturated.

Willingness to accept compensation (WTA): Amount by which individuals would have to be compensated for having to do without something, estimated as an all-or-nothing value or as a marginal value. The amount by which fishermen would have to be compensated to voluntarily forgo fishing in a particular lake, for example, represents the all-or-nothing value of the lake. (Compare *willingness to pay*.)

Willingness to pay (WTP): Amount that people would be willing to pay for a commodity or resource rather than go without it. The WTP for fishing in general is an all-or-nothing value; the all-or-nothing WTP by all consumers of a commodity minus the actual amount paid for the commodity equals the consumer surplus. The WTP for an additional day of fishing or for an additional fish is a marginal value. (Compare *willingness to accept compensation*.)

Windthrow (also blowdown): The uprooting and felling of trees by strong gusts of wind. Also, patches of trees that have been so felled.

Winter-run fish: Anadromous fish that return to fresh water in autumn or winter, migrate to spawning areas, and then spawn in late winter or spring.

Yarding: Hauling of timber from the point of felling to a yard or landing.

Yearling: A 1-year-old individual in its second year of life.

Yellow boy: Ferric hydroxide ($FeOH_3$) precipitated in streams subject to acidic mine effluent. Named for its yellow color.

Yolk-sac fry: See *alevin*.

Young of the year: See *subyearling*.

Zooplankton: Small (often microscopic) aquatic animals suspended or weakly swimming in water.

Glossary References

Bates, R. L., and J. A. Jackson, editors. 1980. Glossary of geology, 2nd edition. American Geological Institute, Falls Church, Virginia.

B.C. (British Columbia) Ministry of Forests, B.C. Ministry of the Environment, Federal Department of Fisheries and Oceans, and Council of Forest Industries. 1988. Coastal fisheries-forestry guidelines, 2nd edition. A joint publication by these agencies, Victoria and Vancouver, British Columbia.

Dadswell, M. J., R. J. Klauda, C. M. Moffitt, R. L. Saunders, R. A. Rulifson, and J. E. Cooper, editors. 1987. Common strategies of anadromous and catadromous fishes. American Fisheries Society Symposium 1.

Ford-Robertson, F. C., editor. 1971. Terminology of forest science, technology, practice and products. Society of American Foresters, Washington, D.C.

Helm, W. T., editor. 1985. Aquatic habitat inventory: glossary and standard methods. American Fisheries Society, Western Division, Bethesda, Maryland.

Huschke, R. E., editor. 1959. Glossary of meteorology. American Meteorological Society, Boston.

Kothmann, M. M., chairman. 1974. A glossary of terms used in range management, 2nd edition. Society for Range Management, Denver.

McCain, M., D. Fuller, L. Decker, and K. Overton. 1989. Stream habitat classification and inventory procedures for northern California. U. S. Forest Service, Pacific Southwest Region, Technical Bulletin, Winter 1989, San Francisco.

Toews, D. A. A., and M. J. Brownlee. 1981. A handbook for fish habitat protection on forest lands in British Columbia. Glossary (pages 103–107). Department of Fisheries and Oceans, Vancouver.

Index